MW00379380

West Academic Publishing's Emeritus Advisory Board

WEST ACADEMIC PUBLISHING'S LAW SCHOOL ADVISORY BOARD

INTELLECTUAL PROPERTY

CASES AND MATERIALS

Sixth Edition

■ ■ ■

Mary LaFrance
IGT Professor of Intellectual Property Law
William S. Boyd School of Law
University of Nevada, Las Vegas

Gary Myers
Earl F. Nelson Professor of Law
University of Missouri School of Law

Lee Ann Wheelis Lockridge
David Weston Robinson Professor of Law
McGlinchey Stafford Professor of Law
Louisiana State University Law Center

AMERICAN CASEBOOK SERIES®

860 Blue Gentian Road, Suite 350
Eagan, MN 55121
1-877-888-1330

Printed in the United States of America

ISBN: 978-1-63659-312-8

The authors dedicate this edition to:

Public higher education in the United States
and academic freedom
and the long-standing relationship
between the two.

AUTHORS' ACKNOWLEDGMENTS

Professor LaFrance acknowledges with gratitude the assistance of the law librarians at the William S. Boyd School of Law.

Professor Myers thanks his research assistant, Kayla Fowler, for her assistance on this edition of the book.

Professor Lockridge thanks staff and student research assistants for their involvement with the Fourth, Fifth, and now Sixth Editions. She appreciates the patience of her family with the weekends and late nights that this book consumes.

PREFACE TO THE SIXTH EDITION

Colleagues who have adopted the past five editions have noted that this book addresses not only the immediate needs of students and instructors but also the eventual concerns of the practitioner. It is grounded in both theory and doctrine. Both adaptable and teachable, the book serves the introductory or survey course beautifully and can engage individuals in specialized study as well.

In this Sixth Edition we therefore retain the essential structure of this adaptable and teachable book while updating it in all relevant ways. We preserved the introductory chapter containing selected materials to initiate students in the basic structure of intellectual property doctrines under the American Constitution. The overall organization of the book continues to follow the earlier pattern: trademark, right of publicity, trade secret, idea protection, patent, and copyright law. Within each of trademark, trade secret, patent, and copyright, we use a sequence that—generally speaking—begins with subject matter and standards for protection and then moves the student through acquisition and ownership, then infringement and defenses, and finally to remedies.

In this updated Sixth Edition, we have included new developments in each area without overburdening the student or instructor with longer readings. We accomplished this by streamlining certain case excerpts, being more selective in some instances, and, in other areas, making judicious use of notes. Each of the "big three" of trademark, patent, and copyright, however, continues to be covered so thoroughly that instructors could build at least a two-credit course around the relevant chapters. Right of publicity, state law protection for ideas, and the federal and state law of trade secret misappropriation each garner a significant chapter, while the final chapter of the book pulls together—as it has in previous editions—a range of cases addressing the complex question of preemption of state law.

SUMMARY OF CONTENTS

PART 3. THE RIGHT OF PUBLICITY

PART 4. CONFIDENTIAL INFORMATION AND IDEAS

PART 5. PATENT LAW

PART 6. COPYRIGHT LAW

TABLE OF CONTENTS

PART 3. THE RIGHT OF PUBLICITY

PART 4. CONFIDENTIAL INFORMATION AND IDEAS

PART 6. COPYRIGHT LAW

TABLE OF CASES

The principal cases are in bold type.

INTELLECTUAL PROPERTY

CASES AND MATERIALS

Sixth Edition

Part 1

Introduction

■ ■ ■

CHAPTER 1

DOCTRINES, ALTERNATIVES, AND THE FIRST AMENDMENT

■ ■ ■

A. BASIC INTELLECTUAL PROPERTY DOCTRINES UNDER THE UNITED STATES CONSTITUTION

The drafters of the U.S. Constitution saw a need for federal authority in the areas of patent and copyright law, which you can find reflected in the eighth clause of Article 1, Section 8 of the Constitution: "The Congress shall have power . . . To promote the progress of science and useful arts, by securing for limited times to authors and inventors the exclusive right to their respective writings and discoveries." The Constitution's provision of federal authority, and Congress's decision to legislate in each of patent and copyright as early as 1790, did not quickly or completely settle questions of the legal and philosophical underpinnings of these intangible rights or their relationships with one another. As you will see in the materials that follow in this chapter, as well as in the remainder of this book, there were then and remain today a number of interesting foundational issues in patent and copyright law, no less than in other areas you will encounter here, such as trademark, trade secret, and rights of publicity.

BAKER V. SELDEN

101 U.S. (11 Otto) 99 (1879).

MR. JUSTICE BRADLEY delivered the opinion of the court.

Charles Selden, the testator of the complainant in this case, in the year 1859 took the requisite steps for obtaining the copyright of a book, entitled "Selden's Condensed Ledger, or Book-keeping Simplified," the object of which was to exhibit and explain a peculiar system of book-keeping. In 1860 and 1861, he took the copyright of several other books, containing additions to and improvements upon the said system. The bill of complaint was filed against the defendant, Baker, for an alleged infringement of these copyrights. The latter, in his answer, denied that Selden was the author or designer of the books, and denied the infringement charged, and contends on the argument that the matter alleged to be infringed is not a lawful subject of copyright.

The book or series of books of which the complainant claims the copyright consists of an introductory essay explaining the system of book-keeping referred to, to which are annexed certain forms or blanks, consisting of ruled lines, and headings, illustrating the system and showing how it is to be used and carried out in practice. This system effects the same results as book-keeping by double entry; but, by a peculiar arrangement of columns and headings, presents the entire operation, of a day, a week, or a month, on a single page, or on two pages facing each other, in an account-book. The defendant uses a similar plan so far as results are concerned; but makes a different arrangement of the columns, and uses different headings. If the complainant's testator had the exclusive right to the use of the system explained in his book, it would be difficult to contend that the defendant does not infringe it, notwithstanding the difference in his form of arrangement; but if it be assumed that the system is open to public use, it seems to be equally difficult to contend that the books made and sold by the defendant are a violation of the copyright of the complainant's book considered merely as a book explanatory of the system. Where the truths of a science or the methods of an art are the common property of the whole world, any author has the right to express the one, or explain and use the other, in his own way. As an author, Selden explained the system in a particular way. It may be conceded that Baker makes and uses account-books arranged on substantially the same system; but the proof fails to show that he has violated the copyright of Selden's book, regarding the latter merely as an explanatory work; or that he has infringed Selden's right in any way, unless the latter became entitled to an exclusive right in the system.

The evidence of the complainant is principally directed to the object of showing that Baker uses the same system as that which is explained and illustrated in Selden's books. It becomes important, therefore, to determine whether, in obtaining the copyright of his books, he secured the exclusive right to the use of the system or method of book-keeping which the said books are intended to illustrate and explain. It is contended that he has secured such exclusive right, because no one can use the system without using substantially the same ruled lines and headings which he has appended to his books in illustration of it. In other words, it is contended that the ruled lines and headings, given to illustrate the system, are a part of the book, and, as such, are secured by the copyright; and that no one can make or use similar ruled lines and headings, or ruled lines and headings made and arranged on substantially the same system, without violating the copyright. And this is really the question to be decided in this case. Stated in another form, the question is, whether the exclusive property in a system of book-keeping can be claimed, under the law of copyright, by means of a book in which that system is explained? The complainant's bill, and the case made under it, are based on the hypothesis that it can be.

It cannot be pretended, and indeed it is not seriously urged, that the ruled lines of the complainant's account-book can be claimed under any special class of objects, other than books, named in the law of copyright existing in 1859. The law then in force was that of 1831, and specified only books, maps, charts, musical compositions, prints, and engravings. An account-book, consisting of ruled lines and blank columns, cannot be called by any of these names unless by that of a book.

There is no doubt that a work on the subject of book-keeping, though only explanatory of well-known systems, may be the subject of a copyright; but, then, it is claimed only as a book. Such a book may be explanatory either of old systems, or of an entirely new system; and, considered as a book, as the work of an author, conveying information on the subject of book-keeping, and containing detailed explanations of the art, it may be a very valuable acquisition to the practical knowledge of the community. But there is a clear distinction between the book, as such, and the art which it is intended to illustrate. The mere statement of the proposition is so evident, that it requires hardly any argument to support it. The same distinction may be predicated of every other art as well as that of book-keeping. A treatise on the composition and use of medicines, be they old or new; on the construction and use of ploughs, or watches, or churns; or on the mixture and application of colors for painting or dyeing; or on the mode of drawing lines to produce the effect of perspective,—would be the subject of copyright; but no one would contend that the copyright of the treatise would give the exclusive right to the art or manufacture described therein. The copyright of the book, if not pirated from other works, would be valid without regard to the novelty, or want of novelty, of its subject-matter. The novelty of the art or thing described or explained has nothing to do with the validity of the copyright. To give to the author of the book an exclusive property in the art described therein, when no examination of its novelty has ever been officially made, would be a surprise and a fraud upon the public. That is the province of letters-patent, not of copyright. The claim to an invention or discovery of an art or manufacture must be subjected to the examination of the Patent Office before an exclusive right therein can be obtained; and it can only be secured by a patent from the government.

The difference between the two things, letters-patent and copyright, may be illustrated by reference to the subjects just enumerated. Take the case of medicines. Certain mixtures are found to be of great value in the healing art. If the discoverer writes and publishes a book on the subject (as regular physicians generally do), he gains no exclusive right to the manufacture and sale of the medicine; he gives that to the public. If he desires to acquire such exclusive right, he must obtain a patent for the mixture as a new art, manufacture, or composition of matter. He may copyright his book, if he pleases; but that only secures to him the exclusive right of printing and publishing his book. So of all other inventions or discoveries.

The copyright of a book on perspective, no matter how many drawings and illustrations it may contain, gives no exclusive right to the modes of drawing described, though they may never have been known or used before. By publishing the book, without getting a patent for the art, the latter is given to the public. The fact that the art described in the book by illustrations of lines and figures, which are reproduced in practice in the application of the art, makes no difference. Those illustrations are the mere language employed by the author to convey his ideas more clearly. Had he used words of description instead of diagrams (which merely stand in the place of words), there could not be the slightest doubt that others, applying the art to practical use, might lawfully draw the lines and diagrams which were in the author's mind, and which he thus described by words in his book.

The copyright of a work on mathematical science cannot give to the author an exclusive right to the methods of operation which he propounds, or to the diagrams which he employs to explain them, so as to prevent an engineer from using them whenever occasion requires. The very object of publishing a book on science or the useful arts is to communicate to the world the useful knowledge which it contains. But this object would be frustrated if the knowledge could not be used without incurring the guilt of piracy of the book. And where the art it teaches cannot be used without employing the methods and diagrams used to illustrate the book, or such as are similar to them, such methods and diagrams are to be considered as necessary incidents to the art, and given therewith to the public; not given for the purpose of publication in other works explanatory of the art, but for the purpose of practical application.

Of course, these observations are not intended to apply to ornamental designs, or pictorial illustrations addressed to the taste. Of these it may be said, that their form is their essence, and their object, the production of pleasure in their contemplation. This is their final end. They are as much the product of genius and the result of composition, as are the lines of the poet or the historian's period. On the other hand, the teachings of science and the rules and methods of useful art have their final end in application and use; and this application and use are what the public derive from the publication of a book which teaches them. But as embodied and taught in a literary composition or book, their essence consists only in their statement. This alone is what is secured by the copyright. The use by another of the same methods of statement, whether in words or illustrations, in a book published for teaching the art, would undoubtedly be an infringement of the copyright.

Recurring to the case before us, we observe that Charles Selden, by his books, explained and described a peculiar system of book-keeping, and illustrated his method by means of ruled lines and blank columns, with proper headings on a page, or on successive pages. Now, whilst no one has a right to print or publish his book, or any material part thereof, as a book intended to convey instruction in the art, any person may practice and use the art itself which he has described and illustrated therein. The use of the art is a totally different thing from a publication of the book explaining it. The copyright of a book on book-keeping cannot secure the exclusive right to make, sell, and use account-books prepared upon the plan set forth in such book. Whether the art might or might not have been patented, is a question which is not before us. It was not patented, and is open and free to the use of the public. And, of course, in using the art, the ruled lines and headings of accounts must necessarily be used as incident to it.

The plausibility of the claim put forward by the complainant in this case arises from a confusion of ideas produced by the peculiar nature of the art described in the books which have been made the subject of copyright. In describing the art, the illustrations and diagrams employed happen to correspond more closely than usual with the actual work performed by the operator who uses the art. Those illustrations and diagrams consist of ruled lines and headings of accounts; and it is similar ruled lines and headings of accounts which, in the application of the art, the book-keeper makes with his pen, or the stationer with his press; whilst in most other cases the diagrams and illustrations can only be represented in concrete forms of wood, metal, stone, or some other physical embodiment. But the principle is the same in all. The description of the art in a book, though entitled to the benefit of copyright, lays no foundation for an exclusive claim to the art itself. The object of the one is explanation; the object of the other is use. The former may be secured by copyright. The latter can only be secured, if it can be secured at all, by letters-patent.

The remarks of Mr. Justice Thompson in the Circuit Court in *Clayton v. Stone & Hall* (2 Paine, 392), in which copyright was claimed in a daily price-current, are apposite and instructive. He says: "In determining the true construction to be given to the act of Congress, it is proper to look at the Constitution of the United States, to aid us in ascertaining the nature of the property intended to be protected. 'Congress shall have power to promote the progress of science and useful arts, by securing for limited times to authors and inventors the exclusive right to their writings and discoveries.' The act in question was passed in execution of the power here given, and the object, therefore, was the promotion of science; and it would certainly be a pretty extraordinary view of the sciences to consider a daily or weekly publication of the state of the market as falling within any class of them. They are of a more fixed, permanent, and durable character. The term 'science' cannot, with any propriety, by applied to a work of so fluctuating and fugitive a form as that of a newspaper or price-current, the subject-matter of which is daily changing, and is of mere temporary use. Although great praise may be due to the plaintiffs for their industry and enterprise in publishing this paper, yet the law does not contemplate their being rewarded in this way: it must seek patronage and protection from its utility to the public, and not a work of science. The title of the act of Congress is, 'for the encouragement of learning,' and was not intended for the encouragement of mere industry, unconnected with learning and the sciences. . . . We are, accordingly, of opinion that the paper in question is not a book the copyright to which can be secured under the act of Congress."

* * *

In *Drury v. Ewing* (1 Bond, 540), which is much relied on by the complainant, a copyright was claimed in a chart of patterns for cutting dresses and basques for ladies, and coats, jackets, & c., for boys. It is obvious that such designs could only be printed and published for information, and not for use in themselves. Their practical use could only be exemplified in cloth on the tailor's board and under his shears; in other words, by the application of a mechanical operation to the cutting of cloth in certain patterns and forms. Surely the exclusive right to this practical use was not reserved to the publisher by his copyright of the chart. Without undertaking to say whether we should or should not concur in the decision in that case, we think it cannot control the present.

The conclusion to which we have come is, that blank account-books are not the subject of copyright; and that the mere copyright of Selden's book did not confer upon him the exclusive right to make and use account-books, ruled and arranged as designated by him and described and illustrated in said book.

NOTES

1. *Baker v. Selden* suggests that copyright protects an author's original expression, but not the utilitarian ends to which that expression may be put. The patent system meanwhile does offer protection to inventive utility. As we will see, these fundamental differences between the two forms of protection give rise to doctrinal distinctions which have separated and divided the fields. Among the most important of these distinctions are differences in the degree to which copyright and patent rights presuppose "originality" or "novelty." In copyright law, originality may mean little more than that the would-be copyright proprietor has not copied the work from an earlier work; historically, no great amount of creativity has been required. *Alfred Bell & Co. v. Catalda Fine Arts*, 191 F.2d 99 (2d Cir. 1951). In patent law, on the other hand, protection for inventions has long required proof of both novelty and nonobviousness, as well as utility. *Graham v. John Deere Co.*, 383 U.S. 1 (1966).

The distinctions observed in *Baker v. Selden* reflect traditional constitutional thinking in American law, based on the Patent and Copyright Clause, U.S. Const. Art. I, § 8, cl. 8. They are quite widely observed, meanwhile, in other legal systems of the world, though typically without any equivalent "constitutional" significance.

2. Charles Selden actually appears to have understood these distinctions. In an introduction to his original work he offered the following observations:

> The author, though always desirous of promoting the public good, does not in this instance, disclaim a hope of pecuniary reward; to this end he has taken steps to secure his right to some personal compensation, for what he thinks, a valuable discovery. In addition to the copyright of this little book, he has applied for a patent right to cover the forms of the publication, and prevent their indiscriminate use by the public.

SELDEN'S CONDENSED LEDGER, OR BOOKKEEPING SIMPLIFIED (1859).[1]

TRADE-MARK CASES: UNITED STATES V. STEFFENS; UNITED STATES V. WITTEMANN; UNITED STATES V. JOHNSON

100 U.S. (10 Otto) 82 (1879).

MR. JUSTICE MILLER delivered the opinion of the court.

The three cases whose titles stand at the head of this opinion are criminal prosecutions for violations of what is known as the trade-mark legislation of Congress. The first two are indictments in the southern district of New York, and the last is an information in the southern district of Ohio. In all of them the judges of the circuit courts in which they are pending have certified to a difference of opinion on what is substantially the same question; namely, are the acts of Congress on the subject of trade-marks founded on any rightful authority in the Constitution of the United States?

The entire legislation of Congress in regard to trade-marks is of very recent origin. It is first seen in sects. 77 to 84, inclusive, of the act of July 8, 1870, entitled "An Act to revise, consolidate, and amend the statutes relating to patents and copyrights." 16 Stat. 198. The part of this act relating to trade-marks is embodied in chap. 2, tit. 60, sects. 4937 to 4947, of the Revised Statutes.

It is sufficient at present to say that they provide for the registration in the Patent Office of any device in the nature of a trade-mark to which

[1] First reprinted in MELVILLE B. NIMMER, COPYRIGHT AND OTHER ASPECTS OF LAWS PERTAINING TO LITERARY, MUSICAL, AND ARTISTIC WORKS ILLUSTRATED 97 (West Publishing Co. Second Edition 1977).

any person has by usage established an exclusive right, or which the person so registering intends to appropriate by that act to his exclusive use; and they make the wrongful use of a trade-mark, so registered, by any other person, without the owner's permission, a cause of action in a civil suit for damages. Six years later we have the act of Aug. 14, 1876 (19 Stat. 141), punishing by fine and imprisonment the fraudulent use, sale, and counterfeiting of trademarks registered in pursuance of the statutes of the United States, on which the informations and indictments are founded in the cases before us.

The right to adopt and use a symbol or a device to distinguish the goods or property made or sold by the person whose mark it is, to the exclusion of use by all other persons, has been long recognized by the common law and the chancery courts of England and of this country, and by the statutes of some of the States. It is a property right for the violation of which damages may be recovered in an action at law, and the continued violation of it will be enjoined by a court of equity, with compensation for past infringement. This exclusive right was not created by the act of Congress, and does not now depend upon it for its enforcement. The whole system of trademark property and the civil remedies for its protection existed long anterior to that act, and have remained in full force since its passage.

These propositions are so well understood as to require neither the citation of authorities nor an elaborate argument to prove them.

As the property in trademarks and the right to their exclusive use rest on the laws of the States, and, like the great body of the rights of person and of property, depend on them for security and protection, the power of Congress to legislate on the subject, to establish the conditions on which these rights shall be enjoyed and exercised, the period of their duration, and the legal remedies for their enforcement, if such power exist at all, must be found in the Constitution of the United States, which is the source of all powers that Congress can lawfully exercise.

In the argument of these cases this seems to be conceded, and the advocates for the validity of the acts of Congress on this subject point to two clauses of the Constitution, in one or in both of which, as they assert, sufficient warrant may be found for this legislation.

The first of these is the eighth clause of sect. 8 of the first article. That section, manifestly intended to be an enumeration of the powers expressly granted to Congress, and closing with the declaration of a rule for the ascertainment of such powers as are necessary by way of implication to carry into efficient operation those expressly given, authorizes Congress, by the clause referred to, "to promote the progress of science and useful arts, by securing for limited times, to authors and inventors, the exclusive right to their respective writings and discoveries."

As the first and only attempt by Congress to regulate the right of trade-marks is to be found in the act of July 8, 1870, to which we have referred, entitled "An Act to revise, consolidate, and amend the statutes relating to patents and copyrights," terms which have long since become technical, as referring, the one to inventions and the other to the writings of authors, it is a reasonable inference that this part of the statute also was, in the opinion of Congress, an exercise of the power found in that clause of the Constitution. It may also be safely assumed that until a critical examination of the subject in the courts became necessary, it was mainly if not wholly to this clause that the advocates of the law looked for its support.

Any attempt, however, to identify the essential characteristics of a trade-mark with inventions and discoveries in the arts and sciences, or with the writings of authors, will show that the effort is surrounded with insurmountable difficulties.

The ordinary trade-mark has no necessary relation to invention or discovery. The trade-mark recognized by the common law is generally the growth of a considerable period of use, rather than a sudden invention. It is often the result of accident rather than design, and when under the act of Congress it is sought to establish it by registration, neither originality, invention, discovery, science, nor art is in any way essential to the right conferred by that act. If we should endeavor to classify it under the head of writings of authors, the objections are equally strong. In this, as in regard to inventions, originality is required. And while the word writings may be liberally construed, as it has been, to include original designs for engravings, prints, & c., it is only such as are original, and are founded in the creative powers of the mind. The writings which are to be protected are the fruits of intellectual labor, embodied in the form of books, prints, engravings, and the like. The trade-mark may be, and generally is, the adoption of something already in existence as the distinctive symbol of the party using it. At common law the exclusive right to it grows out of its use, and not its mere adoption. By the act of Congress this exclusive right attaches upon registration. But in neither case does it depend upon novelty, invention, discovery, or any work of the brain. It requires no fancy or imagination, no genius, no laborious thought. It is simply founded on priority of appropriation. We look in vain in the statute for any other qualification or condition. If the symbol, however plain, simple, old, or well-known, has been first appropriated by the claimant as his distinctive trade-mark, he may by registration secure the right to its exclusive use. While such legislation may be a judicious aid to the common law on the subject of trade-marks, and may be within the competency of legislatures whose general powers embrace that class of subjects, we are unable to see any such power in the constitutional provision concerning authors and inventors, and their writings and discoveries.

The other clause of the Constitution supposed to confer the requisite authority on Congress is the third of the same section, which, read in connection with the granting clause, is as follows: "The Congress shall have power to regulate commerce with foreign nations, and among the several States, and with the Indian tribes."

The argument is that the use of a trademark—that which alone gives it any value—is to identify a particular class or quality of goods as the manufacture, produce, or property of the person who puts them in the general market for sale; that the sale of the article so distinguished is commerce; that the trade-mark is, therefore, a useful and valuable aid or instrument of commerce, and its regulation by virtue of the clause belongs to Congress, and that the act in question is a lawful exercise of this power.

Every species of property which is the subject of commerce, or which is used or even essential in commerce, is not brought by this clause within the control of Congress. The barrels and casks, the bottles and boxes in which alone certain articles of commerce are kept for safety and by which their contents are transferred from the seller to the buyer, do not thereby become subjects of congressional legislation more than other property. *Nathan v. Louisiana,* 8 How. 73. In *Paul v. Virginia* (8 Wall. 168), this court held that a policy of insurance made by a corporation of one State on property situated in another, was not an article of commerce, and did not come within the purview of the clause we are considering. "They are not," says the court, "commodities to be shipped or forwarded from one State to another, and then put up for sale." On the other hand, in *Almy v. State of California* (24 How. 169), it was held that a stamp duty imposed by the legislature of California on bills of lading for gold and silver transported from any place in that State to another out of the State, was forbidden by the Constitution of the United States, because such instruments being a necessity to the transaction of commerce, the duty was a tax upon exports.

The question, therefore, whether the trade-mark bears such a relation to commerce in general terms as to bring it within congressional control, when used or applied to the classes of commerce which fall within that control, is one which, in the present case, we propose to leave undecided. We adopt this course because when this court is called on in the course of the administration of the law to consider whether an act of Congress, or of any other department of the government, is within the constitutional authority of that department, a due respect for a co-ordinate branch of the government requires that we shall decide that it has transcended its powers only when that is so plain that we cannot avoid the duty.

In such cases it is manifestly the dictate of wisdom and judicial propriety to decide no more than is necessary to the case in hand. That such has been the uniform course of this court in regard to statutes passed by Congress will readily appear to any one who will consider the vast amount of argument presented to us assailing them as unconstitutional, and he will count, as he may do on his fingers, the instances in which this court has declared an act of Congress void for want of constitutional power.

Governed by this view of our duty, we proceed to remark that a glance at the commerce clause of the Constitution discloses at once what has been often the subject of comment in this court and out of it, that the power of regulation there conferred on Congress is limited to commerce with foreign nations, commerce among the States, and commerce with the Indian tribes. While bearing in mind the liberal construction, that commerce with foreign nations means commerce between citizens of the United States and citizens and subjects of foreign nations, and commerce among the States means commerce between the individual citizens of different States, there still remains a very large amount of commerce, perhaps the largest, which, being trade or traffic between citizens of the same State, is beyond the control of Congress.

When, therefore, Congress undertakes to enact a law, which can only be valid as a regulation of commerce, it is reasonable to expect to find on the face of the law, or from its essential nature, that it is a regulation of commerce with foreign nations, or among the several States, or with the Indian tribes. If not so limited, it is in excess of the power of Congress. If its main purpose be to establish a regulation applicable to all trade, to commerce at all points, especially if it be apparent that it is designed to govern the commerce wholly between citizens of the same State, it is obviously the exercise of a power not confided to Congress.

We find no recognition of this principle in the chapter on trade-marks in the Revised Statutes. We would naturally look for this in the description of the class of persons who are entitled to register a trade-mark, or in reference to the goods to which it should be applied. If, for instance, the statute described persons engaged in a commerce between the different States, and related to the use of trade-marks in such commerce, it would be evident that Congress believed it was acting under the clause of the Constitution which authorizes it to regulate commerce among the States. So if, when the trade-mark has been registered, Congress had protected its use on goods sold by a citizen of one State to another, or by a citizen of a foreign State to a citizen of the United States, it would be seen that Congress was at least intending to exercise the power of regulation conferred by that clause of the Constitution. But no such idea is found or suggested in this statute. Its language is: "Any person or firm domiciled in the United States, and any corporation created by the United States, or of any State or Territory thereof," or any person residing in a foreign country which by treaty or convention affords similar privileges to our citizens, may by registration obtain protection for his trade-mark. Here is no requirement that such person shall be engaged in the kind of commerce which Congress is authorized to regulate. It is a general declaration that anybody in the United States, and anybody in any other country which permits us to do the like, may, by registering a trade-mark, have it fully protected. So, while the person registering is required to "furnish a statement of the class of merchandise, and the particular description of the goods comprised in such class, by which the trade-mark has been or is intended to be appropriated," there is no hint that the goods are to be transported from one State to another, or between the United States and foreign countries. Sect. 4939 is intended to impose some restriction upon the Commissioner of Patents in the matter of registration, but no limitation is suggested in regard to persons or property engaged in the different classes of commerce mentioned in the Constitution. The remedies provided by the act when the right of the owner of the registered trade-mark is infringed, are not confined to the case of a trade-mark used in foreign or inter-state commerce.

It is therefore manifest that no such distinction is found in the act, but that its broad purpose was to establish a universal system of trade-mark registration, for the benefit of all who had already used a trade-mark, or who wished to adopt one in the future, without regard to the character of the trade to which it was to be applied or the residence of the owner, with the solitary exception that those who resided in foreign countries which extended no such privileges to us were excluded from them here.

* * *

In what we have here said we wish to be understood as leaving untouched the whole question of the treaty-making power over trade-marks, and of the duty of Congress to pass any laws necessary to carry treaties into effect.

* * *

NOTES

1. The Commerce Clause has assumed a leading role in the expansion of Congressional jurisdiction. The Lanham Trademark Act of 1946, 15 U.S.C. §§ 1051–1127, is founded upon this greatly expanded Commerce Clause power, as is the more recent Defend Trade Secrets Act of 2016, Pub. L. No. 114–153, 130 Stat. 376 (2016) (amending 18 U.S.C. § 1831 *et seq.*).

The Trade-Mark Cases were decided at a relatively early moment in the development of American trademark law when the chief function of a trademark was to distinguish goods from other similar goods in direct competition, thereby protecting the public from a likelihood of confusion, mistake or deception in the marketplace. Today, trademark doctrines (and their counterparts in the antecedent, broader and arguably less disciplined arena of unfair competition) extend considerably further, with additional or expanded direct protection for the trademark proprietor against appropriation or dilution of the particular significance in both marks and trade dress. These developments have introduced tensions into the law not present in 1879.

Some contemporary observers now argue that the Patent and Copyright (or "Intellectual Property") Clause (Article I, section 8, clause 8) must take on an expanded role to constrain unacceptable incursions into copyright or patent law, as well as unwise encroachments upon the public domain. *See, e.g.*, Davis, *Copying in the Shadow of the Constitution*, 80 MINN. L. REV. 595 (1996); Pollack, *Unconstitutional Incontestability? The Intersection of the Intellectual Property and Commerce Clause of the Constitution*, 18 PUGET SOUND L. REV. 259 (1995). Others suggest that Congress may now be free to act under the Commerce Clause, essentially without regard for the Patent and Copyright Clause. *See, e.g.*, Goldstein, *Copyright*, 55 LAW & CONTEMP. PROBS. 79 (1992).

Consider also the final paragraph of the Court's opinion above. Does Congress have power to effectuate international treaties affecting intellectual property that are inconsistent with the Patent and Copyright Clause? *See* David Nimmer, *The End of Copyright*, 48 VAND. L. REV. 1385, 1411–12 (1995). Does the treaty power generally authorize compacts with other nations that violate the Constitution? *See* Lange, Weaver & Reed, *Golan v. Holder: Copyright in the Image of the First Amendment*, 11 JOHN MARSHALL REV. OF INTELL. PROP. L. 83 (2011).

2. *The Trade-Mark Cases* continue to have considerable vitality as precedent. Justice O'Connor cited the opinion numerous times, for example, in her own seminal opinion in *Feist Publications v. Rural Telephone Service Co.*, 499 U.S. 340 (1991), in which the Court underscored the continuing importance of the originality requirement in copyright on constitutional as well as statutory grounds.

B. "PROPERTY": SIGNIFICANCE AND ALTERNATIVES

INTERNATIONAL NEWS SERVICE V. ASSOCIATED PRESS

248 U.S. 215, 39 S.Ct. 68 (1918).

MR. JUSTICE PITNEY delivered the opinion of the Court.

The parties are competitors in the gathering and distribution of news and its publication for profit in newspapers throughout the United States. The Associated Press, which was complainant in the District Court, is a co-operative organization, incorporated under the Membership Corporations Law of the state of New York, its members being individuals who are either proprietors or representatives of about 950 daily newspapers published in all parts of the United States. * * * Complainant gathers in all parts of the world, by means of various instrumentalities of its own, by exchange with its members, and by other appropriate means, news and intelligence of current and recent events of interest to newspaper readers and distributes it daily to its members for publication in their newspapers. The cost of the service, amounting approximately to $3,500,000 per annum, is assessed upon the members and becomes a part of their costs of operation, to be recouped, presumably with profit, through the publication of their several newspapers. Under complainant's by-laws each member agrees upon assuming membership that news received through complainant's service is received exclusively for publication in a particular newspaper, language, and place specified in the certificate of membership, that no other use of it shall be permitted, and that no member shall furnish or permit any one in his employ or connected with his newspaper to furnish any of complainant's news in advance of publication to any person not a member. And each member is required to gather the local news of his district and supply it to the Associated Press and to no one else.

Defendant is a corporation organized under the laws of the state of New Jersey, whose business is the gathering and selling of news to its customers and clients, consisting of newspapers published throughout the United States, under contracts by which they pay certain amounts at stated times for defendant's service. It has widespread news-gathering agencies; the cost of its operations amounts, it is said, to more than $2,000,000 per annum; and it serves about 400 newspapers located in the various cities of the United States and abroad, a few of which are represented, also, in the membership of the Associated Press.

The parties are in the keenest competition between themselves in the distribution of news throughout the United States; and so, as a rule, are the newspapers that they serve, in their several districts.

Complainant in its bill, defendant in its answer, have set forth in almost identical terms the rather obvious circumstances and conditions under which their business is conducted. The value of the service, and of the news furnished, depends upon the promptness of transmission, as well as upon the accuracy and impartiality of the news; it being essential that the news be transmitted to members or subscribers as early or earlier than similar information can be furnished to competing newspapers by other news services, and that the news furnished by each agency shall not be furnished to newspapers which do not contribute to the expense of gathering it. And further, to quote from the answer: "Prompt knowledge and publication of worldwide news is essential to the conduct of a modern newspaper, and by reason of the enormous expense incident to the gathering and distribution of such news, the only practical way in which a proprietor of a newspaper can obtain the same is, either through co-operation with a considerable number of other newspaper proprietors in the work of collecting and distributing such news, and the equitable division with them of the expenses thereof, or by the purchase of such news from some existing agency engaged in that business."

The bill was filed to restrain the pirating of complainant's news by defendant in three ways: First, by bribing employees of newspapers published by complainant's members to furnish Associated Press news to defendant before publication, for transmission by telegraph and telephone to defendant's clients for publication by them; second, by inducing Associated Press members to violate its by-laws and permit defendant to obtain news before publication; and, third, by copying news from bulletin boards and from early editions of complainant's newspapers and selling this, either bodily or after rewriting it, to defendant's customers.

* * *

The only matter that has been argued before us is whether defendant may lawfully be restrained from appropriating news taken from bulletins issued by complainant or any of its members, or from newspapers published by them, for the purpose of selling it to defendant's clients. Complainant asserts that defendant's admitted course of conduct in this regard both violates complainant's property right in the news and constitutes unfair competition in business. And notwithstanding the case has proceeded only to the stage of a preliminary injunction, we have deemed it proper to consider the underlying questions, since they go to the very merits of the action and are presented upon facts that are not in dispute. As presented in argument, these questions are: (1) whether there is any property in news; (2) whether, if there be property in news collected for the purpose of being published, it survives the instant of its publication in the first newspaper to which it is communicated by the news-gatherer; and (3) whether defendant's admitted course of conduct in appropriating for commercial use matter taken from bulletins or early editions of Associated Press publications constitutes unfair competition in trade.

The federal jurisdiction was invoked because of diversity of citizenship, not upon the ground that the suit arose under the copyright or other laws of the United States. Complainant's news matter is not copyrighted. It is said that it could not, in practice, be copyrighted, because of the large number of dispatches that are sent daily; and, according to complainant's contention, news is not within the operation of the copyright act. Defendant, while apparently conceding this, nevertheless invokes the analogies of the law of literary property and copyright, insisting as its principal contention that, assuming complainant has a right of property in its news, it can be maintained (unless the copyright act be complied with) only by being kept secret and confidential, and that upon the publication with complainant's consent of uncopyrighted news of any of complainant's members in a newspaper or upon a bulletin board, the right of property is lost, and the subsequent use of the news by the public or by defendant for any purpose whatever becomes lawful.

* * *

In considering the general question of property in news matter, it is necessary to recognize its dual character, distinguishing between the substance of the information and the particular form or collocation of words in which the writer has communicated it.

No doubt news articles often possess a literary quality, and are the subject of literary property at the common law; nor do we question that such an article, as a literary production, is the subject of copyright by the terms of the act as it now stands. In an early case at the circuit Mr. Justice Thompson held in effect that a newspaper was not within the protection of the copyright acts of 1790 (1 Stat. 124) and 1802 (2 Stat. 171). *Clayton v. Stone*, 2 Paine, 382, Fed. Cas. No. 2,872. But the present act is broader; it provides that the works for which copyright may be secured shall include "all the writings of an author," and specifically mentions "periodicals, including newspapers." Act of March 4, 1909, c. 320, §§ 4 and 5, 35 Stat. 1075, 1076 (Comp. St. 1916, §§ 9520, 9521). Evidently this admits to copyright a contribution to a newspaper, notwithstanding it also may convey news; and such is the practice of the copyright office, as the newspapers of the day bear witness. *See* Copyright Office Bulletin No. 15 (1917) pp. 7, 14, 16, 17.

But the news element—the information respecting current events contained in the literary production—is not the creation of the writer, but is a report of matters that ordinarily are publici juris; it is the history of the day. It is not to be supposed that the framers of the Constitution, when they empowered Congress "to promote the progress of science and useful arts, by securing for limited times to authors and inventors the exclusive right to their respective writings and discoveries" (Const. art. 1, § 8, par. 8), intended to confer upon one who might happen to be the first to report a historic event the exclusive right for any period to spread the knowledge of it.

We need spend no time, however, upon the general question of property in news matter at common law, or the application of the copyright act, since it seems to us the case must turn upon the question of unfair competition in business. And, in our opinion, this does not depend upon any general right of property analogous to the common-law right of the proprietor of an unpublished work to prevent its publication without his consent; nor is it foreclosed by showing that the benefits of the copyright act have been waived. We are dealing here not with restrictions upon publication but with the very facilities and processes of publication. The peculiar value of news is in the spreading of it while it is fresh; and it is evident that a valuable property interest in the news, as news, cannot be maintained by keeping it secret. Besides, except for matters improperly disclosed, or published in breach of trust or confidence, or in violation of law, none of which is involved in this branch of the case, the news of current events may be regarded as common property. What we are concerned with is the business of making it known to the world, in which both parties to the present suit are engaged. That business consists in maintaining a prompt, sure, steady, and reliable service designed to place the daily events of the world at the breakfast table of the millions at a price that, while of trifling moment to each reader, is sufficient in the aggregate to afford compensation for the cost of gathering and distributing it, with the added profit so necessary as an incentive to effective action in the commercial world. The service thus performed for newspaper readers is not only innocent but extremely useful in itself, and indubitably constitutes a legitimate business. The parties are competitors in this field; and, on fundamental principles, applicable here as elsewhere, when the rights or privileges of the one are liable to conflict with those of the other, each party is under a duty so to conduct its own business as not unnecessarily or unfairly to injure that of the other. *Hitchman Coal & Coke Co. v. Mitchell*, 245 U.S. 229, 254 (1917).

Obviously, the question of what is unfair competition in business must be determined with particular reference to the character and circumstances of the business. The question here is not so much the rights of either party as against the public but their rights as between themselves. *See Morison v. Moat*, 9 Hare, 241, 258. And, although we may and do assume that neither party has any remaining property interest as against the public in uncopyrighted news matter after the moment of its first publication, it by no means follows that there is no remaining property interest in it as between themselves. For, to both of them alike, news matter, however little susceptible of ownership or dominion in the absolute sense, is stock in trade, to be gathered at the cost of enterprise, organization, skill, labor, and money, and to be distributed and sold to those who will pay money for it, as for any other merchandise. Regarding the news, therefore, as but the material out of which both parties are seeking to make profits at the same time and in the same field, we hardly can fail to recognize that for this purpose, and as between them, it must be regarded as quasi property, irrespective of the rights of either as against the public.

* * *

The question, whether one who has gathered general information or news at pains and expense for the purpose of subsequent publication through the press has such an interest in its publication as may be protected from interference, has been raised many times, although never, perhaps, in the precise form in which it is now presented.

* * *

Not only do the acquisition and transmission of news require elaborate organization and a large expenditure of money, skill, and effort; not only has it an exchange value to the gatherer, dependent chiefly upon its novelty and freshness, the regularity of the service, its reputed reliability and thoroughness, and its adaptability to the public needs; but also, as is evident, the news has an exchange value to one who can misappropriate it.

The peculiar features of the case arise from the fact that, while novelty and freshness form so important an element in the success of the business, the very processes of distribution and publication necessarily occupy a good deal of time. Complainant's service, as well as defendant's, is a daily service to daily newspapers; most of the foreign news reaches this country at the Atlantic seaboard, principally at the city of New York, and because of this, and of time differentials due to the earth's rotation, the distribution of news matter throughout the country is principally from east to west; and, since in speed the telegraph and telephone easily outstrip the rotation of the earth, it is a simple matter for defendant to take complainant's news from bulletins or early editions of complainant's members in the eastern cities and at the mere cost of telegraphic transmission caused it to be published in western papers issued at least as early as those served by complainant. Besides this, and irrespective of time differentials, irregularities in telegraphic transmission on different lines, and the normal consumption of time in printing and distributing the newspaper, result in permitting pirated news to be placed in the hands of defendant's readers sometimes simultaneously with the service of competing Associated Press papers, occasionally even earlier.

Defendant insists that when, with the sanction and approval of complainant, and as the result of the use of its news for the very purpose for which it is distributed, a portion of complainant's members communicate it to the general public by posting it upon bulletin boards so that all may read, or by issuing it to newspapers and distributing it indiscriminately, complainant no longer has the right to control the use to be made of it; that when it thus reaches the light of day it becomes the common possession of all to whom it is accessible; and that any purchaser of a newspaper has the right to communicate the intelligence which it contains to anybody and for any purpose, even for the purpose of selling it for profit to newspapers published for profit in competition with complainant's members.

The fault in the reasoning lies in applying as a test the right of the complainant as against the public, instead of considering the rights of complainant and defendant, competitors in business, as between themselves. The right of the purchaser of a single newspaper to spread knowledge of its contents gratuitously, for any legitimate purpose not unreasonably interfering with complainant's right to make merchandise of it, may be admitted; but to transmit that news for commercial use, in competition with complainant—which is what defendant has done and seeks to justify—is a very different matter. In doing this defendant, by its very act, admits that it is taking material that has been acquired by complainant as the result of organization and the expenditure of labor, skill, and money, and which is salable by complainant for money, and that defendant in appropriating it and selling it as its own is endeavoring to reap where it has not sown, and by disposing of it to newspapers that are competitors of complainant's members is appropriating to itself the harvest of those who have sown. Stripped of all disguises, the process amounts to an unauthorized interference with the normal operation of complainant's legitimate business precisely at the point where the profit is to be reaped, in order to divert a material portion of the profit from those who have earned it to those who have not; with special advantage to defendant in the competition because of the fact that it is not burdened with any part of the expense of gathering the news. The transaction speaks for itself and a court of equity ought not to hesitate long in characterizing it as unfair competition in business.

The underlying principle is much the same as that which lies at the base of the equitable theory of consideration in the law of trusts—that he who has fairly paid the price should have the beneficial use of the property. Pom. Eq. Jur. § 981. It is no answer to say that complainant spends its money for that which is too fugitive or evanescent to be the subject of property. That might, and for the purposes of the discussion we are assuming that it would furnish an answer in a common-law controversy. But in a court of equity, where the question is one of unfair competition, if that which complainant has acquired fairly at substantial cost may be sold fairly at substantial profit, a competitor who is misappropriating it for the purpose of disposing of it to his own profit and to the disadvantage of complainant cannot be heard to say that it is too fugitive or evanescent to be regarded as property. It has all the attributes of property necessary for determining that a misappropriation of it by a competitor is unfair competition because contrary to good conscience.

The contention that the news is abandoned to the public for all purposes when published in the first newspaper is untenable. Abandonment is a question of intent, and the entire organization of the Associated Press negatives such a purpose. The cost of the service would be prohibitive if the reward were to be so limited. No single newspaper, no small group of newspapers, could sustain the expenditure. Indeed, it is one of the most obvious results of defendant's theory that, by permitting indiscriminate publication by anybody and everybody for purposes of profit in competition with the news-gatherer, it would render publication profitless, or so little profitable as in effect to cut off the service by rendering the cost prohibitive in comparison with the return. The practical needs and requirements of the business are reflected in complainant's by-laws which have been referred to. Their effect is that publication by each member must be deemed not by any means an abandonment of the news to the world for any and all purposes, but a publication for limited purposes; for the benefit of the readers of the bulletin or the newspaper as such; not for the purpose of making merchandise of it as news, with the result of depriving complainant's other members of their reasonable opportunity to obtain just returns for their expenditures.

It is to be observed that the view we adopt does not result in giving to complainant the right to monopolize either the gathering or the distribution of the news, or, without complying with the copyright act, to prevent the reproduction of its news articles, but only postpones participation by complainant's competitor in the processes of distribution and reproduction of news that it has not gathered, and only to the extent necessary to prevent that competitor from reaping the fruits of complainant's efforts and expenditure, to the partial exclusion of complainant, and in violation of the principle that underlies the maxim "sic utere tuo," etc.

It is said that the elements of unfair competition are lacking because there is no attempt by defendant to palm off its goods as those of the complainant, characteristic of the most familiar, if not the most typical, cases of unfair competition. *Howe Scale Co. v. Wyckoff, Seamans, etc.*, 198 U.S. 118, 140. But we cannot concede that the right to equitable relief is confined to that class of cases. In the present case the fraud upon complainant's rights is more direct and obvious. Regarding news matter as the mere material from which these two competing parties are endeavoring to make money, and treating it, therefore, as quasi property for the purposes of their business because they are both selling it as such, defendant's conduct differs from the ordinary case of unfair competition in trade principally in this that, instead of selling its own goods as those of complainant, it substitutes misappropriation in the place of misrepresentation, and sells complainant's goods as its own.

Besides the misappropriation, there are elements of imitation, of false pretense, in defendant's practices. The device of rewriting complainant's news articles, frequently resorted to, carries its own comment. The habitual failure to give credit to complainant for that which is taken is significant. Indeed, the entire system of appropriating complainant's news and transmitting it as a commercial product to defendant's clients and patrons amounts to a false representation to them and to their newspaper readers that the news transmitted is the result of defendant's own investigation in the field. But these elements, although accentuating the wrong, are not the essence of it. It is something more than the advantage of celebrity of which complainant is being deprived.

The doctrine of unclean hands is invoked as a bar to relief; it being insisted that defendant's practices against which complainant seeks an injunction are not different from the practice attributed to complainant, of utilizing defendant's news published by its subscribers. At this point it becomes necessary to consider a distinction that is drawn by complainant, and, as we understand it, was recognized by defendant also in the submission of proofs in the District Court, between two kinds of use that may be made by one news agency of news taken from the bulletins and newspapers of the other. The first is the bodily appropriation of a statement of fact or a news article, with or without rewriting, but without independent investigation or other expense. This form of pirating was found by both courts to have been pursued by defendant systematically with respect to complainant's news, and against it the Circuit Court of Appeals granted an injunction. This practice complainant denies having pursued and the denial was sustained by the finding of the District Court. It is not contended by defendant that the finding can be set aside, upon the proofs as they now stand. The other use is to take the news of a rival agency as a "tip" to be investigated, and if verified by independent investigation the news thus gathered is sold. This practice complainant admits that it has pursued and still is willing that defendant shall employ.

Both courts held that complainant could not be debarred on the ground of unclean hands upon the score of pirating defendant's news, because not shown to be guilty of sanctioning this practice.

* * *

In the case before us, in the present state of the pleadings and proofs, we need go no further than to hold, as we do, that the admitted pursuit by complainant of the practice of taking news items published by defendant's subscribers as tips to be investigated, and, if verified, the result of the investigation to be sold—the practice having been followed by defendant also, and by news agencies generally—is not shown to be such as to constitute an unconscientious or inequitable attitude towards its adversary so as to fix upon complainant the taint of unclean hands, and debar it on this ground from the relief to which it is otherwise entitled.

There is some criticism of the injunction that was directed by the District Court upon the going down of the mandate from the Circuit Court of Appeals. In brief, it restrains any taking or gainfully using of the complainant's news, either bodily or in substance from bulletins issued by the complainant or any of its members, or from editions of their newspapers, "*until its commercial value as news to the complainant and all of its members has passed away*." The part complained of is the clause we have italicized; but if this be indefinite, it is no more so than the criticism. Perhaps it would be better that the terms of the injunction be made specific, and so framed as to confine the restraint to an extent consistent with the reasonable protection of complainant's newspapers, each in its own area and for a specified time after its publication, against the competitive use of pirated news by defendant's customers. But the case presents practical difficulties; and we have not the materials, either in the way of a definite suggestion of amendment, or in the way of proofs, upon which to frame a specific injunction; hence, while not expressing approval of the form adopted by the District Court, we decline to modify it at this preliminary stage of the case, and will leave that court to deal with the matter upon appropriate application made to it for the purpose.

The decree of the Circuit Court of Appeals will be affirmed.

MR. JUSTICE HOLMES:

When an uncopyrighted combination of words is published there is no general right to forbid other people repeating them—in other words there is no property in the combination or in the thoughts or facts that the words express. Property, a creation of law, does not arise from value, although exchangeable—a matter of fact. Many exchangeable values may be destroyed intentionally without compensation. Property depends upon exclusion by law from interference, and a person is not excluded from using any combination of words merely because some one has used it before, even if it took labor and genius to make it. If a given person is to be prohibited from making the use of words that his neighbors are free to make some other ground must be found. One such ground is vaguely expressed in the phrase unfair trade. This means that the words are repeated by a competitor in business in such a way as to convey a misrepresentation that materially injures the person who first used them, by appropriating credit of some kind which the first user has earned. The ordinary case is a representation by device, appearance, or other indirection that the defendant's goods come from the plaintiff. But the only reason why it is actionable to make such a representation is that it tends to give the defendant an advantage in his competition with the plaintiff and that it is thought undesirable that an advantage should be gained in that way. Apart from that the defendant may use such unpatented devices and uncopyrighted combinations of words as he likes. The ordinary case, I say, is palming off the defendant's product as the plaintiff's but the same evil may follow from the opposite falsehood—from saying whether in words or by implication that the plaintiff's product is the defendant's, and that, it seems to me, is what has happened here.

Fresh news is got only by enterprise and expense. To produce such news as it is produced by the defendant represents by implication that it has been acquired by the defendant's enterprise and at its expense. When it comes from one of the great news collecting agencies like the Associated Press, the source generally is indicated, plainly importing that credit; and that such a representation is implied may be inferred with some confidence from the unwillingness of the defendant to give the credit and tell the truth. If the plaintiff produces the news at the same time that the defendant does, the defendant's presentation impliedly denies to the plaintiff the credit of collecting the facts and assumes that credit to the defendant. If the plaintiff is later in Western cities it naturally will be supposed to have obtained its information from the defendant. The falsehood is a little more subtle, the injury a little more indirect, than in ordinary cases of unfair trade, but I think that the principle that condemns the one condemns the other. It is a question of how strong an infusion of fraud is necessary to turn a flavor into a poison. The dose seems to me strong enough here to need a remedy from the law. But as, in my view, the only ground of complaint that can be recognized without legislation is the implied misstatement, it can be corrected by stating the truth; and a suitable acknowledgment of the source is all that the plaintiff can require. I think that within the limits recognized by the decision of the Court the defendant should be enjoined from publishing news obtained from the Associated Press for [blank] hours after publication by the plaintiff unless it gives express credit to the Associated Press; the number of hours and the form of acknowledgment to be settled by the District Court.

MR. JUSTICE MCKENNA concurs in this opinion.

MR. JUSTICE BRANDEIS, dissenting.

There are published in the United States about 2,500 daily papers. More than 800 of them are supplied with domestic and foreign news of general interest by the Associated Press—a corporation without capital stock which does not sell news or earn or seek to earn profits, but serves merely as an instrumentality by means of which these papers supply themselves at joint expense with such news. Papers not members of the Associated Press depend for their news of general interest largely upon agencies organized for profit. Among these agencies is the International News Service which supplies news to about 400 subscribing papers. It has, like the Associated Press, bureaus and correspondents in this and foreign countries; and its annual expenditures in gathering and distributing news is about $2,000,000. Ever since its organization in 1909, it has included among the sources from which it gathers news, copies (purchased in the open market) of early editions of some papers published by members of the Associated Press and the bulletins publicly posted by them. These items, which constitute but a small part of the news transmitted to its subscribers, are generally verified by the International News Service before transmission; but frequently items are transmitted without verification; and occasionally even without being re-written. In no case is the fact disclosed that such item was suggested by or taken from a paper or bulletin published by an Associated Press member.

No question of statutory copyright is involved. The sole question for our consideration is this: Was the International News Service properly enjoined from using, or causing to be used gainfully, news of which it acquired knowledge by lawful means (namely, by reading publicly posted bulletins or papers purchased by it in the open market) merely because the news had been originally gathered by the Associated Press and continued to be of value to some of its members, or because it did not reveal the source from which it was acquired?

The "ticker" cases, the cases concerning literary and artistic compositions, and cases of unfair competition were relied upon in support of the injunction. But it is admitted that none of those cases affords a complete analogy with that before us. The question presented for decision is new, and it is important.

News is a report of recent occurrences. The business of the news agency is to gather systematically knowledge of such occurrences of interest and to distribute reports thereof. The Associated Press contended that knowledge so acquired is property, because it costs money and labor to produce and because it has value for which those who have it not are ready to pay; that it remains property and is entitled to protection as long as it has commercial value as news; and that to protect it effectively, the defendant must be enjoined from making, or causing to be made, any gainful use of it while it retains such value. An essential element of individual property is the legal right to exclude others from enjoying it. If the property is private, the right of exclusion may be absolute; if the property is affected with a public interest, the right of exclusion is qualified. But the fact that a product of the mind has cost its producer money and labor, and has a value for which others are willing to pay, is not sufficient to ensure to it this legal attribute of property. The general rule of law is, that the noblest of human productions—knowledge, truths ascertained, conceptions, and ideas—become, after voluntary communication to others, free as the air to common use. Upon these incorporeal productions the attribute of property is continued after such communication only in certain classes of cases where public policy has seemed to demand it. These exceptions are confined to productions which, in some degree, involve creation, invention, or discovery. But by no means all such are endowed with this attribute of property. The creations which are recognized as property by the common law are literary, dramatic, musical, and other artistic creations; and these have also protection under the copyright statutes. The inventions and discoveries upon which this attribute of property is conferred only by statute, are the few comprised within the patent law. There are also many other cases in which courts interfere to prevent curtailment of plaintiff's enjoyment of incorporeal productions; and in which the right to relief is often called a property right, but is such only in a special sense. In those cases, the plaintiff has no absolute right to the protection of his production; he has merely the qualified right to be protected as against the defendant's acts, because of the special relation in which the latter stands or the wrongful method or means employed in acquiring the knowledge or the manner in which it is used. Protection of this character is afforded where the suit is based upon breach of contract or of trust or upon unfair competition.

The knowledge for which protection is sought in the case at bar is not of a kind upon which the law has heretofore conferred the attributes of property; nor is the manner of its acquisition or use nor the purpose to which it is applied, such as has heretofore been recognized as entitling a plaintiff to relief.

* * *

The rule for which the plaintiff contends would effect an important extension of property rights and a corresponding curtailment of the free use of knowledge and of ideas; and the facts of this case admonish us of the danger involved in recognizing such a property right in news, without imposing upon news-gatherers corresponding obligations. A large majority of the newspapers and perhaps half the newspaper readers of the United States are dependent for their news of general interest upon agencies other than the Associated Press. The channel through which about 400 of these papers received, as the plaintiff alleges, "a large amount of news relating to the European war of the greatest importance and of intense interest to the newspaper reading public" was suddenly closed. The closing to the International News Service of these channels for foreign news (if they were closed) was due not to unwillingness on its part to pay the cost of collecting the news, but to the prohibitions imposed by foreign governments upon its securing news from their respective countries and from using cable or telegraph lines running therefrom. For aught that appears, this prohibition may have been wholly undeserved; and at all events the 400 papers and their readers may be assumed to have been innocent. For aught that appears, the International News Service may have sought then to secure temporarily by arrangement with the Associated Press the latter's foreign news service. For aught that appears, all of the 400 subscribers of the International News Service would gladly have then become members of the Associated Press, if they could have secured election thereto. It is possible, also, that a large part of the readers of these papers were so situated that they could not secure prompt access to papers served by the Associated Press. The prohibition of the foreign governments might as well have been extended to the channels through which news was supplied to the more than a thousand other daily papers in the United States not served by the Associated Press; and a large part of their readers may also be so located that they cannot procure prompt access to papers served by the Associated Press.

A Legislature, urged to enact a law by which one news agency or newspaper may prevent appropriation of the fruits of its labors by another, would consider such facts and possibilities and others which appropriate inquiry might disclose. Legislators might conclude that it was impossible to put an end to the obvious injustice involved in such appropriation of news, without opening the door to other evils, greater than that sought to be remedied. Such appears to have been the opinion of our Senate which reported unfavorably a bill to give news a few hours' protection; and which ratified, on February 15, 1911, the convention adopted at the Fourth International American Conference; and such was evidently the view also of the signatories to the International Copyright Union of November 13, 1908, as both these conventions expressly exclude news from copyright protection.

Or legislators dealing with the subject might conclude, that the right to news values should be protected to the extent of permitting recovery of damages for any unauthorized use, but that protection by injunction should be denied, just as courts of equity ordinarily refuse (perhaps in the interest of free speech) to restrain actionable libels, and for other reasons decline to protect by injunction mere political rights; and as Congress has prohibited courts from enjoining the illegal assessment or collection of federal taxes. If a Legislature concluded to recognize property in published news to the extent of permitting recovery at law, it might, with a view to making the remedy more certain and adequate, provide a fixed measure of damages, as in the case of copyright infringement.

Or again, a Legislature might conclude that it was unwise to recognize even so limited a property right in published news as that above indicated; but that a news agency should, on some conditions, be given full protection of its business; and to that end a remedy by injunction as well as one for damages should be granted, where news collected by it is gainfully used without permission. If a Legislature concluded (as at least one court has held, *New York and Chicago Grain and Stock Exchange v. Board of Trade*, 127 Ill. 153, 19 N. E. 855) that under certain circumstances news-gathering is a business affected with a public interest, it might declare that, in such cases, news should be protected against appropriation, only if the gatherer assumed the obligation of supplying it, at reasonable rates and without discrimination, to all papers which applied therefor. If legislators reached that conclusion, they would probably go further, and prescribe the conditions under which and the extent to which the protection should be afforded; and they might also provide the administrative machinery necessary for insuring to the public, the press, and the news agencies, full enjoyment of the rights so conferred.

Courts are ill-equipped to make the investigations which should precede a determination of the limitations which should be set upon any property right in news or of the circumstances under which news gathered by a private agency should be deemed affected with a public interest. Courts would be powerless to prescribe the detailed regulations essential to full enjoyment of the rights conferred or to introduce the machinery required for enforcement of such regulations. Considerations such as these should lead us to decline to establish a new rule of law in the effort to redress a newly disclosed wrong, although the propriety of some remedy appears to be clear.

NOTES

1. The *INS* case has a checkered reputation. Scholars, judges and practitioners alike tend to be suspicious of its uncertain doctrinal underpinnings and concomitant susceptibility to metastasis, as well as its pre-*Erie* origins, and its potential for conflict with the Patent and Copyright Clause or federal doctrinal law. Yet the case is far from dead. The ALI's RESTATEMENT (THIRD) OF UNFAIR COMPETITION, for example, acknowledges its dubious provenance, but also appears to identify three areas of doctrinal law grounded in a theory of misappropriation that is hard to distinguish from the underlying theory recognized in the *INS* case. (These areas include the right of publicity, trade secrets, and common law copyright.) For an extended discussion of this subject, see LANGE AND POWELL, NO LAW: INTELLECTUAL PROPERTY IN THE IMAGE OF AN ABSOLUTE FIRST AMENDMENT 8–24; 149–67 (Stanford University Press 2009).

2. The Second Circuit is said to have cast doubt on the continued viability of the so-called "hot news doctrine" in *Barclays Capital Inc. v. Theflyonthewall.com, Inc.*, 650 F.3d 876 (2d Cir. 2011), a case in which the defendant was engaged in the unauthorized appropriation and dissemination, via the internet, of financial research gathered at considerable expense by the plaintiff banks. The Second Circuit panel held the misappropriation claim to have been preempted by federal copyright. On that ground alone the case can be distinguished from *INS*. But consider whether *INS* itself actually established a "hot news doctrine." Is it not better to see *INS* as a case grounded in a broader concern for "free riding"? And if so, then consider whether (despite the outcome in *Barclays Bank*, in which free riding was explicitly addressed) that concern is ever likely to be entirely subsumed by specific doctrinal limitations and defenses? What recurring tenet in intellectual property law would have to change in order to obviate *INS*'s concern for free riding altogether?

C. INTELLECTUAL PROPERTY AND THE FIRST AMENDMENT

Few topics in the study of intellectual property are as important, or as aggressively disputed, as the relationship between the conventional intellectual property doctrines and the First Amendment. The First Amendment provides (in relevant part) that "Congress shall make no law abridging freedom of speech or of the press. . . . " Although in theory any doctrinal proposition curtailing freedom of expression can justify examination in light of the Amendment, it is copyright—in which authorized expression is always advanced at the expense of disfavored expression under a regime established by Congress—that comes into question most often.

In *Eldred v. Ashcroft*, 537 U.S. 186 (2003), the Supreme Court said that copyright is not "categorically immune" to First Amendment review, as had been suggested erroneously in the Court of Appeals opinion, *Eldred v. Ashcroft*, 255 F.3d 849 (D.C. Cir. 2001), but it still held that the First Amendment was not violated by the term extension at issue in the case. Under *Eldred*, so long as copyright's "traditional contours" remain in place (including the "idea-expression dichotomy" and the "fair use" doctrine), copyright need not be subjected to "heightened scrutiny" under the Amendment. The Court's most recent decision in this context is *Golan v. Holder*, 565 U.S. 302 (2012). The Tenth Circuit had entertained argument addressed to the question whether withdrawing millions of foreign works from the public domain in response to the requirements of the Berne Convention violated the First Amendment. *See Golan v. Holder*, 609 F.3d 1076 (10th Cir. 2010). The works had fallen into the public domain for failure to comply with American copyright formalities prior to American adherence to the Convention, which forbids such formalities. Though willing to consider the question, the Tenth Circuit had upheld the relevant enabling provisions in American law. It held that restoring foreign works to United States copyright protection after they had been in the public domain was a departure from copyright's traditional contours. Applying heightened scrutiny, however, the court found that the legislation enabling restoration was, on balance, a defensible exercise of Congressional discretion. Writing for the majority of the Supreme Court, Justice Ginsburg affirmed the Tenth Circuit's opinion on the First Amendment issue. Justices Breyer and Alito dissented in the case. We include an excerpt from the *Golan* opinion among the materials in our coverage of copyright later in this book.

Professor David Lange comments at length on the future of freedom of expression after *Golan* in a Podcast recorded by the Suffolk Law School, posted on March 1, 2012, and available at the following link. http://legal talknetwork.com/podcasts/suffolk-law/2012/03/david-lange-golan-again/.

NOTES

1. The relationship between copyright and the First Amendment has been the subject of numerous essays. For three classic early treatments, see Robert C. Denicola, *Copyright and Free Speech: Constitutional Limitations on the Protection of Expression*, 67 CALIF.L.REV. 283 (1979); Paul Goldstein, *Copyright and the First Amendment*, 70 COLUM.L.REV. 983 (1970); and Melville B. Nimmer, *Does Copyright Abridge the First Amendment Guarantees to Freedom of Speech and Press?*, 12 UCLA L.REV. 1180 (1970). For still more recent treatments of the subject, see Jed Rubenfeld, *The Freedom Of Imagination: Copyright's Constitutionality*, 112 YALE L.J. 1 (2002), and Yochai

Benkler, *Free As The Air To Common Use: First Amendment Constraints On The Enclosure Of The Public Domain*, 74 N.Y.U. L. REV. 354 (1999). See especially NEIL WEINSTOCK NETANEL, COPYRIGHT'S PARADOX (Oxford Press 2010).

2. The language of the First Amendment suggests that freedom of expression is absolute. Justice Black famously thought that "no law means no law"—though there appears to have been no occasion when he actually said as much in the context of copyright or intellectual property. Should this freedom nevertheless be "balanced" against other interests reflected in intellectual property laws made by Congress? Conventional wisdom (driven in large part by well-established constitutional perspectives attributable to Justice Holmes) so holds.

For book-length treatment of this question, in which the authors advocate an absolute primacy for the Amendment vis-à-vis intellectual property, see DAVID LANGE & H. JEFFERSON POWELL, NO LAW: INTELLECTUAL PROPERTY IN THE IMAGE OF AN ABSOLUTE FIRST AMENDMENT (Stanford University Press 2009). The authors propose "that the First Amendment be read absolutely, in keeping with its first and most obvious meaning: *that Congress shall make no law abridging freedom of speech or of the press by conferring monopolies in expression that otherwise would belong to the universe of discourses in which all are free to share and share alike.* In at least this sense, "no law" should mean *no law.*" *Id.* at 305 (emphasis in original). Lange and Powell endorse a proposal (originally advanced by Jed Rubenfeld in *Freedom of Imagination, supra*) that net revenues resulting from appropriations of expression for commercial purposes can be made the subject of apportioned payments to original creators, according to the value of the appropriated work in the production of the revenues. They argue accordingly that recognizing First Amendment primacy need not mean the end of intellectual property protections:

> The first thing to be said is that they retain (or can retain) their shape to a remarkable degree. The subject matter of the doctrines, the reasons for recognizing them, the disposition of the underlying interests, the incentives and rewards, the acknowledgement of creativity itself—all of these and more remain essentially the same. . . . What will change most dramatically is the single thing that makes intellectual property obviously objectionable under the Constitution at present. Congress will simply have no power to create or recognize monopolies in expression that otherwise would press itself upon the public consciousness at large, and this is so whether the monopolies are justified under the patent and copyright clause, the commerce clause, the treaty power or otherwise.

Id. at 306.

PART 2

TRADEMARK AND UNFAIR COMPETITION LAW

■ ■ ■

CHAPTER 2

THE NATURE AND FUNCTION OF TRADEMARKS

■ ■ ■

A. INTRODUCTION

One broad area of intellectual property involves the protection of distinctive marks: words, names, phrases, slogans, logos, symbols, sounds, shapes, colors, smells, and other indicia of commercial identity. "Distinctiveness" is a sine qua non of trademarks: its purpose is to distinguish the origins of goods and services from others of a similar sort in the marketplace. The classic claim of infringement alleges a likelihood of confusion posed by a second-comer who is using a similar or identical mark, on similar or identical goods or services, in a similar or identical setting in the marketplace. It is sometimes said that the purpose of a trademark is to provide a repository for a merchant's good will. Trademark law protects trademark owners from the economic harm to that good will which would arise from diversion of trade or damage to reputation. It also protects consumers from being misled or confused by false indications of the origin or goods or services.

Under a well-functioning scheme of trademark law, it should not be permissible for an imitator to sell a carbonated beverage using the "Coca-Cola" brand name or to market an automobile under the name "Mercedes-Benz." The firms that manufacture those products have spent considerable resources to develop a high-quality product, which is what consumers have now come to expect when they purchase a soft drink or a car bearing those brand names. The firms have also invested considerable resources in marketing their products and increasing their brand recognition. Indeed, they have been so successful that "Coca-Cola" and "Mercedes-Benz" are now more than merely distinctive: they are marks whose fame is widely recognized around the world. Most of us probably would agree that they deserve some measure of protection. The study of trademark law is an exercise in discerning what "measure" is warranted. When and how should protection for a mark begin? In whom should the right reside? How should we understand infringement? What are the limits of a mark proprietor's rights, whether on a property theory or otherwise? What are the offsetting rights of others, whether competitors, consumers, or the public at large?

Trademark law traces its origins to medieval times, when skilled artisans and craftsmen formed guilds and applied symbols to their products to signify the identity of their makers. The common law generally provided protection for trademarks through actions for deceit. Courts of equity, in contrast, generally protected trademarks based on the likelihood of confusion, regardless of whether the infringer intended to deceive.

Under state laws, trademark owners today can assert traditional trademark infringement claims as well as additional claims grounded in varying theories of unfair competition, including deceit, passing off, or misappropriation, depending upon the jurisdiction and the nature of the violation.

In addition to these claims under state law, there is now an extensive scheme of federal statutes governing trademarks and unfair competition. These statutes are available in settings involving interstate and foreign commerce. Congress enacted the first trademark statute in 1870, but the law was overturned by the Supreme Court on the ground that it exceeded Congress' constitutional powers. *The Trade-Mark Cases*, 100 U.S. (10 Otto) 82 (1879). This case is reproduced in Chapter 1, *supra*. Congress soon enacted new trademark legislation, but expressly based its authority on the Commerce Clause: U.S. CONST. ART. I, § 8, cl. 3. The current version of federal trademark law was enacted in the Lanham Act of 1946, 15 U.S.C. §§ 1051–1127. The Lanham Act has been amended a number of times since then. The Lanham Act provides a scheme of federal trademark registration, with attendant benefits. However, it also protects unregistered marks against unfair competition.

Many states today have statutes recognizing an even broader claim for trademark "dilution." Dilution claims do not require the showing of consumer confusion traditionally expected in trademark infringement cases. In 1995, Congress enacted legislation providing for a federal claim for dilution of widely recognized trademarks; the Act was clarified by amendments in 2006.

Together, these numerous theories of state and federal trademark infringement, unfair competition, and dilution offer substantial overlapping protection. Often, several claims can be asserted on one set of facts. Parties seeking to protect their investment in fair competition thus have a variety of options available in terms of registration and enforcement of their rights.

But of course these claims of right are sometimes a matter of perspective. Among the chief aims of the law of trademarks and unfair competition is the goal of maintaining a balance among competitors, in the interest not only of fair competition, but also the public. The cases often raise difficult questions as to where that balance ought to be struck.

This chapter examines fundamental concepts that apply to *all* trademarks and service marks, regardless of whether they are federally registered at the United States Patent and Trademark Office (PTO). Marks that are not federally registered can be protected by several sources of law: common law, state statutes, and section 43(a) of the Lanham Act. The specific requirements for federal registration are discussed in Chapter 3.

WILLIAM R. WARNER & CO. V. ELI LILLY & CO.

265 U.S. 526, 44 S.Ct. 615 (1924).

MR. JUSTICE SUTHERLAND delivered the opinion of the court:

Respondent is a corporation engaged in the manufacture and sale of pharmaceutical and chemical products. In 1899 it began and has ever since continued to make and sell a liquid preparation of quinine, in combination with other substances, including yerba-santa and chocolate, under the name of Coco-Quinine.

Petitioner also is a pharmaceutical and chemical manufacturer. The Pfeiffer Chemical Company, Searle & Hereth Company, and petitioner are under the same ownership and control. The first-named company, in 1906, began the manufacture of a liquid preparation which is substantially the same as respondent's preparation, and which was put upon the market under the name of Quin-Coco. Two years later the Searle & Hereth Company engaged in the manufacture of the preparation, which ever since has been sold and distributed by petitioner.

This suit was brought in the Federal district court for the eastern district of Pennsylvania by respondent, to enjoin petitioner from continuing to manufacture and sell the preparation if flavored or colored with chocolate; and also from using the name "Quin-Coco," on the ground that it was an infringement of the name "Coco-Quinine," to the use of which respondent had acquired an exclusive right. The district court decided against respondent upon both grounds. On appeal the court of appeals ruled with the district court upon the issue of infringement, but reversed the decree upon that of unfair competition. * * *

First. We agree with the courts below that the charge of [trademark] infringement was not sustained. The name "Coco-Quinine" is descriptive of the ingredients which enter into the preparation. The same is equally true of the name "Quin-Coco." A name which is merely descriptive of the ingredients, qualities, or characteristics of an article of trade cannot be appropriated as a trademark and the exclusive use of it afforded legal protection. The use of a similar name by another to truthfully describe his own product does not constitute a legal or moral wrong, even if its effect be to cause the public to mistake the origin or ownership of the product.

Second. The issue of unfair competition, on which the courts below differed, presents a question of more difficulty. The testimony is voluminous, more than two hundred witnesses having been examined; but, since the question with which we are now dealing is primarily one of fact, we have found it necessary to examine and consider it. Nothing is to be gained by reviewing the evidence at length, and we shall do no more than summarize the facts upon which we have reached our conclusions.

The use of chocolate as an ingredient has a threefold effect: It imparts to the preparation a distinctive color and a distinctive flavor, and, to some extent, operates as a medium to suspend the quinine and prevent its precipitation. It has no therapeutic value, but it supplies the mixture with a quality of palatability for which there is no equally satisfactory substitute. Respondent, by laboratory experiments, first developed the idea of the addition of chocolate to the preparation for the purpose of giving it a characteristic color and an agreeable flavor. There was at the time no liquid preparation of quinine on the market containing chocolate, though there is evidence that it was sometimes so made up by druggists when called for. There is some evidence that petitioner endeavored by experiments to produce a preparation of the exact color and taste of that produced by respondent; and there is evidence in contradiction. We do not, however, regard it as important to determine upon which side lies the greater weight. Petitioner, in fact, did produce a preparation by the use of chocolate so exactly like that of respondent that they were incapable of being distinguished by ordinary sight or taste. By various trade methods an extensive and valuable market for the sale of respondent's preparation already had been established when the preparation of petitioner was put on the market. It is apparent, from a consideration of the testimony, that efforts of petitioner to create a market for Quin-Coco were directed not so much to showing the merits of that preparation as they were to demonstrating its practical identity with Coco-Quinine; and, since it was sold at a lower price, inducing the purchasing druggist, in his own interest, to substitute, as far as he could, the former for the latter. In other words, petitioner sought to avail itself of the favorable repute which had been established for respondent's preparation in order to sell its own. Petitioner's salesmen appeared more anxious to convince the druggists with whom they were dealing that Quin-Coco was a good substitute for Coco-Quinine and was cheaper, than they were to independently demonstrate its merits. The evidence establishes by a fair preponderance that some of petitioner's salesmen suggested that, without danger of detection, prescriptions and orders for Coco-Quinine could be filled by substituting Quin-Coco. More often, however, the feasibility of such a course was brought to the mind of the druggist by pointing out the identity of the two preparations and the enhanced profit to be made by selling Quin-Coco because of its lower price. There is much conflict in the testimony; but, on the whole, it fairly appears that petitioner's agents induced the substitution, either in direct terms or by suggestion or insinuation. Sales to druggists are in original bottles, bearing clearly distinguishing labels, and there is no suggestion of deception in those transactions; but sales to the ultimate purchasers are of the product in its naked form out of the bottle; and the testimony discloses many instances of passing off by retail druggists of petitioner's preparation when respondent's preparation was called for. That no deception was practiced on the retail dealers, and that they knew exactly what they were getting, is of no consequence. The wrong was in designedly enabling the dealers to palm off the preparation as that of the respondent. One who induces another to commit a fraud, and furnishes the means of consummating it, is equally guilty and liable for the injury.

The charge of unfair competition being established, it follows that equity will afford relief by injunction to prevent such unfair competition for the future. Several acts of unfair competition having been shown, we are warranted in concluding that petitioner is willing to continue that course of conduct unless restrained. It remains to consider the character and extent of this relief.

Respondent has no exclusive right to the use of its formula. Chocolate is used as an ingredient not alone for the purpose of imparting a distinctive color, but for the purpose, also, of making the preparation peculiarly agreeable to the palate, to say nothing of its effect as a suspending medium. While it is not a medicinal element in the preparation, it serves a substantial and desirable use, which prevents it from being a mere matter of dress. It does not merely serve the incidental use of identifying the respondent's preparation, and it is doubtful whether it should be called a nonessential. The petitioner or anyone else is at liberty, under the law, to manufacture and market an exactly similar preparation containing chocolate, and to notify the public that it is being done. But the imitator of another's goods must sell them as his own production. He cannot lawfully palm them off on the public as the goods of his competitor. The manufacturer or vendor is entitled to the reputation which his goods have acquired, and the public to the means of distinguishing between them and other goods; and protection is accorded against unfair dealing, whether there be a technical trademark or not. The wrong is in the sale of the goods of one manufacture or vendor as those of another. If petitioner had been content to manufacture the preparation and let it make its own way in the field of open and fair competition, there would be nothing more to be said. It was not thus content, however, but availed itself of unfair means, either expressly or tacitly, to impose its preparation on the ultimate purchaser as and for the product of respondent.

Nevertheless, the right to which respondent is entitled is that of being protected against unfair competition, not of having the aid of a decree to create or support, or assist in creating or supporting, a monopoly of the sale of a preparation which everyone, including petitioner, is free to make and vend. The legal wrong does not consist in the mere use of chocolate as an ingredient, but in the unfair and fraudulent advantage which is taken of such use to pass off the product as that of respondent. The use dissociated from the fraud is entirely lawful, and it is against the petitioner, which has shown by its conduct that it is not to be trusted. Clearly, the relief should extend far enough to enjoin petitioner and its various agents from, directly or indirectly, representing or suggesting to its customers the feasibility or possibility of passing off Quin-Coco for Coco-Quinine. The court of appeals held that petitioner should be unconditionally enjoined from the use of chocolate. We think this goes too far; but, having regard to the past conduct of petitioner, the practices of some druggists to which it has led, and the right of respondent to an effective remedy, we think the decree fairly may require that the original packages sold to druggists shall not only bear labels clearly distinguishing petitioner's bottled product from the bottled product of respondent, but that the preparation is not to be sold or dispensed as Coco-Quinine, or to be used for the latter. With these general suggestions, the details and form of the injunction can be more satisfactorily determined by the district court. The decree of the Court of Appeals is reversed and the cause remanded to the District Court for further proceedings in conformity with this opinion.

NOTES

1. Why did the Court endorse such limited relief in this case? Are there other legal doctrines that might allow the respondent to prevent competitors from using a specific ingredient in their quinine preparations?

2. An action for passing off (or "palming off"), the common law precursor to trademark law, has been defined as follows:

> One is subject to liability to another . . . if, in connection with the marketing of goods or services, the actor makes a representation likely to deceive or mislead prospective purchasers by causing the mistaken belief that the actor's business is the business of the other, or that the actor is the agent, affiliate, or associate of the other, or that the goods or services that the actor markets are produced, sponsored, or approved by the other.

RESTATEMENT (THIRD) OF UNFAIR COMPETITION § 4 (1995). Who engaged in passing off in this case—the petitioner, or the pharmacists to whom the petitioner sold its product? Why did the Court hold the petitioner responsible?

3. Are the rationales for protecting trademarks furthered by the decision in this case? How were consumers potentially harmed by the petitioner's conduct in this case? How was the respondent harmed?

B. VALIDITY OF MARKS—THE "SPECTRUM OF DISTINCTIVENESS"

KING-SEELEY THERMOS CO. V. ALADDIN INDUSTRIES, INC.

321 F.2d 577 (2d Cir. 1963).

LEONARD P. MOORE, CIRCUIT JUDGE.

This action brought by appellant King-Seeley Thermos Co. (King-Seeley) to enjoin the defendant, Aladdin Industries, Incorporated from threatened infringement of eight trademark registrations for the word "Thermos" owned by appellant. Defendant answered, acknowledging its intention to sell its vacuum-insulated containers as "thermos bottles", asserted that the term "thermos" or "thermos bottle" is a generic term in the English language, asked that plaintiff's registrations of its trademark "Thermos" be cancelled and that it be adjudicated that plaintiff have no trademark rights in the word "thermos" on its vacuum bottles. The trial court held that plaintiff's registrations were valid but that the word "thermos" had become "a generic descriptive word in the English language * * * as a synonym for 'vacuum insulated' container."

The facts are set out at great length in the comprehensive and well-reasoned opinion of the district court and will not be detailed here. In that opinion, the court reviewed King-Seeley's corporate history and its use of the trademark "Thermos". He found that from 1907 to 1923, King-Seeley undertook advertising and educational campaigns that tended to make "thermos" a generic term descriptive of the product rather than of its origin. This consequence flowed from the corporation's attempt to popularize "Thermos bottle" as the name of that product without including any of the generic terms then used, such as "Thermos vacuum-insulated bottle". The court found that by 1923 the word "thermos" had acquired firm roots as a descriptive or generic word.

At about 1923, because of the suggestion in an opinion of a district court that "Thermos" might be a descriptive word, King-Seeley adopted the use of the word "vacuum" or "vacuum bottle" with the word "Thermos". Although "Thermos" was generally recognized in the trade as a trademark, the corporation did police the trade and notified those using "thermos" in a descriptive sense that it was a trademark. It failed, however, to take affirmative action to seek out generic uses by non-trade publications and protested only those which happened to come to its attention. Between 1923 and the early 1950's the generic use of "thermos" had grown to a marked extent in non-trade publications and by the end of this period there was wide-spread use by the unorganized public of "thermos" as a synonym for "vacuum insulated." The court concluded that King-Seeley had failed to use due diligence to rescue "Thermos" from becoming a descriptive or generic term.

Between 1954 and 1957, plaintiff showed awareness of the widespread generic use of "thermos" and of the need to educate the public to the word's trademark significance. It diversified its products to include those not directly related to containers designed to keep their contents hot or cold. It changed its name from the American Thermos Bottle Company to The American Thermos Products Company and intensified its policing activities of trade and non-trade publications. The court found, however, that the generic use of "thermos" had become so firmly impressed as a part of the everyday language of the American public that plaintiff's extraordinary efforts commencing in the mid-1950's came too late to keep "thermos" from falling into the public domain. The court also held that appellant's trademarks are valid and because there is an appreciable, though minority, segment of the consumer public which knows and recognizes plaintiff's trademarks, it imposed certain restrictions and limitations on the use of the word "thermos" by defendant.

We affirm the district court's decision that the major significance of the word "thermos" is generic. * * *

Appellant's primary protest on appeal is directed at the district court's finding that "The word 'thermos' became a part of the public domain because of the plaintiff's wide dissemination of the word 'thermos' used as a synonym for 'vacuum-insulated' and as an adjectival-noun, 'thermos', through its educational and advertising campaigns and because of the plaintiff's lack of reasonable diligence in asserting and protecting its trademark rights in the word 'Thermos' among the members of the unorganized public, exclusive of those in the trade, from 1907 to the date of this action."

We are not convinced that the trademark's loss of distinctiveness was the result of some failure on plaintiff's part. Substantial efforts to preserve the trademark significance of the word were made by plaintiff, especially with respect to members of the trade. However, there was little they could do to prevent the public from using "thermos" in a generic rather than a trademark sense. And whether the appropriation by the public was due to highly successful educational and advertising campaigns or to lack of diligence in policing or not is of no consequence; the fact is that the word "thermos" had entered the public domain beyond recall. Even as early as 1910 plaintiff itself asserted that "Thermos had become a household word."

Judge Anderson found that although a substantial majority of the public knows and uses the word "thermos", only a small minority of the public knows that this word has trademark significance. He wrote:

> "The results of the survey (conducted at the behest of the defendant) were that about 75% of adults in the United States who were familiar with containers that keep the contents hot or cold, call such a container a 'thermos'; about 12% of the adult

> American public know that 'thermos' has a trade-mark significance, and about 11% use the term 'vacuum bottle'. This is generally corroborative of the court's conclusions drawn from the other evidence, except that such other evidence indicated that a somewhat larger minority than 12% was aware of the trade-mark meaning of 'thermos'; and a somewhat larger minority than 11% used the descriptive term 'vacuum' bottle or other container."

The record amply supports these findings.

Appellant argues that the court below misapplied the doctrine of the *Aspirin* and *Cellophane* cases. Its primary contention is that in those cases, there was no generic name, such as vacuum bottle, that was suitable for use by the general public. As a result, to protect the use of the only word [that] identified the product in the mind of the public would give the owners of the trademark an unfair competitive advantage. The rule of those cases, however, does not rest on this factor. Judge Learned Hand stated the sole issue in *Aspirin* to be: "What do the buyers understand by the word for whose use the parties are contending? If they understand by it only the kind of goods sold, then, I take it, it makes no difference whatever what efforts the plaintiff has made to get them to understand more." 272 F. at 509. Of course, it is obvious that the fact that there was no suitable descriptive word for either aspirin or cellophane made it difficult, if not impossible, for the original manufacturers to prevent their trademark from becoming generic. But the test is not what is available as an alternative to the public, but what the public's understanding is of the word that it uses. What has happened here is that the public had become accustomed to calling vacuum bottles by the word "thermos". If a buyer walked into a retail store asking for a thermos bottle, meaning any vacuum bottle and not specifically plaintiff's product, the fact that the appellation "vacuum bottle" was available to him is of no significance. The two terms had become synonymous; in fact, defendant's survey showed that the public was far more inclined to use the word "thermos" to describe a container that keeps its contents hot or cold than the phrase "vacuum bottle".

Appellant asserts that the courts in a number of cases have upheld the continued exclusive use of a dual functioning trademark, which both identifies the class of product as well as its source. *See, e.g.*, *Standard Brands v. Smidler*, 151 F.2d 34 (2 Cir.1945) ("V-8"); *Walgreen v. Obear-Nester*, 113 F.2d 956 (8 Cir. 1940)("Pyrex"); *Marks v. Polaroid Corp.*, 129 F.Supp. 243 (D.Mass.1955), *aff'd* 237 F.2d 428 (1 Cir.1956) ("Polaroid"); *Q-Tips v. Johnson & Johnson*, 108 F.Supp. 845 (D.N.J.1952), *aff'd* 206 F.2d 144 (3 Cir. 1953) ("Q-Tips"); *Keebler Weyl Baking Co. v. J. S. Ivins' Son*, 7 F.Supp. 211 (E.D.Pa.1934) ("Club Crackers"); *Barnes v. Pierce*, 164 F. 213 (S.D.N.Y.1908) ("Argyrol"). As this court recently indicated:

> "a mark is not generic merely because it has some significance to the public as an indication of the nature or class of an article. * * * In order to become generic the principal significance of the word must be its indication of the nature or class of an article, rather than an indication of its origin."

Feathercombs, Inc. v. Solo Products Corp., 306 F.2d 251, 256 (2 Cir. 1962). *But see Marks v. Polaroid Corp., supra*, 129 F.Supp. at 270 ("a defendant alleging invalidity of a trademark for genericness must show that to the consuming public as a whole the word has lost all its trademark significance").

Since in this case, the primary significance to the public of the word "thermos" is its indication of the nature and class of an article rather than as an indication of its source, whatever duality of meaning of word still holds for a minority of the public is of little consequence except as a consideration in the framing of a decree. Since the great majority of those members of the public who use the word "thermos" are not aware of any trademark significance, there is not enough dual use to support King-Seeley's claims to monopoly of the word as a trademark.

No doubt, the *Aspirin* and *Cellophane* doctrine can be a harsh one for it places a penalty on the manufacturer who has made skillful use of advertising and has popularized his product. However, King-Seeley has enjoyed a commercial monopoly of the word "thermos" for over fifty years. During that period, despite its efforts to protect the trademark, the public has virtually expropriated it as its own. The word having become part of the public domain, it would be unfair to unduly restrict the right of a competitor of King-Seeley to use the word.

The court below, mindful of the fact that some members of the public and a substantial portion of the trade still recognize and use the word "thermos" as a trademark, framed an eminently fair decree designed to afford King-Seeley as much future protection as was possible. The decree provides that defendant must invariably precede the use of the word "thermos" by the possessive of the name "Aladdin"; that the defendant must confine its use of "thermos" to the lower-case "t"; and that it may never use the words "original" or "genuine" in describing its product. In addition, plaintiff is entitled to retain the exclusive right to all of its present forms of the trademark "Thermos" without change. These conditions provide a sound and proper balancing of the competitive disadvantage to defendants arising out of plaintiff's exclusive use of the word "thermos" and the risk that those who recognize "Thermos" as a trademark will be deceived.

The courts should be ever alert, as the district court said, "to eliminate confusion and the possibility of deceit." The purchasing public is entitled to know the source of the article it desires to purchase. It is not within our province to speculate whether the dire predictions made by appellant in forceful appellate argument will come to pass. Certain it is that the district court made every endeavor in its judgment to give as much protection to plaintiff as possible. The use by defendant of the now generic word "thermos" was substantially curtailed. Plaintiff's trademark "thermos" was protected in every style of printing except the lower case "thermos" and then the use of the word must be preceded by the possessive of defendant's name "Aladdin" or the possessive of "Aladdin" plus one of defendant's brand names. Any doubt about plaintiff's position in the field is removed by the prohibition against the use by defendant in labeling, advertising or publication of the words "genuine" or "original" in referring to the word "thermos". Furthermore, the district court has given both parties the opportunity to apply to it for such orders and directions as may be warranted in the light of changed circumstances and for the enforcement of compliance or for the punishment of violations. In our opinion the trial court has reached a most equitable solution which gives appropriate consideration to the law and the facts.

Affirmed.

NOTES

1. What policies underlie the rule that prohibits a company from maintaining exclusive rights to a generic name? Is the court's focus primarily on the trademark owner's diligence or on the public perception of product names in the marketplace? Will the court's decision and remedy in this case result in some consumer confusion?

2. Was King-Seeley, the trademark owner in this case, doomed by its own marketing success? How can a company prevent its marks from becoming generic?

3. How can one establish that a name is generic? Are such well-known brand names as "Xerox" photocopiers, "Google" for search services, and "Tabasco" brand pepper sauce now generic names as a result of their market success? What about "the sofa & chair company" for furniture? *See In re K-T Zoe Furniture, Inc.*, 16 F.3d 390 (Fed. Cir. 1994). Is the term "self-realization" generic as to the services of a Hindu or yoga spiritual organization? *See Self-Realization Fellowship Church v. Ananda Church of Self-Realization*, 59 F.3d 902 (9th Cir. 1995).

4. In *Anti-Monopoly, Inc. v. General Mills Fun Group, Inc.*, 684 F.2d 1316 (9th Cir. 1982), the makers of a game called "Anti-Monopoly" brought suit to have the trademark for the game "Monopoly" invalidated. The court noted that 63 percent of those polled recognized "Monopoly" as a trademark and 55 percent correctly identified Parker Brothers as the manufacturer of the game. Nonetheless, the court relied upon other survey evidence to conclude that the primary significance of "monopoly" was as a type of product rather than a

brand name, *i.e.*, that "monopoly" was equivalent to terms such as backgammon or poker. Do you agree?

ABERCROMBIE & FITCH CO. V. HUNTING WORLD, INC.

537 F.2d 4 (2d Cir. 1976).

FRIENDLY, CIRCUIT JUDGE:

This action in the District Court for the Southern District of New York by Abercrombie & Fitch Company (A & F), owner of well-known stores at Madison Avenue and 45th Street in New York City and seven places in other states, against Hunting World, Incorporated (HW), operator of a competing store on East 53rd Street, is for infringement of some of A & F's registered trademarks using the word "Safari". It has had a long and, for A & F, an unhappy history. On this appeal from a judgment which not only dismissed the complaint but canceled all of A & F's "Safari" registrations, including several that were not in suit, we relieve A & F of some of its unhappiness but not of all.

I.

The complaint, filed in January, 1970, after describing the general nature of A & F's business, reflecting its motto, "The Greatest Sporting Goods Store in the World," alleged as follows: For many years A & F has used the mark "Safari" on articles "exclusively offered and sold by it." Since 1936 it has used the mark on a variety of men's and women's outer garments. * * *

A & F has spent large sums of money in advertising and promoting products identified with its mark "Safari" and in policing its right in the mark, including the successful conduct of trademark infringement suits. HW, the complaint continued, has engaged in the retail marketing of sporting apparel including hats and shoes, some identified by use of "Safari" alone or by expressions such as "Minisafari" and "Safariland". Continuation of HW's acts would confuse and deceive the public and impair "the distinct and unique quality of the plaintiff's trademark." A & F sought an injunction against infringement and an accounting for damages and profits.

HW filed an answer and counterclaim. This alleged, inter alia, that "the word 'safari' is an ordinary, common, descriptive, geographic, and generic word" which "is commonly used and understood by the public to mean and refer to a journey or expedition, especially for hunting or exploring in East Africa, and to the hunters, guides, men, animals, and equipment forming such an expedition" and is not subject to exclusive appropriation as a trademark. HW sought cancellation of all of A & F's registrations using the word "Safari" on the ground that A & F had fraudulently failed to disclose the true nature of the term to the Patent Office.

* * *

[The district court ruled that "Safari" was descriptive and lacked secondary meaning, and therefore was incapable of distinguishing A & F's products from those of other merchants. Accordingly, it cancelled all of A & F's registrations for the "Safari" mark. A & F appealed.]

II.

It will be useful at the outset to restate some basic principles of trademark law, which, although they should be familiar, tend to become lost in a welter of adjectives.

The cases, and in some instances the Lanham Act, identify four different categories of terms with respect to trademark protection. Arrayed in an ascending order which roughly reflects their eligibility to trademark status and the degree of protection accorded, these classes are (1) generic, (2) descriptive, (3) suggestive, and (4) arbitrary or fanciful. The lines of demarcation, however, are not always bright. Moreover, the difficulties are compounded because a term that is in one category for a particular product may be in quite a different one for another,[6] because a term may shift from one category to another in light of differences in usage through time,[7] because a term may have one meaning to one group of users and a different one to others, and because the same term may be put to different uses with respect to a single product. In various ways, all of these complications are involved in the instant case.

A generic term is one that refers, or has come to be understood as referring, to the genus of which the particular product is a species. At common law neither those terms which were generic nor those which were merely descriptive could become valid trademarks. The same was true under the Trademark Act of 1905, except for marks which had been the subject of exclusive use for ten years prior to its enactment.[10] While, as we shall see, the Lanham Act makes an important exception with respect to those merely descriptive terms which have acquired secondary meaning, *see* § 2(f), 15 U.S.C. § 1052(f), it offers no such exception for generic marks. The Act provides for the cancellation of a registered mark if at any time it "becomes the common descriptive name of an article or substance," § 14(c). This means that even proof of secondary meaning, by virtue of which some

[6] To take a familiar example "Ivory" would be generic when used to describe a product made from the tusks of elephants but arbitrary as applied to soap.

[7] *See, e.g., Haughton Elevator Co. v. Seeberger*, 85 U.S.P.Q. 80 (1950), in which the coined word "Escalator", originally fanciful, or at the very least suggestive, was held to have become generic.

[10] Some protection to descriptive marks which had acquired a secondary meaning was given by the law of unfair competition. The Trademark Act of 1920 permitted registration of certain descriptive marks which had acquired secondary meaning.

"merely descriptive" marks may be registered, cannot transform a generic term into a subject for trademark. * * * The pervasiveness of the principle is illustrated by a series of well known cases holding that when a suggestive or fanciful term has become generic as a result of a manufacturer's own advertising efforts, trademark protection will be denied save for those markets where the term still has not become generic and a secondary meaning has been shown to continue. A term may thus be generic in one market and descriptive or suggestive or fanciful in another.

The term which is descriptive but not generic[11] stands on a better basis. Although § 2(e) of the Lanham Act, 15 U.S.C. § 1052, forbids the registration of a mark which, when applied to the goods of the applicant, is "merely descriptive," § 2(f) removes a considerable part of the sting by providing that "except as expressly excluded in paragraphs (a)–(d) of this section, nothing in this chapter shall prevent the registration of a mark used by the applicant which has become distinctive of the applicant's goods in commerce" and that the Commissioner may accept, as prima facie evidence that the mark has become distinctive, proof of substantially exclusive and continuous use of the mark applied to the applicant's goods for five years preceding the application. As indicated in the cases cited in the discussion of the unregistrability of generic terms, "common descriptive name," as used in §§ 14(c) and 15(4), refers to generic terms applied to products and not to terms that are "merely descriptive." In the former case any claim to an exclusive right must be denied since this in effect would confer a monopoly not only of the mark but of the product by rendering a competitor unable effectively to name what it was endeavoring to sell. In the latter case the law strikes the balance, with respect to registration, between the hardships to a competitor in hampering the use of an appropriate word and those to the owner who, having invested money and energy to endow a word with the good will adhering to his enterprise, would be deprived of the fruits of his efforts.

The category of "suggestive" marks was spawned by the felt need to accord protection to marks that were neither exactly descriptive on the one hand nor truly fanciful on the other a need that was particularly acute because of the bar in the Trademark Act of 1905 (with an exceedingly limited exception noted above) on the registration of merely descriptive marks regardless of proof of secondary meaning. Having created the category the courts have had great difficulty in defining it. * * * [One court has observed] that: "A term is suggestive if it requires imagination, thought

[11] *See, e.g., W. E. Bassett Co. v. Revlon, Inc.*, 435 F.2d 656 (2 Cir.1970). A commentator has illuminated the distinction with an example of the "Deep Bowl Spoon": "Deep Bowl" identifies a significant characteristic of the article. It is "merely descriptive" of the goods, because it informs one that they are deep in the bowl portion. . . . It is not, however, "the common descriptive name" of the article (since) the implement is not a deep bowl, it is a spoon. . . . "Spoon" is not merely descriptive of the article it identifies the article (and therefore) the term is generic. Fletcher, *Actual Confusion as to Incontestability of Descriptive Marks*, 64 Trademark Rep. 252, 260 (1974). On the other hand, "Deep Bowl" would be generic as to a deep bowl.

and perception to reach a conclusion as to the nature of goods. A term is descriptive if it forthwith conveys an immediate idea of the ingredients, qualities or characteristics of the goods." *Stix Prods., Inc. v. United Merchants & Mfrs., Inc.*, 295 F.Supp. 479, 488 (S.D.N.Y. 1968) * * *. Also useful is the approach taken by this court in *Aluminum Fabricating Co. of Pittsburgh v. Season-All Window Corp.*, 259 F.2d 314 (2 Cir.1958), that the reason for restricting the protection accorded descriptive terms, namely the undesirability of preventing an entrant from using a descriptive term for his product, is much less forceful when the trademark is a suggestive word since, as Judge Lumbard wrote, 259 F.2d at 317:

> The English language has a wealth of synonyms and related words with which to describe the qualities which manufacturers may wish to claim for their products and the ingenuity of the public relations profession supplies new words and slogans as they are needed.

If a term is suggestive, it is entitled to registration without proof of secondary meaning. Moreover, as held in the *Season-All* case, the decision of the Patent Office to register a mark without requiring proof of secondary meaning affords a rebuttable presumption that the mark is suggestive or arbitrary or fanciful rather than merely descriptive.

It need hardly be added that fanciful or arbitrary terms[12] enjoy all the rights accorded to suggestive terms as marks without the need of debating whether the term is "merely descriptive" and with ease of establishing infringement.

In the light of these principles we must proceed to a decision of this case.

III.

We turn first to an analysis of A & F's trademarks to determine the scope of protection to which they are entitled. We have reached the following conclusions: (1) applied to specific types of clothing "safari" has become a generic term and "minisafari" may be used for a smaller brim hat; (2) "safari" has not, however, become a generic term for boots or shoes; it is either "suggestive" or "merely descriptive" and is a valid trademark even if "merely descriptive" since it has become incontestable under the Lanham Act; but (3) in light of the justified finding below that "Camel Safari," "Hippo Safari" and "Safari Chukka" were devoted by HW to a purely descriptive use on its boots, HW has a defense against a charge of

[12] As terms of art, the distinctions between suggestive terms and fanciful or arbitrary terms may seem needlessly artificial. Of course, a common word may be used in a fanciful sense; indeed one might say that only a common word can be so used, since a coined word cannot first be put to a bizarre use. Nevertheless, the term "fanciful", as a classifying concept, is usually applied to words invented solely for their use as trademarks. When the same legal consequences attach to a common word, i. e., when it is applied in an unfamiliar way, the use is called "arbitrary."

infringement with respect to these on the basis of "fair use." We now discuss how we have reached these conclusions.

It is common ground that A & F could not apply "Safari" as a trademark for an expedition into the African wilderness. This would be a clear example of the use of "Safari" as a generic term. What is perhaps less obvious is that a word may have more than one generic use. The word "Safari" has become part of a family of generic terms which, although deriving no doubt from the original use of the word and reminiscent of its milieu, have come to be understood not as having to do with hunting in Africa, but as terms within the language referring to contemporary American fashion apparel. These terms name the components of the safari outfit well-known to the clothing industry and its customers: the "Safari hat", a broad flat-brimmed hat with a single, large band; the "Safari jacket", a belted bush jacket with patch pockets and a buttoned shoulder loop; when the jacket is accompanied by pants, the combination is called the "Safari suit". Typically these items are khaki-colored.

This outfit, and its components, were doubtless what Judge Ryan had in mind when he found that "the word 'safari' in connection with wearing apparel is widely used by the general public and people in the trade." The record abundantly supports the conclusion that many stores have advertised these items despite A & F's attempts to police its mark. In contrast, a search of the voluminous exhibits fails to disclose a single example of the use of "Safari", by anyone other than A & F and HW, on merchandise for which A & F has registered "Safari" except for the safari outfit and its components as described above.

What has been thus far established suffices to support the dismissal of the complaint with respect to many of the uses of "Safari" by HW. Describing a publication as a "Safariland Newsletter", containing bulletins as to safari activity in Africa, was clearly a generic use which is nonenjoinable. A & F also was not entitled to an injunction against HW's use of the word in advertising goods of the kind included in the safari outfit as described above. And if HW may advertise a hat of the kind worn on safaris as a safari hat, it may also advertise a similar hat with a smaller brim as a minisafari. Although the issue may be somewhat closer, the principle against giving trademark protection to a generic term also sustains the denial of an injunction against HW's use of "Safariland" as a name of a portion of its store devoted at least in part to the sale of clothing as to which the term "Safari" has become generic.

A & F stands on stronger ground with respect to HW's use of "Camel Safari", "Hippo Safari" and Chukka "Safari" as names for boots imported from Africa. As already indicated, there is no evidence that "Safari" has become a generic term for boots. Since, as will appear, A & F's registration of "Safari" for use on its shoes has become incontestable, it is immaterial (save for HW's contention of fraud which is later rejected) whether A & F's use of "Safari" for boots was suggestive or "merely descriptive."

HW contends, however, that even if "Safari" is a valid trademark for boots, it is entitled to the defense of "fair use" within § 33(b)(4) of the Lanham Act, 15 U.S.C. § 1115(b)(4). That section offers such a defense even as against marks that have become incontestable when the term charged to be an infringement is not used as a trademark "and is used fairly and in good faith only to describe to users the goods and services of such party, or their geographic origin."

Here, Lee Expeditions, Ltd., the parent company of HW, has been primarily engaged in arranging safaris to Africa since 1959; Robert Lee, the president of both companies, is the author of a book published in 1959 entitled "Safari Today The Modern Safari Handbook" and has, since 1961, booked persons on safaris as well as purchased safari clothing in Africa for resale in America. These facts suffice to establish, absent a contrary showing, that defendant's use of "Safari" with respect to boots was made in the context of hunting and traveling expeditions and not as an attempt to garner A & F's good will. The district court here found the HW's use of "Camel Safari", "Hippo Safari", and "Safari Chukka" as names for various boots imported from Africa constituted "a purely descriptive use to apprise the public of the type of product by referring to its origin and use." * * * When a plaintiff has chosen a mark with some descriptive qualities, he cannot altogether exclude some kinds of competing uses even when the mark is properly on the register. * * * It is significant that HW did not use "Safari" alone on its shoes, as it would doubtless have done if confusion had been intended.

We thus hold that the district court was correct in dismissing the complaint.

IV.

We find much greater difficulty in the court's broad invalidation of A & F's trademark registrations. Section 37 of the Lanham Act, 15 U.S.C. § 1119, provides authority for the court to cancel those registrations of any party to an action involving a registered mark. The cases cited above, establish that when a term becomes the generic name of the product to which it is applied, grounds for cancellation exist. * * * The whole of Registration No. 358,781 [for outer garments, including hats] thus was properly canceled. With respect to Registration No. 703,279 [for cloth, sporting goods, and apparel,] only a part has become generic,[14] and cancellation on that ground should be correspondingly limited. Such partial cancellation, specifically recognized by § 37, accords with the rationale by which a court is authorized to cancel a registration, viz, to "rectify" the

[14] To wit, pants, shirts, jackets, coats and hats.

register by conforming it to court judgments which often must be framed in something less than an all-or-nothing way.

There remain eight other registrations and those terms not pared from No. 703,279. Three of these registrations, Nos. 652,098, 768,332 and 770,336, and the non-generic portions of No. 703,279 appear to have become incontestable by virtue of the filing of affidavits under § 15(3), of five years continuous use. There is nothing to suggest that the uses included in these registrations, except the uses described above with respect to 703,279, are the common descriptive names of either current fashion styles or African expeditions. The generic term for A & F's "safari cloth Bermuda shorts", for example, is "Bermuda shorts", not "safari"; indeed one would suppose this garment to be almost ideally unsuited for the forest or the jungle and there is no evidence that it has entered into the family for which "Safari" has become a generic adjective. The same analysis holds for luggage, portable grills, and the rest of the suburban paraphernalia, from swimtrunks and raincoats to belts and scarves, included in these registrations. * * *

We hold also that the registrations which have not become incontestable should not have been canceled. "Safari" as applied to ice chests, axes, tents and smoking tobacco does not describe such items. Rather it is a way of conveying to affluent patrons of A & F a romantic notion of high style, coupled with an attractive foreign allusion. * * * It is even wider of the mark to say that "Safari Mills" "describes" cotton piece goods. Such uses fit into the category of suggestive marks. We need not now decide how valuable they may prove to be; it suffices here that they should not have been canceled.

In sum, we conclude that cancellation should have been directed only with respect to No. 358,781 and portions of No. 703,279 and the New York registration. * * *

NOTES

1. *Fanciful or Arbitrary Marks*. As described in this case, the strength of a trademark is frequently analyzed based upon its distinctiveness. The strongest trademarks are fanciful marks, which are words (or other marks) specially coined to serve as trademarks—*e.g.*, Kodak cameras, Exxon gas, Lenovo computers, and Clorox bleach. Nearly as strong are arbitrary marks, which are words that have no association with the underlying product or service being marketed—*e.g.*, Black & White scotch, Mustang motels, and Amazon.com. Fanciful and arbitrary marks are considered inherently distinctive, and are thus protectable from the outset of their use.

2. *Suggestive Marks*. Suggestive marks have some association with the underlying product or service, but are often said to require some imagination to see the connection. They are also treated as if they are inherently distinctive,

and are therefore also protectable from the outset of their use—*e.g.*, Citibank banking services, At-A-Glance calendars, Gobble Gobble turkey meat, Beetle fishing lures, and Hula-Hoop plastic hoop toys.

3. *Descriptive Marks.* Descriptive marks describe some characteristic of the product or service, and are protectable only upon a showing of secondary meaning (*i.e.*, public perception that the mark signifies origin instead of describing the product or service)—*e.g.*, Food Fair supermarkets, Beef & Brew restaurants, America's Best Popcorn! popcorn snacks, Sharp televisions, Super Glue adhesives.

4. Where do the following marks fall in the "spectrum of distinctiveness"?

APPLE computers

ARM & HAMMER baking soda

CAMEL cigarettes

CHICKEN OF THE SEA tuna

COPPERTONE suntan lotion

HOLIDAY INN motels

HOTELS.COM accommodation booking service

LYFT ride services app

POLAROID cameras

RAISIN BRAN cereal

RICH 'N CHIPS chocolate chip cookies

SANKA coffee

SHAKE SHACK restaurants

SHELL gasoline

SUN bank

WRANGLER jeans

YUBAN coffee

5. Distinguishing between "descriptiveness" and "suggestiveness" is often difficult. Sometimes, courts have laid the difficulty at the feet of the "imagination" test mentioned in Note 2. One alternative is to ask whether competitors need to use the mark in order to compete effectively; another is to ask whether the mark has been used extensively by competitors other than the putative owner. The "competitors' need" and "extent of use" tests are discussed in *Zobmondo Entertainment, LLC v. Falls Media, LLC*, 602 F.3d 1108 (9th Cir. 2010). Is any one of these three tests likely to be more helpful than the others in deciding whether a mark is descriptive or suggestive?

6. Is the name "brick oven" generic as applied to frozen pizzas? *See Schwan's IP, LLC v. Kraft Pizza Co.*, 460 F.3d 971 (8th Cir. 2006). What about "yellow cab" for taxicab services? *See Yellow Cab Co. of Sacramento v. Yellow Cab of Elk Grove, Inc.*, 419 F.3d 925 (9th Cir. 2005).

7. While most courts adhere to *Abercrombie*'s spectrum of distinctiveness, it can be difficult to apply to non-traditional marks, such as three-dimensional objects, sounds, colors, odors, and many forms of trade dress (*e.g.*, packaging, ambience or product design). In *Seabrook Foods, Inc. v. Bar-Well Foods*, 568 F.2d 1342 (C.C.P.A. 1977), where the mark consisted of a stylized leaf design, the court evaluated inherent distinctiveness by asking four questions: "whether it was a 'common' basic shape or design, whether it was unique or unusual in a particular field, whether it was a mere refinement of a commonly-adopted and well-known form of ornamentation for a particular class of goods viewed by the public as a dress or ornamentation for the goods, or whether it was capable of creating a commercial impression distinct from the accompanying words." *Id.* at 1344. Applying the same approach, the Fifth Circuit held in *Amazing Spaces, Inc. v. Metro Mini Storage*, 608 F.3d 225 (5th Cir. 2010) that a variation on a five-pointed star lacked distinctiveness as a matter of law.

8. In *United States Patent and Trademark Office v. Booking.com B.V.*, 140 S.Ct. 2298 (2020), the Supreme Court held that adding ".com" to the term "booking" did not automatically create a term that was generic for on-line hotel reservation services. The PTO therefore erred in refusing to register "booking.com" on the ground that "when a generic term is combined with a generic top-level domain like '.com,' the resulting combination is generic." Instead, consumer perception should determine whether the combination functions as a source indicator.

C. DESCRIPTIVE MARKS AND SECONDARY MEANING

INTERNATIONAL KENNEL CLUB OF CHICAGO, INC. V. MIGHTY STAR, INC.

846 F.2d 1079 (7th Cir. 1988).

COFFEY, CIRCUIT JUDGE.

Plaintiff-appellee International Kennel Club of Chicago, Inc. ("IKC"), brought this action against the defendants-appellants Mighty Star, Inc. ("Mighty Star") and DCN Industries, Inc. ("DCN"), alleging that the defendants' use of the plaintiff's "International Kennel Club" name violates section 43(a) of the Lanham Act, 15 U.S.C. § 1125(a), as well as state statutory and common law. The district court granted the plaintiff's motion for a preliminary injunction against the defendants' use of the name. The defendants appeal. We affirm in part, reverse in part, and remand.

I.

A. Plaintiff's use of the "International Kennel Club" name

The IKC is an Illinois business corporation that sponsors dog shows in Chicago, and is a "show giving member club" of the American Kennel Club ("AKC"), a nationwide organization devoted to furthering the "sport" of showing purebred dogs. In addition to giving dog shows, the IKC serves as an information source for AKC activities in Chicago and provides assistance in the pedigree registration of purebred dogs with the AKC. The IKC also sponsors seminars and contributes funds for animal medical research, the Dog Museum of America, and 4-H programs.

The IKC sponsors two major dog shows each year, with the annual spring show having an attendance of between 20,000 to 30,000 people. An average of 1,500 to 2,000 dogs are entered in plaintiff's shows, and for the spring 1986 show, entries came from 36 different states and various Canadian provinces. Persons who attend the plaintiff's shows are often interested in canine-related paraphernalia. While the IKC does not sell such items, private vendors rent booth space at plaintiff's shows at prices ranging from $600 to $800 per booth and sell dog-related items, including stuffed dogs. In 1985 and 1986, the annual revenue from the rental of booth space averaged $60,000.

In an effort to promote its activities, the IKC spent approximately $60,000 of its total revenue of $231,226 for fiscal year 1986 to hire a full-time staff person to handle the advertising of the dog shows and public relations. The paid advertising of the IKC, consisting of advertisements in magazines with a nationwide circulation such as the American Kennel Club Gazette and Dog World Magazine, as well as advertisements in the Chicago-area media, is primarily designed to reach canine enthusiasts (the dog "fancy" in trade parlance). The activities of the IKC have also been covered in a variety of national and local publications.

B. Defendant's decision to market toy dogs under the name "International Kennel Club"

For almost three decades, defendants DCN and its wholly-owned subsidiary Mighty Star have sold stuffed toys in the United States, Canada, England, Australia and Asia. For many years, defendants used the trademark "Polar Puff" to refer to their top of the line products and prominently displayed the trademark on their products and in their advertisements. In the later part of 1985, the defendants decided to add to their product line of stuffed animals a line of stuffed "pedigree" dogs representing different breeds. The defendants state that at the time they had never heard of the plaintiff, and that they chose the name "International Kennel Club" in part because of the international scope of their business, and also because the products were toy dogs. The defendants utilized a marketing strategy whereby purchasers could "register" their dogs with the "International Kennel Club" and receive an "official International Kennel Club membership and pedigree certificate." Part of the defendants' registration strategy was to emphasize that the stuffed canines represent breeds "sanctioned by the International Kennel Club." Although the defendants' International Kennel Club collection of dogs was marketed in conjunction with their "24K Polar Puff" line of toy animals, the advertising for the stuffed dogs did not always use this second name along with the International Kennel Club name. Defendants' instore advertising included plaques, buttons and counter displays, all of which referred to the "International Kennel Club Center," the "International Kennel Club," or the "IKC" without also referring to the defendants' "Polar Puff" trademark.

After choosing the IKC name for its line of toy dogs, Mighty Star's counsel conducted a search of trade directories in major cities as well as a search of federally registered trademarks. The search disclosed two telephone directory listings in Chicago—one for "international kennel" and one for the "International Kennel Club of Chicago." Nevertheless, counsel advised the defendants that the use of the International Kennel Club name would not infringe upon the plaintiff's name given the local scope of the plaintiff's operations and the fact that the plaintiff did not directly compete with Mighty Star or DCN.[3] Thus, the defendants proceeded to market their line of stuffed dogs under that name without contacting the plaintiff to determine if the use of the International Kennel Club name would present a problem of infringement.

C. Evidence of confusion allegedly caused by the marketing of the defendants' toy dogs under the "International Kennel Club" name

In late March 1986—six months after learning of the plaintiff's existence—the defendants placed a full-page advertisement for their line of stuffed dogs in the April edition of the Good Housekeeping magazine. This advertisement was followed by ads in the June issues of Better Homes and Gardens, Vogue, and Cosmopolitan magazines that reached the public in mid-May. Following the publication of these ads, IKC officials began receiving telephone calls (at a rate of about one per day), letters, and personal inquiries from people expressing confusion as to the plaintiff's relationship to the International Kennel Club stuffed dogs. Prior to the plaintiff's spring 1986 dog show, the IKC's public relations officer, Ms. Johnson, received telephone calls asking to purchase "International Kennel Club stuffed dogs." Ms. Johnson testified that she thought the callers were referring to the stuffed dogs sold by vendors at the plaintiff's shows, and told the callers that the toy dogs would continue to be sold at the show.

---

[3] DCN's president testified that he thought "they . . . [The International Kennel Club of Chicago, Inc. and the International Kennel] were kennels. So I didn't visualize them to be anything more than that."

The IKC learned of the defendants' line of International Kennel Club toys at the plaintiff's spring dog show on March 29 through 30, 1986. Mr. Auslander, the Secretary and Treasurer of the IKC, testified that a vendor at the show brought one of the defendants' ads to his attention, and asked "why I was involved or why our club was involved in a venture of that type." Thereafter, in early April, the IKC began to receive letters of inquiry concerning the defendants' toy canines. Eight letters requested information on purchasing the dogs, and another from a vendor expressed concern about the IKC's apparent competition. The latter wrote that "[w]e are concerned as vendors that this practice [the plaintiff's apparent selling of toy dogs] conflicts with the stated aims of your involvement as a purebred dog club." The defendants' Executive Vice-President Sheldon Bernstein testified that neither Mighty Star nor DCN received any letters indicating confusion as to their relationship with the plaintiff.

After the plaintiff's spring 1986 dog show, Mr. Auslander attended between 15 and 20 other dog shows throughout the country during 1986. Auslander testified that at about half of these shows—including the shows in Florida, Wisconsin, Nebraska, Colorado, Massachusetts, California and Illinois—he was questioned about the relationship between the IKC and Mighty Star's toy dogs. Auslander further recounted that members of the board of directors of the American Kennel Club consulted him, expressing concern that the International Kennel Club might be involved in their sale. According to Auslander's testimony, the President of the American Kennel Club reported to Auslander that it had received questions about whether the toys were a fundraising effort for the Dog Museum of America or the American Kennel Club. Thereafter, at the request of the American Kennel Club, the plaintiff placed an ad disclaiming any relationship to the defendants' toys in the July issue of the American Kennel Club Gazette.

* * *

A. *Likelihood of success on the merits*

In order to prevail in its action under section 43(a) of the Lanham Act, the IKC must establish: (1) that it has a protectible trademark, and (2) a "likelihood of confusion" as to the origin of the defendant's product. * * *

The first step in determining whether an unregistered mark or name is entitled to the protection of the trademark laws is to categorize the name according to the nature of the term itself. Trademarks that are fanciful, arbitrary [i.e. made-up terms like "Kodak"] or suggestive are fully protected, while "descriptive words (e.g., 'bubbly' champagne) may be trademarked only if they have acquired secondary meaning, that is, only if most consumers have come to think of the word not as descriptive at all but as the name of the product." *Blau Plumbing, Inc. v. SOS Fix-It, Inc.*, 781 F.2d 604, 609 (7th Cir.1986). In *Blau*, the court explained that:

> The goal of trademark protection is to allow a firm to affix an identifying mark to its product (or service) offering that will, because it is distinctive and no competitor may use a confusingly similar designation, enable the consumer to discover in the least possible amount of time and with the least possible amount of head scratching whether a particular brand is that firm's brand or a competitor's brand. . . . *To allow a firm to use as a trademark a generic word, or a descriptive word still understood by the consuming public to describe, would make it difficult for competitors to market their own brands of the same product.* Imagine being forbidden to describe a Chevrolet as a "car" or an "automobile" because Ford or Chrysler or Volvo had trademarked these generic words, or an after-shave lotion as "bracing" because the maker of one brand of after-shave lotion had trademarked this descriptive word.

(Emphasis added). Hence, although a term's "primary" meaning is merely descriptive, if through use the public has come to identify the term with a plaintiff's product or service, the words have acquired a "secondary meaning" and would become a protectible trademark. *Gimix, Inc. v. JS & A Group, Inc.,* 699 F.2d 901, 907 (7th Cir. 1983). In other words, " 'secondary meaning' denotes an association in the mind of the consumer between the trade dress [or name] of a product and a particular producer." *Vaughan Manufacturing Co. v. Brikam Intern., Inc.*, 814 F.2d 346, 348 (7th Cir.1987). We agree with the district court that the phrase "International Kennel Club" fits within the category of descriptive words in that it "specifically describes a characteristic or ingredient of an article [or service]." Thus, the "International Kennel Club" name is entitled to trademark protection only if the name has acquired "secondary meaning," i.e. has become distinctive of the plaintiff's goods and/or services.

The defendants claim that the plaintiff's evidence introduced at the preliminary injunction hearing is insufficient to demonstrate that the plaintiff has better than a negligible chance of establishing that the "International Kennel Club" name acquired secondary meaning among the consuming public. "The factors which this court has indicated it will consider on the issue of secondary meaning include '[t]he amount and manner of advertising, volume of sales, the length and manner of use, direct consumer testimony, and consumer surveys.' " *Gimix, Inc.*, 699 F.2d at 907. "Consumer testimony and consumer surveys are the only direct evidence on this question . . . [t]he other factors are relevant in a more circumstantial fashion." *Id.* Not surprisingly, the defendants attack the absence of a consumer survey in the evidence produced by the plaintiff at the preliminary injunction hearing.

Despite this attack, we are not persuaded that the absence of a consumer survey is per se fatal to the plaintiff's request for a preliminary injunction. As noted previously, the trial court merely granted a preliminary injunction; it did not decide the case on the merits after allowing for full discovery. The IKC may be in a better position to produce a survey at a full trial on the merits. Thus, while the lack of survey evidence fails to support the plaintiff's request for preliminary relief, we are convinced that it does not necessarily destroy the plaintiff's entitlement to that relief: the existence of a survey is only one of the variety of factors outlined in *Gimix* as being relevant to the issue of secondary meaning, and the plaintiff may resort to evidence other than a survey in attempting to demonstrate a "better than negligible" chance of establishing secondary meaning. Moreover, *Gimix* was decided at the summary judgment stage, after the parties had completed their discovery. In contrast, the plaintiff's motion in this case was decided under the time pressures characteristic of preliminary injunction hearings and without the benefit of extensive discovery. * * *

The remaining factors articulated in *Gimix* as material to the issue of secondary meaning weigh in favor of the trial court's conclusion that the International Kennel Club of Chicago "has acquired a secondary meaning like that among a small but very well-defined group of people in Chicago and elsewhere." In particular, the "amount and manner of advertising" and the "length and manner of use" of the International Kennel Club name yields a better than negligible chance of establishing secondary meaning. With respect to advertising, the plaintiff introduced evidence supporting the inference that the International Kennel Club has developed and maintained its reputation among canine enthusiasts through advertising carefully targeted to reach persons interested in the sport of showing purebred dogs. It has advertised in publications with a continent-wide circulation that are of interest to dog fanciers, including the American Kennel Club Gazette, Kennel Review, and Dog World. And because its shows are held in Chicago, the plaintiff advertises in regional publications of a more general appeal, including the major Chicago newspapers and magazines, as well as various local periodicals. Moreover, the plaintiff mails out as many as 15,000 "premium lists" prior to each show to persons on its mailing lists, and also employs a full-time public relations professional. In its most recent fiscal year, these advertising and public relations expenses have amounted to almost $60,000, or more than 42 percent of the club's total administrative and operating expenses. Viewed another way, these expenses come to more than 25 percent of the club's total revenues; further, the club's activities are often given extensive free publicity. As an example, both major Chicago newspapers have highlighted the plaintiff's dog shows and have designed and promoted special advertising supplements around those columns.

As evidence of secondary meaning, the International Kennel Club also introduced evidence that the club received a number and a variety of letters and phone calls asking about the defendants' toy dogs. In *A.J. Canfield Co. v. Vess Beverages, Inc.*, 796 F.2d 903 (7th Cir. 1986), the court found similar evidence—letters and phone calls to Canfield "all searching for the elusive diet chocolate fudge drink" (after a competitor advertised its own "Chocolate Fudge" drink)—"sufficient to show that when consumers think of diet chocolate fudge soda they think of Canfield." 796 F.2d at 907. Likewise, the correspondence directed to the plaintiff provides support for the inference that when dog fanciers see the "International Kennel Club" name, they think of the plaintiff. Finally, the plaintiff has operated under and advertised the "International Kennel Club" name continuously for over 50 years. In our view, the club's half-century use of the name, combined with their advertising, substantial free publicity, and wide-ranging activities in support of dog groups, clearly renders the plaintiff's chances of establishing that the International Kennel Club name has acquired secondary meaning better than negligible.

* * *

[The court also concluded that the plaintiff had a "better than negligible" chance of establishing that the defendant's use of a similar mark created a likelihood of confusion.]

AFFIRMED IN PART, REVERSED IN PART, AND REMANDED.

NOTE

Note that this case involved a common law mark—that is, a mark that has not been federally registered at the United States Patent and Trademark Office (PTO). The plaintiff's cause of action therefore arises under section 43(a) of the Lanham Act, which effectively protects the common law mark against a likelihood of confusion on a theory of unfair competition, instead of section 32(1) of the Act, which protects against infringement of a federally registered mark.

D. SURNAMES

DAVID B. FINDLAY, INC. V. FINDLAY

218 N.E.2d 531 (N.Y. 1966).

KEATING, JUDGE.

When should a man's right to use his own name in his business be limited? This is the question before us.

The individual plaintiff David B. Findlay ("David") and the individual defendant Walstein C. Findlay ("Wally") are brothers. The Findlay art business was founded in 1870 by their grandfather in Kansas City. Their father continued and expanded the business with a Chicago branch managed by Wally and a New York branch established and managed by

David on East 57th Street. In 1936 the Kansas City gallery was closed and in 1938, after a dispute, the brothers separated. By agreement David, as president of Findlay Galleries, Inc., and owner of nearly all of the stock of the original Missouri corporation, sold to Wally individually the Chicago gallery and allowed Wally to use the name "Findlay Galleries, Inc." in the conduct of his business in Chicago. Wally organized an Illinois corporation under the name "Findlay Galleries, Inc." in 1938 and has since operated his Chicago gallery. He also opened, in 1961, a Palm Beach, Florida, gallery.

David, since the separation, has operated his gallery on East 57th Street in Manhattan. For many years he has conducted his business on the second floor of 11–13 East 57th Street.

In October, 1963, Wally purchased the premises at 17 East 57th Street and informed David of his plans to open an art gallery. David objected to Wally's use of the name "Findlay" on 57th Street and by letter announced he would "resist any appropriation by you in New York of the name Findlay in connection with a gallery * * * any funds spent by you to establish a gallery at 17 East 57th Street under the name Findlay Galleries, Inc. (or any variation thereof using the name Findlay) are spent at your peril." David also, in self-defense and in an effort to survive, rented additional space at 15 East 57th Street so as to have a street level entrance.

David's objections and pleas seemed to have some effect on Wally. As renovation on the building was carried on from October, 1963 to September, 1964, a large sign proclaimed the coming opening of "W. C. F. Galleries, Inc." There was also a display and listing in the New York Telephone directory under the same name and similar advertisements in other publications. However, in September, 1964 the sign was suddenly changed to announce the imminent opening of "Wally Findlay Galleries" affiliated with "Findlay Galleries, Inc." David immediately sought an injunction. Wally went ahead with his opening and erected a sidewalk canopy from the curb to the building displaying the name "Wally Findlay Galleries."

The trial court made very detailed findings and, based on them, enjoined defendant from using the names "Wally Findlay Galleries", "Findlay Galleries" and any other designation including the name "Findlay" in the conduct on an art gallery on East 57th Street. The Appellate Division has affirmed on the trial court's findings and we find evidence to sustain them.

The trial court concluded that if injunctive relief were not granted, plaintiff would continue to be damaged by confusion and diversion and would suffer great and irreparable loss in his business and in his name and reputation. In his quarter of a century on East 57th Street David has established a valuable good will and reputation as an art dealer. Through hard work, business ability and expenditure of large sums of money, David has reached the level where a significant portion of his business comes from people who have been referred to him by others and told to go to "Findlay's on 57th St."

The effect of Wally's new gallery, with its long canopy, can only be that those looking for "Findlay's on 57th St." will be easily confused and find their way into Wally's rather than David's gallery. Though Wally perhaps did not deliberately set out to exploit David's good will and reputation, the trial court found, and we agree, that such a result would follow if Wally were permitted to operate a gallery under the name "Wally Findlay Galleries" next door to David.

There were numerous instances of people telephoning or asking at David's for personnel of Wally's or for art work exhibited at Wally's. Many regular customers congratulated David on the opening of "his" new gallery next door. Moreover, advertisements frequently appeared on the same pages of the local press for "Findlay Galleries", "Findlay's", or "Wally Findlay Galleries" thus making it very difficult to tell whose advertisement it was. Even the art editors and reporters referred to Wally as "Findlay Galleries"—the name used for many years by David—or as "the new Findlay Gallery."

It is apparent that confusion has and must result from Wally's opening next to David. This is compounded by the fact that both brothers have for years specialized in French impressionist and post-impressionist painters. Therefore, quite naturally, both brothers have in the past dealt in the works of such famous deceased painters as Modigliani, Degas, Renoir, Gauguin, Bonnard, Braque, Monet and many others.

Although someone seeking a Renoir from David is unlikely to purchase a Degas from Wally, it is likely that with respect to some of the lesser-known impressionists such diversion might happen. More important, someone wishing to own a nude by Modigliani, a dancer by Degas or a portrait of a girl by Renoir would not necessarily have a particular painting in mind and would likely purchase any of these species, whether it be in Wally's or David's. The items sold by the two brothers are not unique, nonsubstitutional works.

Moreover, art, particularly modern art, is sold only to those who see it. Works of art are sold to those who cross the threshold of the art gallery and the more people you get into your gallery, the more art you will sell. To this end David has worked hard to develop the name "Findlay's on 57th St." and bring in customers. Many people who have the finances to purchase art do not necessarily have the knowledge to distinguish between the works of all the various painters represented by galleries such as Wally's or David's. For this reason they rely on the reputation of the gallery. David has spent over 25 years in developing satisfied customers who will tell others to go to

"Findlay's on 57th St." This good will brings in customers who look for a work of art that suits their fancy and, if Wally were to continue to use the name Findlay, it is inevitable that some would walk into Wally's by mistake and would have their tastes satisfied there, to David's great harm.

The so-called "sacred right" theory that every man may employ his own name in his business is not unlimited. Moreover, fraud or deliberate intention to deceive or mislead the public are not necessary ingredients to a cause of action.

The present trend of the law is to enjoin the use even of a family name when such use tends or threatens to produce confusion in the public mind. Whether this confusion should be satisfied by misplaced phone calls or confusing advertisements alone we do not decide because there has been a finding that diversion, as well as confusion, will exist if Wally is not enjoined. Thus it is clear that the "confusion" with which we are dealing includes impairment of good will of a business.

In *Meneely v. Meneely*, 62 N.Y. 427, this court noted that one can use his own name provided he does not resort to any artifice or contrivance for the purpose of producing the impression that the establishments are identical, or do anything calculated to mislead the public.

Thirty-five years later, we noted that, as a general principle of law, one's name is his property and he is entitled to its use. However, it was equally a principle of law that no man can sell his goods as those of another. "He may not through unfairness, artifice, misrepresentation or fraud, injure the business of another, or induce the public to believe his product is the product of that other."

* * *

In the present case Wally knew that David had conducted his business and built a reputation under the names "Findlay Galleries" and "Findlay's on 57th St." and that many years of effort and expenses had gone into promoting the name of "Findlay" in the art business on 57th Street. He also knew that people would come into his gallery looking for "Findlay Galleries" and even instructed his employees on this matter before he opened. Nonetheless he opened his gallery next door to David dealing in substantially similar works and using the name Findlay. The *bona fides* of Wally's intentions do not change the applicable principles. The objective facts of this unfair competition and injury to plaintiff's business are determinative, not the defendant's subjective state of mind. Wally's conduct constituted unfair competition and an unfair trade practice, and it is most inequitable to permit Wally to profit from his brother's many years of effort in promoting the name of "Findlay" on 57th Street. Wally should use any name other than "Findlay" in the operation of his business next door to his brother.

In framing its injunction the trial court went no farther than was necessary to avoid the harm threatened. It prevented the use of the name Findlay but limited this to the particular area in which its use would cause confusion and diversion—East 57th Street. It resolved the conflict with as little injury as possible to Wally. The proof showed and the trial court found that many, if not most of the leading art galleries, are now located on Madison Avenue and in the area of the 60's, 70's and 80's in New York City. Wally could probably have found an appropriate place for his New York gallery other than at 17 East 57th Street and can now either find such another location or remain where he is under some name such as "W. C. F. Galleries".

The decision in this case is in accord with the directions of our court: "The defendant has the right to use his name. The plaintiff has the right to have the defendant use it in such a way as will not injure his business or mislead the public. Where there is such a conflict of rights, it is the duty of the court so to regulate the use of his name by the defendant that, due protection to the plaintiff being afforded, there will be as little injury to him as possible. * * *

BURKE, JUDGE (dissenting).

This court decided in *Meneely v. Meneely*, 62 N.Y. 427, 431–432 more than 90 years ago—and the rule, well settled then, has been consistently followed ever since—that "every man has the absolute right to use his own name in his own business, even though he may thereby interfere with or injure the business of another person bearing the same name, provided he does not resort to any artifice or contrivance for the purpose of producing the impression that the establishments are identical, or do anything calculated to mislead. Where the only confusion created is that which results from the similarity of the names the courts will not interfere. A person cannot make a trade mark of his own name, and thus obtain a monopoly of it which will debar all other persons of the same name from using their own names in their own business." * * *

In the case before us, there is not the slightest support for any claim of dishonesty or deceit, not the slightest suggestion of a design on the part of the defendant to defraud or mislead the public or to palm off his business as that of his brother. And this was the view of the Trial Judge below who granted the injunction solely on the strength of the possible confusion which would result from the defendant's use of his own name. Thus, declaring that he did "not believe that Wally set out to deliberately exploit this goodwill and business reputation of the plaintiffs", 47 Misc.2d 649, 652, 262 N.Y.S.2d 1011, the Judge specifically ruled that it was immaterial "whether defendant *intended* to confuse and mislead, if in fact, his conduct tends or threatens to produce confusion." 47 Misc.2d, p. 656, 262 N.Y.S.2d 1015 (italics supplied).

As the decisions cited above establish, proof of confusion—understandably inevitable when there is a similarity of name—is irrelevant since confusion resulting from the honest use of one's own name is not actionable. This is especially appropriate in a case such as this, where the patrons or customers of the plaintiff and the defendant are discriminating and knowledgeable people usually intent on acquiring a particular work of art, people ordinarily fully aware that a desired painting or other work of art can be purchased only at a particular gallery and not apt to be misled into buying by a similarity of dealers' names. Too, the evidence of confusion which, as stated, is the predicate for the injunction in this case—telephone calls to the wrong gallery, misdeliveries, visitors seeking paintings in one gallery exhibited at the other—is not unlike that presented in *Wholesale Serv. Supply Corp. v. Wholesale Bldg. Materials Corp.*, 304 N.Y. 854, 109 N.E.2d 718 (1952), and there held to be insufficient to justify the issuance of an injunction.

Moreover, there is no proof in this case of any actual damage suffered by plaintiff * * *.

Despite the finding of no deceit and in the face of a claim of confusion far weaker than that proven in the cases to which we have referred, the court now refuses to apply the rule of law observed for over a century. The exception rests apparently on the singular circumstance that this competition is between siblings. We are unable to see why that should prompt the court to grant one brother the exclusive right to use the family name in connection with what was originally the family art business. We, therefore, perceive no valid basis for prohibiting the defendant from using his own name in the conduct of his business at 17 East 57th Street in New York City.

NOTES

1. Courts have sometimes extended the rights of trademark owners beyond the immediate market in which they have established good will. In *Sullivan v. Ed Sullivan Radio & T.V., Inc.*, 152 N.Y.S.2d 227 (N.Y. App. Div. 1956), the court held that Ed Sullivan, the host of a well-known television show, was entitled to enjoin Ed Sullivan Radio & TV from engaging in the business of selling and repairing radio and television sets in Buffalo, New York. The court reached this conclusion despite the fact that the local store was owned primarily by an individual named Edward J. Sullivan. The court noted that the plaintiff had "no objection to use of the name 'Sullivan' as such nor even 'E. J. Sullivan', nor the full name 'Edward J. Sullivan', since he feels that such forms of the name would not induce or result in any confusion in the public mind." *Id.* The court held that "[a]lthough, in fact, but one isolated store in Buffalo is involved at the present time, nevertheless the state of facts may so change as to encompass a situation wherein there may be a series or a chain of similar stores throughout the country, in which case indeed, unless

appellant had taken this present, prompt action, he might at a later date encounter great difficulty in obtaining an injunction because of his own laches. Also, at this stage the corporate enterprise would suffer minimal inconvenience in dropping the diminutive prefix, a situation which might not hold true at some future time." *Id.*

Have the courts struck the proper balance between protecting the good will of well known celebrities and permitting persons to use their own names in trade?

2. Ernest and Julio Gallo are brothers who have owned and operated the E. & J. Gallo winery for many years. Their younger brother, Joseph Gallo, seeks to use the "Gallo" name to sell cheese and meat. What result? *See E. & J. Gallo Winery v. Gallo Cattle Co.*, 967 F.2d 1280 (9th Cir. 1992).

3. Should the courts provide relief when an individual sells a business established under his or her own name as an on-going concern to another party and later seeks to establish a new business under the individual's own name? What relief would be appropriate? *See Levitt Corp. v. Levitt*, 593 F.2d 463 (2d Cir.1979) (founder of Levittown, New York, residential development later establishes a residential development called Levittown, Florida).

E. TRADE DRESS

The most traditional trademarks consisted of words, letters, symbols, or combinations thereof. Increasingly, however, merchants have invoked trademark and unfair competition laws to assert that other features associated with their goods or services deserve protection as indications of origin. In the 1924 case of *William R. Warner & Co. v. Eli Lilly & Co.*, reproduced at the start of this chapter, Eli Lilly attempted, unsuccessfully, to assert trade dress protection for the use of chocolate as an ingredient in medicine. While that case was brought under common law, trade dress today is protected by the Lanham Act as well. As illustrated by the cases below, the Supreme Court has taken a strong interest in trade dress protection.

Statutes: 15 U.S.C. §§ 1125(a)(1)(A), 1127

TWO PESOS, INC. V. TACO CABANA, INC.

505 U.S. 763, 112 S.Ct. 2753 (1992).

JUSTICE WHITE delivered the opinion of the Court.

The issue in this case is whether the trade dress[1] of a restaurant may be protected under § 43(a) of the Trademark Act of 1946 (Lanham Act)

[1] The District Court instructed the jury: " '[T]rade dress' is the total image of the business. Taco Cabana's trade dress may include the shape and general appearance of the exterior of the restaurant, the identifying sign, the interior kitchen floor plan, the decor, the menu, the equipment used to serve food, the servers' uniforms and other features reflecting on the total image of the restaurant." The Court of Appeals accepted this definition and quoted from *Blue Bell Bio-Medical*

based on a finding of inherent distinctiveness, without proof that the trade dress has secondary meaning.

I

Respondent Taco Cabana, Inc., operates a chain of fast-food restaurants in Texas. The restaurants serve Mexican food. The first Taco Cabana restaurant was opened in San Antonio in September 1978, and five more restaurants had been opened in San Antonio by 1985. Taco Cabana describes its Mexican trade dress as "a festive eating atmosphere having interior dining and patio areas decorated with artifacts, bright colors, paintings and murals. The patio includes interior and exterior areas with the interior patio capable of being sealed off from the outside patio by overhead garage doors. The stepped exterior of the building is a festive and vivid color scheme using top border paint and neon stripes. Bright awnings and umbrellas continue the theme."

In December 1985, a Two Pesos, Inc., restaurant was opened in Houston. Two Pesos adopted a motif very similar to the foregoing description of Taco Cabana's trade dress. Two Pesos restaurants expanded rapidly in Houston and other markets, but did not enter San Antonio. In 1986, Taco Cabana entered the Houston and Austin markets and expanded into other Texas cities, including Dallas and El Paso where Two Pesos was also doing business.

In 1987, Taco Cabana sued Two Pesos in the United States District Court for the Southern District of Texas for trade dress infringement under § 43(a) of the Lanham Act, 15 U.S.C. § 1125(a), and for theft of trade secrets under Texas common law. The case was tried to a jury, which was instructed to return its verdict in the form of answers to five questions propounded by the trial judge. The jury's answers were: Taco Cabana has a trade dress; taken as a whole, the trade dress is nonfunctional; the trade dress is inherently distinctive; the trade dress has not acquired a secondary meaning in the Texas market; and the alleged infringement creates a likelihood of confusion on the part of ordinary customers as to the source or association of the restaurant's goods or services. Because, as the jury was told, Taco Cabana's trade dress was protected if it either was inherently distinctive or had acquired a secondary meaning, judgment was entered awarding damages to Taco Cabana. In the course of calculating damages, the trial court held that Two Pesos had intentionally and deliberately infringed Taco Cabana's trade dress.

The Court of Appeals ruled that the instructions adequately stated the applicable law and that the evidence supported the jury's findings. In

v. Cin-Bad, Inc., 864 F.2d 1253, 1256 (C.A.5 1989): "The 'trade dress' of a product is essentially its total image and overall appearance." See 932 F.2d 1113, 1118 (C.A.5 1991). It "involves the total image of a product and may include features such as size, shape, color or color combinations, texture, graphics, or even particular sales techniques." *John H. Harland Co. v. Clarke Checks, Inc.*, 711 F.2d 966, 980 (C.A.11 1983).

particular, the Court of Appeals rejected petitioner's argument that a finding of no secondary meaning contradicted a finding of inherent distinctiveness. * * * The Court of Appeals noted that this approach conflicts with decisions of other courts, particularly the holding of the Court of Appeals for the Second Circuit in *Vibrant Sales, Inc. v. New Body Boutique, Inc.*, 652 F.2d 299 (1981), that § 43(a) protects unregistered trademarks or designs only where secondary meaning is shown. We granted certiorari to resolve the conflict among the Courts of Appeals on the question whether trade dress which is inherently distinctive is protectable under § 43(a) without a showing that it has acquired secondary meaning. We find that it is, and we therefore affirm.

II

* * *

A trademark is defined in 15 U.S.C. § 1127 as including "any word, name, symbol, or device or any combination thereof" used by any person "to identify and distinguish his or her goods, including a unique product, from those manufactured or sold by others and to indicate the source of the goods, even if that source is unknown." * * *

Marks which are merely descriptive of a product are not inherently distinctive. When used to describe a product, they do not inherently identify a particular source, and hence cannot be protected. However, descriptive marks may acquire the distinctiveness which will allow them to be protected under the Act. * * * This acquired distinctiveness is generally called "secondary meaning." The concept of secondary meaning has been applied to actions under § 43(a). * * *

* * * There is no persuasive reason to apply to trade dress a general requirement of secondary meaning which is at odds with the principles generally applicable to infringement suits under § 43(a). * * *

Petitioner argues that the jury's finding that the trade dress has not acquired a secondary meaning shows conclusively that the trade dress is not inherently distinctive. The Court of Appeals' disposition of this issue was sound: "Two Pesos' argument—that the jury finding of inherent distinctiveness contradicts its finding of no secondary meaning in the Texas market—ignores the law in this circuit. While the necessarily imperfect (and often prohibitively difficult) methods for assessing secondary meaning address the empirical question of current consumer association, the legal recognition of an inherently distinctive trademark or trade dress acknowledges the owner's legitimate proprietary interest in its unique and valuable informational device, regardless of whether substantial consumer association yet bestows the additional empirical protection of secondary meaning."

* * *

The Fifth Circuit was quite right * * * to follow the *Abercrombie* classifications consistently and to inquire whether trade dress for which protection is claimed under § 43(a) is inherently distinctive. If it is, it is capable of identifying products or services as coming from a specific source and secondary meaning is not required. This is the rule generally applicable to trademark, and the protection of trademarks and trade dress under § 43(a) serves the same statutory purpose of preventing deception and unfair competition. There is no persuasive reason to apply different analysis to the two. * * *

It would be a different matter if there were textual basis in § 43(a) for treating inherently distinctive verbal or symbolic trademarks differently from inherently distinctive trade dress. But there is none. The section does not mention trademarks or trade dress, whether they be called generic, descriptive, suggestive, arbitrary, fanciful, or functional. Nor does the concept of secondary meaning appear in the text of § 43(a). Where secondary meaning does appear in the statute, 15 U.S.C. § 1052, it is a requirement that applies only to merely descriptive marks and not to inherently distinctive ones. We see no basis for requiring secondary meaning for inherently distinctive trade dress protection under § 43(a) but not for other distinctive words, symbols, or devices capable of identifying a producer's product.

Engrafting onto § 43(a) a requirement of secondary meaning for inherently distinctive trade dress also would undermine the purposes of the Lanham Act. Protection of trade dress, no less than of trademarks, serves the Act's purpose to "secure to the owner of the mark the goodwill of his business and to protect the ability of consumers to distinguish among competing producers. National protection of trademarks is desirable, Congress concluded, because trademarks foster competition and the maintenance of quality by securing to the producer the benefits of good reputation." *Park 'N Fly, Inc. v. Dollar Park and Fly, Inc.,* 469 U.S. 189, 198 (1985). By making more difficult the identification of a producer with its product, a secondary meaning requirement for a nondescriptive trade dress would hinder improving or maintaining the producer's competitive position.

Suggestions that under the Fifth Circuit's law, the initial user of any shape or design would cut off competition from products of like design and shape are not persuasive. Only nonfunctional, distinctive trade dress is protected under § 43(a). The Fifth Circuit holds that a design is legally functional, and thus unprotectable, if it is one of a limited number of equally efficient options available to competitors and free competition would be unduly hindered by according the design trademark protection. This serves to assure that competition will not be stifled by the exhaustion of a limited number of trade dresses.

On the other hand, adding a secondary meaning requirement could have anticompetitive effects, creating particular burdens on the start-up of small companies. It would present special difficulties for a business, such as respondent, that seeks to start a new product in a limited area and then expand into new markets. Denying protection for inherently distinctive nonfunctional trade dress until after secondary meaning has been established would allow a competitor, which has not adopted a distinctive trade dress of its own, to appropriate the originator's dress in other markets and to deter the originator from expanding into and competing in these areas.

* * *

We agree with the Court of Appeals that proof of secondary meaning is not required to prevail on a claim under § 43(a) of the Lanham Act where the trade dress at issue is inherently distinctive, and accordingly the judgment of that court is affirmed. * * *

QUALITEX CO. V. JACOBSON PRODUCTS CO., INC.

514 U.S. 159, 115 S.Ct. 1300 (1995).

JUSTICE BREYER delivered the opinion of the Court.

The question in this case is whether the Lanham Trademark Act of 1946 (Lanham Act) permits the registration of a trademark that consists, purely and simply, of a color. We conclude that, sometimes, a color will meet ordinary legal trademark requirements. And, when it does so, no special legal rule prevents color alone from serving as a trademark.

I

The case before us grows out of petitioner Qualitex Company's use (since the 1950's) of a special shade of green-gold color on the pads that it makes and sells to dry cleaning firms for use on dry cleaning presses. In 1989 respondent Jacobson Products (a Qualitex rival) began to sell its own press pads to dry cleaning firms; and it colored those pads a similar green-gold. In 1991 Qualitex registered the special green-gold color on press pads with the Patent and Trademark Office as a trademark. Qualitex subsequently added a trademark infringement count, 15 U.S.C. § 1114(1), to an unfair competition claim, § 1125(a), in a lawsuit it had already filed challenging Jacobson's use of the green-gold color.

Qualitex won the lawsuit in the District Court. But the Court of Appeals for the Ninth Circuit set aside the judgment in Qualitex's favor on the trademark infringement claim because, in that Circuit's view, the Lanham Act does not permit Qualitex, or anyone else, to register "color alone" as a trademark.

The courts of appeals have differed as to whether or not the law recognizes the use of color alone as a trademark. *Compare NutraSweet Co. v. Stadt Corp.*, 917 F.2d 1024, 1028 (C.A.7 1990) (absolute prohibition against protection of color alone), *with In re Owens-Corning Fiberglas Corp.*, 774 F.2d 1116, 1128 (C.A.Fed.1985) (allowing registration of color pink for fiberglass insulation), *and Master Distributors, Inc. v. Pako Corp.*, 986 F.2d 219, 224 (C.A.8 1993) (declining to establish per se prohibition against protecting color alone as a trademark). Therefore, this Court granted certiorari. We now hold that there is no rule absolutely barring the use of color alone, and we reverse the judgment of the Ninth Circuit.

II

The Lanham Act gives a seller or producer the exclusive right to "register" a trademark, 15 U.S.C. § 1052, and to prevent his or her competitors from using that trademark, § 1114(1). Both the language of the Act and the basic underlying principles of trademark law would seem to include color within the universe of things that can qualify as a trademark. The language of the Lanham Act describes that universe in the broadest of terms. It says that trademarks "includ[e] any word, name, symbol, or device, or any combination thereof." § 1127. Since human beings might use as a "symbol" or "device" almost anything at all that is capable of carrying meaning, this language, read literally, is not restrictive. The courts and the Patent and Trademark Office have authorized for use as a mark a particular shape (of a Coca-Cola bottle), a particular sound (of NBC's three chimes), and even a particular scent (of plumeria blossoms on sewing thread). *See, e.g.*, Registration No. 696,147 (Apr. 12, 1960); Registration Nos. 523,616 (Apr. 4, 1950) and 916,522 (July 13, 1971); In re Clarke, 17 U.S.P.Q.2d 1238, 1240 (TTAB 1990). If a shape, a sound, and a fragrance can act as symbols why, one might ask, can a color not do the same?

A color is also capable of satisfying the more important part of the statutory definition of a trademark, which requires that a person "us[e]" or "inten[d] to use" the mark "to identify and distinguish his or her goods, including a unique product, from those manufactured or sold by others and to indicate the source of the goods, even if that source is unknown." 15 U.S.C. § 1127. True, a product's color is unlike "fanciful," "arbitrary," or "suggestive" words or designs, which almost automatically tell a customer that they refer to a brand. The imaginary word "Suntost," or the words "Suntost Marmalade," on a jar of orange jam immediately would signal a brand or a product "source"; the jam's orange color does not do so. But, over time, customers may come to treat a particular color on a product or its packaging (say, a color that in context seems unusual, such as pink on a firm's insulating material or red on the head of a large industrial bolt) as signifying a brand. And, if so, that color would have come to identify and distinguish the goods—i.e. to "indicate" their "source"—much in the way that descriptive words on a product (say, "Trim" on nail clippers or "Car-

Freshner" on deodorizer) can come to indicate a product's origin. In this circumstance, trademark law says that the word (e.g., "Trim"), although not inherently distinctive, has developed "secondary meaning." *See Inwood Laboratories, Inc. v. Ives Laboratories, Inc.*, 456 U.S. 844, 851, n. 11 (1982) ("secondary meaning" is acquired when "in the minds of the public, the primary significance of a product feature . . . is to identify the source of the product rather than the product itself"). Again, one might ask, if trademark law permits a descriptive word with secondary meaning to act as a mark, why would it not permit a color, under similar circumstances, to do the same?

We cannot find in the basic objectives of trademark law any obvious theoretical objection to the use of color alone as a trademark, where that color has attained "secondary meaning" and therefore identifies and distinguishes a particular brand (and thus indicates its "source"). In principle, trademark law, by preventing others from copying a source-identifying mark, "reduce[s] the customer's costs of shopping and making purchasing decisions," 1 J. MCCARTHY, MCCARTHY ON TRADEMARKS AND UNFAIR COMPETITION § 2.01[2], p. 2–3 (3d ed. 1994), for it quickly and easily assures a potential customer that this item—the item with this mark—is made by the same producer as other similarly marked items that he or she liked (or disliked) in the past. At the same time, the law helps assure a producer that it (and not an imitating competitor) will reap the financial, reputation-related rewards associated with a desirable product. The law thereby "encourage[s] the production of quality products," *ibid.*, and simultaneously discourages those who hope to sell inferior products by capitalizing on a consumer's inability quickly to evaluate the quality of an item offered for sale. * * * It is the source-distinguishing ability of a mark—not its ontological status as color, shape, fragrance, word, or sign—that permits it to serve these basic purposes. And, for that reason, it is difficult to find, in basic trademark objectives, a reason to disqualify absolutely the use of a color as a mark.

Neither can we find a principled objection to the use of color as a mark in the important "functionality" doctrine of trademark law. The functionality doctrine prevents trademark law, which seeks to promote competition by protecting a firm's reputation, from instead inhibiting legitimate competition by allowing a producer to control a useful product feature. It is the province of patent law, not trademark law, to encourage invention by granting inventors a monopoly over new product designs or functions for a limited time, 35 U.S.C. §§ 154, 173, after which competitors are free to use the innovation. If a product's functional features could be used as trademarks, however, a monopoly over such features could be obtained without regard to whether they qualify as patents and could be extended forever (because trademarks may be renewed in perpetuity). *See Kellogg Co. v. National Biscuit Co.,* 305 U.S. 111, 119–120 (1938)

(Brandeis, J.); *Inwood Laboratories, Inc.*, 456 U.S., at 863 (White, J., concurring in result) ("A functional characteristic is 'an important ingredient in the commercial success of the product,' and, after expiration of a patent, it is no more the property of the originator than the product itself"). Functionality doctrine therefore would require, to take an imaginary example, that even if customers have come to identify the special illumination-enhancing shape of a new patented light bulb with a particular manufacturer, the manufacturer may not use that shape as a trademark, for doing so, after the patent had expired, would impede competition—not by protecting the reputation of the original bulb maker, but by frustrating competitors' legitimate efforts to produce an equivalent illumination-enhancing bulb. *See, e.g., Kellogg Co.*, 305 U.S., at 119–120 (trademark law cannot be used to extend monopoly over "pillow" shape of shredded wheat biscuit after the patent for that shape had expired). This Court consequently has explained that, "[i]n general terms, a product feature is functional," and cannot serve as a trademark, "if it is essential to the use or purpose of the article or if it affects the cost or quality of the article," that is, if exclusive use of the feature would put competitors at a significant non-reputation-related disadvantage. *Inwood Laboratories, Inc.*, 456 U.S., at 850, n. 10. Although sometimes color plays an important role (unrelated to source identification) in making a product more desirable, sometimes it does not. And, this latter fact—the fact that sometimes color is not essential to a product's use or purpose and does not affect cost or quality—indicates that the doctrine of "functionality" does not create an absolute bar to the use of color alone as a mark. *See Owens-Corning*, 774 F.2d, at 1123 (pink color of insulation in wall "performs no nontrademark function").

It would seem, then, that color alone, at least sometimes, can meet the basic legal requirements for use as a trademark. It can act as a symbol that distinguishes a firm's goods and identifies their source, without serving any other significant function. *See* U.S. DEPT. OF COMMERCE, PATENT AND TRADEMARK OFFICE, TRADEMARK MANUAL OF EXAMINING PROCEDURE § 1202.04(e), p. 1202–13 (2d ed. May, 1993) (approving trademark registration of color alone where it "has become distinctive of the applicant's goods in commerce," provided that "there is [no] competitive need for colors to remain available in the industry" and the color is not "functional"). Indeed, the District Court, in this case, entered findings (accepted by the Ninth Circuit) that show Qualitex's green-gold press pad color has met these requirements. The green-gold color acts as a symbol. Having developed secondary meaning (for customers identified the green-gold color as Qualitex's), it identifies the press pads' source. And, the green-gold color serves no other function. (Although it is important to use some color on press pads to avoid noticeable stains, the court found "no competitive need in the press pad industry for the green-gold color, since other colors are equally usable.") Accordingly, unless there is some special reason that convincingly militates against the use of color alone as a trademark, trademark law would protect Qualitex's use of the green-gold color on its press pads.

III

Respondent Jacobson Products says that there are four special reasons why the law should forbid the use of color alone as a trademark. We shall explain, in turn, why we, ultimately, find them unpersuasive.

First, Jacobson says that, if the law permits the use of color as a trademark, it will produce uncertainty and unresolvable court disputes about what shades of a color a competitor may lawfully use. Because lighting (morning sun, twilight mist) will affect perceptions of protected color, competitors and courts will suffer from "shade confusion" as they try to decide whether use of a similar color on a similar product does, or does not, confuse customers and thereby infringe a trademark. Jacobson adds that the "shade confusion" problem is "more difficult" and "far different from" the "determination of the similarity of words or symbols."

We do not believe, however, that color, in this respect, is special. Courts traditionally decide quite difficult questions about whether two words or phrases or symbols are sufficiently similar, in context, to confuse buyers. They have had to compare, for example, such words as "Bonamine" and "Dramamine" (motion-sickness remedies); "Huggies" and "Dougies" (diapers); "Cheracol" and "Syrocol" (cough syrup); "Cyclone" and "Tornado" (wire fences); and "Mattres" and "1-800-Mattres" (mattress franchisor telephone numbers). Legal standards exist to guide courts in making such comparisons. *See, e.g.*, 2 MCCARTHY § 15.08; 1 MCCARTHY §§ 11.24–11.25 ("[S]trong" marks, with greater secondary meaning, receive broader protection than "weak" marks). We do not see why courts could not apply those standards to a color, replicating, if necessary, lighting conditions under which a colored product is normally sold. Indeed, courts already have done so in cases where a trademark consists of a color plus a design, i.e., a colored symbol such as a gold stripe (around a sewer pipe), a yellow strand of wire rope, or a "brilliant yellow" band (on ampules).

Second, Jacobson argues, as have others, that colors are in limited supply. Jacobson claims that, if one of many competitors can appropriate a particular color for use as a trademark, and each competitor then tries to do the same, the supply of colors will soon be depleted. * * *. By the time one discards colors that, say, for reasons of customer appeal, are not usable, and adds the shades that competitors cannot use lest they risk infringing a similar, registered shade, then one is left with only a handful of possible colors. And, under these circumstances, to permit one, or a few, producers to use colors as trademarks will "deplete" the supply of usable colors to the point where a competitor's inability to find a suitable color will put that competitor at a significant disadvantage.

This argument is unpersuasive, however, largely because it relies on an occasional problem to justify a blanket prohibition. When a color serves as a mark, normally alternative colors will likely be available for similar use by others. *See, e.g., Owens-Corning*, 774 F.2d, at 1121 (pink insulation). Moreover, if that is not so—if a "color depletion" or "color scarcity" problem does arise—the trademark doctrine of "functionality" normally would seem available to prevent the anticompetitive consequences that Jacobson's argument posits, thereby minimizing that argument's practical force.

The functionality doctrine, as we have said, forbids the use of a product's feature as a trademark where doing so will put a competitor at a significant disadvantage because the feature is "essential to the use or purpose of the article" or "affects [its] cost or quality." *Inwood Laboratories, Inc.*, 456 U.S., at 850, n. 10. * * * For example, this Court has written that competitors might be free to copy the color of a medical pill where that color serves to identify the kind of medication (e.g., a type of blood medicine) in addition to its source. *See id.*, at 853, 858, n. 20 ("[S]ome patients commingle medications in a container and rely on color to differentiate one from another"). * * * The Restatement (Third) of Unfair Competition adds that, if a design's "aesthetic value" lies in its ability to "confe[r] a significant benefit that cannot practically be duplicated by the use of alternative designs," then the design is "functional." RESTATEMENT (THIRD) OF UNFAIR COMPETITION § 17, Comment c, pp. 175–176 (1995). The "ultimate test of aesthetic functionality," it explains, "is whether the recognition of trademark rights would significantly hinder competition." *Id.* at 176.

The upshot is that, where a color serves a significant nontrademark function—whether to distinguish a heart pill from a digestive medicine or to satisfy the "noble instinct for giving the right touch of beauty to common and necessary things," G.K. CHESTERTON, SIMPLICITY AND TOLSTOY 61 (1912)—courts will examine whether its use as a mark would permit one competitor (or a group) to interfere with legitimate (nontrademark-related) competition through actual or potential exclusive use of an important product ingredient. That examination should not discourage firms from creating aesthetically pleasing mark designs, for it is open to their competitors to do the same. But, ordinarily, it should prevent the anticompetitive consequences of Jacobson's hypothetical "color depletion" argument, when, and if, the circumstances of a particular case threaten "color depletion."

Third, Jacobson points to many older cases—including Supreme Court cases—in support of its position. * * * [However, Congress subsequently enacted the Lanham Act to "dispense with mere technical prohibitions" and to permit registration of descriptive terms if they had acquired secondary meaning.]

Fourth, Jacobson argues that there is no need to permit color alone to function as a trademark because a firm already may use color as part of a trademark, say, as a colored circle or colored letter or colored word, and may rely upon "trade dress" protection, under § 43(a) of the Lanham Act, if a competitor copies its color and thereby causes consumer confusion regarding the overall appearance of the competing products or their packaging. The first part of this argument begs the question. One can understand why a firm might find it difficult to place a usable symbol or word on a product (say, a large industrial bolt that customers normally see from a distance); and, in such instances, a firm might want to use color, pure and simple, instead of color as part of a design. Neither is the second portion of the argument convincing. Trademark law helps the holder of a mark in many ways that "trade dress" protection does not. *See* 15 U.S.C. § 1124 (ability to prevent importation of confusingly similar goods); § 1072 (constructive notice of ownership); § 1065 (incontestable status); § 1057(b) (prima facie evidence of validity and ownership). Thus, one can easily find reasons why the law might provide trademark protection in addition to trade dress protection.

IV

Having determined that a color may sometimes meet the basic legal requirements for use as a trademark and that respondent Jacobson's arguments do not justify a special legal rule preventing color alone from serving as a trademark (and, in light of the District Court's here undisputed findings that Qualitex's use of the green-gold color on its press pads meets the basic trademark requirements), we conclude that the Ninth Circuit erred in barring Qualitex's use of color as a trademark. For these reasons, the judgment of the Ninth Circuit is

Reversed.

NOTES

1. As a practical matter, can trade dress ever be inherently distinctive? If the trade dress consists of color alone, is secondary meaning required? Why or why not?

2. In *E.R.B.E. Elektromedizin GmbH v. Canady Tech. LLC*, 629 F.3d 1278 (Fed. Cir. 2010), a case involving blue-tipped endoscopic probes used in medical procedures, the court held the color functional as a matter of law when it appeared to "enhance identification of the endoscopic tip [by making it 'more visible' in the course of a procedure], and [when] several companies use blue endoscopic probes." *Id.* at 1289. The court also noted that "the color blue is prevalent in the medical field. . . ." *Id.* How should this additional fact be analyzed? Is it possible to see the color blue as generic, rather than functional, at least in the medical field? In *Sulzer Mixpac AG v. A&N Trading Co.*, 988 F.3d 174 (2d Cir. 2021), the court held that a candy-colored mixing tip on tubes

of products used by dentists was "functional," and therefore unprotected in a trade dress infringement case.

3. Should competitors be able to copy the green color used by a major producer of farm machinery, if farmers prefer their equipment to have matching colors? *See Deere & Co. v. Farmhand, Inc.*, 560 F.Supp. 85, 98 (S.D.Iowa 1982), *aff'd*, 721 F.2d 253 (8th Cir. 1983). Should the color black be protected as trade dress for outboard boat motors, if black makes the motor look smaller and is also compatible with all boat colors? *See Brunswick Corp. v. British Seagull Ltd.*, 35 F.3d 1527, 1532 (Fed. Cir. 1994). Is the blue color of a brand of fertilizer functional because it indicates the presence of nitrogen? *See Nor-Am Chemical v. O.M. Scott & Sons Co.*, 4 U.S.P.Q.2d 1316, 1320 (E.D. Pa. 1987). If the colors of a fishing rod are the natural colors of the high-end materials of which it is composed, can the manufacturer protect this color configuration under trademark law? *See Shakespeare Co. v. Silstar Corp.*, 802 F. Supp. 1386 (D.S.C. 1992), *rev'd on other grounds*, 9 F.3d 1091 (4th Cir. 1993). Are blue and white colors functional in the swimming pool industry? *Polaris Pool Systems, Inc. v. Letro Products, Inc.*, 886 F.Supp. 1513 (C.D.Cal. 1995). Are the shape and color of pills functional if consumers rely on them to identify the type of medication? *See Inwood Labs., Inc. v. Ives Labs., Inc.*, 456 U.S. 844 (1982). Are there different types of functionality, and should all of them be barriers to trademark protection?

4. Can an artist's unique and distinctive style, embodied in a line of fine art posters, be considered trade dress and thereby be protected from imitation by competing artists? *See Romm Art Creations Ltd. v. Simcha International, Inc.*, 786 F.Supp. 1126 (E.D.N.Y. 1992).

5. In listing the advantages of federal trademark registration, the *Qualitex* opinion fails to mention 15 U.S.C. § 1057(c). What benefits does that provision afford to marks registered on the Principal Register?

WAL-MART STORES, INC. V. SAMARA BROTHERS, INC.

529 U.S. 205, 120 S.Ct. 1339 (2000).

SCALIA, J., delivered the opinion for a unanimous Court.

In this case, we decide under what circumstances a product's design is distinctive, and therefore protectible, in an action for infringement of unregistered trade dress under § 43(a) of the Trademark Act of 1946 (Lanham Act).

I

Respondent Samara Brothers, Inc., designs and manufactures children's clothing. Its primary product is a line of spring/summer one-piece seersucker outfits decorated with appliques of hearts, flowers, fruits, and the like. A number of chain stores, including JCPenney, sell this line of clothing under contract with Samara.

Petitioner Wal-Mart Stores, Inc., is one of the nation's best known retailers, selling among other things children's clothing. In 1995, Wal-Mart contracted with one of its suppliers, Judy-Philippine, Inc., to manufacture a line of children's outfits for sale in the 1996 spring/summer season. Wal-Mart sent Judy-Philippine photographs of a number of garments from Samara's line, on which Judy-Philippine's garments were to be based; Judy-Philippine duly copied, with only minor modifications, 16 of Samara's garments, many of which contained copyrighted elements. In 1996, Wal-Mart briskly sold the so-called knockoffs, generating more than $1.15 million in gross profits.

* * *

[Samara sued Wal-Mart for unfair competition under New York law and for infringement of unregistered trade dress under § 43(a) of the Lanham Act. After a jury found in favor of Samara, Wal-mart renewed its motion for judgment as a matter of law, arguing that Samara's clothing designs were not protected by § 43(a). The district court denied the motion, and the Second Circuit affirmed.]

II

* * *

The text of § 43(a) provides little guidance as to the circumstances under which unregistered trade dress may be protected. It does require that a producer show that the allegedly infringing feature is not "functional," *see* § 43(a)(3), and is likely to cause confusion with the product for which protection is sought. Nothing in § 43(a) explicitly requires a producer to show that its trade dress is distinctive, but courts have universally imposed that requirement, since without distinctiveness the trade dress would not "cause confusion . . . as to the origin, sponsorship, or approval of [the] goods," as the section requires. Distinctiveness is, moreover, an explicit prerequisite for registration of trade dress under § 2, and "the general principles qualifying a mark for registration under § 2 of the Lanham Act are for the most part applicable in determining whether an unregistered mark is entitled to protection under § 43(a)." *Two Pesos, Inc. v. Taco Cabana, Inc.*, 505 U.S. 763, 768 (1992).

In evaluating the distinctiveness of a mark under § 2 (and therefore, by analogy, under § 43(a)), courts have held that a mark can be distinctive in one of two ways. First, a mark is inherently distinctive if "[its] intrinsic nature serves to identify a particular source." *Ibid.* In the context of word marks, courts have applied the now-classic test originally formulated by Judge Friendly, in which word marks that are "arbitrary" ("Camel" cigarettes), "fanciful" ("Kodak" film), or "suggestive" ("Tide" laundry detergent) are held to be inherently distinctive. *See Abercrombie & Fitch Co. v. Hunting World, Inc.*, 537 F.2d 4, 10–11 (C.A.2 1976). Second, a mark has acquired distinctiveness, even if it is not inherently distinctive, if it has developed secondary meaning, which occurs when, "in the minds of the public, the primary significance of a [mark] is to identify the source of the product rather than the product itself." *Inwood Laboratories, Inc. v. Ives Laboratories, Inc.*, 456 U.S. 844, 851, n. 11 (1982).

The judicial differentiation between marks that are inherently distinctive and those that have developed secondary meaning has solid foundation in the statute itself. Section 2 requires that registration be granted to any trademark "by which the goods of the applicant may be distinguished from the goods of others"—subject to various limited exceptions. 15 U.S.C. § 1052. It also provides, again with limited exceptions, that "nothing in this chapter shall prevent the registration of a mark used by the applicant which has become distinctive of the applicant's goods in commerce"—that is, which is not inherently distinctive but has become so only through secondary meaning. § 2(f), 15 U.S.C. § 1052(f). Nothing in § 2, however, demands the conclusion that every category of mark necessarily includes some marks "by which the goods of the applicant may be distinguished from the goods of others" without secondary meaning—that in every category some marks are inherently distinctive.

Indeed, with respect to at least one category of mark—colors—we have held that no mark can ever be inherently distinctive. *See Qualitex*, 514 U.S., at 162–163. In *Qualitex*, petitioner manufactured and sold green-gold dry-cleaning press pads. * * * We held that a color could be protected as a trademark, but only upon a showing of secondary meaning. Reasoning by analogy to the *Abercrombie & Fitch* test developed for word marks, we noted that a product's color is unlike a "fanciful," "arbitrary," or "suggestive" mark, since it does not "almost automatically tell a customer that [it] refer[s] to a brand," and does not "immediately . . . signal a brand or a product 'source.'" * * * Because a color, like a "descriptive" word mark, could eventually "come to indicate a product's origin," we concluded that it could be protected upon a showing of secondary meaning.

It seems to us that design, like color, is not inherently distinctive. The attribution of inherent distinctiveness to certain categories of word marks and product packaging derives from the fact that the very purpose of attaching a particular word to a product, or encasing it in a distinctive packaging, is most often to identify the source of the product. Although the words and packaging can serve subsidiary functions—a suggestive word mark (such as "Tide" for laundry detergent), for instance, may invoke positive connotations in the consumer's mind, and a garish form of packaging (such as Tide's squat, brightly decorated plastic bottles for its liquid laundry detergent) may attract an otherwise indifferent consumer's attention on a crowded store shelf—their predominant function remains source identification. Consumers are therefore predisposed to regard those symbols as indication of the producer, which is why such symbols "almost automatically tell a customer that they refer to a brand," *id.*, at 162–163, and "immediately . . . signal a brand or a product 'source,'" *id.*, at 163. And where it is not reasonable to assume consumer predisposition to take an affixed word or packaging as indication of source—where, for example, the affixed word is descriptive of the product ("Tasty" bread) or of a geographic origin ("Georgia" peaches)—inherent distinctiveness will not be found. * * * In the case of product design, as in the case of color, we think consumer predisposition to equate the feature with the source does not exist. Consumers are aware of the reality that, almost invariably, even the most unusual of product designs—such as a cocktail shaker shaped like a penguin—is intended not to identify the source, but to render the product itself more useful or more appealing.

The fact that product design almost invariably serves purposes other than source identification not only renders inherent distinctiveness problematic; it also renders application of an inherent-distinctiveness principle more harmful to other consumer interests. Consumers should not be deprived of the benefits of competition with regard to the utilitarian and esthetic purposes that product design ordinarily serves by a rule of law that facilitates plausible threats of suit against new entrants based upon alleged inherent distinctiveness. How easy it is to mount a plausible suit depends, of course, upon the clarity of the test for inherent distinctiveness, and where product design is concerned we have little confidence that a reasonably clear test can be devised. * * *

It is true, of course, that the person seeking to exclude new entrants would have to establish the nonfunctionality of the design feature, *see* § 43(a)(3)—a showing that may involve consideration of its esthetic appeal, *see Qualitex*, 514 U.S., at 170. Competition is deterred, however, not merely by successful suit but by the plausible threat of successful suit, and given the unlikelihood of inherently source-identifying design, the game of allowing suit based upon alleged inherent distinctiveness seems to us not worth the candle. That is especially so since the producer can ordinarily obtain protection for a design that is inherently source identifying (if any such exists), but that does not yet have secondary meaning, by securing a design patent or a copyright for the design—as, indeed, respondent did for certain elements of the designs in this case. The availability of these other protections greatly reduces any harm to the producer that might ensue from our conclusion that a product design cannot be protected under § 43(a) without a showing of secondary meaning.

Respondent contends that our decision in *Two Pesos* forecloses a conclusion that product-design trade dress can never be inherently distinctive. * * * *Two Pesos* unquestionably establishes the legal principle that trade dress can be inherently distinctive, but it does not establish that product-design trade dress can be. *Two Pesos* is inapposite to our holding here because the trade dress at issue, the decor of a restaurant, seems to us not to constitute product design. It was either product packaging—which, as we have discussed, normally is taken by the consumer to indicate origin—or else some tertium quid that is akin to product packaging and has no bearing on the present case.

Respondent replies that this manner of distinguishing *Two Pesos* will force courts to draw difficult lines between product-design and product-packaging trade dress. There will indeed be some hard cases at the margin: a classic glass Coca-Cola bottle, for instance, may constitute packaging for those consumers who drink the Coke and then discard the bottle, but may constitute the product itself for those consumers who are bottle collectors, or part of the product itself for those consumers who buy Coke in the classic glass bottle, rather than a can, because they think it more stylish to drink from the former. We believe, however, that the frequency and the difficulty of having to distinguish between product design and product packaging will be much less than the frequency and the difficulty of having to decide when a product design is inherently distinctive. To the extent there are close cases, we believe that courts should err on the side of caution and classify ambiguous trade dress as product design, thereby requiring secondary meaning. The very closeness will suggest the existence of relatively small utility in adopting an inherent-distinctiveness principle, and relatively great consumer benefit in requiring a demonstration of secondary meaning.

We hold that, in an action for infringement of unregistered trade dress under § 43(a) of the Lanham Act, a product's design is distinctive, and therefore protectible, only upon a showing of secondary meaning. The judgment of the Second Circuit is reversed, and the case is remanded for further proceedings consistent with this opinion. * * *

NOTES

1. What is the basis for the Court's different treatments of product packaging and product design (also called product configuration)?

2. Should the design of a restaurant or retail store be analyzed as product packaging or product design? What about the brown color of UPS trucks and uniforms?

3. *In re Forney Indus., Inc.*, 955 F.3d 940 (Fed. Cir. 2020), held that multicolored packaging can be inherently distinctive trade dress. The background color of the applicant's packaging consisted of a black horizontal bar above a gradient of horizontal bars starting from yellow and phasing into different shades of orange and finally red at the bottom. Because this was a multicolored mark, it was not subject to the same analysis as the single-color mark at issue in *Qualitex*.

TRAFFIX DEVICES, INC. V. MARKETING DISPLAYS, INC.

532 U.S. 23, 121 S.Ct. 1255 (2001).

JUSTICE KENNEDY delivered the opinion of the Court:

Temporary road signs with warnings like "Road Work Ahead" or "Left Shoulder Closed" must withstand strong gusts of wind. An inventor named Robert Sarkisian obtained two utility patents for a mechanism built upon two springs (the dual-spring design) to keep these and other outdoor signs upright despite adverse wind conditions. The holder of the now-expired Sarkisian patents, respondent Marketing Displays, Inc. (MDI), established a successful business in the manufacture and sale of sign stands incorporating the patented feature. MDI's stands for road signs were recognizable to buyers and users (it says) because the dual-spring design was visible near the base of the sign.

This litigation followed after the patents expired and a competitor, TrafFix Devices, Inc., sold sign stands with a visible spring mechanism that looked like MDI's. * * * [When MDI sued TrafFix for, inter alia, infringement of its trade dress in the dual-spring design, the trial court rejected its claim, but the Sixth Circuit reversed, and the Supreme Court granted certiorari.]

* * *

II

The principal question in this case is the effect of an expired patent on a claim of trade dress infringement. A prior patent, we conclude, has vital significance in resolving the trade dress claim. A utility patent is strong evidence that the features therein claimed are functional. If trade dress protection is sought for those features the strong evidence of functionality based on the previous patent adds great weight to the statutory presumption that features are deemed functional until proved otherwise by the party seeking trade dress protection. Where the expired patent claimed the features in question, one who seeks to establish trade dress protection must carry the heavy burden of showing that the feature is not functional, for instance by showing that it is merely an ornamental, incidental, or arbitrary aspect of the device.

In the case before us, the central advance claimed in the expired utility patents (the Sarkisian patents) is the dual-spring design; and the dual-spring design is the essential feature of the trade dress MDI now seeks to establish and to protect. The rule we have explained bars the trade dress claim, for MDI did not, and cannot, carry the burden of overcoming the strong evidentiary inference of functionality based on the disclosure of the dual-spring design in the claims of the expired patents.

* * *

The rationale for the rule that the disclosure of a feature in the claims of a utility patent constitutes strong evidence of functionality is well illustrated in this case. The dual-spring design serves the important purpose of keeping the sign upright even in heavy wind conditions; and, as confirmed by the statements in the expired patents, it does so in a unique and useful manner. * * * In the course of patent prosecution, it was said that "[t]he use of a pair of spring connections as opposed to a single spring connection . . . forms an important part of this combination" because it "forc[es] the sign frame to tip along the longitudinal axis of the elongated ground-engaging members." The dual-spring design affects the cost of the device as well; it was acknowledged that the device "could use three springs but this would unnecessarily increase the cost of the device." These statements made in the patent applications and in the course of procuring the patents demonstrate the functionality of the design. MDI does not assert that any of these representations are mistaken or inaccurate, and this is further strong evidence of the functionality of the dual-spring design.

III

* * * Discussing trademarks, we have said " '[i]n general terms, a product feature is functional,' and cannot serve as a trademark, 'if it is essential to the use or purpose of the article or if it affects the cost or quality of the article.' " *Qualitex*, 514 U.S., at 165 (quoting *Inwood Laboratories, Inc. v. Ives Laboratories, Inc.*, 456 U.S. 844, 850, n. 10 (1982)). Expanding upon the meaning of this phrase, we have observed that a functional feature is one the "exclusive use of [which] would put competitors at a significant non-reputation-related disadvantage." 514 U.S., at 165. The Court of Appeals in the instant case seemed to interpret this language to mean that a necessary test for functionality is "whether the particular product configuration is a competitive necessity." 200 F.3d, at 940. This was incorrect as a comprehensive definition. As explained in *Qualitex* and *Inwood*, a feature is also functional when it is essential to the use or purpose of the device or when it affects the cost or quality of the device. The *Qualitex* decision did not purport to displace this traditional rule. Instead, it quoted the rule as *Inwood* had set it forth. It is proper to inquire into a "significant non-reputation-related disadvantage" in cases of aesthetic functionality, the question involved in *Qualitex*. Where the design is functional under the *Inwood* formulation there is no need to proceed further to consider if there is a competitive necessity for the feature. In *Qualitex*, by contrast, aesthetic functionality was the central question, there having been no indication that the green-gold color of the laundry press pad had any bearing on the use or purpose of the product or its cost or quality.

* * *

There is no need, furthermore, to engage, as did the Court of Appeals, in speculation about other design possibilities, such as using three or four springs which might serve the same purpose. Here, the functionality of the spring design means that competitors need not explore whether other spring juxtapositions might be used. The dual-spring design is not an arbitrary flourish in the configuration of MDI's product; it is the reason the device works. Other designs need not be attempted.

Because the dual-spring design is functional, it is unnecessary for competitors to explore designs to hide the springs, say by using a box or framework to cover them, as suggested by the Court of Appeals. The dual-spring design assures the user the device will work. If buyers are assured the product serves its purpose by seeing the operative mechanism[,] that in itself serves an important market need. It would be at cross-purposes to those objectives, and something of a paradox, were we to require the manufacturer to conceal the very item the user seeks.

In a case where a manufacturer seeks to protect arbitrary, incidental, or ornamental aspects of features of a product found in the patent claims, such as arbitrary curves in the legs or an ornamental pattern painted on the springs, a different result might obtain. There the manufacturer could perhaps prove that those aspects do not serve a purpose within the terms of the utility patent. The inquiry into whether such features, asserted to be trade dress, are functional by reason of their inclusion in the claims of an expired utility patent could be aided by going beyond the claims and examining the patent and its prosecution history to see if the feature in question is shown as a useful part of the invention. No such claim is made here, however. MDI in essence seeks protection for the dual-spring design alone. The asserted trade dress consists simply of the dual-spring design, four legs, a base, an upright, and a sign. MDI has pointed to nothing arbitrary about the components of its device or the way they are assembled. The Lanham Act does not exist to reward manufacturers for their innovation in creating a particular device; that is the purpose of the patent law and its period of exclusivity. * * * Whether a utility patent has expired or there has been no utility patent at all, a product design which has a particular appearance may be functional because it is "essential to the use or purpose of the article" or "affects the cost or quality of the article." *Inwood*, 456 U.S., at 850, n. 10.

TrafFix and some of its *amici* argue that the Patent Clause of the Constitution, Art. I, § 8, cl. 8, of its own force, prohibits the holder of an expired utility patent from claiming trade dress protection. We need not resolve this question. If, despite the rule that functional features may not be the subject of trade dress protection, a case arises in which trade dress becomes the practical equivalent of an expired utility patent, that will be time enough to consider the matter. The judgment of the Court of Appeals is reversed, and the case is remanded for further proceedings consistent with this opinion.

NOTES

1. What role should the availability of alternative designs play in determining trade dress protection? Is it limited to claims involving aesthetic functionality?

2. Consider the question left open in the last paragraph of the opinion. Should a feature claimed in an expired utility patent be categorically ineligible for trade dress protection? As the Supreme Court noted in *Wal-Mart,* merchants often use design patents to protect designs until they acquire enough secondary meaning to warrant trade dress protection; is this impermissible "double dipping"?

JAY FRANCO & SONS, INC. V. FRANEK

615 F.3d 855 (7th Cir. 2010).

EASTERBROOK, CHIEF JUDGE.

The same year Huey Lewis and the News informed America that it's "Hip To Be Square", Clemens Franek sought to trademark the circular beach towel. His company, CLM Design, Inc., pitched the towel as a fashion statement—"the most radical beach fashion item since the bikini," declared one advertisement. "Bound to be round! Don't be square!" proclaimed another. CLM also targeted lazy sunbathers: "The round shape eliminates the need to constantly get up and move your towel as the sun moves across the sky. Instead merely reposition yourself."

The product enjoyed some initial success. Buoyed by an investment and promotional help from the actor Woody Harrelson (then a bartender on the TV show *Cheers*), CLM had sold more than 30,000 round beach towels in 32 states by the end of 1987. To secure its status as the premier circular-towel maker, the company in 1986 applied for a trademark on the towel's round design. The Patent and Trademark Office registered the "configuration of a round beach towel" as trademark No. 1,502,261 in 1988. But this was not enough to save CLM: Six years later it dissolved. The mark was assigned to Franek, who continues to sell circular towels.

In 2006 Franek discovered that Jay Franco & Sons, a distributor of bath, bedding, and beach accessories, was selling round beach towels. * * * [Franek sued for infringement of his registered trademark under § 32 of the Lanham, Act, 15 U.S.C. § 1114. When the district court granted summary judgment for the defendant on functionality grounds, Franek appealed.]

* * *

TrafFix says that a design is functional when it is "essential to the use or purpose of the device or when it affects the cost or quality of the device," 532 U.S. at 33, a definition cribbed from *Inwood Laboratories, Inc. v. Ives Laboratories, Inc.*, 456 U.S. 844, 850 n. 10 (1982). So if a design enables a product to operate, or improves on a substitute design in some way (such as by making the product cheaper, faster, lighter, or stronger), then the design cannot be trademarked; it is functional because consumers would pay to have it rather than be indifferent toward or pay to avoid it. A qualification is that any pleasure a customer derives from the design's identification of the product's source—the joy of buying a marked good over an identical generic version because the consumer prefers the status conferred by the mark—doesn't count. That broad a theory of functionality would penalize companies for developing brands with cachet to distinguish themselves from competitors, which is the very purpose of trademark law. In short, a design that produces a benefit other than source identification is functional.

Figuring out which designs meet this criterion can be tricky. Utility patents serve as excellent cheat sheets because any design claimed in a patent is supposed to be useful. *See* 35 U.S.C. § 101. For this reason, *TrafFix* held that expired utility patents provide "strong evidence that the features therein claimed are functional." 532 U.S. at 29. The parties in this case wrangle over the relevance of a handful of utility patents that claim circular towels. We need discuss only one (No. 4,794,029), which describes a round beach towel laced with drawstrings that can be pulled to turn the towel into a satchel. This patent's first two claims are:

> 1. A towel-bag construction comprising: a non-rectangular towel;
>
> a casing formed at the perimeter of said towel;
>
> a cord threaded through said casing; and
> a section of relatively non-stretchable fabric of a shape geometrically similar to that of said towel attached with its edges equidistant from the edges of said towel.
>
> 2. A towel-bag construction as set forth in claim 1 wherein said towel is circular in shape, whereby a user while sunbathing may reposition his or her body towards the changing angle of the sun while the towel remains stationary.

Claim 2 sounds like Franek's advertisements, which we quoted above. The patent's specification also reiterates, in both the summary and the detailed description, that a circular towel is central to the invention because of its benefit to lazy sunbathers.

Franek argues that claim 2 does not trigger the *TrafFix* presumption of functionality because his towel does not infringe the '029 patent. * * *

Proving patent infringement can be *sufficient* to show that a trademarked design is useful, as it means that the infringing design is quite similar to a useful invention. But such proof is unnecessary. Functionality is determined by a feature's usefulness, not its patentability or its infringement of a patent. *TrafFix's* ruling that an expired patent (which by definition can no longer be infringed) may evince a design's functionality demonstrates that proof of infringement is unnecessary. * * *

* * *

This "strong evidence" of the round towel's functionality is bolstered by Franek's own advertisements, which highlight two functional aspects of the round beach towel's design. One, also discussed in the '029 patent, is that roundness enables heliotropic sunbathers—tanners who swivel their bodies in unison with the sun's apparent motion in order to maintain an even tan—to remain on their towels as they rotate rather than exert the energy to stand up and reposition their towels every so often, as conventional rectangular towels require.

Franek responds that whatever its shape (golden-ratio rectangle, square, nonagon) any towel can satisfy a heliotropic tanner if it has enough surface area—the issue is size, not shape. That's true, and it is enough to keep the roundness of his towel from being functional under the first prong of *TrafFix's* definition ("essential to the use or purpose of the device") but not the second. For heliotropic sunbathers, a circle surpasses other shapes because it provides the most rotational space without waste. Any non-circle polygon will either limit full rotations (spinning on a normal beach towel leads to sandy hair and feet) or not use all the surface area (a 6′ tall person swiveling on a 6′ by 6′ square towel won't touch the corners). Compared to other shapes that permit full rotations, the round towel requires less material, which makes it easier to fold and carry. That's evidence that the towel's circularity "affects the . . . quality of the device." (The reduction in needed material also suggests that round towels are cheaper to produce than other-shaped towels, though Franek contends that cutting and hemming expenses make them costlier. We express no view on the matter.)

But let us suppose with Franek—who opposed summary judgment and who is thus entitled to all reasonable inferences—that round towels are not measurably better for spinning with the sun. After all, other shapes (squircles, regular icosagons) are similar enough to circles that any qualitative difference may be lost on tanners. Plus, the ability to rotate 180 degrees may be an undesired luxury. Few lie out from dawn 'til dusk (if only to avoid skin cancer) and the daily change in the sun's declination means it will rise due east and set due west just twice a year, during the vernal and autumnal equinoxes. A towel shaped like a curved hourglass that allows only 150 or 120 degrees of rotation (or even fewer) may be all a heliotropic tanner wants. No matter. Franek's mark still is functional.

Franek's advertisements declare that the round towel is a fashion statement. Fashion is a form of function. A design's aesthetic appeal can be as functional as its tangible characteristics. *See Qualitex Co. v. Jacobson Products Co.,* 514 U.S. 159, 169–70 (1995); *Wal-Mart,* 529 U.S. at 214; *TrafFix,* 532 U.S. at 33. And many cases say that fashionable designs can be freely copied unless protected by patent law.

The chief difficulty is distinguishing between designs that are fashionable enough to be functional and those that are merely pleasing. Only the latter group can be protected, because trademark law would be a cruel joke if it limited companies to tepid or repugnant brands that discourage customers from buying the marked wares. * * * The Supreme Court broached the subject in *Qualitex* when it discussed the functionality of the green-gold color of a dry cleaning pad. Unwilling to say that the pad required a green-gold hue or was improved by it, the Court still thought that the color would be functional if its exclusive use by a single designer "would put competitors at a significant non-reputation-related disadvantage." 514 U.S. at 165. This is a problem for Franek's round-towel mark.

Franek wants a trademark on the circle. Granting a producer the exclusive use of a basic element of design (shape, material, color, and so forth) impoverishes other designers' palettes. *See, e.g., Brunswick Corp., v. British Seagull Ltd.,* 35 F.3d 1527 (Fed.Cir.1994) (black color of boat engines is functional because it is compatible with boats of many different colors). *Qualitex's* determination that "color alone, at least sometimes, can meet the basic legal requirements for use as a trademark" (514 U.S. at 166), means that there is no per se rule against this practice. The composition of the relevant market matters. But the more rudimentary and general the element—all six-sided shapes rather than an irregular, perforated hexagon; all labels made from tin rather than a specific tin label; all shades of the color purple rather than a single shade—the more likely it is that restricting its use will significantly impair competition. Franek's towel is of this ilk. He has trademarked the "configuration of a round beach towel." Every other beach towel manufacturer is barred from using the entire shape as well as any other design similar enough that consumers are likely to confuse it with Franek's circle (most regular polygons, for example).

Contrast Franek's mark with the irregular hexagon at issue in *Keene* or the green-gold hue in *Qualitex.* Those marks restrict few design options for competitors. Indeed, they are so distinctive that competitors' only reason to copy them would be to trade on the goodwill of the original designer. That's not so here. A circle is the kind of basic design that a producer like Jay Franco adopts because alternatives are scarce and some consumers want the shape regardless of who manufactures it. There are only so many geometric shapes; few are both attractive and simple enough to fabricate cheaply. *Cf. Qualitex,* 514 U.S. at 168–69 (functionality doctrine invalidates marks that would create color scarcity in a particular market). And some consumers crave round towels-beachgoers who prefer curved edges to sharp corners, those who don't want to be "square," and those who relish the circle's simplicity. A producer barred from selling such towels loses a profitable portion of the market. The record does not divulge much on these matters, but any holes in the evidence are filled by the *TrafFix* presumption that Franek's mark is functional, a presumption he has failed to rebut.

Franek chose to pursue a trademark, not a design patent, to protect the stylish circularity of his beach towel. He must live with that choice. We cannot permit him to keep the indefinite competitive advantage in producing beach towels this trademark creates.

If Franek is worried that consumers will confuse Jay Franco's round beach towels with his, he can imprint a distinctive verbal or pictorial mark on his towels. That will enable him to reap the benefits of his brand while still permitting healthy competition in the beach towel market.

AFFIRMED

NOTE

Which type of functionality figures in Judge Easterbrook's opinion—utilitarian or aesthetic? Is there a meaningful or useful distinction between them?

CHRISTIAN LOUBOUTIN S.A. V. YVES SAINT LAURENT AMERICA HOLDING, INC.

696 F.3d 206 (2d Cir. 2012).

JOSÉ A. CABRANES, CIRCUIT JUDGE:

The question presented is whether a single color may serve as a legally protected trademark in the fashion industry and, in particular, as the mark for a particular style of high fashion women's footwear. Christian Louboutin, a designer of high-fashion women's footwear and accessories, has since 1992 painted the "outsoles" of his women's high-heeled shoes with a high-gloss red lacquer. In 2008, he registered the red lacquered outsole as a trademark with the United States Patent and Trade Office ("PTO"). We are asked to decide whether that mark is protectable under federal trademark law.

* * *

[When Yves Saint Laurent [YSL] began selling a line of monochrome shoes in purple, green, yellow and red, Louboutin sought a preliminary injunction on the ground that YSL's red monochrome shoes infringed Louboutin's registered trademark in the red sole. YSL counterclaimed for cancellation of Louboutin's registration on the grounds that, inter alia, the red sole mark was functional and lacked distinctiveness.]

Interpreting the Supreme Court's holding in *Qualitex,* the District Court explained that color is protectable as a trademark only if it " 'acts as a symbol that distinguishes a firm's goods and identifies their source, *without serving any other significant function.*' " The District Court further observed, albeit without citation to authority, that "whatever commercial purposes may support extending trademark protection to a single color for industrial goods do not easily fit the unique characteristics and needs—the creativity, aesthetics, taste, and seasonal change—that define production of articles of fashion." For that reason, the District Court held that, in the fashion industry, single-color marks are inherently "functional" and that any such registered trademark would likely be held invalid. The Court therefore held that Louboutin was unlikely to be able to prove that the Red Sole Mark was eligible for trademark protection, and denied Louboutin's motion for a preliminary injunction. This appeal followed.

* * *

III. The "Functionality" Defense

As the Supreme Court observed in *Qualitex,* aspects of a product that are "functional" generally "cannot serve as a trademark." We have observed that "[t]he doctrine of functionality prevents trademark law from inhibiting legitimate competition by giving monopoly control to a producer over a useful product." *Nora Beverages, Inc.,* 269 F.3d at 120 n. 4. This is so because functional features can be protected only through the patent system, which grants a limited monopoly over such features until they are released into general use (typically after either 14 or 20 years, depending on the type of patent).

As noted above, two forms of the functionality doctrine are relevant to us today: "traditional" or "utilitarian" functionality, and "aesthetic" functionality. Both forms serve as an affirmative defense to a trademark infringement claim.

A. "Traditional" or "Utilitarian" Functionality

According to our traditional understanding of functionality, a product feature is considered to be "functional" in a utilitarian sense if it is (1) "essential to the use or purpose of the article," or if it (2) "affects the cost or quality of the article." *Inwood Labs.,* 456 U.S. at 850 n. 10. A feature is essential " 'if [it] is dictated by the functions to be performed' " by the article. *LeSportsac, Inc. v. K mart Corp.,* 754 F.2d 71, 76 (2d Cir.1985). It affects the cost or quality of the article where it " 'permits the article to be manufactured at a lower cost' or 'constitutes an improvement in the operation of the goods.' "[14] *Id.* A finding that a product feature is functional according to the *Inwood* test will ordinarily render the feature ineligible for trademark protection.

B. "Aesthetic Functionality"

Generally, "[w]here [a product's] design is functional under the *Inwood* formulation there is no need to proceed further." *TrafFix Devices, Inc. v. Marketing Displays, Inc.*, 532 U.S. 23, 33 (2001). Nevertheless, as the Supreme Court had held in 1995 in *Qualitex*, when the aesthetic design of a product is *itself* the mark for which protection is sought, we may also deem the mark functional if giving the markholder the right to use it exclusively "would put competitors at a significant non-reputation-related disadvantage," *Qualitex*, 514 U.S. at 165. This remains true even if there is "no indication that [the mark has] any bearing on the use or purpose of the product or its cost or quality." *TrafFix*, 532 U.S. at 33; *see Landscape Forms, Inc. v. Colum. Cascade Co.*, 70 F.3d 251, 253 (2d Cir.1995) (when evaluating design trademarks we consider whether "certain features of the design are essential to effective competition in [the] particular market").

As set forth below, the test for aesthetic functionality is threefold: At the start, we address the two prongs of the *Inwood* test, asking whether the design feature is either "essential to the use or purpose" or "affects the cost or quality" of the product at issue. Next, if necessary, we turn to a third prong, which is the competition inquiry set forth in *Qualitex*. In other words, if a design feature would, from a traditional utilitarian perspective, be considered "essential to the use or purpose" of the article, or to affect its cost or quality, then the design feature is functional under *Inwood* and our inquiry ends.[15] But if the design feature is not "functional" from a traditional perspective, it must still pass the fact-intensive *Qualitex* test and be shown not to have a significant effect on competition in order to receive trademark protection.

i. The Development of the Aesthetic Functionality Doctrine

Although the theory of aesthetic functionality was proposed as early as 1938,[16] the first court to adopt the theory as the basis for denial of protection of a design was the United States Court of Appeals for the Ninth Circuit in *Pagliero v. Wallace China Co.*, 198 F.2d 339 (9th Cir.1952). In

[14] In *Warner Brothers*, we cited as examples *Kellogg Co. v. National Biscuit Co.*, 305 U.S. 111, 122 (1938), in which the pillow shape of a shredded wheat biscuit was deemed functional because the cost of the cereal would be increased and its quality lessened by any other form, and *Fisher Stoves Inc. v. All Nighter Stove Works, Inc.*, 626 F.2d 193, 195 (1st Cir.1980), in which a two-tier woodstove design was deemed functional because it improved the operation of the stove.

[15] *See, e.g., Industria Arredamenti Fratelli Saporiti v. Charles Craig, Ltd.*, 725 F.2d 18, 19 (2d Cir.1984) (interlocking design of couch cushions was a visual "label" but served a utilitarian purpose by keeping cushions in place and was therefore functional).

[16] In 1938, the Restatement of Torts stated that "[a] feature of goods is functional . . . if it affects their purpose, action or performance, or the facility or economy of processing, handling or using them; it is non-functional if it does not have any of such effects." Restatement of Torts § 742.

Pagliero, the Court of Appeals determined that the Wallace China Company was not entitled to the exclusive use of a particular floral design on hotel china, despite its "creat[ion of] a substantial market for its products bearing these designs by virtue of extensive advertising." The design, the Court held, was "functional" because it satisfied "a demand for the aesthetic as well as for the utilitarian." Because the "particular feature is an *important ingredient* in the commercial success of the product, the interest in free competition permits its imitation in the absence of a patent or copyright."

Despite its apparent counterintuitiveness (how can the purely aesthetic be deemed functional, one might ask?), our Court has long accepted the doctrine of aesthetic functionality.[17] We have rejected, however, the circular "important ingredient" test formulated by the *Pagliero* court, which inevitably penalized markholders for their success in promoting their product. Instead, we have concluded that "Lanham Act protection does not extend to configurations of ornamental features which would *significantly* limit the range of competitive designs available." *Coach Leatherware Co. v. AnnTaylor, Inc.,* 933 F.2d 162, 171 (2d Cir.1991) (emphasis added). Accordingly, we have held that the doctrine of aesthetic functionality bars protection of a mark that is "necessary to compete in the [relevant] market." *Villeroy & Boch Keramische Werke K.G. v. THC Sys., Inc.,* 999 F.2d 619, 622 (2d Cir.1993).

ii. A Modern Formulation of the Aesthetic Functionality Doctrine

In 1995, the Supreme Court in *Qualitex* gave its imprimatur to the aesthetic functionality doctrine, holding that "[t]he ultimate test of aesthetic functionality . . . is whether the recognition of trademark rights [in an aesthetic design feature] would significantly hinder competition." *Qualitex,* 514 U.S. at 170. Six years later, reiterating its *Qualitex* analysis, the Supreme Court in *TrafFix* declared that where "[a]esthetic functionality [is] the central question," courts must "inquire" as to whether recognizing the trademark "would put competitors at a significant non-reputation-related disadvantage." *TrafFix,* 532 U.S. at 32–33.

---

[17] The doctrine of aesthetic functionality remains controversial in our sister circuits, which have applied the doctrine in varying ways (and some not at all). For example, the Seventh Circuit has applied the doctrine of aesthetic functionality liberally, holding that "[f]ashion is a form of function." *See Jay Franco & Sons, Inc. v. Franek,* 615 F.3d 855, 860 (7th Cir.2010). The Sixth Circuit recently discussed the doctrine, but made clear that it has not yet decided whether or not to adopt it. *See Maker's Mark Distillery, Inc. v. Diageo N. Am., Inc.,* 679 F.3d 410, 417–19 (6th Cir.2012). The Ninth Circuit has applied the doctrine inconsistently. *See* 1 McCarthy on Trademarks § 7:80 (4th ed.) (collecting cases). The Fifth Circuit rejects the doctrine of aesthetic functionality entirely. *Bd. of Supervisors for La. State Univ. Agric. & Mech. Coll. v. Smack Apparel Co.,* 550 F.3d 465, 487–88 (5th Cir.2008) (arguing that the Supreme Court has recognized the aesthetic functionality doctrine only in *dicta,* and that therefore the Fifth Circuit's long-standing rejection of the doctrine was not abrogated by *Qualitex* and *TrafFix*).

Although we have not recently had occasion to apply the doctrine of aesthetic functionality thus enunciated by the Supreme Court, it is clear that the combined effect of *Qualitex* and *TrafFix* was to validate the aesthetic functionality doctrine as it had already been developed by this Court * * *.

On the one hand, " '[w]here an ornamental feature is claimed as a trademark and trademark protection would significantly hinder competition by limiting the range of adequate alternative designs, the aesthetic functionality doctrine denies such protection.' " *Forschner Grp., Inc. v. Arrow Trading Co.,* 124 F.3d 402, 409–10 (2d Cir.1997). But on the other hand, " 'distinctive and arbitrary arrangements of predominantly ornamental features that do *not* hinder potential competitors from entering the same market with differently dressed versions of the product are non-functional[,] and [are] hence eligible for [trademark protection].' " *Fabrication Enters., Inc.,* 64 F.3d at 59 (emphasis added).

In short, a mark is aesthetically functional, and therefore ineligible for protection under the Lanham Act, where protection of the mark *significantly* undermines competitors' ability to compete in the relevant market. *See Knitwaves, Inc. v. Lollytogs Ltd.,* 71 F.3d 996, 1006 (2d Cir.1995) (linking aesthetic functionality to availability of alternative designs for children's fall-themed sweaters); *Landscape Forms, Inc.,* 70 F.3d at 253 (holding that "in order for a court to find a product design functional, it must first find that certain features of the design are essential to effective competition in a particular market"). In making this determination, courts must carefully weigh "the competitive benefits of protecting the source-identifying aspects" of a mark against the "competitive costs of precluding competitors from using the feature." *Fabrication Enters., Inc.,* 64 F.3d at 59.

Finally, we note that a product feature's successful source indication can sometimes be difficult to distinguish from the feature's aesthetic function, if any. Therefore, in determining whether a mark has an aesthetic function so as to preclude trademark protection, we take care to ensure that the mark's very success in denoting (and promoting) its source does not itself defeat the markholder's right to protect that mark. *See Wallace Int'l Silversmiths, Inc.,* 916 F.2d at 80 (rejecting argument that "the commercial success of an aesthetic feature automatically destroys all of the originator's trademark interest in it, notwithstanding the feature's secondary meaning and the lack of any evidence that competitors cannot develop non-infringing, attractive patterns").

Because aesthetic function and branding success can sometimes be difficult to distinguish, the aesthetic functionality analysis is highly fact-specific. In conducting this inquiry, courts must consider both the markholder's right to enjoy the benefits of its effort to distinguish its product and the public's right to the "vigorously competitive market [ ]" protected by the Lanham Act, which an overly broad trademark might hinder. *Yurman Design, Inc.*, 262 F.3d at 115. In sum, courts must avoid jumping to the conclusion that an aesthetic feature is functional merely because it denotes the product's desirable source.

iii. Aesthetic Functionality in the Fashion Industry

We now turn to the *per se* rule of functionality for color marks in the fashion industry adopted by the District Court—a rule that would effectively deny trademark protection to any deployment of a single color in an item of apparel. As noted above, the *Qualitex* Court expressly held that "sometimes [] a color will meet ordinary legal trademark requirements[, a]nd, when it does so, no special legal rule prevents color alone from serving as a trademark." *Qualitex,* 514 U.S. at 161. In other words, the Supreme Court specifically forbade the implementation of a *per se* rule that would deny protection for the use of a single color as a trademark in a particular industrial context. *Qualitex* requires an individualized, fact-based inquiry into the nature of the trademark, and cannot be read to sanction an industry-based *per se* rule. The District Court created just such a rule, on the theory that "there is something unique about the fashion world that militates against extending trademark protection to a single color."

Even if *Qualitex* could be read to permit an industry-specific *per se* rule of functionality (a reading we think doubtful), such a rule would be neither necessary nor appropriate here. We readily acknowledge that the fashion industry, like other industries, has special concerns in the operation of trademark law; it has been argued forcefully that United States law does not protect fashion design adequately. Indeed, the case on appeal is particularly difficult precisely because, as the District Court well noted, in the fashion industry, color can serve as a tool in the palette of a designer, rather than as mere ornamentation.

Nevertheless, the functionality defense does not guarantee a competitor "the greatest range for [his] creative outlet," but only the ability to fairly compete within a given market. *See Wallace Int'l Silversmiths, Inc.*, 916 F.2d at 81 ("It is a first principle of trademark law that an owner may not use the mark as a means of *excluding* competitors from a . . . market." (emphasis added)). The purpose of the functionality defense "is to prevent advances in functional design from being *monopolized* by the owner of [the mark] . . . in order to encourage competition and the broadest dissemination of useful design features." *Fabrication Enters., Inc.*, 64 F.3d at 58 (emphasis added).

In short, "[b]y focusing upon hindrances to legitimate competition, the [aesthetic] functionality test, carefully applied, can accommodate consumers' somewhat conflicting interests in being assured enough product differentiation to avoid confusion as to source and in being afforded the benefits of competition among producers." *Stormy Clime,* 809 F.2d at 978–79.

IV. The Red Sole Mark

Having determined that no *per se* rule governs the protection of single-color marks in the fashion industry, any more than it can do so in any other industry, we turn our attention to the Red Sole Mark. * * *

* * *

A. Distinctiveness

We first address whether the Red Sole Mark "merits protection" as a distinctive mark. As discussed above, distinctiveness may be shown either by proof that the mark is itself inherently distinctive, or by showing that the mark has acquired, through use, secondary meaning in the public eye. For the reasons that follow, we hold that the Red Sole Mark has acquired limited secondary meaning as a distinctive symbol that identifies the Louboutin brand, and that it is therefore a valid and protectable mark as modified below.

Although a single color, standing alone, can almost never be inherently distinctive because it does not "almost automatically tell a customer that [it] refer[s] to a brand," *Qualitex,* 514 U.S. at 162–63 (emphasis omitted), a color as used here is certainly capable of acquiring secondary meaning. * * *

We see no reason why a single-color mark in the specific context of the fashion industry could not acquire secondary meaning—and therefore serve as a brand or source identifier—if it is used so consistently and prominently by a particular designer that it becomes a symbol, "the primary significance" of which is "to identify the source of the product rather than the product itself." *Inwood Labs.,* 456 U.S. at 851 n. 11.

* * *

In light of the evidence in the record, including extensive consumer surveys submitted by both parties during the preliminary injunction proceedings, and of the factual findings of the District Court, we think it plain that Louboutin's marketing efforts have created what the able district judge described as "a . . . brand with worldwide recognition." By placing the color red "in [a] context [that] seems unusual," *Qualitex,* 514 U.S. at 162, and deliberately tying that color to his product, Louboutin has created an identifying mark firmly associated with his brand which, "to those in the know," "instantly" denotes his shoes' source. These findings of fact by the District Court in addressing a motion for a preliminary injunction are not clearly erroneous. We hold that the lacquered red outsole, as applied to a shoe with an "upper" of a different color, has "come to identify and distinguish" the Louboutin brand, and is therefore a distinctive symbol that qualifies for trademark protection.

We further hold that the record fails to demonstrate that the secondary meaning of the Red Sole Mark extends to uses in which the sole *does not* contrast with the upper—in other words, when a red sole is used on a monochromatic red shoe. As the District Court observed, "[w]hen Hollywood starlets cross red carpets and high fashion models strut down runways, and heads turn and eyes drop to the celebrities' feet, lacquered red outsoles on *high-heeled, black shoes* flaunt a glamorous statement that *pops out* at once." (emphasis added). As clearly suggested by the District Court, it is the *contrast* between the sole and the upper that causes the sole to "pop," and to distinguish its creator.

The evidentiary record further demonstrates that the Louboutin mark is closely associated with contrast. For example, Pinault, the chief executive of YSL's parent company, wrote that the "distinctive signature" of the Mark is in its "contrast with the general presentation of the [shoe], particularly its upper." Of the hundreds of pictures of Louboutin shoes submitted to the District Court, only *four* were monochrome red. And Louboutin's own consumer surveys show that when consumers were shown the YSL monochrome red shoe, of those consumers who misidentified the pictured shoes as Louboutin-made, nearly every one cited the red *sole* of the shoe, rather than its general red color. We conclude, based upon the record before us, that Louboutin has not established secondary meaning in an application of a red sole to a red shoe, but *only* where the red sole contrasts with the "upper" of the shoe. The use of a red lacquer on the outsole of a red shoe of the same color is not a use of the Red Sole Mark.

Because we conclude that the secondary meaning of the mark held by Louboutin extends only to the use of a lacquered red outsole that contrasts with the adjoining portion of the shoe, we modify the Red Sole Mark, pursuant to Section 37 of the Lanham Act, 15 U.S.C. § 1119,[26] insofar as it is sought to be applied to any shoe bearing the same color "upper" as the outsole. We therefore instruct the Director of the Patent and Trade Office to limit the registration of the Red Sole Mark to only those situations in which the red lacquered outsole contrasts in color with the adjoining "upper" of the shoe.

In sum, we hold that the Red Sole Mark is valid and enforceable as modified. This holding disposes of the Lanham Act claims brought by both Louboutin and YSL because the red sole on YSL's monochrome shoes is neither a use of, nor confusingly similar to, the Red Sole Mark. We therefore affirm the denial of the preliminary injunction insofar as

[26] 15 U.S.C. § 1119 provides that "[i]n any action involving a registered mark the court may determine the right to registration, order the cancellation of registrations, *in whole or in part,* restore canceled registrations, and otherwise rectify the register with respect to the registrations of any party to the action. * * *

Louboutin could not have shown a likelihood of success on the merits in the absence of an infringing use of the Red Sole Mark by YSL.

A. Likelihood of Confusion and Functionality

Having limited the Red Sole Mark as described above, and having established that the red sole used by YSL is not a use of the Red Sole Mark, it is axiomatic that we need not—and should not—address either the likelihood of consumer confusion or whether the modified Mark is functional.

* * *

NOTES

1. Can a fragrance be protected as a trademark? Does your answer depend on the nature of the goods or services? For example, does it matter whether the product is sewing thread, dishwashing liquid, perfume, or welding compound? *See In re Clarke*, 17 U.S.P.Q.2d 1238 (T.T.A.B. 1990).

2. Can the overall shape of a blender be protectable as a trademark? A gold-fish shaped cracker? A bedroom suite? The shape of a bottle? What if the design is useful in placing the bottle on a bicycle? *Talking Rain Beverage Co. v. South Beach Beverage Co.*, 349 F.3d 601 (9th Cir. 2003).

3. To what extent can trade dress exist in an entire product line? *See Rose Art Industries, Inc. v. Swanson*, 235 F.3d 165 (3d Cir. 2000).

4. Trade dress protection for a design does not preclude copyright or design patent protection for that same design. However, the standards for obtaining protection under each regime are different. Design patents can be especially useful for any trade dress that is treated as a descriptive mark, since the design patent will give the owner the exclusive use of the design for 15 years, during which time the design may acquire sufficient secondary meaning to qualify for trade dress protection.

CHAPTER 3

ESTABLISHING TRADEMARK RIGHTS

■ ■ ■

This chapter examines the rules for establishing a right of priority in an eligible trademark. Part A addresses common law priority. Part B examines the substantive and procedural aspects of federal trademark registration, as well as its benefits. Part C examines the interrelationship between common law priority and priority arising from federal registration. Although states have their own registration systems, state registrations provide different benefits from federal registration, and have their own substantive and procedural rules.

A. COMMON LAW TRADEMARKS

GALT HOUSE, INC. V. HOME SUPPLY CO.

483 S.W.2d 107 (Ky. 1972).

REED, JUDGE.

The plaintiff, Galt House, Inc., instituted this action to enjoin the defendants, Home Supply Company, and its principal officer and stockholder, Al J. Schneider, from operating a new hotel in Louisville, Kentucky, under the assumed trade name "Galt House." * * *

In February 1964, the plaintiff, Galt House, Inc., incorporated under the laws of this state. * * * Plaintiff's president and sole shareholder is Arch Stallard, Sr., a real estate broker in Louisville, Kentucky, who specializes in hotel and motel real estate. Mr. Stallard has on occasions since the date of the filing of plaintiff's articles of incorporation made a few sporadic inquiries concerning possible locations for a hotel and considered engaging in an enterprise by which a franchise operation would be effected. These few efforts came to naught and Mr. Stallard testified that because of illness and death in his family he had been "laying dormant."

* * *

In April 1969, Home Supply Company, through its president Schneider, submitted to the city agency plans of a hotel bearing the name Galt House. This name had been recommended to Schneider by the then mayor of the City of Louisville, Kenneth Schmied, and the chairman of the Riverfront Development Commission, Archibald Cochran. The trial judge found from the evidence that throughout discussions leading up to the bidding, the new hotel was referred to as the Galt House and has been so referred to since. Home Supply Company was the successful bidder, was awarded the contract, and construction commenced in May 1970. A new hotel, 26 stories in height with 714 rooms, is now nearly completed and has affixed a sign bearing the name "The Galt House." The hotel already has scheduled future conventions and room reservations, although it will not open until after May 1972. In April 1971, Home Supply Company applied for and received from the Secretary of State of Kentucky a registration and service mark of the name "The Galt House."

Plaintiff filed suit in August 1971, seeking to enjoin the defendants from any use of the name Galt House. * * *

During the Nineteenth Century the Galt House Hotel was a famous hostelry in Louisville with an excellent and widely recognized reputation. * * *

The Galt House, located on Main Street at Second Street, occupied separate buildings during its existence as a hotel. The second Galt House was destroyed by fire in January 1865 at a reported loss of $1,000,000. The third Galt House, a magnificent structure in its day, was abandoned as a hotel and ceased operations in 1920. Belknap Hardward Company thereafter occupied the site of the last Galt House.

Thus, it would appear that since 1920 there has been no use of the name Galt House in connection with or to describe a hotel. The name doubtless strikes interest when used in the presence of history buffs and among those familiar with the folklore of Louisville. Among such cognoscenti the name encourages remembrance of things past.

As found by the circuit judge, the corporation which operated the last Galt House was formed in 1911 and its formal corporate existence expired in 1961. From 1920 to 1961, however, it did not engage in the hotel business. Therefore, the name Galt House had not been used in connection with a going business for 49 years when defendants undertook to use it as the name of their new hotel in 1969.

The primary argument asserted by the plaintiff actually rests upon a premise that by mere incorporation under a corporate name it retains the right to exclude others from the use of that name so long as the corporation legally exists. * * *

Surely the plaintiff acquires no standing to enjoin under the accepted principles of the law of unfair competition. Under the modern extended scope of the doctrine of unfair competition, its present outer limits afford protection and relief against the unjust appropriation of, or injury to, the good will or business reputation of another, even though he is not a competitor. Plaintiff is concededly a nonuser of the contested name.

Plaintiff has no customers, conducts no real or substantial business and has never held its name out to the public in connection with any going business. Therefore, by its inaction, it could not have established either a good will or reputation which the defendants could be legitimately accused of pirating as a competitor or otherwise. Therefore, if plaintiff has standing to enjoin, its status must rest upon the acquisition of a protectable right by its act of incorporation under the contested name.

* * *

The plaintiff * * * relies upon the case of *Drugs Consolidated v. Drug Incorporated*, 16 Del.Ch. 240, 144 A. 656 (1929). In our view the opinion in that case undertakes to prove too much. There is dictum that the corporation statutes of Delaware, which are substantially similar to the corporation statutes of Kentucky so far as the present point is concerned, assure a right to have the corporate name distinguished from other corporations of like kind subsequently created and that this right does not depend on showing of actual use, in business, of the name, but the right exists as soon as corporate existence is brought into being and as long as it continues; the specific factual findings in the opinion, however, demonstrate that the plaintiff corporation, although it was not yet actually engaged in the business of manufacturing and marketing drugs, had, nevertheless, been engaged in promoting the objects and purposes of its incorporation. Therefore, if this opinion represents a holding that a nonuser of a corporate name retains the right to pre-empt that name during the period of its formal corporate existence without ever having engaged in carrying on any of the objects and purposes of the corporation, it is contrary to the weight of authority concerning that proposition and does not, in our opinion, represent the generally accepted view.

The *Drugs Consolidated* opinion was cited with approval by the Mississippi Supreme Court in *Meridian Yellow Cab Co. v. City Yellow Cabs*, 206 Miss. 812, 41 So.2d 14 (1949). In this case, however, the plaintiff who first incorporated had actually commenced operations at the time it sought to enjoin the defendant who had later incorporated under a similar name. Although the plaintiff did not commence business until after the defendant, it, nevertheless, did actually start active operations in the taxicab business within three years of the date of its incorporation and within two months after the defendant actually operated taxicabs; whether the plaintiff was theretofore engaged in activities to promote the objects and purposes of the corporation is not mentioned. However misplaced that court's reliance on the *Drugs Consolidated* case may have been, its decision, which granted the plaintiff injunctive relief, does not militate against our conclusion in this case that the plaintiff's act of incorporation in a particular name preempts the use of that name by a subsequent user only for a reasonable period in which to allow plaintiff's business to begin. To this extent, incorporation and registration take the place of use[ ] in the case of a trade name. Pre-emption for a reasonable period of time in which to allow the business to begin is not the equivalent of a perpetual monopoly of the trade name without use in trade. * * *

In the instant case, the plaintiff possessed neither good will nor a reasonable prospect to acquire it. Its right to preempt the name by the mere act of incorporation had expired because a reasonable period in which to allow business to begin had passed and the plaintiff neither alleged nor could show reasonable prospect to acquire good will through actively engaging in business. * * *

NOTES

1. As the court points out, neither party in this case was the first to use "Galt House" as a service mark for a hotel in Louisville. In fact, the previous Galt House was quite famous. Will Home Supply actually be able to assert exclusive rights in the mark? Under what theory? Could the renewed use of the mark lead to consumer confusion as to the new hotel's affiliation?

2. Individual states vary as to the kinds of activities that constitute "use" of a mark for purposes of establishing priority. As indicated in *Galt House*, some states may allow a grace period after adoption of a corporate or business name. Others award priority based only on the date on which the goods or services associated with the mark were actually made available to the public for purchase. Others may consider the date on which the mark was first used in advertising the goods or services. Which activities could be considered Home Supply's first use of the Galt House mark?

3. Consider this scenario: At roughly the same time, apparel manufacturers Farah and Blue Bell independently decided to adopt "Time Out" as a trademark for their new lines of men's clothing. On July 3, Farah sent one pair of slacks bearing the "Time Out" mark to each of its twelve regional sales managers; the managers paid for them, and the slacks became their personal property. Advertising began later in July, but the first sales to customers took place in September. In contrast, although Blue Bell intended to use the "Time Out" mark on an entirely new line of men's clothing, initially it attached labels bearing the mark to an existing line of trousers that already bore one of its other marks, "Mr. Hicks," and on July 5 it began shipping these double-tagged items to purchasers that had ordered "Mr. Hicks" slacks. Blue Bell began manufacturing its new "Time Out" merchandise in August, started advertising it in September, and shipped its first orders to customers in October. Under the applicable state law (Texas), trademark priority goes to the first user of the mark, and a mark is "used" when (1) it is affixed to the goods, and (2) the goods are "sold, displayed for sale, or otherwise publicly distributed." Which party has priority for the "Time Out" mark under state law? *See Blue Bell, Inc. v. Farah Manufacturing Co.*, 508 F.2d 1260 (5th Cir. 1975).

4. The Lanham Act has its own rules for determining federal registration priority. These are discussed in Part B below. The problem illustrated by the *Blue Bell* case can also arise in determining priority for federal registration. However, in that context it arises less frequently today than in the past, because Congress created an intent-to-use application, 15 U.S.C. § 1051(b), that enables merchants to establish federal registration priority even before they commence use of their marks. Intent-to-use applications are discussed later in this chapter.

B. FEDERAL REGISTRATION

Chapter 2 examined the generally applicable rules for determining whether a mark is eligible for protection, without regard to whether it is federally registered. In this section, we examine the substantive and procedural requirements for registration on the Principal Register, as well as its benefits.

1. BENEFITS OF FEDERAL REGISTRATION

First, consider the advantages of registering a mark on the Principal Register: 15 U.S.C. § 1124 (ability to prevent importation of confusingly similar goods); § 1072 (constructive notice of ownership); §§ 1065 and 1115 (incontestable status); § 1057(b) (prima facie evidence of validity and ownership); and § 1057(c) (nationwide constructive use as of the applicant's filing date). Applicants must weigh the value of these benefits against the cost of registration, including periodic renewal fees.

In the following case, the Supreme Court explained the benefits of incontestability under sections 1065 and 1115. Incontestable status does not exist at common law; it applies only to marks on the Principal Register. Why is incontestability especially important for descriptive marks? How does a mark achieve this status?

Statutes: 15 U.S.C. §§ 1065, 1115

PARK 'N FLY, INC. V. DOLLAR PARK AND FLY, INC.

469 U.S. 189, 105 S.Ct. 658 (1985).

JUSTICE O'CONNOR delivered the opinion of the Court.

In this case we consider whether an action to enjoin the infringement of an incontestable trade or service mark may be defended on the grounds that the mark is merely descriptive. We conclude that neither the language of the relevant statutes nor the legislative history supports such a defense.

I

[Petitioner operates long-term parking lots near airports in multiple cities. Six years after registering its "Park 'N Fly" service mark on the

Principal Register, Petitioner filed an affidavit with the Patent Office to establish incontestable status. Petitioner also filed an infringement action against Respondent, which provides similar services under the name "Dollar Park and Fly." As a defense, Respondent argued that Petitioner's mark was merely descriptive. Although the district court ruled for Petitioner, the Ninth Circuit reversed, holding that while incontestability protects a mark from being cancelled on descriptiveness grounds, a defendant can still raise descriptiveness as a defense to infringement of that mark.]

* * *

This case requires us to consider the effect of the incontestability provisions of the Lanham Act in the context of an infringement action defended on the grounds that the mark is merely descriptive. Statutory construction must begin with the language employed by Congress and the assumption that the ordinary meaning of that language accurately expresses the legislative purpose. With respect to incontestable trade or service marks, § 33(b) of the Lanham Act states that "registration shall be conclusive evidence of the registrant's exclusive right to use the registered mark" subject to the conditions of § 15 and certain enumerated defenses. Section 15 incorporates by reference subsections (c) and (e) of § 14, 15 U.S.C. § 1064. An incontestable mark that becomes generic may be canceled at any time pursuant to § 14(c). That section also allows cancellation of an incontestable mark at any time if it has been abandoned, if it is being used to misrepresent the source of the goods or services in connection with which it is used, or if it was obtained fraudulently or contrary to the provisions of § 4, 15 U.S.C. § 1054, or §§ 2(a)–(c), 15 U.S.C. §§ 1052(a)–(c).

One searches the language of the Lanham Act in vain to find any support for the offensive/defensive distinction applied by the Court of Appeals. The statute nowhere distinguishes between a registrant's offensive and defensive use of an incontestable mark. On the contrary, § 33(b)'s declaration that the registrant has an "exclusive right" to use the mark indicates that incontestable status may be used to enjoin infringement by others. A conclusion that such infringement cannot be enjoined renders meaningless the "exclusive right" recognized by the statute. Moreover, the language in three of the defenses enumerated in § 33(b) clearly contemplates the use of incontestability in infringement actions by plaintiffs. *See* §§ 33(b)(4)–(6), 15 U.S.C. §§ 1115(b)(4)–(6).

The language of the Lanham Act also refutes any conclusion that an incontestable mark may be challenged as merely descriptive. A mark that is merely descriptive of an applicant's goods or services is not registrable unless the mark has secondary meaning. Before a mark achieves incontestable status, registration provides prima facie evidence of the registrant's exclusive right to use the mark in commerce. § 33(a), 15 U.S.C. § 1115(a). The Lanham Act expressly provides that before a mark becomes incontestable an opposing party may prove any legal or equitable defense which might have been asserted if the mark had not been registered. *Ibid.* Thus, § 33(a) would have allowed respondent to challenge petitioner's mark as merely descriptive if the mark had not become incontestable. With respect to incontestable marks, however, § 33(b) provides that registration is conclusive evidence of the registrant's exclusive right to use the mark, subject to the conditions of § 15 and the seven defenses enumerated in § 33(b) itself. Mere descriptiveness is not recognized by either § 15 or § 33(b) as a basis for challenging an incontestable mark.

* * *

III

Nothing in the legislative history of the Lanham Act supports a departure from the plain language of the statutory provisions concerning incontestability. Indeed, a conclusion that incontestable status can provide the basis for enforcement of the registrant's exclusive right to use a trade or service mark promotes the goals of the statute. The Lanham Act provides national protection of trademarks in order to secure to the owner of the mark the goodwill of his business and to protect the ability of consumers to distinguish among competing producers. National protection of trademarks is desirable, Congress concluded, because trademarks foster competition and the maintenance of quality by securing to the producer the benefits of good reputation. The incontestability provisions, as the proponents of the Lanham Act emphasized, provide a means for the registrant to quiet title in the ownership of his mark. * * * The opportunity to obtain incontestable status by satisfying the requirements of § 15 thus encourages producers to cultivate the goodwill associated with a particular mark. This function of the incontestability provisions would be utterly frustrated if the holder of an incontestable mark could not enjoin infringement by others so long as they established that the mark would not be registrable but for its incontestable status.

* * *

Respondent's argument that enforcing petitioner's mark will not promote the goals of the Lanham Act is misdirected. Arguments similar to those now urged by respondent were in fact considered by Congress in hearings on the Lanham Act. For example, the United States Department of Justice opposed the incontestability provisions and expressly noted that a merely descriptive mark might become incontestable. Hearings on H.R. 82, at 59–60 (statement of the U.S. Dept. of Justice). This result, the Department of Justice observed, would "go beyond existing law in conferring unprecedented rights on trade-mark owners," and would undesirably create an exclusive right to use language that is descriptive of a product. *Id.* at 60. These concerns were answered by proponents of the Lanham Act, who noted that a merely descriptive mark cannot be registered unless the Commissioner finds that it has secondary meaning. Moreover, a mark can be challenged for five years prior to its attaining incontestable status. The supporters of the incontestability provisions further observed that a generic mark cannot become incontestable and that § 33(b)(4) allows the nontrademark use of descriptive terms used in an incontestable mark.

* * *

We conclude that the holder of a registered mark may rely on incontestability to enjoin infringement and that such an action may not be defended on the grounds that the mark is merely descriptive. * * *

NOTE

Incontestability generally renders the existence of secondary meaning irrelevant to the validity of the registered mark. However, under sections 14(3) and (5), 15 U.S.C. §§ 1064(3), (5), the incontestable mark can still be cancelled on other grounds. What are they? *See, e.g., Specialized Seating, Inc. v. Greenwich Industries*, 616 F.3d 722 (7th Cir. 2010) (incontestable mark found to be functional). These grounds can also serve as defenses to infringement of an incontestable mark. *See* 15 U.S.C. § 1115.

2. THE REGISTRATION PROCESS

Statutes: 15 U.S.C. §§ 1051–52

a. Registration Based on Use

B&B HARDWARE, INC. V. HARGIS INDUSTRIES, INC.

575 U.S. 138, 135 S.Ct. 1293 (2015).

JUSTICE ALITO delivered the opinion of the Court.

Sometimes two different tribunals are asked to decide the same issue. When that happens, the decision of the first tribunal usually must be followed by the second, at least if the issue is really the same. Allowing the same issue to be decided more than once wastes litigants' resources and adjudicators' time, and it encourages parties who lose before one tribunal to shop around for another. The doctrine of collateral estoppel or issue preclusion is designed to prevent this from occurring.

This case concerns the application of issue preclusion in the context of trademark law. Petitioner, B & B Hardware, Inc. (B & B), and respondent Hargis Industries, Inc. (Hargis), both use similar trademarks; B & B owns SEALTIGHT while Hargis owns SEALTITE. Under the Lanham Act, an applicant can seek to register a trademark through an administrative process within the United States Patent and Trademark Office (PTO). But if another party believes that the PTO should not register a mark because it is too similar to its own, that party can oppose registration before the Trademark Trial and Appeal Board (TTAB). Here, Hargis tried to register the mark SEALTITE, but B & B opposed SEALTITE's registration. After a lengthy proceeding, the TTAB agreed with B & B that SEALTITE should not be registered.

In addition to permitting a party to object to the registration of a mark, the Lanham Act allows a mark owner to sue for trademark infringement. Both a registration proceeding and a suit for trademark infringement, moreover, can occur at the same time. In this case, while the TTAB was deciding whether SEALTITE should be registered, B & B and Hargis were also litigating the SEALTIGHT versus SEALTITE dispute in federal court. In both registration proceedings and infringement litigation, the tribunal asks whether a likelihood of confusion exists between the mark sought to be protected (here, SEALTIGHT) and the other mark (SEALTITE).

The question before this Court is whether the District Court in this case should have applied issue preclusion to the TTAB's decision that SEALTITE is confusingly similar to SEALTIGHT. Here, the Eighth Circuit rejected issue preclusion for reasons that would make it difficult for the doctrine ever to apply in trademark disputes. We disagree with that narrow understanding of issue preclusion. Instead, consistent with principles of law that apply in innumerable contexts, we hold that a court should give preclusive effect to TTAB decisions if the ordinary elements of issue preclusion are met. We therefore reverse the judgment of the Eighth Circuit and remand for further proceedings.

* * *

Though federal law does not create trademarks, Congress has long played a role in protecting them. In 1946, Congress enacted the Lanham Act, the current federal trademark scheme. As relevant here, the Lanham Act creates at least two adjudicative mechanisms to help protect marks. First, a trademark owner can register its mark with the PTO. Second, a mark owner can bring a suit for infringement in federal court.

Registration is significant. The Lanham Act confers "important legal rights and benefits" on trademark owners who register their marks. * * *

To obtain the benefits of registration, a mark owner files an application with the PTO. § 1051. The application must include, among other things, "the date of the applicant's first use of the mark, the date of the applicant's first use of the mark in commerce, the goods in connection with which the mark is used, and a drawing of the mark." § 1051(a)(2). The usages listed in the application—*i.e.,* those goods on which the mark appears along with, if applicable, their channels of distribution—are critical. *See, e.g.*, 3 McCarthy § 20:24, at 20–83 ("[T]he applicant's right to register must be made on the basis of the goods described in the application"). The PTO generally cannot register a mark which "so resembles" another mark "as to be likely, when used on or in connection with the goods of the applicant, to cause confusion, or to cause mistake, or to deceive." 15 U.S.C. § 1052(d).

If a trademark examiner believes that registration is warranted, the mark is published in the Official Gazette of the PTO. § 1062. At that point, "[a]ny person who believes that he would be damaged by the registration" may "file an opposition." § 1063(a). Opposition proceedings occur before the TTAB (or panels thereof). § 1067(a). The TTAB consists of administrative trademark judges and high-ranking PTO officials, including the Director of the PTO and the Commissioner of Trademarks. § 1067(b).

Opposition proceedings before the TTAB are in many ways "similar to a civil action in a federal district court." TTAB Manual of Procedure § 102.03 (2014) (hereinafter TTAB Manual). These proceedings, for instance, are largely governed by the Federal Rules of Civil Procedure and Evidence. The TTAB also allows discovery and depositions. The party opposing registration bears the burden of proof, and if that burden cannot be met, the opposed mark must be registered, *see* 15 U.S.C. § 1063(b).

The primary way in which TTAB proceedings differ from ordinary civil litigation is that "proceedings before the Board are conducted in writing, and the Board's actions in a particular case are based upon the written record therein." In other words, there is no live testimony. Even so, the TTAB allows parties to submit transcribed testimony, taken under oath and subject to cross-examination, and to request oral argument.

When a party opposes registration because it believes the mark proposed to be registered is too similar to its own, the TTAB evaluates likelihood of confusion by applying some or all of the 13 factors set out in *In re E.I. DuPont DeNemours & Co.*, 476 F.2d 1357 (CCPA 1973). After the TTAB decides whether to register the mark, a party can seek review in the U.S. Court of Appeals for the Federal Circuit, or it can file a new action in district court. *See* 15 U.S.C. § 1071. In district court, the parties can conduct additional discovery and the judge resolves registration *de novo*. § 1071(b).

The Lanham Act, of course, also creates a federal cause of action for trademark infringement. The owner of a mark, whether registered or not, can bring suit in federal court if another is using a mark that too closely resembles the plaintiff's. The court must decide whether the defendant's use of a mark in commerce "is likely to cause confusion, or to cause mistake, or to deceive" with regards to the plaintiff's mark. *See* 15 U.S.C. § 1114(1)(a) (registered marks); § 1125(a)(1)(A) (unregistered marks). In infringement litigation, the district court considers the full range of a mark's usages, not just those in the application.

* * *

[When Hargis sought to register SEALTITE, B&B opposed the registration on the ground that SEALTITE was confusingly similar to B&B's registered mark, SEALTIGHT. The opposition proceedings before the TTAB involved discovery, including depositions. Applying the *DuPont* factors, the TTAB ruled in favor of B&B. Hargis did not seek judicial review. When B&B sued Hargis for infringement, the District Court refused to give the TTAB's decision preclusive effect on the question of likelihood of confusion, and the jury ultimately found no likelihood of confusion. On appeal, the Eighth Circuit affirmed because, *inter alia,* the TTAB and the Eighth Circuit use different factors to assess the likelihood of confusion.]

Although the idea of issue preclusion is straightforward, it can be challenging to implement. The Court, therefore, regularly turns to the Restatement (Second) of Judgments for a statement of the ordinary elements of issue preclusion. The Restatement explains that subject to certain well-known exceptions, the general rule is that "[w]hen an issue of fact or law is actually litigated and determined by a valid and final judgment, and the determination is essential to the judgment, the determination is conclusive in a subsequent action between the parties, whether on the same or a different claim." Restatement (Second) of Judgments § 27, p. 250 (1980); *see also id.*, § 28, at 273 (listing exceptions such as whether appellate review was available or whether there were "differences in the quality or extensiveness of the procedures followed").

* * *

The Eighth Circuit's primary objection to issue preclusion was that the TTAB considers different factors than it does. Whereas the TTAB employs some or all of the *DuPont* factors to assess likelihood of confusion, the Eighth Circuit looks to similar, but not identical, factors identified in *SquirtCo v. Seven-Up Co.*, 628 F.2d 1086, 1091 (C.A.8 1980). The court's instinct was sound: "[I]ssues are not identical if the second action involves application of a different legal standard, even though the factual setting of both suits may be the same." 18 C. Wright, A. Miller, & E. Cooper, Federal Practice & Procedure § 4417, p. 449 (2d ed. 2002). Here, however, the same likelihood-of-confusion standard applies to both registration and infringement.

To begin with, it does not matter that registration and infringement are governed by different statutory provisions. Often a single standard is placed in different statutes; that does not foreclose issue preclusion. *See, e.g., Smith v. Bayer Corp.*, 564 U.S. 299, 307–08 (2011). Neither does it matter that the TTAB and the Eighth Circuit use different factors to assess likelihood of confusion. For one thing, the factors are not fundamentally different, and "[m]inor variations in the application of what is in essence the same legal standard do not defeat preclusion." *Id.*, at 312 n. 9. More important, if federal law provides a single standard, parties cannot escape preclusion simply by litigating anew in tribunals that apply that one standard differently. A contrary rule would encourage the very evils that issue preclusion helps to prevent.

The real question, therefore, is whether likelihood of confusion for purposes of registration is the same standard as likelihood of confusion for purposes of infringement. We conclude it is, for at least three reasons. First, the operative language is essentially the same; the fact that the registration provision separates "likely" from "to cause confusion, or to cause mistake, or to deceive" does not change that reality. Second, the likelihood-of-confusion language that Congress used in these Lanham Act provisions has been central to trademark registration since at least 1881. That could hardly have been by accident. And third, district courts can cancel registrations during infringement litigation, just as they can adjudicate infringement in suits seeking judicial review of registration decisions. *See* 15 U.S.C. § 1119. There is no reason to think that the same district judge in the same case should apply two separate standards of likelihood of confusion.

Hargis responds that the text is not actually the same because the registration provision asks whether the marks "resemble" each other, 15 U.S.C. § 1052(d), while the infringement provision is directed towards the "use in commerce" of the marks, § 1114(1). Indeed, according to Hargis, the distinction between "resembl[ance]" and "use" has been key to trademark law for over a century. There is some force to this argument. It is true that "a party opposing an application to register a mark before the Board often relies only on its federal registration, not on any common-law rights in usages not encompassed by its registration," and "the Board typically analyzes the marks, goods, and channels of trade only as set forth in the application and in the opposer's registration, regardless of whether the actual usage of the marks by either party differs." Brief for United States as *Amicus Curiae* 23; see also *id.*, at 5 (explaining that "the Board typically reviews only the usages encompassed by the registration"); 3 McCarthy § 20:15, at 20–45 (explaining that for registration "it is the mark as shown in the application and as used on the goods described in the application which must be considered, not the mark as actually used"). This means that unlike in infringement litigation, "[t]he Board's determination that a likelihood of confusion does or does not exist will not resolve the confusion issue with respect to non-disclosed usages."

Hargis' argument falls short, however, because it mistakes a reason not to apply issue preclusion in some or even many cases as a reason never to apply issue preclusion. Just because the TTAB does not always consider the *same usages* as a district court does, it does not follow that the Board applies a *different standard* to the usages it does consider. If a mark owner uses its mark in ways that are materially the same as the usages included in its registration application, then the TTAB is deciding the same likelihood-of-confusion issue as a district court in infringement litigation. By contrast, if a mark owner uses its mark in ways that are materially unlike the usages in its application, then the TTAB is not deciding the same issue. Thus, if the TTAB does not consider the marketplace usage of the parties' marks, the TTAB's decision should "have no later preclusive effect in a suit where actual usage in the marketplace is the paramount issue." 6 McCarthy § 32:101, at 32–246.

Materiality, of course, is essential—trivial variations between the usages set out in an application and the use of a mark in the marketplace do not create different "issues," just as trivial variations do not create different "marks." *See generally* 4 *id.*, § 23:50, at 23–265 (explaining that "adding descriptive or non-distinctive" elements to another's mark generally will not negate confusion). Otherwise, a party could escape the preclusive effect of an adverse judgment simply by adding an immaterial feature to its mark. That is not the law.

* * *

Hargis also argues that registration is categorically incompatible with issue preclusion because the TTAB uses procedures that differ from those used by district courts. Granted, "[r]edetermination of issues is warranted if there is reason to doubt the quality, extensiveness, or fairness of procedures followed in prior litigation." But again, this only suggests that sometimes issue preclusion might be inappropriate, not that it always is.

No one disputes that the TTAB and district courts use different procedures. Most notably, district courts feature live witnesses. Procedural differences, by themselves, however, do not defeat issue preclusion. * * * Rather than focusing on whether procedural differences exist—they often will—the correct inquiry is whether the procedures used in the first proceeding were fundamentally poor, cursory, or unfair.

Here, there is no categorical "reason to doubt the quality, extensiveness, or fairness" of the agency's procedures. In large part they are exactly the same as in federal court. For instance, although "[t]he scope of discovery in Board proceedings. . . . is generally narrower than in court proceedings"—reflecting the fact that there are often fewer usages at issue—the TTAB has adopted almost the whole of Federal Rule of Civil Procedure 26. It is conceivable, of course, that the TTAB's procedures may prove ill-suited for a particular issue in a particular case, *e.g.*, a party may have tried to introduce material evidence but was prevented by the TTAB from doing so, or the TTAB's bar on live testimony may materially prejudice a party's ability to present its case. The ordinary law of issue preclusion, however, already accounts for those "rare" cases where a "compelling showing of unfairness" can be made. Restatement (Second) of Judgments § 28, Comments *g* and *j*, at 283–284.

* * *

Hargis also contends that the stakes for registration are so much lower than for infringement that issue preclusion should never apply to TTAB decisions. Issue preclusion may be inapt if "the amount in controversy in the first action [was] so small in relation to the amount in controversy in the second that preclusion would be plainly unfair." Restatement (Second) of Judgments § 28, Comment *j*, at 283–284. * * * Hargis is wrong, however, that this exception to issue preclusion applies to every registration. To the contrary: When registration is opposed, there is good reason to think that both sides will take the matter seriously.

The benefits of registration are substantial. * * *

The importance of registration is undoubtedly why Congress provided for *de novo* review of TTAB decisions in district court. It is incredible to think that a district court's adjudication of particular usages would not have preclusive effect in another district court. Why would unchallenged TTAB decisions be different? Congress' creation of this elaborate registration scheme, with so many important rights attached and backed up by plenary review, confirms that registration decisions can be weighty enough to ground issue preclusion.

V

For these reasons, the Eighth Circuit erred in this case. On remand, the court should apply the following rule: So long as the other ordinary elements of issue preclusion are met, when the usages adjudicated by the TTAB are materially the same as those before the district court, issue preclusion should apply. * * *

QUESTIONS

1. In infringement litigation between the same two parties that participated in an opposition proceeding, if the same marks are involved, when will issue preclusion *not* apply?

2. Should the circuit courts (other than the Federal Circuit) change their likelihood of confusion analysis by adopting the *DuPont* factors?

3. Does issue preclusion also apply to: (1) a district court's de novo review of an *ex parte* TTAB registration decision? (2) a district court's de novo review of a TTAB opposition decision? (3) a direct appeal to the Federal Circuit of a TTAB registration or opposition decision?

4. Recall the *Galt House* and *Blue Bell* cases discussed earlier in this chapter. Both considered whether particular activities constituted "use" of a mark for purposes of establishing common law priority. Under the Lanham Act, what type of activity constitutes a "use in commerce" that qualifies a mark for federal registration? *See* 15 U.S.C. § 1127 (defining "use in commerce" separately for goods and services). Is it sufficient to advertise the goods or services across state lines—*e.g.*, on billboards, television commercials, or the internet? *See Couture v. Playdom, Inc.*, 778 F.3d 1379 (Fed. Cir. 2015) (promoting a service on a website before actually providing it to customers). If a restaurant has only one location, but serves interstate travelers on a busy highway, does the restaurant's mark satisfy the use in commerce requirement for federal registration? *See Larry Harmon Pictures Corp. v. Williams Rest. Corp.*, 929 F.2d 662 (Fed. Cir. 1991).

5. Section 2(d) is the key provision addressing priority rights for federal trademark registration, and should be read carefully. (Additional priority provisions are addressed later in this chapter.) Consider whether a mark can be registered if it would create a likelihood of confusion with:

(a) A mark already in use and not abandoned, which is used only in *intra*state commerce.

(b) A business or corporate name that is not a trademark.

(c) A mark that has been advertised in the U.S. but not yet used on goods and services offered to the public.

(d) A foreign mark that is not used in the United States but is well known to U.S. consumers. *See Belmora LLC v. Bayer Consumer Care AG*, 819 F.3d 697 (4th Cir. 2016) (excerpted in Part B of Chapter 4).

(e) A mark registered on the PTO's Supplemental Register, 15 U.S.C. § 1091, rather than the Principal Register.

(f) A mark that is the subject of an intent-to-use application, 15 U.S.C. § 1051(b) (discussed in the next section).

6. In establishing priority of use for purposes of section 2(d), "tacking" is allowed. This means that a trademark owner or applicant that has made minor changes to its mark over time can rely on the earlier version of its mark if both versions make the same overall commercial impression. *See Hana Financial, Inc. v. Hana Bank*, 574 U.S. 418 (2015).

7. As noted in *B & B Hardware*, the opposition process in 15 U.S.C. § 1063 allows parties to present the Trademark Trial and Appeal Board (TTAB) with reasons why a particular trademark application should be rejected. An application to register may be opposed based on any of the grounds listed in section 2, 15 U.S.C. § 1052. To have standing to oppose a registration, the challenger must have a reasonable basis for believing it will be damaged by the registration. Beyond that, the test for standing depends on the basis asserted for challenging the mark. In most cases, such as section 2(d), the challenger must also have a "real commercial interest in its own marks."

However, only a "direct and personal stake" is required for oppositions under 2(a) which assert that marks falsely suggest an affiliation with a person, institution, or belief. In an opposition based on descriptiveness under section 2(e)(1), the opposer is typically a business with a legitimate interest in using the descriptive term in promoting its own goods or services.

8. Although registration on the Principal Register is prima facie evidence of a mark's validity, 15 U.S.C. § 1057(b), an existing registration can be cancelled on any of the grounds listed in section 14, 15 U.S.C. § 1064. *See, e.g., Quicksilver, Inc. v. Kymsta Corp.*, 466 F.3d 749 (9th Cir. 2006) ("The presumption of validity may be rebutted 'by showing that the registrant had not established valid ownership rights in the mark at the time of registration' "; that is, "if [the non-registrant] can show that [it] used the mark in commerce first, then the registration may be invalidated."). In general, a party that would have had standing to oppose a registration also has standing to seek its cancellation. Several grounds for cancellation apply even if the mark is incontestable. Which ones?

9. Congress enacted the Trademark Modernization Act of 2020, making important changes to trademark examination and maintenance procedures under the Lanham Act. The Act, which took effect on December 18, 2021, facilitates the clearing of registration of unused trademarks and enables the USPTO to move applicants through the registration process more efficiently.

b. Intent-to-Use Applications

B&B Hardware described the process for registering a trademark on the Principal Register based on actual use of the mark in commerce. Use-based applications are governed by section 1(a) of the Lanham Act, 15 U.S.C. § 1051(a).

In addition to use-based applications, section 1(b) of the Lanham Act permits applications based on an applicant's "bona fide intent to use" a particular mark in commerce. 15 U.S.C. § 1051(b). Intent-to-use applications (ITUs) undergo a preliminary examination for registrability. 15 U.S.C. § 1062(a). At this stage, the mark is examined solely in light of the goods or services disclosed in the ITU application. Depending on the circumstances, the examiner may be able to assess whether the proposed mark is generic, inherently distinctive, descriptive, geographic, confusingly similar to an existing mark, or primarily merely a surname. If the examiner finds no basis for rejecting the application, it is then published for opposition. *Id.* If there is no successful opposition, the PTO grants a Notice of Allowance. *Id.* § 1063(b)(2). In contrast, once a use-based application survives the opposition period, the registration will issue. The ITU applicant then has 6 months (or up to 2 years with extensions for good cause) to file a statement verifying and specifying the use in commerce. *Id.* § 1051(d). There follows a second examination that considers the actual use (including specimens); if the examiner is satisfied that the mark is eligible, then registration will be granted.

Note, however, that it can be difficult to successfully oppose an ITU application, because the applicant's mark has not yet been used. Thus, it may be hard to establish that a trademark is deceptive, descriptive, deceptively misdescriptive, or functional when the goods are not yet available for inspection. If the opposer fails to establish grounds to reject the ITU application at this stage, the TTAB will dismiss the opposition without prejudice. However, there is no second opportunity to oppose the registration. Therefore, even if the applicant's actual use of the mark later reveals a basis for opposition, it will be too late to oppose. Of course, the PTO's second examination at this stage may lead to rejection of the application. However, if the PTO allows the mark to be registered, the erstwhile opposer will instead have to petition to cancel the mark.

In *Eastman Kodak Co. v. Bell & Howell Document Management Products Co.*, 994 F.2d 1569 (Fed. Cir. 1993), the Federal Circuit upheld a challenge to the TTAB's policy of requiring oppositions to be filed *before* actual use of the mark in commerce:

> [I]t is clear from the legislative history that Congress, for policy reasons, chose to sequence the opposition process before the use of an intent-to-use mark had commenced. *See* S.Rep. No. 515 at 32, 1988 U.S.C.C.A.N. at 5595 ("Subjecting an intent-to-use application to the opposition process before the applicant makes use of its mark is essential if the system is to achieve its goal of reducing uncertainty before the applicant invests in commercial use of the mark."). Accordingly, Congress knew that some issues of registrability could not be decided in opposition proceedings and would therefore have to be addressed in the post-use PTO examination or challenged in a cancellation proceeding after the mark was registered.

Id. at 1572. With respect to descriptive marks, the court concluded that, in at least some cases, the ITU application would include enough information to establish the mark's descriptiveness even without specimens of use:

> First, there are words and phrases that, as applied to certain goods, the examining attorney in the initial examination could certainly find to be prima facie merely descriptive. For example, an examining attorney could easily find that the term "reader/printer" applied to the microfilm reader/printers at issue here would be merely descriptive or that the term "slow-cooker" was merely descriptive of a Dutch oven.

Id. at 1572–73.

NOTES

1. Some observers have criticized the ITU system. In *Eastman Kodak*, Kodak expressed concern that brand names may be "tied up" through the ITU provision. Is this a legitimate concern? Does the ITU process have sufficient constraints to prevent strategic behavior designed to lock up desirable marks? Why have an ITU system at all?

2. Consider the distinction between numerical product designations that are used as "model numbers" and those that are used as trademarks. Can you think of examples of each? *See generally Arrow Fastener Co. v. Stanley Works*, 59 F.3d 384 (2d Cir. 1995) ("T-50" term used on staple guns could not function as both a trademark and a model designation). What about Levi's 501 jeans?

3. In what circumstances can the descriptiveness of a proposed trademark be determined prior to its actual use? In what circumstances would descriptiveness become evident only after the mark is in use? How would the PTO handle an intent-to-use application for "Soft Sleep" mattresses?

c. Priority Based on Foreign Applications

The Lanham Act grants special registration priority to certain foreign applicants. As a signatory to the International Convention for the Protection of Industrial Property (the "Paris Convention"), the U.S. grants registration priority to foreign nationals from other Paris Convention countries. Under section 44(d) of the Lanham Act, 15 U.S.C. § 1126(d), once the foreign applicant files an application for the same mark in a Paris Convention country, if that applicant files the U.S. application within six months, the effective filing date of the U.S. application will date back to the date of the foreign filing. If the U.S. application succeeds, the foreign filing date will also be the date of the mark's first constructive use in the U.S. The U.S. registration will issue at the earliest of (1) the date the mark is registered in the applicant's country of origin, or (2) the date of the applicant's actual use in commerce. If the former occurs first, the foreign registrant is entitled to maintain the U.S. registration for six years without using the mark in commerce—much longer than under the ITU process.

3. MARKS ELIGIBLE FOR REGISTRATION

Statute: 15 U.S.C. § 1052

a. Bars to Registration

The bars to registering a trademark or service mark on the Principal Register of the PTO are set out in sections 2(a)–(f) of the Lanham Act, 15 U.S.C. §§ 1052(a)–(f). These bars to registration also serve as the grounds for oppositions. The *B & B Hardware* case, reproduced above, has already introduced one of those rules: Under section 2(d), a mark may not be registered if its use would create a likelihood of confusion with other marks already registered, or previously used in the United States by another and not abandoned. The following cases explore some of the other bars to registration.

IN RE BUDGE MANUFACTURING CO., INC.

857 F.2d 773 (Fed. Cir. 1988).

NIES, CIRCUIT JUDGE.

Budge Manufacturing Co., Inc., appeals from the final decision of the United States Trademark Trial and Appeal Board refusing registration of LOVEE LAMB for "automotive seat covers." The basis for rejection is that the term LAMB is deceptive matter within the meaning of section 2(a) of the Lanham Act, 15 U.S.C. § 1052(a), as applied to Budge's goods which are made wholly from synthetic fibers. We affirm.

Opinion

Section 2(a) of the Lanham Act bars registration of a mark which: "Consists of or comprises . . . deceptive . . . matter. . . ." As stated in *In re Automatic Radio Mfg. Co.*, 404 F.2d 1391, 1396 (CCPA 1969): "The proscription [of section 2(a)] is not against misdescriptive terms unless they are also deceptive." Thus, that a mark or part of a mark may be inapt or misdescriptive as applied to an applicant's goods does not make it "deceptive." *Id.* (AUTOMATIC RADIO not a deceptive mark for air conditioners, ignition systems, and antennas). Recognizing that premise, the Trademark Trial and Appeal Board has sought to articulate a standard by which "deceptive matter" under section 2(a) can be judged. In this case, the board applied the three-part test which was stated in *In re Shapely, Inc.*, 231 USPQ 72, 73 (TTAB 1986): (1) whether the term is misdescriptive as applied to the goods, (2) if so, whether anyone would be likely to believe the misrepresentation, and (3) whether the misrepresentation would materially affect a potential purchaser's decision to buy the goods.

Budge argues that the board was bound to follow the standard articulated in *In re Simmons, Inc.*, 192 USPQ 331 (TTAB 1976). Per Budge, *Simmons* sets forth a different standard in that it requires as a minimum that "the mark convey some information, upon which an intended customer may reasonably rely, concerning something about the character, quality, function, composition or use of the goods to induce the purchase thereof, but which information, in fact, is misleadingly false." *Id.* at 332.

The standard applied by the board for determining deceptive matter in section 2(a) cases has not been uniformly articulated in some material respects. For example, in at least one opinion an intent to mislead was required to establish section 2(a) deceptiveness. *See Steinberg Bros., Inc. v. Middletown Rubber Corp.*, 137 USPQ 319, 321 (TTAB 1963). However, while phrased differently, we discern no material difference between the standard set forth in *Shapely* and that in *Simmons*. * * *

* * * Where the issue relates to deceptive misdescriptiveness within the meaning of 2(a), we are in general agreement with the standard set out by the board in *Shapely*, with the following amplification in part drawn from *Simmons*: (1) Is the term misdescriptive of the character, quality, function, composition or use of the goods? (2) If so, are prospective purchasers likely to believe that the misdescription actually describes the goods? (3) If so, is the misdescription likely to affect the decision to purchase?

In ex parte prosecution, the burden is initially on the Patent and Trademark Office (PTO) to put forth sufficient evidence that the mark for which registration is sought meets the above criteria of unregistrability. Mindful that the PTO has limited facilities for acquiring evidence—it cannot, for example, be expected to conduct a survey of the marketplace or obtain consumer affidavits—we conclude that the evidence of record here is sufficient to establish a prima facie case of deceptiveness. That evidence shows with respect to the three-pronged test:

(1) Budge admits that its seat covers are not made from lamb or sheep products. Thus, the term LAMB is misdescriptive of its goods. (2) Seat covers for various vehicles can be and are made from natural lambskin and sheepskin. Applicant itself makes automobile seat covers of natural sheepskin. Lambskin is defined, inter alia, as fine-grade sheep skin. *See* WEBSTER'S THIRD NEW INTERNATIONAL DICTIONARY 639 (unabr. 1976). The board's factual inference is reasonable that purchasers are likely to believe automobile seat covers denominated by the term LAMB or SHEEP are actually made from natural sheep or lamb skins. (3) Evidence of record shows that natural sheepskin and lambskin is more expensive than simulated skins and that natural and synthetic skins have different characteristics. Thus, the misrepresentation is likely to affect the decision to purchase.

Faced with this prima facie case against registration, Budge had the burden to come forward with countering evidence to overcome the rejection. It wholly failed to do so.

Budge argues that its use of LAMB as part of its mark is not misdescriptive when considered in connection with the text in its advertising, which states that the cover is of "simulated sheepskin." Some, but not all, of Budge's specimen labels also have this text. This evidence is unpersuasive. In *R. Neumann & Co. v. Overseas Shipments, Inc.*, 326 F.2d 786 (C.C.P.A. 1964), a similar argument was made that the mark DURA-HYDE on shoes was not deceptive as an indication of leather because of tags affixed to the shoes proclaiming the legend "Outwears leather." In discounting the evidence, the court stated: "The legends constitute advertisement material separate and apart from any trademark significance." *Id.* at 790. * * *

Thus, we conclude that the board properly discounted Budge's advertising and labeling which indicate the actual fabric content. Misdescriptiveness of a term may be negated by its meaning in the context of the whole mark inasmuch as the combination is seen together and makes a unitary impression. *A.F. Gallun & Sons Corp. v. Aristocrat Leather Prods., Inc.*, 135 USPQ 459, 460 (TTAB 1962) (COPY CALF not misdescriptive, but rather suggests imitation of calf skin). The same is not true with respect to explanatory statements in advertising or on labels which purchasers may or may not note and which may or may not always be provided. The statutory provision bars registration of a mark comprising deceptive matter. Congress has said that the advantages of registration may not be extended to a mark which deceives the public. Thus, the mark standing alone must pass muster, for that is what the applicant seeks to register, not extraneous explanatory statements.

Budge next argues that no reasonable purchaser would expect to purchase lambskin automobile seat covers because none made of lambskin are on the market. * * * [We] agree with the board's conclusion that any differences between sheepskin and lambskin would not be readily apparent to potential purchasers of automobile seat covers. The board's finding here that purchasers are likely to believe the misrepresentation is not clearly erroneous. * * *

Finally, we note the evidence of Budge's extensive sales since 1974 under the mark. However, it is too well established for argument that a mark which includes deceptive matter is barred from registration and cannot acquire distinctiveness.

Conclusion

None of the facts found by the board have been shown to be clearly erroneous nor has the board erred as a matter of law. Accordingly, we affirm the board's decision that Budge's mark LOVEE LAMB for automobile seat covers made from synthetic fibers is deceptive within the meaning of 15 U.S.C. § 1052(a) and is, thus, barred from registration.

AFFIRMED.

NOTE

Would the mark "Bahia" be deceptive when used as a trademark for cigars? Bahia is a region in Brazil where cigars are produced, but the cigars in question are not produced in that area. What other information would be pertinent to this determination? *See In re House of Windsor, Inc.*, 221 U.S.P.Q. 53 (T.T.A.B. 1983).

IN RE CALIFORNIA INNOVATIONS, INC.

329 F.3d 1334 (Fed. Cir. 2003).

RADER, CIRCUIT JUDGE.

California Innovations, Inc. (CA Innovations), a Canadian-based corporation, appeals the Trademark Trial and Appeal Board's refusal to register its mark—CALIFORNIA INNOVATIONS. Citing section 2(e)(3) of the Lanham Act, 15 U.S.C. § 1052(e)(3), the Board concluded that the mark was primarily geographically deceptively misdescriptive. Because the Board applied an outdated standard in its analysis under § 1052(e)(3), this court vacates the Board's decision and remands.

I

CA Innovations filed an intent-to-use trademark application, Serial No. 74/650,703, on March 23, 1995, for the composite mark CALIFORNIA INNOVATIONS and Design. The application sought registration for the following goods: automobile visor organizers, namely, holders for personal effects, and automobile trunk organizers for automotive accessories in International Class 12; backpacks in International Class 18; thermal insulated bags for food and beverages, thermal insulated tote bags for food or beverages, and thermal insulated wraps for cans to keep the containers cold or hot in International Class 21; and nylon, vinyl, polyester and/or leather bags for storage and storage pouches in International Class 22.

[The examiner refused registration under § 1052(e)(3), concluding that the mark was primarily geographically deceptively misdescriptive, and the TTAB upheld the refusal. The applicant then appealed to the Federal Circuit, but limited its appeal to the Class 21 items—thermal insulated bags for food and beverages, and thermal insulated wraps for cans.]

* * *

II

The Lanham Act addresses geographical marks in three categories. The first category, § 1052(a), identifies geographically deceptive marks:

> No trademark by which the goods of the applicant may be distinguished from the goods of others shall be refused registration on the principal register on account of its nature unless it—(a) Consists of or comprises immoral, deceptive, or scandalous matter; or matter which may disparage or falsely suggest a connection with persons, living or dead, institutions, beliefs, or national symbols, or bring them into contempt, or disrepute.

15 U.S.C. § 1052(a). Although not expressly addressing geographical marks, § 1052(a) has traditionally been used to reject geographic marks that materially deceive the public. A mark found to be deceptive under

§ 1052(a) cannot receive protection under the Lanham Act. To deny a geographic mark protection under § 1052(a), the PTO must establish that (1) the mark misrepresents or misdescribes the goods, (2) the public would likely believe the misrepresentation, and (3) the misrepresentation would materially affect the public's decision to purchase the goods. *See In re Budge Mfg. Co.*, 857 F.2d 773, 775 (Fed.Cir.1988). This test's central point of analysis is materiality because that finding shows that the misdescription deceived the consumer. *See In re House of Windsor*, 221 USPQ 53, 56–57 (TTAB 1983).

The other two categories of geographic marks are (1) "primarily geographically descriptive" marks and (2) "primarily geographically deceptively misdescriptive" marks under § 1052(e). The North American Free Trade Agreement, as implemented by the NAFTA Implementation Act in 1993, has recently changed these two categories. Before the NAFTA changes, § 1052(e) and (f) stated:

> No trademark by which the goods of the applicant may be distinguished from the goods of others shall be refused registration on the principal register on account of its nature unless it—
>
> (e) Consists of a mark which . . .
>
> (2) when used on or in connection with the goods of the applicant is primarily geographically descriptive or deceptively misdescriptive of them.
>
> * * *
>
> (f) Except as expressly excluded in paragraphs (a)[, (b), (c), and] (d) of this section, nothing in this chapter shall prevent the registration of a mark used by the applicant which has become distinctive of the applicant's goods in commerce.

15 U.S.C. § 1052(e)(2) and (f) (1988).

The law treated these two categories of geographic marks identically. Specifically, the PTO generally placed a "primarily geographically descriptive" or "deceptively misdescriptive" mark on the supplemental register. Upon a showing of acquired distinctiveness, these marks could qualify for the principal register.

Thus, in contrast to the permanent loss of registration rights imposed on deceptive marks under § 1052(a), pre-NAFTA § 1052(e)(2) only required a temporary denial of registration on the principal register. Upon a showing of distinctiveness, these marks could acquire a place on the principal register. * * *

NAFTA and its implementing legislation obliterated the distinction between geographically deceptive marks and primarily geographically deceptively misdescriptive marks. Article 1712 of NAFTA provides:

> 1. Each party [United States, Mexico, Canada] shall provide, in respect of geographical indications, the legal means for interested persons to prevent:
>
> (a) the use of any means in the designation or presentation of a good that indicates or suggests that the good in question originates in a territory, region or locality other than the true place of origin, in a manner that misleads the public as to the geographical origin of the good. . . .

This treaty shifts the emphasis for geographically descriptive marks to prevention of any public deception. Accordingly, the NAFTA Act amended § 1052(e) to read:

> No trademark by which the goods of the applicant may be distinguished from the goods of others shall be refused registration on the principal register on account of its nature unless it—
>
> (e) Consists of a mark which (1) when used on or in connection with the goods of the applicant is merely descriptive or deceptively misdescriptive of them, (2) when used on or in connection with the goods of the applicant is primarily geographically descriptive of them, except as indications of regional origin may be registrable under section 4 [15 USCS § 1054], (3) when used on or in connection with the goods of the applicant is primarily geographically deceptively misdescriptive of them, (4) is primarily merely a surname, or (5) comprises any matter that, as a whole, is functional.
>
> (f) Except as expressly excluded in subsections (a), (b), (c), (d), (e)(3), and (e)(5) of this section, nothing herein shall prevent the registration of a mark used by the applicant which has become distinctive of the applicant's goods in commerce.

15 U.S.C. § 1052(e)–(f) (2000).

Recognizing the new emphasis on prevention of public deception, the NAFTA amendments split the categories of geographically descriptive and geographically deceptively misdescriptive into two subsections (subsections (e)(2) and (e)(3) respectively). Under the amended Lanham Act, subsection (e)(3)—geographically deceptive misdescription—could no longer acquire distinctiveness under subsection (f). Accordingly, marks determined to be primarily geographically deceptively misdescriptive are permanently denied registration, as are deceptive marks under § 1052(a).

* * *

The amended Lanham Act gives geographically deceptively misdescriptive marks the same treatment as geographically deceptive marks under § 1052(a). Because both of these categories are subject to permanent denial of registration, the PTO may not simply rely on lack of distinctiveness to deny registration, but must make the more difficult showing of public deception. In other words, by placing geographically deceptively misdescriptive marks under subsection (e)(3) in the same fatal circumstances as deceptive marks under subsection (a), the NAFTA Act also elevated the standards for identifying those deceptive marks.

Before NAFTA, the PTO identified and denied registration to a primarily geographically deceptively misdescriptive mark with a showing that (1) the primary significance of the mark was a generally known geographic location, and (2) "the public was likely to believe the mark identified the place from which the goods originate and that the goods did not come from there." *In re Loew's*, 769 F.2d at 768. The second prong of the test represents the "goods-place association" between the mark and the goods at issue. This test raised an inference of deception based on the likelihood of a goods-place association that did not reflect the actual origin of the goods. A mere inference, however, is not enough to establish the deceptiveness that brings the harsh consequence of non-registrability under the amended Lanham Act. As noted, NAFTA and the amended Lanham Act place an emphasis on actual misleading of the public.

Therefore, the relatively easy burden of showing a naked goods-place association without proof that the association is material to the consumer's decision is no longer justified, because marks rejected under § 1052(e)(3) can no longer obtain registration through acquired distinctiveness under § 1052(f). To ensure a showing of deceptiveness and misleading before imposing the penalty of non-registrability, the PTO may not deny registration without a showing that the goods-place association made by the consumer is material to the consumer's decision to purchase those goods. This addition of a materiality inquiry equates this test with the elevated standard applied under § 1052(a). * * *

* * *

Thus, due to the NAFTA changes in the Lanham Act, the PTO must deny registration under § 1052(e)(3) if (1) the primary significance of the mark is a generally known geographic location, (2) the consuming public is likely to believe the place identified by the mark indicates the origin of the goods bearing the mark, when in fact the goods do not come from that place, and (3) the misrepresentation was a material factor in the consumer's decision.

As a result of the NAFTA changes to the Lanham Act, geographic deception is specifically dealt with in subsection (e)(3), while deception in general continues to be addressed under subsection (a). Consequently, this court anticipates that the PTO will usually address geographically deceptive marks under subsection (e)(3) of the amended Lanham Act rather than subsection (a). While there are identical legal standards for deception in each section, subsection (e)(3) specifically involves deception involving geographic marks.

III

* * *

The parties agree that CA Innovations' goods do not originate in California.

> Under the first prong of the test—whether the mark's primary significance is a generally known geographic location—a composite mark such as the applicant's proposed mark must be evaluated as a whole. . . . It is not erroneous, however, for the examiner to consider the significance of each element within the composite mark in the course of evaluating the mark as a whole.

Save Venice, 259 F.3d at 1352 (citations omitted).

The Board found that "the word CALIFORNIA is a prominent part of applicant's mark and is not overshadowed by either the word INNOVATIONS or the design element." Although the mark may also convey the idea of a creative, laid-back lifestyle or mindset, the Board properly recognized that such an association does not contradict the primary geographic significance of the mark. Even if the public may associate California with a particular life-style, the record supports the Board's finding that the primary meaning remains focused on the state of California. Nonetheless, this court declines to review at this stage the Board's finding that CA Innovations' composite mark CALIFORNIA INNOVATIONS and Design is primarily geographic in nature. Rather the PTO may apply the entire new test on remand.

The second prong of the test requires proof that the public is likely to believe the applicant's goods originate in California. The Board stated that the examining attorney submitted excerpts from the Internet and the NEXIS database showing "some manufacturers and distributors of backpacks, tote bags, luggage, computer cases, and sport bags . . . headquartered in California." The Board also acknowledged articles "which make reference to companies headquartered in California which manufacture automobile accessories such as auto organizers," as well as the "very serious apparel and sewn products industry" in California.

A great deal of the evidence cited in this case relates to the fashion industry, which is highly prevalent in California due to Hollywood's influence on this industry. However, clothing and fashion have nothing to do with the products in question. * * * At best, the evidence of a connection between California and insulated bags and wraps is tenuous. Even if the evidence supported a finding of a goods-place association, the PTO has yet to apply the materiality test in this case. This court declines to address that issue and apply the new standard in the first instance. Accordingly, this court vacates the finding of the Board that CA Innovations' mark is primarily geographically deceptively misdescriptive, and remands the case for further proceedings. On remand, the Board shall apply the new three-prong standard.

* * *

VACATED and REMANDED.

NOTES

1. In quoting the language of section 2(f), the Federal Circuit's opinion omits some important language that was added by the NAFTA Implementation Act:

> Nothing in this section shall prevent the registration of a mark which, when used on or in connection with the goods of the applicant, is primarily geographically deceptively misdescriptive of them, and which became distinctive of the applicant's goods in commerce before December 8, 1993.

(December 8, 1993, was the effective date of the NAFTA amendments.) Why did Congress add this language? After *California Innovations*, what is its significance? Is the court correct that the NAFTA amendments "obliterated the distinction between geographically deceptive marks and primarily geographically deceptively misdescriptive marks"? Or did the Federal Circuit do this?

2. After *California Innovations*, would it be easier to register "Sweden" as a mark for external kidney units if they were made in Sweden or if they were made in Canada? *See In re Sweden Freezer Mfg. Co.*, 159 U.S.P.Q. 246 (T.T.A.B. 1968). What about "Italian Maide" for canned vegetables produced in Italy or California, respectively? *In re Amerise*, 160 U.S.P.Q. 687, 691 (T.T.A.B. 1969). What about "Swiss Precision" for watches in Switzerland or China, respectively?

3. How would you analyze the use of "Le Marais" for a French kosher restaurant located in New York City? The name is identical to an area of Paris known for having fashionable restaurants (and also known as the Jewish part of the city). *See In re Les Halles de Paris J.V.*, 334 F.3d 1371 (Fed. Cir. 2003), *remanded*, 2004 WL 839413 (T.T.A.B. Apr. 15, 2004). What about "Texas Steak House" for a steak restaurant that is not located in Texas and does not obtain any of its staff, ingredients, or supplies from Texas?

4. As the court notes, CALIFORNIA INNOVATIONS is a composite mark—that is, it consists of more than a single word or symbol. As is common with applications for composite marks, the applicant in this case disclaimed exclusive rights to a portion of the mark that—in this case, the word CALIFORNIA. Applicants often disclaim components of a composite mark that are clearly unregistrable (typically because they are generic or merely descriptive); often the PTO will require this as a condition for registering the mark. (For example, KELLOGG'S CORN FLAKES is a registered mark, but disclaims the generic term CORN FLAKES.) The disclaimer appears as a statement on the registration itself. Note, however, as illustrated in this case, that the use of a disclaimer does not prevent a court or the PTO from considering the import of the disclaimed element in evaluating whether the mark as a whole is deceptive (or deceptively misdescriptive, as the case may be), since the disclaimer does nothing to alleviate the consumer's likelihood of confusion. In *In re Budge*, would the trademark application have succeeded if the applicant had disclaimed LAMB?

5. CALIFORNIA INNOVATIONS appears in all caps because it is registered as a "standard character mark." In the trademark application and registration, such a mark appears in all caps, in block letters, with no special typescript or font, and with no accompanying design. A trademark applicant that registers a word or phrase as a standard character mark generally has priority in all styles and manners of displaying that mark to the public. In contrast, a registrant whose mark is generic or merely descriptive will typically be able to register the mark only in a distinctive form—for example, as part of a composite mark, or in distinctive colors or lettering styles—and may have to disclaim the unregistrable components.

6. Look more closely at the other bars to registration under section 2(e), and the exceptions in section 2(f). Can descriptive marks be federally registered? What about functional marks? How do these rules compare to the common law?

7. How do sections 2(c) and 2(e) restrict the registration of personal names on the Principal Register? Does section 2(c) reflect policies similar to the "right of publicity" that is recognized in the majority of states? Under section 2(e), is there a distinction between full names, first names, and surnames? The Trademark Trial and Appeal Board has ruled that adding "two initials (or more)" to a surname creates a commercial impression of a personal name, with the result that the name "generally will not be primarily a surname." *In re P. J. Fitzpatrick, Inc.*, 95 U.S.P.Q.2d 1412 (T.T.A.B. 2010). How does section 2(e) compare with the common law and section 43(a)?

8. If a putative mark is barred from registration on the Principal Register *only* because it lacks distinctiveness, it can be placed instead on the Supplemental Register. 15 U.S.C. § 1091. This does not confer the same advantages as the Principal Register. However, it can be helpful in two respects. Because the Supplemental Register is a publicly available searchable database, it provides constructive notice that the registrant is using the mark

and attempting to establish secondary meaning. Because anyone doing a trademark search will easily find the mark, this may deter others from adopting a similar mark for similar goods or services. In addition, even though a mark on the Supplemental Register may not have secondary meaning, it can still be cited as the basis for rejecting an application for a similar mark under section 2(d). And once it does acquire secondary meaning, the owner can seek registration on the Principal Register. (Note, however, that ITUs cannot be used for the Supplemental Register.) Which would-be marks are *not* eligible for the Supplemental Register?

MATAL V. TAM

__ U.S. __, 137 S.Ct. 1744 (2017).

JUSTICE ALITO announced the judgment of the Court and delivered the opinion of the Court with respect to Parts I, II, and III-A, and an opinion with respect to Parts III-B, III-C, and IV, in which THE CHIEF JUSTICE, JUSTICE THOMAS, and JUSTICE BREYER join:

This case concerns a dance-rock band's application for federal trademark registration of the band's name, "The Slants." "Slants" is a derogatory term for persons of Asian descent, and members of the band are Asian-Americans. But the band members believe that by taking that slur as the name of their group, they will help to "reclaim" the term and drain its denigrating force.

The Patent and Trademark Office (PTO) denied the application based on a provision of federal law prohibiting the registration of trademarks that may "disparage . . . or bring . . . into contemp[t] or disrepute" any "persons, living or dead." 15 U.S.C. § 1052(a). We now hold that this provision violates the Free Speech Clause of the First Amendment. It offends a bedrock First Amendment principle: Speech may not be banned on the ground that it expresses ideas that offend.

* * *

III

Because the disparagement clause applies to marks that disparage the members of a racial or ethnic group, we must decide whether the clause violates the Free Speech Clause of the First Amendment. And at the outset, we must consider three arguments that would either eliminate any First Amendment protection or result in highly permissive rational-basis review. Specifically, the Government contends (1) that trademarks are government speech, not private speech, (2) that trademarks are a form of government subsidy, and (3) that the constitutionality of the disparagement clause should be tested under a new "government-program" doctrine. We address each of these arguments below.

A

The First Amendment prohibits Congress and other government entities and actors from "abridging the freedom of speech"; the First Amendment does not say that Congress and other government entities must abridge their own ability to speak freely. And our cases recognize that "[t]he Free Speech Clause . . . does not regulate government speech." *Pleasant Grove City v. Summum,* 555 U.S. 460, 467 (2009).

As we have said, "it is not easy to imagine how government could function" if it were subject to the restrictions that the First Amendment imposes on private speech. *Summum, supra,* at 468. " '[T]he First Amendment forbids the government to regulate speech in ways that favor some viewpoints or ideas at the expense of others,' " *Lamb's Chapel v. Center Moriches Union Free School Dist.,* 508 U.S. 384, 394 (1993), but imposing a requirement of viewpoint-neutrality on government speech would be paralyzing. When a government entity embarks on a course of action, it necessarily takes a particular viewpoint and rejects others. The Free Speech Clause does not require government to maintain viewpoint neutrality when its officers and employees speak about that venture.

* * *

But while the government-speech doctrine is important—indeed, essential—it is a doctrine that is susceptible to dangerous misuse. If private speech could be passed off as government speech by simply affixing a government seal of approval, government could silence or muffle the expression of disfavored viewpoints. For this reason, we must exercise great caution before extending our government-speech precedents.

At issue here is the content of trademarks that are registered by the PTO, an arm of the Federal Government. The Federal Government does not dream up these marks, and it does not edit marks submitted for registration. Except as required by the statute involved here, 15 U.S.C. § 1052(a), an examiner may not reject a mark based on the viewpoint that it appears to express. * * *

In light of all this, it is far-fetched to suggest that the content of a registered mark is government speech. * * *

The PTO has made it clear that registration does not constitute approval of a mark. And it is unlikely that more than a tiny fraction of the public has any idea what federal registration of a trademark means. None of our government speech cases even remotely supports the idea that registered trademarks are government speech. In *Johanns v. Livestock Marketing Assn.,* 544 U.S. 550, 553 (2005), we considered advertisements promoting the sale of beef products. A federal statute called for the creation of a program of paid advertising " 'to advance the image and desirability of beef and beef products.' " * * * Noting that "[t]he message set out in the beef promotions [was] from beginning to end the message established by the Federal Government," we held that the ads were government speech. The Government's involvement in the creation of these beef ads bears no resemblance to anything that occurs when a trademark is registered. * * *

This brings us to the case on which the Government relies most heavily, *Walker v. Texas Div., Sons of Confederate Veterans, Inc.*, 576 U.S. ___, ___ (2015), which likely marks the outer bounds of the government-speech doctrine. Holding that the messages on Texas specialty license plates are government speech, the *Walker* Court cited three factors distilled from *Summum*. First, license plates have long been used by the States to convey state messages. Second, license plates "are often closely identified in the public mind" with the State, since they are manufactured and owned by the State, generally designed by the State, and serve as a form of "government ID." Third, Texas "maintain[ed] direct control over the messages conveyed on its specialty plates." As explained above, none of these factors are present in this case.

In sum, the federal registration of trademarks is vastly different from the beef ads in *Johanns*, the monuments in *Summum*, and even the specialty license plates in *Walker*. Holding that the registration of a trademark converts the mark into government speech would constitute a huge and dangerous extension of the government-speech doctrine. For if the registration of trademarks constituted government speech, other systems of government registration could easily be characterized in the same way.

Perhaps the most worrisome implication of the Government's argument concerns the system of copyright registration. If federal registration makes a trademark government speech and thus eliminates all First Amendment protection, would the registration of the copyright for a book produce a similar transformation?

The Government attempts to distinguish copyright on the ground that it is " 'the engine of free expression,' " *Eldred v. Ashcroft*, 537 U.S. 186, 219 (2003), but as this case illustrates, trademarks often have an expressive content. Companies spend huge amounts to create and publicize trademarks that convey a message. It is true that the necessary brevity of trademarks limits what they can say. But powerful messages can sometimes be conveyed in just a few words.

Trademarks are private, not government, speech.

B

We next address the Government's argument that this case is governed by cases in which this Court has upheld the constitutionality of government programs that subsidized speech expressing a particular viewpoint. These cases implicate a notoriously tricky question of constitutional law. "[W]e have held that the Government 'may not deny a benefit to a person on a basis that infringes his constitutionally protected . . . freedom of speech even if he has no entitlement to that benefit.' " *Agency for Int'l Development v. Alliance for Open Society Int'l, Inc.*, 570 U.S. 205, 214 (2013). But at the same time, government is not required to subsidize activities that it does not wish to promote. Determining which of these principles applies in a particular case "is not always self-evident," but no difficult question is presented here.

Unlike the present case, the decisions on which the Government relies all involved cash subsidies or their equivalent. * * *

The federal registration of a trademark is nothing like the programs at issue in these cases. The PTO does not pay money to parties seeking registration of a mark. * * *

The Government responds that registration provides valuable non-monetary benefits that "are directly traceable to the resources devoted by the federal government to examining, publishing, and issuing certificates of registration for those marks." But just about every government service requires the expenditure of government funds. This is true of services that benefit everyone, like police and fire protection, as well as services that are utilized by only some, *e.g.*, the adjudication of private lawsuits and the use of public parks and highways.

Trademark registration is not the only government registration scheme. For example, the Federal Government registers copyrights and patents. State governments and their subdivisions register the title to real property and security interests; they issue driver's licenses, motor vehicle registrations, and hunting, fishing, and boating licenses or permits.

Cases [addressing cash subsidies] are not instructive in analyzing the constitutionality of restrictions on speech imposed in connection with such services.

C

Finally, the Government urges us to sustain the disparagement clause under a new doctrine that would apply to "government-program" cases. For the most part, this argument simply merges our government-speech cases and the previously discussed subsidy cases in an attempt to construct a broader doctrine that can be applied to the registration of trademarks. The only new element in this construct consists of two cases involving a public employer's collection of union dues from its employees. But those cases occupy a special area of First Amendment case law, and they are far removed from the registration of trademarks. * * *

Potentially more analogous are cases in which a unit of government creates a limited public forum for private speech. When government creates such a forum, in either a literal or "metaphysical" sense, some content- and speaker-based restrictions may be allowed. However, even in such cases, what we have termed "viewpoint discrimination" is forbidden.

Our cases use the term "viewpoint" discrimination in a broad sense, and in that sense, the disparagement clause discriminates on the bases of "viewpoint." To be sure, the clause evenhandedly prohibits disparagement of all groups. It applies equally to marks that damn Democrats and Republicans, capitalists and socialists, and those arrayed on both sides of every possible issue. It denies registration to any mark that is offensive to a substantial percentage of the members of any group. But in the sense relevant here, that is viewpoint discrimination: Giving offense is a viewpoint.

We have said time and again that "the public expression of ideas may not be prohibited merely because the ideas are themselves offensive to some of their hearers." *Street v. New York,* 394 U.S. 576, 592 (1969). For this reason, the disparagement clause cannot be saved by analyzing it as a type of government program in which some content- and speaker-based restrictions are permitted.

IV

Having concluded that the disparagement clause cannot be sustained under our government-speech or subsidy cases or under the Government's proposed "government-program" doctrine, we must confront a dispute between the parties on the question whether trademarks are commercial speech and are thus subject to the relaxed scrutiny outlined in *Central Hudson Gas & Elec. Corp. v. Public Serv. Comm'n,* 447 U.S. 557 (1980). The Government and *amici* supporting its position argue that all trademarks are commercial speech. They note that the central purposes of trademarks are commercial and that federal law regulates trademarks to promote fair and orderly interstate commerce. Tam and his *amici,* on the other hand, contend that many, if not all, trademarks have an expressive component. In other words, these trademarks do not simply identify the source of a product or service but go on to say something more, either about the product or service or some broader issue. The trademark in this case illustrates this point. The name "The Slants" not only identifies the band but expresses a view about social issues.

We need not resolve this debate between the parties because the disparagement clause cannot withstand even *Central Hudson* review. Under *Central Hudson,* a restriction of speech must serve "a substantial interest," and it must be "narrowly drawn." This means, among other things, that "[t]he regulatory technique may extend only as far as the interest it serves." The disparagement clause fails this requirement.

It is claimed that the disparagement clause serves two interests. The first is phrased in a variety of ways in the briefs. Echoing language in one of the opinions below, the Government asserts an interest in preventing

" 'underrepresented groups' " from being " 'bombarded with demeaning messages in commercial advertising.' " An *amicus* supporting the Government refers to "encouraging racial tolerance and protecting the privacy and welfare of individuals." But no matter how the point is phrased, its unmistakable thrust is this: The Government has an interest in preventing speech expressing ideas that offend. And, as we have explained, that idea strikes at the heart of the First Amendment. Speech that demeans on the basis of race, ethnicity, gender, religion, age, disability, or any other similar ground is hateful; but the proudest boast of our free speech jurisprudence is that we protect the freedom to express "the thought that we hate." *United States v. Schwimmer,* 279 U.S. 644, 655 (1929) (Holmes, J., dissenting).

The second interest asserted is protecting the orderly flow of commerce. Commerce, we are told, is disrupted by trademarks that "involv[e] disparagement of race, gender, ethnicity, national origin, religion, sexual orientation, and similar demographic classification." *In re Tam,* 808 F.3d at 1380–81 (opinion of Reyna, J.). Such trademarks are analogized to discriminatory conduct, which has been recognized to have an adverse effect on commerce.

A simple answer to this argument is that the disparagement clause is not "narrowly drawn" to drive out trademarks that support invidious discrimination. The clause reaches any trademark that disparages *any person, group, or institution.* It applies to trademarks like the following: "Down with racists," "Down with sexists," "Down with homophobes." It is not an anti-discrimination clause; it is a happy-talk clause. In this way, it goes much further than is necessary to serve the interest asserted.

The clause is far too broad in other ways as well. The clause protects every person living or dead as well as every institution. Is it conceivable that commerce would be disrupted by a trademark saying: "James Buchanan was a disastrous president" or "Slavery is an evil institution"?

There is also a deeper problem with the argument that commercial speech may be cleansed of any expression likely to cause offense. The commercial market is well stocked with merchandise that disparages prominent figures and groups, and the line between commercial and non-commercial speech is not always clear, as this case illustrates. If affixing the commercial label permits the suppression of any speech that may lead to political or social "volatility," free speech would be endangered.

For these reasons, we hold that the disparagement clause violates the Free Speech Clause of the First Amendment. The judgment of the Federal Circuit is affirmed.

It is so ordered.

JUSTICE GORSUCH took no part in the consideration or decision of this case.

JUSTICE KENNEDY, with whom JUSTICE GINSBURG, JUSTICE SOTOMAYOR, and JUSTICE KAGAN join, concurring in part and concurring in the judgment.

* * *

The Court is correct in its judgment, and I join Parts I, II, and III-A of its opinion. This separate writing explains in greater detail why the First Amendment's protections against viewpoint discrimination apply to the trademark here. It submits further that the viewpoint discrimination rationale renders unnecessary any extended treatment of other questions raised by the parties.

I

Those few categories of speech that the government can regulate or punish—for instance, fraud, defamation, or incitement—are well established within our constitutional tradition. Aside from these and a few other narrow exceptions, it is a fundamental principle of the First Amendment that the government may not punish or suppress speech based on disapproval of the ideas or perspectives the speech conveys.

The First Amendment guards against laws "targeted at specific subject matter," a form of speech suppression known as content based discrimination. This category includes a subtype of laws that go further, aimed at the suppression of "particular views . . . on a subject." *Rosenberger v. Rector and Visitors of Univ. of Va.*, 515 U.S. 819, 829 (1995). A law found to discriminate based on viewpoint is an "egregious form of content discrimination," which is "presumptively unconstitutional." *Id.* at 829–30.

At its most basic, the test for viewpoint discrimination is whether—within the relevant subject category—the government has singled out a subset of messages for disfavor based on the views expressed. In the instant case, the disparagement clause the Government now seeks to implement and enforce identifies the relevant subject as "persons, living or dead, institutions, beliefs, or national symbols." Within that category, an applicant may register a positive or benign mark but not a derogatory one. The law thus reflects the Government's disapproval of a subset of messages it finds offensive. This is the essence of viewpoint discrimination.

The Government disputes this conclusion. It argues, to begin with, that the law is viewpoint neutral because it applies in equal measure to any trademark that demeans or offends. This misses the point. A subject that is first defined by content and then regulated or censored by mandating only one sort of comment is not viewpoint neutral. To prohibit all sides from criticizing their opponents makes a law more viewpoint based, not less so. The logic of the Government's rule is that a law would be viewpoint neutral even if it provided that public officials could be praised but not condemned. The First Amendment's viewpoint neutrality principle protects more than the right to identify with a particular side. It protects the right to create and present arguments for particular positions in particular ways, as the speaker chooses. By mandating positivity, the law here might silence dissent and distort the marketplace of ideas.

The Government next suggests that the statute is viewpoint neutral because the disparagement clause applies to trademarks regardless of the applicant's personal views or reasons for using the mark. Instead, registration is denied based on the expected reaction of the applicant's audience. In this way, the argument goes, it cannot be said that Government is acting with hostility toward a particular point of view. For example, the Government does not dispute that respondent seeks to use his mark in a positive way. Indeed, respondent endeavors to use The Slants to supplant a racial epithet, using new insights, musical talents, and wry humor to make it a badge of pride. Respondent's application was denied not because the Government thought his object was to demean or offend but because the Government thought his trademark would have that effect on at least some Asian-Americans.

The Government may not insulate a law from charges of viewpoint discrimination by tying censorship to the reaction of the speaker's audience. The Court has suggested that viewpoint discrimination occurs when the government intends to suppress a speaker's beliefs, but viewpoint discrimination need not take that form in every instance. The danger of viewpoint discrimination is that the government is attempting to remove certain ideas or perspectives from a broader debate. That danger is all the greater if the ideas or perspectives are ones a particular audience might think offensive, at least at first hearing. An initial reaction may prompt further reflection, leading to a more reasoned, more tolerant position. * * *

II

The parties dispute whether trademarks are commercial speech and whether trademark registration should be considered a federal subsidy. The former issue may turn on whether certain commercial concerns for the protection of trademarks might, as a general matter, be the basis for regulation. However that issue is resolved, the viewpoint based discrimination at issue here necessarily invokes heightened scrutiny.

"Commercial speech is no exception," the Court has explained, to the principle that the First Amendment "requires heightened scrutiny whenever the government creates a regulation of speech because of disagreement with the message it conveys." *Sorrell v. IMS Health Inc.*, 564 U.S. 552, 566 (2011). Unlike content based discrimination, discrimination based on viewpoint, including a regulation that targets speech for its offensiveness, remains of serious concern in the commercial context.

To the extent trademarks qualify as commercial speech, they are an example of why that term or category does not serve as a blanket exemption from the First Amendment's requirement of viewpoint neutrality. * * * These marks make up part of the expression of everyday life, as with the names of entertainment groups, broadcast networks, designer clothing, newspapers, automobiles, candy bars, toys, and so on. Nonprofit organizations—ranging from medical-research charities and other humanitarian causes to political advocacy groups—also have trademarks, which they use to compete in a real economic sense for funding and other resources as they seek to persuade others to join their cause. To permit viewpoint discrimination in this context is to permit Government censorship.

This case does not present the question of how other provisions of the Lanham Act should be analyzed under the First Amendment. It is well settled, for instance, that to the extent a trademark is confusing or misleading the law can protect consumers and trademark owners. * * *

A law that can be directed against speech found offensive to some portion of the public can be turned against minority and dissenting views to the detriment of all. The First Amendment does not entrust that power to the government's benevolence. Instead, our reliance must be on the substantial safeguards of free and open discussion in a democratic society.

For these reasons, I join the Court's opinion in part and concur in the judgment.

NOTES

1. THE SLANTS was finally registered (as a standard character mark) on the Principal Register on November 14, 2017, exactly 6 years after the application was filed.

2. In June of 2019, the Supreme Court struck down the § 2(a) bar on registering "immoral" and "scandalous" marks in *Iancu v. Brunetti,* 139 S.Ct. 2294 (2019), on appeal from the Federal Circuit. The Court applied the rationale from *Matal v. Tam,* holding that rejecting marks deemed immoral or scandalous was a form of viewpoint discrimination that violates the First Amendment by disfavoring "ideas that offend." The majority declined to salvage the "scandalous" bar by interpreting it as limited to marks that are lewd, sexually explicit, or profane, a narrowing interpretation that might have passed constitutional muster. Should Congress amend the statute to address these limited categories? Would that pass muster under *Matal*?

3. Do the decisions in *Tam* and *Brunetti* affect bars to registration under section 2(c)? This provision precludes registration of marks consisting of "a name, portrait, or signature identifying a particular living individual except by his written consent, or the name, signature, or portrait of a deceased President of the United States during the life of his widow, if any, except by

the written consent of the widow." *See In re Steve Elster*, 26 F.4th 1328 (Fed. Cir. 2022). *See generally* Gary Myers, *It's Scandalous!—Limiting Profane Trademark Registrations after* Tam *and* Brunetti, 27 J. INTELL. PROP. L. 1 (2020). This issue may land at the Supreme Court in the near future.

b. Service Marks

Marks that are used to identify the origin of services, referred to as "service marks," are generally subject to the same federal registration requirements as trademarks for goods. 15 U.S.C. § 1053. Sometimes, however, it can be hard to distinguish a bona fide service from activities that are merely ancillary to the sale of goods.

Statute: 15 U.S.C. §§ 1053, 1127

IN RE DR. PEPPER CO.

836 F.2d 508 (Fed. Cir. 1987).

NIES, CIRCUIT JUDGE.

Dr Pepper Company appeals from the decision of the Patent and Trademark Office Trademark Trial and Appeal Board affirming the examining attorney's refusal to register the mark PEPPER MAN as a service mark on the ground that applicant's asserted service of sponsoring and operating a particular contest to promote its soft drinks was not a service within the contemplation of sections 3 and 45 of the Trademark Act of 1946, 15 U.S.C. §§ 1053 and 1127. We affirm.

I

Appellant filed an application seeking registration of PEPPER MAN which it asserts is its "service mark for sponsorship and operation of contest services." To promote its DR PEPPER soft drinks, appellant conducts a promotional contest in which cash prizes are awarded to households found to have on hand certain specified quantities of unopened cans or bottles of DR PEPPER soft drinks, or certain coupons called "I'M A PEPPER" cards, which can be obtained free of charge from Dr. Pepper or its bottlers. Appellant displays the name PEPPER MAN on promotional pieces for the contest.

The examining attorney refused registration, and the board affirmed, on the ground that applicant was not rendering a service within the contemplation of the Act. The crux of the board's reasoning is that where, as here, an activity claimed to be a service is incidental to the sale of goods, the activity cannot be separately recognizable as a service unless it is shown that the activity constitutes something clearly different from, or over and above, any activity normally involved in promoting the sale of such goods. The running of a contest to advertise and promote the sale of one's goods is not a service over and above, or materially different from, what would normally be expected from one engaged in the sale of goods.

II

The sole issue raised on appeal is whether conducting a contest to promote the sale of one's own goods is a "service" within the meaning of sections 3 and 45 of the Trademark Act of 1946, 15 U.S.C. §§ 1053, 1127. Appellant maintains that sponsorship and operation of a promotional contest is a "service" to the public because some of them will receive the benefit of cash prizes. Thus, it maintains that the name it uses in promoting the contest is registrable as its service mark.

* * *

Through a series of decisions it has become a settled principle that the rendering of a service which is normally "expected or routine" in connection with the sale of one's own goods is not a registrable service whether denominated by the same or a different name from the trademark for its product. This interpretation is a refinement of the basic principle that the service for which registration is sought must be rendered to others. Merely advertising one's own goods, while, in a sense, an "informational" or in some instances an "entertainment" service to others, was early held not to be a "service" within the purview of sections 3 and 45.

The interpretation that a company's promotional activities are not services to others under the Act was subsequently endorsed in judicial decisions of our predecessor, the Court of Customs and Patent Appeals. *In re Radio Corp. of Am.*, 205 F.2d 180, 182 (CCPA 1953) (supplying radio stations with packaged radio programs of records is mere advertising of record company, not a "service" to consumers). *See also In re Orion Research Inc.*, 523 F.2d 1398, 1400 (CCPA 1975) (Orion I) (the repair or replacement of one's own merchandise or "guaranteeing" same held not a registrable "service" because it is normally expected by purchasers from the purveyor of goods). Thus, our precedent has drawn the line in connection with promotional activities that those which are "ordinary or routine" are not registrable services, despite some extra benefit to the public beyond the existence of the goods themselves. The public does not, per our precedent, perceive such activity as a service to the public but as mere sales activity by and for the benefit of the offerer of the goods.

In several decisions the board has specifically addressed the registrability of the name for a contest promoting the goods of the company conducting the contest. In *In re Johnson Publishing Co.*, 130 USPQ 185 (TTAB 1961), the board held that the publisher of a magazine which offered prizes to readers who submitted at least one paid subscription and solved a puzzle was not providing a registrable service. This interpretation was followed and reaffirmed in *In re Loew's Theatres, Inc.*, 179 USPQ 126, 127 (TTAB 1973), where the board stated:

> The lottery type contest, as conducted by applicant, is incidental to the sale of goods, and it is not a service over and above that normally involved in the promotion and sale of its goods. It is directly related to and tied to applicant's "KENT" cigarettes, and it is nothing more and would not be recognized as anything more than a promotional gimmick or device used to advertise and foster the sale of these cigarettes. Benefits do accrue to winners of the contest, but this is true generally of all promotional devices, but this fact alone cannot serve to obfuscate the true nature and character of applicant's contest.

While the interpretations of the statute by the board are not binding on this court, under general principles of administrative law, deference should be given by a court to the interpretation by the agency charged with its administration. We conclude that the board reasonably has treated promotional contests as "routine" sales activity for a producer's goods.

* * *

Appellant argues that the exclusion of services ordinarily or routinely rendered in connection with the sale of goods will preclude registration of marks for a vast array of activities currently recognized as services under the Act, such as those provided by retail department stores, mail order companies, and gasoline stations. Contrary to appellant's view, this consequence does not follow. Appellant leaves out the key element which is that the activities being questioned here relate to promotion of its own goods. Department stores and gasoline stations are service businesses and provide precisely the types of services intended to be brought under the Act. Indeed, advertising agency services as well as the service of conducting contests for others are within the Act. A parallel nonregistrability situation with a service business would be a refusal to register an asserted service of offering "free" glassware to customers who have made a certain level of purchases at a gasoline station, the service of providing "free" bags for purchasers at a grocery store, or a lottery contest by a new shopping mall. Registration of the marks identifying the services of service businesses is not endangered by continuing to apply the principle that services which are ordinary or routine in the sale of goods (or services), such as promotional activities for one's own business, are not services within the meaning of the Act. As stated by Professor McCarthy:

> The point is that a manufacturer or merchant cannot proliferate registrations by obtaining a trademark registration along with a whole raft of service mark registrations covering each and every "service" which every other competitor also provides as an adjunct to the sale of goods. . . . Thus, even though a given term may

> function as both a trademark and a service mark, the service must constitute more than mere promotion and advertising of one's own goods. The difference lies between those services which are mandatory or common in promoting the sale of this type of merchandise, and those services which are not so mandatory or common.

1 J. MCCARTHY, TRADEMARKS AND UNFAIR COMPETITION § 19.30, at 940 (2d ed. 1984). Such proliferation of registrations by devising ways to describe a sale-of-goods situation as a service has been held not to be within the intendment of the Act. We adhere to that precedent. * * *

III

For the foregoing reasons, we affirm the board's decision refusing registration on the ground that appellant is not rendering a service within the meaning of the Act.

AFFIRMED.

QUESTIONS

1. Can the title, characters, or other distinctive features of a television show be registered as marks for entertainment services? Does it matter if the show is on commercial television, where the programming is interrupted for advertising? Does the Lanham Act's definition of a "service mark" help to answer this question?

2. Suppose that a consumer electronics store offers its customers a service called the Tech Squad, which provides home installation for their purchases and offers free service advice via a 24/7 help desk for 12 months after installation. Can the store register this phrase as a service mark if (1) the service is provided to all of the store's customers free of charge, or (2) customers can purchase the service at the same time they purchase their equipment?

c. Certification and Collective Marks

MIDWEST PLASTIC FABRICATORS, INC. V. UNDERWRITERS LABORATORIES INC.

906 F.2d 1568 (Fed. Cir. 1990).

MICHEL, CIRCUIT JUDGE.

Midwest Plastic Fabricators, Inc. (Midwest) appeals the decision of the United States Patent and Trademark Office, Trademark Trial and Appeal Board (Board), denying Midwest's petition to cancel two certification mark registrations issued to Underwriters Laboratories Inc. (UL). Because the Board's findings that UL did not misuse and did control use of its certification marks are not clearly erroneous, we affirm.

Background

UL, a corporation that promulgates and certifies compliance with safety standards for thousands of consumer and other products, is the owner and federal registrant of the two certification marks at issue in this appeal. Each registration states, in part, that the certification is used by persons authorized by UL to certify that representative samplings of the goods conform to the safety standards or requirements established by UL. A manufacturer that wishes to use the UL marks on its products to indicate compliance with UL safety standards must first submit samples to UL for testing and evaluation. Once those samples are determined to comply with UL standards, the products become eligible for listing with UL. Usually the manufacturer will enter into a listing and follow-up service agreement with UL.

* * *

Midwest is a manufacturer and seller of polyvinyl chloride (PVC) fittings and elbows for use with PVC conduit which encases electrical wiring. The company entered into a listing and follow-up service agreement with UL which provides, in part, that Midwest "agrees that his use of the Listing Mark constitutes his declaration that the products are Listed by [UL] and have been made in compliance with the requirements of [UL]."

Midwest now seeks reversal of the Board's denial of its petition to cancel UL's registrations on the same two bases it presented to the Board. First, Midwest alleged that UL permits use of the certification marks for purposes other than certification, in violation of 15 U.S.C. § 1064(e)(3) (1982). According to Midwest, UL's president testified that application of UL's mark represents not UL's, but merely the manufacturer's declaration that the products meet UL standards. Midwest argued that the failure of UL itself to certify that the products carrying the UL mark meet UL standards demonstrates that UL permits use of the marks for purposes other than certification.

As the second basis for cancellation, Midwest charged UL fails to control the use of its marks. Specifically, Midwest alleged: (1) certain PVC elbows carrying the UL marks failed impact tests performed by its expert, Professor Charles E. Rogers, of Case Western Reserve University; and (2) certain conduit pipe manufactured by a competitor of Midwest, National Pipe Company (National), carried counterfeit UL marks. If UL fails to control its marks, the registrations are subject to cancellation under 15 U.S.C. § 1064(e)(1). Alternatively, Midwest argued to the Board that as UL fails to control use of the marks on PVC conduit, the registrations should be cancelled at least as to such conduit. UL controverted these allegations and asserted that Midwest's cancellation petition was barred by the doctrine of licensee estoppel.

Issue

Whether either the Board's fact finding that UL does not use the marks other than for certification or that UL does control use of its marks is clearly erroneous.

Opinion

I. Use of the Marks for Purposes Other Than to Certify

* * *

A certification mark registration may be cancelled if the mark is not used exclusively as a certification mark. 15 U.S.C. § 1064(e)(3). For example, if a certification mark's owner also allowed the mark to be used as a trademark, there would be a basis for cancellation of the registration.

Midwest argues that UL's registrations must be cancelled because the UL certification marks are not UL's own declarations to consumers that the marked products comply with UL standards, but instead are the manufacturer's declarations. Midwest asserts the failure of UL itself to make that declaration is evidence that UL "permits the use of the certification mark for purposes other than to certify" and therefore the registrations must be cancelled. *See* 15 U.S.C. § 1064(e)(3).

* * *

The statute, however, plainly does not require that, as the registrant, UL itself must test the products and declare to the public that items carrying UL marks meet UL standards. It merely authorizes cancellation of a registration if the registrant allows use of the mark for purposes other than certification. In addition, the general practice, in accord with the statute, allows for a third party to apply the certification mark.

Thus, both registrations at issue here include a provision that the certification marks may be used by "persons authorized by [UL]" to indicate that "representative samplings" of the products conform to safety standards established by UL. The registrations clearly state what the marks do and do not represent to the public. The registrations certainly do not require UL to represent that UL itself tests the items.

* * *

II. Failure to Control Use of the Marks

Midwest also asserts UL does not control the use of the UL marks as required under 15 U.S.C. § 1064(e)(1), and cancellation is thus necessary. Section 1064(e)(1) provides for cancellation if the certification mark registrant "does not control, or is not able legitimately to exercise control over, the use of such mark."

The purpose of requiring a certification mark registrant to control use of its mark is the same as for a trademark registrant: to protect the public from being misled. *Cf. Haymaker Sports, Inc. v. Turian*, 581 F.2d 257, 261 (CCPA 1978) (A trademark licensor "may license his mark if the licensing agreement provides for adequate control by the licensor over the quality of goods or services produced under the mark by a licensee. The purpose of such a requirement is to protect the public from being misled."). In the case of a certification mark registrant, the risk of misleading the public may be even greater because a certification mark registration sets forth specific representations about the manufacture and characteristics of the goods to which the mark is applied.

As the purpose of the control requirement is to protect the public, the requirement places an affirmative obligation on the certification mark owner to monitor the activities of those who use the mark.

To obtain cancellation of the UL certification mark registrations, Midwest has the burden to demonstrate by a preponderance of the evidence that UL failed to exercise control over use of its marks. The statute, however, does not define "control" or otherwise indicate the degree of control that it requires. Clearly, the statutory requirement cannot mean absolute control, because it would be impracticable, if not impossible, to satisfy. The Board stated: "The specific degree of control necessary in determining whether or not a certification mark should be cancelled depends, of course, on the particular facts presented in each case." While interpretation of the statutory term "control" is a question of law which we review de novo, the Board explicated a rule of reasonableness which, because reasonableness cannot be gauged by some abstract standard, will vary depending on the particular facts. The "control" requirement of the statute means the mark owner must take reasonable steps, under all the circumstances of the case, to prevent the public from being misled.

***

The Board found that UL has "a vast network of inspectors making hundreds of thousands of inspections of thousands of different products across the country" and that UL conducts comprehensive follow-up programs to ensure compliance with UL standards. The Board also stated that UL demonstrated "considerable diligence in controlling the use of its marks; that while [the] inspection and follow-up procedures are not 100% accurate or foolproof, we know of no such requirement. . . ."

Midwest relies upon two types of evidence to challenge the Board finding on control. First, it relies on the results of impact tests performed on certain conduit and elbows carrying the UL mark. The Board found the tests were not "shown to be reliable and [are] entitled to very little, if any, probative value." We cannot overturn that finding as clearly erroneous because Midwest's testing of PVC conduit and elbows did not account for the age of the elbows tested or their exposure to sunlight, although it is undisputed that age and sunlight make PVC conduit brittle. Also, impact tests were performed on PVC elbows and Midwest concedes "that the [UL] standards for elbows do not require impact tests." The Board, therefore, appropriately discounted the impact tests.

The second type of evidence Midwest employs to demonstrate UL's failure to control use of its marks is the proven use of counterfeit UL marks on certain conduit manufactured by National, a competitor. The Board concluded that this limited counterfeiting problem was not sufficient to cancel UL's registrations and that UL exercised control over subsequent use of its marks by this company, based on findings about UL's responsiveness and the stringency of its corrective action. It included inspections being done solely by UL personnel and inspection of not just a "representative sampling," all that is required by the registrations, but of 100% of the conduit. These findings have not been shown to be clearly erroneous.

Because Midwest has not shown that the findings supporting the reasonableness of UL's control are clearly erroneous, we must sustain the Board's determination that UL's control avoids cancellation of its registrations in these proceedings.

* * *

NOTES

1. The requirement that certification mark owners exercise control over those licensed to use their marks is closely related to the concept of "naked licensing," discussed in Chapter 5, under which a trademark may be treated as abandoned if its owner does not exercise sufficient quality control over licensees.

2. In addition to certification marks, the Lanham Act provides trademark protection for "collective marks," which are used by members of a cooperative, association, or other collective group to show membership in the group or association. 15 U.S.C. §§ 1054, 1127. Collective marks may be intended primarily to secure "marketing effectiveness" in a relevant industry, and are valid whether or not the cooperative association that owns the mark exercises quality control over the actual sale of goods. *National Pork Board v. Supreme Lobster & Seafood Co.*, 96 U.S.P.Q.2d 1479 (T.T.A.B. 2010) (involving the registered slogan, "The Other White Meat," to be used in promoting the general sale and consumption of pork products throughout the United States, thereby benefiting members of the pork production industry at large).

3. Consider whether the following marks are more likely to be certification or collective marks:

The "Good Housekeeping" seal of approval

The Professional Golfers' Association (PGA)

Roquefort cheese

Sebastian hair salons

C. LIMITED AREA EXCEPTION

Statute: 15 U.S.C. § 1115(b)(5)

THRIFTY RENT-A-CAR SYSTEM, INC. V. THRIFT CARS, INC.

831 F.2d 1177 (1st Cir. 1987).

DAVIS, CIRCUIT JUDGE.

In this trademark infringement suit brought by Thrifty Rent-a-Car System, Inc. (Thrifty), that firm and defendant Thrift Cars, Inc. (Thrift Cars) both appeal the decision of the district court for the District of Massachusetts (Young, J.). After a bench trial, the court enjoined Thrift Cars from conducting a car or truck rental or leasing business outside of Taunton, Massachusetts under the "Thrift Cars" name, and limited Thrift Cars' advertising to those media it had used prior to July 26, 1964, the date that Thrifty obtained federal registration of its own mark. Concomitantly, the court prohibited Thrifty from operating any of its business establishments in East Taunton, Massachusetts or from advertising in any media principally intended to target the East Taunton community. We affirm.

I.

Background

A. Thrifty Rent-a-Car System, Inc.

Thrifty Rent-a-Car System traces its beginnings to March 3, 1958 when L.C. Crow, an individual, began renting cars in Tulsa, Oklahoma, under the trade name "Thrifty." In 1962, Stemmons, Inc., an Oklahoma corporation, purchased Crow's business and expanded the business to Houston, Texas, renting automobiles to customers under the "Thrifty" trade name. Stemmons subsequently changed its name to The Thrifty Rent-a-Car System, Inc. and expanded the business to Wichita, Kansas, Dallas, Texas and St. Louis, Missouri. On July 30, 1962 Thrifty Rent-a-Car made an application to the United States Patent Office to register the service mark "Thrifty Rent-a-Car System" and was granted that mark in July 1964. Thrifty expanded the business through both franchises and directly-owned rental agencies. In December 1967, a Thrifty Rent-a-Car outlet opened in Massachusetts. By the time of trial, Thrifty had become the fifth largest car rental agency worldwide, and operated car rental outlets in 23 locations in Massachusetts.

B. Thrift Cars, Inc.

Thrift Cars' rental business began in October 1962 and was incorporated in Massachusetts as Thrift Cars, Inc. Thrift Cars' owner and proprietor, Peter A. Conlon, at first began a modest car-rental service out of his home in East Taunton, Massachusetts. The East Taunton business was largely limited to what the car-rental industry considers a "tertiary market," that is, the market that serves individuals needing replacement cars to bridge the short term car rental and the longer term automobile lease. Thrift Cars provided customized service, arranging delivery of the rental car to the customer as well as pick-up at the termination of the rental period. In the years immediately following 1962, Thrift Cars delivered automobiles to Boston's Logan Airport and to various cities on Cape Cod and to Nantucket. Prior to Thrifty's federal registration in July 1964, Thrift Cars advertised in the Taunton area yellow pages telephone directory, in The Taunton Daily Gazette, The Cape Cod Times (a newspaper of general circulation servicing Cape Cod, Martha's Vineyard, and Nantucket) and in The Anchor (the newspaper of the Roman Catholic Diocese of Fall River). In 1963 Thrift Cars also advertised in the The Inquirer and Mirror, a Nantucket newspaper. In 1970, some six years after Thrifty had obtained federal registration of its mark, Thrift Cars received a license to operate a car rental facility at the Nantucket airport, and Conlon, Thrift Cars' Chief Executive Officer, moved the major portion of the business to Nantucket.

The Nantucket facility, unlike the operation at East Taunton, was operated largely as a traditional car rental service, servicing the resort market. Customers came directly to the airport to arrange for rental and pick-up of the automobile. Thrift Cars' post-1970 Nantucket operation thus came into a direct clash with Thrifty, which was also operating a car rental facility directed to the resort market in the Cape Cod area.

C. Litigation below.

Thrifty brought this action against Thrift Cars in federal district court, alleging trademark infringement and false designation of title under the Lanham Act. 15 U.S.C. § 1125(a) and §§ 1051–1127. The parties stipulated that the Thrift and Thrifty names are confusingly similar—as, of course, they are. The trial court found that Thrift Cars' business activities as of the critical date of July 26, 1964 (the date of Thrifty's registration) did not extend to areas beyond East Taunton, Massachusetts. The district court then enjoined Thrift Cars from using "Thrift" in conducting a car rental business outside of Taunton. The court also enjoined Thrift Cars from advertising in media directed outside of East Taunton, except in publications in which Thrift Cars had advertised prior to July 26, 1964.

Conversely, the court enjoined Thrifty from operating any business establishment in East Taunton and prohibited it from advertising in any media principally intended to target the East Taunton area.

Both parties appealed. * * *

II.

Discussion

As the district court recognized, disposition of this case revolves around geographical market protection and priority afforded to trademark users under the Lanham Act. Congress passed the Lanham Act in 1946 with the primary purpose of providing some nationwide protection for trademark users. Prior to that time, trademark protection was generally governed by state common law. The normal rule was that the first to appropriate a mark had the exclusive right to use that mark in business. Common law exceptions to the general rule developed as to remote users, but with increased interstate commerce, and the greater mobility of society as a whole, a federal scheme with some consistency was felt to be necessary. * * *

Section 15 of the Lanham Act, 15 U.S.C. § 1065, provides that a party like Thrifty, which has successfully registered and continued using a federal service mark, has an incontestable right to use the mark throughout the United States in connection with the goods or services with which it has been used. Lanham Act registration also puts all would-be users of the mark (or a confusingly similar mark) on constructive notice of the mark. 15 U.S.C. § 1072.

A. "Limited area exception".

However, Lanham Act § 33(b), 15 U.S.C. § 1115(b)(5) declares a "limited area" exception to that general premise of incontestability, an exception which the district court concluded was applicable in this case. The essence of the exception embodied in § 1115(b)(5) is based on common law trademark protection for remote users established by the Supreme Court in *Hanover Star Milling Co. v. Metcalf*, 240 U.S. 403 (1916), and *United Drug Co. v. Theodore Rectanus Co.*, 248 U.S. 90 (1918). Subsection (5) confers upon a junior user, such as Thrift Cars, the right to continued use of an otherwise infringing mark in a remote geographical area if that use was established prior to the other party's federal registration. The junior user is permitted to maintain a proprietary interest in the mark even though it has no general federal protection through registration. To be able to invoke the § 1115(b)(5) exception, however, the junior user must have used the mark continuously in that location and initially in good faith without notice of an infringing mark.

To sustain its "limited area" defense of 15 U.S.C. § 1115(b)(5), Thrift Cars was required to demonstrate (1) that it adopted its mark before

Thrifty's 1964 registration under the Lanham Act, and without knowledge of Thrifty's prior use; (2) the extent of the trade area in which Thrift Cars used the mark prior to Thrifty's registration; and (3) that Thrift Cars has continuously used the mark in the pre-registration trade area. There is no issue that Thrift Cars had adopted its mark in good faith and without notice prior to Thrifty's registration. Rather, the questions are whether Thrift Cars had established a market presence in any locality, the extent of that market presence, and whether that market presence had been continuous within the meaning of § 1115(b)(5). The district court found that Thrift Cars' use of the service mark had been continuous in East Taunton within the meaning of § 1115(b)(5), but also found that it had not established a sufficient market presence outside of East Taunton (i.e., in Nantucket or other areas of southeastern Massachusetts) to establish there a continuous market presence sufficient to confer on Thrift Cars trademark protection under the statute.

As the district court held, the scope of protection afforded by § 1115(b)(5) is limited. A pre-existing good faith user's rights are frozen to the geographical location where the user has established a market penetration as of the date of registration. Such users are unable thereafter to acquire additional protection superior to that obtained by the federal registrant. The district court therefore held that Thrift Cars' expansion into new market areas after the 1964 date of Thrifty's federal registration is not protected under § 1115(b)(5).

* * *

B. Thrift Cars did not demonstrate a continuous presence outside of East Taunton within the meaning of § 1115(b)(5).

The district court found that Thrift Cars had not established a continuous presence in any area outside of East Taunton—prior to July 1964—adequate to satisfy the requirements of § 1115(b)(5). * * *

We also note that the fact that Thrift Cars had desired to expand into the Nantucket market prior to July 1964 by unsuccessfully applying for a license to operate at the airport is not sufficient to meet the requirements of § 1115(b)(5). A mere desire, without more, will not confer upon Thrift Cars the ability to exclude Thrifty from Nantucket. The policy behind the Lanham Act is very strong and the party challenging the federal registrant has the burden of showing a continued and actual market presence in order to qualify for the "limited area" exception under the statute. The trial court permissibly found that Thrift Cars did not meet its burden in this respect.

C. Thrift Cars' activities in East Taunton fall into the "limited area" defense of § 1115(b)(5).

The more difficult question is whether Thrift Cars has established and maintained a continuous market presence in East Taunton so as to sustain an injunction against Thrifty in that region. Under § 1115(b)(5), the junior user must show that it has made continuous use of the mark prior to the issuance of the senior user's registration and must further prove continued use up until trial. Otherwise, the defense "dries up" and the junior user cannot assert rights in the limited trade area.

Here, the district court properly found that Thrift Cars established a significant enough market share in East Taunton prior to Thrifty's 1964 federal registration to constitute continuous use there at least until May 1970, when Conlon opened business operations in Nantucket. The pivotal issue is, however, whether Thrift Cars continued enough of a market presence in East Taunton after May 1970 (to the time of trial) to qualify for the § 1115(b)(5) defense. The district court made no specific findings on this precise matter (though its opinion reveals an implicit affirmative finding), and we think it is a close call whether Thrift Cars conducted a significant amount of business in East Taunton up until trial. Nevertheless, we believe that on this record Thrift Cars should be entitled to continue doing business in East Taunton and Thrifty should be enjoined from establishing a franchise there. First, the record shows that Thrift Cars continually advertised in media directed specifically to the East Taunton area such as the Taunton area telephone yellow pages, even after opening the Nantucket facility. The record also reveals that Thrift Cars made a showing of general reputation in the East Taunton area throughout the period involved by maintaining an East Taunton address and an East Taunton telephone number. We cannot say that the district court's inherent finding of continuous use should be upset.

* * *

E. The district court did not abuse its discretion by allowing Thrift Cars to advertise in those publications it had used prior to Thrifty's registration.

The district court allowed Thrift Cars to continue advertising in those media it had used prior to the critical date of July 26, 1964. Thrifty now urges that the court allowed Thrift Cars too broad an advertising distribution base, because it extended outside East Taunton to Cape Cod and Nantucket. Thrifty says that by permitting both parties to advertise in the major resort area publications, the court abused its discretion because substantial consumer confusion is likely to result.

We reject Thrifty's arguments and agree with the district court that to contract Thrift Cars' advertising base would be a punitive move. The district court did not allow Thrift Cars to advertise in any publications that it had not used prior to Thrifty's registration. On the contrary, the court simply authorized Thrift Cars to use only the same newspapers it had used prior to that critical date. While we recognize that some consumer confusion may result because there will be some overlap in advertising, the

Lanham Act does not require the complete elimination of all confusion. We think, moreover, that the confusion spawned as a result of Thrift Cars' advertising will be minimal and should not significantly interfere with Thrifty's proprietary rights in its mark. Each party shall bear its own costs.

AFFIRMED.

NOTES

1. Will the court's division of the trademark rights in this case result in significant consumer confusion in southeastern Massachusetts? If so, why does the court countenance this result?

2. The "Burger King" chain of restaurants began operations with a single store in Florida, which opened in 1953, and it successfully registered its federal trademark in 1961. Its first Illinois restaurant opened in 1961. Meanwhile, in 1957, a completely independent "Burger King" (hereinafter the "junior user") opened in Mattoon, Illinois. In 1959, the junior user registered the "Burger King" mark under the *Illinois* trademark statute. In 1962, the junior user opened a second restaurant under the same name, this time in Charleston, Illinois. What are the relative rights of the parties? Does the junior user's registration under Illinois law change the analysis? *See Burger King of Florida, Inc. v. Hoots*, 403 F.2d 904 (7th Cir. 1968).

3. Compare the current version of section 1115(b)(5) with the older version as described in *Thrifty*. Suppose that the current version (enacted in 1988) had been in effect at the time these events took place. Would this affect the outcome? What does this tell you about the importance of an applicant's filing date under current law?

CHAPTER 4

CAUSES OF ACTION

■ ■ ■

A wide variety of legal claims may arise from the unauthorized use of trademarks or other indications of origin. These include trademark infringement, trademark dilution, unfair competition, false advertising, and cybersquatting.

Statutes: 15 U.S.C. §§ 1114(1), 1125(a)–(d)

A. INFRINGEMENT

Claims of trademark infringement may arise under state or federal law, and may involve either registered or unregistered trademarks. Infringement claims involving marks that are federally registered are brought under section 32(1) of the Lanham Act, 15 U.S.C. § 1114(1). Even unregistered marks may be the subject of Lanham Act infringement claims; these claims are brought under the federal unfair competition statute, section 43(a) of the Lanham Act, 15 U.S.C. § 1125(a). Under both state and federal law, a claim of trademark infringement requires a plaintiff to prove that the defendant's use of a mark creates a likelihood of confusion. To make this determination, courts use a multi-factor analysis.

CBS INC. V. LIEDERMAN

866 F.Supp. 763 (S.D.N.Y. 1994), *aff'd per curiam*, 44 F.3d 174 (2d Cir.1995).

KEVIN THOMAS DUFFY, DISTRICT JUDGE:

CBS Inc. ("CBS") commenced this action against David and William Liederman ("defendants") alleging trademark infringement, unfair competition, and trademark dilution under the Lanham Act, 15 U.S.C. §§ 1114(1) and 1125(a), and New York statutory and common law. CBS moved for a preliminary injunction and a temporary restraining order preventing the defendants from opening their proposed restaurant, named "Television City."

Since 1952, CBS has owned and operated "Television City," a facility located in Los Angeles, California designed for the production of television shows. On January 26, 1988, the service mark "Television City" was registered on the Principal Register in the United States Patent and Trademark Office in the name of CBS Inc., as U.S. Service Mark

Registration No. 1,474,506. The mark was granted for the following categories: "for television production services" and "for entertainment services, namely the production and distribution of television programs, rental of television production facilities and the providing of tours of production facilities to the public." The facility has a somewhat storied past within American popular culture, having been the home to many of CBS' best television series. Today, many soap operas and game shows are produced at Television City, and hundreds of people descend upon the facility each day in order to be a member of a studio audience. The name "Television City" is shown numerous times each week in connection with these television shows, and can often be heard in the voice-over accompanying each show's introduction. In addition, there is a small retail operation at the facility which sells such memorabilia as T-shirts, pins, watches and the like, each bearing the name "CBS Television City."

The defendants are restauranteurs, who are in the process of opening a restaurant in New York City using the identical mark, "Television City." The proposed restaurant, which is to be a "theme" restaurant celebrating "the world of television" would be located at Sixth Avenue and 50th Street in Manhattan, directly across the street from Radio City Music Hall. The restaurant would not only serve food, but would have an entire section devoted to the sale of television memorabilia, such as T-shirts, sweatshirts, posters, and the like.

CBS asserts that the continued promotion and eventual opening of the proposed restaurant will mislead the general public and convey a false impression as to the restaurant's affiliation with CBS. Thus, CBS seeks to preliminarily enjoin defendants' use of the "Television City" mark in connection with their restaurant.

Discussion

I. Lanham Act Section 32 and Common Law Infringement Claims

Plaintiff claims trademark infringement under both the Lanham Act and the state common law. Infringement of a registered trademark is prohibited by § 32(1) of the Lanham Act. 15 U.S.C. 1114 (1988). Section 32(1) prohibits the use of a registered trademark without permission, in connection with the sale or advertising of goods or services, in a manner that is likely to cause confusion or mistake or to deceive the purchaser as to the source or sponsorship of the goods.

There can be no disputing that CBS is the owner of an incontestable, registered service mark—at least with regard to television production services. The strength of the mark within the television production field is not questioned. The central issue is whether this mark extends from the television production arena to the restaurant arena. The Second Circuit has held that "the strength of an incontestable registered trademark could be overcome by the use of a descriptive or weak portion of the mark."

Gruner & Jahr, 991 F.2d at 1077. *See also W.W.W. Pharmaceutical Co. v. Gillette Co.*, 984 F.2d 567, 576 (2d Cir.1993) (incontestable registered trademark for "Sportstick" lip balm was not infringed by Gillette's "Sport Stick" deodorant); *Pirone v. MacMillan, Inc.*, 894 F.2d 579 (2d Cir.1990) (observing that registration does not remove proper noun from general language or reduce it to exclusive possession of registrant for all purposes). Additionally, "a term that is in one category for a particular product may be in quite a different one for another." *Abercrombie & Fitch Co. v. Hunting World, Inc.*, 537 F.2d 4, 9 (2d Cir.1976).

* * *

(B) Likelihood of Confusion

Likelihood of confusion has been defined as the likelihood that an appreciable number of ordinarily prudent purchasers are likely to be misled, or simply confused, as to the source, sponsorship or affiliation of defendant's goods or services. The law of this circuit with respect to likelihood of confusion was set forth in *Polaroid Corp. v. Polarad Elecs. Corp.*, 287 F.2d 492 (2d Cir. 1961). While not absolutely dispositive, the *Polaroid* factors establish a balancing test consisting of the following factors: (1) the strength of the mark; (2) the degree of similarity between the two marks; (3) the proximity of the two [products]; (4) the likelihood that the senior user of the mark will bridge the gap; (5) evidence of actual confusion; (6) the junior user's bad faith in adopting the mark; (7) the quality of the junior user's [product]; and (8) the sophistication of the relevant consumer group. *Id.* at 495.

(1) Strength of the Mark

The strength of a mark is "its tendency to identify goods sold as emanating from a particular, even if anonymous source." *See Mead Data Central v. Toyota Motor Sales, U.S.A., Inc.*, 702 F.Supp. 1031, 1035 (S.D.N.Y.1988). The strength of the mark is the central issue as it will determine the breadth of the mark's protection.

CBS established the first facility used exclusively for television production in 1952 and named it "Television City." Pursuant to 15 U.S.C. § 1065, CBS used the mark continuously for five consecutive years following its registration and it has become an incontestable mark. Although the mark covers only the words "Television City," the plaintiff uses it almost exclusively as "CBS Television City." In this regard, it seems that public recognition of the mark, to the extent that it is recognized, would be more for "CBS Television City," rather than for "Television City." Moreover, defendants' restaurant will not be broadcasting or producing any television programs. The mere similarity in the subject matter—that they both necessarily involve television—does not grant CBS protection in every area where television is an underlying theme.

Interestingly, there are various registrations similar to plaintiff's mark for the sale and repair of television sets and appliances. These other uses are no more likely to cause confusion with the plaintiff's mark than the defendants' proposed use. The mark is strong within the field of television production, but it is limited to that and related fields.

(2) Similarity of Marks

Because the two marks are identical, this factor overwhelmingly favors CBS. Defendants argue that CBS uses their mark almost exclusively in conjunction with the "CBS" name and corporate logo. While this is true, the fact remains that the registered mark is merely for "Television City," and not for "CBS Television City." The fact that CBS often connects the two marks does not change the fact that defendants are attempting to use the identical mark that CBS has registered and would like to protect.

(3) Proximity

This factor, which is the central issue in this case, measures whether it is likely that consumers will assume either that the junior user's product is associated with the senior user or is a product of the senior user. *See Centaur Communications, Ltd. v. A/S/M Communications, Inc.*, 830 F.2d 1217, 1226 (2d Cir.1987). In determining the proximity of the two "Television Cities," the court considers "content, geographic distribution, market position, and audience appeal." *Major League Baseball v. Sed Non Olet Denarius*, 817 F.Supp. 1103, 1120 (S.D.N.Y.1993).

CBS produces television shows at Television City in California. The mark is to protect the name in that context. The intended use of defendants' proposed restaurant will primarily be serving food. There simply is little or no overlap between the services provided be each of the parties. Additionally, the production site and the proposed restaurant are on opposite coasts. While it is true that an avid fan of television may be attracted to both places, it does not mean that they would visit one at the expense of the other. The individual would have two entirely different experiences. CBS invites the public into CBS Television City to make up the audiences for its game shows and other television programs produced on site. While there, CBS provides a tour of the facility. However, there was testimony that the public is excluded from CBS Television City for all purposes other than for seeing a show produced. * * * There is little overlap of markets between plaintiff's and defendants' services. Accordingly, this factor favors a finding for defendants.

(4) Bridging the Gap

This factor evaluates "whether the senior user of the mark is likely to enter the market in which the junior user is operating." *Centaur Communications, Ltd.*, 880 F.2d at 1227. Trademark law protects a senior user's right to enter into a related field in the future. CBS claims in its papers that it is currently planning to open a full service restaurant near the Ed Sullivan Theater on West 57th Street in Manhattan. This proposed restaurant, which plaintiff has apparently acquired, is to be a "television theme restaurant . . . probably focusing on the history of television." It must be noted that plaintiff's mark is afforded protection in the television production area and related areas only. Plaintiff's announcement that it is looking to enter the restaurant business is irrelevant to this claim. It is a competitive venture to that of the defendants, but since the restaurant business is not "related" to television production, CBS' mark does not necessarily protect this latest endeavor by CBS.

Plaintiff attempts to show that it has already bridged the gap with regard to restaurants because CBS operates an employee cafeteria named "Television City Cafe" at its Los Angeles facility. This establishment is far removed from the type of restaurant proposed by defendants. Additionally, the cafe operated by CBS is located within the CBS' complex in California, and is not open to the public. Defendants' proposed restaurant is in New York City. CBS' maintenance of an on-site cafeteria for its workers is not sufficient to entitle it to protection under its mark. The on-site facility differs dramatically from that of the proposed restaurant, and does not mean that plaintiff has entered the restaurant business. In fact, the cafeteria is not being operated by CBS at all. Rather, it is run by Marriott through a contract with CBS. Clearly, these two eating establishments would not in any way compete with each other, and this argument is without merit.

(5) Actual Confusion

This factor pertains to whether any consumers have actually been misled by the similarity of the two marks. In this case there has been no realistic opportunity for actual confusion because defendants' restaurant has not yet opened. While it was argued that reports of defendants' proposed restaurant have appeared numerous times in the media without mention of CBS' mark, this factor does not seem to favor either side. CBS acted before the restaurant opened and any actual confusion could arise, and it should not be penalized for so doing. Actual confusion is not an essential element in order to prevail under the Lanham Act, since actual confusion is very difficult to prove and the Act requires only a likelihood of confusion as to source. "It would be unfair to penalize appellee for acting to protect its trademark rights before serious damage has occurred." *Lois Sportswear, U.S.A., Inc. v. Levi Strauss & Co.*, 799 F.2d 867, 875 (2d Cir.1986). Therefore, this factor favors neither party.

(6) Junior User's Bad Faith

This factor looks to whether the defendants "adopted its mark with the intention of capitalizing on plaintiff's reputation and goodwill and any confusion between [defendant's] and the senior user's product." *W.W.W.*

Pharmaceutical, 984 F.2d at 575 (quoting *Lang v. Retirement Living Pub. Co.*, 949 F.2d 576, 583 (2d Cir.1991)). In the present case, while CBS argues for bad faith to be inferred, it fails to put forth any evidence that defendants chose this particular mark with the intent of capitalizing on any goodwill which CBS had acquired. * * * Without more, it appears that defendants did not act in bad faith and this factor does not favor either side.

(7) *Quality of Junior User's Product*

While defendants' restaurant is not yet open, there is no evidence to suggest that it will be anything but top quality. CBS acknowledges this fact, yet makes the point that "[A] senior user is entitled 'to protect its reputation even where the infringer's goods are of top quality.'" *Berkshire Fashions, Inc. v. Sara Lee Corp.*, 725 F.Supp. 790, 799 (S.D.N.Y.1989) (quoting *Mobil Oil Corp. v. Pegasus Petroleum Corp.*, 818 F.2d 254, 259–60 (2d Cir.1987)). However, because defendants' restaurant has not yet been opened, any discussion of the quality of the defendants' product would be speculative and the issue will not be addressed.

(8) *Sophistication of the Consumers*

"As a general rule, sophistication of the consumer is a factor that will weigh against a finding of likelihood of confusion." *Comic Strip, Inc.*, 710 F.Supp. at 980 (citation omitted). Defendants' potential customers will be drawn from the general public and thus cannot be said to have unique qualities or sophistication. In fact, the only generalization which it would be possible to make regarding the restaurant's clientele is that many of them will undoubtedly be television watchers. * * *

Applying the *Polaroid* factors to the instant case, the court finds that there is no showing of likelihood of confusion sufficient enough to warrant the issuance of a preliminary injunction. The plaintiff has not demonstrated a likelihood of success on the merits nor sufficiently serious questions warranting litigation. CBS's mark protects it in the field of television production services. The mark does not insure its exclusive use of the mark "Television City" in all markets and all products.

* * *

NOTES

1. Is the correct outcome in this case as clear as the district court makes it appear? Which factors in the "likelihood of confusion" test might weigh more heavily in favor of the plaintiff than the court indicates?

2. Can you predict the outcome if the defendants attempted to open a "Television City" restaurant in Los Angeles? Can the defendants market "Television City" mugs, t-shirts, and other memorabilia at their New York location? Many trademark infringement cases involve fact issues that preclude summary judgment. *See, e.g., Car-Freshner Corp. v. Am. Covers, LLC,* 980 F.3d

314, 319 (2d Cir. 2020) (fact issues as to whether trademark consisting of the words "Black Ice" is infringed by defendant's products labeled with the words "Midnight Black Ice Storm" for the sale of car air fresheners).

3. While there is considerable overlap, each of the federal courts of appeal has articulated its own version of the "likelihood of confusion" factors. The Sixth Circuit, for example, considers the following: "(1) the strength of the plaintiff's mark; (2) the relatedness of the goods; (3) the similarity of the marks; (4) evidence of actual confusion; (5) marketing channels used; (6) the likely degree of purchaser care; (7) the defendants' intent on selecting the its mark; and (8) the likelihood of expansion of the product lines." *Frisch's Restaurants, Inc. v. Elby's Big Boy of Steubenville, Inc.*, 670 F.2d 642 (6th Cir. 1982). The Ninth Circuit uses the *Sleekcraft* factors, as illustrated in the next case. Courts always state that their list of factors is non-exhaustive. Is the ultimate outcome of a case likely to depend on which circuit's test is applied?

4. Although it is not required, evidence of actual confusion is a strong indication that a likelihood of confusion exists. Proof of actual confusion may include survey evidence or anecdotal evidence of specific instances of confused consumers. In *Blockbuster Entertainment Group v. Laylco, Inc.*, 869 F.Supp. 505 (E.D. Mich. 1994). where two video rental stores had similar names (Blockbuster and Video Buster), the plaintiff introduced a survey purporting to show that 14 percent of the Detroit-area public was confused as to the identity or origin between the two stores. Twenty-two percent of people who had visited both stores were shown to be confused. How persuasive is this survey evidence? How might it be refuted? Surveys showing 15–20 percent confusion have been deemed sufficient in other cases. *See e.g., RJR Foods, Inc. v. White Rock Corp.*, 603 F.2d 1058 (2d Cir. 1979); *James Burrough, Ltd. v. Sign of Beefeater, Inc.*, 540 F.2d 266 (7th Cir. 1976). Are these percentages persuasive? If two businesses have been using similar trademarks for an extended period of time, would the absence of actual confusion evidence be significant?

5. Under section 2(d) of the Lanham Act, 15 U.S.C. § 1052(d), the Federal Circuit uses its own version of the likelihood-of-confusion factors when evaluating an application to register a mark. Suppose that Coors Brewing Company seeks to register a new brand name, "Blue Moon," for a line of beer. But "Blue Moon" is already a registered trademark for a restaurant. Should Coors be able to register its mark? *See In re Coors Brewing Co.*, 343 F.3d 1340 (Fed. Cir. 2003).

6. If the PTO rejects an applicant's trademark registration under section 2(d) because it finds a likelihood of confusion with a mark already registered or in use by another party, is the PTO's determination binding on a court that subsequently adjudicates an infringement dispute between the same two parties? Does it matter that the court uses a different set of factors to assess the likelihood of confusion? *See B&B Hardware, Inc. v. Hargis Indus., Inc.*, 575 U.S. 138 (2015), excerpted in Chapter 3.

7. *Post-Sale Confusion:* A likelihood of confusion can be predicated upon the experience of those who observe or use an infringing product, in addition (or as an alternative) to persons who actually purchase the product. *See Georgia-Pacific Consumer Products v. Von Drehle Corp.*, 618 F.3d 441 (4th Cir. 2010) (considering likelihood that restroom visitors would be confused as to source of paper towels where competitor's paper towels were loaded into plaintiff's trademarked dispensers).

8. In the typical trademark infringement case, as illustrated by *CBS v. Liederman,* the senior user asserts that the junior user's infringement will cause the public to believe that the junior user's goods are associated with the senior user. In contrast to this "forward confusion," some disputes arise from "reverse confusion"—where the senior user asserts that a larger junior user has saturated the market with a similar mark, leading the public to believe that the senior user's products come from the junior user, or that the senior user is somehow associated with the junior user. According to the theory of reverse confusion, the senior user is injured because it "loses the value of the trademark—its product identity, corporate identity, control over its goodwill and reputation, and ability to move into new markets." *Ameritech, Inc. v. American Information Technologies Corp.*, 811 F.2d 960, 964 (6th Cir.1987).

9. The likelihood-of-confusion factors were developed long before the advent of the internet. As the next case illustrates, an analytical framework developed for brick-and-mortar commerce can be difficult to apply to the world of e-commerce.

NETWORK AUTOMATION, INC. V. ADVANCED SYSTEMS CONCEPTS, INC.

638 F.3d 1137 (9th Cir. 2011).

WARDLAW, CIRCUIT JUDGE:

* * *

Advanced Systems Concepts ("Systems") is a software engineering and consulting firm founded in 1981. It has used the ActiveBatch trademark since 2000, and it procured federal registration of the mark in 2001. Systems markets ActiveBatch software to businesses, which use the product to centralize and manage disparate tasks. Network Automation ("Network") is a software company founded in 1997 under the name Unisyn. Its signature product, AutoMate, also provides businesses with job scheduling, event monitoring, and related services. * * * There is no dispute that Network and Systems are direct competitors, or that ActiveBatch and AutoMate are directly competing products.

Google AdWords is a program through which the search engine sells "keywords," or search terms that trigger the display of a sponsor's advertisement. When a user enters a keyword, Google displays the links generated by its own algorithm in the main part of the page, along with the advertisements in a separate "sponsored links" section next to or above the objective results. Multiple advertisers can purchase the same keyword, and Google charges sponsors based on the number of times users click on an ad to travel from the search results page to the advertiser's own website. Network purchased "ActiveBatch" as a keyword from Google AdWords and a comparable program offered by Microsoft's Bing search engine.

As a result, consumers searching for business software who enter "ActiveBatch" as a search term would locate a results page where the top objective results are links to Systems' own website and various articles about the product. In the "Sponsored Links" or "Sponsored Sites" section of the page, above or to the right of the regular results, users see Network's advertisement, either alone or alongside Systems' own sponsored link. The text of Network's advertisements begin with phrases such as "Job Scheduler," "Intuitive Job Scheduler," or "Batch Job Scheduling," and end with the company's web site address, www.NetworkAutomation.com. The middle line reads: "Windows Job Scheduling + Much More. Easy to Deploy, Scalable. D/L Trial."

On November 16, 2009, Systems demanded that Network cease and desist from using the ActiveBatch mark in its search engine advertising, as it was not "authorized to use these marks in commerce." In a second letter, Systems explained that Network's use of ActiveBatch in its Google AdWords keyword advertising infringed Systems' trademark rights by deceiving customers into believing that Network's software products were affiliated with Systems' products. Systems threatened litigation unless Network immediately ceased all use of Systems' mark, including removing the mark from the Google AdWords Program. Network responded that its use of the ActiveBatch mark was non-infringing as a matter of law, and filed this lawsuit seeking a declaratory judgment of non-infringement. Systems counterclaimed on February 22, 2010, alleging trademark infringement under the Lanham Act, 15 U.S.C. § 1114(1), and moved for a preliminary injunction against Network's use of the ActiveBatch mark pending trial.

The district court granted injunctive relief on April 30, 2010. Noting that the parties did not dispute the validity or ownership of the ActiveBatch mark, the district court ruled that Systems was likely to succeed in satisfying the Lanham Act's "use in commerce" requirement by showing that Network "used" the mark when it purchased advertisements from search engines triggered by the term "ActiveBatch." Applying the eight-factor *Sleekcraft* test for source confusion, the district court emphasized three factors it viewed as significant for "cases involving the Internet": the similarity of the marks, relatedness of the goods or services, and simultaneous use of the Web as a marketing channel. The district court concluded that all three factors favored Systems: Network used the identical mark to sell a directly competing product, and both advertised on the Internet.

The district court also concluded that Systems' mark was strong because, as a federally registered trademark, ActiveBatch is presumptively distinctive. It concluded that the degree of consumer care suggested likely confusion because "there is generally a low degree of care exercised by Internet consumers." Moreover, Network intentionally used Systems' mark to advertise its own product. Finally, the district court noted that neither party introduced evidence of actual confusion, and that the likelihood of product expansion was not relevant.

The district court also analyzed whether Network infringed Systems' mark by creating initial interest confusion—as opposed to source confusion—which "occurs when the defendant uses the plaintiff's trademark in a manner calculated to capture initial consumer attention, even though no actual sale is finally completed as a result of the confusion." (quoting *Nissan Motor Co. v. Nissan Computer Corp.*, 378 F.3d 1002, 1018 (9th Cir.2004)). Because the district court found that Network's advertisements did not clearly divulge their source, it concluded that consumers might be confused into unwittingly visiting Network's website, allowing the company to "impermissibly capitalize[] on [Systems'] goodwill."

Based on its analysis of the *Sleekcraft* factors and its finding of likely initial interest confusion, the district court concluded that Systems had a strong likelihood of success on the merits of its trademark infringement claim. It then presumed a likelihood of irreparable harm, and concluded that the balance of hardships and the public interest favored Systems. Following entry of the preliminary injunction, Network timely appealed.

* * *

III. DISCUSSION

* * *

Network does not contest the ownership or its use of the mark. We note that the district court correctly found the prerequisite "use in commerce" in Network's use of the mark to purchase keywords to advertise its products for sale on the Internet. Previously we have assumed, without expressly deciding, that the use of a trademark as a search engine keyword that triggers the display of a competitor's advertisement is a "use in commerce" under the Lanham Act. We now agree with the Second Circuit that such use is a "use in commerce" under the Lanham Act. *See Rescuecom Corp. v. Google Inc.*, 562 F.3d 123, 127 (2d Cir.2009) (holding that Google's sale of trademarks as search engine keywords is a use in commerce).

This case, therefore, turns on whether Network's use of Systems' trademark is likely to cause consumer confusion. Network argues that its use of Systems' mark is legitimate "comparative, contextual advertising" which presents sophisticated consumers with clear choices. Systems characterizes Network's behavior differently, accusing it of misleading consumers by hijacking their attention with intentionally unclear advertisements. To resolve this dispute we must apply the *Sleekcraft* test in a flexible manner, keeping in mind that the eight factors it recited are not exhaustive, and that only some of them are relevant to determining whether confusion is likely in the case at hand.

A.

In *Sleekcraft,* we * * * identified eight "relevant" factors for determining whether consumers would likely be confused by related goods: "[1] strength of the mark; [2] proximity of the goods; [3] similarity of the marks; [4] evidence of actual confusion; [5] marketing channels used; [6] type of goods and the degree of care likely to be exercised by the purchaser; [7] defendant's intent in selecting the mark; and [8] likelihood of expansion of the product lines." *AMF Inc. v. Sleekcraft Boats,* 599 F.2d 341, 348–49 (9th Cir. 1979). We also noted that "the list is not exhaustive," and that "[o]ther variables may come into play depending on the particular facts presented." *Id.* at 348 n. 11.

The *Sleekcraft* factors are intended as an adaptable proxy for consumer confusion, not a rote checklist.

When we first confronted issues of trademark infringement and consumer confusion in the Internet context over a decade ago in *Brookfield,* we noted that "[w]e must be acutely aware of excessive rigidity when applying the law in the Internet context; emerging technologies require a flexible approach." *Brookfield Comm'ns, Inc. v. West Coast Ent't Corp.,* 174 F.3d 1036, 1054 (9th Cir. 1999). There, Brookfield, a software company, marketed an entertainment database program under the mark MovieBuff. It sold the software, and offered access to the database, on its website, moviebuffonline.com. West Coast, a video retailer, had registered the mark The Movie Buff's Movie Store. West Coast operated a website using the domain name moviebuff.com, which included a film database that competed with Brookfield's product.

We held that Brookfield was likely to succeed in its claim to be the senior user of MovieBuff, and that there was a likelihood of source confusion stemming from West Coast's use of the mark in its domain name. "Heeding our repeated warnings against simply launching into a mechanical application of the eight-factor *Sleekcraft* test," we determined that three of the eight factors were the most important in analyzing source confusion in the context of Internet domain names: (1) the similarity of the marks; (2) the relatedness of the goods and services offered; and (3) the simultaneous use of the Internet as a marketing channel. Reasoning that the two marks were virtually identical in terms of sight, sound and meaning, that West Coast and Brookfield both offered products and services relating to movies, and that they both used the Web as a marketing and advertising device, we concluded that consumer confusion was likely, particularly given the nature of the consumers at issue, who included casual movie watchers unlikely to realize that they had mistakenly clicked on to West Coast's site when they had intended to reach Brookfield's.

Brookfield also asserted that West Coast infringed its mark by causing initial interest confusion because it had included MovieBuff in its "metatags," code not visible to web users embedded in a website to attract search engines seeking a corresponding keyword.[3] Although were we to apply the same analysis in the metatags context as we did in the domain name context, we would easily reach the same conclusion as to each of the factors (with the possible exception of purchaser care), we declined to do so, reasoning that the "question in the metatags context is quite different." In the metatags context, the question was whether West Coast could use the mark MovieBuff in the metatags of its website to attract search engines to locate its site when the keyword "MovieBuff" was entered, a question analogous to the issue presented here. As in the domain name context, the degree of care and sophistication of the consumer was a key factor, although the outcome differed. We did not find a likelihood of source confusion because the results list from a search for "MovieBuff" would result in a list that included both Brookfield's and West Coast's websites, and if the consumer clicked on West Coast's site its own name was "prominently display[ed]." Thus a consumer was much less likely to be confused about which site he was viewing.

Finding no source confusion, we nonetheless concluded that West Coast's use of MovieBuff in its metatags was likely to cause initial interest confusion. That is, by using Brookfield's mark MovieBuff to direct persons searching for Brookfield's product to the West Coast site, West Coast derived an improper benefit from the goodwill Brookfield developed in its mark.

Five years later in *Playboy,* we considered the practice of "keying"—another situation analogous to that here. Netscape operated a search engine that offered an early version of a keyword advertising program. It sold lists of terms to sponsors, and when users searched for the keywords on the list, the sponsor's advertisement would be displayed on the results page. [*Playboy Enters., Inc. v. Netscape Commcns Corp.,* 354 F.3d 1020, 1022 (9th Cir. 2004).] Netscape required its advertisers from the adult entertainment industry to link their ads to one such list that contained more than 400 terms, including trademarks held by Playboy. Playboy sued, contending that this practice infringed its trademarks in violation of the

[3] Modern search engines such as Google no longer use metatags. Instead they rely on their own algorithms to find websites.

Lanham Act. The district court entered summary judgment in favor of Netscape.

We reversed, holding that summary judgment was inappropriate because genuine issues of material fact existed as to whether Netscape's keying practices constituted actionable infringement. Following *Brookfield,* we analyzed the keying issue in terms of initial interest confusion, "find[ing] insufficient evidence to defeat summary judgment on any other theory." Playboy claimed that Netscape "misappropriated the goodwill of [its] marks by leading Internet users to competitors' websites just as West Coast . . . misappropriated the goodwill of Brookfield's mark." In framing the initial interest confusion inquiry, we stressed that Playboy's infringement claim relied on the fact that the linked banner advertisements were "unlabeled," and were, therefore, more likely to mislead consumers into believing they had followed a link to Playboy's own website.

In *Playboy,* as in *Brookfield,* we applied the *Sleekcraft* test flexibly, determining that evidence of actual confusion was the most important factor. Playboy had introduced an expert study showing that a "statistically significant number" of Internet users searching for the terms "playboy" and "playmate" would think that Playboy itself sponsored the banner advertisements which appeared on the search results page. We noted that this study "alone probably suffices to reverse the grant of summary judgment," but we nonetheless analyzed other relevant *Sleekcraft* factors. As to the strength of the mark, we credited Playboy's expert reports showing it had created strong secondary meanings for "playboy" and "playmate." This suggested that consumers who entered these terms were likely searching for Playboy's products in particular. Analyzing the nature of the goods and consumer, we "presume[d] that the average searcher seeking adult-oriented materials on the Internet is easily diverted from a specific product he or she is seeking if other options, particularly graphic ones, appear more quickly." We concluded that there were genuine issues of material fact with respect to whether consumers were likely to be confused by Netscape's keying practices.

Concurring, Judge Berzon was struck by how analytically similar the keyed advertisements in *Playboy* were to the infringing metatags in *Brookfield.* We agree, and also find similarity to the use of the keyword "ActiveBatch" in this case. Judge Berzon cautioned that a broad reading of *Brookfield*'s metatags holding could result in a finding of initial interest confusion "when a consumer is never confused as to source or affiliation, but instead knows, or should know, from the outset that a product or web link is not related to that of the trademark holder because the list produced by the search engine so informs him." She clarified that the *Playboy* panel's holding was limited to "situations in which the banner advertisements are not labeled or identified."

Judge Berzon analogized the experience of browsing clearly labeled keyword advertisements to shopping at Macy's, explaining that if a shopper en route to the Calvin Klein section is diverted by a prominently displayed Charter Club (Macy's own brand) collection and never reaches the Calvin Klein collection, it could not be said that Macy's had infringed on Calvin Klein's trademark by diverting the customer to it with a clearly labeled, but more prominent display. Therefore, it would be wrong to expand the initial interest confusion theory of infringement beyond the realm of the misleading and deceptive to the context of legitimate comparative and contextual advertising.

B.

Here we consider whether the use of another's trademark as a search engine keyword to trigger one's own product advertisement violates the Lanham Act. We begin by examining the *Sleekcraft* factors that are most relevant to the determination whether the use is likely to cause initial interest confusion.[4] While the district court analyzed each of the *Sleekcraft* factors, it identified the three most important factors as (1) the similarity of the marks, (2) the relatedness of the goods or services, and (3) the simultaneous use of the Web as a marketing channel, for any case addressing trademark infringement on the Internet. * * *

However, we did not intend *Brookfield* to be read so expansively as to forever enshrine these three factors—now often referred to as the "Internet trinity" or "Internet troika"—as the test for trademark infringement on the Internet. *Brookfield* was the first to present a claim of initial interest confusion on the Internet; we recognized at the time it would not be the last, and so emphasized flexibility over rigidity. Depending on the facts of each specific case arising on the Internet, other factors may emerge as more illuminating on the question of consumer confusion. In *Brookfield,* we used the "troika" factors to analyze the risk of source confusion generated by similar domain names, but we did not wholesale adopt them in the metatag analysis. Subsequent courts similarly have found the "troika" helpful to resolve disputes involving websites with similar names or appearances. * * *

Given the multifaceted nature of the Internet and the ever-expanding ways in which we all use the technology, however, it makes no sense to prioritize the same three factors for every type of potential online commercial activity. The "troika" is a particularly poor fit for the question presented here. The potential infringement in this context arises from the risk that while using Systems' mark to search for information about its product, a consumer might be confused by a results page that shows a

[4] Systems' argument rests only on the theory of initial interest confusion. It does not argue source confusion.

competitor's advertisement on the same screen, when that advertisement does not clearly identify the source or its product.

In determining the proper inquiry for this particular trademark infringement claim, we adhere to two long stated principles: the *Sleekcraft* factors (1) are non-exhaustive, and (2) should be applied flexibly, particularly in the context of Internet commerce. Finally, because the *sine qua non* of trademark infringement is consumer confusion, when we examine initial interest confusion, the owner of the mark must demonstrate likely confusion, not mere diversion.

We turn to an examination of each *Sleekcraft* factor to analyze whether there is a likelihood of consumer confusion in this case, assigning each factor appropriate weight in accordance with its relevance to the factual circumstances presented here.

1. Strength of the Mark

"The stronger a mark—meaning the more likely it is to be remembered and associated in the public mind with the mark's owner—the greater the protection it is accorded by the trademark laws." *Brookfield,* 174 F.3d at 1058. Two relevant measurements are conceptual strength and commercial strength. Conceptual strength involves classification of a mark "along a spectrum of generally increasing inherent distinctiveness as generic, descriptive, suggestive, arbitrary, or fanciful." * * * Commercial strength is based on "actual marketplace recognition," and thus "advertising expenditures can transform a suggestive mark into a strong mark."

This factor is probative of confusion here because a consumer searching for a generic term is more likely to be searching for a product category. That consumer is more likely to expect to encounter links and advertisements from a variety of sources. By contrast, a user searching for a distinctive term is more likely to be looking for a particular product, and therefore could be more susceptible to confusion when sponsored links appear that advertise a similar product from a different source. * * *

The district court acknowledged that the parties failed to address the strength of the mark, but it concluded that the factor favors Systems. It reasoned that ActiveBatch is a suggestive mark because it "requires a mental leap from the mark to the product," (quoting *Brookfield,* 174 F.3d at 1058), and as a registered trademark it is "inherently distinctive." We agree. Because the mark is both Systems' product name and a suggestive federally registered trademark, consumers searching for the term are presumably looking for its specific product, and not a category of goods. Nonetheless, that may not be the end of the inquiry about this factor, as the sophistication of the consumers of the product may also play a role. The district court properly declined to consider commercial strength, which, as an evidence-intensive inquiry, is unnecessary at the preliminary injunction stage.

2. Proximity of the Goods

"Related goods are generally more likely than unrelated goods to confuse the public as to the producers of the goods." *Brookfield,* 174 F.3d at 1055. "[T]he danger presented is that the public will mistakenly assume there is an association between the producers of the related goods, though no such association exists." *Sleekcraft,* 599 F.2d at 350. The proximity of goods is measured by whether the products are: (1) complementary; (2) sold to the same class of purchasers; and (3) similar in use and function. *Id.*

The proximity of the goods was relevant in *Playboy,* where unsophisticated consumers were confronted with unlabeled banner advertisements that touted adult-oriented material very similar to Playboy's own products. There, we concluded that under the circumstances, the relatedness of the goods bolstered the likelihood of confusion, and therefore favored Playboy. However, the proximity of the goods would become less important if advertisements are clearly labeled or consumers exercise a high degree of care, because rather than being misled, the consumer would merely be confronted with choices among similar products.

Because the products at issue here are virtually interchangeable, this factor may be helpful, but it must be considered in conjunction with the labeling and appearance of the advertisements and the degree of care exercised by the consumers of the ActiveBatch software. By weighing this factor in isolation and failing to consider whether the parties' status as direct competitors would actually lead to a likelihood of confusion, the district court allowed this factor to weigh too heavily in the analysis.

3. Similarity of the Marks

"[T]he more similar the marks in terms of appearance, sound, and meaning, the greater the likelihood of confusion." *Brookfield,* 174 F.3d at 1054. "Where the two marks are entirely dissimilar, there is no likelihood of confusion." *Id.* "Similarity of the marks is tested on three levels: sight, sound, and meaning. Each must be considered as they are encountered in the marketplace." *Sleekcraft,* 599 F.2d at 351.

In *Sleekcraft,* we concluded that the marks "Sleekcraft" and "Slickcraft" were similar in terms of sight, sound, and meaning by examining the actual situations in which consumers were likely to read, hear, and consider the meaning of the terms. Such an inquiry is impossible here where the consumer does not confront two distinct trademarks. Rather, after entering one company's mark as a search term, the consumer sees a competitor's sponsored link that displays neither company's trademarks. The district court erroneously treated "ActiveBatch," the keyword purchased by Network, as conceptually separate from ActiveBatch the trademark owned by Systems. This is an artificial distinction that does not reflect what consumers "encountered in the marketplace." Again, however, because the consumer keys in Systems' trademark, which results in Network's sponsored link, depending on the labeling and appearance of the advertisement, including whether it identifies Network's own mark, and the degree of care and sophistication of the consumer, it could be helpful in determining initial interest confusion.

4. *Evidence of Actual Confusion*

"[A] showing of actual confusion among significant numbers of consumers provides strong support for the likelihood of confusion." *Playboy,* 354 F.3d at 1026. However, "actual confusion is not necessary to a finding of likelihood of confusion under the Lanham Act." *Academy of Motion Picture Arts & Sciences v. Creative House Promotions, Inc.,* 944 F.2d 1446, 1456 (9th Cir.1991). Indeed, "[p]roving actual confusion is difficult . . . and the courts have often discounted such evidence because it was unclear or insubstantial." *Sleekcraft,* 599 F.2d at 352.

In *Playboy,* the expert report showing a significant number of users were confused by the keying practice at issue was strong evidence that Playboy's infringement claim should be allowed to proceed. *Playboy,* however, was decided at the summary judgment stage, whereas here we examine a sparse record supporting preliminary injunctive relief. As the district court noted, neither Network nor Systems provided evidence regarding actual confusion, which is not surprising given the procedural posture. Therefore, while this is a relevant factor for determining the likelihood of confusion in keyword advertising cases, its importance is diminished at the preliminary injunction stage of the proceedings. The district court correctly concluded that this factor should be accorded no weight.

5. *Marketing Channels*

"Convergent marketing channels increase the likelihood of confusion." *Sleekcraft,* 599 F.2d at 353. In *Sleekcraft,* the two products were sold in niche marketplaces, including boat shows, specialty retail outlets, and trade magazines. However, this factor becomes less important when the marketing channel is less obscure. Today, it would be the rare commercial retailer that did not advertise online, and the shared use of a ubiquitous marketing channel does not shed much light on the likelihood of consumer confusion.

Therefore, the district court's determination that because both parties advertise on the Internet this factor weighed in favor of Systems was incorrect.

6. *Type of Goods and Degree of Care*

"Low consumer care . . . increases the likelihood of confusion." *Playboy,* 354 F.3d at 1028. "In assessing the likelihood of confusion to the public, the standard used by the courts is the typical buyer exercising ordinary caution. . . . When the buyer has expertise in the field, a higher standard is proper though it will not preclude a finding that confusion is likely. Similarly, when the goods are expensive, the buyer can be expected to exercise greater care in his purchases; again, though, confusion may still be likely." *Sleekcraft,* 599 F.2d at 353.

The nature of the goods and the type of consumer is highly relevant to determining the likelihood of confusion in the keyword advertising context. A sophisticated consumer of business software exercising a high degree of care is more likely to understand the mechanics of Internet search engines and the nature of sponsored links, whereas an un-savvy consumer exercising less care is more likely to be confused. The district court determined that this factor weighed in Systems' favor because "there is generally a low degree of care exercised by Internet consumers." However, the degree of care analysis cannot begin and end at the marketing channel. We still must consider the nature and cost of the goods, and whether "the products being sold are marketed primarily to expert buyers." *Brookfield,* 174 F.3d at 1060.

In *Brookfield,* the websites were visited by both sophisticated entertainment industry professionals and amateur film fans, which supported the conclusion that at least some of the consumers were likely to exercise a low degree of care. In *Playboy,* the relevant consumer was looking for cheap, interchangeable adult-oriented material, which similarly led to our court's finding that the consumers at issue would exercise a low degree of care. In both cases, we looked beyond the medium itself and to the nature of the particular goods and the relevant consumers.

We have recently acknowledged that the default degree of consumer care is becoming more heightened as the novelty of the Internet evaporates and online commerce becomes commonplace. In *Toyota Motor Sales v. Tabari,* 610 F.3d 1171 (9th Cir.2010), we vacated a preliminary injunction that prohibited a pair of automobile brokers from using Toyota's "Lexus" mark in their domain names. We determined that it was unlikely that a reasonably prudent consumer would be confused into believing that a domain name that included a product name would necessarily have a formal affiliation with the maker of the product, as "[c]onsumers who use the internet for shopping are generally quite sophisticated about such matters." *Id.* at 1178. * * *

We further explained that we expect consumers searching for expensive products online to be even more sophisticated. *Id.* at 1176 ("Unreasonable, imprudent and inexperienced web-shoppers are not relevant.").

Therefore the district court improperly concluded that this factor weighed in Systems' favor based on a conclusion reached by our court more than a decade ago in *Brookfield* and *GoTo.com* that Internet users on the whole exercise a low degree of care. While the statement may have been accurate then, we suspect that there are many contexts in which it no longer holds true.

7. *Defendant's Intent*

"When the alleged infringer knowingly adopts a mark similar to another's, reviewing courts presume that the defendant can accomplish his purpose: that is, that the public will be deceived." *Sleekcraft,* 599 F.2d at 354. Nevertheless, we have also "recognized that liability for infringement may not be imposed for using a registered trademark in connection with truthful comparative advertising." *Lindy Pen Co., Inc. v. Bic Pen Corp.,* 725 F.2d 1240, 1248 (9th Cir.1984).

Therefore, much like the proximity of the goods, the defendant's intent may be relevant here, but only insofar as it bolsters a finding that the use of the trademark serves to mislead consumers rather than truthfully inform them of their choice of products. The district court incorrectly considered the intent factor in isolation, and concluded that it weighed in Systems' favor without first determining that Network intended to deceive consumers rather than compare its product to ActiveBatch.

8. *Likelihood of Expansion of the Product Lines*

"Inasmuch as a trademark owner is afforded greater protection against competing goods, a 'strong possibility' that either party may expand his business to compete with the other will weigh in favor of finding that the present use is infringing. When goods are closely related, any expansion is likely to result in direct competition." *Sleekcraft,* 599 F.2d at 354. Where two companies are direct competitors, this factor is unimportant. Therefore, the district court correctly declined to consider the likelihood of expansion.

9. *Other Relevant Factors*

The eight *Sleekcraft* factors are "not exhaustive. Other variables may come into play depending on the particular facts presented." In the keyword advertising context the "likelihood of confusion will ultimately turn on what the consumer saw on the screen and reasonably believed, given the context." *Hearts on Fire Co. v. Blue Nile, Inc.,* 603 F.Supp.2d 274, 289 (D.Mass.2009). In *Playboy,* we found it important that the consumers saw banner advertisements that were "confusingly labeled or not labeled at all." 354 F.3d at 1023. We noted that clear labeling "might eliminate the likelihood of initial interest confusion that exists in this case."

The appearance of the advertisements and their surrounding context on the user's screen are similarly important here. The district court correctly examined the text of Network's sponsored links, concluding that the advertisements did not clearly identify their source. However, the district court did not consider the surrounding context. In *Playboy,* we also found it important that Netscape's search engine did not clearly segregate the sponsored advertisements from the objective results. Here, even if Network has not clearly identified itself in the text of its ads, Google and Bing have partitioned their search results pages so that the advertisements appear in separately labeled sections for "sponsored" links. The labeling and appearance of the advertisements as they appear on the results page includes more than the text of the advertisement, and must be considered as a whole.

C.

Given the nature of the alleged infringement here, the most relevant factors to the analysis of the likelihood of confusion are: (1) the strength of the mark; (2) the evidence of actual confusion; (3) the type of goods and degree of care likely to be exercised by the purchaser; and (4) the labeling and appearance of the advertisements and the surrounding context on the screen displaying the results page.

The district court did not weigh the *Sleekcraft* factors flexibly to match the specific facts of this case. It relied on the Internet "troika," which is highly illuminating in the context of domain names, but which fails to discern whether there is a likelihood of confusion in a keywords case. Because the linchpin of trademark infringement is consumer confusion, the district court abused its discretion in issuing the injunction. * * *

NOTE

Where a domain name incorporates or resembles another party's trademark, how should the likelihood-of-confusion factors be applied? As between Delta Faucets and Delta Airlines, both of which had used their trademarks for many years on different goods and services without confusion before the advent of the internet, who should have the superior right to www. delta.com? What if a domain name incorporates another party's trademark but is not being used to offer goods or services to the public? In order to clarify the law regarding unauthorized uses of trademarks in domain names, Congress enacted the Anti-Cybersquatting Protection Act (ACPA), 15 U.S.C. § 1125(d), which is discussed in Part D of this chapter.

LOUIS VUITTON MALLETIER S.A. v. HAUTE DIGGITY DOG, LLC

507 F.3d 252 (4th Cir. 2007).

NIEMEYER, CIRCUIT JUDGE:

* * *

Louis Vuitton Malletier S.A. ("LVM") is a well known manufacturer of luxury luggage, leather goods, handbags, and accessories, which it markets and sells worldwide. In connection with the sale of its products, LVM has adopted trademarks and trade dress that are well recognized and have become famous and distinct. Indeed, in 2006, BusinessWeek ranked LOUIS VUITTON as the 17th "best brand" of all corporations in the world and the first "best brand" for any fashion business.

* * *

Although better known for its handbags and luggage, LVM also markets a limited selection of luxury pet accessories—collars, leashes, and dog carriers—which bear the Monogram Canvas mark and the Multicolor design. These items range in price from approximately $200 to $1600. LVM does not make dog toys.

Haute Diggity Dog, LLC, which is a relatively small and relatively new business located in Nevada, manufactures and sells nationally—primarily through pet stores—a line of pet chew toys and beds whose names parody elegant high-end brands of products such as perfume, cars, shoes, sparkling wine, and handbags. These include—in addition to Chewy Vuiton (LOUIS VUITTON)—Chewnel No. 5 (Chanel No. 5), Furcedes (Mercedes), Jimmy Chew (Jimmy Choo), Dog Perignonn (Dom Perignon), Sniffany & Co. (Tiffany & Co.), and Dogior (Dior). The chew toys and pet beds are plush, made of polyester, and have a shape and design that loosely imitate the signature product of the targeted brand. They are mostly distributed and sold through pet stores, although one or two Macy's stores carries Haute Diggity Dog's products. The dog toys are generally sold for less than $20, although larger versions of some of Haute Diggity Dog's plush dog beds sell for more than $100.

Haute Diggity Dog's "Chewy Vuiton" dog toys, in particular, loosely resemble miniature handbags and undisputedly evoke LVM handbags of similar shape, design, and color. In lieu of the LOUIS VUITTON mark, the dog toy uses "Chewy Vuiton"; in lieu of the LV mark, it uses "CV"; and the other symbols and colors employed are imitations, but not exact ones, of those used in the LVM Multicolor and Cherry designs.

In 2002, LVM commenced this action, naming as defendants Haute Diggity Dog; Victoria D.N. Dauernheim, the principal owner of Haute Diggity Dog; and Woofies, LLC, a retailer of Haute Diggity Dog's products, located in Asburn, Virginia, for trademark, trade dress, and copyright infringement. * * * On cross-motions for summary judgment, the district court granted Haute Diggity Dog's motion and denied LVM's motion, entering judgment in favor of Haute Diggity Dog on all of the claims. It rested its analysis on each count principally on the conclusion that Haute Diggity Dog's products amounted to a successful parody of LVM's marks, trade dress, and copyright.

LVM appealed and now challenges, as a matter of law, virtually every ruling made by the district court.

II

* * *

To prove trademark infringement, LVM must show (1) that it owns a valid and protectable mark; (2) that Haute Diggity Dog uses a "reproduction, counterfeit, copy, or colorable imitation" of that mark in commerce and without LVM's consent; and (3) that Haute Diggity Dog's use is likely to cause confusion. 15 U.S.C. § 1114(1)(a). The validity and protectability of LVM's marks are not at issue in this case, nor is the fact that Haute Diggity Dog uses a colorable imitation of LVM's mark. Therefore, we give the first two elements no further attention. To determine whether the "Chewy Vuiton" product line creates a likelihood of confusion, we have identified several nonexclusive factors to consider: (1) the strength or distinctiveness of the plaintiff's mark; (2) the similarity of the two marks; (3) the similarity of the goods or services the marks identify; (4) the similarity of the facilities the two parties use in their businesses; (5) the similarity of the advertising used by the two parties; (6) the defendant's intent; and (7) actual confusion. *See Pizzeria Uno Corp. v. Temple*, 747 F.2d 1522, 1527 (4th Cir.1984). These *Pizzeria Uno* factors are not always weighted equally, and not all factors are relevant in every case.

Because Haute Diggity Dog's arguments with respect to the *Pizzeria Uno* factors depend to a great extent on whether its products and marks are successful parodies, we consider first whether Haute Diggity Dog's products, marks, and trade dress are indeed successful parodies of LVM's marks and trade dress.

For trademark purposes, "[a] 'parody' is defined as a simple form of entertainment conveyed by juxtaposing the irreverent representation of the trademark with the idealized image created by the mark's owner." *People for the Ethical Treatment of Animals v. Doughney ("PETA")*, 263 F.3d 359, 366 (4th Cir.2001). "A parody must convey two simultaneous—and contradictory—messages: that it is the original, but also that it is not the original and is instead a parody." *Id.* This second message must not only differentiate the alleged parody from the original but must also communicate some articulable element of satire, ridicule, joking, or amusement. Thus, "[a] parody relies upon a difference from the original mark, presumably a humorous difference, in order to produce its desired effect." *Jordache Enterprises, Inc. v. Hogg Wyld, Ltd.*, 828 F.2d 1482, 1486 (10th Cir.1987) (finding the use of "Lardashe" jeans for larger women to be a successful and permissible parody of "Jordache" jeans).

When applying the *PETA* criteria to the facts of this case, we agree with the district court that the "Chewy Vuiton" dog toys are successful parodies of LVM handbags and the LVM marks and trade dress used in connection with the marketing and sale of those handbags. First, the pet chew toy is obviously an irreverent, and indeed intentional, representation of an LVM handbag, albeit much smaller and coarser. The dog toy is shaped roughly like a handbag; its name "Chewy Vuiton" sounds like and rhymes with LOUIS VUITTON; its monogram CV mimics LVM's LV mark; the repetitious design clearly imitates the design on the LVM handbag; and the coloring is similar. In short, the dog toy is a small, plush imitation of an LVM handbag carried by women, which invokes the marks and design of the handbag, albeit irreverently and incompletely. No one can doubt that LVM handbags are the target of the imitation by Haute Diggity Dog's "Chewy Vuiton" dog toys.

At the same time, no one can doubt also that the "Chewy Vuiton" dog toy is not the "idealized image" of the mark created by LVM. The differences are immediate, beginning with the fact that the "Chewy Vuiton" product is a dog toy, not an expensive, luxury LOUIS VUITTON handbag. The toy is smaller, it is plush, and virtually all of its designs differ. Thus, "Chewy Vuiton" is not LOUIS VUITTON ("Chewy" is not "LOUIS" and "Vuiton" is not "VUITTON," with its two Ts); CV is not LV; the designs on the dog toy are simplified and crude, not detailed and distinguished. The toys are inexpensive; the handbags are expensive and marketed to be expensive. And, of course, as a dog toy, one must buy it with pet supplies and cannot buy it at an exclusive LVM store or boutique within a department store. In short, the Haute Diggity Dog "Chewy Vuiton" dog toy undoubtedly and deliberately conjures up the famous LVM marks and trade dress, but at the same time, it communicates that it is not the LVM product.

Finally, the juxtaposition of the similar and dissimilar—the irreverent representation and the idealized image of an LVM handbag—immediately conveys a joking and amusing parody. The furry little "Chewy Vuiton" imitation, as something to be chewed by a dog, pokes fun at the elegance and expensiveness of a LOUIS VUITTON handbag, which must not be chewed by a dog. The LVM handbag is provided for the most elegant and well-to-do celebrity, to proudly display to the public and the press, whereas the imitation "Chewy Vuiton" "handbag" is designed to mock the celebrity and be used by a dog. The dog toy irreverently presents haute couture as an object for casual canine destruction. The satire is unmistakable. The dog toy is a comment on the rich and famous, on the LOUIS VUITTON name and related marks, and on conspicuous consumption in general. This parody is enhanced by the fact that "Chewy Vuiton" dog toys are sold with similar parodies of other famous and expensive brands—"Chewnel No. 5" targeting "Chanel No. 5"; "Dog Perignonn" targeting "Dom Perignon"; and "Sniffany & Co." targeting "Tiffany & Co."

We conclude that the *PETA* criteria are amply satisfied in this case and that the "Chewy Vuiton" dog toys convey "just enough of the original design to allow the consumer to appreciate the point of parody," but stop well short of appropriating the entire marks that LVM claims.

Finding that Haute Diggity Dog's parody is successful, however, does not end the inquiry into whether Haute Diggity Dog's "Chewy Vuiton" products create a likelihood of confusion. *See* 6 J. THOMAS MCCARTHY, TRADEMARKS AND UNFAIR COMPETITION § 31:153 (4th ed. 2010) ("There are confusing parodies and non-confusing parodies. All they have in common is an attempt at humor through the use of someone else's trademark."). The finding of a successful parody only influences the way in which the *Pizzeria Uno* factors are applied. *See, e.g., Anheuser-Busch, Inc. v. L & L Wings, Inc.*, 962 F.2d 316, 321 (4th Cir.1992) (observing that parody alters the likelihood-of-confusion analysis). Indeed, it becomes apparent that an effective parody will actually diminish the likelihood of confusion, while an ineffective parody does not. We now turn to the *Pizzeria Uno* factors.

A

As to the first *Pizzeria Uno* factor, the parties agree that LVM's marks are strong and widely recognized. They do not agree, however, as to the consequences of this fact. LVM maintains that a strong, famous mark is entitled, as a matter of law, to broad protection. While it is true that finding a mark to be strong and famous usually favors the plaintiff in a trademark infringement case, the opposite may be true when a legitimate claim of parody is involved. As the district court observed, "In cases of parody, a strong mark's fame and popularity is precisely the mechanism by which likelihood of confusion is avoided." *Louis Vuitton Malletier*, 464 F.Supp.2d at 499. "An intent to parody is not an intent to confuse the public." *Jordache*, 828 F.2d at 1486.

We agree with the district court. It is a matter of common sense that the strength of a famous mark allows consumers immediately to perceive the target of the parody, while simultaneously allowing them to recognize the changes to the mark that make the parody funny or biting. *See Tommy Hilfiger Licensing, Inc. v. Nature Labs, LLC*, 221 F.Supp.2d 410, 416 (S.D.N.Y.2002) (noting that the strength of the "TOMMY HILFIGER" fashion mark did not favor the mark's owner in an infringement case against "TIMMY HOLEDIGGER" novelty pet perfume). In this case, precisely because LOUIS VUITTON is so strong a mark and so well recognized as a luxury handbag brand from LVM, consumers readily recognize that when they see a "Chewy Vuiton" pet toy, they see a parody. Thus, the strength of LVM's marks in this case does not help LVM establish a likelihood of confusion.

B

With respect to the second *Pizzeria Uno* factor, the similarities between the marks, the usage by Haute Diggity Dog again converts what might be a problem for Haute Diggity Dog into a disfavored conclusion for LVM.

Haute Diggity Dog concedes that its marks are and were designed to be somewhat similar to LVM's marks. But that is the essence of a parody—the invocation of a famous mark in the consumer's mind, so long as the distinction between the marks is also readily recognized. While a trademark parody necessarily copies enough of the original design to bring it to mind as a target, a successful parody also distinguishes itself and, because of the implicit message communicated by the parody, allows the consumer to appreciate it.

In concluding that Haute Diggity Dog has a successful parody, we have impliedly concluded that Haute Diggity Dog appropriately mimicked a part of the LVM marks, but at the same time sufficiently distinguished its own product to communicate the satire. The differences are sufficiently obvious and the parody sufficiently blatant that a consumer encountering a "Chewy Vuiton" dog toy would not mistake its source or sponsorship on the basis of mark similarity.

This conclusion is reinforced when we consider how the parties actually use their marks in the marketplace. The record amply supports Haute Diggity Dog's contention that its "Chewy Vuiton" toys for dogs are generally sold alongside other pet products, as well as toys that parody other luxury brands, whereas LVM markets its handbags as a top-end luxury item to be purchased only in its own stores or in its own boutiques within department stores. These marketing channels further emphasize that "Chewy Vuiton" dog toys are not, in fact, LOUIS VUITTON products.

C

Nor does LVM find support from the third *Pizzeria Uno* factor, the similarity of the products themselves. It is obvious that a "Chewy Vuiton" plush imitation handbag, which does not open and is manufactured as a dog toy, is not a LOUIS VUITTON handbag sold by LVM. Even LVM's most proximate products—dog collars, leashes, and pet carriers—are fashion accessories, not dog toys. As Haute Diggity Dog points out, LVM does not make pet chew toys and likely does not intend to do so in the future. Even if LVM were to make dog toys in the future, the fact remains that the products at issue are not similar in any relevant respect, and this factor does not favor LVM.

D

The fourth and fifth *Pizzeria Uno* factors, relating to the similarity of facilities and advertising channels, have already been mentioned. LVM products are sold exclusively through its own stores or its own boutiques within department stores. It also sells its products on the Internet through an LVM-authorized website. In contrast, "Chewy Vuiton" products are sold primarily through traditional and Internet pet stores, although they might also be sold in some department stores. The record demonstrates that both LVM handbags and "Chewy Vuiton" dog toys are sold at a Macy's department store in New York. As a general matter, however, there is little overlap in the individual retail stores selling the brands.

Likewise with respect to advertising, there is little or no overlap. LVM markets LOUIS VUITTON handbags through high-end fashion magazines, while "Chewy Vuiton" products are advertised primarily through pet-supply channels.

The overlap in facilities and advertising demonstrated by the record is so minimal as to be practically nonexistent. "Chewy Vuiton" toys and LOUIS VUITTON products are neither sold nor advertised in the same way, and the de minimis overlap lends insignificant support to LVM on this factor.

E

The sixth factor, relating to Haute Diggity Dog's intent, again is neutralized by the fact that Haute Diggity Dog markets a parody of LVM products. As other courts have recognized, "An intent to parody is not an intent to confuse the public." *Jordache*, 828 F.2d at 1486. Despite Haute Diggity Dog's obvious intent to profit from its use of parodies, this action does not amount to a bad faith intent to create consumer confusion. To the contrary, the intent is to do just the opposite—to evoke a humorous, satirical association that distinguishes the products. This factor does not favor LVM.

F

On the actual confusion factor, it is well established that no actual confusion is required to prove a case of trademark infringement, although the presence of actual confusion can be persuasive evidence relating to a likelihood of confusion.

While LVM conceded in the district court that there was no evidence of actual confusion, on appeal it points to incidents where retailers misspelled "Chewy Vuiton" on invoices or order forms, using two Ts instead of one. Many of these invoices also reflect simultaneous orders for multiple types of Haute Diggity Dog parody products, which belies the notion that any actual confusion existed as to the source of "Chewy Vuiton" plush toys. The misspellings pointed out by LVM are far more likely in this context to indicate confusion over how to spell the product name than any confusion over the source or sponsorship of the "Chewy Vuiton" dog toys. We conclude that this factor favors Haute Diggity Dog.

In sum, the likelihood-of-confusion factors substantially favor Haute Diggity Dog. But consideration of these factors is only a proxy for the ultimate statutory test of whether Haute Diggity Dog's marketing, sale, and distribution of "Chewy Vuiton" dog toys is likely to cause confusion. Recognizing that "Chewy Vuiton" is an obvious parody and applying the *Pizzeria Uno* factors, we conclude that LVM has failed to demonstrate any likelihood of confusion. Accordingly, we affirm the district court's grant of summary judgment in favor of Haute Diggity Dog on the issue of trademark infringement.

[The court's analysis of Louis Vuitton's dilution claim is reproduced in Part C of this chapter.]

NOTE

Infringement claims involving trademark parodies are common. Although most courts recognize that parodies should be treated differently from garden-variety trademark infringements, their approaches are far from uniform. As this case illustrates, when the parody is commercial in nature, courts typically take the parodic context into consideration as part and parcel of the likelihood of confusion analysis. The more obvious the parody, the less likely it will be to confuse, and the less likely a court will find that it infringes.

Courts tend to take a different approach when the trademark is used in an expressive or artistic work, such as a song, a work of art, or a motion picture. Due to the higher degree of First Amendment protection afforded these works, many (though not all) courts take free speech interests into account more explicitly in such cases, treating the interest in protecting free expression as a countervailing consideration to be weighed carefully against the likelihood of confusion. The treatment of expressive works is addressed in Chapter 5.

B. UNFAIR COMPETITION

Statute: 15 U.S.C. § 1125(a)

The Lanham Act's unfair competition provision, section 43(a), has two components: Section 43(a)(1)(A) addresses confusion as to origin, sponsorship, affiliation or approval (typically called false designation of origin or false endorsement). Section 43(a)(1)(B) addresses false or misleading representations of fact about the characteristics or geographic origin of goods, services, or commercial activities (typically called false advertising). Because both of these provisions are broadly worded, courts are frequently called upon to interpret their scope.

LEXMARK INTERNATIONAL, INC. V. STATIC CONTROL COMPONENTS, INC.

572 U.S. 118, 134 S.Ct. 1377 (2014).

JUSTICE SCALIA delivered the opinion of the Court.

This case requires us to decide whether respondent, Static Control Components, Inc., may sue petitioner, Lexmark International, Inc., for false advertising under the Lanham Act, 15 U.S.C. § 1125(a).

[Although Lexmark designs its laser printers to work only with its own toner cartridges, certain "remanufacturers" refurbish and resell used Lexmark cartridges in competition with Lexmark's new cartridges. In response, Lexmark introduced a "Prebate program" giving its customers a discount for returning their used cartridges to Lexmark. To enforce this agreement, Lexmark included a microchip in each Prebate cartridge that would disable it once it ran out of toner.

Static Control created microchips that mimicked Lexmark's microchips, and sold these to remanufacturers so that they could continue to refurbish and resell used Prebate cartridges. When Lexmark sued Static Control for copyright violations, Static Control counterclaimed for false advertising under section 43(a), alleging, *inter alia,* that Lexmark falsely told remanufacturers that it was illegal to use Static Control's products to refurbish Lexmark cartridges.

The District Court held that Static Controls lacked standing, and that the proper plaintiffs for a false advertising claim were the remanufacturers. The Sixth Circuit reversed, and the Supreme Court granted certiorari.]

* * *

I. Static Control's Right To Sue Under § 1125(a)

[T]his case presents a straightforward question of statutory interpretation: Does the cause of action in § 1125(a) extend to plaintiffs like Static Control? The statute authorizes suit by "any person who believes that he or she is likely to be damaged" by a defendant's false advertising. Read literally, that broad language might suggest that an action is available to anyone who can satisfy the minimum requirements of Article III. No party makes that argument, however, and the "unlikelihood that Congress meant to allow all factually injured plaintiffs to recover persuades us that [§ 1125(a)] should not get such an expansive reading." We reach that conclusion in light of two relevant background principles * * *: zone of interests and proximate causality.

A. Zone of Interests

First, we presume that a statutory cause of action extends only to plaintiffs whose interests "fall within the zone of interests protected by the law invoked." * * *

Identifying the interests protected by the Lanham Act, however, requires no guesswork, since the Act includes an "unusual, and extraordinarily helpful," detailed statement of the statute's purposes. Section 45 of the Act, codified at 15 U.S.C. § 1127, provides:

> The intent of this chapter is to regulate commerce within the control of Congress by making actionable the deceptive and misleading use of marks in such commerce; to protect registered marks used in such commerce from interference by State, or territorial legislation; to protect persons engaged in such commerce against unfair competition; to prevent fraud and deception in such commerce by the use of reproductions, copies, counterfeits, or colorable imitations of registered marks; and to provide rights and remedies stipulated by treaties and conventions respecting trademarks, trade names, and unfair competition entered into between the United States and foreign nations.

Most of the enumerated purposes are relevant to false-association cases; a typical false-advertising case will implicate only the Act's goal of "protect[ing] persons engaged in [commerce within the control of Congress] against unfair competition." Although "unfair competition" was a "plastic" concept at common law, it was understood to be concerned with injuries to business reputation and present and future sales.

We thus hold that to come within the zone of interests in a suit for false advertising under § 1125(a), a plaintiff must allege an injury to a commercial interest in reputation or sales. A consumer who is hoodwinked into purchasing a disappointing product may well have an injury-in-fact cognizable under Article III, but he cannot invoke the protection of the Lanham Act—a conclusion reached by every Circuit to consider the question. Even a business misled by a supplier into purchasing an inferior product is, like consumers generally, not under the Act's aegis.

B. Proximate Cause

Second, we generally presume that a statutory cause of action is limited to plaintiffs whose injuries are proximately caused by violations of the statute. * * *

* * * [T]he proximate-cause requirement generally bars suits for alleged harm that is "too remote" from the defendant's unlawful conduct. That is ordinarily the case if the harm is purely derivative of "misfortunes visited upon a third person by the defendant's acts." In a sense, of course,

all commercial injuries from false advertising are derivative of those suffered by consumers who are deceived by the advertising; but since the Lanham Act authorizes suit only for commercial injuries, the intervening step of consumer deception is not fatal to the showing of proximate causation required by the statute. That is consistent with our recognition that under common-law principles, a plaintiff can be directly injured by a misrepresentation even where "a third party, and not the plaintiff, . . . relied on" it.

We thus hold that a plaintiff suing under § 1125(a) ordinarily must show economic or reputational injury flowing directly from the deception wrought by the defendant's advertising; and that that occurs when deception of consumers causes them to withhold trade from the plaintiff. That showing is generally not made when the deception produces injuries to a fellow commercial actor that in turn affect the plaintiff. For example, while a competitor who is forced out of business by a defendant's false advertising generally will be able to sue for its losses, the same is not true of the competitor's landlord, its electric company, and other commercial parties who suffer merely as a result of the competitor's "inability to meet [its] financial obligations."

C. Proposed Tests

At oral argument, Lexmark agreed that the zone of interests and proximate causation supply the relevant background limitations on suit under § 1125(a). But it urges us to adopt, as the optimal formulation of those principles, a multifactor balancing test * * *. In the alternative, it asks that we adopt a categorical test permitting only direct competitors to sue for false advertising. And although neither party urges adoption of the "reasonable interest" test applied below, several *amici* do so. While none of those tests is wholly without merit, we decline to adopt any of them. We hold instead that a direct application of the zone-of-interests test and the proximate-cause requirement supplies the relevant limits on who may sue.

[The Court found that both the "reasonable interest" test and the multifactor balancing test, which considered factors other than the zone of interests and proximate causation, led to widely divergent results. In addition, the "reasonable interest" test was simply the bare minimum for Article III standing, and did not consider whether the plaintiff's interest was one actually protected by the Lanham Act.]

In contrast * * *, the direct-competitor test provides a bright-line rule; but it does so at the expense of distorting the statutory language. To be sure, a plaintiff who does not compete with the defendant will often have a harder time establishing proximate causation. But a rule categorically prohibiting all suits by noncompetitors would read too much into the Act's reference to "unfair competition" in § 1127. By the time the Lanham Act was adopted, the common-law tort of unfair competition was understood not to be limited to actions between competitors. * * * It is thus a mistake to infer that because the Lanham Act treats false advertising as a form of unfair competition, it can protect *only* the false-advertiser's direct competitors.

* * *

IV. Application

Applying those principles to Static Control's false-advertising claim, we conclude that Static Control comes within the class of plaintiffs whom Congress authorized to sue under § 1125(a).

To begin, Static Control's alleged injuries—lost sales and damage to its business reputation—are injuries to precisely the sorts of commercial interests the Act protects. Static Control is suing not as a deceived consumer, but as a "perso[n] engaged in" "commerce within the control of Congress" whose position in the marketplace has been damaged by Lexmark's false advertising. There is no doubt that it is within the zone of interests protected by the statute.

Static Control also sufficiently alleged that its injuries were proximately caused by Lexmark's misrepresentations. This case, it is true, does not present the "classic Lanham Act false-advertising claim" in which " 'one competito[r] directly injur[es] another by making false statements about his own goods [or the competitor's goods] and thus inducing customers to switch.' " But although diversion of sales to a direct competitor may be the paradigmatic direct injury from false advertising, it is not the only type of injury cognizable under § 1125(a). For at least two reasons, Static Control's allegations satisfy the requirement of proximate causation.

First, Static Control alleged that Lexmark disparaged its business and products by asserting that Static Control's business was illegal. When a defendant harms a plaintiff's reputation by casting aspersions on its business, the plaintiff's injury flows directly from the audience's belief in the disparaging statements. Courts have therefore afforded relief under § 1125(a) not only where a defendant denigrates a plaintiff's product by name, but also where the defendant damages the product's reputation by, for example, equating it with an inferior product. Traditional proximate-causation principles support those results: As we have observed, a defendant who " 'seeks to promote his own interests by telling a known falsehood to *or about* the plaintiff or his product' " may be said to have proximately caused the plaintiff's harm.

The District Court emphasized that Lexmark and Static Control are not direct competitors. But when a party claims reputational injury from disparagement, competition is not required for proximate cause; and that is true even if the defendant's aim was to harm its immediate competitors, and the plaintiff merely suffered collateral damage. Consider two rival carmakers who purchase airbags for their cars from different third-party manufacturers. If the first carmaker, hoping to divert sales from the second, falsely proclaims that the airbags used by the second carmaker are defective, both the second carmaker and its airbag supplier may suffer reputational injury, and their sales may decline as a result. In those circumstances, there is no reason to regard either party's injury as derivative of the other's; each is directly and independently harmed by the attack on its merchandise.

In addition, Static Control adequately alleged proximate causation by alleging that it designed, manufactured, and sold microchips that both (1) were necessary for, and (2) had no other use than, refurbishing Lexmark toner cartridges. It follows from that allegation that any false advertising that reduced the remanufacturers' business necessarily injured Static Control as well. Taking Static Control's assertions at face value, there is likely to be something very close to a 1:1 relationship between the number of refurbished Prebate cartridges sold (or not sold) by the remanufacturers and the number of Prebate microchips sold (or not sold) by Static Control. "Where the injury alleged is so integral an aspect of the [violation] alleged, there can be no question" that proximate cause is satisfied. *Blue Shield of Va. v. McCready,* 457 U.S. 465, 479 (1982).

* * *

To invoke the Lanham Act's cause of action for false advertising, a plaintiff must plead (and ultimately prove) an injury to a commercial interest in sales or business reputation proximately caused by the defendant's misrepresentations. Static Control has adequately pleaded both elements. The judgment of the Court of Appeals is affirmed.

NOTE

In *Lexmark,* the Supreme Court analyzed the purposes of the Lanham Act in order to address the specific question of who has standing to bring a claim under section 43(a). Although the case involved false advertising, the Court's analysis seems to encompass section 43(a) in its entirety.

The next two sections address claims arising under each of the two separate provisions of section 43(a)—false designations of origin under (a)(1)(A), and false advertising under (a)(1)(B).

1. FALSE DESIGNATIONS OF ORIGIN: SECTION 43(a)(1)(A)

In the typical case involving a false designation of origin, the plaintiff asserts ownership of an unregistered trademark, and alleges that the defendant's unauthorized use creates a likelihood of confusion as to origin, sponsorship, affiliation or endorsement. Once the plaintiff establishes ownership of a valid common law mark, the infringement analysis proceeds along the same lines as a case arising under section 32(1), including consideration of the likelihood-of-confusion factors. A typical example is *International Kennel Club, Inc. v. Mighty Star, Inc.*, reproduced in Chapter 2. However, as illustrated by the next case, some courts have interpreted section 43(a)(1)(A) more broadly. After reading *Lexmark*, do you agree with the Fourth Circuit's analysis in this case?

BELMORA LLC V. BAYER CONSUMER CARE AG

819 F.3d 697 (4th Cir. 2016), *cert. denied*, ___ U.S. ___, 137 S.Ct. 1202 (2017).

AGEE, CIRCUIT JUDGE:

In this unfair competition case, we consider whether the Lanham Act permits the owner of a foreign trademark and its sister company to pursue false association, false advertising, and trademark cancellation claims against the owner of the same mark in the United States. Bayer Consumer Care AG ("BCC") owns the trademark "FLANAX" in Mexico and has sold naproxen sodium pain relievers under that mark in Mexico (and other parts of Latin America) since the 1970s. Belmora LLC owns the FLANAX trademark in the United States and has used it here since 2004 in the sale of its naproxen sodium pain relievers. BCC and its U.S. sister company Bayer Healthcare LLC ("BHC," and collectively with BCC, "Bayer") contend that Belmora used the FLANAX mark to deliberately deceive Mexican-American consumers into thinking they were purchasing BCC's product.

BCC successfully petitioned the U.S. Trademark Trial and Appeal Board ("TTAB") to cancel Belmora's registration for the FLANAX mark based on deceptive use. Belmora appealed the TTAB's decision to the district court. In the meantime, BCC filed a separate complaint for false association against Belmora under § 43 of the Lanham Act, 15 U.S.C. § 1125, and in conjunction with BHC, a claim for false advertising. After the two cases were consolidated, the district court reversed the TTAB's cancellation order and dismissed the false association and false advertising claims.

Bayer appeals those decisions. For the reasons outlined below, we vacate the judgment of the district court and remand this case for further proceedings consistent with this opinion.

* * *

A. False Association and False Advertising Under Section 43(a)

The district court dismissed Bayer's false association and false advertising claims because, in its view, the claims failed to satisfy the standards set forth by the Supreme Court in *Lexmark International, Inc. v. Static Control Components, Inc.*, 134 S.Ct. 1377 (2014). At the core of the district court's decision was its conclusion that 1) Bayer's claims fell outside the Lanham Act's "zone of interests"—and are not cognizable—"because Bayer does not possess a protectable interest in the FLANAX mark in the United States," and 2) that a "cognizable economic loss under the Lanham Act" cannot exist as to a "mark that was not used in United States commerce."

On appeal, Bayer contends these conclusions are erroneous as a matter of law because they conflict with the plain language of § 43(a) and misread *Lexmark*.

1.

"While much of the Lanham Act addresses the registration, use, and infringement of trademarks and related marks, § 43(a) . . . goes beyond trademark protection." *Dastar Corp. v. Twentieth Century Fox Film Corp.*, 539 U.S. 23, 28–29 (2003). Written in terms of the putative defendant's conduct, § 43(a) sets forth unfair competition causes of action for false association and false advertising.

Subsection A, which creates liability for statements as to "affiliation, connection, or association" of goods, describes the cause of action known as "false association." Subsection B, which creates liability for "misrepresent[ing] the nature, characteristics, qualities, or geographic origin" of goods, defines the cause of action for "false advertising."

Significantly, the plain language of § 43(a) does not require that a plaintiff possess or have used a trademark in U.S. commerce as an element of the cause of action. Section 43(a) stands in sharp contrast to Lanham Act § 32, which is titled as and expressly addresses "infringement." 15 U.S.C. § 1114 (requiring for liability the "use in commerce" of "any reproduction, counterfeit, copy, or colorable imitation of a registered mark"). Under § 43(a), it is the defendant's use in commerce—whether of an offending "word, term, name, symbol, or device" or of a "false or misleading description [or representation] of fact"—that creates the injury under the terms of the statute. And here the alleged offending "word, term, name, symbol, or device" is Belmora's FLANAX mark.

What § 43(a) does require is that Bayer was "likely to be damaged" by Belmora's "use[ ] in commerce" of its FLANAX mark and related advertisements. The Supreme Court recently considered the breadth of this "likely to be damaged" language in *Lexmark*, a false advertising case arising from a dispute in the used-printer-cartridge market. * * *

As a threshold matter, the Supreme Court noted that courts must be careful not to import requirements into this analysis that Congress has not included in the statute * * *.

The Court concluded that § 43(a)'s broad authorization—permitting suit by "any person who believes that he or she is or is likely to be damaged"—should not be taken "literally" to reach the limits of Article III standing, but is framed by two "background principles," which may overlap.

First, a plaintiff's claim must fall within the "zone of interests" protected by the statute. The scope of the zone of interests is not "especially demanding," and the plaintiff receives the "benefit of any doubt." Because the Lanham Act contains an "unusual, and extraordinarily helpful" purpose statement in § 45, identifying the statute's zone of interests "requires no guesswork." * * *

The second *Lexmark* background principle is that "a statutory cause of action is limited to plaintiffs whose injuries are proximately caused by violations of the statute." The injury must have a "sufficiently close connection to the conduct the statute prohibits." In the § 43(a) context, this means "show[ing] economic or reputational injury flowing directly from the deception wrought by the defendant's advertising; and that that occurs when deception of consumers causes them to withhold trade from the plaintiff."

* * *

2.

a.

We first address the position, pressed by Belmora and adopted by the district court, that a plaintiff must have initially used its own mark in commerce within the United States as a condition precedent to a § 43(a) claim. In dismissing BCC's § 43(a) claims, the district court found dispositive that "Bayer failed to plead facts showing that it used the FLANAX mark in commerce in [the] United States." Upon that ground, the district court held "that Bayer does not possess a protectable interest in the [FLANAX] mark."

As noted earlier, such a requirement is absent from § 43(a)'s plain language and its application in *Lexmark*. Under the statute, the defendant must have "use[d] in commerce" the offending "word, term, name, [or] symbol," but the plaintiff need only "believe[ ] that he or she is or is likely to be damaged by such act."

It is important to emphasize that this is an unfair competition case, not a trademark infringement case. Belmora and the district court conflated the Lanham Act's infringement provision in § 32 (which authorizes suit only "by the registrant," and thereby requires the plaintiff to have used its own mark in commerce) with unfair competition claims pled in this case under § 43(a). Section 32 makes clear that Congress knew how to write a precondition of trademark possession and use into a Lanham Act cause of action when it chose to do so. It has not done so in § 43(a).

Given that *Lexmark* advises courts to adhere to the statutory language, "apply[ing] traditional principles of statutory interpretation," *Lexmark*, 134 S.Ct. at 1388, we lack authority to introduce a requirement into § 43(a) that Congress plainly omitted. Nothing in *Lexmark* can be read to suggest that § 43(a) claims have an unstated requirement that the plaintiff have first used its own mark (word, term, name, symbol, or device) in U.S. commerce before a cause of action will lie against a defendant who is breaching the statute.

The district court thus erred in requiring Bayer, as the plaintiff, to have pled its prior use of its own mark in U.S. commerce when it is the defendant's use of a mark or misrepresentation that underlies the § 43(a) unfair competition cause of action. Having made this foundational error, the district court's resolution of the issues requires reversal.

Admittedly, some of our prior cases appear to have treated a plaintiff's use of a mark in United States commerce as a prerequisite for a false association claim. *See Lamparello v. Falwell*, 420 F.3d 309, 313 (4th Cir.2005) ("Both infringement [under § 32] and false designation of origin [under § 43(a)] have [the same] five elements."); *People for the Ethical Treatment of Animals v. Doughney*, 263 F.3d 359, 364 (4th Cir.2001) (same); *Int'l Bancorp*, 329 F.3d 361 n. 2 ("[T]he tests for trademark infringement and unfair competition . . . are identical."); *Lone Star Steakhouse & Saloon v. Alpha of Va., Inc.*, 43 F.3d 922, 930 (4th Cir.1995) ("[T]o prevail under §§ 32(1) and 43(a) of the Lanham Act for trademark infringement and unfair competition, respectively, a complainant must demonstrate that it has a valid, protectible trademark[.]"). However, none of these cases made that consideration the ratio decidendi of its holding or analyzed whether the statute in fact contains such a requirement. Moreover, all of these cases predate *Lexmark*, which provides the applicable Supreme Court precedent interpreting § 43(a).

Although the plaintiffs' use of a mark in U.S. commerce was a fact in common in the foregoing cases, substantial precedent reflects that § 43(a) unfair competition claims come within the statute's protectable zone of interests without the preconditions adopted by the district court and advanced by Belmora. As the Supreme Court has pointed out, § 43(a) "goes beyond trademark protection." *Dastar Corp.*, 539 U.S. at 29. For example, a plaintiff whose mark has become generic—and therefore not protectable—may plead an unfair competition claim against a competitor that uses that generic name and "fail[s] adequately to identify itself as distinct from the first organization" such that the name causes "confusion or a likelihood of confusion." *Blinded Veterans Ass'n v. Blinded Am. Veterans Found.*, 872 F.2d 1035, 1043 (D.C.Cir.1989); *see also Kellogg Co. v. Nat'l Biscuit Co.*, 305 U.S. 111, 118–19 (1938) (requiring the defendant to "use reasonable care to inform the public of the source of its product" even though the plaintiff's "shredded wheat" mark was generic and therefore unprotectable); *Singer Mfg. Co. v. June Mfg. Co.*, 163 U.S. 169, 203–04 (1896) (same, for "Singer" sewing machines).

Likewise, in a "reverse passing off" case, the plaintiff need not have used a mark in commerce to bring a § 43(a) action.[7] A reverse-passing-off plaintiff must prove four elements: "(1) that the work at issue originated with the plaintiff; (2) that origin of the work was falsely designated by the defendant; (3) that the false designation of origin was likely to cause consumer confusion; and (4) that the plaintiff was harmed by the defendant's false designation of origin." *Universal Furniture Int'l, Inc. v. Collezione Europa USA, Inc.*, 618 F.3d 417, 438 (4th Cir. 2010). Thus, the plaintiff in a reverse passing off case must plead and prove only that the work "originated with" him—not that he used the work (which may or may not be associated with a mark) in U.S. commerce.

The generic mark and reverse passing off cases illustrate that § 43(a) actions do not require, implicitly or otherwise, that a plaintiff have first used its own mark in United States commerce. If such a use were a condition precedent to bringing a § 43(a) action, the generic mark and reverse passing off cases could not exist.

In sum, the Lanham Act's plain language contains no unstated requirement that a § 43(a) plaintiff have used a U.S. trademark in U.S. commerce to bring a Lanham Act unfair competition claim. * * *.[8]

As Bayer is not barred from making a § 43(a) claim, the proper *Lexmark* inquiry is twofold. Did the alleged acts of unfair competition fall within the Lanham Act's protected zone of interests? And if so, did Bayer plead proximate causation of a cognizable injury? We examine the false association and false advertising claims in turn.

b.

i.

As to the zone of interests, *Lexmark* advises that "[m]ost of the [Lanham Act's] enumerated purposes are relevant to false-association cases." One such enumerated purpose is "making actionable the deceptive

---

[7] Reverse passing off occurs when a "producer misrepresents someone else's goods or services as his own," in other words, when the defendant is selling the plaintiff's goods and passing them off as originating with the defendant.

[8] A plaintiff who relies only on foreign commercial activity may face difficulty proving a cognizable false association injury under § 43(a). A few isolated consumers who confuse a mark with one seen abroad, based only on the presence of the mark on a product in this country and not other misleading conduct by the mark holder, would rarely seem to have a viable § 43(a) claim.

The story is different when a defendant, as alleged here, has—as a cornerstone of its business—intentionally passed off its goods in the United States as the same product commercially available in foreign markets in order to influence purchases by American consumers. *See M. Kramer Mfg. Co. v. Andrews*, 783 F.2d 421, 448 (4th Cir.1986) ("[E]vidence of intentional, direct copying establishes a prima facie case of secondary meaning sufficient to shift the burden of persuasion to the defendant on that issue."). Such an intentional deception can go a long way toward establishing likelihood of confusion.

and misleading use of marks" in "commerce within the control of Congress." Lanham Act § 45, 15 U.S.C. § 1127. As pled, BCC's false association claim advances that purpose.

The complaint alleges Belmora's misleading association with BCC's FLANAX has caused BCC customers to buy the Belmora FLANAX in the United States instead of purchasing BCC's FLANAX in Mexico. For example, the complaint alleges that BCC invested heavily in promoting its FLANAX to Mexican citizens or Mexican-Americans in border areas. Those consumers cross into the United States and may purchase Belmora FLANAX here before returning to Mexico. And Mexican-Americans may forego purchasing the FLANAX they know when they cross the border to visit Mexico because Belmora's alleged deception led them to purchase the Belmora product in the United States.

In either circumstance, BCC loses sales revenue because Belmora's deceptive and misleading use of FLANAX conveys to consumers a false association with BCC's product. Further, by also deceiving distributors and vendors, Belmora makes its FLANAX more available to consumers, which would exacerbate BCC's losses. See J.A. 196 (stating in a brochure for distributors that "Flanax is now made in the U.S." and "acts as a powerful attraction for Latinos"); J.A. 410 (noting a distributor's concern that the product "is legal to sell in the US"). In each scenario, the economic activity would be "within the control of Congress" to regulate.

We thus conclude that BCC has adequately pled a § 43(a) false association claim for purposes of the zone of interests prong. Its allegations reflect [that] the claim furthers the § 45 purpose of preventing "the deceptive and misleading use of marks" in "commerce within the control of Congress."

ii.

Turning to *Lexmark*'s second prong, proximate cause, BCC has also alleged injuries that "are proximately caused by [Belmora's] violations of the [false association] statute." * * * As reflected in the zone of interests discussion, BCC FLANAX customers in Mexico near the border may be deceived into foregoing a FLANAX purchase in Mexico as they cross the border to shop and buy the Belmora product in the United States. Second, Belmora is alleged to have targeted Mexican-Americans in the United States who were already familiar with the FLANAX mark from their purchases from BCC in Mexico. We can reasonably infer that some subset of those customers would buy BCC's FLANAX upon their return travels to Mexico if not for the alleged deception by Belmora. Consequently, BCC meets the *Lexmark* pleading requirement as to proximate cause.

* * *

c.

BCC and BHC both assert § 43(a)(1)(B) false advertising claims against Belmora. BHC's claim represents a "typical" false advertising case: it falls within the Act's zone of interests by "protecting persons engaged in commerce within the control of Congress against unfair competition." *Lexmark,* 134 S.Ct. at 1389. As a direct competitor to Belmora in the United States, BHC sufficiently alleges that Belmora engaged in Lanham Act unfair competition by using deceptive advertisements that capitalized on BCC's goodwill. If not for Belmora's statements that its FLANAX was the same one known and trusted in Mexico, some of its consumers could very well have instead purchased BHC's ALEVE brand. These lost customers likewise satisfy *Lexmark*'s second prong: they demonstrate an injury to sales or reputation proximately caused by Belmora's alleged conduct.

* * *

d.

We thus conclude that the Lanham Act permits Bayer to proceed with its claims under § 43(a)—BCC with its false association claim and both BCC and BHC with false advertising claims. It is worth noting, as the Supreme Court did in *Lexmark,* that "[a]lthough we conclude that [Bayer] has alleged an adequate basis to proceed under [§ 43(a)], it cannot obtain relief without evidence of injury proximately caused by [Belmora's alleged misconduct]. We hold only that [Bayer] is entitled to a chance to prove its case."

In granting Bayer that chance, we are not concluding that BCC has any specific trademark rights to the FLANAX mark in the United States. Belmora owns that mark. But trademark rights do not include using the mark to deceive customers as a form of unfair competition, as is alleged here. Should Bayer prevail and prove its § 43(a) claims, an appropriate remedy might include directing Belmora to use the mark in a way that does not sow confusion. *See* Lanham Act § 34(a), 15 U.S.C. § 1116(a) (authorizing injunctions based on "principles of equity"). Of course, the precise remedy would be a determination to be made by the district court in the first instance upon proper evidence.[11] * * *

B. Cancellation Under Section 14(3)

The TTAB ordered the cancellation of Belmora's FLANAX trademark under § 14(3), finding that the preponderance of the evidence "readily establishe[d] blatant misuse of the FLANAX mark in a manner calculated to trade in the United States on the reputation and goodwill of petitioner's

[11] For example, a remedy might include altering the font and color of the packaging or the "ready remedy" of attaching the manufacturer's name to the brand name. *Blinded Veterans,* 872 F.2d at 1047. Another option could be for the packaging to display a disclaimer—to correct for any deliberately created actual confusion.

mark created by its use in Mexico." In reversing that decision and granting Belmora's motion for judgment on the pleadings, the district court found that BCC, as the § 14(3) complainant, "lack[ed] standing to sue pursuant to *Lexmark*" under both the zone of interests and the proximate cause prongs. The district court also reversed the TTAB's holding that Belmora was using FLANAX to misrepresent the source of its goods "because Section 14(3) requires use of the mark in United States commerce and Bayer did not use the FLANAX mark in the United States."

On appeal, Bayer argues that the district court erred in overturning the TTAB's § 14(3) decision because it "read a use requirement into the section that is simply not there." For reasons that largely overlap with the preceding § 43(a) analysis, we agree with Bayer.

1.

Section 14(3) of the Lanham Act creates a procedure for petitioning to cancel the federal registration of a mark that the owner has used to misrepresent the source of goods. * * * Lanham Act § 14(3), 15 U.S.C. § 1064(3). The petitioner must establish that the "registrant deliberately sought to pass off its goods as those of petitioner." *See* 3 McCarthy, § 20:30 (4th ed.2002).

If successful, the result of a § 14(3) petition "is the cancellation of a registration, not the cancellation of a trademark." *Id.* § 20:40. Cancellation of registration strips an owner of "important legal rights and benefits" that accompany federal registration, but it "does not invalidate underlying common law rights in the trademark." *Id.* § 20:68; *see also B & B Hardware Inc. v. Hargis Indus., Inc.*, ___ U.S. ___, ___, 135 S.Ct. 1293, 1300 (2015).

To determine what parties § 14(3) authorizes to petition for cancellation, we again apply the *Lexmark* framework. The relevant language in § 14(3) closely tracks similar language from § 43(a) that the Supreme Court considered in *Lexmark*: "[A]ny person who believes that he is or will be damaged" by the mark's registration may petition for cancellation under § 14(3), just as "any person who believes that he or she is or is likely to be damaged" may bring an unfair competition action under § 43(a). The same two-prong inquiry from *Lexmark* provides the mode of analysis.

To determine if a petitioner falls within the protected zone of interests, we note that § 14(3) pertains to the same conduct targeted by § 43(a) false association actions—using marks so as to misrepresent the source of goods. Therefore, "[m]ost of the [Lanham Act's] enumerated purposes are relevant" to § 14(3) claims as well. *See Lexmark*, 134 S.Ct. at 1389. As for proximate cause, we once again consider whether the plaintiff has "show[n] economic or reputational injury flowing directly from the deception wrought by the defendant's [conduct]." *Id.* at 1391. As with § 43(a), neither

§ 14(3) nor *Lexmark* mandate that the plaintiff have used the challenged mark in United States commerce as a condition precedent to its claim.

2.

Applying the framework from *Lexmark,* we conclude that the Lanham Act authorizes BCC to bring its § 14(3) action against Belmora. BCC's cancellation claim falls within the Lanham Act's zone of interests because it confronts the "deceptive and misleading use of marks." And BCC has also adequately pled a proximately caused injury to survive Belmora's Rule 12(c) motion for the same reasons previously discussed for the false association and false advertising claims. The district court thus erred in reversing the TTAB's decision cancelling the registration of Belmora's FLANAX mark.

III.

For the foregoing reasons, we conclude that Bayer is entitled to bring its unfair competition claims under Lanham Act § 43(a) and its cancellation claim under § 14(3). The district court's judgment is vacated and the case remanded for further proceedings consistent with this opinion.

NOTES

1. Although the *Belmora* court acknowledged that many of its own precedents stated that plaintiffs bringing § 43(a)(1)(A) claims must own a valid trademark, it noted that none of those cases "made that consideration the ratio decidendi of its holding or analyzed whether the statute in fact contains such a requirement," and also that all of them predated *Lexmark*. Pre-*Lexmark* case law from other circuits typically states the same requirement—that ownership of a valid common law trademark is a prerequisite to bringing a claim under § 43(a)(1)(A). Do you agree with the Fourth Circuit that this requirement—if it ever was a valid interpretation of § 43(a)(1)(A)—was eliminated by *Lexmark*?

2. In general, U.S. trademark law incorporates the territoriality principle—that is, the principle that a trademark owner establishes a right of priority in the United States only by actually using its mark in the United States. *Belmora,* therefore, represents an exception to this approach. Like the Fourth Circuit, the Ninth Circuit has also recognized an exception to the territoriality principle. In *Grupo Gigante S.A. De C.V. v. Dallo & Co., Inc.*, 391 F.3d 1088 (9th Cir. 2004), the Ninth Circuit became the only federal court of appeals to expressly adopt the "famous marks doctrine," which permits the owner of a mark used exclusively outside the U.S. to bring a section 43(a) claim where an unauthorized domestic use of the mark creates a likelihood of confusion. According to the Ninth Circuit, the famous marks exception applies only if the foreign mark (1) has secondary meaning in the relevant U.S. market, and (2) "a substantial percentage of consumers in the relevant American market is familiar with the foreign mark." The court explained:

> In making this determination, the court should consider such factors as the intentional copying of the mark by the defendant, and whether customers of the American firm are likely to think they are patronizing the same firm that uses the mark in another country. While these factors are not necessarily determinative, they are particularly relevant because they bear heavily on the risks of consumer confusion and fraud, which are the reasons for having a famous-mark exception.

Id. at 1098. Secondary meaning alone was not enough, the court held, because "[t]his interpretation of the exception would effectively eliminate the territoriality principle by eliminating any effect of international borders on protectability." *Id.* at 1097. Is there a meaningful difference between the Fourth and Ninth Circuit approaches? In contrast, the Second Circuit adheres to a strict territoriality approach, and has expressly held that the Lanham Act does not incorporate the famous marks doctrine. *ITC Ltd. v. Punchgini, Inc.*, 482 F.3d 135 (2d Cir. 2007) (disagreeing with *Grupo Gigante*).

3. If a party uses its trademark exclusively outside the United States, can it oppose the registration of a similar mark on the Principal Register under any of the grounds listed in section 2, 15 U.S.C. § 1052?

4. If a business serves customers only outside of the United States, but uses its trademark in advertising within the United States, can it protect its trademark against infringers in the United States? Can it register its mark on the Principal Register? Does it matter whether travelers from the United States actually purchase its goods or services? *See International Bancorp, LLC v. Societe des Bains De Mer et du Cercle des Etrangers a Monaco*, 329 F.3d 359 (4th Cir. 2003).

DASTAR CORPORATION V. TWENTIETH CENTURY FOX FILM CORPORATION

539 U.S. 23, 123 S.Ct. 2041 (2003).

JUSTICE SCALIA delivered the opinion of the Court in which all other Members joined, except BREYER, J., who took no part in the consideration or decision of the case.

In this case, we are asked to decide whether § 43(a) of the Lanham Act, 15 U.S.C. § 1125(a), prevents the unaccredited copying of a work * * *.

I

In 1948, three and a half years after the German surrender at Reims, General Dwight D. Eisenhower completed *Crusade in Europe*, his written account of the allied campaign in Europe during World War II. Doubleday published the book, registered it with the Copyright Office in 1948, and granted exclusive television rights to an affiliate of respondent Twentieth Century Fox Film Corporation (Fox). Fox, in turn, arranged for Time, Inc., to produce a television series, also called *Crusade in Europe*, based on the book, and Time assigned its copyright in the series to Fox. The television series, consisting of 26 episodes, was first broadcast in 1949. It combined a soundtrack based on a narration of the book with film footage from the United States Army, Navy, and Coast Guard, the British Ministry of Information and War Office, the National Film Board of Canada, and unidentified "Newsreel Pool Cameramen." In 1975, Doubleday renewed the copyright on the book as the " 'proprietor of copyright in a work made for hire.' " Fox, however, did not renew the copyright on the *Crusade* television series, which expired in 1977, leaving the television series in the public domain.

In 1988, Fox reacquired the television rights in General Eisenhower's book, including the exclusive right to distribute the *Crusade* television series on video and to sub-license others to do so. Respondents SFM Entertainment and New Line Home Video, Inc., in turn, acquired from Fox the exclusive rights to distribute *Crusade* on video. SFM obtained the negatives of the original television series, restored them, and repackaged the series on videotape; New Line distributed the videotapes.

Enter petitioner Dastar. In 1995, Dastar decided to expand its product line from music compact discs to videos. Anticipating renewed interest in World War II on the 50th anniversary of the war's end, Dastar released a video set entitled *World War II Campaigns in Europe*. To make *Campaigns*, Dastar purchased eight beta cam tapes of the *original* version of the *Crusade* television series, which is in the public domain, copied them, and then edited the series. Dastar's *Campaigns* series is slightly more than half as long as the original *Crusade* television series. Dastar substituted a new opening sequence, credit page, and final closing for those of the *Crusade* television series; inserted new chapter-title sequences and narrated chapter introductions; moved the "recap" in the *Crusade* television series to the beginning and retitled it as a "preview;" and removed references to and images of the book. Dastar created new packaging for its *Campaigns* series and (as already noted) a new title.

Dastar manufactured and sold the *Campaigns* video set as its own product. The advertising states: "Produced and Distributed by: *Entertainment Distributing*" (which is owned by Dastar), and makes no reference to the *Crusade* television series. Similarly, the screen credits state "DASTAR CORP presents" and "an ENTERTAINMENT DISTRIBUTING Production," and list as executive producer, producer, and associate producer, employees of Dastar. The *Campaigns* videos themselves also make no reference to the *Crusade* television series, New Line's Crusade videotapes, or the book. Dastar sells its *Campaigns* videos to Sam's Club, Costco, Best Buy, and other retailers and mail-order companies for $25 per set, substantially less than New Line's video set.

In 1998, respondents Fox, SFM, and New Line brought this action alleging that Dastar's sale of its *Campaigns* video set infringes Doubleday's copyright in General Eisenhower's book and, thus, their exclusive television rights in the book. Respondents later amended their complaint to add claims that Dastar's sale of *Campaigns* "without proper credit" to the *Crusade* television series constitutes "reverse passing off" in violation of § 43(a) of the Lanham Act, 15 U.S.C. § 1125(a), and in violation of state unfair-competition law. On cross-motions for summary judgment, the District Court found for respondents on all three counts, treating its resolution of the Lanham Act claim as controlling on the state-law unfair-competition claim because "the ultimate test under both is whether the public is likely to be deceived or confused." The court awarded Dastar's profits to respondents and doubled them pursuant to § 35 of the Lanham Act, 15 U.S.C. § 1117(a), to deter future infringing conduct by petitioner.

The Court of Appeals for the Ninth Circuit affirmed the judgment for respondents on the Lanham Act claim* * *. [T]he Court of Appeals reasoned that "Dastar copied substantially the entire *Crusade* in Europe series created by Twentieth Century Fox, labeled the resulting product with a different name and marketed it without attribution to Fox[, and] therefore committed a 'bodily appropriation' of Fox's series." It concluded that "Dastar's 'bodily appropriation' of Fox's original [television] series is sufficient to establish the reverse passing off." * * *

II

The Lanham Act was intended to make "actionable the deceptive and misleading use of marks," and "to protect persons engaged in . . . commerce against unfair competition." 15 U.S.C. § 1127. While much of the Lanham Act addresses the registration, use, and infringement of trademarks and related marks, § 43(a), 15 U.S.C. § 1125(a) is one of the few provisions that goes beyond trademark protection. As originally enacted, § 43(a) created a federal remedy against a person who used in commerce either "a false designation of origin, or any false description or representation" in connection with "any goods or services." 60 Stat. 441. As the Second Circuit accurately observed with regard to the original enactment, however—and as remains true after the 1988 revision—§ 43(a) "does not have boundless application as a remedy for unfair trade practices," *Alfred Dunhill, Ltd. v. Interstate Cigar Co.*, 499 F.2d 232, 237 (C.A.2 1974). "[B]ecause of its inherently limited wording, § 43(a) can never be a federal 'codification' of the overall law of 'unfair competition,' " 4 J. MCCARTHY, TRADEMARKS AND UNFAIR COMPETITION § 27:7, p.27–14 (4th ed. 2002) (MCCARTHY), but can apply only to certain unfair trade practices prohibited by its text.

Although a case can be made that a proper reading of § 43(a), as originally enacted, would treat the word "origin" as referring only "to the geographic location in which the goods originated," the Courts of Appeals considering the issue, beginning with the Sixth Circuit, unanimously concluded that it "does not merely refer to geographical origin, but also to origin of source or manufacture," *Federal-Mogul-Bower Bearings, Inc. v. Azoff*, 313 F.2d 405, 408 (C.A.6 1963), thereby creating a federal cause of action for traditional trademark infringement of unregistered marks. Moreover, every Circuit to consider the issue found § 43(a) broad enough to encompass reverse passing off. The Trademark Law Revision Act of 1988 made clear that § 43(a) covers origin of production as well as geographic origin. Its language is amply inclusive, moreover, of reverse passing off—if indeed it does not implicitly adopt the unanimous court-of-appeals jurisprudence on that subject.

Thus, as it comes to us, the gravamen of respondents' claim is that, in marketing and selling *Campaigns* as its own product without acknowledging its nearly wholesale reliance on the *Crusade* television series, Dastar has made a "false designation of origin, false or misleading description of fact, or false or misleading representation of fact, which . . . is likely to cause confusion . . . as to the origin . . . of his or her goods." That claim would undoubtedly be sustained if Dastar had bought some of New Line's *Crusade* videotapes and merely repackaged them as its own. Dastar's alleged wrongdoing, however, is vastly different: it took a creative work in the public domain—the *Crusade* television series—copied it, made modifications (arguably minor), and produced its very own series of videotapes. If "origin" refers only to the manufacturer or producer of the physical "goods" that are made available to the public (in this case the videotapes), Dastar was the origin. If, however, "origin" includes the creator of the underlying work that Dastar copied, then someone else (perhaps Fox) was the origin of Dastar's product. At bottom, we must decide what § 43(a)(1)(A) of the Lanham Act means by the "origin" of "goods."

III

The dictionary definition of "origin" is "[t]he fact or process of coming into being from a source," and "[t]hat from which anything primarily proceeds; source." WEBSTER'S NEW INTERNATIONAL DICTIONARY 1720–1721 (2d ed.1949). And the dictionary definition of "goods" (as relevant here) is "[w]ares; merchandise." *Id.*, at 1079. We think the most natural understanding of the "origin" of "goods"—the source of wares—is the producer of the tangible product sold in the marketplace, in this case the physical *Campaigns* videotape sold by Dastar. The concept might be stretched (as it was under the original version of § 43(a)) to include not only the actual producer, but also the trademark owner who commissioned or assumed responsibility for ("stood behind") production of the physical product. But as used in the Lanham Act, the phrase "origin of goods" is in our view incapable of connoting the person or entity that originated the ideas or communications that "goods" embody or contain. Such an extension would not only stretch the text, but it would be out of accord with the history and purpose of the Lanham Act and inconsistent with precedent.

Section 43(a) of the Lanham Act prohibits actions like trademark infringement that deceive consumers and impair a producer's goodwill. It forbids, for example, the Coca-Cola Company's passing off its product as Pepsi-Cola or reverse passing off Pepsi-Cola as its product. But the brand-loyal consumer who prefers the drink that the Coca-Cola Company or PepsiCo sells, while he believes that that company produced (or at least stands behind the production of) that product, surely does not necessarily believe that that company was the "origin" of the drink in the sense that it was the very first to devise the formula. The consumer who buys a branded product does not automatically assume that the brand-name company is the same entity that came up with the idea for the product, or designed the product—and typically does not care whether it is. The words of the Lanham Act should not be stretched to cover matters that are typically of no consequence to purchasers.

It could be argued, perhaps, that the reality of purchaser concern is different for what might be called a communicative product—one that is valued not primarily for its physical qualities, such as a hammer, but for the intellectual content that it conveys, such as a book or, as here, a video. The purchaser of a novel is interested not merely, if at all, in the identity of the producer of the physical tome (the publisher), but also, and indeed primarily, in the identity of the creator of the story it conveys (the author). And the author, of course, has at least as much interest in avoiding passing-off (or reverse passing-off) of his creation as does the publisher. For such a communicative product (the argument goes) "origin of goods" in § 43(a) must be deemed to include not merely the producer of the physical item (the publishing house Farrar, Straus and Giroux, or the video producer Dastar) but also the creator of the content that the physical item conveys (the author Tom Wolfe, or—assertedly—respondents).

The problem with this argument according special treatment to communicative products is that it causes the Lanham Act to conflict with the law of copyright, which addresses that subject specifically. The right to copy, and to copy without attribution, once a copyright has expired, like "the right to make [an article whose patent has expired]—including the right to make it in precisely the shape it carried when patented—passes to the public." *Sears, Roebuck & Co. v. Stiffel Co.*, 376 U.S. 225, 230 (1964. "In general, unless an intellectual property right such as a patent or copyright protects an item, it will be subject to copying." *TrafFix Devices, Inc. v. Marketing Displays, Inc.*, 532 U.S. 23, 29 (2001). The rights of a patentee or copyright holder are part of a "carefully crafted bargain," *Bonito Boats, Inc. v. Thunder Craft Boats, Inc.*, 489 U.S. 141, 150–151 (1989), under which, once the patent or copyright monopoly has expired, the public may use the invention or work at will and without attribution. Thus, in construing the Lanham Act, we have been "careful to caution against misuse or over-extension" of trademark and related protections into areas traditionally occupied by patent or copyright. *TrafFix*, 532 U.S., at 29. "The Lanham Act," we have said, "does not exist to reward manufacturers for their innovation in creating a particular device; that is the purpose of the patent law and its period of exclusivity." *Id.*, at 34. Federal trademark law "has no necessary relation to invention or discovery," *In re Trade-Mark Cases*, 100 U.S. 82, 94 (1879), but rather, by preventing competitors from copying "a source-identifying mark," "reduce[s] the customer's costs of shopping and making purchasing decisions," and "helps assure a producer that it (and not an imitating competitor) will reap the financial, reputation-related rewards associated with a desirable product," *Qualitex Co. v. Jacobson Products Co.*, 514 U.S. 159, 163–164 (1995). Assuming for the sake of argument that Dastar's representation of itself as the "Producer" of its videos amounted to a representation that it originated the creative work conveyed by the videos, allowing a cause of action under § 43(a) for that representation would create a species of mutant copyright law that limits the public's "federal right to 'copy and to use,'" expired copyrights, *Bonito Boats, supra*, at 165.

When Congress has wished to create such an addition to the law of copyright, it has done so with much more specificity than the Lanham Act's ambiguous use of "origin." The Visual Artists Rights Act of 1990, § 603(a), 104 Stat. 5128, provides that the author of an artistic work "shall have the right . . . to claim authorship of that work." 17 U.S.C. § 106A(a)(1)(A). That express right of attribution is carefully limited and focused: It attaches only to specified "work[s] of visual art," § 101, is personal to the artist, §§ 106A(b) and (e), and endures only for "the life of the author," at § 106A(d)(1). Recognizing in § 43(a) a cause of action for misrepresentation of authorship of noncopyrighted works (visual or otherwise) would render these limitations superfluous. A statutory interpretation that renders another statute superfluous is of course to be avoided.

Reading "origin" in § 43(a) to require attribution of uncopyrighted materials would pose serious practical problems. Without a copyrighted work as the basepoint, the word "origin" has no discernable limits. A video of the MGM film *Carmen Jones*, after its copyright has expired, would presumably require attribution not just to MGM, but to Oscar Hammerstein II (who wrote the musical on which the film was based), to Georges Bizet (who wrote the opera on which the musical was based), and to Prosper Merimee (who wrote the novel on which the opera was based). In many cases, figuring out who is in the line of "origin" would be no simple task. Indeed, in the present case it is far from clear that respondents have that status. Neither SFM nor New Line had anything to do with the production of the *Crusade* television series—they merely were licensed to distribute the video version. While Fox might have a claim to being in the line of origin, its involvement with the creation of the television series was limited at best. Time, Inc., was the principal if not the exclusive creator, albeit under arrangement with Fox. And of course it was neither Fox nor Time, Inc., that shot the film used in the *Crusade* television series. Rather, that footage came from the United States Army, Navy, and Coast Guard, the British Ministry of Information and War Office, the National Film Board of Canada, and unidentified "Newsreel Pool Cameramen." If anyone has a claim to being the *original* creator of the material used in both the *Crusade* television series and the *Campaigns* videotapes, it would be those groups, rather than Fox. We do not think the Lanham Act requires this search for the source of the Nile and all its tributaries.

Another practical difficulty of adopting a special definition of "origin" for communicative products is that it places the manufacturers of those products in a difficult position. On the one hand, they would face Lanham Act liability for failing to credit the creator of a work on which their lawful copies are based; and on the other hand they could face Lanham Act liability for crediting the creator if that should be regarded as implying the creator's "sponsorship or approval" of the copy, 15 U.S.C. § 1125(a)(1)(A). In this case, for example, if Dastar had simply "copied [the television series] as *Crusade in Europe* and sold it as *Crusade in Europe*," without changing the title or packaging (including the original credits to Fox), it is hard to have confidence in respondents' assurance that they "would not be here on a Lanham Act cause of action."

Finally, reading § 43(a) of the Lanham Act as creating a cause of action for, in effect, plagiarism—the use of otherwise unprotected works and inventions without attribution—would be hard to reconcile with our previous decisions. For example, in *Wal-Mart Stores, Inc. v. Samara Brothers, Inc.*, 529 U.S. 205 (2000), we considered whether product-design trade dress can ever be inherently distinctive. * * * We concluded that the designs could not be protected under § 43(a) without a showing that they had acquired "secondary meaning," so that they " 'identify the source of the product rather than the product itself,' " *id.*, at 211. This carefully considered limitation would be entirely pointless if the "original" producer could turn around and pursue a reverse-passing-off claim under exactly the same provision of the Lanham Act. * * *

Similarly under respondents' theory, the "origin of goods" provision of § 43(a) would have supported the suit that we rejected in *Bonito Boats*, 489 U.S. 141, where the defendants had used molds to duplicate the plaintiff's unpatented boat hulls (apparently without crediting the plaintiff). And it would have supported the suit we rejected in *TrafFix*, 532 U.S. 23: The plaintiff, whose patents on flexible road signs had expired, and who could not prevail on a trade-dress claim under § 43(a) because the features of the signs were functional, would have had a reverse-passing-off claim for unattributed copying of his design.

In sum, reading the phrase "origin of goods" in the Lanham Act in accordance with the Act's common-law foundations (which were *not* designed to protect originality or creativity), and in light of the copyright and patent laws (which were), we conclude that the phrase refers to the producer of the tangible goods that are offered for sale, and not to the author of any idea, concept, or communication embodied in those goods. *Cf.* 17 U.S.C. § 202 (distinguishing between a copyrighted work and "any material object in which the work is embodied"). To hold otherwise would be akin to finding that § 43(a) created a species of perpetual patent and copyright, which Congress may not do. *See Eldred v. Ashcroft*, 537 U.S. 186, 208 (2003).

The creative talent of the sort that lay behind the *Campaigns* videos is not left without protection. The original film footage used in the *Crusade* television series could have been copyrighted, *see* 17 U.S.C. § 102(a)(6), as was copyrighted (as a compilation) the *Crusade* television series, even though it included material from the public domain, *see* § 103(a). Had Fox renewed the copyright in the *Crusade* television series, it would have had an easy claim of copyright infringement. And respondents' contention that *Campaigns* infringes Doubleday's copyright in General Eisenhower's book is still a live question on remand. If, moreover, the producer of a video that substantially copied the *Crusade* series were, in advertising or promotion, to give purchasers the impression that the video was quite different from that series, then one or more of the respondents might have a cause of action—not for reverse passing off under the "confusion . . . as to the origin" provision of § 43(a)(1)(A), but for misrepresentation under the "misrepresents the nature, characteristics [or] qualities" provision of § 43(a)(1)(B). For merely saying it is the producer of the video, however, no Lanham Act liability attaches to Dastar.

* * *

NOTES

1. On remand in *Dastar*, Twentieth Century Fox prevailed on copyright grounds, based on a finding that General Eisenhower's book had been written as a "work for hire" and was therefore still under copyright protection. *See Twentieth Century Fox Film Corp. v. Entertainment Distributing*, 429 F.3d 869, 882 (9th Cir. 2005).

2. How should these cases be resolved under *Dastar*?

(a) A writer/editor/director brings a section 43(a) claim against a film producer for failing to give him screen credit. *See Williams v. UMG Recordings, Inc.*, 281 F.Supp.2d 1177 (C.D. Ca. 2003), *aff'd*, 2006 WL 1307922 (9th Cir. 2006).

(b) An actor brings a section 43(a) claim against a film distributor for removing his name from the screen credits and substituting a different name in the credits and advertising materials. *See Smith v. Montoro*, 648 F.2d 602 (9th Cir. 1981),

(c) A comedy troupe brings a section 43(a) claim against a television network that edited their television show for the insertion of commercials, even though (1) the troupe had retained the copyright in their underlying script, and (2) their contract with the show's prohibited any editing of the program without their consent. *See Gilliam v. ABC*, 538 F.2d 14 (2d Cir. 1976),

(d) Famed writer Stephen King sold the film rights to his story *The Lawnmower Man*, but had no involvement in making the resulting film. Upon viewing a rough cut of the film, he finds that his name appears in a "possessory credit" over the film's title—*i.e.*, "Stephen King's *The Lawnmower Man*." He brings a section 43(a) claim for an injunction prohibiting the producers from (1) using his name in the possessory credit, and (2) stating in the film's credits and advertising materials that the film is "based on a story by Stephen King." *See King v. Innovation Books*, 976 F.2d 824 (2d Cir. 1992).

3. Although *Dastar* is a case about the Lanham Act, it suggests a broader principle—that the Court will not construe federal legislation undertaken outside of the Patent and Copyright Clause power to alter the scope of patent or copyright protection. Under the Supremacy Clause of the Constitution, state laws that conflict with the federal patent and copyright regime are typically preempted. *Dastar*'s principle might be characterized as a type of quasi-preemption, which prevents parties from avoiding the constraints of patent and copyright laws by instead invoking laws that Congress enacted under its Commerce Clause power. Should a similar principle prevent Congress from using its Commerce Clause power to avoid the restrictions of the Patent and Copyright Clause? Consider, for example, 17 U.S.C. § 1101, which grants exclusive rights to musical performers to prevent the unauthorized copying or transmitting of their unfixed (and therefore uncopyrightable) live musical performances, and which was enacted by Congress pursuant to its Commerce Clause power.

2. FALSE ADVERTISING

CASTROL, INC. V. QUAKER STATE CORP.

977 F.2d 57 (2d Cir. 1992).

WALKER, CIRCUIT JUDGE:

A Quaker State television commercial asserts that "tests prove" its 10W-30 motor oil provides better protection against engine wear at start-up. In a thoughtful opinion reported at 1992 WL 47981 (S.D.N.Y. March 2, 1992), the United States District Court for the Southern District of New York (Charles S. Haight, Judge) held that plaintiff-appellee Castrol, Inc. ("Castrol") had proven this advertised claim literally false pursuant to

§ 43(a) of the Lanham Act, 15 U.S.C. § 1125(a) (1988). The district court issued a March 20, 1992 Order preliminarily enjoining defendants-appellants Quaker State Corporation, Quaker State Oil Refining Corporation, and Grey Advertising Inc., ("Quaker State"), from airing the commercial. We agree that Castrol has shown a likelihood of success in proving the commercial literally false. We accordingly affirm.

* * *

The voiceover to Quaker State's 10W-30 motor oil commercial states:

> Warning: Up to half of all engine wear can happen when you start your car. At this critical time, tests prove Quaker State 10W-30 protects better than any other leading 10W-30 motor oil. In an overwhelming majority of engine tests, Quaker State 10W-30 flowed faster to all vital parts. In all size engines tested, Quaker State protected faster, so it protected better. Get the best protection against start up wear. Today's Quaker State! It's one tough motor oil.

Visually, the commercial begins with a man entering a car and then shows a bottle of Quaker State 10W-30 motor oil. Large, block letters, superimposed over the bottle, "crawl" across the screen with the words: AT START UP QUAKER STATE 10W-30 PROTECTS BETTER THAN ANY OTHER LEADING 10W-30 MOTOR OIL. Originally, this "crawl" used the words "tests prove" instead of "at start up," but shortly after the filing of the current lawsuit Quaker State revised the message. The commercial then shows an engine, superimposed over which are bottles of Quaker State and four competing motor oils (including Castrol GTX 10W-30) and a bar graph depicting the speed with which each oil flowed to components of a Chrysler engine. The Quaker State bar is higher than all four competitors indicating that it flowed faster. The commercial closes with the words: "ONE TOUGH MOTOR OIL."

Polymethacrylate or "PMA," an additive intended to quicken oil flow to engine parts, is the source of Quaker State's superiority claim. The competitors listed in its commercial use olefin copolymer or "OCP," another additive. Two laboratory tests, the first run in 1987 and the second in 1991, have compared Quaker State's PMA-based oil with competing OCP-based oils. Rohm and Haas, the Pennsylvania corporation which manufactures PMA, conducted both tests.

Rohm and Haas' 1987 tests measured two performance indicators: "oiling time," or the time it takes for oil to reach distant parts in a just-started engine, and engine wear, measured through the amount of metal debris observed in the oil after the engine had run. Rohm and Haas technicians filled engines, in all other respects similar, with either Quaker State's PMA-based 10W-30 oil, or with a generic OCP-based oil known as

"Texstar." During numerous engine starts, Quaker State's oil demonstrated a substantially faster oiling time, reaching distant engine parts as much as 100 seconds earlier than the Texstar competitor. Contrary to expectations, however, this did not translate into reduced engine wear. A Rohm and Haas report stated that "[a]fter 64 starts . . . the Quaker State oil gave marginally better results, but there was no significant difference in wear metals accumulation between the two oils."

Rohm and Haas initially attributed the poor engine wear results to the presence of "residual oil" remaining from the prior engine starts. They theorized that this oil might be lubricating the engine in the period between ignition and arrival of the new oil, and so might be preventing the faster flowing Quaker State oil from demonstrating better protection that is statistically significant. To address this, they conducted additional engine starts with a warm-up between each run so as to burn off the residual oil. The Rohm and Haas report, however, concluded that "[w]ear metals analysis for this test cycle also failed to differentiate significantly between the two oils. . . ." Thus, while the 1987 Rohm and Haas tests demonstrated faster oil flow, they could not prove better protection against engine wear that is statistically significant.

The 1991 Rohm and Haas tests compared Quaker State's oiling time with that of four leading OCP-based competitors, including Castrol GTX 10W-30. Again, Quaker State's PMA-based oil flowed significantly faster to engine parts. * * * In the 1991 tests, as opposed to the 1987 studies, Rohm and Haas made no attempt to measure whether this faster oiling time resulted in reduced engine wear.

Quaker State broadcast their commercial in November, 1991. On December 19, 1991, Castrol initiated the present action. Castrol asserted that no studies supported the commercial's claim that "tests prove" Quaker State's oil provides better protection, and that this claim of test-proven superiority constituted false advertising. * * * At the hearing on the motion for a preliminary injunction, Quaker State relied on the Rohm and Haas tests. It argued that the Rohm and Haas oiling time findings support the advertised claim of better protection because oil which flows faster to engine parts necessarily protects them better. Dr. Elmer Klaus, Quaker State's sole expert witness, * * * concluded that the faster the new oil flows to the engine parts, the better job it does of minimizing this second period of boundary lubrication. Faster oil flow, therefore, means better protection.

Castrol's three experts focused on the role of residual oil. They testified that the small amount of residual oil left from a prior running of an engine provides more than adequate lubrication at the next start-up. Moreover, they asserted that this residual oil remains functional for a significant period of time so that both PMA-based and OCP-based 10W-30 motor oils reach the engine parts before this residual oil burns off. Thus, they maintained, there is no second boundary lubrication period and Quaker State's faster oiling time is irrelevant to engine wear.

* * *

Judge Haight concluded that because residual oil "holds the fort," Rohm and Haas' faster oiling time findings did not necessarily prove better protection. He consequently held that "Castrol has established the likelihood of proving at trial the falsity of Quaker State's claim that tests prove its oil protects better against start-up engine wear." * * *

Section 43(a) of the Lanham Act, 15 U.S.C. § 1125(a) (1988), pursuant to which Castrol brings this false advertising claim, provides that

> Any person who, on or in connection with any goods or services . . . uses in commerce any . . . false or misleading description of fact, or false or misleading representation of fact, which—* * * (2) in commercial advertising or promotion, misrepresents the nature, characteristics, qualities, or geographic origin of his or her or another person's goods, services, or commercial activities, shall be liable in a civil action by any person who believes that he or she is or is likely to be damaged by such act.

To succeed under § 43(a), a plaintiff must demonstrate that "an advertisement is either literally false or that the advertisement, though literally true, is likely to mislead and confuse consumers. . . . Where the advertising claim is shown to be literally false, the court may enjoin the use of the claim 'without reference to the advertisement's impact on the buying public.'" *McNeil-P.C.C., Inc. v. Bristol-Myers Squibb Co.*, 938 F.2d 1544, 1549 (2d Cir.1991). Here, Castrol contends that the challenged advertisement is literally false. It bears the burden of proving this to a "likelihood of success" standard.

As we have on two occasions explained, plaintiff bears a different burden in proving literally false the advertised claim that tests prove defendant's product superior, than it does in proving the falsity of a superiority claim which makes no mention of tests. In *Procter & Gamble Co. v. Chesebrough-Pond's, Inc.*, 747 F.2d 114 (2d Cir.1984), for example, Chesebrough alleged the literal falsity of Procter's advertised claim that "clinical tests" proved its product superior. Procter, in return, challenged as literally false a Chesebrough commercial which, making no mention of tests, asserted that its lotion was equal in effectiveness to any leading brand. We explained that in order to prove literally false Procter's claim of "test-proven superiority," Chesebrough bore the burden of "showing that the tests referred to by P & G were not sufficiently reliable to permit one to conclude with reasonable certainty that they established the proposition for which they were cited." We held that Procter could prove false

Chesebrough's advertisement, however, "only upon adducing evidence" that affirmatively showed Chesebrough's claim of parity to be false.

We drew this same distinction in *McNeil-P.C.C., Inc. v. Bristol-Myers Squibb Co.*, 938 F.2d 1544 (2d Cir.1991). Bristol-Myers initially advertised to trade professionals that "clinical studies" had shown its analgesic provided better relief than McNeil's. Bristol-Myers' later televised commercial made the product superiority claim but "did not refer to clinical studies." We held that, with respect to the initial trade advertising, "McNeil could . . . meet its burden of proof by demonstrating that these studies did not establish that AF Excedrin provided superior pain relief." With respect to the televised commercial, however, McNeil bore the burden of generating "scientific proof that the challenged advertisement was false."

A plaintiff's burden in proving literal falsity thus varies depending on the nature of the challenged advertisement. Where the defendant's advertisement claims that its product is superior, plaintiff must affirmatively prove defendant's product equal or inferior. Where, as in the current case, defendant's ad explicitly or implicitly represents that tests or studies prove its product superior, plaintiff satisfies its burden by showing that the tests did not establish the proposition for which they were cited. We have held that a plaintiff can meet this burden by demonstrating that the tests were not sufficiently reliable to permit a conclusion that the product is superior. The *Procter* "sufficiently reliable" standard of course assumes that the tests in question, if reliable, would prove the proposition for which they are cited. If the plaintiff can show that the tests, even if reliable, do not establish the proposition asserted by the defendant, the plaintiff has obviously met its burden. In such a case, tests which may or may not be "sufficiently reliable," are simply irrelevant.

The district court held that Castrol had met this latter burden * * *.

I. The district court committed no errors of law.

Quaker State contends that the district court improperly shifted the burden of proof to the defendant when it stated that "the claim that tests demonstrate . . . superiority is false because no test does so and [Dr.] Klaus' analysis fails to fill the gap." It argues that plaintiff bears the burden in a false advertising action and there should be no "gap" for defendant to fill.

Where a plaintiff challenges a test-proven superiority advertisement, the defendant must identify the cited tests. Plaintiff must then prove that these tests did not establish the proposition for which they were cited. *McNeil*, 938 F.2d at 1549. At the hearing, Quaker State cited the 1987 and 1991 Rohm and Haas oiling time tests in conjunction with Dr. Klaus' theory of engine wear at the second boundary lubrication period. Castrol's burden was to prove that neither the Rohm and Haas tests alone, nor the tests in conjunction with Dr. Klaus' theory, permitted the conclusion to a reasonable certainty that Quaker State's oil protected better at start-up.

The district court's statement that "no test [demonstrates superiority] and Klaus' analysis fails to fill the gap" is a finding that Castrol, through its residual oil theory, met its burden. It is, in substance, a finding that the Quaker State tests, which proved faster oiling time, are irrelevant to their claim that Quaker State's oil protects better at start-up. Therefore, we need not consider the tests' reliability. The district court's statement does not shift the burden to defendant. * * *

III. Is the district court's injunction overly broad?

In a March 20, 1992 memorandum opinion accompanying its simultaneously-issued Order of Preliminary Injunction, the district court explained its intent "to enjoin preliminarily Quaker State from claiming 'that tests prove its oil protects better against start-up engine wear.'" The injunction, however, goes beyond this limited intent. Paragraph 2 of the injunction states that

> Defendants ... are preliminarily enjoined from broadcasting, publishing or disseminating, in any manner or in any medium, any advertisement, commercial, or promotional matter ... that claims, directly or by clear implication, that: (a) Quaker State 10W-30 motor oil provides superior protection against engine wear at start-up; (b) Quaker State 10W-30 motor oil provides better protection against engine wear at start-up than other leading 10W-30 motor oils, including Castrol GTX 10W-30; or (c) Castrol GTX 10W-30 motor oil provides inferior protection against engine wear at start-up.

This paragraph enjoins Quaker State from distributing any advertisement claiming that its oil provides superior protection against engine wear at start-up, whether or not the ad claims test-proven superiority. As explained above, Castrol bears a different burden of proof with respect to this broader injunction than it does in seeking to enjoin only commercials which make the test-proven superiority claim.

The district court expressly found that Castrol had met its burden with respect to any test-proven superiority advertisement. It stated that "Castrol has established the likelihood of proving at trial the falsity of Quaker State's claim that tests prove its oil protects better. . . ." Its injunction would be too broad, however, absent the additional finding that Castrol had met its burden with respect to superiority advertisements that omit the "tests prove" language. As we have noted above, Castrol meets this burden by adducing proof that Quaker State's oil is not, in fact, superior.

Judge Haight made this additional finding. Castrol submitted the report from the 1987 Rohm and Haas tests as proof that Quaker State's oil did not protect better. * * * The district court, referring to this document, stated that "the record makes it crystal clear that to the extent tests were performed to demonstrate better wear protection (as opposed to faster flowing), *the tests contradict, rather than support* the claim. * * * These statements amount to a finding that Castrol has met the additional burden. The injunction is not overly broad.

* * *

NOTES

1. What advertising claims can Quaker State still make in light of the injunction? More generally, are claims about a product's "great performance," "superior performance," or "high quality" actionable under section 43(a)?

2. If further testing establishes that Quaker State's oil does in fact provide better protection than its competitors' products, will Quaker State be able to obtain relief from the injunction?

3. Would a competitor's assertion that a manufacturer of consumer products was affiliated with Satan worshippers be actionable? *See Proctor & Gamble Co. [Sic] v. Haugen*, 222 F.3d 1262 (10th Cir. 2000).

TIFFANY (N.J.) INC. V. EBAY INC.

600 F.3d 93 (2d Cir. 2010).

SACK, CIRCUIT JUDGE:

[Tiffany, the world-famous jewelry company, became aware that counterfeit Tiffany merchandise was being sold on eBay. It brought suit against eBay, alleging, inter alia, false advertising and contributory trademark infringement. The portion of the opinion addressing contributory liability is reproduced in Chapter 6.]

* * *

A. *Principles*

Section 43(a) of the Lanham Act prohibits any person from, "in commercial advertising or promotion, misrepresent[ing] the nature, characteristics, qualities, or geographic origin of his or her or another person's goods, services, or commercial activities." 15 U.S.C. § 1125(a)(1)(B). A claim of false advertising may be based on at least one of two theories: "that the challenged advertisement is literally false, *i.e.*, false on its face," or "that the advertisement, while not literally false, is nevertheless likely to mislead or confuse consumers." *Time Warner Cable, Inc. v. DIRECTV, Inc.*, 497 F.3d 144, 153 (2d Cir.2007).

In either case, the "injuries redressed in false advertising cases are the result of public deception." *Johnson & Johnson * Merck Consumer Pharm. Co. v. Smithkline Beecham Corp.*, 960 F.2d 294, 298 (2d Cir.1992) ("*Merck*"). And "[u]nder either theory, the plaintiff must also demonstrate that the false or misleading representation involved an inherent or material quality of the product." *Time Warner Cable,* 497 F.3d at 153 n. 3.

Where an advertising claim is literally false, "the court may enjoin the use of the claim without reference to the advertisement's impact on the buying public." *McNeil-P.C.C., Inc. v. Bristol-Myers Squibb Co.,* 938 F.2d 1544, 1549 (2d Cir.1991). To succeed in a likelihood-of-confusion case where the statement at issue is not literally false, however, a plaintiff "must demonstrate, by extrinsic evidence, that the challenged commercials tend to mislead or confuse consumers," and must "demonstrate that a statistically significant part of the commercial audience holds the false belief allegedly communicated by the challenged advertisement." *Merck,* 960 F.2d at 297, 298; *Time Warner Cable,* 497 F.3d at 153 ("[W]hereas plaintiffs seeking to establish a literal falsehood must generally show the substance of what is conveyed, . . . a district court *must* rely on extrinsic evidence [of consumer deception or confusion] to support a finding of an implicitly false message.").

B. *Discussion*

eBay advertised the sale of Tiffany goods on its website in various ways. Among other things, eBay provided hyperlinks to "Tiffany," "Tiffany & Co. under $150," "Tiffany & Co.," "Tiffany Rings," and "Tiffany & Co. under $50." eBay also purchased advertising space on search engines, in some instances providing a link to eBay's site and exhorting the reader to "Find **tiffany** items at low prices." (bold face type in original). Yet the district court found, and eBay does not deny, that "eBay certainly had generalized knowledge that Tiffany products sold on eBay were often counterfeit." Tiffany argues that because eBay advertised the sale of Tiffany goods on its website, and because many of those goods were in fact counterfeit, eBay should be liable for false advertising.

The district court rejected this argument. The court first concluded that the advertisements at issue were not literally false "[b]ecause authentic Tiffany merchandise is sold on eBay's website," even if counterfeit Tiffany products are sold there, too. The court then considered whether the advertisements, though not literally false, were nonetheless misleading. It concluded they were not for three reasons. First, the court found that eBay's use of Tiffany's mark in its advertising was "protected, nominative fair use." Second, the court found that "Tiffany has not proven that eBay had specific knowledge as to the illicit nature of individual listings," implying that such knowledge would be necessary to sustain a false advertising claim. Finally, the court reasoned that "to the extent that the advertising was false, the falsity was the responsibility of third party sellers, not eBay."

We agree with the district court that eBay's advertisements were not literally false inasmuch as genuine Tiffany merchandise was offered for sale through eBay's website. But we are unable to affirm on the record before us the district court's further conclusion that eBay's advertisements were not "likely to mislead or confuse consumers." *Time Warner Cable*, 497 F.3d at 153.

As noted, to evaluate Tiffany's claim that eBay's advertisements misled consumers, a court must determine whether extrinsic evidence indicates that the challenged advertisements were misleading or confusing. The reasons the district court gave for rejecting Tiffany's claim do not seem to reflect this determination, though. The court's first rationale was that eBay's advertisements were nominative fair use of Tiffany's mark.

But, even if that is so, it does not follow that eBay did not use the mark in a misleading advertisement. It may, after all, constitute fair use for Brand X Coffee to use the trademark of its competitor, Brand Y Coffee, in an advertisement stating that "In a blind taste test, 9 out of 10 New Yorkers said they preferred Brand X Coffee to Brand Y Coffee." But if 9 out of 10 New Yorkers in a statistically significant sample did *not* say they preferred X to Y, or if they were paid to say that they did, then the advertisement would nonetheless be literally false in the first example, or misleading in the second.

There is a similar difficulty with the district court's reliance on the fact that eBay did not know which particular listings on its website offered counterfeit Tiffany goods. That is relevant * * * to whether eBay committed contributory trademark infringement. But it sheds little light on whether the advertisements were misleading insofar as they implied the genuineness of Tiffany goods on eBay's site.

Finally, the district court reasoned that if eBay's advertisements were misleading, that was only because the sellers of counterfeits made them so by offering inauthentic Tiffany goods. Again, this consideration is relevant to Tiffany's direct infringement claim, but less relevant, if relevant at all, here. It is true that eBay did not itself sell counterfeit Tiffany goods; only the fraudulent vendors did, and that is in part why we conclude that eBay did not infringe Tiffany's mark. But eBay did affirmatively advertise the goods sold through its site as Tiffany merchandise. The law requires us to hold eBay accountable for the words that it chose insofar as they misled or confused consumers.

eBay and its amici warn of the deterrent effect that will grip online advertisers who are unable to confirm the authenticity of all of the goods they advertise for sale. We rather doubt that the consequences will be so dire. An online advertiser such as eBay need not cease its advertisements for a kind of goods only because it knows that not all of those goods are authentic. A disclaimer might suffice. But the law prohibits an advertisement that implies that all of the goods offered on a defendant's website are genuine when in fact, as here, a sizeable proportion of them are not.

Rather than vacate the judgment of the district court as to Tiffany's false advertising claim, we think it prudent to remand the cause so that the district court, with its greater familiarity with the evidence, can reconsider the claim in light of what we have said. The case is therefore remanded * * *.

NOTES

1. What exactly is the District Court to do when it "reconsiders the claim in light of what [the Second Circuit] has said?"

2. Do consumers have standing under the Lanham Act to sue a merchant for false advertising? Should they?

3. If a food or beverage label complies with the labeling requirements of the federal Food and Drug Administration, should this immunize the merchant from a Lanham Act false advertising claim alleging that the label is misleading to consumers? *See Pom Wonderful LLC v. Coca-Cola Co.*, 573 U.S. 102 (2014) (defendant used the words "pomegranate blueberry" on an FDA-compliant label for a juice drink that contained .3% pomegranate juice and .2% blueberry juice).

C. DILUTION

Statute: 15 U.S.C. § 1125(c)

Many trademark owners—especially the owners of famous marks—believe that their marks can be damaged by unauthorized uses even when those uses do not create a likelihood of confusion or deception. In response to this concern, many states began to recognize a cause of action for trademark "dilution." Eventually, Congress decided to expand the Lanham Act to permit dilution claims under federal law.

In 1995, Congress enacted the Federal Trademark Dilution Act (FTDA), section 43(c) of the Lanham Act, to protect "famous marks" against dilution. The Supreme Court interpreted the 1995 Act to require proof of "actual dilution"—meaning proof that the plaintiff's famous mark had actually been damaged by the unauthorized use. *See Moseley v. V Secret Catalogue, Inc.*, 537 U.S. 418 (2003). In 2006, Congress responded to this and other decisions that revealed ambiguities in the FTDA by enacting the Trademark Dilution Reform Act (TDRA). The 2006 amendments clarified, among other things, that a federal dilution plaintiff need only prove a *likelihood* of dilution rather than actual dilution. The amendments also clarified the test for fame: "[A] mark is famous if it is widely recognized by the general consuming public of the United States as a designation of source of the goods or services of the mark's owner." § 43(c)(2)(A). The

TDRA expressly recognizes two kinds of dilution: dilution by "blurring" (an "association arising from the similarity between a mark or trade name and a famous mark that impairs the distinctiveness of the famous mark") and dilution by "tarnishment" (an "association arising from the similarity between a mark or tradename and a famous mark that harms the reputation of the famous mark"). § 43(c)(2)(B), (C). The 2006 revisions also clarified and expanded the range of activities that are exempt from federal dilution liability. These now include the fair use ("other than as a designation of source for [the user's] own goods or services") of a famous mark for purposes of comparative advertising, parody, criticism or commentary regarding the mark; news reporting or commentary; and noncommercial uses. § 43(c)(3).

The following decision was the first case to apply the 2006 TDRA.

LOUIS VUITTON MALLETIER S.A. v. HAUTE DIGGITY DOG, LLC

507 F.3d 252 (4th Cir. 2007).

NIEMEYER, CIRCUIT JUDGE:

[The factual background of this case appears in the earlier excerpt addressing trademark infringement, reproduced in Part A of this chapter.]

LVM also contends that Haute Diggity Dog's advertising, sale, and distribution of the "Chewy Vuiton" dog toys dilutes its LOUIS VUITTON, LV, and Monogram Canvas marks, which are famous and distinctive, in violation of the Trademark Dilution Revision Act of 2006 ("TDRA"), 15 U.S.C.A. § 1125(c). It argues, "Before the district court's decision, Vuitton's famous marks were unblurred by any third party trademark use." "Allowing defendants to become the first to use similar marks will obviously blur and dilute the Vuitton Marks." It also contends that "Chewy Vuiton" dog toys are likely to tarnish LVM's marks because they "pose a choking hazard for some dogs."

Haute Diggity Dog urges that, in applying the TDRA to the circumstances before us, we reject LVM's suggestion that a parody "automatically" gives rise to "actionable dilution." Haute Diggity Dog contends that only marks that are "identical or substantially similar" can give rise to actionable dilution, and its "Chewy Vuiton" marks are not identical or sufficiently similar to LVM's marks. It also argues that "[its] spoof, like other obvious parodies," " 'tends to increase public identification' of [LVM's] mark with [LVM]," quoting *Jordache*, 828 F.2d at 1490, rather than impairing its distinctiveness, as the TDRA requires. As for LVM's tarnishment claim, Haute Diggity Dog argues that LVM's position is at best based on speculation and that LVM has made no showing of a likelihood of dilution by tarnishment.

Claims for trademark dilution are authorized by the TDRA, a relatively recent enactment, which provides in relevant part:

> Subject to the principles of equity, the owner of a famous mark . . . shall be entitled to an injunction against another person who . . . commences use of a mark or trade name in commerce that is likely to cause dilution by blurring or dilution by tarnishment of the famous mark, regardless of the presence or absence of actual or likely confusion, of competition, or of actual economic injury.

15 U.S.C.A. § 1125(c)(1). A mark is "famous" when it is "widely recognized by the general consuming public of the United States as a designation of source of the goods or services of the mark's owner." *Id.* § 1125(c)(2)(A). Creating causes of action for only dilution by blurring and dilution by tarnishment, the TDRA defines "dilution by blurring" as the "association arising from the similarity between a mark or trade name and a famous mark that impairs the distinctiveness of the famous mark." *Id.* § 1125(c)(2)(B). It defines "dilution by tarnishment" as the "association arising from the similarity between a mark or trade name and a famous mark that harms the reputation of the famous mark." *Id.* § 1125(c)(2)(C).

Thus, to state a dilution claim under the TDRA, a plaintiff must show:

(1) that the plaintiff owns a famous mark that is distinctive;

(2) that the defendant has commenced using a mark in commerce that allegedly is diluting the famous mark;

(3) that a similarity between the defendant's mark and the famous mark gives rise to an association between the marks; and

(4) that the association is likely to impair the distinctiveness of the famous mark or likely to harm the reputation of the famous mark.

In the context of blurring, distinctiveness refers to the ability of the famous mark uniquely to identify a single source and thus maintain its selling power. *See N.Y. Stock Exch. v. N.Y., N.Y. Hotel LLC*, 293 F.3d 550, 558 (2d Cir.2002) (observing that blurring occurs where the defendant's use creates "the possibility that the [famous] mark will lose its ability to serve as a unique identifier of the plaintiff's product"). In proving a dilution claim under the TDRA, the plaintiff need not show actual or likely confusion, the presence of competition, or actual economic injury. *See* 15 U.S.C.A. § 1125(c)(1).

The TDRA creates three defenses based on the defendant's (1) "fair use" (with exceptions); (2) "news reporting and news commentary"; and (3) "noncommercial use." *Id.* § 1125(c)(3).

A

We address first LVM's claim for dilution by blurring.

The first three elements of a trademark dilution claim are not at issue in this case. LVM owns famous marks that are distinctive; Haute Diggity Dog has commenced using "Chewy Vuiton," "CV," and designs and colors that are allegedly diluting LVM's marks; and the similarity between Haute Diggity Dog's marks and LVM's marks gives rise to an association between the marks, albeit a parody. The issue for resolution is whether the association between Haute Diggity Dog's marks and LVM's marks is likely to impair the distinctiveness of LVM's famous marks.

In deciding this issue, the district court correctly outlined the six factors to be considered in determining whether dilution by blurring has been shown. But in evaluating the facts of the case, the court did not directly apply those factors it enumerated. It held simply:

> [The famous mark's] strength is not likely to be blurred by a parody dog toy product. Instead of blurring Plaintiff's mark, the success of the parodic use depends upon the continued association with LOUIS VUITTON.

Louis Vuitton Malletier, 464 F.Supp.2d at 505. The amicus supporting LVM's position in this case contends that the district court, by not applying the statutory factors, misapplied the TDRA to conclude that simply because Haute Diggity Dog's product was a parody meant that "there can be no association with the famous mark as a matter of law." Moreover, the amicus points out correctly that to rule in favor of Haute Diggity Dog, the district court was required to find that the "association" did not impair the distinctiveness of LVM's famous mark.

LVM goes further in its own brief, however, and contends:

> When a defendant uses an imitation of a famous mark in connection with related goods, a claim of parody cannot preclude liability for dilution.
>
> * * *
>
> The district court's opinion utterly ignores the substantial goodwill VUITTON has established in its famous marks through more than a century of exclusive use. Disregarding the clear Congressional mandate to protect such famous marks against dilution, the district court has granted [Haute Diggity Dog] permission to become the first company other than VUITTON to use imitations of the famous VUITTON Marks.

In short, LVM suggests that any use by a third person of an imitation of its famous marks dilutes the famous marks as a matter of law. This contention misconstrues the TDRA.

The TDRA prohibits a person from using a junior mark that is likely to dilute (by blurring) the famous mark, and blurring is defined to be an impairment to the famous mark's distinctiveness. "Distinctiveness" in turn refers to the public's recognition that the famous mark identifies a single source of the product using the famous mark.

To determine whether a junior mark is likely to dilute a famous mark through blurring, the TDRA directs the court to consider all factors relevant to the issue, including six factors that are enumerated in the statute:

> (i) The degree of similarity between the mark or trade name and the famous mark.
>
> (ii) The degree of inherent or acquired distinctiveness of the famous mark.
>
> (iii) The extent to which the owner of the famous mark is engaging in substantially exclusive use of the mark.
>
> (iv) The degree of recognition of the famous mark.
>
> (v) Whether the user of the mark or trade name intended to create an association with the famous mark.
>
> (vi) Any actual association between the mark or trade name and the famous mark.

15 U.S.C.A. § 1125(c)(2)(B). Not every factor will be relevant in every case, and not every blurring claim will require extensive discussion of the factors. But a trial court must offer a sufficient indication of which factors it has found persuasive and explain why they are persuasive so that the court's decision can be reviewed. The district court did not do this adequately in this case. Nonetheless, after we apply the factors as a matter of law, we reach the same conclusion reached by the district court.

We begin by noting that parody is not automatically a complete defense to a claim of dilution by blurring where the defendant uses the parody as its own designation of source, i.e., as a trademark. Although the TDRA does provide that fair use is a complete defense and allows that a parody can be considered fair use, it does not extend the fair use defense to parodies used as a trademark. As the statute provides:

> The following shall not be actionable as dilution by blurring or dilution by tarnishment under this subsection:
>
> (A) Any fair use . . . *other than as a designation of source for the person's own goods or services,* including use in connection with . . . parodying. . . .

15 U.S.C.A. § 1125(c)(3)(A)(ii) (emphasis added). Under the statute's plain language, parodying a famous mark is protected by the fair use defense only if the parody is not "a designation of source for the person's own goods or services."

The TDRA, however, does not require a court to ignore the existence of a parody that is used as a trademark, and it does not preclude a court from considering parody as part of the circumstances to be considered for determining whether the plaintiff has made out a claim for dilution by blurring. Indeed, the statute permits a court to consider "all relevant factors," including the six factors supplied in § 1125(c)(2)(B).

Thus, it would appear that a defendant's use of a mark as a parody is relevant to the overall question of whether the defendant's use is likely to impair the famous mark's distinctiveness. Moreover, the fact that the defendant uses its marks as a parody is specifically relevant to several of the listed factors. For example, factor (v) (whether the defendant intended to create an association with the famous mark) and factor (vi) (whether there exists an actual association between the defendant's mark and the famous mark) directly invite inquiries into the defendant's intent in using the parody, the defendant's actual use of the parody, and the effect that its use has on the famous mark. While a parody intentionally creates an association with the famous mark in order to be a parody, it also intentionally communicates, if it is successful, that it is not the famous mark, but rather a satire of the famous mark. That the defendant is using its mark as a parody is therefore relevant in the consideration of these statutory factors.

Similarly, factors (i), (ii), and (iv)—the degree of similarity between the two marks, the degree of distinctiveness of the famous mark, and its recognizability—are directly implicated by consideration of the fact that the defendant's mark is a successful parody. Indeed, by making the famous mark an object of the parody, a successful parody might actually enhance the famous mark's distinctiveness by making it an icon. The brunt of the joke becomes yet more famous. *See Hormel Foods*, 73 F.3d at 506 (observing that a successful parody "tends to increase public identification" of the famous mark with its source); *see also Yankee Publ'g Inc. v. News Am. Publ'g Inc.*, 809 F.Supp. 267, 272–82 (S.D.N.Y.1992) (suggesting that a sufficiently obvious parody is unlikely to blur the targeted famous mark).

In sum, while a defendant's use of a parody as a mark does not support a "fair use" defense, it may be considered in determining whether the plaintiff-owner of a famous mark has proved its claim that the defendant's use of a parody mark is likely to impair the distinctiveness of the famous mark.

In the case before us, when considering factors (ii), (iii), and (iv), it is readily apparent, indeed conceded by Haute Diggity Dog, that LVM's marks are distinctive, famous, and strong. The LOUIS VUITTON mark is well known and is commonly identified as a brand of the great Parisian fashion house, Louis Vuitton Malletier. So too are its other marks and designs, which are invariably used with the LOUIS VUITTON mark. It may not be too strong to refer to these famous marks as icons of high fashion.

While the establishment of these facts satisfies essential elements of LVM's dilution claim, *see* 15 U.S.C.A. § 1125(c)(1), the facts impose on LVM an increased burden to demonstrate that the distinctiveness of its famous marks is likely to be impaired by a successful parody. Even as Haute Diggity Dog's parody mimics the famous mark, it communicates simultaneously that it is not the famous mark, but is only satirizing it. And because the famous mark is particularly strong and distinctive, it becomes more likely that a parody will not impair the distinctiveness of the mark. In short, as Haute Diggity Dog's "Chewy Vuiton" marks are a successful parody, we conclude that they will not blur the distinctiveness of the famous mark as a unique identifier of its source.

It is important to note, however, that this might not be true if the parody is so similar to the famous mark that it likely could be construed as actual use of the famous mark itself. Factor (i) directs an inquiry into the "degree of similarity between the junior mark and the famous mark." If Haute Diggity Dog used the actual marks of LVM (as a parody or otherwise), it could dilute LVM's marks by blurring, regardless of whether Haute Diggity Dog's use was confusingly similar, whether it was in competition with LVM, or whether LVM sustained actual injury. Thus, "the use of DUPONT shoes, BUICK aspirin, and KODAK pianos would be actionable" under the TDRA because the unauthorized use of the famous marks themselves on unrelated goods might diminish the capacity of these trademarks to distinctively identify a single source. *Moseley v. V Secret Catalogue, Inc.*, 537 U.S. 418, 431 (2003) (quoting H.R.Rep. No. 104–374, at 3 (1995)). This is true even though a consumer would be unlikely to confuse the manufacturer of KODAK film with the hypothetical producer of KODAK pianos.

But in this case, Haute Diggity Dog mimicked the famous marks; it did not come so close to them as to destroy the success of its parody and, more importantly, to diminish the LVM marks' capacity to identify a single source. Haute Diggity Dog designed a pet chew toy to imitate and suggest, but not use, the marks of a high-fashion LOUIS VUITTON handbag. It used "Chewy Vuiton" to mimic "LOUIS VUITTON"; it used "CV" to mimic "LV"; and it adopted imperfectly the items of LVM's designs. We conclude that these uses by Haute Diggity Dog were not so similar as to be likely to impair the distinctiveness of LVM's famous marks.

In a similar vein, when considering factors (v) and (vi), it becomes apparent that Haute Diggity Dog intentionally associated its marks, but only partially and certainly imperfectly, so as to convey the simultaneous message that it was not in fact a source of LVM products. Rather, as a parody, it separated itself from the LVM marks in order to make fun of them.

In sum, when considering the relevant factors to determine whether blurring is likely to occur in this case, we readily come to the conclusion, as did the district court, that LVM has failed to make out a case of trademark dilution by blurring by failing to establish that the distinctiveness of its marks was likely to be impaired by Haute Diggity Dog's marketing and sale of its "Chewy Vuiton" products.

B

LVM's claim for dilution by tarnishment does not require an extended discussion. To establish its claim for dilution by tarnishment, LVM must show, in lieu of blurring, that Haute Diggity Dog's use of the "Chewy Vuiton" mark on dog toys harms the reputation of the LOUIS VUITTON mark and LVM's other marks. LVM argues that the possibility that a dog could choke on a "Chewy Vuiton" toy causes this harm. LVM has, however, provided no record support for its assertion. It relies only on speculation about whether a dog could choke on the chew toys and a logical concession that a $10 dog toy made in China was of "inferior quality" to the $1190 LOUIS VUITTON handbag. The speculation begins with LVM's assertion in its brief that "defendant Woofie's admitted that 'Chewy Vuiton' products pose a choking hazard for some dogs. Having prejudged the defendant's mark to be a parody, the district court made light of this admission in its opinion, and utterly failed to give it the weight it deserved," citing to a page in the district court's opinion where the court states:

> At oral argument, plaintiff provided only a flimsy theory that a pet may some day choke on a Chewy Vuiton squeak toy and incite the wrath of a confused consumer against LOUIS VUITTON.

Louis Vuitton Malletier, 464 F.Supp.2d at 505. The court was referring to counsel's statement during oral argument that the owner of Woofie's stated that "she would not sell this product to certain types of dogs because there is a danger they would tear it open and choke on it." There is no record support, however, that any dog has choked on a pet chew toy, such as a "Chewy Vuiton" toy, or that there is any basis from which to conclude that a dog would likely choke on such a toy.

We agree with the district court that LVM failed to demonstrate a claim for dilution by tarnishment. * * *

The judgment of the district court is AFFIRMED.

NOTES

1. Does a prima facie case of dilution presuppose substantial similarity between the marks in contention? The TDRA provisions on blurring and tarnishment require some "similarity" between the marks, without specifying

the degree. Are "Starbucks" and "Charbucks" similar enough to support a dilution claim? *See Starbucks v. Wolfe's Borough Coffee, Inc.*, 588 F.3d 97 (2d Cir. 2009).

2. In addition to federal dilution law, most states have enacted their own dilution statutes. Some are modeled after the 1995 FDTA, some reflect the changes in the 2006 TDRA, and others (typically those that were enacted before 1995 and which have not been significantly revised) do not resemble the federal statute at all. For example, the New York dilution statute provides:

> Likelihood of injury to business reputation or of dilution of the distinctive quality of a mark or trade name shall be a ground for injunctive relief in cases of infringement of a mark registered or not registered or in cases of unfair competition, notwithstanding the absence of competition between the parties or the absence of confusion as to the source of goods or services.

New York Gen. Bus. L. § 360–*l*. Does this statute encompass blurring? Tarnishment? Must the plaintiff's mark be famous? Would the use of a plaintiff's mark in parody, comparative advertising, news reporting, criticism, or commentary give rise to liability?

3. An application to register a mark on the PTO's Principal Register can be opposed on dilution grounds under 15 U.S.C. §§ 1052(f) and 1063, and the registration of a dilutive mark can be cancelled under 15 U.S.C. § 1064 (for the Principal Register) or 1092 (for the Supplemental Register).

D. CYBERSQUATTING

Statute: 15 U.S.C. § 1125(d)

The ability to use valuable trademarks as domain names has led to the practice of "cybersquatting," in which one party registers a domain name that incorporates another party's mark with the eventual hope of turning a profit, usually by selling the domain name to the mark owner's owner. In the earliest cybersquatting cases, courts attempted to use traditional trademark law and dilution analysis. In 1999, however, Congress enacted the Anticybersquatting Consumer Protection Act (ACPA), Pub. L. No. 106–113 (1999) (codified at 15 U.S.C. § 1125(d)(1)(A)), which added section 43(d) to the Lanham Act in order to provide more effective remedies in this situation.

LAHOTI V. VERICHECK, INC.

586 F.3d 1190 (9th Cir. 2009).

GOULD, CIRCUIT JUDGE:

David Lahoti appeals the district court's bench trial judgment that his use of the "VeriCheck" Georgia state service mark owned by Vericheck, Inc. violated the Anti-Cybersquatting Consumer Protection Act ("ACPA"), 15

U.S.C. § 1125(d), the Lanham Act, 15 U.S.C. §§ 1051 et seq., the Washington Consumer Protection Act ("WCPA"), Wash. Rev.Code § 19.86, and various Washington common law doctrines. Lahoti, who has previously been found liable for cybersquatting activities, obtained the domain name "vericheck.com," but did not use the website to offer any goods or services. We conclude that the district court's factual decision that the "VeriCheck" mark was a distinctive, legally protectable mark under the ACPA and federal trademark law was based in part on reasoning contrary to federal trademark law and based in part on reasoning that could support the district court's conclusion. Because we believe the district court should decide the issue of distinctiveness in light of the principles we explain, we vacate the district court's opinion and remand for further proceedings not inconsistent with this opinion.

I

Vericheck, Inc. ("Vericheck") is a Georgia corporation that provides electronic financial transaction processing services, including check verification, check guarantee, check collection, account verification, automated check handling, and payment processing services. Vericheck has advertised itself on its website as "[t]he leader in Check Verification and Guarantee Services," and check verification underlies a large part of its operations. Vericheck operates a website at vericheck.net * * *.

David Lahoti considers himself an "Internet entrepreneur." Lahoti claims that in the late 1990s he contemplated going into the business of transaction verification and security. As a preliminary move, as he tells it, he began registering a number of domain names with the "veri-" prefix. Lahoti successfully acquired the vericheck.com domain name in 2003, but he never developed a transaction verification service. Instead, the vericheck.com website consisted only of a few lines of code redirecting visitors to a different website with search result links, including links to Vericheck's competitors. Lahoti earned income when visitors to vericheck.com clicked on links at the website to which they were redirected.

Vericheck frequently received calls from its customers complaining that they were confused because they visited vericheck.com but could not find information on Vericheck. Lahoti told the district court that before registering the Domain Name in 2003 he performed a trademark search and Internet search and he concluded that his use of the Domain Name would not be a trademark issue. He also said that when he reserved the Domain Name he was not aware of Vericheck's existence.

This case does not reflect the first time Lahoti has registered domain names that were similar to the names or trademarks of other companies. Lahoti had previously registered more than four hundred domain names containing the trademarks of other companies, including nissan.org, 1800 mattress.com, and ebays.com. * * *

In 2004 Vericheck contacted Lahoti and offered to purchase the vericheck.com domain name. Doubtless this fit into Lahoti's business plan as an Internet entrepreneur. Lahoti first asked for $72,500, and then reduced his demand to $48,000, but negotiations soon ended. In 2006 Vericheck filed an arbitration complaint pursuant to the Uniform Domain-Name Dispute-Resolution Policy. The arbitrator ordered the transfer of the Domain Name to Vericheck, but instead of complying, Lahoti sought a declaratory judgment in the district court that he did not violate the Lanham Act's cybersquatting or trademark infringement provisions. Vericheck counterclaimed that Lahoti's actions violated the Lanham Act, the ACPA, the WCPA, and Washington state common law. Thus the issues were first framed in the district court.

Both parties moved for summary judgment. The district court granted summary judgment to Vericheck, but only on the question of whether Lahoti acted in bad faith. The district court found that Lahoti did not use the Domain Name to sell goods or services or for a legitimate non-commercial use, and it stated that the Domain Name linked to several of Vericheck's competitors. It also noted Lahoti's past cybersquatting activities. The district court concluded that Lahoti "acted in a bad faith attempt to profit" from his use of the Domain Name and that no reasonable jury could decide otherwise.

After a bench trial on the remaining issues, the district court decided for Vericheck on all claims and counterclaims. The district court determined that the Disputed Mark was inherently distinctive, which was necessary for Vericheck to prevail on any of its trademark or ACPA claims. The district court concluded that Vericheck had established the other elements of its counterclaims, granted Vericheck injunctive relief and statutory damages, and awarded Vericheck attorneys' fees under both the WCPA and the Lanham Act. Lahoti appeals the district court's merits decision and its award of attorneys' fees.

* * *

III

To show trademark infringement, Vericheck "must demonstrate that it owns a valid mark, and thus a protectable interest," and it must show that Lahoti's "use of the mark 'is likely to cause confusion, or to cause mistake, or to deceive.' " * * * Federal trademark registration is not a prerequisite for protection under the Lanham Act, and for infringement claims such as Vericheck's, "the same standard applies to both registered and unregistered trademarks." * * * On its ACPA claim, Vericheck also must prove that Lahoti acted "with a bad faith intent to profit" from the Disputed Mark. 15 U.S.C. § 1125(d)(1)(A)(i).

* * *

B

Lahoti contests the district court's determination on summary judgment that he acted with "a bad faith intent to profit" from the use of the Disputed Mark. 15 U.S.C. § 1125(d)(1)(A)(i). We review the district court's grant of summary judgment *de novo*.

"A finding of 'bad faith' is an essential prerequisite to finding an ACPA violation," though it is not required for general trademark liability. *Interstellar Starship Servs., Ltd. v. Epix, Inc.*, 304 F.3d 936, 946 (9th Cir.2002). Evidence of bad faith may arise well after registration of the domain name. *See Storey v. Cello Holdings, LLC*, 347 F.3d 370, 385 (2d Cir.2003) ("Congress intended the cybersquatting statute to make rights to a domain-name registration contingent on ongoing conduct rather than to make them fixed at the time of registration.").

Congress has enumerated nine nonexclusive factors for courts to consider in determining whether bad faith exists. *See* 15 U.S.C. § 1125(d)(1)(B)(i). "We need not, however, march through the nine factors seriatim because the ACPA itself notes that use of the listed criteria is permissive." *Virtual Works, Inc. v. Volkswagen of Am., Inc.*, 238 F.3d 264, 269 (4th Cir.2001). "[I]nstead, the most important grounds for finding bad faith are the unique circumstances of the case. . . ." *Interstellar Starship*, 304 F.3d at 946. Congress has said that in evaluating bad faith, courts may consider a person's prior cybersquatting activities. *See* 15 U.S.C. § 1125(d)(1)(B)(i)(VIII) (providing that courts may consider "the person's registration or acquisition of multiple domain names which the person knows are identical or confusingly similar to marks of others that are distinctive"). Also, Congress has provided a safe harbor for ACPA defendants who "believed and had reasonable grounds to believe that the use of the domain name was a fair use or otherwise lawful." *Id.* § 1125(d)(1)(B)(ii).

Viewing the evidence in the light most favorable to Lahoti, the record still supports the district court's summary judgment determination that Lahoti was motivated by a bad faith intent to profit from his use of the Disputed Mark. Lahoti never used the Domain Name in connection with a bona fide offering of goods and services. Instead, Lahoti earned income when customers clicked on links when visiting the Domain Name website, some of which directed them to Vericheck's competitors. Lahoti then asked for as much as $72,500 to sell the Domain Name to Vericheck even though Lahoti had no interests associated with the "Vericheck" name. Finally, it is undisputed that Lahoti is a repeat cybersquatter who has registered hundreds of domain names resembling distinctive or famous trademarks and has been admonished by judicial bodies for doing so. Lahoti's response is a vague objection that the district court did not consider the facts in the light most favorable to him. But even in this favorable light, Lahoti's behavior shows "the sort of misconduct that Congress sought to discourage" by enacting the ACPA. *Virtual Works,* 238 F.3d at 270.

Lahoti argues that he is entitled to protection under the bad faith safe harbor because he reasonably believed his use of the Domain Name was lawful. *See* 15 U.S.C. § 1125(d)(1)(B)(ii). However, courts should "make use of this 'reasonable belief' defense very sparingly and only in the most unusual cases." *Audi AG v. D'Amato,* 469 F.3d 534, 549 (6th Cir.2006). Otherwise, the defense would "undermine the rest of the statute" because "[a]ll but the most blatant cybersquatters will be able to put forth at least some lawful motives for their behavior." *Virtual Works,* 238 F.3d at 270. We agree with the Fourth Circuit, which, in affirming a summary judgment determination of bad faith, has held that "[a] defendant who acts even partially in bad faith in registering a domain name is not, as a matter of law, entitled to benefit from the [ACPA's] safe harbor provision." *Id.* As we see the record, there is no genuine appellate issue on Lahoti's bad faith. He has made his cybersquatter bed and now cannot persuasively challenge the district court's conclusion that he must lie in it. A different case might be presented if Lahoti had a genuine business marketing service for which the Vericheck name was an aid, but there was no credible evidence of that here, nothing but his self-serving affidavit.

A reasonable person in Lahoti's position—that is, a reasonable person who had previously been declared a cybersquatter in a judicial proceeding—should have known that his actions might be unlawful. Lahoti has previously advanced, unsuccessfully, the same trademark defenses he argues here, including the claim that the mark at issue was only descriptive and that he is entitled to the safe harbor. Lahoti's failed defenses in these other cases make it unlikely that he legitimately believed that his use of the Domain Name was wholly lawful in this case. *See Coca-Cola Co. v. Purdy,* 382 F.3d 774, 788 (8th Cir.2004) (rejecting the defendant's safe harbor defense because the defendant had previously been enjoined in a prior Internet trademark case while advancing a similar defense). Although Lahoti may have believed that Vericheck's Disputed Mark was descriptive, his use of the Domain Name to link to Vericheck's competitors and his willingness to sell the Domain Name only for an exorbitant profit are quintessential cybersquatting practices. Lahoti acted at least "partially in bad faith" in gambling that the district court would agree with his interpretation of trademark law, and he knew or should have known that he would risk cybersquatting liability if his gamble failed. *Virtual Works,* 238 F.3d at 270. Lahoti is not entitled to the safe harbor. We affirm the district court's grant of summary judgment that Lahoti acted in bad faith.

* * *

NOTES

1. Would there be a valid claim for cybersquatting where a defendant used the plaintiff's mark in a domain name for a website devoted to criticizing the plaintiff's goods or services? What about a fan who uses a famous entertainer's name as a domain name for a site devoted to photos and commentaries on the entertainer?

2. Suppose that a trademark owner has a valid cybersquatting claim, but the court cannot exercise personal jurisdiction over the cybersquatter because the latter provided false contact information in registering the domain name and therefore cannot be located. Can the trademark owner still obtain a remedy under section 43(d)?

3. An alternative avenue for obtaining relief against cybersquatters is through the Uniform Domain Name Dispute Resolution Policy (UDRP), which is administered by the Internet Corporation for Assigned Names and Numbers (ICANN). Trademark owners can submit their complaints for arbitration, and if the trademark owner is successful, the offending domain name will be transferred to the trademark owner. This procedure is faster and cheaper than litigation, although no monetary remedies are available. If the arbitrator rules in favor of the domain name registrant, the trademark owner still has the option of filing an ACPA claim. Domain name registrants must agree to the arbitration procedure as a condition of registration.

CHAPTER 5

DEFENSES AND LIMITATIONS ON RIGHTS

■ ■ ■

In some infringement suits, the defendant will challenge the validity of the plaintiff's trademark or registration on the grounds discussed in Chapters 2 and 3. For example, the defendant may argue that the mark is generic, functional, or not distinctive, or that the plaintiff lacks priority in the mark. In other cases, however, the defendant will invoke defensive doctrines such as fair use, abandonment, comparative advertising, and the First Amendment. These and other defenses are considered below.

Statutes: 15 U.S.C. §§ 1115(b)(4), 1127

A. FAIR USE

KP PERMANENT MAKE-UP, INC. V. LASTING IMPRESSION I, INC., ET AL.

543 U.S. 111, 125 S.Ct. 542 (2004).

JUSTICE SOUTER delivered the opinion of the Court.

The question here is whether a party raising the statutory affirmative defense of fair use to a claim of trademark infringement, 15 U.S.C. § 1115(b)(4), has a burden to negate any likelihood that the practice complained of will confuse consumers about the origin of the goods or services affected. We hold it does not.

I

Each party to this case sells permanent makeup, a mixture of pigment and liquid for injection under the skin to camouflage injuries and modify nature's dispensations, and each has used some version of the term "micro color" (as one word or two, singular or plural) in marketing and selling its product. Petitioner KP Permanent Make-Up, Inc., claims to have used the single-word version since 1990 or 1991 on advertising flyers and since 1991 on pigment bottles. * * * In 1992, Lasting Impression I ("Lasting") applied to the United States Patent and Trademark Office (PTO) under 15 U.S.C. § 1051 for registration of a trademark consisting of the words "Micro Colors" in white letters separated by a green bar within a black square. The PTO registered the mark to Lasting in 1993, and in 1999 the registration became incontestable. § 1065.

It was also in 1999 that KP produced a 10-page advertising brochure using "microcolor" in a large, stylized typeface, provoking Lasting to demand that KP stop using the term. Instead, KP sued Lasting in the Central District of California, seeking, on more than one ground, a declaratory judgment that its language infringed no such exclusive right as Lasting claimed. Lasting counterclaimed, alleging, among other things, that KP had infringed Lasting's "Micro Colors" trademark.

KP sought summary judgment on the infringement counterclaim, based on the statutory affirmative defense of fair use, 15 U.S.C. § 1115(b)(4). After finding that Lasting had conceded that KP used the term only to describe its goods and not as a mark, the District Court held that KP was acting fairly and in good faith because undisputed facts showed that KP had employed the term "microcolor" continuously from a time before Lasting adopted the two-word, plural variant as a mark. Without inquiring whether the practice was likely to cause confusion, the court concluded that KP had made out its affirmative defense under § 1115(b)(4) and entered summary judgment for KP on Lasting's infringement claim.

On appeal, the Court of Appeals for the Ninth Circuit * * * took the view that no use could be recognized as fair where any consumer confusion was probable, and although the court did not pointedly address the burden of proof, it appears to have placed it on KP to show absence of consumer confusion. Since it found there were disputed material facts relevant under the Circuit's eight-factor test for assessing the likelihood of confusion, it reversed the summary judgment and remanded the case.

We granted KP's petition for certiorari to address a disagreement among the Courts of Appeals on the significance of likely confusion for a fair use defense to a trademark infringement claim, and the obligation of a party defending on that ground to show that its use is unlikely to cause consumer confusion. * * * We now vacate the judgment of the Court of Appeals.

II

A

* * *

The holder of a registered mark (incontestable or not) has a civil action against anyone employing an imitation of it in commerce when "such use is likely to cause confusion, or to cause mistake, or to deceive." § 1114(1). Although an incontestable registration is "conclusive evidence . . . of the registrant's exclusive right to use the . . . mark in commerce," § 1115(b), the plaintiff's success is still subject to "proof of infringement as defined in section 1114," § 1115(b). And that, as just noted, requires a showing that the defendant's actual practice is likely to produce confusion in the minds of consumers about the origin of the goods or services in question. This plaintiff's burden has to be kept in mind when reading the relevant portion of the further provision for an affirmative defense of fair use, available to a party whose "use of the name, term, or device charged to be an infringement is a use, otherwise than as a mark, . . . of a term or device which is descriptive of and used fairly and in good faith only to describe the goods or services of such party, or their geographic origin. . . ." § 1115(b)(4).

Two points are evident. Section 1115(b) places a burden of proving likelihood of confusion (that is, infringement) on the party charging infringement even when relying on an incontestable registration. And Congress said nothing about likelihood of confusion in setting out the elements of the fair use defense in § 1115(b)(4).

Starting from these textual fixed points, it takes a long stretch to claim that a defense of fair use entails any burden to negate confusion. It is just not plausible that Congress would have used the descriptive phrase "likely to cause confusion, or to cause mistake, or to deceive" in § 1114 to describe the requirement that a markholder show likelihood of consumer confusion, but would have relied on the phrase "used fairly" in § 1115(b)(4) in a fit of terse drafting meant to place a defendant under a burden to negate confusion. * * *

Finally, a look at the typical course of litigation in an infringement action points up the incoherence of placing a burden to show nonconfusion on a defendant. If a plaintiff succeeds in making out a prima facie case of trademark infringement, including the element of likelihood of consumer confusion, the defendant may offer rebutting evidence to undercut the force of the plaintiff's evidence on this (or any) element, or raise an affirmative defense to bar relief even if the prima facie case is sound, or do both. * * * [I]t is only when a plaintiff has shown likely confusion by a preponderance of the evidence that a defendant could have any need of an affirmative defense, but under Lasting's theory the defense would be foreclosed in such a case. * * * Nor would it make sense to provide an affirmative defense of no confusion plus good faith, when merely rebutting the plaintiff's case on confusion would entitle the defendant to judgment, good faith or not.

* * *

B

Since the burden of proving likelihood of confusion rests with the plaintiff, and the fair use defendant has no free-standing need to show confusion unlikely, it follows (contrary to the Court of Appeals's view) that some possibility of consumer confusion must be compatible with fair use, and so it is. The common law's tolerance of a certain degree of confusion on the part of consumers followed from the very fact that in cases like this one an originally descriptive term was selected to be used as a mark, not to mention the undesirability of allowing anyone to obtain a complete monopoly on use of a descriptive term simply by grabbing it first. The Lanham Act adopts a similar leniency, there being no indication that the statute was meant to deprive commercial speakers of the ordinary utility of descriptive words. "If any confusion results, that is a risk the plaintiff accepted when it decided to identify its product with a mark that uses a well known descriptive phrase." *Cosmetically Sealed Industries, Inc. v. Chesebrough-Pond's USA Co.*, 125 F.3d, at 30. This right to describe is the reason that descriptive terms qualify for registration as trademarks only after taking on secondary meaning as "distinctive of the applicant's goods," 15 U.S.C. § 1052(f), with the registrant getting an exclusive right not in the original, descriptive sense, but only in the secondary one associated with the markholder's goods.

While we thus recognize that mere risk of confusion will not rule out fair use, we think it would be improvident to go further in this case, for deciding anything more would take us beyond the Ninth Circuit's consideration of the subject. It suffices to realize that our holding that fair use can occur along with some degree of confusion does not foreclose the relevance of the extent of any likely consumer confusion in assessing whether a defendant's use is objectively fair. * * *

Since we do not rule out the pertinence of the degree of consumer confusion under the fair use defense, we likewise do not pass upon the position of the United States, as amicus, that the "used fairly" requirement in § 1115(b)(4) demands only that the descriptive term describe the goods accurately. Accuracy of course has to be a consideration in assessing fair use, but the proceedings in this case so far raise no occasion to evaluate some other concerns that courts might pick as relevant, quite apart from attention to confusion. The Restatement raises possibilities like commercial justification and the strength of the plaintiff's mark. RESTATEMENT (THIRD) OF UNFAIR COMPETITION, § 28. As to them, it is enough to say here that the door is not closed.

III

In sum, a plaintiff claiming infringement of an incontestable mark must show likelihood of consumer confusion as part of the prima facie case, 15 U.S.C. § 1115(b), while the defendant has no independent burden to negate the likelihood of any confusion in raising the affirmative defense that a term is used descriptively, not as a mark, fairly, and in good faith, § 1115(b)(4).

* * *

NOTE

In a case like this, how much likelihood of confusion should be sufficient to overcome the fair use defense? Having taken the case, was the Supreme Court right to leave that question open?

TOYOTA MOTOR SALES, U.S.A., INC. V. TABARI

610 F.3d 1171 (9th Cir. 2010).

KOZINSKI, CHIEF JUDGE:

In this trademark infringement case, we consider the application of the nominative fair use doctrine to internet domain names. * * *

Farzad and Lisa Tabari are auto brokers—the personal shoppers of the automotive world. They contact authorized dealers, solicit bids and arrange for customers to buy from the dealer offering the best combination of location, availability and price. * * * Until recently, the Tabaris offered this service at buy-a-lexus.com and buyorleaselexus.com.

Toyota Motor Sales U.S.A. ("Toyota") is the exclusive distributor of Lexus vehicles in the United States, and jealous guardian of the Lexus mark. * * *

Toyota objected to the Tabaris' use on their website of copyrighted photography of Lexus vehicles and the circular "L Symbol Design mark." Toyota also took umbrage at the Tabaris' use of the string "lexus" in their domain names, which it believed was "likely to cause confusion as to the source of [the Tabaris'] web site." The Tabaris removed Toyota's photography and logo from their site and added a disclaimer in large font at the top. But they refused to give up their domain names. Toyota sued, and the district court found infringement after a bench trial. It ordered the Tabaris to cease using their domain names and enjoined them from using the Lexus mark in any other domain name. Pro se as they were at trial, the Tabaris appeal.

NOMINATIVE FAIR USE

When customers purchase a Lexus through the Tabaris, they receive a genuine Lexus car sold by an authorized Lexus dealer, and a portion of the proceeds ends up in Toyota's bank account. Toyota doesn't claim the business of brokering Lexus cars is illegal or that it has contracted with its dealers to prohibit selling through a broker. Instead, Toyota is using this trademark lawsuit to make it more difficult for consumers to use the Tabaris to buy a Lexus.

The district court applied the eight-factor test for likelihood of confusion articulated in *AMF Inc. v. Sleekcraft Boats,* 599 F.2d 341, 348–49 (9th Cir.1979), and found that the Tabaris' domain names—buy-a-lexus.com and buyorleaselexus.com—infringed the Lexus trademark. But we've held that the *Sleekcraft* analysis doesn't apply where a defendant uses the mark to refer to the trademarked good itself. *See Playboy Enters., Inc. v. Welles,* 279 F.3d 796, 801 (9th Cir.2002); *New Kids on the Block v. News Am. Publ'g, Inc.*, 971 F.2d 302, 308 (9th Cir.1992).[1] The Tabaris are using the term Lexus to describe their business of brokering Lexus automobiles; when they say Lexus, they mean Lexus. We've long held that such use of the trademark is a fair use, namely nominative fair use. And fair use is, by definition, not infringement. The Tabaris did in fact present a nominative fair use defense to the district court.

In cases where a nominative fair use defense is raised, we ask whether (1) the product was "readily identifiable" without use of the mark; (2) defendant used more of the mark than necessary; or (3) defendant falsely suggested he was sponsored or endorsed by the trademark holder. *Welles,* 279 F.3d at 801. This test "evaluates the likelihood of confusion in nominative use cases." It's designed to address the risk that nominative use of the mark will inspire a mistaken belief on the part of consumers that the speaker is sponsored or endorsed by the trademark holder. The third factor speaks directly to the risk of such confusion, and the others do so indirectly: Consumers may reasonably infer sponsorship or endorsement if a company uses an unnecessary trademark or "more" of a mark than necessary. But if the nominative use satisfies the three-factor *New Kids* test, it doesn't infringe. If the nominative use does not satisfy all the *New Kids* factors, the district court may order defendants to modify their use of the mark so that all three factors are satisfied; it may not enjoin nominative use of the mark altogether.

A. The district court enjoined the Tabaris from using "any . . . domain name, service mark, trademark, trade name, meta tag or other commercial indication of origin that includes the mark LEXUS." A trademark injunction, particularly one involving nominative fair use, can raise serious First Amendment concerns because it can interfere with truthful communication between buyers and sellers in the marketplace. * * * To uphold the broad injunction entered in this case, we would have to be convinced that consumers are likely to believe a site is sponsored or endorsed by a trademark holder whenever the domain name contains the string of letters that make up the trademark.

* * *

The district court reasoned that the fact that an internet domain contains a trademark will "generally" suggest sponsorship or endorsement

[1] This is no less true where, as here, "the defendant's ultimate goal is to describe his own product." *Cairns v. Franklin Mint Co.,* 292 F.3d 1139, 1151 (9th Cir.2002). In *Welles,* for instance, we applied our nominative fair use analysis to a former playmate's use of the Playboy mark to describe herself and her website. 279 F.3d at 801. We observed that, in those circumstances, "application of the *Sleekcraft* test, which focuses on the similarity of the mark used by the plaintiff and the defendant, would lead to the incorrect conclusion that virtually all nominative uses are confusing." *Id.*

by the trademark holder. When a domain name consists *only* of the trademark followed by .com, or some other suffix like .org or .net, it will typically suggest sponsorship or endorsement by the trademark holder.[4] * * *

But the case where the URL consists of nothing but a trademark followed by a suffix like .com or .org is a special one indeed. The importance ascribed to trademark.com in fact suggests that far less confusion will result when a domain making nominative use of a trademark includes characters in addition to those making up the mark. Because the official Lexus site is almost certain to be found at lexus.com (as, in fact, it is), it's far less likely to be found at other sites containing the word Lexus. On the other hand, a number of sites make nominative use of trademarks in their domains but are not sponsored or endorsed by the trademark holder: You can preen about your Mercedes at mercedesforum.com and mercedestalk.net, read the latest about your double-skim-no-whip latte at starbucksgossip.com and find out what goodies the world's greatest electronics store has on sale this week at fryselectronics-ads.com. * * *

When a domain name making nominative use of a mark does not actively suggest sponsorship or endorsement, the worst that can happen is that some consumers may arrive at the site uncertain as to what they will find. But in the age of FIOS, cable modems, DSL and T1 lines, reasonable, prudent and experienced internet consumers are accustomed to such exploration by trial and error. * * * So long as the site as a whole does not suggest sponsorship or endorsement by the trademark holder, such momentary uncertainty does not preclude a finding of nominative fair use.

Toyota argues it is entitled to exclusive use of the string "lexus" in domain names because it spends hundreds of millions of dollars every year making sure everyone recognizes and understands the word "Lexus." But "[a] large expenditure of money does not in itself create legally protectable rights." *Smith v. Chanel, Inc.*, 402 F.2d 562, 568 (9th Cir.1968). Indeed, it is precisely because of Toyota's investment in the Lexus mark that "[m]uch useful social and commercial discourse would be all but impossible if speakers were under threat of an infringement lawsuit every time they

[4] Of course, not every trademark.com domain name is likely to cause consumer confusion. See *Interstellar Starship*, 304 F.3d at 944–46. For instance, we observed in *Interstellar Starship* that an apple orchard could operate at the website apple.com without risking confusion with Apple Computers, in light of the vast difference between their products. *Id.* at 944. "If, however, the apple grower . . . competed directly with Apple Computer by selling computers, initial interest confusion probably would result," as the apple grower would be using the apple.com domain to appropriate the goodwill Apple Computer had developed in its trademark. *Id.*

When a website deals in goods or services related to a trademarked brand, as in this case, it is much closer to the second example, where apple.com competes with Apple Computers. If a company that repaired iPods, iPads and iPhones were to set up at apple.com, for instance, consumers would naturally assume that the company was sponsored or endorsed by Apple (or, more likely, that it *was* Apple). Where a site is used to sell goods or services related to the trademarked brand, a trademark.com domain will therefore suggest sponsorship or endorsement and will not generally be nominative fair use.

made reference to [Lexus] by using its trademark." *New Kids,* 971 F.2d at 307. It is the wholesale prohibition of nominative use in domain names that would be unfair. It would be unfair to merchants seeking to communicate the nature of the service or product offered at their sites. And it would be unfair to consumers, who would be deprived of an increasingly important means of receiving such information. As noted, this would have serious First Amendment implications. The only winners would be companies like Toyota, which would acquire greater control over the markets for goods and services related to their trademarked brands, to the detriment of competition and consumers. The nominative fair use doctrine is designed to prevent this type of abuse of the rights granted by the Lanham Act.

B. Toyota asserts that, even if the district court's injunction is overbroad, it can be upheld if limited to the Tabaris' actual domain names: buyorleaselexus.com and buy-a-lexus.com. We therefore apply the three-part *New Kids* test to the domain names, and we start by asking whether the Tabaris' use of the mark was "necessary" to describe their business. Toyota claims it was not, because the Tabaris could have used a domain name that did not contain the Lexus mark. It's true they could have used some other domain name like autobroker.com or fastimports.com, or have used the text of their website to explain their business. But it's enough to satisfy our test for necessity that the Tabaris needed to communicate that they specialize in Lexus vehicles, and using the Lexus mark in their domain names accomplished this goal. * * * In *Volkswagenwerk,* for instance, we affirmed the right of a mechanic to put up a sign advertising that he specialized in repairing Volkswagen cars, although he could have used a sandwich board, distributed leaflets or shouted through a megaphone.[9] One way or the other, the Tabaris need to let consumers know that they are brokers of Lexus cars, and that's nearly impossible to do without mentioning Lexus, be it via domain name, metatag, radio jingle, telephone solicitation or blimp.

The fact that the Tabaris also broker other types of cars does not render their use of the Lexus mark unnecessary. * * * The Tabaris are entitled to decide what automotive brands to emphasize in their business, and the district court found that the Tabaris do in fact specialize in Lexus vehicles.

* * * We therefore conclude that the Tabaris easily satisfy the first *New Kids* factor.

---

[9] The Seventh Circuit has similarly upheld the right of a seller of Beanie Babies to operate at "bargainbeanies.com" on the grounds that "[y]ou can't sell a branded product without using its brand name." *Ty Inc.,* 306 F.3d at 512. In a prophetic choice of examples, Judge Posner remarked that prohibiting such a domain name "would amount to saying that if a used car dealer truthfully advertised that it sold Toyotas, or if a muffler manufacturer truthfully advertised that it specialized in making mufflers for installation in Toyotas, Toyota would have a claim of trademark infringement." *Id.*

As for the second and third steps of our nominative fair use analysis, Toyota suggests that use of the stylized Lexus mark and "Lexus L" logo was more use of the mark than necessary and suggested sponsorship or endorsement by Toyota. This is true: The Tabaris could adequately communicate their message without using the visual trappings of the Lexus brand. Moreover, those visual cues might lead some consumers to believe they were dealing with an authorized Toyota affiliate. Imagery, logos and other visual markers may be particularly significant in cyberspace, where anyone can convincingly recreate the look and feel of a luxury brand at minimal expense. It's hard to duplicate a Lexus showroom, but it's easy enough to ape the Lexus site.

But the Tabaris submitted images of an entirely changed site at the time of trial: The stylized mark and "L" logo were gone, and a disclaimer appeared in their place. The disclaimer stated, prominently and in large font, "We are not an authorized Lexus dealer or affiliated in any way with Lexus. We are an Independent Auto Broker." While not required, such a disclaimer is relevant to the nominative fair use analysis. * * * Reasonable consumers would arrive at the Tabaris' site agnostic as to what they would find. Once there, they would immediately see the disclaimer and would promptly be disabused of any notion that the Tabaris' website is sponsored by Toyota. Because there was no risk of confusion as to sponsorship or endorsement, the Tabaris' use of the Lexus mark was fair.

* * *

C. When considering the scope and timing of any infringement on remand, the district court must eschew application of *Sleekcraft* and analyze the case solely under the rubric of nominative fair use. The district court treated nominative fair use as an affirmative defense to be established by the Tabaris only after Toyota showed a likelihood of confusion under *Sleekcraft*. This was error; nominative fair use "replaces" *Sleekcraft* as the proper test for likely consumer confusion whenever defendant asserts to have referred to the trademarked good itself.

On remand, Toyota must bear the burden of establishing that the Tabaris' use of the Lexus mark was *not* nominative fair use. A finding of nominative fair use is a finding that the plaintiff has failed to show a likelihood of confusion as to sponsorship or endorsement. * * * A defendant seeking to assert nominative fair use as a defense need only show that it used the mark to refer to the trademarked good, as the Tabaris undoubtedly have here. The burden then reverts to the plaintiff to show a likelihood of confusion.

* * *

NOTES

1. Judge Kozinski originated the concept of "nominative fair use" in the *New Kids On The Block* case, cited in *Tabari*. It has won increasing acceptance outside of the Ninth Circuit, although courts are far from uniform in their approaches. In particular, outside of the Ninth Circuit, the nominative fair use factors do not replace the likelihood-of-confusion factors; instead, courts treat nominative fair use as an affirmative defense. Which approach represents better policy?

2. Does nominative fair use permit a bar or restaurant to advertise a "Super Bowl Party"? Can a television show about the annual 26-mile footrace in Boston use the words "Boston Marathon"? *See WCVB-TV v. Boston Athletic Ass'n*, 926 F.2d 42 (1st Cir. 1991). Can eBay advertise that Nike and Louis Vuitton products are available from the merchants on its website? Note that all of these terms are registered trademarks.

3. How does nominative fair use apply to a federal dilution claim? *See* 15 U.S.C. § 1125(c)(3)(A). How would it apply, if at all, to a dilution claim arising under state law?

B. ABANDONMENT

Even if a party at one time owned a valid mark, if the mark becomes abandoned then that party will lose ownership of the mark, and others will be free to use it. The Lanham Act's definition of abandonment (in 15 U.S.C. § 1127) is vaguely worded. Courts generally interpret it narrowly to incorporate the various grounds on which a mark may be found abandoned at common law. Some of these grounds are discussed in the cases below.

BARCAMERICA INTERN. USA TRUST V. TYFIELD IMPORTERS, INC.

289 F.3d 589 (9th Cir. 2002).

O'SCANNLAIN, CIRCUIT JUDGE.

We must decide whether a company engaged in "naked licensing" of its trademark, thus resulting in abandonment of the mark and ultimately its cancellation.

I

This case involves a dispute over who may use the "Leonardo Da Vinci" trademark for wines.

A

Barcamerica International USA Trust ("Barcamerica") traces its rights in the Leonardo Da Vinci mark to a February 14, 1984 registration granted by the United States Patent and Trademark Office ("PTO"), on an application filed in 1982. On August 7, 1989, the PTO acknowledged the mark's "incontestability." *See* 15 U.S.C. § 1115(b). Barcamerica asserts that it has used the mark continuously since the early 1980s. * * *

In 1988, Barcamerica entered into a licensing agreement with Renaissance Vineyards ("Renaissance"). Under the agreement, Barcamerica granted Renaissance the nonexclusive right to use the "Da Vinci" mark for five years or 4,000 cases, "whichever comes first," in exchange for $2,500. The agreement contained no quality control provision. In 1989, Barcamerica and Renaissance entered into a second agreement in place of the 1988 agreement. The 1989 agreement granted Renaissance an exclusive license to use the "Da Vinci" mark in the United States for wine products or alcoholic beverages. The 1989 agreement was drafted by Barcamerica's counsel and, like the 1988 agreement, it did not contain a quality control provision. In fact, the only evidence in the record of any efforts by Barcamerica to exercise "quality control" over Renaissance's wines comprised (1) Barcamerica principal George Gino Barca's testimony that he occasionally, informally tasted of the wine, and (2) Barca's testimony that he relied on the reputation of a "world-famous winemaker" employed by Renaissance at the time the agreements were signed. (That winemaker is now deceased, although the record does not indicate when he died.) * * *

B

Cantine Leonardo Da Vinci Soc. Coop. a.r.l. ("Cantine"), an entity of Italy, is a wine producer located in Vinci, Italy. Cantine has sold wine products bearing the "Leonardo Da Vinci" tradename since 1972; it selected this name and mark based on the name of its home city, Vinci. Cantine began selling its "Leonardo Da Vinci" wine to importers in the United States in 1979. Since 1996, however, Tyfield Importers, Inc. ("Tyfield") has been the exclusive United States importer * * *.

[After Cantine petitioned to cancel Barcamerica's trademark registration, Barcamerica sued Tyfield and Cantine for infringement. The district court granted summary judgement for the defendants, concluding that Barcamerica had abandoned the mark through naked licensing. Barcamerica appealed.]

* * *

III

We now turn to the merits of the appeal. Barcamerica first challenges the district court's conclusion that Barcamerica abandoned its trademark by engaging in naked licensing. It is well-established that "[a] trademark owner may grant a license and remain protected provided quality control of the goods and services sold under the trademark by the licensee is maintained." *Moore Bus. Forms, Inc. v. Ryu*, 960 F.2d 486, 489 (5th Cir.1992). But "[u]ncontrolled or 'naked' licensing may result in the trademark ceasing to function as a symbol of quality and controlled source." McCarthy on Trademarks and Unfair Competition § 18:48, at 18–79 (4th ed.2001). Consequently, where the licensor fails to exercise adequate quality control over the licensee, "a court may find that the trademark owner has abandoned the trademark, in which case the owner would be estopped from asserting rights to the trademark." *Moore*, 960 F.2d at 489. Such abandonment "is purely an 'involuntary' forfeiture of trademark rights," for it need not be shown that the trademark owner had any subjective intent to abandon the mark. McCarthy § 18:48, at 18–79. Accordingly, the proponent of a naked license theory "faces a stringent standard" of proof.

A

Judge Damrell's analysis of this issue in his memorandum opinion and order is correct and well-stated, and we adopt it as our own. As that court explained,

* * *

> The lack of an express contract right to inspect and supervise a licensee's operations is not conclusive evidence of lack of control."[T]here need not be formal quality control where 'the particular circumstances of the licensing arrangement [indicate] that the public will not be deceived.' " *Moore Bus. Forms, Inc.*, 960 F.2d at 489. Indeed, "[c]ourts have upheld licensing agreements where the licensor is familiar with and relies upon the licensee's own efforts to control quality." *Morgan Creek Prods., Inc. v. Capital Cities/ABC,* Inc., 22 U.S.P.Q.2d 1881, 1884 (C.D.Cal.1991).
>
> Here, there is no evidence that [Barcamerica] is familiar with or relied upon Renaissance's efforts to control quality. Mr. Barca represents that Renaissance's use of the mark is "controlled by" plaintiff "with respect to the nature and quality of the wine sold under the license," and that "[t]he nature and quality of Renaissance wine sold under the trademark is good." [Barcamerica]'s sole evidence of any such control is Mr. Barca's own apparently random tastings and his reliance on Renaissance's reputation. According to Mr. Barca, the quality of Renaissance's wine is "good" and at the time plaintiff began licensing the mark to Renaissance, Renaissance's winemaker was Karl Werner, a "world famous" winemaker.
>
> Mr. Barca's conclusory statements as to the existence of quality controls is insufficient to create a triable issue of fact on the issue of naked licensing. While Mr. Barca's tastings perhaps demonstrate a minimal effort to monitor quality, Mr. Barca fails

to state when, how often, and under what circumstances he tastes the wine. Mr. Barca's reliance on the reputation of the winemaker is no longer justified as he is deceased. Mr. Barca has not provided any information concerning the successor winemaker(s). While Renaissance's attorney, Mr. Goldman, testified that Renaissance "strive[s] extremely hard to have the highest possible standards," he has no knowledge of the quality control procedures utilized by Renaissance with regard to testing wine. Moreover, according to Renaissance, Mr. Barca never "had any involvement whatsoever regarding the quality of the wine and maintaining it at any level." [Barcamerica] has failed to demonstrate any knowledge of or reliance on the actual quality controls used by Renaissance, nor has it demonstrated any ongoing effort to monitor quality.

[Barcamerica] and Renaissance did not and do not have the type of close working relationship required to establish adequate quality control in the absence of a formal agreement. *See, e.g., Taco Cabana Int'l, Inc. v. Two Pesos, Inc.*, 932 F.2d 1113 1121 (5th Cir. 1991) (licensor and licensee enjoyed close working relationship for eight years). No such familiarity or close working relationship ever existed between [Barcamerica] and Renaissance. Both the terms of the licensing agreements and the manner in which they were carried out show that [Barcamerica] engaged in naked licensing of the "Leonardo Da Vinci" mark. Accordingly, [Barcamerica] is estopped from asserting any rights in the mark.

Barcamerica, No. CV–98–00206–FCD, at 9–13 (E.D.Cal. filed Apr.13, 2000).

B

On appeal, Barcamerica does not seriously contest any of the foregoing. Instead, it argues essentially that because Renaissance makes good wine, the public is not deceived by Renaissance's use of the "Da Vinci" mark, and thus, that the license was legally acceptable. This novel rationale, however, is faulty. Whether Renaissance's wine was objectively "good" or "bad" is simply irrelevant. What matters is that Barcamerica played no meaningful role in holding the wine to a standard of quality-good, bad, or otherwise. As McCarthy explains,

It is important to keep in mind that "quality control" does not necessarily mean that the licensed goods or services must be of "high" quality, but merely of equal quality, whether that quality is high, low or middle. *The point is that customers are entitled to assume that the nature and quality of goods and services sold under the mark at all licensed outlets will be consistent and predictable.*

McCarthy § 18:55, at 18–94 (emphasis added). And "it is well established that where a trademark owner engages in naked licensing, without any control over the quality of goods produced by the licensee, such a practice is inherently deceptive and constitutes abandonment of any rights to the trademark by the licensor." *First Interstate Bancorp v. Stenquist*, 16 U.S.P.Q.2d 1704, 1706, 1990 WL 300321 (N.D.Cal.1990).

Certainly, "[i]t is difficult, if not impossible to define in the abstract exactly how much control and inspection is needed to satisfy the requirement of quality control over trademark licensees." McCarthy, § 18:55, at 18–94. And we recognize that "[t]he standard of quality control and the degree of necessary inspection and policing by the licensor will vary with the wide range of licensing situations in use in the modern marketplace." *Id.*, at 18–95. But in this case we deal with a relatively simple product: wine. Wine, of course, is bottled by season. Thus, at the very least, one might have expected Barca to sample (or to have some designated wine connoisseur sample) on an annual basis, in some organized way, some adequate number of bottles of the Renaissance wines which were to bear Barcamerica's mark to ensure that they were of sufficient quality to be called "Da Vinci." But Barca did not make even this minimal effort.

C

We therefore agree with Judge Damrell, and hold that Barcamerica engaged in naked licensing of its "Leonardo Da Vinci" mark—and that by so doing, Barcamerica forfeited its rights in the mark. We also agree that cancellation of Barcamerica's registration of the mark was appropriate.

* * *

SANDS, TAYLOR & WOOD COMPANY V. THE QUAKER OATS COMPANY

978 F.2d 947 (7th Cir. 1992).

CUDAHY, CIRCUIT JUDGE.

Sands, Taylor & Wood Company (STW) brought this action against The Quaker Oats Company (Quaker) for federal trademark infringement and related state-law claims, alleging that Quaker's use of the words "Thirst Aid" in its advertising slogan "Gatorade is Thirst Aid" infringed STW's registered trademark for THIRST-AID. The district court agreed, and entered judgment for STW in the amount of $42,629,399.09, including prejudgment interest and attorney's fees. The court also permanently enjoined Quaker from using the words "Thirst Aid." Not surprisingly, Quaker appeals.

I.

Plaintiff STW is a small, Vermont-based company that for the past 180 years has sold bagged flour at retail under the brand name "King Arthur Flour." In 1973, STW acquired Joseph Middleby, Jr., Inc. (Middleby), a manufacturer of soft drinks, soda fountain syrups and ice cream toppings. STW thereby became the owner of three trademarks registered to Middleby: (1) THIRST-AID "First Aid for Your Thirst," issued October 10, 1950, for use on "nonalcoholic maltless beverages, sold as soft drinks, and syrups therefor"; (2) THIRST-AID, issued August 26, 1952, for use on various ice cream toppings as well as "fruits and sauces used in the making of ice cream"; and (3) THIRST-AID, issued March 24, 1953, for use on "soda fountain syrups used in the preparation of maltless soft drinks."

From 1921 to 1973, Middleby used the THIRST-AID mark on a wide variety of beverage products and syrups that it sold to soda fountains, ice cream parlors and food service outlets. Middleby also supplied its THIRST-AID customers with various items displaying the name THIRST-AID, including streamers, banners, glasses and pitchers, for in-store advertising and promotion. STW continued these activities after it acquired Middleby, which it operated as a wholly-owned subsidiary.

In the late 1970s sales of THIRST-AID soft drinks declined as consumers turned increasingly to bottles and cans rather than soda fountains and ice cream parlors for their soft drinks. * * * In the spring of 1980, Pet, Inc. (Pet) negotiated with STW a nationwide license to use the name THIRST-AID on a new isotonic beverage intended to compete with the very popular Gatorade. Pet began test-marketing the product in twenty stores in Columbia, South Carolina in June of 1980. * * * Nevertheless, for reasons that are not important here, Pet decided not to enter the market with the new product and in June of 1981 its license to use the name THIRST-AID expired.

In December of 1981, STW sold the assets of Middleby to L. Karp & Sons (Karp), a distributor of bakery products. As part of the sale, STW assigned to Karp all of the registered THIRST-AID trademarks. STW obtained a simultaneous exclusive license back for retail use of the trademark on certain "Products" defined as "jams, jellies, pie fillings" and various other bakery supplies.

In August of 1983, Stokely, the manufacturer of Gatorade, was acquired by Quaker. Shortly thereafter, Quaker solicited proposals for a new advertising campaign intended to educate consumers about Gatorade's ability to quench thirst and replace fluids and minerals lost by the human body through strenuous exercise. One of the candidates was the slogan "Gatorade is Thirst Aid for That Deep Down Body Thirst."

[Lannin, Quaker's in-house counsel, belatedly performed a trademark search, and discovered Middleby's three THIRST-AID registrations and the sale of the marks to Karp. At Lannin's request, a paralegal telephoned Karp and was told that the company was not marketing any products under that name. However, once Quaker began running its "Gatorade is Thirst Aid" commercials, both Karp and STW accused Quaker of infringing their marks.]

* * *

Quaker did not hear from either Karp or STW again until the commencement of this litigation. In the interim, STW entered into a written agreement with Karp under which STW paid Karp $1 for an assignment of Karp's trademark registrations. Sands filed suit one week later, alleging that the slogan "Gatorade is Thirst Aid for That Deep Down Body Thirst" infringed its registrations and constituted unfair competition under the Lanham Act, 15 U.S.C. §§ 1051 et seq., state common law and various state statutes. * * *

* * *

III.

Because trademark rights derive from the use of a mark in commerce and not from mere registration of the mark, the owner of a mark will lose his exclusive rights if he fails actually to use it. 15 U.S.C. § 1127. A mark is deemed to be thus "abandoned" when "its use has been discontinued with intent not to resume such use." *Id.* Two years of nonuse create a prima facie case of abandonment, which may be rebutted by "evidence explaining the nonuse or demonstrating the lack of an intent not to resume use." *Roulo v. Russ Berrie & Co.*, 886 F.2d 931, 938 (7th Cir.1989). Quaker argues that the district court erred in finding that STW or its predecessors had not abandoned through nonuse the THIRST-AID mark for a beverage sold at retail. Alternatively, Quaker contends that Karp abandoned the THIRST-AID marks through its 1984 assignment of those marks to STW.

A. Nonuse

1. Middleby Abandoned the Mark

Quaker contends that STW has no registration rights covering the use of THIRST-AID on a beverage because the trademark THIRST-AID "First Aid for Your Thirst," the only mark registered for use on "beverages" as opposed to "beverage syrups," has not been used since 1949. We reject this argument for two reasons. First, the fact that STW and its predecessors have not used the entire slogan THIRST-AID "First Aid for Your Thirst" since 1949 does not necessarily mean that the registration has been abandoned. "[M]inor changes in a mark which do not change the basic, overall commercial impression created on buyers will not constitute any abandonment." 1 MCCARTHY, *supra* § 17:10, at 787. So long as the owner continues use of the "key element" of the registered mark, courts generally will not find abandonment. *Id.* Further, "the dropping of a non-essential word from a mark" has been held not to constitute abandonment. *Id.*; *see, e.g.*, *Puritan Sportswear Corp. v. Shure*, 307 F.Supp. 377 (W.D.Pa.1969) (change from PURITAN SPORTSWEAR, THE CHOICE OF ALL AMERICANS to PURITAN not abandonment). Certainly, the key element of what Quaker calls the "beverage slogan registration" is the term THIRST-AID. In fact, the trademark registration for the slogan explicitly states that no claim of ownership is made as to the words "First Aid for Your Thirst" apart from the mark as it appears in the registration. * * * Second, even if we were to find that Middleby had abandoned the mark THIRST-AID "First Aid for Your Thirst," we would not conclude that STW therefore had no registration rights covering the use of THIRST-AID on beverages. We do not see the wide gulf between a trademark for beverage syrups and a trademark for beverages, on which Quaker relies. * * *

2. *Intent Not to Resume Use*

Alternatively, Quaker argues that even if Middleby had not abandoned the "beverage slogan registration," any right to use the THIRST-AID marks for a beverage was abandoned by Karp, which acquired the marks in December 1981. * * * While it is true that Karp did not use THIRST-AID for a beverage, it is also the case that, approximately 1½ years after acquiring the marks, Karp hired a consultant for the specific purpose of attempting to license THIRST-AID for use on a beverage. "[T]he owner of the trademark need only produce evidence to rebut the presumption [of abandonment] while the ultimate burden of persuasion rests on the defendant." *Roulo v. Russ Berrie & Co., Inc.*, 886 F.2d 931, 938 (7th Cir. 1989). The district court found that STW's efforts to license THIRST-AID for use on a soft drink during this period were sufficient evidence of intent to resume use to rebut a prima facie case of abandonment. * * * Karp did not abandon the right to use THIRST-AID for a beverage.

B. *Abandonment Through Assignment in Gross*

As the district court noted, "[t]he transfer of a trademark apart from the good will of the business which it represents is an invalid 'naked' or 'in gross' assignment," which passes no rights to the assignee. Quaker contends that the court erred in concluding that the September 1984 assignment of the THIRST-AID trademarks from Karp to STW was not an invalid assignment in gross. Quaker recognizes that transfer of a mark need not be accompanied by the transfer of any physical or tangible assets in order to be valid. "All that is necessary is the transfer of the goodwill to which the mark pertains." *Visa, U.S.A., Inc. v. Birmingham Trust Nat'l Bank*, 696 F.2d 1371, 1377 (Fed.Cir.1982). According to Quaker, however, any good will associated with the THIRST-AID mark existed only in the institutional market, and therefore could not support the transfer of the right to use THIRST-AID on a beverage at retail. We disagree with both Quaker's characterization of the facts and its conclusion.

Quaker's argument that any good will associated with THIRST-AID could exist only in the institutional market simply ignores STW's evidence, accepted by the district court, that from 1921 until at least 1976 the THIRST-AID mark was used in retail, in-store advertising and promotional materials provided to soda fountains that sold beverages made from THIRST-AID syrups. As the district court found, this use of the mark, as well as its use on the Pet product, created good will associated with THIRST-AID at the retail level. This good will, built up over more than fifty years, could not dissipate during the three and one-half years between the Pet test-market and the assignment of the marks from Karp to STW.

The 1981 agreement between STW and Karp, the validity of which Quaker does not challenge, assigned to Karp "all of [STW's] right, title, ownership and interest in and to the Trademarks *and all goodwill appurtenant thereto*." (Emphasis added.) The agreement then licensed back to STW "the exclusive right and license" to use the marks in connection with certain defined "Products" in the retail trade only. None of the defined products were beverages or beverage-related. Thus, as the district court correctly found, the 1981 agreement conferred on Karp "extremely broad rights of ownership," including the exclusive right to use THIRST-AID on beverages and the good will associated with that use.

Under the 1984 agreement between STW and Karp, Karp assigned to STW "all right, title and interest in and to the trademark and the said registrations including the continued exclusive right to use the trademark THIRST-AID in the retail trade field only, together with any goodwill of the business symbolized by the trademark. . . ." Karp retained the "exclusive right and license in perpetuity to use the trademark THIRST-AID in connection with the manufacture, marketing, sale and other commercialization of the Products in institutional trade only and not in retail trade." Thus, the 1984 agreement transferred back to STW the exclusive right to use THIRST-AID on a beverage, together with the good will associated with that use. As we have already noted, that good will existed at the retail as well as at the institutional level, and it was not dissipated during the three and one-half years between the Pet test-market and the 1984 assignment. The district court did not err in finding that the assignment from Karp to STW was valid.

* * *

NOTES

1. To avoid an assignment in gross, the assigned mark should be continuously used, and should be assigned in combination with any goodwill associated with the mark. *See generally Money Store v. Harriscorp. Finance, Inc.*, 689 F.2d 666, 675 (7th Cir. 1982). The Lanham Act expressly requires any assignment of a registered mark (or marks with a pending application) to be

in writing, and to include a transfer of the associated goodwill. 15 U.S.C. § 1060.

2. The Los Angeles Dodgers brought an infringement claim challenging the use of "The Brooklyn Dodger" as the name of a restaurant in Brooklyn, New York. The restaurant opened in 1988. Given that the "Brooklyn Dodgers" baseball team left Brooklyn for Los Angeles in 1958, are the Los Angeles Dodgers entitled to prevent the restaurant from using this name? Would it matter that the Los Angeles Dodgers licensed t-shirts and advertisements bearing the "Brooklyn Dodgers" name and logo beginning in 1981? *See Major League Baseball Properties, Inc. v. Sed Non Olet Denarius, Ltd.*, 817 F.Supp. 1103 (S.D.N.Y. 1993), *vacated pursuant to settlement*, 859 F.Supp. 80 (S.D.N.Y. 1994).

3. Under the Lanham Act's definition of "abandonment," a rebuttable presumption of abandonment arises after 3 years of non-use. 15 U.S.C. § 1127. (*Sands, Taylor & Woods* references an earlier version of the statute, when the presumption arose after only 2 years.). The trademark owner can rebut this presumption with proof of intent to resume use or significant efforts to license the mark during the period of non-use. No such presumption exists at common law.

4. In some cases, a trademark owner can rebut a claim of abandonment due to non-use by showing that it has merely made minor changes in the mark over time, and that the later version makes the same overall commercial impression. This is known as "tacking." *See Hana Financial, Inc. v. Hana Bank*, 574 U.S. 418 (2015).

5. If a mark is deemed abandoned, the mark becomes available for other parties to adopt as their own. (Recall the *Galt House* case from Chapter 3.) Could this lead to consumer confusion? Is confusion more likely where abandonment is caused by naked licensing or an assignment in gross, or where it arises from cessation of use?

6. In *Mission Product Holdings, Inc. v. Tempnology, LLC*, 139 S.Ct. 1652 (2019), the Supreme Court held that if a trademark licensor files for Chapter 11 bankruptcy and opts to reject the license agreement, the licensee can either continue using the mark pursuant to the terms of the license or treat the rejection as a breach of contract and sue for damages.

7. In *Perry v. H. J. Heinz Co. Brands, L.L.C.*, 994 F.3d 466, 469 (5th Cir. 2021), a small business owner sold a small amount of mayonnaise-ketchup blend under the name Metchup and "testified that he hoped to sell more," the court found that "a finder of fact should determine whether his incontestable trademark should be deemed abandoned."

C. COMPARATIVE ADVERTISING

R.G. SMITH V. CHANEL, INC.

402 F.2d 562 (9th Cir. 1968).

BROWNING, CIRCUIT JUDGE:

Appellant R. G. Smith, doing business as Ta'Ron, Inc., advertised a fragrance called "Second Chance" as a duplicate of appellees' "Chanel No. 5," at a fraction of the latter's price. Appellees were granted a preliminary injunction prohibiting any reference to Chanel No. 5 in the promotion or sale of appellants' product. This appeal followed.

The action rests upon a single advertisement published in "Specialty Salesmen," a trade journal directed to wholesale purchasers. The advertisement offered "The Ta'Ron Line of Perfumes" for sale. It gave the seller's address as "Ta'Ron Inc., 26 Harbor Cove, Mill Valley, Calif." It stated that the Ta'Ron perfumes "duplicate 100% Perfect the exact scent of the world's finest and most expensive perfumes and colognes at prices that will zoom sales to volumes you have never before experienced." It repeated the claim of exact duplication in a variety of forms.

The advertisement suggested that a "Blindfold Test" be used "on skeptical prospects," challenging them to detect any difference between a well known fragrance and the Ta'Ron "duplicate." One suggested challenge was, "We dare you to try to detect any difference between Chanel #5 (25.00) and Ta'Ron's 2nd Chance $7.00."

In an order blank printed as part of the advertisement each Ta'Ron fragrance was listed with the name of the well known fragrance which it purportedly duplicated immediately beneath. Below "Second Chance" appeared "*(Chanel #5)." The asterisk referred to a statement at the bottom of the form reading "Registered Trade Name of Original Fragrance House."

Appellees conceded below and concede here that appellants "have the right to copy, if they can, the unpatented formula of appellees' product."[3] Moreover, for the purposes of these proceedings, appellees assume that "the products manufactured and advertised by (appellants) are in fact equivalents of those products manufactured by appellees." Finally, appellees disclaim any contention that the packaging or labeling of appellants' "Second Chance" is misleading or confusing.[4]

---

[3] *Sears, Roebuck & Co. v. Stiffel Co.*, 376 U.S. 225, 231–233 (1964); *Compco Corp. v. Day-Brite Lighting, Inc.*, 376 U.S. 234, 237–238 (1964).

[4] Appellants' product was packaged differently from appellees', and the only words appearing on the outside of appellants' packages were "Second Chance Perfume by Ta'Ron." The same words appeared on the front of appellants' bottles; the words "Ta'Ron trademark by International Fragrances, Inc., of Dallas and New York" appeared on the back.

I

The principal question presented on this record is whether one who has copied an unpatented product sold under a trademark may use the trademark in his advertising to identify the product he has copied. We hold that he may, and that such advertising may not be enjoined under either the Lanham Act, 15 U.S.C. 1125(a), or the common law of unfair competition, so long as it does not contain misrepresentations or create a reasonable likelihood that purchasers will be confused as to the source, identity, or sponsorship of the advertiser's product.

* * *

In *Saxlehner v. Wagner*, 216 U.S. 375 (1910), the copied product was a "bitter water" drawn from certain privately owned natural springs. The plaintiff sold the natural water under the name "Hunyadi Janos," a valid trademark. The defendant was enjoined from using plaintiff's trademark to designate defendant's "artificial" water, but was permitted to use it to identify plaintiff's natural water as the product which defendant was copying.

Justice Holmes wrote:

> We see no reason for disturbing the finding of the courts below that there was no unfair competition and no fraud. The real intent of the plaintiff's bill, it seems to us, is to extend the monopoly of such trademark or tradename as she may have to a monopoly of her type of bitter water, by preventing manufacturers from telling the public in a way that will be understood, what they are copying and trying to sell. But the plaintiff has no patent for the water, and the defendants have a right to reproduce it as nearly as they can. They have a right to tell the public what they are doing, and to get whatever share they can in the popularity of the water by advertising that they are trying to make the same article, and think that they succeed. If they do not convey, but, on the contrary, exclude, the notion that they are selling the plaintiff's goods, it is a strong proposition that when the article has a well-known name they have not the right to explain by that name what they imitate. By doing so, they are not trying to get the good will of the name, but the good will of the goods.

216 U.S. at 380–381.

In *Viavi Co. v. Vimedia Co.*, 245 F. 289 (8th Cir. 1917), plaintiff sold unpatented proprietary medicinal preparations under the registered trademark "Viavi," and local sellers of defendant's medicinal preparations represented to prospective purchasers that Vimedia products "were the same or as good as Viavi" preparations. The court held, "in the absence of such a monopoly as a patent confers, any persons may reproduce the articles, if they can, and may sell them under the representation that they are the same article, if they exclude the notion that they are the plaintiff's goods." 245 F. at 292.

* * * The Lanham Act does not prohibit a commercial rival's truthfully denominating his goods a copy of a design in the public domain, though he uses the name of the designer to do so. Indeed it is difficult to see any other means that might be employed to inform the consuming public of the true origin of the design.

* * *

We have found no holdings by federal or California appellate courts contrary to the rule of these three cases. Moreover, the principle for which they stand—that use of another's trademark to identify the trademark owner's product in comparative advertising is not prohibited by either statutory or common law, absent misrepresentation regarding the products or confusion as to their source or sponsorship—is also generally approved by secondary authorities.

* * *

Preservation of the trademark as a means of identifying the trademark owner's products, implemented both by the Lanham Act and the common law, serves an important public purpose. It makes effective competition possible in a complex, impersonal marketplace by providing a means through which the consumer can identify products which please him and reward the producer with continued patronage. Without some such method of product identification, informed consumer choice, and hence meaningful competition in quality, could not exist.

On the other hand, it has been suggested that protection of trademark values other than source identification would create serious anti-competitive consequences with little compensating public benefit. This is said to be true for the following reasons.

The object of much modern advertising is "to impregnate the atmosphere of the market with the drawing power of a congenial symbol." *Mishawaka Rubber & Woolen Mfg. Co. v. S. S. Kresge Co.*, 316 U.S. 203, 205 (1942), rather than to communicate information as to quality or price. The primary value of the modern trademark lies in the "conditioned reflex developed in the buyer by imaginative or often purely monotonous selling of the mark itself." Derring, *Trademarks on Noncompetitive Products*, 36 OR.L.REV. 1, 2 (1956). To the extent that advertising of this type succeeds, it is suggested, the trademark is endowed with sales appeal independent of the quality or price of the product to which it is attached; economically irrational elements are introduced into consumer choices; and the trademark owner is insulated from the normal pressures of price and quality competition. In consequence the competitive system fails to perform its function of allocating available resources efficiently.

Moreover, the economically irrelevant appeal of highly publicized trademarks is thought to constitute a barrier to the entry of new competition into the market. "The presence of irrational consumer allegiances may constitute an effective barrier to entry. Consumer allegiances built over the years with intensive advertising, trademarks, trade names, copyrights and so forth extend substantial protection to firms already in the market. In some markets this barrier to entry may be insuperable." Papandreou, *The Economic Effects of Trademarks*, 44 CALIF.L.REV. 503, 508–09 (1956). High barriers to entry tend, in turn, to produce "high excess profits and monopolistic output restriction" and "probably * * * high and possibly excessive costs of sales promotion." J. BAIN, BARRIERS TO NEW COMPETITION 203 (1955).

* * *

Against these considerations, two principal arguments are made for protection of trademark values other than source identification.

The first of these, as stated in the findings of the district court, is that the creation of the other values inherent in the trademark require "the expenditure of great effort, skill and ability," and that the competitor should not be permitted "to take a free ride" on the trademark owner's "widespread goodwill and reputation."

A large expenditure of money does not in itself create legally protectable rights. Appellees are not entitled to monopolize the public's desire for the unpatented product, even though they themselves created that desire at great effort and expense. As we have noted, the most effective way (and in some cases the only practical way) in which others may compete in satisfying the demand for the product is to produce it and tell the public they have done so, and if they could be barred from this effort appellees would have found a way to acquire a practical monopoly in the unpatented product to which they are not legally entitled.

Disapproval of the copyist's opportunism may be an understandable first reaction, "but this initial response to the problem has been curbed in deference to the greater public good." *American Safety Table Co. v. Schreiber*, 269 F.2d at 272. By taking his "free ride," the copyist, albeit unintentionally, serves an important public interest by offering comparable goods at lower prices. On the other hand, the trademark owner, perhaps equally without design, sacrifices public to personal interests by seeking immunity from the rigors of competition.

Moreover, appellees' reputation is not directly at stake. Appellants' advertisement makes it clear that the product they offer is their own. If it proves to be inferior, they, not appellees, will bear the burden of consumer disapproval.[25]

The second major argument for extended trademark protection is that even in the absence of confusion as to source, use of the trademark of another "creates a serious threat to the uniqueness and distinctiveness" of the trademark, and "if continued would create a risk of making a generic or descriptive term of the words" of which the trademark is composed.

The contention has little weight in the context of this case. Appellants do not use appellees' trademark as a generic term. They employ it only to describe appellees' product, not to identify their own. They do not label their product "Ta'Ron's Chanel No. 5," as they might if appellees' trademark had come to be the common name for the product to which it is applied. Appellants' use does not challenge the distinctiveness of appellees' trademark, or appellees' exclusive right to employ that trademark to indicate source or sponsorship. For reasons already discussed, we think appellees are entitled to no more. * * *

Reversed and remanded for further proceedings.

NOTE

Are comparative advertising and nominative fair use based on the same underlying principle? If so, which offers the broader defense? Are they subject to comparable limitations?

D. FIRST SALE

Under the first sale principle, the purchaser of lawfully made trademarked goods is generally free to display, offer and sell those goods under their original trademark. This principle does not apply, however, under circumstances where the use of the mark would mislead consumers as to the origin of the goods or the affiliation of the seller.

CHAMPION SPARK PLUG CO. V. SANDERS

331 U.S. 125, 67 S.Ct. 1136 (1947).

MR. JUSTICE DOUGLAS delivered the opinion of the Court.

Petitioner is a manufacturer of spark plugs which it sells under the trade mark "Champion." Respondents collect the used plugs, repair and recondition them, and resell them. Respondents retain the word "Champion" on the repaired or reconditioned plugs. The outside box or carton in which the plugs are packed has stamped on it the word

---

[25] In addition, if appellants' specific claims of equivalence are false, appellees may have a remedy under 43(a) of the Lanham Act, 15 U.S.C. 1125(a) (1964), which provides a civil remedy to a person injured by "any false description or representation, including words or other symbols * * *[,]" of goods in interstate commerce. A common-law remedy may also be available. * * *

"Champion," together with the letter and figure denoting the particular style or type. They also have printed on them "Perfect Process Spark Plugs Guaranteed Dependable" and "Perfect Process Renewed Spark Plugs." Each carton contains smaller boxes in which the plugs are individually packed. These inside boxes also carry legends indicating that the plug has been renewed. But respondent company's business name or address is not printed on the cartons. It supplies customers with petitioner's charts containing recommendations for the use of Champion plugs. On each individual plug is stamped in small letters, blue on black, the word "Renewed," which at times is almost illegible.

Petitioner brought this suit in the District Court, charging infringement of its trade mark and unfair competition. The District Court found that respondents had infringed the trade mark. It enjoined them from offering or selling any of petitioner's plugs which had been repaired or reconditioned unless (a) the trade mark and type and style marks were removed, (b) the plugs were repainted with a durable grey, brown, orange, or green paint, (c) the word "Repaired" was stamped into the plug in letters of such size and depth as to retain enough white paint to display distinctly each letter of the word, (d) the cartons in which the plugs were packed carried a legend indicating that they contained used spark plugs originally made by petitioner and repaired and made fit for use up to 10,000 miles by respondent company.[2] The District Court denied an accounting.

The Circuit Court of Appeals * * * modified the decree in the following respects: (a) it eliminated the provision requiring the trade mark and type and style marks to be removed from the repaired or reconditioned plugs; (b) it substituted for the requirement that the word "Repaired" be stamped into the plug, etc., a provision that the word "Repaired" or "Used" be stamped and baked on the plug by an electrical hot press in a contrasting color so as to be clearly and distinctly visible, the plug having been completely covered by permanent aluminum paint or other paint or lacquer; and (c) it eliminated the provision specifying the precise legend to be printed on the cartons and substituted therefore a more general one.[3] * * *

There is no challenge here to the findings as to the misleading character of the merchandising methods employed by respondents, nor to the conclusion that they have not only infringed petitioner's trade mark

[2] The prescribed legend read: "Used spark plug(s) originally made by Champion Spark Plug Company repaired and made fit for use up to 10,000 miles by Perfect Recondition Spark Plug Co., 1133 Bedford Avenue, Brooklyn, N.Y." The decree also provided: "the name and address of the defendants to be larger and more prominent than the legend itself, and the name of plaintiff may be in slightly larger type than the rest of the body of the legend."

[3] "The decree shall permit the defendants to state on cartons and containers, selling and advertising material, business records, correspondence and other papers, when published, the original make and type numbers provided it is made clear that any plug referred to therein is used and reconditioned by the defendants, and that such material contains the name and address of defendants."

but have also engaged in unfair competition. The controversy here relates to the adequacy of the relief granted, particularly the refusal of the Circuit Court of Appeals to require respondents to remove the word "Champion" from the repaired or reconditioned plugs which they resell.

* * *

We are dealing here with second-hand goods. The spark plugs, though used, are nevertheless Champion plugs and not those of another make. There is evidence to support what one would suspect, that a used spark plug which has been repaired or reconditioned does not measure up to the specifications of a new one. But the same would be true of a second-hand Ford or Chevrolet car. And we would not suppose that one could be enjoined from selling a car whose valves had been reground and whose piston rings had been replaced unless he removed the name Ford or Chevrolet. *Prestonettes, Inc. v. Coty*, 264 U.S. 359 (1924), was a case where toilet powders had as one of their ingredients a powder covered by a trade mark and where perfumes which were trade marked were rebottled and sold in smaller bottles. The Court sustained a decree denying an injunction where the prescribed labels told the truth. Mr. Justice Holmes stated, "A trade-mark only gives the right to prohibit the use of it so far as to protect the owner's good will against the sale of another's product as his. * * * When the mark is used in a way that does not deceive the public we see no such sanctity in the word as to prevent its being used to tell the truth. It is not taboo." 264 U.S. at page 368.

Cases may be imagined where the reconditioning or repair would be so extensive or so basic that it would be a misnomer to call the article by its original name, even though the words "used" or "repaired" were added. But no such practice is involved here. The repair or reconditioning of the plugs does not give them a new design. It is no more than a restoration, so far as possible, of their original condition. * * * And there is evidence that the reconditioned plugs are inferior so far as heat range and other qualities are concerned. But inferiority is expected in most second-hand articles. Indeed, they generally cost the customer less. That is the case here. Inferiority is immaterial so long as the article is clearly and distinctively sold as repaired or reconditioned rather than as new. The result is, of course, that the second-hand dealer gets some advantage from the trade mark. But under the rule of *Prestonettes, Inc. v. Coty, supra,* that is wholly permissible so long as the manufacturer is not identified with the inferior qualities of the product resulting from wear and tear or the reconditioning by the dealer. Full disclosure gives the manufacturer all the protection to which he is entitled.

The decree as shaped by the Circuit Court of Appeals is fashioned to serve the requirements of full disclosure. * * * We cannot say that the conduct of respondents in this case, or the nature of the article involved and the characteristics of the merchandising methods used to sell it, called for more stringent controls than the Circuit Court of Appeals provided. * * *

Affirmed.

NOTES

1. If a seller represents that goods are new when in fact they are used or reconditioned, in addition to incurring liability for trademark infringement, for what other cause of action might the seller be liable?

2. Can an independent retailer advertise that it sells new or used trademarked goods by making use of the manufacturer's trademark? *Scott Fetzer Co. v. House of Vacuums Inc.*, 381 F.3d 477 (5th Cir. 2004). Does it matter if the claim is for dilution rather than infringement? *See Tiffany (N.J.), Inc. v. eBay, Inc.*, 600 F.3d 93 (2d Cir. 2010).

3. Gray market goods are trademarked products which the trademark owner has authorized exclusively for foreign sale, but which are imported and sold in the United States without the trademark owner's consent. (Thus, they differ from counterfeit goods, which are goods to which a trademark has been affixed without the authority of the trademark owner.) Often, these unauthorized imports are priced more cheaply than the goods sold by authorized retailers. Should the importation and sale of such goods constitute trademark infringement? Would if matter if the imported goods are "materially different" from their domestic counterparts?

E. FIRST AMENDMENT

MATTEL, INC. V. MCA RECORDS, INC.

296 F.3d 894 (9th Cir. 2002).

KOZINSKI, CIRCUIT JUDGE:

If this were a sci-fi melodrama, it might be called Speech-Zilla meets Trademark Kong.

I

Barbie was born in Germany in the 1950s as an adult collector's item. Over the years, Mattel transformed her from a doll that resembled a "German street walker," as she originally appeared, into a glamorous, long-legged blonde. Barbie has been labeled both the ideal American woman and a bimbo. She has survived attacks both psychic (from feminists critical of her fictitious figure) and physical (more than 500 professional makeovers). She remains a symbol of American girlhood, a public figure who graces the aisles of toy stores throughout the country and beyond. With Barbie, Mattel created not just a toy but a cultural icon.

With fame often comes unwanted attention. Aqua is a Danish band that has, as yet, only dreamed of attaining Barbie-like status. In 1997, Aqua produced the song Barbie Girl on the album *Aquarium*. In the song, one bandmember impersonates Barbie, singing in a high-pitched, doll-like voice; another bandmember, calling himself Ken, entices Barbie to "go party." (The lyrics are in the Appendix.) Barbie Girl singles sold well and, to Mattel's dismay, the song made it onto Top 40 music charts.

Mattel brought this lawsuit against the music companies who produced, marketed and sold Barbie Girl: MCA Records, Inc., Universal Music International Ltd., Universal Music A/S, Universal Music & Video Distribution, Inc. and MCA Music Scandinavia AB (collectively, "MCA"). * * * [The district court granted MCA's motion for summary judgment on Mattel's claims for trademark infringement and dilution.]

Mattel appeals the district court's ruling that Barbie Girl is a parody of Barbie and a nominative fair use; that MCA's use of the term Barbie is not likely to confuse consumers as to Mattel's affiliation with Barbie Girl or dilute the Barbie mark * * *.

III

* * *

Our likelihood-of-confusion test generally strikes a comfortable balance between the trademark owner's property rights and the public's expressive interests. But when a trademark owner asserts a right to control how we express ourselves—when we'd find it difficult to describe the product any other way (as in the case of aspirin), or when the mark (like Rolls Royce) has taken on an expressive meaning apart from its source-identifying function—applying the traditional test fails to account for the full weight of the public's interest in free expression.

The First Amendment may offer little protection for a competitor who labels its commercial good with a confusingly similar mark, but "[t]rademark rights do not entitle the owner to quash an unauthorized use of the mark by another who is communicating ideas or expressing points of view." *L.L. Bean, Inc. v. Drake Publishers, Inc.*, 811 F.2d 26, 29 (1st Cir.1987). Were we to ignore the expressive value that some marks assume, trademark rights would grow to encroach upon the zone protected by the First Amendment. Simply put, the trademark owner does not have the right to control public discourse whenever the public imbues his mark with a meaning beyond its source-identifying function.

There is no doubt that MCA uses Mattel's mark: Barbie is one half of Barbie Girl. But Barbie Girl is the title of a song about Barbie and Ken, a reference that—at least today—can only be to Mattel's famous couple. We expect a title to describe the underlying work, not to identify the producer, and Barbie Girl does just that.

The Barbie Girl title presages a song about Barbie, or at least a girl like Barbie. The title conveys a message to consumers about what they can expect to discover in the song itself; it's a quick glimpse of Aqua's take on their own song. The lyrics confirm this: The female singer, who calls herself Barbie, is "a Barbie girl, in [her] Barbie world." She tells her male counterpart (named Ken), "Life in plastic, it's fantastic. You can brush my hair, undress me everywhere/Imagination, life is your creation." And off they go to "party." The song pokes fun at Barbie and the values that Aqua contends she represents. The female singer explains, "I'm a blond bimbo girl, in a fantasy world/Dress me up, make it tight, I'm your dolly."

The song does not rely on the Barbie mark to poke fun at another subject but targets Barbie herself. *See Dr. Seuss Ents., L.P. v. Penguin Books USA, Inc.,* 109 F.3d 1394, 1400 (9th Cir.1997). This case is therefore distinguishable from *Dr. Seuss,* where we held that the book *The Cat NOT in the Hat!* borrowed Dr. Seuss's trademarks and lyrics to get attention rather than to mock *The Cat in the Hat!* The defendant's use of the Dr. Seuss trademarks and copyrighted works [for a satirical commentary on O.J. Simpson's murder trial] had "no critical bearing on the substance or style of" *The Cat in the Hat!,* and therefore could not claim First Amendment protection. *Dr. Seuss* recognized that, where an artistic work targets the original and does not merely borrow another's property to get attention, First Amendment interests weigh more heavily in the balance.

The Second Circuit has held that "in general the [Lanham] Act should be construed to apply to artistic works only where the public interest in avoiding consumer confusion outweighs the public interest in free expression." *Rogers v. Grimaldi,* 875 F.2d 994, 999 (2d Cir.1989). *Rogers* considered a challenge by the actress Ginger Rogers to the film *Ginger and Fred.* The movie told the story of two Italian cabaret performers who made a living by imitating Ginger Rogers and Fred Astaire. Rogers argued that the film's title created the false impression that she was associated with it.

At first glance, Rogers certainly had a point. Ginger was her name, and Fred was her dancing partner. If a pair of dancing shoes had been labeled Ginger and Fred, a dancer might have suspected that Rogers was associated with the shoes (or at least one of them), just as Michael Jordan has endorsed Nike sneakers that claim to make you fly through the air. But *Ginger and Fred* was not a brand of shoe; it was the title of a movie and, for the reasons explained by the Second Circuit, deserved to be treated differently.

A title is designed to catch the eye and to promote the value of the underlying work. Consumers expect a title to communicate a message about the book or movie, but they do not expect it to identify the publisher or producer. If we see a painting titled "Campbell's Chicken Noodle Soup," we're unlikely to believe that Campbell's has branched into the art business. Nor, upon hearing Janis Joplin croon "Oh Lord, won't you buy me a Mercedes-Benz?," would we suspect that she and the carmaker had entered into a joint venture. A title tells us something about the underlying work but seldom speaks to its origin:

> Though consumers frequently look to the title of a work to determine what it is about, they do not regard titles of artistic works in the same way as the names of ordinary commercial products. Since consumers expect an ordinary product to be what the name says it is, we apply the Lanham Act with some rigor to prohibit names that misdescribe such goods. But most consumers are well aware that they cannot judge a book solely by its title any more than by its cover.

Rogers, 875 F.2d at 1000 (citations omitted).

Rogers concluded that literary titles do not violate the Lanham Act "unless the title has no artistic relevance to the underlying work whatsoever, or, if it has some artistic relevance, unless the title explicitly misleads as to the source or the content of the work." *Id.* at 999. We agree with the Second Circuit's analysis and adopt the *Rogers* standard as our own.

Applying *Rogers* to our case, we conclude that MCA's use of Barbie is not an infringement of Mattel's trademark. Under the first prong of *Rogers,* the use of Barbie in the song title clearly is relevant to the underlying work, namely, the song itself. As noted, the song is about Barbie and the values Aqua claims she represents. The song title does not explicitly mislead as to the source of the work; it does not, explicitly or otherwise, suggest that it was produced by Mattel. The *only* indication that Mattel might be associated with the song is the use of Barbie in the title; if this were enough to satisfy this prong of the *Rogers* test, it would render *Rogers* a nullity. We therefore agree with the district court that MCA was entitled to summary judgment on this ground. * * *

IV

Mattel separately argues that, under the Federal Trademark Dilution Act ("FTDA"), MCA's song dilutes the Barbie mark in two ways: It diminishes the mark's capacity to identify and distinguish Mattel products, and tarnishes the mark because the song is inappropriate for young girls. *See* 15 U.S.C. § 1125(c).

* * * Barbie easily qualifies under the FTDA as a famous and distinctive mark, and reached this status long before MCA began to market the Barbie Girl song. The commercial success of Barbie Girl establishes beyond dispute that the Barbie mark satisfies each of these elements.

We are also satisfied that the song amounts to a "commercial use in commerce." Although this statutory language is ungainly, its meaning seems clear: It refers to a use of a famous and distinctive mark to sell goods other than those produced or authorized by the mark's owner. That is precisely what MCA did with the Barbie mark: It created and sold to consumers in the marketplace commercial products (the Barbie Girl single and the *Aquarium* album) that bear the Barbie mark.

MCA's use of the mark is dilutive. MCA does not dispute that, while a reference to Barbie would previously have brought to mind only Mattel's doll, after the song's popular success, some consumers hearing Barbie's name will think of both the doll and the song, or perhaps of the song only. This is a classic blurring injury and is in no way diminished by the fact that the song itself refers back to Barbie the doll. To be dilutive, use of the mark need not bring to mind the junior user alone. The distinctiveness of the mark is diminished if the mark no longer brings to mind the senior user alone.

We consider next the applicability of the FTDA's three statutory exemptions. These are uses that, though potentially dilutive, are nevertheless permitted: comparative advertising; news reporting and commentary; and noncommercial use. 15 U.S.C. § 1125(c)(4)(B). The first two exemptions clearly do not apply; only the exemption for noncommercial use need detain us.

* * *

To determine whether Barbie Girl falls within this exemption, we look to our definition of commercial speech under our First Amendment caselaw. "Although the boundary between commercial and noncommercial speech has yet to be clearly delineated, the 'core notion of commercial speech' is that it 'does no more than propose a commercial transaction.'" *Hoffman v. Capital Cities/ABC, Inc.,* 255 F.3d 1180, 1184 (9th Cir.2001). If speech is not "purely commercial"—that is, if it does more than propose a commercial transaction—then it is entitled to full First Amendment protection.

In *Hoffman,* a magazine published an article featuring digitally altered images from famous films. Computer artists modified shots of Dustin Hoffman, Cary Grant, Marilyn Monroe and others to put the actors in famous designers' spring fashions; a still of Hoffman from the movie "Tootsie" was altered so that he appeared to be wearing a Richard Tyler evening gown and Ralph Lauren heels. Hoffman, who had not given permission, sued under the Lanham Act and for violation of his right to publicity.

The article featuring the altered image clearly served a commercial purpose: "to draw attention to the for-profit magazine in which it appear[ed]" and to sell more copies. *Id.* at 1186. Nevertheless, we held that the article was fully protected under the First Amendment because it included protected expression: "humor" and "visual and verbal editorial comment on classic films and famous actors." *Id.* at 1185. Because its commercial purpose was "inextricably entwined with [these] expressive elements," the article and accompanying photographs enjoyed full First Amendment protection.

Hoffman controls: Barbie Girl is not purely commercial speech, and is therefore fully protected. To be sure, MCA used Barbie's name to sell copies of the song. However, as we've already observed, the song also lampoons the Barbie image and comments humorously on the cultural values Aqua claims she represents. Use of the Barbie mark in the song Barbie Girl therefore falls within the noncommercial use exemption to the FTDA. For precisely the same reasons, use of the mark in the song's title is also exempted.

AFFIRMED.

NOTE

Courts have applied a variety of approaches to analyzing First Amendment defenses to claims of trademark infringement involving expressive works. The *Rogers* balancing test has been applied not only to titles, but also to the contents of such works. *See, e.g., Brown v. Electronic Arts, Inc.*, 724 F.3d 1235 (9th Cir. 2013) (rejecting § 43(a) claim arising from use of football players' likenesses in videogame).

Some courts, however, take a more restrictive approach to expressive works. The Eighth Circuit, for example, recognizes a First Amendment defense to trademark infringement only where the defendant had "no alternative avenues" for conveying its message. *See, e.g., Mutual of Omaha Ins. Co. v. Novak*, 836 F.2d 397, 402 (8th Cir. 1987) (no First Amendment protection for maker of novelty T-shirts promoting "Mutant of Omaha" insurance against nuclear disasters, because same ideas could be expressed in editorial commentaries).

F. ELEVENTH AMENDMENT

Although the Lanham Act expressly permits states to be sued for Lanham Act violations in federal court, a series of decisions by the Supreme Court has made clear that this provision violates the Eleventh Amendment, which precludes federal courts from exercising jurisdiction over suits against states or state actors. *See College Savings Bank v. Florida Prepaid Postsecondary Education Expense Bd.*, 527 U.S. 666 (1999); *Florida Prepaid Postsecondary Education Expense Bd. v. College Savings Bank*, 527 U.S. 627 (1999); *City of Boerne v. Flores*, 521 U.S. 507 (1997). Accordingly, states and state actors are immune from Lanham Act claims in federal courts. However, the Court has not ruled out the possibility that, under *Ex parte Young*, 209 U.S. 123 (1908), a federal court could enjoin a Lanham Act violation by an individual state official acting within his or her official capacity.

Note, however, that federal courts do not have exclusive jurisdiction over Lanham Act claims, and the Eleventh Amendment does not curtail the jurisdiction of state courts. What strategies might a potential plaintiff consider if it has a meritorious trademark or unfair competition claim against a state or state actor?

G. EQUITABLE DEFENSES

A number of equitable defenses can also apply to trademark claims. *Laches* is the most common defense, requiring the defendant to prove that (1) the plaintiff had knowledge of the defendant's unauthorized use of a confusingly similar mark; (2) the plaintiff unreasonably delayed taking action; and (3) the defendant was unduly prejudiced as a result of the plaintiff's delay. *See Brittingham v. Jenkins*, 914 F.2d 447, 456 (4th Cir. 1990). *Estoppel* occurs when the plaintiff knowingly acquiesced or encouraged the defendant's use of a mark. *TMT North America, Inc. v. Magic Touch GmbH*, 124 F.3d 876, 885–86 (7th Cir. 1997). A *waiver* occurs when the plaintiff knowingly relinquishes an existing legal right. Finally, the plaintiff may be barred by the doctrine of *unclean hands*. *See Havana Club Holding, S.A. v. Galleon, S.A.*, 49 U.S.P.Q.2d 1296 (S.D.N.Y. 1998), *aff'd on other grounds*, 203 F.3d 116 (2d Cir.2000); RESTATEMENT (THIRD) OF UNFAIR COMPETITION § 32 (1995) ("If a designation used as a trademark, trade name, collective mark, or certification mark is deceptive, or if its use is otherwise in violation of public policy, or if the owner of the designation has engaged in other substantial misconduct directly related to the owner's assertion of rights in the trademark, trade name, collective mark, or certification mark, the owner may be barred in whole or in part from the relief that would otherwise be available. . . .").

CHAPTER 6

SECONDARY LIABILITY AND REMEDIES

■ ■ ■

A. SECONDARY LIABILITY

INWOOD LABORATORIES, INC. V. IVES LABORATORIES, INC.

456 U.S. 844, 102 S.Ct. 2182 (1982).

JUSTICE O'CONNOR delivered the opinion of the Court.

This action requires us to consider the circumstances under which a manufacturer of a generic drug, designed to duplicate the appearance of a similar drug marketed by a competitor under a registered trademark, can be held vicariously liable for infringement of that trademark by pharmacists who dispense the generic drug.

I

In 1955, respondent Ives Laboratories, Inc. (Ives), received a patent on the drug cyclandelate, a vasodilator used in long-term therapy for peripheral and cerebral vascular diseases. Until its patent expired in 1972, Ives retained the exclusive right to make and sell the drug, which it did under the registered trademark CYCLOSPASMOL. Ives marketed the drug, a white powder, to wholesalers, retail pharmacists, and hospitals in colored gelatin capsules. Ives arbitrarily selected a blue capsule, imprinted with "Ives 4124," for its 200 mg dosage and a combination blue-red capsule, imprinted with "Ives 4148," for its 400 mg dosage.

After Ives' patent expired, several generic drug manufacturers, including petitioners Premo Pharmaceutical Laboratories, Inc., Inwood Laboratories, Inc., and MD Pharmaceutical Co., Inc. (collectively the generic manufacturers), began marketing cyclandelate. They intentionally copied the appearance of the CYCLOSPASMOL capsules, selling cyclandelate in 200 mg and 400 mg capsules in colors identical to those selected by Ives.[3]

* * *

[3] Initially, the generic manufacturers did not place any identifying mark on their capsules. After Ives initiated this action, Premo imprinted "Premo" on its capsules and Inwood imprinted "Inwood 258."

A pharmacist, regardless of whether he is dispensing CYCLOSPASMOL or a generic drug, removes the capsules from the container in which he receives them and dispenses them to the consumer in the pharmacist's own bottle with his own label attached. Hence, the final consumer sees no identifying marks other than those on the capsules themselves.

II

* * *

Ives' claim under § 32 derived from its allegation that some pharmacists had dispensed generic drugs mislabeled as CYCLOSPASMOL.[8] Ives contended that the generic manufacturers' use of look-alike capsules and of catalog entries comparing prices and revealing the colors of the generic capsules induced pharmacists illegally to substitute a generic drug for CYCLOSPASMOL and to mislabel the substitute drug CYCLOSPASMOL. Although Ives did not allege that the petitioners themselves applied the Ives trademark to the drug products they produced and distributed, it did allege that the petitioners contributed to the infringing activities of pharmacists who mislabeled generic cyclandelate.

Ives' claim under § 43(a) alleged that the petitioners falsely designated the origin of their products by copying the capsule colors used by Ives and by promoting the generic products as equivalent to CYCLOSPASMOL. In support of its claim, Ives argued that the colors of its capsules were not functional and that they had developed a secondary meaning for the consumers.

Contending that pharmacists would continue to mislabel generic drugs as CYCLOSPASMOL so long as imitative products were available, Ives asked that the court enjoin the petitioners from marketing cyclandelate capsules in the same colors and form as Ives uses for CYCLOSPASMOL. * * *

III

A

As the lower courts correctly discerned, liability for trademark infringement can extend beyond those who actually mislabel goods with the mark of another. Even if a manufacturer does not directly control others in the chain of distribution, it can be held responsible for their infringing activities under certain circumstances. Thus, if a manufacturer

---

[8] The claim involved two types of infringements. The first was "direct" infringement, in which druggists allegedly filled CYCLOSPASMOL prescriptions marked "dispense as written" with a generic drug and mislabeled the product as CYCLOSPASMOL. The second, "intermediate" infringement, occurred when pharmacists, although authorized by the prescriptions to substitute, allegedly mislabeled a generic drug as CYCLOSPASMOL. * * *

or distributor intentionally induces another to infringe a trademark, or if it continues to supply its product to one whom it knows or has reason to know is engaging in trademark infringement, the manufacturer or distributor is contributorially responsible for any harm done as a result of the deceit.

It is undisputed that those pharmacists who mislabeled generic drugs with Ives' registered trademark violated § 32. However, whether these petitioners were liable for the pharmacists' infringing acts depended upon whether, in fact, the petitioners intentionally induced the pharmacists to mislabel generic drugs or, in fact, continued to supply cyclandelate to pharmacists whom the petitioners knew were mislabeling generic drugs. The District Court concluded that Ives made neither of those factual showings. * * *

IV

In reversing the District Court's judgment, the Court of Appeals initially held that the trial court failed to give sufficient weight to the evidence Ives offered to show a "pattern of illegal substitution and mislabeling in New York. . . ." * * * Because the trial court's findings concerning the significance of the instances of mislabeling were not clearly erroneous, they should not have been disturbed.

Next, after completing its own review of the evidence, the Court of Appeals concluded that the evidence was "clearly sufficient to establish a § 32 violation." In reaching its conclusion, the Court of Appeals was influenced by several factors. First, it thought the petitioners reasonably could have anticipated misconduct by a substantial number of the pharmacists who were provided imitative, lower priced products which, if substituted for the higher priced brand name without passing on savings to consumers, could provide an economic advantage to the pharmacists.[17] Second, it disagreed with the trial court's finding that the mislabeling which did occur reflected confusion about state law requirements. Third, it concluded that illegal substitution and mislabeling in New York are neither de minimis nor inadvertent. Finally, the Court of Appeals indicated it was further influenced by the fact that the petitioners did not offer "any persuasive evidence of a legitimate reason unrelated to CYCLOSPASMOL" for producing an imitative product. *Ibid.*[20]

* * *

[17] The Court of Appeals cited no evidence to support its conclusion, which apparently rests upon the assumption that a pharmacist who has been provided an imitative generic drug will be unable to resist the temptation to profit from illegal activity. * * *.

[20] The Court of Appeals reached that conclusion despite the District Court's express finding that, for purposes of § 43(a), the capsule colors were functional. As the dissent below noted, the Court of Appeals' majority either disregarded the District Court's finding of functionality or implicitly rejected that finding as not "persuasive." While the precise basis for the Court of Appeals' ruling on this issue is unclear, it is clear that the Court of Appeals erred. * * *

V

The Court of Appeals erred in setting aside findings of fact that were not clearly erroneous. Accordingly, the judgment of the Court of Appeals that the petitioners violated § 32 of the Lanham Act is reversed. * * *

NOTES

1. Given that the Lanham Act lacks a statutory provision providing for secondary liability (in contrast to the Patent Act), why have the courts expanded liability beyond what Congress has expressly provided?

2. Note that contributory infringement must be predicated on some evidence of direct infringement, though the plaintiff need not sue the direct infringer in order to bring a claim against the contributory infringer. Why?

HARD ROCK CAFE LICENSING CORP. V. CONCESSION SERVICES, INC.

955 F.2d 1143 (7th Cir. 1992).

CUDAHY, CIRCUIT JUDGE.

The Hard Rock Cafe Licensing Corporation (Hard Rock) owns trademarks on several clothing items, including t-shirts and sweatshirts, and apparently attempts to exploit its trademark monopoly to the full. In the summer of 1989, Hard Rock sent out specially trained private investigators to look for counterfeit Hard Rock Cafe merchandise. The investigators found Iqbal Parvez selling counterfeit Hard Rock t-shirts from stands in the Tri-State Swap-O-Rama and the Melrose Park Swap-O-Rama, flea markets owned and operated by Concession Services Incorporated (CSI). The investigators also discovered that Harry's Sweat Shop (Harry's) was selling similar items. Hard Rock brought suit against Parvez, CSI, Harry's and others not relevant to this appeal under the Lanham Trademark Act, 15 U.S.C. § 1051 et seq. (1988). Most of the defendants settled, including Parvez, who paid Hard Rock some $30,000. CSI and Harry's went to trial. * * *

All of the parties who participated in the trial appealed. CSI believes that it is not liable and that, in any event, entry of the injunction was inappropriate. Hard Rock wants attorney's fees from both defendants. Harry's appealed from the finding of liability and the entry of the injunction as well, but filed its appeal one day too late; its appeal has therefore been dismissed. Finding errors of law and a fatal ambiguity in the findings of fact, we vacate the judgment against CSI, vacate the denial of attorney's fees and remand for further proceedings.

I.

* * *

A. The Parties and Their Practices

1. Concession Services, Inc.

* * *

CSI generates revenue from a flea market in four ways. First, it rents space to vendors for flat fees that vary by the day of the week and the location of the space. Second, CSI charges a reservation and storage fee to those vendors who want to reserve the same space on a month-to-month basis. Third, CSI charges shoppers a nominal 75 cents admission charge. Fourth, CSI runs concession stands inside the market. To promote its business, CSI advertises the markets, announcing "BARGAINS" to be had, but does not advertise the presence of any individual vendors or any particular goods.

Supervision of the flea markets is minimal. CSI posts a sign at the Tri-State prohibiting vendors from selling "illegal goods." It also has "Rules For Sellers" which prohibit the sale of food or beverages, alcohol, weapons, fireworks, live animals, drugs and drug paraphernalia and subversive or un-American literature. Other than these limitations, vendors can, and do, sell almost any conceivable item. Two off-duty police officers provide security and crowd control (an arrangement that does not apply to the other markets). These officers also have some duty to ensure that the vendors obey the Sellers' Rules. The manager of the Tri-State, Albert Barelli, walks around the flea market about five times a day, looking for problems and violations of the rules. No one looks over the vendors' wares before they enter the market and set up their stalls, and any examination after that is cursory. Moreover, Barelli does not keep records of the names and addresses of the vendors. The only penalty for violating the Seller's Rules is expulsion from the market.

James Pierski, the vice president in charge of CSI's flea markets, testified that CSI has a policy of cooperating with any trademark owner that notifies CSI of possible infringing activity. But there is no evidence that this policy has ever been carried into effect. * * *

* * *

3. Hard Rock Licensing Corp.

Hard Rock owns the rights to a variety of Hard Rock trademarks. The corporation grants licenses to use its trademarks to the limited partnerships that own and operate the various Hard Rock Cafe restaurants. These restaurants are the only authorized distributors of Hard Rock Cafe merchandise, but apparently this practice of exclusivity is neither publicized nor widely known. The shirts themselves are produced by Winterland Productions, which prints logos on blank, first quality t-shirts that it buys from Hanes, Fruit-of-the-Loom and Anvil. According to the manager of the Chicago Hard Rock Cafe, Scott Floersheimer,

Winterland has an agreement with Hard Rock to retain all defective Hard Rock shirts. Thus, if Winterland performs as agreed, all legitimate Hard Rock shirts sold to the public are well-made and cleanly printed.

The Chicago Hard Rock Cafe has done very well from its business. Since 1986, it has sold over 500,000 t-shirts at an average gross profit of $10.12 per shirt.

B. The Investigation

* * * The investigators visited both the Melrose Park and the Tri-State Swap-O-Ramas and observed Iqbal Parvez (or his employees) offering more than a hundred Hard Rock t-shirts for sale. Cynthia Myers, the chief investigator on the project, testified that these shirts were obviously counterfeit. The shirts were poor quality stock, with cut labels and were being sold for $3 apiece (a legitimate Hard Rock shirt, we are told, goes for over $14). * * *

At no point before filing suit did Hard Rock warn * * * CSI (or Parvez, whose supplier Hard Rock was trying to track down) that the shirts were counterfeits.

C. The District Court Proceedings

* * * After a bench trial, the district court entered permanent injunctions against both defendants * * *.

The court's reasoning is crucial to the resolution of this appeal. Accordingly, we think it appropriate to quote from it at some length. The court concluded that both defendants were "guilty of willful blindness that counterfeit goods were being sold on [their] premises." Another sentence follows, however, which somewhat dilutes the impact of the preceding finding: "Neither defendant took reasonable steps to detect or prevent the sale of Hard Rock Cafe counterfeit T-shirts on its premise [sic]." This suggests mere negligence.

Willful blindness, the court said, "is a sufficient basis for a finding of violation of the Lanham Act. *Louis Vuitton S.A. v. Lee*, 875 F.2d 584, 590 (7th Cir.1989)." As to CSI's argument that it did not actually sell the offending goods, the court observed that CSI is not "merely a landlord; it also advertises and promoted the activity on its premises, sells admission tickets to buyers and supervises the premises. Under these circumstances it must also take reasonable precautions against the sale of counterfeit products."

II.

* * *

A. *Secondary Liability*

The most interesting issue in this case is CSI's liability for Parvez's sales. Hard Rock argues that CSI has incurred both contributory and vicarious liability for the counterfeits, and we take the theories of liability in that order.

It is well established that "if a manufacturer or distributor intentionally induces another to infringe a trademark, or if it continues to supply its product to one whom it knows or has reason to know is engaging in trademark infringement, the manufacturer or distributor is contributorially responsible for any harm done as a result of the deceit." *Inwood Labs.,* 456 U.S. at 854. Despite this apparently definitive statement, it is not clear how the doctrine applies to people who do not actually manufacture or distribute the good that is ultimately palmed off as made by someone else. A temporary help service, for example, might not be liable if it furnished Parvez the workers he employed to erect his stand, even if the help service knew that Parvez would sell counterfeit goods. Thus we must ask whether the operator of a flea market is more like the manufacturer of a mislabeled good or more like a temporary help service supplying the purveyor of goods. To answer questions of this sort, we have treated trademark infringement as a species of tort and have turned to the common law to guide our inquiry into the appropriate boundaries of liability.

CSI characterizes its relationship with Parvez as that of landlord and tenant. Hard Rock calls CSI a licensor, not a landlord. Either way, the Restatement of Torts tells us that CSI is responsible for the torts of those it permits on its premises "knowing or having reason to know that the other is acting or will act tortiously. . . ." RESTATEMENT (SECOND) OF TORTS § 877(c) & cmt. d (1979). The common law, then, imposes the same duty on landlords and licensors that the Supreme Court has imposed on manufacturers and distributors. In the absence of any suggestion that a trademark violation should not be treated as a common law tort, we believe that the *Inwood Labs.* test for contributory liability applies. CSI may be liable for trademark violations by Parvez if it knew or had reason to know of them. But the factual findings must support that conclusion.

The district court found CSI to be willfully blind. Since we have held that willful blindness is equivalent to actual knowledge for purposes of the Lanham Act, *Lee,* 875 F.2d at 590, this finding should be enough to hold CSI liable (unless clearly erroneous). But we very much doubt that the district court defined willful blindness as it should have. To be willfully blind, a person must suspect wrongdoing and deliberately fail to investigate. The district court, however, made little mention of CSI's state of mind and focused almost entirely on CSI's failure to take precautions against counterfeiting. In its conclusions of law, the court emphasized that

CSI had a duty to take reasonable precautions. In short, it looks as if the district court found CSI to be negligent, not willfully blind.

This ambiguity in the court's findings would not matter if CSI could be liable for failing to take reasonable precautions. But CSI has no affirmative duty to take precautions against the sale of counterfeits. Although the "reason to know" part of the standard for contributory liability requires CSI (or its agents) to understand what a reasonably prudent person would understand, it does not impose any duty to seek out and prevent violations. We decline to extend the protection that Hard Rock finds in the common law to require CSI, and other landlords, to be more dutiful guardians of Hard Rock's commercial interests. Thus the district court's findings do not support the conclusion that CSI bears contributory liability for Parvez's transgressions.

Before moving on, we should emphasize that we have found only that the district court applied an incorrect standard. We have not found that the evidence cannot support the conclusion that CSI was in fact willfully blind. At the Tri-State, Barelli saw Parvez's shirts and had the opportunity to note that they had cut labels and were being sold cheap. Further, Barelli testified that he did not ask vendors whether their goods were counterfeit because they were sure to lie to him. One might infer from these facts that Barelli suspected that the shirts were counterfeits but chose not to investigate.

On the other hand, we do not wish to prejudge the matter. For it is undisputed that Hard Rock made no effort to broadcast the information that legitimate Hard Rock t-shirts could only be found in Hard Rock Cafes. Moreover, there does not seem to be any particular reason to believe that inexpensive t-shirts with cut labels are obviously counterfeit, no matter what logo they bear. *Cf. Lee*, 875 F.2d at 590 (genuine Vuitton and Gucci bags unlikely to display poor workmanship or purple vinyl linings). The circumstantial evidence that Barelli suspected the shirts to be counterfeit is, at best, thin. On remand, the district court may choose to develop this issue more fully.

Perhaps recognizing that the district court's opinion is unclear, Hard Rock urges us to find CSI vicariously liable for Parvez's sales, regardless of its knowledge of the counterfeiting. Indeed, if we accept this theory, CSI is liable for Parvez's sales even if it was not negligent. *See, e.g., Shapiro, Bernstein & Co. v. H.L. Green Co.*, 316 F.2d 304, 309 (2d Cir.1963).

We have recognized that a joint tortfeasor may bear vicarious liability for trademark infringement by another. This theory of liability requires a finding that the defendant and the infringer have an apparent or actual partnership, have authority to bind one another in transactions with third parties or exercise joint ownership or control over the infringing product.

The case before us does not fit into the joint tortfeasor model, and Hard Rock does not argue that it does.

Instead, Hard Rock wants us to apply the more expansive doctrine of vicarious liability applicable to copyright violations. Under the test developed by the Second Circuit, a defendant is vicariously liable for copyright infringement if it has "the right and ability to supervise the infringing activity and also has a direct financial interest in such activities." *Gershwin Publishing Corp. v. Columbia Artists Management, Inc.*, 443 F.2d 1159, 1162 (2d Cir.1971) (hereinafter CAMI). The purpose of the doctrine is to prevent an entity that profits from infringement from hiding behind undercapitalized "dummy" operations when the copyright owner eventually sues. *Shapiro, Bernstein*, 316 F.2d at 309.

The parties have argued vigorously about the application of this doctrine to the facts.[4] But we need not decide the question; for the Supreme Court tells us that secondary liability for trademark infringement should, in any event, be more narrowly drawn than secondary liability for copyright infringement. *Sony Corp. of America v. Universal City Studios, Inc.*, 464 U.S. 417, 439 n. 19 (1984) (citing "fundamental differences" between copyright and trademark law). If Hard Rock referred us to some principle of common law that supported its analogy to copyright, we would be more understanding of its claims. But it has not. Further, there is no hint that CSI is playing at the sort of obfuscation that inspired the Second Circuit to develop its more expansive form of vicarious copyright liability. Hard Rock must look to Congress to provide the level of protection it demands of CSI here.

In sum, we find that CSI may bear contributory liability for Parvez's unlawful sales, but we see no evidence on the record that would support a finding that CSI is vicariously liable. Accordingly, because the district court's findings fail to establish that CSI knew or had reason to know that Parvez was selling counterfeits, we must vacate the judgment against CSI and remand for further proceedings. * * *

---

4 We are inclined to favor CSI's side of the dispute. CSI neither hired Parvez to entertain its customers, cf. *Dreamland Ball Room*, 36 F.2d at 355, nor did it take a percentage of his sales, cf. *Shapiro, Bernstein*, 316 F.2d at 306 (department store took 10%–12% of record department's gross receipts); *CAMI*, 443 F.2d at 1161 (management company took percentage of infringer's performance fees). Further, whether CSI is a landlord or a licensor, CSI exercises no more control over its tenants than any landlord concerned with the safety and convenience of visitors and of its tenants as a group. *Deutsch v. Arnold*, 98 F.2d 686, 688 (2d Cir.1938) (ignorant landlord not liable for copyright infringement by tenant).

TIFFANY (N.J.) INC. V. EBAY INC.

600 F.3d 93 (2d Cir. 2010).

SACK, CIRCUIT JUDGE:

* * *

BACKGROUND

By opinion dated July 14, 2008, following a week-long bench trial, the United States District Court for the Southern District of New York (Richard J. Sullivan, Judge) set forth its findings of fact and conclusions of law. *Tiffany (NJ) Inc. v. eBay, Inc.*, 576 F.Supp.2d 463 (S.D.N.Y.2008) ("*Tiffany*"). * * *

eBay

eBay is the proprietor of www.ebay.com, an Internet-based marketplace that allows those who register with it to purchase goods from and sell goods to one another. * * *

* * *

Tiffany

Tiffany is a world-famous purveyor of, among other things, branded jewelry. Since 2000, all new Tiffany jewelry sold in the United States has been available exclusively through Tiffany's retail stores, catalogs, and website, and through its Corporate Sales Department. It does not use liquidators, sell overstock merchandise, or put its goods on sale at discounted prices. It does not—nor can it, for that matter—control the "legitimate secondary market in authentic Tiffany silvery jewelry," i.e., the market for second-hand Tiffany wares. The record developed at trial "offere[d] little basis from which to discern the actual availability of authentic Tiffany silver jewelry in the secondary market."

Sometime before 2004, Tiffany became aware that counterfeit Tiffany merchandise was being sold on eBay's site. * * * The [district court] decided that during the period in which the Buying Programs were in effect, a "significant portion of the 'Tiffany' sterling silver jewelry listed on the eBay website . . . was counterfeit," and that eBay knew "that some portion of the Tiffany goods sold on its website might be counterfeit." The court found, however, that "a substantial number of authentic Tiffany goods are [also] sold on eBay."

* * *

Anti-Counterfeiting Measures

Because eBay facilitates many sales of Tiffany goods, genuine and otherwise, and obtains revenue on every transaction, it generates substantial revenues from the sale of purported Tiffany goods, some of which are counterfeit. * * *

Because eBay "never saw or inspected the merchandise in the listings," its ability to determine whether a particular listing was for counterfeit goods was limited. Even had it been able to inspect the goods, moreover, in many instances it likely would not have had the expertise to determine whether they were counterfeit.

Notwithstanding these limitations, eBay spent "as much as $20 million each year on tools to promote trust and safety on its website." For example, eBay and PayPal set up "buyer protection programs," under which, in certain circumstances, the buyer would be reimbursed for the cost of items purchased on eBay that were discovered not to be genuine. eBay also established a "Trust and Safety" department, with some 4,000 employees "devoted to trust and safety" issues, including over 200 who "focus exclusively on combating infringement" and 70 who "work exclusively with law enforcement."

By May 2002, eBay had implemented a "fraud engine," "which is principally dedicated to ferreting out illegal listings, including counterfeit listings." * * * In addition to identifying items actually advertised as counterfeit, the engine also incorporates various filters designed to screen out less-obvious instances of counterfeiting using "data elements designed to evaluate listings based on, for example, the seller's Internet protocol address, any issues associated with the seller's account on eBay, and the feedback the seller has received from other eBay users." In addition to general filters, the fraud engine incorporates "Tiffany-specific filters," including "approximately 90 different keywords" designed to help distinguish between genuine and counterfeit Tiffany goods. During the period in dispute, eBay also "periodically conducted [manual] reviews of listings in an effort to remove those that might be selling counterfeit goods, including Tiffany goods."

For nearly a decade, including the period at issue, eBay has also maintained and administered the "Verified Rights Owner ('VeRO') Program"—a " 'notice-and-takedown' system" allowing owners of intellectual property rights, including Tiffany, to "report to eBay any listing offering potentially infringing items, so that eBay could remove such reported listings." Any such rights-holder with a "good-faith belief that [a particular listed] item infringed on a copyright or a trademark" could report the item to eBay, using a "Notice Of Claimed Infringement form or NOCI form." During the period under consideration, eBay's practice was to remove reported listings within twenty-four hours of receiving a NOCI, but eBay in fact deleted seventy to eighty percent of them within twelve hours of notification.

On receipt of a NOCI, if the auction or sale had not ended, eBay would, in addition to removing the listing, cancel the bids and inform the seller of the reason for the cancellation. If bidding had ended, eBay would retroactively cancel the transaction. In the event of a cancelled auction, eBay would refund the fees it had been paid in connection with the auction.

In some circumstances, eBay would reimburse the buyer for the cost of a purchased item, provided the buyer presented evidence that the purchased item was counterfeit. During the relevant time period, the district court found, eBay "never refused to remove a reported Tiffany listing, acted in good faith in responding to Tiffany's NOCIs, and always provided Tiffany with the seller's contact information."

* * *

In 2003 or early 2004, eBay began to use "special warning messages when a seller attempted to list a Tiffany item." These messages "instructed the seller to make sure that the item was authentic Tiffany merchandise and informed the seller that eBay 'does not tolerate the listing of replica, counterfeit, or otherwise unauthorized items' and that violation of this policy 'could result in suspension of [the seller's] account.' " The messages also provided a link to Tiffany's "About Me" page with its "buyer beware" disclaimer. If the seller "continued to list an item despite the warning, the listing was flagged for review."

In addition to cancelling particular suspicious transactions, eBay has also suspended from its website " 'hundreds of thousands of sellers every year,' tens of thousands of whom were suspected [of] having engaged in infringing conduct." eBay primarily employed a " 'three strikes rule' " for suspensions, but would suspend sellers after the first violation if it was clear that "the seller 'listed a number of infringing items,' and '[selling counterfeit merchandise] appears to be the only thing they've come to eBay to do.' " But if "a seller listed a potentially infringing item but appeared overall to be a legitimate seller, the 'infringing items [were] taken down, and the seller [would] be sent a warning on the first offense and given the educational information, [and] told that . . . if they do this again, they will be suspended from eBay.' "

By late 2006, eBay had implemented additional anti-fraud measures: delaying the ability of buyers to view listings of certain brand names, including Tiffany's, for 6 to 12 hours so as to give rights-holders such as Tiffany more time to review those listings; developing the ability to assess the number of items listed in a given listing; and restricting one-day and three-day auctions and cross-border trading for some brand-name items.

The district court concluded that "eBay consistently took steps to improve its technology and develop anti-fraud measures as such measures became technologically feasible and reasonably available."

* * *

Tiffany appeals from the district court's judgment for eBay.

DISCUSSION

I. Direct Trademark Infringement

[The court rejected Tiffany's claim of "direct" trademark infringement, holding that it was lawful for eBay to use Tiffany's trademark "to describe accurately the genuine Tiffany goods offered for sale on its website," because eBay did nothing to suggest "that Tiffany affiliated itself with eBay or endorsed the sale of its products through eBay's website.]

* * *

II. Contributory Trademark Infringement

The more difficult issue, and the one that the parties have properly focused our attention on, is whether eBay is liable for contributory trademark infringement—i.e., for culpably facilitating the infringing conduct of the counterfeiting vendors. Acknowledging the paucity of case law to guide us, we conclude that the district court correctly granted judgment on this issue in favor of eBay.

A. Principles

Contributory trademark infringement is a judicially created doctrine that derives from the common law of torts. * * * The Supreme Court most recently dealt with the subject in *Inwood Laboratories, Inc. v. Ives Laboratories, Inc.*, 456 U.S. 844 (1982). * * *

Inwood's test for contributory trademark infringement applies on its face to manufacturers and distributors of goods. Courts have, however, extended the test to providers of services.

The Seventh Circuit applied *Inwood* to a lawsuit against the owner of a swap meet, or "flea market," whose vendors were alleged to have sold infringing Hard Rock Café T-shirts. *See Hard Rock Café*, 955 F.2d at 1148–49. The court "treated trademark infringement as a species of tort," *id.* at 1148, and analogized the swap meet owner to a landlord or licensor, on whom the common law "imposes the same duty . . . [as *Inwood*] impose[s] on manufacturers and distributors," *id.* at 1149; *see also Fonovisa, Inc. v. Cherry Auction, Inc.*, 76 F.3d 259 (9th Cir.1996) (adopting *Hard Rock Café*'s reasoning and applying *Inwood* to a swap meet owner).

Speaking more generally, the Ninth Circuit concluded that *Inwood*'s test for contributory trademark infringement applies to a service provider if he or she exercises sufficient control over the infringing conduct. *Lockheed Martin Corp. v. Network Solutions, Inc.*, 194 F.3d 980, 984 (9th Cir.1999). * * *

The limited case law leaves the law of contributory trademark infringement ill-defined. Although we are not the first court to consider the application of *Inwood* to the Internet, *see, e.g., Lockheed*, 194 F.3d 980 (Internet domain name registrar), we are apparently the first to consider its application to an online marketplace.

B. Discussion

* * *

The question that remains, then, is whether eBay is liable under the *Inwood* test on the basis of the services it provided to those who used its website to sell counterfeit Tiffany products. As noted, when applying *Inwood* to service providers, there are two ways in which a defendant may become contributorially liable for the infringing conduct of another: first, if the service provider "intentionally induces another to infringe a trademark," and second, if the service provider "continues to supply its [service] to one whom it knows or has reason to know is engaging in trademark infringement." *Inwood*, 456 U.S. at 854. Tiffany does not argue that eBay induced the sale of counterfeit Tiffany goods on its website—the circumstances addressed by the first part of the *Inwood* test. It argues instead, under the second part of the *Inwood* test, that eBay continued to supply its services to the sellers of counterfeit Tiffany goods while knowing or having reason to know that such sellers were infringing Tiffany's mark.

[The court agreed with the district court that eBay was not liable for the listings that it terminated promptly upon learning that they were for counterfeits.] * * *

Tiffany disagrees vigorously, however, with the district court's further determination that eBay lacked sufficient knowledge of trademark infringement by sellers behind other, non-terminated listings to provide a basis for *Inwood* liability. Tiffany argued in the district court that eBay knew, or at least had reason to know, that counterfeit Tiffany goods were being sold ubiquitously on its website. * * * Tiffany urged that eBay be held contributorially liable on the basis that despite that knowledge, it continued to make its services available to infringing sellers.

The district court rejected this argument. It acknowledged that "[t]he evidence produced at trial demonstrated that eBay had *generalized* notice that some portion of the Tiffany goods sold on its website might be counterfeit." The court characterized the issue before it as "whether eBay's *generalized* knowledge of trademark infringement on its website was sufficient to meet the 'knowledge or reason to know' prong of the *Inwood* test." eBay had argued that "such generalized knowledge is insufficient, and that the law demands more specific knowledge of individual instances of infringement and infringing sellers before imposing a burden upon eBay to remedy the problem."

The district court concluded that "while eBay clearly possessed general knowledge as to counterfeiting on its website, such generalized knowledge is insufficient under the *Inwood* test to impose upon eBay an affirmative duty to remedy the problem." The court reasoned that *Inwood*'s language explicitly imposes contributory liability on a defendant who "continues to supply its product[—in eBay's case, its service—]to *one* whom it knows or has reason to know is engaging in trademark infringement." The court also noted that plaintiffs "bear a high burden in establishing 'knowledge' of contributory infringement," and that courts have

> been reluctant to extend contributory trademark liability to defendants where there is some uncertainty as to the extent or the nature of the infringement. In *Inwood*, Justice White emphasized in his concurring opinion that a defendant is not "require[d] . . . to refuse to sell to dealers who merely *might pass off its goods*."

Tiffany at 508–09 (quoting *Inwood*, 456 U.S. at 861) (White, J., concurring) (emphasis and alteration in original).

Accordingly, the district court concluded that for Tiffany to establish eBay's contributory liability, Tiffany would have to show that eBay "knew or had reason to know of specific instances of actual infringement" beyond those that it addressed upon learning of them. Tiffany failed to make such a showing.

* * *

We agree with the district court. For contributory trademark infringement liability to lie, a service provider must have more than a general knowledge or reason to know that its service is being used to sell counterfeit goods. Some contemporary knowledge of which particular listings are infringing or will infringe in the future is necessary.

* * * [W]e agree with the district court that "Tiffany's general allegations of counterfeiting failed to provide eBay with the knowledge required under *Inwood*." Tiffany's demand letters * * * did not identify particular sellers who Tiffany thought were then offering or would offer counterfeit goods. And although the NOCIs and buyer complaints gave eBay reason to know that certain sellers had been selling counterfeits, those sellers' listings were removed and repeat offenders were suspended from the eBay site. Thus Tiffany failed to demonstrate that eBay was supplying its service to individuals who it knew or had reason to know were selling counterfeit Tiffany goods.

Accordingly, we affirm the judgment of the district court insofar as it holds that eBay is not contributorially liable for trademark infringement.

3. *Willful Blindness.*

Tiffany and its amici express their concern that if eBay is not held liable except when specific counterfeit listings are brought to its attention, eBay will have no incentive to root out such listings from its website. They argue that this will effectively require Tiffany and similarly situated retailers to police eBay's website—and many others like it—"24 hours a day, and 365 days a year." They urge that this is a burden that most mark holders cannot afford to bear.

First, and most obviously, we are interpreting the law and applying it to the facts of this case. We could not, even if we thought it wise, revise the existing law in order to better serve one party's interests at the expense of the other's.

But we are also disposed to think, and the record suggests, that private market forces give eBay and those operating similar businesses a strong incentive to minimize the counterfeit goods sold on their websites. eBay received many complaints from users claiming to have been duped into buying counterfeit Tiffany products sold on eBay. The risk of alienating these users gives eBay a reason to identify and remove counterfeit listings. Indeed, it has spent millions of dollars in that effort.

Moreover, we agree with the district court that if eBay had reason to suspect that counterfeit Tiffany goods were being sold through its website, and intentionally shielded itself from discovering the offending listings or the identity of the sellers behind them, eBay might very well have been charged with knowledge of those sales sufficient to satisfy *Inwood*'s "knows or has reason to know" prong. A service provider is not, we think, permitted willful blindness. When it has reason to suspect that users of its service are infringing a protected mark, it may not shield itself from learning of the particular infringing transactions by looking the other way. *See, e.g., Hard Rock Café,* 955 F.2d at 1149 ("To be willfully blind, a person must suspect wrongdoing and deliberately fail to investigate."); *Fonovisa,* 76 F.3d at 265 (applying *Hard Rock Café*'s reasoning to conclude that "a swap meet can not disregard its vendors' blatant trademark infringements with impunity"). In the words of the Seventh Circuit, "willful blindness is equivalent to actual knowledge for purposes of the Lanham Act." *Hard Rock Café,* 955 F.2d at 1149.

eBay appears to concede that it knew as a general matter that counterfeit Tiffany products were listed and sold through its website. Without more, however, this knowledge is insufficient to trigger liability under *Inwood.* The district court found, after careful consideration, that eBay was not willfully blind to the counterfeit sales. That finding is not clearly erroneous. eBay did not ignore the information it was given about counterfeit sales on its website.

* * *

CONCLUSION

For the foregoing reasons, we affirm the judgment of the district court with respect to the claims of trademark infringement * * *.

NOTES

1. Does the *Tiffany* decision allocate responsibility for preventing infringement in a manner that properly balances the public interest in avoiding consumer confusion against the public interest in efficient e-commerce? Does eBay have a sufficient incentive to vigorously enforce its rules against counterfeit sales?

2. The court's analysis of Tiffany's false advertising claim is included in Chapter 4.

B. REMEDIES

Statutes: 15 U.S.C. §§ 1116, 1117

SANDS, TAYLOR & WOOD COMPANY V. THE QUAKER OATS COMPANY

978 F.2d 947 (7th Cir. 1992).

[The portion of this opinion addressing infringement and abandonment can be found in Chapter 5.]

The district court awarded STW ten percent of Quaker's profits on sales of Gatorade for the period during which the "Thirst Aid" campaign ran—$24,730,000—based on its finding that Quaker had acted in bad faith. The court also ordered Quaker to pay STW's attorney's fees, again based on the finding of bad faith, as well as prejudgment interest on the award of profits beginning from May 12, 1984. Quaker challenges all three of these rulings.

A. Profits

Quaker argues that an award of its profits was inappropriate here because there was no evidence that Quaker intended to trade on STW's good will or reputation; indeed, such an intent is necessarily absent in a reverse confusion case. According to Quaker, an award of the defendant's profits is justified only where the defendant has been unjustly enriched by appropriating the plaintiff's good will. There is some support for this position in the case law. "To obtain an accounting of profits, the courts usually require that defendant's infringement infer some connotation of 'intent,' or a knowing act denoting an intent, to infringe or reap the harvest of another's mark and advertising." 2 MCCARTHY, *supra* § 30:25, at 498. The law of this circuit is not, however, so limited. As we stated in *Roulo*:

> The Lanham Act specifically provides for the awarding of profits in the discretion of the judge subject only to principles of equity. As stated by this Court, "The trial court's primary function is to make violations of the Lanham Act unprofitable to the infringing party." Other than general equitable considerations, there is no express requirement that the parties be in direct competition or that the infringer wilfully infringe the trade dress to justify an award of profits. Profits are awarded under different rationales including unjust enrichment, deterrence, and compensation.

886 F.2d at 941. This broader view seems to be more consistent with the language of the Lanham Act than is the narrower (though perhaps more logical) rule espoused by Quaker. We decline to adopt Quaker's restrictive interpretation in light of Seventh Circuit precedent.

Nevertheless, we are mindful of the fact that awards of profits are to be limited by "equitable considerations." The district court justified the award of profits based on its finding that Quaker acted in bad faith. The evidence of bad faith in this case, however, is pretty slim. The court based its finding on (1) Quaker's "failure to conduct a basic trademark search until days before the airing of the Thirst Aid commercial," and its "anonymous, cursory investigations" of Karp's use of the mark once it obtained such a search; (2) Quaker's decision to continue with the "Thirst Aid" campaign after it discovered Karp's registrations; (3) the fact that Quaker did not seek a formal legal opinion regarding potential trademark issues until after the first "Thirst Aid" commercials were aired; and (4) Quaker's failure to take "reasonable precautions" to avoid the likelihood of confusion.

None of these facts is particularly good evidence of bad faith. For example, Quaker's in-house counsel, Lannin, testified at trial that his review of the "Thirst Aid" campaign in February or March of 1984 did not include a trademark search because he concluded that the proposed advertisements used the words "Thirst Aid" descriptively, and not as a trademark, and therefore did not raise any trademark issues. The district court apparently accepted this testimony, but nonetheless found Quaker's failure to investigate indicative of bad faith. Further, the court stated that it is a "close question" whether "Thirst Aid" is a descriptive term. Indeed, this court has found that the district court erred in concluding that "Thirst Aid" was not descriptive as a matter of law. A party who acts in reasonable reliance on the advice of counsel regarding a close question of trademark law generally does not act in bad faith.

Nor does Quaker's decision to proceed with the "Thirst Aid" campaign once it learned of Karp's registrations necessarily show bad faith. Based both on his earlier conclusion that "Thirst Aid" was descriptive and on his investigation into Karp's use of the term, which revealed that Karp was not currently using the THIRST-AID mark on any products sold at retail, Lannin concluded that Quaker's ads did not infringe Karp's rights in its marks. * * * Even the defendant's refusal to cease using the mark upon demand is not necessarily indicative of bad faith. Absent more, courts should "not make an inference of bad faith from evidence of conduct that is compatible with a good faith business judgment." *Munters Corp. v. Matsui America, Inc.*, 730 F.Supp. 790, 799–800 (N.D.Ill.1989), *aff'd*, 909 F.2d 250 (7th Cir.1990).

Quaker's failure to obtain a formal legal opinion from outside counsel until after the "Thirst Aid" campaign began is similarly weak evidence of bad faith. Given Lannin's sincere, reasonable conclusion that Quaker's ads used "Thirst Aid" descriptively, so that no trademark issue was raised, Quaker had no reason to seek the opinion of outside trademark counsel. Similarly, Quaker had no reason to take any precautions to avoid likelihood of confusion; Quaker's research had revealed that there was no product about which people were likely to be confused.

A determination of bad faith is a finding of fact subject to the clearly erroneous standard of review. We cannot say on this record that the district court's conclusion was clearly erroneous. We do think, however, that the evidence of bad faith here is marginal at best. Further, this is not a case where the senior user's trademark is so well-known that the junior user's choice of a confusingly similar mark, out of the infinite number of marks in the world, itself supports an inference that the junior user acted in bad faith. There is no question that Quaker developed the "Thirst Aid" campaign entirely independently, with no knowledge of STW's marks. In such a case, an award of $24 million in profits is not "equitable"; rather, it is a windfall to the plaintiff. Quaker may have been unjustly enriched by using STW's mark without paying for it, but the award of profits bears no relationship to that enrichment. A reasonable royalty, perhaps related in some way to the fee STW was paid by Pet, would more accurately reflect both the extent of Quaker's unjust enrichment and the interest of STW that has been infringed. We therefore reverse the district court's award of profits and remand for a redetermination of damages. * * *

B. Attorney's Fees

The Lanham Act provides for recovery of attorney's fees by the prevailing party in "exceptional cases." 15 U.S.C. § 1117(a). The district court concluded that this was such an exceptional case based on its finding that Quaker acted in bad faith. Because we affirm that finding, we also affirm the award of attorney's fees. The "equitable considerations" which lead us to reverse the award of profits do not apply to this issue. * * *

NOTES

1. The Lanham Act authorizes both injunctive relief, 15 U.S.C. § 1116, and recovery of the plaintiff's damages, the infringer's profits, and costs, 15 U.S.C. § 1117. Courts have discretion to enhance the damages award where necessary to compensate the plaintiff; awards of profits may be either enhanced or reduced, as the court finds just. *Id.* There are additional penalties for counterfeiting (including treble damages or statutory damages), *id.*, as well as provisions permitting the destruction of infringing articles and prohibiting the importation of infringing goods. 15 U.S.C. §§ 1118, 1124.

2. Punitive damages may be available under state law for certain forms of unfair competition, although these awards are subject to constitutional constraints. *See Cooper Industries, Inc. v. Leatherman Tool Group, Inc.*, 532 U.S. 424 (2001) (assessing constitutionality of punitive damages award for unfair competition and false advertising).

3. Under the Lanham Act, attorneys' fees are awarded to the prevailing party "in exceptional cases," as well as in any case involving intentional and knowing use of a counterfeit mark. *See* 15 U.S.C. § 1117(a), (b). To determine which cases are exceptional, most circuits have adopted the same test that the Supreme Court developed for awarding attorneys' fees in patent cases: A case is exceptional if it "stands out from others with respect to the substantive strength of a party's litigating position . . . or the unreasonable manner in which the case was litigated . . . considering the totality of the circumstances." *Octane Fitness LLC v. Icon Health and Fitness, Inc.*, 572 U.S. 545 (2014). For trademark claims arising under state law, the standards for attorneys' fees may be different.

4. *Notice:* If the action involves infringement of a federally registered mark, no damages or profits will be awarded unless the defendant had notice of the registration. 15 U.S.C. § 1111. This typically takes the form of a trademark notice displayed in connection with the goods or services. Absent such marking, the plaintiff can recover damages or profits only if the defendant has actual notice of the registration. However, several courts have held that the notice requirement does not apply to statutory damages for counterfeiting.

5. In *Romag Fasteners, Inc. v. Fossil, Inc.*, 140 S.Ct. 1492 (2020), the Supreme Court resolved a circuit split by holding that willfulness is not a prerequisite to awarding the defendant's profits. However, since all awards of damages or profits under § 1117(a) are subject to "principles of equity," the defendant's mental state remains a "highly important" consideration.

6. In a case of first impression, *Hard Candy v. Anastasia Beverly Hills*, 921 F.3d 1343 (11th Cir. 2019), the Eleventh Circuit held that the Seventh Amendment right to a jury trial does not apply to an action to recover a defendant's profits arising from the sale of infringing goods, where the plaintiff sought profits in lieu of actual damages, because a profits award is an equitable remedy.

7. In practice, injunctions are routinely awarded to trademark plaintiffs once a likelihood of confusion (or dilution) is established, based largely on the presumption of irreparable harm. In patent cases, the Supreme Court held in *eBay, Inc. v. MercExchange L.L.C.*, 547 U.S. 388 (2006) (excerpted in Chapter 12.D.1., *infra*) that a plaintiff must demonstrate irreparable harm in order to obtain injunctive relief; such harm cannot be presumed. The question whether the *eBay* rule also applied to Lanham Act claims initially divided the federal courts. However, Congress resolved the issue in the Trademark Modernization Act of 2020, amending section 1116(a) to give Lanham Act plaintiffs the benefit of a rebuttable presumption of irreparable harm for purposes of awarding preliminary or permanent injunctive relief.

PART 3

THE RIGHT OF PUBLICITY

■ ■ ■

CHAPTER 7

THE RIGHT OF PUBLICITY

■ ■ ■

Although the scope of the right varies by state, the right of publicity generally protects an individual's right to prevent the unauthorized use of his or her identity for commercial gain. The right is closely related to the right of privacy, but the nature of the injury is different. Whereas privacy claims are based on injury to feelings or disclosure of personal information, right of publicity claims are based on a commercial injury. In *Haelan Laboratories, Inc. v. Topps Chewing Gum, Inc.*, 202 F.2d 866, 868 (2d Cir. 1953), the Second Circuit explained the right as follows:

> * * * We think that, in addition to and independent of that right of privacy (which in New York derives from statute), a man has a right in the publicity value of his photograph, i.e., the right to grant the exclusive privilege of publishing his picture, and that such a grant may validly be made 'in gross,' i.e., without an accompanying transfer of a business or of anything else. Whether it be labelled a 'property' right is immaterial; for here, as often elsewhere, the tag 'property' simply symbolizes the fact that courts enforce a claim which has pecuniary worth.
>
> This right might be called a 'right of publicity.' For it is common knowledge that many prominent persons (especially actors and ball-players), far from having their feelings bruised through public exposure of their likenesses, would feel sorely deprived if they no longer received money for authorizing advertisements, popularizing their countenances, displayed in newspapers, magazines, busses, trains and subways. This right of publicity would usually yield them no money unless it could be made the subject of an exclusive grant which barred any other advertiser from using their pictures.

Often, the same facts that give rise to a right of publicity claim can also support a claim for false designation of origin under section 43(a) of the Lanham Act. As a result, many plaintiffs pursue remedies under both theories.

A. NATURE AND SCOPE

MIDLER V. FORD MOTOR CO.

849 F.2d 460 (9th Cir. 1988).

NOONAN, CIRCUIT JUDGE:

This case centers on the protectibility of the voice of a celebrated chanteuse from commercial exploitation without her consent. Ford Motor Company and its advertising agency, Young & Rubicam, Inc., in 1985 advertised the Ford Lincoln Mercury with a series of nineteen 30 or 60 second television commercials in what the agency called "The Yuppie Campaign." The aim was to make an emotional connection with Yuppies, bringing back memories of when they were in college. Different popular songs of the seventies were sung on each commercial. The agency tried to get "the original people," that is, the singers who had popularized the songs, to sing them. Failing in that endeavor in ten cases the agency had the songs sung by "sound alikes." Bette Midler, the plaintiff and appellant here, was done by a sound alike.

Midler is a nationally known actress and singer. She won a Grammy as early as 1973 as the Best New Artist of that year. Records made by her since then have gone Platinum and Gold. She was nominated in 1979 for an Academy award for Best Female Actress in The Rose, in which she portrayed a pop singer. Newsweek in its June 30, 1986 issue described her as an "outrageously original singer/comedian." Time hailed her in its March 2, 1987 issue as "a legend" and "the most dynamic and poignant singer-actress of her time."

When Young & Rubicam was preparing the Yuppie Campaign it presented the commercial to its client by playing an edited version of Midler singing "Do You Want To Dance," taken from the 1973 Midler album, "The Divine Miss M." After the client accepted the idea and form of the commercial, the agency contacted Midler's manager, Jerry Edelstein. The conversation went as follows: "Hello, I am Craig Hazen from Young and Rubicam. I am calling you to find out if Bette Midler would be interested in doing . . .?" Edelstein: "Is it a commercial?" "Yes." "We are not interested."

Undeterred, Young & Rubicam sought out Ula Hedwig, whom it knew to have been one of "the Harlettes" a backup singer for Midler for ten years. Hedwig was told by Young & Rubicam that "they wanted someone who could sound like Bette Midler's recording of [Do You Want To Dance]." She was asked to make a "demo" tape of the song if she was interested. She made an a capella demo and got the job.

At the direction of Young & Rubicam, Hedwig then made a record for the commercial. The Midler record of "Do You Want To Dance" was first played to her. She was told to "sound as much as possible like the Bette Midler record," leaving out only a few "aahs" unsuitable for the commercial. Hedwig imitated Midler to the best of her ability.

After the commercial was aired Midler was told by "a number of people" that it "sounded exactly" like her record of "Do You Want To Dance." Hedwig was told by "many personal friends" that they thought it was Midler singing the commercial. Ken Fritz, a personal manager in the entertainment business not associated with Midler, declares by affidavit that he heard the commercial on more than one occasion and thought Midler was doing the singing.

Neither the name nor the picture of Midler was used in the commercial; Young & Rubicam had a license from the copyright holder to use the song. At issue in this case is only the protection of Midler's voice. The district court described the defendants' conduct as that "of the average thief." They decided, "If we can't buy it, we'll take it." The court nonetheless believed there was no legal principle preventing imitation of Midler's voice and so gave summary judgment for the defendants. Midler appeals.

The First Amendment protects much of what the media do in the reproduction of likenesses or sounds. A primary value is freedom of speech and press. *Time, Inc. v. Hill*, 385 U.S. 374, 388 (1967). The purpose of the media's use of a person's identity is central. If the purpose is "informative or cultural" the use is immune; "if it serves no such function but merely exploits the individual portrayed, immunity will not be granted." Felcher and Rubin, *Privacy, Publicity and the Portrayal of Real People by the Media*, 88 YALE L.J. 1577, 1596 (1979). Moreover, federal copyright law preempts much of the area. "Mere imitation of a recorded performance would not constitute a copyright infringement even where one performer deliberately sets out to simulate another's performance as exactly as possible." Notes of Committee on the Judiciary, 17 U.S.C.A. § 114(b). It is in the context of these First Amendment and federal copyright distinctions that we address the present appeal.

Nancy Sinatra once sued Goodyear Tire and Rubber Company on the basis of an advertising campaign by Young & Rubicam featuring "These Boots Are Made For Walkin'," a song closely identified with her; the female singers of the commercial were alleged to have imitated her voice and style and to have dressed and looked like her. The basis of Nancy Sinatra's complaint was unfair competition; she claimed that the song and the arrangement had acquired "a secondary meaning" which, under California law, was protectible. This court noted that the defendants "had paid a very substantial sum to the copyright proprietor to obtain the license for the use of the song and all of its arrangements." To give Sinatra damages for their use of the song would clash with federal copyright law. Summary judgment for the defendants was affirmed. *Sinatra v. Goodyear Tire & Rubber Co.*,

435 F.2d 711, 717–718 (9th Cir.1970). If Midler were claiming a secondary meaning to "Do You Want To Dance" or seeking to prevent the defendants from using that song, she would fail like Sinatra. But that is not this case. Midler does not seek damages for Ford's use of "Do You Want To Dance," and thus her claim is not preempted by federal copyright law. Copyright protects "original works of authorship fixed in any tangible medium of expression." 17 U.S.C. § 102(a). A voice is not copyrightable. The sounds are not "fixed." What is put forward as protectible here is more personal than any work of authorship.

Bert Lahr once sued Adell Chemical Co. for selling Lestoil by means of a commercial in which an imitation of Lahr's voice accompanied a cartoon of a duck. Lahr alleged that his style of vocal delivery was distinctive in pitch, accent, inflection, and sounds. The First Circuit held that Lahr had stated a cause of action for unfair competition, that it could be found "that defendant's conduct saturated plaintiff's audience, curtailing his market." *Lahr v. Adell Chemical Co.*, 300 F.2d 256, 259 (1st Cir.1962). That case is more like this one. But we do not find unfair competition here. One-minute commercials of the sort the defendants put on would not have saturated Midler's audience and curtailed her market. Midler did not do television commercials. The defendants were not in competition with her.

California Civil Code section 3344 is also of no aid to Midler. The statute affords damages to a person injured by another who uses the person's "name, voice, signature, photograph or likeness, in any manner." The defendants did not use Midler's name or anything else whose use is prohibited by the statute. The voice they used was Hedwig's, not hers. The term "likeness" refers to a visual image not a vocal imitation. The statute, however, does not preclude Midler from pursuing any cause of action she may have at common law; the statute itself implies that such common law causes of action do exist because it says its remedies are merely "cumulative." *Id.* § 3344(g).

* * * Appropriation of common law rights is a tort in California. *Motschenbacher v. R.J. Reynolds Tobacco Co.*, 498 F.2d 821 (9th Cir.1974). In that case what the defendants used in their television commercial for Winston cigarettes was a photograph of a famous professional racing driver's racing car. The number of the car was changed and a wing-like device known as a "spoiler" was attached to the car; the car's features of white pinpointing, an oval medallion, and solid red coloring were retained. The driver, Lothar Motschenbacher, was in the car but his features were not visible. Some persons, viewing the commercial, correctly inferred that the car was his and that he was in the car and was therefore endorsing the product. The defendants were held to have invaded a "proprietary interest" of Motschenbacher in his own identity.

Midler's case is different from Motschenbacher's. He and his car were physically used by the tobacco company's ad; he made part of his living out of giving commercial endorsements. But, as Judge Koelsch expressed it in *Motschenbacher*, California will recognize an injury from "an appropriation of the attributes of one's identity." *Id.* at 824. It was irrelevant that Motschenbacher could not be identified in the ad. The ad suggested that it was he. The ad did so by emphasizing signs or symbols associated with him. In the same way the defendants here used an imitation to convey the impression that Midler was singing for them.

Why did the defendants ask Midler to sing if her voice was not of value to them? Why did they studiously acquire the services of a sound-alike and instruct her to imitate Midler if Midler's voice was not of value to them? What they sought was an attribute of Midler's identity. Its value was what the market would have paid for Midler to have sung the commercial in person.

A voice is more distinctive and more personal than the automobile accoutrements protected in *Motschenbacher*. A voice is as distinctive and personal as a face. The human voice is one of the most palpable ways identity is manifested. We are all aware that a friend is at once known by a few words on the phone. At a philosophical level it has been observed that with the sound of a voice, "the other stands before me." D. IHDE, LISTENING AND VOICE 77 (1976). A fortiori, these observations hold true of singing, especially singing by a singer of renown. The singer manifests herself in the song. To impersonate her voice is to pirate her identity.

We need not and do not go so far as to hold that every imitation of a voice to advertise merchandise is actionable. We hold only that when a distinctive voice of a professional singer is widely known and is deliberately imitated in order to sell a product, the sellers have appropriated what is not theirs and have committed a tort in California. Midler has made a showing, sufficient to defeat summary judgment, that the defendants here for their own profit in selling their product did appropriate part of her identity.

NOTES

1. On these facts, could Bette Midler have also brought a claim under section 43(a) of the Lanham Act? Would the analysis differ, and if so, how?

2. Would the right of publicity be implicated when figures resembling characters from the television series "Cheers" are placed in airport bars licensed by the producers of Cheers? *See Wendt v. Host International, Inc.*, 125 F.3d 806 (9th Cir. 1997). By use of a basketball star's former name, Lew Alcindor, in an advertisement for automobile? *See Abdul-Jabbar v. General Motors Corp.*, 85 F.3d 407 (9th Cir. 1996). By use of the phrase "Here's Johnny" (which was used to introduce talk-show host Johnny Carson) in connection

with the sale of portable toilets? *See Carson v. Here's Johnny Portable Toilets, Inc.*, 698 F.2d 831 (6th Cir. 1983).

3. Most states recognize the right of publicity—many by statute, some by common law, and California by both—but there is wide variation in their scope. Some states do not recognize claims for voice imitations or for postmortem rights. What features of a person's identity should the right encompass—names, nicknames, facial features, digital avatars, caricatures, body shape, posture, voice, vocal styles, mannerisms, speech patterns, catch phrases, hairstyles, fashion styles, jersey numbers, musical instruments, race car markings, or a song made famous by a specific performer?

4. State laws differ on whether the right of publicity is assignable, and also on the existence, scope, and duration of a descendible postmortem right. Would resolution of these issues depend on the policy underpinning the right of publicity? If the right persists after death, how long should it endure, and under what conditions? Who should have standing to bring a postmortem claim, or the authority to grant licenses? Should individuals be allowed to assign their rights of publicity, even though they might later regret that decision? Should these questions be answered by courts or by legislatures?

5. Because of the wide variation in right of publicity laws, there can be significant conflict of law problems when a claim involves a celebrity domiciled in one jurisdiction but the allegedly infringing conduct took place in a different jurisdiction. For example, the estates of Marilyn Monroe, Jimi Hendrix and Diana, Princess of Wales, have all encountered difficulty in asserting right of publicity claims, even in states that recognize the postmortem right, because at the time of their deaths all three were domiciled in jurisdictions that do not recognize a postmortem right. Can conflict of laws principles resolve these problems? Should a federal statute be enacted to establish uniformity? If so, should it preempt state laws completely?

6. Would professional baseball players' publicity rights with regard to the broadcast of copyrighted baseball games be preempted by federal copyright law? Is this situation different from *Midler*? *See National Basketball Ass'n v. Motorola*, 105 F.3d 841 (2d Cir. 1997). Could a performer bring a right of publicity claim based on unauthorized images of a character that he or she played in a copyrighted film or television show?

7. Although there is no federal law recognizing a generally-applicable right of publicity, the anti-bootlegging provisions in 17 U.S.C. § 1101 offer a limited version of the right. Who is protected, and under what circumstances?

B. LIMITATIONS

ETW CORP. V. JIREH PUBLISHING, INC.

332 F.3d 915 (6th Cir. 2003).

GRAHAM, DISTRICT JUDGE.

Plaintiff-Appellant ETW Corporation ("ETW") is the licensing agent of Eldrick "Tiger" Woods ("Woods"), one of the world's most famous professional golfers. Woods, chairman of the board of ETW, has assigned to it the exclusive right to exploit his name, image, likeness, and signature, and all other publicity rights. ETW owns a United States trademark registration for the mark "TIGER WOODS" (Registration No. 2,194,381) for use in connection with "art prints, calendars, mounted photographs, notebooks, pencils, pens, posters, trading cards, and unmounted photographs."

Defendant-Appellee Jireh Publishing, Inc. ("Jireh") of Tuscaloosa, Alabama, is the publisher of artwork created by Rick Rush ("Rush"). Rush, who refers to himself as "America's sports artist," has created paintings of famous figures in sports and famous sports events. A few examples include Michael Jordan, Mark McGuire, Coach Paul "Bear" Bryant, the Pebble Beach Golf Tournament, and the America's Cup Yacht Race. Jireh has produced and successfully marketed limited edition art prints made from Rush's paintings.

In 1998, Rush created a painting entitled The Masters of Augusta, which commemorates Woods's victory at the Masters Tournament in Augusta, Georgia, in 1997. At that event, Woods became the youngest player ever to win the Masters Tournament, while setting a 72-hole record for the tournament and a record 12-stroke margin of victory. In the foreground of Rush's painting are three views of Woods in different poses. In the center, he is completing the swing of a golf club, and on each side he is crouching, lining up and/or observing the progress of a putt. To the left of Woods is his caddy, Mike "Fluff" Cowan, and to his right is his final round partner's caddy. Behind these figures is the Augusta National Clubhouse. In a blue background behind the clubhouse are likenesses of famous golfers of the past looking down on Woods. These include Arnold Palmer, Sam Snead, Ben Hogan, Walter Hagen, Bobby Jones, and Jack Nicklaus. Behind them is the Masters leader board.

The limited edition prints distributed by Jireh consist of an image of Rush's painting which includes Rush's signature at the bottom right hand corner. Beneath the image of the painting, in block letters, is its title, "The Masters Of Augusta." Beneath the title, in block letters of equal height, is the artist's name, "Rick Rush," and beneath the artist's name, in smaller upper and lower case letters, is the legend "Painting America Through Sports."

As sold by Jireh, the limited edition prints are enclosed in a white envelope, accompanied with literature which includes a large photograph of Rush, a description of his art, and a narrative description of the subject painting. On the front of the envelope, Rush's name appears in block letters inside a rectangle, which includes the legend "Painting America Through Sports." Along the bottom is a large reproduction of Rush's signature two inches high and ten inches long. On the back of the envelope, under the flap, are the words "Masters of Augusta" in letters that are three-eighths of an inch high, and "Tiger Woods" in letters that are one-fourth of an inch high. Woods's name also appears in the narrative description of the painting where he is mentioned twice in twenty-eight lines of text. The text also includes references to the six other famous golfers depicted in the background of the painting as well as the two caddies. Jireh published and marketed two hundred and fifty 22″ × 30″ serigraphs and five thousand 9″ × 11″ lithographs of The Masters of Augusta at an issuing price of $700 for the serigraphs and $100 for the lithographs.

* * *

ETW filed suit against Jireh [alleging] violation of Woods's right of publicity under Ohio common law. Jireh counterclaimed, seeking a declaratory judgment that Rush's art prints are protected by the First Amendment * * *. Both parties moved for summary judgment. [The district court granted the defendant's motion, and ETW appealed.]

* * *

D. Right of Publicity Claim

ETW claims that Jireh's publication and marketing of prints of Rush's painting violates Woods's right of publicity. The right of publicity is an intellectual property right of recent origin which has been defined as the inherent right of every human being to control the commercial use of his or her identity. The right of publicity is a creature of state law and its violation gives rise to a cause of action for the commercial tort of unfair competition.

The right of publicity is, somewhat paradoxically, an outgrowth of the right of privacy. A cause of action for violation of the right was first recognized in *Haelan Laboratories, Inc. v. Topps Chewing Gum, Inc.*, 202 F.2d 866 (2nd Cir.1953), where the Second Circuit held that New York's common law protected a baseball player's right in the publicity value of his photograph, and in the process coined the phrase "right of publicity" as the name of this right.

The Ohio Supreme Court recognized the right of publicity in 1976 in *Zacchini v. Scripps-Howard Broadcasting Co.* 351 N.E.2d 454 (Ohio 1976).

In *Zacchini*, which involved the videotaping and subsequent rebroadcast on a television news program of plaintiff's human cannonball act, the Ohio Supreme Court held that Zacchini's right of publicity was trumped by the First Amendment. On appeal, the Supreme Court of the United States reversed, holding that the First Amendment did not insulate defendant from liability for violating Zacchini's state law right of publicity where defendant published the plaintiff's entire act. *See Zacchini v. Scripps-Howard Broadcasting Co.*, 433 U.S. 562 (1977). *Zacchini* is the only United States Supreme Court decision on the right of publicity.

* * *

In § 47, Comment c, the authors of the RESTATEMENT (THIRD) OF UNFAIR COMPETITION note, "The right of publicity as recognized by statute and common law is fundamentally constrained by the public and constitutional interest in freedom of expression." In the same comment, the authors state that "[t]he use of a person's identity primarily for the purpose of communicating information or expressing ideas is not generally actionable as a violation of the person's right of publicity." Various examples are given, including the use of the person's name or likeness in news reporting in newspapers and magazines. The RESTATEMENT recognizes that this limitation on the right is not confined to news reporting but extends to use in "entertainment and other creative works, including both fiction and non-fiction." The authors list examples of protected uses of a celebrity's identity, likeness or image, including unauthorized print or broadcast biographies and novels, plays or motion pictures. According to the RESTATEMENT, such uses are not protected, however, if the name or likeness is used solely to attract attention to a work that is not related to the identified person, and the privilege may be lost if the work contains substantial falsifications.

We believe the courts of Ohio would follow the principles of the RESTATEMENT in defining the limits of the right of publicity. The Ohio Supreme Court's decision in *Zacchini* suggests that Ohio is inclined to give substantial weight to the public interest in freedom of expression when balancing it against the personal and proprietary interests recognized by the right of publicity. * * *

This court first encountered the right of publicity in *Memphis Development Foundation v. Factors Etc., Inc.*, 616 F.2d 956 (6th Cir.1980), where the issue presented was whether the heirs of Elvis Presley retained his right of publicity after his death. We concluded that they did not. We held that under Tennessee law, "[t]he famous have an exclusive legal right during life to control and profit from the commercial use of their name and personality." *Id.* at 957. Noting that the Tennessee courts had not addressed the issue, we decided the case "in the light of practical and policy considerations, the treatment of other similar rights in our legal system, the relative weight of the conflicting interests of the parties, and certain moral presuppositions concerning death, privacy, inheritability and economic opportunity." *Id.* at 958.

In *Carson v. Here's Johnny Portable Toilets, Inc.*, 698 F.2d 831 (6th Cir.1983), a majority of this court, with Judge Kennedy dissenting, held that television comedian and talk show host Johnny Carson's right of publicity was invaded when defendant used the phrase with which Carson was commonly introduced on his television program. In *Carson*, we held that "a celebrity has a protected pecuniary interest in the commercial exploitation of his identity." *Id.* at 835.

In *Landham v. Lewis Galoob Toys, Inc.*, 227 F.3d 619, 625–26 (6th Cir. 2000), this court held that Landham, a fringe actor who played supporting roles in several motion pictures, had failed to show a violation of his right of publicity when defendant marketed an action figure of a character he had played but which did not bear a personal resemblance to him. This court found that Landham had failed to show that his persona had significant value or that the toy invoked his persona as distinct from that of the fictional character he played.

There is an inherent tension between the right of publicity and the right of freedom of expression under the First Amendment. This tension becomes particularly acute when the person seeking to enforce the right is a famous actor, athlete, politician, or otherwise famous person whose exploits, activities, accomplishments, and personal life are subject to constant scrutiny and comment in the public media. In *Memphis Development Foundation*, 616 F.2d at 959, this court discussed the problems of judicial line drawing that would arise if it should recognize the inheritability of publicity rights, including the question "[a]t what point does the right collide with the right of free expression guaranteed by the First Amendment?" In *Carson*, after noting that the First Amendment protects commercial speech, Judge Kennedy opined in her dissent that "public policy requires that the public's interest in free enterprise and free expression take precedence over any interest Johnny Carson may have in a phrase associated with his person." *Carson*, 698 F.2d at 841. In *Landham*, we noted "the careful balance that courts have gradually constructed between the right of publicity and the First Amendment[.]" 227 F.3d at 626.

In a series of recent cases, other circuits have been called upon to establish the boundaries between the right of publicity and the First Amendment. In *Rogers v. Grimaldi*, 875 F.2d 994 (2d Cir. 1989), the Second Circuit affirmed the district court's grant of summary judgment on Rogers' right of publicity claim, noting that commentators have "advocated limits on the right of publicity to accommodate First Amendment concerns." 875 F.2d at 1004 n. 11. That court also cited three cases in which state courts refused to extend the right of publicity to bar the use of a celebrity's name in the title and text of a fictional or semi-fictional book or movie.

In *White v. Samsung Electronics America, Inc.*, 971 F.2d 1395 (9th Cir. 1992), television celebrity Vanna White, brought suit against Samsung Electronics, alleging that its television advertisement which featured a female-shaped robot wearing a long gown, blonde wig, large jewelry, and turning letters in what appeared to be the "Wheel of Fortune" game show set, violated her California common law right of publicity and her rights under the Lanham Act. The Ninth Circuit, with Judge Alarcon dissenting in part, reversed the grant of summary judgment to defendant, holding that White had produced sufficient evidence that defendant's advertisement appropriated her identity in violation of her right of publicity, and that the issue of confusion about White's endorsement of defendant's product created a jury issue which precluded summary judgment on her Lanham Act claim. In so holding, the court rejected the defendant's parody defense which posited that the advertisement was a parody of White's television act and was protected speech.

A suggestion for rehearing en banc failed. Three judges dissented from the order rejecting the suggestion for a rehearing en banc. *See White v. Samsung Electronics America, Inc.*, 989 F.2d 1512 (9th Cir.1993). Judge Kozinski, writing the dissenting opinion, observed, "Something very dangerous is going on here. . . . Overprotecting intellectual property is as harmful as underprotecting it. Creativity is impossible without a rich public domain." 989 F.2d at 1513. Later, he commented:

> Intellectual property rights aren't free: They're imposed at the expense of future creators and of the public at large. . . . This is why intellectual property law is full of careful balances between what's set aside for the owner and what's left in the public domain for the rest of us[.]

Id. at 1516. In *Landham*, this court declined to follow the majority in *White* and, instead, cited Judge Kozinski's dissent with approval.

In *Cardtoons, L.C. v. Major League Baseball Players Assoc.*, 95 F.3d 959 (10th Cir.1996), the Tenth Circuit held that the plaintiff's First Amendment right to free expression outweighed the defendant's proprietary right of publicity. The plaintiff in *Cardtoons* contracted with a political cartoonist, a sports artist, and a sports author and journalist to design a set of trading cards which featured readily identifiable caricatures of major league baseball players with a humorous commentary about their careers on the back. The cards ridiculed the players using a variety of themes. The cards used similar names, recognizable caricatures, distinctive team colors and commentaries about individual players which left no doubt about their identity. The Tenth Circuit held that the defendant's use of the player's likenesses on its trading cards would violate their rights of publicity under an Oklahoma statute. Addressing the defendant's First Amendment claim, the court held:

> Cardtoons' parody trading cards receive full protection under the First Amendment. The cards provide social commentary on public figures, major league baseball players, who are involved in a significant commercial enterprise, major league baseball. While not core political speech . . . this type of commentary on an important social institution constitutes protected expression.

Cardtoons, 95 F.3d at 969. The Tenth Circuit rejected the reasoning of the panel majority in *White*, and expressed its agreement with the dissenting opinions of Judges Alarcon and Kozinski. *See* 95 F.3d at 970 ("We disagree with the result in [*White*] for reasons discussed in the two dissents that it engendered."). In striking the balance between the players' property rights and the defendant's First Amendment rights, the court in *Cardtoons* commented on the pervasive presence of celebrities in the media, sports and entertainment. The court noted that celebrities are an important part of our public vocabulary and have come to symbolize certain ideas and values * * *. *Cardtoons*, 95 F.3d at 972. * * * The Tenth Circuit affirmed the district court's ruling that the trading cards were expression protected by the First Amendment.

* * *

In *Comedy III Productions, Inc. v. Gary Saderup, Inc.*, 21 P.3d 797 (Cal. 2001), the California Supreme Court adopted a transformative use test in determining whether the artistic use of a celebrity's image is protected by the First Amendment. Saderup, an artist with over twenty-five years experience in making charcoal drawings of celebrities, created a drawing of the famous comedy team, The Three Stooges. The drawings were used to create lithographic and silk screen masters, which were then used to produce lithographic prints and silk screen images on T-shirts. Comedy III, the owner of all rights to the former comedy act, brought suit against Saderup under a California statute, which grants the right of publicity to successors in interest of deceased celebrities.

The California Supreme Court found that Saderup's portraits were entitled to First Amendment protection because they were "expressive works and not an advertisement or endorsement of a product." * * *

The court rejected the proposition that Saderup's lithographs and T-shirts lost their First Amendment protection because they were not original single works of art, but were instead part of a commercial enterprise designed to generate profit solely from the sale of multiple reproductions of likenesses of The Three Stooges:

> [T]his position has no basis in logic or authority. No one would claim that a published book, because it is one of many copies,

> receives less First Amendment protection than the original manuscript. . . . [A] reproduction of a celebrity image that, as explained above, contains significant creative elements is entitled to as much First Amendment protection as an original work of art.

Id. at 810.

Borrowing part of the fair use defense from copyright law, the California court proposed the following test for distinguishing between protected and unprotected expression when the right of publicity conflicts with the First Amendment:

> When artistic expression takes the form of a literal depiction or imitation of a celebrity for commercial gain, directly trespassing on the right of publicity without adding significant expression beyond that trespass, the state law interest in protecting the fruits of artistic labor outweighs the expressive interests of the imitative artist.
>
> On the other hand, when a work contains significant transformative elements, it is not only especially worthy of First Amendment protection, but it is also less likely to interfere with the economic interest protected by the right of publicity. . . .
>
> Accordingly, First Amendment protection of such works outweighs whatever interest the state may have in enforcing the right of publicity.

Id. at 808. Later in its opinion, the California court restated the test as follows:

> Another way of stating the inquiry is whether the celebrity likeness is one of the "raw materials" from which an original work is synthesized, or whether the depiction or imitation of the celebrity is the very sum and substance of the work in question.

Id. at 809.

Finally, citing the art of Andy Warhol, the court noted that even literal reproductions of celebrity portraits may be protected by the First Amendment.

> Through distortion and the careful manipulation of context, Warhol was able to convey a message that went beyond the commercial exploitation of celebrity images and became a form of ironic social comment on the dehumanization of celebrity itself. . . . Although the distinction between protected and unprotected expression will sometimes be subtle, it is no more so than other distinctions triers of fact are called on to make in First Amendment jurisprudence.

Id. at 811.

We conclude that in deciding whether the sale of Rush's prints violate Woods's right of publicity, we will look to the Ohio case law and the RESTATEMENT (THIRD) OF UNFAIR COMPETITION. In deciding where the line should be drawn between Woods's intellectual property rights and the First Amendment, we find ourselves in agreement with the dissenting judges in *White*, the Tenth Circuit's decision in *Cardtoons*, and the Ninth Circuit's decision in *Hoffman*, and we will follow them in determining whether Rush's work is protected by the First Amendment. Finally, we believe that the transformative elements test adopted by the Supreme Court of California in *Comedy III Productions*, will assist us in determining where the proper balance lies between the First Amendment and Woods's intellectual property rights. We turn now to a further examination of Rush's work and its subject.

E. *Application of the Law to the Evidence in this Case*

The evidence in the record reveals that Rush's work consists of much more than a mere literal likeness of Woods. It is a panorama of Woods's victory at the 1997 Masters Tournament, with all of the trappings of that tournament in full view, including the Augusta clubhouse, the leader board, images of Woods's caddy, and his final round partner's caddy. These elements in themselves are sufficient to bring Rush's work within the protection of the First Amendment. The Masters Tournament is probably the world's most famous golf tournament and Woods's victory in the 1997 tournament was a historic event in the world of sports. A piece of art that portrays a historic sporting event communicates and celebrates the value our culture attaches to such events. It would be ironic indeed if the presence of the image of the victorious athlete would deny the work First Amendment protection. Furthermore, Rush's work includes not only images of Woods and the two caddies, but also carefully crafted likenesses of six past winners of the Masters Tournament: Arnold Palmer, Sam Snead, Ben Hogan, Walter Hagen, Bobby Jones, and Jack Nicklaus, a veritable pantheon of golf's greats. Rush's work conveys the message that Woods himself will someday join that revered group.

* * *

In regard to the Ohio law right of publicity claim, we conclude that Ohio would construe its right of publicity as suggested in the RESTATEMENT (THIRD) OF UNFAIR COMPETITION, Chapter 4, Section 47, Comment d., which articulates a rule analogous to the rule of fair use in copyright law. Under this rule, the substantiality and market effect of the use of the celebrity's image is analyzed in light of the informational and creative content of the defendant's use. Applying this rule, we conclude that Rush's work has substantial informational and creative content which outweighs any adverse effect on ETW's market and that Rush's work does not violate Woods's right of publicity.

We further find that Rush's work is expression which is entitled to the full protection of the First Amendment and not the more limited protection afforded to commercial speech. When we balance the magnitude of the speech restriction against the interest in protecting Woods's intellectual property right, we encounter precisely the same considerations weighed by the Tenth Circuit in *Cardtoons*. These include consideration of the fact that through their pervasive presence in the media, sports and entertainment celebrities have come to symbolize certain ideas and values in our society and have become a valuable means of expression in our culture. As the Tenth Circuit observed "[c]elebrities . . . are an important element of the shared communicative resources of our cultural domain."

* * *

After balancing the societal and personal interests embodied in the First Amendment against Woods's property rights, we conclude that the effect of limiting Woods's right of publicity in this case is negligible and significantly outweighed by society's interest in freedom of artistic expression.

Finally, applying the transformative effects test adopted by the Supreme Court of California in *Comedy III*, we find that Rush's work does contain significant transformative elements which make it especially worthy of First Amendment protection and also less likely to interfere with the economic interest protected by Woods' right of publicity. Unlike the unadorned, nearly photographic reproduction of the faces of The Three Stooges in *Comedy III*, Rush's work does not capitalize solely on a literal depiction of Woods. Rather, Rush's work consists of a collage of images in addition to Woods's image which are combined to describe, in artistic form, a historic event in sports history and to convey a message about the significance of Woods's achievement in that event. Because Rush's work has substantial transformative elements, it is entitled to the full protection of the First Amendment. In this case, we find that Woods's right of publicity must yield to the First Amendment.

* * *

NOTE

The plaintiff in *ETW* also brought several Lanham Act claims—for infringement, dilution, and false advertising—based on the unauthorized use of Tiger Woods' likeness as well as the registered trademark TIGER WOODS. How would the analysis of these Lanham Act claims differ from the right of publicity analysis?

IN RE NCAA STUDENT-ATHLETE NAME & LIKENESS LICENSING LITIGATION (KELLER V. ELECTRONIC ARTS)

724 F.3d 1268 (9th Cir. 2013).

BYBEE, CIRCUIT JUDGE:

Video games are entitled to the full protections of the First Amendment, because "[l]ike the protected books, plays, and movies that preceded them, video games communicate ideas—and even social messages—through many familiar literary devices (such as characters, dialogue, plot, and music) and through features distinctive to the medium (such as the player's interaction with the virtual world)." *Brown v. Entm't Merchs. Ass'n,* 564 U.S. 786, 790 (2011). Such rights are not absolute, and states may recognize the right of publicity to a degree consistent with the First Amendment. *Zacchini v. Scripps-Howard Broad. Co.,* 433 U.S. 562, 574–75 (1977). In this case, we must balance the right of publicity of a former college football player against the asserted First Amendment right of a video game developer to use his likeness in its expressive works.

The district court concluded that the game developer, Electronic Arts ("EA"), had no First Amendment defense against the right-of-publicity claims of the football player, Samuel Keller. We affirm. Under the "transformative use" test developed by the California Supreme Court, EA's use does not qualify for First Amendment protection as a matter of law because it literally recreates Keller in the very setting in which he has achieved renown. The other First Amendment defenses asserted by EA do not defeat Keller's claims either.

I

Samuel Keller was the starting quarterback for Arizona State University in 2005 before he transferred to the University of Nebraska, where he played during the 2007 season. EA is the producer of the *NCAA Football* series of video games, which allow users to control avatars representing college football players as those avatars participate in simulated games. In *NCAA Football,* EA seeks to replicate each school's entire team as accurately as possible. Every real football player on each team included in the game has a corresponding avatar in the game with the player's actual jersey number and virtually identical height, weight, build, skin tone, hair color, and home state. EA attempts to match any unique, highly identifiable playing behaviors by sending detailed questionnaires to team equipment managers. Additionally, EA creates realistic virtual versions of actual stadiums; populates them with the virtual athletes, coaches, cheerleaders, and fans realistically rendered by EA's graphic artists; and incorporates realistic sounds such as the crunch of the players' pads and the roar of the crowd.

EA's game differs from reality in that EA omits the players' names on their jerseys and assigns each player a home town that is different from the actual player's home town. However, users of the video game may upload rosters of names obtained from third parties so that the names do appear on the jerseys. In such cases, EA allows images from the game containing athletes' real names to be posted on its website by users. Users can further alter reality by entering "Dynasty" mode, where the user assumes a head coach's responsibilities for a college program for up to thirty seasons, including recruiting players from a randomly generated pool of high school athletes, or "Campus Legend" mode, where the user controls a virtual player from high school through college, making choices relating to practices, academics, and social life.

In the 2005 edition of the game, the virtual starting quarterback for Arizona State wears number 9, as did Keller, and has the same height, weight, skin tone, hair color, hair style, handedness, home state, play style (pocket passer), visor preference, facial features, and school year as Keller. In the 2008 edition, the virtual quarterback for Nebraska has these same characteristics, though the jersey number does not match, presumably because Keller changed his number right before the season started.

Objecting to this use of his likeness, Keller filed a putative class-action complaint in the Northern District of California asserting, as relevant on appeal, that EA violated his right of publicity under California Civil Code § 3344 and California common law.

* * * EA did not contest before the district court and does not contest here that Keller has stated a right-of-publicity claim under California common and statutory law. Instead, EA raises four affirmative defenses derived from the First Amendment: the "transformative use" test, the *Rogers* test, the "public interest" test, and the "public affairs" exemption. EA argues that, in light of these defenses, it is not reasonably probable that Keller will prevail on his right-of-publicity claim. This appeal therefore centers on the applicability of these defenses. We take each one in turn.

A

The California Supreme Court formulated the transformative use defense in *Comedy III Productions, Inc. v. Gary Saderup, Inc.*, 25 Cal.4th 387 (2001). The defense is "a balancing test between the First Amendment and the right of publicity based on whether the work in question adds significant creative elements so as to be transformed into something more than a mere celebrity likeness or imitation." *Id.* The California Supreme Court explained that "when a work contains significant transformative elements, it is not only especially worthy of First Amendment protection, but it is also less likely to interfere with the economic interest protected by the right of publicity." The court rejected the wholesale importation of the copyright "fair use" defense into right-of-publicity claims, but recognized that some aspects of that defense are "particularly pertinent."

Comedy III gives us at least five factors to consider in determining whether a work is sufficiently transformative to obtain First Amendment protection. First, if "the celebrity likeness is one of the 'raw materials' from which an original work is synthesized," it is more likely to be transformative than if "the depiction or imitation of the celebrity is the very sum and substance of the work in question." Second, the work is protected if it is "primarily the defendant's own expression"—as long as that expression is "something other than the likeness of the celebrity." This factor requires an examination of whether a likely purchaser's primary motivation is to buy a reproduction of the celebrity, or to buy the expressive work of that artist. Third, to avoid making judgments concerning "the quality of the artistic contribution," a court should conduct an inquiry "more quantitative than qualitative" and ask "whether the literal and imitative or the creative elements predominate in the work." Fourth, the California Supreme Court indicated that "a subsidiary inquiry" would be useful in close cases: whether "the marketability and economic value of the challenged work derive primarily from the fame of the celebrity depicted." Lastly, the court indicated that "when an artist's skill and talent is manifestly subordinated to the overall goal of creating a conventional portrait of a celebrity so as to commercially exploit his or her fame," the work is not transformative.

* * *

California courts have applied the transformative use test in relevant situations in four cases. First, in *Comedy III* itself, the California Supreme Court applied the test to T-shirts and lithographs bearing a likeness of The Three Stooges and concluded that it could "discern no significant transformative or creative contribution." The court reasoned that the artist's "undeniable skill is manifestly subordinated to the overall goal of creating literal, conventional depictions of The Three Stooges so as to exploit their fame." "[W]ere we to decide that [the artist's] depictions were protected by the First Amendment," the court continued, "we cannot perceive how the right of publicity would remain a viable right other than in cases of falsified celebrity endorsements."

Second, in *Winter v. DC Comics,* the California Supreme Court applied the test to comic books containing characters Johnny and Edgar Autumn, "depicted as villainous half-worm, half-human offspring" but evoking two famous brothers, rockers Johnny and Edgar Winter. 30 Cal.4th 881, 134 Cal.Rptr.2d 634, 69 P.3d 473, 476 (2003). The court held that "the comic books are transformative and entitled to First Amendment protection." It reasoned that the comic books "are not just conventional depictions of plaintiffs but contain significant expressive content other than plaintiffs' mere likenesses." "To the extent the drawings of the Autumn brothers resemble plaintiffs at all, they are distorted for purposes of lampoon, parody, or caricature." *Id.* Importantly, the court relied on the fact that the brothers "are but cartoon characters . . . in a larger story, which is itself quite expressive."

Third, in *Kirby v. Sega of America, Inc.*, the California Court of Appeal applied the transformative use test to a video game in which the user controls the dancing of "Ulala," a reporter from outer space allegedly based on singer Kierin Kirby, whose " 'signature' lyrical expression . . . is 'ooh la la.' " 144 Cal.App.4th 47, 50 Cal.Rptr.3d 607, 609–10 (2006). The court held that "Ulala is more than a mere likeness or literal depiction of Kirby," pointing to Ulala's "extremely tall, slender computer-generated physique," her "hairstyle and primary costume," her dance moves, and her role as "a space-age reporter in the 25th century," all of which were "unlike any public depiction of Kirby." "As in *Winter,* Ulala is a 'fanciful, creative character' who exists in the context of a unique and expressive video game."

Finally, in *No Doubt v. Activision Publishing, Inc.*, the California Court of Appeal addressed Activision's *Band Hero* video game. 192 Cal.App.4th 1018, 122 Cal.Rptr.3d 397, 400 (2011). In *Band Hero,* users simulate performing in a rock band in time with popular songs. Users choose from a number of avatars, some of which represent actual rock stars, including the members of the rock band No Doubt. Activision licensed No Doubt's likeness, but allegedly exceeded the scope of the license by permitting users to manipulate the No Doubt avatars to play any song in the game, solo or with members of other bands, and even to alter the avatars' voices. The court held that No Doubt's right of publicity prevailed despite Activision's First Amendment defense because the game was not "transformative" under the *Comedy III* test. It reasoned that the video game characters were "literal recreations of the band members," doing "the same activity by which the band achieved and maintains its fame." * * * The court concluded that "the expressive elements of the game remain manifestly subordinated to the overall goal of creating a conventional portrait of No Doubt so as to commercially exploit its fame."

We have also had occasion to apply the transformative use test. In *Hilton v. Hallmark Cards,* we applied the test to a birthday card depicting Paris Hilton in a manner reminiscent of an episode of Hilton's reality show *The Simple Life.* 599 F.3d at 899. We observed some differences between the episode and the card, but noted that "the basic setting is the same: we see Paris Hilton, born to privilege, working as a waitress." We reasoned that "[w]hen we compare Hallmark's card to the video game in *Kirby,* which transported a 1990s singer (catchphrases and all) into the 25th century and transmogrified her into a space-age reporter, . . . the card falls far short of the level of new expression added in the video game." As a result, we concluded that "there is enough doubt as to whether Hallmark's card is transformative under our case law that we cannot say Hallmark is entitled to the defense as a matter of law."

With these cases in mind as guidance, we conclude that EA's use of Keller's likeness does not contain significant transformative elements such that EA is entitled to the defense as a matter of law. The facts of *No Doubt* are very similar to those here. EA is alleged to have replicated Keller's physical characteristics in *NCAA Football,* just as the members of No Doubt are realistically portrayed in *Band Hero*. Here, as in *Band Hero,* users manipulate the characters in the performance of the same activity for which they are known in real life—playing football in this case, and performing in a rock band in *Band Hero*. The context in which the activity occurs is also similarly realistic—real venues in *Band Hero* and realistic depictions of actual football stadiums in *NCAA Football*. As the district court found, Keller is represented as "what he was: the starting quarterback for Arizona State" and Nebraska, and "the game's setting is identical to where the public found [Keller] during his collegiate career: on the football field."

EA argues that the district court erred in focusing primarily on Keller's likeness and ignoring the transformative elements of the game as a whole. Judge Thomas, our dissenting colleague, suggests the same. We are unable to say that there was any error, particularly in light of *No Doubt,* which reasoned much the same as the district court in this case * * *. EA suggests that the fact that *NCAA Football* users can alter the characteristics of the avatars in the game is significant. Again, our dissenting colleague agrees. In *No Doubt,* the California Court of Appeal noted that *Band Hero* "d[id] not permit players to alter the No Doubt avatars in any respect." *Id.* at 410. The court went on to say that the No Doubt avatars "remain at all times immutable images of the real celebrity musicians, in stark contrast to the 'fanciful, creative characters' in *Winter* and *Kirby*." * * * Judge Thomas says that "[t]he Court of Appeal cited character immutability as a chief factor distinguishing [*No Doubt*] from *Winter* and *Kirby*." Though *No Doubt* certainly mentioned the immutability of the avatars, we do not read the California Court of Appeal's decision as turning on the inability of users to alter the avatars. The key contrast with *Winter* and *Kirby* was that in those games the public figures were transformed into "fanciful, creative characters" or "portrayed as . . . entirely new character[s]." *No Doubt,* 122 Cal.Rptr.3d at 410. On this front, our case is clearly aligned with *No Doubt,* not with *Winter* and *Kirby*. We believe *No Doubt* offers a persuasive precedent that cannot be materially distinguished from Keller's case.

The Third Circuit came to the same conclusion in *Hart v. Electronic Arts, Inc.,* 717 F.3d 141 (3d Cir.2013). In *Hart,* EA faced a materially identical challenge under New Jersey right-of-publicity law, brought by former Rutgers quarterback Ryan Hart. Though the Third Circuit was tasked with interpreting New Jersey law, the court looked to the transformative use test developed in California. Applying the test, the court held that "the *NCAA Football* . . . games at issue . . . do not sufficiently transform [Hart]'s identity to escape the right of publicity claim," reversing the district court's grant of summary judgment to EA.

As we have, the Third Circuit considered the potentially transformative nature of the game as a whole, and the user's ability to alter avatar characteristics. Asserting that "the lack of transformative context is even more pronounced here than in *No Doubt,*" *id.* at 166, and that "the ability to modify the avatar counts for little where the appeal of the game lies in users' ability to play as, or alongside [,] their preferred players or team," *id.* at 168, the Third Circuit agreed with us that these changes do not render the *NCAA Football* games sufficiently transformative to defeat a right-of-publicity claim.

* * *

B

EA urges us to adopt for right-of-publicity claims the broader First Amendment defense that we have previously adopted in the context of false endorsement claims under the Lanham Act: the *Rogers* test.

Rogers v. Grimaldi is a landmark Second Circuit case balancing First Amendment rights against claims under the Lanham Act. 875 F.2d 994 (2d Cir.1989). The case involved a suit brought by the famous performer Ginger Rogers against the producers and distributors of *Ginger and Fred,* a movie about two fictional Italian cabaret performers who imitated Rogers and her frequent performing partner Fred Astaire. Rogers alleged both a violation of the Lanham Act for creating the false impression that she endorsed the film and infringement of her common law right of publicity.

The *Rogers* court recognized that "[m]ovies, plays, books, and songs are all indisputably works of artistic expression and deserve protection," but that "[t]he purchaser of a book, like the purchaser of a can of peas, has a right not to be misled as to the source of the product." "Consumers of artistic works thus have a dual interest: They have an interest in not being misled and they also have an interest in enjoying the results of the author's freedom of expression." *Id.* at 998. The *Rogers* court determined that titles of artistic or literary works were less likely to be misleading than "the names of ordinary commercial products," and thus that Lanham Act protections applied with less rigor when considering titles of artistic or literary works than when considering ordinary products. The court concluded that "in general the Act should be construed to apply to artistic works only where the public interest in avoiding consumer confusion outweighs the public interest in free expression." *Id.* at 999. The court therefore held:

> In the context of allegedly misleading titles using a celebrity's name, that balance will normally not support application of the [Lanham] Act unless the title has no artistic relevance to the underlying work whatsoever, or, if it has some artistic relevance, unless the title explicitly misleads as to the source or the content of the work.

* * *

In this case, EA argues that we should extend this test, created to evaluate Lanham Act claims, to apply to right-of-publicity claims because it is "less prone to misinterpretation" and "more protective of free expression" than the transformative use defense. Although we acknowledge that there is some overlap between the transformative use test formulated by the California Supreme Court and the *Rogers* test, we disagree that the *Rogers* test should be imported wholesale for right-of-publicity claims. Our conclusion on this point is consistent with the Third Circuit's rejection of EA's identical argument in *Hart.* As the history and development of the *Rogers* test makes clear, it was designed to protect consumers from the risk of consumer confusion—the hallmark element of a Lanham Act claim. The right of publicity, on the other hand, does not primarily seek to prevent consumer confusion. Rather, it primarily "protects a form of intellectual property [in one's person] that society deems to have some social utility." *Comedy III,* 106 Cal.Rptr.2d 126, 21 P.3d at 804. * * *

The right of publicity protects the *celebrity,* not the *consumer.* Keller's publicity claim is not founded on an allegation that consumers are being illegally misled into believing that he is endorsing EA or its products. Indeed, he would be hard-pressed to support such an allegation absent evidence that EA explicitly misled consumers into holding such a belief. Instead, Keller's claim is that EA has appropriated, without permission and without providing compensation, his talent and years of hard work on the football field. The reasoning of the *Rogers* and *Mattel* courts—that artistic and literary works should be protected unless they explicitly mislead consumers—is simply not responsive to Keller's asserted interests here. * * *

C

California has developed two additional defenses aimed at protecting the reporting of factual information under state law. One of these defenses only applies to common law right-of-publicity claims while the other only applies to statutory right-of-publicity claims. *Montana v. San Jose Mercury News, Inc.,* 34 Cal.App.4th 790, 40 Cal.Rptr.2d 639, 640 (1995). Liability will not lie for common law right-of-publicity claims for the "publication of matters in the public interest." *Id.* at 640–41. Similarly, liability will not lie for statutory right-of-publicity claims for the "use of a name, voice, signature, photograph, or likeness in connection with any news, public affairs, or sports broadcast or account, or any political campaign." Cal. Civ.Code § 3344(d). Although these defenses are based on First Amendment concerns, they are not coextensive with the Federal Constitution, and their application is thus a matter of state law.

EA argues that these defenses give it the right to "incorporate athletes' names, statistics, and other biographical information" into its expressive works, as the defenses were "designed to create 'extra breathing space' for the use of a person's name in connection with matters of public interest." Keller responds that the right of publicity yields to free use of a public figure's likeness only to the extent reasonably required to report information to the public or publish factual data, and that the defenses apply only to broadcasts or accounts of public affairs, not to EA's *NCAA Football* games, which do not contain or constitute such reporting about Keller.

California courts have generally analyzed the common law defense and the statutory defense separately, but it is clear that both defenses protect only the act of publishing or reporting. By its terms, § 3344(d) is limited to a "broadcast or account," and we have confirmed that the common law defense is about a publication or reporting of newsworthy items. *Hilton,* 599 F.3d at 912. However, most of the discussion by California courts pertains to whether the subject matter of the communication is of "public interest" or related to "news" or "public affairs," leaving little guidance as to when the communication constitutes a publication or reporting.

For instance, in *Dora v. Frontline Video, Inc.,* a wellknown surfer sued the producer of a documentary on surfing entitled "The Legends of Malibu," claiming misappropriation of his name and likeness. 15 Cal.App.4th 536, 18 Cal.Rptr.2d 790, 791 (1993). The court held that the documentary was protected because it was "a fair comment on real life events which have caught the popular imagination." The court explained that surfing "has created a lifestyle that influences speech, behavior, dress, and entertainment," has had "an economic impact," and "has also had a significant influence on the popular culture," such that "[i]t would be difficult to conclude that a surfing documentary does not fall within the category of public affairs." Similarly, in *Gionfriddo v. Major League Baseball,* retired professional baseball players alleged that Major League Baseball violated their right of publicity by displaying "factual data concerning the players, their performance statistics, and verbal descriptions and video depictions of their play" in game programs and on its website. 94 Cal.App.4th 400, 114 Cal.Rptr.2d 307, 314 (2001). The court reasoned that "[t]he recitation and discussion of factual data concerning the athletic performance of these plaintiffs command a substantial public interest, and, therefore, is a form of expression due substantial constitutional protection." And in *Montana v. San Jose Mercury News, Inc.*, former NFL quarterback Joe Montana brought a right-of-publicity action against a newspaper for selling posters containing previously published pages from the newspaper depicting the many Super Bowl victories by Montana and the San Francisco 49ers. *Montana,* 40 Cal.Rptr.2d at 639–40. The court found that "[p]osters portraying the 49'ers' [sic] victories are . . . a form of public interest presentation to which protection must be extended."

We think that, unlike in *Gionfriddo, Montana,* and *Dora,* EA is not publishing or reporting factual data. EA's video game is a means by which users can play their own virtual football games, not a means for obtaining information about real-world football games. Although EA has incorporated certain actual player information into the game (height, weight, etc.), its case is considerably weakened by its decision not to include the athletes' names along with their likenesses and statistical data. EA can hardly be considered to be "reporting" on Keller's career at Arizona State and Nebraska when it is not even using Keller's name in connection with his avatar in the game. Put simply, EA's interactive game is not a publication of facts about college football; it is a game, not a reference source. These state law defenses, therefore, do not apply.

III

Under California's transformative use defense, EA's use of the likenesses of college athletes like Samuel Keller in its video games is not, as a matter of law, protected by the First Amendment. We reject EA's suggestion to import the *Rogers* test into the right-of-publicity arena, and conclude that state law defenses for the reporting of information do not protect EA's use.

NOTES

1. On the same day, in a case presenting similar facts (but involving a professional rather than collegiate football player), Judge Bybee applied the *Rogers* balancing test to the plaintiff's Lanham Act claims, and ruled for the defendant. *Brown v. Electronic Arts,* 724 F.3d 1235 (9th Cir. 2013). Does it make sense to have opposite outcomes arising from the same facts?

2. If a court applied the *Rogers* balancing test to Tiger Woods' Lanham Act claims in the *ETW* case, what would be the result?

3. Major new development are now taking place directly related the right of amateur athletes to license their "name, image, and likeness" (NIL). Consider the extent to which courts and the NCAA should recognize the rights of college athletes in the same manner as professionals.

SARVER V. CHARTIER

813 F.3d 891 (9th Cir. 2016).

O'SCANNLAIN, CIRCUIT JUDGE:

We must decide whether the district court properly applied California's Anti-Strategic Lawsuit Against Public Participation (anti-SLAPP) statute when it dismissed Army Sergeant Jeffrey Sarver's lawsuit relating to the Oscar-winning film *The Hurt Locker*.

I

A

Sergeant Jeffrey Sarver joined the United States Army in 1991. During parts of 2004 and 2005, he served as one of approximately 150 Explosive Ordnance Disposal (EOD) technicians in Iraq. Sarver led one of three teams in the 788th Ordnance Company whose principal duty was to identify, make safe, and dispose of improvised explosive devices.

In December 2004, Mark Boal, a journalist working for *Playboy* magazine, was embedded with the 788th out of Camp Victory in Baghdad, Iraq. Boal followed Sarver for a significant amount of time and took photographs and video of him while he was on and off duty. After Sarver returned to the United States, Boal conducted additional interviews with him in Wisconsin.

Boal wrote an article focused on Sarver's life and experiences in Iraq, which was published in the August/September 2005 issue of *Playboy*. A condensed version of that article was later published in *Reader's Digest*. The *Playboy* article contained two photographs of Sarver in addition to other personal information about him. Sarver alleges that he never consented to the use of his name and likeness in the *Playboy* article, that he objected to it after reviewing an advance copy, and that he attempted to have portions of the article removed before its publication in *Reader's Digest*.

Boal later wrote the screenplay for the film that became *The Hurt Locker*, which was released in June 2009 while Sarver was stationed at the Picatinny Arsenal in New Jersey. Sarver contends that Will James, the movie's main character, is based on his life and experiences, pointing to characteristics of James and events in the movie that allegedly mirror his life story. Sarver asserts that he did not consent to such use and that several scenes in the film falsely portray him in a way that has harmed his reputation.

* * *

[Sarver filed suit for, inter alia, infringement of his right of publicity. The district court first undertook a conflict of laws analysis, concluding that California law should apply rather than the law of New Jersey, the state which Sarver claimed as his domicile. The court then dismissed all claims against the filmmakers under California's anti-SLAPP statute, holding that the film was protected by the First Amendment. Sarver appealed.]

[E]ven assuming for the sake of argument that Sarver can establish all elements of his claim, the defendants contend that their production of the film is nevertheless protected under the First Amendment. That is, they argue that allowing Sarver to pursue his right of publicity action against them would infringe their constitutional right to free speech. Because it is dispositive, we consider that argument first.

The First Amendment, applicable to the states through the Fourteenth Amendment, forbids laws "abridging the freedom of speech." State laws, including state common law, may not "restrict expression because of its message, its ideas, its subject matter, or its content." *Police Dep't of City of Chi. v. Mosley,* 408 U.S. 92, 95 (1972). "Content-based laws—those that target speech based on its communicative content—are presumptively unconstitutional and may be justified only if the government proves that they are narrowly tailored to serve compelling state interests." *Reed,* 135 S.Ct. at 2226.

By its terms, California's right of publicity law clearly restricts speech based upon its content. The Supreme Court has reviewed the constitutionality of a state's right of publicity law only once, concluding that application of such a law to prevent the broadcast of a performer's entire performance did not violate the First Amendment. In *Zacchini v. Scripps-Howard Broadcasting Co.,* a journalist videotaped and broadcasted Zacchini's entire 15-second "human cannonball" act. 433 U.S. 562, 563–64 (1977). Zacchini brought an action against the television station for violation of his right of publicity under Ohio law. In rejecting the station's First Amendment defense, the Court first considered the nature of Ohio's interest in enforcing the law. According to the Court, the state's right of publicity law was aimed at protecting "the proprietary interest of the individual in his act" and "prevent[ing] unjust enrichment by the theft of good will," in order to provide "an economic incentive for [the individual] to make the investment required to produce a performance of interest to the public." *Id.* at 573, 576. The Court analogized this interest to those which "underlie[ ] the patent and copyright laws long enforced by this Court," as opposed to reputational and privacy-based interests which underlie torts like defamation. *Id.* at 573–76.

The Court balanced this state interest against the station's countervailing First Amendment interests in broadcasting Zacchini's performance. It determined that the First Amendment interest in broadcasting the *entire* performance (as opposed to just using Zacchini's name or picture) was minimal because "[n]o social purpose [was] served by having the defendant get free some aspect of the plaintiff that would have market value and for which he would normally pay." *Id.* The Court explained that such a broadcast is tantamount to "preventing [Zacchini] from charging an admission fee" to view what was "the product of [his] own talents and energy, the end result of much time, effort, and expense." *Id.* at 575–76. Thus, because the "broadcast of a film of [Zacchini]'s entire act pose[d] a substantial threat to the economic value of that performance," and protection provided an "economic incentive" for him to develop such a performance of public interest, the Court held that the First Amendment did not prevent Ohio from protecting Zacchini's right of publicity. *Id.* at 575–79. The Court has not revisited the question of when a state's right of publicity law is consistent with the First Amendment since *Zacchini.*

We, however, have interpreted *Zacchini* to uphold the right of publicity in a variety of contexts where the defendant appropriates the economic value that the plaintiff has built in an identity or performance. For example, in *Hilton v. Hallmark Cards,* we held that Paris Hilton could pursue a right of publicity claim for Hallmark's use of her image and catch phrase ("that's hot") from her television show in one of its greeting cards. 599 F.3d at 899. In doing so, we suggested that "merely merchandising a celebrity's image without that person's consent, the prevention of which is the core of the right of publicity," is not protected by the First Amendment. Similarly, in *Keller v. Electronic Arts, Inc.,* we upheld an action by a college football player who sought to prevent the use of his likeness in EA's video game. 724 F.3d at 1268. We noted that the video game "literally recreates [the football player] in the very setting in which he has achieved renown," and interferes with his ability "to capitalize on his athletic success," which took "talent and years of hard work on the football field" to build.

Likewise, we have upheld actions involving celebrities challenging the use of their images in commercial advertising. *See, e.g., Newcombe v. Adolf Coors Co.,* 157 F.3d 686, 691–94 (9th Cir.1998) (California's right of publicity law applied to use of Dodgers pitcher Don Newcombe's image in printed beer advertisement); *White v. Samsung Elecs. Am., Inc.,* 971 F.2d 1395, 1397–99, 1401 n. 3 (9th Cir.1992) (same for use of Vanna White's likeness as a robot in an advertisement for VCRs). Although we have not explicitly applied *Zacchini* in these cases, our opinions indicate that the state's interest is in preventing "the exploitation of celebrity to sell products, and an attempt to take a free ride on a celebrity's celebrity value." *White,* 971 F.2d at 1401 n. 3.

In sum, our precedents have held that speech which either appropriates the economic value of a performance or persona or seeks to capitalize off a celebrity's image in commercial advertisements is unprotected by the First Amendment against a California right-of-publicity claim.

Such lines of cases are not applicable here.

First, *The Hurt Locker* is not speech proposing a commercial transaction. Accordingly, our precedents relying on the lesser protection afforded to commercial speech are inapposite. Second, and critically, unlike the plaintiffs in *Zacchini, Hilton,* and *Keller,* Sarver did not "make the investment required to produce a performance of interest to the public," *Zacchini,* 433 U.S. at 576, or invest time and money to build up economic value in a marketable performance or identity.

Rather, Sarver is a private person who lived his life and worked his job. Indeed, while Sarver's life and story may have proven to be of public interest, Sarver has expressly disavowed the notion that he sought to attract public attention to himself. Neither the journalist who initially told Sarver's story nor the movie that brought the story to life stole Sarver's "entire act" or otherwise exploited the economic value of any performance or persona he had worked to develop. The state has no interest in giving Sarver an economic incentive to live his life as he otherwise would.

In sum, *The Hurt Locker* is speech that is fully protected by the First Amendment, which safeguards the storytellers and artists who take the raw materials of life—including the stories of real individuals, ordinary or extraordinary—and transform them into art, be it articles, books, movies, or plays. If California's right of publicity law applies in this case, it is simply a content-based speech restriction. As such, it is presumptively unconstitutional, and cannot stand unless Sarver can show a compelling state interest in preventing the defendants' speech. Because Sarver cannot do so, applying California's right of publicity in this case would violate the First Amendment.

Accordingly, Sarver cannot "state and substantiate a legally sufficient" right of publicity claim, *Hilton,* 599 F.3d at 908, and the district court did not err in granting the defendants' anti-SLAPP motions regarding such claim.

* * *

NOTES

1. How persuasive is the court's argument that Sarver cannot bring a right of publicity claim because he did not seek public attention for himself? If the defendant had featured digitally-altered footage of Sarver in a videogame about defusing bombs, would the court have reached the same result?

2. When a right of publicity claim is based on the depiction of events from a person's life, should it matter whether the individual is a celebrity or a private person? Whether the work is strictly factual or partly fictionalized?

PART 4

CONFIDENTIAL INFORMATION AND IDEAS

■ ■ ■

CHAPTER 8

TRADE SECRET LAW

■ ■ ■

A. INTRODUCTION

Trade secret law is, along with patent law, one of the principal ways to protect inventions and other proprietary information. Like other areas of intellectual property, trade secret law requires a balancing of interests. It is important to reward and protect research and development efforts, but—on the other hand—imitation of a competitor's successful products and services is the essence of competition. Trade secret doctrine strikes its balance between these competing interests by managing the scope of protectable subject matter (*i.e.*, not all information claimed to be confidential is a "trade secret") and by distinguishing between a party's improper and proper access to or use of information (*i.e.*, not all acquisitions or uses of information constitute "misappropriation").

If one can prove ownership of a trade secret and misappropriation by another, both state and federal civil actions and remedies will generally be available. Before 2016, civil trade secret enforcement in the United States was the exclusive domain of state law, and all the states had for many years provided civil actions for the unauthorized acquisition or use of trade secret information. State criminal sanctions for trade secret theft are also and have been generally potentially available, with some state laws containing criminal statutes specific to trade secrets and others using non-specific criminal theft or larceny statutes. From 1996 until 2016, federal law offered criminal sanctions for intentional usurpation of trade secrets (with a nexus to interstate commerce, including foreign commerce). *See* Economic Espionage Act of 1996, Pub. L. No. 104–359, 110 Stat. 3488 (1996) (codified as amended at 18 U.S.C. §§ 1831–39) (establishing criminal penalties for theft of trade secrets). Then in 2016, despite the widespread availability of civil actions and remedies at the state level for misappropriation of a trade secret, Congress made a significant addition to the landscape of trade secret law in the United States by creating a federal civil trade secret action. *See* Defend Trade Secrets Act of 2016, Pub. L. No. 114–153, 130 Stat. 376 (2016) (amending 18 U.S.C. § 1831 *et seq.*) (DTSA). Only litigants whose secrets have no nexus to interstate commerce—if any such situations exist under current case law—will have access to state law alone.

Although state law and jurisdictional variations dominated the law of trade secrecy for many years, and even though Congress in the DTSA elected not to preempt state law even when federal law applies, one can gain a general understanding of the basic principles and doctrines of trade secret law across the country. First, there are a limited number of common sources for trade secret law today, as further explained below. Second, there are similarities among these sources, and therefore also among state laws and the new federal law.

State and federal laws providing for civil protection of trade secrets are today based largely—but not exclusively—on the Uniform Trade Secrets Act (UTSA). The UTSA is the work of the Uniform Law Commission, a non-profit association made up of members of the bar appointed by each state. The aim of a "uniform" act from the Commission is for it to be adopted by all U.S. states, the District of Columbia, Puerto Rico, and the U.S. Virgin Islands. The UTSA, promulgated in 1979 and amended in 1985, has been enacted in all but two U.S. jurisdictions, although some states modified the statutory language (to varying degrees) before adoption. The remaining two non-UTSA states (as of mid-2022) were North Carolina and New York (whose protection remains common law, based on the RESTATEMENT (FIRST)). North Carolina's statutory trade secret protection bears a number of similarities to the UTSA. Bills proposing the adoption of the UTSA have been introduced in New York, but not passed, in recent years. And while state law is the focus of the Uniform Law Commission, the new provisions for federal trade secret protection in the DTSA use a basic framework that is essentially the same as the UTSA, and some UTSA language appears verbatim. (The federal DTSA also includes some novel and controversial provisions related to ex parte seizure of a defendant's property.) The DTSA is so close in the definition of the key issues, trade secret subject matter and misappropriation, that courts who take up state trade secret and DTSA claims in the same case may not often feel compelled to distinguish between them in their analysis. *See, e.g., RGIS, LLC v. Gerdes*, 817 F. App'x 158, 162 (6th Cir. 2020)(treating the DTSA as sufficiently consonant with a state's implementation of the UTSA so as to eliminate the need to separately analyze trade secret claims brought under state and federal law under the same facts); *compare Compulife Software Inc. v. Newman*, 959 F.3d 1288, 1311 n.13 (11th Cir. 2020) (noting the DTSA's express exclusion of "reverse engineering, independent derivation, or any other lawful means of acquisition" from the definition of "improper means" and therefore "misappropriation"; although the language is not present in the text of the UTSA, it is fundamental to the law of trade secrecy and is contained in case law applying and interpreting the UTSA).

The UTSA crafted by the Uniform Law Commission was based in large part on the principles contained in the RESTATEMENT OF TORTS, which like other "Restatements" of law was the work of the American Law Institute, a different non-profit organization made up of lawyers, judges, and academics. The RESTATEMENT provisions on trade secrets prevailed in most jurisdictions for many years following their promulgation in 1939. *See* RESTATEMENT OF TORTS §§ 757–59 (1939) (hereinafter RESTATEMENT or RESTATEMENT (FIRST)). Direct application of the principles from the RESTATEMENT (FIRST) has declined in the past forty years in favor of the UTSA, although it remains in use, albeit indirectly, in some jurisdictions that have adopted the UTSA (*e.g.*, in Wisconsin, as demonstrated by the first case in this chapter), as well as more directly in New York. Another influence on the development of trade secret law is the more recently promulgated RESTATEMENT (THIRD) OF UNFAIR COMPETITION, which includes provisions on trade secret law. *See* RESTATEMENT (THIRD) OF UNFAIR COMPETITION §§ 39–45 (1995) (hereinafter RESTATEMENT (THIRD)).

A leading treatise in the field is R. MILGRIM, MILGRIM ON TRADE SECRETS. Another useful source is BRIAN M. MALSBERGER, TRADE SECRETS: A STATE-BY-STATE SURVEY (2021), BNA.

B. PROTECTABLE SUBJECT MATTER AND REQUIREMENTS

The first step in exploring trade secret law is to understand what information is protectable as a trade secret—*i.e.*, is protectable subject matter. As noted early in the introduction above, not all information claimed to be confidential is a "trade secret." Putative trade secret owners must be able to identify what information they seek to protect and prove why it falls within the definition of a "trade secret" under applicable law. The following case demonstrates a fairly typical analysis of what information will be treated as a trade secret. Note in particular how the court included in its decision the factors from the RESTATEMENT (FIRST) even after Wisconsin adopted the UTSA.

MINUTEMAN, INC. V. ALEXANDER

434 N.W.2d 773 (Wis. 1989).

DAY, JUSTICE.

[The trial court denied plaintiff Minuteman, Inc.'s motion for temporary injunction to prevent misappropriation of trade secrets by the defendants, L.D. Alexander, George Cash, and Amity, Inc. The court of appeals affirmed in part and reversed in part, and this appeal to the Wisconsin Supreme Court followed.]

The basic question to be answered in this review is: what is the proper test for determining what is a "trade secret?" The answer is to be found in sec. 134.90, Stats. We do find, however, that our holding in *Corroon &*

Black v. Hosch, 325 N.W.2d 883 (Wis. 1982), still provides helpful guidance in determining what are trade secrets under sec. 134.90.

Several other issues are raised: (A)(1) What remedy, if any, is available if a trade secret is improperly acquired, but not subsequently used, by a wrongful taker? We conclude that under section 134.90(2)(a), Stats., an improper acquisition is enough to constitute a misappropriation of a trade secret, and therefore, all remedies in sec. 134.90 are available. (2) What effect, if any, does the possibility of reverse engineering[1] the chemical formula of a trade secret have on remedies available under sec. 134.90? We hold the possibility of reverse engineering is not enough to prevent a temporary injunction from being issued, but rather should be considered when determining the length of the temporary injunction.

(B) What is the trade secret status of customer lists and lists of persons who have made inquiries as a result of a businesses' [sic] advertisements? We conclude these lists may be eligible for trade secret protection under sec. 134.90, Stats.

* * *

Minuteman and Amity, Inc., (Amity) are both engaged in the furniture stripping business. Both sell products to people in the furniture restoration business, usually small enterprises. Chemicals, tubs for dipping the furniture, and other related products are sold to customers mostly from catalogs. Their products are essentially the same and both companies consider the other a direct competitor.

This case arises out of events occurring during March and April of 1986. Some facts are in dispute. In March, 1986, Defendants L.D. Alexander (Alexander) and George Cash (Cash) were employed by Minuteman. Alexander was vice president and general manager. Cash was the vice president in charge of Research and Development. Both were employees at will and had not signed any form of non-competition or non-disclosure agreement with Minuteman.

In late March, Alexander and Cash met with Jerry Cook, president of Amity. It is unclear what was discussed, but Minuteman alleged that Alexander and Cash discussed the possibility of leaving Minuteman to join Amity.

On April 7, 1986, the president of Minuteman, Jim Gauthier (Gauthier), returned from a two week vacation. Upon his return to work he was allegedly met by Alexander and Cash who gave him their immediate resignations. Gauthier stated he did not take the two seriously and told them to take that day off.

1 "Reverse engineering" is "starting with a known product and working backward to find the method by which [the item] was developed." Note, 1985 Wis. Act 236, sec. 6.

On the morning of April 8, Alexander was observed removing boxes of materials from Minuteman's premises. Shortly thereafter, Minuteman allegedly discovered both Cash's and Alexander's work stations completely empty of normal business materials. Minuteman claimed it was unable to locate various business related items. They thought Cash and Alexander had taken the materials.

Several days later, Alexander and Cash began working for Amity. Immediately thereafter, Minuteman filed a complaint against the Defendants. Minuteman claimed numerous causes of action against the Defendants, four of which are the subject of this review. The first allegation claimed the Defendants had misappropriated the trade secret formula for Minuteman's Stripper '76 (formula). The second allegation claimed the Defendants had misappropriated a list of inquiries made in response to Minuteman's advertisements (Inquiry list). The third allegation claimed the Defendants had misappropriated a list of Minuteman's customers which included information about what and how much each customer had ordered (Customer list). The fourth allegation claimed the Defendants had misappropriated various computer data from Minuteman. None of the items involved were protected by trademarks or patents.

* * *

A three day hearing was later held on the matter which included conflicting testimony about what happened. There was testimony about Cash's and Alexander's behavior just before they left Minuteman. In early March 1986, Alexander had requested a printout of the entire Inquiry list. Alexander told Minuteman's computer operator he needed the list for promotional reasons. A complete printout of the list had never been prepared for anyone before, nor had there ever been a complete printed copy of the list routinely maintained in the office. There was also testimony that Minuteman took some security measures to protect the contents of the list from being known by those outside the company. The list was provided to Alexander because of his executive position within Minuteman. After Alexander left Minuteman, it is claimed the list was never found.

There was also testimony that in early April of 1986, Cash had contacted one of Minuteman's two suppliers of Stripper '76. Cash asked for a copy of the formula of Stripper '76 and the supplier complied. The supplier had a record that it had sent the formula directly to Cash, but Minuteman claimed it never found the formula in its files. Cash admitted contacting the supplier for the formula, but said he did so at the request of Gauthier and that he left it on Gauthier's desk when he quit. Minuteman's second supplier of Stripper '76 testified that he considered the formula a trade secret and that he would not have disclosed it to Cash. There was evidence that other steps were taken to keep the formula a secret. There was also testimony that Stripper '76 could possibly be reverse engineered and that the elements of Stripper '76 could have been analyzed to discover its ingredients.

Minuteman asserted additional computer data assigned to Cash and Alexander by Minuteman were also discovered missing, including a recent printout of the Customer list.

A list of Amity's business solicitation mailings made by Cash and Alexander, on April 16 and 17, 1986, was also introduced into evidence. Minuteman argued this list was based on the Customer and Inquiry lists allegedly taken by Cash and Alexander. Minuteman's computer manager testified that the list was in the same sequence as Minuteman's Customer and Inquiry lists and that Minuteman's lists were the sources of Amity's list. Both Minuteman's and Amity's lists were basically in the same zip code order with some random additions in Amity's list. There were also similar mistakes in spelling and addressing on each list. Alexander stated he had written a list for his personal use while he was at Minuteman and used this personal list as the basis for the Amity mailings.

* * *

The first question is: what is the proper test for determining what is a trade secret? In *Corroon & Black*, this court established the definition of trade secret based on the 4 RESTATEMENT (FIRST) OF TORTS, sec. 757.

> In discussing the definition of a trade secret, we quoted with approval the following language from RESTATEMENT, 4 TORTS, sec. 757, comment b (1939): Some factors to be considered in determining whether given information is one's trade secret are: (1) the extent to which the information is known outside of his business; (2) the extent to which it is known by employees and others involved in his business; (3) the extent of measures taken by him to guard the secrecy of the information; (4) the value of the information to him and to his competitors; (5) the amount of effort or money expended by him in developing the information; (6) the ease or difficulty with which the information could be properly acquired or duplicated by others.

This court required that all six of the RESTATEMENT elements be met before the material could be defined as a trade secret.

In 1986, however, the legislature passed the Wisconsin version of the Uniform Trade Secret Act (UTSA). Section 134.90, Stats., created a new definition of trade secret as well as establishing possible remedies available to those injured by trade secret misappropriation. The basic question before this court is how the passage of the UTSA affects this court's decision in *Corroon & Black*, and what is the current definition of "trade secret" in Wisconsin.

* * *

The new definition of trade secret is found in sec. 134.90(1)(c), Stats., which states:

> Uniform trade secrets act. . . . (c) 'Trade secret' means information, including a formula, pattern, compilation, program, device, method, technique or process to which all of the following apply:
>
> 1. The information derives independent economic value, actual or potential, from not being generally known to, and not being readily ascertainable by proper means by, other persons who can obtain economic value from its disclosure or use.
>
> 2. The information is the subject of efforts to maintain its secrecy that are reasonable under the circumstances.

The Commissioners of the Uniform Laws Commission who drafted the UTSA, as well as our legislature, noted "[t]hat the definition of 'trade secret' contains a reasonable departure from the RESTATEMENT OF TORTS (first) definition which required that a trade secret be 'continuously used in one's business.' "

We still find, however, the RESTATEMENT'S definition helpful. The RESTATEMENT was the basic source of the UTSA's definition of trade secret. In addition, the UTSA's Comments state it "codifies the results of the better reasoned cases concerning the remedies for trade secret misappropriation." We hold that although all six elements of the RESTATEMENT'S test are no longer required, the RESTATEMENT requirements still provide helpful guidance in deciding whether certain materials are trade secrets under our new definition. *See* R. MILGRIM, MILGRIM ON TRADE SECRETS, sec. 201[1] (1987).

* * *

When examining an alleged violation of sec. 134.90, Stats., three questions arise. First, whether the material complained about is a trade secret under sec. 134.90(1)(c), Stats. Second, whether a misappropriation has occurred in violation of sec. 134.90(2). And finally, if both of the above requirements are met, what type of relief is appropriate under sec. 134.90(3) or (4). *See also Electro-Craft Corp. v. Controlled Motion, Inc.*, 332 N.W.2d 890 (Minn. 1983) (same analysis is followed).

A. STRIPPER '76 FORMULA

As to Minuteman's first allegation, both the circuit court and court of appeals determined that the formula for Stripper '76 is a trade secret. The Defendants do not challenge this finding. What is in contention is whether the Defendants misappropriated the formula, and if so, what type of relief should be granted to Minuteman.

The circuit court found that "Cash obtained the formula without permission" but that there was insufficient evidence that it was turned over to Amity. Section 134.90(2), Stats., defines misappropriation as:

> Uniform trade secrets act.... (2) MISAPPROPRIATION. No person, including the state, may misappropriate or threaten to misappropriate a trade secret by doing any of the following:
>
> (a) Acquiring the trade secret of another by means which the person knows or has reason to know constitute improper means....

The circuit court's finding that "Cash obtained the formula without permission" constitutes an "improper means" as defined in sec. 134.90(1)(a), Stats.[4] The circuit court acknowledges that this section "may have been violated by Cash in obtaining the formula." The circuit court held, however, that sec. 134.90(2)(b) [disclosure to another] also had to be violated. We disagree. The statute only requires a violation of one of the subsections. It states "any of the following" will constitute a misappropriation of a trade secret. *See also* Uniform Trade Secret Act, sec. 1, 14 U.L.A.1988 pocket part 332 (1985).

* * *

This court notes * * * that the possibility of reverse engineering is not enough to deny a temporary injunction as the circuit court had held. The Commissioners' comments to the UTSA note that discovery by reverse engineering is a proper means to discover a trade secret.

The *possibility* of reverse engineering a trade secret, however, is not a factor in determining whether an item is a trade secret, but rather it is a factor in deciding how long the injunctive relief should last:

> The general principle of section 2(a) and (b) is that an injunction should last for as long as is necessary, but no longer than is necessary, to eliminate the commercial advantage of 'lead time' with respect to good faith competitors that a person has obtained through misappropriation. Subject to any additional period of restraint necessary to negate lead time, an injunction accordingly should terminate when a former trade secret becomes either generally known to good faith competitors or generally knowable to them because of the lawful availability of products that can be reverse engineered to reveal a trade secret.
>
> For example, assume that A has a valuable trade secret of which B and C, the other industry members, are originally unaware. If

[4] Section 134.90(1)(a), Stats., provides:

Uniform trade secrets act. (1) DEFINITIONS. In this section: (a) "Improper means" includes espionage, theft, bribery, misrepresentation and breach or inducement of a breach of duty to maintain secrecy.

> B subsequently misappropriates the trade secret and is enjoined from use, but C later lawfully reverse engineers the trade secret, the injunction restraining B is subject to termination as soon as B's lead time has been dissipated. All of the persons who could derive economic value from use of the information are now aware of it, and there is no longer a trade secret under section 1(4). It would be anti-competitive to continue to restrain B after any lead time that B had derived from misappropriation had been removed.

Commissioners' Comments, Uniform Trade Secrets Act, sec. 2, 14 U.L.A. 544–45 (1985).

> If the trade secret could have been independently developed or discovered by reverse engineering or otherwise, the maximum appropriate duration of the injunction would be that amount of time which the misappropriator would have needed to discover the trade secret using "proper means." In most cases, the amount of lead time that the defendant would have taken is debatable. A comparison can be made of the time taken by other competitors to develop the trade secret independently, if one or more of them had done so.

Klitzke, *Uniform Trade Secrets Act*, 64 MARQ.L.REV. 277, 302–03 (1980).

B. THE CUSTOMER AND INQUIRY LISTS

Although the lists are distinct, both the circuit court and the court of appeals decided the second and third allegations in a similar fashion. Both courts interpreted sec. 134.90, Stats., as still embodying the trade secret definition in *Corroon* which required all six factors of the RESTATEMENT test be met before a trade secret could be found. As discussed above, the *Corroon* test no longer embodies the definition of trade secret. We, therefore, reverse the court of appeals' decision and remand for further determination using the statutory definition in sec. 134.90, Stats.

Some customer lists are afforded protection under the UTSA:

> This is not to say that every customer list would be denied trade secret status under the uniform act. We are well aware, for example, . . . that in certain sectors of the business community identical or nearly identical products and/or services are sold to a small, fixed group of purchasers. In such an intensely purchaser-oriented market, a supplier's customer list could well constitute a trade secret.

Steenhoven v. College Life Ins. Co. of Am., 460 N.E.2d 973, 974, n. 5 (Ind. Ct. App. 1984).

In *Kozuch v. CRA-MAR Video Center, Inc.*, 478 N.E.2d 110 (Ind. Ct. App. 1985), the customer list of a video rental club was found to constitute a trade secret under the Indiana version of the UTSA. An injunction was permitted to stop the use of the misappropriated trade secret. Others have noted the possibility of trade secret protection for Customer Lists under the UTSA. *See American Paper & Packaging Products, Inc. v. Kirgan*, 228 Cal. Rptr. 713 (Cal. App. 1986); Klitzke, *The Uniform Trade Secret Act*, 64 MARQ. L. REV. 277, 285 (1980). Decisions by other jurisdictions on questions involving the UTSA are to be given careful consideration by the courts in Wisconsin. Section 134.90(7), Stats.

The court of appeals is reversed on this issue and the cause is remanded for an inquiry as to whether the lists are trade secrets as defined in sec. 134.90, Stats.

* * *

NOTES

1. *Factors as a Guide:* Observe that while the *Minuteman* court uses the six RESTATEMENT (FIRST) factors, those factors were applied as a tool, or a guide, rather than a list of six required elements of trade secrecy that all must be satisfied or found to be favorable to the plaintiff. *Accord Learning Curve Toys, Inc. v. PlayWood Toys, Inc.*, 342 F.3d 714, 722 (7th Cir. 2003) (applying the factors to guide its decision as "instructive guidelines" to ascertain trade secret status under the Illinois Trade Secrets Act).

2. *Customer Lists:* Customer lists, like other types of information (including formulas, manufacturing processes, business plans, etc.), are not either categorically excluded or included in the subject matter protected by trade secret law. Determining whether trade secret law protects a list requires a rich factual evaluation. Consider, for example, a tailoring shop's customer list. *See Elmer Miller, Inc. v. Landis*, 625 N.E.2d 338 (Ill. App. 1993). What about a propane dealer's customer list? *See AmeriGas Propane, L.P. v. T-Bo Propane, Inc.*, 972 F.Supp. 685 (S.D. Ga. 1997).

The Eighth Circuit affirmed a district court's refusal to grant a preliminary injunction against an oil field equipment and service company that had been formed by former employees of the plaintiff company, even when those former employees admitted taking "limited" records with them when they left the plaintiff's employment: "It appears undisputed that the potential customers for [plaintiff] and [defendant] in the area surrounding Dickinson [North Dakota] are a small collection of easily identifiable, locally operating oilfield companies. Information about these companies would be easily obtainable, if not already known, by relevant actors in the local oilfield service and equipment industry." *CDI Energy Services Inc. v. West River Pumps, Inc.*, 567 F.3d 398, 402 (8th Cir. 2009). One district court found a trade secret likely to exist on the facts available at the preliminary injunction stage (but denied the preliminary injunction for other reasons), explaining that the evidence introduced indicated the claimed trade secrets, customer contacts downloaded by defendant (a former employee) from the plaintiff's customer database, "could not have been gathered without substantial effort and time" and, while defendant learned and retained significant client information during his employment, "it cannot be contended that [he] had personal knowledge of all the customer information he forwarded to [his new employer], which constituted the 'names, addresses, e-mail addresses, and phone numbers for 60,000 contacts located in [seven states].'" *Tanium Inc. v. Yago*, 2021 WL 5033452 (N.D. Ga. July 28, 2021). *See also* Note 5 in Part D. of this Chapter 8, *infra* page 339.

1. DERIVING ECONOMIC VALUE FROM SECRECY

For information to be found to be a trade secret, the UTSA, the DTSA, and both RESTATEMENTS require that the information be both economically valuable and relatively secret, with secrecy to be determined vis-a-vis others who could apply the information and extract value from it. *See* UTSA § 1(4)(i); 18 U.S.C. § 1839(3)(B); RESTATEMENT (FIRST) § 757 cmt. b; RESTATEMENT (THIRD) § 39 cmt. e–f. Information that is easily discerned, widely known, or obvious will not satisfy the requirements of trade secret law. *Kewanee Oil Co. v. Bicron Corp.*, 416 U.S. 470 (1974).

a. Not Generally Known

It is important to note that trade secret law requires only relative secrecy. The information must be sufficiently secret that it accords an advantage to those competitors or others who do not possess it, but it need not be maintained in absolute secrecy or remain completely unknown to others. The secrecy requirement is satisfied if others who could exploit the information would find it difficult or costly to obtain it. Put another way, although the information must not be widely known, it need not be completely novel or new. *See Kewanee Oil Co. v. Bicron Corp.*, 416 U.S. 470 (1974); RESTATEMENT (THIRD) § 39, cmt. f. If several competitors lawfully possess a trade secret, while several others do not, the information can still qualify as a trade secret. Look for the court's discussion of this element in the next case in this chapter.

In addition, a trade secret owner may make limited, confidential disclosures of the information to third parties without destroying trade secret status. Licensing the trade secret may be the best route to commercialization, or the trade secret may be relevant to negotiating the sale of a business that uses it. *See, e.g., Metallurgical Industries, Inc. v. Fourtek, Inc.*, 790 F.2d 1195, 1200 (5th Cir. 1986).

b. Not Readily Ascertainable by Proper Means

In the *Minuteman* decision the court states that "[t]he *possibility* of reverse engineering a trade secret . . . is not a factor in determining whether an item is a trade secret." This statement deserves further attention. While a mere possibility of reverse engineering does not eliminate trade secret status, the ease or likelihood of successful reverse engineering (*i.e.*, the probability of it) can in fact be used to assess whether the information is "readily ascertainable by proper means," one of the issues in trade secret status under the UTSA and the DTSA. Consider first a situation where information can be easily reverse engineered by using publicly available information, such as by analyzing a product already being marketed to the public by the plaintiff. Then compare that situation to one where information is only theoretically subject to reverse engineering from public information, or where information would only be subject to reverse engineering in the future, upon later public sale of a product. If the asserted trade secret is easily obtainable, then the issue of reverse engineering is indeed a factor in determining whether the information is a trade secret, rather than only a factor in determining the length of injunctive relief. *See* RESTATEMENT (THIRD) § 39 cmt. f. Look for the court's discussion of this element in the next case in this chapter.

2. SUBJECT OF REASONABLE EFFORTS TO MAINTAIN SECRECY

Trade secret information must be both a (relative) secret and be the subject of reasonable efforts to maintain that secrecy. *See* UTSA § 1(4)(ii); 18 U.S.C. § 1839(3)(A). As you can see in the *Minuteman* case, the RESTATEMENT (FIRST) also directs courts to consider the "extent of measures taken by [the owner] to guard the secrecy of the information." *See also* RESTATEMENT (FIRST) § 757 cmt. b; RESTATEMENT (THIRD) § 39 cmt. g. What efforts are reasonable or the extent of the measures that must be taken, however, varies with the facts of each case. As stated in a case later in this chapter, "Our tolerance of the espionage game must cease when the protections required to prevent another's spying cost so much that the spirit of inventiveness is dampened. . . . Reasonable precautions against predatory eyes we may require, but an impenetrable fortress is an unreasonable requirement . . . ." *E.I. duPont deNemours & Co. v. Christopher*, 431 F.2d 1012, 1016–17 (5th Cir. 1970).

In the next case excerpt, the court briefly assesses whether the information was generally known or readily ascertainable and whether the information derived independent value from its relative secrecy before turning to a more extensive analysis of reasonable efforts to maintain secrecy.

ELECTRO-CRAFT CORP. V. CONTROLLED MOTION, INC.

332 N.W.2d 890 (Minn. 1983).

COYNE, JUSTICE.

Respondent Electro-Craft Corporation ("ECC") sued appellants Controlled Motion, Inc. ("CMI") and CMI's president, John Mahoney, (a former employee of ECC) for misappropriation of trade secrets. ECC claimed that CMI and Mahoney improperly copied the designs of ECC's electric motors. * * *

* * *

THE EVENTS

In May of 1980, John Mahoney, while employed by ECC, began to explore the possibility of starting his own business. Mahoney already had many contacts in the business, including people at Storage Technology and at IBM—ECC customers for the ECC 1125–03–003 and brushless motors. Mahoney had also guided development of the IBM project and the Ford project. On June 12, 1980, Mahoney hired an attorney as counsel for the proposed new business, and counsel helped Mahoney prepare a prospectus which was circulated to prospective investors. Mahoney met with several prospective investors during June and July but apparently received no investments before August 1980.

The prospectus indicates that Mahoney proposed to compete with ECC in its IBM and Ford applications. Mahoney planned to complete prototypes for IBM in twelve weeks and obtain IBM approval in another week. Mahoney planned to try eventually to enter the market for the Ford systems. The prospectus projected revenues in the third month from sales of the prototype brushless motors but projected no research and development expenses for the first few months.

In June of 1980 Mahoney met with several of his fellow ECC employees about their joining the new business. On August 6, 1980, Mahoney resigned from ECC. Mahoney and ECC's president, Kelen, met briefly regarding trade secrets and Mahoney told Kelen not to worry. On September 16, 1980, four other ECC employees resigned in order to work for Mahoney's company, now called CMI. * * *

All of these employees, as well as Mahoney, had signed confidentiality agreements[1] when hired by ECC. None of these agreements, however, included a non-competition clause. When these four employees left ECC, ECC's management conducted exit interviews. The employees were asked to sign acknowledgment forms which outlined the areas that ECC considered confidential; only [one] signed the acknowledgment.

[1] The agreements were part of the employment agreements, reading in part as follows: FOURTH—Employee shall not directly or indirectly disclose or use at any time, either during or subsequent to the said employment, any secret or confidential information, knowledge, or data of Employer (whether or not obtained, acquired or developed by Employee) unless he shall first secure the written consent of Employer. Upon termination of his employment Employee shall turn over to Employer all notes, memoranda, notebooks, drawings or other documents made, compiled by or delivered to him concerning any product, apparatus or process manufactured, used or developed or investigated by Employer during the period of his employment; it being agreed that the same and all information contained therein are at all times the property of the Employer.

* * *

On September 18, Mahoney traveled to Colorado to meet representatives of Storage Technology Co. Mahoney received the specifications for a moving coil motor to meet Storage Technology's application, at that time supplied by the ECC 1125–03–003 and a Honeywell motor. Mahoney delivered prototypes of a CMI motor, the CMI 440, to Storage Technology on December 15, 1980; the motor was finally approved on March 1, 1981.

The evidence is conflicting as to how CMI produced the 440. The CMI 440 is almost identical in dimensions and tolerances[2] to the ECC 1125–03–003. William Craighill, the former ECC employee who developed the CMI 440, testified that he did not copy, nor even possess, an ECC 1125 motor when he designed the CMI 440. Craighill claimed that he used only a similar Honeywell motor, the Storage Technology specifications, and his own calculations to develop the CMI 440. On the other hand, circumstantial evidence pointed to the conclusion that CMI employees copied the ECC 1125. The similarity of the motors suggests copying, although the motors are not absolutely identical. Furthermore, the manufacturing processes, adhesives, and other materials are nearly identical. Expert testimony differed as to how long it should have taken CMI to "reverse engineer" the motor by taking apart an ECC 1125, measuring the parts and testing the material, and putting the plans together. A CMI expert estimated that it should have taken two to three months to develop a prototype motor. An expert for ECC estimated that the process would take at least six months to a year. Kelen estimated it would take a year.

* * *

THE ACTION

On September 26, 1980, about six weeks after Mahoney's resignation, ECC sued CMI and Mahoney (hereinafter referred to together as "CMI") claiming that CMI misappropriated ECC's trade secrets. * * *

A trial was held before Judge Arthur, without a jury, from June 15, 1981 to July 7, 1981. By order of October 19, 1981, Judge Arthur found that CMI had misappropriated ECC's trade secrets and enjoined CMI from producing or selling any "brushless or low inertia electric motor or tachometer" with dimensions within 10% of the dimensions of ECC's 1125 motor or ECC's brushless motor produced for IBM. The injunction was to be in effect for 12 months after the expiration of the last stay of execution

---

[2] Tolerances are the allowable manufacturing errors in dimension which still allow a working product. For example, a part may be required to be five one-thousandths of an inch in diameter, plus or minus one ten-thousandth of an inch.

of the order. The court also awarded ECC $50.00 in exemplary damages (but no compensatory damages) for each offending motor sold.

* * *

A. TRADE SECRET STATUS

* * *

In order to determine the existence of trade secrets, we must first determine what trade secrets are claimed by ECC and what trade secrets were found by the district court. CMI claims that neither ECC nor the district court were specific enough in defining ECC's trade secrets. CMI also claims that ECC's definition of its trade secrets changed during the course of the litigation. Therefore, according to CMI the district court should be reversed due to lack of specificity.

Regarding the brushless motor, we agree with CMI that ECC did not specify its trade secrets at trial. Nor did ECC even introduce the dimensions, tolerances, etc. of the brushless motor into evidence. The trial court found trade secrets in the general "design procedures" for the brushless motor. The court then enjoined CMI with respect to duplication of only the dimensions of the brushless motors. This lack of clarity is fatal to ECC's claim. On the record before us, ECC did not meet its burden of showing that certain features of the brushless motor were protectable trade secrets which might be misappropriated in the future. Furthermore, given ECC's lack of specificity, it was impossible for the district court to fashion a meaningful injunction which would not overly restrict legitimate competition for the IBM project.

With respect to the moving coil motors, however, ECC claims that the dimensions, tolerances, adhesives, and manufacturing processes of the ECC 1125–03–003 motor are trade secrets. The thrust of ECC's claim is that the specific combination of details and processes for the 1125 motor is a trade secret, and the evidence of the specific features of the 1125 motor sold to Storage Technology adequately identifies the information which ECC claims constitutes a trade secret. We believe that ECC's claim was specific enough in identifying its trade secrets to support a misappropriation action with respect to the 1125.

* * *

(a) *Not generally known, readily ascertainable.* The trial court found the information regarding the ECC 1125–03–003 to be secret. This finding was not clearly erroneous. First, the trial court found on conflicting evidence that CMI could not readily (i.e. quickly) reverse engineer a motor with exactly the same dimensions, tolerances, and materials as the ECC 1125–03–003. This finding was not clearly erroneous. Reverse engineering time is certainly a factor in determining whether information is readily ascertainable. *ILG Industries, Inc. v. Scott*, 273 N.E.2d 393, 396 (Ill. 1971); *Kubik, Inc. v. Hull*, 224 N.W.2d 80, 92–93 (Mich. App. 1974). The complexity and detail of dimensional data also bears on its ascertainability. *A.H. Emery Co. v. Marcan Products Corp.*, 389 F.2d 11, 16 (2d Cir.1968) ("[I]t is well settled that detailed manufacturing drawings and tolerance data are prima facie trade secrets.").

Second, the district court found that the exact combination of features of the 1125–03–003 is unique, even though none of the processes or features are unique in the industry and the 1125–03–003 is not the only way to achieve the required performance. Novelty is not a requirement for trade secrets to the same extent as for patentability. *E.g., Clark v. Bunker*, 453 F.2d 1006, 1009 (9th Cir. 1972). On the other hand, some novelty is required; mere variations on widely used processes cannot be trade secrets. Thus, in *Jostens*, a type of computer system was held not to be secret where it merely combined known subsystems (and where defendant had produced a different system). In the present case the exact combination of features of the 1125–03–003 could be characterized as a unique solution to the needs of one customer in the industry.

* * * Therefore, the finding of the trial court, that the features of the motor are not generally known or readily ascertainable, is supported by substantial evidence and is not clearly erroneous.

* * *

(b) *Independent economic value from secrecy*. This statutory element carries forward the common law requirement of competitive advantage. The trial court found ECC to have a competitive advantage in the ECC 1125–03–003, not over all competitors, but over "any company which has not, through its own efforts or through license, obtained similar information." CMI claims that ECC was required to show a competitive advantage over all competitors, including those competitors already successfully producing motors.

The statute requires that a trade secret "[derive] independent economic value . . . from not being generally known . . . and not being readily ascertainable. . . ." Minn. Stat. § 325C.01, subd. 5(i). This does not mean, as CMI contends, that the owner of the trade secret must be the only one in the market. Several developers of the same information, for example, may have trade secret rights in the information. Uniform Trade Secrets Act § 1, Commissioner's Comment, 14 U.L.A. 542–43 (1979). If an outsider would obtain a valuable share of the market by gaining certain information, then that information may be a trade secret if it is not known or readily ascertainable.

* * *

(c) *Reasonable efforts to maintain secrecy.* It is this element upon which ECC's claim founders. The district court found that, even though ECC had no "meaningful security provisions," ECC showed an intention to keep its data and processes secret. This finding does not bear upon the statutory requirement that ECC use "efforts that are reasonable under the circumstances to maintain . . . secrecy." Minn. Stat. § 325C.01, subd. 5(ii). The "intention" language used by the district court comes from the common law test for trade secret status. However, even under the common law, more than an "intention" was required—the plaintiff was required to show that it had manifested that intention by making some effort to keep the information secret.

This element of trade secret law does not require maintenance of absolute secrecy; only partial or qualified secrecy has been required under the common law. *Radium Remedies Co. v. Weiss*, 217 N.W. 339, 341 (Minn. 1928). What is actually required is conduct which will allow a court acting in equity to enforce plaintiff's rights. In speaking of the requirement, one commentator has stated:

> It would appear, from the standpoint of a broad overview, that the policy goal of the doctrine is to preclude employee liability unless the employer can establish that his treatment of the knowledge in issue has been adequate to indicate a breach of the confidential relationship. It might also be said that the goal is to preclude vindictive employers from placing employees in mental bondage.

Sloan, *Trade Secrets: Real Toads in a Conceptual Garden*, 1 W.ST.U.L.REV. 113, 145 (1973). To put it another way, the employer must come into court with clean hands; the employer cannot complain of the employee's use of information if the employer has never treated the information as secret.

It is this aspect of trade secret law which truly sets it apart from the other two means through which employers can protect information—patents, and employment contracts containing a non-competition clause. The latter two remedies depend on only a single act by the employer. Trade secret protection, on the other hand, depends upon a continuing course of conduct by the employer, a course of conduct which creates a confidential relationship. This relationship, in turn, creates a reciprocal duty in the employee to treat the information as confidential insofar as the employer has so treated it * * *.

In the present case, even viewing the evidence most favorably to the findings below, we hold that ECC did not meet its burden of proving that it used reasonable efforts to maintain secrecy as to the ECC 1125–03–003. We acknowledge that ECC took minimal precautions in screening its handbook and publications for confidential information and by requiring some of its employees to sign a confidentiality agreement,[13] but these were not enough.

First, ECC's physical security measures did not demonstrate any effort to maintain secrecy. By "security" we mean the protection of information from discovery by outsiders. Security was lax in this case. For example, the main plant had a few guarded entrances, but seven unlocked entrances existed without signs warning of limited access. Employees were at one time required to wear badges, but that system was abandoned by the time of the events giving rise to this case. The same was generally true of the Amery, Wisconsin plant where ECC 1125 and brushless motors were manufactured. One sign was posted at each plant, however, marking the research and development lab at Hopkins and the machine shop at Amery as restricted to "authorized personnel." Discarded drawings and plans for motors were simply thrown away, not destroyed. Documents such as motor drawings were not kept in a central or locked location, although some design notebooks were kept locked.

The relaxed security by itself, however, does not preclude a finding of reasonable efforts by ECC to maintain secrecy. Other evidence did not indicate that industrial espionage is a major problem in the servo motor industry. Therefore, "security" measures may not have been needed,[14] and the trial court could have found trade secrets if ECC had taken other reasonable measures to preserve secrecy.

However, ECC's "confidentiality" procedures were also fatally lax, and the district court was clearly in error in finding ECC's efforts to be reasonable. By "confidentiality" in this case we mean the procedures by which the employer signals to its employees and to others that certain information is secret and should not be disclosed. Confidentiality was important in this case, for testimony demonstrated that employees in the servo motor business frequently leave their employers in order to produce similar or identical devices for new employers. ECC has hired many employees from other corporations manufacturing similar products.[16] If

[13] Thus, this case is not as extreme as was *United Wild Rice, Inc. v. Nelson*, 313 N.W.2d 628 (Minn. 1982), in which plaintiff itself publicly disclosed the supposedly confidential information.

[14] *Compare E.I. duPont deNemours & Co., Inc. v. Christopher*, 431 F.2d 1012 (5th Cir. 1970), cert. denied 400 U.S. 1024 (1971) (not reasonably necessary to guard against aerial reconnaissance flight, which showed plaintiff's plant design during construction of plant), *with Capsonic Group, Inc. v. Plas-Met Corp.*, 361 N.E.2d 41 (1977) (secrecy not reasonably maintained where plant had no guard, no passes were required, drawings were not kept locked, and people on tours were not told that any information was confidential).

[16] One ECC employee actually prided himself on the information he had brought with him from his former employer. One day, just before that employee left ECC to join another company, the president of ECC found him copying documents after hours. ECC never questioned the employee or warned him or his new employer that certain information was confidential.

ECC wanted to prevent its employees from doing the same thing, it had an obligation to inform its employees that certain information was secret.[17]

ECC's efforts were especially inadequate because of the nonintuitive nature of ECC's claimed secrets here. The dimensions, etc., of ECC's motors are not trade secrets in as obvious a way as a "secret formula" might be. ECC should have let its employees know in no uncertain terms that those features were secret.

Instead, ECC treated its information as if it were not secret. None of its technical documents were marked "Confidential", and drawings, dimensions and parts were sent to customers and vendors without special marking. Employee access to documents was not restricted. ECC never issued a policy statement outlining what it considered to be secret. Many informal tours were given to vendors and customers without warnings as to confidential information. Further, two plants each had an "open house" at which the public was invited to observe manufacturing processes.

The district court relied on certain contrary evidence to show ECC's "intention," but this evidence does not demonstrate reasonable efforts to maintain confidentiality. There was no showing that a 1977 memo from the president of ECC to its managerial employees, warning them to restrict unannounced laboratory tours in the interests of protecting secrets, had ever been enforced. The confidentiality agreements signed by the employees were too vague to apprise the employees of specific "secrets." (*See* note 1, *supra*).

The exit interviews also did not constitute reasonable efforts to maintain secrecy. The exit interviews, a procedure initiated by ECC only after it became clear that the employees were about to work for Mahoney, occurred a mere ten days before the commencement of this litigation. These "interviews" were little more than attempts to intimidate or threaten employees, to prevent them from leaving ECC and engaging in legitimate competition using their skill and expertise. Such thinly-veiled threats certainly do not qualify as ongoing efforts to maintain the secrecy of specific information. The law of trade secrets does not condone, and this court certainly will not reward, ECC's conduct.

In summary, ECC has not met its burden of proof in establishing the existence of any trade secrets. The evidence does not show that ECC was ever consistent in treating the information here as secret.

---

[17] *See Future Plastics, Inc. v. Ware Shoals Plastics, Inc.*, 340 F. Supp. 1376 (D.S.C. 1972) (where plaintiff company's engineer had left plaintiff and formed new competing company and plaintiff had never objected, plaintiff had not treated processes as confidential and could not enjoin defendant employee, who joined other competitor); *Sun Dial Corp. v. Rideout*, 102 A.2d 90 (N.J. Super.), aff'd 108 A.2d 442 (N.J. 1954) (even though plaintiff conducted limited plant tours and published vague articles about secret process, reasonable confidentiality was maintained where other efforts were taken to protect secret information).

B. MISAPPROPRIATION

Since no trade secrets existed to be misappropriated, we technically need not reach the issue of whether misappropriation occurred. However, as we noted above the concept of trade secret status and the concept of misappropriation should not be artificially separated. * * * Misappropriation involves the acquisition, disclosure, or use of a trade secret through improper means. Minn. Stat. § 325C.01, subd. 3. "Improper means" are defined as

> [T]heft, bribery, misrepresentation, breach or inducement of breach of a duty to maintain secrecy, or espionage through electronic or other means.

Minn. Stat. § 325C.01, subd. 2. In the employer-employee context of the present case, ECC was required to show some duty on the part of the employee not to disclose the information. ECC claims that the employees' duty here arose from the employee agreements and from a confidential employer-employee relationship.

However, a common law duty of confidentiality arises out of the employer-employee relationship only as to information which the employer has treated as secret:

> [T]he employee is entitled to fair notice of the confidential nature of the relationship and what material is to be kept confidential.

Jostens, supra, 318 N.W.2d at 702 (citing ELLIS, TRADE SECRETS 79 (1953)). Therefore, in the present case, ECC's failure to make reasonable efforts to maintain secrecy, discussed above, was fatal to its claim of a confidential relationship. The employees were never put on notice of any duty of confidentiality. The employee agreements do not help ECC's claim for the same reason—ECC never treated specific information as secret. Therefore, the agreements' vague language prohibiting the employee from taking "secrets" did not create a duty of confidentiality in the employee, and no misappropriation occurred.

* * *

NOTES

1. *Balancing Reasonableness of Efforts:* The inquiry into secrecy measures will be fact intensive because it may require the judge or jury to balance the costs and benefits of the measures the plaintiff took against more stringent precautions it could have taken. In *Learning Curve Toys, Inc. v. PlayWood Toys, Inc.*, 342 F.3d 714, 725–26 (7th Cir. 2003), the Seventh Circuit reinstated a jury verdict of misappropriation of a trade secret even though the court noted, in its discussion of the secrecy measures undertaken by the plaintiff PlayWood, that "PlayWood might have done more to protect its secret" beyond its sole precaution, a non-specific oral confidentiality agreement.

Although using only an oral agreement was "a decision that proved unwise in hindsight," the court still ruled that the "jury was entitled to conclude that PlayWood's reliance on the oral confidentiality agreement was reasonable under the circumstances of this case." The oral agreement created a confidential relationship that imposed upon the defendant the duty to maintain the information in secrecy and "as part of the reasonableness inquiry, the jury could have considered the size and sophistication of the parties, as well as the relevant industry."

2. *Efforts Not Taken:* In *Hertz v. Luzenac Group*, 576 F.3d 1103 (10th Cir. 2009), the Tenth Circuit reversed the district court's grant of summary judgment (and remanded the case for further proceedings) where the lower court had, in denying trade secret status to the production process for a product, focused on secrecy measures that were not taken by the plaintiff, rather than the reasonableness of the secrecy measures that the plaintiff company did take:

> [T]here are always more security precautions that can be taken. Just because there is something else that Luzenac *could* have done does not mean that their efforts were unreasonable under the circumstances. In light of undisputed precautions that Luzenac took, we do not think that the record demonstrates beyond dispute that Luzenac's measures to protect the secrecy of 604AV were merely 'superficial.' Whether these precautions were, in fact, reasonable, will have to be decided by a jury.

Id. at 1113 (citations omitted).

3. *Disclosure in Confidence:* The need to maintain secrecy does not mean that a trade secret owner will never license the trade secret for use by another company or disclose the trade secret information as part of business negotiations. The obligation to take reasonable measures to preserve secrecy does mean that a careful trade secret owner will limit disclosures to the extent possible and will require—before the owner reveals the information—the recipient to agree to contractual restrictions on the use and disclosure of the trade secret information.

4. *Asking the Right Questions:* What questions would you ask a client that was seeking to ensure, from both a legal and practical standpoint, that it is taking sufficient measures to protect its trade secrets?

C. OWNERSHIP

Determinations of ownership or proprietary interests under trade secret law have typically resulted in less thorny analyses than those that often arise in patent, trademark, or copyright law. Consider how the UTSA and DTSA direct attention to the concept of proper possession, and to protection from misappropriation, rather than to the concepts of initial conception and individual ownership, emphasizing that rights are relative rather than absolute. In certain situations, the identity of the party with the right to control the information may be hotly contested. One example would be when two parties possess the same information and came into that possession simultaneously or through a relationship between them, such as in cases involving the joint development of valuable information or in certain situations involving employees and employers. *See* RESTATEMENT (THIRD) § 42 cmt. e. In many instances, however, if a trade secret is determined to exist, the plaintiff's right to enforce the trade secret will not be in question, even when the defendant's acts remain in dispute.

In determining which of two parties is the rightful owner or possessor when both claim the right to the same information to the exclusion of the other, courts may look to considerations such as: which party was actively engaged in the use of the information; whether one controlled the development of the information; which party maintained secrecy measures protecting the information; what contractual relationships, if any, existed between the two parties; and fiduciary duties existing between the parties at the time of development or use. *See, e.g., Khazai v. Watlow Elec. Mfg. Co.*, 201 F. Supp. 2d 967, 974 (E.D. Mo. 2001) (ruling that where an employee's work in developing valuable information was performed in the course of his employment, and where the written employment agreement provided that the data and information resulting from that employment would belong to the employer, the employee owned no rights in the trade secret despite the fact that employee utilized, in the development process, information and knowledge he possessed before his employment); *Tlapek v. Chevron Oil Co.*, 407 F.2d 1129, 1134 (8th Cir. 1969) (applying Arkansas law to rule that the employer, and not the developing employee, owned trade secret rights in a valuable and unique theory of the existence and commercial viability of a drilling prospect). One well-known case holding that the employer could not claim ownership of the chemical formulas developed by a chemist during his employment is *Wexler v. Greenberg*, 160 A.2d 430, 436–37 (Pa. 1960). The court assessed the factual circumstances surrounding the employee-employer relationship, the employee's skill, and the development of the information in dispute to hold that the employee's post-employment use of the formulas should be unrestricted.

In some states, statutes may govern employee-employer ownership of information and inventions. *See, e.g.*, Cal. Lab. Code §§ 2860, 2870. In others, the courts have used other legal principles, including equity, as a guide. While patent and trade secret law are distinct, and patent law does not govern rights in trade secrets, courts needing guidance have sometimes looked to state law on employee-employer ownership of rights in patentable inventions. For example, in a criminal trade secret theft case where state law did not separately establish a default ownership rule for trade secret disputes, a Texas court examined the specific employee-employer relationship in question and referred to a number of patent law cases before concluding that the employer did not own the alleged trade secrets to the exclusion of the former employee. *McClain v. State*, 269 S.W.3d 191, 197–99 (Tex. App. 2008) (assuming without deciding that certain "improvements" could be trade secrets, yet rejecting the State's arguments that the employer owned the improvements: "When the trade secret originates from the employee," and there is no "express contract restricting its use or . . . special confidential relationship of the parties," which relationship includes an employee "hired to invent or devise" the information, then the employee rather than employer owns the trade secret). More information on an employee's obligation to assign patentable inventions to the employer in certain circumstances can be found in Chapter 11.A.4. on page 545, *infra*, along with discussion of alternate circumstances in which an employer may hold an equitable "shop right" in certain employee inventions.

D. MISAPPROPRIATION AND DEFENSES

Misappropriation hinges, generally speaking, on a finding that "improper means" were used to obtain trade secret information or that an unauthorized disclosure or use of trade secret information was made when that information was subject to an obligation of secrecy or confidentiality. *See* UTSA § 1(2); 18 U.S.C. § 1839(5); RESTATEMENT (FIRST) § 757 (including comments f–o); RESTATEMENT (THIRD) §§ 40–43 (including associated comments). Just as the "definition" of a trade secret does not include precise criteria and requires the balancing of factors and interests, the scope of liability-creating "misappropriation" also eludes precise definition.

Misappropriation can take many forms, and it is important to note that unauthorized or improper acquisition of a trade secret can lead to liability, even without commercial use of the secret in competition with the rightful possessor. *See* UTSA § 1(2); 18 U.S.C. § 1839(5)(A). Under the older RESTATEMENT (FIRST), liability required both misappropriation and use of the trade secret; the "use" required, however, was sometimes inferred from access or construed broadly to include an exercise of control and dominion over the information to the detriment of its owner or the benefit of the defendant. *See, e.g., Metallurgical Industries, Inc. v. Fourtek, Inc.*, 790 F.2d 1195, 1200 (5th Cir. 1986); *University Computing Co. v. Lykes-Youngstown Corp.*, 504 F.2d 518 (5th Cir. 1974).

The following case arose under Texas law before that state adopted the UTSA. The drafters of the UTSA adopted the opinion's analysis of "improper means" in their comments, and the decision continues to be influential and widely cited today.

E.I. DUPONT DENEMOURS & CO. V. CHRISTOPHER

431 F.2d 1012 (5th Cir. 1970).

GOLDBERG, CIRCUIT JUDGE:

This is a case of industrial espionage in which an airplane is the cloak and a camera the dagger. The defendants-appellants, Rolfe and Gary Christopher, are photographers in Beaumont, Texas. The Christophers were hired by an unknown third party to take aerial photographs of new construction at the Beaumont plant of E. I. duPont deNemours & Company, Inc. Sixteen photographs of the DuPont facility were taken from the air on March 19, 1969, and these photographs were later developed and delivered to the third party.

DuPont employees apparently noticed the airplane on March 19 and immediately began an investigation to determine why the craft was circling over the plant. By that afternoon the investigation had disclosed that the craft was involved in a photographic expedition and that the Christophers were the photographers. DuPont contacted the Christophers that same afternoon and asked them to reveal the name of the person or corporation requesting the photographs. The Christophers refused to disclose this information, giving as their reason the client's desire to remain anonymous.

Having reached a dead end in the investigation, DuPont subsequently filed suit against the Christophers, alleging that the Christophers had wrongfully obtained photographs revealing DuPont's trade secrets which they then sold to the undisclosed third party. DuPont contended that it had developed a highly secret but unpatented process for producing methanol, a process which gave DuPont a competitive advantage over other producers. This process, DuPont alleged, was a trade secret developed after much expensive and time-consuming research, and a secret which the company had taken special precautions to safeguard. The area photographed by the Christophers was the plant designed to produce methanol by this secret process, and because the plant was still under construction parts of the process were exposed to view from directly above the construction area. Photographs of that area, DuPont alleged, would enable a skilled person to deduce the secret process for making methanol. DuPont thus contended that the Christophers had wrongfully appropriated DuPont trade secrets by taking the photographs and delivering them to the undisclosed third party. In its suit DuPont asked for damages to cover the loss it had already sustained as a result of the wrongful disclosure of the trade secret and sought temporary and permanent injunctions prohibiting any further circulation of the photographs already taken and prohibiting any additional photographing of the methanol plant.

* * *

On June 5, 1969, the trial court held a hearing on all pending motions and an additional motion by the Christophers for summary judgment. The court denied the Christophers' motions to dismiss for want of jurisdiction and failure to state a claim and also denied their motion for summary judgment. The court granted DuPont's motion to compel the Christophers to divulge the name of their client. Having made these rulings, the court then granted the Christophers' motion for an interlocutory appeal under 28 U.S.C.A. 1292(b) to allow the Christophers to obtain immediate appellate review of the court's finding that DuPont had stated a claim upon which relief could be granted. Agreeing with the trial court's determination that DuPont had stated a valid claim, we affirm the decision of that court.

This is a case of first impression, for the Texas courts have not faced this precise factual issue, and sitting as a diversity court we must sensitize our *Erie* antennae to divine what the Texas courts would do if such a situation were presented to them. The only question involved in this interlocutory appeal is whether DuPont has asserted a claim upon which relief can be granted. The Christophers argued both at trial and before this court that they committed no "actionable wrong" in photographing the DuPont facility and passing these photographs on to their client because they conducted all of their activities in public airspace, violated no government aviation standard, did not breach any confidential relation, and did not engage in any fraudulent or illegal conduct. In short, the Christophers argue that for an appropriation of trade secrets to be wrongful there must be a trespass, other illegal conduct, or breach of a confidential relationship. We disagree.

It is true, as the Christophers assert, that the previous trade secret cases have contained one or more of these elements. However, we do not think that the Texas courts would limit the trade secret protection exclusively to these elements. On the contrary, in *Hyde Corporation v. Huffines*, 314 S.W.2d 763 (Tex. 1958), the Texas Supreme Court specifically adopted the rule found in the RESTATEMENT OF TORTS which provides:

> One who discloses or uses another's trade secret, without a privilege to do so, is liable to the other if (a) he discovered the secret by improper means, or (b) his disclosure or use constitutes a breach of confidence reposed in him by the other in disclosing the secret to him * * *.

RESTATEMENT OF TORTS § 757 (1939).

Thus, although the previous cases have dealt with a breach of a confidential relationship, a trespass, or other illegal conduct, the rule is much broader than the cases heretofore encountered. Not limiting itself to specific wrongs, Texas adopted subsection (a) of the RESTATEMENT which recognizes a cause of action for the discovery of a trade secret by any "improper" means.

* * *

The question remaining, therefore, is whether aerial photography of plant construction is an improper means of obtaining another's trade secret. We conclude that it is and that the Texas courts would so hold. The Supreme Court of that state has declared that "the undoubted tendency of the law has been to recognize and enforce higher standards of commercial morality in the business world." *Hyde Corporation v. Huffines, supra* 314 S.W.2d at 773. That court has quoted with approval articles indicating that the proper means of gaining possession of a competitor's secret process is "through inspection and analysis" of the product in order to create a duplicate. *K & G Oil Tool & Service Co. v. G & G Fishing Tool Service*, 314 S.W.2d 782, 783, 788 (Tex. 1958). * * *

We think, therefore, that the Texas rule is clear. One may use his competitor's secret process if he discovers the process by reverse engineering applied to the finished product; one may use a competitor's process if he discovers it by his own independent research; but one may not avoid these labors by taking the process from the discoverer without his permission at a time when he is taking reasonable precautions to maintain its secrecy. To obtain knowledge of a process without spending the time and money to discover it independently is improper unless the holder voluntarily discloses it or fails to take reasonable precautions to ensure its secrecy.

In the instant case the Christophers deliberately flew over the DuPont plant to get pictures of a process which DuPont had attempted to keep secret. The Christophers delivered their pictures to a third party who was certainly aware of the means by which they had been acquired and who may be planning to use the information contained therein to manufacture methanol by the DuPont process. The third party has a right to use this process only if he obtains this knowledge through his own research efforts, but thus far all information indicates that the third party has gained this knowledge solely by taking it from DuPont at a time when DuPont was making reasonable efforts to preserve its secrecy. In such a situation DuPont has a valid cause of action to prohibit the Christophers from improperly discovering its trade secret and to prohibit the undisclosed third party from using the improperly obtained information.

We note that this view is in perfect accord with the position taken by the authors of the RESTATEMENT. In commenting on improper means of discovery the savants of the RESTATEMENT said:

> 'f. Improper means of discovery. The discovery of another's trade secret by improper means subjects the actor to liability independently of the harm to the interest in the secret. Thus, if one uses physical force to take a secret formula from another's pocket, or breaks into another's office to steal the formula, his

> conduct is wrongful and subjects him to liability apart from the rule stated in this Section. Such conduct is also an improper means of procuring the secret under this rule. But means may be improper under this rule even though they do not cause any other harm than that to the interest in the trade secret. Examples of such means are fraudulent misrepresentations to induce disclosure, tapping of telephone wires, eavesdropping or other espionage. A complete catalogue of improper means is not possible. In general they are means which fall below the generally accepted standards of commercial morality and reasonable conduct.'

RESTATEMENT OF TORTS 757, comment f at 10 (1939).

In taking this position we realize that industrial espionage of the sort here perpetrated has become a popular sport in some segments of our industrial community. However, our devotion to free wheeling industrial competition must not force us into accepting the law of the jungle as the standard of morality expected in our commercial relations. Our tolerance of the espionage game must cease when the protections required to prevent another's spying cost so much that the spirit of inventiveness is dampened. Commercial privacy must be protected from espionage which could not have been reasonably anticipated or prevented. We do not mean to imply, however, that everything not in plain view is within the protected vale, nor that all information obtained through every extra optical extension is forbidden. Indeed, for our industrial competition to remain healthy there must be breathing room for observing a competing industrialist. A competitor can and must shop his competition for pricing and examine his products for quality, components, and methods of manufacture. Perhaps ordinary fences and roofs must be built to shut out incursive eyes, but we need not require the discoverer of a trade secret to guard against the unanticipated, the undetectable, or the unpreventable methods of espionage now available.

In the instant case DuPont was in the midst of constructing a plant. Although after construction the finished plant would have protected much of the process from view, during the period of construction the trade secret was exposed to view from the air. To require DuPont to put a roof over the unfinished plant to guard its secret would impose an enormous expense to prevent nothing more than a school boy's trick. * * * Reasonable precautions against predatory eyes we may require, but an impenetrable fortress is an unreasonable requirement, and we are not disposed to burden industrial inventors with such a duty in order to protect the fruits of their efforts. "Improper" will always be a word of many nuances, determined by time, place, and circumstances. We therefore need not proclaim a catalogue of commercial improprieties. Clearly, however, one of its commandments does say "thou shall not appropriate a trade secret through deviousness under circumstances in which countervailing defenses are not reasonably available."

Having concluded that aerial photography, from whatever altitude, is an improper method of discovering the trade secrets exposed during construction of the DuPont plant, we need not worry about whether the flight pattern chosen by the Christophers violated any federal aviation regulations. Regardless of whether the flight was legal or illegal in that sense, the espionage was an improper means of discovering DuPont's trade secret.

* * *

NOTES

1. *Scope of "Improper Means":* As noted before the case, both the UTSA and DTSA use the concept of "improper means" within the definition of misappropriation. Does the *DuPont v. Christopher* decision provide a workable standard or guideline for determining when a competitor or other party is using improper means?

Would searching through a competitor's trash constitute improper means? For further discussion of improper means, see RESTATEMENT (THIRD) OF UNFAIR COMPETITION § 43 (1995).

2. *Connection to Reasonable Efforts:* Note that the measures taken by a company to protect its secrets weigh in the balance when a court is determining the existence of a trade secret, *see, e.g., Electro-Craft Corp. v. Controlled Motion, Inc., supra*, and might also become part of the calculus when a court assesses whether the means a third party used to acquire the secret were proper or improper, as in the case above.

3. *Receipt of Information:* A trade secret violation can also occur if someone receives trade secret information knowing (or having reason to know based on the circumstances) that it is improperly revealed (*i.e.*, revealed as a result of a breach of confidence or use of improper means) or sometimes even accidentally revealed. What purposes does this rule serve? *See Lamb v. Turbine Designs, Inc.*, 207 F.3d 1259 (11th Cir. 2000). For further discussion of the scope of trade secret violations, see RESTATEMENT (THIRD) OF UNFAIR COMPETITION §§ 40–42 (1995).

4. *Defenses:* Common defenses to a claim of trade secret misappropriation include arguments that there was no trade secret, or no duty of confidence, as well as proof of independent development of the information or development through reverse engineering of a publicly available product or by using other public information. Notice also that innocent use of information wrongfully acquired from the trade secret owner, but not wrongfully acquired by the defendant, may not lead to liability. *See* UTSA § 1(2); 18 U.S.C. 1839(5); RESTATEMENT (FIRST) § 758; RESTATEMENT (THIRD) § 40 cmt. d–e. More

general equitable doctrines, such as the plaintiff's unclean hands or estoppel, might also apply in certain circumstances.

The statute of limitations can also provide a defense in some cases. The UTSA and DTSA both limit claims to those brought within three years of the time of discovery of the misappropriation or the time by which, with reasonable diligence, the misappropriation should have been discovered. *See* UTSA § 6; 18 U.S.C. § 1836(d) (each also stating that a continuing misappropriation constitutes a single claim, as opposed to being a continuing wrong).

5. *Mental Misappropriation:* An argument that no tangible copies of trade secret information were taken, and that the information is instead only within the alleged misappropriator's memory—and thus not wrongfully acquired or otherwise not subject to protection as a trade secret—may not create a viable defense to a misappropriation claim when the claim is based on use of the mentally retained information. *See, e.g., Al Minor & Associates v. Martin*, 881 N.E.2d 850 (Ohio 2008); *Ed Nowogroski Ins., Inc. v. Rucker*, 971 P.2d 936 (Wash. 1999). Customer list cases are inconsistent with respect to remembered information; in some instances, the mentally reconstructed list of customer names might be deemed not to be a trade secret at all. *See, e.g., Renee Beauty Salons, Inc. v. Blose-Venable*, 652 A.2d 1345, 1349 (Pa. Super. Ct. 1995) (acknowledging that detailed customer information could be a trade secret but rejecting trade secret status where hairstylists had, after leaving one hair salon, reconstructed from memory a list of the names of their regular customers).

Has there been potential misappropriation if an ex-employee does not take a customer list, either physically or electronically, away from the employer when the employment ends, but instead utilizes customer or client information within a list of contacts the employee developed during the employment period by using online social media or an online professional networking site?

E. REMEDIES

Under the UTSA and the DTSA, a successful trade secret plaintiff may obtain injunctive relief as well as an award of actual damages (including lost profits), and it may also be able to obtain the defendant's profits resulting from the misappropriation. UTSA §§ 2–3; 18 U.S.C. § 1836(b)(3) (both allowing damages for "actual loss caused" and any "unjust enrichment caused" by the misappropriation). *See also* RESTATEMENT (THIRD) § 44 cmt. i & § 45 cmt. m. A reasonable royalty for past use may instead be appropriate, such as in cases where the trade secret has not been destroyed by the defendant's actions and the plaintiff cannot show other specific injury or loss. UTSA § 3(a); 18 U.S.C. § 1836(b)(3)(B)(ii); *see also* RESTATEMENT (THIRD) § 45 cmt. d, g. In addition to seeking permanent injunctive relief at the close of a case, plaintiffs generally seek preliminary injunctive relief upon or immediately after filing a trade secret complaint so as to avoid additional damage to the trade secret(s) before trial. For one limit on injunctive relief in the DTSA, see Note 1 on page 353, following the final case in this chapter.

The following decision includes one court's discussion of the geographic scope of an injunction and the calculation of the appropriate temporal length of the injunction, both with respect to the facts of the case before it.

LAMB-WESTON, INC. V. MCCAIN FOODS, LTD.

941 F.2d 970 (9th Cir. 1991).

EUGENE A. WRIGHT, CIRCUIT JUDGE:

Lamb-Weston's attempt to spiral ahead of its competitors was allegedly thwarted by the misappropriation by McCain of Lamb-Weston's trade secrets for manufacturing curlicue french fries. To keep Lamb-Weston from being left to twist in the wind before the trial on the merits, an eight-month preliminary injunction was imposed, barring McCain from producing or selling products made with the technology in question. McCain appeals and we affirm.

I

Lamb-Weston, a potato processor, began in 1986 to develop the technology for producing curlicue french fries. The unique process involved a helical blade and water-feed system. McCain, a competitor, began work on a manufacturing process for curlicue fries in 1989.

In January 1990, McCain approached several Lamb-Weston employees to help its development. At that time, Richard Livermore, who had helped create the Lamb-Weston blade and process, allegedly gave McCain a copy of Lamb-Weston's confidential patent application. Livermore later went to work for McCain. Subsequently, Jerry Ross, the independent contractor who fabricated the Lamb-Weston blade, was hired by McCain to craft a helical blade for it. McCain left the decisions about the specifications, materials and manufacturing process to Ross, knowing he was still working on Lamb-Weston's blades.

Lamb-Weston was issued two patents for its blade system on May 22, 1990. In August, after discovering Ross was working for McCain, Lamb-Weston had him sign a confidentiality agreement. Contemporaneously, it sent a letter to McCain asserting concern that McCain was misappropriating its trade secrets. In October, Lamb-Weston insisted Ross sign an exclusivity agreement. McCain then requested and received from Ross all the information he had on the McCain blade.

According to Lamb-Weston, with the help of Ross and Livermore, McCain built a prototype before the patents issued in May 1990. By June, McCain had the blades hooked up to a prototype water-feed system and by December was producing curlicue fries.

During the following month, Lamb-Weston sued for misappropriation of trade secrets. The parties consented to proceedings before a magistrate judge, who entered an eight-month preliminary injunction against McCain in March 1991.

II

McCain * * * contends that it had no reason to know that trade secrets were being transmitted through Ross, as he was an independent contractor who assured McCain that there would be no confidentiality problems.

Misappropriation of trade secrets under Oregon law requires a showing of (1) a valuable commercial design, (2) a confidential relationship between the party asserting trade secret protection and the party who disclosed the information, and (3) the key features of the design that were the creative product of the party asserting protection.

* * *

Circumstantial evidence supports the court's preliminary conclusion that despite Ross's assurance he would not breach confidentiality, McCain knew that he would. McCain hired him knowing he was working on Lamb-Weston's blade. McCain told him to build a helical blade but said nothing about how he was to do it. In contrast, Lamb-Weston had specified what materials, dimensions and process to use. As a practical matter, it would be difficult for a person developing the same technology for two clients not to use knowledge gained from the first project in producing the second. This is obviously true here because McCain left the development to Ross.

McCain points to Ross's testimony that he left both the McCain and Lamb-Weston blades in the open where anyone could see them. McCain argues this shows that Lamb-Weston knew Ross was working on a McCain blade but was unconcerned about breaches of confidence. It was not clear error for the court to reject this proposition. Ross's failure to keep the blades segregated suggests he was using the same information to build both blades.

Furthermore, Lamb-Weston employees testified that they did not see the McCain blade at Ross's shop and that, when they learned in August 1990 that Ross was working for McCain, Lamb-Weston had him sign a confidentiality agreement. This demonstrates Lamb-Weston was concerned about protecting its trade secrets.

Probable success in showing misappropriation is also supported by testimony that Livermore gave McCain a copy of the confidential patent application five months before the patent issued. McCain did not challenge this testimony.[2]

---

[2] In its reply brief, McCain argues that the Lamb-Weston information Ross had was not confidential. We decline to address arguments not raised in the appellant's opening brief.

* * *

III

McCain argues that the court abused its discretion by imposing a geographically overbroad injunction. The court enjoined it from selling curlicue french fries worldwide even though Lamb-Weston's foreign market is limited.[3] Arguing that Lamb-Weston cannot be harmed in countries where it is not selling, McCain urges this court to limit the injunction to those countries where Lamb-Weston actually sells its product.

* * *

McCain's reliance on *Mantek Div. of NCH Corp. v. Share Corp.*, 780 F.2d 702 (7th Cir. 1986), is not persuasive. The case involved violations of covenants not to compete signed by the plaintiff's former employees. The injunction barred the defendants from calling on the plaintiff's actual and potential customers. Noting that the injunction was to protect the goodwill the plaintiff had built up with its customers through its sales staff and reasoning that the plaintiff had no goodwill with respect to unsolicited but potential customers, the court held enjoining the defendants from approaching the unsolicited ones was an abuse of discretion. *Id.* at 710–11.

The interest protected here is fundamentally different. An injunction in a trade secret case seeks to protect the secrecy of misappropriated information and to eliminate any unfair head start the defendant may have gained. *Winston Research Corp. v. Minnesota Mining and Mfg.*, 350 F.2d 134, 141 (9th Cir. 1965). A worldwide injunction here is consistent with those goals because it "place[s the defendant] in the position it would have occupied if the breach of confidence had not occurred prior to the public disclosure, . . ." *Id.* at 142.

Lamb-Weston alleged that without the worldwide injunction it will be irreparably harmed because its novel french fries are important in creating a niche for its products. According to Lamb-Weston, this novelty will enable it to compete more effectively with McCain, which apparently has a more

---

Were we to view this argument as part of McCain's assertion that it did not know Ross was breaching any confidentiality and address it, we would find no clear error. McCain acknowledges that at the outset Ross orally agreed to keep Lamb-Weston's information confidential. It also does not challenge the finding that the blade and the fabrication process were trade secrets.

In addition, Lamb-Weston's efforts to secure first a written confidentiality agreement and then an exclusivity agreement show it believed the information Ross had was confidential. *See Holland Dev. v. Manufacturers Consultants*, 724 P.2d 844, 847–48 (Or. App. 1986) (finding a confidential relationship existed and noting that the employer would not invest time and money to develop a project simply to allow its employee to turn around and use the developed technology for personal benefit); *E.V. Prentice Dryer Co. v. Northwest Dryer & Machinery Co.*, 424 P.2d 227, 229 (Or. 1967) (finding no confidentiality agreement where the information was not of a confidential nature and there was nothing in the employment relationship indicating that the plaintiff wanted it to be secret).

[3] McCain contends that Lamb-Weston's only foreign markets are in England, Japan and Canada. Lamb-Weston claims that it also has sold or attempted to sell its fries in Europe, Australia and Brazil.

established distribution system. Allowing McCain to sell the french fries at all will permit it to profit from its head start and to shut Lamb-Weston out of new markets it is trying to reach.

The geographic scope of the injunction was not an abuse of discretion.

IV

McCain argues that the court erred by failing to make specific findings about the length of its alleged head start. McCain also contends the injunction was an abuse of discretion because it is too long.

* * *

"[T]he appropriate duration for the injunction should be the period of time it would have taken [the defendant], either by reverse engineering or by independent development, to develop [the product] legitimately without use of [plaintiff's] trade secrets." *K-2 Ski Co. v. Head Ski Co.*, 506 F.2d 471, 474 (9th Cir. 1974).

McCain argues that April 19, 1990 is the only date for which there is evidence of misappropriation and that at most it had a one-year advantage beginning on that date. It asserts that with a one-year head start, the injunction imposed on March 27, 1991, should have ended on April 19, 1991, one year from the misappropriation date.

If we were to accept McCain's argument that the misappropriation was April 19 and the head start should be calculated from that date, the injunction imposed was not an abuse of discretion simply because it ended a year and seven months after that date. Lamb-Weston presented testimony that its development time for the materials, dimensions and fabricating process for the blade was about a year and a half. Additional testimony was given about Lamb-Weston's reputation for ingenuity and its development time for the blade design.

We reject McCain's argument that if the misappropriation through Ross occurred on April 19, it had only a 33-day head start because Lamb-Weston's patents were issued May 22. Although the shape of the blade and the slicing process was public on May 22, the specifications, materials and manufacturing process for making the blade were still trade secrets because they were not included in the patent applications.

Oregon law affords broad protection to trade secrets so public disclosure of the blade shape did not exonerate McCain from previous illegal use of that trade secret or the subsequent illegal use of the remaining trade secrets. Although a defendant may ask the court to vacate an injunction after the trade secret is public, "the injunction may be continued for an additional reasonable period of time in order to eliminate commercial advantage that otherwise would be derived from the misappropriation." 1989 Or. Laws 646.463(1); *Kamin v. Kuhnau*, 374 P.2d 912, 921–22 (Or. 1962).

The eight-month injunction was not an abuse of discretion.

AFFIRMED.

NOTES

1. *Monetary Relief:* The theories underlying monetary relief vary, including compensatory damages (plaintiff's loss, such as plaintiff's lost profits, a reasonable royalty, or the fair market value of a trade secret that has been destroyed), and restitutionary awards (defendant's gain, including its profits or unjust enrichment). Monetary awards require a temporal analysis similar to that performed to determine the length of injunctive relief so that, for example, the reasonable royalty awarded is calculated only for the period before the secret could be properly ascertained by lawful reverse engineering or would be disclosed publicly, such as through the publication of a patent or patent application. *See* RESTATEMENT (THIRD) § 45 cmt. h.

In some states punitive or exemplary damages may also be available in certain circumstances. The UTSA and DTSA, however, limit exemplary damages to cases of "willful and malicious misappropriation," when a court may award an additional amount that is up to twice the amount otherwise awarded. UTSA § 3(b); 18 U.S.C. § 1836(b)(3)(C). Both the UTSA and DTSA provide for attorneys' fees in certain instances of "bad faith" on the part of either the plaintiff or the defendant, including willful and malicious misappropriation. *See* UTSA § 4; 18 U.S.C. § 1836(b)(3)(D).

2. *Length of Injunction:* Would an injunction be appropriate if other competitors in the industry in question already (rightfully) possessed the asserted trade secret process or other information? Compare the last paragraph in *Lamb-Weston*, above (noting that once the trade secret has been made public, the defendant may ask for an injunction to be vacated), with the older case of *Hyde Corp. v. Huffines*, 314 S.W.2d 763, 778–81 (Tex. 1958) (upholding a permanent injunction against a defendant who breached a covenant not to make the plaintiff's tool even though the tool was later described in an issued patent).

3. *Reasonable Efforts Revisited:* Was the plaintiff in *Lamb-Weston* vigilant in identifying and protecting its trade secrets? Both the trial and appellate courts, at this preliminary stage of the litigation, refused to credit McCain's argument that Lamb-Weston lost any potential trade secret rights by failing to adequately secure a confidential relationship with the contractor, Ross, before he began his work on the McCain blade. Compare these facts to those in *Electro-Craft Corp. v. Controlled Motion, Inc.*, *supra*.

4. *Connection to Patents:* Why might the plaintiff in *Lamb-Weston* obtain patents for some of its inventions (the cutting blade and the slicing process) but not seek a patent on the process for making the blade (the specifications, materials, and manufacturing steps involved)?

F. NON-COMPETITION AGREEMENTS

Beyond trade secret law, non-competition or "non-compete" agreements, also referred to as covenants not to compete, provide an alternate or supplementary means of protecting a business from a competitor who may have inside information about that business that could give the competitor an unfair advantage. The potential competitor subject to a non-competition agreement is often an ex-employee but may also be the former owner of or partner in a business, or a participant in a joint venture. Each state has its own statutory or judicial restrictions on a business's freedom to restrict others from engaging in competition with it. Some states provide firm temporal limitations on employment-related non-competition agreements, *see, e.g.* La. Rev. Stat. Ann. § 23:921(C) (setting a limit of two years after termination of employment), while other states limit the term and scope of these agreements by a standard of reasonableness. Other state laws take different approaches when there has been a desire to restrict use of these agreements. For example, in 2016 Illinois began to prohibit covenants not to compete between an employer and a "low-wage employee" (defined as an employee earning no more than the greater of $13 per hour or the applicable state, federal, or local minimum wage); with further amendments effective January 1, 2022, however, the state eliminated "low-wage employee" from the Act and now limits covenants not to compete to those employees earning, or expected to earn, at least $75,000 a year (with an escalating minimum salary built into the statute). *See* 820 Ill Comp. Stat. §§ 90/5, 90/10 (also invalidating covenants not to solicit for employees earning less than $45,000 a year). In California, meanwhile, non-competition agreements with former employees are generally unenforceable no matter how narrowly drawn. *See Edwards v. Arthur Andersen LLP*, 189 P.3d 285, 288–92 (Cal. 2008). At the same time, a non-competition agreement obtained in the sale or dissolution of a corporation, partnership, or limited liability company may be enforced in California. *See* Cal. Bus. & Prof. Code § 16600–16602.5.

As noted above, many states use a reasonableness standard for many or most noncompetition agreements. The following case explores, in a fairly typical way, whether the geographic and temporal restrictions within an employee's covenant not to compete, as well as the scope of activities curtailed, were "reasonable" and thus enforceable. It is important to bear in mind that each state's approach varies from other states to a greater or lesser extent and that each state's law on non-competition agreements may be governed by statute as well as being guided by state-specific case law.

COMPREHENSIVE TECHNOLOGIES INTERNATIONAL v. SOFTWARE ARTISANS, INC.

3 F.3d 730 (4th Cir. 1993).

WILLIAMS, CIRCUIT JUDGE:

Comprehensive Technologies International, Inc. (CTI), brought this action for copyright infringement against former employees Dean Hawkes, Igor A. Filippides, Randall L. Sterba, Richard T. Hennig, and David R. Bixler (the Defendant employees). CTI also named as defendants Alvan S. Bixler and Software Artisans, Inc. (SA), a corporation formed by Alvan Bixler and several of the Defendant employees shortly after their departure from CTI. CTI contended that "Transend," a computer program developed by the Defendants, infringed upon the copyrights CTI held in its "Claims Express" and "EDI Link" computer programs. CTI appended numerous state law causes of action, including trade secret misappropriation, breach of confidentiality, and breach of contract. CTI also alleged that Hawkes breached his covenant not to compete with CTI by performing services for SA, soliciting CTI's customers, and hiring CTI's former employees. After a bench trial, the district court entered judgment for the Defendants on all counts.

* * * CTI challenges the district court's conclusion that Hawkes's covenant not to compete with CTI is unreasonable and hence unenforceable under Virginia law. * * *

***

Each of the Defendant employees except Hawkes signed CTI's standard Confidentiality and Proprietary Information Agreement. Under the Agreement, each employee agreed not to disclose or use, directly or indirectly, during his employment and for three years thereafter any confidential, proprietary, or software-related information belonging to CTI. The Agreement specifically identified the Claims Express and EDI Link projects as confidential. Although Hawkes did not sign a Confidentiality and Proprietary Information Agreement, he did sign an Employment Agreement that contained similar but more restrictive provisions. In addition to promising confidentiality, Hawkes agreed that during the term of his employment he would not compete with CTI, solicit CTI's customers, or employ CTI's current or former employees.

The Software Products Group undertook to develop two software packages for personal computers. The first, Claims Express, is an electronic medical billing system. * * * The program has been successfully marketed. CTI's second software package, EDI Link, is not specific to the health care industry. It is designed to permit users to create generic forms, enter data on the forms electronically, test that data for errors, and store both the forms and the data on a computer. Although CTI expended substantial effort on EDI Link, at the time of trial the program had not been completed and had never been sold or marketed. * * *

In February 1991, all of the Defendant employees left CTI. Hawkes executed a formal Termination Agreement with CTI. In that Agreement, Hawkes agreed to rescind his Employment Agreement in return for $50,000 and more than $20,000 worth of equipment. Hawkes also agreed that he would not disclose or use CTI's confidential information, and that, for a period of one year following his departure, he would not (1) compete with CTI, (2) solicit CTI's customers, or (3) hire CTI's employees.

In April 1991, the Defendants incorporated Software Artisans, Inc., located in Fairfax, Virginia. By July 1991, SA had developed and begun to market its own program called Transend. According to its User's Manual, Transend creates a "paperless office environment" by enabling its users to process business forms on a computer. Transend is similar to Claims Express and EDI Link in that it is designed to prepare forms for transmission by EDI. Transend permits the user to input data, check the data for errors, and prepare the data for transmission by EDI.

* * *

III. TRADE SECRETS

* * *

In denying CTI's claim for trade secret misappropriation, the district court found that CTI did not possess any trade secrets and that, even if CTI did possess trade secrets, the Defendants had not misappropriated them. The court found no evidence that CTI's purported trade secrets * * * derived independent economic value from not being generally known or were not readily ascertainable by proper means. * * *

* * *

IV. COVENANT NOT TO COMPETE

CTI next argues that the district court should have enforced Dean Hawkes's covenant not to compete. In his Termination Agreement, Hawkes agreed that, for a period of twelve months following his departure from CTI, he would not

> engage directly or indirectly in any business within the United States (financially as an investor or lender or as an employee, director, officer, partner, independent contractor, consultant or owner or in any other capacity calling for the rendition of personal services or acts of management, operation or control) which is in competition with the business of CTI. For purposes of this Agreement, the "business of CTI" shall be defined as the design, development, marketing, and sales of CLAIMS EXPRESS[TM] and

EDI LINK[TM] type PC-based software with the same functionality and methodology. . . .

Virginia has established a three-part test for assessing the reasonableness of restrictive employment covenants. Under the test, the court must ask the following questions:

"(1) Is the restraint, from the standpoint of the employer, reasonable in the sense that it is no greater than is necessary to protect the employer in some legitimate business interest?

(2) From the standpoint of the employee, is the restraint reasonable in the sense that it is not unduly harsh and oppressive in curtailing his legitimate efforts to earn a livelihood?

(3) Is the restraint reasonable from the standpoint of a sound public policy?"

Blue Ridge Anesthesia & Critical Care, Inc. v. Gidick, 389 S.E.2d 467, 469 (Va. 1990) (citation omitted). If a covenant not to compete meets each of these standards of reasonableness, it must be enforced. *Roanoke Eng'g Sales Co. v. Rosenbaum*, 290 S.E.2d 882, 884 (Va. 1982). As a general rule, however, the Virginia courts do not look favorably upon covenants not to compete and will strictly construe them against the employer. *Grant [v. Carotek, Inc.]*, 737 F.2d [410, 411 (4th Cir. 1984)]. The employer bears the burden of demonstrating that the restraint is reasonable.

The district court refused to enforce the covenant not to compete because it concluded that the covenant was broader than necessary to protect CTI's legitimate business interests. * * *

We review the enforceability of the covenant not to compete de novo.

CTI asserts that under the facts of this case the employment restrictions were reasonably necessary to protect its business interests.

Although the district court believed that the covenant was categorically overbroad because it precluded Hawkes from working for a competitor of CTI in any capacity, the Virginia Supreme Court has enforced similarly broad restrictions. In *Roanoke Engineering*, the Court enforced a three-year restriction on an employee's right to "own, manage, operate, control, *be employed by*, participate in, or be associated in any manner with the ownership, management, operation or control of any business similar to the type of business conducted by" the employer. In *Blue Ridge*, the Court upheld a three-year covenant under which the employee could not "open or be employed by or act on behalf of any competitor of Employer which renders the same or similar services as Employer". The covenant in Hawkes's agreement properly restricts him from competitive employment that would, in all likelihood, substantially interfere with CTI's business. *See Stoneman v. Wilson*, 192 S.E. 816, 819 (Va. 1938); *cf. Grant*, 737 F.2d at 412 (covenant which restrained more than direct competition with the employer was unreasonable).

Moreover, as Vice President of CTI's Software Products Group, Hawkes necessarily came in contact with confidential information concerning both CTI's products and its customers. Hawkes's access to such confidential information makes the covenant not to compete more reasonable. As the Virginia Supreme Court has noted,

> [t]he fact that the employment is of such a character as to inform the employee of business methods and trade secrets which, if brought to the knowledge of a competitor, would prejudice the interests of the employer, tends to give an element of reasonableness to a contract that the employee will not engage in a similar business for a limited time after the termination of his employment, and is always regarded as a strong reason for upholding the contract.

Stoneman, 192 S.E. at 819; *Meissel [v. Finley],* 95 S.E.2d [186] at 191 [(Va.1956)] (possession of trade secrets and confidential information is an "important consideration" in testing the reasonableness of a restrictive covenant); *cf. Community Counselling Serv., Inc. v. Reilly,* 317 F.2d 239, 244 (4th Cir.1963) (even in absence of covenant not to compete, employee may not appropriate trade secrets and confidential information rightfully belonging to his former employer). Similarly, in *Roanoke Engineering,* an employee had access to confidential financial records, lists of customers and suppliers, and detailed knowledge of overhead factors, pricing policies, and bidding techniques. The Virginia Supreme Court held that this information enabled the employee to become a "formidable competitor" of his former employer, and concluded that a restriction barring the employee from working for competitors in any capacity was no greater than necessary to protect the employer's legitimate business interests.

Hawkes poses a similar danger to CTI's business. As the individual primarily responsible for the design, development, marketing and sale of CTI's software, Hawkes became intimately familiar with every aspect of CTI's operation, and necessarily acquired information that he could use to compete with CTI in the marketplace. When an employee has access to confidential and trade secret information crucial to the success of the employer's business, the employer has a strong interest in enforcing a covenant not to compete because other legal remedies often prove inadequate. It will often be difficult, if not impossible, to prove that a competing employee has misappropriated trade secret information belonging to his former employer. On the facts of this case, we conclude that the scope of the employment restrictions is no broader than necessary to protect CTI's legitimate business interests.

As a second ground for invalidating the covenant not to compete, the district court concluded that the geographic scope of the employment restrictions—"within the United States"—was greater than necessary to protect CTI's business. The district court merely noted that CTI had marketed Claims Express in only three states and therefore did not have a national market for its product.

The district court clearly erred in concluding that CTI did not have a national market for Claims Express. CTI licensed Claims Express in at least ten states: California, Colorado, Connecticut, Florida, Iowa, Kansas, Maryland, Nebraska, New York, and Oregon. This list alone demonstrates that CTI's customers were dispersed throughout the country and not concentrated in any particular geographic area. CTI's operation was neither local nor regional, but national. Other evidence of a national market for Claims Express was similarly compelling. * * * CTI presented Claims Express and EDI Link (albeit in preliminary form) at national EDIA trade shows in both 1989 and 1990. Finally, CTI presented evidence that it faced direct competition from companies located in California, Colorado, Georgia, Idaho, Illinois, Indiana, Kansas, Maryland, Michigan, Minnesota, New Jersey, Ohio, Oregon, South Carolina, Texas, Utah, and Virginia, and that it faced potential competition from companies in Arizona, California, Georgia, Maryland, North Dakota, Ohio, Oklahoma, Tennessee, and Texas. Given the breadth of the market for Claims Express, we cannot see how anything less than a nationwide prohibition could conceivably protect CTI's business interests. Because CTI had a national market for its product, the restrictions on Hawkes's employment throughout the United States were no greater than necessary to protect it from competition by Hawkes. *See Roanoke Eng'g*, 290 S.E.2d at 885 (restriction geographically coterminous with territory in which employer did business was reasonable); *see also National Homes Corp. v. Lester Indus., Inc.*, 404 F.2d 225, 227 (4th Cir.1968) (under Virginia law, injunctive relief against former employee should be extended to entire state, even though employer had record of sales in only widely scattered sections of the state). CTI fully satisfied the first test of reasonableness.

Having determined that the covenant not to compete is reasonable from CTI's point of view, we must next determine whether the covenant is reasonable from Hawkes's point of view, i.e., whether the curtailment on Hawkes's ability to earn a living is unduly harsh or oppressive. Although the agreement applies throughout the United States, it restricts Hawkes from engaging in only an extremely narrow category of business. Hawkes may not render personal services to, or perform acts of management, operation, or control for, any business in competition with "the business of CTI," which the agreement defines as "the design, development, marketing and sales of CLAIMS EXPRESS[TM] and EDI LINK[TM] type PC-based software with the same functionality and methodology." The agreement therefore permits Hawkes to design, develop, market and sell any software of a type different from Claims Express or EDI Link, any software of the same type having a different functionality or methodology, or any software of the same type having the same functionality and methodology that is not designed to run on personal computers. Hawkes is also free to compete with any other branch of CTI's business. Because Hawkes retains broad employability under the agreement, the agreement is not unduly harsh or oppressive.

In light of the foregoing, we conclude that the covenant not to compete is no greater than necessary to protect CTI's business and is not unduly harsh or oppressive. Hawkes does not suggest, and we do not find, that the covenant is unreasonable from the standpoint of public policy. We therefore hold that the covenant is enforceable.

* * *

MURNAGHAN, CIRCUIT JUDGE, concurring in part and dissenting in part:

While I fully concur with the majority opinion insofar as it disallows recovery on a copyright or trade secrets basis, I reluctantly come to another conclusion with respect to whether CTI, as employer, could enforce as reasonable and not unduly harsh or oppressive the Hawkes covenant not to compete. The covenant not to compete held valid by the majority is operable "within the United States." The district court found that a reasonable covenant would restrict competition only in "Virginia, Nebraska and perhaps one other state." The majority has enhanced CTI's claim to proof of reasonableness by naming 31 states in which CTI has licenses, clients, or potential clients, but that still leaves 19 others, every one of which, it seems to me, is "within the United States." While the majority characterizes CTI's business as "national," it has provided no justification for calling it all inclusive.

The question of validity or not of the non-compete undertaking is one to be decided by the law of the Commonwealth of Virginia. The decision announced by the majority, that a company with business in only 31 states may enforce a non-compete clause in all 50, is a mathematically dubious one on a Virginia point of law. However, the same decision, if announced by the Virginia Supreme Court, would carry more authority than any decision on the point announced by the Fourth Circuit. I feel and have suggested that the question should be certified to the Supreme Court of Virginia. Unfortunately, my colleagues on the panel feel otherwise. Hence, I must make as educated a guess as possible as to what the Virginia law is.[2]

---

[2] In that I have the assistance of the district judge, who has had intimate relationship with Virginia law. "As we have noted in the past 'in determining state law in diversity cases where there is no clear precedent,' we accord 'substantial deference to the opinion of a federal district

A restraint on an employee is unreasonable if it is greater than is necessary to protect the employer in its legitimate business interest and unreasonable from the employee's standpoint as unduly harsh in curtailing his legitimate efforts to earn his livelihood. * * *

> Because restraints of trade are disfavored in Virginia, we must give effect to the language of the agreement, strictly construed. We construe the agreement, reading it literally and construing it favorably to the employee, as an attempt to impose a post-employment restraint upon Gress [employee] without geographic or other limitation. We must therefore decline Alston's [employer's] invitation to read into the agreement limitations which simply are not there.

Alston Studios, Inc. v. Lloyd V. Gress & Associates, 492 F.2d 279, 285 (4th Cir. 1974). "Conceivably the non-competition clause could be interpreted more narrowly, but Virginia law requires that it be strictly construed against the employer. . . ." *Grant v. Carotek, Inc.*, 737 F.2d 410, 412 (4th Cir. 1984).

The Supreme Court of Virginia has never approved a non-compete clause that restricts employment "within the United States." To the contrary, Virginia courts have repeatedly held that non-compete clauses should be limited to a geographical area no greater than is necessary to protect the employer's legitimate business interests. Where Virginia courts have enforced non-compete contracts, the contracts have restricted competition only within "quite narrow and well defined geographic limitations." *Alston Studios*, 492 F.2d at 283 n. 5. *See, e.g., Blue Ridge*, 389 S.E.2d 467 at 469 (covenant that prohibited employment only in territories serviced by the former employee, not in the company's entire market area, enforced); *Roanoke Eng'g*, 290 S.E.2d at 884 (three year restriction that broadly limited an employee's right to be employed by any similar business enforced; court specifically noted that the restriction was reasonable because it was geographically co-terminous with the territory in which the employer did business, which involved only two states); *Meissel v. Finley*, 95 S.E.2d 186, 190 (Va. 1956) (covenant with restrictions that applied only within a radius of 50 miles of Norfolk enforced); *Worrie v. Boze*, 62 S.E.2d 876, 879–81 (Va. 1951) (covenant that restricted competition within 25 miles of dance studio enforced); *Stoneman*, 192 S.E. at 818 (agreement of employee not to go into the hardware business for five years within a limited geographical radius enforced); *Power Distribution, Inc. v. Emergency Power Eng'g*, 569 F. Supp. 54 (E.D. Va. 1983) (non-compete

---

judge because of his familiarity with the state law which must be applied.'" *National Bank of Washington v. Pearson*, 863 F.2d 322, 327 (4th Cir. 1988). My panel colleagues hail from South Carolina and West Virginia and I from Maryland. The district judge, acting in the Eastern District of Virginia, refused to enforce the covenant because it was geographically overbroad and unreasonably curtailed the employee's legitimate efforts to earn a living.

contract that restrained former employee from employment with anyone in competition with employer found too broad because area in which plaintiff competed was not fixed and thus the limitation could extend "to every location where plaintiff might potentially compete, which included at least the entire United States").

Perhaps the Virginia Supreme Court would agree that the noncompete clause applicable to the employee, Hawkes, was reasonable, but in doing so it would have severely to limit, curtail or even contradict what it has said before. I do not accept that we are free to treat a controlling state rule of law applied by the highest court in the Commonwealth of Virginia so cavalierly.

Accordingly, I would hold the non-compete clause overbroad and hence invalid. I would uphold the district court throughout. So to that extent I dissent.

NOTES

1. *Inevitable Disclosure:* Some, but certainly not all, states have recognized a doctrine of "inevitable disclosure" within their trade secret law. Under the doctrine, if an employer (or other trade secret owner) has proven the existence of a trade secret within the possession of (including intangibly, such as within the memory of) a former employee (or business partner, perhaps), a court may enjoin the person from working for a direct competitor of the employer by reasoning that disclosure or use of the trade secret information is "inevitable" under the circumstances. *See, e.g., PepsiCo v. Redmond,* 54 F.3d 1262 (7th Cir. 1995) (affirming a district court's five-month preliminary injunction preventing PepsiCo's ex-employee Redmond from assuming his duties with a new employer, a direct competitor, where PepsiCo claimed and the court agreed that "Redmond cannot help but rely on [PepsiCo's] trade secrets as he helps plot [competitor's] new course, and that these secrets will enable [competitor] to achieve a substantial advantage by knowing exactly how [PepsiCo] will price, distribute, and market its sports drinks and new age drinks and being able to respond strategically."). The DTSA's remedial provisions constrain use of the theory somewhat, in that they allow a court to "prevent any actual or threatened misappropriation" but do not permit entry of an order to "prevent a person from entering into an employment relationship," cautioning "that conditions placed on such employment shall be based on evidence of threatened misappropriation and not merely on the information the person knows." 18 U.S.C. § 1836 (b)(3)(A)(i)(I).

If an employer could have, but did not, require a high-level employee to enter into a non-competition agreement during employment, is that employer well-positioned to seek an injunction against competitive employment of that employee under inevitable disclosure theory? Would a possibility that the employee could recall and use trade secret information justify the broad imposition of an injunction against competitive employment? Or a narrow injunction prohibiting the employee from taking a specific position of employment with a named competitor? Or neither? One court highlighted a company's failure to use a non-competition employment agreement when it refused to issue a preliminary injunction after expiration of a temporary restraining order; this meant the court would no longer bar a former employee from continuing in a particular new position pending trial. *See American Airlines, Inc. v. Imhof*, 620 F. Supp. 2d 574, 587 (S.D.N.Y. 2009). The court relied largely on the vagueness of the asserted confidential information and the balancing of hardships between the parties, even though the court acknowledged the "inevitable disclosure" theory and the court assumed "for purposes of analysis that [employee Imhof] has retained some information that American [Airlines] properly regards as secret and competitively sensitive, and ... that Mr. Imhof would be unable, even in the best of good faith, to put everything of that nature that he recalls out of his mind in doing his job at Delta [Airlines]." *Id.* at 585.

2. *Protecting Non-Secret Interests:* Notice that the Fourth Circuit in the case above affirmed the district court's ruling that the employer did not prove it possessed trade secret information misappropriated by the departing employees, yet it reversed the district court and remanded for further proceedings to determine whether departing employee Hawkes had breached the enforceable covenant not to compete. When information does not fall within the scope of a state's trade secret law, does an employer possess a protectable interest in that information justifying a restriction on an ex-employee's future employment or business activities? Would a confidentiality agreement contractually restraining use of that information by contract be sufficient, or are restraints on employee mobility necessary to protect valid business interests—in that information or otherwise?

3. *Non-Solicitation Agreement:* Some businesses utilize non-solicitation agreements in conjunction with, or in place of, non-competition agreements. Under a non-solicitation agreement, the party being restrained (often, but not exclusively, an employee) agrees that upon termination of the parties' relationship, that party will not solicit or induce the customers or employees of the business to terminate their relationships with the business.

A broad non-solicitation agreement may restrain competition in a manner akin to a non-competition agreement; as a result, these agreements should be, and often are, subject to an analysis similar to that of a non-competition agreement under relevant state law. Thus in California, where non-competition agreements with former employees are generally unenforceable, and the doctrine of inevitable disclosure of trade secrets is not recognized, non-solicitation agreements protecting trade secret information may be enforced, while non-solicitation agreements unrelated to trade secret information generally will not be enforced.

4. *Non-Disclosure Agreements:* Would a non-disclosure agreement with an unlimited term be considered akin to a covenant not to compete? In certain circumstances, or in all cases? When would such an agreement be enforceable? *See, e.g., Gary Van Zeeland Talent, Inc. v. Sandas*, 267 N.W.2d 242 (Wis. 1978)

(refusing post-employment enforcement of a portion of the employee's nondisclosure agreement relating to customer list after finding the list not to constitute a trade secret and finding the agreement, which was unlimited geographically and temporally, to constitute an unreasonable restraint of trade).

5. *Efficacy of Alternate Measures:* What measures should a company take to protect its information from acquisition and use by a third party? How might you assist a client in deciding what measures to pursue? Consider the efficacy of trade secret protection, confidentiality agreements (which presume access but legally limit disclosure via contract), non-competition agreements, physical security measures (such as the ones suggested in *Electro-Craft*), electronic security measures (such as encryption, passwords, network security protocols, and other means of controlling access to electronically stored information), and patents (which eliminate the secret through public disclosure but provide alternate protection as further set forth in later chapters of this book).

6. *Public Policy Concerns:* Covenants not to compete in the practice of law or of medicine raise particular public policy concerns in light of the special relationship of trust and confidence between attorneys or physicians and their clients or patients. As a result, a noncompetition agreement that might be reasonable if it related to a business supplying goods or services may, if applied to a physician or attorney, not be reasonable or may flatly contravene public policy or related state laws or regulations. *See, e.g.*, *Cohen v. Lord, Day & Lord*, 550 N.E.2d 410 (N.Y. 1989) (law); Tex. Bus. & Com. Code § 15.50(b) (providing that covenants not to compete may be enforced against physicians if the covenant conforms to statutory requirements).

7. *Resource:* For more information on non-competition and related agreements, see BRIAN M. MALSBERGER, COVENANTS NOT TO COMPETE: A STATE-BY-STATE SURVEY (2021), BNA.

CHAPTER 9

PROTECTING IDEAS

■ ■ ■

The protection of ideas that have not ripened, so to speak, into a recognized form of intellectual property—such as copyright-protected expression, an invention for which patent protection is sought, a secret protected by trade secret law, or the like—does not rely on a single body of law. Protection, to the extent it is available to the possessor of an idea, arises through one or more of the following legal theories, all of which are state-law claims or theories of recovery rather than rights recognized by federal law: misappropriation (or conversion), breach of contract (either express or implied), or unjust enrichment (sometimes called quasi-contract). Not all states recognize a claim for misappropriation of an idea, and the requirements for a successful claim in any of these areas may vary from state to state. In some situations, the state law misappropriation or unjust enrichment claim may be preempted by the state's trade secret law. *See* UTSA § 7(a). Moreover, state law claims related to the use of an idea embodied in a work of authorship may be preempted by federal copyright law, an issue that is explored further in Chapter 19, *infra*.

A. MISAPPROPRIATION

BAER V. CHASE

392 F.3d 609 (3d Cir. 2004).

GREENBERG, CIRCUIT JUDGE.

This matter comes on before this court on Robert V. Baer's ("Baer") appeal from an order of the district court entered February 20, 2004, granting summary judgment to the defendants, David Chase and DC Enterprises, Inc. (together called "Chase"), pursuant to Federal Rule of Civil Procedure 56(c). This dispute centers on the creation and development of the well-known television series, *The Sopranos*. Through this action, Baer seeks compensation for what he perceives was his role in the creation and development of the popular and financially successful television series.

I. FACTUAL AND PROCEDURAL HISTORY

Chase, who originally was from New Jersey, but relocated to Los Angeles in 1971, is the creator, producer, writer and director of *The*

Sopranos. Chase has numerous credits for other television productions as well. Before Chase met Baer, Chase had worked on a number of projects involving organized crime activities based in New Jersey, including a script for "a mob boss in therapy," a concept that, in part, would become the basis for *The Sopranos.*

In 1995, Chase was producing and directing a *Rockford Files* "movie-of-the-week" when he met Joseph Urbancyk who was working on the set as a camera operator and temporary director of photography. Chase mentioned to Urbancyk that he was looking for new material and for writers who could develop feature film screenplays that Chase later might re-write and direct. Urbancyk also overheard Chase say that the creators of *The Rockford Files* were looking to assign additional writers for their "movie of the week" project.

Urbancyk became the connection between Chase and Baer as a result of Urbancyk's long-time friendship with Baer and his knowledge of Baer's interest in pursuing a career in writing, directing and producing. Baer, who was a New Jersey attorney, recently had left his employment in the Union County Prosecutor's Office in Elizabeth, New Jersey, where he had worked for the previous six years.

Urbancyk urged Baer to write a script for *The Rockford Files.* Baer did so and gave it to Urbancyk who passed it on to Chase. Chase considered Baer's work "interesting" and asked Urbancyk if Baer had any plans to be in Los Angeles. Upon hearing of Chase's interest, Baer flew to Los Angeles to meet with Chase.

Chase, Urbancyk and Baer met for lunch on June 20, 1995. At that time Chase informed Baer that he would be unable to use Baer's screenplay, as the remaining slots in *The Rockford Files* had been filled. The lunch continued, however, with Baer describing his experience as a prosecutor. Baer also pitched the idea to shoot "a film or television shows about the New Jersey Mafia." At that time Baer was unaware of Chase's previous work involving mob activity premised in New Jersey. At the lunch there was no reference to any payment that Chase might make to Baer for the latter's services and the parties agree that they did not reach any agreement on that day.

In October 1995, Chase visited New Jersey for three days. During this "research visit" Baer arranged meetings for Chase with Detective Thomas Koczur, Detective Robert A. Jones, and Tony Spirito who provided Chase with information, material and personal stories about their experiences with organized crime [including situations and characters similar to some that appeared in episodes of *The Sopranos*]. * * * Baer does not dispute that virtually all of the ideas and locations that he "contributed" to Chase existed in the public record.

After returning to Los Angeles, Chase sent Baer a copy of a draft of a *Sopranos* screenplay that he had written, which was dated December 20, 1995. Baer asserts that after he read it he called Chase and made various comments with regard to it. Baer claims that the two spoke at least four times during the following year and that he sent a letter to Chase dated February 10, 1997, discussing *The Sopranos* script. Baer ensured that Chase received the letter by confirming its arrival with Chase's assistant. On this appeal we accept Baer's allegations regarding his input into *The Sopranos* draft.

* * *

Baer asserts that he and Chase orally agreed on three separate occasions that if the show became a success, Chase would "take care of" Baer, and "remunerate [Baer] in a manner commensurate to the true value of [his services]." According to Baer, he and Chase first made this oral agreement on the telephone during one of their first two or three conversations during the summer of 1995. The second occasion was on the telephone and occurred immediately prior to Chase's October 1995 visit to New Jersey. The third time the parties reached the agreement was in person when they met in New Jersey in October 1995.

Baer claims that on each of these occasions the parties had the same conversation in which Chase offered to pay Baer, stating "you help me; I pay you." Baer always rejected Chase's offer, reasoning that Chase would be unable to pay him "for the true value of the services [Baer] was rendering." Each time Baer rejected Chase's offer he did so with a counteroffer, "that I would perform the services while assuming the risk that if the show failed [Chase] would owe me nothing. If, however, the show succeeded he would remunerate me in a manner commensurate to the true value of my services." Baer acknowledges that this counteroffer, which in these proceedings we treat as having become the parties' agreement, always was oral and did not include any fixed term of duration or price. There is no other evidence in the record of any other discussion between Baer and Chase regarding the terms of the contract. For purposes of the motion for summary judgment, Chase accepts Baer's version of the events as true and thus concedes there was an oral agreement to the extent that Baer sets it forth. Notwithstanding this agreement, insofar as we can ascertain, other than Baer's calls to Chase after he received the *Sopranos* script, the next time Baer heard anything from or about Chase was when he received a phone call from Detective Koczur telling him that Chase was in Elizabeth shooting *The Sopranos*. In fact, Chase has not paid Baer for his services.

* * *

[Baer sued for breach of contract and misappropriation of his idea, among other claims. Chase eventually moved for summary judgment, which the district court granted. The appellate court affirmed summary judgment for Chase on the contract-based claims; the contract portion of the case is excerpted in Part B. of this chapter. After dispensing with the contract issue, the court then turned to the misappropriation claim.]

Baer next raises the issue of whether the district court erred in holding that the fact that the ideas he advanced existed in the public domain precluded those ideas, alone or in combination, from possessing the requisite novelty so that their use cannot be the basis for a claim for common law idea misappropriation. The cause of action of "misappropriation" is based on tort principles rather than on contract law. RESTATEMENT (THIRD) OF UNFAIR COMPETITION § 40, cmt. a. The premise behind the tort is that when a party misappropriates another's confidential idea or some other type of property, the law imposes an obligation on that party to pay the other restitution for its improper use.

There is no dispute between the parties that this case is governed by the leading precedent on the misappropriation of ideas in New Jersey, *Flemming v. Ronson Corp.*, 258 A.2d 153, 156–57 (N.J. Super. Ct. Law Div. 1969), *aff'd*, 275 A.2d 759 (N.J. Super. Ct. App. Div. 1971). The court in *Flemming* articulated the test for determining whether the law will imply an obligation to pay for a confidentially submitted idea: When "a person communicates a novel idea to another with the intention that the latter may use the idea and compensate him for such use, the other party is liable for such use and must pay compensation if . . . (1) the idea was novel; (2) it was made in confidence [to the defendant]; and (3) it was adopted and made use of [by the defendant in connection with his own activities]."

Thus, the misappropriation issue on appeal is whether the ideas Baer provided were novel. While novelty is clearly a prerequisite to establish a misappropriation claim in New Jersey, the courts have not articulated clearly the test for determining whether an idea is sufficiently novel to warrant protection. Two leading cases dealing with the parameters of New Jersey misappropriation law arose in federal courts deciding state law issues, *Duffy* [*v. Charles Schwab & Co.*], 123 F. Supp. 2d 802 [(D.N.J. 2001)], and *Bergin v. Century 21 Real Estate Corp.*, 2000 WL 223833 (S.D.N.Y. Feb.25, 2000), *aff'd*, 234 F.3d 1261 (2d Cir.2000) (table).

* * *

The predicates on which a property right in an idea may be based are novelty and originality. *See Downey v. General Foods Corp.*, 286 N.E.2d 257, 259 (N.Y. 1972). A misappropriation claim, unlike a contract-based claim, only can arise from the taking of an idea that is original or novel because the law of property does not protect against the appropriation of that which is free and available to all. *Nadel* [*v. Play-by-Play Toys & Novelties, Inc.*], 208 F.3d [368] at 378 [(2d Cir. 2000)]. Therefore, anyone may use ideas in the public domain freely with impunity. *See Ed Graham Prods., Inc. v. National Broad. Co.,* 347 N.Y.S.2d 766 (N.Y.Sup.Ct.1973).

The district court here acknowledged *Duffy's* observation that the law of "unfair competition 'is an amorphous area of jurisprudence' and 'knows of no clear boundaries.'" For example, the court in *Duffy* noted that the *Flemming* court, "did not discuss a specific test that should be used to determine whether an idea is novel."

The present facts, however, do not compel us to set forth a broad description of what is novel in our disposition of Baer's misappropriation claim. Though *Flemming* did not articulate a test for affirmatively determining when an idea is "novel," the court did cite examples of ideas that would *not* be novel. The *Flemming* court recognized that even an otherwise novel idea would lose its novelty if it was "in the domain of public knowledge" before the defendant used it. The *Duffy* court expanded on this conclusion by noting "[a]n idea will not satisfy [the novelty requirement] if it is not significantly different from, or is an obvious adaptation or combination of ideas in the public domain." The Court of Appeals for the Second Circuit, applying New Jersey law, also noted in *Bergin v. Century 21 Real Estate Corp.,* 234 F.3d 1261 (2d Cir.2000) (table), *available at* 2000 WL 1678777, at *3, that "[s]ummary judgment is appropriate where the defendant knew of the idea or the idea was 'a matter[ ] in the domain of public knowledge before the plaintiff disclosed it to the defendant.'" Other jurisdictions have taken like positions. *See Educational Sales Programs, Inc. v. Dreyfus Corp.,* 317 N.Y.S.2d 840, 844 (N.Y.Sup.Ct.1970) ("The idea need not reflect the 'flash of genius,' but it must shown [sic] genuine novelty and invention, and not a merely clever or useful adaptation of existing knowledge."); *Oasis Music, Inc. v. 900 U.S.A., Inc.,* 614 N.Y.S.2d 878, 882–84 (N.Y.Sup.Ct.1994) (declining to attribute novelty where ideas were variations and adaptations of existing knowledge in the public domain). We conclude, similarly, that the New Jersey Supreme Court, if addressed with the issue, would hold that ideas lose their novelty if they are in the domain of public knowledge before use. Such ideas cannot be misappropriated.

Baer admits that all of the locations he identified to Chase exist in the public domain.[7] In addition, many of the stories and potential plot lines that Baer "provided" Chase existed in the public record. Moreover, as the district court noted, the additional ideas and stories that Baer claims were misappropriated were not *his* stories; "associates" of Baer actually told them to Chase:

> In particular, the Plaintiff seeks compensation for *Spirito's story* of rivalry with his uncles in the aftermath of his father's death, that *Koczur's account* to Chase that many waste management

[7] Baer "introduced" Chase to the City of Elizabeth, The Pulaski Skyway, and Centanni's Meat Market.

> companies were alleged to be involved with organized crime, *Spirito's story* of his experiences with a 'loan shark' and *Jones's description* of the way in which organized crime uses loan shark debts to take over a business, *Jones's description* of the operation of 'cutout' schemes used by organized crime, *Koczur's information* regarding the involvement of the DeCavalcante crime family in Saint Anthony's Church in Elizabeth, and a *story told to Chase by Jones* about Morris Levy's horse farm.

(emphasis added). It is clear that virtually all of Baer's alleged contributions either existed in the public domain or concerned stories and facts he did not provide.

Baer argues that he did not simply introduce these third-parties to Chase, but rather "the majority of ideas were suggested by Plaintiff prior to the meeting." Baer alleges that his aggregating and combining of ideas was essential in "put[ting] it all together" and "creat[ing] the 'template' for *The Sopranos*." Baer alleges that it is "their combination that gives these ideas originality." In other words, Baer's contribution in essence was "choosing" which ideas, existing in the public domain, he would present to Chase.

Aggregation of ideas and expression do not by themselves create novelty. In *Duffy* the plaintiff argued that "its idea was novel because [it] spent many months deciding the organization and layout of the data so its products could be readily understood by nonprofessional investors. . . . [It] stated that it was the format that made Duffy's reports unique and proprietary to [it]." The plaintiff in *Duffy* took data, fields and information in the public domain and organized them to create a "mutual fund report card." The court held that, though the organization and layout of the data may involve some originality, this articulation of originality went more to an idea's expression than to the idea itself. It is well-established that an idea's expression is not entitled to protection under a state's misappropriation law. As the court in *Duffy* recognized, "To the extent a state's law purports to impose liability for the misappropriation of an idea's expression, such a law would be preempted by federal copyright law." Despite Baer's creativity in combining stories and facts existing in the public domain, New Jersey does not protect this mode of originality under its misappropriation law. Thus, the district court correctly granted Chase summary judgment on Baer's misappropriation claim.

* * *

NOTE

Novelty for Idea Misappropriation Claims: Among states allowing enforcement of a claim for misappropriation of an idea, a requirement of novelty is fairly strictly enforced—although exactly what "novelty" means in the idea context is not always entirely clear. Breach-of-contract claims related to idea submission and idea sharing also often turn on "novelty"—as you will see in Part B. of this chapter—but the meaning of the term can vary. In contrast, patent law requires "novelty" under a statutorily defined standard, as further explained in Chapter 10.C., *infra.*

In *Nadel v. Play-by-Play Toys & Novelties, Inc.*, 208 F.3d 368 (2d Cir. 2000), the Second Circuit explained its view of the level of novelty that supports a misappropriation claim, as contrasted with the novelty that it held could support a contract claim.

> In contrast to contract-based claims, a misappropriation claim can only arise from the taking of an idea that is original or novel in absolute terms, because the law of property does not protect against the misappropriation or theft of that which is free and available to all. *See Murray v. National Broad. Co.*, 844 F.2d 988, 993 (2d Cir. 1988) ("Since . . . non-novel ideas are not protectible as property, they cannot be stolen."); *cf. Ed Graham Prods., Inc. v. National Broad. Co.*, 347 N.Y.S.2d 766, 769 (N.Y. Sup. Ct. 1973) ("Ideas such as those presented by the plaintiff are in the public domain and may freely be used by anyone with impunity."); *Educational Sales Programs, Inc. v. Dreyfus Corp.*, 317 N.Y.S.2d 840, 843 (N.Y. Sup. Ct. 1970) ("An idea is impalpable, intangible, incorporeal, yet it may be a stolen gem of great value, or mere dross of no value at all, depending on its novelty and uniqueness.").
>
> [A]lthough the legal requirements for contract-based claims and property-based claims are well-defined, we note that the determination of novelty in a given case is not always clear. *Cf. AEB & Assocs. Design Group, Inc. v. Tonka Corp.*, 853 F.Supp. 724, 734 (S.D.N.Y.1994) ("In establishing an idea's originality, a plaintiff cannot rest on mere assertions, but must demonstrate some basis in fact for its claims."). The determination of whether an idea is original or novel depends upon several factors, including, inter alia, the idea's specificity or generality (is it a generic concept or one of specific application?), its commonality (how many people know of this idea?), its uniqueness (how different is this idea from generally known ideas?), and its commercial availability (how widespread is the idea's use in the industry?). *Cf. Murray*, 844 F.2d at 993 ("In assessing whether an idea is in the public domain, the central issue is the uniqueness of the creation."); *AEB & Assocs.*, 853 F.Supp. at 734 ("[N]ovelty cannot be found where the idea consists of nothing more than a variation on a basic theme."); *Educational Sales Programs*, 317 N.Y.S.2d at 844 (noting that an idea "must show[ ] genuine novelty and invention, and not a merely clever or useful adaptation of existing knowledge" in order to be considered original or novel). Thus, for example, a once original or novel idea may become so widely disseminated over the course of time that it enters the body of common knowledge. When this occurs, the idea ceases to be novel or

original. *See, e.g., Murray*, 844 F.2d at 989, 991–92 (affirming district court's finding that plaintiff's idea for a television sitcom about "Black American family life" was not novel or original because it "merely combined two ideas which had been circulating in the industry for a number of years—namely, the family situation comedy, which was a standard formula, and the casting of black actors in non-stereotypical roles," even though "the portrayal of a nonstereotypical black family on television was indeed a breakthrough").

Moreover, in assessing the interrelationship between originality and novelty to the buyer [Ed. Note: "novelty to the buyer" arises in contract cases], we note that in some cases an idea may be so unoriginal or lacking in novelty that its obviousness bespeaks widespread and public knowledge of the idea, and such knowledge is therefore imputed to the buyer. *See Soule*, 195 N.Y.S. at 575 (noting that the idea that an increase in the wholesale price of groceries would result in an increase in profits was "not new" in 1922, "not original," and left the court "at a loss to understand how it could be deemed valuable"). In such cases, a court may conclude, as a matter of law, that the idea lacks both the originality necessary to support a misappropriation claim and the novelty to the buyer necessary to support a contract claim. *See id.* at 576 ("No person can by contract monopolize an idea that is common and general to the whole world."); *Ed Graham Prods.*, 347 N.Y.S.2d at 769 ("[W]here plaintiff's idea is wholly lacking in novelty, no cause of action in contract or tort can stand. . . .") (emphasis added); *Educational Sales Programs*, 317 N.Y.S.2d at 843–44 ("Nothing is bestowed if the facts of a 'secret' imparted in confidence are already the subject of general knowledge.").

208 F.3d at 378–79. The portion of *Nadel* discussing the level of novelty required in the context of breach-of-contract claims related to ideas is excerpted *infra* in Note 4 following the next case.

B. BREACH OF CONTRACT (EXPRESS OR IMPLIED)

BAER V. CHASE

392 F.3d 609 (3d Cir. 2004).

GREENBERG, CIRCUIT JUDGE.

[The facts of the case are set forth in the case excerpt in Part A. of this chapter, *supra*.]

III. DISCUSSION

A. Baer's Implied-In-Fact Contract Claim

Baer predicates his contract claim on this appeal on an implied-in-fact contract rather than on the oral agreement he reached with Chase. The issue with respect to the implied-in-fact contract claim concerns whether Chase and Baer entered into an enforceable contract for services Baer rendered that aided in the creation and production of *The Sopranos*. In the district court Baer offered two alternative theories in which a purported contract was formed: the "oral agreement/success contingency" and an implied-in-fact contract.

The parties agree for purposes of the summary judgment motion that there was a contingent oral agreement providing for Chase to compensate Baer, depending on Chase's "success," in exchange for the aid Baer provided in the creation and production of *The Sopranos*. As we noted above, the parties reached the oral agreement in three exchanges in which Baer proposed: "that I would perform the services while assuming the risk that if the show failed [Chase] would owe me nothing. If, however, the show succeeded he would remunerate me in a manner commensurate to the true value of my services." As we have indicated, for purposes of the summary judgment motion only, Chase accepts this version of the events so we will regard the existence of the oral agreement as not in dispute.

The district court held, and Baer concedes on appeal, that this oral agreement was "too vague to be enforced" as an express contract. ("The contract as articulated by the Plaintiff lacks essential terms, and is vague, indefinite and uncertain; no version of the alleged agreement contains sufficiently precise terms to constitute an enforceable contract.") This description of the oral agreement leaves at issue Baer's contention that the district court overlooked the existence of an enforceable implied-in-fact contract, rendering Chase liable for the services that Baer provided.

1. The Distinction Between Express And Implied-In-Fact Contracts

The distinction between express and implied contracts rests on alternative methods of contract formation. Contracts are "express" when the parties state their terms and "implied" when the parties do not state their terms. The distinction is based not on the contracts' legal effect but on the way the parties manifest their mutual assent. *In re Penn. Cent. Transp. Co.*, 831 F.2d 1221, 1228 (3d Cir.1987) ("An implied-in-fact contract, therefore, is a true contract arising from mutual agreement and intent to promise, but in circumstances in which the agreement and promise have not been verbally expressed. The agreement is rather inferred from the conduct of the parties."). In other words, the terms "express" and "implied" do not denote different kinds of contracts, but rather reference the evidence by which the parties demonstrate their agreement.

Baer's attempt to find an implied-in-fact contract in his dealings with Chase does not strengthen his claim that Chase breached his contract with him. There is only one contract at issue, Chase's promise to compensate Baer for services he rendered which aided in the creation and production of *The Sopranos*. Chase's stipulation that there was such a contract has the consequence of making Baer's attempts to label this agreement "implied" rather than "express" to advance a distinction without a difference as the mode of contract formation, as we will explain, is immaterial to the disposition of the breach of contract claim. In other words, inasmuch as the parties agree for purposes of these summary judgment proceedings that there was an agreement, the manner in which they formed the contract is immaterial because different legal consequences do not flow from analyzing the alleged contract as implied-in-fact rather than express. * * *

Moreover, Baer's claim of an implied-in-fact contract, in the face of an express agreement governing the same subject matter, is legally untenable. There cannot be an implied-in-fact contract if there is an express contract that covers the same subject matter. In other words, express contract and implied-in-fact contract theories are mutually exclusive.

* * *

The question is not whether Chase entered into an agreement with Baer or whether Chase utilized his ideas. We already deem these matters, for the purposes of the motion for summary judgment and this appeal, as established. The question is whether Chase's nonverbal actions prove there was a contract distinct from the express agreement or expanding on the terms of the agreement to make it enforceable. The answer is clearly that the actions do not do so. The alleged implied-in-fact contract completely mirrors the acknowledged express contract's subject matter. Baer nowhere demonstrates that the subject matter of the alleged implied-in-fact contract is distinct, more definite in terms of price and duration, or covers a subject matter divergent from the oral agreement. The district court, therefore, would have erred if it had analyzed this case on the basis that there was a separate implied-in-fact contract distinct from the express contract that governed the identical subject matter.

2. Definitiveness As To Price and Duration In An "Idea Submission" Case

Even assuming that Baer had been able to demonstrate that he had an implied-in-fact contract with Chase, his contention that an implied-in-fact contract claim in an idea submission case need not be definite as to price and duration, would be incorrect. Baer asserts that the district court's holding "that the absence of a price and duration term render[s] an implied contract in an idea submission scenario too vague to be enforced . . . is contrary to the law in virtually every jurisdiction that has ever considered the issue." Baer's claim fails on three grounds: (1) there is no distinction between express and implied contracts, aside from issues of contract formation; (2) definiteness with respect to price and duration is necessary for idea submission cases under New Jersey contract law; and (3) the district court was correct in holding that the contract Baer alleges existed was too ambiguous and indefinite to be enforceable.

a. An Implied-In-Fact Contract Has The Same Legal Consequences As An Express Contract.

In fact there are no distinctions in legal effect, at least in the context of this case, when a promise is implied rather than express. No rationale exists to conclude that definiteness as to the essential terms of a contract could be an exception from this fundamental principle. We therefore determine if in any "idea submission case," whether predicated on an express or implied contract, definiteness is a requirement to create an enforceable contract.

b. A Contract Involving An Idea Submission Must Be Definite With Respect To All Essential Terms To Be Enforceable Under New Jersey Contract Law.

In fact "[a] contract arises from offer and acceptance, and must be sufficiently definite so 'that the performance to be rendered by each party can be ascertained with reasonable certainty.' " Therefore parties create an enforceable contract when they agree on its essential terms and manifest an intent that the terms bind them. If parties to an agreement do not agree on one or more essential terms of the purported agreement courts generally hold it to be unenforceable.

New Jersey contract law focuses on the performance promised when analyzing an agreement to determine if it is too vague to be enforced. "An agreement so deficient in the specification of its essential terms that the performance by each party cannot be ascertained with reasonable certainty is not a contract, and clearly is not an enforceable one." A contract, therefore, is unenforceable for vagueness when its essential terms are too indefinite to allow a court to determine with reasonable certainty what each party has promised to do.

New Jersey law deems the price term, i.e., the amount of compensation, an essential term of any contract. An agreement lacking definiteness of price, however, is not unenforceable if the parties specify a practicable method by which they can determine the amount. *Moorestown Mgmt., Inc. v. Moorestown Bookshop, Inc.*, 104 N.J. Super. 250, 249 A.2d 623, 628 (1969). However, in the absence of an agreement as to the manner or method of determining compensation the purported agreement is invalid. Additionally, the duration of the contract is deemed an essential term and therefore any agreement must be sufficiently definitive to allow a court to determine the agreed upon length of the contractual relationship. *Lo Bosco* [*v. Kure Eng'g Ltd.*], 891 F. Supp. [1020] at 1026 [(D.N.J. 1995)]("With regard to contracts for services in return for a percentage of some yet-to-be-determined number, such as profits, sales, etc., the courts [of and in New Jersey] look to whether there are certain dates of commencement and termination.").

The New Jersey Supreme Court explicitly has held that an implied-in-fact contract "must be sufficiently definite [so] that the performance to be rendered by each party can be ascertained with reasonable certainty." If possible, courts will "attach a sufficiently definite meaning to the terms of a bargain to make it enforceable[,]"and in doing so may refer to "commercial practice or other usage or custom." But the courts recognize that a contract is "unenforceable for vagueness when its terms are too indefinite to allow a court to determine with reasonable certainty what each party has promised to do."

Baer premises his argument on his view that New Jersey should disregard the well-established requirement of definiteness in its contract law when the subject-matter of the contract is an "idea submission." He cites extensively to a string of cases from various jurisdictions which he urges support his contention. * * *

Baer's argument is inaccurate and misleading. * * * None of the cases Baer cites holds that there is not a definiteness requirement necessary to create an enforceable contract in idea submission cases. * * *

New Jersey precedent does not support Baer's attempt to carve out an exception to traditional principles of contract law for submission-of-idea cases. The New Jersey courts have not provided even the slightest indication that they intend to depart from their well-established requirement that enforceability of a contract requires definiteness with respect to the essential terms of that contract. Accordingly, we will not relax the need for Baer to demonstrate definiteness as to price and duration with respect to the contract he entered into with Chase.

3. The Alleged "Contract" Regardless Of Labels Is Too Vague To Be Enforced.

The final question with respect to the Baer's contract claim, therefore, is whether his contract is enforceable in light of the traditional requirement of definitiveness in New Jersey contract law for a contract to be enforceable. A contract may be expressed in writing, or orally, or in acts, or partly in one of these ways and partly in others. There is a point, however, at which interpretation becomes alteration. In this case, even when all of the parties' verbal and non-verbal actions are aggregated and viewed most favorably to Baer, we cannot find a contract that is distinct and definitive enough to be enforceable.

Nothing in the record indicates that the parties agreed on how, how much, where, or for what period Chase would compensate Baer. The parties did not discuss who would determine the "true value" of Baer's services, when the "true value" would be calculated, or what variables would go into such a calculation. There was no discussion or agreement as to the meaning of "success" of The Sopranos. There was no discussion how "profits" were to be defined. There was no contemplation of dates of commencement or termination of the contract. And again, nothing in Baer's or Chase's conduct, or the surrounding circumstances of the relationship, shed light on, or answers, any of these questions. The district court was correct in its description of the contract between the parties: "The contract as articulated by the Plaintiff lacks essential terms, and is vague, indefinite and uncertain; no version of the alleged agreement contains sufficiently precise terms to constitute an enforceable contract." We therefore will affirm the district court's rejection of Baer's claim to recover under a theory of implied-in-fact contract.

NOTES

1. *Concreteness or Specificity of the Idea:* In *Sellers v. American Broadcasting Co.*, 668 F.2d 1207 (11th Cir. 1982), Larry Sellers had sued ABC and its investigative reporter Geraldo Rivera for breach of contract (and other claims) related to his disclosure to Rivera of his theory concerning the death of Elvis Presley. Before he discussed his research and ideas with Rivera, Sellers required Rivera to sign a contract that would give Sellers copyright privileges in the story and require public credit as the source of the story. Sellers recorded the entire meeting with Rivera. The primary theory of Presley's death disclosed by Sellers in the meeting was that Presley's physician and bodyguard intentionally replaced (with a placebo) cortisone that had been taken by Presley for three years before his death, and that this intentional cortisone deprivation caused Presley's cardiovascular system to collapse. In the alternative, Sellers hypothesized that Presley might have been suffocated by either man. After ABC—without crediting Sellers—later aired an hour-long special in which Presley's death was argued to have been due to the interaction of prescription drugs, and not cardiac arrhythmia (the official cause of death), Sellers filed suit. In affirming summary judgment for the defendants, the appellate court explained:

> Sellers asserts that he informed Rivera not only of the possibility that Presley might have been murdered through a deprivation of cortisone, but also that the cause of death might have been the interaction of numerous prescription drugs, that the singer's personal physician may have been grossly negligent in overprescribing drugs for Presley and that there had been a cover-up of the true cause of death. Assuming without deciding that Sellers did present these additional theories to Rivera,[3] we nonetheless conclude that they are so vague and uncertain as to be unenforceable as a matter of law.

[3] A review of the transcribed meeting between the parties reflects that Sellers never specifically told Rivera that the personal physician may have been grossly negligent in overprescribing drugs for Presley. Moreover, the lone reference at the meeting to the possibility

> Under New York law, a contract will not be enforced if an essential element is vague, indefinite or incomplete. A complete review of the transcribed meeting between the parties shows that at best Sellers made broad, general statements concerning the possibility of overdose, gross negligence by the personal physician and a cover-up. The transcript demonstrates that plaintiff failed to provide any substantiating details for these vague allegations. He did not make clear whether Presley's death resulted from a single drug or a combination of drugs. He made no effort to provide the name of any specific drug that had been overprescribed by the personal physician. Nor did plaintiff show that medication unnecessary for the treatment of the singer's illnesses was prescribed for Presley. Finally, references to books and newspaper articles[5] constituted the only support for these vague and uncertain statements. Sellers' theory that Presley was murdered by a withdrawal of cortisone may well have been specific enough to give rise to an enforceable agreement. The district court, however, concluded that the defendants did not utilize the cortisone-murder theory in any of their broadcasts and did not, therefore, breach the agreement. Plaintiff does not challenge this conclusion on appeal.

Notice the difference in the basis of the *Sellers* court's conclusion on breach of contract with respect to plaintiff's specific theory of cortisone withdrawal versus the basis of its conclusion on breach of contract with respect to his general theories of overdose, medical negligence, and a cover-up.

2. *Time of Contract Formation:* A 1975 case, *Smith v. Recrion Corp.*, 51 P. 2d 663 (Nev. 1975), provides a cautionary tale to would-be idea submitters. An employee of the Stardust Hotel in Las Vegas, Nevada, conceived of the idea that an RV park would be a profitable addition to the hotel's offerings. He arranged to meet with the general manager (GM) of the hotel and disclosed the idea to the GM in the meeting. He then told the GM that he expected to be compensated for the idea. The GM did not at that time express interest in the idea, nor had the GM either solicited the idea from the employee or asked for the meeting. Two years later, the Stardust Hotel opened an RV park next to the hotel. The employee demanded compensation, and when none was forthcoming, he sued on a variety of theories, including breach of contract. The Nevada Supreme Court affirmed the grant of summary judgment in favor of the hotel defendant.

> Prior to the time Smith and Sachs first met to discuss Smith's idea, Sachs had no knowledge of the purpose of the meeting. Smith's idea was entirely unsolicited and he voluntarily disclosed his idea before the subject of compensation had been discussed. Even if Sachs

that Presley died of the interaction of drugs in his body was made by Sellers in passing and appears to be nothing more than background information. * * *

[5] We note that at least a portion of plaintiff's "exclusive story", particularly the theory that Presley died from an interaction of drugs, appeared in a number of newspaper articles prior to his discussion with Rivera. * * *

subsequently promised Smith compensation, the promise would be unenforceable for the reason that it would have been unsupported by consideration. Past consideration is the legal equivalent to no consideration. *Murray v. Lichtman*, 339 F.2d 749, 752 n. 5 (D.C. Cir. 1964). An abstract idea cannot be protected by an express or implied contract unless the contract was made before the disclosure of the idea. *See e.g., Hampton v. La Salle Hat Company*, 88 F. Supp. 153 (S.D.N.Y.1949); *Desny v. Wilder*, 299 P.2d 257 (Cal. 1956).

3. *Novelty for Breach-of-Contract Claims:* Should novelty of an idea play a substantive role, or only an evidentiary role, in a claim based on breach of contract? Or should novelty play a role at all? When a contract is formed before an idea is disclosed, is the conveying party providing a service to the receiving party (the act of disclosing) or delivering property to the receiving party (the idea itself)? What about a post-disclosure contract?

4. *State Law Variation:* There is significant state-to-state variation on the question of whether novelty is required for contract-based protection of an idea. Not all states require any form of novelty. *See, e.g., Reeves v. Alyeska Pipeline Serv. Co.*, 926 P.2d 1130 (Alaska 1996); *Wrench LLC v. Taco Bell Corp.*, 256 F.3d 446 (6th Cir. 2001) (interpreting *Sarver v. Detroit Edison Co.*, 571 N.W.2d 759 (Mich. Ct. App. 1997) to allow a plaintiff to rely on a breach of contract claim under Michigan law even if the idea conveyed pursuant to a contract was not novel). Two important states for the entertainment field, New York and California, diverge significantly.

New York: There is some disagreement as to the role of novelty in a contract claim in New York, but in any event, some amount of novelty is required if the idea seller wishes to enforce a *pre*-disclosure contract for the disclosure of the idea. According to the Second Circuit in *Nadel v. Play-by-Play Toys & Novelties, Inc.*, 208 F.3d 368 (2d Cir. 2000), New York law requires an idea to be novel to the buyer in order for a *pre*-disclosure contract to be enforced. The opinion appears to conclude that the idea must also be novel to the buyer in order to support a *post*-disclosure contract under New York law, but other courts in New York have disagreed. *See Lapine v. Seinfeld*, 918 N.Y.S.2d 313, 320–21 (N.Y. Sup. Ct. 2011) (disagreeing with the *Nadel* court's "novelty to the buyer" reading of the case law, and distinguishing the idea novelty required for pre-disclosure contracts (absolute novelty required) and post-disclosure contracts (no novelty required)).

The following excerpt is from *Nadel v. Play-by-Play*, in which plaintiff Nadel had submitted to toy company Play-by-Play an idea for a spinning toy monkey with a specific type of spinning mechanism.

> Nadel's factual allegations present a familiar submission-of-idea case: (1) the parties enter into a pre-disclosure confidentiality agreement; (2) the idea is subsequently disclosed to the prospective buyer; (3) there is no post-disclosure contract for payment based on use; and (4) plaintiff sues defendant for allegedly using the disclosed idea under either a contract-based or property-based theory. For the

reasons that follow, we conclude that a finding of novelty as to Play-By-Play can suffice to provide consideration for Nadel's contract claims against Play-By-Play. Accordingly, because we also find that there exists a genuine issue of material fact as to whether Nadel's idea was novel to Play-By-Play at the time of his October 1996 disclosure, we vacate the district court's grant of summary judgment on Nadel's contract claims. * * *

* * * *Apfel* [*v. Prudential-Bache Securities, Inc.*, 616 N.E.2d 1095 (N.Y. 1993)] clarified an important distinction between the requirement of "novelty to the buyer" for contract claims, on the one hand, and "originality" (or novelty generally) for misappropriation claims, on the other hand.

* * *

In rejecting defendant's argument [that a disclosed idea must be novel or original generally to constitute legal consideration for a contract], the Court of Appeals held that there was sufficient consideration to support plaintiff's contract claim because the idea at issue had value to the defendant at the time the parties concluded their post-disclosure agreement. The *Apfel* court noted that "traditional principles of contract law" provide that parties "are free to make their bargain, even if the consideration exchanged is grossly unequal or of dubious value," and that, so long as the "defendant received something of value" under the contract, the contract would not be void for lack of consideration. *See also id.* at 478. ("[T]he buyer knows what he or she is buying and has agreed that the idea has value, and the Court will not ordinarily go behind that determination.").

* * *

The *Apfel* court first noted that "novelty as an element of an idea seller's claim" is a distinct element of proof with respect to both (1) "a claim based on a property theory" and (2) "a claim based on a contract theory." The court then proceeded to discuss how the leading submission-of-idea case—*Downey v. General Foods Corp.*, 31 N.Y.2d 56 (N.Y. 1972)—treated novelty with respect to property-based and contract-based claims. First, the *Apfel* court explained that the plaintiff's property-based claims for misappropriation were dismissed in *Downey* because "the elements of novelty and originality [were] absent," i.e., the ideas were so common as to be unoriginal and known generally. *Apfel*, 81 N.Y.2d at 477 (quoting *Downey*, 31 N.Y.2d at 61) (alteration in original); accord *Downey*, 31 N.Y.2d at 61–62 (holding that the submitted idea—marketing Jell-O to children under the name "Mr. Wiggle"—was "lacking in novelty and originality" because the idea was merely the "use of a word ('wiggley' or 'wiggle') descriptive of the most obvious characteristic of Jell-O, with the prefix 'Mr.' added"). Second, the *Apfel* court explained that the plaintiff's contract claims in *Downey* had been dismissed on the separate ground that the "defendant possessed plaintiff's ideas prior to plaintiff's disclosure [and thus], the ideas could have no value to defendant and could not supply consideration for any agreement between the parties." *Apfel*, 81 N.Y.2d at 477; accord *Downey*, 31 N.Y.2d at 62 (finding that, where defendant had used the words "wiggles" and "wigglewam" in prior advertising, defendant could "rel[y] on its own previous experience" and "was free to make use of 'Mr. Wiggle' without being obligated to compensate the plaintiff").

By distinguishing between the two types of claims addressed in *Downey* and the different bases for rejecting each claim, the New York Court of Appeals clarified that the novelty requirement in submission-of-idea cases is different for misappropriation of property and breach of contract claims. * * *

* * * [T]he *Apfel* court clarified that the longstanding requirement that an idea have originality or general novelty in order to support a misappropriation claim does not apply to contract claims. For contract-based claims in submission-of-idea cases, a showing of novelty to the buyer will supply sufficient consideration to support a contract.

Moreover, *Apfel* made clear that the "novelty to the buyer" standard is not limited to cases involving an express post-disclosure contract for payment based on an idea's use. The *Apfel* court explicitly discussed the pre-disclosure contract scenario present in the instant case, where "the buyer and seller contract for disclosure of the idea with payment based on use, but no separate postdisclosure contract for the use of the idea has been made." In such a scenario, a seller might, as Nadel did here, bring an action against a buyer who allegedly used his ideas without payment, claiming both misappropriation of property and breach of an express or implied-in-fact contract. The *Apfel* court recognized that these cases present courts with the difficult problem of determining "whether the idea the buyer was using was, in fact, the seller's." Specifically, the court noted that, with respect to a misappropriation of property claim, it is difficult to "prove that the buyer obtained the idea from [the seller] and nowhere else." With respect to a breach of contract claim, the court noted that it would be inequitable to enforce a contract if "it turns out upon disclosure that the buyer already possessed the idea." The court then concluded that, with respect to these cases, "[a] showing of novelty, at least novelty as to the buyer" should address these problems.

We note, moreover, that the "novelty to the buyer" standard comports with traditional principles of contract law. While an idea may be unoriginal or non-novel in a general sense, it may have substantial value to a particular buyer who is unaware of it and

> therefore willing to enter into contract to acquire and exploit it. As the *Apfel* court emphasized, "the buyer may reap benefits from such a contract in a number of ways—for instance, by not having to expend resources pursuing the idea through other channels or by having a profit-making idea implemented sooner rather than later."

208 F.3d at 373–77. The court concluded its long summary and analysis of New York contract law related to ideas as follows:

> In sum, we find that New York law in submission-of-idea cases is governed by the following principles: Contract-based claims require only a showing that the disclosed idea was novel to the buyer in order to find consideration.[10] Such claims involve a fact-specific inquiry that focuses on the perspective of the particular buyer. By contrast, misappropriation claims require that the idea at issue be original and novel in absolute terms. This is so because unoriginal, known ideas have no value as property and the law does not protect against the use of that which is free and available to all. Finally, an idea may be so unoriginal or lacking in novelty generally that, as a matter of law, the buyer is deemed to have knowledge of the idea. In such cases, neither a property-based nor a contract-based claim for uncompensated use of the idea may lie.

208 F.3d at 380.

California: The courts in California focus on the circumstances surrounding the express or implied contract, rather than on the novelty of the idea. The following excerpt is from *Desny v. Wilder*, 299 P.2d 257 (Cal. 1956), which emphasized the importance of the context in which an idea disclosure is made.

> From what has been shown respecting the law of ideas and of contracts we conclude that conveyance of an idea can constitute valuable consideration and can be bargained for before it is disclosed to the proposed purchaser, but once it is conveyed, i.e., disclosed to him and he has grasped it, it is henceforth his own and he may work with it and use it as he sees fit. In the field of entertainment the producer may properly and validly agree that he will pay for the service of conveying to him ideas which are valuable and which he can put to profitable use. * * * But, assuming legality of consideration, the idea purveyor cannot prevail in an action to recover compensation for an abstract idea unless (a) before or after

---

[10] Of course, the mere formation of a contract in a submission-of-idea case does not necessarily mean that the contract has been breached by the defendant upon his use of the idea. In order to recover for breach of contract, a plaintiff must demonstrate some nexus or causal connection between his or her disclosure and the defendant's use of the idea, i.e., where there is an independent source for the idea used by the defendant, there may be no breach of contract, and the plaintiff's claim for recovery may not lie. *See, e.g.*, *Ferber*, 51 N.Y.2d at 784 (noting that, even if plaintiff's idea were novel to the defendant at the time of disclosure, his claim would have been extinguished when the idea subsequently fell into the public domain through the issuance of patents disclosing the idea).

> disclosure he has obtained an express promise to pay, or (b) the circumstances preceding and attending disclosure, together with the conduct of the offeree acting with knowledge of the circumstances, show a promise of the type usually referred to as 'implied' or 'implied-in-fact.' That is, if the idea purveyor has clearly conditioned his offer to convey the idea upon an obligation to pay for it if it is used by the offeree and the offeree, knowing the condition before he knows the idea, voluntarily accepts its disclosure (necessarily on the specified basis) and finds it valuable and uses it, the law will either apply the objective test and hold that the parties have made an express (sometimes called implied-in-fact) contract, or under those circumstances, as some writers view it, the law itself, to prevent fraud and unjust enrichment, will imply a promise to compensate.
>
> Such inferred or implied promise, if it is to be found at all, must be based on circumstances which were known to the producer at and preceding the time of disclosure of the idea to him and he must voluntarily accept the disclosure, knowing the conditions on which it is tendered. Section 1584 of the Civil Code ('[T]he acceptance of the consideration offered with a proposal, is an acceptance of the proposal') can have no application unless the offeree has an opportunity to reject the consideration—the proffered conveyance of the idea—before it is conveyed. Unless the offeree has opportunity to reject he cannot be said to accept. The idea man who blurts out his idea without having first made his bargain has no one but himself to blame for the loss of his bargaining power. The law will not in any event, from demands stated subsequent to the unconditioned disclosure of an abstract idea, imply a promise to pay for the idea, for its use, or for its previous disclosure. The law will not imply a promise to pay for an idea from the mere facts that the idea has been conveyed, is valuable, and has been used for profit; this is true even though the conveyance has been made with the hope or expectation that some obligation will ensue. * * *

Desny v. Wilder, 299 P.2d at 269–270. The 1970 California Court of Appeal (Second District) decision in *Blaustein v. Burton*, 88 Cal.Rptr. 319 (Cal. Ct. App. 1970), relied on *Desny v. Wilder* when it reversed summary judgment for a contract defendant even where the movie ideas conveyed by the plaintiff were not—even according to plaintiff's own testimony—unique or unusual.

> It is held that " * * * if a producer obligates himself to pay for the disclosure of an idea, whether it is for protectible or unprotectible material, in return for a disclosure thereof he should be compelled to hold to his promise. There is nothing unreasonable in the assumption that a producer would obligate himself to pay for the disclosure of an idea which he would otherwise be legally free to use, but which in fact, he would be unable to use but for the disclosure." [*Chandler v. Roach*, 319 P.2d 776, 781 (Cal. Ct. App. 1957).]

> "The producer and the writer should be free to make any contract they desire to make with reference to the buying of the ideas of the writer; the fact that the producer may later determine, with a little thinking, that he could have had the same ideas and could thereby have saved considerable money for himself, is no defense against the claim of the writer. This is so even though the material to be purchased is abstract and unprotected material." [*Id.*] An idea which can be the subject matter of a contract need not be novel or concrete.

88 Cal.Rptr. at 333–34. *See also Desny v. Wilder*, 299 P.2d 257 (Cal. 1956) (prior disclosure of idea can give rise to contractual obligation to pay when promise is made to do so, even though prior disclosure could be considered "past consideration"). Similarly, writer Art Buchwald prevailed in a suit against Paramount Pictures based on his contract providing for payment if Paramount made a film based on his idea, which was concededly not an original one. When Paramount made "Coming to America," it found itself held liable for damages under California contract law. *See* Gail D. Cox, *African Kings, Movie Studios, and Rip-offs?*, National Law Journal, Jan. 15, 1990, p. 7.

Consider the policies at play on either side of the novelty requirement for a contract-based claim for disclosure of an idea. Should the novelty of the idea disclosed play a role in a contract claim? If so, should it play a different role where a pre-disclosure contract is concerned than it would in the case of a post-disclosure contract?

C. UNJUST ENRICHMENT OR QUASI-CONTRACT

MATARESE V. MOORE-MCCORMACK LINES, INC.

158 F.2d 631 (2d Cir. 1946).

CLARK, CIRCUIT JUDGE.

This appeal raises the issue whether a corporation may be required to pay the reasonable value of the use of certain inventive ideas disclosed by an employee to an agent of the corporation in the expectation of payment where an express contract fails for want of proof of the agent's authority. Here the plaintiff, being refused compensation, brought suit upon an alleged express contract to pay one-third of the savings realized by the defendants through the use of his devices. * * * During the trial plaintiff abandoned his theory and, over the objections of defendants, amended his complaint by adding a prayer for recovery of quantum meruit upon the theory of unjust enrichment. The court submitted the case to the jury upon this theory, and it returned a verdict for plaintiff for $90,000. This, upon motion, the district judge ordered set aside unless the plaintiff consented to its reduction to the sum of $40,000. The plaintiff so consented, judgment was entered for the latter sum, and defendants appeal.

The plaintiff is a man of little education, who, emigrating to this country from Italy some forty-six years ago, had always worked around the docks and in 1938 was employed as a part-time stevedore on defendants' pier. His case, which the jury quite obviously must have accepted in full, was that in August of that year he informed Furey, defendants' agent in charge of the pier, that he had something which would facilitate cargo loading and unloading, thus saving the defendants much money and preventing the numerous accidents ordinarily occurring at the pier. So, at plaintiff's invitation, Furey made a special trip to plaintiff's home in the Coney Island section of Brooklyn and was there shown models of devices for loading and unloading cargo which the plaintiff had invented. Present were not only plaintiff and Furey, but also plaintiff's son and a friend named Devereaux, all of whom handled the models in an operational demonstration. All of these were witnesses at the trial; and even Furey, testifying for the defendants, admitted the visit to plaintiff's home and the demonstration of the models, while denying any further commitments upon his part. According to plaintiff and his witnesses, however, Furey expressed his satisfaction with the models and promised the plaintiff one-third of what the defendants would save by use of the device. He suggested that plaintiff patent his device and offered to be the plaintiff's partner in exploiting it. He also offered the plaintiff the job of supervising the construction of his devices for defendants on the defendants' premises and with the defendants' materials. Plaintiff accepted the job and continued to receive longshoreman's pay until the end of the year, when, presumably, he received gearman's pay. After a full-scale test of plaintiff's devices, defendants put a great number of them into use at the pier under Furey's charge and at other piers subsequently acquired by them. From time to time plaintiff asked Furey about his money, and Furey always assured him that he would be compensated in the future. In 1941, however, Furey sent plaintiff to another agent of the defendants, who discharged him from his job. This action was commenced in April, 1943.

Meanwhile on January 28, 1939, plaintiff applied for a patent. The application was divided in the patent office in 1940, and on March 18, 1941, plaintiff was issued two patents. One was for a "cargo loading and unloading apparatus," consisting of a reversible 5′ x 4′ wooden pallet, and a flexible bridle, a guiding frame, a mesh net, and lifting bars to transport the pallet between ship and pier. The other was for a "cargo loading and unloading platform," or stationary wooden platform attached to, and extending out from, the pier. Defendants objected to the admission of these patents in evidence, asserting that they were "secretly after-acquired" grants which were invalid for want of invention and that their admission was highly prejudicial on plaintiff's claim of novel invention. But the question of validity of the patents was not involved, and the court very carefully explained to the jury that it was not. The patents, however, were properly admitted, as part of the history of events between the parties, taken pursuant to Furey's direction and plan of retaining the benefit to defendants alone.

The main legal issue of the appeal turns, therefore, upon the validity of plaintiff's claim of unjust enrichment under the circumstances of this case. * * * [Defendants] claim that, since Furey was not shown to have been authorized in the premises, none of the negotiations were admissible in evidence. * * * But the showing of grounds for a reasonable expectation of compensation was a necessary part of the plaintiff's case, as he conceived it* * *.

The doctrine of unjust enrichment or recovery in quasi-contract obviously does not deal with situations in which the party to be charged has by word or deed legally consented to assume a duty toward the party seeking to charge him. Instead, it applies to situations where as a matter of fact there is no legal contract, but where the person sought to be charged is in possession of money or property which in good conscience and justice he should not retain, but should deliver to another. Where this is true the courts impose a duty to refund the money or the use value of the property to the person to whom in good conscience it ought to belong. The doctrine is applicable to a situation where, as here, the product of an inventor's brain is knowingly received and used by another to his own great benefit without compensating the inventor. This is recognized in the leading New York case of *Bristol v. Equitable Life Assur. Soc. of United States*, 132 N.Y. 264, 267. In that case the New York Court of Appeals dismissed a complaint based on the use by defendant of an advertising scheme of which plaintiff had apprised it, because the scheme was not original and because it was not alleged to be marketable. The court, however, was careful to distinguish the situation in which an invention is involved, saying: "In such cases (of inventions) there is a production which can by multiplying copies be put to marketable use, * * *. Whoever infringes takes benefits or profits which otherwise would naturally come to the producer." * * *

Courts have justly been assiduous in defeating attempts to delve into the pockets of business firms through spurious claims for compensation for the use of ideas. Thus to be rejected are attempts made by telephoning or writing vague general ideas to business corporations and then seizing upon some later general similarity between their products and the notions propounded as a basis for damages. Such schemes are quite different from the situation envisaged in the *Bristol* case, *supra*, and that at bar. Here the relationship between the parties before and after the disclosure, the seeking of disclosure by Furey, Furey's promise of compensation, the specific character, novelty, and patentability of plaintiff's invention, the subsequent use made of it by defendants, and the lack of compensation given the plaintiff—all indicate that the application of the principle of unjust enrichment is required.

Defendants, relying upon the concession of lack of proof of Furey's authority to make the contract as originally alleged, claim a like lack of authority to accept the benefit of plaintiff's ideas to such an extent as to make them liable to pay reasonable compensation therefor. Such liability, they assert, could be based only on an extensive and fearsome corporate responsibility to pay for all chance ideas of an employee unwittingly utilized by the corporation. We may pass the interesting question how far an unwitting appropriation of property in ideas may create liability, since the case was presented and submitted to the jury on the theory of valuable services rendered by the plaintiff either to the knowledge of the defendants or "at the instance of someone authorized to obtain such services for the defendant." * * *

This charge, it seems to us, was justified upon the record. There was evidence that plaintiff was authorized by Furey to manufacture his devices using defendants' workmen and materials; that his devices were demonstrated on the pier in the presence of Furey "and all the rest of the officials, foreman and all"; that he was directed to go ahead with the manufacture of the pallets, something with which previously he had nothing to do; that he then went to work full time for defendants; and that Furey was promoted in the fall of 1938 from Stevedore Superintendent to Chief of Operations, an executive position with wide powers and an increase of pay. Furey's denial that these changes and advances were due to the utilization of plaintiff's ideas was of course offset not merely by plaintiff's testimony, but by such matters as Furey's specific written direction to plaintiff on December 20, 1938, for the making up of twenty-four pallets, together with numerous wire nets, frames, and bridles, for delivery by Saturday morning, December 30. Moreover, Commodore Lee, defendants' executive vice-president, visited the docks regularly at least once a week, knew the plaintiff and spoke to him at work, and saw the extensive use of his devices at this period. It would seem that an inference of actual knowledge by Lee would be justifiable under the circumstances; but in any event Furey's position by that time in the corporate structure was surely sufficiently high to justify his accepting for the company the benefits of more efficient stevedoring. It is true that defendants presented some evidence of use by them of pallets and loading platforms similar to plaintiff's on other operations in Philadelphia and perhaps in New York as early as 1937; but the evaluation of this evidence was of course for the jury, who may indeed have been unfavorably impressed by the somewhat halting and vague nature of the testimony from a responsible company official as to a matter which would seem capable of definite and exact proof.

With the issue of unjust enrichment settled in favor of plaintiff, the final major issue was as to the rate of compensation. The judge properly charged that recovery must be based upon the "reasonable value of the use" of the devices and the "reasonable value of the services" rendered by the plaintiff. Defendants contend that there was not sufficient proof of damages, either in fact or in amount, to justify submission of the case to the jury.

Plaintiff's evidence was, however, adequate to show extensive gross savings earned for the defendants by his devices. Thus the loading platforms attached to the piers saved the defendants expense of additional labor, since they remained stationary and level with the pier, despite the movements of the tide. * * *

[The court then summarized the manner in which the defendant's operations were streamlined and the consequent reduction in labor and materials.] Thus the amount of money saved per pier a year by the use of plaintiff's pallets in the actual loading and unloading operations only could be found to be about $140,000. The defendants in 1941 operated ten piers, and the plaintiff's devices were used on all of them. Moreover, the period of time for which damages were recovered extends to the date on which the verdict was given, in December, 1945. The total gross savings from the use of both platforms and unloading apparatus on all piers were obviously much higher than the yearly per pier figures.

Since the amounts thus indicated are much higher than the award as finally made, the only question arises because plaintiff did not offer evidence on the cost to the defendants of producing the plaintiff's devices. Records containing this information were of course in the possession of the defendants. Plaintiff did, however, prove the fact of damages; and the amount of damages could be determined as a matter of just and reasonable inference from the plaintiff's evidence. * * * The rule which proscribes the recovery of uncertain and speculative damages applies where the fact of damages is uncertain, not where the amount is uncertain. Where the fact of damages is certain, the uncertainty of the amount will not prevent their being assessed. * * * [T]he failure of defendants to introduce their cost records as part of their case tends to indicate that the cost of production might not be very high relative to the savings effected through the use of plaintiff's devices. Under the relevant principles of law here stated and the evidence introduced at the trial, the damages ultimately awarded were not excessive.

Affirmed.

NOTES

1. *Likelihood of Success:* What specific showing must a plaintiff make in order to recover under the legal theory presented in this case? Will plaintiffs be able to make this showing very often?

2. *Connection to Patents:* How are Matarese's patents relevant in this case? Why does patent law not provide him with a remedy against his former

employer? Reconsider this question after reading *Teets v. Chromalloy Gas Turbine Corp.*, excerpted in Chapter 11.A.4., *infra.*

3. *Providing Advice:* In light of the series of decisions presented in this chapter, under the varying theories used to protect ideas, what advice would you give to an individual seeking to submit an idea in return for compensation? What advice would you give to companies seeking to avoid baseless claims from idea submitters?

4. *INS v. AP Reconsidered:* Think back to the misappropriation theory as set forth in *INS v. AP* in Chapter 1, *supra*. Would it be effective in protecting innovative ideas? The American Law Institute's RESTATEMENT (THIRD) OF UNFAIR COMPETITION endorses the view that this legal theory should be abolished. *See* RESTATEMENT (THIRD) OF UNFAIR COMPETITION, § 38, comments b & c; *see also* Gary Myers, *The Restatement's Rejection of the Misappropriation Tort: A Victory for the Public Domain*, 47 S.C. L. REV. 673 (1996). *See National Basketball Association v. Motorola, Inc.*, 105 F.3d 841 (2d Cir.1997) (finding that only a narrow misappropriation claim for "hot news" survives preemption by the Copyright Act) (excerpted in Chapter 19.A., *infra*).

PART 5

PATENT LAW

■ ■ ■

CHAPTER 10

PATENT PROTECTION FOR INVENTIONS

■ ■ ■

A. BRIEF INTRODUCTION AND SHORT HISTORY

Patent law in the United States offers exclusive rights to the creator of a useful product or process, an ornamental design, or a plant. In contrast to trade secret law, patent protection requires disclosure of the invention to the public. In return for disclosure, the inventor enjoys during the statutory period the exclusive right to exclude others not only from copying the subject matter of the invention claimed in the patent, but also from exploiting any independently developed subject matter which is identical to, or the equivalent of, the claimed invention. Trade secret law, explained in the previous chapter, does not block independent development or reverse engineering from publicly available sources. Copyright law protects against copying a work of authorship but provides the copyright owner no rights against persons who independently create similar or identical subject matter.

Patent protection is broader in scope than trademark, trade secret, unfair competition, or copyright protection, but also shorter in duration and more difficult to obtain. To be patentable, an innovation must meet stringent statutory requirements. Among the most significant of these is the requirement of novelty. To meet this standard, an invention must differ from any subject matter in the "prior art," or the publicly available or commercially exploited products or processes. See more in Part C. of this Chapter 10. This stands in sharp contrast to trademark, trade secret, and copyright law (the latter of which requires not novelty but originality, meaning simply that the work must not itself have been copied and must possess only a very minimal degree of creativity, *see infra* Chapter 14). A claimed invention must even be "nonobvious," which requires it to be even a step (or more) beyond mere "novelty." See more in Part D. of this Chapter 10. Because the statutory standards of patent law are so demanding, the process of obtaining patent protection is more rigorous than the process of obtaining any other form of intellectual property protection, and the patent, once issued, is more vulnerable to legal challenge.

The foundation of United States patent law derives, as a historical matter, from English patent law. In sixteenth-century England, the Crown issued numerous "letters patent" giving individuals monopolies over production, importation, and/or sales of particular items within the kingdom regardless of their novelty or previous availability. The resulting shortages and price increases eventually led Parliament to enact the Statute of Monopolies, 21 Jac. I, c. 3 (1623), declaring all monopolies "contrary to the laws of this Realm" and "utterly void and of none Effect." The law, however, excepted patents of 14 years to "the true and first Inventor and Inventors" of "new Manufactures" that were "not contrary to the Law, nor mischievous to the State, by raising Prices of Commodities at home, or Hurt of Trade, or generally inconvenient." An exception parallel to the Statute of Monopolies for short-term exclusive rights for inventors appears in Article I, Section 8, Clause 8 of the United States Constitution, which grants Congress the power "To promote the Progress of Science and useful Arts, by securing for limited Times to Authors and Inventors the exclusive Right to their respective Writings and Discoveries."

Congress first exercised its patent authority in the Patent Act of 1790 and then broadened those provisions in 1793. The 1836 Patent Act created the Patent Office and introduced the rule that no invention could be patented without first being examined to determine that it satisfied the novelty requirement. Congress added protection for ornamental designs in 1842. Other significant developments in United States patent law during the nineteenth and early twentieth centuries involved judicial interpretation. Then, in the Patent Act of 1952, Congress codified some of these judicially created doctrines such as the nonobviousness requirement now contained in section 103. It legislatively overruled others. In 1930 and 1954, Congress enacted plant patent legislation. Later in the twentieth century, Congress changed the term of utility patents and otherwise revised the patent statutes in response to the commercialization of new technologies and increasing emphasis on international harmonization of patent policy and practice in connection with international trade negotiations.

One aspect of U.S. law, the rules for judging novelty or newness of an invention, remained out of step with other nations for many years. In most patent systems, the question of novelty addresses only the novelty of a claimed invention as of the effective filing date of the application containing the claim. If more than one person invents the same invention, the *first inventor to file* a patent application is the rightful recipient of the patent grant. Which person was the *first to invent* does not affect patent ownership. For ease of reference, these systems are called "first to file." Until 2013, the United States applied a set of rules effectuating a different policy, one that can be called "first to invent." In that "first to invent" system, which person was the first to invent a specific invention significantly affected (although it did not in all cases conclusively determine) the rightful ownership of the patent covering that invention.

In September 2011, the "America Invents Act" (AIA) was passed by Congress and signed by the President. Pub. L. No. 112–29, 125 Stat. 284

(2011) (hereinafter "AIA"). Among other reforms, beginning in March 2013 the AIA converted the U.S. from a "first-to-invent" system to a "first-inventor-to-file" system—although as you will see later in this chapter, a more accurate characterization might be "first inventor to file or to disclose publicly." Thus the AIA eliminated the longstanding policy of awarding the U.S. patent rights in an invention to the first person to invent it and instead focused on the inventor who first filed a patent application (or who first disclosed the invention to the public, followed by an application within one year).

The AIA resulted from over six years of proposals and negotiations in Congress, and it contains the most significant changes to U.S. patent law since the passage of the Patent Act of 1952. It brought the U.S. into greater harmony with the patent systems of other nations. Complete harmonization was not attempted, however, nor is complete harmonization required by international agreements.

For a number of years, the Patent and Trademark Office (PTO) and the federal courts have encountered difficulty in determining how existing patent statutes can be applied to inventions the nature of which was not even contemplated when those statutes were enacted: inventions such as computer software, biotechnological products and processes, and certain engineered living organisms. While the AIA modified and updated the patent statutes, it did not solve some of the more difficult practical, technological, and, sometimes, philosophical issues.

Two additional introductory notes will help the reader to understand and appreciate the cases and materials that follow.

First, one must understand that patent law is dominated by the "claims" within the patent application and the issued patent. In order to obtain a utility patent from the United States Patent & Trademark Office (PTO) for a new invention, the patent applicant must file a written application that includes, among other requirements, a complete description of the invention and how to make and use it, as well as "one or more claims particularly pointing out and distinctly claiming the subject matter" that has been invented. Each claim provides the basis on which the PTO and the courts assess the patentability of the invention being claimed; the claim also defines the scope of the patentee's exclusive rights in the invention. When a court refers to "the invention," and whether "the invention" is useful, novel, or nonobvious, or is patentable subject matter in the first instance, the court is referring to "the invention" as it has been delineated in a particular patent claim. Patent applications and issued patents generally include more than one separate claim, each of which is separately considered during both the application process and any infringement actions.

Second, one should note that substantive patent law is wholly the province of federal law. A patent issue may come before a federal court through two separate paths, depending on whether it arises during the patent prosecution process or another administrative procedure within the PTO, or instead arises from a patentee's later claim for infringement.

Patent claims are examined and either rejected or granted by patent examiners within the PTO, a federal administrative agency. The patent examination process, called "patent prosecution," is discussed further in Chapter 11.B., *infra*. At this point, it suffices to understand an examiner may reject a claim for failure to meet any requirement of patentability and a disappointed patent applicant may appeal an examiner's final rejection of a claim or claims. That appeal goes in the first instance to the Patent Trial and Appeal Board (formerly called the Board of Patent Appeals and Interferences), which is an administrative court within the PTO (not an Article III court). The decision of the Board may be (and generally is) appealed directly to the U.S. Court of Appeals for the Federal Circuit. (An action in district court is also now an option.) Before the Federal Circuit was created, however, an applicant could appeal the decision of the Board to the Court of Customs and Patent Appeals (CCPA).

Patent owners file any complaints for patent infringement with a federal district court. Before 1982, appeals in infringement actions went to the regional federal courts of appeals—using the same path as any other federal case. Since that time, however, appeals of most substantive patent law issues have gone to the Federal Circuit. *See infra* Chapter 12.C.1. Appeals from district court decisions in infringement actions can include the issue of validity, or patentability, of a claim, since invalidity is one of the affirmative defenses in an infringement action.

The patent cases excerpted in this casebook present a mix of both infringement litigation and appeals of PTO rejections. Most are from either the Supreme Court or the Federal Circuit, while a few older cases illustrating a specific issue are from the CCPA or a regional court of appeals.

B. PATENTABLE SUBJECT MATTER

Statutes: 35 U.S.C. §§ 100, 101, 161, 171

United States patent law provides for three separate types of patents: utility (§ 101), design (§ 171), and plant (§ 161). Utility patents protect a "useful process, machine, manufacture, or composition of matter," while design patents provide exclusive rights in an "ornamental design for an article of manufacture." Plant patents create exclusivity in certain asexually reproduced (but not tuber-propagated) plants. According to the most recent five years of complete data available from the PTO (2016–2020), just under 91% of issued U.S. patents (excluding reissued patents) were utility patents, almost 9% were design patents, and only 0.36% were plant patents. Across ten years (2011–2020), the figures are similar, although the trend is that design patents are growing slightly faster than other two types. Total numbers of all grants are up over the past ten years.

In this chapter as well as those that follow, utility patents are addressed first and provide the focus for each topic or issue; when needed, this coverage is accompanied by additional material specific to design patents and plant patents.

1. UTILITY PATENT SUBJECT MATTER

Statutes: 35 U.S.C. § 100, 101

Under § 101 of the Patent Act:

> Whoever invents or discovers any new and useful process, machine, manufacture, or composition of matter, or any new and useful improvement thereof, may obtain a patent therefor, subject to the conditions and requirements of this title.

In order for a valid patent to issue under § 101, then, it seems as if the claimed invention must fall within one of the four categories of statutory subject matter: process, machine, manufacture, or composition of matter. Improvements falling in one of those categories may also be patented. As long as the claimed invention falls within at least one category, neither the PTO nor the courts are required to determine which particular category applies. Cases, treatises, and other analyses of patentable subject matter often speak of all of machines, manufactures, or compositions of matter as "products," creating two basic types of (useful) inventions: products and processes. Reconsider the importance of the four categories in section 101 after reading the next few cases and associated notes.

After the invention has been determined to satisfy the subject matter requirement, it must also be found to satisfy the other conditions of patentability: utility, novelty, and nonobviousness, which are the subjects of subsequent parts of this chapter.

a. Products

DIAMOND V. CHAKRABARTY

447 U.S. 303, 100 S.Ct. 2204 (1980).

MR. CHIEF JUSTICE BURGER delivered the opinion of the Court.

[Respondent Chakrabarty filed a patent application for a human-made, genetically engineered bacterium of the genus *Pseudomonas*, containing at least two stable plasmids capable of breaking down hydrocarbons. Plasmids are circular strands of DNA separate from a bacterium's chromosomal DNA. This bacterium, because it contained these different plasmids, was capable of breaking down multiple components of crude oil so as to aid in cleaning up oil spills more efficiently than existing methods, which relied on naturally occurring bacteria. The patent examiner held that the genetically engineered bacteria were not patentable subject matter under 35 U.S.C. § 101 because (1) they were "products of nature" and (2) they were living things. The Patent Office Board of Appeals affirmed, concluding that while the human-made bacteria were not "products of nature" (because their plasmid content was different from naturally occurring bacteria), nonetheless section 101 was not intended to cover living things. The Court of Customs and Patent Appeals reversed, relying on its decision in *In re Bergy*, 563 F.2d 1031, 1038 (1977), noting that "the fact that the microorganisms . . . are alive" is "without legal significance" for patent law purposes.]

* * *

The Constitution grants Congress broad power to legislate to "promote the Progress of Science and useful Arts, by securing for limited Times to Authors and Inventors the exclusive Right to their respective Writings and Discoveries." Art. I, § 8, cl. 8. The patent laws promote this progress by offering inventors exclusive rights for a limited period as an incentive for their inventiveness and research efforts. *Kewanee Oil Co. v. Bicron Corp.*, 416 U.S. 470, 480–481 (1974); *Universal Oil Co. v. Globe Co.*, 322 U.S. 471, 484 (1944). The authority of Congress is exercised in the hope that "[the] productive effort thereby fostered will have a positive effect on society through the introduction of new products and processes of manufacture into the economy, and the emanations by way of increased employment and better lives for our citizens." *Kewanee, supra,* at 480.

The question before us in this case is a narrow one of statutory interpretation requiring us to construe 35 U.S.C. § 101 * * *. Specifically, we must determine whether respondent's micro-organism constitutes a "manufacture" or "composition of matter" within the meaning of the statute.

III

* * *

[In the absence of a statutory definition,] this Court has read the term "manufacture" in § 101 in accordance with its dictionary definition to mean "the production of articles for use from raw or prepared materials by giving to these materials new forms, qualities, properties, or combinations, whether by hand-labor or by machinery." *American Fruit Growers, Inc. v. Brogdex Co.*, 283 U.S. 1, 11 (1931). Similarly, "composition of matter" has been construed consistent with its common usage to include "all compositions of two or more substances and . . . all composite articles, whether they be the results of chemical union, or of mechanical mixture, or whether they be gases, fluids, powders or solids." *Shell Development Co. v. Watson*, 149 F.Supp. 279, 280 (D.C.1957). In choosing such expansive terms as "manufacture" and "composition of matter," modified by the comprehensive "any," Congress plainly contemplated that the patent laws would be given wide scope.

The relevant legislative history also supports a broad construction. The Patent Act of 1793, authored by Thomas Jefferson, defined statutory subject matter as "any new and useful art, machine, manufacture, or composition of matter, or any new or useful improvement [thereof]." The Act embodied Jefferson's philosophy that "ingenuity should receive a liberal encouragement." 5 WRITINGS OF THOMAS JEFFERSON 75–76 (Washington ed. 1871). Subsequent patent statutes in 1836, 1870, and 1874 employed this same broad language. In 1952, when the patent laws were recodified, Congress replaced the word "art" with "process," but otherwise left Jefferson's language intact. The Committee Reports accompanying the 1952 Act inform us that Congress intended statutory subject matter to "include anything under the sun that is made by man." S. Rep. No. 1979, 82d Cong., 2d Sess., 5 (1952); H. R. Rep. No. 1923, 82d Cong., 2d Sess., 6 (1952).

This is not to suggest that § 101 has no limits or that it embraces every discovery. The laws of nature, physical phenomena, and abstract ideas have been held not patentable. *See Parker v. Flook*, 437 U.S. 584 (1978); *Gottschalk v. Benson*, 409 U.S. 63, 67 (1972); *Funk Brothers Seed Co. v. Kalo Inoculant Co.*, 333 U.S. 127, 130 (1948); *O'Reilly v. Morse*, 15 How. 62, 112–121 (1854); *Le Roy v. Tatham*, 14 How. 156, 175 (1853). Thus, a new mineral discovered in the earth or a new plant found in the wild is not patentable subject matter. Likewise, Einstein could not patent his celebrated law that $E=mc^2$; nor could Newton have patented the law of gravity. Such discoveries are "manifestations of . . . nature, free to all men and reserved exclusively to none." *Funk, supra*, at 130.

Judged in this light, respondent's micro-organism plainly qualifies as patentable subject matter. His claim is not to a hitherto unknown natural phenomenon, but to a nonnaturally occurring manufacture or composition of matter—a product of human ingenuity "having a distinctive name, character [and] use." *Hartranft v. Wiegmann*, 121 U.S. 609, 615 (1887). The point is underscored dramatically by comparison of the invention here with that in *Funk*. There, the patentee had discovered that there existed in nature certain species of root-nodule bacteria which did not exert a mutually inhibitive effect on each other. He used that discovery to produce a mixed culture capable of inoculating the seeds of leguminous plants. Concluding that the patentee had discovered "only some of the handiwork of nature," the Court ruled the product nonpatentable:

"Each of the species of root-nodule bacteria contained in the package infects the same group of leguminous plants which it always infected. No species acquires a different use. The combination of species produces no new bacteria, no change in the six species of bacteria, and no enlargement of the range of their utility. Each species has the same effect it always had. The bacteria perform in their natural way. Their use in combination does not improve in any way their natural functioning. They serve the ends nature originally provided and act quite independently of any effort of the patentee." 333 U.S., at 131.

Here, by contrast, the patentee has produced a new bacterium with markedly different characteristics from any found in nature and one having the potential for significant utility. His discovery is not nature's handiwork, but his own; accordingly it is patentable subject matter under § 101.

IV

Two contrary arguments are advanced, neither of which we find persuasive.

(A)

The petitioner's first argument rests on the enactment of the 1930 Plant Patent Act, which afforded patent protection to certain asexually reproduced plants, and the 1970 Plant Variety Protection Act, which authorized protection for certain sexually reproduced plants but excluded bacteria from its protection. In the petitioner's view, the passage of these Acts evidences congressional understanding that the terms "manufacture" or "composition of matter" do not include living things; if they did, the petitioner argues, neither Act would have been necessary.

We reject this argument. Prior to 1930, two factors were thought to remove plants from patent protection. The first was the belief that plants, even those artificially bred, were products of nature for purposes of the patent law. This position appears to have derived from the decision of the Patent Office in *Ex parte Latimer*, 1889 Dec. Com. Pat. 123, in which a patent claim for fiber found in the needle of the *Pinus australis* was rejected. The Commissioner reasoned that a contrary result would permit "patents [to] be obtained upon the trees of the forest and the plants of the earth, which of course would be unreasonable and impossible." *Id.*, at 126. The *Latimer* case, it seems, came to "[set] forth the general stand taken in these matters" that plants were natural products not subject to patent protection. Thorne, *Relation of Patent Law to Natural Products*, 6 J. PAT. OFF. SOC. 23, 24 (1923). The second obstacle to patent protection for plants was the fact that plants were thought not amenable to the "written description" requirement of the patent law. *See* 35 U.S.C.A. § 112. Because new plants may differ from old only in color or perfume, differentiation by written description was often impossible.

In enacting the Plant Patent Act, Congress addressed both of these concerns. It explained at length its belief that the work of the plant breeder "in aid of nature" was patentable invention. And it relaxed the written description requirement in favor of "a description . . . as complete as is reasonably possible." 35 U.S.C. § 162. * * *

> "There is a clear and logical distinction *between the discovery of a new variety of plant and certain inanimate things*, such, for example, as a new and useful natural mineral. The mineral is created wholly by nature unassisted by man. . . . On the other hand, a plant discovery resulting from cultivation is unique, isolated, and is not repeated by nature, nor can it be reproduced by nature unaided by man. . . ." S. Rep. No. 315, *supra*, at 6; H. R. Rep. No. 1129, *supra*, at 7 (emphasis added).

Congress thus recognized that the relevant distinction was not between living and inanimate things, but between products of nature, whether living or not, and human-made inventions. Here, respondent's micro-organism is the result of human ingenuity and research. Hence, the passage of the Plant Patent Act affords the Government no support.

Nor does the passage of the 1970 Plant Variety Protection Act support the Government's position. As the Government acknowledges, sexually reproduced plants were not included under the 1930 Act because new varieties could not be reproduced true-to-type through seedlings. By 1970, however, it was generally recognized that true-to-type reproduction was possible and that plant patent protection was therefore appropriate. The 1970 Act extended that protection. There is nothing in its language or history to suggest that it was enacted because § 101 did not include living things.

In particular, we find nothing in the exclusion of bacteria from plant variety protection to support the petitioner's position. The legislative history gives no reason for this exclusion. As the Court of Customs and Patent Appeals suggested, it may simply reflect congressional agreement with the result reached by that court in deciding *In re Arzberger*, 112 F.2d 834 (C.C.P.A. 1940), which held that bacteria were not plants for the purposes of the 1930 Act. Or it may reflect the fact that prior to 1970 the Patent Office had issued patents for bacteria under § 101. In any event, absent some clear indication that Congress "focused on [the] issues . . . directly related to the one presently before the Court," *SEC v. Sloan*, 436 U.S. 103, 120–121 (1978), there is no basis for reading into its actions an intent to modify the plain meaning of the words found in § 101.

(B)

The petitioner's second argument is that micro-organisms cannot qualify as patentable subject matter until Congress expressly authorizes such protection. His position rests on the fact that genetic technology was unforeseen when Congress enacted § 101. From this it is argued that resolution of the patentability of inventions such as respondent's should be left to Congress. The legislative process, the petitioner argues, is best equipped to weigh the competing economic, social, and scientific considerations involved, and to determine whether living organisms produced by genetic engineering should receive patent protection. In support of this position, the petitioner relies on our recent holding in *Parker v. Flook*, 437 U.S. 584 (1978), and the statement that the judiciary "must proceed cautiously when . . . asked to extend patent rights into areas wholly unforeseen by Congress." *Id.*, at 596.

It is, of course, correct that Congress, not the courts, must define the limits of patentability; but it is equally true that once Congress has spoken it is "the province and duty of the judicial department to say what the law is." *Marbury v. Madison*, 1 Cranch 137, 177 (1803). Congress has performed its constitutional role in defining patentable subject matter in § 101; we perform ours in construing the language Congress has employed. In so doing, our obligation is to take statutes as we find them, guided, if ambiguity appears, by the legislative history and statutory purpose. Here, we perceive no ambiguity. The subject-matter provisions of the patent law have been cast in broad terms to fulfill the constitutional and statutory goal of promoting "the Progress of Science and the useful Arts" with all that means for the social and economic benefits envisioned by Jefferson. * * *

* * * *Flook* did not announce a new principle that inventions in areas not contemplated by Congress when the patent laws were enacted are unpatentable per se.

To read that concept into *Flook* would frustrate the purposes of the patent law. This Court frequently has observed that a statute is not to be confined to the "particular [applications] . . . contemplated by the legislators." *Barr v. United States*, 324 U.S. 83, 90 (1945). This is especially true in the field of patent law. A rule that unanticipated inventions are without protection would conflict with the core concept of the patent law that anticipation undermines patentability. *See Graham v. John Deere Co.*, 383 U.S., at 12–17. Mr. Justice Douglas reminded that the inventions most benefiting mankind are those that "push back the frontiers of chemistry, physics, and the like." Congress employed broad general language in drafting § 101 precisely because such inventions are often unforeseeable.

* * *

ASSOCIATION FOR MOLECULAR PATHOLOGY v. MYRIAD GENETICS, INC.

569 U.S. 576, 133 S.Ct. 2107 (2013).

JUSTICE THOMAS delivered the opinion of the Court.

Respondent Myriad Genetics, Inc. (Myriad), discovered the precise location and sequence of two human genes, mutations of which can substantially increase the risks of breast and ovarian cancer. Myriad obtained a number of patents based upon its discovery. This case involves claims from three of them and requires us to resolve whether a naturally occurring segment of deoxyribonucleic acid (DNA) is patent eligible under 35 U.S.C. § 101 by virtue of its isolation from the rest of the human genome. We also address the patent eligibility of synthetically created DNA known as complementary DNA (cDNA), which contains the same protein-coding information found in a segment of natural DNA but omits portions within the DNA segment that do not code for proteins. For the reasons that follow, we hold that a naturally occurring DNA segment is a product of nature and not patent eligible merely because it has been isolated, but that cDNA is patent eligible because it is not naturally occurring. We, therefore, affirm in part and reverse in part the decision of the United States Court of Appeals for the Federal Circuit.

I

A

Genes form the basis for hereditary traits in living organisms. The human genome consists of approximately 22,000 genes packed into 23 pairs of chromosomes. Each gene is encoded as DNA, which takes the shape of the familiar "double helix" that Doctors James Watson and Francis Crick first described in 1953. Each "cross-bar" in the DNA helix consists of two chemically joined nucleotides. The possible nucleotides are adenine (A), thymine (T), cytosine (C), and guanine (G), each of which binds naturally with another nucleotide: A pairs with T; C pairs with G. The nucleotide cross-bars are chemically connected to a sugar-phosphate backbone that forms the outside framework of the DNA helix. Sequences of DNA nucleotides contain the information necessary to create strings of amino acids, which in turn are used in the body to build proteins. Only some DNA nucleotides, however, code for amino acids; these nucleotides are known as "exons." Nucleotides that do not code for amino acids, in contrast, are known as "introns."

Creation of proteins from DNA involves two principal steps, known as transcription and translation. In transcription, the bonds between DNA nucleotides separate, and the DNA helix unwinds into two single strands. A single strand is used as a template to create a complementary ribonucleic acid (RNA) strand. The nucleotides on the DNA strand pair naturally with their counterparts, with the exception that RNA uses the nucleotide base uracil (U) instead of thymine (T). Transcription results in a single strand RNA molecule, known as pre-RNA, whose nucleotides form an inverse image of the DNA strand from which it was created. Pre-RNA still contains nucleotides corresponding to both the exons and introns in the DNA molecule. The pre-RNA is then naturally "spliced" by the physical removal of the introns. The resulting product is a strand of RNA that contains nucleotides corresponding only to the exons from the original DNA strand. The exons-only strand is known as messenger RNA (mRNA), which creates amino acids through translation. In translation, cellular structures known as ribosomes read each set of three nucleotides, known as codons, in the mRNA. Each codon either tells the ribosomes which of the 20 possible amino acids to synthesize or provides a stop signal that ends amino acid production.

DNA's informational sequences and the processes that create mRNA, amino acids, and proteins occur naturally within cells. Scientists can, however, extract DNA from cells using well known laboratory methods. These methods allow scientists to isolate specific segments of DNA—for instance, a particular gene or part of a gene—which can then be further studied, manipulated, or used. It is also possible to create DNA synthetically through processes similarly well known in the field of genetics. One such method begins with an mRNA molecule and uses the natural bonding properties of nucleotides to create a new, synthetic DNA molecule. The result is the inverse of the mRNA's inverse image of the original DNA, with one important distinction: Because the natural creation of mRNA involves splicing that removes introns, the synthetic DNA created from mRNA also contains only the exon sequences. This synthetic DNA created in the laboratory from mRNA is known as complementary DNA (cDNA).

Changes in the genetic sequence are called mutations. Mutations can be as small as the alteration of a single nucleotide—a change affecting only one letter in the genetic code. Such small-scale changes can produce an entirely different amino acid or can end protein production altogether. Large changes, involving the deletion, rearrangement, or duplication of hundreds or even millions of nucleotides, can result in the elimination, misplacement, or duplication of entire genes. Some mutations are harmless, but others can cause disease or increase the risk of disease. As a result, the study of genetics can lead to valuable medical breakthroughs.

B

This case involves patents filed by Myriad after it made one such medical breakthrough. Myriad discovered the precise location and sequence of what are now known as the BRCA1 and BRCA2 genes. Mutations in these genes can dramatically increase an individual's risk of developing breast and ovarian cancer. The average American woman has a 12- to 13-percent risk of developing breast cancer, but for women with certain genetic mutations, the risk can range between 50 and 80 percent for breast cancer and between 20 and 50 percent for ovarian cancer. Before Myriad's discovery of the BRCA1 and BRCA2 genes, scientists knew that heredity played a role in establishing a woman's risk of developing breast and ovarian cancer, but they did not know which genes were associated with those cancers.

Myriad identified the exact location of the BRCA1 and BRCA2 genes on chromosomes 17 and 13. Chromosome 17 has approximately 80 million nucleotides, and chromosome 13 has approximately 114 million. Within those chromosomes, the BRCA1 and BRCA2 genes are each about 80,000 nucleotides long. If just exons are counted, the BRCA1 gene is only about 5,500 nucleotides long; for the BRCA2 gene, that number is about 10,200. Knowledge of the location of the BRCA1 and BRCA2 genes allowed Myriad to determine their typical nucleotide sequence.[1] That information, in turn, enabled Myriad to develop medical tests that are useful for detecting mutations in a patient's BRCA1 and BRCA2 genes and thereby assessing whether the patient has an increased risk of cancer.

Once it found the location and sequence of the BRCA1 and BRCA2 genes, Myriad sought and obtained a number of patents. Nine composition claims from three of those patents are at issue in this case.[2] Claims 1, 2, 5, and 6 from the '282 patent are representative. The first claim asserts a patent on "[a]n isolated DNA coding for a BRCA1 polypeptide," which has "the amino acid sequence set forth in SEQ ID NO:2." SEQ ID NO:2 sets forth a list of 1,863 amino acids that the typical BRCA1 gene encodes. Put differently, claim 1 asserts a patent claim on the DNA code that tells a cell to produce the string of BRCA1 amino acids listed in SEQ ID NO:2. [A dependent claim, Claim 5, claimed "isolated DNA having at least 15 nucleotides" of the same sequence of claim 1 (from the typical BRCA1 gene), which meant even mutated BRCA1 genes would likely contain at least one (infringing) segment of 15 nucleotides.]

Claim 2 of the '282 patent operates similarly. It claims "[t]he isolated DNA of claim 1, wherein said DNA has the nucleotide sequence set forth in SEQ ID NO:1." Like SEQ ID NO:2, SEQ ID NO:1 sets forth a long list of data, in this instance the sequence of cDNA that codes for the BRCA1 amino acids listed in claim 1. Importantly, SEQ ID NO:1 lists only the cDNA exons in the BRCA1 gene, rather than a full DNA sequence

---

[1] Technically, there is no "typical" gene because nucleotide sequences vary between individuals, sometimes dramatically. Geneticists refer to the most common variations of genes as "wild types."

[2] At issue are claims 1, 2, 5, 6, and 7 of U.S. Patent 5,747,282 (the '282 patent), claim 1 of U.S. Patent 5,693,473 (the '473 patent), and claims 1, 6, and 7 of U.S. Patent 5,837,492 (the '492 patent).

containing both exons and introns. As a result, the Federal Circuit recognized that claim 2 asserts a patent on the cDNA nucleotide sequence listed in SEQ ID NO:1, which codes for the typical BRCA1 gene.

* * *

C

Myriad's patents would, if valid, give it the exclusive right to isolate an individual's BRCA1 and BRCA2 genes (or any strand of 15 or more nucleotides within the genes) by breaking the covalent bonds that connect the DNA to the rest of the individual's genome. The patents would also give Myriad the exclusive right to synthetically create BRCA cDNA. In Myriad's view, manipulating BRCA DNA in either of these fashions triggers its "right to exclude others from making" its patented composition of matter under the Patent Act. 35 U.S.C. § 154(a)(1).

But isolation is necessary to conduct genetic testing, and Myriad was not the only entity to offer BRCA testing after it discovered the genes. The University of Pennsylvania's Genetic Diagnostic Laboratory (GDL) and others provided genetic testing services to women. Petitioner Dr. Harry Ostrer, then a researcher at New York University School of Medicine, routinely sent his patients' DNA samples to GDL for testing. After learning of GDL's testing and Ostrer's activities, Myriad sent letters to them asserting that the genetic testing infringed Myriad's patents. In response, GDL agreed to stop testing and informed Ostrer that it would no longer accept patient samples. Myriad also filed patent infringement suits against other entities that performed BRCA testing, resulting in settlements in which the defendants agreed to cease all allegedly infringing activity. Myriad, thus, solidified its position as the only entity providing BRCA testing.

Some years later, petitioner Ostrer, along with medical patients, advocacy groups, and other doctors, filed this lawsuit seeking a declaration that Myriad's patents are invalid under 35 U.S.C. § 101. * * * The District Court * * * granted summary judgment to petitioners on the composition claims at issue in this case based on its conclusion that Myriad's claims, including claims related to cDNA, were invalid because they covered products of nature. The Federal Circuit reversed, and this Court granted the petition for certiorari, vacated the judgment, and remanded the case in light of *Mayo Collaborative Services v. Prometheus Laboratories, Inc.*, 566 U.S. [66] (2012). [Ed. note: An excerpt from *Mayo* can be found later in this chapter.]

On remand, the Federal Circuit affirmed the District Court in part and reversed in part, with each member of the panel writing separately. * * * [Two of the three panel members found the isolated DNA to be patent eligible, but they disagreed on the rationale. All three panel members agreed that the claims to cDNA were eligible under § 101.]

* * *

II

A

Section 101 of the Patent Act provides:

> "Whoever invents or discovers any new and useful . . . composition of matter, or any new and useful improvement thereof, may obtain a patent therefor, subject to the conditions and requirements of this title."

We have "long held that this provision contains an important implicit exception[:] Laws of nature, natural phenomena, and abstract ideas are not patentable." Rather, " 'they are the basic tools of scientific and technological work' " that lie beyond the domain of patent protection. As the Court has explained, without this exception, there would be considerable danger that the grant of patents would "tie up" the use of such tools and thereby "inhibit future innovation premised upon them." This would be at odds with the very point of patents, which exist to promote creation.

The rule against patents on naturally occurring things is not without limits, however, for "all inventions at some level embody, use, reflect, rest upon, or apply laws of nature, natural phenomena, or abstract ideas," and "too broad an interpretation of this exclusionary principle could eviscerate patent law." As we have recognized before, patent protection strikes a delicate balance between creating "incentives that lead to creation, invention, and discovery" and "imped[ing] the flow of information that might permit, indeed spur, invention." We must apply this well-established standard to determine whether Myriad's patents claim any "new and useful . . . composition of matter," § 101, or instead claim naturally occurring phenomena.

B

It is undisputed that Myriad did not create or alter any of the genetic information encoded in the BRCA1 and BRCA2 genes. The location and order of the nucleotides existed in nature before Myriad found them. Nor did Myriad create or alter the genetic structure of DNA. Instead, Myriad's principal contribution was uncovering the precise location and genetic sequence of the BRCA1 and BRCA2 genes within chromosomes 17 and 13. The question is whether this renders the genes patentable.

Myriad recognizes that our decision in *Chakrabarty* is central to this inquiry. * * * The *Chakrabarty* bacterium was new "with markedly different characteristics from any found in nature" due to the additional plasmids and resultant "capacity for degrading oil." In this case, by contrast, Myriad did not create anything. To be sure, it found an important and useful gene, but separating that gene from its surrounding genetic material is not an act of invention.

Groundbreaking, innovative, or even brilliant discovery does not by itself satisfy the § 101 inquiry. * * * Myriad found the location of the BRCA1 and BRCA2 genes, but that discovery, by itself, does not render the BRCA genes "new . . . composition[s] of matter," § 101, that are patent eligible.

Indeed, Myriad's patent descriptions highlight the problem with its claims. For example, a section of the '282 patent's Detailed Description of the Invention indicates that Myriad found the location of a gene associated with increased risk of breast cancer and identified mutations of that gene that increase the risk.[4] In subsequent language Myriad explains that the location of the gene was unknown until Myriad found it among the approximately eight million nucleotide pairs contained in a subpart of chromosome 17. The '473 and '492 patents contain similar language as well. Many of Myriad's patent descriptions simply detail the "iterative process" of discovery by which Myriad narrowed the possible locations for the gene sequences that it sought.[6] Myriad seeks to import these extensive research efforts into the § 101 patent-eligibility inquiry. But extensive effort alone is insufficient to satisfy the demands of § 101.

Nor are Myriad's claims saved by the fact that isolating DNA from the human genome severs chemical bonds and thereby creates a nonnaturally occurring molecule. Myriad's claims are simply not expressed in terms of chemical composition, nor do they rely in any way on the chemical changes that result from the isolation of a particular section of DNA. Instead, the

---

[4] The full relevant text of the Detailed Description of the Patent is as follows:

"It is a discovery of the present invention that the BRCA1 locus which predisposes individuals to breast cancer and ovarian cancer, is a gene encoding a BRCA1 protein, which has been found to have no significant homology with known protein or DNA sequences. . . . It is a discovery of the present invention that mutations in the BRCA1 locus in the germline are indicative of a predisposition to breast cancer and ovarian cancer. Finally, it is a discovery of the present invention that somatic mutations in the BRCA1 locus are also associated with breast cancer, ovarian cancer and other cancers, which represents an indicator of these cancers or of the prognosis of these cancers. The mutational events of the BRCA1 locus can involve deletions, insertions and point mutations."

Notwithstanding Myriad's repeated use of the phrase "present invention," it is clear from the text of the patent that the various discoveries *are* the "invention."

[6] Myriad first identified groups of relatives with a history of breast cancer (some of whom also had developed ovarian cancer); because these individuals were related, scientists knew that it was more likely that their diseases were the result of genetic predisposition rather than other factors. Myriad compared sections of their chromosomes, looking for shared genetic abnormalities not found in the general population. It was that process which eventually enabled Myriad to determine where in the genetic sequence the BRCA1 and BRCA2 genes reside.

claims understandably focus on the genetic information encoded in the BRCA1 and BRCA2 genes. * * *

Finally, Myriad argues that the PTO's past practice of awarding gene patents is entitled to deference. * * * [In the scenario and case cited by Myriad, which related to § 101 eligibility of plant breeds,] Congress had recognized and endorsed that position in a subsequent Patent Act amendment. In this case, however, Congress has not endorsed the views of the PTO in subsequent legislation. * * *

Further undercutting the PTO's practice, the United States argued in the Federal Circuit and in this Court that isolated DNA was not patent eligible under § 101, and that the PTO's practice was not "a sufficient reason to hold that isolated DNA is patent-eligible." These concessions weigh against deferring to the PTO's determination.[7]

C

cDNA does not present the same obstacles to patentability as naturally occurring, isolated DNA segments. As already explained, creation of a cDNA sequence from mRNA results in an exons-only molecule that is not naturally occurring.[8] Petitioners concede that cDNA differs from natural DNA in that "the non-coding regions have been removed." They nevertheless argue that cDNA is not patent eligible because "[t]he nucleotide sequence of cDNA is dictated by nature, not by the lab technician." That may be so, but the lab technician unquestionably creates something new when cDNA is made. cDNA retains the naturally occurring exons of DNA, but it is distinct from the DNA from which it was derived. As a result, cDNA is not a "product of nature" and is patent eligible under § 101, except insofar as very short series of DNA may have no intervening introns to remove when creating cDNA. In that situation, a short strand of cDNA may be indistinguishable from natural DNA.[9]

III

It is important to note what is *not* implicated by this decision. First, there are no method claims before this Court. Had Myriad created an innovative method of manipulating genes while searching for the BRCA1 and BRCA2 genes, it could possibly have sought a method patent. But the processes used by Myriad to isolate DNA were well understood by geneticists at the time of Myriad's patents "were well understood, widely

---

[7] Myriad also argues that we should uphold its patents so as not to disturb the reliance interests of patent holders like itself. Concerns about reliance interests arising from PTO determinations, insofar as they are relevant, are better directed to Congress.

[8] Some viruses rely on an enzyme called reverse transcriptase to reproduce by copying RNA into cDNA. * * * The possibility that an unusual and rare phenomenon *might* randomly create a molecule similar to one created synthetically through human ingenuity does not render a composition of matter nonpatentable.

[9] We express no opinion whether cDNA satisfies the other statutory requirements of patentability. *See, e.g.*, 35 U.S.C. §§ 102, 103, and 112.

used, and fairly uniform insofar as any scientist engaged in the search for a gene would likely have utilized a similar approach," and are not at issue in this case.

Similarly, this case does not involve patents on new *applications* of knowledge about the BRCA1 and BRCA2 genes. Judge Bryson [of the Federal Circuit] aptly noted that, "[a]s the first party with knowledge of the [BRCA1 and BRCA2] sequences, Myriad was in an excellent position to claim applications of that knowledge. Many of its unchallenged claims are limited to such applications."

Nor do we consider the patentability of DNA in which the order of the naturally occurring nucleotides has been altered. Scientific alteration of the genetic code presents a different inquiry, and we express no opinion about the application of § 101 to such endeavors. We merely hold that genes and the information they encode are not patent eligible under § 101 simply because they have been isolated from the surrounding genetic material.

For the foregoing reasons, the judgment of the Federal Circuit is affirmed in part and reversed in part.

NOTES

1. *Natural or Unnatural?* Suppose an inventor develops a method for producing a sterile oyster. Its utility lies in the fact that a nonreproducing oyster remains edible year-round. Is the oyster itself patentable subject matter?

2. *Utility Patents for Useful Plants:* As noted above in *Chakrabarty*, Congress has enacted separate measures to protect certain new plants—but some new, human-created plants might, like the new, human-created bacterium of *Chakrabarty*, also be useful and fall within the Court's broad interpretation of "manufacture" and "composition of matter." The question thus arose whether plants that fall within the subject matter of the more specific protections for plants should be excluded from protection under § 101. The PTO's Board of Patent Appeals and Interferences applied *Chakrabarty* to hold that plants, seeds, and plant tissue cultures are patentable subject matter under § 101, even though the same subject matter might also be eligible for a plant patent or a plant variety protection certificate. *Ex Parte Hibberd*, 227 U.S.P.Q. 443 (B.P.A.I. 1985).

In 2001 the Supreme Court addressed the argument that utility patents could not issue on plants because alternate avenues of plant protection provided by Congress excluded plants from the purview of § 101. Referring to the 1985 Board decision in *Hibberd*, the Court stated:

> It has been the unbroken practice of the PTO since that time to confer utility patents for plants. To obtain utility patent protection, a plant breeder must show that the plant he has developed is new, useful, and non-obvious. 35 U.S.C. §§ 101–103. In addition, the plant must

meet the specifications of § 112, which require a written description of the plant and a deposit of seed that is publicly accessible.

Petitioners do not allege that Pioneer's patents are invalid for failure to meet the requirements for a utility patent. Nor do they dispute that plants otherwise fall within the terms of § 101's broad language that includes "manufacture" or "composition of matter." Rather, petitioners argue that the PPA [Plant Patent Act, applicable to asexually reproduced plants] and the PVPA [Plant Variety Protection Act, applicable to certain sexually reproduced plants] provide the exclusive means of protecting new varieties of plants, and so awarding utility patents for plants upsets the scheme contemplated by Congress. We disagree. * * *

* * *

The PPA's enactment and the then-existing state of the art in plant breeding] does not mean, however, that prior to 1930 plants could not have fallen within the subject matter of § 101. Rather, it illustrates only that in 1930 Congress believed that plants were not patentable under § 101, both because they were living things and because in practice they could not meet the stringent description requirement. Yet these premises were disproved over time. As this Court held in *Chakrabarty*, "the relevant distinction" for purposes of § 101 is not "between living and inanimate things, but between products of nature, whether living or not, and human-made inventions." In addition, advances in biological knowledge and breeding expertise have allowed plant breeders to satisfy § 101's demanding description requirement.

* * *

Petitioners essentially ask us to deny utility patent protection for sexually reproduced plants because it was unforeseen in 1930 that such plants could receive protection under § 101. Denying patent protection under § 101 simply because such coverage was thought technologically infeasible in 1930, however, would be inconsistent with the forward-looking perspective of the utility patent statute. As we noted in *Chakrabarty*, "Congress employed broad general language in drafting § 101 precisely because [new types of] inventions are often unforeseeable."

* * *

By passing the PVPA in 1970, Congress specifically authorized limited patent-like protection for certain sexually reproduced plants. Petitioners therefore argue that this legislation evidences Congress' intent to deny broader § 101 utility patent protection for such plants. Petitioners' argument, however, is unavailing for two reasons. First, nowhere does the PVPA purport to provide the exclusive statutory means of protecting sexually reproduced plants. Second, the PVPA and § 101 can easily be reconciled. Because it is harder to qualify for a utility patent than for a Plant Variety Protection (PVP) certificate, it only makes sense that utility patents would confer a greater scope of protection.

J.E.M. Ag Supply, Inc. v. Pioneer Hi-Bred Int'l, Inc., 534 U.S. 124, 131–42 (2001). Additional coverage of protection for plants can be found in Part B.3. of this Chapter 10, *infra*.

3. *Patenting Humans:* Controversy has for some time surrounded the patentability of human gene sequences (*see Myriad* above), cloning methods that could be applied to human beings, and genetic alterations of human beings. Section 33 of the AIA provides that after September 16, 2011, "[n]otwithstanding any other provision of law, no patent may issue on a claim directed to or encompassing a human organism," whether the application was pending on, or filed on or after that date. A ban similar to that in the AIA was part of a few earlier appropriations bills.[1] A September 2011 PTO memorandum addressed to the patent examining corps takes the position that the AIA provision:

> does not change existing law or long-standing USPTO policy that a claim encompassing a human being is not patentable. This long-standing policy is reflected in MPEP [Manual of Patent Examining Procedure] § 2105, which currently provides that:
>
> > If the broadest reasonable interpretation of the claimed invention as a whole encompasses a human being, then a rejection under 35 U.S.C. 101 must be made * * *.

What does "directed to or encompassing a human organism" mean? Is this limited to prohibiting a claim that, as a whole, claims a (multicellular, living, breathing) human being? Could it apply to a claim directed to treating illness in humans? Might it prohibit patenting of modified human stem cells?

Setting aside the interpretation issues presented by section 101 of the Patent Act and section 33 of the AIA, what kinds of policy questions are presented by patents involving humans or other animals, and who should resolve them?

b. Processes

Over the five-year period spanning 2010 to 2014, the Supreme Court thrice tackled processes as patentable subject matter under section 101. Together with *Association for Molecular Pathology v. Myriad Genetics, Inc.*, *see* page 395, *supra*, the Court was quite busy with patentable subject

---

[1] In 1999, the PTO rejected claims for a method of combining human and animal material to produce an animal-human embryo. *See* 58 Patent Trademark & Copyright Journal (BNA) 203 (June 17, 1999). Notwithstanding the appropriations bans, the PTO in 2004 granted a patent on methods for cloning mammals, some of the claims of which could be construed to apply to the cloning of humans. An earlier cloning patent that arguably encompassed humans was granted in 2001.

matter over that period. As with *AMP v. Myriad*, which upset some expectations in the biotechnology field, the process cases have now reset some expectations and changed practices related to process patents, particularly in software, business or financial methods, medical treatments or processes, and any intersections of those areas.

As you can see below, the majority opinion from the Supreme Court in *Bilski v. Kappos* (2010) shied away from providing any wide-ranging rules of patentability—such as a ruling that no business method could be patentable—despite the urging of the four-judge group joining in a concurring opinion by Justice Stevens. Instead, as further set forth in the excerpt below, it relied on a more general subject matter eligibility concept. Just two years later, the Supreme Court handed down another decision with respect to process patents, *Mayo Collaborative Services v. Prometheus Laboratories, Inc.* (2012), but in a factual situation far from so-called "business methods": a process for helping assess proper doses of a particular drug for patients with gastrointestinal autoimmune diseases by measuring the drug's metabolites. Then in 2014, the Court was back to reviewing a method of engaging in certain business transactions mediated by computers, in *Alice Corp. v. CLS Bank International*. By the end of the series of three process cases, the Court had developed a two-step "test" for eligibility that the Federal Circuit calls the *Alice/Mayo* test, which in turn rests on *Bilski v. Kappos*.

BILSKI V. KAPPOS

561 U.S. 593, 130 S.Ct. 3218 (2010).

JUSTICE KENNEDY delivered the opinion of the Court, except as to Parts II-B-2 and II-C-2.*

The question in this case turns on whether a patent can be issued for a claimed invention designed for the business world. The patent application claims a procedure for instructing buyers and sellers how to protect against the risk of price fluctuations in a discrete section of the economy. Three arguments are advanced for the proposition that the claimed invention is outside the scope of patent law: (1) it is not tied to a machine and does not transform an article; (2) it involves a method of conducting business; and (3) it is merely an abstract idea. The Court of Appeals ruled that the first mentioned of these, the so-called machine-or-

* Justice Scalia does not join Parts II-B-2 and II-C-2. [Ed. note: Because Parts II-B-2 and II-C-2 have been omitted from this edited version of the case, the portions of the Kennedy opinion set forth here represent the opinion of a majority of the Court. Not included in this case excerpt are two opinions concurring in the judgment, one authored by Justice Stevens (representing four justices) and one by Justice Breyer (representing two justices). No justices dissented from the Court's judgment, but the concurring opinions demonstrated that the majority opinion represented only the reasoning of five justices.]

transformation test, was the sole test to be used for determining the patentability of a "process" under the Patent Act, 35 U.S.C. § 101.

I

Petitioners' application seeks patent protection for a claimed invention that explains how buyers and sellers of commodities in the energy market can protect, or hedge, against the risk of price changes. The key claims are claims 1 and 4. Claim 1 describes a series of steps instructing how to hedge risk. Claim 4 puts the concept articulated in claim 1 into a simple mathematical formula. Claim 1 consists of the following steps:

(a) initiating a series of transactions between said commodity provider and consumers of said commodity wherein said consumers purchase said commodity at a fixed rate based upon historical averages, said fixed rate corresponding to a risk position of said consumers;

(b) identifying market participants for said commodity having a counter-risk position to said consumers; and

(c) initiating a series of transactions between said commodity provider and said market participants at a second fixed rate such that said series of market participant transactions balances the risk position of said series of consumer transactions.

The remaining claims explain how claims 1 and 4 can be applied to allow energy suppliers and consumers to minimize the risks resulting from fluctuations in market demand for energy. For example, claim 2 claims "[t]he method of claim 1 wherein said commodity is energy and said market participants are transmission distributors." Some of these claims also suggest familiar statistical approaches to determine the inputs to use in claim 4's equation. For example, claim 7 advises using well-known random analysis techniques to determine how much a seller will gain "from each transaction under each historical weather pattern."

The patent examiner rejected petitioners' application, explaining that it " 'is not implemented on a specific apparatus and merely manipulates [an] abstract idea and solves a purely mathematical problem without any limitation to a practical application, therefore, the invention is not directed to the technological arts.' " The Board of Patent Appeals and Interferences affirmed, concluding that the application involved only mental steps that do not transform physical matter and was directed to an abstract idea.

* * *

II

A

Section 101 defines the subject matter that may be patented under the Patent Act:

> Whoever invents or discovers any new and useful process, machine, manufacture, or composition of matter, or any new and useful improvement thereof, may obtain a patent therefor, subject to the conditions and requirements of this title.

Section 101 thus specifies four independent categories of inventions or discoveries that are eligible for protection: processes, machines, manufactures, and compositions of matter. "In choosing such expansive terms . . . modified by the comprehensive 'any,' Congress plainly contemplated that the patent laws would be given wide scope." *Diamond v. Chakrabarty*, 447 U.S. 303, 308 (1980). * * *

The Court's precedents provide three specific exceptions to § 101's broad patent-eligibility principles: "laws of nature, physical phenomena, and abstract ideas." *Chakrabarty, supra*, at 309. While these exceptions are not required by the statutory text, they are consistent with the notion that a patentable process must be "new and useful." And, in any case, these exceptions have defined the reach of the statute as a matter of statutory stare decisis going back 150 years. The concepts covered by these exceptions are "part of the storehouse of knowledge of all men . . . free to all men and reserved exclusively to none." *Funk Brothers Seed Co. v. Kalo Inoculant Co.*, 333 U.S. 127, 130 (1948).

The § 101 patent-eligibility inquiry is only a threshold test. Even if an invention qualifies as a process, machine, manufacture, or composition of matter, in order to receive the Patent Act's protection the claimed invention must also satisfy "the conditions and requirements of this title." § 101. Those requirements include that the invention be novel, *see* § 102, nonobvious, *see* § 103, and fully and particularly described, *see* § 112.

The present case involves an invention that is claimed to be a "process" under § 101. Section 100(b) defines "process" as:

> process, art or method, and includes a new use of a known process, machine, manufacture, composition of matter, or material.

The Court first considers two proposed categorical limitations on "process" patents under § 101 that would, if adopted, bar petitioners' application in the present case: the machine-or-transformation test and the categorical exclusion of business method patents.

B

1

Under the Court of Appeals' formulation, an invention is a "process" only if: "(1) it is tied to a particular machine or apparatus, or (2) it transforms a particular article into a different state or thing." This Court has "more than once cautioned that courts 'should not read into the patent laws limitations and conditions which the legislature has not expressed.' " *Diamond v. Diehr*, 450 U.S. 175, 182 (1981) (quoting *Chakrabarty*, *supra*, at 308). In patent law, as in all statutory construction, "[u]nless otherwise defined, 'words will be interpreted as taking their ordinary, contemporary, common meaning.' " *Diehr, supra*, at 182. The Court has read the § 101 term "manufacture" in accordance with dictionary definitions, and approved a construction of the term "composition of matter" consistent with common usage.

Any suggestion in this Court's case law that the Patent Act's terms deviate from their ordinary meaning has only been an explanation for the exceptions for laws of nature, physical phenomena, and abstract ideas. *See Parker v. Flook*, 437 U.S. 584, 588–589 (1978). This Court has not indicated that the existence of these well-established exceptions gives the Judiciary carte blanche to impose other limitations that are inconsistent with the text and the statute's purpose and design. Concerns about attempts to call any form of human activity a "process" can be met by making sure the claim meets the requirements of § 101.

Adopting the machine-or-transformation test as the sole test for what constitutes a "process" (as opposed to just an important and useful clue) violates these statutory interpretation principles. Section 100(b) provides that "[t]he term 'process' means process, art or method, and includes a new use of a known process, machine, manufacture, composition of matter, or material." The Court is unaware of any " 'ordinary, contemporary, common meaning,' " *Diehr, supra*, at 182, of the definitional terms "process, art or method" that would require these terms to be tied to a machine or to transform an article. * * *

* * *

C

1

Section 101 similarly precludes the broad contention that the term "process" categorically excludes business methods. The term "method," which is within § 100(b)'s definition of "process," at least as a textual matter and before consulting other limitations in the Patent Act and this Court's precedents, may include at least some methods of doing business. *See, e.g.*, WEBSTER'S NEW INTERNATIONAL DICTIONARY 1548 (2d ed. 1954) (defining "method" as "[a]n orderly procedure or process . . . regular way or manner of doing anything; hence, a set form of procedure adopted in investigation or instruction"). The Court is unaware of any argument that the " 'ordinary, contemporary, common meaning' " of "method" excludes business methods. Nor is it clear how far a prohibition on business method patents would reach, and whether it would exclude technologies for conducting a business more efficiently.

The argument that business methods are categorically outside of § 101's scope is further undermined by the fact that federal law explicitly contemplates the existence of at least some business method patents. Under 35 U.S.C. § 273(b)(1), if a patent-holder claims infringement based on "a method in [a] patent," the alleged infringer can assert a defense of prior use. [Ed. note: Section 273 has since been amended by the AIA, *see infra* Chapter 12.B.5.] For purposes of this defense alone, "method" is defined as "a method of doing or conducting business." In other words, by allowing this defense the statute itself acknowledges that there may be business method patents. Section 273's definition of "method," to be sure, cannot change the meaning of a prior-enacted statute. But what § 273 does is clarify the understanding that a business method is simply one kind of "method" that is, at least in some circumstances, eligible for patenting under § 101.

A conclusion that business methods are not patentable in any circumstances would render § 273 meaningless. This would violate the canon against interpreting any statutory provision in a manner that would render another provision superfluous. * * * Finally, while § 273 appears to leave open the possibility of some business method patents, it does not suggest broad patentability of such claimed inventions.

* * *

III

Even though petitioners' application is not categorically outside of § 101 under the two broad and atextual approaches the Court rejects today, that does not mean it is a "process" under § 101. Petitioners seek to patent both the concept of hedging risk and the application of that concept to energy markets. Rather than adopting categorical rules that might have wide-ranging and unforeseen impacts, the Court resolves this case narrowly on the basis of this Court's decisions in *Benson*, *Flook*, and *Diehr*, which show that petitioners' claims are not patentable processes because they are attempts to patent abstract ideas. Indeed, all members of the Court agree that the patent application at issue here falls outside of § 101 because it claims an abstract idea.

In *Benson*, the Court considered whether a patent application for an algorithm to convert binary-coded decimal numerals into pure binary code was a "process" under § 101. The Court first explained that " '[a] principle, in the abstract, is a fundamental truth; an original cause; a motive; these cannot be patented, as no one can claim in either of them an exclusive right.' " The Court then held the application at issue was not a "process," but an unpatentable abstract idea. "It is conceded that one may not patent an idea. But in practical effect that would be the result if the formula for converting . . . numerals to pure binary numerals were patented in this case." A contrary holding "would wholly pre-empt the mathematical formula and in practical effect would be a patent on the algorithm itself."

In *Flook*, the Court considered the next logical step after *Benson*. The applicant there attempted to patent a procedure for monitoring the conditions during the catalytic conversion process in the petrochemical and oil-refining industries. The application's only innovation was reliance on a mathematical algorithm. *Flook* held the invention was not a patentable "process." The Court conceded the invention at issue, unlike the algorithm in *Benson*, had been limited so that it could still be freely used outside the petrochemical and oil-refining industries. Nevertheless, *Flook* rejected "[t]he notion that post-solution activity, no matter how conventional or obvious in itself, can transform an unpatentable principle into a patentable process." The Court concluded that the process at issue there was "unpatentable under § 101, not because it contain[ed] a mathematical algorithm as one component, but because once that algorithm [wa]s assumed to be within the prior art, the application, considered as a whole, contain[ed] no patentable invention." As the Court later explained, *Flook* stands for the proposition that the prohibition against patenting abstract ideas "cannot be circumvented by attempting to limit the use of the formula to a particular technological environment" or adding "insignificant postsolution activity."

Finally, in *Diehr*, the Court established a limitation on the principles articulated in *Benson* and *Flook*. The application in *Diehr* claimed a previously unknown method for "molding raw, uncured synthetic rubber into cured precision products," using a mathematical formula to complete some of its several steps by way of a computer. *Diehr* explained that while an abstract idea, law of nature, or mathematical formula could not be patented, "an application of a law of nature or mathematical formula to a known structure or process may well be deserving of patent protection." *Diehr* emphasized the need to consider the invention as a whole, rather than "dissect[ing] the claims into old and new elements and then . . . ignor[ing] the presence of the old elements in the analysis." Finally, the Court concluded that because the claim was not "an attempt to patent a mathematical formula, but rather [was] an industrial process for the molding of rubber products," it fell within § 101's patentable subject matter.

In light of these precedents, it is clear that petitioners' application is not a patentable "process." Claims 1 and 4 in petitioners' application explain the basic concept of hedging, or protecting against risk: "Hedging is a fundamental economic practice long prevalent in our system of commerce and taught in any introductory finance class." 545 F.3d, at 1013 (Rader, J., dissenting). The concept of hedging, described in claim 1 and reduced to a mathematical formula in claim 4, is an unpatentable abstract idea, just like the algorithms at issue in *Benson* and *Flook*. Allowing petitioners to patent risk hedging would preempt use of this approach in all fields, and would effectively grant a monopoly over an abstract idea.

Petitioners' remaining claims are broad examples of how hedging can be used in commodities and energy markets. *Flook* established that limiting an abstract idea to one field of use or adding token postsolution components did not make the concept patentable. That is exactly what the remaining claims in petitioners' application do. These claims attempt to patent the use of the abstract idea of hedging risk in the energy market and then instruct the use of well-known random analysis techniques to help establish some of the inputs into the equation. Indeed, these claims add even less to the underlying abstract principle than the invention in *Flook* did, for the *Flook* invention was at least directed to the narrower domain of signaling dangers in operating a catalytic converter.

* * *

Today, the Court once again declines to impose limitations on the Patent Act that are inconsistent with the Act's text. The patent application here can be rejected under our precedents on the unpatentability of abstract ideas. The Court, therefore, need not define further what constitutes a patentable "process," beyond pointing to the definition of that term provided in § 100(b) and looking to the guideposts in *Benson*, *Flook*, and *Diehr*.

* * *

MAYO COLLABORATIVE SERVS. V. PROMETHEUS LABS., INC.

566 U.S. 66, 132 S.Ct. 1289 (2012).

JUSTICE BREYER delivered the opinion of the Court.

Section 101 of the Patent Act defines patentable subject matter. It says:

> "Whoever invents or discovers any new and useful process, machine, manufacture, or composition of matter, or any new and useful improvement thereof, may obtain a patent therefor, subject to the conditions and requirements of this title." 35 U.S.C. § 101.

The Court has long held that this provision contains an important implicit exception. "[L]aws of nature, natural phenomena, and abstract ideas" are not patentable. * * *

* * *

The Court has recognized, however, that too broad an interpretation of this exclusionary principle could eviscerate patent law. For all inventions at some level embody, use, reflect, rest upon, or apply laws of nature, natural phenomena, or abstract ideas. Thus, in *Diehr* the Court pointed out that " 'a process is not unpatentable simply because it contains a law of nature or a mathematical algorithm.' " 450 U.S., at 187 (quoting *Parker v. Flook,* 437 U.S. 584, 590 (1978)). It added that "an *application* of a law of nature or mathematical formula to a known structure or process may well be deserving of patent protection." *Diehr, supra,* at 187. * * *

Still, as the Court has also made clear, to transform an unpatentable law of nature into a patent-eligible *application* of such a law, one must do more than simply state the law of nature while adding the words "apply it."

The case before us lies at the intersection of these basic principles. It concerns patent claims covering processes that help doctors who use thiopurine drugs to treat patients with autoimmune diseases determine whether a given dosage level is too low or too high. The claims purport to apply natural laws describing the relationships between the concentration in the blood of certain thiopurine metabolites and the likelihood that the drug dosage will be ineffective or induce harmful side-effects. We must determine whether the claimed processes have transformed these unpatentable natural laws into patent-eligible applications of those laws. We conclude that they have not done so and that therefore the processes are not patentable.

Our conclusion rests upon an examination of the particular claims before us in light of the Court's precedents. * * * And [our precedents] insist that a process that focuses upon the use of a natural law also contain other elements or a combination of elements, sometimes referred to as an "inventive concept," sufficient to ensure that the patent in practice amounts to significantly more than a patent upon the natural law itself.

We find that the process claims at issue here do not satisfy these conditions. In particular, the steps in the claimed processes (apart from the natural laws themselves) involve well-understood, routine, conventional activity previously engaged in by researchers in the field. At the same time, upholding the patents would risk disproportionately tying up the use of the underlying natural laws, inhibiting their use in the making of further discoveries.

I

A

The patents before us concern the use of thiopurine drugs in the treatment of autoimmune diseases, such as Crohn's disease and ulcerative colitis. When a patient ingests a thiopurine compound, his body metabolizes the drug, causing metabolites to form in his bloodstream. Because the way in which people metabolize thiopurine compounds varies, the same dose of a thiopurine drug affects different people differently, and it has been difficult for doctors to determine whether for a particular patient a given dose is too high, risking harmful side effects, or too low, and so likely ineffective.

At the time the discoveries embodied in the patents were made, scientists already understood that the levels in a patient's blood of certain metabolites, including, in particular, 6-thioguanine and its nucleotides (6-TG) and 6-methyl-mercaptopurine (6-MMP), were correlated with the likelihood that a particular dosage of a thiopurine drug could cause harm or prove ineffective. But those in the field did not know the precise correlations between metabolite levels and likely harm or ineffectiveness. The patent claims at issue here set forth processes embodying researchers' findings that identified these correlations with some precision.

More specifically, the patents—U.S. Patent No. 6,355,623 ('623 patent) and U.S. Patent No. 6,680,302 ('302 patent)—embody findings that concentrations in a patient's blood of 6-TG or of 6-MMP metabolite beyond a certain level (400 and 7000 picomoles per $8x10^8$ red blood cells, respectively) indicate that the dosage is likely too high for the patient, while concentrations in the blood of 6-TG metabolite lower than a certain level (about 230 picomoles per $8x10^8$ red blood cells) indicate that the dosage is likely too low to be effective.

The patent claims seek to embody this research in a set of processes. Like the Federal Circuit we take as typical claim 1 of the '623 Patent, which describes one of the claimed processes as follows:

> "A method of optimizing therapeutic efficacy for treatment of an immune-mediated gastrointestinal disorder, comprising:
>
> "(a) administering a drug providing 6-thioguanine to a subject having said immune-mediated gastrointestinal disorder; and
>
> "(b) determining the level of 6-thioguanine in said subject having said immune-mediated gastrointestinal disorder,
>
> "wherein the level of 6-thioguanine less than about 230 pmol per $8x10^8$ red blood cells indicates a need to increase the amount of said drug subsequently administered to said subject and

"wherein the level of 6-thioguanine greater than about 400 pmol per 8x10[8] red blood cells indicates a need to decrease the amount of said drug subsequently administered to said subject." '623 patent, col.20, ll.10–20, 2 App. 16.

For present purposes we may assume that the other claims in the patents do not differ significantly from claim 1.

* * *

II

Prometheus' patents set forth laws of nature—namely, relationships between concentrations of certain metabolites in the blood and the likelihood that a dosage of a thiopurine drug will prove ineffective or cause harm. Claim 1, for example, states that *if* the levels of 6-TG in the blood (of a patient who has taken a dose of a thiopurine drug) exceed about 400 pmol per 8x10[8] red blood cells, *then* the administered dose is likely to produce toxic side effects. While it takes a human action (the administration of a thiopurine drug) to trigger a manifestation of this relation in a particular person, the relation itself exists in principle apart from any human action. The relation is a consequence of the ways in which thiopurine compounds are metabolized by the body—entirely natural processes. And so a patent that simply describes that relation sets forth a natural law.

The question before us is whether the claims do significantly more than simply describe these natural relations. To put the matter more precisely, do the patent claims add *enough* to their statements of the correlations to allow the processes they describe to qualify as patent-eligible processes that *apply* natural laws? We believe that the answer to this question is no.

A

If a law of nature is not patentable, then neither is a process reciting a law of nature, unless that process has additional features that provide practical assurance that the process is more than a drafting effort designed to monopolize the law of nature itself. A patent, for example, could not simply recite a law of nature and then add the instruction "apply the law." Einstein, we assume, could not have patented his famous law by claiming a process consisting of simply telling linear accelerator operators to refer to the law to determine how much energy an amount of mass has produced (or vice versa). Nor could Archimedes have secured a patent for his famous principle of flotation by claiming a process consisting of simply telling boat builders to refer to that principle in order to determine whether an object will float.

What else is there in the claims before us? The process that each claim recites tells doctors interested in the subject about the correlations that the researchers discovered. In doing so, it recites an "administering" step, a "determining" step, and a "wherein" step. These additional steps are not themselves natural laws but neither are they sufficient to transform the nature of the claim.

First, the "administering" step simply refers to the relevant audience, namely doctors who treat patients with certain diseases with thiopurine drugs. That audience is a pre-existing audience; doctors used thiopurine drugs to treat patients suffering from autoimmune disorders long before anyone asserted these claims. In any event, the "prohibition against patenting abstract ideas 'cannot be circumvented by attempting to limit the use of the formula to a particular technological environment.'" *Bilski,* 130 S.Ct., at 3230 (quoting *Diehr,* 450 U.S., at 191–192).

Second, the "wherein" clauses simply tell a doctor about the relevant natural laws, at most adding a suggestion that he should take those laws into account when treating his patient. That is to say, these clauses tell the relevant audience about the laws while trusting them to use those laws appropriately where they are relevant to their decisionmaking (rather like Einstein telling linear accelerator operators about his basic law and then trusting them to use it where relevant).

Third, the "determining" step tells the doctor to determine the level of the relevant metabolites in the blood, through whatever process the doctor or the laboratory wishes to use. As the patents state, methods for determining metabolite levels were well known in the art. Indeed, scientists routinely measured metabolites as part of their investigations into the relationships between metabolite levels and efficacy and toxicity of thiopurine compounds. Thus, this step tells doctors to engage in well-understood, routine, conventional activity previously engaged in by scientists who work in the field. Purely "conventional or obvious" "[pre]-solution activity" is normally not sufficient to transform an unpatentable law of nature into a patent-eligible application of such a law. *Flook,* 437 U.S., at 590; *see also Bilski,* 130 S.Ct., at 3230 ("[T]he prohibition against patenting abstract ideas 'cannot be circumvented by' . . . adding 'insignificant post-solution activity' ").

Fourth, to consider the three steps as an ordered combination adds nothing to the laws of nature that is not already present when the steps are considered separately. *See Diehr, supra,* at 188 ("[A] new combination of steps in a process may be patentable even though all the constituents of the combination were well known and in common use before the combination was made"). Anyone who wants to make use of these laws must first administer a thiopurine drug and measure the resulting metabolite concentrations, and so the combination amounts to nothing significantly more than an instruction to doctors to apply the applicable laws when treating their patients.

The upshot is that the three steps simply tell doctors to gather data from which they may draw an inference in light of the correlations. To put the matter more succinctly, the claims inform a relevant audience about certain laws of nature; any additional steps consist of well-understood, routine, conventional activity already engaged in by the scientific community; and those steps, when viewed as a whole, add nothing significant beyond the sum of their parts taken separately. For these reasons we believe that the steps are not sufficient to transform unpatentable natural correlations into patentable applications of those regularities.

B

1

A more detailed consideration of the controlling precedents reinforces our conclusion. The cases most directly on point are *Diehr* and *Flook,* two cases in which the Court reached opposite conclusions about the patent eligibility of processes that embodied the equivalent of natural laws. [Ed. note: *Bilski* also discussed these cases.] The *Diehr* process (held patent eligible) set forth a method for molding raw, uncured rubber into various cured, molded products [and included process steps involving the mold or press for the rubber, measuring the temperature, a computer, and a "device" that would automatically open the press when signaled by the computer]. * * *

* * * And so the patentees did not "seek to pre-empt the use of [the] equation," but sought "only to foreclose from others the use of that equation in conjunction with all of the other steps in their claimed process." These other steps apparently added to the formula something that in terms of patent law's objectives had significance—they transformed the process into an inventive application of the formula.

The process in *Flook* (held not patentable) provided a method for adjusting "alarm limits" in the catalytic conversion of hydrocarbons. * * *

The Court * * * characterized the claimed process as doing nothing other than "provid[ing] a[n unpatentable] formula for computing an updated alarm limit." * * * And so the other steps in the process did not limit the claim to a particular application. Moreover, [the process steps in the claim] were all "well known," to the point where, putting the formula to the side, there was no "inventive concept" in the claimed application of the formula. "[P]ost-solution activity" that is purely "conventional or obvious," the Court wrote, "can[not] transform an unpatentable principle into a patentable process."

The claim before us presents a case for patentability that is weaker than the (patent-eligible) claim in *Diehr* and no stronger than the (unpatentable) claim in *Flook.* Beyond picking out the relevant audience, namely those who administer doses of thiopurine drugs, the claim simply tells doctors to: (1) measure (somehow) the current level of the relevant metabolite, (2) use particular (unpatentable) laws of nature (which the claim sets forth) to calculate the current toxicity/inefficacy limits, and (3) reconsider the drug dosage in light of the law. These instructions add nothing specific to the laws of nature other than what is well-understood, routine, conventional activity, previously engaged in by those in the field. And since they are steps that must be taken in order to apply the laws in question, the effect is simply to tell doctors to apply the law [of nature] somehow when treating their patients. The process in *Diehr* was not so characterized; that in *Flook* was characterized in roughly this way.

* * *

III

We have considered several further arguments in support of Prometheus' position. But they do not lead us to adopt a different conclusion. First, the Federal Circuit, in upholding the patent eligibility of the claims before us, relied on this Court's determination that "[t]ransformation and reduction of an article 'to a different state or thing' is *the clue* to the patentability of a process claim that does not include particular machines." * * *

* * * Regardless, in stating that the "machine-or-transformation" test is an "*important and useful clue*" to patentability, we have neither said nor implied that the test trumps the "law of nature" exclusion. *Bilski, supra* (emphasis added). That being so, the test fails here.

Second, Prometheus argues that, because the particular laws of nature that its patent claims embody are narrow and specific, the patents should be upheld. * * *

But the underlying functional concern here is a *relative* one. * * *And, as we have previously pointed out, even a narrow law of nature (such as the one before us) can inhibit future research.

In any event, our cases have not distinguished among different laws of nature according to whether or not the principles they embody are sufficiently narrow. And this is understandable. Courts and judges are not institutionally well suited to making the kinds of judgments needed to distinguish among different laws of nature. And so the cases have endorsed a bright-line prohibition against patenting laws of nature, mathematical formulas and the like, which serves as a somewhat more easily administered proxy for the underlying "building-block" concern.

Third, the Government argues that virtually any step beyond a statement of a law of nature itself should transform an unpatentable law of nature into a potentially patentable application sufficient to satisfy § 101's demands. The Government does not necessarily believe that claims that (like the claims before us) extend just minimally beyond a law of nature should receive patents. But in its view, other statutory provisions—those that insist that a claimed process be novel, 35 U.S.C. § 102, that it not be "obvious in light of prior art," § 103, and that it be "full[y], clear[ly], concise[ly], and exact[ly]" described, § 112—can perform this screening function. In particular, it argues that these claims likely fail for lack of novelty under § 102.

This approach, however, would make the "law of nature" exception to § 101 patentability a dead letter. The approach is therefore not consistent with prior law. The relevant cases rest their holdings upon section 101, not later sections.

We recognize that, in evaluating the significance of additional steps, the § 101 patent-eligibility inquiry and, say, the § 102 novelty inquiry might sometimes overlap. But that need not always be so. And to shift the patent-eligibility inquiry entirely to these later sections risks creating significantly greater legal uncertainty, while assuming that those sections can do work that they are not equipped to do.

* * *

Fourth, Prometheus, supported by several *amici,* argues that a principle of law denying patent coverage here will interfere significantly with the ability of medical researchers to make valuable discoveries, particularly in the area of diagnostic research. That research, which includes research leading to the discovery of laws of nature, is expensive; it "ha[s] made the United States the world leader in this field"; and it requires protection.

Other medical experts, however, argue strongly against a legal rule that would make the present claims patent eligible, invoking policy considerations that point in the opposite direction. * * *

We do not find this kind of difference of opinion surprising. Patent protection is, after all, a two-edged sword. * * * Patent law's general rules must govern inventive activity in many different fields of human endeavor, with the result that the practical effects of rules that reflect a general effort to balance these considerations may differ from one field to another.

In consequence, we must hesitate before departing from established general legal rules lest a new protective rule that seems to suit the needs of one field produce unforeseen results in another. And we must recognize the role of Congress in crafting more finely tailored rules where necessary. *Cf.* 35 U.S.C. §§ 161–164 (special rules for plant patents). We need not determine here whether, from a policy perspective, increased protection for discoveries of diagnostic laws of nature is desirable.

* * *

ALICE CORP. PTY. LTD. V. CLS BANK INT'L

573 U.S. 208, 134 S.Ct. 2347, 2354–60 (2014).

[In *Alice Corp. Pty. Ltd. v. CLS Bank Int'l*, the Supreme Court relied heavily on its decision in *Mayo* when addressing the patent eligibility of claims based on a method of mitigating "settlement risk" in financial transactions, the risk that one of the parties to a financial transaction will fail to fulfill its obligations. The patent claims included claims to: (1) a method for exchanging obligations through a neutral intermediary, which would permit completion of a transaction only when both parties have sufficient funds to fulfill the obligations of the transaction; (2) a computer system configured to perform the method; and (3) a computer-readable medium on which computer code for performing the method has been stored. In its opinion, the Supreme Court first referred to its oft-repeated list of implicit exceptions to patentable subject matter under section 101: laws of nature, natural or physical phenomena, and abstract ideas. The Court summarized its rationale for the exceptions as follows:]

We have described the concern that drives this exclusionary principle as one of pre-emption. Laws of nature, natural phenomena, and abstract ideas are the basic tools of scientific and technological work. Monopolization of those tools through the grant of a patent might tend to impede innovation more than it would tend to promote it, thereby thwarting the primary object of the patent laws. We have repeatedly emphasized this concern that patent law not inhibit further discovery by improperly tying up the future use of these building blocks of human ingenuity.

At the same time, we tread carefully in construing this exclusionary principle lest it swallow all of patent law. At some level, all inventions embody, use, reflect, rest upon, or apply laws of nature, natural phenomena, or abstract ideas. Thus, an invention is not rendered ineligible for patent simply because it involves an abstract concept. Applications of such concepts to a new and useful end, we have said, remain eligible for patent protection.

Accordingly, in applying the § 101 exception, we must distinguish between patents that claim the building blocks of human ingenuity and those that integrate the building blocks into something more, thereby transforming them into a patent-eligible invention. The former would risk disproportionately tying up the use of the underlying ideas, and are therefore ineligible for patent protection. The latter pose no comparable risk of pre-emption, and therefore remain eligible for the monopoly granted under our patent laws.

* * *

[The Court then summarized its method for analyzing claims under those exceptions:]

In *Mayo Collaborative Services v. Prometheus Laboratories, Inc.*, 566 U.S. [66] (2012), we set forth a framework for distinguishing patents that claim laws of nature, natural phenomena, and abstract ideas from those that claim patent-eligible applications of those concepts. First, we determine whether the claims at issue are directed to one of those patent-ineligible concepts. If so, we then ask, "[w]hat else is there in the claims before us?" To answer that question, we consider the elements of each claim both individually and "as an ordered combination" to determine whether the additional elements "transform the nature of the claim" into a patent-eligible application. We have described step two of this analysis as a search for an " 'inventive concept' "—*i.e.*, an element or combination of elements that is "sufficient to ensure that the patent in practice amounts to significantly more than a patent upon the [ineligible concept] itself."

* * *

[Using that framework, the Court first determined that the claims in the case at hand were directed to an abstract idea:]

It follows from our prior cases, and *Bilski* in particular, that the claims at issue here are directed to an abstract idea. Petitioner's claims involve a method of exchanging financial obligations between two parties using a third-party intermediary to mitigate settlement risk. The intermediary creates and updates "shadow" records to reflect the value of each party's actual accounts held at "exchange institutions," thereby permitting only those transactions for which the parties have sufficient resources. At the end of each day, the intermediary issues irrevocable instructions to the exchange institutions to carry out the permitted transactions.

On their face, the claims before us are drawn to the concept of intermediated settlement, *i.e.*, the use of a third party to mitigate settlement risk. Like the risk hedging in *Bilski*, the concept of intermediated settlement is " 'a fundamental economic practice long prevalent in our system of commerce.' " *Ibid.; see, e.g.*, Emery, *Speculation on the Stock and Produce Exchanges of the United States*, in 7 Studies in History, Economics and Public Law 283, 346–356 (1896) (discussing the use of a "clearing-house" as an intermediary to reduce settlement risk). The use of a third-party intermediary (or "clearing house") is also a building block of the modern economy. *See, e.g.*, Yadav, *The Problematic Case of Clearinghouses in Complex Markets*, 101 Geo. L.J. 387, 406–412 (2013); J. HULL, RISK MANAGEMENT AND FINANCIAL INSTITUTIONS 103–104 (3d ed. 2012). Thus, intermediated settlement, like hedging, is an "abstract idea" beyond the scope of § 101.

* * *

[The Court then addressed whether the claims contained additional features to ensure that the claim would not simply monopolize the abstract idea, rejecting the idea that applying the ineligible method on a computer created a patent-eligible claim or otherwise altered the analysis under *Mayo* and prior case law.]

[T]he mere recitation of a generic computer cannot transform a patent-ineligible abstract idea into a patent-eligible invention. Stating an abstract idea "while adding the words 'apply it' " is not enough for patent eligibility. *Mayo, supra,* at 72. Nor is limiting the use of an abstract idea " 'to a particular technological environment.' " *Bilski, supra,* at 610–611. Stating an abstract idea while adding the words "apply it with a computer" simply combines those two steps, with the same deficient result. * * * Given the ubiquity of computers, wholly generic computer implementation is not generally the sort of "additional featur[e]" that provides any "practical assurance that the process is more than a drafting effort designed to monopolize the [abstract idea] itself." *Mayo,* 566 U.S., at [77].

The fact that a computer "necessarily exist[s] in the physical, rather than purely conceptual, realm," Brief for Petitioner 39, is beside the point. There is no dispute that a computer is a tangible system (in § 101 terms, a "machine"), or that many computer-implemented claims are formally addressed to patent-eligible subject matter. But if that were the end of the § 101 inquiry, an applicant could claim any principle of the physical or social sciences by reciting a computer system configured to implement the relevant concept. Such a result would make the determination of patent eligibility "depend simply on the draftsman's art," *Flook, supra,* at 593, thereby eviscerating the rule that " '[l]aws of nature, natural phenomena, and abstract ideas are not patentable,' " *Myriad,* 569 U.S., at [589].

* * *

Taking the [method] claim elements separately, the function performed by the computer at each step of the process is purely conventional. Using a computer to create and maintain "shadow" accounts amounts to electronic recordkeeping—one of the most basic functions of a computer. The same is true with respect to the use of a computer to obtain data, adjust account balances, and issue automated instructions; all of these computer functions are "well-understood, routine, conventional activit[ies]" previously known to the industry. *Mayo,* 566 U.S., at [73]. In short, each step does no more than require a generic computer to perform generic computer functions.

* * *

Petitioner's claims to a computer system and a computer-readable medium fail for substantially the same reasons. Petitioner conceded below that its media claims rise or fall with its method claims. As to its system claims, petitioner emphasizes that those claims recite "specific hardware" configured to perform "specific computerized functions." But what petitioner characterizes as specific hardware—a "data processing system" with a "communications controller" and "data storage unit"—is purely functional and generic. Nearly every computer will include a "communications controller" and "data storage unit" capable of performing the basic calculation, storage, and transmission functions required by the method claims. *See* 717 F.3d, at 1290 (Lourie, J., concurring). As a result, none of the hardware recited by the system claims "offers a meaningful limitation beyond generally linking 'the use of the [method] to a particular technological environment,' that is, implementation via computers." *Id.*, at 1291 (quoting *Bilski*, 561 U.S., at 610–611).

* * *

NOTES

1. *Justification for Exclusions:* Why does patent law not protect abstract ideas, such as mathematical formulas? What is the basis for excluding laws of nature and natural phenomena from patentability, even if newly discovered? Does the Patent Act exclude them? The Constitution? Some explanations can be found throughout the cases. If Congress chose to offer such protection, would that exceed Congress's power under the Intellectual Property Clause? Could Congress enact such a law under any other provision of the Constitution?

2. *New Process, Old Product:* Can a new process be section 101 subject matter if it produces a known or naturally occurring product? What if a known product can be used in a new process with new effects?

According to section 100(b) of the Patent Act, "[t]he term 'process' means process, art, or method, and includes a new use of a known process, machine, manufacture, composition of matter, or material." This means that a person who invents or discovers a new use for a known product, including a chemical composition that is discovered to have previously unknown therapeutic qualities, may obtain a process patent on a new process of using the product or chemical composition, including a new method of treating human disease using that chemical composition. As stated in an extended hypothetical by Judge Rader of the Federal Circuit:

> Inventor A invents a shoe polish for shining shoes (which, for the sake of example, is novel, useful, and nonobvious). Inventor A receives a patent having composition claims for shoe polish. Indeed, the preamble of these hypothetical claims recites "a composition for polishing shoes." Clearly, Inventor B could not later secure a patent with composition claims on the same composition because it would not be novel. Likewise, Inventor B could not secure claims on the method of using the composition for shining shoes because the use is not a "new use" of the composition but, rather, the same use shining shoes.

Suppose Inventor B discovers that the polish also repels water when rubbed onto shoes. Inventor B could not likely claim a method of using the polish to repel water on shoes because repelling water is inherent in the normal use of the polish to shine shoes. In other words, Inventor B has not invented a "new" use by rubbing polish on shoes to repel water. Upon discovering, however, that the polish composition grows hair when rubbed on bare human skin, Inventor B can likely obtain method claims directed to the new use of the composition to grow hair. *See* 35 U.S.C. § 101 (1994) ("Whoever invents or discovers any new and useful process . . . may obtain a patent therefor."); 35 U.S.C. § 100(b) (1994) ("The term 'process' means process, art or method, and includes a new use of a known process, machine, manufacture, composition of matter, or material."). Hence, while Inventor B may obtain a blocking patent on the use of Inventor A's composition to grow hair, this method patent does not bestow on Inventor B any right with respect to the patented composition. Even though Inventor A's claim recites "a composition for polishing shoes," Inventor B cannot invoke this use limitation to limit Inventor A's composition claim because that preamble phrase states a use or purpose of the composition and does not impose a limit on Inventor A's claim.

Catalina Marketing International, Inc. v. Coolsavings.com, Inc., 289 F.3d 801, 809–10 (Fed. Cir. 2002).

3. *Printed Matter:* In *C R Bard Inc. v. AngioDynamics, Inc.*, 979 F.3d 1372 (Fed. Cir. 2020), the Federal Circuit took up the so-called "printed matter" doctrine within patent law and combined it with the two-step *Alice/Mayo* test for patentable subject matter. As the court observed, "While historically 'printed matter' referred to claim elements that literally encompassed 'printed' material, the doctrine has evolved over time to guard against attempts to monopolize the conveyance of information using any medium." 979 F.3d at 1381. Patentee C R Bard asserted both product and process claims (in the patents, the products or devices were denoted as "assemblies" or "systems"), all of which featured improved vascular injection access ports. The improved ports, which could accommodate higher pressure and flow rates, could (usefully) be identified and distinguished from lower-capacity injection ports even after subcutaneous implantation because radiographic markers had been etched on the devices, and those markers could be seen using a CT scan at the beginning of an injection procedure. The court determined that although the claims in the case contained printed matter, the claims as a whole could remain patent eligible under the two-step test even though the printed matter was not "functionally related" to its "substrate," which would have also created eligibility. The court emphasized that the claims, when taken as a whole, did not focus solely on the content of the information or printed matter (the flow rate/pressure info), but also on the means of conveying that information. *Id.* at 1382–84. The court found that defendant AngioDynamics had not demonstrated that the means for conveying the information were routine and

conventional, or routinely conducted in the prior art, leaving the assembly and method claims patent-eligible (patentable subject matter) at step two. *Id.*

4. *Categorizing Methods?* A divided Federal Circuit panel decided *Illumina, Inc. v. Ariosa Diagnostics, Inc.*, 967 F.3d 1319 (Fed. Cir. Aug. 3, 2020) (modified opinion), cert. dismissed 141 S.Ct. 2171 (May 21, 2021) (cert. dismissed following agreement of parties), using the two-step *Alice/Mayo* "test" for eligibility. The panel candidly observed that Federal Circuit panels have "consistently held diagnostic claims unpatentable" under *Mayo* while simultaneously noting, "we have held that method of treatment claims are patent-eligible." In the case, the court found the claims to present a "method of preparation" rather than either of the other types of claims; as a result, it considered them under the two steps of *Alice* and *Mayo* (and found patentable subject matter on the facts). These three "categories" of methods may be superficially tidy.

5. *Mental Steps:* The Federal Circuit ruled in *CyberSource Corp. v. Retail Decisions, Inc.*, 654 F.3d 1366 (Fed. Cir. 2011), that a claimed process was an unpatentable abstract idea, where the process determined the validity of a credit card transaction by (a) obtaining information about other transactions that have utilized the same internet address as the questioned transaction, (b) creating a map or list of credit card numbers used in those other transactions, and (c) using the map or list of numbers to determine if the credit card transaction is valid.

> [C]laim 3's steps can all be performed in the human mind. Such a method that can be performed by human thought alone is merely an abstract idea and is not patent-eligible under § 101. Methods which can be performed entirely in the human mind are unpatentable not because there is anything wrong with claiming mental method steps as part of a process containing non-mental steps, but rather because computational methods which can be performed entirely in the human mind are the types of methods that embody the "basic tools of scientific and technological work" that are free to all men and reserved exclusively to none.

Id. at 1373. The Federal Circuit characterized another clam in the case as "nothing more than a computer readable medium containing program instructions for executing the method of [the unpatentable, abstract claim 3, above]." *Id.* at 1374. The court ruled this "machine" claim an unpatentably abstract process as well, although it was not written as a "process" claim. *Id.* at 1375.

6. *Section 101 Categories:* In *In re Nuijten*, 500 F.3d 1346 (Fed. Cir. 2007), the Federal Circuit held that a "signal" related to digital watermarking was not statutory subject matter. The claimed signal included "physical but transitory forms of signal transmission such as radio broadcasts, electrical signals through a wire, and light pulses through a fiber optic cable." It did not constitute statutory subject matter, however, because it did not fit within any of the four categories listed in section 101: process, machine, manufacture, and

composition of matter. Is it important which category of subject matter is involved after *Chakrabarty* and the other section 101 cases you have read? Can an invention be "made by [hu]man" per *Chakrabarty* and not involve a "law of nature, physical phenomena, [or] abstract ideas," yet still not constitute statutory subject matter?

7. *Business Methods, Tax Planning, and the AIA:* Some so-called business methods claims are not as broad and will continue to pass muster as patentable subject matter under *Bilski* and *Alice Corp.* There are and have been, nevertheless, concerns that such claims are or should be invalid for failure to satisfy the requirements of novelty or nonobviousness. This concern arises at least in part as a result of the limited ability of the PTO to uncover the relevant prior art, particularly prior use by others of the claimed invention. Congress addressed some (but not all) of the prior-art based concerns related to business method patents in the 2011 AIA, *see* H.R. Rep. No. 112–98, pt. 1, at 54 (2011), when it created transitional, or temporary post-grant review procedures for existing business method patents.[2] (The reviews set up were available for an eight-year period.) The AIA drafters skirted the question of statutory subject matter by expressly providing the following "rule of construction": "Nothing in this section shall be construed as amending or interpreting categories of patent-eligible subject matter set forth under section 101 [of the Patent Act]." AIA § 18(e).

In addition, the 2011 AIA responded to controversy that had arisen in the previous decade as to the patentability of tax planning strategies. If tax strategies were patentable, tax preparers, accountants, lawyers and taxpayers would risk being sued for infringement if they did not conduct a patent search before implementing a tax planning strategy.[3] Section 14 of the AIA attacked patentability of tax planning strategies through novelty (§ 102) and nonobviousness (§ 103) rather than through statutory subject matter (§ 101): "any strategy for reducing, avoiding, or deferring tax liability, whether known or unknown at the time of the invention or application for patent, shall be deemed insufficient to differentiate a claimed invention from the prior art." AIA § 14(a). The provision applies to any patent application pending on September 16, 2011, or filed on or after that date, as well as any patent that is issued on or after that date. A "rule of construction" accompanying the tax strategy provision provides that "Nothing in this section shall be construed to imply that other business methods are patentable or that other business

[2] Under section 18 of the AIA, the PTO implemented "transitional post-grant review" proceedings for review of "covered business method patents," *id.* § 18(a)(1); persons sued for or charged with infringement of a such a patent could request review of the patent's validity by filing a petition between September 16, 2012, and September 16, 2020. Not all petitions met the standard for instituting a Board review, and the parties settled many that did (leading to termination without a Board decision), but many proceeded to a written decision. All moved quickly, with the last written decisions issuing in 2021.

[3] According to the House Report prepared in connection with the AIA, "Critics assert that it is not fair to permit patents on techniques used to satisfy a government mandate, such as compliance with the Internal Revenue Code. * * * The ability to interpret the tax law and implement such interpretations should remain in the public domain, available to all taxpayers and their advisors." H.R. Rep. No. 112–98, pt. 1, at 51 (2011).

method patents are valid." *Id.* § 14(d). Might this be a response to the *Bilski* majority's treatment of the section 273 prior user defense for good faith prior users of business methods? Compare this rule of construction to the one above.

It is interesting to note that in *Bilski v. Kappos,* the Court was one justice away from applying a "business methods" exclusion instead of the "abstract ideas" exclusion. Three concurring justices in *Alice Corp v. CLS Bank* would have used a business methods exclusion invalidate the claims. These concurring opinions reflect some of the issues and concerns surrounding patentability of so-called "business methods."

8. *Medical Procedures:* Although many countries prohibit patents on medical and surgical procedures except where they are a necessary component of a patentable device or product, the United States until recently imposed no special limitations on the patentability of such inventions. Thus, for example, patents have issued for the use of ultrasound (as opposed to the ultrasound apparatus itself) to determine the gender of a fetus by visualizing its genital structure, and for the use of a frown-shaped incision for a particular operation. Patents may even be granted for emergency medical procedures. In 1996, Congress added subsection (c) to section 287, denying holders of patents on medical and surgical procedures the right to sue medical practitioners for the unauthorized use of those procedures in medical activities. A competing bill would have made process patents unavailable for certain medical procedures, but while the American Medical Association supported this proposal, the bill failed in the face of strong opposition, most notably that of the PTO and the pharmaceutical and biotech industries.

Should patent protection be unavailable, or more limited in scope, for certain lifesaving or medically significant inventions? Should the answer be different for products (such as new vaccines, medicines, chemotherapy drugs, stents, artificial joints, or other medical devices) than for processes (such as surgical procedures, radiation treatment methods, or the like)? Is section 287(c) an appropriate compromise?

c. The Utility Requirement

The following excerpt from a 1966 decision of the Supreme Court continues to guide the PTO and courts today. As you read, consider the trade-offs of granting exclusivity to an invention at a stage of development when it is believed to be promising but before it has been made "useful" within the meaning of the term under section 101.

BRENNER V. MANSON

383 U.S. 519, 86 S.Ct. 1033 (1966).

MR. JUSTICE FORTAS delivered the opinion of the Court.

* * *

[The Patent Office rejected Manson's patent application for a chemical process that produces certain known steroids, basing its rejection on Manson's failure "to disclose any utility for" the steroids as required by 35 U.S.C. § 101, even though Manson had established that a closely related steroid had tumor-inhibiting effects in mice. The Board of Appeals affirmed the rejection and stated that "the statutory requirement of usefulness of a product cannot be presumed merely because it happens to be closely related to another compound which is known to be useful." The Court of Customs and Patent Appeals (CCPA) reversed, holding that "where a claimed process produces a known product it is not necessary to show utility for the product," so long as the product is not "detrimental to the public interest." The government appealed the CCPA's decision.]

* * *

It is not remarkable that differences arise as to how the test of usefulness is to be applied to chemical processes. Even if we knew precisely what Congress meant in 1790 when it devised the "new and useful" phraseology and in subsequent re-enactments of the test, we should have difficulty in applying it in the context of contemporary chemistry where research is as comprehensive as man's grasp and where little or nothing is wholly beyond the pale of "utility"—if that word is given its broadest reach.

Respondent does not—at least in the first instance—rest upon the extreme proposition, advanced by the court below, that a novel chemical process is patentable so long as it yields the intended product and so long as the product is not itself "detrimental." Nor does he commit the outcome of his claim to the slightly more conventional proposition that any process is "useful" within the meaning of § 101 if it produces a compound whose potential usefulness is under investigation by serious scientific researchers, although he urges this position, too, as an alternative basis for affirming the decision of the CCPA. Rather, he begins with the much more orthodox argument that * * * an adjacent homologue of the steroid yielded by his process has been demonstrated to have tumor-inhibiting effects in mice, and that this discloses the requisite utility. We do not accept any of these theories as an adequate basis for overriding the determination of the Patent Office that the "utility" requirement has not been met.

Even on the assumption that the process would be patentable were respondent to show that the steroid produced had a tumor-inhibiting effect in mice,[17] we would not overrule the Patent Office finding that respondent has not made such a showing. The Patent Office held that, despite the reference to the adjacent homologue, respondent's papers did not disclose

[17] In light of our disposition of the case, we express no view as to the patentability of a process whose sole demonstrated utility is to yield a product shown to inhibit the growth of tumors in laboratory animals. * * *

a sufficient likelihood that the steroid yielded by his process would have similar tumor-inhibiting characteristics. * * *

The second and third points of respondent's argument present issues of much importance. Is a chemical process "useful" within the meaning of § 101 either (1) because it works—*i.e.,* produces the intended product? or (2) because the compound yielded belongs to a class of compounds now the subject of serious scientific investigation? These contentions present the basic problem for our adjudication. Since we find no specific assistance in the legislative materials underlying § 101, we are remitted to an analysis of the problem in light of the general intent of Congress, the purposes of the patent system, and the implications of a decision one way or the other.

In support of his plea that we attenuate the requirement of "utility," respondent relies upon Justice Story's well-known statement that a "useful" invention is one "which may be applied to a beneficial use in society, in contradistinction to an invention injurious to the morals, health, or good order of society, or frivolous and insignificant"[20]—and upon the assertion that to do so would encourage inventors of new processes to publicize the event for the benefit of the entire scientific community, thus widening the search for uses and increasing the fund of scientific knowledge. Justice Story's language sheds little light on our subject. Narrowly read, it does no more than compel us to decide whether the invention in question is "frivolous and insignificant"—a query no easier of application than the one built into the statute. Read more broadly, so as to allow the patenting of any invention not positively harmful to society, it places such a special meaning on the word "useful" that we cannot accept it in the absence of evidence that Congress so intended. There are, after all, many things in this world which may not be considered "useful" but which, nevertheless, are totally without a capacity for harm.

It is true, of course, that one of the purposes of the patent system is to encourage dissemination of information concerning discoveries and inventions. And it may be that inability to patent a process to some extent discourages disclosure and leads to greater secrecy than would otherwise be the case. The inventor of the process, or the corporate organization by which he is employed, has some incentive to keep the invention secret while uses for the product are searched out. However, in light of the highly developed art of drafting patent claims so that they disclose as little useful information as possible—while broadening the scope of the claim as widely as possible—the argument based upon the virtue of disclosure must be warily evaluated. Moreover, the pressure for secrecy is easily exaggerated, for if the inventor of a process cannot himself ascertain a "use" for that which his process yields, he has every incentive to make his invention

[20] Note on the Patent Laws, 3 Wheat. App. 13, 24. *See also* Justice Story's decisions on circuit in *Lowell v. Lewis,* 15 Fed.Cas. 1018 (No. 8568) (C.C.D.Mass.), and *Bedford v. Hunt,* 3 Fed.Cas. 37 (No. 1217) (C.C.D.Mass.).

known to those able to do so. Finally, how likely is disclosure of a patented process to spur research by others into the uses to which the product may be put? To the extent that the patentee has power to enforce his patent, there is little incentive for others to undertake a search for uses.

Whatever weight is attached to the value of encouraging disclosure and of inhibiting secrecy, we believe a more compelling consideration is that a process patent in the chemical field, which has not been developed and pointed to the degree of specific utility, creates a monopoly of knowledge which should be granted only if clearly commanded by the statute. Until the process claim has been reduced to production of a product shown to be useful, the metes and bounds of that monopoly are not capable of precise delineation. It may engross a vast, unknown, and perhaps unknowable area. Such a patent may confer power to block off whole areas of scientific development, without compensating benefit to the public. The basic quid pro quo contemplated by the Constitution and the Congress for granting a patent monopoly is the benefit derived by the public from an invention with substantial utility. Unless and until a process is refined and developed to this point—where specific benefit exists in currently available form—there is insufficient justification for permitting an applicant to engross what may prove to be a broad field.

These arguments for and against the patentability of a process which either has no known use or is useful only in the sense that it may be an object of scientific research would apply equally to the patenting of the product produced by the process. * * * We find absolutely no warrant for the proposition that although Congress intended that no patent be granted on a chemical compound whose sole "utility" consists of its potential role as an object of use-testing, a different set of rules was meant to apply to the process which yielded the unpatentable product. * * *

This is not to say that we mean to disparage the importance of contributions to the fund of scientific information short of the invention of something "useful," or that we are blind to the prospect that what now seems without "use" may tomorrow command the grateful attention of the public. But a patent is not a hunting license. It is not a reward for the search, but compensation for its successful conclusion. "[A] patent system must be related to the world of commerce rather than to the realm of philosophy. * * * "

NOTES

1. *Patenting Versus Secrecy:* Evaluate the Supreme Court's response to the disclosure argument in *Brenner v. Manson*. Is it persuasive? What might be the impact of the court's standard of utility on pharmaceutical or biotechnological research?

2. *Utility and Reduction to Practice:* Where an invention has actually been reduced to practice (that is, constructed and made to function in the intended manner), utility is determined by the effects of that reduction to practice. Where there is only a constructive reduction to practice (that is, a complete patent application), utility is determined by the disclosures of the patent. *See Yasuko Kawai v. Metlesics*, 480 F.2d 880 (C.C.P.A. 1973).

3. *Utility Before Final Testing:* In *In re Brana*, 51 F.3d 1560 (Fed.Cir.1995), the Federal Circuit held that the utility of a drug intended for humans could be adequately demonstrated by animal testing, even if human testing was a prerequisite for approval by the Food and Drug Administration. The court reaffirmed the view asserted by its predecessor court:

> [O]ne who has taught the public that a compound exhibits some desirable pharmaceutical property in a standard experimental animal has made a significant and useful contribution to the art, even though it may eventually appear that the compound is without value in the treatment [of] humans.

51 F.3d at 1567 (citing *In re Krimmel*, 292 F.2d 948, 953 (C.C.P.A. 1961)). The Federal Circuit added:

> Usefulness in patent law, and in particular in the context of pharmaceutical inventions, necessarily includes the expectation of further research and development. The stage at which an invention in this field becomes useful is well before it is ready to be administered to humans. Were we to require [human] testing in order to prove utility, the associated costs would prevent many companies from obtaining patent protection on promising new inventions, thereby eliminating an incentive to pursue, through research and development, potential cures in many crucial areas such as the treatment of cancer.

51 F.3d at 1568. These and other principles are reflected in the Manual of Patent Examining Procedure's [MPEP] explanation of the utility requirement in § 2107.01:

> [C]ourts have found utility for therapeutic inventions despite the fact that an applicant is at a very early stage in the development of a pharmaceutical product or therapeutic regimen based on a claimed pharmacological or bioactive compound or composition. The Federal Circuit, in *Cross v. Iizuka*, 753 F.2d 1040, 1051 (Fed. Cir. 1985), commented on the significance of data from *in vitro* testing that showed pharmacological activity:
>
> > We perceive no insurmountable difficulty, under appropriate circumstances, in finding that the first link in the screening chain, *in vitro* testing, may establish a practical utility for the compound in question. Successful *in vitro* testing will marshal resources and direct the expenditure of effort to further *in vivo* testing of the most potent compounds, thereby providing an

> immediate benefit to the public, analogous to the benefit provided by the showing of an *in vivo* utility.
>
> The Federal Circuit has reiterated that therapeutic utility sufficient under the patent laws is not to be confused with the requirements of the FDA with regard to safety and efficacy of drugs to [be] marketed in the United States. * * * Accordingly, Office personnel should not construe 35 U.S.C. 101, under the logic of "practical" utility or otherwise, to require that an applicant demonstrate that a therapeutic agent based on a claimed invention is a safe or fully effective drug for humans.

U.S. PATENT & TRADEMARK OFFICE, MANUAL OF PATENT EXAMINING PROCEDURE § 2107.01 (9th ed. 2019, rev. June 2020) (citations omitted).

4. *"Specific and Substantial" Utility:* In *In re Fisher*, 421 F.3d 1365 (Fed. Cir. 2005), the Federal Circuit affirmed the rejection of claims for failure to meet the utility requirement, holding that a "substantial" utility is "practical" and "real world" utility providing an immediate benefit to the public. Inventions that may prove useful in the future do not meet the "substantial" utility requirement. The "specific" utility requirement means that the use must not be "so vague as to be meaningless"; the claimed invention must be capable of being used to provide a well-defined and particular benefit to the public. According to the Federal Circuit, a "specific utility is particular to the subject matter claimed and would not be applicable to a broad class of invention."

The Federal Circuit applied the "specific and substantial" utility requirement to an applicant's claimed invention of five particular expressed sequence tags, or ESTs, which are short sequences of nucleotides (adenine, guanine, cytosine, and thymine, the building blocks of DNA) created by isolating and sequencing a small portion of a synthetically produced DNA. The applicant had sequenced the ESTs, which correspond to existing genes, by studying particular tissue of the maize plant. The applicant did not know, however, the precise structure or function of either the genes or the proteins encoded for by those genes. The applicant asserted that the claimed ESTs showed utility because they could be used in a variety of ways: (1) serving as a molecular marker for mapping the entire maize genome, (2) measuring the level of mRNA in a tissue sample to provide information about gene expression; and (3) several other uses, all of which relate to using ESTs to learn more about the genetic makeup of, or to manipulate protein expression within maize and other plants or animal tissue samples.

> Regarding the seven uses asserted by Fisher, we observe that each claimed EST uniquely corresponds to the single gene from which it was transcribed ("underlying gene"). As of the filing date of the '643 application, Fisher admits that the underlying genes have no known functions. Fisher, nevertheless, claims that this fact is irrelevant because the seven asserted uses are not related to the functions of the underlying genes. We are not convinced by this contention. Essentially, the claimed ESTs act as no more than research

> intermediates that may help scientists to isolate the particular underlying protein-encoding genes and conduct further experimentation on those genes. The overall goal of such experimentation is presumably to understand the maize genome * * *. Accordingly, the claimed ESTs are, in words of the Supreme Court, mere "objects of use-testing," to wit, objects upon which scientific research could be performed with no assurance that anything useful will be discovered in the end. *Brenner,* 383 U.S. at 535.
>
> * * *
>
> * * * Here, granting a patent to Fisher for its five claimed ESTs would amount to a hunting license because the claimed ESTs can be used only to gain further information about the underlying genes and the proteins encoded for by those genes. The claimed ESTs themselves are not an end of Fisher's research effort, but only tools to be used along the way in the search for a practical utility. Thus, while Fisher's claimed ESTs may add a noteworthy contribution to biotechnology research, our precedent dictates that the '643 application does not meet the utility requirement of § 101 because Fisher does not identify the function for the underlying protein-encoding genes. Absent such identification, we hold that the claimed ESTs have not been researched and understood to the point of providing an immediate, well-defined, real world benefit to the public meriting the grant of a patent.

421 F.3d at 1373–76.

5. *Operability:* If the claimed invention is inoperable—because it does not work as claimed—then it is not "useful" and is unpatentable under section 101. Cases of invalidity based on inoperability are fact-specific and rare. Consider the explanation in the PTO's Manual of Patent Examining Procedure:

> [A]s the Federal Circuit has stated, "[t]o violate [35 U.S.C.] 101 the claimed device must be <u>totally incapable of achieving a useful result</u>." If an invention is only partially successful in achieving a useful result, a rejection of the claimed invention as a whole based on a lack of utility is not appropriate.
>
> Situations where an invention is found to be "inoperative" and therefore lacking in utility are rare, and rejections maintained solely on this ground by a federal court even rarer. * * * [T]he underlying finding by the court in these cases was that, <u>based on the factual record of the case</u>, it was clear that the invention could not and did not work as the inventor claimed it did. * * * Examples of such cases include: an invention asserted to change the taste of food using a magnetic field, a perpetual motion machine, a flying machine operating on "flapping or flutter function", a "cold fusion" process for producing energy, a method for increasing the energy output of fossil

> fuels upon combustion through exposure to a magnetic field, uncharacterized compositions for curing a wide array of cancers, and a method of controlling the aging process.

U.S. PATENT & TRADEMARK OFFICE, MANUAL OF PATENT EXAMINING PROCEDURE § 2107.01 (9th ed. 2019, rev. June 2020) (citations omitted).

The fairly low bar set for utility in section 101 is exemplified by Justice Story's formulation in *Bedford v. Hunt,* 3 Fed.Cas. 37, 37 (No. 1217) (C.C.D.Mass.1817). Consider the following while knowing in advance its characterization with respect to "sound morals" has been modified over the years, as explained in the case below.

> By useful invention, in the statute, is meant such a one as may be applied to some beneficial use in society, in contradistinction to an invention, which is injurious to the morals, the health, or the good order of society. * * * The law, however, does not look to the degree of utility; it simply requires, that it shall be capable of use, and that the use is such as sound morals and policy do not discountenance or prohibit. * * *

See also Lowell v. Lewis, 15 Fed.Cas. 1018 (No. 8568) (C.C.D.Mass.1817) (rejecting the argument that, for a pump to be patentable, "it must be, for the public, a better pump than the common pump").

Does *Brenner v. Manson* impose limits on Justice Story's broad standard for utility? Does Story's view permit patents on impractical or inefficient inventions? Does *Brenner v. Manson* do so? Should it?

JUICY WHIP, INC. V. ORANGE BANG, INC.

185 F.3d 1364 (Fed. Cir. 1999).

BRYSON, CIRCUIT JUDGE.

[The claimed invention was a "post-mix beverage dispenser" designed to look like a "pre-mix beverage dispenser." In a post-mix dispenser, syrup and water are mixed together immediately before the beverage is dispensed. In a pre-mix dispenser, a mixture of beverage syrup and water is both displayed and dispensed, with the visual display of beverage thought to stimulate impulse buying. The drawback of a pre-mix dispenser is that the display (and thus the dispenser) has limited capacity and greater possibility of bacterial or other contamination, compared to a post-mix dispenser. The claimed invention contained a transparent bowl filled with a fluid that looked like the beverage being sold but was resistant to bacterial growth. The claimed invention made it seem that the liquid being displayed was the principal source of the dispensed beverage, although in fact the beverage was mixed immediately before it was dispensed, as in conventional post-mix dispensers.]

The [district] court concluded that the invention lacked utility because its purpose was to increase sales by deception, *i.e.*, through imitation of another product. The court explained that the purpose of the invention "is to create an illusion, whereby customers believe that the fluid contained in the bowl is the actual beverage that they are receiving, when of course it is not." * * *

Section 101 of the Patent Act of 1952, 35 U.S.C. § 101, provides that "[w]hoever invents or discovers any new and useful process, machine, manufacture, or composition of matter, or any new and useful improvement thereof," may obtain a patent on the invention or discovery. The threshold of utility is not high: An invention is "useful" under section 101 if it is capable of providing some identifiable benefit.

To be sure, since Justice Story's opinion in *Lowell v. Lewis,* 15 F. Cas. 1018 (C.C.D.Mass.1817), it has been stated that inventions that are "injurious to the well-being, good policy, or sound morals of society" are unpatentable. As examples of such inventions, Justice Story listed "a new invention to poison people, or to promote debauchery, or to facilitate private assassination." Courts have continued to recite Justice Story's formulation, but the principle that inventions are invalid if they are principally designed to serve immoral or illegal purposes has not been applied broadly in recent years. For example, years ago courts invalidated patents on gambling devices on the ground that they were immoral, but that is no longer the law.

* * *

It is not at all unusual for a product to be designed to appear to viewers to be something it is not. For example, cubic zirconium is designed to simulate a diamond, imitation gold leaf is designed to imitate real gold leaf, synthetic fabrics are designed to simulate expensive natural fabrics, and imitation leather is designed to look like real leather. In each case, the invention of the product or process that makes such imitation possible has "utility" within the meaning of the patent statute, and indeed there are numerous patents directed toward making one product imitate another. *See, e.g.,* U.S. Pat. No. 5,762,968 (method for producing imitation grill marks on food without using heat); U.S. Pat. No. 5,899,038 (laminated flooring imitating wood); U.S. Pat. No. 5,571,545 (imitation hamburger). Much of the value of such products resides in the fact that they appear to be something they are not. Thus, in this case the claimed post-mix dispenser meets the statutory requirement of utility by embodying the features of a post-mix dispenser while imitating the visual appearance of a pre-mix dispenser.

* * * The requirement of "utility" in patent law is not a directive to the Patent and Trademark Office or the courts to serve as arbiters of deceptive trade practices. Other agencies, such as the Federal Trade Commission and the Food and Drug Administration, are assigned the task of protecting consumers from fraud and deception in the sale of food products. *Cf. In re Watson,* 517 F.2d 465, 474–76 (C.C.P.A. 1975) (stating that it is not the province of the Patent Office to determine, under section 101, whether drugs are safe). * * *

Of course, Congress is free to declare particular types of inventions unpatentable for a variety of reasons, including deceptiveness. *Cf.* 42 U.S.C. § 2181(a) (exempting from patent protection inventions useful solely in connection with special nuclear material or atomic weapons). Until such time as Congress does so, however, we find no basis in section 101 to hold that inventions can be ruled unpatentable for lack of utility simply because they have the capacity to fool some members of the public. * * *

NOTES

1. *Utility's Low Bar—in General:* As noted before the case excerpt from *Juicy Whip v. Orange Bang,* the older characterizations of utility as connected to "sound morals" have changed over time, although the general idea of merely requiring "some beneficial use" without regard to "degree of utility" remains. Is this the right path for patent policy?

2. *Utility's Low Bar—Applied:* Is the utility requirement satisfied where an invention (a) performs some, but not all, of the useful functions that the patent specification asserts that it performs? (b) is a toy or game? (c) is useful for causing injury?

2. DESIGN PATENT SUBJECT MATTER

Statute: 35 U.S.C. § 171

Under § 171 of the Patent Act:

> Whoever invents any new, original and ornamental design for an article of manufacture may obtain a patent therefor, subject to the conditions and requirements of this title.

As explained in the following excerpts, the purpose of design patents is simply to encourage manufacturers to give a pleasing appearance to articles of manufacture: this is a "meritorious service" to us, the purchasing public.

> The acts of Congress which authorize the grant of patents for designs were plainly intended to give encouragement to the decorative arts. They contemplate not so much utility as appearance, and that, not an abstract impression, or picture, but an aspect given to those objects mentioned in the acts. It is a new

> and original design for a manufacture, whether of metal or other material; * * * a new and useful pattern, print, or picture, to be either worked into, or on, any article of manufacture; or a new and original shape or configuration of any article of manufacture—it is one or all of these that the law has in view. And the thing invented or produced, for which a patent is given, is that which gives a peculiar or distinctive appearance to the manufacture, or article to which it may be applied, or to which it gives form. The law manifestly contemplates that giving certain new and original appearances to a manufactured article may enhance its salable value, may enlarge the demand for it, and may be a meritorious service to the public. It therefore proposes to secure for a limited time to the ingenious producer of those appearances the advantages flowing from them.

Gorham Mfg. Co. v. White, 81 U.S. (14 Wall.) 511 (1871).

Design patents are quite different from utility patents in that they may not claim "useful" features as such. Because design patents claim the "ornamental design for an article of manufacture," the subject matter of design patents may overlap with the protection provided by other intellectual property laws (as illustrated in the *Yardley* excerpt below).

APPLICATION OF RICHARD Q. YARDLEY

493 F.2d 1389 (C.C.P.A. 1974).

LANE, JUDGE.

[Yardley appealed from the PTO Board of Appeals' decision rejecting his claim for an ornamental design for a watch face. The design comprised a watch face depicting a caricatured figure whose extended arms and hands serve as the watch's hour and minute hands. The basis for the rejection was estoppel in view of prior copyright registrations for the design. The Board took the position that copyright and design patent protection could not be obtained for the same subject matter.]

* * *

Under the power granted to the Congress in Art. I, § 8, cl. 8 of the Constitution, the Congress has enacted the copyright statute as Title 17, United States Code, and the patent statute as Title 35, United States Code. In the two statutes, the Congress has created an area of overlap with regard to at least one type of subject matter.

Thus, the Congress has provided that subject matter of the type involved in the instant appeal is "statutory subject matter" under the copyright statute and "statutory subject matter" under the design patent statute. The statutory language clearly shows the intent of Congress.

* * *

The Supreme Court has recognized that an area of overlapping "statutory subject matter" exists between copyrights and design patents. In *Mazer v. Stein*, 347 U.S. 201, 217 (1954), the Court stated:

> * * * We do hold that the patentability of the statuettes, fitted as lamps or unfitted, does not bar copyright as works of art. Neither the Copyright Statute nor any other says that because a thing is patentable it may not be copyrighted. We should not so hold.

* * *

The existence of an area of overlap was accepted by the examiner and the board. Nevertheless, both held that an author-inventor must elect between securing a copyright or securing a design patent. We disagree.

We believe that the "election of protection" doctrine is in direct conflict with the clear intent of Congress manifested in the two statutory provisions quoted above. The Congress has provided that subject matter of the type involved in this appeal is "statutory subject matter" under the copyright statute and is "statutory subject matter" under the design patent statute, but the Congress has not provided that an author-inventor must elect between securing a copyright or securing a design patent. Therefore, we conclude that it would be contrary to the intent of Congress to hold that an author-inventor must elect between the two available modes of securing exclusive rights.

* * *

[One of the rationales advanced by the Board in affirming the examiner's rejection was] that "[the] framers of the Constitution presumably recognized the difference between the endeavors of authors and inventors, because they used the word 'respective' in reference to their 'writings and discoveries.' "

We agree with the board's view that the framers of the Constitution recognized a distinction between "authors" and "inventors" and "writings" and "discoveries." But, we do not think that the constitutional provision requires an election. The Congress, through its legislation under the authority of the Constitution, has interpreted the Constitution as authorizing an area of overlap where a certain type of creation may be the subject matter of a copyright and the subject matter of a design patent. We see nothing in that legislation which is contradictory and repugnant to the intent of the framers of the Constitution. Congress has not required an author-inventor to elect between the two modes which it has provided for securing exclusive rights on the type of subject matter here involved. If anything, the concurrent availability of both modes of securing exclusive rights aids in achieving the stated purpose of the constitutional provision.

* * *

NOTE

Design patent subject matter may also overlap with trade dress protection if the ornamental design in question serves a source-identifying function and satisfies other requirements.

a. "Design for an Article of Manufacture"

Although the design patent statutes do not define "design," the PTO employs the following definition:

> In a design patent application, the subject matter which is claimed is the design embodied in or applied to an article of manufacture (or portion thereof) and not the article itself. *Ex parte Cady*, 1916 C.D. 62, 232 O.G. 621 (Comm'r Pat. 1916). "[35 U.S.C.] 171 refers, not to the design of an article, but to the design for an article, and is inclusive of ornamental designs of all kinds including surface ornamentation as well as configuration of goods." *In re Zahn*, 617 F.2d 261 (C.C.P.A. 1980).
>
> The design for an article consists of the visual characteristics embodied in or applied to an article.
>
> Since a design is manifested in appearance, the subject matter of a design patent application may relate to the configuration or shape of an article, to the surface ornamentation applied to an article, or to the combination of configuration and surface ornamentation.
>
> Design is inseparable from the article to which it is applied and cannot exist alone merely as a scheme of surface ornamentation. It must be a definite, preconceived thing, capable of reproduction and not merely the chance result of a method.

U.S. Patent & Trademark Office, MANUAL OF PATENT EXAMINING PROCEDURE § 1502 (9th ed. 2019, rev. June 2020). The term "article of manufacture," also undefined in the statutes, has been broadly construed at times. *See, e.g.*, *In re Hruby*, 373 F.2d 997 (C.C.P.A. 1967) (reversing PTO's rejection of design patent application for fountain; although design was "a fleeting product of nozzle arrangements," and thus observable only when the water was flowing, "a manufacture is anything made 'by the hands of man' from raw materials, whether literally by hand or by machinery or by art.").

b. The Ornamentality Requirement

As the cases below will further explain, for design patents the requirement of ornamentality replaces that of utility. The term "ornamental" in Section 171 has been construed to require not only that ornamentation be the primary purpose of the design, but also that the design have an aesthetically pleasing effect. *See Bonito Boats, Inc. v. Thunder Craft Boats, Inc.*, 489 U.S. 141, 148 (1989) (ornamental design "must present an aesthetically pleasing appearance that is not dictated by function alone").

AVIA GROUP INTERNATIONAL, INC. V. L.A. GEAR CALIFORNIA, INC.

853 F.2d 1557 (Fed. Cir. 1988).[4]

NIES, CIRCUIT JUDGE.

L.A. Gear California, Inc. (LAG) appeals the decision of the United States District Court for the Central District of California, *Pensa, Inc. v. L.A. Gear of California, Inc.*, 4 USPQ2d 1016 (C.D.Cal.1987), granting the motion of Avia Group International, Inc. (formerly Pensa, Inc.) for summary judgment holding United States Design Patent Nos. 284,420 ('420) and 287,301 ('301) valid as between the parties and willfully infringed, and the case exceptional under 35 U.S.C. § 285 (1982). We affirm.

I
BACKGROUND

Avia owns the '420 patent, claiming an ornamental design for an athletic shoe outer sole, and the '301 patent, claiming an ornamental design for an athletic shoe upper, by assignment from the inventor, James Tong. * * * Avia filed suit against LAG alleging, inter alia, that both of LAG's models infringed its '420 design patent and that LAG's Hi-Top model also infringed the '301 design. LAG counterclaimed for a declaratory judgment that the two patents were not infringed and were invalid because the designs were both obvious and functional. Avia moved for partial summary judgment on the patent validity and infringement issues and for attorney fees.

Finding no bona fide dispute as to any material fact and that Avia had shown entitlement to judgment as a matter of law, the court granted Avia's motion after a hearing. * * *

* * *

III
VALIDITY OF '420 AND '301 DESIGN PATENTS

* * *

[4] This case was abrogated on the grounds not related to the excerpt above by *Egyptian Goddess, Inc. v. Swisa, Inc.*, 543 F. 3d 665 (Fed. Cir. 2008), excerpted *infra* page 624.

The patents in suit are design patents. Under 35 U.S.C. § 171 (1982), a patent may be obtained on the design of an article of manufacture which is "new, original and ornamental" and "nonobvious" within the meaning of section 103, which is incorporated by reference into section 171. LAG attacks the validity of the patents for the subject designs covering parts of shoes on the grounds (1) that the designs are primarily functional rather than ornamental and (2) that the designs would have been obvious from the prior art.

A. *Ornamental versus Functional Designs*

* * *

LAG correctly asserts that if a patented design is "primarily functional," rather than primarily ornamental, the patent is invalid. When function dictates a design, protection would not promote the decorative arts, a purpose of the design patent statute. There is no dispute that shoes are functional and that certain features of the shoe designs in issue perform functions. However, a distinction exists between the functionality of an article or features thereof and the functionality of the particular design of such article or features thereof that perform a function. Were that not true, it would not be possible to obtain a design patent on a utilitarian article of manufacture, *see, e.g., Pacific Furniture Mfg. Co. v. Preview Furniture Corp.*, 800 F.2d 1111 (Fed.Cir.1986) (design patent for chairs), or to obtain both design and utility patents on the same article, *see, e.g., Carman Indus., Inc. v. Wahl*, 724 F.2d 932, 938–39 (Fed.Cir.1983); *In re Dubois & Will*, 262 F.2d 88, 90 (C.C.P.A. 1958).

With respect to functionality of the design of the '301 patent, the court stated:

> [LAG] has taken each little aspect of the upper and pointed out that many of the aspects or features of the upper have a function. Even if, arguendo, true[,] that would not make the design primarily functional. If the functional aspect or purpose could be accomplished in many other ways that [sic] is involved in this very design, that fact is enough to destroy the claim that this design is primarily functional. There are many things in the ['301] patent on the upper which are clearly ornamental and nonfunctional such as the location of perforations and how they are arranged, and the stitching and how it's arranged, and the coloration of elements between black and white colors.
>
> The overall aesthetics of the various components and the way they are combined are quite important and are not functional. They are purely aesthetic. . . .

Pensa, Inc., 4 USPQ2d at 1019.

On the design of the '420 patent, the court made a similar analysis of various features and concluded:

> But every function which [LAG] says is achieved by one of the component aspects of the sole in this case could be and has been achieved by different components. And that is a very persuasive rationale for the holding that the design overall is not primarily functional. Moreover, there is no function which even defendant assigns to the swirl effect around the pivot point, which swirl effect is a very important aspect of the design.
>
> . . . .
>
> . . . [T]his is a unique and pleasing design and [its] patentability in my view is not offset or destroyed by the fact that the utility patent is utilized and incorporated in this aesthetically pleasing design.
>
> Plaintiff has given us evidence of other shoes that incorporate the utility patent and its concavity—others of its own shoes—but with a totally different design, and has thus established that the utility patent does not make the design patent invalid in this case.

Pensa, Inc., 4 USPQ2d at 1019–20. We agree that the designs in suit have not persuasively been shown to be functional and that no genuine issue of material fact is present with respect to this issue. [The court also rejected the argument that Avia's patents were invalid on obviousness grounds, finding no genuine issue of material fact or error of law on the part of the district court, and affirmed the district court's opinion.]

* * *

Drawings from the two design patents in *Avia Group* are shown below:

The '420 patent:

The '301 patent:

IN RE CARLETTI

328 F.2d 1020 (C.C.P.A. 1964).

RICH, JUDGE.

This appeal is from the decision of the Patent Office Board of Appeals affirming the rejection of the claim in an application for a design patent, serial No. 56,122, filed May 28, 1959, for "GASKET."

* * *

One of the examiner's principal grounds of rejection was that the differences between appellants' gasket and the prior art, to which differences we must look in deciding whether patentable invention exists, are *dictated by functional requirements*, "i.e., to make the article fit the place where it is to be used and to increase the functional utility thereof rather than to appeal to the esthetic sense." * * * The board affirmed this rejection saying:

> The instant design *differs* from the [prior art] * * * essentially by the plurality of concentric annular ribs and by the recessed groove. These features, however, are added to the Somerville citation [disclosure] essentially for *purely functional purposes*, the ribs to effect better sealing action and the groove primarily to prevent a fileting action in the mold. It has been held in Court decisions including *Connecticut Paper Products Co. v. New York Paper Co.*, 127 F.(2d) 423, 53 USPQ 271, that the addition of features placed upon an old design for *purely functional purposes* does not ordinarily render a design patentable. [Emphasis added.]

* * *

It is thus seen that the *functionality* of the elements asserted to *distinguish* the design from the prior art—as distinguished from the obviousness of those features—was a ground, if not a principal ground, of rejection. The Patent Office Solicitor's brief takes the same position.

While it cannot be said that the Patent Office has made out an ironclad case of the functionality of the features relied on for patentability, more than a good case has been made out and the appellants have failed to refute it. In the first place we have in the record the military specification covering this gasket, MIL–P–40068, 9 June 1959, containing engineering drawings in great detail, specifying the exact position, dimensions, and tolerances of the grooves and ribs etc., without the slightest suggestion that they serve in any way as ornamentation. In the second place, appellants' brief says:

> The design was created at the U.S. Army Quartermaster Research and Engineering Center, Natick, Massachusetts, in the course of appellants' employment by the Government of the United States as technologists. Its intended use is as a component of a closure assembly for containers, such as gasoline drums.

The record further shows such drums to be the common 55 gal. drums and the gasket to be for the threaded plug which closes the bung hole therein.

It seems naive in the extreme to believe that anyone would try to "ornament" the rubber gasket on the under side of the bung cap for a gasoline drum, notwithstanding the seriocomic legal arguments presented by counsel for the Department of the Army. Common sense and but a slight familiarity with the requirements of gaskets both point to the obvious functionality of the groove and ribs on the gasket. In a letter to the Commissioner of Patents in this application on August 1, 1960, appellants' counsel said:

> [T]he current design resulted from a development program which was inaugurated more than a year prior to publication of MIL–P–40068. Numerous gaskets were *designed* and subjected to *severe testing* under all service conditions including tropical and arctic. Only a device which passes all tests and experiments is finally standardized in a procurement specification. [Emphasis added.]

The gasket at bar was standardized in a specification. This does not bespeak the existence of design in anything other than the sense of engineering "design," and certainly contraindicates the existence of the "ornamental design" referred to in 35 U.S.C. § 171 under which a patent is here sought.

It is clear that appellants never invented an "ornamental design." The appearance of appellants' gasket seems as much dictated by functional considerations as is the appearance of a piece of rope, which, too, has ribs and grooves nicely arranged. The fact that it is attractive or pleasant to behold is not enough. Many well-constructed articles of manufacture whose configurations are dictated solely by function are pleasing to look upon, for example a hex-nut, a ball bearing, a golf club, or a fishing rod, the pleasure depending largely on one's interests. But it has long been settled that when a configuration is the result of functional considerations only, the resulting design is not patentable as an ornamental design for the simple reason that it is not "ornamental"—was not created for the purpose of ornamenting. [T]his court has said:

> It is true * * * that a design may embody functional features and still be patentable, but in order to attain this legal status under these circumstances, the design *must have an unobvious appearance, distinct from that dictated solely by functional considerations*. [Emphasis added.]

That is the principle which is believed to apply here.

Neither does it suffice to argue, as appellants do, that the ribs and grooves *could* have been less gracefully arranged than they are in their actual "balanced relationship." If obviousness enters into this case, it is at this point. If it is desired to employ a groove for flexibility and three concentric ribs to make a good seal on a flat drum head, what is more obvious than to arrange them with approximately equal spacing, as was done? But it was done without thought of ornament. The creation or origination of an ornamental design does not reside in the mere *avoidance* of dissymmetry.

For the foregoing reasons the decision is affirmed.

NOTES

1. *Alternative Designs and Ornamentality:* According to the Federal Circuit, the existence of alternative designs is an important factor, but not the sole factor, in determining whether a particular design is primarily ornamental:

> The presence of alternative designs may or may not assist in determining whether the challenged design can overcome a functionality challenge. Consideration of alternative designs, if present, is a useful tool that may allow a court to conclude that a challenged design is not invalid for functionality. As such, alternative designs join the list of other appropriate considerations for assessing whether the patented design as a whole—its overall appearance—was dictated by functional considerations. Other appropriate considerations might include: whether the protected design represents the best design; whether alternative designs would adversely affect the utility of the specified article; whether there are any concomitant utility patents; whether the advertising touts particular features of the design as having specific utility; and whether there are any elements in the design or an overall appearance clearly not dictated by function.

Berry Sterling Corp. v. Prescor Plastics, Inc., 122 F.3d 1452, 1456 (Fed. Cir. 1997).

2. *Aesthetically Pleasing Designs:* Under the ornamentality standard, an aesthetically poor design, no matter how original or creative, will be ineligible for design patent protection, although it may be copyrightable (*see infra* Chapter 14.A. & C.4.) and/or protectible under trademark and unfair competition law if it acquires secondary meaning (*see supra* Chapter 2.C. & E.). Not surprisingly, courts examining the validity of design patents display considerable variation in their aesthetic judgments. Does the standard requiring "aesthetic appeal" or "appeal[ing] to the eye as a thing of beauty," *see Bentley v. Sunset House Distrib. Corp.*, 359 F.2d 140, 145 (9th Cir.1966) represent sound policy? Is it appropriate to ask the PTO and the courts to make these judgments? For example, if a court finds that a design is non-functional, but also aesthetically unappealing, is it appropriate to deny design patent protection?

3. *Questions:* Should design patent protection be available for a decorative design (a) on the outer surface of a mattress? (b) on an artificial hip joint designed to be surgically implanted inside the human body?

3. PLANT PATENT SUBJECT MATTER

Statute: 35 U.S.C. § 161

Under § 161 of the Patent Act, the subject matter scope of plant patents is restricted to asexually reproduced varieties of plants:

> Whoever invents or discovers and asexually reproduces any distinct and new variety of plant, including cultivated sports, mutants, hybrids, and newly found seedlings, other than a tuber propagated plant or a plant found in an uncultivated state, may obtain a patent therefor, subject to the conditions and requirements of this title.

Although this provision expressly precludes protection for plants found in an uncultivated state, it permits the grant of a patent for a plant found in a cultivated state, even if the "inventor" did no more than discover the plant, recognize its patentable characteristics, and asexually reproduce it.

As discussed in Note 2 on page 402, *supra*, inventors of new and nonobvious plants that are useful and can be described in a manner satisfying the written description and enablement requirements of patentability may elect to seek utility protection under section 101 (example: a hybrid seed for corn that produces superior yield or displays other advantageous qualities). Other non-patent, but patent-like protection is available under the Plant Variety Protection Act for certain sexually reproduced, tuber propagated, or asexually reproduced plant varieties.

NOTE: PLANT VARIETY PROTECTION CERTIFICATES

The patent-like protection available for plants under the Plant Variety Protection Act of 1970 (PVPA), 7 U.S.C. § 2321 *et seq.* allows the breeder of "new, . . . distinct, . . . uniform, . . . [and] stable" sexually reproduced, tuber propagated, or asexually reproduced plant varieties to obtain plant variety protection certificates issued by the Department of Agriculture (rather than the PTO). The certificate holder enjoys the exclusive right to market, sell, reproduce, import or export the plant variety, to use it in producing hybrids or different varieties, to tuber propagate it as a step in marketing, to condition the variety for propagation (except for farmers replanting their own holdings), and to stock the variety for any purpose which would be infringing. Under the most recent amendments to the PVPA, the term of protection is 20 years (25 years for trees and vines).

The Supreme Court has compared and contrasted utility patents and protection under the PVPA as follows:

> To be sure, there are differences in the requirements for, and coverage of, utility patents and PVP certificates issued pursuant to the PVPA. These differences, however, do not present irreconcilable conflicts because the requirements for obtaining a utility patent under § 101 are more stringent than those for obtaining a PVP certificate, and the protections afforded by a utility patent are greater than those afforded by a PVP certificate. Thus, there is a parallel relationship between the obligations and the level of protection under each statute.
>
> It is much more difficult to obtain a utility patent for a plant than to obtain a PVP certificate because a utility patentable plant must be new, useful, and nonobvious, 35 U.S.C. §§ 101–103. In addition, to obtain a utility patent, a breeder must describe the plant with sufficient specificity to enable others to "make and use" the invention after the patent term expires. § 112. The disclosure required by the Patent Act is "the *quid pro quo* of the right to exclude." *Kewanee Oil Co. v. Bicron Corp.*, 416 U.S. 470, 484 (1974). The description requirement for plants includes a deposit of biological material, for example, seeds, and mandates that such material be accessible to the public. *See* 37 CFR §§ 1.801–1.809 (2001).
>
> By contrast, a plant variety may receive a PVP certificate without a showing of usefulness or nonobviousness. *See* 7 U.S.C. § 2402(a) (requiring that the variety be only new, distinct, uniform, and stable). Nor does the PVPA require a description and disclosure as extensive as those required under § 101. The PVPA requires a "description of the variety setting forth its distinctiveness, uniformity and stability and a description of the genealogy and breeding procedure, when known." 7 U.S.C. § 2422(2). It also requires a deposit of seed in a public depository, § 2422(4), but neither the statute nor the applicable regulation mandates that such material be accessible

to the general public during the term of the PVP certificate. *See* 7 CFR § 97.6 (2001).

Because of the more stringent requirements, utility patent holders receive greater rights of exclusion than holders of a PVP certificate. Most notably, there are no exemptions for research or saving seed under a utility patent. Additionally, although Congress increased the level of protection under the PVPA in 1994, a PVP certificate still does not grant the full range of protections afforded by a utility patent. For instance, a utility patent on an inbred plant line protects that line as well as all hybrids produced by crossing that inbred with another plant line. Similarly, the PVPA now protects "any variety whose production requires the repeated use of a protected variety." 7 U.S.C. § 2541(c)(3). Thus, one cannot use a protected plant variety to produce a hybrid for commercial sale. PVPA protection still falls short of a utility patent, however, because a breeder can use a plant that is protected by a PVP certificate to "develop" a new inbred line while he cannot use a plant patented under § 101 for such a purpose. *See* 7 U.S.C. § 2541(a)(4) (infringement includes "use [of] the variety in producing (as distinguished from developing) a hybrid or different variety therefrom").

J.E.M. Ag Supply, Inc. v. Pioneer Hi-Bred Int'l, Inc., 534 U.S. 124, 142–43 (2001).

C. NOVELTY

Statutes: 35 U.S.C. § 102 (both pre-AIA and post-AIA)

The novelty material in this chapter first introduces "novelty" and some foundational issues. It then explains the basic landscape of pre-AIA and post-AIA novelty rules and notes areas where the two enjoy significant continuity. It then works through the primary prior art concepts that are shared by pre-AIA and post-AIA section 102. The chapter continues to use primary cases from before the AIA because, as will be further explained, the AIA did not change the meaning of the concepts being interpreted and applied in those cases. This section of the chapter then moves to a brief discussion of new aspects of post-AIA section 102; the novelty material concludes with an exploration of other important issues and rules imbedded in pre-section 102.

1. INTRODUCTION

The novelty requirement of patent law raises a significant obstacle to patentability for all patents, whether utility, design, or plant. An invention is not patentable for lack of novelty unless it differs from each publicly available or commercially exploited product and process, known as "prior art." The inventor's knowledge or awareness of the prior art does not affect novelty. Thus, even if the invention was independently created, it will be unpatentable if the same invention can be found within the prior art.

Some cases use the term "anticipation" in discussing novelty; they note that a novel invention cannot be found within or "anticipated" by the prior art. This "anticipation" must be specific rather than broad or general, no matter which type of patent is at issue; for a utility patent, an individual patent claim avoids anticipation and remains novel unless all claim elements in that claim are present in one pieces of prior art. Novelty is not destroyed if all the prior art taken together contains the claim elements, or if a generalized notion of the invention would appear to be anticipated. "Anticipation under 35 U.S.C. § 102 requires the presence in a *single* prior art disclosure of *each and every element* of a claimed invention." *Lewmar Marine, Inc. v. Barient, Inc.*, 827 F.2d 744, 747 (Fed. Cir.1987) (emphasis added). The test for anticipation—or lack of novelty—is the same as the test for literal infringement: "That which would literally infringe if later in time anticipates if earlier than the [critical date]." *Id.*

Section 102 of the Patent Act gives specific content to the novelty requirement in part by defining the prior art and in part by defining the critical date or dates. The AIA, enacted in September 2011, amended section 102 in its entirety, but it did so only prospectively, for applications filed after March 16, 2013. (One important caveat to the effective date of the changes to section 102 is explained below on pages 485–486 in Chapter 10.C.6.b., *infra*.) We look to pre-AIA section 102 when judging the novelty of a claimed invention in a patent issuing from an application containing only claims with effective filing dates before March 16, 2013.

The issue of novelty can arise more than once in the life of a patent. The novelty of a patent claim is first addressed by the patent examiner during the prosecution of the patent application. It arises again in litigation when an alleged infringer defends itself by arguing that a claim in the infringement suit is invalid for lack of novelty. It may also arise during review and reexamination proceedings conducted within the patent office. Pre-AIA section 102 will continue to govern the validity of patent claims in litigation and other proceedings if it governed their validity during patent prosecution. Because the term of a patent under current law generally extends 20 years from the date of filing (*see infra* Chapter 11.C.), both the pre-AIA and post-AIA versions of section 102 will remain vital for over 20 years after the AIA's passage in 2011.

2. PRE-AIA SECTION 102

Pre-AIA section 102 contains two types of provisions. One type deals with the novelty of the invention on the date of its invention by the patent applicant. The other type asks whether the invention is still novel as of the date of filing of the application, or whether instead the applicant waited "too long" to file the application such that it is barred by the statute. Taken together, they mean that an invention must be *both* novel as of the date of invention *and* not subject, as of the date of filing, to what have been called "statutory bars." Pre-AIA section 102 is reproduced in full in a footnote below for your ease of reference.[5]

a. Pre-AIA Date-of-Invention Provisions

The four date-of-invention novelty provisions, 35 U.S.C. § 102(a), (e), (f), and (g), focus on the state of the art at the moment of invention by the inventor named in the patent application. Because they look at the art before the current inventor conceived of the invention, they can be triggered only by the activities of persons other than the named inventor; an inventor's own work cannot be prior art under these provisions. Section 102(a) and (e) are focused entirely on whether this inventor was the first to invent the invention described in the patent claim. Section 102(g) might be more accurately characterized as a priority provision since it provides a means of selecting between two inventors whose inventive activity overlaps in time. Section 102(f) is designed to deny a patent to persons who are not

---

[5] Pre-AIA § 102—Conditions for patentability; novelty and loss of right to patent.

A person shall be entitled to a patent unless—

(a) the invention was known or used by others in this country, or patented or described in a printed publication in this or a foreign country, before the invention thereof by the applicant for patent, or

(b) the invention was patented or described in a printed publication in this or a foreign country or in public use or on sale in this country, more than one year prior to the date of the application for patent in the United States, or

(c) he has abandoned the invention, or

(d) the invention was first patented or caused to be patented, or was the subject of an inventor's certificate, by the applicant or his legal representatives or assigns in a foreign country prior to the date of the application for patent in this country on an application for patent or inventor's certificate filed more than twelve months before the filing of the application in the United States, or

(e) the invention was described in—

(1) an application for patent, published under section 122(b), by another filed in the United States before the invention by the applicant for patent or

(2) a patent granted on an application for patent by another filed in the United States before the invention by the applicant for patent, except that an international application filed under the treaty defined in section 351(a) shall have the effects for the purposes of this subsection of an application filed in the United States only if the international application designated the United States and was published under Article 21(2) of such treaty in the English language; or

(f) he did not himself invent the subject matter sought to be patented, or

(g) (1) during the course of an interference conducted under section 135 or section 291, another inventor involved therein establishes, to the extent permitted in section 104, that before such person's invention thereof the invention was made by such other inventor and not abandoned, suppressed, or concealed, or

(2) before such person's invention thereof, the invention was made in this country by another inventor who had not abandoned, suppressed, or concealed it. In determining priority of invention under this subsection, there shall be considered not only the respective dates of conception and reduction to practice of the invention, but also the reasonable diligence of one who was first to conceive and last to reduce to practice, from a time prior to conception by the other.

true inventors and who instead derived the claimed invention from another.

This focus on the prior art in existence before the date of invention by the named inventor requires one to determine, sometimes with precision, the date of invention. Where section 102(a), (e) or (f) is concerned, courts and the PTO will focus on the inventor's conception of the invention. More on the question of "conception" of an invention can be found in Chapter 11.A., *infra*. (*See Burroughs Wellcome Co. v. Barr Labs., Inc.* and associated Notes.) The law presumes that the filing date is the date of invention unless the applicant proves an earlier date.

Priority is more complex under section 102(g), as those determinations involve two inventors with overlapping periods of inventive activity. Merely conceiving the invention first does not establish priority under section 102(g). To establish priority of invention, a party must either (1) reduce the invention to practice first or (2) conceive the invention first and exercise reasonable diligence in reducing it to practice. To reduce the invention to practice means to demonstrate that it is suitable for its intended purpose.

A reduction to practice may be actual or constructive. In the *Telephone Cases*, 126 U.S. 1 (1888), the Supreme Court rejected the argument that actual reduction to practice is a prerequisite to patentability:

> The law does not require that a discoverer or inventor, in order to get a patent for a process, must have succeeded in bringing his art to the highest degree of perfection; it is enough if he describes his method with sufficient clearness and precision to enable those skilled in the matter to understand what the process is, and if he points out some practicable way of putting it into operation.

Id. at 783. An actual reduction to practice requires a physical embodiment that includes all limitations of the claims. If an inventor does not actually construct a complete embodiment of the invention at issue, then a "constructive reduction to practice" is deemed to take place at the time of filing the patent application that eventually leads to issuance of the patent. *See, e.g., Automatic Weighing Machine Co. v. Pneumatic Scale Corp., Ltd.*, 166 F. 288 (1st Cir.1909) (reasoning that sufficient reduction to practice has occurred once an inventor "has done all that he is required to do to obtain a valid patent").

Just as actual reduction to practice is not a prerequisite to an inventor's full conception of an invention or its patentability, it is also not a prerequisite to a determination that the invention was present within the prior art, destroying novelty for a later inventor, as demonstrated by the *Borst* case, excerpted below.

b. Pre-AIA Date-of-Filing Provisions

The remaining subsections of pre-AIA section 102, 35 U.S.C. § 102(b), (c) and (d), focus on events that occur after the named inventor's date of invention but before the patent application was filed. These pre-filing events can, in effect, cause a forfeiture of the right to receive a patent, regardless of the invention's utility, novelty, and nonobviousness at the time of its conception. They set forth circumstances in which Congress has determined that, because the inventor has not proceeded diligently toward applying for a United States patent, the underlying public purpose of the patent monopoly will not be served by issuing a patent. In other words, an invention may have been novel at the time of invention and yet is still unpatentable under the statute as a result of a delay in filing. For this reason, these provisions, particularly section 102(b), have been said to create a "statutory bar" to patentability. Either a third party's or an inventor's own activities can create invalidating prior art for purposes of section 102(b), while only the inventor's own activities (or an assignee's or representative's) can trigger section 102(c) or (d).

The section 102(b) and (d) statutory bars provide a grace period of one year for an application to be filed after the potentially invalidating activity. In other words, in order for an event to invalidate a utility or plant patent under section 102(b) or (d), the event must take place more than one year before the patent application is filed. (In the case of design patents, the statutory grace period under section 102(d) is 6 months. *See* 35 U.S.C. § 172.)

Section 102(c) does not refer to a specific critical date, but it is certainly a statutory bar rather than a novelty provision. As further explained below, it refers to abandonment of an invention after conception but before filing. It has rarely been applied.

c. Pre-AIA Geographic Distinctions

A final overarching note on pre-AIA section 102 is to highlight the geographic discrimination with respect to certain types of prior art in subsections (a) and (b), as well as in priority contests in (g). Prior knowledge or use by others in foreign countries (in subsection (a)) and prior public use or offering for sale in foreign countries (in subsection (b)) do not enter into the analysis of novelty or a statutory bar. By contrast, printed publications describing the invention and patents on the invention serve as invalidating prior art whether occurring in this or a foreign country. Subsection (g) also contains some differentiation between domestic inventive activity and foreign inventive activity, with (g)(1) allowing for foreign activity to create priority in the interference context but (g)(2) considering solely domestic activity when assessing the relative priority of two true inventors outside the interference context.

In addition, pre-AIA section 104 provides that a patent applicant may not establish a date of conception or reduction to practice (for any purpose, even outside a priority contest) by relying on knowledge, use or other activity with respect to the invention in foreign countries that do not belong to the North American Free Trade Agreement (NAFTA) or the World Trade Organization (WTO), except for certain persons performing overseas duties on behalf of the United States or a NAFTA or WTO member, or where a foreign filing qualifies as a constructive reduction to practice under section 119 (and section 365, where applicable). Section 104 will not apply to applications subject to the post-AIA novelty rules.

What purpose was served by these geographic restrictions? Does pre-AIA law unfairly discriminate against foreign inventors? Post-AIA section 102 eliminates these geographic distinctions, placing domestic and foreign prior art on equal footing, regardless of type or category, *see* section 102(a)(1), other than prior-filed patent applications, *see* section 102(a)(2).

3. POST-AIA SECTION 102

We look to post-AIA section 102 when judging the novelty of an invention in an application (or later, a patent issuing from such an application) that contains, or contained at any time, a claim to a claimed invention with an effective filing date on or after March 16, 2013. Post-AIA section 102 does not concern itself with whether an invention was new, or novel, as of the date of invention by the applicant. Its goal is, among other things, to encourage the early filing of an application by a true inventor, or at least the early public disclosure of the invention by a true inventor. Post-AIA section 102 is reproduced in full in a footnote below for your ease of reference.[6]

---

[6] Post-AIA § 102—Conditions for patentability; novelty

(a) NOVELTY; PRIOR ART.—A person shall be entitled to a patent unless—

(1) the claimed invention was patented, described in a printed publication, or in public use, on sale, or otherwise available to the public before the effective filing date of the claimed invention; or

(2) the claimed invention was described in a patent issued under section 151, or in an application for patent published or deemed published under section 122(b), in which the patent or application, as the case may be, names another inventor and was effectively filed before the effective filing date of the claimed invention.

(b) EXCEPTIONS.—

(1) DISCLOSURES MADE 1 YEAR OR LESS BEFORE THE EFFECTIVE FILING DATE OF THE CLAIMED INVENTION.—A disclosure made 1 year or less before the effective filing date of a claimed invention shall not be prior art to the claimed invention under subsection (a)(1) if—

(A) the disclosure was made by the inventor or joint inventor or by another who obtained the subject matter disclosed directly or indirectly from the inventor or a joint inventor; or

(B) the subject matter disclosed had, before such disclosure, been publicly disclosed by the inventor or a joint inventor or another who obtained the subject matter disclosed directly or indirectly from the inventor or a joint inventor.

(2) DISCLOSURES APPEARING IN APPLICATIONS AND PATENTS.—A disclosure shall not be prior art to a claimed invention under subsection (a)(2) if—

Notice how the post-AIA section 102 sections interact. Section 102(a)(1) first sets a novelty rule in place that effectuates a policy of barring patents on inventions that have been previously publicly disclosed by anyone, or commercially exploited by the applicant. Novelty is measured as of the effective filing date rather than either the date of invention or a year before the filing date, as in pre-AIA section 102. Section 102(a)(2) then puts in place a basic first-to-file rule by giving priority to the first application filed that discloses an invention. But unlike some other first-to-file patent systems, the post-AIA system provides in 102(b) two different grace periods that soften the effect of the emphasis in 102(a) on the effective filing date. These grace periods are discussed further in Chapter 10.C.5., *infra*.

a. Post-AIA Critical Date

The critical date in post-AIA section 102, "the effective filing date" for a claimed invention, is defined in section 100(i)(1):

> (A) if subparagraph (B) does not apply, the actual filing date of the patent or the application for the patent containing a claim to the invention; or
>
> (B) the filing date of the earliest application for which the patent or application is entitled, as to such invention, to a right of priority

---

(A) the subject matter disclosed was obtained directly or indirectly from the inventor or a joint inventor;

(B) the subject matter disclosed had, before such subject matter was effectively filed under subsection (a)(2), been publicly disclosed by the inventor or a joint inventor or another who obtained the subject matter disclosed directly or indirectly from the inventor or a joint inventor; or

(C) the subject matter disclosed and the claimed invention, not later than the effective filing date of the claimed invention, were owned by the same person or subject to an obligation of assignment to the same person.

(c) COMMON OWNERSHIP UNDER JOINT RESEARCH AGREEMENTS.—Subject matter disclosed and a claimed invention shall be deemed to have been owned by the same person or subject to an obligation of assignment to the same person in applying the provisions of subsection (b)(2)(C) if—

(1) the subject matter disclosed was developed and the claimed invention was made by, or on behalf of, 1 or more parties to a joint research agreement that was in effect on or before the effective filing date of the claimed invention;

(2) the claimed invention was made as a result of activities undertaken within the scope of the joint research agreement; and

(3) the application for patent for the claimed invention discloses or is amended to disclose the names of the parties to the joint research agreement.

(d) PATENTS AND PUBLISHED APPLICATIONS EFFECTIVE AS PRIOR ART.—For purposes of determining whether a patent or application for patent is prior art to a claimed invention under subsection (a)(2), such patent or application shall be considered to have been effectively filed, with respect to any subject matter described in the patent or application—

(1) if paragraph (2) does not apply, as of the actual filing date of the patent or the application for patent; or

(2) if the patent or application for patent is entitled to claim a right of priority under section 119, 365(a), or 365(b), or to claim the benefit of an earlier filing date under section 120, 121, or 365(c), based upon 1 or more prior filed applications for patent, as of the filing date of the earliest such application that describes the subject matter.

under section 119, 365(a), or 365(b) or to the benefit of an earlier filing date under section 120, 121, or 365(c).

A basic, although admittedly incomplete, understanding of the "effective filing date" proceeds in two parts. First, the "effective filing date" for a claim to an invention within a patent application (and there are usually multiple claims in each application) may simply be the actual date on which the application containing that claim was filed with the PTO. Alternately, the claim may instead gain filing priority from a date earlier than the actual U.S. filing date of the current application and instead may be able to take the earlier filing date of an earlier application containing the same invention—which becomes the critical "effective filing date." The earlier application whose filing date provides the claim with an earlier "effective filing date" could be a foreign application (§ 119), PCT (Patent Cooperation Treaty) application (§ 365), a domestic provisional application (§ 119(e)), or an earlier domestic application that has been continued (§ 120) or divided (§ 121), provided that the requirements applicable to those sections are met. *See infra* Chapter 11.B.1.

b. Post-AIA Continuity

The AIA left in place many aspects of U.S. patent law while altering the critical dates to accomplish a significant change in focus of the U.S. patent application and granting system away from early inventive activity and toward early filing of patent applications (or other early public disclosure of the invention by the inventor). Much of the basic landscape of relevant *types* of prior art remains in place (on sale, in public use, patents and patent applications, etc.). The technical nature of the novelty inquiry (barring patenting of inventions where there is complete anticipation in one piece of prior art) remains as it was before, as does the essence of the nonobviousness analysis (barring patenting of inventions made obvious by the prior art, even if novel). In addition, the nature and analysis of infringing acts, as well as the available remedies for infringement, are all untouched.

For some inventors and inventions this may mean the AIA created a major contrast to pre-AIA law. The most fundamental change is in judging novelty or anticipation based only on the effective filing date (with some grace periods for the inventor's own public disclosures)—prioritizing early filing and ignoring early invention—rather than judging novelty or anticipation based in large part on the date of invention. By moving the date upon which novelty (and nonobviousness) are judged later in time (focusing on the effective filing date), and by abandoning a preference for early invention in favor of early filing, the AIA may alter the patentability of some inventors' inventions by making more critical an inventor's time delay between the time of invention and filing. For inventors who take the changed legal landscape into account and proceed to file patent applications as soon as possible (even if that is sooner than they would have otherwise done under pre-AIA law), the ultimate effect may not be significant.

4. SECTION 102 PUBLIC PRIOR ART

As explained earlier, this section of the chapter examines the "prior art" that is common to both pre- and post-AIA section 102.

a. "Known or Used" or in "Public Use"

Notice how pre-AIA section 102 bars patenting of a claimed invention if the invention was in the prior art by virtue of being "known or used by others" before the date of invention (§ 102(a)) *or* if the invention was "in public use" more than a year before the filing date of the application (§ 102(b)). Despite the difference in statutory language between mere knowledge or use "by others" and "public" use, courts have required the knowledge or use "by others" under section 102(a) to be comparable in availability or accessibility to a "public use" under section 102(b).

In re Borst, an important 1965 decision of the Court of Customs and Patent Appeals (the "CCPA," one of the Federal Circuit's predecessor courts), confirmed and overruled different aspects of one of its earlier decisions related to prior knowledge or use.

> [One] aspect of the court's discussion in *Schlittler* [234 F.2d 882 (C.C.P.A. 1956)] involved the well-established principle that "prior knowledge of a patented invention would not invalidate a claim of the patent unless such knowledge was available to the public." * * *
>
> * * * Although that portion of the *Schlittler* opinion is clearly dictum, we think it just as clearly represents the settled law. The knowledge contemplated by section 102(a) must be accessible to the public. * * *
>
> * * *
>
> [The cited prior art reference, a memorandum that described an as-yet-untested idea, included all elements of four of the applicant's claims.] The remaining consideration regarding the status of [the memorandum] as evidence of prior knowledge directly calls into question the correctness of the unequivocal holding in *Schlittler* that the knowledge must be of a reduction to practice, either actual or constructive. After much deliberation, we have concluded that such a requirement is illogical and anomalous, and to the extent *Schlittler* is inconsistent with the decision in this case, it is hereby expressly overruled.

> The mere fact that a disclosure is contained in a patent or application and thus 'constructively' reduced to practice, or that it is found in a printed publication, does not make the disclosure itself any more meaningful to those skilled in the art (and thus, ultimately, to the public). Rather, the criterion should be whether the disclosure is sufficient to enable one skilled in the art to reduce the disclosed invention to practice. In other words, the disclosure must be such as will give possession of the invention to the person of ordinary skill. Even the act of publication or the fiction of constructive reduction to practice will not suffice if the disclosure does not meet this standard.

In re Borst, 345 F.2d 851 (C.C.P.A. 1965).

The district court in *Oak Industries, Inc. v. Zenith Electronics Corp.*, 726 F.Supp. 1525 (N.D.Ill.1989), later summarized the prevailing interpretation of "known or used by others" under pre-AIA section 102(a) as follows:

> Courts construe this phrase to mean that the public must have access to the knowledge of the prior art. While there is no per se rule on the number of persons who must have knowledge of, or who used the prior invention, it appears that more than just a few persons must know or use the invention for it to be publicly known. However, where those skilled in the relevant art know of or use an invention, courts may infer the knowledge will become known to a sufficient number of people to become "public." Furthermore, the court may find a public use where there is a "non-secret use of a claimed process in the usual course of producing articles for commercial purposes."

726 F.Supp. at 1537 (citations omitted).

The following case explores two primary issues with finding that "the invention" was in public use or was known or used by others: (1) just how "public" the knowledge or use must be; and (2) the rigid rule that "the invention" that is known or used must contain all elements of the patent claim.

BENNETT REGULATOR GUARDS, INC. V. CANADIAN METER CO. INC.

184 Fed. Appx. 977 (Fed. Cir. 2006).

PROST, CIRCUIT JUDGE.

[Bennett's patent claimed a spray cover for a natural gas regulator pressure valve. The spray cover prevented the valve from failing due to ice formation. Accused infringers American Meter Co. and Canadian Meter Co., related companies together referred to as "Meter" by the court, argued that their own activities prior to the patentholder's 1994 invention date invalidated the claims at issue on the grounds of prior public knowledge and public use under 35 U.S.C. § 102(a) and (b).]

I.

* * *

Meter alleged that its own activities relating to the Splash Guard anticipated Bennett's patent. Specifically, in the 1980s, Meter began searching for the cause of a few catastrophic failures of gas regulating valves. As a result of that research, Meter realized that the old style regulators had malfunctioned when, during freezing conditions, water splashed and subsequently froze onto the screens of the regulators. Canadian Meter then developed a product called the Splash Guard that kept water from splashing up onto the screen and thereby prevented malfunctioning due to ice formation. While Meter never patented its Splash Guard, in the early 1990s, Meter undertook a number of activities relating to its Splash Guard product. These efforts are the factual basis for Meter's theories of anticipation upon which Meter filed a motion for summary judgment of invalidity.[1]

* * *

The district court [granted] the motion for summary judgment as to Meter's last two theories, namely that the patent was anticipated by prior public use and public knowledge. First, Meter contended that, in October 1991, it conducted regulatory testing of the Splash Guard with the Canadian Gas Association ("CGA") in Nebraska City, Nebraska to certify that the Splash Guard met CGA safety standards. The testing was evidenced by affidavits describing the tests, by memos discussing the tests, by the certificate resulting from the CGA testing, and by the test results. Meter contended that the testing was not confidential and was accessible to the public and therefore the Nebraska City testing of the Splash Guard constituted an anticipatory public use under 35 U.S.C. § 102(a) and (b).

Second, Meter contended that the Splash Guard was publicly known in the United States, and thus anticipated under 35 U.S.C. § 102(a). In support, Meter submitted statements from employees attesting to their knowledge of the Splash Guard product demonstrating, according to Meter, that the Splash Guard was known in the United States. The statements also state that Meter's knowledge about the Splash Guard was publicly

---

[1] In this case, the accused infringing device, the Splash Guard, is also the device that allegedly provides the anticipatory use or knowledge. Thus, absent a dispute as to whether the complete Splash Guard device was involved in the anticipatory act, we agree with the district court that "[w]hen the anticipatory reference is the accused product, the Defendant's burden [of showing that the anticipatory reference contains each and every claim element] is satisfied by the Plaintiff's infringement allegations in the Complaint that the accused product embodies the claimed invention."

accessible. Furthermore, Meter submitted a letter sent to the Bay State Gas Company, another letter to the Vermont Gas Company, and an inter-office memo. The letters tell the gas companies that Meter would be "pleased to offer any information [they] may require" regarding the Splash Guard. The inter-office memo asks American Meter to relay customer feedback regarding the Splash Guard. Meter contended that these documents evidence that American Meter's knowledge about the Splash Guard was publicly accessible and therefore the '029 patent is invalid due to anticipation by public knowledge under 35 U.S.C. § 102(a).

As to these last two theories, the district court found that Meter presented clear and convincing evidence that the Splash Guard was both publicly known and used prior to the earliest potential date of invention for the '029 patent. First, the district court found that the CGA 1991 testing of the Splash Guard in Nebraska City, Nebraska, was a corroborated public use. Reinforcing the testimony relating to the testing, the district court held that "the certification document not only demonstrates public use, but also corroborates the other documents and statements referencing the Nebraska City testing." Second, as to public knowledge, the district court held that "[t]here can be no dispute that the claimed invention, embodied in the Splash Guard product, was known 'in this country'. [Bennett] cannot argue that Defendant American Meter lacked knowledge of the accused product. . . . The issue, therefore, is whether the Defendants' knowledge . . . was 'public.'" The district court found that the letters from [sic] Bay State Gas Company and Vermont Gas Company along with an inter-office memo demonstrated that Meter's knowledge about the Splash Guard was not secret or confidential. The district court concluded that "the corroborative documentary evidence of public knowledge . . . is substantial and constitutes clear and convincing evidence of invalidity." As a result, the district court granted Meter's motion for summary judgment of invalidity. Bennett appealed and we have jurisdiction pursuant to 28 U.S.C. § 1295(a)(1).

II.

* * *

A.

Bennett contends that, as to the public use of the Splash Guard, it raised a genuine issue of fact as to the public nature of the Nebraska City testing and that there is a genuine issue of fact as to whether the product tested in Nebraska City possessed each and every element of the asserted claims in the patent. In response, Meter contends that its testing of the Splash Guard in Nebraska City with a team from the CGA was not confidential. Meter contends that the CGA was under no obligations to keep information about the Splash Guard secret and therefore the testing constitutes a public use under § 102(a) or (b). Further, Meter contends that the complete Splash Guard was tested in Nebraska City and therefore there is no question as to the identity of the public use in regards to the claim elements.

We conclude that there exists a genuine issue of material fact as to the public nature of the testing in Nebraska City. As pointed out by Bennett, a Vice President from Meter testified that "I believe in my opinion, the Canadian Gas Association views [the CGA testing] as being proprietary." Read in the light most favorable to Bennett, this testimony raises a genuine issue of material fact as to the publicness of the Nebraska City testing.

Furthermore, there exists a genuine issue of material fact as to whether the device used in the Nebraska City testing contained each and every element of the asserted claims. In particular, there is a question as to whether the tested device included the baffling means element required by the claims. Bennett highlights that an inter-office memo by Meter stated that the Nebraska City tests were performed "with the prototype . . . vent shield, and no device or screen installed." Bennett argues that this memo creates a genuine issue of fact as to the identity of the tested device. Bennett points to Meter's drawings it submitted to the CGA. In those drawings, the "Vent Shield" is only the outer skirt of the Splash Guard without the baffling insert. Because the memo suggests that only the Vent Shield was tested, Bennett argues that the memo demonstrates that the device tested in Nebraska City cannot anticipate as a prior use because the tested device did not contain a baffling means as required by the claims. Although it is not clear what device was tested, the memo does create a genuine issue of fact as to whether the device tested in Nebraska City met the claim limitation requiring "a baffle means." Thus, the Nebraska City testing cannot, on summary judgment, support a judgment of invalidity.

B.

There is also a genuine issue of fact underlying Meter's theory of anticipation via 35 U.S.C. § 102(a) public knowledge. There is little dispute that American Meter knew about the Splash Guard. In other words, the Splash Guard was known in the United States prior to the '029 invention date because American Meter certainly knew about its own product. Rather, the parties dispute whether that knowledge was accessible to the public as required by our caselaw. In support of its contention that its knowledge was publicly known, Meter submitted affidavits and testimony describing its efforts at contacting customers in the United States regarding the Splash Guard highlighting that it did not attempt to keep information about the Splash Guard secret and confidential from the public.

As described above, under § 102(a), knowledge must be publicly accessible. In support of its grant of summary judgment of invalidity as to public knowledge, the district court primarily relied on two pieces of evidence. First, the district court relied on a memorandum sent from Canadian Meter to American Meter that referred to the transfer of forty units of the Splash Guard product and that asked for "future requirements and customer feedback" as to the Splash Guard. Because it referenced customer feedback in regards to the Splash Guard, Meter argues that this memorandum shows that Meter was making its knowledge of the Splash Guard publicly accessible. Second, in March of 1992 and April of 1994, Meter sent letters to the Vermont Gas Company and to Bay State Gas Company respectively, telling these gas companies of the Splash Guard. Both letters concluded by stating that the gas companies could contact Meter for "any information you may require" about the Splash Guard. Meter argues that these letters evidence that it was not keeping the Splash Guard secret and Meter's knowledge about the Splash Guard was accessible to the public. Meter argues that the district court properly granted the motion for summary judgment based on these documents.

However, in our view, there does exist a genuine issue of fact as to whether Meter's letters and memos establish that Meter's knowledge was accessible to the public. As argued by Bennett, the reference in the letters to "any information you may require" or the reference to customer feedback could be taken to mean a wide variety of things relating to the Splash Guard—"prices, product availability, or lack thereof, test results, expected standards to be enacted in the United States, etc." Certainly the letter and memo do suggest that Meter intended to publicize the Splash Guard but, in the light most favorable to Bennett, it does not establish that Meter intended to make its technical knowledge about the structure and function of the Splash Guard publicly accessible. One can publicize that a new product exists while still keeping an enabling disclosure of the structure and function of the product secret. Thus, when viewed in the light most favorable to Bennett, the internal memorandum asking for "customer feedback" or the letters to customers offering "any information you may require" do not establish by clear and convincing evidence that Meter's knowledge about the Splash Guard was accessible to the public. Rather, there exists a genuine issue of material fact as to the public accessibility of Meter's knowledge of the Splash Guard and it cannot properly support summary judgment of invalidity.

III.

When viewed in the light most favorable to Bennett, summary judgment was not properly granted. There exist genuine issues of material fact as to the confidentiality of the Nebraska City testing and the identity of the product tested there that preclude a finding of a public use. Further, when all inferences are drawn in favor of Bennett, the memorandum and letters are not enough to establish that Meter's knowledge of the Splash Guard was accessible to the public. Therefore, we find the grant of summary judgment was improper and we vacate the judgment and remand for further proceedings consistent with this opinion.

NOTES

1. *"Public Use" and "Otherwise Available to the Public":* Post-AIA section 102 continues to give prior art status to activities by which an invention is "in public use" before the effective filing date, and it adds to the prior art activities that make the claimed invention "otherwise available to the public." Because Congress used the same "in public use" language in the AIA, without express alteration of the meaning in pre-AIA section 102(b), courts and the PTO are likely to continue to apply pre-AIA interpretations of "public use." See also Note 4, below.

2. *Geographic Scope of "Public Use":* A significant change is the elimination of the geographic limit on "public use" prior art, as noted above. Post-AIA section 102 considers public uses anywhere in the world, while pre-AIA law only examines public uses in this country.

3. *Timing of "Public Use":* Under pre-AIA section 102, an inventor has up to one year, called the grace period, in which to file an application after a public use, whether the use was by the inventor or by a third party. Under post-AIA section 102, however, the third-party public use bar will be immediate unless the third-party public use was preceded by a public disclosure by the inventor. *See* post-AIA § 102(a) & (b)(1)(B). The inventor's own first public use will continue to gain the benefit of a one-year grace period in which an application may be filed. *See* post-AIA § 102(b)(1)(A). The distinction in post-AIA section 102 between a "disclosure" and a "public disclosure" that will create a grace period is open to interpretation. Consult Chapter 10.C.5., *infra*, for further discussion.

4. *Distinction Between the Inventor and a Third Party:* If a device is used only in a factory from which the general public is excluded, does this constitute a "public use" of the device under section 102(a)? Is it a "public use" if a device is being publicly used, but not all aspects of the invention claimed in a patent or patent application are visible to the public?

How "public" the public use must be in order to create a public use novelty bar may depend on whether the relevant acts are those of the patentee or a third party. One rationale for the public use bar in the case of the *patentee* (or applicant) is that an inventor should not be allowed to commercially exploit or benefit from the invention for more than a year after it is ready for patenting. As a result of this motivating policy, a *commercial* use by the patentee will likely be deemed a "public use" even if the aspects of the invention visible or disclosed to the public (such as a product produced by a claimed process) do not constitute an enabling disclosure of the full invention. *See Metallizing Eng'g Co. v. Kenyon Bearing & Auto. Parts Co.*, 153 F.2d 516 (2d Cir.1946). Activities authorized by the patentee will be treated the same. In other words, a *commercial use* by the *patentee* need not fully disclose all aspects of the invention *to the public*, as long as all elements were present, in order to create a public use bar.

Another rationale for the public use bar is against removing information from the public store of knowledge, except in the limited circumstances prescribed in the Patent Act. Pre-AIA, the policy was for the public not to have access to an invention, in an enabling manner, for more than one year before a patent application is filed. Post-AIA, the policy is for the public's access to an invention via a third party to create an immediate bar. In the case of third parties, whether unauthorized and pirated, or independent, the public use bar is motivated by solicitude for the public's access to—and potential reliance upon the invention. In the case of third parties, then, the public use bar is not motivated by a desire to prohibit the patentee from inappropriately extending the exclusive rights provided by a patent, and as a result, third party uses fall within the public use bar only when the activities in fact disclose the invention to the public. The public use bar of section 102(b) does apply to third-party disclosures regardless of whether the unauthorized use was independent of the patentee or a pirated use derived from the patentee without its consent. *Lorenz v. Colgate-Palmolive-Peet Co.*, 167 F.2d 423, 429–30 (3d Cir.1948) (pirated public use was a bar); *Electric Storage Battery Co. v. Shimadzu*, 307 U.S. 5, 19–20 (1939) (use of independently developed invention in factory, with no effort at secrecy, was a bar). Where a party acting without the inventor's authority makes secret commercial use of the invention, however, such as selling articles made by the method or device sought to be patented, courts have generally held that the public use bar will not apply unless the invention is disclosed by the articles sold, even though the bar would have applied to those same activities if undertaken with the inventor's consent.

5. *Totality of the Circumstances:* In *Baxter International, Inc. v. Cobe Laboratories, Inc.*, 88 F.3d 1054 (Fed.Cir.1996), the Federal Circuit noted that "[i]n considering whether a particular use was a public use within the meaning of section 102(b), we consider the totality of the circumstances in conjunction with the policies underlying the public use bar," and reiterated the policies it had identified in *Tone Bros., Inc. v. Sysco Corp.*, 28 F.3d 1192, 1198 (Fed.Cir.1994) as the underlying purposes of the public use bar:

> (1) discouraging the removal, from the public domain, of inventions that the public reasonably has come to believe are freely available; (2) favoring the prompt and widespread disclosure of inventions; (3) allowing the inventor a reasonable amount of time following sales activity to determine the potential economic value of a patent; and (4) prohibiting the inventor from commercially exploiting the invention for a period greater than the statutorily prescribed time.

Baxter International, 88 F.3d at 1058 (quoting *Tone Bros.*, 28 F.3d at 1198). In light of these purposes, should the public use bar apply where a party other than the inventor, acting independently, develops the same invention and uses it in a research laboratory where the persons observing the invention are under no legal or ethical obligation of confidentiality?

6. *Exception for Public "Experimental" Uses:* An inventor's experimental use of an invention will not trigger the "public use" bar even if the use discloses the invention to the public. In *Elizabeth v. American Nicholson Pavement Co.*, 97 U.S. (7 Otto) 126 (1877), which held that installing pavement on a public street for testing purposes was not an invalidating public use, the Court discussed the scope of "experimental use":

> That the use of the pavement in question was public in one sense cannot be disputed. But can it be said that the invention was in public use? The use of an invention by the inventor himself, or of any other person under his direction, by way of experiment, and in order to bring the invention to perfection, has never been regarded as such a use.
>
> * * *
>
> It would not be necessary, in such a case, that the machine should be put up and used only in the inventor's own shop or premises. He may have it put up and used in the premises of another, and the use may inure to the benefit of the owner of the establishment. Still, if used under the surveillance of the inventor, and for the purpose of enabling him to test the machine, and ascertain whether it will answer the purpose intended, and make such alterations and improvements as experience demonstrates to be necessary, it will still be a mere experimental use, and not a public use, within the meaning of the statute.
>
> Whilst the supposed machine is in such experimental use, the public may be incidentally deriving a benefit from it. If it be a grist-mill, or a carding-machine, customers from the surrounding country may enjoy the use of it by having their grain made into flour, or their wool into rolls, and still it will not be in public use, within the meaning of the law.
>
> But if the inventor allows his machine to be used by other persons generally, either with or without compensation, or if it is, with his consent, put on sale for such use, then it will be in public use and on public sale, within the meaning of the law.
>
> * * *
>
> It is sometimes said that an inventor acquires an undue advantage over the public by delaying to take out a patent, inasmuch as he thereby preserves the monopoly to himself for a longer period than is allowed by the policy of the law; but this cannot be said with justice when the delay is occasioned by a bona fide effort to bring his invention to perfection, or to ascertain whether it will answer the purpose intended. His monopoly only continues for the allotted period, in any event; and it is the interest of the public, as well as himself, that the invention should be perfect and properly tested, before a patent is granted for it. Any attempt to use it for a profit, and

> not by way of experiment, for a longer period than two years [Ed. note: now one year] before the application, would deprive the inventor of his right to a patent.

Id. at 134–37.

Subsequent case law has emphasized the degree of control exercised by the inventor over any parties making experimental use of the invention. In *Allen Eng'g Corp. v. Bartell Indus., Inc.*, 299 F.3d 1336 (Fed.Cir. 2002), the Federal Circuit listed the factors that, in previous cases, have been instructive in identifying experimental uses:

> (1) the necessity for public testing, (2) the amount of control over the experiment retained by the inventor, (3) the nature of the invention, (4) the length of the test period, (5) whether payment was made, (6) whether there was a secrecy obligation, (7) whether records of the experiment were kept, (8) who conducted the experiment, (9) the degree of commercial exploitation during testing, (10) whether the invention reasonably requires evaluation under actual conditions of use, (11) whether testing was systematically performed, (12) whether the inventor continually monitored the invention during testing, and (13) the nature of contacts made with potential customers.

Id. at 1353 (quotation and alteration marks omitted). In some cases, the inventor's lack of control over the alleged experiment has been dispositive. *Atlanta Attachment Co. v. Leggett & Platt, Inc.*, 516 F.3d 1361, 1366 (Fed.Cir. 2008). The purpose of the experimental use must be to determine whether the claimed invention is ready for patenting. Market testing to determine the consumer demand for or commercial viability of the invention, rather than to confirm functionality of the invention, is not an experimental use and will therefore be a "public use" under section 102.

7. *Experimental Use Questions:* Should the experimental use exception apply (1) where the use is by a party, other than the patent applicant, who independently produced the same invention; or (2) where the experimentation is directed to non-claimed features of the invention?

8. *Anticipation by Inherency:* It is possible for a product or process to be unpatentable due to anticipation even though the creator of the prior art product or process did not fully appreciate or recognize the utility or properties of that creation; this is known as anticipation by inherency. "In order for a claim to be inherent in the prior art it is not sufficient that a person following the disclosure sometimes obtain the result set forth in the claim, it must invariably happen." *Standard Oil v. Montedison*, 664 F.2d 356, 372 (3d Cir.1981). Where the prior art reference is a written description that is silent about the allegedly inherent characteristic, the Federal Circuit has permitted resort to extrinsic evidence in order to establish that "the missing descriptive matter is necessarily present in the thing described in the reference, and that it would be so recognized by persons of ordinary skill." *Continental Can Co. USA, Inc. v. Monsanto Co.*, 948 F.2d 1264, 1269 (Fed.Cir.1991). In *Galderma*

Labs., L.P. v. Teva Pharms. USA, Inc., 799 Fed. Appx. 838 (Fed. Cir. 2020), the Federal Circuit rejected the district court's inherency analysis on the facts of the case, as not necessarily present or invariably resulting in relation to the proffered prior art reference:

> It is true that anticipation is not defeated by a showing that the allegedly anticipating reference also discloses non-anticipating alternatives. But that is not the question before us. The inquiry here is whether the claimed efficacy limitations [of the patent being challenged] are an inherent result of practicing [the prior art reference's] disclosed methods. The answer is no because: (1) [the prior art reference] does not disclose the specific [formulation relevant to the patent claim]; and (2) as [defendant's] expert acknowledged, variation in formulation parameters will undoubtedly affect the results achieved from the use of [the] disclosed formulations. [Defendant] has provided no basis for us to conclude with certainty that all [relevant] formulations within the scope of [the prior art reference's] disclosure will inevitably achieve the claimed efficacy limitations.

Id. at 846. In *Schering Corp. v. Geneva Pharmaceuticals, Inc.*, 339 F.3d 1373 (Fed. Cir. 2003), the Federal Circuit held that anticipation by inherency occurred where the invention sought to be patented was itself a metabolite of a patented pharmaceutical, and was necessarily formed whenever the latter was put to its intended use (ingestion by humans) under normal conditions. Anticipation did not depend on whether a person of ordinary skill in the art would have recognized this inherent disclosure.

b. "Described in a Printed Publication"

The statutory phrase "described in a printed publication" appears in both post-AIA section 102 and pre-AIA section 102. *In re Hall*, reproduced below, applies pre-AIA section 102(b), but the courts have ascribed the same meaning to this phrase each time it appears. Congress did not alter the words in post-AIA section 102, and there is no reason to think Congress intended the meaning to change, nor have courts begun to alter the interpretation. In pre-AIA section 102(b) there was a one-year grace period in which to file after any printed publication disclosed an invention to the public; under post-AIA section 102, third-party printed publications are excluded from the one-year grace period retained for the inventor's own publications.

IN RE HALL

781 F.2d 897 (Fed. Cir. 1986).

BALDWIN, CIRCUIT JUDGE.

This is an appeal from the decision of the U.S. Patent and Trademark Office's (PTO) former Board of Appeals, adhered to on reconsideration by the Board of Patent Appeals and Interferences (board), sustaining the final rejection of claims 1–25 of reissue Application No. 343,922, filed January 29, 1982, based principally on a "printed publication" bar under 35 U.S.C. §§ 102(b). The reference is a doctoral thesis. Because appellant concedes that his claims are un-patentable if the thesis is available as a "printed publication" more than one year prior to the application's effective filing date of February 27, 1979, the only issue is whether the thesis is available as such a printed publication. On the record before us, we affirm the board's decision.

BACKGROUND

A protest was filed during prosecution of appellant's reissue application which included in an appendix a copy of the dissertation "1,4-a-Glucanglukohydrolase ein amylotylisches Enzym . . ." by Peter Foldi (Foldi thesis or dissertation). The record indicates that in September 1977, Foldi submitted his dissertation to the Department of Chemistry and Pharmacy at Freiburg University in the Federal Republic of Germany, and that Foldi was awarded a doctorate degree on November 2, 1977.

Certain affidavits from Dr. Erich Will, who is the director and manager of the Loan Department of the Library of Freiburg University, have been relied upon by the examiner and the board in reaching their decisions. One document, styled a "Declaration" and signed by Dr. Will, states that:

> [I]n November 1977 copies of the dissertation FOLDI . . . were received in the library of Freiburg University, and in . . . December 1977 copies of the said dissertation were freely made available to the faculty and student body of Freiburg University as well as to the general public.

In an August 28, 1981 letter responding to an inquiry from a German corporation, Dr. Will said that the Freiburg University library was able to make the Foldi dissertation "available to our readers as early as 1977."

The examiner made a final rejection of the application claims. He said: "On the basis of the instant record it is reasonable to assume that the Foldi thesis was available (accessible) prior to February 27, 1979." He also pointed out that there was no evidence to the contrary and asked the appellant to state his "knowledge of any inquiry which may have been made regarding 'availability' beyond that presently referred to in the record." Appellant did not respond.

By letter, the PTO's Scientific Library asked Dr. Will whether the Foldi dissertation was made available to the public by being cataloged and placed in the main collection. Dr. Will replied in an October 20, 1983 letter, as translated:

> Our dissertations, thus also the Foldi dissertation, are indexed in a special dissertations catalogue, which is part of the general

users' catalogue. In the stacks they are likewise set apart in a special dissertation section, which is part of the general stacks.

In response to a further inquiry by the PTO's Scientific Library requesting (1) the exact date of indexing and cataloging of the Foldi dissertation or (2) "the time such procedures normally take," Dr. Will replied in a June 18, 1984 letter:

> The Library copies of the Foldi dissertation were sent to us by the faculty on November 4, 1977. Accordingly, the dissertation most probably was available for general use toward the beginning of the month of December, 1977.

The board held that the unrebutted evidence of record was sufficient to conclude that the Foldi dissertation had an effective date as prior art more than one year prior to the filing date of the appellant's initial application. In rejecting appellant's argument that the evidence was not sufficient to establish a specific date when the dissertation became publicly available, the board said:

> We rely on the librarian's affidavit of express facts regarding the *specific* dissertation of interest and his description of the routine treatment of dissertations in general, in the ordinary course of business in his library.

On appeal, appellant raises two arguments: (1) the § 102(b) "printed publication" bar requires that the publication be accessible to the interested public, but there is no evidence that the dissertation was properly indexed in the library catalog prior to the critical date; and (2) even if the Foldi thesis were cataloged prior to the critical date, the presence of a single cataloged thesis in one university library does not constitute sufficient accessibility of the publication's teachings to those interested in the art exercising reasonable diligence.

OPINION

The "printed publication" bar is found in 35 U.S.C. § 102:

> A person shall be entitled to a patent unless—
>
> (b) the invention was patented or described in a printed publication in this or a foreign country . . . more than one year prior to the date of the application for patent in the United States. . . .

The bar is grounded on the principle that once an invention is in the public domain, it is no longer patentable by anyone. *In re Bayer*, 568 F.2d 1357, 1361 (C.C.P.A. 1978).

The statutory phrase "printed publication" has been interpreted to give effect to ongoing advances in the technologies of data storage, retrieval, and dissemination. *In re Wyer*, 655 F.2d 221, 226 (C.C.P.A. 1981).

Because there are many ways in which a reference may be disseminated to the interested public, "public accessibility" has been called the touchstone in determining whether a reference constitutes a "printed publication" bar under 35 U.S.C. § 102(b). *See, e.g., In re Bayer*, 568 F.2d at 1359; *In re Wyer*, 655 F.2d at 224. The § 102 publication bar is a legal determination based on underlying fact issues, and therefore must be approached on a case-by-case basis. The proponent of the publication bar must show that prior to the critical date the reference was sufficiently accessible, at least to the public interested in the art, so that such a one by examining the reference could make the claimed invention without further research or experimentation.

Relying on *In re Bayer*, appellant argues that the Foldi thesis was not shown to be accessible because Dr. Will's affidavits do not say when the thesis was indexed in the library catalog and do not chronicle the procedures for receiving and processing a thesis in the library.

As the board pointed out in its decision, the facts in *Bayer* differ from those here. Bayer, who was himself the author of the dissertation relied upon by the PTO, submitted a declaration from the university librarian which detailed the library's procedures for receiving, cataloging, and shelving of theses and attested to the relevant dates that Bayer's thesis was processed. The evidence showed that cataloging and shelving thesis copies routinely took many months from the time they were first received from the faculty and that during the interim the theses were accumulated in a private library office accessible only to library employees. In particular, processing of Bayer's thesis was shown to have been completed after the critical date.

On those facts the CCPA held that Bayer's thesis was not sufficiently accessible and could not give rise to the § 102(b) publication bar. But the court did not hold, as appellant would have it, that accessibility can only be shown by evidence establishing a specific date of cataloging and shelving before the critical date. While such evidence would be desirable, in lending greater certainty to the accessibility determination, the realities of routine business practice counsel against requiring such evidence. The probative value of routine business practice to show the performance of a specific act has long been recognized. Therefore, we conclude that competent evidence of the general library practice may be relied upon to establish an approximate time when a thesis became accessible.

In the present case, Dr. Will's affidavits give a rather general library procedure as to indexing, cataloging, and shelving of theses. Although no specific dates are cited (except that the thesis was received on November 4, 1977), Dr. Will's affidavits consistently maintain that inasmuch as the Foldi dissertation was received by the library in early November 1977, the dissertation "most probably was available for general use toward the beginning of the month of December, 1977." The only reasonable interpretation of the affidavits is that Dr. Will was relying on his library's general practice for indexing, cataloging, and shelving theses in estimating the time it would have taken to make the dissertation available to the interested public. Dr. Will's affidavits are competent evidence, and in these circumstances, persuasive evidence that the Foldi dissertation was accessible prior to the critical date. Reliance on an approximation found in the affidavits such as "toward the beginning of the month of December, 1977" works no injustice here because the critical date, February 27, 1978, is some two and one half months later. Moreover, it is undisputed that appellant proffered no rebuttal evidence.

Based on what we have already said concerning "public accessibility," and noting that the determination rests on the facts of each case, we reject appellant's legal argument that a single cataloged thesis in one university library does not constitute sufficient accessibility to those interested in the art exercising reasonable diligence.

We agree with the board that the evidence of record consisting of Dr. Will's affidavits establishes a prima facie case for unpatentability of the claims under the § 102(b) publication bar. It is a case which stands unrebutted.

Accordingly, the board's decision sustaining the rejection of appellant's claims is *affirmed*.

NOTES

1. *Scope of "Printed Publication":* Consider the language "known . . . by others" (pre-AIA § 102(a) only), "described in a printed publication" (pre-AIA and post-AIA), and "otherwise available to the public" (post-AIA only). Does *In re Hall* assist you in identifying a difference between "known by others" and "described in a printed publication"? Can you imagine circumstances when any difference would be important? What role do you anticipate for "otherwise available to the public" in light of the breadth of "printed publication" under a case like *In re Hall*?

2. *Enabling Publications:* In order to invalidate a patent under section 102, a "printed publication" must contain a disclosure that is "enabling"—that is, complete enough to enable a person of ordinary skill in the art to make the invention. *See, e.g., Paperless Accounting, Inc. v. Bay Area Rapid Transit Sys.*, 804 F.2d 659, 665 (Fed.Cir.1986) (construing section 102(b)). A non-enabling disclosure, however, may still be considered prior art for purposes of determining obviousness under section 103 (discussed in Chapter 10.D., *infra*).

3. *Beyond Indexing:* In *In re Klopfenstein*, 380 F.3d 1345 (Fed. Cir. 2004), another pre-AIA section 102(b) case, the Federal Circuit expanded on its approach to determining whether a document is sufficiently publicly accessible to be a "printed publication." While noting that distribution and

indexing are helpful "proxies for public accessibility," the court cautioned that these are not the sole measures of public accessibility, and that the determination instead requires "a case-by-case inquiry into the facts and circumstances surrounding the reference's disclosure to members of the public." *Id.* at 1350. In *Klopfenstein,* where the material in question was displayed to members of the public, but never distributed, factors considered by the court included "the length of time the display was exhibited, the expertise of the target audience, the existence (or lack thereof) of reasonable expectations that the material displayed would not be copied, and the simplicity or ease with which the material displayed could have been copied." *Id.; see also M&K Holdings, Inc. v. Samsung Electronics Co., Ltd.*, 985 F.3d 1376 (Fed. Cir. 2021) (affirming two references as printed publications by upholding findings that: a standards-setting organization as a whole was prominent among the community of skilled artisans in the relevant art, and interested users of the organization's website could have located the references through reasonable diligence due to the structure and organization of the site plus the title-search functionality of papers hosted on the site).

In *Bruckelmyer v. Ground Heaters, Inc.*, 445 F.3d 1374 (Fed. Cir. 2006), the Federal Circuit held that a Canadian patent application was an invalidating "printed publication" under pre-AIA section 102(b) where the invention in question was disclosed in two figures that were contained in the underlying application but not in the issued patent. The court reached this conclusion because the issued patent was classified and indexed, the application was publicly accessible as part of the issued patent's underlying file wrapper, and the issued patent stated a possible use for the claimed invention that was illustrated by the two figures in the application.

4. *Questions:* Consider whether the following references should be deemed to anticipate as a printed publication. (Assume that each contains an enabling disclosure of the invention in question.)

(a) a single copy of a document, deposited in a library or archive?

(b) a "classified" or "secret" government document?

(c) a device manufactured for, and delivered to, the federal government under conditions of secrecy?

(d) a United States patent that describes, but does not claim, the subject matter of the invention?

(e) a company's confidential internal memorandum distributed to a small group of researchers and executives?

(f) a manuscript delivered to a publisher but not yet published?

c. "On Sale"

Both pre- and post-AIA versions of section 102 give prior art status to activities that place a claimed invention "on sale." The differences are the critical date and the location of the activity (*i.e.*, pre-AIA "on sale" prior art must be in the United States). What does it mean for an invention to be "on sale"? Must a sale be consummated? Will an offer suffice? What if an offer to sell an invention is made before the object embodying the invention is physically ready for delivery or before the process is actually able to be performed in a commercially viable way?

In the following case, the Supreme Court ruled on the question of whether an inventor's offer to sell an invention not yet reduced to practice placed the invention "on sale" within the meaning of section 102.

PFAFF V. WELLS ELECTRONICS, INC.

525 U.S. 55, 119 S.Ct. 304 (1998).

JUSTICE STEVENS delivered the opinion of the Court.

Section 102(b) of the Patent Act of 1952 provides that no person is entitled to patent an "invention" that has been "on sale" more than one year before filing a patent application. We granted certiorari to determine whether the commercial marketing of a newly invented product may mark the beginning of the 1-year period even though the invention has not yet been reduced to practice.[2]

I

On April 19, 1982, petitioner, Wayne Pfaff, filed an application for a patent on a computer chip socket. Therefore, April 19, 1981, constitutes the critical date for purposes of the on-sale bar of 35 U.S.C. § 102(b); if the 1-year period began to run before that date, Pfaff lost his right to patent his invention.

Pfaff commenced work on the socket in November 1980, when representatives of Texas Instruments asked him to develop a new device for mounting and removing semiconductor chip carriers. In response to this request, he prepared detailed engineering drawings that described the design, the dimensions, and the materials to be used in making the socket. Pfaff sent those drawings to a manufacturer in February or March 1981.

Prior to March 17, 1981, Pfaff showed a sketch of his concept to representatives of Texas Instruments. On April 8, 1981, they provided Pfaff with a written confirmation of a previously placed oral purchase order for 30,100 of his new sockets for a total price of $91,155. In accord with his normal practice, Pfaff did not make and test a prototype of the new device before offering to sell it in commercial quantities.

The manufacturer took several months to develop the customized tooling necessary to produce the device, and Pfaff did not fill the order until

[2] "A process is reduced to practice when it is successfully performed. A machine is reduced to practice when it is assembled, adjusted and used. A manufacture is reduced to practice when it is completely manufactured. A composition of matter is reduced to practice when it is completely composed." *Corona Cord Tire Co. v. Dovan Chemical Corp.*, 276 U.S. 358, 383 (1928).

July 1981. The evidence therefore indicates that Pfaff first reduced his invention to practice in the summer of 1981. The socket achieved substantial commercial success before Patent No. 4,491,377 (the '377 patent) issued to Pfaff on January 1, 1985.

* * *

[After the patent issued, Pfaff brought an infringement action against respondent, Wells Electronics, Inc., a competing socket manufacturer. The District Court found that claims 7, 10 and 11 of the patent were infringed, and] rejected respondent's § 102(b) defense because Pfaff had filed the application for the '377 patent less than a year after reducing the invention to practice.

The Court of Appeals reversed, finding all six claims invalid. 124 F.3d 1429 (C.A.Fed.1997). Four of the claims (1, 6, 7, and 10) described the socket that Pfaff had sold to Texas Instruments prior to April 8, 1981. Because that device had been offered for sale on a commercial basis more than one year before the patent application was filed on April 19, 1982, the court concluded that those claims were invalid under § 102(b). That conclusion rested on the court's view that as long as the invention was "substantially complete at the time of sale," the 1-year period began to run, even though the invention had not yet been reduced to practice. Id., at 1434. The other two claims (11 and 19) described a feature that had not been included in Pfaff's initial design, but the Court of Appeals concluded as a matter of law that the additional feature was not itself patentable because it was an obvious addition to the prior art. Given the court's § 102(b) holding, the prior art included Pfaff's first four claims.

Because other courts have held or assumed that an invention cannot be "on sale" within the meaning of § 102(b) unless and until it has been reduced to practice, and because the text of § 102(b) makes no reference to "substantial completion" of an invention, we granted certiorari.

II

The primary meaning of the word "invention" in the Patent Act unquestionably refers to the inventor's conception rather than to a physical embodiment of that idea. The statute does not contain any express requirement that an invention must be reduced to practice before it can be patented. Neither the statutory definition of the term in § 100 nor the basic conditions for obtaining a patent set forth in § 101 make any mention of "reduction to practice." The statute's only specific reference to that term is found in § 102(g), which sets forth the standard for resolving priority contests between two competing claimants to a patent. That subsection provides:

> "In determining priority of invention there shall be considered not only the respective dates of conception and reduction to practice

of the invention, but also the reasonable diligence of one who was first to conceive and last to reduce to practice, from a time prior to conception by the other."

Thus, assuming diligence on the part of the applicant, it is normally the first inventor to conceive, rather than the first to reduce to practice, who establishes the right to the patent.

It is well settled that an invention may be patented before it is reduced to practice. In 1888, this Court upheld a patent issued to Alexander Graham Bell even though he had filed his application before constructing a working telephone. Chief Justice Waite's reasoning in that case merits quoting at length:

> "It is quite true that when Bell applied for his patent he had never actually transmitted telegraphically spoken words so that they could be distinctly heard and understood at the receiving end of his line, but in his specification he did describe accurately and with admirable clearness his process, that is to say, the exact electrical condition that must be created to accomplish his purpose, and he also described, with sufficient precision to enable one of ordinary skill in such matters to make it, a form of apparatus which, if used in the way pointed out, would produce the required effect, receive the words, and carry them to and deliver them at the appointed place. The particular instrument which he had, and which he used in his experiments, did not, under the circumstances in which it was tried, reproduce the words spoken, so that they could be clearly understood, but the proof is abundant and of the most convincing character, that other instruments, carefully constructed and made exactly in accordance with the specification, without any additions whatever, have operated and will operate successfully. A good mechanic of proper skill in matters of the kind can take the patent and, by following the specification strictly, can, without more, construct an apparatus which, when used in the way pointed out, will do all that it is claimed the method or process will do. . . .
>
> "The law does not require that a discoverer or inventor, in order to get a patent for a process, must have succeeded in bringing his art to the highest degree of perfection. It is enough if he describes his method with sufficient clearness and precision to enable those skilled in the matter to understand what the process is, and if he points out some practicable way of putting it into operation." The Telephone Cases, 126 U.S. 1 (1888).[10]

---

[10] This Court has also held a patent invalid because the invention had previously been disclosed in a prior patent application, although that application did not claim the invention and

When we apply the reasoning of *The Telephone Cases* to the facts of the case before us today, it is evident that Pfaff could have obtained a patent on his novel socket when he accepted the purchase order from Texas Instruments for 30,100 units. At that time he provided the manufacturer with a description and drawings that had "sufficient clearness and precision to enable those skilled in the matter" to produce the device. The parties agree that the sockets manufactured to fill that order embody Pfaff's conception as set forth in claims 1, 6, 7, and 10 of the '377 patent. We can find no basis in the text of § 102(b) or in the facts of this case for concluding that Pfaff's invention was not "on sale" within the meaning of the statute until after it had been reduced to practice.

III

Pfaff nevertheless argues that longstanding precedent, buttressed by the strong interest in providing inventors with a clear standard identifying the onset of the 1-year period, justifies a special interpretation of the word "invention" as used in § 102(b). We are persuaded that this nontextual argument should be rejected.

As we have often explained, most recently in *Bonito Boats, Inc. v. Thunder Craft Boats*, Inc., 489 U.S. 141, 151 (1989), the patent system represents a carefully crafted bargain that encourages both the creation and the public disclosure of new and useful advances in technology, in return for an exclusive monopoly for a limited period of time. The balance between the interest in motivating innovation and enlightenment by rewarding invention with patent protection on the one hand, and the interest in avoiding monopolies that unnecessarily stifle competition on the other, has been a feature of the federal patent laws since their inception. As this Court explained in 1871:

> "Letters patent are not to be regarded as monopolies . . . but as public franchises granted to the inventors of new and useful improvements for the purpose of securing to them, as such inventors, for the limited term therein mentioned, the exclusive right and liberty to make and use and vend to others to be used their own inventions, as tending to promote the progress of science and the useful arts, and as matter of compensation to the inventors for their labor, toil, and expense in making the inventions, and reducing the same to practice for the public benefit, as contemplated by the Constitution and sanctioned by the laws of Congress." *Seymour v. Osborne*, 78 U.S. 516.

Consistent with these ends, § 102 of the Patent Act serves as a limiting provision, both excluding ideas that are in the public domain from patent

the first invention apparently had not been reduced to practice. *Alexander Milburn Co. v. Davis-Bournonville Co.*, 270 U.S. 390, 401–402 (1926).

protection and confining the duration of the monopoly to the statutory term.

We originally held that an inventor loses his right to a patent if he puts his invention into public use before filing a patent application. "His voluntary act or acquiescence in the public sale and use is an abandonment of his right" *Pennock v. Dialogue*, 2 Pet. 1, 24 (1829) (Story, J.). A similar reluctance to allow an inventor to remove existing knowledge from public use undergirds the on-sale bar.

Nevertheless, an inventor who seeks to perfect his discovery may conduct extensive testing without losing his right to obtain a patent for his invention—even if such testing occurs in the public eye. The law has long recognized the distinction between inventions put to experimental use and products sold commercially. In 1878, we explained why patentability may turn on an inventor's use of his product.

> "It is sometimes said that an inventor acquires an undue advantage over the public by delaying to take out a patent, inasmuch as he thereby preserves the monopoly to himself for a longer period than is allowed by the policy of the law; but this cannot be said with justice when the delay is occasioned by a bona fide effort to bring his invention to perfection, or to ascertain whether it will answer the purpose intended. His monopoly only continues for the allotted period, in any event; and it is the interest of the public, as well as himself, that the invention should be perfect and properly tested, before a patent is granted for it. *Any attempt to use it for a profit, and not by way of experiment, for a longer period than two years before the application, would deprive the inventor of his right to a patent.*" *Elizabeth v. Pavement Co.*, 97 U.S. 126, 137 (emphasis added).

The patent laws therefore seek both to protect the public's right to retain knowledge already in the public domain and the inventor's right to control whether and when he may patent his invention. The Patent Act of 1836, 5 Stat. 117, was the first statute that expressly included an on-sale bar to the issuance of a patent. Like the earlier holding in *Pennock*, that provision precluded patentability if the invention had been placed on sale at any time before the patent application was filed. In 1839, Congress ameliorated that requirement by enacting a 2-year grace period in which the inventor could file an application. 5 Stat. 353.

In *Andrews v. Hovey*, 123 U.S. 267, 274 (1887), we noted that the purpose of that amendment was "to fix a period of limitation which should be certain"; it required the inventor to make sure that a patent application was filed "within two years from the completion of his invention." In 1939, Congress reduced the grace period from two years to one year.

Petitioner correctly argues that these provisions identify an interest in providing inventors with a definite standard for determining when a patent application must be filed. A rule that makes the timeliness of an application depend on the date when an invention is "substantially complete" seriously undermines the interest in certainty.[11] Moreover, such a rule finds no support in the text of the statute. Thus, petitioner's argument calls into question the standard applied by the Court of Appeals, but it does not persuade us that it is necessary to engraft a reduction to practice element into the meaning of the term "invention" as used in § 102(b).

The word "invention" must refer to a concept that is complete, rather than merely one that is "substantially complete." It is true that reduction to practice ordinarily provides the best evidence that an invention is complete. But just because reduction to practice is sufficient evidence of completion, it does not follow that proof of reduction to practice is necessary in every case. Indeed, both the facts of the *Telephone Cases* and the facts of this case demonstrate that one can prove that an invention is complete and ready for patenting before it has actually been reduced to practice.[12]

We conclude, therefore, that the on-sale bar applies when two conditions are satisfied before the critical date.

First, the product must be the subject of a commercial offer for sale. An inventor can both understand and control the timing of the first commercial marketing of his invention. The experimental use doctrine, for example, has not generated concerns about indefiniteness,[13] and we perceive no reason why unmanageable uncertainty should attend a rule that measures the application of the on-sale bar of § 102(b) against the date when an invention that is ready for patenting is first marketed commercially. In this case the acceptance of the purchase order prior to

---

[11] The Federal Circuit has developed a multifactor, "totality of the circumstances" test to determine the trigger for the on-sale bar. As the Federal Circuit itself has noted, this test "has been criticized as unnecessarily vague."

[12] Several of this Court's early decisions stating that an invention is not complete until it has been reduced to practice are best understood as indicating that the invention's reduction to practice demonstrated that the concept was no longer in an experimental phase. *See, e.g., Seymour v. Osborne*, 78 U.S. 516 (1870) ("Crude and imperfect experiments are not sufficient to confer a right to a patent; but in order to constitute an invention, the party must have proceeded so far as to have reduced his idea to practice, and embodied it in some distinct form"); *Clark Thread Co. v. Willimantic Linen Co.*, 140 U.S. 481, 489 (1891) (describing how inventor continued to alter his thread winding machine until July 1858, when "he put it in visible form in the shape of a machine. . . . It is evident that the invention was not completed until the construction of the machine"); *Corona Cord Tire Co. v. Dovan Chemical Corp.*, 276 U.S. at 382–383 (stating that an invention did not need to be subsequently commercialized to constitute prior art after the inventor had finished his experimentation. "It was the fact that it would work with great activity as an accelerator that was the discovery, and that was all, and the necessary reduction to use is shown by instances making clear that it did so work, and was a completed discovery").

[13] *See, e.g.*, Rooklidge & Jensen, *Common Sense, Simplicity and Experimental Use Negation of the Public Use and On Sale Bars to Patentability*, 29 JOHN MARSHALL L. REV. 1, 29 (1995) (stating that "whether a particular activity is experimental is often clear").

April 8, 1981, makes it clear that such an offer had been made, and there is no question that the sale was commercial rather than experimental in character.

Second, the invention must be ready for patenting. That condition may be satisfied in at least two ways: by proof of reduction to practice before the critical date; or by proof that prior to the critical date the inventor had prepared drawings or other descriptions of the invention that were sufficiently specific to enable a person skilled in the art to practice the invention.[14] In this case the second condition of the on-sale bar is satisfied because the drawings Pfaff sent to the manufacturer before the critical date fully disclosed the invention.

The evidence in this case thus fulfills the two essential conditions of the on-sale bar. As succinctly stated by Learned Hand:

> "It is a condition upon an inventor's right to a patent that he shall not exploit his discovery competitively after it is ready for patenting; he must content himself with either secrecy, or legal monopoly." *Metallizing Engineering Co. v. Kenyon Bearing & Auto Parts Co.*, 153 F.2d 516, 520 (C.A.2 1946).

The judgment of the Court of Appeals finds support not only in the text of the statute but also in the basic policies underlying the statutory scheme, including § 102(b). When Pfaff accepted the purchase order for his new sockets prior to April 8, 1981, his invention was ready for patenting. The fact that the manufacturer was able to produce the socket using his detailed drawings and specifications demonstrates this fact. Furthermore, those sockets contained all the elements of the invention claimed in the '377 patent. Therefore, Pfaff's '377 patent is invalid because the invention had been on sale for more than one year in this country before he filed his patent application. Accordingly, the judgment of the Court of Appeals is affirmed.

It is so ordered.

NOTES

1. *Post-AIA Meaning of "On Sale"*: In *Helsinn Healthcare S.A. v. Teva Pharmaceuticals USA, Inc.*, 139 S.Ct. 628 (2019), the Supreme Court interpreted for the first time the basic novelty provision of the AIA, 35 U.S.C. § 102(a)(1), barring a patent when an invention "was patented, described in a

---

[14] The Solicitor General has argued that the rule governing on-sale bar should be phrased somewhat differently. In his opinion, "if the sale or offer in question embodies the invention for which a patent is later sought, a sale or offer to sell that is primarily for commercial purposes and that occurs more than one year before the application renders the invention unpatentable." It is true that evidence satisfying this test might be sufficient to prove that the invention was ready for patenting at the time of the sale if it is clear that no aspect of the invention was developed after the critical date. However, the possibility of additional development after the offer for sale in these circumstances counsels against adoption of the rule proposed by the Solicitor General.

printed publication, or in public use, on sale, or otherwise available to the public before the effective filing date of the claimed invention." At issue in the case was the meaning of "on sale," specifically whether the meaning of "on sale" had changed in the AIA in comparison to its pre-AIA meaning. Petitioner-patentee Helsinn's primary argument before the Court was that the addition of "otherwise available to the public"—language not present in pre-AIA § 102(b)—altered the meaning of "on sale" to exclude any sales that did not make the invention "available to the public." (See also Note 2 below.) In other words, the petitioner argued that adding "otherwise available to the public" to the end of the list of novelty bars changed the meaning of the preceding words or phrases, even though all preceding wording was present in pre-AIA § 102 and had been interpreted by courts over a period of many years before being otherwise identically reenacted in post-AIA § 102. The Court disagreed. It held that the meaning of "on sale" did not change when reenacted in the AIA.

> Congress enacted the AIA in 2011 against the backdrop of a substantial body of law interpreting § 102's on-sale bar. * * *
>
> Although this Court has never addressed the precise question presented in this case, our precedents suggest that a sale or offer of sale need not make an invention available to the public. For instance, we held in *Pfaff* that an offer for sale could cause an inventor to lose the right to patent, without regard to whether the offer discloses each detail of the invention. Other cases focus on whether the invention had been sold, not whether the details of the invention had been made available to the public or whether the sale itself had been publicly disclosed. *E.g., Consolidated Fruit-Jar Co. v. Wright*, 94 U.S. 92, 94 (1877) ("[A] single instance of sale or of use by the patentee may, under the circumstances, be fatal to the patent . . ."); *cf. Smith & Griggs Mfg. v. Sprague*, 123 U.S. 249, 257 (1887) ("A single sale to another . . . would certainly have defeated his right to a patent . . ."); *Elizabeth v. Pavement Co.*, 97 U.S. 126, 136 (1878) ("It is not a public knowledge of his invention that precludes the inventor from obtaining a patent for it, but a public use or sale of it").
>
> The Federal Circuit—which has "exclusive jurisdiction" over patent appeals, 28 U.S.C. § 1295(a)—has made explicit what was implicit in our precedents. It has long held that "secret sales" can invalidate a patent. *E.g.*, * * * *Woodland Trust v. Flowertree Nursery, Inc.*, 148 F.3d 1368, 1370 (1998) ("Thus an inventor's own prior commercial use, albeit kept secret, may constitute a public use or sale under § 102(b), barring him from obtaining a patent").
>
> In light of this settled pre-AIA precedent on the meaning of "on sale," we presume that when Congress reenacted the same language in the AIA, it adopted the earlier judicial construction of that phrase. The new § 102 retained the exact language used in its predecessor statute ("on sale") and, as relevant here, added only a new catchall clause ("or otherwise available to the public"). As *amicus* United

States noted at oral argument, if "on sale" had a settled meaning before the AIA was adopted, then adding the phrase "or otherwise available to the public" to the statute "would be a fairly oblique way of attempting to overturn" that "settled body of law." Tr. of Oral Arg. 28. The addition of "or otherwise available to the public" is simply not enough of a change for us to conclude that Congress intended to alter the meaning of the reenacted term "on sale."

Helsinn disagrees, arguing that our construction reads "otherwise" out of the statute. * * * Helsinn contends that the associated-words canon requires us to read "otherwise available to the public" to limit the preceding terms in § 102 to disclosures that make the claimed invention available to the public.

As an initial matter, neither of the cited decisions addresses the reenactment of terms that had acquired a well-settled judicial interpretation. And Helsinn's argument places too much weight on § 102's catchall phrase. Like other such phrases, "otherwise available to the public" captures material that does not fit neatly into the statute's enumerated categories but is nevertheless meant to be covered. Given that the phrase "on sale" had acquired a well-settled meaning when the AIA was enacted, we decline to read the addition of a broad catchall phrase to upset that body of precedent.

Helsinn does not ask us to revisit our pre-AIA interpretation of the on-sale bar. Nor does it dispute the Federal Circuit's determination that the invention claimed in the '219 patent was "on sale" within the meaning of the pre-AIA statute. Because we determine that Congress did not alter the meaning of "on sale" when it enacted the AIA, we hold that an inventor's sale of an invention to a third party who is obligated to keep the invention confidential can qualify as prior art under § 102(a).

Helsinn Healthcare S.A. v. Teva Pharm. USA, Inc., 139 S.Ct. 628, 633–34 (2019). Similar arguments could be made about a change of meaning to longstanding interpretations of the inventor's own "public use," *see* Note 4 on page 461, but for reasons parallel to those above, one might anticipate them to be similarly unsuccessful.

2. *Distinction Between the Inventor and a Third Party:* In most cases, courts apply to the on-sale bar an analysis similar to that used for the public use bar, when considering whether the product on sale must disclose the invention to the public in order to bar a patent under pre-AIA § 102(b). Review Note 4 on page 461, which discusses the "public use" bar. In short, the on-sale bar applies to *all* "on sale" activities *of the inventor* and those acting with the inventor's authority, regardless of whether the activity discloses the invention to the public. *See also* Note 1 above. It also applies to the activities of *other parties*, even where those activities are independent, *if the activity discloses the invention* to the public, although in those cases the courts may also consider the disclosing sale to implicate public use:

> An offer for sale, sale, or public use, if more than one year before the patent application was filed, will bar patenting of the product, even if the sale was not authorized by the patentee. *See In re Caveney*, 761 F.2d 671, 675 (Fed.Cir.1985) ("[S]ales or offers by one person of a claimed invention will bar another party from obtaining a patent if the sale or offer to sell is made over a year before the latter's filing date. An exception to this general rule exists where a patented method is kept secret and remains secret after a sale of the unpatented product of the method. Such a sale prior to the critical date is a bar if engaged in by the patentee or patent applicant, but not if engaged in by another.") (citations omitted). As the court explained in *Caveney*, "The 'on sale' provision of 35 U.S.C. § 102(b) is directed at precluding an inventor from commercializing his invention for over a year before he files his application. Sales or offers made by others and disclosing the claimed invention implicate the 'public use' provision of 35 U.S.C. § 102(b)."

ResQNet.com, Inc. v. Lansa, Inc., 594 F.3d 860, 866 (Fed. Cir. 2010). In reading the excerpt, recall this is a pre-AIA case, and post-AIA there will be no one-year grace period following third party prior art sales and uses.

3. *License Versus Sale:* In *Elan Corp., PLC v. Andrx Pharmaceuticals, Inc.*, 366 F.3d 1336 (Fed. Cir. 2004), the Federal Circuit held that the section 102(b) on-sale bar was not implicated by an offer to license the right to manufacture an invention:

> Following *Pfaff*, this court held in *Group One*[, *Ltd. v. Hallmark Cards, Inc.*, 254 F.3d 1041, 1045–46 (Fed.Cir. 2001)] that "[o]nly an offer which rises to the level of a commercial offer for sale, one which the other party could make into a binding contract by simple acceptance . . ., constitutes an offer for sale under § 102(b)." 254 F.3d at 1048. We further explained that "a sale of rights in a patent, as distinct from a sale of the invention itself, is not within the scope of the statute, and thus does not implicate the on-sale bar." *Id.* at 1049. In *In re Kollar*, 286 F.3d 1326 (Fed.Cir. 2002), we held that an offer to license a patent claiming an invention after future research and development had occurred, without more, is not an offer to sell the invention.
>
> Based on the principles articulated in *Pfaff*, *Group One*, and *Kollar*, we conclude that the district court erred in concluding that Elan's product was the subject of a commercial offer for sale based on Elan's letter to Lederle. An offer to enter into a license under a patent for future sale of the invention covered by the patent when and if it has been developed, which is what the Lederle letter was, is not an offer to sell the patented invention that constitutes an on-sale bar. *Kollar*, 286 F.3d at 1331. The letter to Lederle is clear on its face that Elan was not offering to sell naproxen tablets to Lederle, but rather granting a license under the patent and offering Lederle the

> opportunity to become its partner in the clinical testing and eventual marketing of such tablets at some indefinite point in the future. * * * [T]he dollar amounts recited in the fourth paragraph of the letter to Lederle are clearly not price terms for the sale of tablets, but rather the amount that Elan was requesting to form and continue a partnership with Lederle. Indeed, the letter explicitly refers to the total as a "licensing fee."
>
> Of course, if Elan had simply disguised a sales price as a licensing fee it would not avoid triggering the on-sale bar. Nonetheless, that is not what Elan did here. If Lederle had accepted Elan's offer, it would have owed Elan $500,000 at contract signing and additional amounts at various milestones in the collaboration. There is no statement in the letter of how many tablets Elan would supply in exchange for those funds, and there is no suggestion that the number of tablets supplied would depend in any way on those payments (although the payments were to be keyed to the number of patients enrolled in clinical trials per the fifth paragraph of the letter).

366 F.3d at 1341. Where the invention in question is a process, the Federal Circuit has held that the on-sale bar is triggered by the sale of a product made by that process, and by performing (or offering to perform) the process itself for consideration, but not by a license of the right to practice the process. *In re Kollar*, 286 F.3d 1326, 1332 (Fed. Cir. 2002).

4. *Selling While Experimenting:* The experimental use doctrine (discussed in Note 6 on pages 463–464, *supra*) also applies to the "on sale" bar; as in cases involving the "public use" bar, the doctrine applies only where the evidence demonstrates a bona fide experimental purpose, and factors such as those discussed in *Elizabeth* and *Baxter International* should have equal relevance in the sale context. *See, e.g., In re Hamilton*, 882 F.2d 1576, 1581 (Fed.Cir.1989) (discussing experimental use in the context of the on-sale bar). Should the experimental use exception apply where a sale serves both an experimental and a commercial purpose?

5. *Geographic Scope of "On Sale":* A significant change in the AIA is the elimination of the geographic limit on "on sale" prior art, as noted earlier in the chapter. Post-AIA section 102 considers "on sale" prior art anywhere in the world, while pre-AIA law only examines sales in this country. That means under pre-AIA section 102(b), placing a claimed invention on sale in a foreign country more than a year before the date of application does not bar a patent in this country, although identical domestic sales activity would bar the patent; post-AIA, the location of the sale will be irrelevant.

6. *Questions:* Should the "on sale" bar be triggered by: (a) the sale, merger or reorganization of a going concern which includes an invention (or the products thereof)? (b) the transfer of an invention (or the products thereof) by a corporation to its parent, subsidiary, or other corporate affiliate?

d. "Patented"

Under pre-AIA section 102, if the claimed invention has been "patented" anywhere either before the date of invention (pre-AIA § 102(a)) or more than one year before the filing date (pre-AIA § 102(b)), the earlier patent anticipates the claimed invention and bars the issuance of a patent to the applicant on that invention. Under post-AIA section 102, the timing will change, but the question of patenting will remain the same. Post-AIA, the question becomes whether the claimed invention has been patented anywhere, at any time, before the effective filing date.

At the highest level, this is easy enough to understand. Patents are exclusionary rights granted by the government in exchange for public disclosure of inventions, and it makes little sense for the government to grant one party an exclusionary right if an invention has already been patented and therefore publicly disclosed by, another inventor. When it comes to applying the provision in some cases, however, an issue may arise as to the date on which the invention in question became subject to a foreign patent, because the date on which a foreign patent officially issues may differ from the date on which it becomes accessible to the public, the date on which some or all of the inventor's rights become exclusive, or the date on which the patentee is entitled to enforce the patent. Finally, where a foreign grant conveys rights which are significantly different from those conveyed by United States patents, courts must determine whether to treat the foreign grant as a patent at all. *See, e.g., In re Carlson*, 983 F.2d 1032 (Fed.Cir.1992) (treating German design patent as anticipatory subject matter even though the rights conveyed more closely resembled a copyright).

Pre-AIA section 102(d) is a provision also relating to earlier foreign patents—but it only relates to the applicant's own filings (or applicant's legal representatives or assigns). Its purpose was to encourage rapid U.S. filing after a foreign filing; it specifically discouraged inventors from delaying the filing of a U.S. patent application for more than one year after a foreign filing for the same invention. *See In re Kathawala*, 9 F.3d 942 (Fed. Cir. 1993). It invalidates a pre-AIA U.S. patent if the applicant for the U.S. patent filed a foreign application more than one year before the U.S. application and the related foreign patent issued before the U.S. filing date.

5. FIRST TO FILE (OR TO PUBLICLY DISCLOSE)

As mentioned earlier, in the introduction to post-AIA section 102, unlike some other first-to-file systems, the U.S. system contains two grace periods cutting away at the focus on the effective filing date. In contrast with pre-AIA section 102, the first-filing inventor does not enjoy a general one-year grace period in which to file an application after all public disclosures. One grace period is confined to the first-filing inventor's own activities, while the other one requires the first-filing inventor to have publicly disclosed the invention before the third party's act.

One of the grace periods in post-AIA section 102(b) is in a sense, personal to the inventor, while the other is absolute. The personal, or tentative grace period in section 102(b)(1)(A) gives inventors up to one year (before filing) in which their own disclosures of any type will not bar a patent. Section 102(b)(1)(A) does not protect the right to file against a third party's disclosures into the prior art. The absolute grace period of section 102(b)(1)(B) & (b)(2)(B), on the other hand, requires a *public* disclosure rather than a mere disclosure, and it acts as a shield to protect the inventor's right to file for one year by barring a third party's later-filed application and preventing any third-party disclosures from becoming prior art to the inventor's own application. If the inventor's disclosure does not reveal the invention to the public, the inventor is not protected against a third party's filing of an application for the invention. As to Inventor A, a public use or printed publication by Inventor B is an absolute bar at the moment it occurs *unless* A had already publicly disclosed or filed an application for the invention. As to Inventor B, however, that same public use or publication begins a one-year grace period in which intervening disclosures by other persons will not become invalidating prior art to Inventor B's application.

The first-to-file aspect of post-AIA 102(a)(2) relies on two different filing dates. First is the "effective filing date" of the application under immediate examination, *see supra* page 453 (post-AIA § 100(i)(1)), while the second is the similarly, but not identically defined date on which the novelty-defeating piece of prior art was "effectively filed," *see* post-AIA § 102(a)(2) & (d). The date by which a novelty-defeating patent or application will be judged under section 102(a)(2) is the actual filing date of the application (or the application on which the patent was granted) or, if applicable, the filing date of certain earlier, but related applications, such as a prior foreign application that provided priority to the U.S. application, *see* post-AIA § 102(d)(2), as long as the "subject matter" in question is described in the earlier application. These patents or applications "effectively filed" before the "effective filing date" of the claimed invention need not claim the subject matter in order to defeat the novelty of the claimed invention (in the application under immediate examination). One distinction between the "effective filing date" and the date on which prior art was "effectively filed" is that an effective filing date is claim-specific (one application can include multiple claims with different effective filing dates), while the date on which a prior art application was "effectively filed" is not claim-specific but instead relates to subject matter disclosed or described.

Post-AIA section 102(a)(2)'s implementation of the "first to file" rule also comes with protection in section 102(b)(2)(C) designed to prevent applications subject to common ownership (including merely a joint research agreement, *see* § 102(c)) from invalidating one another. This feature can be particularly important when section 102 prior art is applied in the section 103 obviousness analysis, the subject of Part D of this chapter, below.

After the examination system fully transitions to post-AIA section 102, there will be no section 102(g)-type priority determinations in which priority is based on a date of invention (discussed further in the next part of this chapter). But a different type of fact-specific priority determination will still need to be made during the examination of an application (or when an invalidity defense is raised). Post-AIA section 102 can provide an absolute one-year grace period after a *public* disclosure by an inventor—with the public disclosure absolutely barring an application by another inventor. *See* post-AIA § 102(b) (creating an exception from the 102(a) novelty rule for third-party disclosures of subject matter when the inventor (or certain other parties) has previously publicly disclosed the same subject matter). As a result, while priority will not be based on the date of invention under post-AIA law, the effective filing date alone will not govern whether the first-filed application will be given priority over later applications. The AIA's failure to rely solely on effective filing dates means that post-AIA conflicts between competing inventors will not all be resolved easily, without in-depth factual inquiries. These conflicts between co-pending applications will not be subject to section 135 interferences within the PTO, however, when both applications contain only claims with effective filing dates after March 16, 2013.

Questions still unresolved include, but are certainly not limited to: (1) what is within "otherwise available to the public" that is not included in the other types of listed prior art (recall the breadth of "printed publication," for example, and see Note 1 on page 469 after *In re Hall*, *supra*); (2) the difference between a "disclosure" and a "public disclosure" with respect to gaining the absolute one-year grace period (compare § 102(b)(1)(A) with § 102(b)(1)(B)); and (3) what it means for a disclosure to come "directly or indirectly" from the applicant, such that it can be excluded from the prior art.

6. OTHER OBSTACLES AND ISSUES IN SECTION 102

a. Non-Public Prior Art in Prior-Filed Applications

Almost all prior art addressed thus far, whether pre-AIA or post-AIA, requires some element of public accessibility before a bar will apply. An exception is when an inventor's uses or sales have an element of secrecy but allow commercialization more than a year before the filing date. See *supra* discussions in Note 4 on page 461 after *Bennett Regulator Guards, Inc. v. Canadian Meter Co.* and in Note 2 on page 479 after *Pfaff v. Wells Electronics, Inc.* One type of entirely non-public prior art exists, however, in both pre-AIA and post-AIA section 102: certain prior-filed patent applications describing the invention and filed by others.

Pre-AIA section 102(e) gives prior art status to (and thus eliminates novelty based on) certain patent applications that describe the invention and are filed by others before the applicant's date of invention. Review pre-AIA section 102(e) for details. The fact that these applications may not have been available to the public or the applicant before the applicant's date of invention is not relevant under 102(e). A prior-filed application describing the same invention (even if it does not claim it) demonstrates that the current inventor was not the first, making this novelty bar is entirely logical in light of the pre-AIA policy goal of preferring to award a patent to the first inventor to invent.

Now compare pre-AIA section 102(e) with post-AIA section 102(a)(2). Observe that under the AIA, prior-filed application-based non-public prior art continues to invalidate the later-filed application. This is simply the first-to-file rule, which is discussed further above in Chapter 10.C.5.

b. Priority Determinations

The question of "priority" under the AIA is addressed by novelty rule, including the rule of first-to-file (or to publicly disclose). Pre-AIA section 102(g) contains two separate priority-based provisions addressing pre-AIA invention priority when a later-filing inventor claims to be the first to invent; these provisions address when an earlier inventor gains (and does not gain) priority over a competing, true inventor. *See, e.g., Paulik v. Rizkalla*, 760 F.2d 1270 (Fed. Cir. 1985) (holding a long period of inactivity did not always create forfeiture under section 102(g) for the first inventor (and second filer) if the first inventor resumed work on the invention before a second inventor enters the field and files the first patent application). In section 102(g)(1), which is applicable when two applicants (or an applicant and a patentee) are competing in an interference for priority to a claimed invention, the first person to invent gains priority unless deemed to have "abandoned, suppressed, or concealed" the invention. Inventive activity in the U.S. or a NAFTA or WTO member country can be used to prove the earliest date of invention under 102(g)(1). Under section 102(g)(2), however, which applies in any validity determination, not merely in the interference context, only inventive activity in this country may be applied to deny priority to the patentee or patent applicant.

Pre-AIA 102(g), as you will recall, continues to apply to applications containing claims with effective filing dates before March 16, 2013. Thus, section 102(g) priority determinations will continue for some time. Interference proceedings under pre-AIA section 135 will remain available for patents and applications containing at least one claim with an effective filing date before March 16, 2013 (which is when the first-to-invent novelty and priority rules cease to apply and the first-to-file priority rules come into effect). Some unusual issues arise from the transition between the first-to-invent system to the first-to-file (or publicly disclose) system of the AIA. One such issue is the fact that an application containing at least one claim with a pre-March 16, 2013 effective filing date and at least one claim with a post-March 16, 2013 effective filing date (*see infra* Chapter 11.B.1.c., continuation-in-part applications) will be examined for "basic" novelty purposes under post-AIA section 102, yet that same application may also become subject to a pre-AIA section 135 interference, which in turn will utilize pre-AIA section 102(g). *Compare* AIA § 3(n)(1) *with* § 3(n)(2); *see also* MPEP § 2301.04.

NOTES

1. *Same-Day Filing:* What should the PTO do if two inventors independently file an application on the same date claiming the same invention? Do you think this is likely to occur in practice?

2. *Pre-AIA Inventorship Overlap:* Under pre-AIA section 102(a), (e) & (g), invalidating prior art does not include work by the same inventorship entity (that is, the same sole inventor or the same group of co-inventors) as in the later patent application. In contrast, while the matter is not entirely free from doubt, it appears that work by another inventorship entity with partially overlapping membership *would* constitute prior art under these provisions. *See generally* D. CHISUM, 1–3 CHISUM ON PATENTS § 3.08[2][a] (collecting cases).

c. Derivation of the Invention from Another

Both pre- and post-AIA law contain features requiring a patent to be awarded only to a "true" inventor or that person's assignee, rather than to one who learns of or derives an invention from another person's inventive activity.

Pre-AIA section 102(f) might be called either a "true inventor" or "anti-derivation" novelty rule. It bars a patent to an applicant "when he did not himself invent the subject matter sought to be patented." In *Applegate v. Scherer*, 332 F.2d 572 (C.C.P.A. 1964), for example, the question of derivation arose in an interference, which is a pre-AIA proceeding instituted within the PTO to settle a conflict over an invention created by a pending application. *See* pre-AIA 35 U.S.C. § 135. (Not all interferences present questions of derivation; more common would be conflicting claims, yet independently developed inventions.) In *Applegate v. Scherer* each party had applied for a patent on the same method for controlling sea lampreys, which were causing "havoc" in the Great Lakes and surrounding fresh water streams, by using a specific chemical composition to treat streams where lamprey spawn. The PTO declared an interference between the conflicting (or interfering) applications under 35 U.S.C. § 135. Reducing the facts to their simplest essence, Scherer had the idea and disclosed it to Applegate, who tested it and confirmed it worked as expected. Both filed for patents. Applegate's theory to defend the patent from invalidation for derivation—that without a reduction to practice, Scherer's conception of the full invention was incomplete—was rejected. The underlying finding of derivation under 102(f) was affirmed.

Pre-AIA section 102(f) issues can also arise in infringement litigation when an accused infringer challenges the validity of a patent claim based on failure to name the true inventor. The accused infringer need not be the true inventor to raise the 102(f) issue in litigation.

Post-AIA law does not contain a direct analogue in section 102, but it retains the basic principle that a patent should only go to a "true" inventor or that person's assignee, rather than one who learns or derives an invention from another person's inventive activity. The true inventor or anti-derivation principle appears today in the Patent Act in various ways: section 115's requirement of an oath or declaration from named inventors that they believe themselves to be the original or an original joint inventor of the claimed invention, section 100(f)'s definition of "inventor," section 135's new Board proceeding called a "derivation proceeding," and section 291's civil action for derivation.[7] Note also the possible constitutional dimension to the true inventor or anti-derivation principle: Article I, § 8 provides that "Congress shall have Power. . . To promote the Progress of. . . useful Arts, by securing for limited Times *to. . . Inventors* the exclusive Right to *their. . . Discoveries*" (emphasis added).

Derivation proceedings under post-AIA section 135 are applicable to patents and applications containing claims with effective filing dates after March 16, 2013. The end result of a successful derivation proceeding, which must be filed by a later applicant who claims the same invention as an earlier applicant, will be that the earlier applicant will be refused a patent on the affected, derived claims. *See* 35 U.S.C. § 135. A true inventor may also have a civil action for relief under post-AIA section 291, which will provide the owner of a later-filed patent with a civil action against the owner of an earlier-filed patent claiming the same invention and naming a deriving non-true inventor. Post-AIA section 291 limits the filing of actions to the first year after issuance of the patent containing a claim to the derived invention. In keeping with the change from a first-to-file system to a first-to-invent(-or-publicly-disclose) system, neither section 135 nor section 291 addresses, post-AIA, which inventor was "first." The sole question for post-AIA patents will be "true" inventorship and derivation of

[7] The derivation proceeding before the Patent Trial and Appeal Board replaces the interference proceedings, previously codified at § 135, although those proceedings will continue to exist for some time for pre-AIA applications; The civil action for derived patents replaces at § 291 the former civil action for interfering patents.

the invention from the person challenging the earlier-filed application. For more on who is an "inventor," go to Chapter 11.A., *infra*.

d. Abandoning the Invention

Pre-AIA section 102(c) bars a patent when the inventor "has abandoned the invention." Post-AIA section 102 eliminates abandonment from consideration and relies on the "first to file" rule to spur inventors to seek a patent or risk loss of that option. Beyond being seemingly unnecessary in a first-to-file (or to publicly disclose) system, the abandonment provision was almost never successfully used to invalidate a patent as a practical matter—because other arguments were better in many cases. If the inventor has used the invention commercially during a period of delay between inventing and filing an application, there is a clearer-cut argument for invalidity under pre-AIA 102(b) than under 102(c). As explained above in Parts C.4.a. and C.4.c. of this Chapter 10, even secret use of an invention by the inventor, if commercially exploited for more than a year before filing, eliminates novelty under either the public use bar or the on-sale bar. The activities and timing under pre-AIA 102(b) are relatively clear, making a more difficult argument of "abandoned" patent rights unnecessary. If the inventor has not used the invention during the period of delay, however, then a pre-AIA 102(b) argument cannot be substituted.

If the inventor has not used the invention while delaying, and has done nothing more than delay, the section 102(c) meaning of an "abandoned" invention may well not apply. Mere non-use of an invention does not create an "abandoned" invention under pre-AIA section 102(c), nor does secret but noncommercial use. In *Moore v. United States*, 194 U.S.P.Q. (BNA) 423 (Ct. Cl. 1977), the infringement defendant argued that patentholder Moore's patent was invalid under section 102(c) because there was a near-14-year delay between the plaintiff's 1942 reduction to practice and the filing of his initial patent application in 1955. The Court of Claims stated:

> Abandonment is an affirmative defense which must be proven by clear and convincing evidence. Abandonment, under 35 U.S.C. § 102(c), presupposes a deliberate, though not necessarily an express, surrender of any rights to a patent. To abandon the invention, the inventor must intend a dedication to the public. *This intent may be express, as by a declaration by the inventor, or implied as by the actions or inactions of the inventor. Delay alone is not a sufficient basis from which to infer the requisite intent.*
>
> In the present case, abandonment has not been proven. Particularly, defendant has not shown that plaintiff intended to dedicate his invention to the public. To the extent that defendant relies solely upon the mere delay by Moore in filing for a patent, no matter how long, defendant has not shown an express intent

> by plaintiff to abandon his invention. Moreover, the absence of some other facts, events, or circumstances which make intent to dedicate to the public the only reasonable explanation of Moore's "inaction" is fatal to defendant's position that plaintiff has by implication abandoned his invention.

Moore v. United States, 194 U.S.P.Q. (BNA) 423 (Ct. Cl. 1977) (emphasis added).

7. NOVELTY OF DESIGN PATENTS

The section 102 novelty requirements (both pre- and post-AIA) apply to design patents to the same extent that they apply to utility patents. However, novelty itself must be defined somewhat differently in this context.

INTERNATIONAL SEAWAY TRADING CORP. V. WALGREENS CORP.

589 F.3d 1233 (Fed. Cir. 2009).

DYK, CIRCUIT JUDGE.

* * *

Plaintiff-Appellant Seaway is an Ohio corporation that acts as a buyer's agent and/or importer of footwear to mass merchandise retailers, as well as to footwear, apparel, and sporting goods stores. Seaway also creates its own shoe and boot designs and pursues design patents for them. Defendant-Appellee Walgreens is an Illinois corporation with retail drug stores across the country that sell footwear, among other products. Defendant-Appellee Touchsport is a California corporation that, like Seaway, serves as a buyer's agent and/or importer of footwear to retailers, including Walgreens.

Seaway's '263, '032, and '033 patents (collectively "the patents-in-suit") claim designs for casual, lightweight footwear, which are typically referred to as "clogs." The '263 patent application was filed on February 18, 2005, and issued on October 3, 2006. The '032 and '033 patents were filed as continuations-in-part of the '263 patent in February 2006, and both issued on June 26, 2007. It is undisputed that the '032 and '033 patents are "substantially the same as the '263 patent design" except that the heel strap is in a forward position overlying a portion of the clog upper in the '032 patent and that the heel strap is not part of the claimed design for the '033 patent.

A single Patent Office Examiner examined and allowed each of the three patents-in-suit. During prosecution of the '263 patent application, the examiner considered and found the '263 patent design patentable over: (a) four pages from the website of Crocs that depicted various models of Crocs clogs, including the Beach model clog; (b) five pages of photographs of the Crocs Beach model clog; and (c) a December 2002 archival version of the Crocs website, depicting various views of a Crocs clog. In the examination of the '263 patent application, the examiner did not have the benefit of the Crocs '789 patent, which depicted the Crocs Beach model clog, even though the '789 patent issued before the examination was concluded. For the '032 and '033 patent applications, the examiner considered and found the '032 and '033 designs patentable over the references considered during the '263 prosecution as well as the '789 patent.

[Seaway sued Walgreens and Touchsport for infringement, and the defendants moved for summary judgment on the basis that] Seaway's patents were invalid as anticipated under 35 U.S.C. § 102(a) & (e) by the Crocs Beach and Cayman model clogs and/or the Crocs '789 patent, or as obvious under 35 U.S.C. § 103 in view of the Crocs Beach and Cayman model clogs and/or the Crocs '789 patent. Figures depicting the design in the '789 patent, and the design in the '263 patent, which is representative of the designs in the '032 and '033 patents, are set forth below.

Figure 1 in the '789 Patent

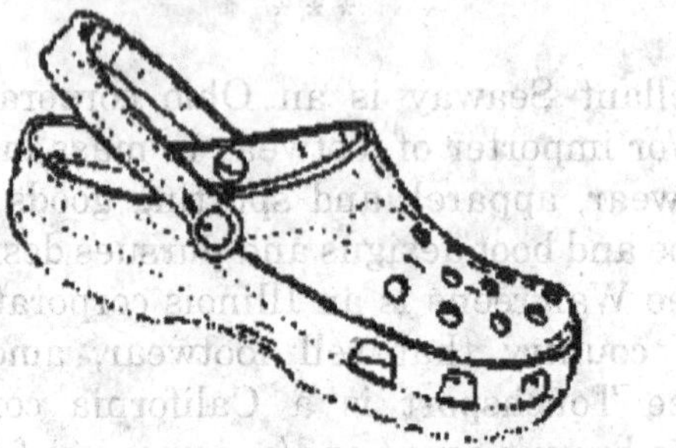

Figure 2 in the '263 Patent

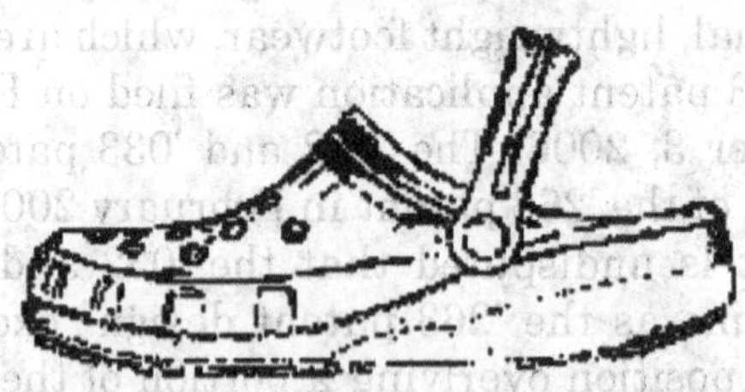

On January 22, 2009, the district court granted summary judgment of anticipation, finding that the three Seaway patents were anticipated by the Crocs '789 patent. The district court held that the ordinary observer test was the sole test of design patent invalidity under 35 U.S.C. § 102. In granting summary judgment, the district court considered and compared the exterior portions of the designs of the patents-in-suit, but not the insoles of the designs, to the prior art. The district court concluded that comparison of the insoles was not required, holding "that the law requires a court to consider only those portions of the product that are visible during normal use, regardless of whether those portions are visible during the point of sale." The court then explained its rationale:

> When a shoe is in use, it's [sic] insole is, obviously, hidden by the user's foot. The sole of the shoe, however is sometimes visible while a person is sitting or walking. As such, this Court will not consider any aspects of the insoles of the shoes, but will consider the sole of the shoes as those are visible during use.

* * *

Section 171 of Title 35 provides the criteria for obtaining a design patent. It provides that: "Whoever invents any new, original and ornamental design for an article of manufacture may obtain a patent therefor, subject to the conditions and requirements of this title." 35 U.S.C. § 171. There are two differences in wording between the requirements for a design patent under § 171 and for a utility patent under 35 U.S.C. § 101. Section 171 excludes the word "useful" (to distinguish design patents from utility patents) and adds the word "original." The originality requirement in § 171 dates back to 1842 when Congress enacted the first design patent law. The purpose of incorporating an originality requirement is unclear; it likely was designed to incorporate the copyright concept of originality-requiring that the work be original with the author, although this concept did not find its way into the language of the Copyright Act until 1909. *See* 1–2 MELVILLE B. NIMMER & DAVID NIMMER, NIMMER ON COPYRIGHT § 2.01 (2005) (subject matter of copyright). In any event, the courts have not construed the word "original" as requiring that design patents be treated differently than utility patents. Section 171 requires that the "conditions and requirements of this title" be applied to design patents, thus requiring application of the provisions of sections 102 (anticipation) and 103 (invalidity). * * *

* * *

While our cases have utilized the point of novelty test for infringement and anticipation, as we pointed out in *Egyptian Goddess*, 543 F.3d at 672, this test was not mandated by *Smith v. Whitman Saddle Co.*, 148 U.S. 674 (1893), or precedent from other courts. In *Whitman*, the Supreme Court utilized only the ordinary observer test for determining infringement and invalidity * * *.

Moreover, it has been well established for over a century that the same test must be used for both infringement and anticipation.[4] This general rule derives from the Supreme Court's proclamation 120 years ago in the context of utility patents: "[t]hat which infringes, if later, would anticipate, if earlier." The same rule applies for design patents.

In *Egyptian Goddess*, we abandoned the point of novelty test for design patent infringement and held that the ordinary observer test should serve as the sole test for design patent infringement. The ordinary observer test originated in 1871 when the Supreme Court held

> that if, in the eye of an ordinary observer, giving such attention as a purchaser usually gives, two designs are substantially the same, if the resemblance is such as to deceive such an observer, inducing him to purchase one supposing it to be the other, the first one patented is infringed by the other.

Gorham Mfg. Co. v. White, 81 U.S. 511, 528 (1871). In *Egyptian Goddess*, we also refined the ordinary observer test by characterizing the ordinary observer as being "deemed to view the differences between the patented design and the accused product in the context of the prior art." We explained:

> When the differences between the claimed and accused design are viewed in light of the prior art, the attention of the hypothetical ordinary observer will be drawn to those aspects of the claimed design that differ from the prior art. And when the claimed design is close to the prior art designs, small differences between the accused design and the claimed design are likely to be important to the eye of the hypothetical ordinary observer.

We further determined that the point of novelty test, as a second and free-standing requirement for proof of design patent infringement, was inconsistent with the ordinary observer test laid down in *Gorham* and was not mandated by Supreme Court cases or other precedent.

In light of Supreme Court precedent and our precedent holding that the same tests must be applied to infringement and anticipation, and our holding in *Egyptian Goddess* that the ordinary observer test is the sole test for infringement, we now conclude that the ordinary observer test must logically be the sole test for anticipation as well. In doing so, we will prevent an inconsistency from developing between the infringement and anticipation analyses, and we will continue our well-established practice of maintaining identical tests for infringement and anticipation.

* * *

---

[4] One possible exception is product by process claims. *See Amgen Inc. v. F. Hoffman-LA Roche, Ltd.*, 580 F.3d 1340, 1370 (Fed.Cir.2009) ("For product-by-process claims, that which anticipates if earlier does not necessarily infringe if later.")

Seaway's second contention is that, even if the ordinary observer test is found to be the sole and proper test for anticipation under § 102, the district court misapplied the ordinary observer test by failing to compare the entirety of the patented designs, including the clogs' insoles, with the Crocs '789 patent. The district court, relying on *Contessa*, held "that the law requires a court to consider only those portions of the product that are visible during normal use, regardless of whether those portions are visible during the point of sale." The court did "not consider any aspects of the insoles of the shoes" because the insoles are "hidden by the user's foot." We conclude that the district court erred, and we vacate and remand for a determination of whether the differences between the insole patterns in the patents-in-suit and in the prior Crocs art bar a finding of anticipation or obviousness.

In *Contessa*, we considered the issue of infringement with regard to a shrimp serving tray. The district court held that "any reasonable fact finder would conclude that the competing designs are substantially similar despite the minor differences in tray structure." The district court did not consider the undersides of the trays because they were not visible at the time of sale. On appeal, we stated: "Our precedent makes clear that all of the ornamental features illustrated in the figures must be considered in evaluating design patent infringement." We found that the district court in *Contessa* erred by limiting its infringement inquiry to those features visible at the time of sale, rather than to those features visible at any time in the "normal use" lifetime of the accused product. We explained that "normal use" in the design patent context extends from the completion of manufacture or assembly until the ultimate destruction, loss, or disappearance of the article. The same test necessarily applies to anticipation.

The district court here misconstrued *Contessa* as requiring that the normal use of a clog be limited to the time when it is worn. *Contessa* did not exclude the point of sale from the normal use of a product. Rather, it emphasized that normal use should not be limited to only one phase or portion of the normal use lifetime of an accused product. The sale of a clog occurs after it has been manufactured and before it is ultimately destroyed. Thus, the point of sale for a clog clearly occurs during its normal use lifetime. At the point of sale, the insole is visible to potential purchasers when the clog is displayed on a shelf or rack and when the clog is picked up for examination. Similarly, removing a clog from a wearer's foot also occurs after manufacture and before destruction of the clog, so it also falls squarely within the clog's normal use lifetime. The wearer may remove the clog temporarily to stretch out his or her toes, leave the clogs on the beach to go for a swim, or engage in countless other activities that would leave the insole exposed.

Walgreens and Touchsport acknowledge that the district court misinterpreted *Contessa* but argue that it was harmless error. They assert that it was a harmless error because insoles have an insignificant effect on the overall visual appearance of the clogs. They claim there is a "universal truth that consumers buy shoes primarily for their exterior appearance. The insole therefore contributes little to the overall appearance of the shoe to an ordinary observer with knowledge of the prior art." We reject this argument. The burden is on an accused infringer to show by clear and convincing evidence facts supporting the conclusion that the patent is invalid. Hence, Walgreens and Touchsport had the burden to establish by clear and convincing evidence that consumers do not consider the insoles of shoes to be significant. The appellees failed to present any evidence in support of this argument.

Walgreens and Touchsport also argue that the district court's error was harmless because the asserted differences between the insoles of the patents-in-suit and the prior art "were at most slight variations of design elements already present in the Crocs prior art." We disagree. The insole pattern for the patents-in-suit is distinctly different than the Crocs insole pattern.

Figure 6 in the '789 Patent

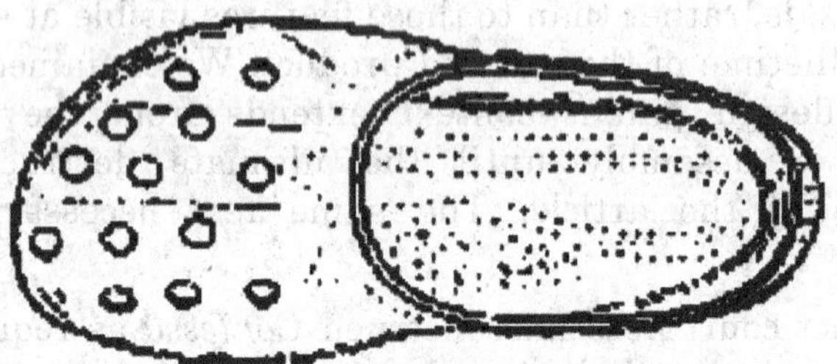

Figure 6 in the '263 Patent

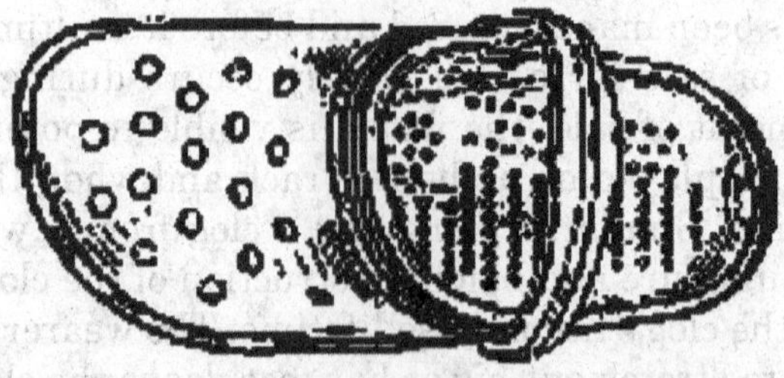

The Crocs '789 patent, as shown above in the figure on the left, contains a long, U-shaped dimpling pattern on the insole. In contrast, the patents-in-suit, as demonstrated above in the figure on the right, have a dimpling pattern that includes multiple short rows of dimples. Because we cannot say that these differences are insignificant as a matter of law, a genuine issue of material fact exists as to whether the designs would be viewed as substantially similar in the eyes of the ordinary observer armed with the knowledge of the prior art.

* * *

8. NOVELTY OF PLANT PATENTS

Under section 161, the section 102 novelty requirements (both pre- and post-AIA) apply to plant patents to the same extent that they apply to utility and design patents, but plant patents are subject to the additional, related requirement of "distinctness": "Whoever invents or discovers and asexually reproduces any distinct and new variety of plant . . . may obtain a patent therefor, subject to the conditions and requirements of this title." A patentable plant need not be either "useful" or "ornamental."

In *Yoder Bros., Inc. v. California-Florida Plant Corp.*, 537 F.2d 1347, 1377–78 (5th Cir.1976), the Fifth Circuit discussed the novelty and distinctness requirements as applied to plant patents under section 161:

> Normally, the three requirements for patentability are novelty, utility, and non-obviousness. For plant patents, the requirement of distinctness replaces that of utility, and the additional requirement of asexual reproduction is introduced.
>
> The concept of novelty refers to novelty of conception, rather than novelty of use; no single prior art structure can exist in which all of the elements serve substantially the same function. * * * As applied to plants, the Patent Office Board of Appeals held that a "new" plant had to be one that literally had not existed before, rather than one that had existed in nature but was newly found, such as an exotic plant from a remote part of the earth. *Ex parte Foster*, 90 U.S.P.Q. 16 (1951). In *Application of Greer*, [484 F.2d 488 (C.C.P.A. 1973)], the court indicated that the Board believed that novelty was to be determined by a detailed comparison with other known varieties.
>
> The legislative history of the Plant Patent Act is of considerable assistance in defining "distinctness." The Senate Report said:
>
>> In order for the new variety to be distinct it must have characteristics clearly distinguishable from those of existing varieties and it is immaterial whether in the judgment of the Patent Office the new characteristics are inferior or superior to those of existing varieties. Experience has shown the

> absurdity of many views held as to the value of new varieties at the time of their creation.
>
> The characteristics that may distinguish a new variety would include, among others, those of habit; immunity from disease; or soil conditions; color of flower, leaf, fruit or stems; flavor; productivity, including ever-bearing qualities in case of fruits; storage qualities; perfume; form; and ease of asexual reproduction. Within any one of the above or other classes of characteristics the differences which would suffice to make the variety a distinct variety, will necessarily be differences of degree.
>
> S.Rep. 315, 71st Cong., 2d Sess. (1930). (Emphasis omitted.) A definition of "distinctness" as the aggregate of the plant's distinguishing characteristics seems to us a sensible and workable one.

537 F.2d at 1377–78 (footnote omitted). In a footnote, the court added:

> In order for a plant to have "existed" before in nature, we think that it must have been capable of reproducing itself. Thus, we have concluded that the mere fact that a sport [i.e., bud mutation] of a plant had appeared in the past would not be sufficient to preclude the patentability of the plant on novelty grounds, since each sport is a one-time phenomenon absent human intervention.

Id. at 1378 n. 34.

NOTES

1. *Policy of Distinctness:* Why do you think a patentable plant must be both "distinct" and novel rather than either "useful" or "ornamental" (and novel)?

2. *Plant Novelty:* In the case of a plant patent under section 161, consider which of the following disclosures, if known to the public, would give rise to a novelty bar under section 102(a): (a) a detailed description of the plant's novel characteristics, with photographs; (b) a description of the steps taken in breeding the plant; (c) availability of seeds for purchase. Would your answers be different in the case of a utility patent for a plant? *See, e.g., Application of LeGrice*, 301 F.2d 929 (C.C.P.A. 1962); *In re Elsner*, 381 F.3d 1125 (Fed. Cir. 2004).

3. *Plant Discovery:* Is a plant patent subject to a derivation proceeding under post-AIA section 135 if the patent claimant discovered the plant growing in another person's cultivated tract and then reproduced the plant asexually? (Or invalid under pre-AIA § 102(f)?) What if, in addition, the claimant did not recognize the distinctive features of the plant until they were pointed out by another party?

D. NONOBVIOUSNESS

Statute: 35 U.S.C. § 103

Case law before the 1952 Patent Act developed a requirement that a patentable invention be not merely novel, or differentiable from each individual prior art reference, but instead represent something more than a mere incremental advance beyond the prior art. The characterization of this "something more" varied, however, and often focused on the nature of "invention," contrasting "invention" and an "inventor" with a modest advance created by a skilled mechanic. In the 1952 Patent Act, Congress used the term "obvious" rather than focusing on the nature of "invention" to expressly include in the statute this long-standing additional requirement beyond novelty. The AIA moved the timing of the inquiry from the "time the invention was made"[8] to the "effective filing date of the claimed invention,"[9] but it did not alter the basic substance of the section 103 requirement of nonobviousness, which still requires the differences between the invention in the patent claim and the prior art to be such that the claimed invention would not have been "obvious" to a "person having ordinary skill in the art," or the field to which the invention in the patent claim belongs. In the case below, the Supreme Court addressed for the first time the meaning of nonobviousness and the appropriate structure for the nonobviousness inquiry.

1. THE OBVIOUSNESS INQUIRY

GRAHAM V. JOHN DEERE CO.; CALMAR, INC. V. COOK CHEMICAL CO.

383 U.S. 1, 86 S.Ct. 684 (1966).

MR. JUSTICE CLARK delivered the opinion of the Court.

[Two separate patent cases before the Supreme Court in the same term presented the Court with its first opportunity to interpret section 103's requirement of nonobviousness. The Court heard oral argument on the cases on the same day and ultimately issued a consolidated opinion. In

---

[8] Pre-AIA § 103—Conditions for patentability; non-obvious subject matter. (a) A patent may not be obtained though the invention is not identically disclosed or described as set forth in section 102 of this title, if the differences between the subject matter sought to be patented and the prior art are such that the subject matter as a whole would have been obvious at the time the invention was made to a person having ordinary skill in the art to which said subject matter pertains. Patentability shall not be negatived by the manner in which the invention was made.

[9] Post-AIA § 103—Conditions for patentability; non-obvious subject matter. (a) A patent for a claimed invention may not be obtained, notwithstanding that the claimed invention is not identically disclosed as set forth in section 102, if the differences between the claimed invention and the prior art are such that the claimed invention as a whole would have been obvious before the effective filing date of the claimed invention to a person having ordinary skill in the art to which the claimed invention pertains. Patentability shall not be negated by the manner in which the invention was made.

addressing these challenges to patent validity, the Court carefully considered the effect of Congress's codification of the judicially developed test of nonobviousness.]

* * *

At the outset it must be remembered that the federal patent power stems from a specific constitutional provision which authorizes the Congress "To promote the Progress of . . . useful Arts, by securing for limited Times to . . . Inventors the exclusive Right to their . . . Discoveries." Art. I, § 8, cl. 8. The clause is both a grant of power and a limitation. This qualified authority, unlike the power often exercised in the sixteenth and seventeenth centuries by the English Crown, is limited to the promotion of advances in the "useful arts." It was written against the backdrop of the practices—eventually curtailed by the Statute of Monopolies—of the Crown in granting monopolies to court favorites in goods or businesses which had long before been enjoyed by the public. The Congress in the exercise of the patent power may not overreach the restraints imposed by the stated constitutional purpose. Nor may it enlarge the patent monopoly without regard to the innovation, advancement or social benefit gained thereby. Moreover, Congress may not authorize the issuance of patents whose effects are to remove existent knowledge from the public domain, or to restrict free access to materials already available. Innovation, advancement, and things which add to the sum of useful knowledge are inherent requisites in a patent system which by constitutional command must "promote the Progress of . . . useful Arts." * * *

* * *

As a member of the patent board for several years [and the author of the 1793 Patent Act, Thomas] Jefferson saw clearly the difficulty in "drawing a line between the things which are worth to the public the embarrassment of an exclusive patent, and those which are not." * * * Although the Patent Act was amended, revised or codified some 50 times between 1790 and 1950, Congress steered clear of a statutory set of requirements other than the bare novelty and utility tests reformulated in Jefferson's draft of the 1793 Patent Act.

* * *

III.

The difficulty of formulating conditions for patentability was heightened by the generality of the constitutional grant and the statutes implementing it, together with the underlying policy of the patent system that "the things which are worth to the public the embarrassment of an exclusive patent," as Jefferson put it, must outweigh the restrictive effect of the limited patent monopoly. The inherent problem was to develop some means of weeding out those inventions which would not be disclosed or devised but for the inducement of a patent.

This Court formulated a general condition of patentability in 1851 in *Hotchkiss v. Greenwood*, 11 How. 248. The patent involved a mere substitution of materials—porcelain or clay for wood or metal in doorknobs—and the Court condemned it, holding:

> "[U]nless more ingenuity and skill . . . were required . . . than were possessed by an ordinary mechanic acquainted with the business, there was an absence of that degree of skill and ingenuity which constitute essential elements of every invention. In other words, the improvement is the work of the skilful mechanic, not that of the inventor." At p. 267.

Hotchkiss, by positing the condition that a patentable invention evidence more ingenuity and skill than that possessed by an ordinary mechanic acquainted with the business, merely distinguished between new and useful innovations that were capable of sustaining a patent and those that were not. * * * The language in the case, and in those which followed, gave birth to "invention" as a word of legal art signifying patentable inventions. * * * In practice, *Hotchkiss* has required a comparison between the subject matter of the patent, or patent application, and the background skill of the calling. It has been from this comparison that patentability was in each case determined.

IV.

The 1952 Patent Act.

The Act sets out the conditions of patentability in three sections. An analysis of the structure of these three sections indicates that patentability is dependent upon three explicit conditions: novelty and utility as articulated and defined in § 101 and § 102, and nonobviousness, the new statutory formulation, as set out in § 103. * * *

* * *

The first sentence of [section 103] * * * is strongly reminiscent of the language in *Hotchkiss.* Both formulations place emphasis on the pertinent art existing at the time the invention was made and both are implicitly tied to advances in that art. The major distinction is that Congress has emphasized "nonobviousness" as the operative test of the section, rather than the less definite "invention" language of *Hotchkiss* that Congress thought had led to "a large variety" of expressions in decisions and writings. In the title itself the Congress used the phrase "Conditions for patentability; *non-obvious subject matter*" (italics added), thus focusing upon "non-obviousness" rather than "invention." The Senate and House Reports reflect this emphasis in these terms:

> 'Section 103, for the first time in our statute, provides a condition which exists in the law and has existed for more than 100 years, but only by reason of decisions of the courts. An invention which has been made, and which is new in the sense that the same thing has not been made before, may still not be patentable if the difference between the new thing and what was known before is not considered sufficiently great to warrant a patent. That has been expressed in a large variety of ways in decisions of the courts and in writings. Section 103 states this requirement in the title. It refers to the difference between the subject matter sought to be patented and the prior art, meaning what was known before as described in section 102. If this difference is such that the subject matter as a whole would have been obvious at the time to a person skilled in the art, then the subject matter cannot be patented.
>
> 'That provision paraphrases language which has often been used in decisions of the courts, and the section is added to the statute for uniformity and definiteness. This section should have a stabilizing effect and minimize great departures which have appeared in some cases.'

* * *

We believe that this legislative history, as well as other sources, shows that the revision was not intended by Congress to change the general level of patentable invention. We conclude that the section was intended merely as a codification of judicial precedents embracing the *Hotchkiss* condition, with congressional directions that inquiries into the obviousness of the subject matter sought to be patented are a prerequisite to patentability.

V.

Approached in this light, the § 103 additional condition, when followed realistically, will permit a more practical test of patentability. The emphasis on nonobviousness is one of inquiry, not quality, and, as such, comports with the constitutional strictures.

While the ultimate question of patent validity is one of law, the § 103 condition, which is but one of three conditions, each of which must be satisfied, lends itself to several basic factual inquiries. Under § 103, the scope and content of the prior art are to be determined; differences between the prior art and the claims at issue are to be ascertained; and the level of ordinary skill in the pertinent art resolved. Against this background, the obviousness or nonobviousness of the subject matter is determined. Such secondary considerations as commercial success, long felt but unsolved needs, failure of others, etc., might be utilized to give light to the circumstances surrounding the origin of the subject matter sought to be patented. As indicia of obviousness or nonobviousness, these inquiries may have relevancy.

* * *

Although we conclude here that the inquiry which the Patent Office and the courts must make as to patentability must be beamed with greater intensity on the requirements of § 103, it bears repeating that we find no change in the general strictness with which the overall test is to be applied. We have been urged to find in § 103 a relaxed standard, supposedly a congressional reaction to the "increased standard" applied by this Court in its decisions over the last 20 or 30 years. The standard has remained invariable in this Court. Technology, however, has advanced—and with remarkable rapidity in the last 50 years. Moreover, the ambit of applicable art in given fields of science has widened by disciplines unheard of a half century ago. It is but an evenhanded application to require that those persons granted the benefit of a patent monopoly be charged with an awareness of these changed conditions. The same is true of the less technical, but still useful arts. He who seeks to build a better mousetrap today has a long path to tread before reaching the Patent Office.

VI.

We now turn to the application of the conditions found necessary for patentability to the cases involved here:

A. The Patent in Issue in No. 11, Graham v. John Deere Co.

This patent, No. 2,627,798 (hereinafter called the '798 patent) relates to a spring clamp which permits plow shanks to be pushed upward when they hit obstructions in the soil, and then springs the shanks back into normal position when the obstruction is passed over. * * *

When the chisel hits a rock or other obstruction in the soil, the obstruction forces the chisel and the rear portion of the shank to move upward. * * * When the obstruction is passed over, the upward force on the chisel disappears and the spring pulls the shank and hinge plate back into their original position. * * *

In practical use, a number of spring-hinge-shank combinations are clamped to a plow frame, forming a set of ground-working chisels capable of withstanding the shock of rocks and other obstructions in the soil without breaking the shanks.

Background of the Patent.

Chisel plows, as they are called, were developed for plowing in areas where the ground is relatively free from rocks or stones. Originally, the shanks were rigidly attached to the plow frames. When such plows were used in the rocky, glacial soils of some of the Northern States, they were found to have serious defects. As the chisels hit buried rocks, a vibratory motion was set up and tremendous forces were transmitted to the shank near its connection to the frame. The shanks would break. Graham, one of the petitioners, sought to meet that problem, and in 1950 obtained a patent, U.S. No. 2,493,811 (hereinafter '811), on a spring clamp which solved some of the difficulties. Graham and his companies manufactured and sold the '811 clamps. In 1950, Graham modified the '811 structure and filed for a patent. That patent, the one in issue, was granted in 1953. This suit against competing plow manufacturers resulted from charges by petitioners that several of respondents' devices infringed the '798 patent.

The Prior Art.

Five prior patents indicating the state of the art were cited by the Patent Office in the prosecution of the '798 application. Four of these patents, 10 other United States patents and two prior-use spring-clamp arrangements not of record in the '798 file wrapper were relied upon by respondents as revealing the prior art. The District Court and the Court of Appeals found that the prior art "as a whole in one form or another contains all of the mechanical elements of the 798 Patent." One of the prior-use clamp devices not before the Patent Examiner—Glencoe—was found to have "all of the elements."

We confine our discussion to the prior patent of Graham, '811, and to the Glencoe clamp device, both among the references asserted by respondents. The Graham '811 and '798 patent devices are similar in all elements, save two: (1) the stirrup and the bolted connection of the shank to the hinge plate do not appear in '811; and (2) the position of the shank is reversed, being placed in patent '811 above the hinge plate, sandwiched between it and the upper plate. The shank is held in place by the spring rod which is hooked against the bottom of the hinge plate passing through a slot in the shank. Other differences are of no consequence to our examination. In practice the '811 patent arrangement permitted the shank to wobble or fishtail because it was not rigidly fixed to the hinge plate; moreover, as the hinge plate was below the shank, the latter caused wear on the upper plate, a member difficult to repair or replace.

Graham's '798 patent application contained 12 claims. All were rejected as not distinguished from the Graham '811 patent. The inverted position of the shank was specifically rejected as was the bolting of the shank to the hinge plate. The Patent Office examiner found these to be "matters of design well within the expected skill of the art and devoid of invention." Graham withdrew the original claims and substituted the two new ones which are substantially those in issue here. His contention was that wear was reduced in patent '798 between the shank and the heel or rear of the upper plate. He also emphasized several new features, the relevant one here being that the bolt used to connect the hinge plate and shank maintained the upper face of the shank in continuing and constant contact with the underface of the hinge plate.

Graham did not urge before the Patent Office the greater "flexing" qualities of the '798 patent arrangement which he so heavily relied on in the courts. The sole element in patent '798 which petitioners argue before us is the interchanging of the shank and hinge plate and the consequences flowing from this arrangement. The contention is that this arrangement—which petitioners claim is not disclosed in the prior art—permits the shank to flex under stress for its entire length. * * * Petitioners say that this difference in flex, though small, effectively absorbs the tremendous forces of the shock of obstructions whereas prior art arrangements failed.

The Obviousness of the Differences.

We cannot agree with petitioners. We assume that the prior art does not disclose such an arrangement as petitioners claim in patent '798. Still we do not believe that the argument on which petitioners' contention is bottomed supports the validity of the patent. The tendency of the shank to flex is the same in all cases. If free-flexing, as petitioners now argue, is the crucial difference above the prior art, then it appears evident that the desired result would be obtainable by not boxing the shank within the confines of the hinge. The only other effective place available in the arrangement was to attach it below the hinge plate and run it through a stirrup or bracket that would not disturb its flexing qualities. Certainly a person having ordinary skill in the prior art, given the fact that the flex in the shank could be utilized more effectively if allowed to run the entire length of the shank, would immediately see that the thing to do was what Graham did, *i. e.*, invert the shank and the hinge plate.

* * *

We find no nonobvious facets in the '798 arrangement. The wear and repair claims were sufficient to overcome the patent examiner's original conclusions as to the validity of the patent. However, some of the prior art, notably Glencoe, was not before him. There the hinge plate is below the shank but, as the courts below found, all of the elements in the '798 patent are present in the Glencoe structure. Furthermore, even though the position of the shank and hinge plate appears reversed in Glencoe, the mechanical operation is identical. The shank there pivots about the underside of the stirrup, which in Glencoe is above the shank. In other words, the stirrup in Glencoe serves exactly the same function as the heel of the hinge plate in '798. The mere shifting of the wear point to the heel of the '798 hinge plate from the stirrup of Glencoe—itself a part of the hinge plate—presents no operative mechanical distinctions, much less nonobvious differences.

B. The Patent in Issue in No. 37, Calmar, Inc. v. Cook Chemical Co., and in No. 43, Colgate-Palmolive Co. v. Cook Chemical Co.

The single patent involved in these cases relates to a plastic finger sprayer with a "hold-down" lid used as a built-in dispenser for containers or bottles packaging liquid products, principally household insecticides. * * *

* * *

[For many years, insecticide makers had tried unsuccessfully to develop sprayers that could be integrated with the containers in which the insecticides were marketed. In 1956, Scoggin, an officer of Cook Chemical, developed the finger-operated shipper-sprayer in suit, an integrated sprayer that could be mounted directly on each container during the packaging process and which would not leak during shipment or handling. The patent examiner allowed the claims, based solely on the novelty of the sealing mechanism, and a patent issued to Cook Chemical as Scoggin's assignee in 1959. In the meantime, Calmar also developed a shipper-sprayer, which it began marketing in 1958. When the Scoggin patent issued, Cook Chemical charged Calmar with infringement. The validity of the patent was upheld by the district court and the court of appeals.]

The Invalidity of the Patent.

* * *

The substitution of a rib built into a collar [as a component of the device's sealing mechanism] * * * presents no patentable difference above the prior art. It was fully disclosed and dedicated to the public in the [prior art] Livingstone patent. Cook Chemical argues, however, that Livingstone is not in the pertinent prior art because it relates to liquid containers having pouring spouts rather than pump sprayers. Apart from the fact that respondent made no such objection to similar references cited by the Examiner, so restricted a view of the applicable prior art is not justified. The problems confronting Scoggin and the insecticide industry were not insecticide problems; they were mechanical closure problems. Closure devices in such a closely related art as pouring spouts for liquid containers are at the very least pertinent references.

Cook Chemical insists, however, that the development of a workable shipper-sprayer eluded Calmar, who had long and unsuccessfully sought to solve the problem. And, further, that the long-felt need in the industry for a device such as Scoggin's together with its wide commercial success supports its patentability. These legal inferences or subtests do focus attention on economic and motivational rather than technical issues and are, therefore, more susceptible of judicial treatment than are the highly technical facts often present in patent litigation. Such inquiries may lend a helping hand to the judiciary which, as Mr. Justice Frankfurter observed, is most ill-fitted to discharge the technological duties cast upon it by patent legislation. They may also serve to "guard against slipping into use of hindsight," and to resist the temptation to read into the prior art the teachings of the invention in issue.

However, these factors do not, in the circumstances of this case, tip the scales of patentability. The Scoggin invention, as limited by the Patent Office and accepted by Scoggin, rests upon exceedingly small and quite nontechnical mechanical differences in a device which was old in the art. At the latest, those differences were rendered apparent in 1953 by the appearance of the Livingstone patent, and unsuccessful attempts to reach a solution to the problems confronting Scoggin made before that time became wholly irrelevant. It is also irrelevant that no one apparently chose to avail himself of knowledge stored in the Patent Office and readily available by the simple expedient of conducting a patent search—a prudent and nowadays common preliminary to well organized research. To us, the limited claims of the Scoggin patent are clearly evident from the prior art as it stood at the time of the invention.

We conclude that the claims in issue in the Scoggin patent must fall as not meeting the test of § 103, since the differences between them and the pertinent prior art would have been obvious to a person reasonably skilled in that art.

* * *

NOTES

1. *Secondary Considerations:* As the Supreme Court recognized in *Graham v. John Deere Co.*, various secondary considerations can offer relevant, and relatively non-technical, evidence on the question of whether an invention represents a nonobvious solution to the particular problem at issue. The secondary factors which various courts have treated as evidence of nonobviousness include: failure of others to solve the problem in spite of long-felt need for a solution; the commercial success of the invention (or of infringements); acquiescence of competitors through licensing (or, conversely, nonacquiescence through copying); the favorable comments of experts in the field (or, in some cases, of the accused infringer); and an accused infringer's attempt to patent the technology. Obviousness, in contrast, is suggested where several persons independently develop similar solutions at almost the same time.

2. *Scope of the Prior Art—Analogous Arts:* As illustrated by the Court's discussion in *Calmar Inc. v. Cook Chemical Co.*, the case consolidated with *Graham v. John Deere Co.*, obviousness cases often raise questions of which prior art should be included in the assessment of whether the invention represents a merely obvious advance beyond the prior art. In *Calmar* the Court found a patented shipper-sprayer device for insecticides to be obvious in light of prior art in the "closely related art" of "pouring spouts for liquid containers,"

which involved the questions of what the field of endeavor or invention is and how closely related the fields must be for subject matter in one field of endeavor to be rendered obvious by prior art from another field.

The Federal Circuit employs a "field of endeavor" test to identify "analogous arts" and thus define the proper scope of the relevant prior art. That test inquires:

> (1) whether the art is from the same field of endeavor, regardless of the problem addressed and, (2) if the reference is not within the field of the inventor's endeavor, whether the reference still is reasonably pertinent to the particular problem.

In re Deminski, 796 F.2d 436, 442 (Fed. Cir. 1986). As the Federal Circuit has more recently explained:

> This test for analogous art requires the PTO to determine the appropriate field of endeavor by reference to explanations of the invention's subject matter in the patent application, including the embodiments, function, and structure of the claimed invention.

In re Bigio, 381 F.3d 1320, 1325 (Fed. Cir. 2004). The test is intended to be objective, employing the "person of ordinary skill" standard:

> In that vein, this court has previously "reminded . . . the PTO that it is necessary to consider 'the reality of the circumstances'—in other words, common sense—in deciding in which fields a person of ordinary skill would reasonably be expected to look for a solution to the problem facing the inventor." Accordingly, the examiner and the Board must consider the "circumstances" of the application—the full disclosure—and weigh those circumstances from the vantage point of the common sense likely to be exerted by one of ordinary skill in the art in assessing the scope of the endeavor. Those factual determinations are neither unbridled nor wholly subjective. Instead this test rests on an assessment of the nature of the application and claimed invention in addition to the level of ordinary skill in the art.

Id. at 1326 (citations omitted).

Under this test, would a toothbrush and a hairbrush be analogous arts? *Compare id.* at 1327 (Rader, J., for the majority) *with id.* at 1327–28 (Newman, J. dissenting).

3. *Scope of the Prior Art—Pertinent to the Problem: Stratoflex, Inc. v. Aeroquip Corp.*, 713 F.2d 1530 (Fed. Cir. 1983), can be used to illustrate the second part of the Federal Circuit's test for "analogous arts," namely references "reasonably pertinent to the problem." In *Stratoflex* the Federal Circuit addressed a patentee's argument that its patent should be held valid despite an obviousness defense, with one vital aspect of the argument being that the scope of the prior art should have been more narrowly defined. The patented invention related to a composite, layered PTFE tubing, formed of an inner layer of electrically conductive PTFE having particles such as carbon black, a

conductor, uniformly distributed in it and an outer layer of essentially pure non-conductive PTFE. The conductivity of the inner layer was desirable for various reasons, but conductive PTFE tube alone (a single composition throughout, rather than layers), was susceptible to the development of pin holes as a result of arcing of electrostatic charges through the tube walls. Conductive PTFE tubing was used in aircraft engines, and the fuel being conveyed through the tubing leaked through the pin holes—an undesirable consequence to be sure. The inventor of the patent-in-suit conceived of the dual-layered PTFE tube which allowed the non-conductive outer layer to contain any fuel that might leak through pin holes in the conductive inner layer. In ruling the invention obvious, the district judge had included in the prior art, among other things, a patent on a particular composite rubber hose wherein each layer of the composite was arranged to take advantage of its particular properties. That patent suggested carbon black as a filler, but not as a conductor. The use of carbon black as a conductor in PTFE hose or tubing was also within the prior art.

> Aeroquip contends that the scope of the relevant prior art excludes rubber hose because PTFE is a unique material, possessing properties that differ significantly from rubber, and that, because the claims are limited to PTFE, the rubber hose art could at most be peripherally relevant as background information.
>
> The scope of the prior art has been defined as that "reasonably pertinent to the particular problem with which the inventor was involved." The problem confronting Slade [the inventor] was preventing electrostatic buildup in PTFE tubing caused by hydrocarbon fuel flow while precluding leakage of fuel. None of the unique properties of PTFE would change the nature of that problem. Nor would anything of record indicate that one skilled in the art would not include the rubber hose art in his search for a solution to that problem.
>
> Indeed, Slade himself referred to a standard textbook on conductive carbon black in rubber when he began his search for a solution. Judge Boyle correctly found Slade's act an acknowledgement by the problem solver of what he considered relevant prior art.
>
> The examiner cited two prior art references in the rubber hose art, one disclosing the problem of electrostatic buildup caused by fuel flow. The Abbey-Upham report, though concerned with PTFE, included a conductivity comparison with carbon black filled rubber hose, and its bibliography listed several articles on electrostatic buildup in rubber. The record reflects that PTFE and rubber are used by the same hose manufacturers to make hoses and that the same and similar problems have been experienced with both. There is no basis for finding that a solution found for a problem experienced with one material would not be looked to when facing a problem with the

other. The finding that the rubber hose art is relevant and thus within the scope of the art was not clearly erroneous.

Stratoflex, Inc. v. Aeroquip Corp., 713 F.2d 1530, 1532–35 (Fed. Cir. 1983).

2. OBVIOUS TO COMBINE OR TO TRY

Before the following case, *KSR International*, the Federal Circuit had begun to require the party challenging a patent under section 103 to present affirmative evidence in the prior art of a "teaching, suggestion or motivation" to combine prior art elements, and its approach had become increasingly formalistic. The arguable, although not certain, benefit of this formalism was some amount of predictability. In *KSR International* the Supreme Court rejected sole reliance on "teaching, suggestion or motivation" and set out a broader (and therefore more challenging) analysis of nonobviousness.

How much guidance does the Court provide to lower courts and to potential litigants needing to evaluate the validity of a patent under § 103? What does it mean to say that a combination was "obvious to try"? When you read the Supreme Court's summary of the District Court's obviousness analysis, notice how the district court followed the *Graham v. John Deere* framework. Note also how fact-specific the obviousness analysis is and how it requires the court to apply the perspective of a person other than the judge.

KSR INTERNATIONAL CO. V. TELEFLEX INC.

550 U.S. 398, 127 S.Ct. 1727 (2007).

JUSTICE KENNEDY delivered the opinion of the Court.

Teleflex Incorporated and its subsidiary Technology Holding Company—both referred to here as Teleflex—sued KSR International Company for patent infringement. The patent at issue, United States Patent No. 6,237,565 B1, is entitled "Adjustable Pedal Assembly With Electronic Throttle Control." The patentee is Steven J. Engelgau, and the patent is referred to as "the Engelgau patent." Teleflex holds the exclusive license to the patent.

Claim 4 of the Engelgau patent describes a mechanism for combining an electronic sensor with an adjustable automobile pedal so the pedal's position can be transmitted to a computer that controls the throttle in the vehicle's engine. When Teleflex accused KSR of infringing the Engelgau patent by adding an electronic sensor to one of KSR's previously designed pedals, KSR countered that claim 4 was invalid under the Patent Act, 35 U.S.C. § 103, because its subject matter was obvious.

Section 103 forbids issuance of a patent when "the differences between the subject matter sought to be patented and the prior art are such that the subject matter as a whole would have been obvious at the time the invention was made to a person having ordinary skill in the art to which said subject matter pertains."

In *Graham v. John Deere Co. of Kansas City,* 383 U.S. 1 (1966), the Court set out a framework for applying the statutory language of § 103, language itself based on the logic of the earlier decision in *Hotchkiss v. Greenwood,* 11 How. 248 (1851), and its progeny. The analysis is objective:

> "Under § 103, the scope and content of the prior art are to be determined; differences between the prior art and the claims at issue are to be ascertained; and the level of ordinary skill in the pertinent art resolved. Against this background the obviousness or nonobviousness of the subject matter is determined. Such secondary considerations as commercial success, long felt but unsolved needs, failure of others, etc., might be utilized to give light to the circumstances surrounding the origin of the subject matter sought to be patented."

While the sequence of these questions might be reordered in any particular case, the factors continue to define the inquiry that controls. If a court, or patent examiner, conducts this analysis and concludes the claimed subject matter was obvious, the claim is invalid under § 103.

Seeking to resolve the question of obviousness with more uniformity and consistency, the Court of Appeals for the Federal Circuit has employed an approach referred to by the parties as the "teaching, suggestion, or motivation" test (TSM test), under which a patent claim is only proved obvious if "some motivation or suggestion to combine the prior art teachings" can be found in the prior art, the nature of the problem, or the knowledge of a person having ordinary skill in the art. KSR challenges that test, or at least its application in this case. Because the Court of Appeals addressed the question of obviousness in a manner contrary to § 103 and our precedents, we granted certiorari. We now reverse.

I

A

In car engines without computer-controlled throttles, the accelerator pedal interacts with the throttle via cable or other mechanical link. The pedal arm acts as a lever rotating around a pivot point. In a cable-actuated throttle control the rotation caused by pushing down the pedal pulls a cable, which in turn pulls open valves in the carburetor or fuel injection unit. The wider the valves open, the more fuel and air are released, causing combustion to increase and the car to accelerate. When the driver takes his foot off the pedal, the opposite occurs as the cable is released and the valves slide closed.

In the 1990's it became more common to install computers in cars to control engine operation. Computer-controlled throttles open and close valves in response to electronic signals, not through force transferred from the pedal by a mechanical link. Constant, delicate adjustments of air and fuel mixture are possible. The computer's rapid processing of factors beyond the pedal's position improves fuel efficiency and engine performance.

For a computer-controlled throttle to respond to a driver's operation of the car, the computer must know what is happening with the pedal. A cable or mechanical link does not suffice for this purpose; at some point, an electronic sensor is necessary to translate the mechanical operation into digital data the computer can understand.

Before discussing sensors further we turn to the mechanical design of the pedal itself. In the traditional design a pedal can be pushed down or released but cannot have its position in the footwell adjusted by sliding the pedal forward or back. As a result, a driver who wishes to be closer or farther from the pedal must either reposition himself in the driver's seat or move the seat in some way. In cars with deep footwells these are imperfect solutions for drivers of smaller stature. To solve the problem, inventors, beginning in the 1970's, designed pedals that could be adjusted to change their location in the footwell. Important for this case are two adjustable pedals disclosed in U.S. Patent Nos. 5,010,782 (filed July 28, 1989) (Asano) and 5,460,061 (filed Sept. 17, 1993) (Redding). The Asano patent reveals a support structure that houses the pedal so that even when the pedal location is adjusted relative to the driver, one of the pedal's pivot points stays fixed. The pedal is also designed so that the force necessary to push the pedal down is the same regardless of adjustments to its location. The Redding patent reveals a different, sliding mechanism where both the pedal and the pivot point are adjusted.

We return to sensors. Well before Engelgau applied for his challenged patent, some inventors had obtained patents involving electronic pedal sensors for computer-controlled throttles. These inventions, such as the device disclosed in U.S. Patent No. 5,241,936 (filed Sept. 9, 1991) ('936), taught that it was preferable to detect the pedal's position in the pedal assembly, not in the engine. The '936 patent disclosed a pedal with an electronic sensor on a pivot point in the pedal assembly. U.S. Patent No. 5,063,811 (filed July 9, 1990) (Smith) taught that to prevent the wires connecting the sensor to the computer from chafing and wearing out, and to avoid grime and damage from the driver's foot, the sensor should be put on a fixed part of the pedal assembly rather than in or on the pedal's footpad.

In addition to patents for pedals with integrated sensors inventors obtained patents for self-contained modular sensors. A modular sensor is designed independently of a given pedal so that it can be taken off the shelf and attached to mechanical pedals of various sorts, enabling the pedals to be used in automobiles with computer-controlled throttles. One such sensor was disclosed in U.S. Patent No. 5,385,068 (filed Dec. 18, 1992) ('068). In 1994, Chevrolet manufactured a line of trucks using modular sensors "attached to the pedal support bracket, adjacent to the pedal and engaged with the pivot shaft about which the pedal rotates in operation."

The prior art contained patents involving the placement of sensors on adjustable pedals as well. For example, U.S. Patent No. 5,819,593 (filed Aug. 17, 1995) (Rixon) discloses an adjustable pedal assembly with an electronic sensor for detecting the pedal's position. In the Rixon pedal the sensor is located in the pedal footpad. The Rixon pedal was known to suffer from wire chafing when the pedal was depressed and released.

This short account of pedal and sensor technology leads to the instant case.

B

KSR, a Canadian company, manufactures and supplies auto parts, including pedal systems. Ford Motor Company hired KSR in 1998 to supply an adjustable pedal system for various lines of automobiles with cable-actuated throttle controls. KSR developed an adjustable mechanical pedal for Ford and obtained U.S. Patent No. 6,151,976 (filed July 16, 1999) ('976) for the design. In 2000, KSR was chosen by General Motors Corporation (GMC or GM) to supply adjustable pedal systems for Chevrolet and GMC light trucks that used engines with computer-controlled throttles. To make the '976 pedal compatible with the trucks, KSR merely took that design and added a modular sensor.

Teleflex is a rival to KSR in the design and manufacture of adjustable pedals. As noted, it is the exclusive licensee of the Engelgau patent. Engelgau filed the patent application on August 22, 2000 as a continuation of a previous application for U.S. Patent No. 6,109,241, which was filed on January 26, 1999. He has sworn he invented the patent's subject matter on February 14, 1998. The Engelgau patent discloses an adjustable electronic pedal described in the specification as a "simplified vehicle control pedal assembly that is less expensive, and which uses fewer parts and is easier to package within the vehicle." * * *

We agree with the District Court that [claim 4] discloses "a position-adjustable pedal assembly with an electronic pedal position sensor attached to the support member of the pedal assembly. Attaching the sensor to the support member allows the sensor to remain in a fixed position while the driver adjusts the pedal."

Before issuing the Engelgau patent the U.S. Patent and Trademark Office (PTO) rejected one of the patent claims that was similar to, but broader than, the present claim 4. The claim did not include the requirement that the sensor be placed on a fixed pivot point. The PTO concluded the claim was an obvious combination of the prior art disclosed in Redding and Smith, explaining:

> " 'Since the prior ar[t] references are from the field of endeavor, the purpose disclosed . . . would have been recognized in the pertinent art of Redding. Therefore it would have been obvious . . . to provide the device of Redding with the . . . means attached to a support member as taught by Smith.' "

In other words Redding provided an example of an adjustable pedal and Smith explained how to mount a sensor on a pedal's support structure, and the rejected patent claim merely put these two teachings together.

Although the broader claim was rejected, claim 4 was later allowed because it included the limitation of a fixed pivot point, which distinguished the design from Redding's. Engelgau had not included Asano among the prior art references, and Asano was not mentioned in the patent's prosecution. Thus, the PTO did not have before it an adjustable pedal with a fixed pivot point. The patent issued on May 29, 2001 and was assigned to Teleflex.

Upon learning of KSR's design for GM, Teleflex sent a warning letter informing KSR that its proposal would violate the Engelgau patent. " 'Teleflex believes that any supplier of a product that combines an adjustable pedal with an electronic throttle control necessarily employs technology covered by one or more' " of Teleflex's patents. KSR refused to enter a royalty arrangement with Teleflex; so Teleflex sued for infringement, asserting KSR's pedal infringed the Engelgau patent and two other patents. Teleflex later abandoned its claims regarding the other patents and dedicated the patents to the public. The remaining contention was that KSR's pedal system for GM infringed claim 4 of the Engelgau patent. Teleflex has not argued that the other three claims of the patent are infringed by KSR's pedal, nor has Teleflex argued that the mechanical adjustable pedal designed by KSR for Ford infringed any of its patents.

C

The District Court granted summary judgment in KSR's favor. After reviewing the pertinent history of pedal design, the scope of the Engelgau patent, and the relevant prior art, the court considered the validity of the contested claim. By direction of 35 U.S.C. § 282, an issued patent is presumed valid. The District Court applied *Graham*'s framework to determine whether under summary-judgment standards KSR had overcome the presumption and demonstrated that claim 4 was obvious in light of the prior art in existence when the claimed subject matter was invented. *See* § 102(a).

The District Court determined, in light of the expert testimony and the parties' stipulations, that the level of ordinary skill in pedal design was " 'an undergraduate degree in mechanical engineering (or an equivalent amount of industry experience) [and] familiarity with pedal control systems for vehicles.' " The court then set forth the relevant prior art, including the patents and pedal designs described above.

Following *Graham*'s direction, the court compared the teachings of the prior art to the claims of Engelgau. It found "little difference." Asano taught everything contained in claim 4 except the use of a sensor to detect the pedal's position and transmit it to the computer controlling the throttle. That additional aspect was revealed in sources such as the '068 patent and the sensors used by Chevrolet.

Under the controlling cases from the Court of Appeals for the Federal Circuit, however, the District Court was not permitted to stop there. The court was required also to apply the TSM test. The District Court held KSR had satisfied the test. It reasoned (1) the state of the industry would lead inevitably to combinations of electronic sensors and adjustable pedals, (2) Rixon provided the basis for these developments, and (3) Smith taught a solution to the wire chafing problems in Rixon, namely locating the sensor on the fixed structure of the pedal. This could lead to the combination of Asano, or a pedal like it, with a pedal position sensor.

* * *

With principal reliance on the TSM test, the Court of Appeals reversed. It ruled the District Court had not been strict enough in applying the test, having failed to make " 'finding[s] as to the specific understanding or principle within the knowledge of a skilled artisan that would have motivated one with no knowledge of [the] invention' . . . to attach an electronic control to the support bracket of the Asano assembly." The Court of Appeals held that the District Court was incorrect that the nature of the problem to be solved satisfied this requirement because unless the "prior art references address[ed] the precise problem that the patentee was trying to solve," the problem would not motivate an inventor to look at those references.

Here, the Court of Appeals found, the Asano pedal was designed to solve the " 'constant ratio problem' "—that is, to ensure that the force required to depress the pedal is the same no matter how the pedal is adjusted—whereas Engelgau sought to provide a simpler, smaller, cheaper adjustable electronic pedal. As for Rixon, the court explained, that pedal suffered from the problem of wire chafing but was not designed to solve it. In the court's view Rixon did not teach anything helpful to Engelgau's purpose. Smith, in turn, did not relate to adjustable pedals and did not "necessarily go to the issue of motivation to attach the electronic control on the support bracket of the pedal assembly." When the patents were interpreted in this way, the Court of Appeals held, they would not have led a person of ordinary skill to put a sensor on the sort of pedal described in Asano.

That it might have been obvious to try the combination of Asano and a sensor was likewise irrelevant, in the court's view, because " '[o]bvious to try" has long been held not to constitute obviousness.' "

* * *

The Court of Appeals further held that genuine issues of material fact precluded summary judgment. Teleflex had proffered statements from one expert that claim 4 " 'was a simple, elegant, and novel combination of features,' " compared to Rixon, and from another expert that claim 4 was nonobvious because, unlike in Rixon, the sensor was mounted on the support bracket rather than the pedal itself. This evidence, the court concluded, sufficed to require a trial.

II

A

We begin by rejecting the rigid approach of the Court of Appeals. Throughout this Court's engagement with the question of obviousness, our cases have set forth an expansive and flexible approach inconsistent with the way the Court of Appeals applied its TSM test here. To be sure, *Graham* recognized the need for "uniformity and definiteness." Yet the principles laid down in *Graham* reaffirmed the "functional approach" of *Hotchkiss,* 11 How. 248. To this end, *Graham* set forth a broad inquiry and invited courts, where appropriate, to look at any secondary considerations that would prove instructive.

Neither the enactment of § 103 nor the analysis in *Graham* disturbed this Court's earlier instructions concerning the need for caution in granting a patent based on the combination of elements found in the prior art. For over a half century, the Court has held that a "patent for a combination which only unites old elements with no change in their respective functions . . . obviously withdraws what is already known into the field of its monopoly and diminishes the resources available to skillful men." *Great Atlantic & Pacific Tea Co. v. Supermarket Equipment Corp.,* 340 U.S. 147, 152 (1950). This is a principal reason for declining to allow patents for what is obvious. The combination of familiar elements according to known methods is likely to be obvious when it does no more than yield predictable results. [C]ases decided after *Graham* illustrate the application of this doctrine.

In *United States v. Adams,* 383 U.S. 39, 40 (1966), a companion case to *Graham,* the Court considered the obviousness of a "wet battery" that varied from prior designs in two ways: It contained water, rather than the acids conventionally employed in storage batteries; and its electrodes were magnesium and cuprous chloride, rather than zinc and silver chloride. The Court recognized that when a patent claims a structure already known in the prior art that is altered by the mere substitution of one element for another known in the field, the combination must do more than yield a predictable result. It nevertheless rejected the Government's claim that Adams's battery was obvious. The Court relied upon the corollary principle that when the prior art teaches away from combining certain known elements, discovery of a successful means of combining them is more likely to be nonobvious. When Adams designed his battery, the prior art warned that risks were involved in using the types of electrodes he employed. The fact that the elements worked together in an unexpected and fruitful manner supported the conclusion that Adams's design was not obvious to those skilled in the art.

In *Anderson's-Black Rock, Inc. v. Pavement Salvage Co.*, 396 U.S. 57 (1969), the Court elaborated on this approach. The subject matter of the patent before the Court was a device combining two pre-existing elements: a radiant-heat burner and a paving machine. The device, the Court concluded, did not create some new synergy: The radiant-heat burner functioned just as a burner was expected to function; and the paving machine did the same. The two in combination did no more than they would in separate, sequential operation. In those circumstances, "while the combination of old elements performed a useful function, it added nothing to the nature and quality of the radiant-heat burner already patented," and the patent failed under § 103.

In *Sakraida v. AG Pro, Inc.*, 425 U.S. 273 (1976), the Court derived from the precedents the conclusion that when a patent "simply arranges old elements with each performing the same function it had been known to perform" and yields no more than one would expect from such an arrangement, the combination is obvious.

The principles underlying these cases are instructive when the question is whether a patent claiming the combination of elements of prior art is obvious. When a work is available in one field of endeavor, design incentives and other market forces can prompt variations of it, either in the same field or a different one. If a person of ordinary skill can implement a predictable variation, § 103 likely bars its patentability. * * *

Following these principles may be more difficult in other cases than it is here because the claimed subject matter may involve more than the simple substitution of one known element for another or the mere application of a known technique to a piece of prior art ready for the improvement. Often, it will be necessary for a court to look to interrelated teachings of multiple patents; the effects of demands known to the design community or present in the marketplace; and the background knowledge possessed by a person having ordinary skill in the art, all in order to determine whether there was an apparent reason to combine the known elements in the fashion claimed by the patent at issue. To facilitate review, this analysis should be made explicit. As our precedents make clear, however, the analysis need not seek out precise teachings directed to the specific subject matter of the challenged claim, for a court can take account of the inferences and creative steps that a person of ordinary skill in the art would employ.

B

When it first established the requirement of demonstrating a teaching, suggestion, or motivation to combine known elements in order to show that the combination is obvious, the Court of Customs and Patent Appeals captured a helpful insight. As is clear from cases such as *Adams,* a patent composed of several elements is not proved obvious merely by demonstrating that each of its elements was, independently, known in the prior art. Although common sense directs one to look with care at a patent application that claims as innovation the combination of two known devices according to their established functions, it can be important to identify a reason that would have prompted a person of ordinary skill in the relevant field to combine the elements in the way the claimed new invention does. This is so because inventions in most, if not all, instances rely upon building blocks long since uncovered, and claimed discoveries almost of necessity will be combinations of what, in some sense, is already known.

Helpful insights, however, need not become rigid and mandatory formulas; and when it is so applied, the TSM test is incompatible with our precedents. The obviousness analysis cannot be confined by a formalistic conception of the words teaching, suggestion, and motivation, or by overemphasis on the importance of published articles and the explicit content of issued patents. The diversity of inventive pursuits and of modern technology counsels against limiting the analysis in this way. In many fields it may be that there is little discussion of obvious techniques or combinations, and it often may be the case that market demand, rather than scientific literature, will drive design trends. Granting patent protection to advances that would occur in the ordinary course without real innovation retards progress and may, in the case of patents combining previously known elements, deprive prior inventions of their value or utility.

In the years since the Court of Customs and Patent Appeals set forth the essence of the TSM test, the Court of Appeals no doubt has applied the test in accord with these principles in many cases. There is no necessary inconsistency between the idea underlying the TSM test and the *Graham* analysis. But when a court transforms the general principle into a rigid rule that limits the obviousness inquiry, as the Court of Appeals did here, it errs.

C

The flaws in the analysis of the Court of Appeals relate for the most part to the court's narrow conception of the obviousness inquiry reflected in its application of the TSM test. In determining whether the subject matter of a patent claim is obvious, neither the particular motivation nor the avowed purpose of the patentee controls. What matters is the objective reach of the claim. If the claim extends to what is obvious, it is invalid under § 103. One of the ways in which a patent's subject matter can be proved obvious is by noting that there existed at the time of invention a known problem for which there was an obvious solution encompassed by the patent's claims.

The first error of the Court of Appeals in this case was to foreclose this reasoning by holding that courts and patent examiners should look only to the problem the patentee was trying to solve. The Court of Appeals failed to recognize that the problem motivating the patentee may be only one of many addressed by the patent's subject matter. The question is not whether the combination was obvious to the patentee but whether the combination was obvious to a person with ordinary skill in the art. Under the correct analysis, any need or problem known in the field of endeavor at the time of invention and addressed by the patent can provide a reason for combining the elements in the manner claimed.

The second error of the Court of Appeals lay in its assumption that a person of ordinary skill attempting to solve a problem will be led only to those elements of prior art designed to solve the same problem. The primary purpose of Asano was solving the constant ratio problem; so, the court concluded, an inventor considering how to put a sensor on an adjustable pedal would have no reason to consider putting it on the Asano pedal. Common sense teaches, however, that familiar items may have obvious uses beyond their primary purposes, and in many cases a person of ordinary skill will be able to fit the teachings of multiple patents together like pieces of a puzzle. Regardless of Asano's primary purpose, the design provided an obvious example of an adjustable pedal with a fixed pivot point; and the prior art was replete with patents indicating that a fixed pivot point was an ideal mount for a sensor. The idea that a designer hoping to make an adjustable electronic pedal would ignore Asano because Asano was designed to solve the constant ratio problem makes little sense. A person of ordinary skill is also a person of ordinary creativity, not an automaton.

The same constricted analysis led the Court of Appeals to conclude, in error, that a patent claim cannot be proved obvious merely by showing that the combination of elements was "obvious to try." When there is a design need or market pressure to solve a problem and there are a finite number of identified, predictable solutions, a person of ordinary skill has good

reason to pursue the known options within his or her technical grasp. If this leads to the anticipated success, it is likely the product not of innovation but of ordinary skill and common sense. In that instance the fact that a combination was obvious to try might show that it was obvious under § 103.

The Court of Appeals, finally, drew the wrong conclusion from the risk of courts and patent examiners falling prey to hindsight bias. A factfinder should be aware, of course, of the distortion caused by hindsight bias and must be cautious of arguments reliant upon *ex post* reasoning. Rigid preventative rules that deny factfinders recourse to common sense, however, are neither necessary under our case law nor consistent with it.

* * * [T]he fundamental misunderstandings identified above led the Court of Appeals in this case to apply a test inconsistent with our patent law decisions.

III

When we apply the standards we have explained to the instant facts, claim 4 must be found obvious. We agree with and adopt the District Court's recitation of the relevant prior art and its determination of the level of ordinary skill in the field. As did the District Court, we see little difference between the teachings of Asano and Smith and the adjustable electronic pedal disclosed in claim 4 of the Engelgau patent. A person having ordinary skill in the art could have combined Asano with a pedal position sensor in a fashion encompassed by claim 4, and would have seen the benefits of doing so.

* * *

The District Court was correct to conclude that, as of the time Engelgau designed the subject matter in claim 4, it was obvious to a person of ordinary skill to combine Asano with a pivot-mounted pedal position sensor. There then existed a marketplace that created a strong incentive to convert mechanical pedals to electronic pedals, and the prior art taught a number of methods for achieving this advance. The Court of Appeals considered the issue too narrowly by, in effect, asking whether a pedal designer writing on a blank slate would have chosen both Asano and a modular sensor similar to the ones used in the Chevrolet truckline and disclosed in the '068 patent. * * * The proper question to have asked was whether a pedal designer of ordinary skill, facing the wide range of needs created by developments in the field of endeavor, would have seen a benefit to upgrading Asano with a sensor.

* * *

For a designer starting with Asano, the question was where to attach the sensor. The consequent legal question, then, is whether a pedal designer of ordinary skill starting with Asano would have found it obvious to put the sensor on a fixed pivot point. The prior art discussed above leads us to the conclusion that attaching the sensor where both KSR and Engelgau put it would have been obvious to a person of ordinary skill.

The '936 patent taught the utility of putting the sensor on the pedal device, not in the engine. Smith, in turn, explained to put the sensor not on the pedal's footpad but instead on its support structure. And from the known wire-chafing problems of Rixon, and Smith's teaching that "the pedal assemblies must not precipitate any motion in the connecting wires," the designer would know to place the sensor on a nonmoving part of the pedal structure. The most obvious nonmoving point on the structure from which a sensor can easily detect the pedal's position is a pivot point. The designer, accordingly, would follow Smith in mounting the sensor on a pivot, thereby designing an adjustable electronic pedal covered by claim 4.

Just as it was possible to begin with the objective to upgrade Asano to work with a computer-controlled throttle, so too was it possible to take an adjustable electronic pedal like Rixon and seek an improvement that would avoid the wire-chafing problem. Following similar steps to those just explained, a designer would learn from Smith to avoid sensor movement and would come, thereby, to Asano because Asano disclosed an adjustable pedal with a fixed pivot.

* * *

Like the District Court, finally, we conclude Teleflex has shown no secondary factors to dislodge the determination that claim 4 is obvious. Proper application of *Graham* and our other precedents to these facts therefore leads to the conclusion that claim 4 encompassed obvious subject matter. As a result, the claim fails to meet the requirement of § 103.

* * *

NOTES

1. *Post-AIA Date of Obviousness and Prior Art:* Under section 103 as amended by the AIA, the statutory text zeroes in the effective filing date for assessing the content of the prior art. When an application contains a claim whose effective filing date is on or after March 16, 2013, a claimed invention within that application will be unpatentable if the invention as a whole would have been obvious (in light of the prior art) before the effective filing date. Section 102(a) provides the basic scope of "prior art," and section 102(b) details what will not constitute prior art (for example, certain disclosures made within one year of the date of application and either made by the inventor or a joint inventor, or by a third party after the inventor had already publicly disclosed the invention).

2. *Pre-AIA Date of Obviousness and Prior Art:* The statutory text of pre-AIA section 103 focuses on the "time the invention was made," or the date of

invention, for the obviousness analysis. This fairly evidently includes all relevant prior art under section 102(a), (e), and (g), since those references (by statutory language) must arise before the date of invention; any section 102(e), (f), or (g) prior art subject to common ownership with the claimed invention (or common obligation of assignment) is, however, excluded from the prior art under section 103(c). Less obviously included within the scope of prior art available for the obviousness analysis under pre-AIA section 103 would be prior art arising under section 102(b), whose critical date (by statute) is one year before the filing date rather than the date of invention. The issue was settled, however, by the Court of Customs and Patent Appeals in *In re Foster*, 343 F.2d 980 (C.C.P.A. 1965), which held that section 102(b) prior art with an effective date more than a year before the filing date remained included within the obviousness analysis under section 103. The *Foster* court noted that its conclusion was consistent with the history of both sections 102(b) and 103:

> As to what the law has been, more particularly what it was prior to 1953, when the new patent act and its section 103 became effective, there is a paucity of direct precedents on the precise problem. We think there is a reason for this. Under the old law (R.S. 4886, where 102(b) finds its origin) patents were refused or invalidated on references dated more than a year before the filing date [Ed. note: exactly the potential outcome if 102(b) references are part of the 103 analysis] because the invention was anticipated or, if they were not, then because there was no "invention," the latter rejection being based either on (a) a single non-anticipatory reference plus the skill of the art or (b) on a plurality of references. There was no need to seek out the precise statutory basis because it was R.S. 4886 in any event, read in the light of the Supreme Court's interpretation of the law that there must always be "invention." * * *
>
> * * *
>
> * * * [S]ection 103 had but a single purpose which was to add to the statute a provision to take the place of the judge-made "requirement for invention." In doing that, the history also shows, the words "at the time the invention was made" were included for the sole purpose of precluding the use of hindsight in deciding whether an invention is obvious. We are sure Congress had no intent thereby to modify the law respecting loss of right based on the existence of a time-bar. * * *

343 F.2d at 988–89, 990 (footnote omitted).

3. Is it obvious to combine, or to try to combine, features from various prior art references for a multi-camera imaging system for detecting diseases of human tissue (predominantly but perhaps not exclusively skin cancer), wherein the patient's imaging position is at the central axis or intersection of the array of cameras/imaging devices, and the prior art references range from (1) a skin cancer imaging and screening system where the patient stood against a wall; (2) an apparatus (kiosk) for imaging the surface of a person from

multiple sides and angles to create a computer avatar of that person; (3) a 3D body-imaging system for use in making made-to-measure apparel, and for other applications related to body measurement, having six imaging sensors (a light projector plus camera) positioned at two heights on three towers to surround the body and image and measure all sides? Why or why not, and what facts are most relevant under *KSR*? *See Canfield Scientific, Inc. v. Melanoscan, LLC,* 987 F.3d 1375, 1383 (Fed. Cir. 2021) (including patent claim and diagrams of prior art reference systems).

3. NONOBVIOUSNESS OF DESIGN PATENTS

Section 171 expressly applies the nonobviousness requirement to design patents. When assessing obviousness, just as with novelty, the visual impression of the claimed design must be considered as a whole. In *High Point Design LLC v. Buyers Direct, Inc.*, 730 F.3d 1301 (Fed. Cir. 2013), the Federal Circuit explained judicial analysis of the obviousness of a claimed design as follows:

> When assessing the potential obviousness of a design patent, a finder of fact employs two distinct steps: first, "one must find a single reference, a something in existence, the design characteristics of which are basically the same as the claimed design"; second, "[o]nce this primary reference is found, other references may be used to modify it to create a design that has the same overall visual appearance as the claimed design." *Durling v. Spectrum Furniture Co.,* 101 F.3d 100, 103 (Fed. Cir. 1996) (internal quotations omitted); *see also Apple, Inc. v. Samsung Elecs. Co.,* 678 F.3d 1314, 1329 (Fed. Cir. 2012).
>
> Under the first step, a court must both "(1) discern the correct visual impression created by the patented design as a whole; and (2) determine whether there is a single reference that creates 'basically the same' visual impression." *Durling,* 101 F.3d at 103. The ultimate inquiry in an obviousness analysis is "whether the claimed design would have been obvious to a designer of ordinary skill who designs articles of the type involved." *Id., quoted in Apple,* 678 F.3d at 1329.[2]
>
> * * *
>
> Although obviousness is assessed from the vantage point of an ordinary designer in the art, "an expert's opinion on the legal conclusion of obviousness is neither necessary nor controlling." *Avia Grp.*, 853 F.2d at 1564. That said, an expert's opinion may

[2] We do not believe our decision in *International Seaway Trading Corp. v. Walgreens Corp.*, 589 F.3d 1233, 1240 (Fed. Cir. 2009), cited by the district court, compels a contrary conclusion. The *International Seaway* court may in fact have had the "designer of ordinary skill" standard in mind when it used the term "ordinary observer." . . . .

> be relevant to the factual aspects of the analysis leading to that legal conclusion. *See Petersen Mfg. Co., Inc. v. Cent. Purchasing, Inc.*, 740 F.2d 1541, 1547 (Fed. Cir.1984), *abrogated on other grounds by Beatrice Foods Co. v. New England Printing and Lithographing Co.*, 899 F.2d 1171, 1177–78 (Fed. Cir.1990) ("In civil litigation involving a design [patent], an expert's testimony is most helpful, as in the determination of obviousness with respect to any other type of invention, to explain the technology, the scope and content of the prior art, the differences between the prior art and the invention, and the level of skill in the art.").

730 F.3d 1301, 1311–14 (footnotes and some citations omitted).

4. NONOBVIOUSNESS OF PLANT PATENTS

Section 161 appears to make the nonobviousness requirement applicable to plant patents. In *Yoder Bros., Inc. v. California-Florida Plant Corp.*, 537 F.2d 1347 (5th Cir.1976), the Fifth Circuit attempted to determine the meaning of nonobviousness with respect to plant patents. The court rejected the argument that obviousness could be established merely by showing that the distinct chrysanthemum "sport" (a bud mutation) claimed in the challenged patent had recurred naturally. The court reasoned that recurrence only indicated that the particular mutation would be predictable to those skilled in the art, and that the legislative history of the plant patent statutes indicated that Congress intended to extend protection to new plant mutations regardless of whether they were predictable. 537 F.2d at 1381–82. This approach, the court concluded, did not disregard the requirements of the Intellectual Property Clause:

> The only way that the Constitution would be offended by permitting patents on recurring sports would be if such leniency indicated that no "invention" was present. We do not think that sport recurrence would negate invention, however. An infinite number of a certain sized sport could appear on a plant, but until someone recognized its uniqueness and difference and found that the traits could be preserved by asexual reproduction in commercial quantities, no patentable plant would exist. An objective judgment of the value of the sport's new and different characteristics—*i.e.* nutritive value, ornamental value, hardiness, longevity, etc.—would not depend in any way on whether a similar sport had appeared in the past, or whether that particular sport was predictable.

Id. at 1382 (footnote omitted). The court also attempted to formulate an affirmative statement of what "nonobviousness" means in the context of plant patents:

Rephrasing the *John Deere* tests for the plant world, we might ask about (1) the characteristics of prior plants of the same general type, both patented and nonpatented, and (2) the differences between the prior plants and the claims at issue. We see no meaningful way to apply the third criterion to plants—*i.e.* the level of ordinary skill in the prior art. Criteria one and two are reminiscent of the "distinctness" requirement already in the Plant Patent Act. Thus, if we are to give obviousness an independent meaning, it must refer to something other than observable characteristics.

We think that the most promising approach toward the obviousness requirement for plant patents is reference to the underlying constitutional standard that it codifies—namely, invention.

The general thrust of the "invention" requirement is to ensure that minor improvements will not be granted the protection of a seventeen year monopoly by the state. In the case of plants, to develop or discover a new variety that retains the desirable qualities of the parent stock and adds significant improvements, and to preserve the new specimen by asexually reproducing it constitutes no small feat.

This Court's case dealing with the patent on the chemical compound commonly known as the drug "Darvon" provides some insight into the problem of how to apply the "invention" requirement to a new and esoteric subject matter. The court first noted that

> [a]nalogical reasoning is necessarily restricted in many chemical patent cases because of the necessity for physiological experimentation before any use can be determined.

> In fact, such lack of predictability of useful result from the making of even the slightest variation in the atomic structure or spatial arrangement of a complex molecule . . . deprives the instant claims of obviousness and anticipation of most of their vitality. . . .

460 F.2d [1096] at 1101. The court resolved the apparent dilemma by looking to the therapeutic value of the new drug instead of to its chemical composition:

> [R]eason compels us to agree that novelty, usefulness and non-obviousness inhere in the true discovery that a chemical compound exhibits a new needed medicinal capability, even

> though it be closely related in structure to a known or patented drug.

460 F.2d at 1103.

> The same kind of shift in focus would lead us to a more productive inquiry for plant patents. If the plant is a source of food, the ultimate question might be its nutritive content or its prolificacy. A medicinal plant might be judged by its increased or changed therapeutic value. Similarly, an ornamental plant would be judged by its increased beauty and desirability in relation to the other plants of its type, its usefulness in the industry, and how much of an improvement it represents over prior ornamental plants, taking all of its characteristics together.

Id. at 1379 (footnotes omitted). Compare the *Yoder Bros.* court's discussion of novelty and distinctness, reproduced on pages 495–496, *supra*. Do you agree with the court's interpretation of nonobviousness?

E. THE WRITTEN SPECIFICATION

Statute: 35 U.S.C. § 112

Section 101 of the Patent Act, which requires that an invention be "new and useful," also notes that the grant of a patent is "subject to the conditions and requirements" of the remainder of the Patent Act. Section 112 sets forth certain of those additional requirements:

> The specification shall contain a written description of the invention, and of the manner and process of making and using it, in such full, clear, concise, and exact terms as to enable any person skilled in the art to which it pertains, or with which it is most nearly connected, to make and use the same, and shall set forth the best mode contemplated by the inventor or joint inventor of carrying out the invention.
>
> * * *
>
> The specification shall conclude with one or more claims particularly pointing out and distinctly claiming the subject matter which the inventor or a joint inventor regards as the invention.

The "specification" whose features are described in section 112 is one of the mandatory portions of the patent application under section 111. As discussed in Chapter 11.B.1., *infra*, Patent Act sections 111–121 (including other portions of section 112 not reproduced here) also set forth additional requirements that must be satisfied by each patent applicant.

The AIA's changes to section 112 were minimal. In addition to some nomenclature changes, the AIA created separate subsections ((a), (b), etc.), which will avoid in the future what were previously awkward paragraph-based references, such as "§ 112, ¶ 2."

1. ENABLEMENT

The first portion of section 112 reproduced above has long been understood to mandate a "full, clear, concise, and exact" description of the invention in the specification, sufficient to "enable a person skilled in the art to make and use the claimed invention." *In re Wands*, 858 F.2d 731, 735 (Fed. Cir. 1988). Because it is written for an audience composed of persons skilled in the relevant art, the "patent need not disclose what is well known in the art." *Id.* The skilled person should merely be able to make and use the invention without "undue experimentation."

> Factors to be considered in determining whether a disclosure would require undue experimentation * * * include (1) the quantity of experimentation necessary, (2) the amount of direction or guidance presented, (3) the presence or absence of working examples, (4) the nature of the invention, (5) the state of the prior art, (6) the relative skill of those in the art, (7) the predictability or unpredictability of the art, and (8) the breadth of the claims.

Id. at 737.

2. WRITTEN DESCRIPTION

In *Ariad Pharmaceuticals, Inc. v. Eli Lilly & Co.*, 598 F.3d 1336 (Fed. Cir. 2010), the Federal Circuit, sitting *en banc*, "reaffirmed" that the first portion of section 112 quoted above contains both a written description requirement and an enablement requirement, which should each be analyzed separately.

> Perhaps there is little difference in some fields between describing an invention and enabling one to make and use it, but that is not always true of certain inventions * * * Thus, although written description and enablement often rise and fall together, requiring a written description of the invention plays a vital role in curtailing claims that do not require undue experimentation to make and use, and thus satisfy enablement, but that have not been invented, and thus cannot be described.

598 F.3d at 1352. The standard the court set forth for assessing compliance with the written description requirement was not concise, despite the court's reference to a "fairly uniform standard":

> Since its inception, this court has consistently held that § 112, first paragraph, contains a written description requirement separate from enablement, and we have articulated a "fairly uniform standard," which we now affirm. Specifically, the

> description must "clearly allow persons of ordinary skill in the art to recognize that [the inventor] invented what is claimed." In other words, the test for sufficiency is whether the disclosure of the application relied upon reasonably conveys to those skilled in the art that the inventor had possession of the claimed subject matter as of the filing date.
>
> The term "possession," however, has never been very enlightening. It implies that as long as one can produce records documenting a written description of a claimed invention, one can show possession. But the hallmark of written description is disclosure. Thus, "possession as shown in the disclosure" is a more complete formulation. Yet whatever the specific articulation, the test requires an objective inquiry into the four corners of the specification from the perspective of a person of ordinary skill in the art. Based on that inquiry, the specification must describe an invention understandable to that skilled artisan and show that the inventor actually invented the invention claimed.
>
> This inquiry, as we have long held, is a question of fact. Thus, we have recognized that determining whether a patent complies with the written description requirement will necessarily vary depending on the context. Specifically, the level of detail required to satisfy the written description requirement varies depending on the nature and scope of the claims and on the complexity and predictability of the relevant technology. * * *
>
> * * *
>
> There are, however, a few broad principles that hold true across all cases. We have made clear that the written description requirement does not demand either examples or an actual reduction to practice; a constructive reduction to practice that in a definite way identifies the claimed invention can satisfy the written description requirement. Conversely, we have repeatedly stated that actual "possession" or reduction to practice outside of the specification is not enough. Rather, as stated above, it is the specification itself that must demonstrate possession. And while the description requirement does not demand any particular form of disclosure, or that the specification recite the claimed invention *in haec verba*, a description that merely renders the invention obvious does not satisfy the requirement.

Id. at 1351–52 (citations omitted). The court also spoke to the purpose of the written description requirement, as separated from the enablement requirement:

> A description of the claimed invention allows the [PTO] to examine applications effectively; courts to understand the invention, [to] determine compliance with the statute, and to construe the claims; and the public to understand and improve upon the invention and to avoid the claimed boundaries of the patentee's exclusive rights.

Id. at 1345. In response to the argument that the written description requirement, as constituted by the court, would disadvantage universities and others engaged in basic research, the court emphasized its view of the policy underlying patent law:

> But the patent law has always been directed to the "useful Arts," meaning inventions with a practical use. Much university research relates to basic research, including research into scientific principles and mechanisms of action, and universities may not have the resources or inclination to work out the practical implications of all such research, i.e., finding and identifying compounds able to affect the mechanism discovered. That is no failure of the law's interpretation, but its intention. Patents are not awarded for academic theories, no matter how groundbreaking or necessary to the later patentable inventions of others. "[A] patent is not a hunting license. It is not a reward for the search, but compensation for its successful conclusion." Requiring a written description of the invention limits patent protection to those who actually perform the difficult work of "invention"—that is, conceive of the complete and final invention with all its claimed limitations—and disclose the fruits of that effort to the public.
>
> That research hypotheses do not qualify for patent protection possibly results in some loss of incentive, although Ariad presents no evidence of any discernable impact on the pace of innovation or the number of patents obtained by universities. But claims to research plans also impose costs on downstream research, discouraging later invention. The goal is to get the right balance, and the written description doctrine does so by giving the incentive to actual invention and not "attempt[s] to preempt the future before it has arrived." As this court has repeatedly stated, the purpose of the written description requirement is to "ensure that the scope of the right to exclude, as set forth in the claims, does not overreach the scope of the inventor's contribution to the field of art as described in the patent specification." It is part of the *quid pro quo* of the patent grant and ensures that the public receives a meaningful disclosure in exchange for being excluded from practicing an invention for a period of time.

Id. at 1353–54. *See also Centocor Ortho Biotech, Inc. v. Abbott Labs.*, 636 F.3d 1341, 1348 (Fed.Cir. 2011) ("A mere wish or plan for obtaining the claimed invention is not adequate written description.") (internal quotation omitted).

3. DEFINITENESS

Section 112 contains additional requirements for a valid patent beyond an enabling written description that demonstrates the inventor's possession of the claimed subject matter. As shown above, section 112 also mandates that that the claims be definite: "The specification shall conclude with one or more claims *particularly pointing out and distinctly claiming* the subject matter which the inventor or a joint inventor regards as the invention." 35 U.S.C.A. § 112(b) (emphasis added).

In *Nautilus, Inc. v. Biosig Instruments, Inc.*, 572 U.S. 898 (2014), the Supreme Court held that "a patent is invalid for indefiniteness if its claims, read in light of the specification delineating the patent, and the prosecution history, fail to inform, with reasonable certainty, those skilled in the art about the scope of the invention." In its examination of "definiteness," the Court first noted several points of agreement between the parties (largely supported by citations to previous Court decisions):

> First, definiteness is to be evaluated from the perspective of someone skilled in the relevant art. Second, in assessing definiteness, claims are to be read in light of the patent's specification and prosecution history. Third, definiteness is measured from the viewpoint of a person skilled in the art at the time the patent was filed.

572 U.S. at 908 (internal citations, quotation marks, and emphasis omitted). It then expanded upon the competing policies at stake:

> Section 112, we have said, entails a delicate balance. On the one hand, the definiteness requirement must take into account the inherent limitations of language. Some modicum of uncertainty, the Court has recognized, is the price of ensuring the appropriate incentives for innovation. One must bear in mind, moreover, that patents are not addressed to lawyers, or even to the public generally, but rather to those skilled in the relevant art.
>
> At the same time, a patent must be precise enough to afford clear notice of what is claimed, thereby apprising the public of what is still open to them. Otherwise there would be a zone of uncertainty which enterprise and experimentation may enter only at the risk of infringement claims. * * * [T]he patent drafter is in the best position to resolve the ambiguity in patent claims.

Id. at 909–10 (internal citations and quotation marks omitted). The Court ruled that to satisfy definiteness, the patent claims, "viewed in light of the specification and prosecution history, [must] inform those skilled in the art about the scope of the invention with reasonable certainty." *Id.* at 910. The Court reasoned that this "reasonable certainty" standard should give sufficient and workable guidance to lower courts while reconciling the "unattainable" nature of "absolute precision" with the need for "clarity" for the public and would-be competitors. *Id.*

The *Nautilus* case involved a heart-rate monitor for exercise equipment. One claim limitation for the monitor required two electrodes "mounted . . . in spaced relationship with each other" within a cylindrical bar to be gripped by the person exercising on the equipment. The District Court had ruled that the term "spaced relationship" was indefinite, and the Federal Circuit reversed and remanded. In reviewing the Federal Circuit decision, the Supreme Court expanded on the demands of § 112 as noted above, but it declined to apply its definition of definiteness to the patent at issue. It instead vacated the Federal Circuit's decision and remanded the case for further proceedings. On remand, the Federal Circuit found the claim to be sufficiently definite (as it also had before the Supreme Court heard the case). *See* 783 F.3d 1374 (Fed. Cir. 2015).

4. BEST MODE

The first paragraph of section 112 also includes a third requirement beyond enablement and written description: the inventor must set forth in the patent specification the "best mode contemplated by the inventor of carrying out the invention." Although the "best mode" requirement exists as a matter of patent prosecution meaning the PTO examiner will demand it, for proceedings commenced on or after September 16, 2011 (the AIA's effective date), failure to disclose the best mode cannot be the basis of an invalidity determination during post-issuance litigation. *See* 35 U.S.C. § 282. Failure to satisfy any other requirement of section 112, however, including enablement and written description, can supply the basis of an invalidity determination either during prosecution or after grant.

NOTE

A patentee may choose broad language for its claims. But although broad claim language may increase the scope of infringement (the subject of Chapter 12, *infra*), such claim language can also increase the likelihood that the claim will be held invalid under section 112, as further set forth above. For example, the patent in *Sitrick v. Dreamworks*, 516 F.3d 993 (Fed.Cir. 2008), claimed an entertainment system that could integrate user-provided images and audio into existing audiovisual works. At the claim construction phase of its infringement lawsuit (*see infra* Chapter 12.A.1.), the patentee persuaded the district court to hold that its claims encompassed not only video games but motion pictures as well. This claim scope would have likely included the defendant's activities. Unfortunately, for the patentee, however, the court ruled that the specification did not enable the claim with respect to motion pictures, and the Federal Circuit affirmed.

> The full scope of the claimed invention must be enabled. The rationale for this statutory requirement is straightforward. Enabling the full scope of each claim is "part of the *quid pro quo* of the patent bargain." A patentee who chooses broad claim language must make sure the broad claims are fully enabled. "The scope of the claims must be less than or equal to the scope of the enablement" to "ensure[ ] that the public knowledge is enriched by the patent specification to a degree at least commensurate with the scope of the claims."
>
> * * *
>
> An enablement analysis begins with the disclosure in the specification. Neither patent specification in this case teaches how the substitution and integration of a user image would be accomplished in movies. Claim 56 of the '864 patent and claims 1, 20, 49, 57, 58, 62, 64, and 69 of the '825 patent provide for the "integration" or "substitution" of a visual or audio "user image" in place of a "pre-defined character image" or "character function" within a "presentation" such as a motion picture. After thoroughly analyzing both patents, the district court determined that the specifications do not disclose how the IAIS or Controller 260C would function for movies. We agree. The patents do not teach how to implement the "intercept logic functioning" of Controller 260C in the context of movies. The patents do not teach how the IAIS and its Controller 260C would perform such necessary steps as "selecting" and "analyzing" the predefined character image in a movie, or "integrat[ing]" or "substituting" the image in movies. As the district court recognized, "[m]ovies do not have easily separable character functions, as video games do, and the patent does not explain how the IAIS either selects the character functions to be substituted for a user image or intercepts signals in order to effectuate the substitution."
>
> Defendants' two experts explained that one skilled in the art would not to be able to take the teachings regarding video games and apply them to movies. Both experts explained that movies and video games are technically different. The experts opined that the claims are not enabled because the analysis techniques described in the specification for identifying character functions or intercepting character signals have no relevance to movies. Defendants thus carried their burden of showing by clear and convincing evidence that the claims are not enabled for "integrating" or substituting a "user image" in movies. With respect to audio substitution, the district court determined that Defendants showed by clear, convincing, and undisputed evidence that it is difficult, if not impossible, to "isolate

> any one voice [from] the rest of the sounds" in soundtracks in pre-existing movies.

Id. at 999–1001. Accordingly, the claims were invalid because their full scope was not enabled by the specification.

CHAPTER 11

INVENTORSHIP, OWNERSHIP, AND PROSECUTION

■ ■ ■

As in the previous chapter, any reference to the "AIA" in this chapter refers to the America Invents Act, Pub. L. No. 112–29, 125 Stat. 284 (2011).

A. INVENTORSHIP AND OWNERSHIP

Statutes: 35 U.S.C. §§ 101, 111(a)(1), 115–18, 256, 261–62

1. NATURE OF INVENTORSHIP

A patent must name as inventors all the individuals who participated in the conception of the inventions claimed therein, and no other persons. This rule flows from the fundamental inventorship requirement of section 101 ("Whoever invents or discovers . . . may obtain a patent therefor") as well as pre-AIA section 102(f) ("[A person shall be entitled to a patent unless] he did not himself invent the subject matter sought to be patented") and post-AIA section 100(f) ("The term 'inventor' means the individual or, if a joint invention, the individuals collectively who invented or discovered the subject matter of the invention."). Moreover, under section 115, every application must be accompanied by an oath or declaration from each inventor or joint inventor that "such individual believes himself or herself to be the original inventor or an original joint inventor of a claimed invention in the application." Sections 116 and 256 allow for correction of inventorship errors during the application process and after the patent issues, respectively.[1] The nature of inventorship, including the roles of conception, experimentation, and collaboration, is explored in the following case and notes.

[1] In proceedings commenced before September 15, 2012, the operative language related to correcting inventorship included a long-standing proviso, which only allowed for correction if the improper identification of inventors occurred "without any deceptive intention" on the part of the true inventor(s). Under the proviso, if the inventors were improperly named with deceptive intention, no correction could be made and the patent could be invalidated.

BURROUGHS WELLCOME CO. V. BARR LABORATORIES, INC.

40 F.3d 1223 (Fed. Cir. 1994).

MAYER, CIRCUIT JUDGE.

Barr Laboratories, Inc., Novopharm, Inc., and Novopharm, Ltd., appeal the order of the United States District Court for the Eastern District of North Carolina, *Burroughs Wellcome Co. v. Barr Lab., Inc.*, 828 F.Supp. 1208 (E.D.N.C.1993), granting the motion of Burroughs Wellcome Co. for judgment as a matter of law that six United States patents were not invalid and were infringed. We affirm in part, vacate in part, and remand.

Background

Burroughs Wellcome Co. is the owner of six United States patents that cover various preparations of 3'-azidothymidine (AZT) and methods for using that drug in the treatment of persons infected with the human immunodeficiency virus (HIV). Each of these patents names the same five inventors—Janet Rideout, David Barry, Sandra Lehrman, Martha St. Clair, and Phillip Furman (Burroughs Wellcome inventors)—all of whom were employed by Burroughs Wellcome at the time the inventions were alleged to have been conceived. The defendants-appellants concede that all five are properly named as inventors on the patents.

* * *

In the early 1980s, scientists began to see patients with symptoms of an unknown disease of the immune system, now known as AIDS. The disease attacks and destroys certain white blood cells known as CD4 T-lymphocytes or T-cells, which form an important component of the body's immune system. The level of destruction eventually becomes so great that the immune system is no longer able to mount an effective response to infections that pose little threat to a healthy person.

In mid-1984, scientists discovered that AIDS was caused by a retrovirus, known as HTLV III or, more commonly today, HIV. After the identification of HIV, Burroughs Wellcome began to search for a cure, screening compounds for antiretroviral activity using two murine (or mouse) retroviruses, the Friend leukemia virus and the Harvey sarcoma virus.

At about this time, scientists at the National Institutes of Health (NIH), led by Samuel Broder, were looking for effective AIDS therapies as well. Unlike Burroughs Wellcome, Broder and his colleagues used live HIV, and were able to develop a test that could demonstrate a compound's effectiveness against HIV in humans using a unique line of T-cell clones (the ATH8 cell line). The NIH scientists began to seek compounds from private pharmaceutical companies for screening in their cell line. After Burroughs Wellcome contacted Broder in the fall of 1984, he agreed to accept compounds from Burroughs Wellcome under code for testing against live HIV.

Burroughs Wellcome's Rideout selected AZT and a number of other compounds for testing in the murine screens on October 29, 1984. The tests, performed at Burroughs Wellcome facilities by St. Clair, showed that AZT had significant activity against both murine retroviruses at low concentrations.

In light of these positive results, the Burroughs Wellcome inventors met on December 5, 1984, to discuss patenting the use of AZT in the treatment of AIDS. Burroughs Wellcome's patent committee thereafter recommended that the company prepare a patent application for future filing. By February 6, 1985, the company had prepared a draft application for filing in the United Kingdom. The draft disclosed using AZT to treat patients infected with HIV, and set out various pharmaceutical formulations of the compound in an effective dosage range to treat HIV infection.

Two days earlier, on February 4, 1985, Burroughs Wellcome had sent a sample of AZT, identified only as Compound S, to Broder at NIH. In an accompanying letter, Lehrman told Broder of the results of the murine retrovirus tests and asked that he screen the compound for activity against HIV in the ATH8 cell line. Another NIH scientist, Hiroaka Mitsuya, performed the test in mid-February 1985, and found that Compound S was active against HIV. Broder informed Lehrman of the results by telephone on February 20, 1985. Burroughs Wellcome filed its patent application in the United Kingdom on March 16, 1985.

After Burroughs Wellcome learned that AZT was active against HIV, it began the process of obtaining Food and Drug Administration (FDA) approval for AZT as an AIDS therapy. As a part of the clinical trials leading to FDA approval, Broder and another NIH scientist, Robert Yarchoan, conducted a Phase I human patient study which showed that treatment with AZT could result in an increase in the patient's T-cell count. Broder reported this result to Lehrman on July 23, 1985. In 1987, the FDA approved AZT for marketing by Burroughs Wellcome; Burroughs Wellcome markets the drug for treatment of HIV infection under the trademark Retrovir.

On March 19, 1991, Barr Laboratories, Inc. (Barr) sought FDA approval to manufacture and market a generic version of AZT by filing an Abbreviated New Drug Application (ANDA) pursuant to 21 U.S.C. § 355(j) (1988). As part of the process, Barr certified to the FDA that Burroughs Wellcome's patents were invalid or were not infringed by the product described in its ANDA. After Barr informed Burroughs Wellcome of its action, Burroughs Wellcome commenced this case for patent infringement against Barr on May 14, 1991, alleging technical infringement of its patents under 35 U.S.C. § 271(e)(2)(A) (1988).

Barr filed a counterclaim under 35 U.S.C. § 256 (1988) seeking correction of the patents to list Broder and Mitsuya as coinventors. Barr admitted that its AZT product would infringe the patents, but contended that it did not because Barr had obtained a license to manufacture and sell AZT from the government, which should be deemed the owner of the interest of coinventors Broder and Mitsuya in the AZT patents. Burroughs Wellcome denied that Broder and Mitsuya were coinventors and also responded that the assertion of any rights of Broder, Mitsuya, or the government in the patents was barred by laches, estoppel, and waiver.

Thereafter, Novopharm, Ltd. filed an ANDA of its own, seeking approval to manufacture and market its generic version of AZT. Burroughs Wellcome filed infringement suits against Novopharm, Ltd. and its American subsidiary Novopharm, Inc., which were consolidated with the suit against Barr. Like Barr, Novopharm, Ltd. admitted that its AZT product would infringe the claims of the six patents, but for the failure of Burroughs Wellcome to name the NIH scientists as coinventors of the subject matter of the patents. Although Novopharm, Inc. agreed to be bound by any injunction issued against its parent, it argued that it had not infringed the patents because it had not filed an ANDA and had no AZT product of its own. Novopharm contended that Broder and Mitsuya should have been named as inventors on five of the patents, and contended that Broder and Yarchoan were coinventors of the '750 patent. It maintained that the patents were invalid because of the alleged nonjoinder, and because Burroughs Wellcome had omitted the coinventors with deceptive intent, the patents were unenforceable for inequitable conduct.

After more than three weeks of trial, while Burroughs Wellcome was still in the process of presenting its case, the district court granted Burroughs Wellcome's motion for judgment as a matter of law against all of the defendants, concluding that the Burroughs Wellcome inventors had conceived of the subject matter of the inventions at some time before February 6, 1985, without the assistance of Broder, Mitsuya, or Yarchoan. The court rejected the arguments of Barr and Novopharm that they should be allowed to present evidence that the Burroughs Wellcome inventors had no reasonable belief that the inventions would actually work—that AZT was in fact active against HIV—until they were told the results of the NIH testing.

* * *

Discussion

The arguments of both Barr and Novopharm are directed to when the inventors conceived the invention. Burroughs Wellcome says it was before they learned the results of the NIH tests; Barr and Novopharm say that confirmation of the inventions' operability, which came from the NIH tests, was an essential part of the inventive process. If Burroughs Wellcome is right, then the patents name the proper inventors, they are not invalid, and the appellants are liable for infringement. If Barr and Novopharm are correct, then Broder, Mitsuya, and Yarchoan should have been named as joint inventors and the resolution of Burroughs Wellcome's infringement suits is premature.

* * *

A joint invention is the product of a collaboration between two or more persons working together to solve the problem addressed. 35 U.S.C. § 116 (1988); *Kimberly-Clark Corp. v. Procter & Gamble Distrib. Co.*, 973 F.2d 911, 917 (Fed.Cir.1992). People may be joint inventors even though they do not physically work on the invention together or at the same time, and even though each does not make the same type or amount of contribution. 35 U.S.C. § 116. The statute does not set forth the minimum quality or quantity of contribution required for joint inventorship.

Conception is the touchstone of inventorship, the completion of the mental part of invention. It is "the formation in the mind of the inventor, of a definite and permanent idea of the complete and operative invention, as it is hereafter to be applied in practice." Conception is complete only when the idea is so clearly defined in the inventor's mind that only ordinary skill would be necessary to reduce the invention to practice, without extensive research or experimentation. *Sewall* [*v. Walters*], 21 F.3d at 415 [(Fed. Cir. 1994)]; *see also Coleman v. Dines,* 754 F.2d 353, 359 (Fed.Cir.1985) (conception must include every feature of claimed invention). Because it is a mental act, courts require corroborating evidence of a contemporaneous disclosure that would enable one skilled in the art to make the invention. *Coleman v. Dines,* 754 F.2d at 359.

Thus, the test for conception is whether the inventor had an idea that was definite and permanent enough that one skilled in the art could understand the invention; the inventor must prove his conception by corroborating evidence, preferably by showing a contemporaneous disclosure. An idea is definite and permanent when the inventor has a specific, settled idea, a particular solution to the problem at hand, not just a general goal or research plan he hopes to pursue. *See Amgen, Inc. v. Chugai Pharm. Co.*, 927 F.2d 1200, 1206 (Fed. Cir. 1991) (no conception of chemical compound based solely on its biological activity). The conception analysis necessarily turns on the inventor's ability to describe his invention with particularity. Until he can do so, he cannot prove possession of the complete mental picture of the invention. These rules ensure that patent rights attach only when an idea is so far developed that the inventor can point to a definite, particular invention.

But an inventor need not know that his invention will work for conception to be complete. *Applegate v. Scherer*, 332 F.2d 571, 573 (CCPA 1964). He need only show that he had the idea; the discovery that an invention actually works is part of its reduction to practice. *Id.*

Barr and Novopharm suggest that the inventor's definite and permanent idea must include a reasonable expectation that the invention will work for its intended purpose. They argue that this expectation is of paramount importance when the invention deals with uncertain or experimental disciplines, where the inventor cannot reasonably believe an idea will be operable until some result supports that conclusion. Without some experimental confirmation, they suggest, the inventor has only a hope or an expectation, and has not yet conceived the invention in sufficiently definite and permanent form. But this is not the law. An inventor's belief that his invention will work or his reasons for choosing a particular approach are irrelevant to conception.

To support their reasonable expectation rule, Barr and Novopharm point to a line of cases starting with *Smith v. Bousquet*, 111 F.2d 157 (CCPA 1940), establishing the so-called doctrine of simultaneous conception and reduction to practice. *Smith* was an interference priority contest between alleged inventors of the use of two known compounds as insecticides. Both parties asserted priority based on testing of the compounds against selected insect species. Noting the unpredictability of the experimental sciences of chemistry and biology, in particular the uncertain relationship between chemical structure and biological activity, *Smith* declined to find conception until the invention had been reduced to practice by the filing of the first patent application. *Id.* at 162. Barr and Novopharm read this and subsequent cases to establish, or at least support, their rule that conception of an invention in an unpredictable field occurs only when the inventor has reasonable grounds to believe the invention will work.

But these cases do not stand for the proposition that an inventor can never conceive an invention in an unpredictable or experimental field until reduction to practice. In rejecting the asserted evidence of conception, *Smith* said as to one of the compounds:

> it is apparent from the record that neither [party] had in mind at the time the suggestions were originally made, nor at any time thereafter, until successful tests, if any, were made, what insects, if any, it might be effective against, or how it might be applied to produce the desired results. Accordingly, neither party had a definite idea of the "complete and operative invention" here involved prior to a successful reduction—actual or constructive—of it to practice.

Id. Thus, in awarding priority to Smith based on his constructive reduction to practice, the court relied not on the inherent unpredictability of the science, but on the absence of any evidence to corroborate an earlier conception for either of the parties.

It is undoubtedly true that "[i]n some instances, an inventor is unable to establish a conception until he has reduced the invention to practice through a successful experiment." *Amgen,* 927 F.2d at 1206; *Alpert v. Slatin,* 305 F.2d 891, 894 (CCPA 1962) (no conception "where results at each step do not follow as anticipated, but are achieved empirically by what amounts to trial and error"). But in such cases, it is not merely because the field is unpredictable; the alleged conception fails because, as in *Smith,* it is incomplete. Then the event of reduction to practice in effect provides the only evidence to corroborate conception of the invention.

Under these circumstances, the reduction to practice can be the most definitive corroboration of conception, for where the idea is in constant flux, it is not definite and permanent. A conception is not complete if the subsequent course of experimentation, especially experimental failures, reveals uncertainty that so undermines the specificity of the inventor's idea that it is not yet a definite and permanent reflection of the complete invention as it will be used in practice. *See Amgen,* 927 F.2d at 1207 (no conception until reduction to practice where others tried and failed to clone gene using suggested strategy); *Rey-Bellet v. Engelhardt,* 493 F.2d 1380, 1387 (CCPA 1974) (focusing on nature of subsequent research as indicator that inventors encountered no perplexing intricate difficulties). It is this factual uncertainty, not the general uncertainty surrounding experimental sciences, that bears on the problem of conception.

Barr and Novopharm argue for a broader reading of *Amgen* and *Fiers* in support of their reasonable expectation rule. Both of these cases involve conception of a DNA encoding a human protein—a chemical compound. Conception of a chemical substance includes knowledge of both the specific chemical structure of the compound and an operative method of making it. The alleged inventors in *Fiers* and *Amgen* claimed conception of their respective inventions before they knew relevant chemical structure—the nucleotide sequence—so the courts found no conception until experimentation finally revealed that structure. Here, though, Burroughs Wellcome's inventions use a compound of known structure; the method of making the compound is also well known.

We emphasize that we do not hold that a person is precluded from being a joint inventor simply because his contribution to a collaborative effort is experimental. Instead, the qualitative contribution of each collaborator is the key—each inventor must contribute to the joint arrival at a definite and permanent idea of the invention as it will be used in practice.

Nor do we suggest that a bare idea is all that conception requires. The idea must be definite and permanent in the sense that it involves a specific approach to the particular problem at hand. It must also be sufficiently precise that a skilled artisan could carry out the invention without undue experimentation. And, of course, the alleged conception must be supported by corroborating evidence. On the facts before us, it is apparent that the district court correctly ruled against Barr and Novopharm as to five of the patents, but that the court's judgment as to the sixth, the '750 patent, was premature.

The '232, '838, '130, '208, and '538 patents encompass compositions and methods of using AZT to treat AIDS. The Burroughs Wellcome inventors claim conception of these inventions prior to the NIH experiments, based on the draft British patent application. That document is not itself a conception, for conception occurs in the inventors' minds, not on paper. The draft simply corroborates the claim that they had formulated a definite and permanent idea of the inventions by the time it was prepared.

The Burroughs Wellcome inventors set out with the general goal of finding a method to treat AIDS, but by the time Broder confirmed that AZT was active against HIV, they had more than a general hope or expectation. They had thought of the particular antiviral agent with which they intended to address the problem, and had formulated the idea of the inventions to the point that they could express it clearly in the form of a draft patent application, which Barr and Novopharm concede would teach one skilled in the art to practice the inventions. The draft expressly discloses the intended use of AZT to treat AIDS. It sets out the compound's structure, which, along with at least one method of preparation, was already well known. The draft also discloses in detail both how to prepare a pharmaceutical formulation of AZT and how to use it to treat a patient infected with HIV. The listed dosages, dose forms, and routes of administration conform to those eventually approved by the FDA. The draft shows that the idea was clearly defined in the inventors' minds; all that remained was to reduce it to practice—to confirm its operability and bring it to market. *See Haskell v. Colebourne,* 671 F.2d 1362, 1365–66 (CCPA 1982) (enabling draft patent application sufficient to corroborate conception).

An examination of the events that followed the preparation of Burroughs Wellcome's draft confirms the soundness of the conception. Broder and Mitsuya received from Burroughs Wellcome a group of compounds, known to Broder and Mitsuya only by code names, selected for testing by the Burroughs Wellcome inventors. They then tested those compounds for activity against HIV in their patented cell line. The test results revealed for the first time that one of the compounds, later revealed to be AZT, was exceptionally active against the virus.

Here, though, the testing was brief, simply confirming the operability of what the draft application disclosed. True, the science surrounding HIV and AIDS was unpredictable and highly experimental at the time the Burroughs Wellcome scientists made the inventions. But what matters for conception is whether the inventors had a definite and permanent idea of the operative inventions. In this case, no prolonged period of extensive research, experiment, and modification followed the alleged conception. By all accounts, what followed was simply the normal course of clinical trials that mark the path of any drug to the marketplace.

That is not to say, however, that the NIH scientists merely acted as a "pair of hands" for the Burroughs Wellcome inventors. Broder and Mitsuya exercised considerable skill in conducting the tests, using their patented cell line to model the responses of human cells infected with HIV. Lehrman did suggest initial concentrations to Broder, but she hardly controlled the conduct of the testing, which necessarily involved interpretation of results for which Broder and Mitsuya, and very few others, were uniquely qualified. But because the testing confirmed the operability of the inventions, it showed that the Burroughs Wellcome inventors had a definite and permanent idea of the inventions. It was part of the reduction to practice and inured to the benefit of Burroughs Wellcome.

Barr and Novopharm allege error in the district court's refusal to hear their evidence of the poor predictive value of the murine retrovirus screens for activity against HIV. Regardless of the predictive value of the murine tests, however, the record shows that soon after those tests, the inventors determined, for whatever reason, to use AZT as a treatment for AIDS, and they prepared a draft patent application that specifically set out the inventions, including an enabling disclosure. Obviously, enablement and conception are distinct issues, and one need not necessarily meet the enablement standard of 35 U.S.C. § 112 to prove conception. *See Fiers,* 984 F.2d at 1169. But the enabling disclosure does suffice in this case to confirm that the inventors had concluded the mental part of the inventive process—that they had arrived at the final, definite idea of their inventions, leaving only the task of reduction to practice to bring the inventions to fruition.

The question is not whether Burroughs Wellcome reasonably believed that the inventions would work for their intended purpose, the focus of the evidence offered by Barr and Novopharm, but whether the inventors had formed the idea of their use for that purpose in sufficiently final form that only the exercise of ordinary skill remained to reduce it to practice. *See MacMillan v. Moffett,* 432 F.2d at 1239 (Inventor's "reasons or lack of reasons for including U-5008 are not relevant to the question of conception. The important thing is that he did think in definite terms of the method claimed."). Whether or not Burroughs Wellcome believed the inventions would in fact work based on the mouse screens is irrelevant.

We do not know precisely when the inventors conceived their inventions, but the record shows that they had done so by the time they prepared the draft patent application that thoroughly and particularly set out the inventions as they would later be used. The district court correctly ruled that on this record, the NIH scientists were not joint inventors of these inventions.

* * *

NOTES

1. *More on Burroughs Wellcome:* Another patent at issue in *Burroughs-Wellcome* was a process patent claiming the use of AZT to increase the number of T-lymphocytes in a human infected with HIV. Novopharm argued that the use of AZT to treat HIV by halting the continuing destruction of T-lymphocytes was patentably distinct from the use of AZT to affirmatively *raise* depleted T-lymphocyte counts and restore immune function. Furthermore, it argued, AZT's ability to raise T-lymphocyte counts was unknown to the Burroughs-Wellcome scientists until it was revealed by the Phase I human patient study conducted by NIH scientists. The Federal Circuit remanded this aspect of the case because these arguments, if true, suggested that the Burroughs-Wellcome scientists did not conceive of this invention before they received the results of the NIH tests, and that this patent should therefore have named the NIH scientists as joint inventors. *Burroughs-Wellcome*, 40 F.3d at 1231–32.

2. *Who or What Can Be an Inventor?* The material introducing the "nature of inventorship" on the first page of this chapter is written with the implicit assumption that an "inventor" must be a natural person, or a human being, rather than a legal person (which includes entities). But what happens if an AI system generates patentable inventions? Can the AI system itself become the inventor? *See Thaler v. Vidal*, 43 F.4th 1207 (Fed. Cir. 2022). Does the creator of the AI system become the "inventor"? Review post-AIA section 100(f) ("The term 'inventor' means the individual or, if a joint invention, the individuals collectively who invented or discovered the subject matter of the invention.") as well as other language in the Patent Act. If the statutory language does not allow for the AI system to be an "inventor" today, could Congress revise the Patent Act to include AI as "inventors," if that would "promote the progress of . . . the useful arts"?

3. *Inventors Versus Assignees as Applicants:* For patent applications filed before September 16, 2012, the inventor or joint inventors of an invention were the only proper applicants for an application claiming that invention. Section 115 in effect until that date required that the "applicant shall make oath that he believes himself to be the original and first inventor." The inventor or inventors could, however, assign their right to the invention to another person at any time.

For patent applications filed on or after that date, the AIA altered the rules governing who may properly apply for a patent. Section 118, as revised by the AIA, allows an application to be filed by a "person to whom the inventor has assigned or is under an obligation to assign the invention." Revised section 115 requires that an application name the inventor of any invention claimed in the application and requires a declaration or oath of inventorship from each inventor, but if an inventor under an obligation to assign the invention refuses to make the required declaration, the applicant/assignee may submit a prescribed substitute statement for that inventor. *See* § 115(d).

4. *Corroboration of Conception:* Why is corroboration important in establishing the date of conception? What form(s) might such corroboration take? How does corroboration differ from reduction to practice? Might they ever coincide?

5. *Requirement of Collaboration in Joint Inventorship:* Congress added the second sentence of section 116 in 1984. The language clarified that physical collaboration is not required, nor are equal contributions. In *Kimberly-Clark Corp. v. Procter & Gamble Distributing Co.*, 973 F.2d 911 (Fed. Cir. 1992), Procter & Gamble argued that the new language also removed a requirement that the joint inventors be aware of one another or interact in some fashion. The Federal Circuit disagreed.

> What is clear is that the statutory word "jointly" is not mere surplusage. For persons to be joint inventors under Section 116, there must be some element of joint behavior, such as collaboration or working under common direction, one inventor seeing a relevant report and building upon it or hearing another's suggestion at a meeting. Here there was nothing of that nature. Individuals cannot be joint inventors if they are completely ignorant of what each other has done until years after their individual independent efforts. They cannot be totally independent of each other and be joint inventors.
>
> We therefore hold that joint inventorship under Section 116 requires at least some quantum of collaboration or connection.

6. *Collective Conception of the Invention:* In *Vanderbilt University v. ICOS Corp.*, 601 F.3d 1297 (Fed. Cir. 2010), the Federal Circuit further clarified the proper standard of joint inventorship under section 116:

> A primary focus of section 116 has thus always been on collaboration and joint behavior. A person must contribute to the conception of the claimed invention to qualify as a joint inventor. Yet, each contributor need not have their own contemporaneous picture of the final claimed invention in order to qualify as joint inventors. Rather, "the qualitative contribution of each collaborator is the key—each inventor must contribute to the joint arrival at a definite and permanent idea of the invention as it will be used in practice." The interplay between conception and collaboration requires that each co-inventor engage with the other co-inventors to contribute to a joint conception.

601 F.3d at 1303 (citations omitted).

7. *Standard for Correction:* The court in *Vanderbilt Univ. v. ICOS* also affirmed its requirement that a party seeking to correct the inventorship of a patent by claiming joint invention must demonstrate its contribution to the claimed invention with clear and convincing evidence. In multiple cases, the Federal Circuit has emphasized that the testimony of an alleged co-inventor (or co-inventors) cannot, standing alone, suffice to overcome the presumption that the inventors named on an issued patent are the true and only inventors. Corroborating evidence beyond the inventor's testimony is required. *See, e.g., Hess v. Advanced Cardiovascular Sys., Inc.*, 106 F.3d 976, 980 (Fed. Cir. 1997); *Ethicon, Inc. v. United States Surgical Corp.*, 135 F.3d 1456, 1461 (Fed. Cir. 1998).

2. RIGHTS OF OWNERS

Inventorship and ownership are separate questions. The inventor of the inventions claimed in a patent is the first presumptive owner that patent. Section 261 provides that patents have the "attributes of personal property." It also notes that "[a]pplications for patent, patents, or any interest therein" may be assigned "by an instrument in writing." The rule of a writing also applies to exclusive licenses. Patent owners can thus assign their rights to patents, in whole or in part. Section 261 requires a patent assignment to be recorded in the PTO if the assignee wishes to establish priority over subsequent conflicting transfers for consideration and without notice.

3. RIGHTS OF JOINT OWNERS

If the requirements of section 116 are satisfied and joint inventorship is established for one or more of the inventions claimed in a patent, the properly named joint inventors are co-owners of that patent. This is true even when each co-inventor did not contribute to each and every claim within the patent. Joint or co-ownership's default rule leads to full exploitation rights in each owner under section 262, which provides:

> In the absence of any agreement to the contrary, each of the joint owners of a patent may make, use, offer to sell, or sell the patented invention within the United States, or import the patented invention into the United States, without the consent of and without accounting to the other owners.

The Federal Circuit has ruled that, in the absence of an agreement to the contrary, each co-owner of a patent "presumptively owns a pro rata undivided interest in the entire patent." *Ethicon, Inc. v. United States Surgical Corp.*, 135 F.3d 1456 (Fed. Cir. 1998). This is true whether co-ownership arises through joint inventorship or later assignment of a partial interest in the patent, and the pro rata undivided interest rule applies to all joint inventors "no matter what their respective contributions." *Id.* As the Federal Circuit explained:

> This freedom to exploit the patent without a duty to account to other co-owners also allows co-owners to freely license others to exploit the patent without the consent of other co-owners. Thus, the congressional policy expressed by section 262 is that patent co-owners are "at the mercy of each other." *Willingham v. Lawton*, 555 F.2d 1340, 1344 (6th Cir. 1977).

Ethicon, 135 F.3d 1456. In *Ethicon*, over a strong dissent related to the pro rata undivided interest awarded to a joint inventor who contributed to only some of the claims, a Federal Circuit panel applied all of the above principles to hold that when one joint inventor of a patent, who was a co-inventor only of claims 33 and 47 of the patent, could validly license the entire patent to a third party who was accused by a co-owner of the patent of infringing claims 34 and 50.

Joint inventors may, as a result of these principles and the Federal Circuit's application of them, wish to enter into an "agreement to the contrary" to determine in advance the relative rights of the joint inventors, and thus co-owners, of the patent.

NOTE

Why Separate Exploitation? Joint ownership of a patent may arise through joint invention or by assignment. What purpose is served by allowing one owner of a jointly owned patent to exploit the invention without the consent of the other joint owner(s) and without any duty of accounting?

4. INVENTION BY EMPLOYEES

As explained above in relation to ownership, inventorship and ownership are separate questions. Although the inventor of an invention is the first presumptive owner of a patent claiming that invention, the inventor can assign or license any right or interest in the invention or patent to anyone else—including the inventor's employer. And while patent rights are federal, contracts, and the contractual relationship between an employee and employer are generally a matter of state law. As a result, state law governs the determination of whether the parties to an employment relationship have entered a contract (either express or implied in fact) granting the employer rights to the employee's inventions.

TEETS V. CHROMALLOY GAS TURBINE CORP.

83 F.3d 403 (Fed. Cir. 1996).

RADER, CIRCUIT JUDGE.

Chromalloy Gas Turbine Corporation (Chromalloy) and J. Michael Teets dispute ownership of an invention called the hot forming process (HFP). Following a bench trial, the United States District Court for the

Southern District of Florida concluded that Teets solely owned the HFP and enjoined Chromalloy from certain uses of the HFP. Because the district court erred in concluding Teets owned the process, this court reverses.

BACKGROUND

The General Electric Aircraft Company (GE) developed a more powerful and fuel efficient jet engine called the GE90. In conjunction with this development, GE designed a composite turbine engine fan blade which was lighter than existing metal fan blades. These lightweight blades, however, fractured more frequently from contact with birds, freezing rain, and other debris.

GE tried to solve this problem by fitting the leading edge of the blade with a hard protective covering of electroform nickel. After initially failing to manufacture the edge internally, GE asked DRB Industries, a division of Chromalloy, to devise a method of manufacturing the leading edge for the new composite blades. GE specified that DRB should make the leading edge of one piece of titanium. In fact, GE offered DRB a long-term contract if it was successful.

DRB labelled this project the GE90 Project. Less than a month later, in November 1991, Douglas R. Burnham, General Manager of DRB, assigned Teets as the Chief Engineer on the GE90 Project. Teets spent at least 70% of his time on the GE90 Project. At this time, Teets was an employee at will and had no written employment contract addressing ownership of inventive work. Burnham, on the other hand, had contractually agreed to assign any inventive rights to DRB.

On November 1, 1991, DRB proposed several initial manufacturing designs. All the proposals involved welding or diffusion bonding several pieces together to form the leading edge. On November 12, 1991, GE agreed to purchase some welded and bonded fan blades [but also continued to ask DFB to work on a one-piece leading edge—not only a welded or bonded one.]

[Problems with the welded edges appeared early 1992, design changes followed, and in a mid-March 1992 meeting,] Teets showed Burnham sketches he had drawn at home depicting Teets's initial idea for the HFP. Burnham thought the idea had potential. Nonetheless he instructed Teets to make changes in the welding process because GE would not alter its delivery schedule for design changes. Teets refined the HFP idea while still working on GE's changes to the welding process. Other employees at DRB assisted Teets in his refinement of the HFP process

On April 21, 1992, Teets submitted a more detailed sketch of the HFP idea to Douglas Burnham and to Nigel Bond, GE's lead engineer on the GE90 Project. DRB also proposed other new approaches at this meeting. GE rejected all of the proposals

In July 1992, GE tested the welded leading edges. Test results showed a complete composite failure. By August 1992, however, Teets had successfully tested the HFP at DRB. On the basis of this test data, DRB gained approval from GE. In October 1992, GE ordered 450 pieces using the HFP. Thereafter, GE continued to order one-piece leading edges manufactured with the HFP. In fact, GE still uses the HFP to manufacture leading edges for its GE90 engines

In late 1992, Teets discussed with Burnham the need to seek patent protection for the HFP. On January 25, 1993, Teets sent a letter describing the HFP to Mitchell Bittman, patent counsel for Sequa Corporation, Chromalloy's parent company. In that letter, Teets states that DRB developed the HFP. On January 26, 1993, Teets and Burnham completed an invention disclosure form in preparation for a patent application. Teets identifies Burnham as co-inventor on that form. Both Teets and Burnham later assisted Bittman in the prosecution of a patent application for the HFP. The record in this appeal does not indicate if a patent has issued.

[After Teets sued for a declaration of ownership of the HFP, the district court ruled he solely owned the process while Chromalloy had a shop right in it.]

DISCUSSION

* * *

Ownership springs from invention. The patent laws reward individuals for contributing to the progress of science and the useful arts. As part of that reward, an invention presumptively belongs to its creator. This simple proposition becomes more complex when one creates while employed by another person.

Consistent with the presumption that the inventor owns his invention, an individual owns the patent rights even though the invention was conceived and/or reduced to practice during the course of employment. At the same time, however, the law recognizes that employers may have an interest in the creative products of their employees. For example, an employer may obtain a shop right in employee inventions where it has contributed to the development of the invention. A shop right permits the employer to use the employee's invention without liability for infringement.

In addition, contract law allows individuals to freely structure their transactions and employee relationships. An employee may thus freely consent by contract to assign all rights in inventive ideas to the employer.

Without such an express assignment, employers may still claim an employee's inventive work where the employer specifically hires or directs the employee to exercise inventive faculties. When the purpose for employment thus focuses on invention, the employee has received full compensation for his or her inventive work. To apply this contract principle, a court must examine the employment relationship at the time of the inventive work to determine if the parties entered an implied-in-fact contract to assign patent rights.

An implied-in-fact contract is an agreement "founded upon a meeting of the minds, which, although not embodied in an express contract, is inferred, as a fact from conduct of the parties showing, in the light of the surrounding circumstances, their tacit understanding." *Baltimore & Ohio R.R. v. United States*, 261 U.S. 592, 597 (1923). By comparison, an implied-in-law contract is a "fiction of law where a promise is imputed to perform a legal duty, as to repay money obtained by fraud or duress." *Hercules Inc. v. United States*, 516 U.S. 417, [424] (1996).

As a matter of common law, after the Supreme Court's decision in *Erie Railroad v. Tompkins*, 304 U.S. 64 (1938), state contract principles provide the rules for identifying and enforcing implied-in-fact contracts. Florida, however, like most states, follows pre-*Erie* Supreme Court decisions involving ownership of inventive rights. Under these rules, a Florida employer cannot claim ownership of an employee's invention "unless the contract of employment by express terms or unequivocal inference shows that the employee was hired for the express purpose of producing the thing patented." *State v. Neal*, 152 Fla. 582, 12 So.2d 590, 591 (1943). Thus, when an employer hires a person for general service and the employee invents on the side, the invention belongs to the employee. However, the employer may claim ownership of the invention if the employer hires a person for the "specific purpose of making the invention." *Id.*, 12 So.2d at 591. Even if hired for a general purpose, an employee with the specific task of developing a device or process may cede ownership of the invention from that task to the employer. *Id.*

The existence of an implied-in-fact contract to assign inventive rights is a question of fact. * * *

Returning now to Teets, the specific goal of his project was to develop a one-piece leading edge. GE approached DRB to propose ways to apply a leading edge to turbine blades in its new engine. GE specifically and repeatedly expressed a desire for a one-piece solution. Faced with GE's requests, DRB, through Burnham, assigned Teets as the chief engineer on the GE90 project. Teets spent 70% of his time on that project. After undertaking the GE90 project and attempting several solutions to GE's problem, Teets developed the HFP. Teets reduced the invention to practice using DRB's resources—DRB's employees, DRB's shop tools and materials, and DRB's time. DRB has paid and continues to pay for the prosecution of a patent application for the HFP.

Most important, as recognized by the trial court, Teets repeatedly acknowledged DRB's role in the development of the HFP. He stated "DRB devised or developed" the HFP. In fact, the patent application lists another

DRB employee, Burnham, as a co-inventor. Thus, Teets himself recognized DRB's role in the inventive activity.

These undisputed facts show an implied-in-fact contract of assignment between Teets and DRB. DRB specifically directed Teets to devise a one-piece leading edge for GE. Having directed Teets to that task, compensated him for his efforts, paid for the refinement of the process, and paid for the patent protection, Chromalloy owns the patent rights in the HFP. The Florida Supreme Court's decision in *Neal* governs this case and compels the conclusion that Teets entered an implied-in-fact contract to assign patent rights to Chromalloy.

* * *

NOTES

1. *Role of State Versus Federal Law:* If an implied-in-fact assignment, or an express oral assignment of rights to an employee's patentable inventions is held enforceable under state law, does that law conflict with section 261, which requires a written assignment of a patent or patent application? Under the general Supremacy Clause principle that federal law preempts conflicting state laws, should these state laws be deemed preempted by section 261? For some thoughts on the interplay of implied obligations to assign an employee's inventions and section 261, read Judge O'Malley's concurring opinion in *Vapor Point LLC v. Moorhead*, 832 F.3d 1343, 1351–55 (Fed. Cir. 2016) (O'Malley, concurring).

State statutes may restrict the enforceability of employee preinvention assignment agreements in some situations, even when they are in writing. For example, some states may invalidate contracts granting an employer the exclusive rights in employee-made inventions: (a) made on employees' own time, (b) with their own resources, and (c) not reasonably pertinent to the employer's business. What policy arguments can you make both for and against such a position?

2. *Shop Rights:* A shop right—the employer's equitable, non-exclusive right to use an invention developed by an employee using the employer's time, facilities and materials—is a defense to a claim of infringement by the employee or assignee of rights to the employee's invention, but it does not give the holder of the right standing to sue for infringement. (Shop rights are also governed by state law.) Although a shop right is generally not assignable, it has been held to be assignable as part of the entire business of the employer; in addition, there is authority allowing delegation of an employer's shop right to another party acting on the employer's behalf. Case law diverges on whether shop rights are confined to a true employer/employee relationship or also apply to independent contractors. What equitable principles underlie the shop right doctrine? *See McElmurry v. Arkansas Power & Light Co.*, 995 F.2d 1576 (Fed.Cir.1993). To what extent would those same principles apply in the case of an independent contractor?

Compare the relative rights of employees and employers to inventions created in the course of an employee's employment with the relative rights of those same parties with respect to any copyright-protected works that may be created during the course of the employee's employment. *See infra* Chapter 15.A.1.b.

3. *Promise to Assign Versus Present Assignment:* In *Board of Trustees of the Leland Stanford Junior Univ. v. Roche Molecular Sys., Inc.*, 583 F.3d 832 (Fed. Cir. 2009) (affirmed on other grounds, see Note 5 below), the Federal Circuit held one of Stanford's research employees assigned his rights in a later invention to a third party company as part of the company's "Visitor's Confidentiality Agreement," despite a pre-existing and continuing contractual obligation of the research employee to assign his patent rights to Stanford. The court ruled that the researcher's agreement with the university, in which he "agree[d] to assign or confirm in writing to Stanford . . . that right, title and interest in . . . such inventions as required by Contracts or Grants," was a mere promise to assign rights in the future, not an immediate transfer of expectant interests. As such, the court held that while the language may have given Stanford equitable rights against the researcher, it did not transfer title to any future inventions. The researcher's subsequent agreement with the third-party company, where the researcher had gone to learn certain processes related to the invention later developed, contained the language "will assign and do hereby assign to [third-party company] my right, title, and interest in each of the ideas, inventions and improvements" developed "as a consequence" of work done with the third party. The Federal Circuit ruled this language created a present assignment of future inventions, giving the third party immediate equitable title to the researcher's inventions. With immediate equitable title assigned to the third party under that agreement, ownership rights immediately passed to the third party when the invention was made. This left nothing for the researcher to assign to Stanford in the future under its agreement. Stanford also argued it was a bona fide purchaser of the rights under section 261, based on an assignment the researcher signed in connection with the later patent application, but the Federal Circuit rejected that argument on the basis that agency principles applied to charge Stanford with knowledge of its employee's assignments. The university therefore had notice of the unrecorded assignment to the third party and section 261 did not protect it as a bona fide purchaser.

4. *Federal Employees:* At one point, the patent rights of federal government employees were no different from those of private sector employees, *see United States v. Dubilier Condenser Corp.*, 289 U.S. 178 (1933). But that changed in 1950. Executive Order 10096, *codified as amended at* 37 C.F.R. § 501.6, provides that the United States is entitled to the entire domestic rights to any invention which a federal employee makes during working hours, or makes with resources contributed by the government, or which either bears a direct relation to the inventor's official duties or is made in consequence of those duties. The Order establishes a rebuttable presumption that these conditions are satisfied whenever the inventor is

employed for the specific purpose of research or invention. Where the conditions are found not to be satisfied, the United States nonetheless is entitled to an irrevocable, royalty-free, nonexclusive license in the invention.

5. *Ownership of Federally Funded Inventions:* The Bayh-Dole University and Small Business Patent Procedure Act of 1980, 35 U.S.C. § 200 *et seq.*, which addresses rights in inventions arising from federally funded research, is especially relevant to universities. Under the Act, institutions engaged in federally funded research are required to disclose the resulting inventions to the federal government. The contracting institutions may elect to retain ownership of the inventions, and are free to license them, provided that they (1) share the royalties with their employee-inventors, and (2) use the remaining proceeds to fund further research and development. The government retains an irrevocable paid-up license in such inventions.

In *Board of Trustees of the Leland Stanford Junior Univ. v. Roche Molecular Sys., Inc.*, 563 U.S. 776 (2011), the Supreme Court addressed Stanford University's claim that the Bayh-Dole Act vested ownership in federally funded inventions in the federal contractor. The Supreme Court disagreed and reaffirmed that initial ownership of an invention lies with the inventor or inventors:

> Stanford and the United States as amicus curiae contend that the Bayh-Dole Act reorders the normal priority of rights in an invention when the invention is conceived or first reduced to practice with the support of federal funds. In their view, the Act moves inventors from the front of the line to the back by vesting title to federally funded inventions in the inventor's employer—the federal contractor.

563 U.S. at 786–87. After analyzing the language of the Bayh-Dole Act, the Court concluded:

> But because the Bayh-Dole Act, including § 210(a), applies only to "subject inventions"—"inventions of the contractor"—it does not displace an inventor's antecedent title to his invention. Only when an invention belongs to the contractor does the Bayh-Dole Act come into play. The Act's disposition of rights—like much of the rest of the Bayh-Dole Act—serves to clarify the order of priority of rights between the Federal Government and a federal contractor in a federally funded invention that already belongs to the contractor. Nothing more.

563 U.S. at 790. The Supreme Court's decision in *Stanford v. Roche* did not address the Federal Circuit's ruling in the case, discussed in Note 3 above, with respect to the relative rights of two parties with whom the inventor in question had executed agreements related to the invention. *See* 563 U.S. at 784 n.2 ("Because the Federal Circuit's interpretation of the relevant assignment agreements is not an issue on which we granted certiorari, we have no occasion to pass on the validity of the lower court's construction of those agreements.").

5. INVENTORSHIP OF DESIGN PATENTS

HOOP V. HOOP

279 F.3d 1004 (Fed. Cir. 2002).

MAYER, CHIEF JUDGE.

Mark R. and Lisa J. Hoop appeal the preliminary injunction entered by the United States District Court for the Southern District of Ohio enjoining them from acts which would constitute infringement of Jeffrey W. and Stephen E. Hoop's U.S. Design Patent No. 428,831. Because the district court did not abuse its discretion in determining that Jeffrey and Stephen Hoop would likely succeed in sustaining the validity of their patent, we affirm.

Background

In 1998, Jeffrey and Stephen Hoop ("Hoop brothers") conceived of a pair of eagle-shaped motorcycle fairing guards. Fairings are clear glass or plastic structures mounted above motorcycle handlebars to reduce wind drag. The eagle-shaped guards attach to the fairings to prevent damage to the fairings if the motorcycle tips over. The Hoop brothers created sketches of the eagle design. * * * Lacking drawing and casting expertise, they hired Lisa Hoop, a graphic designer, and Mark Hoop (their cousin and Lisa's ex-husband), a metal die caster, ("Mark and Lisa") to create detailed drawings and three-dimensional models for a patent application. Mark and Lisa signed nondisclosure agreements and prepared sketches and molds. * * *

In November of 1999, the Hoop brothers applied for a design patent. After discussions over a manufacturing agreement between the parties failed, in March of 2000, Mark and Lisa also applied for a design patent, using the same drawings they had prepared for the Hoop brothers. The Hoop brothers' patent issued on August 1, 2000, as U.S. Design Patent No. 428,831, and Mark and Lisa's identical patent issued on September 26, 2000, as U.S. Design Patent No. 431,211. [The Hoop brothers successfully used reexamination to have Mark and Lisa's patent claim invalidated. Mark and Lisa then filed suit to invalidate the Hoop brothers' patent, among other claims. The brothers filed counterclaims for patent infringement. The district court found the Hoop brothers to be the true inventors of the design and granted their motion for preliminary injunction. This appeal followed.]

Discussion

The question here is whether the refinements made by Mark and Lisa rise to the level of inventorship, so as to displace the Hoop brothers as patentees. Mark and Lisa argue that they are the true inventors because they perfected the original design by adding detail to the design sketches and creating the three-dimensional molds. Accordingly, they assert that the trial court erred in finding the Hoop brothers likely to succeed in sustaining the validity of their patent. We do not agree.

Design patents may be obtained by "[w]hoever invents any new, original and ornamental design for an article of manufacture." 35 U.S.C. § 171 (1994). We apply the same standard of inventorship to design patents that we require for utility patents. An inventor under the patent laws is the "person or persons who conceived the patented invention." An inventor may then "use the services, ideas, and aid of others in the process of perfecting his invention without losing his right to a patent." The facts are undisputed that the Hoop brothers were the first to conceive of the eagle-shaped fairing guards, and brought the concept to Mark and Lisa for assistance. Thus in the absence of the inventive quality required for a patentable design on the part of Mark and Lisa, the Hoop brothers remain the true inventors.

One may not qualify as a joint inventor, or as here, a new inventor, by "merely assisting the actual inventor *after conception* of the claimed invention." *Ethicon[, Inc. v. United States Surgical Corp.]*, 135 F.3d [1456] at 1460 [(Fed. Cir. 1998)] (emphasis added). Minor differences between the prior art and the new claim will not suffice. The differences here must be substantial and not just superficial; the new design must contain an inventive concept. The ultimate test for design-patent inventorship, like the test for anticipation and infringement, is whether the second asserted invention is "substantially similar" to the first. Substantial similarity is a question of fact.

The district court found that Mark and Lisa's drawing lacked an "independent," which we read as inventive, concept. The court summarized [Mark and Lisa's] improvements over the Hoop brothers' sketch as increased detailed feathering and an overall less triangular shape. Noting the strong similarity between the drawings, the court reasoned that Mark and Lisa merely refined and perfected the Hoop brothers' concept. Therefore, the two designs were not separate inventions. Mark and Lisa did remove the suggestion of the eagle's tail, * * *, but the two eagles have the same proportions, body size, orientation, three rows of feathers, head and beak shape, and eye placement. We agree that the trial court could permissibly conclude at the preliminary injunction stage that the second design was likely to be found to be merely a more refined version of the first. However, final resolution of this factual question must await a trial on the merits. The court's determination that the Hoop brothers are likely to be found to be the true inventors and that they are likely to succeed in sustaining the validity of their patent is sustained.

* * *

LOURIE, CIRCUIT JUDGE, dissenting.

I respectfully dissent. I would reverse the district court's grant of a preliminary injunction on the ground that the district court applied the wrong legal standard in determining inventorship of a design patent and that the court's determination that the Hoop brothers had proved a likelihood of success on the question of validity was therefore flawed. I would remand for a redetermination of the likelihood of success under the proper standard.

* * *

The undisputed facts are that the Hoop brothers made a sketch of an eagle fairing design and asked Mark and Lisa to make three-dimensional drawings and models of that design. In doing so, Mark and Lisa made a different design, one that differed from the original design of the brothers in several respects. Both parties then filed patent applications and obtained the grant of patents on the design of Mark and Lisa. The majority opinion does not note that the design that accompanied the brothers' patent application and constituted its claim * * * was Mark and Lisa's design [not the Hoop brothers' original sketch].

* * *

Design patents do not claim concepts. They claim specific designs set forth in their claims, which invariably refer to the appearance of what is illustrated in the patent's drawings. Contrary to the conclusion of the district court, as the invention is not the concept of an eagle design, but only the specific claimed representation of that eagle, the "concept" of the design is not what one must look at in determining whether the inventions are one and the same or separate. One must look at the differences between the overall appearance of the eagles to determine inventorship of the specific design. *See KeyStone Retaining Wall Sys. v. Westrock, Inc.,* 997 F.2d 1444, 1450 (Fed.Cir.1993) ("[I]t is the appearance of a design as a whole which is controlling in determining questions of patentability and infringement."). When a design is changed, the result may be a new design.

It is undisputed that both patents claim the same design, a design consisting of the specific appearance of the eagle shown in the patents, which is different from that in the sketch made by the Hoop brothers and identical to that made by Mark and Lisa * * *. Quite possibly, one could reasonably conclude that the changes are significant enough to constitute a new design. * * *

* * *

* * * What matters in determining whether the brothers are the inventors of the claimed design is whether, from the standpoint of an ordinary designer, the claimed design is the same as or different and patentably distinct from the brothers' original design. *See In re Nalbandian,* 661 F.2d 1214, 1215 (CCPA 1981) (adopting an "ordinary

designer" standard for patentability of designs, as opposed to an "ordinary observer" test for infringement of design patents).

Because we are not designers of ordinary skill, we cannot make the conclusive factual evaluations necessary to determine whether the original brothers' design and Mark and Lisa's design are patentably distinct. I would therefore reverse the grant of the injunction and remand this case for the trial court to focus on the appearance of the respective designs and decide whether they are sufficiently different in a nonobviousness sense that it can be concluded that the brothers are not the inventors of the design claimed in their patent. If so, then they cannot show a likelihood of success in sustaining the validity of their patent under 35 U.S.C. § 102(f) so as to justify the grant of the preliminary injunction.

NOTE

Which opinion above—majority or dissent—is more convincing to you? If the two designs in *Hoop* are not patentably distinct, which patent is valid, and who are the inventors?

B. PROCESS FOR OBTAINING A PATENT

Statutes: 35 U.S.C. §§ 111, 119–22, 131–35, 141, 145–46, 151, 172, 251–52

1. PATENT PROSECUTION

The mandatory contents of a patent application are set forth in section 111(a). The application must include a specification meeting the requirements of section 112, a drawing under section 113 if necessary for understanding the subject matter claimed, the required filing fee, and an oath or declaration from the inventor as prescribed in section 115. The inventor was required to make the application—at least technically—before September 16, 2012. Now, applications can be made by the assignee of the invention or a person to whom the inventor is obligated to assign the invention—see Note 3 on page 542. The application must name all inventors and joint inventors of the claimed invention and include an oath or declaration from each named inventor.

Section 112 mandates that the application include an enabling specification with a full written description, as further discussed in Chapter 10.E., *supra*, and it requires that the specification conclude with "one or more claims particularly pointing out and distinctly claiming the subject matter" regarded to be the invention. A claim that fails to meet this requirement is invalid due to "indefiniteness."

After an application is filed, it is examined by a patent examiner at the Patent and Trademark Office ("PTO"), who makes an initial determination of patentability for each claim in the application. If the patent examiner rejects some or all of the claims, which is common, the examiner provides reasons for the rejection in a response to the applicant called an "office action." In response to the first office action, the applicant may dispute the examiner's grounds for rejection, amend or cancel those claims, amend the patent's disclosures to support the challenged claims (although 35 U.S.C. § 132 prohibits adding "new matter," meaning matter unsupported by the original disclosure), file a continuation or continuation-in-part application in order to add new claims, or abandon the application.

If the patent examiner twice rejects the disputed claims, the applicant can appeal in the first instance to the Board. 35 U.S.C. § 134. If that appeal is unsuccessful, the applicant may seek judicial review either by appealing the Board's decision to the United States Court of Appeals for the Federal Circuit (in which case review is limited to the PTO record) or by filing a civil action against the Director of the PTO in the District Court for the Eastern District of Virginia, which conducts a full trial. The plaintiff-applicant may introduce new evidence in that action even if the evidence could have been presented to the PTO in the first instance. And if new evidence is introduced, the district court "must make *de novo* factual findings that take account of both the new evidence and the administrative record before the PTO." *Kappos v. Hyatt*, 566 U.S. 431, 446 (2012). The outcome of the trial is appealable to the Federal Circuit. Rather than appeal the examiner's second rejection of its claims, the applicant can alternatively elect to file a continuation application, discussed below in a separate subsection.

Section 122 requires the PTO to publish certain pending patent applications 18 months after filing. Publication is mandatory if the inventor has filed foreign patent applications for the same invention that will be published within 18 months of the foreign filing (which includes virtually all foreign applications). The publication rules do not apply to provisional patent applications (see below), which have no foreign filing counterparts, or to design patent applications. Applicants who have not filed foreign applications (and do not intend to) may elect to avoid PTO publication, which then keeps the application confidential unless and until the patent issues. All applications were kept confidential and remained unpublished by the PTO until the Patent Reform Act of 1999 took effect in November of 2000. Pre-AIA section 102(e) and post-AIA section 102(a)(2) treat published applications as anticipating subject matter (and, thus, as prior art for section 103 purposes) as of their filing dates (not the later publication date), and naturally a published application would constitute a printed publication under either pre- or post-AIA section 102. Section 154 grants provisional royalty rights to inventors whose applications are published under the new rule.

Under sections 133 and 111(a)(4), if an applicant fails to prosecute an application in a timely manner (as specified by the statute) after any action by the PTO, such as issuance of an office action, the application will be deemed abandoned, unless the applicant can demonstrate that the delay was unavoidable.

a. Provisional Patent Applications

Section 111 allows inventors to file provisional patent applications ("PPAs"), which require specifications and drawings but no claims. The filing fee for a PPA is lower than a regular utility application. If the PPA is not followed by a complete application within one year, it will be deemed abandoned, unless the applicant has, in the interim, asked for the PPA to be treated as a nonprovisional application under section 111(a).

Under section 119(e)(1), the filing date of the PPA will apply to the complete utility patent application, provided the latter is filed within one year, names at least one of the same inventors, and contains a specific reference to the provisional application. Thus, a PPA may be filed to create domestic priority (for examination under sections 102 and 103) as of the date the PPA is filed, although the patent term is calculated from the filing date of the nonprovisional application. *See* 35 U.S.C. § 154(a)(2)–(3). A PPA is not entitled to priority based on any other patent application or filing date under sections 119, 120, 121, 365(a) or 365(c). Under section 172, PPAs cannot establish priority for design patents.

The provisional application is not examined for patentability and cannot be placed in interference; as just noted, it also cannot benefit from the priority or filing date of any earlier application under sections 119–21 or 365. Under PTO Rule 53(b), 37 C.F.R. § 1.53(b), within one year of filing a complete patent application, an applicant may, for a fee, convert that application to a provisional application, but the applicant then loses the benefit of any earlier-filed applications from which the nonprovisional application had derived its priority or filing date.

b. Establishing Priority by Filing Date of Foreign Application

Under section 119(a), a patent applicant can establish priority based on the filing date of the *earliest* foreign patent application disclosing (even if not claiming) the same invention. The foreign application must have been filed by the same applicant (or the applicant's legal representatives or assigns) in a foreign country that provides reciprocity to United States citizens and patent applications, and it may not predate the filing of the United States patent application by more than twelve months (six months for design patents, under section 172). It is not necessary that the foreign patent actually issue.

Filing-date priority granted under section 119 on the basis of a prior-filed *foreign* application can be invoked only in favor of a patent applicant. It cannot be used to create an earlier reference date for patent-defeating prior art under pre-AIA sections 102(e) and 102(g). *See In re Hilmer*, 359 F.2d 859, 862 (C.C.P.A. 1966); *In re Hilmer*, 424 F.2d 1108, 1112–12 (C.C.P.A. 1970).

c. Continuation and Divisional Applications

Under section 120, a patent applicant may file a second application containing the same disclosure as the previous (or "parent") application while receiving the benefit of the earlier filing date. Such a "continuation" application is used to add new claims and establish a right to further consideration by the patent examiner. It receives the benefit of the parent application's filing date, which may be crucial for establishing novelty and nonobviousness, only if four requirements are met:

> First, the invention described in the new application must be "disclosed . . . in an application previously filed in the United States." Second, the application must be "filed by an inventor or inventors named in the previously filed application." [Ed. note: the AIA requires naming of these inventors, rather than filing by them.] Third, the application must be co-pending with the earlier application, or "filed before the patenting or abandonment of or termination of proceedings on the first application." Fourth, the application must "contain[ ] or [be] amended to contain a specific reference to the earlier filed application."

Encyclopaedia Britannica, Inc. v. Alpine Electronics of America, Inc., 609 F.3d 1345, 1349–50 (Fed. Cir. 2010). Each continuation application in a chain of applications—not just the final application that ultimately issues as a patent—must meet the four requirements of section 120. Any faulty application in a series of continuation applications will break the chain that provides a later continuation application with priority. *Id.* at 1349–51.

A "continuation-in-part" application is one that contains claims unsupported by the disclosure of the parent application. To support the new claims, the applicant adds new matter to the disclosure. Thus, in a priority dispute involving a continuation-in-part application, the claims supported by the parent application's disclosure receive the benefit of the earlier, parent application's filing date, but claims supported by the new matter only found in the continuation-in-part application's disclosure are entitled only to the later filing date.

A "divisional" application under section 121 is a later application for an invention that was originally included in, but was later separated from, the claims of the parent application. To be entitled to the parent's filing date, the divisional application must disclose or claim only subject matter that was disclosed in the parent application. Both a "continuation-in-part" and a "divisional" application must have at least one inventor in common with their respective parent applications.

A "substitute" application, which duplicates a previously abandoned application, is not entitled to the earlier filing date of the abandoned application (even if the "substitute" is identical to the one abandoned), because the applications were not co-pending.

d. Reissue Applications

When a patent is found to be wholly or partly invalid or inoperative as a result of defects in the specification or drawing(s), or claims that are too broad or too narrow, under section 251 a patentee may obtain a corrected, or "reissue," patent for the remainder of the patent term, provided that the defects in the original patent were the result of "error."[2] However, a patentee may not use this procedure to introduce "new matter" into the patent specification or to claim an invention that was not disclosed in the original patent.

To the extent that the claims in the reissue patent are substantially identical to those in the original patent, the reissue patent is treated like a continuation patent and is effective retroactively to the issue date of the original patent. Where a reissue patent broadens the claims of the original patent, the reissue application must be filed within two years of the granting of the original patent. New or amended claims (which as noted must be based on the disclosure in the original patent) are effective only from the date of reissue. In addition, the statute and related case law protect the "intervening rights" of certain parties by entitling the patentee to damages only from the date of reissuance. A party is protected from broadened scope when a party's prior activity comes within the broadened (but not the original) scope of the claims. Where the claims of the reissue patent are narrower than the claims of the original patent, the doctrine of intervening rights also protects a party that relied on the invalidity of the original overbroad claims.

2. THIRD-PARTY CHALLENGES

Responding to criticism and concern about the quality of issued patents, the AIA reformed certain aspects of the PTO's review of patent applications and issued patents, including: (1) modifying *inter partes* patent reexamination proceedings (and renaming them "*inter partes* review"); (2) establishing a post-grant review procedure available for nine months after the date of the grant of the patent (or issuance of a reissue patent); and (3) permitting third party submissions of relevant prior art in the form of patents and printed publications at any time during the life of a patent application or issued patent, which submissions may be

[2] In addition to revising claims that are too broad or too narrow, reissue patents have been permitted to remedy defects in claims to priority, and to amend claims that are invalid due to ambiguity. Until September 16, 2012, section 251 limited reissue proceedings to errors made "without deceptive intention."

accompanied by a written explanation of the relevance of the prior art to patentability. As explained in Chapter 10 in Note 7 on pages 425–426, *supra*, the AIA also created a transitional post-grant review proceeding for the review of "covered business method patents."

Sections 301 through 318, as amended in 2002, set forth the procedures for PTO reexamination of the validity of one or more claims in an issued patent. Such reexamination procedures are typically less costly than challenging the validity of a patent through litigation. Under the still-existing *ex parte* reexamination provisions, 35 U.S.C. §§ 301–307, any person may petition the PTO for reexamination of an issued patent based on prior art patents or printed publications, or the PTO Director may reexamine the patent on the Director's own initiative. The patent owner is entitled to respond to the validity challenge, and to appeal an adverse determination to the Patent Trial and Appeal Board and then to the Federal Circuit. The patent owner can also request reexamination of its own patent through this procedure. The party requesting reexamination has a very limited opportunity to participate in the reexamination process and has no right of appeal.[3] "Intervening rights" also protect certain parties when a reexamination changes the scope of a patent's claims. (*See* discussion of reissue applications immediately above.)

The AIA introduced two types of proceedings in which a third party can challenge a patent's validity: *inter partes* review, which replaced a previous *inter partes* reexamination, (35 U.S.C. §§ 311–319), and post-grant review, an entirely new post-grant opposition proceeding (35 U.S.C. §§ 321–329). As noted in Chapter 10.A., *supra*, the Patent Trial and Appeal Board (called Board of Patent Appeals and Interferences before being renamed in the AIA) (the "Board") is an administrative tribunal within the PTO, not an Article III court. In *Oil States Energy Services, LLC v. Greene's Energy Group, LLC*, 138 S.Ct. 1365 (2018), the Court ruled *inter partes* review did not violate Article III or the Seventh Amendment even with the Board's non-Article III status. That ruling did not prevent the Court from later ruling in *United States v. Arthrex, Inc.*, 141 S.Ct. 1970 (2021) that another aspect of the PTAB was problematic. On its face, 35 U.S.C. § 6(c), limits to the Board itself the power to grant rehearing of a Board decision. In *Arthrex*, the Court ruled that the method of appointment of the judges on the Board (by the Secretary of Commerce and not by the President with advice and consent of the Senate) meant the Board's judges were unable to issue final decisions unreviewable within the agency. The remedy in *Arthrex* was not to invalidate the entire scheme of Board review of patents

[3] Before September 16, 2012, a person other than the patent owner could request an *inter partes* reexamination of a patent based on prior art patents or printed publications. This reexamination, like the *ex parte* reexamination, took place before a patent examiner. The requester could participate by submitting written comments related to issues raised in the examination process and the responses filed by the patentee. *See* pre-AIA §§ 311–318. Appeals went first to the Board and then the Federal Circuit.

but instead to exempt the Director of the PTO from section 6(c) and to remand the matter to the Acting Director (with no confirmed Director in place at the time) to decide whether to rehear the case. Since *Arthrex* the PTO has created and revised a process for Director review of any issue of fact or law in any final written decision issued in a PTAB AIA proceeding: inter partes reviews, post-grant reviews and covered business method patent reviews. More implementation work will surely be done after this book is published.

The *inter partes* review proceeding is available to third parties from nine months after issuance of the patent (or termination of post-grant review, discussed below) until the end of the patent term. The proceeding may be based only on a ground that could be raised under sections 102 or 103 and only on the basis of patents or printed publications (thus, not public uses or sales). Any patent, whether issued under pre-AIA or post-AIA novelty rules, is subject to the new proceeding. The threshold for instituting the review is whether the requester demonstrates a "reasonable likelihood" that one or more claims will be found invalid. The PTO's decision to open or not to open a review proceeding cannot be appealed. 35 U.S.C. § 314(d) ("The determination by the Director whether to institute an inter partes review under this section shall be final and nonappealable.")

If the requester has filed a declaratory judgment seeking invalidation of the patent, it may not institute *inter partes* review, and if a declaratory judgment action is filed by the requester during review, the review will be stayed unless the patent owner counterclaims for infringement. A requester has a year after being sued for infringement to file a request for *inter partes* review. In *inter partes* review the PTO uses the claim's "broadest reasonable construction in light of the specification of the patent in which it appears," while district courts use a patent claim's "ordinary meaning . . . as understood by a person of skill in the art." *See Cuozzo Speed Techs., LLC v. Lee*, 579 U.S. 261, 276 (2016). As a result of the PTO's broader rule of construction, the PTO is more likely to find a claim invalid during *inter partes* review than a district court is during litigation. In *Cuozzo*, the Court rebuffed a challenge to the PTO's broader standard on the basis that Congress had given the PTO the authority under § 316 to issue rules governing review, and the "broadest reasonable construction" standard and rule were properly created in the reasonable exercise of the PTO's rulemaking authority. *See id.* at 276–83.

Inter partes review proceedings take place before the Patent Trial and Appeal Board, not before a patent examiner, and include some limited discovery and the possibility of an oral hearing. If a review is instituted and a written decision issued by the Board, a requester may not raise in litigation any assertion of invalidity that was or could have been raised during review (which was also true of the prior *inter partes* reexamination).

Decisions of the Board may be appealed to the Federal Circuit. As noted above, parties may also use a new process for Director review of any issue of fact or law in the Board's final written decision in an *inter partes* review.

Post-grant review is the entirely new opposition proceeding under the AIA for patents examined under the post-AIA novelty rules. In a post-grant review, the petitioner may challenge the validity of any or all claims on any ground, including lack of patentable subject matter, utility, novelty, obviousness, or failure to satisfy section 112 (except best mode). The petition for post-grant review must be filed within nine months of issuance of the patent. The standard for instituting a post-grant review is whether the information presented indicates that it is "more likely than not" that at least one claim is unpatentable or whether it presents a novel or unsettled, and important legal question. The information presented must include a specific, written explanation of the grounds on which the challenge to patentability is made as well as copies of the patents and printed publications relied upon and any affidavits or declarations if the petitioner relies on other factual evidence.

The burden of proof in post-grant reviews may make this early opportunity to challenge the validity of an issued patent more appealing than filing a declaratory judgment action for invalidity or waiting for the patentee to sue for infringement. In a post-grant review, a preponderance of the evidence is required, while in litigation the challenger must present clear and convincing evidence of invalidity. The interaction between post-grant review proceedings and litigation mirrors that of the new *inter partes* review proceeding, and refusals by the PTO to open a post-grant review are similarly unappealable.

In addition, since September 17, 2012, any person has been able to submit certain prior art to the PTO within six months of the date of publication of a patent application under section 122 or before the first rejection during examination (or the date of mailing of the notice of allowance, if earlier). 35 U.S.C. § 122(e). That prior art may include patents, published patent applications, and printed publications "of potential relevance to the examination of the application," and the submission must be accompanied by an explanation of each document's relevance. The goal is to improve the information available to examiners during the examination process. *Cf.* 35 U.S.C. § 301 (providing for post-issuance submissions of prior art, which are placed in the file after a patent has already been granted).

NOTES

1. *Deference to the PTO:* In *Dickinson v. Zurko,* 527 U.S. 150 (1999), the Supreme Court held that section 706 of the Administrative Procedure Act (APA), 5 U.S.C. § 706 (1999), governs the standard of review applicable to judicial review of findings of fact made by the PTO in patent examinations.

The APA permits a reviewing court to set aside an administrative agency's "actions, findings and conclusions" only where they are found to be "arbitrary, capricious, an abuse of discretion, or otherwise not in accordance with law, [or] unsupported by substantial evidence."

2. *Government as "Person" for Board Review of Patents:* The Board's several AIA patent review proceedings allow any "person" to petition the PTO for review. Applying the presumption that a statutory reference to a "person" does not include the Government, the Supreme Court held in 2019 that the Government and its agencies did not qualify as a "person" for the purposes of the AIA *inter partes* review provisions, as the Postal Service could provide nothing in the context of the AIA to demand otherwise. *See Return Mail v. United States Postal Service*, 139 S.Ct. 1853 (2019). The Government can still challenge validity of a patent if sued for infringement, but it cannot challenge the validity of a patent, post-issuance, through the Patent Trial and Appeal Board.

3. *Sovereign Immunity and IPRs:* The Federal Circuit has now held that PTAB *inter partes* proceedings are not barred by either state or tribal sovereign immunity; the Supreme Court denied certiorari in both cases. *Regents of the University of Minnesota. v. LSI Corp.*, 926 F.3d 1327 (Fed. Cir. 2019) (state sovereign immunity); *Saint Regis Mohawk Tribe v. Mylan Pharmaceuticals Inc.*, 896 F.3d 1322 (Fed. Cir. 2018) (tribal sovereign immunity).

C. TERM OF PATENT PROTECTION

Statutes: 35 U.S.C. §§ 119(e), 154, 156, 173

As part of U.S. obligations under international agreements designed to create greater harmony between the patent systems of different nations, Congress amended section 154 to change the term of protection for utility and plant patents from a fixed term of 17 years from issuance to a term that begins on issuance and ends 20 years from filing.[4] The change affected patents with U.S. application dates on or after June 8, 1995. Limited extensions of the 20-year terms are permitted where prosecution of a patent is delayed beyond 3 years by interferences, appeals, secrecy orders, or PTO processing delays. Under a provision of the Hatch-Waxman Act,[5] the term of a patent involving a drug product, medical device, or food or color additive may be extended one additional time (upon application), separately from section 154(b), if the patentholder did not receive the full benefit of the statutory patent term because FDA regulatory review

---

[4] The amendment came in the Uruguay Round Agreements Act, which implemented the "TRIPS Agreement," (Trade Related Aspects of Intellectual Property), one of the mandatory agreements for all members of the World Trade Organization. *See* Pub. L. No. 103–465, 108 Stat. 4809 (December 8, 1994).

[5] Drug Price Competition and Patent Term Restoration Act of 1984 (the Hatch-Waxman Act), codified at 35 U.S.C. § 156. In *Merck & Co. v. Kessler*, 80 F.3d 1543 (Fed.Cir.1996), the Federal Circuit held that section 156 extensions may be added to the end of the new 20-year patent term.

delayed the marketing of the product in question. Section 156 contains detailed provisions regarding the length of such extensions.

For design patents issuing from applications filed on or after May 13, 2015, the term of the patentee's exclusive rights is 15 years from the date of issuance of the patent (not the date of filing). *See* 35 U.S.C. § 173. For design patent applications filed before that date, the term of any resulting patent is 14 years. *See* Patent Law Treaties Implementation Act of 2012, Pub. L. No. 112–211, §§ 102–103.

NOTES

1. *Policy Behind Term Measures:* What policy arguments support measuring the patent term from (a) the date the application is filed? (b) the date the patent issues?

2. *Transition to New Terms:* At some time in the future, all existing patents will be subject to the 20-year term. Although pre-1995 pending applications are typically confidential (publication of applications did not begin until 2000), due to a variety of circumstances, including litigation between one prolific applicant and the PTO as well as Congressional hearings, we know that in or around 2014–15, there were over 400 pending applications with a filing date before June 8, 1995. If these result in an issued patent, it would still be subject (in the first instance) to the previous term of 17 years from issue. Is there a specific future date after which all patents will be subject to the 20-year term?

For more on the possible effects of a long-pending application, *see Symbol Technologies, Inc. v. Lemelson Medical, Education and Research Found. LP*, 422 F.3d 1378 (Fed. Cir. 2005) (affirming use of equitable defense of prosecution laches to render patents unenforceable when patents issued only after unreasonable and unexplained delay in prosecution, specifically including refiling an application solely containing previously allowed claims for the business purpose of delaying issuance, with the delay prejudicing the public and the opposing party, which had invested in the technology described in the applications during their long and confidential pendency at the PTO).

3. *No Post-Patent-Term Royalties:* In *Kimble v. Marvel Entm't, LLC*, 576 U.S. 446 (2015), which involved a patent on a web-shooting toy licensed to Marvel for use in a Spider Man toy, the Supreme Court addressed and rejected a challenge to its 1964 decision barring post-patent-term royalties.

> In *Brulotte v. Thys Co.*, 379 U.S. 29 (1964), this Court held that a patent holder cannot charge royalties for the use of his invention after its patent term has expired. The sole question presented here is whether we should overrule *Brulotte*. Adhering to principles of *stare decisis*, we decline to do so. Critics of the *Brulotte* rule must seek relief not from this Court but from Congress.

* * *

> Patents endow their holders with certain superpowers, but only for a limited time. In crafting the patent laws, Congress struck a balance between fostering innovation and ensuring public access to discoveries. While a patent lasts, the patentee possesses exclusive rights to the patented article—rights he may sell or license for royalty payments if he so chooses. *See* 35 U.S.C. § 154(a)(1). But a patent typically expires 20 years from the day the application for it was filed. *See* § 154(a)(2). And when the patent expires, the patentee's prerogatives expire too, and the right to make or use the article, free from all restriction, passes to the public. *See Sears, Roebuck & Co. v. Stiffel Co.*, 376 U.S. 225, 230 (1964).
>
> This Court has carefully guarded that cut-off date, just as it has the patent laws' subject-matter limits: In case after case, the Court has construed those laws to preclude measures that restrict free access to formerly patented, as well as unpatentable, inventions. * * * By virtue of federal law, we [have] reasoned, "an article on which the patent has expired," like an unpatentable article, "is in the public domain and may be made and sold by whoever chooses to do so." *Sears*, 376 U.S., at 231. In a related line of decisions, we have deemed unenforceable private contract provisions limiting free use of such inventions. In *Scott Paper Co. v. Marcalus Mfg.* Co., 326 U.S. 249 (1945), for example, we determined that a manufacturer could not agree to refrain from challenging a patent's validity [because that] "would deprive . . . the consuming public of the advantage to be derived" from free exploitation of the discovery. And to permit such a result, whether or not authorized "by express contract," would impermissibly undermine the patent laws.
>
> *Brulotte* was brewed in the same barrel. There, an inventor licensed his patented hop-picking machine to farmers in exchange for royalties from hop crops harvested both before and after his patents' expiration dates. The Court (by an 8–1 vote) held the agreement unenforceable—"unlawful per se"—to the extent it provided for the payment of royalties "accru[ing] after the last of the patents incorporated into the machines had expired." * * * Emphasizing that a patented invention "become[s] public property once [that term] expires," the Court then quoted from *Scott Paper*: Any attempt to limit a licensee's post-expiration use of the invention, "whatever the legal device employed, runs counter to the policy and purpose of the patent laws."

576 U.S. at 449–53 (some citations omitted). The Court went on to acknowledge that post-expiration royalties might be desired for legitimate business reasons, and it suggested several possible "ways around" the rule against post-expiration royalties that might accomplish the same legitimate business goals. *Id.* at 453–54.

CHAPTER 12

PATENT INFRINGEMENT, DEFENSES, AND REMEDIES

■ ■ ■

A. INFRINGEMENT

Statutes: 35 U.S.C. §§ 154(a), 271

During the patent term, the holder of a utility or design patent has the right to exclude others from making, using, selling, or offering to sell the invention throughout the United States, and from importing the invention into this country. *See* §§ 154(a) & 271(a). Where the invention is a process, the exclusive rights extend also to the sale and import of any products produced by the patented process. *See* § 271(g). A patent holder may, under certain circumstances, exclude others from exporting components of a patented combination for assembly abroad. *See* § 271(f).

A direct infringer of a patent is the person who performs the acts described above, such as making or selling a product or using a process. Persons who induce or contribute to the direct infringement of a patent are also made liable as infringers in certain circumstances. *See* § 271(b)–(c). The first question in any infringement action is whether *anyone* is making, using, selling (or offering), or importing *the invention*.

As discussed in the readings below, to constitute *literal infringement*, an accused product or process must literally embody every limitation in the claim(s) alleged to have been infringed. Under the *doctrine of equivalents*, however, minor departures from the literal claims of a patent will not necessarily bar a finding of infringement. After exploring how courts determine whether *the invention* is present either literally or through equivalents, the material below moves to the nature of the varied acts that constitute infringement, such as making and using the invention, as well as the acts that create liability for inducing or contributing to infringement. Forms of infringement that encompass activity not confined within the United States are also more briefly addressed.

Due to differences in how ornamental designs are claimed, courts have adjusted the legal standard applied when assessing whether an accused infringer is making, using, selling, offering to sell, or importing "the invention." Infringement of "the invention" claimed by a design patent is addressed in Part A.4. of this chapter. Note also that section 271 does not govern infringement of a plant patent; this chapter therefore separately addresses plant patent infringement in Part E.

1. LITERAL INFRINGEMENT

The first step in any infringement action is the interpretation of the claim language. Claim construction or interpretation is the process by which a court construes the language of the patent claim and determines the scope of the literal language of each claim, as further explained in the *Autogiro* case below and the accompanying notes. (Design patent claim construction is distinct, as noted in Part A.4. below.)

After claim construction, the scope of the allegedly infringed claim must be compared with the allegedly infringing, or "accused" product or process. The *Autogiro* case calls this "reading the claims on the accused structures." A finding of literal infringement requires that the accused product or process embody or contain all elements or limitations of the claim as construed by the court. Equivalency comes into play if literal infringement is not present.

AUTOGIRO COMPANY OF AMERICA V. THE UNITED STATES

384 F.2d 391 (Ct. Cl. 1967).[1]

DURFEE, JUDGE.

* * *

I

The Patent Act of 1952, 35 U.S.C. § 1 et seq., which applies to all patents granted on or before January 1, 1953, is the controlling law in this case. No previous patent act contained a section on infringement. Congress had always allowed the courts to settle the issue without any legislative guidelines. Section 271(a) which covers the type of infringement alleged here was not inserted in the Act to clarify any legal problems, but only as a codification of existing judicial determinations. * * *

The claims of the patent provide the concise formal definition of the invention. They are the numbered paragraphs which "particularly [point] out and distinctly [claim] the subject matter which the applicant regards as his invention." 35 U.S.C. § 112. It is to these wordings that one must look to determine whether there has been infringement. Courts can neither broaden nor narrow the claims to give the patentee something different than what he has set forth. No matter how great the temptations of fairness or policy making, courts do not rework claims. They only interpret them.

---

[1] Under 28 U.S.C. § 1498, claims of patent infringement based on use or manufacture of an invention by or for the United States, the patentee's remedy is to bring an action against the United States in the Court of Federal Claims. The Court of Claims from which this decision issued was a predecessor court to the modern Court of Federal Claims.

Although courts are confined by the language of the claims, they are not, however, confined to the language of the claims in interpreting their meaning.

Courts occasionally have confined themselves to the language of the claims. When claims have been found clear and unambiguous, courts have not gone beyond them to determine their content. Courts have also held that the fact that claims are free from ambiguity is no reason for limiting the material which may be inspected for the purpose of better understanding the meaning of claims. We find both approaches to be hypothetical. Claims cannot be clear and unambiguous on their face. A comparison must exist. The lucidity of a claim is determined in light of what ideas it is trying to convey. Only by knowing the idea, can one decide how much shadow encumbers the reality.

The very nature of words would make a clear and unambiguous claim a rare occurrence. Writing on statutory interpretation, Justice Frankfurter commented on the inexactitude of words:

> They are symbols of meaning. But unlike mathematical symbols, the phrasing of a document, especially a complicated enactment, seldom attains more than approximate precision. If individual words are inexact symbols, with shifting variables, their configuration can hardly achieve invariant meaning or assured definiteness.

Frankfurter, *Some Reflections on the Reading of Statutes*, 47 COL.L.REV. 527, 528 (1947). *See, also, A Re-Evaluation of the Use of Legislative History in the Federal Courts*, 52 COL.L.REV. 125 (1952).

The inability of words to achieve precision is none the less extant with patent claims than it is with statutes. The problem is likely more acute with claims. Statutes by definition are the reduction of ideas to print. Since the ability to verbalize is crucial in statutory enactment, legislators develop a facility with words not equally developed in inventors. An invention exists most importantly as a tangible structure or a series of drawings. A verbal portrayal is usually an afterthought written to satisfy the requirements of patent law. This conversion of machine to words allows for unintended idea gaps which cannot be satisfactorily filled. Often the invention is novel and words do not exist to describe it. The dictionary does not always keep abreast of the inventor. It cannot. Things are not made for the sake of words, but words for things. To overcome this lag, patent law allows the inventor to be his own lexicographer. Allowing the patentee verbal license only augments the difficulty of understanding the claims. The sanction of new words or hybrids from old ones not only leaves one unsure what a rose is, but also unsure whether a rose is a rose. Thus we find that a claim cannot be interpreted without going beyond the claim itself. No matter how clear a claim appears to be, lurking in the background are documents that may completely disrupt initial views on its meaning.

The necessity for a sensible and systematic approach to claim interpretation is axiomatic. The Alice-in-Wonderland view that something means whatever one chooses it to mean makes for enjoyable reading, but bad law. Claims are best construed in connection with the other parts of the patent instrument and with the circumstances surrounding the inception of the patent application. In utilizing all the patent documents, one should not sacrifice the value of these references by the 'unimaginative adherence to well-worn professional phrases.' Frankfurter, *supra,* at 529. Patent law is replete with major canons of construction of minor value which have seldom provided useful guidance in the unraveling of complex claims. Instead, these canons have only added confusion to the problem of claim interpretation.

* * *

II

In deriving the meaning of a claim, we inspect all useful documents and reach what Justice Holmes called the "felt meaning" of the claim. In seeking this goal, we make use of three parts of the patent: the specification, the drawings, and the file wrapper.

Specification.—Section 112 of the 1952 Patent Act requires the specification to describe the manner and process of making and using the invention so that any person skilled in the patent's art may utilize it. In serving its statutory purpose, the specification aids in ascertaining the scope and meaning of the language employed in the claims inasmuch as words must be used in the same way in both the claims and the specification. The use of the specification as a concordance for the claims is accepted by almost every court, and is a basic concept of patent law. * * *

The specification "set[s] forth the best mode contemplated by the inventor of carrying out his invention." 35 U.S.C. § 112. This one embodiment of the invention does not restrict the claims. Claim interpretation must not make use of "best mode" terms inasmuch as the patentee need not guard against infringement by listing every possible infringing device in the specification. But where the specification does not refer to an embodiment or a class of embodiments in terms of "best mode," such reference may be of value in claim interpretation. This would be where the patentee describes an embodiment as being the invention itself and not only one way of utilizing it.

Drawings.—The patent may contain drawings. 35 U.S.C. § 113. In those instances where a visual representation can flesh out words, drawings may be used in the same manner and with the same limitations as the specification.

File wrapper.—The file wrapper contains[2] the entire record of the proceedings in the Patent Office from the first application papers to the issued patent. Since all express representations of the patent applicant made to induce a patent grant are in the file wrapper, this material provides an accurate charting of the patent's pre-issuance history. One use of the file wrapper is file wrapper estoppel, which is the application of familiar estoppel principles to Patent Office prosecution and patent infringement litigation. [Ed. note: The "file wrapper" contained the patent's "prosecution history," and today "file wrapper estoppel" is more commonly known as "prosecution history estoppel," as demonstrated in later cases.] The patent applicant must convince the patent examiner that his invention meets the statutory requirements; otherwise, a patent will not be issued. When the application is rejected, the applicant will insert limitations and restrictions for the purpose of inducing the Patent Office to grant his patent. When the patent is issued, the patentee cannot disclaim these alterations and seek an interpretation that would ignore them. He cannot construe the claims narrowly before the Patent Office and later broadly before the courts. File wrapper estoppel serves two functions in claim interpretation; the applicant's statements not only define terms, but also set the barriers within which the claim's meaning must be kept. These results arise when the file wrapper discloses either what the claim covers or what it does not cover.

The file wrapper also has a broader and more general use. This is its utilization, like the specification and drawings, to determine the scope of claims. For example, the prior art cited in the file wrapper is used in this manner. In file wrapper estoppel, it is not the prior art that provides the guidelines, but the applicant's acquiescence with regard to the prior art. In its broader use as source material, the prior art cited in the file wrapper gives clues as to what the claims do not cover.

III

The use of the various parts of the patent to determine the meaning of the claims is only half the process of determining patent infringement. The other half is "reading the claims on the accused structures." If the claims read literally on the accused structures, an initial hurdle in the test for infringement has been cleared. [Ed. note: See Note 4 following the case for a rarely applied exception to this statement.] * * *

If the claims do not read literally on the accused structures, infringement is not necessarily ruled out. The doctrine of equivalence [now

[2] [Ed. Note: At the time of this case and for a number of years, although not today, patent applications were maintained in paper files, each of which had an outer cover or "file wrapper" that listed all the steps and actions taken on the application along the way from filing to issuance. As explained above, the full details behind each step or action (including any amendments or representations made by the applicant) were permanently maintained inside that file wrapper, leading to the name "file wrapper" estoppel. With the demise of paper files, perhaps, came the rise of the substitute terminology "prosecution history estoppel."]

called "doctrine of equivalents"] casts around a claim a penumbra which also must be avoided if there is to be no infringement. * * * [Ed. note: See the next cases for an explanation of and current constraints upon the doctrine of equivalents.] * * * The rationale behind equivalence was set forth by the Supreme Court in *Graver Tank & Mfg. Co. v. Linde Air Products Co.*, [339 U.S. 605, 607 (1950)]:

> [T]o permit imitation of a patented invention which does not copy every literal detail would be to convert the protection of the patent grant into a hollow and useless thing. Such a limitation would leave room for—indeed encourage—the unscrupulous copyist to make unimportant and unsubstantial changes and substitutions in the patent which, though adding nothing, would be enough to take the copied matter outside the claim, and hence outside the reach of the law.

* * *

IV

In summary, the determination of patent infringement is a two-step process. First, the meaning of the claims in issue must be determined by a study of all relevant patent documents. Secondly, the claims must be read on the accused structures. In doing this, it is of little value that they read literally on the structures. * * * This is the general approach which this court uses to determine the infringement of all the patent claims properly before it in this case.

* * *

NOTES

1. *Claim Construction:* Ordinarily, the test for interpreting the meaning of a claim term is determined from the vantage point of one skilled in the art. *See SmithKline Diagnostics, Inc. v. Helena Lab. Corp.*, 859 F.2d 878, 882 (Fed.Cir.1988). In *Markman v. Westview Instruments, Inc.*, 517 U.S. 370 (1996), the Supreme Court held that the judge, rather than the jury, should decide questions of claim interpretation in an infringement action. The Court emphasized that judges are better trained than juries in "the construction of written instruments," and noted that patent construction, in particular, requires specialized training and discipline. The Court took special note of "the importance of uniformity in the treatment of a given patent:"

> As we noted in *General Elec. Co. v. Wabash Appliance Corp.*, 304 U.S. 364, 369 (1938), "the limits of a patent must be known for the protection of the patentee, the encouragement of the inventive genius of others and the assurance that the subject of the patent will be dedicated ultimately to the public." Otherwise, a "zone of uncertainty which enterprise and experimentation may enter only at the risk of infringement claims would discourage invention only a little less than

> unequivocal foreclosure of the field," *United Carbon Co. v. Binney & Smith Co.*, 317 U.S. 228, 236 (1942), and "[t]he public [would] be deprived of rights supposed to belong to it, without being clearly told what it is that limits these rights." *Merrill v. Yeomans*, 94 U.S. 568, 573 (1877).

517 U.S. at 390.

2. *Primary Sources in Claim Construction:* In *Phillips v. AWH Corp.*, 415 F.3d 1303 (Fed. Cir. 2005) (en banc), the Federal Circuit reheard, en banc, a case in which the members of the original panel had differed on the use of a dictionary definition of a crucial term in the claims ("baffle"). The majority had held that the term "baffle" in the claims should be construed in light of the specification (*see* § 112, including written description) to have a narrower meaning than the dictionary definition of that term, while the dissent argued that the dictionary definition should govern. *Phillips v. AWH Corp.*, 363 F.3d 1207 (Fed. Cir. 2004). The en banc court reaffirmed that the primary sources for claim construction are (1) the language of the claim, (2) the written description, and (3) the prosecution history (referred to in *Autogiro*, above, as the file wrapper). The court rejected the suggestion in some earlier case law that dictionaries should be the starting point for claim interpretation, although it did not preclude their use altogether. Technical dictionaries "or comparable sources are often useful to assist in understanding the commonly understood meaning of words" and may therefore be used, if needed, to supplement the interpretation of the claims based on the primary sources. *Id.*

3. *Both De Novo and Clear Error Review of Claim Construction:* As noted above, the Supreme Court's *Markman* ruling provides that claim construction is a matter for a judge, not a jury. Until the 2015 decision in *Teva Pharmaceuticals USA, Inc. v. Sandoz, Inc.*, 574 U.S. 318 (2015), the Federal Circuit reasoned that because claim construction was a matter of law, a district court's claim construction, including factual questions underlying the claim construction, should be subjected to de novo review. *See Cybor Corp. v. FAS Technologies, Inc.*, 138 F.3d 1448 (Fed. Cir. 1998). In its *Teva* decision, the Supreme Court rejected de novo appellate review of all matters pertinent to claim construction.

> Federal Rule of Civil Procedure 52(a)(6) states that a court of appeals "must not . . . set aside" a district court's "[f]indings of fact" unless they are "clearly erroneous." In our view, this rule and the standard it sets forth must apply when a court of appeals reviews a district court's resolution of subsidiary factual matters made in the course of its construction of a patent claim. * * *
>
> * * *
>
> Our opinion in *Markman* neither created, nor argued for, an exception to Rule 52(a). The question presented in that case was a Seventh Amendment question: Should a jury or a judge construe patent claims? We pointed out that history provides no clear answer.

> The task primarily involves the construction of written instruments. And that task is better matched to a judge's skills. * * *
>
> * * *
>
> * * * We recognize that a district court's construction of a patent claim, like a district court's interpretation of a written instrument, often requires the judge only to examine and to construe the document's words without requiring the judge to resolve any underlying factual disputes. As all parties agree, when the district court reviews only evidence intrinsic to the patent (the patent claims and specifications, along with the patent's prosecution history), the judge's determination will amount solely to a determination of law, and the Court of Appeals will review that construction *de novo*.
>
> In some cases, however, the district court will need to look beyond the patent's intrinsic evidence and to consult extrinsic evidence in order to understand, for example, the background science or the meaning of a term in the relevant art during the relevant time period. *See, e.g., Seymour v. Osborne*, 11 Wall. 516, 546 (1871) (a patent may be "so interspersed with technical terms and terms of art that the testimony of scientific witnesses is indispensable to a correct understanding of its meaning"). In cases where those subsidiary facts are in dispute, courts will need to make subsidiary factual findings about that extrinsic evidence. These are the "evidentiary underpinnings" of claim construction that we discussed in *Markman*, and this subsidiary factfinding must be reviewed for clear error on appeal.

574 U.S. at 324–32 (some citations omitted).

4. *Reverse Doctrine of Equivalents:* In a passage in *Autogiro* not included above, the court observed that:

> [C]laims must not only read literally on the accused structures, but also the structures must "do the same work, in substantially the same way, and accomplish substantially the same result." This approach of making literal overlap only a step and not the entire test of infringement has been consistently applied by the courts * * *.

In other words, a product or process that literally reads on the claims of a patent may be found non-infringing because it is not the "equivalent" of the patented invention. The *Autogiro* court noted that this doctrine is designed to protect the accused infringer, while the doctrine of equivalents (the subject of Part A.2. of this chapter) is designed to protect the patentee.

It is important to note that in practice, the reverse doctrine of equivalents is rarely applied to excuse conduct falling within the literal scope of a claim. *See DePuy Spine Inc. v. Medtronic Sofamor Danek, Inc.*, 567 F.3d 1314, 1338 (Fed. Cir. 2009) ("We have explained that the reverse doctrine of equivalents is an equitable doctrine designed to prevent unwarranted extension of the claims beyond a fair scope of the patentee's invention. Because the reverse doctrine of equivalents requires a fundamental change in the basic principle by which the device operates, the doctrine is rarely invoked and virtually never sustained.") (internal quotations omitted). If a claim in a patent being asserted appears to be exceptionally broad and, as a result, might cover devices or processes that the patent does not enable or fully describe, what might an accused infringer choose to pursue as its litigation strategy rather than relying on the reverse doctrine of equivalents? *See* §§ 112 & 282.

The case below was not selected by the Federal Circuit for publication, which indicates the panel issuing the opinion determined it did not add significantly to the legal issues at stake. It does provide, however, a fairly simple mechanical device—a birdfeeder—and claim language devoid of difficult technicalities. This makes the case a nice environment in which to understand and apply literal infringement.

The Federal Circuit's brief review and discussion of the claim construction of one claim term appears below, along with two disputed portions of the claim. A sketch representative of some of defendant's accused products appears after the case. It was created for this Casebook based on some product photographs. Information drawn from that sketch and from a typical website sales description, which may assist in comparing the claim and claim elements to the accused product, appears in the first note after the case.

BACKYARD NATURE PRODS., INC. V. WOODLINK, LTD.

81 F. App'x 729, 733 (Fed. Cir. 2003).

PROST, CIRCUIT JUDGE.

Backyard Nature Products, Inc. ("Backyard"), appeals the decision of the United States District Court for the Eastern District of Wisconsin granting Woodlink Ltd.'s ("Woodlink's") motions for summary judgment of non-infringement of U.S. Patent Nos. 5,927,231 and 6,095,087 ("the '231 patent" and "the '087 patent," respectively). Woodlink cross-appeals the district court's denial of summary judgment as to the invalidity of the '231 patent in light of U.S. Patent No. 5,269,255 issued to Finn. Because the district court properly construed the patent claims and correctly found no genuine issues of material fact on the question of infringement, and because the district court did not abuse its discretion in dismissing Woodlink's invalidity arguments as moot, we *affirm*.

I. Background

Backyard sued Woodlink for infringement of [both patents]. As to each patent, Woodlink filed a motion for summary judgment of non-infringement.

[Discussion of the '231 patent omitted.]

With respect to the '087 patent, the district court granted Woodlink's motion for summary judgment of non-infringement, both literally and under the doctrine of equivalents. Again, in considering the motion, the district court first construed the asserted claims of the '087 patent. The representative independent claim 1 provides in relevant part, with the disputed claim terms [italicized]:

> 1. A bird feeder comprising:
>
> a first wall portion defining a first *vertical* surface;
>
> a second wall portion defining a second *vertical* surface;
>
> a third wall portion defining a third *vertical* surface;
>
> a fourth wall portion defining a fourth *vertical* surface;
>
> said first, second, third and fourth *vertical* surfaces of said first, second, third and fourth wall portions, respectively, being assembled together to define a bird feed retaining portion of said bird feeder, . . .
>
> . . .
>
> an apertured floor member, said *apertured floor member* extending to said first, second, third, and fourth *vertical* surfaces . . .

the '087 patent, col. 4, I. 60—col. 5, I. 32 (emphasis added). The district court found that the claim language "apertured floor member" requires at least one raised edge. Moreover, it construed "vertical" to require walls perpendicular to the birdfeeder's floor.

Based on its construction of the claims, the district court found that Woodlink's birdfeeders do not infringe Backyard's asserted patent claims, either literally or under the doctrine of equivalents. First, it found no issue as to literal infringement because Woodlink's birdfeeders have neither a removable apertured floor member nor vertical walls. Second, because an apertured floor member is not equivalent to a sheet, the court found no possible infringement under the doctrine of equivalents.

Backyard filed a timely appeal. Jurisdiction in this court is proper under 28 U.S.C. § 1295(a)(1).

II. Discussion

* * *

B. The '087 Patent

On appeal, Backyard argues that the term "apertured floor member" does not require an upturned edge, but could cover a flat sheet. Backyard relies on both the intrinsic evidence and the doctrine of claim differentiation in making its argument.

[A] *de novo* review of the district court's claim construction of "apertured floor member" reveals that it correctly found the claim language to require at least one upturned edge. First, the specification states that "the term 'apertured floor member' means a tray-like member" Moreover, the dictionary definitions of "tray"[2] imply something more than a flat surface. Two of the four definitions used by the district court require a raised edge or rim, while the other two note the prevalence of this characteristic. Moreover, the specification states that a sheet "may be used for *forming* the apertured floor member." (emphasis added). By disclosing some kind of forming process performed on a flat sheet, the specification suggests that a simple, unformed sheet does not amount to a tray-like member. Finally, the drawings also illustrate an upturned edge. Thus, we affirm the district court's claim construction requiring an upturned edge.

Backyard further argues that the doctrine of claim differentiation precludes such a construction of "apertured floor member." Specifically, Backyard submits that we should not read in the limitation from dependent claim 3—"The bird feeder of claim 2, wherein the apertured floor member further comprises at least one upturned edge." We conclude that the presumption of claim differentiation is overcome here by the intrinsic evidence, which favors construing the "apertured floor member" as requiring at least one upturned edge.

Based on its claim construction with respect to the '087 patent, the district court correctly found no infringement, literally or under the doctrine of equivalents. Because Woodlink uses a flat sheet in all of its accused birdfeeders, and not a "tray" with at least one upturned edge, there is no literal infringement. [See Note 2 below for the court's brief statement on the doctrine of equivalents.]

Lacking the "apertured floor member" element, Woodlink's birdfeeders cannot infringe. Consequently, we need not address the "vertical" claim-construction issue.

* * *

[2] The district court used the following definitions of "tray" in construing the term:

1. "[A] shallow flat receptacle with a raised edge or rim." *American Heritage Dictionary* 1837 (4th ed.2000).

2. "[A] utensil of the form of a flat board with a raised rim." *Oxford English Dictionary* 1837 (2d ed.1989).

3. "[A] flat receptacle made of wood, metal, glass, plastic, etc., often with slightly raised edges." *Webster's New World College Dictionary* 1524 (4th ed.2001).

Sketch by Sofia Lockridge

NOTES

1. *Applying the All-Elements Rule:* Review the claim elements of independent claim 1 from the '087 patent as provided in the decision above (which eliminated some portions of the claim). Compare the claim elements to the birdfeeder in the sketch, using the following information modified from a sales description to help you understand the features of the birdfeeder in the sketch above (*note—this is not claim language*): (1) Two cedar uprights each contain grooves to hold two plastic panels; (2) the uprights and the plastic panels together create a reservoir holding over a quart of birdseed, and a hinge across the top of the roof allows one side to open, enabling easy filling of the reservoir; (3) the grooves in the uprights hold the clear panels at an inward angle, directing the seed down to the base of the feeder; (4) each plastic panel has a gap cut into the bottom to allow the seed to spread out onto the base of the birdfeeder; (5) the birdfeeder base is a flat, metal mesh screen, which allows water to drain away from the seed; (6) the flat mesh screen base is neatly fitted into grooves in the cedar trim edging for crisp, finished look. Use the "all elements" rule to identify which elements of the claim are and are not literally present in the birdfeeder, and why.

2. *No Equivalents:* You may wish to come back to this note after reading the next case, *Warner-Jenkinson Co. v. Hilton Davis Chemical Co.*, 520 U.S. 17 (1997), and learning more about the doctrine of equivalents. In *Backyard Nature Products* (above), the Federal Circuit panel opinion tersely addressed the argument of equivalency as to the "apertured floor member" claim element not found to be literally present in the defendant's products: "In addition, as applied to the facts of this case, there is no equivalence; trays are not equivalent to sheets because they have a lip (which helps contain the contents)

and increased rigidity (as a consequence of the bend)." The patent owner had argued that a flat sheet present as the "floor" in defendant's products was equivalent to the "apertured floor member" in the claim. Recall, however, that in the district court's claim construction affirmed by the Federal Circuit, the "apertured floor member" had been interpreted as "tray-like" and therefore requiring at least one upturned edge (due to, among other things, the drawings and language in the specification).

2. INFRINGEMENT BY EQUIVALENTS

a. The Doctrine of Equivalents and Prosecution History Estoppel

WARNER-JENKINSON COMPANY, INC. V. HILTON DAVIS CHEMICAL CO.

520 U.S. 17, 117 S.Ct. 1040 (1997).

JUSTICE THOMAS delivered the opinion of the Court.

Nearly 50 years ago, this Court in *Graver Tank & Mfg. Co. v. Linde Air Products Co.*, 339 U.S. 605 (1950), set out the modern contours of what is known in patent law as the "doctrine of equivalents." Under this doctrine, a product or process that does not literally infringe upon the express terms of a patent claim may nonetheless be found to infringe if there is "equivalence" between the elements of the accused product or process and the claimed elements of the patented invention. *Id.*, at 609. Petitioner, which was found to have infringed upon respondent's patent under the doctrine of equivalents, invites us to speak the death of that doctrine. We decline that invitation. The significant disagreement within the Court of Appeals for the Federal Circuit concerning the application of *Graver Tank* suggests, however, that the doctrine is not free from confusion. We therefore will endeavor to clarify the proper scope of the doctrine.

I

* * *

[Respondent Hilton Davis's patent (the '746 patent) claims an "ultrapurification" process for purifying dyes, utilizing a specified range of hydrostatic pressure and a pH range of "approximately 6.0 to 9.0." The upper pH limit of 9.0 was added during patent prosecution to distinguish prior art (the "Booth patent") which used pH levels above 9.0. When Warner-Jenkinson began commercial use of a similar process using a pH of 5.0, Hilton Davis sued for patent infringement.]

As trial approached, Hilton Davis conceded that there was no literal infringement, and relied solely on the doctrine of equivalents. Over Warner-Jenkinson's objection that the doctrine of equivalents was an equitable doctrine to be applied by the court, the issue of equivalence was included among those sent to the jury. The jury found that the '746 patent was not invalid and that Warner-Jenkinson infringed upon the patent under the doctrine of equivalents. * * * A fractured en banc Court of Appeals for the Federal Circuit affirmed.

The majority below held that the doctrine of equivalents continues to exist and that its touchstone is whether substantial differences exist between the accused process and the patented process. The court also held that the question of equivalence is for the jury to decide and that the jury in this case had substantial evidence from which it could conclude that the Warner-Jenkinson process was not substantially different from the ultrafiltration process disclosed in the '746 patent.

There were three separate dissents, commanding a total of 5 of 12 judges. Four of the five dissenting judges viewed the doctrine of equivalents as allowing an improper expansion of claim scope, contrary to this Court's numerous holdings that it is the claim that defines the invention and gives notice to the public of the limits of the patent monopoly. The fifth dissenter, the late Judge Nies, was able to reconcile the prohibition against enlarging the scope of claims and the doctrine of equivalents by applying the doctrine to each element of a claim, rather than to the accused product or process "overall." As she explained it, "[t]he 'scope' is not enlarged if courts do not go beyond the substitution of equivalent elements." All of the dissenters, however, would have found that a much narrowed doctrine of equivalents may be applied in whole or in part by the court.

We granted certiorari, and now reverse and remand.

II

In *Graver Tank* we considered the application of the doctrine of equivalents to an accused chemical composition for use in welding that differed from the patented welding material by the substitution of one chemical element. The substituted element did not fall within the literal terms of the patent claim, but the Court nonetheless found that the "question which thus emerges is whether the substitution [of one element for the other] . . . is a change of such substance as to make the doctrine of equivalents inapplicable; or conversely, whether under the circumstances the change was so insubstantial that the trial court's invocation of the doctrine of equivalents was justified." The Court also described some of the considerations that go into applying the doctrine of equivalents:

> "What constitutes equivalency must be determined against the context of the patent, the prior art, and the particular circumstances of the case. Equivalence, in the patent law, is not the prisoner of a formula and is not an absolute to be considered in a vacuum. It does not require complete identity for every purpose and in every respect. In determining equivalents, things

> equal to the same thing may not be equal to each other and, by the same token, things for most purposes different may sometimes be equivalents. Consideration must be given to the purpose for which an ingredient is used in a patent, the qualities it has when combined with the other ingredients, and the function which it is intended to perform. An important factor is whether persons reasonably skilled in the art would have known of the interchangeability of an ingredient not contained in the patent with one that was." *Id.* at 609.

Considering those factors, the Court viewed the difference between the chemical element claimed in the patent and the substitute element to be "colorable only," and concluded that the trial court's judgment of infringement under the doctrine of equivalents was proper.

A

Petitioner's primary argument in this Court is that the doctrine of equivalents, as set out in *Graver Tank* in 1950, did not survive the 1952 revision of the Patent Act, 35 U.S.C. § 100 *et seq.*, because it is inconsistent with several aspects of that Act. In particular, petitioner argues: (1) the doctrine of equivalents is inconsistent with the statutory requirement that a patentee specifically "claim" the invention covered by a patent, 35 U.S.C. § 112; (2) the doctrine circumvents the patent reissue process—designed to correct mistakes in drafting or the like—and avoids the express limitations on that process, 35 U.S.C. §§ 251–252; (3) the doctrine is inconsistent with the primacy of the Patent and Trademark Office (PTO) in setting the scope of a patent through the patent prosecution process; and (4) the doctrine was implicitly rejected as a general matter by Congress' specific and limited inclusion of the doctrine in one section regarding "means" claiming, 35 U.S.C. § 112, ¶ 6. All but one of these arguments were made in *Graver Tank* in the context of the 1870 Patent Act, and failed to command a majority.

The 1952 Patent Act is not materially different from the 1870 Act with regard to claiming, reissue, and the role of the PTO. *Compare, e.g.,* 35 U.S.C. § 112 ("The specification shall conclude with one or more claims particularly pointing out and distinctly claiming the subject matter which the applicant regards as his invention") *with* The Consolidated Patent Act of 1870, ch. 230, § 26, 16 Stat. 198, 201 (the applicant "shall particularly point out and distinctly claim the part, improvement, or combination which he claims as his invention or discovery"). Such minor differences as exist between those provisions in the 1870 and the 1952 Acts have no bearing on the result reached in *Graver Tank,* and thus provide no basis for our overruling it. * * *

Petitioner's fourth argument for an implied congressional negation of the doctrine of equivalents turns on the reference to "equivalents" in the "means" claiming provision of the 1952 Act. Section 112, ¶ 6, a provision not contained in the 1870 Act, states:

> "An element in a claim for a combination may be expressed as a means or step for performing a specified function without the recital of structure, material, or acts in support thereof, and such claim shall be construed to cover the corresponding structure, material, or acts described in the specification *and equivalents thereof.*" (Emphasis added.)

Thus, under this new provision, an applicant can describe an element of his invention by the result accomplished or the function served, rather than describing the item or element to be used (*e.g.*, "a means of connecting Part A to Part B," rather than "a two-penny nail"). Congress enacted § 112, ¶ 6 in response to *Halliburton Oil Well Cementing Co. v. Walker*, which rejected claims that "do not describe the invention but use 'conveniently functional language at the exact point of novelty,' " 329 U.S. 1, 8 (1946) (citation omitted). Section 112, ¶ 6 now expressly allows so-called "means" claims, with the proviso that application of the broad literal language of such claims must be limited to only those means that are "equivalent" to the actual means shown in the patent specification. This is an application of the doctrine of equivalents in a restrictive role, narrowing the application of broad literal claim elements. We recognized this type of role for the doctrine of equivalents in *Graver Tank* itself. The added provision, however, is silent on the doctrine of equivalents as applied where there is no literal infringement.

Because § 112, ¶ 6 was enacted as a targeted cure to a specific problem, and because the reference in that provision to "equivalents" appears to be no more than a prophylactic against potential side effects of that cure, such limited congressional action should not be overread for negative implications. Congress in 1952 could easily have responded to *Graver Tank* as it did to the *Halliburton* decision. But it did not. Absent something more compelling than the dubious negative inference offered by petitioner, the lengthy history of the doctrine of equivalents strongly supports adherence to our refusal in *Graver Tank* to find that the Patent Act conflicts with that doctrine. Congress can legislate the doctrine of equivalents out of existence any time it chooses. The various policy arguments now made by both sides are thus best addressed to Congress, not this Court.

B

We do, however, share the concern of the dissenters below that the doctrine of equivalents, as it has come to be applied since *Graver Tank*, has taken on a life of its own, unbounded by the patent claims. There can be no denying that the doctrine of equivalents, when applied broadly, conflicts with the definitional and public-notice functions of the statutory claiming requirement. Judge Nies identified one means of avoiding this conflict:

"[A] distinction can be drawn that is not too esoteric between substitution of an equivalent for a component *in* an invention and enlarging the metes and bounds of the invention *beyond* what is claimed.

* * *

"Where a claim to an invention is expressed as a combination of elements, as here, 'equivalents' in the sobriquet 'Doctrine of Equivalents' refers to the equivalency of an *element* or *part* of the invention with one that is substituted in the accused product or process.

* * *

"This view that the accused device or process must be more than 'equivalent' *overall* reconciles the Supreme Court's position on infringement by equivalents with its concurrent statements that 'the courts have no right to enlarge a patent beyond the scope of its claims as allowed by the Patent Office.' [Citations omitted.] The 'scope' is not enlarged if courts do not go beyond the substitution of equivalent elements." 62 F.3d, at 1573–1574 (Nies, J., dissenting) (emphasis in original).

We concur with this apt reconciliation of our two lines of precedent. Each element contained in a patent claim is deemed material to defining the scope of the patented invention, and thus the doctrine of equivalents must be applied to individual elements of the claim, not to the invention as a whole. It is important to ensure that the application of the doctrine, even as to an individual element, is not allowed such broad play as to effectively eliminate that element in its entirety. So long as the doctrine of equivalents does not encroach beyond the limits just described, or beyond related limits to be discussed *infra*, * * * we are confident that the doctrine will not vitiate the central functions of the patent claims themselves.

III

Understandably reluctant to assume this Court would overrule *Graver Tank*, petitioner has offered alternative arguments in favor of a more restricted doctrine of equivalents than it feels was applied in this case. We address each in turn.

A

Petitioner first argues that *Graver Tank* never purported to supersede a well-established limit on nonliteral infringement, known variously as "prosecution history estoppel" and "file wrapper estoppel." According to petitioner, any surrender of subject matter during patent prosecution, regardless of the reason for such surrender, precludes recapturing any part of that subject matter, even if it is equivalent to the matter expressly claimed. Because, during patent prosecution, respondent limited the pH element of its claim to pH levels between 6.0 and 9.0, petitioner would have those limits form bright lines beyond which no equivalents may be claimed. Any inquiry into the reasons for a surrender, petitioner claims, would undermine the public's right to clear notice of the scope of the patent as embodied in the patent file.

We can readily agree with petitioner that *Graver Tank* did not dispose of prosecution history estoppel as a legal limitation on the doctrine of equivalents. But petitioner reaches too far in arguing that the reason for an amendment during patent prosecution is irrelevant to any subsequent estoppel. In each of our cases cited by petitioner and by the dissent below, prosecution history estoppel was tied to amendments made to avoid the prior art, or otherwise to address a specific concern—such as obviousness—that arguably would have rendered the claimed subject matter unpatentable. Thus, in *Exhibit Supply Co. v. Ace Patents Corp.*, Chief Justice Stone distinguished inclusion of a limiting phrase in an original patent claim from the "very different" situation in which "the applicant, in order to meet objections in the Patent Office, *based on references to the prior art,* adopted the phrase as a substitute for the broader one" previously used. 315 U.S. 126, 136 (1942) (emphasis added). Similarly, in *Keystone Driller Co. v. Northwest Engineering Corp.*, 294 U.S. 42 (1935), estoppel was applied where the initial claims were "rejected on the prior art," *id.*, at 48, n. 6, and where the allegedly infringing equivalent element was outside of the revised claims and within the prior art that formed the basis for the rejection of the earlier claims, *id.*, at 48.

It is telling that in each case this Court probed the reasoning behind the Patent Office's insistence upon a change in the claims. In each instance, a change was demanded because the claim as otherwise written was viewed as not describing a patentable invention at all—typically because what it described was encompassed within the prior art. But, as the United States informs us, there are a variety of other reasons why the PTO may request a change in claim language. And if the PTO has been requesting changes in claim language without the intent to limit equivalents or, indeed, with the expectation that language it required would in many cases allow for a range of equivalents, we should be extremely reluctant to upset the basic assumptions of the PTO without substantial reason for doing so. Our prior cases have consistently applied prosecution history estoppel only where claims have been amended for a limited set of reasons, and we see no substantial cause for requiring a more rigid rule invoking an estoppel regardless of the reasons for a change.

In this case, the patent examiner objected to the patent claim due to a perceived overlap with the Booth patent, which revealed an ultrafiltration process operating at a pH above 9.0. In response to this objection, the phrase "at a pH from approximately 6.0 to 9.0" was added to the claim.

While it is undisputed that the upper limit of 9.0 was added in order to distinguish the Booth patent, the reason for adding the lower limit of 6.0 is unclear. The lower limit certainly did not serve to distinguish the Booth patent, which said nothing about pH levels below 6.0. Thus, while a lower limit of 6.0, by its mere inclusion, became a material element of the claim, that did not necessarily preclude the application of the doctrine of equivalents as to that element. Where the reason for the change was not related to avoiding the prior art, the change may introduce a new element, but it does not necessarily preclude infringement by equivalents of that element.

We are left with the problem, however, of what to do in a case like the one at bar, where the record seems not to reveal the reason for including the lower pH limit of 6.0. In our view, holding that certain reasons for a claim amendment may avoid the application of prosecution history estoppel is not tantamount to holding that the absence of a reason for an amendment may similarly avoid such an estoppel. Mindful that claims do indeed serve both a definitional and a notice function, we think the better rule is to place the burden on the patentholder to establish the reason for an amendment required during patent prosecution. The court then would decide whether that reason is sufficient to overcome prosecution history estoppel as a bar to application of the doctrine of equivalents to the element added by that amendment. Where no explanation is established, however, the court should presume that the PTO had a substantial reason related to patentability for including the limiting element added by amendment. In those circumstances, prosecution history estoppel would bar the application of the doctrine [of] equivalents as to that element. The presumption we have described, one subject to rebuttal if an appropriate reason for a required amendment is established, gives proper deference to the role of claims in defining an invention and providing public notice, and to the primacy of the PTO in ensuring that the claims allowed cover only subject matter that is properly patentable in a proffered patent application. Applied in this fashion, prosecution history estoppel places reasonable limits on the doctrine of equivalents, and further insulates the doctrine from any feared conflict with the Patent Act.

Because respondent has not proffered in this Court a reason for the addition of a lower pH limit, it is impossible to tell whether the reason for that addition could properly avoid an estoppel. Whether a reason in fact exists, but simply was not adequately developed, we cannot say. On remand, the Federal Circuit can consider whether reasons for that portion of the amendment were offered or not and whether further opportunity to establish such reasons would be proper.

B

Petitioner next argues that even if *Graver Tank* remains good law, the case held only that the absence of substantial differences was a necessary element for infringement under the doctrine of equivalents, not that it was sufficient for such a result. Relying on *Graver Tank*'s references to the problem of an "unscrupulous copyist" and "piracy," 339 U.S., at 607, petitioner would require judicial exploration of the equities of a case before allowing application of the doctrine of equivalents. To be sure, *Graver Tank* refers to the prevention of copying and piracy when describing the benefits of the doctrine of equivalents. That the doctrine produces such benefits, however, does not mean that its application is limited only to cases where those particular benefits are obtained.

Elsewhere in *Graver Tank* the doctrine is described in more neutral terms. And the history of the doctrine as relied upon by *Graver Tank* reflects a basis for the doctrine not so limited as petitioner would have it. In *Winans v. Denmead*, 15 How. 330, 343 ([U.S.] 1854), we described the doctrine of equivalents as growing out of a legally implied term in each patent claim that "the claim extends to the thing patented, however its form or proportions may be varied." Under that view, application of the doctrine of equivalents involves determining whether a particular accused product or process infringes upon the patent claim, where the claim takes the form—half express, half implied—of "X and its equivalents."

* * *

Petitioner also points to *Graver Tank*'s seeming reliance on the absence of independent experimentation by the alleged infringer as supporting an equitable defense to the doctrine of equivalents. * * *

But another explanation is available that does not require a divergence from generally objective principles of patent infringement. In both instances in *Graver Tank* where we referred to independent research or experiments, we were discussing the known interchangeability between the chemical compound claimed in the patent and the compound substituted by the alleged infringer. The need for independent experimentation thus could reflect knowledge—or lack thereof—of interchangeability possessed by one presumably skilled in the art. The known interchangeability of substitutes for an element of a patent is one of the express objective factors noted by *Graver Tank* as bearing upon whether the accused device is substantially the same as the patented invention. Independent experimentation by the alleged infringer would not always reflect upon the objective question whether a person skilled in the art would have known of the interchangeability between two elements, but in many cases it would likely be probative of such knowledge.

Although *Graver Tank* certainly leaves room for petitioner's suggested inclusion of intent-based elements in the doctrine of equivalents, we do not read it as requiring them. The better view, and the one consistent with *Graver Tank*'s predecessors and the objective approach to infringement, is that intent plays no role in the application of the doctrine of equivalents.

C

Finally, petitioner proposes that in order to minimize conflict with the notice function of patent claims, the doctrine of equivalents should be limited to equivalents that are disclosed within the patent itself. A milder version of this argument, which found favor with the dissenters below, is that the doctrine should be limited to equivalents that were known at the time the patent was issued, and should not extend to after-arising equivalents.

As we have noted, with regard to the objective nature of the doctrine, a skilled practitioner's knowledge of the interchangeability between claimed and accused elements is not relevant for its own sake, but rather for what it tells the fact-finder about the similarities or differences between those elements. Much as the perspective of the hypothetical "reasonable person" gives content to concepts such as "negligent" behavior, the perspective of a skilled practitioner provides content to, and limits on, the concept of "equivalence." Insofar as the question under the doctrine of equivalents is whether an accused element is equivalent to a claimed element, the proper time for evaluating equivalency—and thus knowledge of interchangeability between elements—is at the time of infringement, not at the time the patent was issued. And rejecting the milder version of petitioner's argument necessarily rejects the more severe proposition that equivalents must not only be known, but must also be actually disclosed in the patent in order for such equivalents to infringe upon the patent.

* * *

V

All that remains is to address the debate regarding the linguistic framework under which "equivalence" is determined. Both the parties and the Federal Circuit spend considerable time arguing whether the so-called "triple identity" test—focusing on the function served by a particular claim element, the way that element serves that function, and the result thus obtained by that element—is a suitable method for determining equivalence, or whether an "insubstantial differences" approach is better. * * *

In our view, the particular linguistic framework used is less important than whether the test is probative of the essential inquiry: Does the accused product or process contain elements identical or equivalent to each claimed element of the patented invention? Different linguistic frameworks may be more suitable to different cases, depending on their particular facts. A focus on individual elements and a special vigilance against allowing the concept of equivalence to eliminate completely any such elements should reduce considerably the imprecision of whatever language is used. * * *

VI

Today we adhere to the doctrine of equivalents. The determination of equivalence should be applied as an objective inquiry on an element-by-element basis. Prosecution history estoppel continues to be available as a defense to infringement, but if the patent-holder demonstrates that an amendment required during prosecution had a purpose unrelated to patentability, a court must consider that purpose in order to decide whether an estoppel is precluded. Where the patentholder is unable to establish such a purpose, a court should presume that the purpose behind the required amendment is such that prosecution history estoppel would apply. Because the Court of Appeals for the Federal Circuit did not consider all of the requirements as described by us today, particularly as related to prosecution history estoppel and the preservation of some meaning for each element in a claim, we reverse and remand for further proceedings consistent with this opinion.

It is so ordered.

NOTES

1. *Fact Question:* Equivalence is a question of fact. *Graver Tank & Mfg. Co. v. Linde Air Prods. Co.*, 339 U.S. 605, 609 (1950).

In *Graver Tank* the Supreme Court considered whether a patented welding flux containing magnesium was infringed by the defendant's welding flux, which was identical except that it substituted manganese for magnesium. The Court held that the substitution of manganese infringed the patent under the doctrine of equivalents, based on the trial court's finding that the compositions were "substantially identical in operation and in result." The Court observed:

> It is difficult to conceive of a case more appropriate for application of the doctrine of equivalents. The disclosures of the prior art made clear that manganese silicate was a useful ingredient in welding compositions. Specialists familiar with the problems of welding compositions understood that manganese was equivalent to and could be substituted for magnesium in the composition of the patented flux and their observations were confirmed by the literature of chemistry. * * *

Id. at 612.

2. *All Elements or Limitations:* Literal infringement requires that the accused process or product possess or include each and every element or limitation of the infringed claim. Similarly, a finding of infringement by

equivalents requires a one-to-one correspondence with respect to *every* limitation in the claim that has been infringed. *See Forest Laboratories, Inc. v. Abbott Laboratories*, 239 F.3d 1305, 1313 (Fed.Cir.2001) (ruling that infringement of a respiratory drug patent is not proved without proving all the elements). (Recall also from Chapter 10.C.1., *supra*, that a patent claim is not invalid for lack of novelty unless one piece of prior art contains each and every element or limitation of the claim in question.)

3. *Relationship to Obviousness:* Equivalence is generally found where the accused product would have been obvious in light of the plaintiff's patent. For example, equivalence was found where a patent for a playpen claimed a pair of holes in the side fabric through which two drawstrings could be pulled to adjust the side webbing, and the accused product had a single hole for the drawstrings. *See Tigrett Indus., Inc. v. Standard Indus., Inc.*, 162 U.S.P.Q. 32, 36 (W.D.Tenn.1967), *aff'd*, 411 F.2d 1218 (6th Cir.1969), *aff'd by an equally divided court*, 397 U.S. 586 (1970).

4. *Pioneer Versus Improvement:* It is frequently said that "the range of equivalents depends upon and varies with the degree of invention." *Continental Paper Bag Co. v. Eastern Paper Bag Co.*, 210 U.S. 405 (1908). Thus, a "pioneer" patent is entitled to a broader range of equivalents than a patent for a narrow improvement.

> Another guide is the notion that pioneer patents are to be given wider ranges of equivalence than minor improvement patents. This statement is less a canon of construction and more a shorthand expression for the dictates of the law and the patents themselves. The doctrine of equivalence is subservient to file wrapper estoppel. It may not include within its range anything that would vitiate limitations expressed before the Patent Office. Thus a patent that has been severely limited to avoid the prior art will only have a small range between it and the point beyond which it violates file wrapper estoppel. Similarly a patent which is a major departure from the prior art will have a larger range in which equivalence can function. The scope of the patents also influences the range of equivalence. A pioneer patent which occupies symbolically a six-inch circle will have three inches of equivalence if its range is fifty percent. An improvement patent occupying a two-inch circle has only one inch of equivalence with the same range. Thus with relatively identical ranges, the scope of the patent provides the pioneer patent with absolutely a larger range of equivalence.

Autogiro Co. of Am. v. United States, 384 F.2d 391 (Ct. Cl. 1967).

5. *Means-Plus-Function Claims:* As briefly discussed in *Warner-Jenkinson v. Hilton Davis*, section 112 allows for a particular form of patent claim, referred to as a "means-plus-function" claim. This form permits a patent applicant to express an element in a combination claim as a means for performing a function. The applicant need not recite structure, material, or acts in the claim's means-plus-function limitation. For example, one element

of a (unrealistic) claim might recite "a means for attaching two papers" rather than a list of the various structural attachment devices that can be used to attach two papers (staples, metal paper clip, plastic paper clip, binder clip, tape, etc.). Section 112 does not allow, however, patent applicants to leave these "means" for performing the specified functions altogether unlimited. The applicant must describe in the patent specification a structure or structures that can perform the specified function. The court must construe the functional claim language "to cover the corresponding structure, material, or acts described in the specification *and equivalents thereof*." Thus the concept of equivalency embodied in section 112 (namely equivalency of the means (structure) in the accused device compared to the structures recited in the patent specification) plays a role in *limiting* the literal scope of the otherwise broad "means" component of a means-plus-function claim. Equivalency in section 112 is not an application of the "doctrine of equivalents," which is used in the infringement analysis to broaden a patentee's rights beyond a claim's literal scope.

For literal infringement to be found, the structure of the accused device fulfilling the "means" must be equivalent to that in the specification and must perform a function identical to that recited in the claim. If the structure in the accused device is equivalent, but does not perform a function identical to that in the claim, the court may then move to the question of infringement under the doctrine of equivalents. Infringement by equivalency would be found if the function is "substantially the same" as the function in the claim. The doctrine of equivalents is generally not applied to the structure. *See, e.g., WMS Gaming, Inc. v. International Game Technology,* 184 F.3d 1339 (Fed. Cir. 1999); *Valmont Indus., Inc. v. Reinke Mfg. Co., Inc.,* 983 F.2d 1039 (Fed.Cir.1993). *See also Chiuminatta Concrete Concepts, Inc. v. Cardinal Indus. Inc.*, 145 F.3d 1303 (Fed. Cir. 1998) (allowing recourse to the doctrine of equivalents on the structural or means element of a means-plus-function claim, although it would normally not be permitted, in the limited circumstance of after-arising technology).

b. Limitations on Equivalents

As noted in *Autogiro* and *Hilton Davis*, the range of equivalents with respect to a particular claim may be limited by the doctrine of prosecution history estoppel (also known as "file wrapper estoppel" as noted above and in *Warner-Jenkinson*). Consider how the scope of prosecution history estoppel has been affected by the Supreme Court's 2002 decision in *Festo Corporation v. Shoketsu Kinzoku Kogyo Kabushiki Co.*

FESTO CORP. V. SHOKETSU KINZOKU KOGYO KABUSHIKI CO.

535 U.S. 722, 122 S.Ct. 1831 (2002).

JUSTICE KENNEDY delivered the opinion of the Court.

* * *

Petitioner Festo Corporation owns two patents for an improved magnetic rodless cylinder, a piston-driven device that relies on magnets to move objects in a conveying system. The device has many industrial uses and has been employed in machinery as diverse as sewing equipment and the Thunder Mountain ride at Disney World. Although the precise details of the cylinder's operation are not essential here, the prosecution history must be considered.

Petitioner's patent applications, as often occurs, were amended during the prosecution proceedings. The application for the first patent, the Stoll Patent (U.S. Patent No. 4,354,125), was amended after the patent examiner rejected the initial application because the exact method of operation was unclear and some claims were made in an impermissible way. (They were multiply dependent.) 35 U.S.C. § 112 (1994 ed.). The inventor, Dr. Stoll, submitted a new application designed to meet the examiner's objections and also added certain references to prior art. 37 CFR § 1.56 (2000). The second patent, the Carroll Patent (U.S. Patent No. 3,779,401), was also amended during a reexamination proceeding. The prior art references were added to this amended application as well. Both amended patents added a new limitation—that the inventions contain a pair of sealing rings, each having a lip on one side, which would prevent impurities from getting on the piston assembly. The amended Stoll Patent added the further limitation that the outer shell of the device, the sleeve, be made of a magnetizable material.

After Festo began selling its rodless cylinder, respondents (whom we refer to as SMC) entered the market with a device similar, but not identical, to the ones disclosed by Festo's patents. SMC's cylinder, rather than using two one-way sealing rings, employs a single sealing ring with a two-way lip. Furthermore, SMC's sleeve is made of a nonmagnetizable alloy. SMC's device does not fall within the literal claims of either patent, but petitioner contends that it is so similar that it infringes under the doctrine of equivalents.

SMC contends that Festo is estopped from making this argument because of the prosecution history of its patents. The sealing rings and the magnetized alloy in the Festo product were both disclosed for the first time in the amended applications. In SMC's view, these amendments narrowed the earlier applications, surrendering alternatives that are the very points of difference in the competing devices—the sealing rings and the type of alloy used to make the sleeve. As Festo narrowed its claims in these ways in order to obtain the patents, says SMC, Festo is now estopped from saying that these features are immaterial and that SMC's device is an equivalent of its own.

The United States District Court for the District of Massachusetts disagreed. It held that Festo's amendments were not made to avoid prior art, and therefore the amendments were not the kind that give rise to estoppel. * * *

The en banc [Federal Circuit] reversed, holding that prosecution history estoppel barred Festo from asserting that the accused device infringed its patents under the doctrine of equivalents. The court held, with only one judge dissenting, that estoppel arises from any amendment that narrows a claim to comply with the Patent Act, not only from amendments made to avoid prior art. More controversial in the Court of Appeals was its further holding: When estoppel applies, it stands as a complete bar against any claim of equivalence for the element that was amended. * * * In the court's view a complete-bar rule, under which estoppel bars all claims of equivalence to the narrowed element, would promote certainty in the determination of infringement cases.

* * *

We agree with the Court of Appeals that a narrowing amendment made to satisfy any requirement of the Patent Act may give rise to an estoppel. As that court explained, a number of statutory requirements must be satisfied before a patent can issue. The claimed subject matter must be useful, novel, and not obvious. 35 U.S.C. §§ 101–103 (1994 ed. and Supp. V). In addition, the patent application must describe, enable, and set forth the best mode of carrying out the invention. § 112 (1994 ed.). These latter requirements must be satisfied before issuance of the patent, for exclusive patent rights are given in exchange for disclosing the invention to the public. What is claimed by the patent application must be the same as what is disclosed in the specification; otherwise the patent should not issue. The patent also should not issue if the other requirements of § 112 are not satisfied, and an applicant's failure to meet these requirements could lead to the issued patent being held invalid in later litigation.

Petitioner contends that amendments made to comply with § 112 concern the form of the application and not the subject matter of the invention. The PTO might require the applicant to clarify an ambiguous term, to improve the translation of a foreign word, or to rewrite a dependent claim as an independent one. In these cases, petitioner argues, the applicant has no intention of surrendering subject matter and should not be estopped from challenging equivalent devices. While this may be true in some cases, petitioner's argument conflates the patentee's reason for making the amendment with the impact the amendment has on the subject matter.

Estoppel arises when an amendment is made to secure the patent and the amendment narrows the patent's scope. If a § 112 amendment is truly cosmetic, then it would not narrow the patent's scope or raise an estoppel. On the other hand, if a § 112 amendment is necessary and narrows the patent's scope—even if only for the purpose of better description—estoppel may apply. A patentee who narrows a claim as a condition for obtaining a patent disavows his claim to the broader subject matter, whether the amendment was made to avoid the prior art or to comply with § 112. We must regard the patentee as having conceded an inability to claim the broader subject matter or at least as having abandoned his right to appeal a rejection. In either case estoppel may apply.

Petitioner concedes that the limitations at issue—the sealing rings and the composition of the sleeve—were made for reasons related to § 112, if not also to avoid the prior art. Our conclusion that prosecution history estoppel arises when a claim is narrowed to comply with § 112 gives rise to the second question presented: Does the estoppel bar the inventor from asserting infringement against any equivalent to the narrowed element or might some equivalents still infringe? The Court of Appeals held that prosecution history estoppel is a complete bar, and so the narrowed element must be limited to its strict literal terms. Based upon its experience the Court of Appeals decided that the flexible-bar rule is unworkable because it leads to excessive uncertainty and burdens legitimate innovation. For the reasons that follow, we disagree with the decision to adopt the complete bar.

Though prosecution history estoppel can bar challenges to a wide range of equivalents, its reach requires an examination of the subject matter surrendered by the narrowing amendment. The complete bar avoids this inquiry by establishing a *per se* rule; but that approach is inconsistent with the purpose of applying the estoppel in the first place—to hold the inventor to the representations made during the application process and to the inferences that may reasonably be drawn from the amendment. By amending the application, the inventor is deemed to concede that the patent does not extend as far as the original claim. It does not follow, however, that the amended claim becomes so perfect in its description that no one could devise an equivalent. After amendment, as before, language remains an imperfect fit for invention. The narrowing amendment may demonstrate what the claim is not; but it may still fail to capture precisely what the claim is. There is no reason why a narrowing amendment should be deemed to relinquish equivalents unforeseeable at the time of the amendment and beyond a fair interpretation of what was surrendered. Nor is there any call to foreclose claims of equivalence for aspects of the invention that have only a peripheral relation to the reason the amendment was submitted. The amendment does not show that the inventor suddenly had more foresight in the drafting of claims than an inventor whose application was granted without amendments having been submitted. It shows only that he was familiar with the broader text and with the difference between the two. As a result, there is no more reason for holding the patentee to the literal terms of an amended claim than there is for abolishing the doctrine of equivalents altogether and holding every patentee to the literal terms of the patent.

* * *

In *Warner-Jenkinson* we struck the appropriate balance by placing the burden on the patentee to show that an amendment was not for purposes of patentability:

> "Where no explanation is established, however, the court should presume that the patent application had a substantial reason related to patentability for including the limiting element added by amendment. In those circumstances, prosecution history estoppel would bar the application of the doctrine of equivalents as to that element." *Id.*, at 33.

When the patentee is unable to explain the reason for amendment, estoppel not only applies but also "bar[s] the application of the doctrine of equivalents as to that element." *Ibid.* These words do not mandate a complete bar; they are limited to the circumstance where "no explanation is established." They do provide, however, that when the court is unable to determine the purpose underlying a narrowing amendment—and hence a rationale for limiting the estoppel to the surrender of particular equivalents—the court should presume that the patentee surrendered all subject matter between the broader and the narrower language.

Just as *Warner-Jenkinson* held that the patentee bears the burden of proving that an amendment was not made for a reason that would give rise to estoppel, we hold here that the patentee should bear the burden of showing that the amendment does not surrender the particular equivalent in question. This is the approach advocated by the United States, and we regard it to be sound. The patentee, as the author of the claim language, may be expected to draft claims encompassing readily known equivalents. A patentee's decision to narrow his claims through amendment may be presumed to be a general disclaimer of the territory between the original claim and the amended claim. There are some cases, however, where the amendment cannot reasonably be viewed as surrendering a particular equivalent. The equivalent may have been unforeseeable at the time of the application; the rationale underlying the amendment may bear no more than a tangential relation to the equivalent in question; or there may be some other reason suggesting that the patentee could not reasonably be expected to have described the insubstantial substitute in question. In those cases the patentee can overcome the presumption that prosecution history estoppel bars a finding of equivalence.

This presumption is not, then, just the complete bar by another name. Rather, it reflects the fact that the interpretation of the patent must begin with its literal claims, and the prosecution history is relevant to construing those claims. When the patentee has chosen to narrow a claim, courts may presume the amended text was composed with awareness of this rule and that the territory surrendered is not an equivalent of the territory claimed. In those instances, however, the patentee still might rebut the presumption that estoppel bars a claim of equivalence. The patentee must show that at the time of the amendment one skilled in the art could not reasonably be expected to have drafted a claim that would have literally encompassed the alleged equivalent.

* * *

NOTE

Analysis of Prosecution History Estoppel: On remand the case from the Supreme Court, the Federal Circuit issued a new en banc opinion, *Festo Corp. v. Shoketsu Kinzoku Kogyo Kabushiki Co.*, 344 F.3d 1359 (Fed. Cir. 2003) (en banc), in which it outlined the correct post-*Festo* multi-step procedure for analyzing the effect of a narrowing amendment:

> [T]he *Warner-Jenkinson* and *Festo* presumptions operate together in the following manner: The first question in a prosecution history estoppel inquiry is whether an amendment filed in the Patent and Trademark Office ("PTO") has narrowed the literal scope of a claim. If the amendment was not narrowing, then prosecution history estoppel does not apply. But if the accused infringer establishes that the amendment was a narrowing one, then the second question is whether the reason for that amendment was a substantial one relating to patentability. When the prosecution history record reveals no reason for the narrowing amendment, *Warner-Jenkinson* presumes that the patentee had a substantial reason relating to patentability; consequently, the patentee must show that the reason for the amendment was not one relating to patentability if it is to rebut that presumption. In this regard, we reinstate our earlier holding that a patentee's rebuttal of the *Warner-Jenkinson* presumption is restricted to the evidence in the prosecution history record. If the patentee successfully establishes that the amendment was not for a reason of patentability, then prosecution history estoppel does not apply.
>
> If, however, the court determines that a narrowing amendment has been made for a substantial reason relating to patentability—whether based on a reason reflected in the prosecution history record or on the patentee's failure to overcome the *Warner-Jenkinson*

> presumption—then the third question in a prosecution history estoppel analysis addresses the scope of the subject matter surrendered by the narrowing amendment. At that point *Festo*[ ] imposes the presumption that the patentee has surrendered all territory between the original claim limitation and the amended claim limitation. The patentee may rebut that presumption of total surrender by demonstrating that it did not surrender the particular equivalent in question according to the criteria discussed below. Finally, if the patentee fails to rebut the *Festo* presumption, then prosecution history estoppel bars the patentee from relying on the doctrine of equivalents for the accused element. If the patentee successfully rebuts the presumption, then prosecution history estoppel does not apply and the question whether the accused element is in fact equivalent to the limitation at issue is reached on the merits.

344 F.3d at 1366–67. In considering whether to apply the presumption of a total surrender of subject matter in the territory between the original and the narrowed claim limitation, or instead to apply a limited estoppel under the prosecution history, the court will generally look for evidence related to the following criteria: (1) whether an alleged equivalent would have been, as an objective matter, unforeseeable to a person having ordinary skill in the art at the time of the amendment and therefore not fairly interpreted to have been surrendered at the time of amendment (*e.g.*, the alleged equivalent represents later-developed technology); (2) whether the patentee can show that the reason for narrowing the claim was only tangentially related to the equivalent in question (*i.e.*, the reason reflected in the prosecution history for the narrowing amendment was not directly relevant to the alleged equivalent); and (3) whether the patentee can establish another reason that the patent claim could not reasonably be expected to have described the insubstantial substitute or equivalent in question (*e.g.*, shortcomings of language at the time of prosecution of the patent prevented description of the alleged equivalent). 344 F.3d at 1368–70.

Because the question whether a patentee has rebutted the *Festo* presumption of surrender is a question of law, the Federal Circuit subjects these determinations to *de novo* review. If one of the goals of prosecution history estoppel is to provide competitors with greater certainty regarding the scope of patent claims and their range of equivalents, has *Festo* advanced that goal?

3. INFRINGING ACTIVITIES

a. Direct Infringement: Making, Using, Selling, and Offering to Sell

Statute: 35 U.S.C. § 271(a)

As briefly noted in the introduction to this chapter, section 271(a) provides the primary list of directly infringing acts, including making, using, offering to sell, selling, and importing the invention. While some cases of "making," "using," or "selling" are clear, others are not.

The next two cases are related to one another. The patent covered a convertible top's combination or assembly but not any individual part, such as the fabric. In both *Aro* decisions, the defendant Aro Manufacturing was accused of contributory infringement through making and selling replacement fabric for the tops; the direct infringement to which it allegedly contributed was the "making" of the invention when the convertible owner replaced the fabric and thereby (re-)made the convertible top. In each case, if replacing the fabric was "making" the invention (direct infringement), then Aro could have been a contributory infringer—and the Court would need to interpret and apply § 271(c).

In the first *Aro* decision below, *Aro I* (which related to licensed 1952–54 GM convertibles), the Court addressed whether replacing the fabric in a licensed convertible automobile top "made" the invention within the meaning of section 271(a) ("whoever without authority makes, uses, ..."). Depending on the facts, for the owner of a licensed, legitimate product, there may not always be a simple answer: the owner of a legitimate, noninfringing copy or unit of a patented product does not have the authority—just by virtue of ownership—to make another copy of the patented product.

In the second *Aro* decision below, *Aro II* (which related to unlicensed 1952–54 Ford convertibles), the Court addressed the effect of the unlicensed status of the original convertible tops being repaired with Aro's fabric before turning to other issues raised by the accusation of contributory infringement, including the knowledge Aro must have under § 271(c).

ARO MANUFACTURING CO., INC. V. CONVERTIBLE TOP REPLACEMENT CO., INC.

365 U.S. 336, 81 S.Ct. 599 (1961).

MR. JUSTICE WHITTAKER delivered the opinion of the Court.

* * *

[Respondent Convertible Top Replacement Co.'s '724 combination patent covered a convertible folding top for an automobile, consisting of a flexible fabric top and supporting apparatus. Individual components of the patented combination, such as the fabric, were not covered by the patent. Aro Manufacturing Co. made and sold replacement fabric for the convertible tops. The district court ruled that Aro's acts constituted contributory infringement because a person who replaced the worn-out fabric infringed by reconstructing the patented combination, *i.e.*, the person *made* the invention anew when replacing the fabric. The court of appeals affirmed, and this appeal followed.]

* * *

Since the patentees never claimed the fabric or its shape as their invention, and the claims made in the patent are the sole measure of the grant, the fabric is no more than an unpatented element of the combination which was claimed as the invention, and the patent did not confer a monopoly over the fabric or its shape. * * *

It follows that petitioners' manufacture and sale of the fabric is not a direct infringement under 35 U.S.C. § 271(a). But the question remains whether petitioners' manufacture and sale of the fabric constitute a contributory infringement of the patent under 35 U.S.C. § 271(c). It is admitted that petitioners know that the purchasers intend to use the fabric for replacement purposes on automobile convertible tops which are covered by the claims of respondent's combination patent, and such manufacture and sale with that knowledge might well constitute contributory infringement under § 271(c), if, but only if, such a replacement by the purchaser himself would in itself constitute a direct infringement under § 271(a), for it is settled that if there is no direct infringement of a patent there can be no contributory infringement. * * * The determinative question, therefore, comes down to whether the car owner would infringe the combination patent by replacing the worn-out fabric element of the patented convertible top on his car, or even more specifically, whether such a replacement by the car owner is infringing "reconstruction" or permissible "repair."

This Court's decisions specifically dealing with whether the replacement of an unpatented part, in a patented combination, that has worn out, been broken or otherwise spent, is permissible "repair" or infringing "reconstruction," have steadfastly refused to extend the patent monopoly beyond the terms of the grant. *Wilson v. Simpson*, 9 How. 109—doubtless the leading case in this Court that deals with the distinction—concerned a patented planing machine which included, as elements, certain cutting knives which normally wore out in a few months' use. The purchaser was held to have the right to replace those knives without the patentee's consent. The Court held that, although there is no right to "rebuild" a patented combination, the entity "exists" notwithstanding the fact that destruction or impairment of one of its elements renders it inoperable; and that, accordingly, replacement of that worn-out essential part is permissible restoration of the machine to the original use for which it was bought. The Court explained that it is "the use of the whole" of the combination which a purchaser buys, and that repair or replacement of the worn-out, damaged or destroyed part is but an exercise of the right "to give duration to that which he owns, or has a right to use as a whole."

The distilled essence of the *Wilson* case was stated by Judge Learned Hand in *United States v. Aluminum Co. of America*, 148 F.2d 416, 425 (C. A. 2d Cir.): "The [patent] monopolist cannot prevent those to whom he sells from . . . reconditioning articles worn by use, unless they in fact make a new article." * * *

* * *

No element, not itself separately patented, that constitutes one of the elements of a combination patent is entitled to patent monopoly, however essential it may be to the patented combination and no matter how costly or difficult replacement may be. While there is language in some lower court opinions indicating that "repair" or "reconstruction" depends on a number of factors, it is significant that each of the three cases of this Court, cited for that proposition, holds that a license to use a patented combination includes the right "to preserve its fitness for use so far as it may be affected by wear or breakage." We hold that maintenance of the "use of the whole" of the patented combination through replacement of a spent, unpatented element does not constitute reconstruction.

The decisions of this Court require the conclusion that reconstruction of a patented entity, comprised of unpatented elements, is limited to such a true reconstruction of the entity as to "in fact make a new article," after the entity, viewed as a whole, has become spent. In order to call the monopoly, conferred by the patent grant, into play for a second time, it must, indeed, be a second creation of the patented entity * * *. Mere replacement of individual unpatented parts, one at a time, whether of the same part repeatedly or different parts successively, is no more than the lawful right of the owner to repair his property. Measured by this test, the replacement of the fabric involved in this case must be characterized as permissible "repair," not "reconstruction."

Reversed.

NOTES

1. *"Making" by Reconstruction:* The distinction between infringing reconstruction and permissible repairs under *Aro I* was further explored in *Sandvik Aktiebolag v. E.J. Co.*, 121 F.3d 669 (Fed.Cir.1997). In holding that

the replacement of a spent drill tip was an infringing reconstruction of the patented drill, the court explained:

> There are a number of factors to consider in determining whether a defendant has made a new article, after the device has become spent, including the nature of the actions by the defendant, the nature of the device and how it is designed (namely, whether one of the components of the patented combination has a shorter useful life than the whole), whether a market has developed to manufacture or service the part at issue and objective evidence of the intent of the patentee. Under the totality of the circumstances, we hold in this case that E.J.'s actions are a reconstruction.
>
> By E.J.'s own admission, the drill is "spent" when the tip can no longer be resharpened unless it is retipped. In fact, the record reveals that E.J.'s customers may elect not to retip and inform E.J. to discard the drill instead.
>
> Moreover, the nature of the work done by E.J. shows that retipping is more like reconstruction than repair. E.J. does not just attach a new part for a worn part, but rather must go through several steps to replace, configure and integrate the tip onto the shank. It has to break the worn or damaged tip from the shank by heating it to 1300 degrees Fahrenheit. It brazes to the shank a new rectangular block of carbide and grinds and machines it to the proper diameter and creates the point. Thereafter, the tip is honed and sharpened, grinding the rake surfaces and the center of the point and honing the edges. These actions are effectively a re-creation of the patented invention after it is spent.
>
> This is not a case where it is clear that the patented device has a useful life much longer than that of certain parts which wear out quickly. For example, in *Wilson v. Simpson*, 13 L.Ed. 66 (1850), in determining that a repair had occurred, the Supreme Court focused specifically on the fact that the [patented planing] machine was designed so that the knives had to be replaced long before the other components * * * [every sixty or ninety days]. * * *
>
> The drill tip in this case is not a part like the detachable knives in *Wilson* that have to be replaced periodically over the useful life of the planing machine. The drill tip was not manufactured to be a replaceable part, although it could be resharpened a number of times to extend its life. It was not intended or expected to have a life of temporary duration in comparison to the drill shank. And finally, the tip was not attached to the shank in a manner to be easily detachable.
>
> In *Aro I*, the Supreme Court also noted that "the consequent demand for replacement fabrics has given rise to a substantial industry." Evidence of development in the industry could also be a factor tending to prove that there is a reasonable expectation that the

> part of the patented combination wears out quickly and requires frequent replacement. In this case, there is no evidence of a substantial market for drill retipping of the sort required for the Sandvik drill. There is no evidence of large numbers of customers retipping these drills or of companies (other than E.J.) offering to retip these drills. No one manufactures replacement tips for Sandvik's drill and although some customers opt to retip the drill only a small percentage of all drills manufactured are retipped.
>
> Finally, there was no intent evidenced by the patentee that would support E.J.'s argument that replacement of the tips is a repair. *See Kendall Co.*, 85 F.3d at 1575 (replacing the sleeve in a medical device which applies pressure to patients' limbs was a repair noting that the manufacturer "clearly intended to permit its customers to replace the sleeves" and actually sold replacement sleeves); *Sage Prods.*, 45 F.3d at 1578–79 (evidence that patentee intended the inner containers to be replaced, that it manufactures replacement parts and instructs customers to replace supports holding such replacement a permissible repair); *Porter*, 790 F.2d at 885–86 (considering that the patentee sold replacement cutting disks for its tomato harvester). The evidence shows that Sandvik never intended for its drills to be retipped. It did not manufacture or sell replacement drill tips. It did not publish instructions on how to retip its patented drills or suggest that the drills could or should be retipped. Sandvik was aware that the drill tip would need occasional resharpening and instructed its customer on how to resharpen the tip. There is, therefore, no objective evidence that Sandvik's drill tip was intended to be a replaceable part. Although the repair or reconstruction issue does not turn on the intention of the patentee alone, the fact that no replacement drill tips have ever been made or sold by the patentee is consistent with the conclusion that replacement of the carbide tip is not a permissible repair.

121 F.3d at 673–74.

2. *Multiple Repairs and "Making":* Would infringing reconstruction occur where sequential repairs to a patented combination led, over time, to replacement of all or substantially all of its unpatented components?

3. *"Use" in the United States:* Has there been "use" of a system *in the United States* for purposes of 271(a) when some components of an allegedly infringing system are located in the United States but others not? What about the "use" of a method or process, when at least one step of a multi-step method claim is performed in another country?

The Federal Circuit in *NTP, Inc. v. Research in Motion, Ltd.*, 418 F.3d 1282 (Fed. Cir. 2005), examined defendant Research in Motion's ("RIM") Blackberry wireless system, which integrated electronic mail systems ("wireline" systems) with radio frequency ("RF") wireless communication networks so as to enable mobile users to receive email over a wireless network.

Some components of the defendant's system were located in the United States, while others were located in Canada. Distinguishing between the system (or product) claims and the method (or process) claims of the patent in question, the court decided that, for purposes of section 271(a), the place where a system is "used" is "the place where control of the system is exercised and beneficial use of the system obtained." *Id.* at 1317. In the case, because the defendant's "customers located within the United States controlled the transmission of the originated information and also benefited from such an exchange of information," the defendant's system was used in the United States. *Id.* However, the court reached a different conclusion with respect to the method claims, deciding "that a process cannot be used 'within' the United States as required by section 271(a) unless each of the steps is performed within this country." *Id.* at 1318. In this case, each of the method claims in question involved a step utilizing an "interface" or "interface switch," which was satisfied only by the use of the defendant's relay, which was located in Canada. The court held, therefore, that the claimed methods were not infringed. *Id.* In addition, the court held that the defendant's *sales* within the United States of the Blackberry *devices used to receive* its wireless transmissions did not constitute infringing *sales of the patented method* for purposes of section 271(a). *Id.* at 1319.

4. *Divided "Use" of a Product:* Has there been "use" of a system or apparatus claim where the accused direct infringer does not interact with or control each component of the system? In *Centillion Data Sys., LLC v. Qwest Commc'ns Int'l, Inc.*, 631 F.3d 1279 (Fed. Cir. 2011), the Federal Circuit held that "to 'use' a system for purposes of infringement [under 271(a)], a party must put the invention into service, *i.e.*, control the system as a whole and obtain benefit from it . . . . . [but] a party [need not] exercise physical or direct control over each individual element of the system." *Id.* at 1284. "[D]irect infringement by 'use' of a system claim 'requires a party . . . to use each and every element of a claimed [system].' In order to 'put the system into service,' the end user must be using all portions of the claimed invention." *Id.*

5. *Divided "Use" of a Process:* Analyzing infringement of a process or method patent, wherein a claim comprises a series of steps, brings with it additional questions regarding what it means to "use" the patented invention—and who is using it. Infringement of a method patent containing a number of steps requires, in all instances, for all of those steps to be carried out. When all of the steps are carried out by one party, either literally or via equivalents, finding an infringing "use" of the patent should be simple enough. But if no one party performs all of the steps of a multi-step process claim—yet all of the steps are being performed and are connected in some fashion with one another—can the acts of more than one party be aggregated to prove that all of the steps have been performed and create infringement liability? And if so, by what standard should courts judge the necessary connection or relationship between different parties when determining whether acts by those parties may be aggregated to find direct infringement?

Until recently, the Federal Circuit refused to find infringement where no one actor performed, or closely directed or controlled, all of the steps in the patented process. In a 2015 en banc decision, however, the Federal Circuit broadened the circumstances in which the acts of multiple parties may be aggregated in finding liability for direct infringement.

> Direct infringement under § 271(a) occurs where all steps of a claimed method are performed by or attributable to a single entity. Where more than one actor is involved in practicing the steps, a court must determine whether the acts of one are attributable to the other such that a single entity is responsible for the infringement. We will hold an entity responsible for others' performance of method steps in two sets of circumstances: (1) where that entity directs or controls others' performance, and (2) where the actors form a joint enterprise.
>
> To determine if a single entity directs or controls the acts of another, we continue to consider general principles of vicarious liability. In the past, we have held that an actor is liable for infringement under § 271(a) if it acts through an agent (applying traditional agency principles) or contracts with another to perform one or more steps of a claimed method. We conclude, on the facts of this case, that liability under § 271(a) can also be found when an alleged infringer conditions participation in an activity or receipt of a benefit upon performance of a step or steps of a patented method and establishes the manner or timing of that performance. In those instances, the third party's actions are attributed to the alleged infringer such that the alleged infringer becomes the single actor chargeable with direct infringement. * * *
>
> Alternatively, where two or more actors form a joint enterprise, all can be charged with the acts of the other, rendering each liable for the steps performed by the other as if each is a single actor. *See* Restatement (Second) of Torts § 491 cmt. b ("The law . . . considers that each is the agent or servant of the others, and that the act of any one within the scope of the enterprise is to be charged vicariously against the rest."). A joint enterprise requires proof of four elements:
>
> (1) an agreement, express or implied, among the members of the group;
>
> (2) a common purpose to be carried out by the group;
>
> (3) a community of pecuniary interest in that purpose, among the members; and
>
> (4) an equal right to a voice in the direction of the enterprise, which gives an equal right of control.
>
> *Id.* § 491 cmt. c. * * *
>
> * * * Section 271(a) is not limited solely to principal-agent relationships, contractual arrangements, and joint enterprise, as the

> vacated panel decision held. Rather, to determine direct infringement, we consider whether all method steps can be attributed to a single entity.

Akamai Techs., Inc. v. Limelight Networks, Inc., 797 F.3d 1020, 1022–23 (Fed. Cir. 2015) (en banc) (footnotes and some citations omitted). The court noted that "to the extent our prior cases formed the predicate for the vacated panel decision, those decisions are also overruled." *Id.* at 1023 n.3. *See also Eli Lilly and Co. v. Teva Parenteral Meds., Inc.*, 845 F.3d 1357 (Fed. Cir. 2017) (applying *Akamai* to a method of treatment patent where one step was performed by the patient under instructions by the physician who would not allow treatment to continue without it due to the risks, and attributing that step to the physician to create § 271(a) liability via "condition[ing] participation in an activity or receipt of a benefit upon performance of a step or steps of a patented method and establishes the manner or timing of that performance").

6. *Questions:* Suppose that various auto makers install patented intermittent windshield wipers without the consent of the patentee. Does the car dealer infringe the patent by selling the car so equipped? Does the buyer of the car infringe when using the patented intermittent function of the wipers? What if the buyer operates the car without using the wipers at all? Or just without using their patented intermittent function? Does your answer change if the wipers themselves do not infringe a patent, but are manufactured using an infringing process? If a car owner incurred liability for patent infringement by normal operation of the car, would the owner have any action against the seller of the car?

b. Contributing to or Inducing Infringement

Statute: 35 U.S.C. § 271(b)–(c)

Section 271 creates infringement liability beyond the person making, using, selling, etc. in certain circumstances. Review section 271(b)–(c) in particular. As explained before the *Aro I* decision, the case immediately above and the one below are related. Be sure to review the material before *Aro I* as well as that decision, noting carefully that the convertible tops in question in *Aro I* had been licensed by the patentee (on 1952–54 GM convertibles), while the convertible tops in the case below, *Aro II*, had not been licensed by the patentee (on 1952–54 Ford convertibles). What difference does that make to the Court's analysis in *Aro II*?

ARO MANUFACTURING CO., INC. V. CONVERTIBLE TOP REPLACEMENT CO., INC.

377 U.S. 476, 84 S.Ct. 1526 (1964).

MR. JUSTICE BRENNAN delivered the opinion of the Court.

[As in the previous adjudication between these parties (*Aro I*, *supra* page 597), the plaintiff here alleged that Aro's act of supplying replacement fabric for use in repairing its patented convertible tops was a contributory infringement, because the repair itself was a direct infringement. However, in this case (*Aro II*) the tops had been installed without a license from the patentee. Thus, the Court was asked to decide whether repair of the infringing tops constituted direct infringement, and whether the manufacture and sale of the replacement fabric used in that repair constituted contributory infringement.]

* * *

Section 271(a) provides that "whoever without authority makes, uses or sells any patented invention . . . infringes the patent." It is not controverted—nor could it be—that Ford infringed by making and selling cars embodying the patented top-structures without any authority from the patentee. If Ford had had such authority, its purchasers would not have infringed by using the automobiles, for it is fundamental that sale of a patented article by the patentee or under his authority carries with it an "implied license to use." *United States v. Univis Lens Co.*, 316 U.S. 241, 249, 250–251. But with Ford lacking authority to make and sell, it could by its sale of the cars confer on the purchasers no implied license to use, and their use of the patented structures was thus "without authority" and infringing under § 271(a). Not only does that provision explicitly regard an unauthorized user of a patented invention as an infringer, but it has often and clearly been held that unauthorized use, without more, constitutes infringement.

If the owner's *use* infringed, so also did his *repair* of the top-structure, as by replacing the worn-out fabric component. Where use infringes, repair does also, for it perpetuates the infringing use. * * * Consequently replacement of worn-out fabric components with fabrics sold by Aro, held in *Aro I* to constitute "repair" rather than "reconstruction" and thus to be permissible in the case of licensed General Motors cars, was not permissible here in the case of unlicensed Ford cars. Here, as was not the case in *Aro I*, the direct infringement by the car owners that is prerequisite to contributory infringement by Aro was unquestionably established.

We turn next to the question whether Aro, as supplier of replacement fabrics for use in the infringing repair by the Ford car owners, was a contributory infringer under § 271(c) of the Patent Code. * * * We think Aro was indeed liable under this provision.

Such a result would plainly have obtained under the contributory-infringement case law that § 271 (c) was intended to codify. Indeed, most of the law was established in cases where, as here, suit was brought to hold liable for contributory infringement a supplier of replacement parts specially designed for use in the repair of infringing articles. In *Union Tool Co. v. Wilson*, [259 U.S. 107, 113–114], the Court held that where use of the patented machines themselves was not authorized,

"There was, consequently, no implied license to use the spare parts in these machines. As such use, unless licensed, clearly constituted an infringement, the sale of the spare parts to be so used violated the injunction [enjoining infringement]."

As early as 1897, Circuit Judge Taft, as he then was, thought it "well settled" that

"where one makes and sells one element of a combination covered by a patent with the intention and for the purpose of bringing about its use in such a combination he is guilty of contributory infringement and is equally liable to the patentee with him who in fact organizes the complete combination." *Thomson-Houston Elec. Co. v. Ohio Brass Co.*, 80 F. 712, 721 (C.A. 6th Cir. 1897).

While conceding that in the case of a machine purchased from the patentee, one "may knowingly assist in assembling, repairing, and renewing a patented combination by furnishing some of the needed parts," Judge Taft added: "but, when he does so, he must ascertain, if he would escape liability for infringement, that the one buying and using them for this purpose has a license, express or implied, to do so." *Id.*, at 723. * * *

"The right of one, other than the patentee, furnishing repair parts of a patented combination, can be no greater than that of the user, and he is bound to see that no other use of such parts is made than that authorized by the user's license." *National Malleable Casting Co. v. American Steel Foundries*, 182 F. 626, 641 (C.C.D.N.J.1910).

In enacting § 271(c), Congress clearly succeeded in its objective of codifying this case law. The language of the section fits perfectly Aro's activity of selling "a component of a patented . . . combination . . ., constituting a material part of the invention, . . . especially made or especially adapted for use in an infringement of such patent, and not a staple article or commodity of commerce suitable for substantial noninfringing use." Indeed, this is the almost unique case in which the component was hardly suitable for *any* noninfringing use.[7] On this basis both the District Court originally, 119 U.S.P.Q., at 124, and the Court of Appeals in the instant case, 312 F.2d, at 57, held that Aro was a contributory infringer within the precise letter of § 271(c). *See also Aro I*, 365 U.S., at 341.

However, the language of § 271(c) presents a question, apparently not noticed by the parties or the courts below, concerning the element of knowledge that must be brought home to Aro before liability can be imposed. It is only sale of a component of a patented combination "*knowing*

[7] Aro's factory manager admitted that the fabric replacements in question not only were specially designed for the Ford convertibles but would not, to his knowledge, fit the top-structures of any other cars.

the same to be especially made or especially adapted for use in an infringement of such patent" that is contributory infringement under the statute. Was Aro "knowing" within the statutory meaning because—as it admits, and as the lower courts found—it knew that its replacement fabrics were especially designed for use in the 1952–1954 Ford convertible tops and were not suitable for other use? Or does the statute require a further showing that Aro knew that the tops were patented, and knew also that Ford was not licensed under the patent so that any fabric replacement by a Ford car owner constituted infringement?

On this question a majority of the Court is of the view that § 271(c) does require a showing that the alleged contributory infringer knew that the combination for which his component was especially designed was both patented and infringing. With respect to many of the replacement-fabric sales involved in this case, Aro clearly had such knowledge. For by letter dated January 2, 1954, AB informed Aro that it held the [relevant] patent; that it had granted a license under the patent to General Motors but to no one else; and that "It is obvious, from the foregoing and from an inspection of the convertible automobile sold by the Ford Motor Company, that anyone selling ready-made replacement fabrics for these automobiles would be guilty of contributory infringement of said patent." Thus the Court's interpretation of the knowledge requirement affords Aro no defense with respect to replacement-fabric sales made after January 2, 1954. It would appear that the overwhelming majority of the sales were in fact made after that date, since the oldest of the cars were 1952 models and since the average life of a fabric top is said to be three years. With respect to any sales that were made before that date, however, Aro cannot be held liable in the absence of a showing that at that time it had already acquired the requisite knowledge that the Ford car tops were patented and infringing. When the case is remanded, a finding of fact must be made on this question by the District Court, and, unless Aro is found to have had such prior knowledge, the judgment imposing liability must be vacated as to any sales made before January 2, 1954. As to subsequent sales, however, we hold, in agreement with the lower courts, that Aro is liable for contributory infringement within the terms of [section] 271(c).

[The Court went on to analyze the effect of a July 1955 license agreement with Ford, which ultimately eliminated liability for a large portion of the Ford tops sold because it meant that subsequent use and repair of the tops by owners of the Ford cars would not infringe—a question of exhaustion addressed in Part B.2. of this chapter.]

* * *

NOTES

1. *Knowledge for Inducement:* Section 271(b) provides another avenue by which a party other than the direct infringer may become liable for the infringement: "Whoever actively induces infringement of a patent shall be liable as an infringer." The Supreme Court ruled on the knowledge element of inducement in *Global-Tech Appliances, Inc. v. SEB S.A.*, 563 U.S. 754 (2011), where it relied on *Aro II*'s interpretation of 271(c), as well as the close historical relationship of the infringing acts separated by Congress into § 271(b) & (c), to reach the conclusion that the same knowledge—knowledge of the patent—is required under both § 271(b) & (c). Liability under section 271(b), then, requires that the inducing party act with specific intent to encourage the *infringement*, and not merely to induce the *acts* which are ultimately determined to constitute infringement, entailing proof (1) that an act of direct infringement occurred, (2) that the defendant's conduct actually induced the infringing act, (3) that the defendant knew of the existence of the patent, and (4) that the defendant knew or should have known that its actions would induce actual infringement.

An additional question in *GlobalTech* was by what standard the knowledge must be proven. The Court ruled that willful blindness as to the infringing nature of the acts being induced would satisfy the requirement of knowledge, but that deliberate indifference to a known risk was insufficient. Willful blindness in this context "require[s] active efforts by an inducer to avoid knowing about the infringing nature of the activities." The Court held that the evidence in the case satisfied the willful blindness requirement: "[The] evidence was more than sufficient for a jury to find that Pentalpha subjectively believed there was a high probability that SEB's fryer was patented [it copied all but the cosmetic features of the innovative SEB fryer after buying a unit overseas, which the Court noted would not bear U.S. patent markings], that Pentalpha took deliberate steps to avoid knowing that fact [by obtaining a non-infringement opinion from a patent attorney without notifying him that the product had been copied from SEB], and that it therefore willfully blinded itself to the infringing nature of [its customer] Sunbeam's sales." Would the manufacturer of the units, Pentalpha, have fared better if it had not obtained a noninfringement opinion?

2. *Knowledge, Intent, and Opinions of Counsel:* Under section 298 (added by the AIA):

> The failure of an infringer to obtain the advice of counsel with respect to any allegedly infringed patent, or the failure of the infringer to present such advice to the court or jury, may not be used to prove that the accused infringer willfully infringed the patent or that the infringer intended to induce infringement of the patent.

35 U.S.C. § 298. The section applies to infringement actions filed on or after January 14, 2013 (the effective date of a technical corrections act, *see* PL 112–274, § 1(a), 126 Stat. 2456 (Jan. 14, 2013). Congress was motivated to add section 298 by a contrary opinion by the Federal Circuit, which held that

failure to obtain an opinion of counsel as to infringement may constitute circumstantial evidence of intent to induce infringement. *See Broadcom Corp. v. Qualcomm, Inc.*, 543 F.3d 683, 699–700 (Fed. Cir. 2008) (superseded by statute).

3. *Role of Good-Faith Belief:* As both the statutes and decisions make clear, indirect infringement liability requires both the existence of direct infringement and certain connections between that direct infringement and the indirect infringer, as further specified in either section 271(b) (inducement) or section 271(c) (contributory infringement). And liability for direct infringement requires a *valid* patent to have been *infringed* (via one or more of the activities listed in section 271(a)).

Under the Supreme Court's interpretation of both 271(b) and 271(c), a good faith belief that the underlying act in question was *noninfringing* is a good defense to indirect infringement liability, a conclusion that follows from the knowledge requirement for indirect infringement liability under the decisions in *Aro II* ("[Section] 271(c) does requires a showing that the alleged contributory infringer knew that the combination for which his component was especially designed was both patented and infringing.") and *Global-Tech* ("[T]he same knowledge is needed for induced infringement under § 271(b) [as for contributory infringement under § 271(c).] . . . . Accordingly, we now hold that induced infringement under § 271(b) requires knowledge that the induced acts constitute patent infringement."). Why, then, might a good faith belief that the underlying patent is *invalid* not similarly serve as a good defense to indirect infringement liability? Read the following excerpt and consider whether you agree:

> The question the Court confronts today concerns whether a defendant's belief regarding patent validity is a defense to a claim of induced infringement. It is not. The scienter element for induced infringement concerns infringement; that is a different issue than validity. Section 271(b) requires that the defendant "actively induce[d] infringement." That language requires intent to "bring about the desired result," which is infringement. [*Global-Tech,*] 131 S.Ct., at 2065. And because infringement and validity are separate issues under the Act, belief regarding validity cannot negate the scienter required under § 271(b).
>
> * * *
>
> Indeed, the issues of infringement and validity appear in separate parts of the Patent Act. Part III of the Act deals with "Patents and Protection of Patent Rights," including the right to be free from infringement. §§ 251–329. Part II, entitled "Patentability of Inventions and Grants of Patents," defines what constitutes a valid patent. §§ 100–212. Further, noninfringement and invalidity are listed as two separate defenses, *see* §§ 282(b)(1), (2), and defendants are free to raise either or both of them. *See Cardinal, supra*, at 98.

> Were this Court to interpret § 271(b) as permitting a defense of belief in invalidity, it would conflate the issues of infringement and validity.
>
> Allowing this new defense would also undermine a presumption that is a "common core of thought and truth" reflected in this Court's precedents for a century. Under the Patent Act, and the case law before its passage, a patent is "presumed valid." § 282(a). That presumption takes away any need for a plaintiff to prove his patent is valid to bring a claim. But if belief in invalidity were a defense to induced infringement, the force of that presumption would be lessened to a drastic degree, for a defendant could prevail if he proved he reasonably believed the patent was invalid.

Commil USA, LLC v. Cisco Systems, Inc., 575 U.S. 632, 642–44 (2015) (some citations omitted). The dissenting opinion in *Commil* sharply disagreed with the reasoning of the majority opinion. In part, the dissent reasoned as follows:

> Infringing a patent means invading a patentee's exclusive right to practice his claimed invention. Only valid patents confer this right to exclusivity—invalid patents do not. *FTC v. Actavis, Inc.*, 133 S.Ct. 2223, 2230–31 (2013). It follows, as night the day, that only valid patents can be infringed. To talk of infringing an invalid patent is to talk nonsense.
>
> Induced infringement, we have said, "requires knowledge that the induced acts constitute patent infringement." *Global-Tech Appliances, Inc. v. SEB S. A.*, 131 S.Ct. 2060, 2068 (2011). Because only valid patents can be infringed, anyone with a good-faith belief in a patent's invalidity necessarily believes the patent cannot be infringed. And it is impossible for anyone who believes that a patent cannot be infringed to induce actions that he knows will infringe it. A good-faith belief that a patent is invalid is therefore a defense to induced infringement of that patent.

575 U.S. at 648 (Scalia, J., dissenting).

4. *Requirement of Direct Infringement:* In another inducement case, *Limelight Networks, Inc. v. Akamai Technologies, Inc.*, 572 U.S. 915 (2014), the Supreme Court focused on the existence of an underlying act of direct infringement—which of course must include all elements of the patent claim in question. In the decision below, the Federal Circuit had concluded that a defendant could be held liable under § 271(b) if it carried out some of the steps within a claimed process and induced other parties to carry out the remaining steps in the claimed process—even if no single party could be held liable as a direct infringer. *See Akamai Technologies, Inc. v. Limelight Networks, Inc.*, 692 F.3d 1301, 1308–18 (Fed. Cir. 2012) (en banc) (per curiam). The Supreme Court disagreed with the Federal Circuit on the question of whether liability may be found under § 271(b) for inducing infringement when there is no single actor that can be charged with liability for direct infringement of the patent. It first referred to the decision in *Aro I*, reproduced in part on page 597, *supra*, noting

that "our case law leaves no doubt that inducement liability may arise 'if, but only if, [there is] . . . direct infringement.' " 572 U.S. at 921. The Court emphasized the vital importance of each element in a patent claim, which means that "a patentee's rights extend only to the claimed combination of elements, and no further." *Id.* It then rejected all attempts to expand the scope of inducement liability under § 271(b) to aggregate and capture the acts of multiple parties whose performance of individual elements of a process claim cannot be combined for direct infringement liability.

The Supreme Court did *not*, however, address the merits of the question of *when* and *how* the acts of multiple parties properly *may be combined or aggregated* to show direct infringement. The Court remanded the case to the Federal Circuit for further proceedings. The latest Federal Circuit opinion in the case, briefly excerpted in Note 5 on pages 602–604, *supra*, addresses the matter of combining or aggregating the acts of multiple parties for direct infringement liability under § 271(a).

5. *"Natural" Infringement:* Suppose a manufacturer makes a drug which, after ingestion by humans, is converted by the human body into a patented compound. Would the manufacturer be liable for patent infringement? What about the consumer?

6. *Direct Infringer Knowledge:* Must a direct infringer know that a process or product is patented and infringing in order to be held liable? *Compare* § 271(a) *with* §§ 271(c) & 287(a). Why should such knowledge be a prerequisite to liability for contributory infringement or inducement? Note that the majority in *Aro II* rejected the dissent's suggestion that the knowledge requirement could be satisfied by establishing that the defendant knew "that the component was especially designed for use in a combination and was not a staple article suitable for substantial other use," without necessarily knowing that the combination was either patented or infringing. 377 U.S. at 491 n.8. Which interpretation would better serve the purposes of the patent monopoly? Which would be easier to apply in practice?

7. *Supply Without Direct Infringement:* If the defendant sells a component part specially designed for an infringing use, but the buyer does not in fact use the part in any infringing way, is the seller still liable for contributory infringement?

8. *Multiple-Use Components:* Would the analysis in *Aro II* have been different if the replacement fabric had been designed to fit both the infringing and the noninfringing convertible tops? Suppose it fit the infringing tops, did not fit the noninfringing tops, but could also be used as a tarp to keep firewood dry?

9. *Pre- and Post-Term Activities:* Suppose parts that the seller knows are suitable for use in an infringing combination are sold before the combination patent issues and are assembled into the infringing combination after the patent issues? Alternatively, what if such parts are sold shortly before the patent term expires and are assembled after expiration?

10. *Officer Liability:* Under familiar principles of tort law, a principal (for example, a corporation) can be held liable for patent infringement by its agent (for example, an employee) acting within the scope of the agent-principal relationship. *See, e.g., Westinghouse Elec. & Mfg. Co. v. Independent Wireless Tel. Co.*, 300 F. 748 (S.D.N.Y.1924). Under what circumstances, if any, should corporate officers be held personally liable for a corporation's direct infringement in which they do not individually participate?

11. *Generic Drug Applications:* In 1984, Congress created a new, and somewhat artificial, act of infringement, with limited remedies, by adding sections 271(e)(2) and (e)(4) to the patent statutes. Under section 271(e)(2), it is an infringement of a drug patent to file certain applications for streamlined regulatory approval of generic equivalents (an Abbreviated New Drug Application, or ANDA) which the applicant believes will not infringe the patent on the brand-name drug (for example, because the applicant believes the patent is invalid). If the patentee fails to commence an infringement action within 45 days after the filing of the ANDA (and timely notice to the patentee), the FDA may approve the generic drug for marketing. 21 U.S.C. § 355(c)(3)(C). Where the generic drug applicant is found liable for infringement under section 271(e)(2), the limited remedies set forth in section 271(e)(4) are exclusive. Why did Congress create this new act of infringement, and then deny the plaintiff access to the full range of remedies?

In 2003, Congress added a new section subsection (e)(5) to section 271 to provide that, if a brand name drug manufacturer does not sue a generic drug maker for infringement arising from the latter's ANDA within 45 days of receiving notice of the ANDA filing, the generic drug maker may seek a declaratory judgment that the patent for the drug is invalid or not infringed. The declaratory judgment sought by the generic drug maker must satisfy the Article III case or controversy rule, as applied by the Supreme Court in *MedImmune, Inc. v. Genentech, Inc.* (excerpted later in this chapter): "This means that [the generic drug maker] is only required to satisfy Article III, which includes standing and ripeness, by showing under 'all the circumstances' an actual or imminent injury caused by the defendant that can be redressed by judicial relief and that is of 'sufficient immediacy and reality to warrant the issuance of a declaratory judgment.' " *Teva Pharmaceuticals USA, Inc. v. Novartis Pharmaceuticals Corp.*, 482 F.3d 1330, 1338–39 (Fed. Cir. 2007) (overruling prior Federal Circuit case law requiring the generic maker to show that the patent owner had taken action giving the generic maker a "reasonable apprehension" of suit, in addition to satisfying the requirements of § 271(e)(5)).

c. Cross-Border Infringement

Statute: 35 U.S.C. § 271(f)–(g)

Liability for infringement of United States patent laws generally arises only when an act of direct infringement takes place within United States territory, which reflects a jurisdictional principle called territoriality. (Look back at the language of section 271(a).) There are, however, some limited exceptions to the prevailing rule of territoriality in U.S. patent law. Section 271(f) and (g) describe activities that take place partly in the United States and partly overseas and create infringement liability under U.S. patent law for those activities.

In two relatively recent cases, the Supreme Court has addressed issues related to the scope of section 271(f).

MICROSOFT CORP. v. AT&T CORP.

550 U.S. 437, 127 S.Ct. 1746 (2007).

JUSTICE GINSBURG delivered the opinion of the Court, except as to footnote 14.

It is the general rule under United States patent law that no infringement occurs when a patented product is made and sold in another country. There is an exception. Section 271(f) of the Patent Act, adopted in 1984, provides that infringement does occur when one "supplies . . . from the United States," for "combination" abroad, a patented invention's "components." 35 U.S.C. § 271(f)(1). This case concerns the applicability of § 271(f) to computer software first sent from the United States to a foreign manufacturer on a master disk, or by electronic transmission, then copied by the foreign recipient for installation on computers made and sold abroad.

AT&T holds a patent on an apparatus for digitally encoding and compressing recorded speech. Microsoft's Windows operating system, it is conceded, has the potential to infringe AT&T's patent, because Windows incorporates software code that, when installed, enables a computer to process speech in the manner claimed by that patent. It bears emphasis, however, that uninstalled Windows software does not infringe AT&T's patent any more than a computer standing alone does; instead, the patent is infringed only when a computer is loaded with Windows and is thereby rendered capable of performing as the patented speech processor. * * *

The master disk or electronic transmission Microsoft sends from the United States is never installed on any of the foreign-made computers in question. Instead, copies made abroad are used for installation. Because Microsoft does not export from the United States the copies actually installed, it does not "suppl[y] . . . from the United States" "components" of the relevant computers, and therefore is not liable under § 271(f) as currently written.

Plausible arguments can be made for and against extending § 271(f) to the conduct charged in this case as infringing AT&T's patent. Recognizing that § 271(f) is an exception to the general rule that our patent law does not apply extraterritorially, we resist giving the language in which Congress cast § 271(f) an expansive interpretation. Our decision leaves to

Congress' informed judgment any adjustment of § 271(f) it deems necessary or proper.

I

Our decision some 35 years ago in *Deepsouth Packing Co. v. Laitram Corp.*, 406 U.S. 518 (1972), a case about a shrimp deveining machine, led Congress to enact § 271(f). In that case, Laitram, holder of a patent on the time-and-expense-saving machine, sued Deepsouth, manufacturer of an infringing deveiner. Deepsouth conceded that the Patent Act barred it from making and selling its deveining machine in the United States, but sought to salvage a portion of its business: Nothing in United States patent law, Deepsouth urged, stopped it from making in the United States the *parts* of its deveiner, as opposed to the machine itself, and selling those *parts* to foreign buyers for assembly and use abroad. *Id.*, at 522–524. We agreed.

Interpreting our patent law as then written, we reiterated in *Deepsouth* that it was "not an infringement to make or use a patented product outside of the United States." *Id.*, at 527; *see* 35 U.S.C. § 271(a) (1970 ed.) ("[W]hoever without authority makes, uses or sells any patented invention, within the United States during the term of the patent therefor, infringes the patent."). Deepsouth's foreign buyers did not infringe Laitram's patent, we held, because they assembled and used the deveining machines outside the United States. Deepsouth, we therefore concluded, could not be charged with inducing or contributing to an infringement. 406 U.S., at 526–527. Nor could Deepsouth be held liable as a direct infringer, for it did not make, sell, or use the patented invention—the fully assembled deveining machine—within the United States. The parts of the machine were not themselves patented, we noted, hence export of those parts, unassembled, did not rank as an infringement of Laitram's patent. *Id.*, at 527–529.

Laitram had argued in *Deepsouth* that resistance to extension of the patent privilege to cover exported parts "derived from too narrow and technical an interpretation of the [Patent Act]." *Id.*, at 529. Rejecting that argument, we referred to prior decisions holding that "a combination patent protects only against the operable assembly of the whole and not the manufacture of its parts." *Id.*, at 528. Congress' codification of patent law, we said, signaled no intention to broaden the scope of the privilege. *Id.*, at 530 ("When, as here, the Constitution is permissive, the sign of how far Congress has chosen to go can come only from Congress."). And we again emphasized that

> "[o]ur patent system makes no claim to extraterritorial effect; these acts of Congress do not, and were not intended to, operate beyond the limits of the United States; and we correspondingly reject the claims of others to such control over our markets." *Id.*,

at 531 (quoting *Brown v. Duchesne,* 19 How. 183, 195 ([U.S.] 1857)).

Absent "a clear congressional indication of intent," we stated, courts had no warrant to stop the manufacture and sale of the parts of patented inventions for assembly and use abroad. 406 U.S., at 532.

Focusing its attention on *Deepsouth,* Congress enacted § 271(f). The provision expands the definition of infringement to include supplying from the United States a patented invention's components:

> "(1) Whoever without authority supplies or causes to be supplied in or from the United States all or a substantial portion of the components of a patented invention, where such components are uncombined in whole or in part, in such manner as to actively induce the combination of such components outside of the United States in a manner that would infringe the patent if such combination occurred within the United States, shall be liable as an infringer.
>
> "(2) Whoever without authority supplies or causes to be supplied in or from the United States any component of a patented invention that is especially made or especially adapted for use in the invention and not a staple article or commodity of commerce suitable for substantial noninfringing use, where such component is uncombined in whole or in part, knowing that such component is so made or adapted and intending that such component will be combined outside of the United States in a manner that would infringe the patent if such combination occurred within the United States, shall be liable as an infringer." 35 U.S.C. § 271(f).

II

Windows is designed, authored, and tested at Microsoft's Redmond, Washington, headquarters. Microsoft sells Windows to end users and computer manufacturers, both foreign and domestic. Purchasing manufacturers install the software onto the computers they sell. Microsoft sends to each of the foreign manufacturers a master version of Windows, either on a disk or via encrypted electronic transmission. The manufacturer uses the master version to generate copies. Those copies, not the master sent by Microsoft, are installed on the foreign manufacturer's computers. Once assembly is complete, the foreign-made computers are sold to users abroad.

AT&T's patent ('580 patent) is for an apparatus (as relevant here, a computer) capable of digitally encoding and compressing recorded speech. Windows, the parties agree, contains software that enables a computer to process speech in the manner claimed by the '580 patent. In 2001, AT&T filed an infringement suit in the United States District Court for the

Southern District of New York, charging Microsoft with liability for domestic and foreign installations of Windows. [Microsoft contested liability based on the foreign installations while acknowledging domestic infringement.]

* * *

III

A

This case poses two questions: First, when, or in what form, does software qualify as a "component" under § 271(f)? Second, were "components" of the foreign-made computers involved in this case "supplie[d]" by Microsoft "from the United States"?[7]

As to the first question, no one in this litigation argues that software can *never* rank as a "component" under § 271(f). The parties disagree, however, over the stage at which software becomes a component. Software, the "set of instructions, known as code, that directs a computer to perform specified functions or operations," *Fantasy Sports Properties, Inc. v. Sportsline.com, Inc.*, 287 F.3d 1108, 1118 (C.A.Fed.2002), can be conceptualized in (at least) two ways. One can speak of software in the abstract: the instructions themselves detached from any medium. (An analogy: The notes of Beethoven's Ninth Symphony.) One can alternatively envision a tangible "copy" of software, the instructions encoded on a medium such as a CD-ROM. (Sheet music for Beethoven's Ninth.) AT&T argues that software in the abstract, not simply a particular copy of software, qualifies as a "component" under § 271(f). Microsoft and the United States argue that only a copy of software, not software in the abstract, can be a component.

The significance of these diverse views becomes apparent when we turn to the second question: Were components of the foreign-made computers involved in this case "supplie[d]" by Microsoft "from the United States"? If the relevant components are the copies of Windows actually installed on the foreign computers, AT&T could not persuasively argue that those components, though generated abroad, were "supplie[d] . . . from the United States" as § 271(f) requires for liability to attach. If, on the other hand, Windows in the abstract qualifies as a component within § 271(f)'s compass, it would not matter that the master copies of Windows software dispatched from the United States were not themselves installed abroad as working parts of the foreign computers.

[7] The record leaves unclear which paragraph of § 271(f) AT & T's claim invokes. While there are differences between § 271(f)(1) and (f)(2), the parties do not suggest that those differences are outcome determinative. *Cf. infra*, at 14–15, n. 16 (explaining why both paragraphs yield the same result). For clarity's sake, we focus our analysis on the text of § 271(f)(1).

With this explanation of the relationship between the two questions in view, we further consider the twin inquiries.

B

First, when, or in what form, does software become a "component" under § 271(f)? We construe § 271(f)'s terms "in accordance with [their] ordinary or natural meaning." *FDIC v. Meyer,* 510 U.S. 471, 476 (1994). Section 271(f) applies to the supply abroad of the "components of a patented invention, where *such components* are uncombined in whole or in part, in such manner as to actively induce the combination of *such components.*" § 271(f)(1) (emphasis added). The provision thus applies only to "such components" as are combined to form the "patented invention" at issue. The patented invention here is AT&T's speech-processing computer.

* * *

Because it is so easy to encode software's instructions onto a medium that can be read by a computer, AT&T intimates, that extra step should not play a decisive role under § 271(f). But the extra step is what renders the software a usable, combinable part of a computer; easy or not, the copy-producing step is essential. Moreover, many tools may be used easily and inexpensively to generate the parts of a device. A machine for making sprockets might be used by a manufacturer to produce tens of thousands of sprockets an hour. That does not make the machine a "component" of the tens of thousands of devices in which the sprockets are incorporated, at least not under any ordinary understanding of the term "component." Congress, of course, might have included within § 271(f)'s compass, for example, not only combinable "components" of a patented invention, but also "information, instructions, or tools from which those components readily may be generated." It did not. In sum, a copy of Windows, not Windows in the abstract, qualifies as a "component" under § 271(f).

C

The next question, has Microsoft "supplie[d] . . . from the United States" components of the computers here involved? Under a conventional reading of § 271(f)'s text, the answer would be "No," for the foreign-made copies of Windows actually installed on the computers were "supplie[d]" from places outside the United States. * * *

* * *

Section 271(f) prohibits the supply of components "from the United States . . . in such manner as to actively induce the combination of *such components.*" § 271(f)(1) (emphasis added). Under this formulation, the very components supplied from the United States, and not copies thereof, trigger § 271(f) liability when combined abroad to form the patented invention at issue. Here, as we have repeatedly noted, the copies of Windows actually installed on the foreign computers were not themselves supplied from the United States.[14] Indeed, those copies did not exist until they were generated by third parties outside the United States. Copying software abroad, all might agree, is indeed easy and inexpensive. But the same could be said of other items: "Keys or machine parts might be copied from a master; chemical or biological substances might be created by reproduction; and paper products might be made by electronic copying and printing." Brief for United States as *Amicus Curiae* 24. *See also supra,* at 11–12 (rejecting argument similarly based on ease of copying in construing "component"). Section 271(f) contains no instruction to gauge when duplication is easy and cheap enough to deem a copy in fact made abroad nevertheless "supplie[d] . . . from the United States." The absence of anything addressing copying in the statutory text weighs against a judicial determination that replication abroad of a master dispatched from the United States "supplies" the foreign-made copies from the United States within the intendment of § 271(f).

D

Any doubt that Microsoft's conduct falls outside § 271(f)'s compass would be resolved by the presumption against extraterritoriality, on which we have already touched. *See supra,* at 2, 4. The presumption that United States law governs domestically but does not rule the world applies with particular force in patent law. The traditional understanding that our patent law "operate [s] only domestically and d[oes] not extend to foreign activities," is embedded in the Patent Act itself, which provides that a patent confers exclusive rights in an invention within the United States. 35 U.S.C. § 154(a)(1) (patentee's rights over invention apply to manufacture, use, or sale "throughout the United States" and to importation "into the United States").

As a principle of general application, moreover, we have stated that courts should "assume that legislators take account of the legitimate sovereign interests of other nations when they write American laws." Thus, the United States accurately conveyed in this case: "Foreign conduct is [generally] the domain of foreign law," and in the area here involved, in particular, foreign law "may embody different policy judgments about the relative rights of inventors, competitors, and the public in patented inventions." * * *

* * *

* * * In short, foreign law alone, not United States law, currently governs the manufacture and sale of components of patented inventions in

[14] In a footnote, Microsoft suggests that even a disk shipped from the United States, and used to install Windows directly on a foreign computer, would not give rise to liability under § 271(f) if the disk were removed after installation. We need not and do not reach that issue here.

foreign countries. If AT&T desires to prevent copying in foreign countries, its remedy today lies in obtaining and enforcing foreign patents.

* * *

For the reasons stated, the judgment of the Court of Appeals for the Federal Circuit is

Reversed.

LIFE TECHNOLOGIES CORP. V. PROMEGA CORP.

580 U.S. 140, 137 S.Ct. 734 (2017).

JUSTICE SOTOMAYOR delivered the opinion of the Court.

This case concerns the intersection of international supply chains and federal patent law. Section 271(f)(1) of the Patent Act of 1952 prohibits the supply from the United States of "all or a substantial portion" of the components of a patented invention for combination abroad. We granted certiorari to determine whether a party that supplies a single component of a multicomponent invention for manufacture abroad can be held liable for infringement under § 271(f)(1). We hold that a single component does not constitute a substantial portion of the components that can give rise to liability under § 271(f)(1). Because only a single component of the patented invention at issue here was supplied from the United States, we reverse and remand.

I

A

We begin with an overview of the patent in dispute. Although the science behind the patent is complex, a basic understanding suffices to resolve the question presented by this case.

The Tautz patent, U.S. Reissue Patent No. RE 37,984, claims a toolkit for genetic testing. [The kit takes small samples of DNA and copies or amplifies the sequences to create DNA profiles useful for forensic law enforcement work or in clinical and research work.] For purposes of this litigation, the parties agree that the kit covered by the Tautz patent contains five components: (1) a mixture of primers that mark the part of the DNA strand to be copied; (2) nucleotides for forming replicated strands of DNA; (3) an enzyme known as Taq polymerase; (4) a buffer solution for the amplification; and (5) control DNA. [The parties agreed that the invention was made up of only these five components, so the Court did not consider the broader question of how to identify components of a patent or how to relate "components" to the elements of a patent claim. Although the defendant had a license to the patent, the license only covered making and selling kits for law enforcement use. The patent infringement suit claimed that the defendant had infringed by going outside the scope of the license and selling in clinical and research markets.]

* * *

II

The question before us is whether the supply of a single component of a multicomponent invention is an infringing act under 35 U.S.C. § 271(f)(1). We hold that it is not.

A

The threshold determination to be made is whether § 271(f)(2)'s requirement of "a substantial portion" of the components of a patented invention refers to a quantitative or qualitative measurement. Life Technologies and the United States argue that the text of § 271(f)(1) establishes a quantitative threshold, and that the threshold must be greater than one. Promega defends the Federal Circuit's reading of the statute, arguing that a "substantial portion" of the components includes a single component if that component is sufficiently important to the invention.

We look first to the text of the statute. The Patent Act itself does not define the term "substantial," and so we turn to its ordinary meaning. Here we find little help. All agree the term is ambiguous and, taken in isolation, might refer to an important portion or to a large portion. "Substantial," as it is commonly understood, may refer either to qualitative importance or to quantitatively large size. *See, e.g.,* WEBSTER'S THIRD NEW INTERNATIONAL DICTIONARY 2280 (defs. 1c, 2c) (1981) (WEBSTER'S THIRD) ("important, essential," or "considerable in amount, value, or worth"); 17 OXFORD ENGLISH DICTIONARY 67 (defs. 5a, 9) (2d ed. 1989) (OED) ("That is, constitutes, or involves an essential part, point, or feature; essential, material," or "Of ample or considerable amount, quantity, or dimensions").

The context in which "substantial" appears in the statute, however, points to a quantitative meaning here. Its neighboring terms are the first clue. "[A] word is given more precise content by the neighboring words with which it is associated." *United States v. Williams*, 553 U.S. 285, 294 (2008). Both "all" and "portion" convey a quantitative meaning. "All" means the entire quantity, without reference to relative importance. *See, e.g.*, WEBSTER'S THIRD 54 (defs. 1a, 2a, 3) ("that is the whole amount or quantity of," or "every member or individual component of," or "the whole number or sum of "); 1 OED 324 (def. 2) ("The entire number of; the individual components of, without exception"). "Portion" likewise refers to some quantity less than all. WEBSTER'S THIRD 1768 (defs. 1, 3a) ("an individual's part or share of something," or "a part of a whole"); 12 OED 154, 155 (def. 1a, 5a) ("The part (of anything) allotted or belonging to one person," or "A part of any whole"). Conversely, there is nothing in the neighboring text to ground a qualitative interpretation.

Moreover, the phrase "substantial portion" is modified by "of the components of a patented invention." It is the supply of all or a substantial portion "of the components" of a patented invention that triggers liability for infringement. But if "substantial" has a qualitative meaning, then the more natural way to write the opening clause of the provision would be to not reference "the components" at all. Instead, the opening clause of § 271(f)(1) could have triggered liability for the supply of "all or a substantial portion of . . . a patented invention, where [its] components are uncombined in whole or in part." A qualitative reading would render the phrase "of the components" unnecessary the first time it is used in § 271(f)(1). Whenever possible, however, we should favor an interpretation that gives meaning to each statutory provision. *See Hibbs v. Winn*, 542 U.S. 88, 101 (2004). Only the quantitative approach does so here. Thus, "substantial," in the context of § 271(f)(1), is most reasonably read to connote a quantitative measure.

* * *

* * * Promega reads § 271(f)(1) to mean that the answer to whether a given portion of the components is "substantial" depends not only on the number of components involved but also on their qualitative importance to the invention overall. At first blush, there is some appeal to the idea that, in close cases, a subjective analysis of the qualitative importance of a component may help determine whether it is a "substantial portion" of the components of a patent. But, for the reasons discussed above, the statute's structure provides little support for a qualitative interpretation of the term.

Nor would considering the qualitative importance of a component necessarily help resolve close cases. To the contrary, it might just as easily complicate the factfinder's review. Surely a great many components of an invention (if not every component) are important. * * * How are courts—or, for that matter, market participants attempting to avoid liability—to determine the relative importance of the components of an invention? Neither Promega nor the Federal Circuit offers an easy way to make this decision. Accordingly, we conclude that a quantitative interpretation hews most closely to the text of the statute and provides an administrable construction.

B

Having determined that the term "substantial portion" refers to a quantitative measurement, we must next decide whether, as a matter of law, a single component can ever constitute a "substantial portion" so as to trigger liability under § 271(f)(1). The answer is no.

As before, we begin with the text of the statute. Section 271(f)(1) consistently refers to "components" in the plural. The section is targeted toward the supply of all or a substantial portion "of the *components*," where "such *components*" are uncombined, in a manner that actively induces the combination of "such *components*" outside the United States. Text specifying a substantial portion of "components," plural, indicates that multiple components constitute the substantial portion.

The structure of § 271(f) reinforces this reading. Section 271(f)(2), which is § 271(f)(1)'s companion provision, reads as follows:

> "Whoever without authority supplies or causes to be supplied in or from the United States any component of a patented invention that is especially made or especially adapted for use in the invention and not a staple article or commodity of commerce suitable for substantial noninfringing use, where such component is uncombined in whole or in part, knowing that such component is so made or adapted and intending that such component will be combined outside of the United States in a manner that would infringe the patent if such combination occurred within the United States, shall be liable as an infringer."

Reading § 271(f)(1) to refer to more than one component allows the two provisions to work in tandem. Whereas § 271(f)(1) refers to "components," plural, § 271(f)(2) refers to "any component," singular. And, whereas § 271(f)(1) speaks to whether the components supplied by a party constitute a substantial portion of the components, § 271(f)(2) speaks to whether a party has supplied "any" noncommodity component "especially made or especially adapted for use in the invention."

We do not disagree with the Federal Circuit's observation that the two provisions concern different scenarios. *See* 773 F. 3d, at 1354. As this Court has previously observed, §§ 271(f)(1) and 271(f)(2) "differ, among other things, on the quantity of components that must be 'supplie[d] . . . from the United States' for liability to attach." *Microsoft Corp. v. AT&T Corp.*, 550 U.S. 437, 454, n. 16 (2007). But we do not draw the Federal Circuit's conclusion from these different but related provisions. Reading § 271(f)(1) to cover *any* single component would not only leave little room for § 271(f)(2), but would also undermine § 271(f)(2)'s express reference to a single component "especially made or especially adapted for use in the invention." Our conclusion that § 271(f)(1) prohibits the supply of components, plural, gives each subsection its unique application.

Taken alone, § 271(f)(1)'s reference to "components" might plausibly be read to encompass "component" in the singular. *See* 1 U.S.C. § 1 (instructing that "words importing the plural include the singular," "unless the context indicates otherwise"). But § 271(f)'s text, context, and structure leave us to conclude that when Congress said "components," plural, it meant plural, and when it said "component," singular, it meant singular. We do not today define how close to "all" of the components "a substantial portion" must be. We hold only that one component does not constitute "all or a substantial portion" of a multicomponent invention under § 271(f)(1). This is all that is required to resolve the question presented.

* * *

NOTES

1. *Steps in a Process:* Two years before the Supreme Court's 2007 decision in *Microsoft v. AT&T*, the Federal Circuit addressed arguments related to section 271(f) & (g) as well as arguments related to cross-border infringement under section 271(a) (*see supra* Note 3 on pages 601–602). *See NTP, Inc. v. Research in Motion, Ltd.* ["RIM"], 418 F.3d 1282 (Fed. Cir. 2005). In the portion of the decision applying section 271(f), the Federal Circuit rejected the patent holder's argument that defendant RIM's sales of the Blackberry devices constituted "supplying" a "component" of the patented *method or process*: "By merely supplying *products* to its customers in the United States, RIM is not supplying or causing to be supplied in this country any *steps of a patented process* invention for combination outside the United States and cannot infringe NTP's asserted *method* claims under section 271(f) as a matter of law." *Id.* at 1322–23 (emphasis added).

Then, two years after *Microsoft v. AT&T*, the Federal Circuit more directly ruled that section 271(f) cannot apply to method claims because there is no physical "component" to supply in or from this country. *See Cardiac Pacemakers, Inc. v. St. Jude Medical, Inc.*, 576 F.3d 1348, 1360–65 (Fed. Cir. 2009) (en banc) (overruling a 2005 decision to the contrary). The court reasoned that while method or process patents have "components," those components are the steps of the method or process, not materials or other tangible articles used in practicing the patented method or process. The court stated that the ordinary "meanings [of 'supply'] imply the transfer of a physical object. Supplying an intangible step is thus a physical impossibility." 576 F.3d at 1364.

2. *Knowledge:* If parts with no substantial noninfringing use are sold in the United States and assembled into an infringing device overseas, is the seller of the parts liable for contributory infringement? Does it matter whether the seller knows what they are to be used for?

3. *Supplying Components from Abroad:* If parts are sold overseas for assembly into infringing devices in the United States, can the foreign seller be held liable for contributory infringement?

4. *Section 271(g) Products from Processes:* If a French drug manufacturer makes an unpatented compound using a process which is patented in the United States but not in France, is the process patent infringed by importation of that compound into the United States without the patentee's permission? What if the process is patented in France as well as the United

States, and the manufacturer has a license from the patentee to use the process in France?

In *NTP v. Research in Motion*, discussed in Note 1 above, the Federal Circuit held that the defendant's activities did not involve the importation of a *product* made by a patented process, 35 U.S.C. § 271(g), even though the defendant used a patented method to deliver *wireless emails* to customers within the United States. Citing its prior holding in *Bayer AG v. Housey Pharmaceuticals, Inc.*, 340 F.3d 1367 (Fed.Cir.2003), which held that section 271(g) applies only to the production of physical articles, not intangibles such as information, the Federal Circuit decided that an email is merely a transmission of information, and is therefore not a "product" within the meaning of section 271(g). *Id.* at 1323–24.

4. INFRINGEMENT OF DESIGN PATENTS

Owners of design patents hold, like owners of utility patents on products, the right to make, use, sell, and offer for sale the patented design within the United States, and to import the patented design into the United States.

In *Richardson v. Stanley Works, Inc.*, 597 F.3d 1288, 1293–94 (Fed. Cir. 2010), the Federal Circuit addressed the role of claim construction in design patent infringement analysis (and, one presumes, validity determinations as well). It noted that although "the preferable course ordinarily will be for a district court not to attempt to construe a design patent claim," in cases where a design patent claims an ornamental design that also includes functional elements, the design claim should be narrowly construed. In those cases, a court may "properly factor[ ] out the functional aspects of [the] design as part of its claim construction." "If the patented design is primarily functional rather than ornamental, the patent is invalid. However, when the design also contains ornamental aspects, it is entitled to a design patent whose scope is limited to those aspects alone and does not extend to any functional elements of the claimed article."

With or without claim construction, however, the question remains how to determine whether an accused product contains "the invention" for purposes of assessing design patent infringement.

EGYPTIAN GODDESS, INC. V. SWISA, INC.

543 F.3d 665 (Fed. Cir. 2008)(en banc).

BRYSON, CIRCUIT JUDGE.

We granted rehearing en banc in this design patent case to address the appropriate legal standard to be used in assessing claims of design patent infringement.

Appellant Egyptian Goddess, Inc., ("EGI") brought this action in the United States District Court for the Northern District of Texas, alleging that Swisa, Inc., and Dror Swisa (collectively, "Swisa") had infringed EGI's U.S. Design Patent No. 467,389 ("the '389 patent"). The patent claimed a design for a nail buffer, consisting of a rectangular, hollow tube having a generally square cross-section and featuring buffer surfaces on three of its four sides. Swisa's accused product consists of a rectangular, hollow tube having a square cross-section, but featuring buffer surfaces on all four of its sides.

* * *

Swisa * * * moved for summary judgment of noninfringement. The district court granted the motion. Citing precedent of this court, the district court stated that the plaintiff in a design patent case must prove both (1) that the accused device is "substantially similar" to the claimed design under what is referred to as the "ordinary observer" test, and (2) that the accused device contains "substantially the same points of novelty that distinguished the patented design from the prior art." After comparing the claimed design and the accused product, the court held that Swisa's allegedly infringing product did not incorporate the "point of novelty" of the '389 patent, which the court identified as "a fourth, bare side to the buffer."

The district court noted that the parties disagreed as to the points of novelty in the '389 patent. EGI identified four elements in its design, and for each element it identified prior art that did not embody that element. EGI therefore contended that the point of novelty of the '389 patent is the combination of those four elements. The district court, however, declined to address the question whether the point of novelty could be found in the combination of elements not present in various prior art references, because the court found that a single prior art reference, United States Design Patent No. 416,648 ("the Nailco patent"), contained all but one of the elements of the '389 design. The court described the Nailco Patent as disclosing "a nail buffer with an open and hollow body, raised rectangular pads, and open corners." The only element of the '389 patent design that was not present in the Nailco patent, according to the district court, was "the addition of the fourth side without a pad, thereby transforming the equilateral triangular cross-section into a square." Because the Swisa product does not incorporate the point of novelty of the '389 patent—a fourth side without a pad-the court concluded that there was no infringement.

EGI appealed, and a panel of this court affirmed. The panel agreed with the district court that there was no issue of material fact as to whether the accused Swisa buffer "appropriates the point of novelty of the claimed design." *Egyptian Goddess, Inc. v. Swisa, Inc.*, 498 F.3d 1354, 1355 (Fed.Cir.2007). In reaching that conclusion, the panel stated that the point of novelty in a patented design "can be either a single novel design element or a combination of elements that are individually known in the prior art." The panel added, however, that in order for a combination of individually known design elements to constitute a point of novelty, "the combination must be a nontrivial advance over the prior art."

The panel noted that EGI's asserted point of novelty was a combination of four of the claimed design's elements: (1) an open and hollow body, (2) a square cross-section, (3) raised rectangular buffer pads, and (4) exposed corners. The panel agreed with the district court's observation that the Nailco prior art patent contained each of those elements except that the body was triangular, rather than square, in cross-section. In light of the prior art, the panel determined that "no reasonable juror could conclude that EGI's asserted point of novelty constituted a non-trivial advance over the prior art."

The panel further observed that the various design elements of the claimed design "were each individually disclosed in the prior art." The Swisa buffers, the panel noted, have raised, abrasive pads on all four sides, not just on three of the four sides, as in the claimed design, in which the fourth side is bare. The panel then concluded that "[w]hen considering the prior art in the nail buffer field, this difference between the accused design and the patented design cannot be considered minor." The panel therefore concluded that summary judgment was appropriate.

* * *

This court granted rehearing en banc and asked the parties to address several questions, including whether the "point of novelty" test should continue to be used as a test for infringement of a design patent * * *.

I

The starting point for any discussion of the law of design patents is the Supreme Court's decision in *Gorham Co. v. White*, 81 U.S. 511 (1871). That case involved a design patent for the handles of tablespoons and forks. In its analysis of claim infringement, the Court stated that the test of identity of design "must be sameness of appearance, and mere difference of lines in the drawing or sketch . . . or slight variances in configuration . . . will not destroy the substantial identity." Identity of appearance, the Court explained, or "sameness of effect upon the eye, is the main test of substantial identity of design"; the two need not be the same "to the eye of an expert," because if that were the test, "[t]here never could be piracy of a patented design, for human ingenuity has never yet produced a design, in all its details, exactly like another, so like, that an expert could not distinguish them.".

The *Gorham* Court then set forth the test that has been cited in many subsequent cases: "[I]f, in the eye of an ordinary observer, giving such attention as a purchaser usually gives, two designs are substantially the same, if the resemblance is such as to deceive such an observer, inducing him to purchase one supposing it to be the other, the first one patented is infringed by the other." In the case before it, the Court concluded that "whatever differences there may be between the plaintiffs' design and those of the defendant in details of ornament, they are still the same in general appearance and effect, so much alike that in the market and with purchasers they would pass for the same thing-so much alike that even persons in the trade would be in danger of being deceived."

* * *

Swisa counters that this court may not, and should not, abandon the point of novelty test. According to Swisa, the point of novelty test was adopted by the Supreme Court in *Smith v. Whitman Saddle Co.*, 148 U.S. 674 (1893). * * *

We disagree with Swisa's submission. * * * We conclude that the point of novelty test, as a second and free-standing requirement for proof of design patent infringement, is inconsistent with the ordinary observer test laid down in *Gorham*, is not mandated by *Whitman Saddle* * * *, and is not needed to protect against unduly broad assertions of design patent rights.

* * *

In [*Whitman Saddle*], the Court characterized the patented saddle design as a combination of elements from two saddle designs that were well known in the art. The Court explained that the patented design consisted of a combination of the front half of the so-called Granger saddle and the back end of the so-called Jenifer saddle. The design differed from a simple combination of the two known saddles, according to the Court, only in that the front end of the design had "a nearly perpendicular drop of some inches at the rear of the pommel," unlike in the Granger saddle.

Although the trial court, sitting in equity, concluded that the design was patentable, the Supreme Court disagreed. The Court wrote, "Nothing more was done in this instance (except as hereafter noted) than to put the two halves of these saddles together in the exercise of the ordinary skill of workmen of the trade, and in the way and manner ordinarily done." The Court noted that there was a difference between the pommel of the designed saddle and the pommel of the Granger saddle, and it added that the "shape of the front end being old, the sharp drop of the pommel at the rear seems to constitute what was new and to be material." That feature, however, was not present in the defendants' saddle. * * *

Because *Whitman Saddle* was an action in equity, the Court did not distinguish sharply between its analysis of patentability and its discussion of infringement. Within the same passage, the Court moved from stating that it could not agree with the trial court that the design in issue was patentable to the conclusion that if the design were patentable because of the drop at the rear of the pommel, there was no infringement. Nothing in the Court's opinion suggested that it was fashioning a separate point of novelty test for infringement. The point the Court was making was that, viewed in light of the similarities between the prior art and the patented design, the accused design did not contain the single feature that would have made it appear distinctively similar to the patented design rather than like the numerous prior art designs. For that reason, the Court held, the accused design did not infringe.

Subsequent cases applied that principle, interpreting the ordinary observer test of *Gorham* to require that the perspective of the ordinary observer be informed by a comparison of the patented design and the accused design in light of the prior art, so as to enable the fact-finder to determine whether the accused design had appropriated the inventiveness of the patented design. * * *

* * *

* * * When the differences between the claimed and accused design are viewed in light of the prior art, the attention of the hypothetical ordinary observer will be drawn to those aspects of the claimed design that differ from the prior art. And when the claimed design is close to the prior art designs, small differences between the accused design and the claimed design are likely to be important to the eye of the hypothetical ordinary observer. It was for that reason that the Supreme Court in *Whitman Saddle* focused on the one feature of the patented saddle design that departed from the prior art—the sharp drop at the rear of the pommel. To an observer familiar with the multitude of prior art saddle designs, * * * the sharp drop at the rear of the pommel would be important to the overall appearance of the design and would serve to distinguish the accused design, which did not possess that feature, from the claimed design.

* * *

Not only is this approach consistent with the precedents discussed above, but it makes sense as a matter of logic as well. Particularly in close cases, it can be difficult to answer the question whether one thing is like another without being given a frame of reference. The context in which the claimed and accused designs are compared, *i.e.*, the background prior art, provides such a frame of reference and is therefore often useful in the process of comparison. Where the frame of reference consists of numerous similar prior art designs, those designs can highlight the distinctions between the claimed design and the accused design as viewed by the ordinary observer.

* * *

* * * Our rejection of the point of novelty test does not mean, of course, that the differences between the claimed design and prior art designs are irrelevant. To the contrary, examining the novel features of the claimed design can be an important component of the comparison of the claimed design with the accused design and the prior art. But the comparison of the designs, including the examination of any novel features, must be conducted as part of the ordinary observer test, not as part of a separate test focusing on particular points of novelty that are designated only in the course of litigation.

* * * [I]n accordance with *Gorham* and subsequent decisions, we hold that the "ordinary observer" test should be the sole test for determining whether a design patent has been infringed. Under that test, as this court has sometimes described it, infringement will not be found unless the accused article "embod[ies] the patented design or any colorable imitation thereof."

In some instances, the claimed design and the accused design will be sufficiently distinct that it will be clear without more that the patentee has not met its burden of proving the two designs would appear "substantially the same" to the ordinary observer, as required by *Gorham*. In other instances, when the claimed and accused designs are not plainly dissimilar, resolution of the question whether the ordinary observer would consider the two designs to be substantially the same will benefit from a comparison of the claimed and accused designs with the prior art, as in many of the cases discussed above and in the case at bar. Where there are many examples of similar prior art designs, as in a case such as *Whitman Saddle*, differences between the claimed and accused designs that might not be noticeable in the abstract can become significant to the hypothetical ordinary observer who is conversant with the prior art.

We emphasize that although the approach we adopt will frequently involve comparisons between the claimed design and the prior art, it is not a test for determining validity, but is designed solely as a test of infringement. Thus, as is always the case, the burden of proof as to infringement remains on the patentee. However, if the accused infringer elects to rely on the comparison prior art as part of its defense against the claim of infringement, the burden of production of that prior art is on the accused infringer. * * * Under the ordinary observer test, however, it makes sense to impose the burden of production as to any comparison prior art on the accused infringer. The accused infringer is the party with the motivation to point out close prior art, and in particular to call to the court's attention the prior art that an ordinary observer is most likely to regard as highlighting the differences between the claimed and accused design. Regardless of whether the accused infringer elects to present prior art that it considers pertinent to the comparison between the claimed and accused design, however, the patentee bears the ultimate burden of proof to demonstrate infringement by a preponderance of the evidence. As in our recent decision in *In re Seagate Technology, LLC*, we "leave it to future cases to further develop the application of this standard."

* * *

IV

We now turn to the facts of this case. It is agreed that the general shape of the accused nail buffer at issue in this case is the same as that of the patented buffer design. The difference between the two is that the accused buffer has raised buffing pads on all four sides, while the patented buffer has buffing pads on only three sides. The two closest prior art nail buffers before the court were the Falley nail buffer, which has a solid, rectangular cross section with slightly raised buffers on all sides, and the Nailco patent, which shows a nail buffer design having a triangular shape and a hollow cross section, and in which raised buffing pads are located on all three sides. The four nail buffers are pictured below:

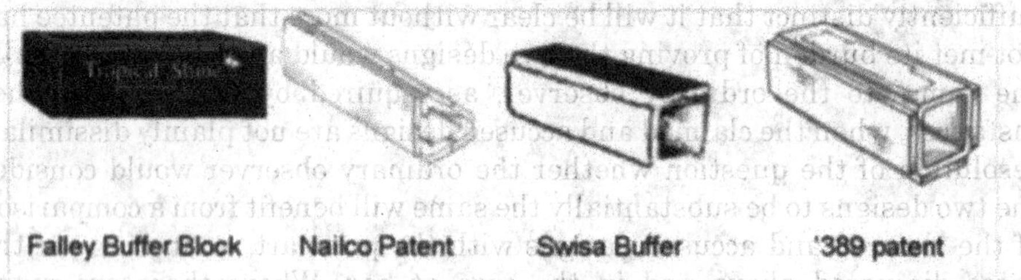

Falley Buffer Block Nailco Patent Swisa Buffer '389 patent

The question before this court under the standard we have set forth above is whether an ordinary observer, familiar with the prior art Falley and Nailco designs, would be deceived into believing the Swisa buffer is the same as the patented buffer. EGI argues that such an observer would notice a difference between the prior art and the '389 patent, consisting of "the hollow tube that is square in cross section and that has raised pads with exposed gaps at the corners."

* * *

Swisa counters that the '389 patent closely tracks the design of the Nailco nail buffer, except that it "add[s] a fourth side without an abrasive pad, resulting in square ends." In light of the close prior art buffers, including a number having square cross-sections, Swisa argues that an ordinary observer would notice the difference between the claimed and accused designs. * * *

* * *

In light of the similarity of the prior art buffers to the accused buffer, we conclude that no reasonable fact-finder could find that EGI met its burden of showing, by a preponderance of the evidence, that an ordinary observer, taking into account the prior art, would believe the accused design to be the same as the patented design. In concluding that a reasonable fact-finder could not find infringement in this case, we reach the same conclusion that the district court reached, and for many of the same reasons. Although we do so by using the ordinary observer test as informed by the prior art, rather than by applying the point of novelty test, our analysis largely tracks that of the district court. After analyzing the Nailco patent and the claimed design, as they related to the accused design, the district court concluded that "in the context of nail buffers, a fourth side without a pad is not substantially the same as a fourth side with a pad." While the district court focused on the differences in the particular feature at issue rather than the effect of those differences on the appearance of the design as a whole, we are satisfied that the difference on which the district court focused is important, viewed in the context of the prior art.

Finally, * * * we note that our analysis under the ordinary observer test is parallel to the panel's approach in an essential respect. The panel focused on viewing the difference between the claimed and accused designs in light of the prior art, as we do. The panel wrote: "The Swisa buffers have raised, abrasive pads on all four sides. When considering the prior art in the nail buffer field, this difference between the accused design and the patented design cannot be considered minor." That point captures the essence of the rationale of our decision today, even though the panel decision employed a different analytical approach. For the foregoing reasons, we sustain the district court's entry of summary judgment of no infringement, but we do so under the ordinary observer test in the form that we have adopted, and without using the point of novelty test that we have disapproved. In the language used by the Supreme Court in *Gorham*, 81 U.S. at 528, we hold that the accused design could not reasonably be viewed as so similar to the claimed design that a purchaser familiar with the prior art would be deceived by the similarity between the claimed and accused designs, "inducing him to purchase one supposing it to be the other."

AFFIRMED.

NOTES

1. *Standard for the Ordinary Observer:* Does the ordinary observer test for infringement require consumer confusion? Should it?

2. *Ordinary Observer Versus Obviousness:* What is the difference between the ordinary observer test for novelty and infringement, and the analysis of obviousness?

B. DEFENSES

Statutes: 35 U.S.C. §§ 282, 296

Read section 282 before going further. Defenses available to a patent infringement defendant, beyond noninfringement, include: invalidity of the claims in question (*see supra* Chapter 10); shop rights (*see supra* Chapter 11.A.4.); exhaustion; patent misuse; de minimis or experimental use; inequitable conduct in procuring the patent; and estoppel. The plaintiff's rights will also be subject to special limitations where the defendant is acting on behalf of the federal government or a state government, or, in the case of medical procedure patents, where the defendant is a medical practitioner (35 U.S.C. § 287(c)).

1. INVALIDITY

Under 35 U.S.C. § 282, a patent is presumed valid, but a defendant may plead the invalidity of an asserted claim as a defense to an action for infringement. Invalidity may be asserted on any condition of patentability (*e.g.*, novelty and nonobviousness) or on the patentee's failure to comply with the requirements of section 112 (other than best mode). The burden of proving invalidity falls on the infringement defendant, who must show by "clear and convincing evidence" that the claims in question are invalid. *Microsoft Corp. v. i4i Limited Partnership*, 564 U.S. 91 (2011).

In *Blonder-Tongue Laboratories, Inc. v. University of Illinois Foundation*, 402 U.S. 313 (1971), the Supreme Court held that once a federal court has ruled a particular patent invalid the patentee is estopped from relitigating the issue of patent validity unless the patentee had not had "a full and fair chance to litigate the validity of his patent" in the earlier case. *Id.* at 333. Overruling the contrary holding of *Triplett v. Lowell*, 297 U.S. 638 (1936), the Court observed:

> [T]he expense of patent litigation has two principal consequences if the *Triplett* rule is maintained. First, assuming that a perfectly sound judgment of invalidity has been rendered in an earlier suit involving the patentee, a second infringement action raising the same issue and involving much of the same proof has a high cost to the individual parties. The patentee is expending funds on litigation to protect a patent which is by hypothesis invalid. These moneys could be put to better use, such as further research and development. The alleged infringer—operating as he must against the presumption of validity—is forced to divert substantial funds to litigation that is wasteful.
>
> The second major economic consideration is far more significant. Under *Triplett*, only the comity restraints flowing from an adverse prior judgment operate to limit the patentee's

> right to sue different defendants on the same patent. In each successive suit the patentee enjoys the statutory presumption of validity, and so may easily put the alleged infringer to his expensive proof. As a consequence, prospective defendants will often decide that paying royalties under a license or other settlement is preferable to the costly burden of challenging the patent.
>
> * * *
>
> The tendency of *Triplett* to multiply the opportunities for holders of invalid patents to exact licensing agreements or other settlements from alleged infringers must be considered in the context of other decisions of this Court. Although recognizing the patent system's desirable stimulus to invention, we have also viewed the patent as a monopoly which, although sanctioned by law, has the economic consequences attending other monopolies. A patent yielding [licensing or settlement] returns for a device that fails to meet the congressionally imposed criteria of patentability is anomalous.

402 U.S. at 338, 342–43 (footnotes omitted). The *Blonder-Tongue* rule is based on collateral estoppel, a doctrine that bars re-litigation of issues presented and determined in a separate, prior lawsuit when the party against whom the estoppel is asserted had a full and fair opportunity to litigate the issue in the earlier proceeding. As a result, when applied to the issue of invalidity, it generally operates only against the patentee whose claim has previously been ruled invalid. The rule does not prohibit a person sued for infringement of a patent from asserting the affirmative defense of invalidity simply because the patent was ruled valid in a separate lawsuit to which the current defendant was not a party.

NOTE: ASSIGNOR ESTOPPEL

In some cases, the assignor of an invention, a patent application, or a patent (or a party closely affiliated with the assignor) is later accused of infringing one or more claims in the patent and becomes the defendant in the resulting patent infringement lawsuit. The question then arises whether such a defendant may raise all theoretically available invalidity defenses, as can other defendants, or whether instead such a defendant has more limited options due to its relationship to the patent and the plaintiff patent owner. The doctrine of assignor estoppel has been used for many years to limit assignor (and closely related party) invalidity defenses. At the same time, assignors have been allowed to submit evidence to support favorable or narrowing claim construction for assigned patents.

The Supreme Court in *Minerva Surgical, Inc. v. Hologic, Inc.*, 141 S.Ct. 2298 (2021) reexamined and upheld assignor estoppel but also limited its use.

The Court explained the doctrine's grounding in what it referred to as "centuries-old fairness principles."

> "If one lawfully conveys to another a patented right," the Court reasoned [in *Westinghouse Elec. v. Formica Insulation*, 266 U.S. 342 (1924)], "fair dealing should prevent him from derogating from the title he has assigned." After all, the "grantor purports to convey the right to exclude others"; how can he later say, given that representation, that the grantee in fact possesses no such right? The Court supported that view of equity by referring to estoppel by deed. Under that doctrine, the Court explained, "a grantor of a deed of land" cannot "impeach [ ] the effect of his solemn act" by later claiming that the grantee's title is no good. . . . In the [patent] context too, the Court held, the assignor could not fairly "attack" the validity of a right he had formerly sold.

141 S.Ct. at 2305–06. The Court's 5–4 majority more than once emphasized issues related to the defense's scope, noting that if a given assignor makes neither an "explicit or implicit" representation or assurance as to validity when assigning the rights, then it would not be unfair for that assignor to raise an invalidity defense—and assignor estoppel does not apply. It also explained how a patent assignor's mere silence at the time of assignment, on the other hand, leaves room to apply the assignor estoppel doctrine: "When a person sells his patent rights, he makes an (at least) implicit representation to the buyer that the patent at issue is valid . . . In later raising an invalidity defense, the assignor disavows that implied warranty." *Id.* at 2309.

So, then, under what circumstances may inventors assign their patent rights and not make a contradiction by later challenging validity? The Court identified three examples when no contradiction between the sale of rights and a later invalidity defense exists, making assignor estoppel inapplicable: (1) when the sale of rights or assignment occurs before an application or patent exists, which is the not-uncommon situation of the invention assignment, and is particularly common in employee-employer agreements wherein new employees assign all rights to future inventions; (2) when an after-arising change of law "renders irrelevant" the warranty made through the act of assignment; and (3) when a post-assignment amendment of the patent claims eliminates the basis for applying the doctrine, such as when a patent application (not a patent) has been assigned, and the claims have been thereafter materially broadened by the assignee. *Id.* at 2310.

> Assuming that the new claims are materially broader than the old claims, the assignor did not warrant to the new claims' validity. And if he made no such representation, then he can challenge the new claims in litigation: Because there is no inconsistency in his positions, there is no estoppel.

Id. Other questions have been addressed in other decisions, including how closely affiliated the assignor and another party must be for assignor estoppel to apply to another party, and whether receipt of only nominal consideration for an assignment can support assignor estoppel in later litigation.

In contrast to continued vitality of assignor estoppel, the Supreme Court abolished the doctrine of licensee estoppel in *Lear v. Adkins*, 395 U.S. 653 (1969). Before *Lear*, licensee estoppel had barred a patent licensee from contesting the validity of the licensed patent if sued for infringement. Why would patent licensees and patent assignors be subject to different estoppel rules? *Cf. MedImmune, Inc. v. Genentech, Inc.*, 549 U.S. 118 (2007) (excerpted later in this chapter).

2. EXHAUSTION

Under the "first sale" or "exhaustion of rights" doctrine of patent law, the authorized sale of a patented article is said to "exhaust" certain of the patentee's rights in that tangible item. Thus, use or resale of that particular tangible article by the purchaser does not infringe. *See, e.g., Adams v. Burke,* 84 U.S. (17 Wall.) 453 (1873) (use); *Keeler v. Standard Folding-Bed Co.,* 157 U.S. 659 (1895) (resale). The authorized sale of the patented article does not affect the patentee's right to make or manufacture the article. *Cf. Aro I* (examining repair versus reconstruction), excerpted earlier in this chapter.

Although the basic "first sale" doctrine as applied to patented devices has long been established, both the limits of exhaustion and the contours of related doctrines continue to develop.

IMPRESSION PRODS, INC. V. LEXMARK INT'L, INC.

581 U.S. ___, 137 S.Ct. 1523 (2017).

CHIEF JUSTICE ROBERTS delivered the opinion of the Court.

A United States patent entitles the patent holder (the "patentee"), for a period of 20 years, to "exclude others from making, using, offering for sale, or selling [its] invention throughout the United States or importing the invention into the United States." 35 U.S.C. § 154(a). Whoever engages in one of these acts "without authority" from the patentee may face liability for patent infringement. § 271(a).

When a patentee sells one of its products, however, the patentee can no longer control that item through the patent laws—its patent rights are said to "exhaust." The purchaser and all subsequent owners are free to use or resell the product just like any other item of personal property, without fear of an infringement lawsuit.

This case presents two questions about the scope of the patent exhaustion doctrine: First, whether a patentee that sells an item under an express restriction on the purchaser's right to reuse or resell the product may enforce that restriction through an infringement lawsuit. And second, whether a patentee exhausts its patent rights by selling its product outside the United States, where American patent laws do not apply. We conclude that a patentee's decision to sell a product exhausts all of its patent rights in that item, regardless of any restrictions the patentee purports to impose or the location of the sale.

I

The underlying dispute in this case is about laser printers—or, more specifically, the cartridges that contain the powdery substance, known as toner, that laser printers use to make an image appear on paper. Respondent Lexmark International, Inc. designs, manufactures, and sells toner cartridges to consumers in the United States and around the globe. It owns a number of patents that cover components of those cartridges and the manner in which they are used.

When toner cartridges run out of toner they can be refilled and used again. This creates an opportunity for other companies—known as remanufacturers—to acquire empty Lexmark cartridges from purchasers in the United States and abroad, refill them with toner, and then resell them at a lower price than the new ones Lexmark puts on the shelves.

Not blind to this business problem, Lexmark structures its sales in a way that encourages customers to return spent cartridges. It gives purchasers two options: One is to buy a toner cartridge at full price, with no strings attached. The other is to buy a cartridge at roughly 20-percent off through Lexmark's "Return Program." A customer who buys through the Return Program still owns the cartridge but, in exchange for the lower price, signs a contract agreeing to use it only once and to refrain from transferring the empty cartridge to anyone but Lexmark. To enforce this single-use/no-resale restriction, Lexmark installs a microchip on each Return Program cartridge that prevents reuse once the toner in the cartridge runs out.

Lexmark's strategy just spurred remanufacturers to get more creative. Many kept acquiring empty Return Program cartridges and developed methods to counteract the effect of the microchips. With that technological obstacle out of the way, there was little to prevent the remanufacturers from using the Return Program cartridges in their resale business. After all, Lexmark's contractual single-use/no-resale agreements were with the initial customers, not with downstream purchasers like the remanufacturers.

Lexmark, however, was not so ready to concede that its plan had been foiled. In 2010, it sued a number of remanufacturers, including petitioner Impression Products, Inc., for patent infringement with respect to two groups of cartridges. One group consists of Return Program cartridges that Lexmark sold within the United States. Lexmark argued that, because it expressly prohibited reuse and resale of these cartridges, the remanufacturers infringed the Lexmark patents when they refurbished and resold them. The other group consists of all toner cartridges that Lexmark sold abroad and that remanufacturers imported into the country. Lexmark claimed that it never gave anyone authority to import these cartridges, so the remanufacturers ran afoul of its patent rights by doing just that.

Eventually, the lawsuit was whittled down to one defendant, Impression Products, and one defense: that Lexmark's sales, both in the United States and abroad, exhausted its patent rights in the cartridges, so Impression Products was free to refurbish and resell them, and to import them if acquired abroad. Impression Products filed separate motions to dismiss with respect to both groups of cartridges. The District Court granted the motion as to the domestic Return Program cartridges, but denied the motion as to the cartridges Lexmark sold abroad. Both parties appealed.

The Federal Circuit considered the appeals en banc and ruled for Lexmark with respect to both groups of cartridges.

* * *

We granted certiorari to consider the Federal Circuit's decisions with respect to both domestic and international exhaustion and now reverse.

II

A

First up are the Return Program cartridges that Lexmark sold in the United States. We conclude that Lexmark exhausted its patent rights in these cartridges the moment it sold them. The single-use/no-resale restrictions in Lexmark's contracts with customers may have been clear and enforceable under contract law, but they do not entitle Lexmark to retain patent rights in an item that it has elected to sell.

The Patent Act grants patentees the "right to exclude others from making, using, offering for sale, or selling [their] invention[s]." 35 U.S.C. § 154(a). For over 160 years, the doctrine of patent exhaustion has imposed a limit on that right to exclude. *See Bloomer v. McQuewan*, 14 How. 539 (1853). The limit functions automatically: When a patentee chooses to sell an item, that product "is no longer within the limits of the monopoly" and instead becomes the "private, individual property" of the purchaser, with the rights and benefits that come along with ownership. A patentee is free to set the price and negotiate contracts with purchasers, but may not, "by virtue of his patent, control the use or disposition" of the product after ownership passes to the purchaser. *United States v. Univis Lens Co.*, 316 U.S. 241, 250 (1942) (emphasis added). The sale "terminates all patent rights to that item." *Quanta Computer, Inc. v. LG Electronics, Inc.*, 553 U.S. 617, 625 (2008).

This well-established exhaustion rule marks the point where patent rights yield to the common law principle against restraints on alienation. The Patent Act "promote[s] the progress of science and the useful arts by granting to [inventors] a limited monopoly" that allows them to "secure the financial rewards" for their inventions. But once a patentee sells an item, it has "enjoyed all the rights secured" by that limited monopoly. *Keeler v. Standard Folding Bed Co.*, 157 U.S. 659, 661 (1895). Because "the purpose of the patent law is fulfilled . . . when the patentee has received his reward for the use of his invention," that law furnishes "no basis for restraining the use and enjoyment of the thing sold."

We have explained in the context of copyright law that exhaustion has "an impeccable historic pedigree," tracing its lineage back to the "common law's refusal to permit restraints on the alienation of chattels." *Kirtsaeng v. John Wiley & Sons, Inc.*, 568 U.S. 519, 538 (2013). As Lord Coke put it in the 17th century, if an owner restricts the resale or use of an item after selling it, that restriction "is voide, because . . . it is against Trade and Traffique, and bargaining and contracting betweene man and man." 1 E. COKE, INSTITUTES OF THE LAWS OF ENGLAND § 360, p. 223 (1628); *see* J. GRAY, RESTRAINTS ON THE ALIENATION OF PROPERTY § 27, p. 18 (2d ed. 1895) ("A condition or conditional limitation on alienation attached to a transfer of the entire interest in personalty is as void as if attached to a fee simple in land").

This venerable principle is not, as the Federal Circuit dismissively viewed it, merely "one common-law jurisdiction's general judicial policy at one time toward anti-alienation restrictions." 816 F.3d, at 750. Congress enacted and has repeatedly revised the Patent Act against the backdrop of the hostility toward restraints on alienation. That enmity is reflected in the exhaustion doctrine. The patent laws do not include the right to "restrain [] . . . further alienation" after an initial sale; such conditions have been "hateful to the law from Lord Coke's day to ours" and are "obnoxious to the public interest." *Straus v. Victor Talking Machine Co.*, 243 U.S. 490, 501 (1917). "The inconvenience and annoyance to the public that an opposite conclusion would occasion are too obvious to require illustration." *Keeler*, 157 U.S. at 667.

But an illustration never hurts. Take a shop that restores and sells used cars. The business works because the shop can rest assured that, so long as those bringing in the cars own them, the shop is free to repair and resell those vehicles. That smooth flow of commerce would sputter if companies that make the thousands of parts that go into a vehicle could keep their patent rights after the first sale. Those companies might, for instance, restrict resale rights and sue the shop owner for patent infringement. And even if they refrained from imposing such restrictions, the very threat of patent liability would force the shop to invest in efforts to protect itself from hidden lawsuits. Either way, extending the patent rights beyond the first sale would clog the channels of commerce, with little benefit from the extra control that the patentees retain. And advances in technology, along with increasingly complex supply chains, magnify the problem. *See* Brief for Intel Corp. et al. as Amici Curiae 17, n. 5 ("A generic smartphone assembled from various high-tech components could practice an estimated 250,000 patents").

This Court accordingly has long held that, even when a patentee sells an item under an express restriction, the patentee does not retain patent rights in that product. In *Boston Store of Chicago v. American Graphophone Co.*, for example, a manufacturer sold graphophones—one of the earliest devices for recording and reproducing sounds—to retailers under contracts requiring those stores to resell at a specific price. When the manufacturer brought a patent infringement suit against a retailer who sold for less, we concluded that there was "no room for controversy" about the result: By selling the item, the manufacturer placed it "beyond the confines of the patent law, [and] could not, by qualifying restrictions as to use, keep [it] under the patent monopoly."

Two decades later, we confronted a similar arrangement in *United States v. Univis Lens Co.* There, a company that made eyeglass lenses authorized an agent to sell its products to wholesalers and retailers only if they promised to market the lenses at fixed prices. The Government filed an antitrust lawsuit, and the company defended its arrangement on the ground that it was exercising authority under the Patent Act. We held that the initial sales "relinquish[ed] . . . the patent monopoly with respect to the article[s] sold," so the "stipulation . . . fixing resale prices derive[d] no support from the patent and must stand on the same footing" as restrictions on unpatented goods.

It is true that *Boston Store* and *Univis* involved resale price restrictions that, at the time of those decisions, violated the antitrust laws. But in both cases it was the sale of the items, rather than the illegality of the restrictions, that prevented the patentees from enforcing those resale price agreements through patent infringement suits. And if there were any lingering doubt that patent exhaustion applies even when a sale is subject to an express, otherwise lawful restriction, our recent decision in *Quanta Computer, Inc. v. LG Electronics, Inc.* settled the matter. [Ed. Note: *Quanta* is excerpted in Note 1 following this case.] In that case, a technology company—with authorization from the patentee—sold microprocessors under contracts requiring purchasers to use those processors with other parts that the company manufactured. One buyer disregarded the restriction, and the patentee sued for infringement. Without so much as mentioning the lawfulness of the contract, we held that the patentee could not bring an infringement suit because the "authorized sale . . . took its products outside the scope of the patent monopoly."

Turning to the case at hand, we conclude that this well-settled line of precedent allows for only one answer: Lexmark cannot bring a patent infringement suit against Impression Products to enforce the single-use/no-resale provision accompanying its Return Program cartridges. Once sold, the Return Program cartridges passed outside of the patent monopoly, and whatever rights Lexmark retained are a matter of the contracts with its purchasers, not the patent law.

B

The Federal Circuit reached a different result largely because it got off on the wrong foot. The "exhaustion doctrine," the court believed, "must be understood as an interpretation of" the infringement statute, which prohibits anyone from using or selling a patented article "without authority" from the patentee. Exhaustion reflects a default rule that a patentee's decision to sell an item "*presumptively* grant[s] 'authority' to the purchaser to use it and resell it." 816 F. 3d, at 742. But, the Federal Circuit explained, the patentee does not have to hand over the full "bundle of rights" every time. *Id.*, at 741 (internal quotation marks omitted). If the patentee expressly withholds a stick from the bundle—perhaps by restricting the purchaser's resale rights—the buyer never acquires that withheld authority, and the patentee may continue to enforce its right to exclude that practice under the patent laws.

The misstep in this logic is that the exhaustion doctrine is not a presumption about the authority that comes along with a sale; it is instead a limit on "the scope of the *patentee's rights.*" *United States v. General Elec. Co.*, 272 U.S. 476, 489 (1926) (emphasis added). The right to use, sell, or import an item exists independently of the Patent Act. What a patent adds—and grants exclusively to the patentee—is a limited right to prevent others from engaging in those practices. Exhaustion extinguishes that exclusionary power. As a result, the sale transfers the right to use, sell, or import because those are the rights that come along with ownership, and the buyer is free and clear of an infringement lawsuit because there is no exclusionary right left to enforce.

The Federal Circuit also expressed concern that preventing patentees from reserving patent rights when they sell goods would create an artificial distinction between such sales and sales by licensees. Patentees, the court explained, often license others to make and sell their products, and may place restrictions on those licenses. A computer developer could, for instance, license a manufacturer to make its patented devices and sell them only for non-commercial use by individuals. If a licensee breaches the license by selling a computer for commercial use, the patentee can sue the licensee for infringement. * * *

The Federal Circuit's concern is misplaced. A patentee can impose restrictions on licensees because a license does not implicate the same concerns about restraints on alienation as a sale. Patent exhaustion reflects the principle that, when an item passes into commerce, it should not be shaded by a legal cloud on title as it moves through the marketplace. But a license is not about passing title to a product, it is about changing the contours of the patentee's monopoly: The patentee agrees not to exclude a licensee from making or selling the patented invention, expanding the club of authorized producers and sellers. Because the patentee is exchanging rights, not goods, it is free to relinquish only a portion of its bundle of patent protections.

A patentee's authority to limit *licensees* does not, as the Federal Circuit thought, mean that patentees can use licenses to impose post-sale restrictions on *purchasers* that are enforceable through the patent laws. So long as a licensee complies with the license when selling an item, the patentee has, in effect, authorized the sale. That licensee's sale is treated, for purposes of patent exhaustion, as if the patentee made the sale itself. The result: The sale exhausts the patentee's rights in that item. A license may require the licensee to impose a restriction on purchasers, like the license limiting the computer manufacturer to selling for non-commercial use by individuals. But if the licensee does so—by, perhaps, having each customer sign a contract promising not to use the computers in business—the sale nonetheless exhausts all patent rights in the item sold. The purchasers might not comply with the restriction, but the only recourse for the licensee is through contract law, just as if the patentee itself sold the item with a restriction.

General Talking Pictures [cited by the Federal Circuit in support of its decision] involved a fundamentally different situation * * * [and] stands for the modest principle that, if a patentee has not given authority for a licensee to make a sale, that sale cannot exhaust the patentee's rights.

In sum, patent exhaustion is uniform and automatic. Once a patentee decides to sell—whether on its own or through a licensee—that sale exhausts its patent rights, regardless of any post-sale restrictions the patentee purports to impose, either directly or through a license.

III

Our conclusion that Lexmark exhausted its patent rights when it sold the domestic Return Program cartridges goes only halfway to resolving this case. Lexmark also sold toner cartridges abroad and sued Impression Products for patent infringement for "importing [Lexmark's] invention into the United States." 35 U.S.C. § 154(a). Lexmark contends that it may sue for infringement with respect to all of the imported cartridges—not just those in the Return Program—because a foreign sale does not trigger patent exhaustion unless the patentee "expressly or implicitly transfer[s] or license[s]" its rights. The Federal Circuit agreed, but we do not. An authorized sale outside the United States, just as one within the United States, exhausts all rights under the Patent Act.

This question about international exhaustion of intellectual property rights has also arisen in the context of copyright law. [Ed. note: *See Kirtsaeng* decision on page 990.] * * * We began with the text of § 109(a), but it was not decisive * * *. What helped tip the scales for global exhaustion was the fact that the first sale doctrine originated in "the common law's refusal to permit restraints on the alienation of chattels." That "common-law doctrine makes no geographical distinctions." * * *

Applying patent exhaustion to foreign sales is just as straightforward. Patent exhaustion, too, has its roots in the antipathy toward restraints on alienation, *see supra*, and nothing in the text or history of the Patent Act shows that Congress intended to confine that borderless common law principle to domestic sales. In fact, Congress has not altered patent exhaustion at all; it remains an unwritten limit on the scope of the patentee's monopoly. *See Astoria Fed. Sav. & Loan Assn. v. Solimino*, 501 U.S. 104, 108 (1991) ("[W]here a common-law principle is well established, ... courts may take it as given that Congress has legislated with an expectation that the principle will apply except when a statutory purpose to the contrary is evident" (internal quotation marks omitted)). And differentiating the patent exhaustion and copyright first sale doctrines would make little theoretical or practical sense: The two share a "strong similarity ... and identity of purpose," *Bauer & Cie v. O'Donnell*, 229 U.S. 1, 13 (1913), and many everyday products—"automobiles, microwaves, calculators, mobile phones, tablets, and personal computers"—are subject to both patent and copyright protections, *see Kirtsaeng*, 568 U.S., at 545. There is a "historic kinship between patent law and copyright law," *Sony Corp. of America v. Universal City Studios, Inc.*, 464 U.S. 417, 439 (1984), and the bond between the two leaves no room for a rift on the question of international exhaustion.

Lexmark sees the matter differently. The Patent Act, it points out, limits the patentee's "right to exclude others" from making, using, selling, or importing its products to acts that occur in the United States. 35 U.S.C. § 154(a). A domestic sale, it argues, triggers exhaustion because the sale compensates the patentee for "surrendering [those] *U.S.* rights." A foreign sale is different [according to Lexmark]: The Patent Act does not give patentees exclusionary powers abroad. Without those powers, a patentee selling in a foreign market may not be able to sell its product for the same price that it could in the United States, and therefore is not sure to receive "the reward guaranteed by U.S. patent law." Absent that reward, says Lexmark, there should be no exhaustion. In short, there is no patent exhaustion from sales abroad because there are no patent rights abroad to exhaust.

* * * [The territorial limit does not] support the premise of Lexmark's argument. Exhaustion is a separate limit on the patent grant, and does not depend on the patentee receiving some undefined premium for selling the right to access the American market. A purchaser buys an item, not patent rights. And exhaustion is triggered by the patentee's decision to give that item up and receive whatever fee it decides is appropriate "for the article and the invention which it embodies." *Univis*, 316 U.S., at 251. The patentee may not be able to command the same amount for its products abroad as it does in the United States. But the Patent Act does not guarantee a particular price, much less the price from selling to American consumers. Instead, the right to exclude just ensures that the patentee receives one reward—of whatever amount the patentee deems to be "satisfactory compensation," *Keeler*, 157 U.S., at 661—for every item that passes outside the scope of the patent monopoly.

* * *

* * * Exhaustion does not arise because of the parties' expectations about how sales transfer patent rights. More is at stake when it comes to patents than simply the dealings between the parties, which can be addressed through contract law. Instead, exhaustion occurs because, in a sale, the patentee elects to give up title to an item in exchange for payment. Allowing patent rights to stick remora-like to that item as it flows through the market would violate the principle against restraints on alienation. Exhaustion does not depend on whether the patentee receives a premium for selling in the United States, or the type of rights that buyers expect to receive. As a result, restrictions and location are irrelevant; what matters is the patentee's decision to make a sale.

* * *

JUSTICE GINSBURG, concurring in part and dissenting in part.

I concur in the Court's holding regarding domestic exhaustion—a patentee who sells a product with an express restriction on reuse or resale may not enforce that restriction through an infringement lawsuit, because the U.S. sale exhausts the U.S. patent rights in the product sold. I dissent, however, from the Court's holding on international exhaustion. A foreign sale, I would hold, does not exhaust a U.S. inventor's U.S. patent rights.

Patent law is territorial. When an inventor receives a U.S. patent, that patent provides no protection abroad. A U.S. patentee must apply to each country in which she seeks the exclusive right to sell her invention. And patent laws vary by country; each country's laws "may embody different policy judgments about the relative rights of inventors, competitors, and the public in patented inventions."

Because a sale abroad operates independently of the U.S. patent system, it makes little sense to say that such a sale exhausts an inventor's U.S. patent rights. * * *

* * *

NOTES

1. *Exhaustion via Sales by Licensees—Processes and Products:* In *Quanta Computer, Inc. v. LG Electronics, Inc.*, 553 U.S. 617 (2008), the Supreme Court addressed exhaustion in complex circumstances involving a license for a large patent portfolio. LG (the plaintiff) had licensed its patents to Intel, and Quanta (the defendant) had purchased products from Intel that it then used in manufacturing computers. LG objected to the fact that Quanta had combined the Intel parts in combination with non-Intel parts in ways that practiced the LG patents. On the facts of the case, the Court found that the relevant patent rights, including both product and process claims, were exhausted by the first sale of the products that were produced under the license. The Court first dispensed with the argument that method patents could not be exhausted, explaining both that its precedent did not differentiate between method and product patents when considering exhaustion via sale of an item and that removing exhaustion from method patents would conflict with the policy of exhaustion:

> This case illustrates the danger of allowing such an end-run around exhaustion. On LGE's theory, although Intel is authorized to sell a completed computer system that practices the LGE Patents, any downstream purchasers of the system could nonetheless be liable for patent infringement. Such a result would violate the longstanding principle that, when a patented item is "once lawfully made and sold, there is no restriction on [its] use to be implied for the benefit of the patentee." We therefore reject LGE's argument that method claims, as a category, are never exhaustible.

553 U.S. at 630. The Court then turned to a prior case, *United States v. Univis Lens Co.*, 316 U.S. 241 (1942), as it considered "the extent to which a product must embody a patent in order to trigger exhaustion." In *Univis*, the owner of a patent on eyeglass lenses licensed the manufacture and sale of lens blanks for bi- and tri-focal lenses. Wholesalers were licensed to grind the blanks into the patented finished lenses and to sell them to licensed prescription retailers for resale. Finishing retailers were similarly licensed, but for sale to consumers. Univis fixed the prices or rates for the sales at each level. The United States brought an antitrust suit, and the issue for the *Univis* court was whether the patents had been exhausted by the authorized sales or whether the patent rights could protect Univis's pricing scheme from antitrust scrutiny. The *Quanta* decision examined the case for its applicability to the licensed Intel products:

First, *Univis* held that "the authorized sale of an article which is capable of use only in practicing the patent is a relinquishment of the patent monopoly with respect to the article sold." *Id.,* at 249. * * * Here, LGE has suggested no reasonable use for the Intel Products other than incorporating them into computer systems that practice the LGE Patents. Nor can we discern one: A microprocessor or chipset cannot function until it is connected to buses and memory. And here, as in *Univis,* the only apparent object of Intel's sales to Quanta was to permit Quanta to incorporate the Intel Products into computers that would practice the patents.

Second, the lens blanks in *Univis* "embodie[d] essential features of [the] patented invention." *Id.,* at 250–251. The essential, or inventive, feature of the Univis lens patents was the fusing together of different lens segments to create bi- and tri-focal lenses. The finishing process performed by the [licensees] after the fusing was not unique. * * * [It was] incidental to the invention, noting, for example, that "[t]he blank is then ground in the usual manner" * * *.

Like the Univis lens blanks, the Intel Products constitute a material part of the patented invention and all but completely practice the patent. Here, as in *Univis,* the incomplete article substantially embodies the patent because the only step necessary to practice the patent is the application of common processes or the addition of standard parts. * * * The Intel Products were specifically designed to function only when memory or buses are attached; Quanta was not required to make any creative or inventive decision when it added those parts. Indeed, Quanta had no alternative but to follow Intel's specifications in incorporating the Intel Products into its computers because it did not know their internal structure, which Intel guards as a trade secret. Intel all but practiced the patent itself by designing its products to practice the patents, lacking only the addition of standard parts.

* * *

With regard to LGE's argument that exhaustion does not apply across patents, we agree on the general principle: The sale of a device that practices patent A does not, by virtue of practicing patent A, exhaust patent B. But if the device practices patent A *while substantially embodying* patent B, its relationship to patent A does not prevent exhaustion of patent B. For example, if the Univis lens blanks had been composed of shatter-resistant glass under patent A, the blanks would nonetheless have substantially embodied, and therefore exhausted, patent B for the finished lenses. This case is no different. While each Intel microprocessor and chipset practices thousands of individual patents, including some LGE patents not at issue in this case, the exhaustion analysis is not altered by the fact that more than one patent is practiced by the same product. The

> relevant consideration is whether the Intel Products that partially practice a patent—by, for example, embodying its essential features—exhaust *that* patent.

553 U.S. at 631–35. The Court concluded by addressing the question of whether the first sale was, in fact, authorized under the license. The license agreement from LGE to Intel "broadly permit[ted] Intel to 'make, use, [or] sell' products free of LGE's patent claims," and "[n]othing in the License Agreement restrict[ed] Intel's right to sell its microprocessors and chipsets to purchasers who intend[ed] to combine them with non-Intel parts." At the same time, the license did not expressly provide a license to Intel's downstream customers who purchased products, such as Quanta, and it expressly denied that a license had been granted for those customers to combine the Intel parts with non-Intel parts. (A "master agreement" between the parties required Intel to notify its customers that LGE had not licensed the patents to the customers.) The Court determined that the product sales by Intel to Quanta were authorized by license agreement from LGE to Intel, meaning those first sales exhausted the patent rights.

> The authorized sale of an article that substantially embodies a patent exhausts the patent holder's rights and prevents the patent holder from invoking patent law to control postsale use of the article. Here, LGE licensed Intel to practice any of its patents and to sell products practicing those patents. Intel's microprocessors and chipsets substantially embodied the LGE Patents because they had no reasonable noninfringing use and included all the inventive aspects of the patented methods. Nothing in the License Agreement limited Intel's ability to sell its products practicing the LGE Patents. Intel's authorized sale to Quanta thus took its products outside the scope of the patent monopoly, and as a result, LGE can no longer assert its patent rights against Quanta.

553 U.S. at 638.

2. *When Using Includes Making:* What effect should exhaustion have on a self-replicating invention, meaning an invention whose normal and foreseeable use results in the replication of the invention—whose normal use therefore results in a new making? Should the "exhaustion" that follows the unrestricted and noninfringing sale of a product embodying all inventions—which exhausts the right to exclude others from use and (re)sale of the original unit of the product—allow the "fruits" of the use of the product to also be used, sold, and resold outside of the control of patent law?

In *Bowman v. Monsanto*, 569 U.S. 278 (2013), the Supreme Court addressed one self-replicating invention, the Monsanto Co.'s patented "Roundup Ready" soybean seeds. When used (planted), the Roundup Ready seeds grow into plants that can survive application of the herbicide glyphosate (sold by Monsanto under its "Roundup" trademark); those plants in turn make new seeds bearing the same trait. The Roundup-resistant trait arises from a genetic modification invented by Monsanto. Monsanto sued Bowman, an

Indiana soybean farmer, for patent infringement based on his growing of soybean crops from "commodity seed" he purchased from a grain elevator. Commodity seed is typically used for consumption by either humans or animals; many or most of the commodity soybeans in question contained the Roundup Ready modification due to widespread use by other farmers of licensed Roundup Ready soybeans. Bowman argued for application of an exhaustion defense because the commodity seeds he used had initially been produced from licensed Roundup Ready seeds (a first sale licensed by Monsanto), by the farmers who grew and sold them to the grain elevator.

> Bowman principally argues that exhaustion should apply here because seeds are meant to be planted. The exhaustion doctrine, he reminds us, typically prevents a patentee from controlling the use of a patented product following an authorized sale. And in planting Roundup Ready seeds, Bowman continues, he is merely using them in the normal way farmers do. Bowman thus concludes that allowing Monsanto to interfere with that use would "creat[e] an impermissible exception to the exhaustion doctrine" for patented seeds and other "self-replicating technologies."
>
> But it is really Bowman who is asking for an unprecedented exception—to what he concedes is the "well settled" rule that "the exhaustion doctrine does not extend to the right to 'make' a new product." Reproducing a patented article no doubt "uses" it after a fashion. But as already explained, we have always drawn the boundaries of the exhaustion doctrine to exclude that activity, so that the patentee retains an undiminished right to prohibit others from making the thing his patent protects. * * * [E]xhaustion applies only to the particular item sold, and not to reproductions.

569 U.S. at 287. The Court expressly stated that its holding was limited to the specific situation of the claimed invention in the case, rather than all self-replicating inventions or products incorporating those inventions.

3. PATENT MISUSE

Patent misuse is a judicially created affirmative defense designed to bar enforcement of a patent when the patentee has attempted to broaden in an impermissible manner the "physical or temporal scope" of the patent grant. *See Windsurfing Int'l, Inc. v. AMF, Inc.*, 782 F.2d 995, 1001 (Fed. Cir. 1986) (quoting *Blonder-Tongue Labs., Inc. v. Univ. of Illinois Found.*, 402 U.S. 313, 343 (1971)). In *Princo Corp. v. International Trade Comm'n*, 616 F.3d 1318 (Fed. Cir. 2010) (en banc), the Federal Circuit explained the basis of patent misuse as follows:

> The doctrine of patent misuse is [ ] grounded in the policy-based desire to prevent a patentee from using the patent to obtain market benefit beyond that which inheres in the statutory patent right. It follows that the key inquiry under the patent misuse

> doctrine is whether, by imposing the condition in question, the patentee has impermissibly broadened the physical or temporal scope of the patent grant *and has done so in a manner that has anticompetitive effects.* Where the patentee has not leveraged its patent beyond the scope of rights granted by the Patent Act, misuse has not been found.
>
> In determining whether a particular licensing condition has the effect of impermissibly broadening the patent grant, courts have noted that the patentee begins with substantial rights under the patent grant—including the right to suppress the invention while continuing to prevent all others from using it, to license others, or to refuse to license, to charge such royalty as the leverage of the patent monopoly permits, and to limit the scope of the license to a particular field of use. Given that the patent grant entitles the patentee to impose a broad range of conditions in licensing the right to practice the patent, the doctrine of patent misuse has largely been confined to a handful of specific practices by which the patentee seemed to be trying to extend his patent grant beyond its statutory limits.

Id. at 1327–29 (internal quotations omitted) (emphasis added). The major patent law treatise lists three "classic acts of misuse":

> (1) requiring the purchase of unpatented goods for use with patented apparatus or processes, (2) prohibiting production or sale of competing goods, and (3) conditioning the granting of a license under one patent upon the acceptance of another and different license.

6A Chisum on Patents § 19.04 (2022). Congress narrowed patent misuse in section 271(d), which lists five types of acts or conduct that may not form the basis of a patent misuse defense. One, for example, narrows a tying-based claims of misuse, such as "classic acts" (1) and (3) above, since it bars a misuse finding when the patentee has "conditioned the license of any rights to the patent or the sale of the patented product on the acquisition of a license to rights in another patent or purchase of a separate product, unless, in view of the circumstances, the patent owner has market power in the relevant market for the patent or patented product on which the license or sale is conditioned." 35 U.S.C. § 271(d)(5). Under section 271(d)(4), the patentee does not risk a finding of misuse on the basis that it has "refused to license or use any rights to the patent." For more on misuse, see 6A Chisum on Patents § 19.04 (2022).

NOTES

1. *What Is Misuse?* Should patent misuse be found where a license requires payment of royalties to continue even after the patent term expires?

Where a license is entered into while the patent application is pending, and specifies that royalties will be payable even if the patent does not issue? Where a condition of the license is that the licensor receive a license to exploit any improvements on the invention which are developed by the licensee?

2. *Direct Effect Required?* Should an infringement defendant be entitled to invoke the patent misuse defense based on anticompetitive provisions contained in patent licenses to which the defendant was not bound?

3. *Tying:* The principles underlying the narrow view of wrongful tying in section 271(d)(5), quoted above, are reflected in the Supreme Court's antitrust decision in *Illinois Tool Works Inc. v. Independent Ink, Inc.*, 547 U.S. 28 (2006), where the Court held unanimously that, for purposes of a tying claim under section 1 of the Sherman Act, courts may no longer presume that a patent confers monopoly power, and that in all tying cases a plaintiff must prove that the defendant has market power in the tying product.

4. EXPERIMENTAL USE

The unauthorized use of a patented product or process even for noncommercial purposes is an infringement. Courts have excluded from infringement, however, the making or using of a patented invention purely for purposes of experimentation or research if there is no purpose of commercial advantage and the activity is on a small enough scale to qualify as truly de minimis. Federal Circuit law narrowly interprets this common law "experimental use" exception. In *Madey v. Duke University*, 307 F.3d 1351 (Fed. Cir. 2002), Madey, formerly a lab director in a Duke University research laboratory, sued the university for infringement when it continued to use his patented laser technology in its research after he was removed from his position. The Federal Circuit disagreed with the district court that Duke's use was experimental and thus excused as a result of Duke's status as a non-profit educational institution with a stated primary mission of teaching, research, and expansion of knowledge:

> * * * [We have admonished] that the experimental use defense is very narrow and strictly limited. * * * [The defense is] very narrow and limited to actions performed "for amusement, to satisfy idle curiosity, or for strictly philosophical inquiry." Further, use does not qualify for the experimental use defense when it is undertaken in the "guise of scientific inquiry" but has "definite, cognizable, and not insubstantial commercial purposes." * * * [U]se is disqualified from the defense if it has the "slightest commercial implication." Moreover, use in keeping with the legitimate business of the alleged infringer does not qualify for the experimental use defense. * * *

* * *

> Our precedent clearly does not immunize use that is in any way commercial in nature. Similarly, our precedent does not immunize any conduct that is in keeping with the alleged infringer's legitimate business, regardless of commercial implications. For example, major research universities, such as Duke, often sanction and fund research projects with arguably no commercial application whatsoever. However, these projects unmistakably further the institution's legitimate business objectives, including educating and enlightening students and faculty participating in these projects. These projects also serve, for example, to increase the status of the institution and lure lucrative research grants, students and faculty.
>
> In short, regardless of whether a particular institution or entity is engaged in an endeavor for commercial gain, so long as the act is in furtherance of the alleged infringer's legitimate business and is not solely for amusement, to satisfy idle curiosity, or for strictly philosophical inquiry, the act does not qualify for the very narrow and strictly limited experimental use defense. Moreover, the profit or non-profit status of the user is not determinative.
>
> In the present case, the district court attached too great a weight to the non-profit, educational status of Duke, effectively suppressing the fact that Duke's acts appear to be in accordance with any reasonable interpretation of Duke's legitimate business objectives. On remand, the district court will have to significantly narrow and limit its conception of the experimental use defense. The correct focus should not be on the non-profit status of Duke but on the legitimate business Duke is involved in and whether or not the use was solely for amusement, to satisfy idle curiosity, or for strictly philosophical inquiry.

Id. at 1362–63. The Federal Circuit also confirmed that the burden of establishing experimental use lies with the defendant. *Id.* at 1361.

NOTES

1. *Important Distinction:* Note that the experimental use defense is an entirely different doctrine from the experimental use exception to the public use bar in section 102, discussed in Chapter 10.C.4., *supra* (in Note 6 on page 463).

2. *Protecting Academic Experimentation:* Would it be possible to craft an experimental use provision that would shelter at least some academic activities from infringement liability? Which activities should be covered, and which should be excluded?

3. *Specific Exception for FDA-Related Experimentation:* In *Roche Products, Inc. v. Bolar Pharmaceutical Co.*, 733 F.2d 858 (Fed.Cir.1984), the Federal Circuit held that the defendant's commercial purpose made the experimental use privilege inapplicable where a generic drug maker used samples of a patented drug (acquired from a foreign source) in connection with FDA-required testing of the generic equivalent which it intended to market when the patent expired. Concerned that this result would delay the marketing of many generic drugs, Congress immediately enacted the narrowly defined experimentation privilege of section 271(e)(1), which the Supreme Court later held applicable activities related to FDA approval of both drugs and medical devices. *Eli Lilly & Co. v. Medtronic, Inc.*, 496 U.S. 661 (1990). (At the same time, Congress enacted sections 271(e)(2) and (e)(4), discussed at page 612–612, *supra*, which added an "artificial" act of infringement when an unlicensed person submits certain applications for FDA approval before the end of a patent's term.)

The section 271(e)(1) safe harbor provision makes the making, using, importing, selling, or offering to sell certain patented inventions noninfringing, if the acts are performed "solely for uses reasonably related to the development and submission of information under a Federal law which regulates the manufacture, use, or sale of drugs or veterinary biological products." The chief purpose and effect of section 271(e)(1) is to enable generic drug makers to establish bioequivalence with patented drugs as part of the FDA approval process without having to delay their testing activities until the expiration of the patent term.

5. GOOD FAITH PRIOR USE

The Patent Reform Act of 1999 added a new section 273 to Title 35, establishing a first inventor—or "prior user"—defense against patent infringement claims involving "methods of doing or conducting business." Congress chose not to enact a broader prior user defense that would have applied to subject matter other than business methods, because of significant opposition by parties concerned about the conflict between trade secret rights and the patent policy favoring prompt disclosure of new technology. It was claimed that a broad prior user defense could discourage some inventors from filing patent applications and encourage them to rely on trade secret protection instead, by insulating them from the risk of infringement liability where another inventor later obtains a patent on the same invention. Should these concerns preclude a broad prior user defense? The 1999 version of the section 273 defense for business methods was almost never asserted, and there are no reported decisions applying it to excuse infringement.

In 2011, Congress expanded (in the AIA) the good faith prior user defense for any patent issued on or after September 16, 2011. The expanded defense does not, however, apply either to all good faith prior uses or to all types of inventions. Instead, section 273 was broadened to include (1) "subject matter consisting of a process, or consisting of a machine, manufacture, or composition of matter used in a manufacturing or other commercial process, that would otherwise infringe a claimed invention being asserted," when that subject matter was (2) "commercially used" by a person "acting in good faith" in connection with "an internal commercial use or an actual arm's length sale or other arm's length commercial transfer of a useful end result of such commercial use," if the commercial use (3) occurred at least one year before the earlier of the effective filing date of the claimed invention or the date of public disclosure of the claimed invention under an exception in post-AIA section 102(b). *See* 35 U.S.C. § 273(a). The defense is personal to the prior commercial user (and an entity that controls, is controlled by, or under common control with that person), and is non-transferable and non-licensable, except that it may be assigned in connection with the assignment of the entire line of business to which it relates. As with the earlier (1999) defense, this good faith prior user defense is not available to a person who has abandoned use of the invention in the past or a person who derived the invention from the patentee. If the good faith prior user whose use is excused from infringement under this new provision sells the "useful end result" to another, the patentee's rights as to that "useful end result" are exhausted in the same way they would be under the first sale doctrine if the patentee had itself made that sale. Is there reason to anticipate that the new section 273 defense will be put to greater use than the 1999 version? Why or why not?

6. INEQUITABLE CONDUCT

A patent applicant has a duty of candor in dealing with the Patent and Trademark Office, and intentional misrepresentations, omissions, or misleading statements that violate the duty can constitute "inequitable conduct" or "fraud" that renders the *entire patent* unenforceable. This breadth makes inequitable conduct unlike validity defenses in litigation, which are claim-specific (leaving other patent claims untouched), and unlike some other defects, it cannot be cured by reissue or reexamination proceedings. The inequitable conduct defense was narrowed in 2011 by *Therasense, Inc. v. Becton, Dickinson & Co.*, 649 F.3d 1276 (Fed. Cir. 2011) (en banc). In *Therasense*, the Federal Circuit restricted inequitable conduct to cases where the patentee (1) omits or misrepresents *material* information during prosecution and (2) does so deliberately, with specific *intent to deceive* the PTO; the decision made clear that materiality and intent are separate requirements. *Id.* at 1290–91. The materiality of the omission or misrepresentation must generally constitute "but-for" materiality, which means that the court must determine whether the PTO would have allowed a claim if it had been aware of the undisclosed reference or the true facts that were misrepresented. Some examples of information that might, in certain circumstances, be material include the identity of the inventor, prior art, existence of any facts constituting a statutory bar, and (under pre-AIA novelty rules) the date of invention. The intent requirement may be proved by indirect or circumstantial evidence, except that it may not be inferred solely from materiality. Clear and convincing evidence is required to establish inequitable conduct.

7. ESTOPPEL AND LACHES

Estoppel: The Federal Circuit has applied the general equitable defense of estoppel as an equitable defense available under section 282. When established, equitable estoppel may entirely bar the patentee's claim. In *A.C. Aukerman Co. v. R.L. Chaides Const. Co.*, 960 F.2d 1020 (Fed. Cir. 1992) (en banc), the court stated:

> Three elements must be established to bar a patentee's suit by reason of equitable estoppel:
>
> a. The patentee, through misleading conduct, leads the alleged infringer to reasonably infer that the patentee does not intend to enforce its patent against the alleged infringer. "Conduct" may include specific statements, action, inaction, or silence where there was an obligation to speak.
>
> b. The alleged infringer relies on that conduct.
>
> c. Due to its reliance, the alleged infringer will be materially prejudiced if the patentee is allowed to proceed with its claim.
>
> No presumption is applicable to the defense of equitable estoppel.

A.C. Aukerman, 960 F.2d at 1028. Note that equitable estoppel can bar all relief (injunctive and monetary) for both past and future infringement.

Laches: Another general equitable defense often discussed in older patent cases is laches, but today laches only applies to the equitable remedy of an injunction (if at all), rather than being used to bar damages. The Patent Act contains a six-year limitation on damages in section 286: "Except as otherwise provided by law, no recovery shall be had for any infringement committed more than six years prior to the filing of the complaint or counterclaim for infringement in the action." In *SCA Hygiene Prods. v. First Quality Baby Prods.*, 580 U.S. 328, 137 S.Ct. 954 (2017), the Supreme Court explained why laches, while potentially available to bar injunctive relief, should not be applied to a claim for damages. "Laches is a gap-filling doctrine, and where there is a statute of limitations, there is no gap to fill." Section 286 does not operate like a typical statute of limitations, barring the action in full, but it does bar "recovery" (of monetary damages) for infringement outside the limitations period. Said the Court:

> Laches provides a shield against untimely claims, and statutes of limitations serve a similar function. When Congress enacts a statute of limitations, it speaks directly to the issue of timeliness and provides a rule for determining whether a claim is timely enough to permit relief. The enactment of a statute of limitations necessarily reflects a congressional decision that the timeliness of covered claims is better judged on the basis of a generally hard and fast rule rather than the sort of case-specific judicial determination that occurs when a laches defense is asserted.

137 S.Ct. at 960 (citations omitted). The Supreme Court's decision in *SCA Hygiene Products* did not address the contours of the defense of equitable estoppel, and it expressly noted that "the doctrine of equitable estoppel provides protection against some of the problems that First Quality highlights, namely, unscrupulous patentees inducing potential targets of infringement suits to invest in the production of arguably infringing products." *Id.* at 967.

8. INFRINGEMENT BY GOVERNMENT ENTITIES

Federal Government: Under 28 U.S.C. § 1498, a patentholder's exclusive remedy for infringing use by or for the federal government (including use by a government contractor where authorized by the federal government) is a suit for reasonable compensation in the United States Court of Federal Claims. See also Note 6 on page 669, *infra*.

State Governments: After a series of conflicting court rulings on the question whether states were immune from suit for patent infringement, Congress in 1992 clarified its intent to abrogate state immunity from patent infringement suits, *see* 35 U.S.C. §§ 271(h), 296(a), specifying that in doing so it was acting upon its authority under the Intellectual Property Clause, the Commerce Clause, and section 5 of the Fourteenth Amendment. The Supreme Court's subsequent decision in *Seminole Tribe v. Florida*, 517 U.S. 44 (1996), however, suggested that only the last of these constitutional provisions is a valid source of authority for such abrogation, thus placing the validity of the 1992 amendments in question.

In 1999, the Supreme Court held the 1992 amendments invalid in *Florida Prepaid Postsecondary Education Expense Board v. College Savings Bank*, 527 U.S. 627 (1999). The Court held that Congress was not acting within the scope of its authority under section 5 of the Fourteenth Amendment when it abrogated Eleventh Amendment immunity for purposes of patent infringement suits, because there was no evidence that states had engaged in a historical pattern of infringing patents and providing inadequate remedies for those infringements. Because the federal courts have exclusive jurisdiction over patent infringement suits (under 28 U.S.C. § 1338(a)), this holding appears to immunize states from damages liability for patent infringement. However, the Eleventh Amendment allows federal courts to enjoin individual state actors from continuing to infringe. *Pennington Seed Inc. v. Produce Exchange No. 299,* 457 F.3d 1334 (Fed. Cir. 2006). Moreover, when a state actor initiates a patent infringement suit, thus voluntarily subjecting itself to federal court jurisdiction, this constitutes a waiver of its immunity with respect to any compulsory counterclaims. *Regents of Univ. of New Mexico v. Knight*, 321 F.3d 1111 (Fed. Cir. 2003). Legislation has been proposed, but never enacted, to respond to *College Savings* by denying certain federal intellectual property rights to states that fail to waive their immunity to infringement suits.

C. INFRINGEMENT ADJUDICATION

1. JURISDICTION AND VENUE

Exclusive Federal Jurisdiction: Under 28 U.S.C. § 1338(a), the federal district courts have exclusive jurisdiction over "any claim for relief *arising under* any Act of Congress relating to patents, plant variety protection, or copyrights" (emphasis added). This is not to say that federal courts have jurisdiction over all claims for relief *related to* patents. For example, the Supreme Court ruled in *Gunn v. Minton*, 568 U.S. 251 (2013), that inventor Minton's claim for legal malpractice in the prosecution of his patent application did not fall within the exclusive patent jurisdiction of the federal courts under 28 U.S.C. § 1338(a) because it did not "arise under" federal law—even in the special category of cases with disputed and substantial federal issues but without a federal cause of action. Issues related to the validity or interpretation of contracts, such as patent assignment agreements, similarly do not create federal subject matter jurisdiction.

Appellate Jurisdiction: Under 28 U.S.C. § 1295(a)(1), the Federal Circuit has exclusive appellate jurisdiction over a district court's final decision "in any civil action arising under, or in any civil action in which a party has asserted a compulsory counterclaim arising under any Act of Congress related to patents or plant variety protection." The Federal Circuit was created in large part to consolidate patent-related appeals (although it also has responsibility for a wider, and significant, variety of other matters), and it now hears all appeals of substantive patent law issues decided in infringement actions as well as the appeals from the PTO's administrative tribunal. At its creation in 1982, the Federal Circuit adopted as binding precedent the decisions of its predecessor courts, the United States Court of Claims and the Court of Customs and Patent Appeals. Although the Federal Circuit follows these and its own precedents regarding matters over which it has exclusive jurisdiction, in cases involving a mix of patent and nonpatent issues, it follows the precedents of the United States Court of Appeals for the Circuit which would otherwise have had jurisdiction over the appeal when it addresses any nonpatent issues in the case.

Venue: Patent and copyright cases have a specific venue provision—28 U.S.C. § 1400—rather than only using the general venue provision in 28 U.S.C. § 1391. Section 1400 provides that:

> (a) Civil actions, suits, or proceedings arising under any Act of Congress relating to copyrights or exclusive rights in mask works or designs may be instituted in the district in which the defendant or his agent resides or may be found.
>
> (b) Any civil action for patent infringement may be brought in the judicial district where the defendant resides, or where the defendant has committed acts of infringement and has a regular and established place of business.

The Supreme Court interpreted the "where the defendant resides" portion of the patent venue provision in *TC Heartland, LLC v. Kraft Foods Group Brands, LLC*, 137 S.Ct. 1514 (2017), applying *Fourco Glass Co. v. Transmirra Products Corp.*, 353 U.S. 222, 226 (1957), which held that for purposes of § 1400(b) a domestic corporation "resides" only in its State of incorporation. 137 S.Ct. at 1517 (2017). The Federal Circuit had been using a different interpretation, relying on broad language related to corporate residence in some intervening amendments to the general venue statute, 28 U.S.C. § 1391, but the Supreme Court rejected that interpretation. The Court did not address the second basis for venue under § 1400(b), "where the defendant has committed acts of infringement and has a regular and established place of business." It also did not address whether, when a domestic entity is organized in a state with multiple judicial districts, venue is proper in all of the judicial districts of that state.

2. PROPER PLAINTIFFS AND DEFENDANTS

a. Standing to Bring Infringement Actions

Under 35 U.S.C. § 281, standing to bring an infringement claim is limited to patent owners (unless they have assigned all significant rights under the patent), their assignees, and, in some cases, their exclusive licensees. Ordinarily, an exclusive licensee has standing to bring suit independently only when the licensee holds all substantial rights in the patent; otherwise, the licensee may sue only by joining the patent owner as an indispensable co-plaintiff. However, an exception is recognized where the infringer is the patent owner. *See Mentor H/S, Inc. v. Medical Device Alliance, Inc.*, 240 F.3d 1016, 1017 (Fed.Cir.2001). Furthermore, an exclusive licensee has standing to sue an infringer only if the rights infringed are within the scope of the license. Where patent rights have been transferred, standing belongs to the party that owned the infringed rights at the time of the infringement.

Where parties share undivided co-ownership of patent rights (as joint inventors, for example), the traditional rule is that an infringement action can proceed only if all co-owners join voluntarily as plaintiffs. A few decisions, however, have departed from that rule. *See, e.g., Willingham v. Lawton*, 555 F.2d 1340 (6th Cir.1977) (allowing action to proceed where co-owner was joined as involuntary plaintiff, and where co-owners had agreed by contract that either could sue an infringer even if the other did not join).

b. Proper Joinder of Defendants

Until the AIA, multi-defendant patent litigation had become quite common. A patentee would often join in one lawsuit all defendants against whom it had a claim of infringement of a given patent, even when the defendants were unrelated to one another and had not acted together in any way. This reduced litigation costs for the patentee. Effective for all civil actions filed on or after September 16, 2011, however, accused infringers may be joined in one action only if: (1) the patentee proceeds against the parties jointly, severally or in the alternative, and the infringing acts relate to or arise out of the same transaction, occurrence, or series of transactions or occurrences involving the same accused product or process; and (2) questions of fact common to all defendants will arise in the action. *See* 35 U.S.C. § 299.

c. Declaratory Judgment Actions

On the principle that the best defense is a good offense, a party that anticipates being sued for patent infringement may seek to take the offensive by asking a federal court to issue a declaratory judgment that the claims in question are invalid or are not infringed. Such a determination may help a potential infringer decide whether to make a substantial investment in the technology necessary to produce the product or service in question. When filing an action seeking a declaratory judgment of invalidity or non-infringement of a patent, one generally determines the proper declaratory judgment defendants by looking to the rules on proper standing to sue for infringement.

Although a declaratory judgment can sometimes benefit a potential infringer, not every would-be declaratory judgment plaintiff presents a "case" or "controversy" that is justiciable by the federal courts. Pursuant to Article III of the Constitution and the Declaratory Judgment Act, federal courts will not rule on hypothetical scenarios, requiring instead that an actual case or controversy exist. In the 2007 case that follows, the Supreme Court clarified the standards for determining when a potential patent infringer may obtain a declaratory judgment, articulating a more liberal policy than the Federal Circuit had earlier embraced.

MEDIMMUNE, INC. V. GENENTECH, INC.

549 U.S. 118, 127 S.Ct. 764 (2007).

JUSTICE SCALIA delivered the opinion of the Court.

We must decide whether Article III's limitation of federal courts' jurisdiction to "Cases" and "Controversies," reflected in the "actual controversy" requirement of the Declaratory Judgment Act, 28 U.S.C. § 2201(a), requires a patent licensee to terminate or be in breach of its license agreement before it can seek a declaratory judgment that the underlying patent is invalid, unenforceable, or not infringed.

I

[Respondent patent owner Genentech entered an agreement to license its then-pending patent (the "Cabilly II" patent) to petitioner MedImmune. MedImmune agreed to pay royalties on sales of products which would, in the absence of the license, infringe one or more claims in the patent until the patent expired or the claims were held invalid. The licensing agreement gave MedImmune the right to terminate upon six months' written notice. When the patent issued, Genentech demanded that MedImmune begin paying royalties. Although MedImmune believed that the patent was invalid, it paid the royalties "under protest and with reservation of all of [its] rights." MedImmune then commenced this declaratory judgment action. The district court dismissed the declaratory judgment claims, relying on Federal Circuit case law that held that patent licensees had no justiciable case or controversy when in good standing under the license because such licensees had no reasonable apprehension of being sued. The Federal Circuit affirmed.]

* * *

III

The Declaratory Judgment Act provides that, "[i]n a case of actual controversy within its jurisdiction . . . any court of the United States . . . may declare the rights and other legal relations of any interested party seeking such declaration, whether or not further relief is or could be sought." 28 U.S.C. § 2201(a). There was a time when this Court harbored doubts about the compatibility of declaratory-judgment actions with Article III's case-or-controversy requirement. We dispelled those doubts, however, in *Nashville, C. & St. L.R. Co. v. Wallace,* 288 U.S. 249 (1933), holding (in a case involving a declaratory judgment rendered in state court) that an appropriate action for declaratory relief *can* be a case or controversy under Article III. The federal Declaratory Judgment Act was signed into law the following year, and we upheld its constitutionality in *Aetna Life Ins. Co. v. Haworth,* 300 U.S. 227 (1937). Our opinion explained that the phrase "case of actual controversy" in the Act refers to the type of "Cases" and "Controversies" that are justiciable under Article III.

Aetna and the cases following it do not draw the brightest of lines between those declaratory-judgment actions that satisfy the case-or-controversy requirement and those that do not. Our decisions have required that the dispute be "definite and concrete, touching the legal relations of parties having adverse legal interests"; and that it be "real and substantial" and "admi[t] of specific relief through a decree of a conclusive character, as distinguished from an opinion advising what the law would be upon a hypothetical state of facts." * * * "Basically, the question in each case is whether the facts alleged, under all the circumstances, show that there is a substantial controversy, between parties having adverse legal interests, of sufficient immediacy and reality to warrant the issuance of a declaratory judgment."

There is no dispute that these standards would have been satisfied if petitioner had taken the final step of refusing to make royalty payments under the 1997 license agreement. Respondents claim a right to royalties under the licensing agreement. Petitioner asserts that no royalties are owing because the Cabilly II patent is invalid and not infringed; and alleges (without contradiction) a threat by respondents to enjoin sales if royalties are not forthcoming. The factual and legal dimensions of the dispute are well defined and, but for petitioner's continuing to make royalty payments, nothing about the dispute would render it unfit for judicial resolution. Assuming (without deciding) that respondents here could not claim an anticipatory breach and repudiate the license, the continuation of royalty payments makes what would otherwise be an imminent threat at least remote, if not nonexistent. As long as those payments are made, there is no risk that respondents will seek to enjoin petitioner's sales. Petitioner's own acts, in other words, eliminate the imminent threat of harm. The question before us is whether this causes the dispute no longer to be a case or controversy within the meaning of Article III.

Our analysis must begin with the recognition that, where threatened action by *government* is concerned, we do not require a plaintiff to expose himself to liability before bringing suit to challenge the basis for the threat—for example, the constitutionality of a law threatened to be enforced. The plaintiff's own action (or inaction) in failing to violate the law eliminates the imminent threat of prosecution, but nonetheless does not eliminate Article III jurisdiction. * * * [Choosing to avoid violating the law does] not preclude subject-matter jurisdiction because the threat-eliminating behavior [is] effectively coerced. The dilemma posed by that coercion—putting the challenger to the choice between abandoning his rights or risking prosecution—is "a dilemma that it was the very purpose of the Declaratory Judgment Act to ameliorate."

Supreme Court jurisprudence is more rare regarding application of the Declaratory Judgment Act to situations in which the plaintiff's self-avoidance of imminent injury is coerced by threatened enforcement action of *a private party* rather than the government. Lower federal courts, however (and state courts interpreting declaratory judgment Acts requiring "actual controversy"), have long accepted jurisdiction in such cases.

The only Supreme Court decision in point is, fortuitously, close on its facts to the case before us. *Altvater v. Freeman,* 319 U.S. 359 (1943), held that a licensee's failure to cease its payment of royalties did not render nonjusticiable a dispute over the validity of the patent. In that litigation, several patentees had sued their licensees to enforce territorial restrictions in the license. The licensees filed a counterclaim for declaratory judgment that the underlying patents were invalid, in the meantime paying "under protest" royalties required by an injunction the patentees had obtained in an earlier case. The patentees argued that "so long as [licensees] continue to pay royalties, there is only an academic, not a real controversy, between the parties." We rejected that argument and held that the declaratory-judgment claim presented a justiciable case or controversy: "The fact that royalties were being paid did not make this a 'difference or dispute of a hypothetical or abstract character.' " The royalties "were being paid under protest and under the compulsion of an injunction decree," and "[u]nless the injunction decree were modified, the only other course [of action] was to defy it, and to risk not only actual but treble damages in infringement suits." We concluded that "the requirements of [a] case or controversy are met where payment of a claim is demanded as of right and where payment is made, but where the involuntary or coercive nature of the exaction preserves the right to recover the sums paid or to challenge the legality of the claim."

The Federal Circuit [has] distinguished *Altvater* on the ground that it involved the compulsion of an injunction. But *Altvater* cannot be so readily dismissed. Never mind that the injunction had been privately obtained and was ultimately within the control of the patentees, who could permit its modification. More fundamentally, and contrary to the Federal Circuit's conclusion, *Altvater* did not say that the coercion dispositive of the case was governmental, but suggested just the opposite. The opinion acknowledged that the licensees had the option of stopping payments in defiance of the injunction, but explained that the *consequence* of doing so would be to risk "actual [and] treble damages in infringement suits" by the patentees. It significantly did not mention the threat of prosecution for contempt, or any other sort of governmental sanction. Moreover, it cited approvingly a treatise which said that an "actual or threatened serious injury to business or employment" by a private party can be as coercive as other forms of coercion supporting restitution actions at common law; and that "[t]o imperil a man's livelihood, his business enterprises, or his solvency, [was] ordinarily quite as coercive" as, for example, "detaining his property." F.

WOODWARD, THE LAW OF QUASI CONTRACTS § 218 (1913), cited in *Altvater, supra,* at 365.

* * *

Respondents assert that the parties in effect settled this dispute when they entered into the 1997 license agreement. When a licensee enters such an agreement, they contend, it essentially purchases an insurance policy, immunizing it from suits for infringement so long as it continues to pay royalties and does not challenge the covered patents. Permitting it to challenge the validity of the patent without terminating or breaking the agreement alters the deal, allowing the licensee to continue enjoying its immunity while bringing a suit, the elimination of which was part of the patentee's *quid pro quo.* Of course even if it were valid, this argument would have no force with regard to petitioner's claim that the agreement does not call for royalties because their product does not infringe the patent. But even as to the patent invalidity claim, the point seems to us mistaken. To begin with, it is not clear where the prohibition against challenging the validity of the patents is to be found. It can hardly be implied from the mere promise [in the license at issue] to pay royalties on patents "which have neither expired nor been held invalid by a court or other body of competent jurisdiction from which no appeal has been or may be taken." Promising to pay royalties on patents that have not been held invalid does not amount to a promise *not to seek* a holding of their invalidity.

* * *

We hold that petitioner was not required, insofar as Article III is concerned, to break or terminate its 1997 license agreement before seeking a declaratory judgment in federal court that the underlying patent is invalid, unenforceable, or not infringed. The Court of Appeals erred in affirming the dismissal of this action for lack of subject-matter jurisdiction.

The judgment of the Court of Appeals is reversed, and the cause is remanded for proceedings consistent with this opinion.

It is so ordered.

NOTES

1. *Motivation to Challenge:* After *MedImmune,* are patent licensees more likely to seek declaratory judgments? What factors might influence a licensee's decision?

2. *Agreement Not to Challenge:* If a patent license contains a clause in which the licensee expressly agrees not to seek a declaratory judgment of invalidity or non-infringement, should the clause be enforceable?

3. *Influence on Royalty Structure:* How might *MedImmune* affect a potential licensor's decisions to seek a running royalty (*e.g.*, an annual royalty based on the licensee's annual revenues from use of the patented product or process during the term of the license) as opposed to a one-time lump sum royalty payable upon execution of the licensing agreement?

4. *Alternative Avenues:* Like an action for infringement, a declaratory judgment action can involve expensive and protracted litigation. Congress has expanded the opportunities for third parties to file administrative challenges to the validity of patents and pending applications, as explained further in Chapter 11.B.2., *supra*.

5. *Pre-License Declaratory Judgment Action:* The Federal Circuit applied *MedImmune* in *Sandisk Corp. v. STMicroelectronics, Inc.*, 480 F.3d 1372 (Fed. Cir. 2007), where it allowed an action for declaratory judgment of patent invalidity and non-infringement to proceed even before the parties had entered into a licensing agreement. It was sufficient, the court held, that the parties had engaged in licensing negotiations, and that the party seeking the declaratory judgment was engaged in an activity that could give rise to an infringement action:

> In the context of conduct prior to the existence of a license, declaratory judgment jurisdiction generally will not arise merely on the basis that a party learns of the existence of a patent owned by another or even perceives such a patent to pose a risk of infringement, without some affirmative act by the patentee. But Article III jurisdiction may be met where the patentee takes a position that puts the declaratory judgment plaintiff in the position of either pursuing arguably illegal behavior or abandoning that which he claims a right to do. We need not define the outer boundaries of declaratory judgment jurisdiction, which will depend on the application of the principles of declaratory judgment jurisdiction to the facts and circumstances of each case. We hold only that where a patentee asserts rights under a patent based on certain identified ongoing or planned activity of another party, and where that party contends that it has the right to engage in the accused activity without license, an Article III case or controversy will arise and the party need not risk a suit for infringement by engaging in the identified activity before seeking a declaration of its legal rights.

Id. at 1380–81. The court held further that a patentee's declaration that it has no intent to sue for infringement does not eliminate the justiciable controversy, if the patentee has "engaged in a course of conduct that shows a preparedness and willingness to enforce its patent rights." *Id.* at 1383.

6. *Litigation Burdens:* The patentee bears the burden of persuasion when it brings a claim for patent infringement (while a defendant, as noted previously, *see* page 632, bears the burden of persuasion on invalidity and other affirmative defenses). The patentee retains the burden of persuasion on the question of infringement even when the patentee is the defendant in a

declaratory judgment action brought by a plaintiff seeking a noninfringement ruling. In *Medtronic, Inc. v. Mirowski Family Ventures, LLC*, 571 U.S. 191, 200 (2014), the Supreme Court reaffirmed the burden and noted, among other relevant factors underlying its decision, that a patentee who has accused another of infringement—even when that other party is its licensee—is "in a better position than an alleged infringer to know, and to be able to point out, just where, how, and why a product (or process) infringes a claim of [a complex patent containing many pages of claims and limitations]."

D. REMEDIES

The Patent Act allows a court to grant injunctive relief "to prevent the violation of any right secured by patent" and damages "adequate to compensate for the infringement." Attorney's fees may be available to the prevailing party (either patentee or defendant), but only if the case is "exceptional."

1. INJUNCTIONS

Statute: 35 U.S.C. § 283

The grant of an injunction against infringement remains a typical—although not automatic—remedy awarded to a successful patent plaintiff. Until the Supreme Court decision below, the Federal Circuit applied a "general rule" that a permanent injunction would issue against infringement absent "exceptional circumstances."

EBAY, INC. V. MERCEXCHANGE, L.L.C.

547 U.S. 388, 126 S.Ct. 1837 (2006).

JUSTICE THOMAS delivered the opinion of the Court.

Ordinarily, a federal court considering whether to award permanent injunctive relief to a prevailing plaintiff applies the four-factor test historically employed by courts of equity. Petitioners eBay Inc. and Half.com, Inc., argue that this traditional test applies to disputes arising under the Patent Act. We agree and, accordingly, vacate the judgment of the Court of Appeals.

I

Petitioner eBay operates a popular Internet Web site that allows private sellers to list goods they wish to sell, either through an auction or at a fixed price. Petitioner Half.com, now a wholly owned subsidiary of eBay, operates a similar Web site. Respondent MercExchange, L.L.C., holds a number of patents, including a business method patent for an electronic market designed to facilitate the sale of goods between private individuals by establishing a central authority to promote trust among participants. *See* U.S. Patent No. 5,845,265. MercExchange sought to license its patent to eBay and Half.com, as it had previously done with other companies, but the parties failed to reach an agreement. MercExchange subsequently filed a patent infringement suit against eBay and Half.com * * *. A jury found that MercExchange's patent was valid, that eBay and Half.com had infringed that patent, and that an award of damages was appropriate. [The district court denied a permanent injunction, and the Federal Circuit reversed.]

* * *

II

According to well-established principles of equity, a plaintiff seeking a permanent injunction must satisfy a four-factor test before a court may grant such relief. A plaintiff must demonstrate: (1) that it has suffered an irreparable injury; (2) that remedies available at law, such as monetary damages, are inadequate to compensate for that injury; (3) that, considering the balance of hardships between the plaintiff and defendant, a remedy in equity is warranted; and (4) that the public interest would not be disserved by a permanent injunction. The decision to grant or deny permanent injunctive relief is an act of equitable discretion by the district court, reviewable on appeal for abuse of discretion.

These familiar principles apply with equal force to disputes arising under the Patent Act. As this Court has long recognized, "a major departure from the long tradition of equity practice should not be lightly implied." Nothing in the Patent Act indicates that Congress intended such a departure. To the contrary, the Patent Act expressly provides that injunctions "may" issue "in accordance with the principles of equity." 35 U.S.C. § 283.

To be sure, the Patent Act also declares that "patents shall have the attributes of personal property," § 261, including "the right to exclude others from making, using, offering for sale, or selling the invention," § 154(a)(1). According to the Court of Appeals, this statutory right to exclude alone justifies its general rule in favor of permanent injunctive relief. But the creation of a right is distinct from the provision of remedies for violations of that right. Indeed, the Patent Act itself indicates that patents shall have the attributes of personal property "[s]ubject to the provisions of this title," 35 U.S.C. § 261, including, presumably, the provision that injunctive relief "may" issue only "in accordance with the principles of equity," § 283.

This approach is consistent with our treatment of injunctions under the Copyright Act. Like a patent owner, a copyright holder possesses "the right to exclude others from using his property." *Fox Film Corp. v. Doyal*, 286 U.S. 123, 127 (1932); *see also id.*, at 127–128 ("A copyright, like a patent, is at once the equivalent given by the public for benefits bestowed by the genius and meditations and skill of individuals, and the incentive to further efforts for the same important objects" (internal quotation marks omitted)). Like the Patent Act, the Copyright Act provides that courts "may" grant injunctive relief "on such terms as it may deem reasonable to prevent or restrain infringement of a copyright." 17 U.S.C. § 502(a). And as in our decision today, this Court has consistently rejected invitations to replace traditional equitable considerations with a rule that an injunction automatically follows a determination that a copyright has been infringed. *See, e.g., New York Times Co. v. Tasini,* 533 U.S. 483, 505 (2001) (citing *Campbell v. Acuff-Rose Music, Inc.,* 510 U.S. 569, 578, n. 10 (1994)).

Neither the District Court nor the Court of Appeals below fairly applied these traditional equitable principles in deciding respondent's motion for a permanent injunction. Although the District Court recited the traditional four-factor test, it appeared to adopt certain expansive principles suggesting that injunctive relief could not issue in a broad swath of cases. Most notably, it concluded that a "plaintiff's willingness to license its patents" and "its lack of commercial activity in practicing the patents" would be sufficient to establish that the patent holder would not suffer irreparable harm if an injunction did not issue. *Id.,* at 712. But traditional equitable principles do not permit such broad classifications. For example, some patent holders, such as university researchers or self-made inventors, might reasonably prefer to license their patents, rather than undertake efforts to secure the financing necessary to bring their works to market themselves. Such patent holders may be able to satisfy the traditional four-factor test, and we see no basis for categorically denying them the opportunity to do so. To the extent that the District Court adopted such a categorical rule, then, its analysis cannot be squared with the principles of equity adopted by Congress. The court's categorical rule is also in tension with *Continental Paper Bag Co. v. Eastern Paper Bag Co.,* 210 U.S. 405, 422–430 (1908), which rejected the contention that a court of equity has no jurisdiction to grant injunctive relief to a patent holder who has unreasonably declined to use the patent.

In reversing the District Court, the Court of Appeals departed in the opposite direction from the four-factor test. The court articulated a "general rule," unique to patent disputes, "that a permanent injunction will issue once infringement and validity have been adjudged." The court further indicated that injunctions should be denied only in the "unusual" case, under "exceptional circumstances" and " 'in rare instances . . . to protect the public interest.' " Just as the District Court erred in its categorical denial of injunctive relief, the Court of Appeals erred in its categorical grant of such relief. *Cf. Roche Products v. Bolar Pharmaceutical Co.,* 733 F.2d 858, 865 (C.A.Fed.1984) (recognizing the "considerable discretion" district courts have "in determining whether the facts of a situation require it to issue an injunction").

Because we conclude that neither court below correctly applied the traditional four-factor framework that governs the award of injunctive relief, we vacate the judgment of the Court of Appeals, so that the District Court may apply that framework in the first instance. In doing so, we take no position on whether permanent injunctive relief should or should not issue in this particular case, or indeed in any number of other disputes arising under the Patent Act. We hold only that the decision whether to grant or deny injunctive relief rests within the equitable discretion of the district courts, and that such discretion must be exercised consistent with traditional principles of equity, in patent disputes no less than in other cases governed by such standards.

Accordingly, we vacate the judgment of the Court of Appeals, and remand for further proceedings consistent with this opinion.

It is so ordered.

CHIEF JUSTICE ROBERTS, with whom JUSTICE SCALIA and JUSTICE GINSBURG join, concurring.

I agree with the Court's holding that "the decision whether to grant or deny injunctive relief rests within the equitable discretion of the district courts, and that such discretion must be exercised consistent with traditional principles of equity, in patent disputes no less than in other cases governed by such standards," *ante*, at 1841, and I join the opinion of the Court. That opinion rightly rests on the proposition that "a major departure from the long tradition of equity practice should not be lightly implied."

From at least the early 19th century, courts have granted injunctive relief upon a finding of infringement in the vast majority of patent cases. This "long tradition of equity practice" is not surprising, given the difficulty of protecting a right to *exclude* through monetary remedies that allow an infringer to *use* an invention against the patentee's wishes—a difficulty that often implicates the first two factors of the traditional four-factor test. This historical practice, as the Court holds, does not *entitle* a patentee to a permanent injunction or justify a *general rule* that such injunctions should issue. * * * At the same time, there is a difference between exercising equitable discretion pursuant to the established four-factor test and writing on an entirely clean slate. "Discretion is not whim, and limiting discretion according to legal standards helps promote the basic principle of justice that like cases should be decided alike." When it comes to discerning and applying those standards, in this area as others, "a page of history is worth a volume of logic."

JUSTICE KENNEDY, with whom JUSTICE STEVENS, JUSTICE SOUTER, and JUSTICE BREYER join, concurring.

The Court is correct, in my view, to hold that courts should apply the well-established, four-factor test—without resort to categorical rules—in deciding whether to grant injunctive relief in patent cases. The Chief Justice is also correct that history may be instructive in applying this test. *Ante,* at 1841–1842 (concurring opinion). The traditional practice of issuing injunctions against patent infringers, however, does not seem to rest on "the difficulty of protecting a right to *exclude* through monetary remedies that allow an infringer to *use* an invention against the patentee's wishes." *Ante,* at 1841 (ROBERTS, C.J., concurring). Both the terms of the Patent Act and the traditional view of injunctive relief accept that the existence of a right to exclude does not dictate the remedy for a violation of that right. *Ante,* at 1839–1840 (opinion of the Court). To the extent earlier cases establish a pattern of granting an injunction against patent infringers almost as a matter of course, this pattern simply illustrates the result of the four-factor test in the contexts then prevalent. The lesson of the historical practice, therefore, is most helpful and instructive when the circumstances of a case bear substantial parallels to litigation the courts have confronted before.

In cases now arising trial courts should bear in mind that in many instances the nature of the patent being enforced and the economic function of the patent holder present considerations quite unlike earlier cases. An industry has developed in which firms use patents not as a basis for producing and selling goods but, instead, primarily for obtaining licensing fees. *See* FTC, To Promote Innovation: The Proper Balance of Competition and Patent Law and Policy, ch. 3, pp. 38–39 (Oct.2003), available at http://www.ftc.gov/os/2003/10/innovationrpt.pdf (as visited May 11, 2006, and available in Clerk of Court's case file). For these firms, an injunction, and the potentially serious sanctions arising from its violation, can be employed as a bargaining tool to charge exorbitant fees to companies that seek to buy licenses to practice the patent. *See ibid.* When the patented invention is but a small component of the product the companies seek to produce and the threat of an injunction is employed simply for undue leverage in negotiations, legal damages may well be sufficient to compensate for the infringement and an injunction may not serve the public interest. In addition injunctive relief may have different consequences for the burgeoning number of patents over business methods, which were not of much economic and legal significance in earlier times. The potential vagueness and suspect validity of some of these patents may affect the calculus under the four-factor test.

The equitable discretion over injunctions, granted by the Patent Act, is well suited to allow courts to adapt to the rapid technological and legal developments in the patent system. For these reasons it should be recognized that district courts must determine whether past practice fits the circumstances of the cases before them. With these observations, I join the opinion of the Court.

NOTES

1. *Withholding Injunctive Relief:* Under what circumstances would it be appropriate to withhold permanent injunctive relief against a patent infringer? Do the majority and concurring opinions in *eBay v. MercExchange* agree? The Federal Circuit, while clearly acknowledging the *eBay* decision, remains noticeably in favor of injunctive relief. *See Robert Bosch LLC v. Pylon Mfg. Corp.*, 659 F.3d 1142, 1149 (Fed. Cir. 2011):

> We . . . confirm that *eBay* jettisoned the presumption of irreparable harm as it applies to determining the appropriateness of injunctive relief . . . . . [Nevertheless,] it does not follow that courts should entirely ignore the fundamental nature of patents as property rights granting the owner the right to exclude . . . . . Although the Supreme Court disapproved of this court's absolute reliance on the patentee's right to exclude as a basis for our prior rule favoring injunctions, that does not mean that the nature of patent rights has no place in the appropriate equitable analysis.

The Federal Circuit has also, since *eBay*, affirmed the denial of permanent injunctive relief. For example, in *Nichia Corp. v. Everlight Americas, Inc.*, 855 F.3d 1328 (Fed. Cir. 2017), it affirmed a district court's denial of an injunction where the district court had found the patentee failed to establish irreparable harm because it had not demonstrated: the infringer and patentee were "meaningful competitors"; any sales were lost as a result of the infringement; or erosion of the patentee's prices due to the infringement.

2. *Non-Practicing or Patent Assertion Entities: eBay v. MercExchange* involved a patent holder that (1) had not practiced or licensed the patent invention, and (2) had probably acquired the patent only for the purpose of suing infringers. Such patent holders are sometimes referred to as "patent trolls," although less pejorative terminology might be "non-practicing entity" or "patent assertion entity." (Can you match each of those terms to the two different characteristics of the *eBay* plaintiff?) Under the Court's decision, should the availability of a permanent injunction depend on whether the patent holder is exploiting the patent, including by licensing it to others in return for royalties, or whether the patent owner is the original assignee of the patent?

3. *Effect on Licensing:* How might the decision in *eBay v. MercExchange* influence settlement negotiations between patent holders and alleged infringers?

4. *Post-Term Injunction:* Where the term of a patent expires during the infringement litigation, should an injunction be awarded in order to effectively extend the patent term against the losing defendant?

5. *Preliminary Injunctions:* In determining when to grant a preliminary injunction (as opposed to a permanent injunction) in a patent infringement proceeding, a court must evaluate: (1) whether the plaintiff has demonstrated a reasonable likelihood of success on the merits, (2) whether irreparable harm will occur if injunctive relief is denied, (3) whether the balance of hardships tips in the plaintiff's favor, and (4) whether issuing an injunction is in the public interest. No one factor is dispositive. *See, e.g., Chrysler Motors Corp. v. Auto Body Panels of Ohio, Inc.*, 908 F.2d 951, 953 (Fed.Cir.1990). In a case where the defendant challenges the validity of the patent in suit, the plaintiff seeking a preliminary injunction cannot rely solely on the statutory presumption of patent validity under section 282 with respect to "likelihood of success"; according to the Federal Circuit, the plaintiff must make a "clear showing" that the defendant's challenge to the patent's validity will fail. *See, e.g., Chrysler Motors*, 908 F.2d at 954; *Atlas Powder Co. v. Ireco Chemicals*, 773 F.2d 1230, 1232–33 (Fed.Cir.1985). And as to "irreparable harm," the Federal Circuit requires proof of a causal nexus between the allegedly infringing features of the accused infringer's products and consumer demand for those products (as opposed to consumer demand unrelated to the alleged infringement). On one of the several occasions for the Federal Circuit to decide an issue in the long-lived dispute between Apple and Samsung related to smart phone design and technology, the Federal Circuit explained:

> To show irreparable harm, it is necessary to show that the infringement caused harm in the first place. Sales lost to an infringing product cannot irreparably harm a patentee if consumers buy that product for reasons other than the patented feature. If the patented feature does not drive the demand for the product, sales would be lost even if the offending feature were absent from the accused product. Thus, a likelihood of irreparable harm cannot be shown if sales would be lost regardless of the infringing conduct.

Apple, Inc. v. Samsung Electronics Co., 678 F.3d 1314, 1324 (Fed. Cir. 2012).

6. *Remedies for Infringement by United States:* Under 28 U.S.C. § 1498, an infringement plaintiff may not obtain an injunction against unauthorized use or manufacture of the patented invention "by or for the United States" (including use or manufacture by a government contractor or subcontractor "with the authorization or consent" of the government). The plaintiff's remedies are limited to a suit for "reasonable and entire compensation" in the United States Court of Federal Claims.

2. DAMAGES

Statutes: 35 U.S.C. §§ 284, 286, 287(a)

As observed at the start of this Part D of the chapter, the Patent Act mandates damages "adequate to compensate for the infringement" whenever infringement has been found. It also allows the court to "increase the damages up to three times the amount found or assessed" and provides a floor on damages of a "reasonable royalty for the use made of the invention by the infringer." How to measure the patent owner's damages in the form of lost profits caused by the infringement is the subject of regular disputes.

RITE-HITE CORPORATION V. KELLEY COMPANY, INC.

56 F.3d 1538 (Fed. Cir. 1995).

LOURIE, CIRCUIT JUDGE.

[Patentee Rite-Hite's '847 patent covered its own MDL-55 device which secures a vehicle to a loading dock. Rite-Hite's ADL-100 truck restraint was an older model that did not incorporate the patented invention but did incorporate one or more Rite-Hite patents other than the '847 patent. The district court found that Kelley's "Truk-Stop" product infringed the '847 patent. It held that Rite-Hite was entitled to lost profits for lost sales not only of the MDL-55 truck restraint but also of the ADL-100 because the Truk-Stop also directly competed with the ADL-100. The district court also awarded lost profits for lost sales of Rite-Hite's dock levelers, which did not compete directly with Kelley's infringing Truk-Stop device but which were often sold in a package with the ADL-100 and MDL-55 devices. Kelley appealed, arguing that the patent statute does not provide for damages for lost sales of products (here, the ADL-100 and the dock levelers) not covered by the patent in suit.]

* * *

I. Lost Profits on the ADL-100 Restraints

The district court's decision to award lost profits damages pursuant to 35 U.S.C. § 284 turned primarily upon the quality of Rite-Hite's proof of actual lost profits. The court found that, "but for" Kelley's infringing Truk Stop competition, Rite-Hite would have sold 3,243 additional ADL-100 restraints and 80 additional MDL-55 restraints. The court reasoned that awarding lost profits fulfilled the patent statute's goal of affording complete compensation for infringement and compensated Rite-Hite for the ADL-100 sales that Kelley "anticipated taking from Rite-Hite when it marketed the Truk Stop against the ADL-100." The court stated, "the rule applied here therefore does not extend Rite-Hite's patent rights excessively, because Kelley could reasonably have foreseen that its infringement of the '847 patent would make it liable for lost ADL-100 sales in addition to lost MDL-55 sales." The court further reasoned that its decision would avoid what it referred to as the "whip-saw" problem, whereby an infringer could avoid paying lost profits damages altogether by developing a device using a first patented technology to compete with a device that uses a second patented technology and developing a device using the second patented technology to compete with a device that uses the first patented technology.

Kelley maintains that Rite-Hite's lost sales of the ADL-100 restraints do not constitute an injury that is legally compensable by means of lost profits. It has uniformly been the law, Kelley argues, that to recover damages in the form of lost profits a patentee must prove that, "but for" the infringement, it would have sold a product covered by the patent in suit to the customers who bought from the infringer. Under the circumstances of this case, in Kelley's view, the patent statute provides only for damages calculated as a reasonable royalty. Rite-Hite, on the other hand, argues that the only restriction on an award of actual lost profits damages for patent infringement is proof of causation-in-fact. A patentee, in its view, is entitled to all the profits it would have made on any of its products "but for" the infringement. Each party argues that a judgment in favor of the other would frustrate the purposes of the patent statute. Whether the lost profits at issue are legally compensable is a question of law, which we review de novo.

Our analysis of this question necessarily begins with the patent statute. Implementing the constitutional power under Article I, section 8, to secure to inventors the exclusive right to their discoveries, Congress has provided in 35 U.S.C. § 284 as follows:

> Upon finding for the claimant the court shall award the claimant damages adequate to compensate for the infringement, but in no event less than a reasonable royalty for the use made of the invention by the infringer, together with interest and costs as fixed by the court.

35 U.S.C. § 284 (1988). The statute thus mandates that a claimant receive damages "adequate" to compensate for infringement. Section 284 further instructs that a damage award shall be "in no event less than a reasonable royalty"; the purpose of this alternative is not to direct the form of compensation, but to set a floor below which damage awards may not fall. Thus, the language of the statute is expansive rather than limiting. It affirmatively states that damages must be adequate, while providing only a lower limit and no other limitation.

The Supreme Court spoke to the question of patent damages in *General Motors*, stating that, in enacting § 284, Congress sought to "ensure that the patent owner would in fact receive full compensation for 'any damages' [the patentee] suffered as a result of the infringement." *General Motors Corp.* [*v. Devex Corp.*, 461 U.S. 648,] 654 [(1983)]. Thus, while the statutory text states tersely that the patentee receive "adequate" damages, the Supreme Court has interpreted this to mean that "adequate" damages should approximate those damages that will fully compensate the patentee for infringement. Further, the Court has cautioned against imposing limitations on patent infringement damages, stating: "When Congress wished to limit an element of recovery in a patent infringement action, it said so explicitly." *General Motors*, 461 U.S. at 653 (refusing to impose limitation on court's authority to award interest).

In *Aro Mfg. Co. v. Convertible Top Replacement Co.*, 377 U.S. 476 (1964), the Court discussed the statutory standard for measuring patent infringement damages, explaining:

> The question to be asked in determining damages is "how much had the Patent Holder and Licensee suffered by the infringement. And that question [is] primarily: had the Infringer not infringed, what would the Patentee Holder-Licensee have made?"

377 U.S. at 507 (plurality opinion) (citations omitted). This surely states a "but for" test. In accordance with the Court's guidance, we have held that the general rule for determining actual damages to a patentee that is itself producing the patented item is to determine the sales and profits lost [by] the patentee because of the infringement. *See State Indus., Inc. v. Mor-Flo Indus., Inc.*, 883 F.2d 1573, 1577 (Fed.Cir.1989) (award of damages may be split between lost profits as actual damages to the extent they are proven and a reasonable royalty for the remainder). To recover lost profits damages, the patentee must show a reasonable probability that, "but for" the infringement, it would have made the sales that were made by the infringer.

Panduit Corp. v. Stahlin Bros. Fibre Works, Inc., 575 F.2d 1152 (6th Cir.1978), articulated a four-factor test that has since been accepted as a useful, but non-exclusive, way for a patentee to prove entitlement to lost profits damages. The *Panduit* test requires that a patentee establish: (1) demand for the patented product; (2) absence of acceptable non-infringing substitutes; (3) manufacturing and marketing capability to exploit the demand; and (4) the amount of the profit it would have made. *Panduit*, 575 F.2d at 1156. A showing under *Panduit* permits a court to reasonably infer that the lost profits claimed were in fact caused by the infringing sales, thus establishing a patentee's prima facie case with respect to "but for" causation. A patentee need not negate every possibility that the purchaser might not have purchased a product other than its own, absent the infringement. The patentee need only show that there was a reasonable probability that the sales would have been made "but for" the infringement. When the patentee establishes the reasonableness of this inference, *e.g.*, by satisfying the *Panduit* test, it has sustained the burden of proving entitlement to lost profits due to the infringing sales. The burden then shifts to the infringer to show that the inference is unreasonable for some or all of the lost sales.

Applying *Panduit*, the district court found that Rite-Hite had established "but for" causation. In the court's view, this was sufficient to prove entitlement to lost profits damages on the ADL-100. Kelley does not challenge that Rite-Hite meets the *Panduit* test and therefore has proven "but for" causation; rather, Kelley argues that damages for the ADL-100, even if in fact caused by the infringement, are not legally compensable because the ADL-100 is not covered by the patent in suit.

Preliminarily, we wish to affirm that the "test" for compensability of damages under § 284 is not solely a "but for" test in the sense that an infringer must compensate a patentee for any and all damages that proceed from the act of patent infringement. Notwithstanding the broad language of § 284, judicial relief cannot redress every conceivable harm that can be traced to an alleged wrongdoing. For example, remote consequences, such as a heart attack of the inventor or loss in value of shares of common stock of a patentee corporation caused indirectly by infringement are not compensable. Thus, along with establishing that a particular injury suffered by a patentee is a "but for" consequence of infringement, there may also be a background question whether the asserted injury is of the type for which the patentee may be compensated.

* * *

We believe that under § 284 of the patent statute, the balance between full compensation, which is the meaning that the Supreme Court has attributed to the statute, and the reasonable limits of liability encompassed by general principles of law can best be viewed in terms of reasonable, objective foreseeability. If a particular injury was or should have been reasonably foreseeable by an infringing competitor in the relevant market, broadly defined, that injury is generally compensable absent a persuasive reason to the contrary. Here, the court determined that Rite-Hite's lost sales of the ADL-100, a product that directly competed with the infringing product, were reasonably foreseeable. We agree with that conclusion. Being responsible for lost sales of a competitive product is surely foreseeable; such losses constitute the full compensation set forth by Congress, as interpreted by the Supreme Court, while staying well within the traditional meaning of proximate cause. Such lost sales should therefore clearly be compensable.

Recovery for lost sales of a device not covered by the patent in suit is not of course expressly provided for by the patent statute. Express language is not required, however. Statutes speak in general terms rather than specifically expressing every detail. Under the patent statute, damages should be awarded "where necessary to afford the plaintiff full compensation for the infringement." *General Motors,* 461 U.S. at 654. Thus, to refuse to award reasonably foreseeable damages necessary to make Rite-Hite whole would be inconsistent with the meaning of § 284.

* * *

Kelley further asserts that, as a policy matter, inventors should be encouraged by the law to practice their inventions. This is not a meaningful or persuasive argument, at least in this context. A patent is granted in exchange for a patentee's disclosure of an invention, not for the patentee's use of the invention. There is no requirement in this country that a patentee make, use, or sell its patented invention. If a patentee's failure to practice a patented invention frustrates an important public need for the invention, a court need not enjoin infringement of the patent. *See* 35 U.S.C. § 283 (1988) (courts may grant injunctions in accordance with the principles of equity). Accordingly, courts have in rare instances exercised their discretion to deny injunctive relief in order to protect the public interest. *See, e.g., Hybritech Inc. v. Abbott Lab.*, 4 U.S.P.Q.2D (BNA) 1001 (C.D.Cal.1987) (public interest required that injunction not stop supply of medical test kits that the patentee itself was not marketing), *aff'd*, 849 F.2d 1446 (Fed.Cir.1988); *City of Milwaukee v. Activated Sludge, Inc.*, 21 U.S.P.Q. (BNA) 69 (7th Cir.1934) (injunction refused against city operation of sewage disposal plant because of public health danger). * * *

Kelley next argues that to award lost profits damages on Rite-Hite's ADL-100s would be contrary to precedent. Citing *Panduit,* Kelley argues that case law regarding lost profits uniformly requires that "the intrinsic value of the patent in suit is the only proper basis for a lost profits award." Kelley argues that each prong of the Panduit test focuses on the patented invention; thus, Kelley asserts, Rite-Hite cannot obtain damages consisting of lost profits on a product that is not the patented invention.

Generally, the *Panduit* test has been applied when a patentee is seeking lost profits for a device covered by the patent in suit. However, *Panduit* is not the sine qua non for proving "but for" causation. If there are other ways to show that the infringement in fact caused the patentee's lost profits, there is no reason why another test should not be acceptable. Moreover, other fact situations may require different means of evaluation, and failure to meet the *Panduit* test does not ipso facto disqualify a loss from being compensable.

* * *

Kelley has thus not provided, nor do we find, any justification in the statute, precedent, policy, or logic to limit the compensability of lost sales of a patentee's device that directly competes with the infringing device if it is proven that those lost sales were caused in fact by the infringement. Such lost sales are reasonably foreseeable and the award of damages is necessary to provide adequate compensation for infringement under 35 U.S.C. § 284. Thus, Rite-Hite's ADL-100 lost sales are legally compensable and we affirm the award of lost profits on the 3,283 sales lost to Rite-Hite's wholesale business in ADL-100 restraints.

II. Damages on the Dock Levelers

Based on the "entire market value rule," the district court awarded lost profits on 1,692 dock levelers that it found Rite-Hite would have sold with the ADL-100 and MDL-55 restraints. Kelley argues that this award must be set aside because Rite-Hite failed to establish that the dock levelers were eligible to be included in the damage computation under the entire market value rule. We agree.

When a patentee seeks damages on unpatented components sold with a patented apparatus, courts have applied a formulation known as the "entire market value rule" to determine whether such components should be included in the damage computation, whether for reasonable royalty purposes or for lost profits purposes. Early cases invoking the entire market value rule required that for a patentee owning an "improvement patent" to recover damages calculated on sales of a larger machine incorporating that improvement, the patentee was required to show that the entire value of the whole machine, as a marketable article, was "properly and legally attributable" to the patented feature. Subsequently, our predecessor court held that damages for component parts used with a patented apparatus were recoverable under the entire market value rule if the patented apparatus "was of such paramount importance that it substantially created the value of the component parts." We have held that the entire market value rule permits recovery of damages based on the value of a patentee's entire apparatus containing several features when the patent-related feature is the "basis for customer demand."

The entire market value rule has typically been applied to include in the compensation base unpatented components of a device when the unpatented and patented components are physically part of the same machine. The rule has been extended to allow inclusion of physically separate unpatented components normally sold with the patented components. However, in such cases, the unpatented and patented components together were considered to be components of a single assembly or parts of a complete machine, or they together constituted a functional unit.

* * *

Thus, the facts of past cases clearly imply a limitation on damages, when recovery is sought on sales of unpatented components sold with patented components, to the effect that the unpatented components must function together with the patented component in some manner so as to produce a desired end product or result. All the components together must be analogous to components of a single assembly or be parts of a complete machine, or they must constitute a functional unit. Our precedent has not extended liability to include items that have essentially no functional relationship to the patented invention and that may have been sold with an infringing device only as a matter of convenience or business advantage. We are not persuaded that we should extend that liability. Damages on such items would constitute more than what is "adequate to compensate for the infringement."

The facts of this case do not meet this requirement. The dock levelers operated to bridge the gap between a loading dock and a truck. The patented vehicle restraint operated to secure the rear of the truck to the loading dock. Although the two devices may have been used together, they did not function together to achieve one result and each could effectively have been used independently of each other. * * * [Although] customers frequently solicited package bids for the simultaneous installation of restraints and dock levelers, they did so because such bids facilitated contracting and construction scheduling, and because both Rite-Hite and Kelley encouraged this linkage by offering combination discounts. The dock levelers were thus sold by Kelley with the restraints only for marketing reasons, not because they essentially functioned together. We distinguish our conclusion to permit damages based on lost sales of the unpatented (not covered by the patent in suit) ADL-100 devices, but not on lost sales of the unpatented dock levelers, by emphasizing that the Kelley Truk Stops were devices competitive with the ADL-100s, whereas the dock levelers were merely items sold together with the restraints for convenience and business advantage. * * *

* * *

NOTES

1. *Reasonable Royalty:* Even where a patentee cannot prove it has been damaged by losing profits due to infringement (for example, where the patentee does not sell a competing product, or where the defendant's customers might have purchased noninfringing substitute goods if the infringing goods had not been offered), under section 284 courts must still award the patentee, at a minimum, a reasonable royalty on sales of the infringing goods. A reasonable royalty may even be, in practice, the predominant measure of damages in patent infringement cases—but that does not mean it is easy to prove. It is often determined on the basis of a hypothetical negotiation occurring between the parties at the time the infringement began. The patentee bears the burden of proof on damages and must satisfy the court that there is a basis in fact to associate the evidence being analyzed by a damages expert (such as royalty rates used in prior licenses) and submitted to the court with the particular hypothetical negotiation at issue in the case. Recent cases have restricted the use of license agreements not specifically related to the patents in suit (within the same industry was not sufficient) and licenses that, while related to the patents in suit as well as other patents, used a different royalty basis (running royalty versus lump sum payment) or contained no information about how the license amount or rate was determined, or what

products were to be produced under the license. *See Uniloc USA, Inc. v. Microsoft Corp.*, 632 F.3d 1292 (Fed. Cir. 2011); *Wordtech Systems, Inc. v. Integrated Networks Solutions, Inc.*, 609 F.3d 1308 (Fed.Cir.2010); *ResQNet.com, Inc. v. Lansa, Inc.*, 594 F.3d 860 (Fed.Cir.2010); *Lucent Techs., Inc. v. Gateway, Inc.*, 580 F.3d 1301 (Fed.Cir.2009).

2. *Alternative Proof of Lost Profits:* As noted in *Rite-Hite*, the *Panduit* test is not the exclusive test of damages in the form of the patent owner's lost profits. Lost profits may be awarded in any situation where the patentee establishes that the infringement caused economic harm. For example, even if the patentee does not establish that particular sales were lost to the infringer, lost profits may be awarded where the infringer's competition forces the patentee to lower its prices or forego a price increase. In a case where the second *Panduit* factor is not satisfied—for example, where a third party offers acceptable noninfringing substitutes—lost profits may be established by showing that the infringement caused a drop in the patentee's market share.

3. *Absence or Presence of Noninfringing Substitutes:* In *King Instruments Corp. v. Perego*, 65 F.3d 941 (Fed.Cir.1995), the Federal Circuit extended the reasoning of *Rite-Hite* to award lost profits where the defendant's infringing product competed *only* with the patentee's unpatented product, because the patentee had opted not to exploit its patented invention at all:

> The 1952 Act, § 154, clarified that a patent empowered its owner "to *exclude others* from making, using, or selling" the invention. 35 U.S.C. § 154 (1952) (emphasis added). The 1952 amendment should have corrected any mistaken belief that patent rights somehow hinged upon the patentee's exploitation of the invention. Inventors possess the natural right to exploit their inventions (subject to the patent rights of others in a dominant patent) apart from any Government grant. Therefore, patent rights do not depend upon the exercise of rights already in the patentee's possession. Thus, the 1952 Act clarified that a patent confers the right to exclude others from exploiting an invention. It does not confer the right to exploit the invention already possessed by the inventor.
>
> This understanding of the right protected by section 284 informs the purpose and scope of the damages provision. Section 284 protects the right to exclude others from exploiting an invention. To invoke that protection, a patentee need not have exercised its natural right to itself make, use, or sell the invention. The damages section, section 284, protects the right to exclude, not the right to exploit. A patentee qualifies for damages adequate to compensate for infringement without exploiting its patent.
>
> * * *
>
> * * * The language of the Patent Act recognizes that the value of a claim to the patentee, and the extent of harm from infringement, do not depend on whether the patentee markets the claimed device.

> To adequately compensate for infringement of the right to exclude, as section 284 requires, "damages" includes lost profits on competing products not covered by the infringed claims.

65 F.3d at 949–52. In *Presidio Components, Inc. v. Am. Technical Ceramics Corp.*, 875 F.3d 1369 (Fed. Cir. 2017), the infringer sold two types of capacitors—one that infringed the patent and one that did not—and the Federal Circuit found that the defendant's non-infringing capacitor was an acceptable non-infringing alternative to the product sold by the patentee (both less expensive than the patentee's product and, for some uses, better performing). The court set aside the jury's award of lost profits and remanded for a determination of a reasonable royalty.

4. *Foreign Lost Profits:* In *WesternGeco LLC v. ION Geophysical Corp.*, 138 S.Ct. 2129 (2018), the Supreme Court held that the presumption against extraterritoriality—stated another way, the presumption that federal statutes apply only within the territorial jurisdiction of the U.S.—did not prevent recovery of lost foreign profits under § 284 for a patent owner who proves infringement under § 271(f)(2). In *WesternGeco*, patentee WesternGeco owned patents covering a system for surveying the ocean floor, which it did not license but instead used to provide services to oil & gas companies who wanted such surveys. Infringer ION manufactured components for a competing survey system and then exported those components to its customers abroad, who competed with WesternGeco in providing surveying services. A jury awarded WesternGeco $12.5 million in royalties and $93.4 million in lost profits related to 10 survey contracts; ION argued that the lost profits award was improper since those contracts were foreign, making the associated losses entirely extraterritorial and beyond the reach of U.S. patent law, even under § 271(f). In holding that the foreign lost profits were not outside the reach of § 284, the Court emphasized that the focus of § 284 is to remedy or compensate for "the infringement" that has occurred, and to do so as completely as possible. The Court majority combined that focus with § 271(f)(2), which the Court argued contains domestic conduct at its heart (the supply of a non-staple component from the U.S. with particular knowledge and intent). As such, it decided that the foreign lost profits damages remained a domestic application of the statute. Stated another way, the majority seemed to be saying that the award of lost foreign profits compensated the plaintiff for defendant's domestic conduct, although the profits were lost on overseas contracts.

5. *Time Limit on Damages Awards:* Section 286 bars damages awards for infringements occurring more than six years before commencement of the infringement suit. It is not a statute of limitations barring suit but merely a limit on monetary recovery. In determining whether the six-year time limit for damages awards has expired in a case of contributory infringement, should the determinative date be that of the direct infringement or the action constituting contributory infringement?

6. *Enhanced Damages:* Section 284 gives a court authority to increase the damage award up to three times the amount found as actual damages. This

grant of remedial authority is discretionary. Over the years, the Federal Circuit had provided district courts with guidance in exercising this discretion and had, in doing so, narrowed the permissible exercise of discretion. The Supreme Court, however, emphasized the broad discretion in the statute in a 2016 case overturning that line of Federal Circuit case law. *Halo Elecs., Inc. v. Pulse Elecs., Inc.*, 579 U.S. 93 (2016).

While "[d]iscretion is not whim," the Court emphasized that there should nevertheless be no rule or formula for enhanced damages under section 284. In the past, the Federal Circuit required the patentee to prove, at a minimum, "objective recklessness" on the part of the infringer before damages could be enhanced. In *Halo*, however, the Court rejected that standard for the enhancement of damages as "unduly rigid." For example, it observed that "[t]he subjective willfulness of a patent infringer, intentional or knowing, may warrant enhanced damages, without regard to whether his infringement was objectively reckless." *Id.* at 105. The Court eliminated the narrow objective recklessness standard and instead instructed that a district court should simply be mindful of the "considerations" underlying Congress's decision to allow for enhanced damages. One noted "consideration" related to the discretionary, rather than mandatory, enhancement of damages was "the 'injustice' of subjecting a 'defendant who acted in ignorance or good faith' to the same treatment as the 'wanton and malicious pirate.'" *Id.* at 97–98 (quoting *Seymour v. McCormick*, 16 How. 480, 488 (1854)).

> Awards of enhanced damages under the Patent Act over the past 180 years establish that they are not to be meted out in a typical infringement case, but are instead designed as a "punitive" or "vindictive" sanction for egregious infringement behavior. The sort of conduct warranting enhanced damages has been variously described in our cases as willful, wanton, malicious, bad-faith, deliberate, consciously wrongful, flagrant, or—indeed—characteristic of a pirate. District courts enjoy discretion in deciding whether to award enhanced damages, and in what amount. But through nearly two centuries * * * "the channel of discretion ha[s] narrowed," so that such damages are generally reserved for egregious cases of culpable behavior.

Id. at 103–04 (citations omitted). The Court did observe that the Federal Circuit's test "sound[ly] recogni[zed]" that enhancement should generally be limited to "egregious" cases. *Id.* at 104. The majority opinion ended by emphasizing that the principles guiding patent law and its remedies for infringement "channel the exercise of discretion, limiting the award of enhanced damages to egregious cases of misconduct beyond typical infringement." *Id.* at 110. The standard of proof for enhanced damages under section 284 is simply a preponderance of the evidence, and the district court's decision should be reviewed under an abuse-of-discretion standard. *Halo*, 136 S.Ct. at 107.

7. *Interest:* Although not mandatory, prejudgment interest is normally awarded on the amount found to be the patentee's damages in order to ensure that the total damages award satisfies section 284's goal of full compensation for infringement. However, courts have held that it is not appropriate to award prejudgment interest on enhanced damages.

8. *Marking:* Section 287(a) imposes a duty to mark patented articles; if the patentee does not satisfy the marking requirement, then damages may be recovered only for infringements that occur after the infringer receives notice of the infringement (a requirement which may be satisfied by filing the infringement suit). "[O]nce marking has begun, it must be substantially consistent and continuous in order for the party to avail itself of the constructive notice provisions of the statute." *American Medical Sys., Inc. v. Medical Eng'g Corp.*, 6 F.3d 1523, 1537 (Fed.Cir.1993). In *Maxwell v. J. Baker, Inc.*, 86 F.3d 1098 (Fed.Cir.1996), the Federal Circuit applied a "rule of reason" test to determine whether a third party's (*e.g.*, a licensee's) failure to mark should affect the patentee's damages entitlement:

> When the failure to mark is caused by someone other than the patentee, the court may consider whether the patentee made reasonable efforts to ensure compliance with the marking requirements. The rule of reason is consistent with the purpose of the constructive notice provision—to encourage patentees to mark their products in order to provide notice to the public of the existence of the patent and to prevent innocent infringement.

86 F.3d at 1111–12 (citing *American Medical*, 6 F.3d at 1538). Marking is a matter of constructive notice; it does not guarantee that a particular defendant has encountered the marked article (for example, where the defendant independently produces the same invention or acquires the infringing article without knowledge that it is infringing).

Is it fair to hold a defendant liable in damages for use or sale of an infringing article without knowledge that it infringes? Is the marking prerequisite inconsistent with the holding of *Rite-Hite* that lost profits may be awarded even where the patentee has not exploited the infringed patent?

The marking requirement does not apply to limit recovery when an infringement suit asserts *only* method claims, even if the patent as a whole contains both method and apparatus claims. *See Crown Packaging v. Rexam Beverage Can Co.*, 559 F.3d 1308 (Fed. Cir. 2009).

> The purpose behind the marking statute is to encourage the patentee to give notice to the public of the patent. The reason that the marking statute does not apply to method claims is that, ordinarily, where the patent claims are directed to only a method or process there is nothing to mark. Where the patent contains both apparatus and method claims, however, to the extent that there is a tangible item to mark by which notice of the asserted method claims can be given, a

party is obliged to do so if it intends to avail itself of the constructive notice provisions of section 287(a).

American Medical Systems, Inc. v. Medical Engineering Corp., 6 F.3d 1523, 1538–39 (Fed.Cir.1993).

> In this case, *both apparatus and method claims of the '765 patent were asserted* and there was a physical device produced by the claimed method that was capable of being marked. Therefore, we conclude that AMS was required to mark its product pursuant to section 287(a) in order to recover damages under its method claims prior to actual or constructive notice being given to MEC.

Id. at 1539 (emphasis added).

9. *False Marking:* Penalties for false marking are set forth in section 292. Before the AIA, the statute allowed any person to sue for a fine of up to $500 for every false marking offense, with half going to the litigant and half to the government. After a brief burst of private qui tam actions, however, the 2011 AIA revised the statute to narrow private enforcement to "a person who has suffered a competitive injury" as a result of false marking; that person may recover "damages adequate to compensate for the injury." AIA § 16(b). The government retains the ability to sue for the $500 penalty for each false marking offense. The amendment applied to pending and future cases. False marking is not a strict liability offense; instead, it requires a showing of intent to deceive the public.

3. ADDITIONAL REMEDIES

Statutes: 35 U.S.C. §§ 285, 289

Attorney's Fees: Section 285 permits courts in "exceptional cases" to award attorneys' fees to prevailing infringement litigants. This provision, like section 284, is discretionary. Under section 285, the Federal Circuit had limited the scope of "exceptional" cases for purposes of awarding attorneys' fees to: (1) cases in which there had been "material inappropriate conduct related to the matter in litigation, such as willful infringement, fraud or inequitable conduct in procuring the patent, misconduct during litigation, vexatious or unjustified litigation, conduct that violates Fed. R. Civ. P. 11, or like infractions"; or (2) situations in which *both* (a) the patentee had brought the litigation in subjective bad faith and (b) the litigation was objectively baseless. *Brooks Furniture Mfg., Inc. v. Dutailier Int'l, Inc.*, 393 F.3d 1378, 1381 (Fed. Cir. 2005). In *Octane Fitness, LLC v. Icon Health & Fitness, Inc.*, 572 U.S. 545 (2014), however, the Supreme Court rejected that formulation because it "superimposes an inflexible framework onto statutory text that is inherently flexible" and "it is so demanding that it would appear to render § 285 largely superfluous." *Id.* at 555, 557. The Court construed section 285 largely by reference to the "ordinary meaning" of "exceptional," which it determined to mean a case "that stands out from others with respect to the substantive strength of a party's litigating position (considering both the governing law and the facts of the case) or the unreasonable manner in which the case was litigated." *Id.* at 553–54. It stated that "District courts may determine whether a case is 'exceptional' in the case-by-case exercise of their discretion, considering the totality of the circumstances." *Id.* at 554. The standard of proof for shifting fees under section 285 is simply a preponderance of the evidence, *id.* at 557–58, and district court fee-shifting decisions are subject to appellate review for an abuse of discretion, *Highmark Inc. v. Allcare Health Mgmt. Sys., Inc.*, 572 U.S. 559, 563–64 (2014).

Additional Remedy for Design Patents: The same remedial provisions that apply to utility patents apply equally to design patents. In addition, however, the design patentee may recover the infringer's total profit, with a minimum award of $250. 35 U.S.C. § 289. In *Samsung Electronics Co. v. Apple Inc.*, 580 U.S. 53, 137 S.Ct. 429 (2016), the Supreme Court addressed section 289 and its award of "total profit" for design patent infringement.

> Section 289 allows a patent holder to recover the total profit an infringer makes from the infringement. It does so by first prohibiting the unlicensed "appli[cation]" of a "patented design, or any colorable imitation thereof, to any article of manufacture for the purpose of sale" or the unlicensed sale or exposure to sale of "any article of manufacture to which [a patented] design or colorable imitation has been applied." 35 U.S.C. § 289. It then makes a person who violates that prohibition "liable to the owner to the extent of his total profit, but not less than $250." *Ibid.* "Total," of course, means all. *See* American Heritage Dictionary 1836 (5th ed. 2011) ("[t]he whole amount of something; the entirety"). The "total profit" for which § 289 makes an infringer liable is thus all of the profit made from the prohibited conduct, that is, from the manufacture or sale of the "article of manufacture to which [the patented] design or colorable imitation has been applied."
>
> Arriving at a damages award under § 289 thus involves two steps. First, identify the "article of manufacture" to which the infringed design has been applied. Second, calculate the infringer's total profit made on that article of manufacture.
>
> This case requires us to address a threshold matter: the scope of the term "article of manufacture." The only question we resolve today is whether, in the case of a multicomponent product, the relevant "article of manufacture" must always be the end product sold to the consumer or whether it can also be a component of that product. * * *

> The text resolves this case. The term "article of manufacture," as used in § 289, encompasses both a product sold to a consumer and a component of that product.
>
> * * *
>
> * * * That a component may be integrated into a larger product * * * does not put it outside the category of articles of manufacture.
>
> This reading of article of manufacture in § 289 is consistent with 35 U.S.C. § 171(a), which makes "new, original and ornamental design[s] for an article of manufacture" eligible for design patent protection. The Patent Office and the courts have understood § 171 to permit a design patent for a design extending to only a component of a multicomponent product. * * *
>
> * * *
>
> * * * [R]eading "article of manufacture" in § 289 to cover only an end product sold to a consumer gives too narrow a meaning to the phrase.
>
> The parties ask us to go further and resolve whether, for each of the design patents at issue here, the relevant article of manufacture is the smartphone, or a particular smartphone component. Doing so would require us to set out a test for identifying the relevant article of manufacture. * * * We decline to lay out a test for the first step of the § 289 damages inquiry in the absence of adequate briefing by the parties. Doing so is not necessary to resolve the question presented in this case, and the Federal Circuit may address any remaining issues on remand.

137 S.Ct. at 434–36.

Section 337 Proceedings: In a situation involving importation of infringing goods into the United States, an additional remedy may be obtained in a section 337 proceeding before the U.S. International Trade Commission (ITC). Where infringement is found, the ITC is empowered to issue an exclusion order instructing the U.S. Customs Service to prevent the infringing goods from entering the country. 19 U.S.C. § 1337. Section 337 relief may be pursued in place of, or in addition to, an infringement action in district court.

E. INFRINGEMENT OF PLANT PATENTS

Unlike design and utility patents, infringement of a plant patent is not governed by section 271. Instead, it is governed by section 163, which grants to the owner of the plant patent "the right to exclude others from asexually reproducing the plant, and from using, offering for sale, or selling the plant so reproduced, or any of its parts, throughout the United States, or from importing the plant to reproduced or any parts thereof, into the United States." In *Imazio Nursery, Inc. v. Dania Greenhouses*, 69 F.3d 1560 (Fed. Cir. 1995), the Federal Circuit faced the questions of (a) the scope of section 161's protection of a "distinct and new variety of plant" and (b) the nature of the infringing acts in section 163 and whether independent creation is a defense to infringement of a plant patent.

> The parties dispute the meaning of the term "variety" in section 161. The meaning of that term may inform the scope of protection of plant patents inasmuch as such patents are granted to "whoever invents or discovers and asexually reproduces any distinct and new *variety* of plant." 35 U.S.C. § 161 (emphasis added). Imazio argues that in providing plant patent protection for "any distinct and new variety of plant," it was intended that a plant patent cover "all plants of that new and distinct variety, i.e., all plants having the same essential and distinctive characteristics." Thus, argues Imazio, "variety" should be construed in its technical, taxonomical sense and should be interpreted to encompass more than just clones of a single plant. [Defendant] Coastal, on the other hand, contends that "variety" should be construed in the vernacular sense as "something different from others of the same general kind." Coastal maintains that by use of the term "variety" Congress did not intend to afford plant patent protection to a range of plants but intended only to protect a single plant.
>
> * * *
>
> Although the legislative history does not answer the question of what "variety" means in terms of whether a single plant or a range of plants is protected by a plant patent, in addition to being distinct and new, a patentable plant must also be asexually reproduced. 35 U.S.C. § 161; *see Yoder Bros., Inc. v. California-Florida Plant Corp.*, 537 F.2d 1347, 1377 (5th Cir.1976) ("For plant patents . . . the additional requirement of asexual reproduction is introduced."); Senate Report [No. 315, 71st Cong., 2d Sess. (1930) (hereinafter "Senate Report")] at 5 ("It is not only necessary that the new and distinct variety of plant shall have been invented or discovered, but it is also necessary that it shall have been asexually reproduced prior to the application for patent."). As discussed below, this additional requirement informs the scope of protection of plant patents and hence directs the meaning of "variety" in § 161.
>
> * * *

Due to the asexual reproduction prerequisite, plant patents cover a single plant and its asexually reproduced progeny. *See* Senate Report at 6 (Plant patent protection encourages "those who own the single specimen to reproduce it asexually and create an adequate supply."). Thus, the term "variety" in section 161 must be interpreted consistently with this requirement. Accordingly, "variety" in section 161 cannot be read as affording plant patent protection to a range of plants, as asserted by Imazio.

* * *

Section 163 grants to plant patentees the right to exclude others from asexually reproducing the plant or selling or using the plant so reproduced. As stated above, the trial court held that asexual reproduction is shown if the patentee can prove that the alleged infringing plant has the same essential characteristics as the patented plant. We disagree.

* * *

The "asexual reproduction question" * * * is critical to the infringement analysis. In construing section 161, we held above that the scope of a plant patent is the asexual reproduction of the plant shown and described in the specification. Asexual reproduction, in terms of section 161, means the progeny of the patented plant via "grafting, budding, cuttings, layering, division and the like, but not by seeds." Senate Report at 1.

We must construe the term "asexual reproduction" in section 163 in the same way as we did in section 161. Thus, for purposes of plant patent infringement, the patentee must prove that the alleged infringing plant is an asexual reproduction, that is, that it is the progeny of the patented plant. *Yoder*, 537 F.2d at 1380 ("It is quite possible that infringement of a plant patent would occur only if stock obtained is used, given the extreme unlikelihood that any other plant could actually infringe.").

* * *

We must reject the trial court's analysis of the independent creation defense because it is contrary to the plain meaning of the statute. The statute requires asexual reproduction of the patented plant for there to be infringement. It is necessarily a defense to plant patent infringement that the alleged infringing plant is not an asexual reproduction of the patented plant. Part of this proof could be, thus, that the defendant independently developed the allegedly infringing plant. However, the sine qua non is asexual reproduction. That is what the patentee must prove and what the defendant will seek to disprove.

NOTES

1. *Nature and Time of Infringing Acts:* At what point in the asexual reproduction process should infringement of a plant patent be deemed to occur: When cuttings are first taken? When the cuttings mature into adult plants? When the resulting plants are offered for sale? Would it be an infringement to propagate a plant asexually for personal noncommercial use only?

2. *Term of a Plant Patent:* As noted in Chapter 11.C., *supra*, the term of a plant patent is the same as a utility patent—20 years from filing.

3. *Remedies for Infringement of Plant Patents:* The same remedial provisions that apply to utility patents apply equally to plant patents.

4. *Relationship of Plant Patents to the PVPA:* Although the plant patent statutes do not define "variety," the *Imazio* court declined to import the definition assigned to that term under the Plant Variety Protection Act of 1970, 7 U.S.C. § 2401(a)(9) (defining a variety as a group of plants sharing certain genetically-dictated characteristics and capable of being propagated unchanged):

> It is true that both the Plant Patent Act and the PVPA use the term "variety" and grant some form of intellectual property protection. However, the two statutes differ significantly in their purposes. The Plant Patent Act grants a plant patent to one who "invents or discovers and asexually reproduces any distinct and new variety of plant." 35 U.S.C.A. § 161. Conversely, one is entitled to plant variety protection under the PVPA if he has sexually reproduced the variety and has otherwise met the requirements of 7 U.S.C.A. § 2402(a). The term "variety" in both statutes cannot be read divorced from the very different circumstances in which that term is used.
>
> Those circumstances, asexual reproduction in the case of plant patents, and sexual reproduction in the case of plant variety protection, mandate the protection afforded under these different statutory provisions. Asexual reproduction is the cornerstone of plant patent protection, while sexual reproduction is the distinguishing feature of plant variety protection. Indeed, this is why the PVPA was enacted, to afford protection for sexually reproduced plants. The result of asexual reproduction is a plant that is genetically identical to its parent. The result of sexual reproduction is a plant that combines the characteristics of the parents, but is a different plant.
>
> It follows from this that the scope of protection afforded as a result of sexual versus asexual reproduction must be different; in the case of asexual reproduction, the same plant is produced, but in the case of sexual reproduction, a different plant, albeit like the parent plants, is produced. Given this, we reject Imazio's contention that the meaning of variety in the Plant Patent Act and the PVPA must be the same.

69 F.3d at 1568.

5. *Remedies Under the Plant Variety Protection Act:* The remedial rules of the PVPA closely parallel those of the patent statutes, including damage awards "adequate to compensate but in no event less than a reasonable royalty," the possibility of trebled damages, discretionary attorney's fees in exceptional cases, a six-year time limit on damages awards (but with the earlier limit "or known to the owner more than one year"), and a requirement of actual notice as a prerequisite to damages where the certificate holder has not complied with the PVPA's marking provisions. *See* 7 U.S.C. §§ 2561–67.

PART 6

COPYRIGHT LAW

■ ■ ■

CHAPTER 13

INTRODUCTION AND A SHORT HISTORY

■ ■ ■

Copyright law in the United States grants limited exclusive rights to the authors of a wide variety of expressive and creative works. Though some rights (sometimes called "common law copyright," or the right of first publication) can arise under state law, almost all forms of copyright today are governed by federal law. Under current federal law, when an original work of authorship eligible for copyright (such as a novel) is fixed in a tangible medium of embodiment (such as a written manuscript or an electronic file), its author automatically enjoys the exclusive rights available to that category of work under the copyright statute. Rights can vary somewhat by categories, as we will see. For example, musical compositions carry performance rights that are unavailable to many sound recordings. What this means is that the DJ who plays a recording of a song at a party needs a license to play the song itself but not to play the recording of the song. In this sense (and many others) copyright can seem wonderfully complex. And yet there is a certain simplicity to the subject as well. In contrast to a patent, for example, no formalities are required to obtain a copyright, and the examination process that leads to a registration is relatively uncomplicated; the scope and duration of the exclusive rights in copyright differ significantly from patent rights as well.

As the following short history reveals, Anglo-American copyright law began as a response to revolutionary changes in the instruments and practices of authorship and expression: notably, first, in the introduction of the printing press into late fifteenth-century England; and then, some two centuries later, in the insistence of the English Parliament upon cessation of the licensing system that had enabled the Tudor monarchs to control dissent by controlling the press. Copyright law has been struggling to keep pace with developments in technology and with evolving understandings of freedom of expression ever since.

A. ENGLISH LAW

Our federal copyright law owes its origins to the copyright laws of England. Until 1709, copyright as such did not exist in England, and certainly not in statutory form, although the English common law was credited somewhat later with having previously recognized the right of authors to prevent the publication of their unpublished manuscripts. Once copies of a work were circulated to the public, however, the author's common law right was exhausted. Thanks to the invention of the printing press, which made it possible to copy works cheaply and quickly, after its initial publication a work could be mass produced without generating any financial return to its author or publisher.

The press itself is said to have been brought to England in 1476 by William Caxton. At first, printing was allowed without effective oversight or legal constraint. By 1556, however, the Crown had subjected all printing to royal control. Eventually the privilege of printing was granted exclusively to a group of publishers known as the Stationers' Company. Any member of the Company wishing to publish a work was required to register it with the Company itself, and upon doing so received in return the exclusive right to publish that work in perpetuity. But these Crown-sponsored privileges and monopolies were repressive and even brutal in practice (the infamous Star Chamber was but one of many instruments of suppression that grew out of these on-going efforts to control the press), and over time the system grew to be much despised. At last, in 1694, in a time of revolutionary fervor and dissent, Parliament allowed the final English Printing Act to expire.

When the restrictions on printing ended at the end of the seventeenth century, members of the Stationers' Company discovered that this newfound freedom of the press had also cost them their exclusive publication rights and, they insisted, their very livelihood. In a dramatic appeal to Parliament that included a parade of wives and children dressed in rags, the erstwhile Stationers asked for statutory protection to restore some of the constraints upon the press that had expired with the Printing Act. Parliament responded in 1709 by enacting the Statute of Anne, 8 Anne c.19 (effective 1710), which bore the title "An Act for the Encouragement of Learning, by Vesting the Copies of Printed Books in the Authors or Purchasers of such Copies, during the Times therein mentioned." The preamble reveals the intent of the act:

> Whereas Printers, Booksellers and other Persons have of late frequently taken the Liberty of Printing, Reprinting, and Publishing . . . Books and other Writings without the Consent of the Authors or Proprietors . . . to their very great Detriment, and too often to the Ruin of them and their Families:
>
> For Preventing therefore such Practices for the future, and for the Encouragement of Learned men to Compose and write useful Books . . .

To accomplish these goals, the Statute of Anne gave authors the exclusive right to publish new works for an initial term of fourteen years, measured from the date of first publication, at the expiration of which a second fourteen-year term would vest in the author if he or she were still living (even if the original term had been conveyed). However, enforcement of these rights was conditioned on registering the work and depositing copies at official libraries. Printing, reprinting or importing a protected work without the author's permission was punishable by a fine and by forfeiture and destruction of the unlawful copies.

This was the state of English copyright law when the American colonies broke away. At the instance of the Continental Congress, and at the urging of Noah Webster, most of the new states enacted copyright statutes shortly after Independence. Most resembled the English Statute of Anne, which had emphasized (in "the encouragement of learned men to compose and write useful books") the public benefits of granting limited monopolies to authors. Others, however, adopted the Continental view of copyright as a "natural right," arising as a moral entitlement in acknowledgment of the very fact of authorship itself. Whatever the underlying jurisprudence might be, as a practical matter lack of uniformity in these copyright laws made it difficult to protect works widely disseminated beyond the borders of an individual state.

B. THE ADVENT OF FEDERAL COPYRIGHT LAW

When the Constitution replaced the Articles of Confederation in 1787, the enactment of federal copyright (and patent) law was facilitated by Article I, section 8, clause 8, variously known as the "Intellectual Property Clause" or the "Patent and Copyright Clause," which grants Congress the power "to Promote the Progress of Science and useful Arts, by securing for limited Times to Authors and Inventors the exclusive Right to their respective Writings and Discoveries." James Madison summarized the goals of this clause in The Federalist No. 43:

> The utility of this power will scarcely be questioned. The copyright of authors has been solemnly adjudged, in Great Britain, to be a right of common law. The right to useful inventions seems with equal reason to belong to inventors. The public good fully coincides in both cases with the claims of individuals. The States cannot separately make effectual provision for either of the cases, and most of them have anticipated the decision of this point, by laws passed at the instance of Congress.

Despite some hint of a dual purpose in this passage from Madison, it is the English view that has come to prevail as the accepted jurisprudence in American copyright under the Constitution. Thus, copyright in the United States is generally said to be justified as a means for encouraging the creation of new works for the benefit of the public, rather than to recognize the more personal natural, or moral, rights of authors. In the conventional understanding, copyright is said to reflect a kind of "*quid pro quo*": authors receive exclusive rights for a limited time, in exchange for eventual contributions of their works to the public domain.

Congress passed the first federal copyright statute in 1790. Since then, the copyright laws have undergone significant changes. These changes generally fall into four categories: (1) broadening the scope of copyrightable subject matter (often in response to technological change, from photography to movies to the internet); (2) lengthening the term of protection; (3) broadening the array of exclusive rights that comprise copyright; and (4) reducing formalities and other barriers to protection. Changes in the fourth category have been particularly important to the internationalization of commerce in copyrights, which in itself may be said to amount to a fifth category of change, especially in the past three decades.

Copyright scholars and practitioners must be mindful of the changes that have taken place in copyright law since its first enactment. Many contemporary controversies require an understanding of the law as it existed prior to the current (1976) Act, since events taking place decades ago (for example, the public distribution of copies lacking adequate copyright notice) can affect the copyright status of a work today. In particular, no student of copyright can afford to give short shrift to the provisions of the 1909 Act, as well as any subsequent legislation.

C. FEDERAL LEGISLATION PRIOR TO THE 1976 ACT

Subject Matter: The 1790 Act provided copyright protection to a narrow range of subject matter—"any map, chart, book or books already printed." Congress soon expanded this list, adding designs, prints, etchings and engravings in 1802, musical compositions in 1831, dramatic compositions in 1856, "photographs and the negatives thereof" in 1865, and "statuary" and "models or designs intended to be perfected as works of the fine arts" in 1870. Not until 1891, however, were works of foreign origin protected.

In the Copyright Act of 1909, Congress took a different approach to defining copyrightable subject matter. Instead of trying to list exhaustively all works eligible for copyright, Congress simply provided that "[t]he works for which copyright may be secured under this title shall include all the writings of an author." The 1909 Act also contained a non-exhaustive list of eligible works in order simply to clarify the meaning of "all the writings of an author." When the advent of motion pictures made further clarification necessary, Congress in 1912 added "motion pictures" to the list of examples. In 1971, Congress added "sound recordings." As discussed in Chapter 16, the chief significance of these categories today lies in defining the scope of the exclusive rights that attach to certain types of copyrighted works that do not enjoy the full panoply of rights afforded to other works.

Prior to the Copyright Act of 1976, federal statutory copyright was unavailable for unpublished works, except for certain works designed for exhibition, performance or oral delivery rather than reproduction (for example, motion pictures), and then only if the works were registered. For other unpublished works, only state law protection was available.

Duration: As Congress broadened the scope of copyrightable subject matter, it also lengthened the term of protection. Under the 1790 Act, the duration of copyright was the same as it had been under the Statute of Anne—fourteen years, renewable for another fourteen if the author was alive at the end of the first term. The 1831 Act lengthened the first term to 28 years, and extended the renewal privilege to the author's surviving spouse and children. The 1909 Act extended the renewal term to 28 years, and starting in 1962 this term was repeatedly extended in order to prevent renewal terms from expiring on the eve of the comprehensive copyright revision that became the Copyright Act of 1976.

Formalities: The 1790 Act had conditioned protection on registering the work and publishing a copy of this registration in a newspaper. The copyright claimant was also required to deposit a copy of the work with the Secretary of State within six months of publication. The 1802 revisions replaced the requirement that the notice of registration be published in a newspaper with the requirement that copyright notice be inserted in each copy of the published work. Although protection was extended to foreign works in 1891, foreign authors were not exempt from these formalities, and often forfeited their U.S. copyrights through inadvertence. The 1909 Act also changed the law to provide that copyright protection for *published* works would commence upon publication with notice, rather than upon registration. Publication without notice led to forfeiture of copyright. The 1909 Act also introduced the rule, still in effect today, that a certificate of registration constitutes prima facie evidence of the facts recorded in the registration—that is, the validity of the registrant's copyright. The 1909 Act also added, in section 16, the now-defunct manufacturing clause, a protectionist provision which required printed books and periodicals in the English language, or by an American author, to be manufactured in the United States rather than imported. Copyright in some works was forfeited for noncompliance.

Rights: The early copyright statutes did not include the full panoply of rights afforded by copyright today. The 1790 Act included only the rights to print, reprint, publish, and sell. It did not include an exclusive right of public performance; this right was added in 1856 for dramatic compositions, in 1897 for musical compositions, and in 1952 for nondramatic literary works. The exclusive right to create derivative works was added in 1870.

D. COMPREHENSIVE REVISION: THE COPYRIGHT ACT OF 1976

The most significant revision of the federal copyright law was the Copyright Act of 1976, the culmination of twenty years of studies, hearings, debates, reports, and revisions. Among other things, the 1976 Act abrogated common law copyright in unpublished works and replaced it with statutory copyright, providing a single federal system of copyright for works of authorship commencing as soon as they were fixed in a tangible medium of expression. The Act relaxed the rule that publication without proper copyright notice resulted in forfeiture of copyright, prescribing steps by which an author could "cure" a publication without notice. The Act eliminated the renewal term in favor of a single term of copyright protection, measured in most cases by the life of the author plus 50 years, but measured as a fixed term from the date of creation (100 years) or publication (75 years), whichever first occurred, in the case of works made for hire and pseudonymous or anonymous works. The Act codified for the first time the judicially created doctrine of fair use, and further limited the copyright owner's exclusive rights by expressly permitting specific nonprofit uses and providing for compulsory licenses in certain other situations. The Act also expressly provided for federal preemption of state laws "equivalent" to copyright, and recognized the concept of divisibility of copyright ownership, which allowed assignees and exclusive licensees of portions of a copyright to sue for infringement of their rights. The 1976 Act introduced the exclusive right of public display, and provided for four copyright compulsory licenses (the cable television license of sec. 111, the mechanical recording license of sec. 115, the jukebox license of sec. 116 (since replaced with a negotiated license), and the public broadcasting license of sec. 118). It also modified the much-criticized manufacturing clause and provided for its eventual repeal (which took effect in 1986).

E. POST-1976 REVISIONS

Although it dramatically altered the copyright landscape, the 1976 Act was by no means the last significant revision of federal copyright. Indeed, compared with the evolution of copyright law prior to 1976, revisions since 1976 have been fast and furious, in keeping with—and, in large part, resulting from—technological change and the increasing internationalization of the marketplace for intellectual property.

Technological Change: While preparing the 1976 revisions, Congress established the National Commission on New Technological Uses of Copyrighted Works (CONTU) to study and make recommendations regarding the provisions needed to make copyright law responsive to significant technological developments such as computers and photocopying. CONTU submitted its final report in 1978, and Congress implemented most of its recommendations soon after—for example, in 1980 revising section 117 to address the copying of computer software.

In 1990, Congress banned the commercial rental of computer software, fearing the ease with which software could be copied by those who rented it; in this legislation Congress echoed earlier concerns that had led it (in 1987) to forbid record rentals on similar grounds. Concerns as to copying grew ever more intense as digital technologies displaced earlier analog technologies, particularly in the case of video and sound recordings. The older technology might well allow for rapid copying, but generally at a considerable cost in quality (measured by the declining signal to noise ratio) in each succeeding generation. In contrast, a digital copy is for most practical purposes indistinguishable from its predecessor in any medium. In the Audio Home Recording Act of 1992, responding to the concerns of music publishers and record companies that digital audio recordings would be widely copied, Congress clarified the permissibility of home audio taping while imposing a royalty on the sale of digital recording media and devices, and requiring all such devices to be equipped with copying controls to prevent serial copying of digital works. (That provision is now virtually obsolete, however, as unauthorized distribution of mp3 files via the internet has displaced home audio taping.) In 1995, responding to concerns that digital transmission of sound recordings would supplant many record purchases, Congress enacted a limited public performance right for sound recordings performed by means of certain digital transmissions.

Even greater pressures have been brought to bear upon the copyright system by the rapid growth of the internet, which enables copyrighted works to be disseminated instantly in digital format throughout the world. It is difficult to exaggerate the number or the complexity of issues this new fact of life raises for copyright proprietors, to whom the net is an unprecedented medium for the exploitation of their works, but a medium in which the threat of digital copying is omnipresent and exponentially magnified. Meanwhile, every issue to be seen from the perspective of proprietors raises a corresponding issue from the perspective of the public domain. In essence the question for the public domain is this: how to realize the enormous possibilities for freedom of expression, creativity, and cultural exchange which inhere in the internet, without unnecessarily undermining copyright as an incentive for continuing intellectual productivity?

Because the stakes are high, and there are no easy answers to these questions, copyright today can resemble a battlefield in which the contest is desperate and the outcome still uncertain. On the one hand, proprietors appear at times to have the edge in Congress, where effective lobbying efforts have led to new legislation aimed at curtailing the worst excesses of digital copying. A number of early successful efforts in this direction have been mentioned above. Perhaps the crowning achievement to date, however, is the Digital Millennium Copyright Act of 1998, a major piece of legislation designed principally to deal with efforts by hackers to circumvent digital security measures (such as the motion picture industry's CSS encryption system, intended to protect on-line movies from unauthorized copying), as well as certain issues affecting the liability of online service providers for copyright infringement arising from postings by others. Against these advances, however, the forces of the public domain can claim some victories as well, though not always victories at law. The achievement of 15-year-old Jon Johanssen, the Norwegian lad who deconstructed the CSS code used for encryption of DVDs, and then posted his results on the internet so that others might make use of his work, suggests the guerrilla nature of some of the public domain resistance. The Napster, Morpheus, and Grokster systems for unauthorized downloads of recorded music were additional examples of the guerrilla movement at work. More recently, YouTube (for streaming performances and downloads) and BitTorrent (for peer-to-peer downloads) have created even more opportunities for unauthorized access to copyrighted content. Other efforts, somewhat more systematically aimed at creating a viable commons, are reflected in the advancing fortunes of the Linux operating system, an alternative to Microsoft's operating systems which, unlike Microsoft's copyrighted computer codes, depends on a so-called "general public license" (or GPL) that is meant to be a deliberate alternative to copyright protection.

Internationalization: The United States first participated in a multilateral copyright treaty in 1952, when it signed the Universal Copyright Convention (UCC). UCC members were required to protect, on a nondiscriminatory basis, works authored by nationals of member nations or first published in member nations. Formalities were waived for unpublished works and works published with proper notice. The UCC was especially attractive to the United States (which had been instrumental in its development) because it demanded little in the way of recognition of moral rights. For that very reason, however, it proved less than successful in attracting adherents. In recent decades its importance has dwindled as the vast majority of its signatories have ratified the more sweeping, moral rights-based Berne Convention for the Protection of Literary and Artistic Works. In 1988 the United States itself finally adhered to the Berne Convention, a move that has had a major impact on U.S. copyright law.

The Berne Convention was originally formed in 1886 and has been periodically revised with ever-expanding membership. The treaty is not self-executing, and therefore Congress has had to make several significant changes in domestic law in order to satisfy the treaty requirements—for example, eliminating the notice requirement (for works first published on or after March 1, 1989), removing registration as a prerequisite to suit for infringement of works originating in Berne countries, eliminating altogether the requirement that copyright transfers be recorded in the Copyright Office as a prerequisite to suit, and phasing out the compulsory license for jukeboxes in favor of negotiated licenses (which were finally eliminated in 1993). Later changes inspired, if not directly required, by Berne include recognition of moral rights for certain works of visual art (section 106A), recognition of copyright in architectural works (section 102(a)(8)), and automatic renewal of copyright (for works published under the 1909 Act).

When the U.S. signed the North American Free Trade Agreement (NAFTA) in 1993, and then subscribed in 1994 to the Uruguay Round of the General Agreement on Tariffs and Trade (GATT) (which established the World Trade Organization, or WTO, and included for the first time specific provisions on Trade Related Aspects of Intellectual Property Rights, or TRIPS) in 1994, yet another round of revisions to the Copyright Act of 1976 also ensued. Some of these revisions were merely technical and of small account, but others were of considerable significance. Particularly notable among the latter, Section 104A, enacted in 1993 and expanded in 1994, restored copyright protection to works originating in countries belonging to the World Trade Organization (WTO) or the Berne Convention which prematurely entered the public domain in the U.S. (often through failure to comply with formalities). Certain protections were built in, however, for parties that relied on such a work's uncopyrighted status. In another significant departure from traditional American copyright law, the GATT-inspired revisions to Title 17 also recognize certain rights in unfixed works, providing civil and criminal penalties for making or "trafficking in" bootleg recordings of live musical performances.

In 1998, the U.S. Senate ratified two new international treaties, the WIPO Copyright Treaty and the WIPO Performances and Phonograms Treaty. The Digital Millennium Copyright Act of 1998 (DMCA), discussed above, amended the 1976 Copyright Act to bring the signatories to the two WIPO treaties into approximate parity under American law with the signatories to Berne and GATT-TRIPS. Of particular note, the DMCA effectively extended the copyright restoration provisions of section 104A to signatories to the new WIPO treaties. Otherwise, these treaties have had little impact on U.S. copyright law.

In 2019, the U.S. ratified WIPO's Marrakesh Treaty to Facilitate Access to Published Works for Persons Who Are Blind, Visually Impaired or Otherwise Print Disabled, which facilitates the production and distribution of books in formats accessible to disabled persons. The U.S. has signed, but not yet ratified, WIPO's Beijing Treaty on Audiovisual Performances, which requires signatory nations to grant certain intellectual property rights to performers with respect to their audiovisual performances. Although the treaty would have little effect on U.S. law, requiring other signatory countries to grant these rights could enhance the competitive position of the U.S. film industry.

Copyright Duration: The Sonny Bono Copyright Term Extension Act (SBCTEA), Pub. L. No. 105–298 (signed Oct. 27, 1998), added 20 years to the terms of most subsisting U.S. copyrights, thus making it possible for U.S. copyright owners to enjoy the maximum term of copyright protection provided by countries belonging to the European Union. Both the extension of the copyright term under the SBCTEA, and the removal of certain foreign works from the public domain under section 104A, have prompted constitutional challenges under the Copyright Clause and the First Amendment. As discussed in Chapter 15, however, in both cases the Supreme Court has given broad deference to Congress's policymaking authority.

CHAPTER 14

THE SUBJECT MATTER OF COPYRIGHT

■ ■ ■

A. INTRODUCTION

Statutes: 17 U.S.C. §§ 101 (as needed, for definitions of material terms), 102–03, 1401

BURROW-GILES LITHOGRAPHIC CO. V. SARONY

111 U.S. 53, 4 S.Ct. 279 (1884).

MR. JUSTICE MILLER delivered the opinion of the Court.

* * *

Plaintiff is a lithographer and defendant a photographer, with large business in those lines in the city of New York.

The suit was commenced by an action at law in which Sarony was plaintiff and the lithographic company was defendant, the plaintiff charging the defendant with violating his copyright in regard to a photograph, the title of which is "Oscar Wilde No. 18." A jury being waived, the court made a finding of facts on which a judgment in favor of the plaintiff was rendered * * *.

* * *

The eighth section of the first article of the Constitution is the great repository of the powers of Congress, and by the eighth clause of that section Congress is authorized:

> "To promote the progress of science and useful arts, by securing, for limited times to authors and inventors, the exclusive right to their respective writings and discoveries."

The argument here is, that a photograph is not a writing nor the production of an author. Under the acts of Congress designed to give effect to this section, the persons who are to be benefited are divided into two classes, authors and inventors. The monopoly which is granted to the former is called a copyright, that given to the latter, letters patent, or, in the familiar language of the present day, patent right.

We have, then, copyright and patent right, and it is the first of these under which plaintiff asserts a claim for relief.

It is insisted in argument, that a photograph being a reproduction on paper of the exact features of some natural object or of some person, is not a writing of which the producer is the author.

Section 4952 of the Revised Statutes places photographs in the same class as things which may be copyrighted with "books, maps, charts, dramatic or musical compositions, engravings, cuts, prints, paintings, drawings, statues, statuary, and models or designs intended to be perfected as works of the fine arts." * * *

* * *

Unless, therefore, photographs can be distinguished in the classification on this point from the maps, charts, designs, engravings, etchings, cuts, and other prints, it is difficult to see why Congress cannot make them the subject of copyright as well as the others.

These statutes certainly answer the objection that books only, or writing in the limited sense of a book and its author, are within the constitutional provision. Both these words are susceptible of a more enlarged definition than this. An author in that sense is "he to whom anything owes its origin; originator; maker; one who completes a work of science or literature." *Worcester.* So, also, no one would now claim that the word writing in this clause of the Constitution, though the only word used as to subjects in regard to which authors are to be secured, is limited to the actual script of the author, and excludes books and all other printed matter. By writings in that clause is meant the literary productions of those authors, and Congress very properly has declared these to include all forms of writing, printing, engraving, etching, & c., by which the ideas in the mind of the author are given visible expression. The only reason why photographs were not included in the extended list in the act of 1802 is probably that they did not exist, as photography as an art was then unknown, and the scientific principle on which it rests, and the chemicals and machinery by which it is operated, have all been discovered long since that statute was enacted.

* * *

We entertain no doubt that the Constitution is broad enough to cover an act authorizing copyright of photographs, so far as they are representatives of original intellectual conceptions of the author.

But it is said that an engraving, a painting, a print, does embody the intellectual conception of its author, in which there is novelty, invention, originality, and therefore comes within the purpose of the Constitution in securing its exclusive use or sale to its author, while the photograph is the mere mechanical reproduction of the physical features or outlines of some object animate or inanimate, and involves no originality of thought or any novelty in the intellectual operation connected with its visible reproduction in shape of a picture. That while the effect of light on the prepared plate may have been a discovery in the production of these pictures, and patents could properly be obtained for the combination of the chemicals, for their application to the paper or other surface, for all the machinery by which the light reflected from the object was thrown on the prepared plate, and for all the improvements in this machinery, and in the materials, the remainder of the process is merely mechanical, with no place for novelty, invention or originality. It is simply the manual operation, by the use of these instruments and preparations, of transferring to the plate the visible representation of some existing object, the accuracy of this representation being its highest merit.

This may be true in regard to the ordinary production of a photograph, and, further, that in such case a copyright is no protection. On the question as thus stated we decide nothing.

In regard, however, to the kindred subject of patents for invention, they cannot by law be issued to the inventor until the novelty, the utility, and the actual discovery or invention by the claimant have been established by proof before the Commissioner of Patents; and when he has secured such a patent, and undertakes to obtain redress for a violation of his right in a court of law, the question of invention, of novelty, of originality, is always open to examination. Our copyright system has no such provision for previous examination by a proper tribunal as to the originality of the book, map, or other matter offered for copyright. A deposit of two copies of the article or work with the Librarian of Congress, with the name of the author and its title page, is all that is necessary to secure a copyright. It is, therefore, much more important that when the supposed author sues for a violation of his copyright, the existence of those facts of originality, of intellectual production, of thought, and conception on the part of the author should be proved, than in the case of a patent right.

In the case before us we think this has been done.

The third finding of facts says, in regard to the photograph in question, that it is a "useful, new, harmonious, characteristic, and graceful picture, and that plaintiff made the same . . . entirely from his own original mental conception, to which he gave visible form by posing the said Oscar Wilde in front of the camera, selecting and arranging the costume, draperies, and other various accessories in said photograph, arranging the subject so as to present graceful outlines, arranging and disposing the light and shade, suggesting and evoking the desired expression, and from such disposition, arrangement, or representation, made entirely by plaintiff, he produced the picture in suit."

These findings, we think, show this photograph to be an original work of art, the product of plaintiff's intellectual invention, of which plaintiff is the author, and of a class of inventions for which the Constitution intended that Congress should secure to him the exclusive right to use, publish and sell, as it has done by section 4952 of the Revised Statutes.

* * *

COPYRIGHT ACT OF 1976

H.R. Rep. No. 94–1476.
94th Cong., 2d Sess. 51–54 (1976).

* * *

Section 102. General Subject Matter of Copyright

"Original Works of Authorship"

The two fundamental criteria of copyright protection—originality and fixation in tangible form—are restated in the first sentence of this cornerstone provision. The phrase "original works of authorship," which is purposely left undefined, is intended to incorporate without change the standard of originality established by the courts under the present copyright statute. This standard does not include requirements of novelty, ingenuity, or esthetic merit, and there is no intention to enlarge the standard of copyright protection to require them.

In using the phrase "original works of authorship," rather than "all the writings of an author" now in section 4 of the statute, the committee's purpose is to avoid exhausting the constitutional power of Congress to legislate in this field, and to eliminate the uncertainties arising from the latter phrase. * * *

The history of copyright law has been one of gradual expansion in the types of works accorded protection * * *.

Authors are continually finding new ways of expressing themselves, but it is impossible to foresee the forms that these new expressive methods will take. The bill does not intend either to freeze the scope of copyrightable subject matter at the present stage of communications technology or to allow unlimited expansion into areas completely outside the present congressional intent. Section 102 implies neither that that subject matter is unlimited nor that new forms of expression within that general area of subject matter would necessarily be unprotected. * * *

* * * [T]here are unquestionably other areas of existing subject matter that this bill does not propose to protect but that future Congresses may want to.

* * *

Categories of copyrightable works

The second sentence of section 102 lists seven broad categories which the concept of "works" of ["]authorship" is said to "include." The use of the word "include," as defined in section 101, makes clear that the listing is "illustrative and not limitative," and that the seven categories do not necessarily exhaust the scope of "original works of authorship" that the bill is intended to protect. Rather, the list sets out the general area of copyrightable subject matter, but with sufficient flexibility to free the courts from rigid or outmoded concepts of the scope of particular categories. The items are also overlapping in the sense that a work falling within one class may encompass works coming within some or all of the other ca[t]egories. * * *

* * * The term "literary works" does not connote any criterion of literary merit or qualitative value: it includes catalogs, directories, and similar factual, reference, or instructional works and compilations of data. It also includes computer data bases, and computer programs to the extent that they incorporate authorship in the programmer's expression of original ideas, as distinguished from the ideas themselves.

* * *

NOTES

1. The Supreme Court has discussed the scope of the constitutional terms "Authors" and "Writings" on several occasions when it has been called upon to address the scope of Congress' power to define copyrightable subject matter. In the *Trade-Mark Cases*, 100 U.S. (10 Otto) 82, 94 (1879), the Court defined "Writings" as "the fruits of intellectual labor," but only those that "are original, and are founded in the creative powers of the mind." After the *Burrow-Giles* decision, the Court held in *Bleistein v. Donaldson Lithographing Co.*, 188 U.S. 239, 249–52 (1903), that Congress was empowered to extend copyright protection to chromolithographs used in printing circus posters, even where the depictions in question were realistic rather than fanciful:

> It is obvious also that the plaintiffs' case is not affected by the fact, if it be one, that the pictures represent actual groups—visible things. They seem from the testimony to have been composed from hints or description, not from sight of a performance. But even if they had been drawn from the life, that fact would not deprive them of protection. The opposite proposition would mean that a portrait by Velasquez or Whistler was common property because others might try their hand on the same face. Others are free to copy the original. They are not free to copy the copy. * * * The copy is the personal reaction of an individual upon nature. Personality always contains something unique. It expresses its singularity even in handwriting, and a very modest grade of art has in it something irreducible, which

> is one man's alone. That something he may copyright unless there is a restriction in the words of the act.
>
> * * *
>
> It would be a dangerous undertaking for persons trained only to the law to constitute themselves final judges of the worth of pictorial illustrations, outside of the narrowest and most obvious limits. At the one extreme some works of genius would be sure to miss appreciation. Their very novelty would make them repulsive until the public had learned the new language in which their author spoke. It may be more than doubted, for instance, whether the etchings of Goya or the paintings of Manet would have been sure of protection when seen for the first time. At the other end, copyright would be denied to pictures which appealed to a public less educated than the judge. Yet if they command the interest of any public, they have a commercial value—it would be bold to say that they have not an aesthetic and educational value—and the taste of any public is not to be treated with contempt. It is an ultimate fact for the moment, whatever may be our hopes for a change.

In 1973, the Supreme Court confirmed that the Intellectual Property Clause empowered Congress to extend copyright protection to audio recordings of musical performances:

> By Art. I, § 8, cl. 8, of the Constitution, the States granted to Congress the power to protect the "Writings" of "Authors." These terms have not been construed in their narrow literal sense but, rather, with the reach necessary to reflect the broad scope of constitutional principles. While an "author" may be viewed as an individual who writes an original composition, the term, in its constitutional sense, has been construed to mean an "originator," "he to whom anything owes its origin." *Burrow-Giles Lithographic Co. v. Sarony*, 111 U.S. 53, 58 (1884). Similarly, although the word "writings" might be limited to script or printed material, it may be interpreted to include any physical rendering of the fruits of creative intellectual or aesthetic labor. *Ibid.*; *Trade-Mark Cases*, 100 U.S. 82, 94 (1879). Thus, recordings of artistic performances may be within the reach of Clause 8.
>
> While the area in which Congress *may* act is broad, the enabling provision of Clause 8 does not require that Congress act in regard to all categories of materials which meet the constitutional definitions. Rather, whether any specific category of "Writings" is to be brought within the purview of the federal statutory scheme is left to the discretion of the Congress. The history of federal copyright statutes indicates that the congressional determination to consider specific classes of writings is dependent, not only on the character of the writing, but also on the commercial importance of the product to the national economy. As our technology has expanded the means

> available for creative activity and has provided economical means for reproducing manifestations of such activity, new areas of federal protection have been initiated.

Goldstein v. California, 412 U.S. 546, 561–62 (1973).

2. Does the Patent and Copyright Clause authorize Congress to extend copyright protection to unposed snapshots? Videotapes or film footage of real-life events? A recording of the sounds of nature? The title "Gone With the Wind"? The name "Coca-Cola"? An invented word, such as "supercalifragilisticexpialidocious"? A simple commercial logo (for example, the Nike "swoosh" symbol)? A federal statute? A typeface? A recipe? A questionnaire? A Halloween costume? The design of a sports car? The design of a golf course? If a category of subject matter is eligible for copyright under the Intellectual Property Clause, may Congress refuse to extend protection to that subject matter? *See Graham v. John Deere Co.*, 383 U.S. 1 (1966). *Cf.* Copyright Office Regulations, 37 C.F.R. § 202.1 (listing material not subject to copyright).

3. Consider Holmes' observations in *Bleistein* as to the question of copyright and aesthetics. Does the Patent and Copyright Clause *require* Congress to extend copyright without regard to the merits of an individual work? Does the Clause allow Congress to extend copyright protection to works which arguably do not "promote the progress of science and useful arts"? *See* Heald & Sherry, *Implied Limits on the Legislative Power: The Intellectual Property Clause as an Absolute Constraint on Congress*, 2000 U.ILL.L.REV. 1119 (2000).

4. In *Teller v. Dogge*, 8 F.Supp.3d 1228 (D. Nev. 2014), the district court granted magician Raymond Teller summary judgment on his copyright infringement claim against a defendant who posted a video of Teller's "Shadows" illusion on YouTube and offered to sell the "secret" for $3,000. The court noted that the illusion could be classified as either a pantomime or a dramatic work. *Id.* at 1233.

5. To be eligible for copyright protection, must a work have a human author? What if an elephant or a monkey creates a painting? What about works produced by artificial intelligence? If any of these works are copyrightable, who would be the author and presumptive copyright owner?

6. Prior to 1972, federal copyright protection did not extend to sound recordings. Congress remedied this in the Sound Recording Act of 1971, Pub. L. 92–140 (Oct. 15, 1971), which took effect on February 15, 1972. *See* 17 U.S.C. § 102(a)(7). However, Congress did not make this protection retroactive. Therefore, until 2018, sound recordings made in the United States before February 15, 1972 ("pre-1972 sound recordings") received no federal protection (although the musical compositions embodied on those recordings were eligible for copyright protection under 17 U.S.C. § 102(a)(2)). During this time, states were free to extend their own copyright-like protection to those sound recordings.

This changed in 2018, when Congress enacted the Hatch-Goodlatte Music Modernization Act, H.R. 1551, Pub. L. No. 115–264 (Oct. 11, 2018). Title II, called the "CLASSICS Protection and Access Act," added a new Chapter 14 to Title 17, consisting of a single code section, 17 U.S.C. § 1401, which establishes a new type of sui generis federal protection for pre-1972 sound recordings. Although technically these recordings are still not eligible for "copyright" protection, the rights granted (and the limitations on those rights) are almost identical to those that apply to federally copyrighted sound recordings, with several notable exceptions (discussed in greater detail in later chapters):

(1) There are no termination rights for the authors of pre-1972 recordings (*see* Chapter 15);

(2) Initial ownership of the rights (as of the enactment date) is determined by state law (*see* Chapter 15);

(3) The term of protection varies depending on the age of the recording (but in each case it is at least 95 years from publication, and even pre-1923 recordings are protected until 2021) (*see* Chapter 15);

(4) A noncommercial use exception permits, with notice, certain limited uses of pre-1972 recordings that are no longer commercially available unless the rights owner promptly objects (*see* Chapter 16); and

(5) Pre-1972 recordings cannot be federally registered, but there is an alternative filing scheme that is a prerequisite to collecting statutory damages and attorney's fees for successful infringement claims (*see* Chapter 18).

Title II also amended 17 U.S.C. § 301(c) to address federal preemption of state law claims involving pre-1972 sound recordings. *See* Chapter 19.

The stated purpose of Title II was to provide financial benefits to recording artists who performed on these older recordings. The artists in question are now entitled to receive their share of the statutory performance royalties paid by music streaming services under §§ 114(f)–(g). As will become evident in Chapter 16, however, the greatest beneficiaries of Title II are the rights owners (technically, not "copyright" owners) of these recordings; in most cases, these are the record labels.

MANNION V. COORS BREWING CO.

377 F.Supp.2d 444 (S.D.N.Y. 2005).

KAPLAN, DISTRICT JUDGE.

The parties dispute whether a photograph used in billboard advertisements for Coors Light beer infringes the plaintiff's copyright in a photograph of a basketball star. The defendants almost certainly imitated the plaintiff's photograph. The major question is whether and to what extent what was copied is protected. The case requires the Court to consider the nature of copyright protection in photographs. The matter is before the Court on cross motions for summary judgment.

Facts

Jonathan Mannion is a freelance photographer who specializes in portraits of celebrity athletes and musicians in the rap and rhythm-and-blues worlds.* * * In 1999 he was hired by SLAM, a basketball magazine, to photograph basketball star Kevin Garnett in connection with an article that the magazine planned to publish about him. The article, entitled "Above the Clouds," appeared as the cover story of the December 1999 issue of the magazine. It was accompanied by a number of Mannion's photographs of Garnett, including the one at issue here (the "Garnett Photograph"), which was printed on a two-page spread introducing the article.

The Garnett Photograph is a three-quarter-length portrait of Garnett against a backdrop of clouds with some blue sky shining through. The view is up and across the right side of Garnett's torso, so that he appears to be towering above earth. He wears a white T-shirt, white athletic pants, a black close-fitting cap, and a large amount of platinum, gold, and diamond jewelry ("bling bling" in the vernacular), including several necklaces, a Rolex watch and bracelet on his left wrist, bracelets on his right wrist, rings on one finger of each hand, and earrings. His head is cocked, his eyes are closed, and his heavily-veined hands, nearly all of which are visible, rest over his lower abdomen, with the thumbs hooked on the waistband of the trousers. The light is from the viewer's left, so that Garnett's right shoulder is the brightest area of the photograph and his hands cast slight shadows on his trousers. As reproduced in the magazine, the photograph cuts off much of Garnett's left arm.

In early 2001, defendant Carol H. Williams Advertising ("CHWA") began developing ideas for outdoor billboards that would advertise Coors Light beer to young black men in urban areas. One of CHWA's "comp boards"—a "comp board" is an image created by an advertising company to convey a proposed design—used a manipulated version of the Garnett Photograph and superimposed on it the words "Iced Out" ("ice" being slang for diamonds) and a picture of a can of Coors Light beer (the "Iced Out Comp Board"). CHWA obtained authorization from Mannion's representative to use the Garnett Photograph for this purpose. The authorization was for "[u]sage in internal corporate merchandising catalog," which Mannion concedes extended to the Iced Out Comp Board. The Iced Out Comp Board * * * used a black-and-white, mirror image of the Garnett Photograph, but with the head cropped out on top and part of the fingers cropped out below. CHWA forwarded its comp boards to, and solicited bids for the photograph for the Coors advertising from, various photographers including Mannion, who submitted a bid but did not receive the assignment.

Coors and CHWA selected for a Coors billboard a photograph (the "Coors Billboard"), reproduced below, that resembles the Iced Out Comp Board. The Coors Billboard depicts, in black-and-white, the torso of a muscular black man, albeit a model other than Garnett, shot against a cloudy backdrop. The pose is similar to that in the Garnett Photograph, and the view also is up and across the left side of the torso. The model in the billboard photograph also wears a white T-shirt and white athletic pants. The model's jewelry is prominently depicted; it includes a necklace of platinum or gold and diamonds, a watch and two bracelets on the right wrist, and more bracelets on the left wrist. The light comes from the viewer's right, so that the left shoulder is the brightest part of the photograph, and the right arm and hand cast slight shadows on the trousers.

Mannion subsequently noticed the Coors Billboard at two locations in the Los Angeles area. He applied for registration of his copyright of the Garnett Photograph in 2003 and brought this action for infringement in February of 2004. The registration was completed in May 2004. The parties each move for summary judgment.

Discussion

* * *

Mannion concededly owns a valid copyright in the Garnett photograph. Access is undisputed. There is ample evidence from which a trier of fact could find that CHWA actually copied the Garnett Photograph for the Coors Billboard. Thus, the major questions presented by these motions are whether a trier of fact could or must find substantial similarity between protected elements of the Garnett Photograph and the Coors Billboard. If no reasonable trier could find such similarity, the defendants' motion must be granted and the plaintiff's denied. If any reasonable trier would be obliged to find such similarity (along with actual copying), the plaintiff's motion must be granted and the defendants' denied. If a reasonable trier could, but would not be required to, find substantial similarity (and actual copying), both motions must be denied.

* * *

C. Determining the Protectible Elements of the Garnett Photograph

The first question must be: in what respects is the Garnett Photograph protectible?

1. Protectible Elements of Photographs

It is well-established that "[t]he sine qua non of copyright is originality" and, accordingly, that "copyright protection may extend only to those components of a work that are original to the author." "Original" in the copyright context "means only that the work was independently created by the author (as opposed to copied from other works), and that it possesses at least some minimal degree of creativity."

It sometimes is said that "copyright in the photograph conveys no rights over the subject matter conveyed in the photograph." But this is not always true. It of course is correct that the photographer of a building or tree or other pre-existing object has no right to prevent others from photographing the same thing. That is because originality depends upon independent creation, and the photographer did not create that object. By contrast, if a photographer arranges or otherwise creates the subject that his camera captures, he may have the right to prevent others from producing works that depict that subject.

Almost any photograph "may claim the necessary originality to support a copyright." Indeed, ever since the Supreme Court considered an 1882 portrait by the celebrity photographer Napoleon Sarony of the 27-year-old Oscar Wilde, courts have articulated lists of potential components of a photograph's originality.

These lists, however, are somewhat unsatisfactory. First, they do not deal with the issue, alluded to above, that the nature and extent of a photograph's protection differs depending on what makes that photograph original. Second, courts have not always distinguished between decisions that a photographer makes in creating a photograph and the originality of the final product. Several cases, for example, have included in lists of the potential components of photographic originality "selection of film and camera," "lens and filter selection," and "the kind of camera, the kind of film, [and] the kind of lens." Having considered the matter fully, however, I think this is not sufficiently precise. Decisions about film, camera, and lens, for example, often bear on whether an image is original. But the fact that a photographer made such choices does not alone make the image original. "Sweat of the brow" is not the touchstone of copyright. Protection derives from the features of the work itself, not the effort that goes into it. This point is illustrated by *Bridgeman Art Library, Ltd. v. Corel Corp.*, 36 F.Supp.2d 191 (S.D.N.Y. 1999), in which this Court held that there was no copyright in photographic transparencies that sought to reproduce precisely paintings in the public domain. To be sure, a great deal of effort and expertise may have been poured into the production of the plaintiff's images, including decisions about camera, lens, and film. But the works were "slavish copies." They did not exhibit the originality necessary for copyright.

The Court therefore will examine more closely the nature of originality in a photograph. In so doing, it draws on the helpful discussion in a leading treatise on United Kingdom copyright law, [HON. SIR HUGH LADDIE ET AL.,

THE MODERN LAW OF COPYRIGHT AND DESIGNS (3d ed. Butterworths 2000)] which is similar to our own with respect to the requirement of originality.

A photograph may be original in three respects. They are not mutually exclusive.

a. Rendition

First, "there may be originality which does not depend on creation of the scene or object to be photographed . . . and which resides [instead] in such specialties as angle of shot, light and shade, exposure, effects achieved by means of filters, developing techniques etc." I will refer to this type of originality as originality in the rendition because, to the extent a photograph is original in this way, copyright protects not what is depicted, but rather how it is depicted.

It was originality in the rendition that was at issue in *SHL Imaging, Inc. v. Artisan House, Inc.*, 117 F.Supp. 2d 301 (S.D.N.Y. 2000). That case concerned photographs of the defendants' mirrored picture frames that the defendants commissioned from the plaintiff. The photographs were to be used by the defendants' sales force for in-person pitches. When the defendants reproduced the photographs in their catalogues and brochures, the court found infringement: "Plaintiff cannot prevent others from photographing the same frames, or using the same lighting techniques and blue sky reflection in the mirrors. What makes plaintiff's photographs original is the totality of the precise lighting selection, angle of the camera, lens and filter selection." Again, what made the photographs original was not the lens and filter selection themselves. It was the effect produced by the lens and filters selected, among other things. In any case, those effects were the basis of the originality of the works at issue in *SHL Imaging*. By contrast, in *Bridgeman Art Library*, the goal was to reproduce exactly other works. The photographs were entirely unoriginal in the rendition, an extremely unusual circumstance. Unless a photograph replicates another work with total or near-total fidelity, it will be at least somewhat original in the rendition.

b. Timing

A photograph may be original in a second respect. "[A] person may create a worthwhile photograph by being at the right place at the right time." I will refer to this type of originality as originality in timing.

One case that concerned originality in timing, among other things, was *Pagano v. Chas. Beseler Co.*, 234 F. 963 (S.D.N.Y.1916), which addressed the copyrightability of a photograph of a scene in front of the New York Public Library at Fifth Avenue and Forty-Second Street: "The question is not, as defendant suggests, whether the photograph of a public building may properly be copyrighted. Any one may take a photograph of a public building and of the surrounding scene. It undoubtedly requires originality to determine just when to take the photograph, so as to bring out the proper setting for both animate and inanimate objects. . . . The photographer caught the men and women in not merely lifelike, but artistic, positions, and this is especially true of the traffic policeman. . . . There are other features, which need not be discussed in detail, such as the motor cars waiting for the signal to proceed." 234 F.Supp.2d at 964.

A modern work strikingly original in timing might be *Catch of the Day*, by noted wildlife photographer Thomas Mangelsen, which depicts a salmon that appears to be jumping into the gaping mouth of a brown bear at Brooks Falls in Katmai National Park, Alaska. An older example is Alfred Eisenstaedt's photograph of a sailor kissing a young woman on VJ Day in Times Square, the memorability of which is attributable in significant part to the timing of its creation.

Copyright based on originality in timing is limited by the principle that copyright in a photograph ordinarily confers no rights over the subject matter. Thus, the copyright in *Catch of the Day* does not protect against subsequent photographs of bears feasting on salmon in the same location. Furthermore, if another photographer were sufficiently skilled and fortunate to capture a salmon at the precise moment that it appeared to enter a hungry bear's mouth—and others have tried, with varying degrees of success—that photographer, even if inspired by Mangelsen, would not necessarily have infringed his work because Mangelsen's copyright does not extend to the natural world he captured.

In practice, originality in timing gives rise to the same type of protection as originality in the rendition. In each case, the image that exhibits the originality, but not the underlying subject, qualifies for copyright protection.

c. *Creation of the Subject*

The principle that copyright confers no right over the subject matter has an important limitation. A photograph may be original to the extent that the photographer created "the scene or subject to be photographed." This type of originality, which I will refer to as originality in the creation of the subject, played an essential role in *Rogers v. Koons*, 960 F.2d 301 (2d Cir. 1992), and *Gross v. Seligman*, 212 F. 930 (2d Cir. 1914).

In *Rogers*, the court held that the copyright in the plaintiff's photograph *Puppies*, which depicted a contrived scene of the photographer's acquaintance, Jim Scanlon, and his wife on a park bench with eight puppies on their laps, protected against the defendants' attempt to replicate precisely, albeit in a three dimensional sculpture, the content of the photograph. Although the Circuit noted that *Puppies* was original because the artist "made creative judgments concerning technical matters with his camera and the use of natural light"—in other words, because it was original in the rendition—its originality in the creation of the subject was more salient. The same is true of the works at issue in *Gross v. Seligman*, in which the Circuit held that the copyright in a photograph named *Grace of Youth* was infringed when the same artist created a photograph named *Cherry Ripe* using "the same model in the identical pose, with the single exception that the young woman now wears a smile and holds a cherry stem between her teeth."

To conclude, the nature and extent of protection conferred by the copyright in a photograph will vary depending on the nature of its originality. Insofar as a photograph is original in the rendition or timing, copyright protects the image but does not prevent others from photographing the same object or scene. Thus, the copyright at issue in *SHL Imaging* does not protect against subsequent photographs of the picture frames because the originality of the plaintiffs' photographs was almost purely in the rendition of those frames, not in their creation or the timing of the scene captured. In *Pagano*, the timing of the capture of the scene in front of the New York Public Library and its rendition were original, but the copyright in the *Pagano* photograph does not protect against future attempts to capture a scene in front of the same building, just as a copyright in *Catch of the Day* would not protect against other photographers capturing images of salmon-eating bears.

By contrast, to the extent that a photograph is original in the creation of the subject, copyright extends also to that subject. Thus, an artist who arranges and then photographs a scene often will have the right to prevent others from duplicating that scene in a photograph or other medium.

2. Originality of the Garnett Photograph

There can be no serious dispute that the Garnett Photograph is an original work. The photograph does not result from slavishly copying another work and therefore is original in the rendition. Mannion's relatively unusual angle and distinctive lighting strengthen that aspect of the photograph's originality. His composition—posing man against sky—evidences originality in the creation of the subject. Furthermore, Mannion instructed Garnett to wear simple and plain clothing and as much jewelry as possible, and "to look 'chilled out.'" His orchestration of the scene contributes additional originality in the creation of the subject.

Of course, there are limits to the photograph's originality and therefore to the protection conferred by the copyright in the Garnett Photograph. For example, Kevin Garnett's face, torso, and hands are not original with Mannion, and Mannion therefore may not prevent others from creating photographic portraits of Garnett. Equally obviously, the existence of a cloudy sky is not original, and Mannion therefore may not prevent others from using a cloudy sky as a backdrop.

The defendants, however, take this line of reasoning too far. They argue that it was Garnett, not Mannion, who selected the specific clothing, jewelry, and pose. In consequence, they maintain, the Garnett Photograph is not original to the extent of Garnett's clothing, jewelry, and pose. They appear to be referring to originality in the creation of the subject.

The defendants complain as well that Mannion's declaration does not mention, among other things, the type of film, camera, and filters that he used to produce the Garnett Photograph. * * * These omissions are irrelevant. As discussed above, originality in the rendition is assessed with respect to the work, not the artist's specific decisions in producing it.

There are two problems with the defendants' argument. The first is that Mannion indisputably orchestrated the scene, even if he did not plan every detail before he met Garnett, and then made the decision to capture it. The second difficulty is that the originality of the photograph extends beyond the individual clothing, jewelry, and pose viewed in isolation. It is the entire image—depicting man, sky, clothing, and jewelry in a particular arrangement—that is at issue here, not its individual components. The Second Circuit has rejected the proposition that: "in comparing designs for copyright infringement, we are required to dissect them into their separate components, and compare only those elements which are in themselves copyrightable. . . . [I]f we took this argument to its logical conclusion, we might have to decide that 'there can be no originality in a painting because all colors of paint have been used somewhere in the past.' " *Knitwaves, Inc. v. Lollytogs Ltd.*, 71 F.3d 996, 1003 (2d Cir.1995) (citation omitted).

3. *The Idea/Expression Difficulty*

Notwithstanding the originality of the Garnett Photograph, the defendants argue that the Coors Billboard does not infringe because the two, insofar as they are similar, share only "the generalized idea and concept of a young African American man wearing a white T-shirt and a large amount of jewelry." It is true that an axiom of copyright law is that copyright does not protect "ideas," only their expression. Furthermore, when "a given idea is inseparably tied to a particular expression" so that "there is a 'merger' of idea and expression," courts may deny protection to the expression in order to avoid conferring a monopoly on the idea to which it inseparably is tied. But the defendants' reliance on these principles is misplaced. The "idea" (if one wants to call it that) postulated by the defendants does not even come close to accounting for all the similarities between the two works, which extend at least to angle, pose, background, composition, and lighting. It is possible to imagine any number of depictions of a black man wearing a white T-shirt and "bling bling" that look nothing like either of the photographs at issue here.

This alone is sufficient to dispose of the defendants' contention that Mannion's claims must be rejected because he seeks to protect an idea rather than its expression. But the argument reveals an analytical difficulty in the case law about which more ought to be said. One of the main cases upon which the defendants rely is *Kaplan v. Stock Market Photo Agency, Inc.*,133 F.Supp.2d 317 (S.D.N.Y. 2001), in which two remarkably similar photographs of a businessman's shoes and lower legs, taken from the top of a tall building looking down on a street below (the plaintiff's and defendants' photographs are reproduced below), were held to be not substantially similar as a matter of law because all of the similarities flowed only from an unprotected idea rather than from the expression of that idea.

But what is the "idea" of Kaplan's photograph? Is it (1) a businessman contemplating suicide by jumping from a building, (2) a businessman contemplating suicide by jumping from a building, seen from the vantage point of the businessman, with his shoes set against the street far below, or perhaps something more general, such as (3) a sense of desperation produced by urban professional life?

If the "idea" is (1) or, for that matter, (3), then the similarities between the two photographs flow from something much more than that idea, for it have would been possible to convey (1) (and (3)) in any number of ways that bear no obvious similarities to Kaplan's photograph. (Examples are a businessman atop a building seen from below, or the entire figure of the businessman, rather than just his shoes or pants, seen from above.) If, on the other hand, the "idea" is (2), then the two works could be said to owe much of their similarity to a shared idea.

To be sure, the difficulty of distinguishing between idea and expression long has been recognized. Judge Learned Hand famously observed in 1930: "Upon any work, and especially upon a play, a great number of patterns of increasing generality will fit equally well, as more and more of the incident is left out. The last may perhaps be no more than the most general statement of what the play is about, and at times might consist only of its title; but there is a point in this series of abstractions where they are no longer protected, since otherwise the playwright could prevent the use of his 'ideas,' to which, apart from their expression, his property is never extended. Nobody has ever been able to fix that boundary, and nobody ever can." *Nichols v. Universal Pictures Corp.*, 45 F.2d 119, 121 (2d Cir. 1930).

This passage is often referred to as the abstractions test, but it is no such thing. Judge Newman has lamented this parlance and the underlying difficulty it elides: "Judge Hand manifestly did not think of his observations as the enunciation of anything that might be called a 'test.' His disclaimer (for himself and everyone else) of the ability to 'fix the boundary' should have been sufficient caution that no 'test' capable of yielding a result was intended." Hon. Jon O. Newman, *New Lyrics for an Old Melody: The Idea/Expression Dichotomy in the Computer Age*, 17 CARDOZO ARTS & ENT. L.J. 691, 694 (1999).

Three decades later, Judge Hand's views were essentially the same: "The test for infringement of a copyright is of necessity vague.... Obviously, no principle can be stated as to when an imitator has gone beyond copying the 'idea,' and has borrowed its 'expression.' Decisions must therefore inevitably be ad hoc." *Peter Pan Fabrics, Inc. v. Martin Weiner Corp.*, 274 F.2d 487, 489 (2d Cir.1960). Since then, the Second Circuit and other authorities repeatedly have echoed these sentiments.

But there is a difference between the sort of difficulty Judge Hand identified in *Nichols* and *Peter Pan Fabrics* and the one presented by the *Kaplan* rationale and the defendants' argument about ideas in this case. The former difficulty is essentially one of line-drawing, and, as Judge Hand taught, is common to most cases in most areas of the law. The latter difficulty, however, is not simply that it is not always clear where to draw the line; it is that the line itself is meaningless because the conceptual categories it purports to delineate are ill-suited to the subject matter.

The idea/expression distinction arose in the context of literary copyright. For the most part, the Supreme Court has not applied it outside that context. The classic Hand formulations reviewed above also were articulated in the context of literary works. And it makes sense to speak of the idea conveyed by a literary work and to distinguish it from its expression. To take a clear example, two different authors each can describe, with very different words, the theory of special relativity. The words will be protected as expression. The theory is a set of unprotected ideas.

In the visual arts, the distinction breaks down. For one thing, it is impossible in most cases to speak of the particular "idea" captured, embodied, or conveyed by a work of art because every observer will have a different interpretation. Furthermore, it is not clear that there is any real distinction between the idea in a work of art and its expression. An artist's idea, among other things, is to depict a particular subject in a particular way. As a demonstration, a number of cases from this Circuit have observed that a photographer's "conception" of his subject is copyrightable. By "conception," the courts must mean originality in the rendition, timing, and creation of the subject-for that is what copyright protects in photography. But the word "conception" is a cousin of "concept," and both are akin to "idea." In other words, those elements of a photograph, or indeed, any work of visual art protected by copyright, could just as easily be labeled "idea" as "expression."

* * *

For all of these reasons, I think little is gained by attempting to distinguish an unprotectible "idea" from its protectible "expression" in a photograph or other work of visual art. It remains, then, to consider just what courts have been referring to when they have spoken of the "idea" in a photograph.

A good example is *Rogers v. Koons*, in which the court observed that "[i]t is not . . . the idea of a couple with eight small puppies seated on a bench that is protected, but rather Rogers' expression of this idea-as caught in the placement, in the particular light, and in the expressions of the subjects. . . ." 960 F.2d at 308. But "a couple with eight small puppies seated on a bench" is not necessarily the idea of *Puppies*, which just as easily could be "people with dogs on their laps," "the bliss of owning puppies," or even a sheepishly ironic thought such as "Ha ha! This might look cute now, but boy are these puppies going to be a lot of work!"

* * * Thus another photographer may pose a couple with eight puppies on a bench, depict a businessman contemplating a leap from an office building onto a street, or take a picture of a black man in white athletic wear and showy jewelry. In each case, however, there would be infringement (assuming actual copying and ownership of a valid copyright) if the subject and rendition were sufficiently like those in the copyrighted work.

* * *

I recognize that those principles sometimes may pose a problem like the one that Judge Hand identified with distinguishing idea from expression in the literary context. As Judge Hand observed, however, such line-drawing difficulties appear in all areas of the law. The important thing is that the categories at issue be useful and relevant, even if their precise boundaries are sometimes difficult to delineate. In the context of photography, the idea/expression distinction is not useful or relevant.

D. *Comparison of the Coors Billboard and the Garnett Photograph*

The next step is to determine whether a trier of fact could or must find the Coors Billboard substantially similar to the Garnett Photograph with respect to their protected elements.

Substantial similarity ultimately is a question of fact. "The standard test for substantial similarity between two items is whether an 'ordinary observer, unless he set out to detect the disparities, would be disposed to overlook them, and regard [the] aesthetic appeal as the same.' " The Second Circuit sometimes has applied a "more discerning observer" test when a work contains both protectible and unprotectible elements. The test "requires the court to eliminate the unprotectible elements from its consideration and to ask whether the protectible elements, standing alone, are substantially similar." The Circuit, however, is ambivalent about this test. In several cases dealing with fabric and garment designs, the Circuit has cautioned that: "a court is not to dissect the works at issue into separate components and compare only the copyrightable elements. . . . To do so would be to take the 'more discerning' test to an extreme, which would result in almost nothing being copyrightable because original works broken down into their composite parts would usually be little more than basic unprotectible elements like letters, colors and symbols."

* * *

The Garnett Photograph is protectible to the extent of its originality in the rendition and creation of the subject. Key elements of the Garnett Photograph that are in the public domain—such as Kevin Garnett's likeness—are not replicated in the Coors Billboard. Other elements arguably in the public domain—such as the existence of a cloudy sky, Garnett's pose, his white T-shirt, and his specific jewelry—may not be copyrightable in and of themselves, but their existence and arrangement in this photograph indisputably contribute to its originality. Thus the fact that the Garnett Photograph includes certain elements that would not be copyrightable in isolation does not affect the nature of the comparison. The question is whether the aesthetic appeal of the two images is the same.

The two photographs share a similar composition and angle. The lighting is similar, and both use a cloudy sky as backdrop. The subjects are wearing similar clothing and similar jewelry arranged in a similar way. The defendants, in other words, appear to have recreated much of the subject that Mannion had created and then, through imitation of angle and lighting, rendered it in a similar way. The similarities here thus relate to the Garnett Photograph's originality in the rendition and the creation of the subject and therefore to its protected elements.

There of course are differences between the two works. The similarity analysis may take into account some, but not all, of these. It long has been the law that "no plagiarist can excuse the wrong by showing how much of his work he did not pirate." Thus the addition of the words "Iced Out" and a can of Coors Light beer may not enter into the similarity analysis.

Other differences, however, are in the nature of changes rather than additions. One image is black and white and dark, the other is in color and bright. One is the mirror image of the other. One depicts only an unidentified man's torso, the other the top three-fourths of Kevin Garnett's body. The jewelry is not identical. One T-shirt appears to fit more tightly than the other. These changes may enter the analysis because "[i]f the points of dissimilarity not only exceed the points of similarity, but indicate that the remaining points of similarity are, within the context of plaintiff's work, of minimal importance . . . then no infringement results."

The parties have catalogued at length and in depth the similarities and differences between these works. In the last analysis, a reasonable jury could find substantial similarity either present or absent. As in *Kisch v. Ammirati & Puris Inc.*, 657 F.Supp. 380, 384 (S.D.N.Y. 1987), which presents facts as close to this case as can be imagined, the images are such that infringement cannot be ruled out-or in-as a matter of law.

Conclusion

The defendants' motion for summary judgment dismissing the complaint is granted to the extent that the complaint seeks relief for violation of the plaintiff's exclusive right to prepare derivative works and otherwise denied. The plaintiff's cross motion for summary judgment is denied.

Appendix

The Garnett Photograph

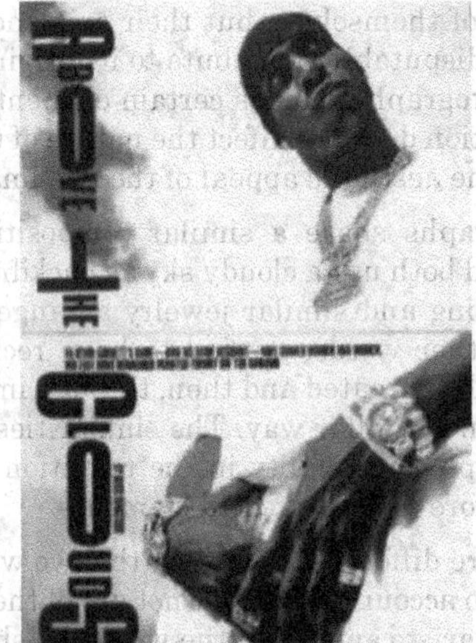

The Iced Out Comp Board

The Coors Billboard [and section of the Coors Billboard]

The plaintiff's photograph in *Kaplan v. Stock Market Photo Agency, Inc.*

The defendants' photograph in *Kaplan*

NOTES

1. At trial, both the advertising agency and Coors were held liable for infringing Mannion's copyright in the photograph, and Mannion was awarded $50,000 in damages. Mannion's motion for a new trial (for an increased damage award) was denied, and the damage award was sustained. *See Mannion v. Coors Brewing Co.*, 530 F. Supp. 2d 543 (S.D.N.Y. 2008).

2. The opinion in *Mannion* suggests how far the law of photography has traveled in the years since *Burrow-Giles*. Does the shift from film to digital photography change the analysis at all?

3. Does *Mannion* clarify the law or provide useful guidance to practitioners and their clients?

B. THE FIXATION REQUIREMENT

COPYRIGHT ACT OF 1976

H.R. Rep. No. 94–1476.
94th Cong., 2d Sess. 52–53 (1976).

Fixation in tangible form

As a basic condition of copyright protection, the bill perpetuates the existing requirement that work be fixed in a "tangible medium of expression," and adds that this medium may be one "now known or later developed," and that the fixation is sufficient if the work "can be perceived, reproduced, or otherwise communicated, either directly or with the aid of a machine or device." This broad language is intended to avoid the artificial and largely unjustifiable distinctions, derived from cases such as *White-Smith Publishing Co. v. Apollo Co.*, 209 U.S. 1 (1908), under which statutory copyrightability in certain cases has been made to depend upon the form or medium in which the work is fixed. Under the bill it makes no difference what the form, manner, or medium of fixation may be—whether it is in words, numbers, notes, sounds, pictures, or any other graphic or symbolic indicia, whether embodied in a physical object in written, printed, photographic, sculptural, punched, magnetic, or any other stable form, and whether it is capable of perception directly or by means of any machine or device "now known or later developed."

Under the bill, the concept of fixation is important since it not only determines whether the provisions of the statute apply to a work, but it also represents the dividing line between common law and statutory protection. As will be noted in more detail in connection with section 301, an unfixed work of authorship, such as an improvisation or an unrecorded choreographic work, performance, or broadcast, would continue to be subject to protection under State common law or statute, but would not be eligible for Federal statutory protection under section 102.

The bill seeks to resolve, through the definition of "fixation" in section 101, the status of live broadcasts—sports, news coverage, live performances of music, etc.—that are reaching the public in unfixed form but that are simultaneously being recorded. When a football game is being covered by four television cameras, with a director guiding the activities of the four cameramen and choosing which of their electronic images are sent out to the public and in what order, there is little doubt that what the cameramen and the director are doing constitutes "authorship." The further question to be considered is whether there has been a fixation. If the images and sounds to be broadcast are first recorded (on a video tape, film, etc.) and then transmitted, the recorded work would be considered a "motion picture" subject to statutory protection against unauthorized reproduction or retransmission of the broadcast. If the program content is transmitted live to the public while being recorded at the same time, the case would be treated the same; the copyright owner would not be forced to rely on common law rather than statutory rights in proceeding against an infringing user of the live broadcast.

Thus, assuming it is copyrightable—as a "motion picture" or "sound recording," for example—the content of a live transmission should be regarded as fixed and should be accorded statutory protection if it is being recorded simultaneously with its transmission. On the other hand, the definition of "fixation" would exclude from the concept purely evanescent or transient reproductions such as those projected briefly on a screen, shown electronically on a television or other cathode ray tube, or captured momentarily in the "memory" of a computer.

Under the first sentence of the definition of "fixed" in section 101, a work would be considered "fixed in a tangible medium of expression" if there has been an authorized embodiment in a copy or phonorecord and if that embodiment "is sufficiently permanent or stable" to permit the work "to be perceived, reproduced, or otherwise communicated for a period of more than transitory duration." The second sentence makes clear that, in the case of "a work consisting of sounds, images, or both, that are being transmitted," the work is regarded as "fixed" if a fixation is being made at the same time as the transmission.

Under this definition "copies" and "phonorecords" together will comprise all of the material objects in which copyrightable works are capable of being fixed. * * * Two essential elements—original work and tangible object—must merge through fixation in order to produce subject matter copyrightable under the statute.

* * *

STERN ELECTRONICS, INC. V. KAUFMAN

669 F.2d 852 (2d Cir. 1982).

NEWMAN, CIRCUIT JUDGE:

[Defendants appeal the district court's grant of a preliminary injunction barring Omni Video Games, Inc., its distributor, and two of its officers, from infringing Stern Electronics' copyright in the electronic video game "Scramble," on the ground that "the visual images and accompanying sounds of the video game fail to satisfy the fixation and originality requirements of the Copyright Act, 17 U.S.C.App. § 102(a) (1976)."]

* * *

* * * To satisfy the statutory requirement for deposit of copies of a work to be copyrighted, 17 U.S.C.App. § 408(b) (1976), [Stern's licensor]

Konami submitted video tape recordings of the "Scramble" game, both in its "attract mode" and in its "play mode."

* * * In April 1981 Omni began to sell a video game called "Scramble" that not only bears the same name as the "Scramble" game Stern was then marketing, but also is virtually identical in both sight and sound. It sold this copy of Stern's "Scramble" game, known in the trade as a "knock-off," for several hundred dollars less than Stern's game.

1. *Copyright Issues*

In challenging the preliminary injunction that bars distribution of its "Scramble" game, Omni does not dispute that Konami and its sub-licensee Stern are entitled to secure some copyright protection for their "Scramble" game. Omni contends that Konami was entitled to copyright only the written computer program that determines the sights and sounds of the game's audiovisual display. While that approach would have afforded some degree of protection, it would not have prevented a determined competitor from manufacturing a "knock-off" of "Scramble" that replicates precisely the sights and sounds of the game's audiovisual display. This could be done by writing a new computer program that would interact with the hardware components of a video game to produce on the screen the same images seen in "Scramble," accompanied by the same sounds. Such replication is possible because many different computer programs can produce the same "results," whether those results are an analysis of financial records or a sequence of images and sounds. A program is simply "a set of statements (i.e., data) or instructions to be used directly or indirectly in a computer in order to bring about a certain result," Pub.L.No. 96–517, § 10(a), 94 Stat. 3015, 3028 (1980) (amending 17 U.S.C.App. § 101 (1976)). To take an elementary example, the result of displaying a "4" can be achieved by an instruction to add 2 and 2, subtract 3 from 7, or in a variety of other ways. Obviously, writing a new program to replicate the play of "Scramble" requires a sophisticated effort, but it is a manageable task.

To secure protection against the risk of a "knock-off" of "Scramble" based upon an original program, Konami eschewed registration of its program as a literary work and chose instead to register the sights and sounds of "Scramble" as an audiovisual work. *See* 17 U.S.C.App. § 102(a)(6) (1976). The Act defines "audiovisual works" as "works that consist of a series of related images which are intrinsically intended to be shown by the use of machines, or devices such as projectors, viewers, or electronic equipment, together with accompanying sounds, if any, regardless of the nature of the material objects, such as films or tapes, in which the works are embodied." 17 U.S.C.App. § 101 (1976). Omni contends that Konami is not entitled to secure a copyright in the sights and sounds of its "Scramble" game because the audiovisual work is neither "fixed in any tangible medium of expression" nor "original" within the meaning of § 102(a). Both contentions arise from the fact that the sequence of some of the images appearing on the screen during each play of the game will vary depending upon the actions taken by the player. For example, if he fails to avoid enemy fire, his spaceship will be destroyed; if he fails to destroy enough fuel depots, his own fuel supply will run out, and his spaceship will crash; if he succeeds in destroying missile sites and enemy planes, those images will disappear from the screen; and the precise course travelled by his spaceship will depend upon his adjustment of the craft's altitude and velocity.

If the content of the audiovisual display were not affected by the participation of the player, there would be no doubt that the display itself, and not merely the written computer program, would be eligible for copyright. The display satisfies the statutory definition of an original "audiovisual work," and the memory devices of the game satisfy the statutory requirement of a "copy" in which the work is "fixed." The Act defines "copies" as "material objects . . . in which a work is fixed by any method now known or later developed, and from which the work can be perceived, reproduced, or otherwise communicated, either directly or with the aid of a machine or device" and specifies that a work is "fixed" when "its embodiment in a copy . . . is sufficiently permanent or stable to permit it to be perceived, reproduced, or otherwise communicated for a period of more than transitory duration." 17 U.S.C.App. § 101 (1976). The audiovisual work is permanently embodied in a material object, the memory devices, from which it can be perceived with the aid of the other components of the game.

We agree with the District Court that the player's participation does not withdraw the audiovisual work from copyright eligibility. No doubt the entire sequence of all the sights and sounds of the game are different each time the game is played, depending upon the route and speed the player selects for his spaceship and the timing and accuracy of his release of his craft's bombs and lasers. Nevertheless, many aspects of the sights and the sequence of their appearance remain constant during each play of the game. These include the appearance (shape, color, and size) of the player's spaceship, the enemy craft, the ground missile bases and fuel depots, and the terrain over which (and beneath which) the player's ship flies, as well as the sequence in which the missile bases, fuel depots, and terrain appears. Also constant are the sounds heard whenever the player successfully destroys an enemy craft or installation or fails to avoid an enemy missile or laser. It is true, as appellants contend, that some of these sights and sounds will not be seen and heard during each play of the game in the event that the player's spaceship is destroyed before the entire course is traversed. But the images remain fixed, capable of being seen and heard each time a player succeeds in keeping his spaceship aloft long enough to permit the appearances of all the images and sounds of a complete play of the game. The repetitive sequence of a substantial portion of the sights and sounds of the game qualifies for copyright protection as an audiovisual work.

* * *

KELLEY V. CHICAGO PARK DISTRICT

635 F.3d 290 (7th Cir. 2011).

SYKES, CIRCUIT JUDGE:

Chapman Kelley is a nationally recognized artist known for his representational paintings of landscapes and flowers—in particular, romantic floral and woodland interpretations set within ellipses. In 1984 he received permission from the Chicago Park District to install an ambitious wildflower display at the north end of Grant Park, a prominent public space in the heart of downtown Chicago. "Wildflower Works" was thereafter planted: two enormous elliptical flower beds, each nearly as big as a football field, featuring a variety of native wildflowers and edged with borders of gravel and steel.

Promoted as "living art," Wildflower Works received critical and popular acclaim, and for a while Kelley and a group of volunteers tended the vast garden, pruning and replanting as needed. But by 2004 Wildflower Works had deteriorated, and the City's goals for Grant Park had changed. So the Park District dramatically modified the garden, substantially reducing its size, reconfiguring the oval flower beds into rectangles, and changing some of the planting material.

Kelley sued the Park District for violating his "right of integrity" under the Visual Artists Rights Act of 1990 ("VARA"), 17 U.S.C. § 106A, and also for breach of contract. The contract claim is insubstantial; the main event here is the VARA claim, which is novel and tests the boundaries of copyright law. Congress enacted this statute to comply with the nation's obligations under the Berne Convention for the Protection of Literary and Artistic Works. VARA amended the Copyright Act, importing a limited version of the civil-law concept of the "moral rights of the artist" into our intellectual-property law. In brief, for certain types of visual art—paintings, drawings, prints, sculptures, and exhibition photographs—VARA confers upon the artist certain rights of attribution and integrity. The latter include the right of the artist to prevent, during his lifetime, any distortion or modification of his work that would be "prejudicial to his . . . honor or reputation," and to recover for any such intentional distortion or modification undertaken without his consent. *See* 17 U.S.C. § 106A(a)(3)(A).

[The district court rejected Kelley's VARA claim on the ground that Wildflower Works lacked sufficient originality to be copyrightable, a prerequisite for protection under VARA. On appeal, the Seventh Circuit agrees that the work is not copyrightable, but on different grounds.]

* * *

I. Background

Kelley is a painter noted for his use of bold, elliptical outlines to surround scenes of landscapes and flowers. In the late-1970s and 1980s, he moved from the canvas to the soil and created a series of large outdoor wildflower displays that resembled his paintings. He planted the first in 1976 alongside a runway at the Dallas-Fort Worth International Airport and the second in 1982 outside the Dallas Museum of Natural History. The wildflower exhibit at the museum was temporary; the one at the airport just "gradually petered out."

In 1983 Kelley accepted an invitation from Chicago-based oil executive John Swearingen and his wife, Bonnie—collectors of Kelley's paintings—to come to Chicago to explore the possibility of creating a large outdoor wildflower display in the area. He scouted sites by land and by air and eventually settled on Grant Park, the city's showcase public space running along Lake Michigan in the center of downtown Chicago. This location suited Kelley's artistic, environmental, and educational mission; it also provided the best opportunity to reach a large audience. Kelley met with the Park District superintendent to present his proposal, and on June 19, 1984, the Park District Board of Commissioners granted him a permit to install a "permanent Wild Flower Floral Display" on a grassy area on top of the underground Monroe Street parking garage in Daley Bicentennial Plaza in Grant Park. Under the terms of the permit, Kelley was to install and maintain the exhibit at his own expense. The Park District reserved the right to terminate the installation by giving Kelley "a 90 day notice to remove the planting."

Kelley named the project "Chicago Wildflower Works I." The Park District issued a press release announcing that "a new form of 'living' art" was coming to Grant Park—"giant ovals of multicolored wildflowers" created by Kelley, a painter and "pioneer in the use of natural materials" who "attracted national prominence for his efforts to incorporate the landscape in artistic creation." The announcement explained that "[o]nce the ovals mature, the results will be two breathtaking natural canvases of Kelley-designed color patterns."

In the late summer of 1984, Kelley began installing the two large-scale elliptical flower beds at the Grant Park site; they spanned 1.5 acres of parkland and were set within gravel and steel borders. A gravel walkway bisected one of the ovals, and each flower bed also accommodated several large, preexisting air vents that were flush with the planting surface, providing ventilation to the parking garage below. For planting material

Kelley selected between 48 and 60 species of self-sustaining wildflowers native to the region. The species were selected for various aesthetic, environmental, and cultural reasons, but also to increase the likelihood that the garden could withstand Chicago's harsh winters and survive with minimal maintenance. Kelley designed the initial placement of the wildflowers so they would blossom sequentially, changing colors throughout the growing season and increasing in brightness towards the center of each ellipse. He purchased the initial planting material—between 200,000 and 300,000 wildflower plugs—at a cost of between $80,000 and $152,000. In September of 1984, a battery of volunteers planted the seedlings under Kelley's direction.

When the wildflowers bloomed the following year, Wildflower Works was greeted with widespread acclaim. Chicago's mayor, the Illinois Senate, and the Illinois Chapter of the American Society of Landscape Artists issued commendations. People flocked to see the lovely display—marketed by the Park District as "living landscape art"—and admiring articles appeared in national newspapers. Wildflower Works was a hit. * * *

For the next several years, Kelley's permit was renewed and he and his volunteers tended the impressive garden. They pruned and weeded and regularly planted new seeds, both to experiment with the garden's composition and to fill in where initial specimen had not flourished. Of course, the forces of nature—the varying bloom periods of the plants; their spread habits, compatibility, and life cycles; and the weather—produced constant change. Some wildflowers naturally did better than others. Some spread aggressively and encroached on neighboring plants. Some withered and died. Unwanted plants sprung up from seeds brought in by birds and the wind. Insects, rabbits, and weeds settled in, eventually taking a toll. * * *

* * *

[Despite Kelley's objections, in 2004 Park District officials reconfigured Wildflower Works, reducing its size by half, and replacing its elliptical flower beds with rectangular beds. Weeds were removed, some flowers were transplanted, and new planting material was added. When Kelley sued for violation of his moral rights under VARA, the district court rejected his claims on the ground that Wildflower Works was insufficiently original for copyright protection, and Kelley appealed.]

II. Discussion

* * *

4. Is Wildflower Works copyrightable?

To merit copyright protection, Wildflower Works must be an "original work[ ] of authorship fixed in a[ ] tangible medium of expression . . . from which [it] can be perceived, reproduced, or otherwise communicated." 17

U.S.C. § 102(a). The district court held that although Wildflower Works was both a painting and a sculpture, it was ineligible for copyright because it lacked originality. There is a contradiction here. As we have explained, VARA supplements general copyright protection and applies only to artists who create the specific subcategories of art enumerated in the statute. VARA-eligible paintings and sculptures comprise a discrete subset of otherwise copyrightable pictorial and sculptural works; the statute designates these works of fine art as worthy of special protection. If a work is so lacking in originality that it cannot satisfy the basic requirements for copyright, then it can hardly qualify as a painting or sculpture eligible for *extra* protection under VARA.

That point aside, the district court's conclusion misunderstands the originality requirement. Originality is "the touchstone of copyright protection today," an implicit constitutional and explicit statutory requirement. *Feist Publ'ns, Inc. v. Rural Tel. Serv. Co.,* 499 U.S. 340, 347, 346 (1991) ("Originality is a constitutional requirement."); *Id.* at 355 (The Copyright Act of 1976 made the originality requirement explicit.). Despite its centrality in our copyright regime, the threshold for originality is minimal. *See Feist,* 499 U.S. at 345. The standard requires "only that the work was independently created by the author (as opposed to copied from other works), and that it possesses at least some minimal degree of creativity." *Feist,* 499 U.S. at 345 (citation omitted). The "requisite level of creativity is extremely low; even a slight amount will suffice. The vast majority of works make the grade quite easily, as they possess some creative spark." *Id.* (citation omitted).

* * *

The real impediment to copyright here is not that Wildflower Works fails the test for originality (understood as "not copied" and "possessing some creativity") but that a living garden lacks the kind of authorship and stable fixation normally required to support copyright. Unlike originality, authorship and fixation are *explicit* constitutional requirements; the Copyright Clause empowers Congress to secure for "authors" exclusive rights in their "writings." U.S. Const. art 1, § 8, cl. 8. The originality requirement is implicit in these express limitations on the congressional copyright power. *See Feist,* 499 U.S. at 346 (The constitutional reference to "authors" and "writings" "presuppose[s] a degree of originality."). The Supreme Court has "repeatedly construed all three terms in relation to one another [or] perhaps has collapsed them into a single concept"; therefore, "[w]ritings are what authors create, but for one to be an author, the writing has to be original." 2 WILLIAM F. PATRY, PATRY ON COPYRIGHT § 3:20 (2010).

"Without fixation," moreover, "there cannot be a 'writing.' " *Id.* § 3:22. The Nimmer treatise elaborates:

> Fixation in tangible form is not merely a statutory condition to copyright. It is also a constitutional necessity. That is, unless a work is reduced to tangible form it cannot be regarded as a "writing" within the meaning of the constitutional clause authorizing federal copyright legislation. Thus, certain works of conceptual art stand outside of copyright protection.

1 MELVILLE B. NIMMER & DAVID NIMMER, NIMMER ON COPYRIGHT § 2.03[B] (2010). A work is "fixed" in a tangible medium of expression "when its embodiment in a copy or phonorecord . . . is sufficiently permanent or stable to permit it to be perceived, reproduced, or otherwise communicated for a period of more than transitory duration." 17 U.S.C. § 101. As William Patry explains:

> Fixation serves two basic roles: (1) easing problems of proof of creation and infringement, and (2) providing the dividing line between state common law protection and protection under the federal Copyright Act, since works that are not fixed are ineligible for federal protection but may be protected under state law. The distinction between the intangible intellectual property (the work of authorship) and its fixation in a tangible medium of expression (the copy) is an old and fundamental and important one. The distinction may be understood by examples of multiple fixations of the same work: A musical composition may be embodied in sheet music, on an audio-tape, on a compact disc, on a computer hard drive or server, or as part of a motion picture soundtrack. In each of the fixations, the intangible property remains a musical composition.

2 PATRY § 3:22.

Finally, "authorship is an entirely human endeavor." *Id.* § 3:19 (2010). Authors of copyrightable works must be human; works owing their form to the forces of nature cannot be copyrighted. *Id.* § 3:19 n. 1; *see also* U.S. Copyright Office, Compendium II: Copyright Office Practices § 503.03(a) ("[A] work must be the product of human authorship" and not the forces of nature.) (1984); *Id.* § 202.02(b).

Recognizing copyright in Wildflower Works presses too hard on these basic principles. We fully accept that the artistic community might classify Kelley's garden as a work of postmodern conceptual art. We acknowledge as well that copyright's prerequisites of authorship and fixation are broadly defined. But the law must have some limits; not all conceptual art may be copyrighted. In the ordinary copyright case, authorship and fixation are not contested; most works presented for copyright are unambiguously authored and unambiguously fixed. But this is not an ordinary case. A living garden like Wildflower Works is neither "authored" nor "fixed" in the senses required for copyright. *See Toney v. L'Oreal USA, Inc.*, 406 F.3d 905,

910 (7th Cir. 2005) ("A person's likeness—her persona—is not authored and it is not fixed.").

Simply put, gardens are planted and cultivated, not authored. A garden's constituent elements are alive and inherently changeable, not fixed. Most of what we see and experience in a garden—the colors, shapes, textures, and scents of the plants—originates in nature, not in the mind of the gardener. At any given moment in time, a garden owes most of its form and appearance to natural forces, though the gardener who plants and tends it obviously assists. All this is true of Wildflower Works, even though it was designed and planted by an artist.

Of course, a human "author"—whether an artist, a professional landscape designer, or an amateur backyard gardener—determines the initial arrangement of the plants in a garden. This is not the kind of authorship required for copyright. To the extent that seeds or seedlings can be considered a "medium of expression," they originate in nature, and natural forces—not the intellect of the gardener—determine their form, growth, and appearance. Moreover, a garden is simply too changeable to satisfy the primary purpose of fixation; its appearance is too inherently variable to supply a baseline for determining questions of copyright creation and infringement. If a garden can qualify as a "work of authorship" sufficiently "embodied in a copy," at what point has fixation occurred? When the garden is newly planted? When its first blossoms appear? When it is in full bloom? How—and at what point in time—is a court to determine whether infringing copying has occurred?

In contrast, when a landscape designer conceives of a plan for a garden and puts it in writing—records it in text, diagrams, or drawings on paper or on a digital-storage device—we can say that his intangible intellectual property has been embodied in a fixed and tangible "copy." This writing is a sufficiently permanent and stable copy of the designer's intellectual expression and is vulnerable to infringing copying, giving rise to the designer's right to claim copyright. The same cannot be said of a garden, which is not a fixed copy of the gardener's intellectual property. Although the planting material is tangible and can be perceived for more than a transitory duration, it is not stable or permanent enough to be called "fixed." Seeds and plants in a garden are naturally in a state of perpetual change; they germinate, grow, bloom, become dormant, and eventually die. This life cycle moves gradually, over days, weeks, and season to season, but the real barrier to copyright here is not *temporal* but *essential*. The essence of a garden is its vitality, not its fixedness. It may endure from season to season, but its nature is one of dynamic change.

We are not suggesting that copyright attaches *only* to works that are static or fully permanent (no medium of expression lasts forever), or that artists who incorporate natural or living elements in their work can *never* claim copyright. Kelley compares Wildflower Works to the Crown Fountain, a sculpture by Spanish artist Jaume Plensa that sits nearby in Chicago's Millennium Park. The surfaces of Plensa's fountain are embedded with LED screens that replay recorded video images of the faces of 1,000 Chicagoans. But the Copyright Act specifically contemplates works that incorporate or consist of sounds or images that are broadcast or transmitted electronically, such as telecasts of sporting events or other live performances, video games, and the like. *See* 17 U.S.C. § 101 (defining "fixed" as including a "work consisting of sounds, images, or both, that are being transmitted . . . if a fixation of the work is being made simultaneously with its transmission"). Wildflower Works does not fit in this category; the Crown Fountain is not analogous.

Though not addressing the requirement of fixation directly, the district court compared Wildflower Works to "[t]he mobiles of Alexander Calder" and "Jeff Koons' 'Puppy,' a 43-foot flowering topiary." These analogies are also inapt. Although the aesthetic effect of a Calder mobile is attributable in part to its subtle movement in response to air currents, the mobile itself is obviously fixed and stable. In "Puppy" the artist assembled a huge metal frame in the shape of a puppy and covered it with thousands of blooming flowers sustained by an irrigation system within the frame. This may be sufficient fixation for copyright (we venture no opinion on the question), but Wildflower Works is quite different. It is quintessentially a garden; "Puppy" is not.

In short, Wildflower Works presents serious problems of authorship and fixation that these and other examples of conceptual or kinetic art do not. Because Kelley's garden is neither "authored" nor "fixed" in the senses required for basic copyright, it cannot qualify for moral-rights protection under VARA.

* * *

NOTES

1. In certain countries, fixation is not a copyright prerequisite. Under United States law, however, fixation generally is conceded (though not entirely without dissent) to be a constitutional requirement under the Intellectual Property Clause, as well as a statutory requirement. What purpose does fixation serve?

2. The Uruguay Round Agreements Act of 1994 added 17 U.S.C. § 1101 and 18 U.S.C. § 2319A, providing civil and criminal remedies for making or trafficking in unauthorized recordings of live musical performances. Does this exceed Congress's power under the Intellectual Property Clause? Is the statute therefore unconstitutional? Two federal appeals courts have upheld various aspects of the bootlegging statutes under the Commerce Clause. In *United States v. Moghadam*, 175 F.3d 1269 (11th Cir. 1999), the court rejected a claim

that providing protection for unfixed works violated the Copyright Clause, because Congress has the power to regulate this conduct under the Commerce Clause. The Second Circuit, in *United States v. Martignon*, 492 F.3d 140 (2d Cir. 2007), vacated a district court's ruling that struck down section 2319A as unconstitutional on the ground that the statute represented an essentially "copyright-like" enactment, and therefore exceeded congressional power under the Copyright Clause by virtue of its failure to impose a limit on the term of protection. The Second Circuit concluded that enactment of § 2319A was a proper exercise of Congress' Commerce Clause power, and therefore the limitations found in the Copyright Clause did not apply. The court remanded the case for consideration of whether enforcement of § 2319A might violate the First Amendment.

3. Outside the context of sections 1101 and 2319A, is it possible to obtain copyright (or similar) protection for a live event (for example, a live stage performance, or a news or sporting event), or any portion thereof? If so, how? (Consider the definition of "fixed" in section 101 of the Copyright Act.)

4. If material is entered into a computer but not saved on the hard drive, is it sufficiently fixed to be copyrightable? Does copyright law protect material in an on-line chat that is not saved by its author? What about a message on Snapchat?

C. "ORIGINAL WORKS OF AUTHORSHIP"

1. ORIGINALITY: THE MINIMUM REQUIREMENT

Absent a statutory definition of the term, courts have labored to determine which works constitute "original works of authorship." The statutes do not define the quantum of originality required. It is clear, in principle, that an erstwhile "author" cannot obtain copyright protection for any portions of a work which consist entirely of material that is copied from a work in the public domain or from another copyrighted work. However, since all works of authorship necessarily are made up of public domain components—such as ideas, facts, words, musical notes, and naturally occurring images and sounds, as well as preexisting works of authorship—applying this general principle in particular cases can be difficult.

FEIST PUBLICATIONS V. RURAL TELEPHONE SERVICE

499 U.S. 340, 111 S.Ct. 1282 (1991).

JUSTICE O'CONNOR delivered the opinion of the Court:

This case requires us to clarify the extent of copyright protection available to telephone directory white pages.

I

Rural Telephone Service Company, Inc., is a certified public utility that provides telephone service to several communities in northwest Kansas. It is subject to a state regulation that requires all telephone companies operating in Kansas to issue annually an updated telephone directory. Accordingly, as a condition of its monopoly franchise, Rural publishes a typical telephone directory, consisting of white pages and yellow pages. The white pages list in alphabetical order the names of Rural's subscribers, together with their towns and telephone numbers. The yellow pages list Rural's business subscribers alphabetically by category and feature classified advertisements of various sizes. Rural distributes its directory free of charge to its subscribers, but earns revenue by selling yellow pages advertisements.

Feist Publications, Inc., is a publishing company that specializes in area-wide telephone directories. Unlike a typical directory, which covers only a particular calling area, Feist's area-wide directories cover a much larger geographical range, reducing the need to call directory assistance or consult multiple directories. The Feist directory that is the subject of this litigation covers 11 different telephone service areas in 15 counties and contains 46,878 white pages listings—compared to Rural's approximately 7,700 listings. Like Rural's directory, Feist's is distributed free of charge and includes both white pages and yellow pages. Feist and Rural compete vigorously for yellow pages advertising.

As the sole provider of telephone service in its service area, Rural obtains subscriber information quite easily. Persons desiring telephone service must apply to Rural and provide their names and addresses; Rural then assigns them a telephone number. Feist is not a telephone company, let alone one with monopoly status, and therefore lacks independent access to any subscriber information. To obtain white pages listings for its area-wide directory, Feist approached each of the 11 telephone companies operating in northwest Kansas and offered to pay for the right to use its white pages listings.

Of the 11 telephone companies, only Rural refused to license its listings to Feist. Rural's refusal created a problem for Feist, as omitting these listings would have left a gaping hole in its area-wide directory, rendering it less attractive to potential yellow pages advertisers. In a decision subsequent to that which we review here, the District Court determined that this was precisely the reason Rural refused to license its listings. The refusal was motivated by an unlawful purpose "to extend its monopoly in telephone service to a monopoly in yellow pages advertising." *Rural Telephone Service Co. v. Feist Publications, Inc.*, 737 F.Supp. 610, 622 (D.Kan. 1990).

Unable to license Rural's white pages listings, Feist used them without Rural's consent. Feist began by removing several thousand listings that fell outside the geographic range of its area-wide directory, then hired personnel to investigate the 4,935 that remained. These employees verified the data reported by Rural and sought to obtain additional information. As a result, a typical Feist listing includes the individual's street address; most of Rural's listings do not. Notwithstanding these additions, however, 1,309 of the 46,878 listings in Feist's 1983 directory were identical to listings in Rural's 1982–1983 white pages. * * * Four of these were fictitious listings that Rural had inserted into its directory to detect copying.

Rural sued for copyright infringement in the District Court for the District of Kansas taking the position that Feist, in compiling its own directory, could not use the information contained in Rural's white pages. Rural asserted that Feist's employees were obliged to travel door-to-door or conduct a telephone survey to discover the same information for themselves. Feist responded that such efforts were economically impractical and, in any event, unnecessary because the information copied was beyond the scope of copyright protection. The District Court granted summary judgment to Rural, explaining that "[c]ourts have consistently held that telephone directories are copyrightable" and citing a string of lower court decisions. In an unpublished opinion, the Court of Appeals for the Tenth Circuit affirmed "for substantially the reasons given by the district court." We granted certiorari to determine whether the copyright in Rural's directory protects the names, towns, and telephone numbers copied by Feist.

II

A

This case concerns the interaction of two well-established propositions. The first is that facts are not copyrightable; the other, that compilations of facts generally are. Each of these propositions possesses an impeccable pedigree. That there can be no valid copyright in facts is universally understood. The most fundamental axiom of copyright law is that "no author may copyright his ideas or the facts he narrates." *Harper & Row, Publishers, Inc. v. Nation Enterprises*, 471 U.S. 539, 556 (1985). Rural wisely concedes this point, noting in its brief that "facts and discoveries, of course, are not themselves subject to copyright protection." Brief for Respondent 24. At the same time, however, it is beyond dispute that compilations of facts are within the subject matter of copyright. Compilations were expressly mentioned in the Copyright Act of 1909, and again in the Copyright Act of 1976.

There is an undeniable tension between these two propositions. Many compilations consist of nothing but raw data—i.e., wholly factual information not accompanied by any original written expression. On what basis may one claim a copyright in such a work? Common sense tells us that 100 uncopyrightable facts do not magically change their status when gathered together in one place. Yet copyright law seems to contemplate that compilations that consist exclusively of facts are potentially within its scope.

The key to resolving the tension lies in understanding why facts are not copyrightable. The sine qua non of copyright is originality. To qualify for copyright protection, a work must be original to the author. *See Harper & Row, supra,* at 547–549. Original, as the term is used in copyright, means only that the work was independently created by the author (as opposed to copied from other works), and that it possesses at least some minimal degree of creativity. 1 M. NIMMER & D. NIMMER, COPYRIGHT §§ 2.01[A], [B] (1990) (hereinafter NIMMER). To be sure, the requisite level of creativity is extremely low; even a slight amount will suffice. The vast majority of works make the grade quite easily, as they possess some creative spark, "no matter how crude, humble or obvious" it might be. *Id.*, § 1.08[C][1]. Originality does not signify novelty; a work may be original even though it closely resembles other works so long as the similarity is fortuitous, not the result of copying. To illustrate, assume that two poets, each ignorant of the other, compose identical poems. Neither work is novel, yet both are original and, hence, copyrightable. *See Sheldon v. Metro-Goldwyn Pictures Corp.*, 81 F. 2d 49, 54 (C.A. 2 1936).

Originality is a constitutional requirement. The source of Congress' power to enact copyright laws is Article I, § 8, cl. 8, of the Constitution, which authorizes Congress to "secure for limited Times to Authors . . . the exclusive Right to their respective Writings." In two decisions from the late 19th century—*The Trade-Mark Cases,* 100 U.S. 82 (1879); and *Burrow-Giles Lithographic Co. v. Sarony*, 111 U.S. 53 (1884)—this Court defined the crucial terms "authors" and "writings." In so doing, the Court made it unmistakably clear that these terms presuppose a degree of originality.

In *The Trade-Mark Cases*, the Court addressed the constitutional scope of "writings." For a particular work to be classified "under the head of writings of authors," the Court determined, "originality is required." 100 U.S., at 94. The Court explained that originality requires independent creation plus a modicum of creativity: "[W]hile the word *writings* may be liberally construed, as it has been, to include original designs for engraving, prints, & c., it is only such as are *original,* and are founded in the creative powers of the mind. The writings which are to be protected are *the fruits of intellectual labor,* embodied in the form of books, prints, engravings, and the like." *Ibid.* (emphasis in original).

In *Burrow-Giles,* the Court distilled the same requirement from the Constitution's use of the word "authors." The Court defined "author," in a constitutional sense, to mean "he to whom anything owes its origin; originator; maker." 111 U.S., at 58 (internal quotation marks omitted). As in *The Trade-Mark Cases,* the Court emphasized the creative component of originality. It described copyright as being limited to "original intellectual conceptions of the author," 111 U.S., at 58, and stressed the importance of requiring an author who accuses another of infringement to prove "the existence of those facts of originality, of intellectual production, of thought, and conception." *Id.*, at 59–60.

The originality requirement articulated in *The Trade-Mark Cases* and *Burrow-Giles* remains the touchstone of copyright protection today. It is the very "premise of copyright law." *Miller v. Universal City Studios, Inc.*, 650 F. 2d 1365, 1368 (5th Cir. 1981). Leading scholars agree on this point. As one pair of commentators succinctly puts it: "The originality requirement is *constitutionally mandated* for all works." Patterson & Joyce, *Monopolizing the Law: The Scope of Copyright Protection for Law Reports and Statutory Compilations,* 36 UCLA L. REV. 719, 763, n. 155 (1989) (emphasis in original) (hereinafter Patterson & Joyce). *Accord, Id.*, at 759–760, and n. 140; NIMMER § 1.06[A] ("Originality is a statutory as well as a constitutional requirement"); *Id.*, § 1.08[C][1] ("[A] modicum of intellectual labor . . . clearly constitutes an essential constitutional element").

It is this bedrock principle of copyright that mandates the law's seemingly disparate treatment of facts and factual compilations. "No one may claim originality as to facts." *Id.*, § 2.11[A], p. 2–157. This is because facts do not owe their origin to an act of authorship. The distinction is one between creation and discovery: The first person to find and report a particular fact has not created the fact; he or she has merely discovered its existence. To borrow from *Burrow-Giles,* one who discovers a fact is not its "maker" or "originator." 111 U.S., at 58. "The discoverer merely finds and records." NIMMER § 2.03[E]. Census takers, for example, do not "create" the population figures that emerge from their efforts; in a sense, they copy these figures from the world around them. Census data therefore do not trigger copyright because these data are not "original" in the constitutional sense. The same is true of all facts—scientific, historical, biographical, and news of the day. "They may not be copyrighted and are part of the public domain available to every person." *Miller, supra,* at 1369.

Factual compilations, on the other hand, may possess the requisite originality. The compilation author typically chooses which facts to include, in what order to place them, and how to arrange the collected data so that they may be used effectively by readers. These choices as to selection and arrangement, so long as they are made independently by the compiler and entail a minimal degree of creativity, are sufficiently original that Congress may protect such compilations through the copyright laws. Thus, even a directory that contains absolutely no protectible written expression, only facts, meets the constitutional minimum for copyright protection if it features an original selection or arrangement.

This protection is subject to an important limitation. The mere fact that a work is copyrighted does not mean that every element of the work may be protected. Originality remains the sine qua non of copyright; accordingly, copyright protection may extend only to those components of a work that are original to the author. Ginsburg, *Creation and Commercial Value: Copyright Protection of Works of Information*, 90 COLUM. L. REV. 1865, 1868 and n.12 (1990) (hereinafter Ginsburg). Thus, if the compilation author clothes facts with an original collocation of words, he or she may be able to claim a copyright in this written expression. Others may copy the underlying facts from the publication, but not the precise words used to present them. In *Harper & Row*, for example, we explained that President Ford could not prevent others from copying bare historical facts from his autobiography, *see* 471 U.S., at 556–557, but that he could prevent others from copying his "subjective descriptions and portraits of public figures." *Id.*, at 563. Where the compilation author adds no written expression but rather lets the facts speak for themselves, the expressive element is more elusive. The only conceivable expression is the manner in which the compiler has selected and arranged the facts. Thus, if the selection and arrangement are original, these elements of the work are eligible for copyright protection. No matter how original the format, however, the facts themselves do not become original through association.

This inevitably means that the copyright in a factual compilation is thin. Notwithstanding a valid copyright, a subsequent compiler remains free to use the facts contained in another's publication to aid in preparing a competing work, so long as the competing work does not feature the same selection and arrangement. As one commentator explains it: "No matter how much original authorship the work displays, the facts and ideas it exposes are free for the taking. . . . The very same facts and ideas may be divorced from the context imposed by the author, and restated or reshuffled by second comers, even if the author was the first to discover the facts or to propose the ideas." Ginsburg, 1868.

It may seem unfair that much of the fruit of the compiler's labor may be used by others without compensation. As Justice Brennan has correctly observed, however, this is not "some unforeseen byproduct of a statutory scheme." *Harper & Row*, 471 U.S. 539, at 589 (dissenting opinion). It is, rather, "the essence of copyright," *ibid.*, and a constitutional requirement. The primary objective of copyright is not to reward the labor of authors, but "to promote the Progress of Science and useful Arts." Art. I, § 8, cl. 8. *Accord, Twentieth Century Music Corp. v. Aiken*, 422 U.S. 151, 156 (1975). To this end, copyright assures authors the right to their original expression, but encourages others to build freely upon the ideas and information conveyed by a work. This principle, known as the idea/

expression or fact/expression dichotomy, applies to all works of authorship. As applied to a factual compilation, assuming the absence of original written expression, only the compiler's selection and arrangement may be protected; the raw facts may be copied at will. This result is neither unfair nor unfortunate. It is the means by which copyright advances the progress of science and art.

This Court has long recognized that the fact/expression dichotomy limits severely the scope of protection in fact-based works. More than a century ago, the Court observed: "The very object of publishing a book on science or the useful arts is to communicate to the world the useful knowledge which it contains. But this object would be frustrated if the knowledge could not be used without incurring the guilt of piracy of the book." *Baker v. Selden,* 101 U.S. 99, 103 (1880). * * *

This, then, resolves the doctrinal tension: Copyright treats facts and factual compilations in a wholly consistent manner. Facts, whether alone or as part of a compilation, are not original and therefore may not be copyrighted. A factual compilation is eligible for copyright if it features an original selection or arrangement of facts, but the copyright is limited to the particular selection or arrangement. In no event may copyright extend to the facts themselves.

B

As we have explained, originality is a constitutionally mandated prerequisite for copyright protection. The Court's decisions announcing this rule predate the Copyright Act of 1909, but ambiguous language in the 1909 Act caused some lower courts temporarily to lose sight of this requirement.

The 1909 Act embodied the originality requirement, but not as clearly as it might have. The subject matter of copyright was set out in §§ 3 and 4 of the Act. Section 4 stated that copyright was available to "all the writings of an author." 35 Stat. 1076. By using the words "writings" and "author"—the same words used in Article I, § 8, of the Constitution and defined by the Court in *The Trade-Mark Cases* and *Burrow-Giles*—the statute necessarily incorporated the originality requirement articulated in the Court's decisions. It did so implicitly, however, thereby leaving room for error.

Section 3 was similarly ambiguous. It stated that the copyright in a work protected only "the copyrightable component parts of the work." It thus stated an important copyright principle, but failed to identify the specific characteristic—originality—that determined which component parts of a work were copyrightable and which were not.

* * *

[Because of these ambiguities, some courts adopted the view that factual compilations were protectible regardless of their originality.] Making matters worse, these courts developed a new theory to justify the protection of factual compilations. Known alternatively as "sweat of the brow" or "industrious collection," the underlying notion was that copyright was a reward for the hard work that went into compiling facts. The classic formulation of the doctrine appeared in *Jeweler's Circular Publishing Co.* [*v. Keystone Publishing Co.*, 281 F. 83 (2d Cir.1922)], at 88:

> "The right to copyright a book upon which one has expended labor in its preparation does not depend upon whether the materials which he has collected consist or not of matters which are publici juris, or whether such materials show literary skill *or originality*, either in thought or in language, or anything more than industrious collection. The man who goes through the streets of a town and puts down the names of each of the inhabitants, with their occupations and their street number, acquires material of which he is the author" (emphasis added).

The "sweat of the brow" doctrine had numerous flaws, the most glaring being that it extended copyright protection in a compilation beyond selection and arrangement—the compiler's original contributions—to the facts themselves. Under the doctrine, the only defense to infringement was independent creation. A subsequent compiler was "not entitled to take one word of information previously published," but rather had to "independently wor[k] out the matter for himself, so as to arrive at the same result from the same common sources of information." *Id.*, at 88–89 (internal quotations omitted). "Sweat of the brow" courts thereby eschewed the most fundamental axiom of copyright law—that no one may copyright facts or ideas. *See Miller v. Universal City Studios, Inc.*, 650 F.2d, at 1372 (criticizing "sweat of the brow" courts because "ensur[ing] that later writers obtain the facts independently . . . is precisely the scope of protection given . . . copyrighted matter, and the law is clear that facts are not entitled to such protection").

Decisions of this Court applying the 1909 Act make clear that the statute did not permit the "sweat of the brow" approach. The best example is *International News Service v. Associated Press*, 248 U.S. 215 (1918). In that decision, the Court stated unambiguously that the 1909 Act conferred copyright protection only on those elements of a work that were original to the author. International News Service had conceded taking news reported by Associated Press and publishing it in its own newspapers. Recognizing that § 5 of the Act specifically mentioned " 'periodicals, including newspapers,' " § 5(b), the Court acknowledged that news articles were copyrightable. *Id.*, at 234. It flatly rejected, however, the notion that the copyright in an article extended to the factual information it contained: "[T]he news element—the information respecting current events contained in the literary production—is not the creation of the writer, but is a report of matters that ordinarily are publici juris; it is the history of the day." *Ibid.*

Without a doubt, the "sweat of the brow" doctrine flouted basic copyright principles. Throughout history, copyright law has "recognize[d] a greater need to disseminate factual works than works of fiction or fantasy." *Harper & Row*, 471 U.S. 539, at 563. But "sweat of the brow" courts took a contrary view; they handed out proprietary interests in facts and declared that authors are absolutely precluded from saving time and effort by relying upon the facts contained in prior works. In truth, "[i]t is just such wasted effort that the proscription against the copyright of ideas and facts . . . [is] designed to prevent." *Rosemont Enterprises, Inc. v. Random House, Inc.*, 366 F.2d 303, 310 (C.A.2 1966). "Protection for the fruits of such research . . . may in certain circumstances be available under a theory of unfair competition. But to accord copyright protection on this basis alone distorts basic copyright principles in that it creates a monopoly in public domain materials without the necessary justification of protecting and encouraging the creation of 'writings' by 'authors.'" NIMMER § 3.04, p. 3–23 (footnote omitted).

C

"Sweat of the brow" decisions did not escape the attention of the Copyright Office. When Congress decided to overhaul the copyright statute and asked the Copyright Office to study existing problems, *see Mills Music, Inc.* v. *Snyder*, 469 U.S. 153, 159 (1985), the Copyright Office promptly recommended that Congress clear up the confusion in the lower courts as to the basic standards of copyrightability. * * *

* * * In enacting the Copyright Act of 1976, Congress dropped the reference to "all the writings of an author" and replaced it with the phrase "original works of authorship." 17 U.S.C. § 102(a). In making explicit the originality requirement, Congress announced that it was merely clarifying existing law * * *. This sentiment was echoed by the Copyright Office: "Our intention here is to maintain the *established standards* of originality. . . ." Supplementary Report of the Register of Copyrights on the General Revision of U.S. Copyright Law, 89th Cong., 1st Sess., pt. 6, p. 3 (H. Judiciary Comm. Print 1965) (emphasis added).

* * *

To ensure that the mistakes of the "sweat of the brow" courts would not be repeated, Congress took additional measures. For example, § 3 of the 1909 Act had stated that copyright protected only the "copyrightable component parts" of a work, but had not identified originality as the basis for distinguishing those component parts that were copyrightable from those that were not. The 1976 Act deleted this section and replaced it with § 102(b), which identifies specifically those elements of a work for which copyright is not available: "In no case does copyright protection for an original work of authorship extend to any idea, procedure, process, system, method of operation, concept, principle, or discovery, regardless of the form in which it is described, explained, illustrated, or embodied in such work." Section 102(b) is universally understood to prohibit any copyright in facts. As with § 102(a), Congress emphasized that § 102(b) did not change the law, but merely clarified it: "Section 102(b) in no way enlarges or contracts the scope of copyright protection under the present law. Its purpose is to restate . . . that the basic dichotomy between expression and idea remains unchanged." H. R. Rep., at 57; S. Rep., at 54.

Congress took another step to minimize confusion by deleting the specific mention of "directories . . . and other compilations" in § 5 of the 1909 Act. * * * In its place, Congress enacted two new provisions. First, to make clear that compilations were not copyrightable per se, Congress provided a definition of the term "compilation." Second, to make clear that the copyright in a compilation did not extend to the facts themselves, Congress enacted § 103.

The definition of "compilation" is found in § 101 of the 1976 Act. It defines a "compilation" in the copyright sense as "a work formed by the collection and assembling of preexisting materials or of data *that* are selected, coordinated, or arranged *in such a way that* the resulting work as a whole constitutes an original work of authorship" (emphasis added).

The purpose of the statutory definition is to emphasize that collections of facts are not copyrightable per se. It conveys this message through its tripartite structure, as emphasized above by the italics. The statute identifies three distinct elements and requires each to be met for a work to qualify as a copyrightable compilation: (1) the collection and assembly of pre-existing material, facts, or data; (2) the selection, coordination, or arrangement of those materials; and (3) the creation, by virtue of the particular selection, coordination, or arrangement, of an "original" work of authorship. "This tripartite conjunctive structure is self-evident, and should be assumed to 'accurately express the legislative purpose.' " Patry 51, quoting *Mills Music* [*Inc. v. Snyder*, 469 U.S. 153, 164 (1985)].

At first glance, the first requirement does not seem to tell us much. It merely describes what one normally thinks of as a compilation—a collection of pre-existing material, facts, or data. What makes it significant is that it is not the sole requirement. It is not enough for copyright purposes that an author collects and assembles facts. To satisfy the statutory definition, the work must get over two additional hurdles. In this way, the plain language indicates that not every collection of facts receives copyright protection. Otherwise, there would be a period after "data."

The third requirement is also illuminating. It emphasizes that a compilation, like any other work, is copyrightable only if it satisfies the originality requirement ("an original work of authorship"). Although § 102 states plainly that the originality requirement applies to all works, the point was emphasized with regard to compilations to ensure that courts would not repeat the mistake of the "sweat of the brow" courts by concluding that fact-based works are treated differently and measured by some other standard. As Congress explained it, the goal was to "make plain that the criteria of copyrightable subject matter stated in section 102 apply with full force to works . . . containing preexisting material." H. R. Rep. [No. 94–1476], at 57; S. Rep. [No. 94–473], at 55.

The key to the statutory definition is the second requirement. It instructs courts that, in determining whether a fact-based work is an original work of authorship, they should focus on the manner in which the collected facts have been selected, coordinated, and arranged. This is a straight-forward application of the originality requirement. Facts are never original, so the compilation author can claim originality, if at all, only in the way the facts are presented. To that end, the statute dictates that the principal focus should be on whether the selection, coordination, and arrangement are sufficiently original to merit protection.

Not every selection, coordination, or arrangement will pass muster. This is plain from the statute. It states that, to merit protection, the facts must be selected, coordinated, or arranged "in such a way" as to render the work as a whole original. This implies that some "ways" will trigger copyright, but that others will not. * * * Otherwise, the phrase "in such a way" is meaningless and Congress should have defined "compilation" simply as "a work formed by the collection and assembly of preexisting materials or data that are selected, coordinated, or arranged." That Congress did not do so is dispositive. In accordance with "the established principle that a court should give effect, if possible, to every clause and word of a statute," *Moskal v. United States*, 498 U.S. 103, 109–110 (1990) (internal quotation marks omitted), we conclude that the statute envisions that there will be some fact-based works in which the selection, coordination, and arrangement are not sufficiently original to trigger copyright protection.

As discussed earlier, however, the originality requirement is not particularly stringent. A compiler may settle upon a selection or arrangement that others have used; novelty is not required. Originality requires only that the author make the selection or arrangement independently (i.e., without copying that selection or arrangement from another work), and that it display some minimal level of creativity. Presumably, the vast majority of compilations will pass this test, but not all will. There remains a narrow category of works in which the creative spark is utterly lacking or so trivial as to be virtually nonexistent. *See generally Bleistein v. Donaldson Lithographing Co.*, 188 U.S. 239, 251

(1903) (referring to "the narrowest and most obvious limits"). Such works are incapable of sustaining a valid copyright.

Even if a work qualifies as a copyrightable compilation, it receives only limited protection. This is the point of § 103 of the Act. Section 103 explains that "the subject matter of copyright . . . includes compilations," § 103(a), but that copyright protects only the author's original contributions—not the facts or information conveyed * * *.

As § 103 makes clear, copyright is not a tool by which a compilation author may keep others from using the facts or data he or she has collected. "The most important point here is one that is commonly misunderstood today: copyright . . . has no effect one way or the other on the copyright or public domain status of the preexisting material." [H.R. Rep. No. 94–1476, 94th Cong., 2d Sess. 57 (1976); S. Rep. No. 94–473, 94th Cong., 1st Sess. 55 (1975)]. The 1909 Act did not require, as "sweat of the brow" courts mistakenly assumed, that each subsequent compiler must start from scratch and is precluded from relying on research undertaken by another. *See, e. g., Jeweler's Circular Publishing Co.* 281 F., at 88–89. Rather, the facts contained in existing works may be freely copied because copyright protects only the elements that owe their origin to the compiler—the selection, coordination, and arrangement of facts.

In summary, the 1976 revisions to the Copyright Act leave no doubt that originality, not "sweat of the brow," is the touchstone of copyright protection in directories and other fact-based works. * * * The revisions explain with painstaking clarity that copyright requires originality, § 102(a); that facts are never original, § 102(b); that the copyright in a compilation does not extend to the facts it contains, § 103(b); and that a compilation is copyrightable only to the extent that it features an original selection, coordination, or arrangement, § 101.

* * *

III

* * *

The selection, coordination, and arrangement of Rural's white pages do not satisfy the minimum constitutional standards for copyright protection. As mentioned at the outset, Rural's white pages are entirely typical. Persons desiring telephone service in Rural's service area fill out an application and Rural issues them a telephone number. In preparing its white pages, Rural simply takes the data provided by its subscribers and lists it alphabetically by surname. The end product is a garden-variety white pages directory, devoid of even the slightest trace of creativity.

Rural's selection of listings could not be more obvious: It publishes the most basic information—name, town, and telephone number—about each person who applies to it for telephone service. This is "selection" of a sort, but it lacks the modicum of creativity necessary to transform mere selection into copyrightable expression. Rural expended sufficient effort to make the white pages directory useful, but insufficient creativity to make it original.

We note in passing that the selection featured in Rural's white pages may also fail the originality requirement for another reason. Feist points out that Rural did not truly "select" to publish the names and telephone numbers of its subscribers; rather, it was required to do so by the Kansas Corporation Commission as part of its monopoly franchise. Accordingly, one could plausibly conclude that this selection was dictated by state law, not by Rural.

Nor can Rural claim originality in its coordination and arrangement of facts. The white pages do nothing more than list Rural's subscribers in alphabetical order. This arrangement may, technically speaking, owe its origin to Rural; no one disputes that Rural undertook the task of alphabetizing the names itself. But there is nothing remotely creative about arranging names alphabetically in a white pages directory. It is an age-old practice, firmly rooted in tradition and so commonplace that it has come to be expected as a matter of course. * * * It is not only unoriginal, it is practically inevitable. This time-honored tradition does not possess the minimal creative spark required by the Copyright Act and the Constitution.

We conclude that the names, towns, and telephone numbers copied by Feist were not original to Rural and therefore were not protected by the copyright in Rural's combined white and yellow pages directory. As a constitutional matter, copyright protects only those constituent elements of a work that possess more than a *de minimis* quantum of creativity. Rural's white pages, limited to basic subscriber information and arranged alphabetically, fall short of the mark. As a statutory matter, 17 U.S.C. § 101 does not afford protection from copying to a collection of facts that are selected, coordinated, and arranged in a way that utterly lacks originality. Given that some works must fail, we cannot imagine a more likely candidate. Indeed, were we to hold that Rural's white pages pass muster, it is hard to believe that any collection of facts could fail.

Because Rural's white pages lack the requisite originality, Feist's use of the listings cannot constitute infringement. This decision should not be construed as demeaning Rural's efforts in compiling its directory, but rather as making clear that copyright rewards originality, not effort. As this Court noted more than a century ago, " 'great praise may be due to the plaintiffs for their industry and enterprise in publishing this paper, yet the law does not contemplate their being rewarded in this way.' " *Baker v. Selden*, 101 U.S., at 105.

The judgment of the Court of Appeals is

Reversed.

NOTES

1. Why did the Court find it necessary to discuss the constitutional standards for copyright protection in *Feist*? Is this discussion part of the holding in the case? Could the decision have been grounded entirely in section 102 of the Act? Should it have been?

2. In *Feist*, the Supreme Court articulated two components of the constitutional requirement of "originality"—independent creation and creativity. How do these concepts differ? Are random images (such as arbitrary paint splatters) copyrightable after *Feist*? Is the standard of originality in copyright law too low? Should a standard approaching novelty be required? Why should copyright be different from patent law?

3. Plaintiff publishes a yellow pages phone directory. Defendant copies the names, subject matter headings, addresses, and phone numbers from plaintiff's directory for its competing directory. Has defendant copied protectible subject matter? Does it matter whether defendant's directory deletes or adds to the plaintiff's listings? Does it matter whether defendant changes some of plaintiff's subject matter headings (for example, consolidating several into one)? *See BellSouth Advertising & Publishing Corp. v. Donnelley Info. Publishing, Inc.*, 999 F.2d 1436 (11th Cir. 1993) (en banc).

4. Does copyright protect West Reporter citations? What about pinpoint cites? Do these reflect West's original "selection and arrangement" of court opinions? In a series of cases, West brought infringement claims against legal database services for inserting West's internal pagination throughout their digital reproductions of court opinions. In resolving those claims, courts reached conflicting conclusions as to whether West's internal pagination satisfied the originality requirement, and whether reproducing that pagination infringed West's copyright. *Compare Matthew Bender & Co., Inc. v. West Pub. Co.*, 158 F.3d 693 (2d Cir. 1998) (holding that West's volume and page numbers were not copyrightable) *with West Pub. Co. v. Mead Data Central, Inc.*, 799 F.2d 1219 (8th Cir.1986) (finding West's pagination copyrightable and infringed) *and Oasis Pub. Co. v. West Pub. Co.*, 924 F.Supp. 918 (D.Minn.1996) (finding West's pagination copyrightable and infringed).

5. In another infringement suit involving the West Reporters, the Second Circuit held that certain of West's enhancements of court opinions, including (1) the arrangement of information specifying the parties, court, and date of decision, (2) the selection of parallel and alternative case citations, (3) the selection and arrangement of attorney information, and (4) the arrangement of information pertaining to subsequent procedural history, were not sufficiently original or creative to warrant copyright protection. (West's headnotes and key numbers were not at issue in this case.) *Matthew Bender & Co., Inc. v. West Publishing Co.*, 158 F.3d 674 (2d Cir. 1998). The majority explained:

> West's editorial work entails considerable scholarly labor and care, and is of distinct usefulness to legal practitioners. Unfortunately for West, however, creativity in the task of creating a useful case report can only proceed in a narrow groove. Doubtless, that is because for West or any other editor of judicial opinions for legal research, faithfulness to the public-domain original is the dominant editorial value, so that the creative is the enemy of the true.
>
> Our decision in this case does not mean that an editor seeking to create the most accurate edition of another work never exercises creativity. As West argues, our decisions establish a low threshold of creativity, even in works involving selection from among facts. But those cases involved the exercise of judgments more evaluative and creative than West exercises in the four elements of the case reports that HyperLaw intends to copy.

Id. at 688 (footnotes omitted).

6. In *Silverstein v. Penguin Putnam, Inc.*, 368 F.3d 77 (2d Cir. 2004), plaintiff Silverstein compiled what he believed to be the authoritative collection of poems written by Dorothy Parker, a prolific American poet. Silverstein's claimed creative effort involved "weeding out of works that he did not consider to be poems and of works he believed Mrs. Parker did not write." Did Silverstein exercise sufficient creativity to merit copyright protection for his selection and arrangement of poems?

MESHWERKS, INC. V. TOYOTA MOTOR SALES U.S.A.

528 F.3d 1258 (10th Cir. 2008).

GORSUCH, CIRCUIT JUDGE.

This case calls on us to apply copyright principles to a relatively new technology: digital modeling. Meshwerks insists that, contrary to the district court's summary judgment determination, its digital models of Toyota cars and trucks are sufficiently original to warrant copyright protection. Meshwerks' models, which form the base layers of computerized substitutes for product photographs in advertising, are unadorned, digital wire-frames of Toyota's vehicles. While fully appreciating that digital media present new frontiers for copyrightable creative expression, in this particular case the uncontested facts reveal that Meshwerks' models owe their designs and origins to Toyota and deliberately do not include anything original of their own; accordingly, we hold that Meshwerks' models are not protected by copyright and affirm.

I

A

In 2003, and in conjunction with Saatchi & Saatchi, its advertising agency, Toyota began work on its model-year 2004 advertising campaign.

Saatchi and Toyota agreed that the campaign would involve, among other things, digital models of Toyota's vehicles for use on Toyota's website and in various other media. These digital models have substantial advantages over the product photographs for which they substitute. With a few clicks of a computer mouse, the advertiser can change the color of the car, its surroundings, and even edit its physical dimensions to portray changes in vehicle styling; before this innovation, advertisers had to conduct new photo shoots of whole fleets of vehicles each time the manufacturer made even a small design change to a car or truck.

To supply these digital models, Saatchi and Toyota hired Grace & Wild, Inc. ("G & W"). In turn, G & W subcontracted with Meshwerks to assist with two initial aspects of the project-digitization and modeling. Digitizing involves collecting physical data points from the object to be portrayed. In the case of Toyota's vehicles, Meshwerks took copious measurements of Toyota's vehicles by covering each car, truck, and van with a grid of tape and running an articulated arm tethered to a computer over the vehicle to measure all points of intersection in the grid. Based on these measurements, modeling software then generated a digital image resembling a wire-frame model. In other words, the vehicles' data points (measurements) were mapped onto a computerized grid and the modeling software connected the dots to create a "wire frame" of each vehicle.

At this point, however, the on-screen image remained far from perfect and manual "modeling" was necessary. Meshwerks personnel fine-tuned or, as the company prefers it, "sculpted," the lines on screen to resemble each vehicle as closely as possible. Approximately 90 percent of the data points contained in each final model, Meshwerks represents, were the result not of the first-step measurement process, but of the skill and effort its digital sculptors manually expended at the second step. For example, some areas of detail, such as wheels, headlights, door handles, and the Toyota emblem, could not be accurately measured using current technology; those features had to be added at the second "sculpting" stage, and Meshwerks had to recreate those features as realistically as possible by hand, based on photographs. Even for areas that were measured, Meshwerks faced the challenge of converting measurements taken of a three-dimensional car into a two-dimensional computer representation; to achieve this, its modelers had to sculpt, or move, data points to achieve a visually convincing result. The purpose and product of these processes, after nearly 80 to 100 hours of effort per vehicle, were two-dimensional wire-frame depictions of Toyota's vehicles that appeared three-dimensional on screen, but were utterly unadorned-lacking color, shading, and other details.

With Meshwerks' wire-frame products in hand, G & W then manipulated the computerized models by, first, adding detail, the result of which appeared on screen as a "tightening" of the wire frames, as though significantly more wires had been added to the frames, or as though they were made of a finer mesh. Next, G & W digitally applied color, texture, lighting, and animation for use in Toyota's advertisements. G & W's digital models were then sent to Saatchi to be employed in a number of advertisements prepared by Saatchi and Toyota in various print, online, and television media.

B

This dispute arose because, according to Meshwerks, it contracted with G & W for only a single use of its models—as part of one Toyota television commercial—and neither Toyota nor any other defendant was allowed to use the digital models created from Meshwerks' wire-frames in other advertisements. Thus, Meshwerks contends defendants improperly—in violation of copyright laws as well as the parties' agreement—reused and redistributed the models created by Meshwerks in a host of other media.

In due course, defendants moved for summary judgment on the theory that Meshwerks' wire-frame models lacked sufficient originality to be protected by copyright. Specifically, defendants argued that any original expression found in Meshwerks' products was attributable to the Toyota designers who conceived of the vehicle designs in the first place; accordingly, defendants' use of the models could not give rise to a claim for copyright infringement.

The district court agreed. It found that the wire-frame models were merely copies of Toyota's products, not sufficiently original to warrant copyright protection * * *. Today, Meshwerks asks us to reverse and hold its digital, wire-frame models sufficiently original to warrant copyright protection.

II

To make a case for copyright infringement, Meshwerks must show (1) it owns a valid copyright, and (2) defendants copied constituent elements of the work that are original to Meshwerks. Our inquiry in this case focuses on the first of these tests—that is, on the question whether Meshwerks held a valid copyright in its digital wire-frame models. Because Meshwerks obtained registration certificates for its models from the Copyright Office, we presume that it holds a valid copyright. At the same time, defendants may overcome this presumption by presenting evidence and legal argument sufficient to establish that the works in question were not entitled to copyright protection.

A

The Constitution authorizes Congress "[t]o promote the Progress of Science and useful Arts, by securing for limited Times to Authors and Inventors the exclusive Right to their respective Writings and Discoveries."

U.S. Const. art. I, § 8, cl. 8. The Supreme Court has emphasized that the power afforded by this provision—namely, to give an author exclusive authority over a work-rests in part on a "presuppos[ition]" that the work contains "a degree of originality." *Feist Publ'ns, Inc. v. Rural Tel. Serv. Co.*, 499 U.S. 340, 346 (1991). Congress has recognized this same point, extending copyright protection only to "*original works* of authorship. . . ." 17 U.S.C. § 102 (emphasis added). Originality, thus, is said to be "[t]he *sine qua non* of copyright." *Feist*, 499 U.S. at 345.

* * *

The parties focus most of their energy in this case on the question whether Meshwerks' models qualify as independent creations, as opposed to copies of Toyota's handiwork. But what can be said, at least based on received copyright doctrine, to distinguish an independent creation from a copy? And how might that doctrine apply in an age of virtual worlds and digital media that seek to mimic the "real" world, but often do so in ways that undoubtedly qualify as (highly) original? While there is little authority explaining how our received principles of copyright law apply to the relatively new digital medium before us, some lessons may be discerned from how the law coped in an earlier time with a previous revolution in technology: photography.

As Judge Pauley admirably recounted in *SHL Imaging, Inc. v. Artisan House, Inc.*, photography was initially met by critics with a degree of skepticism: a photograph, some said, "copies everything and explains nothing," and it was debated whether a camera could do anything more than merely record the physical world. 117 F.Supp.2d 301, 307 (S.D.N.Y. 2000). These largely aesthetic debates migrated into legal territory when Oscar Wilde toured the United States in the 1880s and sought out Napoleon Sarony for a series of publicity photographs to promote the event. Burrow-Giles, a lithography firm, quickly copied one of Sarony's photos and sold 85,000 prints without the photographer's permission. Burrow-Giles defended its conduct on the ground that the photograph was a "mere mechanical reproduction of the physical features" of Wilde and thus not copyrightable. *Burrow-Giles*, 111 U.S. at 59. Recognizing that Oscar Wilde's inimitable visage does not belong, or "owe its origins" to any photographer, the Supreme Court noted that photographs may well sometimes lack originality and are thus not *per se* copyrightable. *Id.* ("the ordinary production of a photograph" may involve "no protection" in copyright). At the same time, the Court held, a copyright may be had to the extent a photograph involves "posing the said Oscar Wilde in front of the camera, selecting and arranging the costume, draperies, and other various accessories in said photograph, arranging the subject so as to present graceful outlines, arranging and disposing the light and shade, suggesting and evoking the desired expression. . . ." *Id.* at 60. Accordingly, the Court indicated, photographs are copyrightable, if only to the extent of their *original* depiction of the subject. Wilde's image is not copyrightable; but to the extent a photograph reflects the photographer's decisions regarding pose, positioning, background, lighting, shading, and the like, those elements can be said to "owe their origins" to the photographer, making the photograph copyrightable, at least to that extent.

As the Court more recently explained in *Feist,* the operative distinction is between, on the one hand, ideas or facts in the world, items that cannot be copyrighted, and a particular expression of that idea or fact, that can be. "This principle, known as the idea/expression or fact/expression dichotomy, applies to all works of authorship. As applied to a factual compilation," the particular matter at issue in *Feist,* "assuming the absence of original written expression, only the compiler's selection and arrangement may be protected; the raw facts may be copied at will. This result is neither unfair nor unfortunate. It is the means by which copyright advances the progress of science and art." *Feist,* 499 U.S. at 350; *see also Id.* at 351 ("In no event may copyright extend to the facts themselves."). So, in the case of photographs, for which Meshwerks' digital models were designed to serve as practically advantageous substitutes, authors are entitled to copyright protection only for the "incremental contribution," *SHL Imaging, Inc.,* 117 F.Supp.2d at 311, represented by their interpretation or expression of the objects of their attention.

B

Applying these principles, evolved in the realm of photography, to the new medium that has come to supplement and even in some ways to supplant it, we think Meshwerks' models are not so much independent creations as (very good) copies of Toyota's vehicles. In reaching this conclusion we rely on (1) an objective assessment of the particular models before us and (2) the parties' purpose in creating them. All the same, we do not doubt for an instant that the digital medium before us, like photography before it, can be employed to create vivid new expressions fully protectable in copyright.

1

Key to our evaluation of this case is the fact that Meshwerks' digital wire-frame computer models depict Toyota's vehicles without any individualizing features: they are untouched by a digital paintbrush; they are not depicted in front of a palm tree, whizzing down the open road, or climbing up a mountainside. Put another way, Meshwerks' models depict nothing more than unadorned Toyota vehicles—the car *as* car. And the unequivocal lesson from *Feist* is that works are not copyrightable to the extent they do not involve any expression apart from the raw facts in the world. As Professor Nimmer has commented in connection with the predecessor technology of photography, "[a]s applied to a photograph of a pre-existing product that bedrock principle [of originality] means that the photographer manifestly cannot claim to have originated the matter depicted therein. . . . The upshot is that the photographer is entitled to copyright solely based on lighting, angle, perspective, and the other ingredients that traditionally apply to that art-form." NIMMER ON COPYRIGHT § 3.03[C][3]. It seems to us that exactly the same holds true with the digital medium now before us: the facts in this case unambiguously show that Meshwerks did not make any decisions regarding lighting, shading, the background in front of which a vehicle would be posed, the angle at which to pose it, or the like—in short, its models reflect none of the decisions that can make depictions of things or facts in the world, whether Oscar Wilde or a Toyota Camry, new expressions subject to copyright protection.

The primary case on which Meshwerks asks us to rely actually reinforces this conclusion. In *Ets-Hokin v. Skyy Spirits, Inc.*, 225 F.3d 1068 (9th Cir.2000) (*Skyy I*), the Ninth Circuit was faced with a suit brought by a plaintiff photographer who alleged that the defendant had infringed on his commercial photographs of a Skyy-brand vodka bottle. The court held that the vodka bottle, as a "utilitarian object," a fact in the world, was not itself (at least usually) copyrightable. *Id.* at 1080 (citing 17 U.S.C. § 101). At the same time, the court recognized that plaintiff's photos reflected decisions regarding "lighting, shading, angle, background, and so forth," *id.* at 1078, and to the extent plaintiff's photographs reflected such original contributions the court held they could be copyrighted. In so holding, the Ninth Circuit reversed a district court's dismissal of the case and remanded the matter for further proceedings, and Meshwerks argues this analysis controls the outcome of its case.

But *Skyy I* tells only half the story. The case soon returned to the court of appeals, and the court held that the defendant's photos, which differed in terms of angle, lighting, shadow, reflection, and background, did *not* infringe on the plaintiff's copyrights. *Ets-Hokin v. Skyy Spirits, Inc.*, 323 F.3d 763, 765 (9th Cir.2003) (*Skyy II*). Why? The only constant between the plaintiff's photographs and the defendant's photographs was the bottle itself, *id.* at 766, and an accurate portrayal of the unadorned bottle could not be copyrighted. Facts and ideas are the public's domain and open to exploitation to ensure the progress of science and the useful arts. Only original expressions of those facts or ideas are copyrightable, leaving the plaintiff in the *Skyy* case with an admittedly "thin" copyright offering protection perhaps only from exact duplication by others. *Id.*; *see also SHL Imaging, Inc.*, 117 F.Supp.2d at 311 ("Practically, the plaintiffs [photos] are only protected from verbatim copying.").

The teaching of *Skyy* I and II, then, is that the vodka bottle, because it did not owe its origins to the photographers, had to be filtered out to determine what copyrightable expression remained. And, by analogy—though not perhaps the one Meshwerks had in mind—we hold that the unadorned images of Toyota's vehicles cannot be copyrighted by Meshwerks and likewise must be filtered out. To the extent that Meshwerks' digital wire-frame models depict only those unadorned vehicles, having stripped away all lighting, angle, perspective, and "other ingredients" associated with an original expression, we conclude that they have left no copyrightable matter.

Confirming this conclusion as well is the peculiar place where Meshwerks stood in the model-creation pecking order. On the one hand, Meshwerks had nothing to do with designing the appearance of Toyota's vehicles, distinguishing them from any other cars, trucks, or vans in the world. That expressive creation took place *before* Meshwerks happened along, and was the result of work done by Toyota and its designers; indeed, at least six of the eight vehicles at issue are still covered by design patents belonging to Toyota and protecting the *appearances* of the objects for which they are issued. On the other hand, how the models Meshwerks created were to be deployed in advertising—including the backgrounds, lighting, angles, and colors—were all matters left to those (G & W, Saatchi, and 3D Recon) who came *after* Meshwerks left the scene. Meshwerks thus played a narrow, if pivotal, role in the process by simply, if effectively, copying Toyota's vehicles into a digital medium so they could be expressively manipulated by others.

Were we to afford copyright protection in this case, we would run aground on one of the bedrock principles of copyright law—namely, that originality, "as the term is used in copyright, means only that the work was independently created by the author (*as opposed to copied from other works*)." *Feist*, 499 U.S. at 345 (emphasis added). * * *

It is certainly true that what Meshwerks accomplished was a peculiar kind of copying. It did not seek to recreate Toyota vehicles outright—steel, rubber, and all; instead, it sought to depict Toyota's three-dimensional physical objects in a two-dimensional digital medium. But we hold, as many before us have already suggested, that, standing alone, "[t]he fact that a work in one medium has been copied from a work in another medium does not render it any the less a 'copy.' " NIMMER ON COPYRIGHT § 8.01[B]. After all, the putative creator who merely shifts the medium in which another's creation is expressed has not necessarily added anything beyond the expression contained in the original. *See Bridgeman Art Library, Ltd.*, 36 F.Supp.2d at 199 (noting that "a copy in a new medium is copyrightable only where, as often but not always is the case, the copier makes some identifiable original contribution").

In reaching this conclusion, we do not for a moment seek to downplay the considerable amount of time, effort, and skill that went into making Meshwerks' digital wire-frame models. But, in assessing the originality of a work for which copyright protection is sought, we look only at the final *product,* not the process, and the fact that intensive, skillful, and even creative labor is invested in the process of creating a product does not guarantee its copyrightability. In the case before us, there is no doubt that transposing the physical appearances of Toyota's vehicles from three dimensions to two, such that computer-screen images accurately reflect Toyota's products, was labor intensive and required a great amount of skill. But because the end-results were unadorned images of Toyota's vehicles, the appearances of which do not owe their origins to Meshwerks, we are unable to reward that skill, effort, and labor with copyright protection.

2

Meshwerks' intent in making its wire-frame models provides additional support for our conclusion. "In theory, the originality requirement tests the putative author's state of mind: Did he have an earlier work in mind when he created his own?" PAUL GOLDSTEIN, GOLDSTEIN ON COPYRIGHT § 2.2.1.1. If an artist affirmatively sets out to be unoriginal—to make a copy of someone else's creation, rather than to create an original work—it is far more likely that the resultant product will, in fact, be unoriginal.

In this case, the undisputed evidence before us leaves no question that Meshwerks set out to copy Toyota's vehicles, rather than to create, or even to add, any original expression.

* * *

C

Although we hold that Meshwerks' digital, wire-frame models are insufficiently original to warrant copyright protection, we do not turn a blind eye to the fact that digital imaging is a relatively new and evolving technology and that Congress extended copyright protection to "original works of authorship fixed in any tangible medium of expression, *now known or later developed.*" 17 U.S.C. § 102(a) (emphasis added). A Luddite might make the mistake of suggesting that digital modeling, as was once said of photography, allows for nothing more than "mechanical reproduction of the physical features or outlines of some object . . . and involves no originality of thought or any novelty in the intellectual operation connected with its visible reproduction in [the] shape of a picture." *Burrow-Giles,* 111 U.S. at 59. Clearly, this is not so.

Digital modeling can be, surely is being, and no doubt increasingly will be used to create copyrightable expressions. Yet, just as photographs *can be,* but are not *per se,* copyrightable, the same holds true for digital models. There's little question that digital models *can* be devised of Toyota cars with copyrightable features, whether by virtue of unique shading, lighting, angle, background scene, or other choices. The problem for Meshwerks in this particular case is simply that the uncontested facts reveal that it wasn't involved in any such process, and indeed contracted to provide completely unadorned digital replicas of Toyota vehicles in a two-dimensional space. For this reason, we do not envision any "chilling effect" on creative expression based on our holding today, and instead see it as applying to digital modeling the same legal principles that have come, in the fullness of time and with an enlightened eye, to apply to photographs and other media.

* * *

Originality is the *sine qua non* of copyright. If the basic design reflected in a work of art does not owe its origin to the putative copyright holder, then that person must add something original to that design, and then only the original addition may be copyrighted. In this case, Meshwerks copied Toyota's designs in creating digital, wire-frame models of Toyota's vehicles. But the models reflect, that is, "express," no more than the depiction of the vehicles *as* vehicles. The designs of the vehicles, however, owe their origins to Toyota, not to Meshwerks, and so we are unable to reward Meshwerks' digital wire-frame models, no doubt the product of significant labor, skill, and judgment, with copyright protection. The judgment of the district court is affirmed, and defendants' request for attorneys' fees is denied.

So ordered.

APPENDIX A

06-4222, Meshwerks v. Toyota

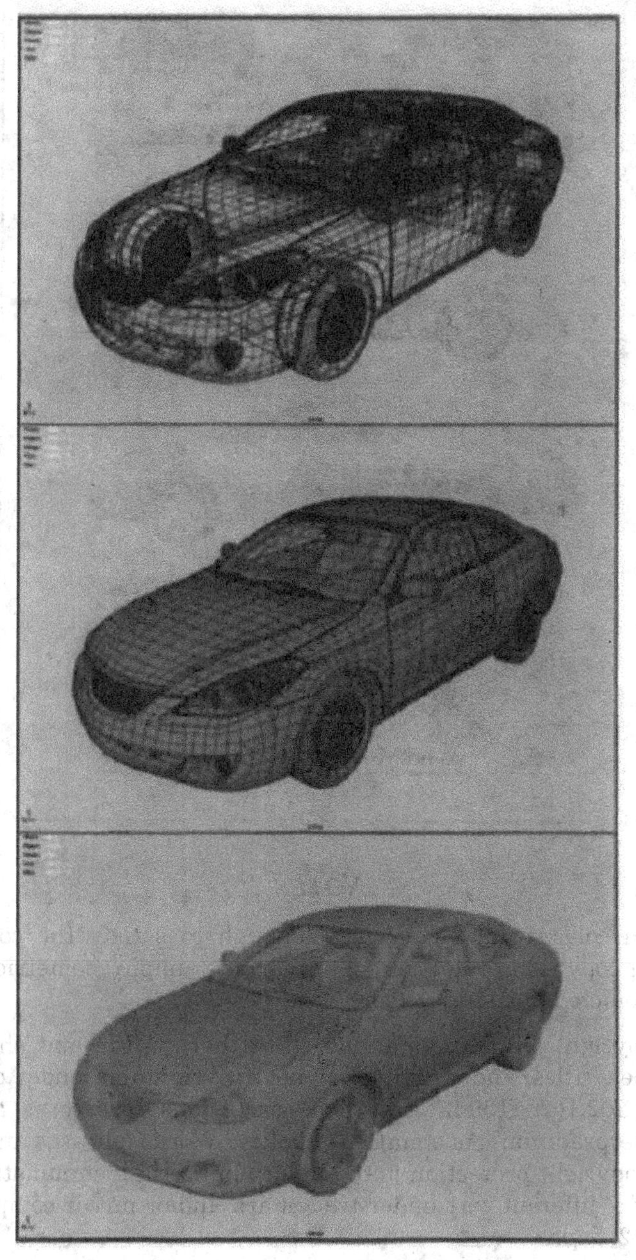

APPENDIX B

06-4222, Meshwerks v. Toyota

NOTES

1. Is a color, by itself, original enough to satisfy the constitutional standards for copyright protection? What about a simple geometric shape such as a circle, depicted in a single color?

2. Copyright Office regulations state that "words and short phrases such as names, titles, and slogans" are not copyrightable under current law. 37 C.F.R. § 202.1(a) (1994). Are these exclusions correct as a matter of statutory interpretation? As a matter of policy? Words, phrases and titles that are denied copyright protection may, under appropriate circumstances, enjoy protection of a different sort under trademark and/or unfair competition law. *See* Chapter 2, *supra*.

3. The Ninth Circuit held that elements of glass-in-glass sculptures of jellyfish that followed from the type of medium used or jellyfish physiology were not copyrightable. In *Satava v. Lowry*, 323 F.3d 805, 811 (9th Cir. 2003), the court held that "a combination of unprotectable elements is eligible for copyright protection only if those elements are numerous enough and their selection and arrangement original enough that their combination constitutes an original work of authorship."

2. DISTINGUISHING EXPRESSION FROM IDEAS AND FACTS

The leading case distinguishing copyrightable expression from non-copyrightable ideas is *Baker v. Selden*, 101 U.S. (11 Otto) 99 (1879). The principles of *Baker v. Selden* are reflected in section 102(b), as noted in the House Report accompanying the 1976 Act:

> Copyright does not preclude others from using the ideas or information revealed by the author's work. It pertains to the literary, musical, graphic, or artistic form in which the author expressed intellectual concepts. Section 102(b) makes clear that copyright protection does not extend to any idea, procedure, process, system, method of operation, concept, principle, or discovery, regardless of the form in which it is described, explained, illustrated, or embodied in such work. Some concern has been expressed lest copyright in computer programs should extend protection to the methodology or processes adopted by the programmer, rather than merely to the 'writing' expressing his ideas. Section 102(b) is intended, among other things, to make clear that the expression adopted by the programmer is the copyrightable element in a computer program, and that the actual processes or methods embodied in the program are not within the scope of the copyright law. Section 102(b) in no way enlarges or contracts the scope of copyright protection under the present law. Its purpose is to restate, in the context of the new single Federal system of copyright, that the basic dichotomy between expression and idea remains unchanged.

H.R. Rep. No. 94–1476, 94th Cong., 2d Sess. 56–57 (1976).

Consider how the principles of section 102(b) apply in the following materials.

HOEHLING V. UNIVERSAL CITY STUDIOS, INC.

618 F.2d 972 (2d Cir. 1980), *cert. denied*, 449 U.S. 841, 101 S.Ct. 121 (1980).

KAUFMAN, CHIEF JUDGE:

A grant of copyright in a published work secures for its author a limited monopoly over the expression it contains. The copyright provides a financial incentive to those who would add to the corpus of existing knowledge by creating original works. Nevertheless, the protection afforded the copyright holder has never extended to history, be it documented fact or explanatory hypothesis. The rationale for this doctrine is that the cause of knowledge is best served when history is the common property of all, and each generation remains free to draw upon the discoveries and insights of the past. Accordingly, the scope of copyright in historical accounts is narrow indeed, embracing no more than the author's original expression of particular facts and theories already in the public domain. As the case before us illustrates, absent wholesale usurpation of another's expression, claims of copyright infringement where works of history are at issue are rarely successful.

I.

This litigation arises from three separate accounts of the triumphant introduction, last voyage, and tragic destruction of the Hindenburg, the colossal dirigible constructed in Germany during Hitler's reign. The zeppelin, the last and most sophisticated in a fleet of luxury airships, which punctually floated its wealthy passengers from the Third Reich to the United States, exploded into flames and disintegrated in 35 seconds as it hovered above the Lakehurst, New Jersey Naval Air Station at 7:25 p. m. on May 6, 1937. Thirty-six passengers and crew were killed but, fortunately, 52 persons survived. Official investigations conducted by both American and German authorities could ascertain no definitive cause of the disaster, but both suggested the plausibility of static electricity or St. Elmo's Fire, which could have ignited the highly explosive hydrogen that filled the airship. Throughout, the investigators refused to rule out the possibility of sabotage.

The destruction of the Hindenburg marked the concluding chapter in the chronicle of airship passenger service, for after the tragedy at Lakehurst, the Nazi regime permanently grounded the Graf Zeppelin I and discontinued its plan to construct an even larger dirigible, the Graf Zeppelin II.

The final pages of the airship's story marked the beginning of a series of journalistic, historical, and literary accounts devoted to the Hindenburg and its fate. * * *

Appellant A. A. Hoehling published *Who Destroyed the Hindenburg?*, a full-length book based on his exhaustive research in 1962. Mr. Hoehling studied the investigative reports, consulted previously published articles and books, and conducted interviews with survivors of the crash as well as others who possessed information about the Hindenburg. His book is presented as a factual account, written in an objective, reportorial style.

The first half recounts the final crossing of the Hindenburg, from Sunday, May 2, when it left Frankfurt, to Thursday, May 6, when it exploded at Lakehurst. Hoehling describes the airship, its role as an instrument of propaganda in Nazi Germany, its passengers and crew, the danger of hydrogen, and the ominous threats received by German officials, warning that the Hindenburg would be destroyed. The second portion, headed The Quest, sets forth the progress of the official investigations, followed by an account of Hoehling's own research. In the final chapter, spanning eleven pages, Hoehling suggests that all proffered explanations of the explosion, save deliberate destruction, are unconvincing. He concludes that the most likely saboteur is one Eric Spehl, a "rigger" on the Hindenburg crew who was killed at Lakehurst.

According to Hoehling, Spehl had motive, expertise, and opportunity to plant an explosive device, constructed of dry-cell batteries and a flashbulb, in "Gas Cell 4," the location of the initial explosion. An amateur photographer with access to flashbulbs, Spehl could have destroyed the Hindenburg to please his ladyfriend, a suspected communist dedicated to exploding the myth of Nazi invincibility.

Ten years later appellee Michael MacDonald Mooney published his book, *The Hindenburg*. Mooney's endeavor might be characterized as more literary than historical in its attempt to weave a number of symbolic themes through the actual events surrounding the tragedy. His dominant theme contrasts the natural beauty of the month of May, when the disaster occurred, with the cold, deliberate progress of "technology." The May theme is expressed not simply by the season, but also by the character of Spehl, portrayed as a sensitive artisan with needle and thread. The Hindenburg, in contrast, is the symbol of technology, as are its German creators and the Reich itself. The destruction is depicted as the ultimate triumph of nature over technology, as Spehl plants the bomb that ignites the hydrogen. Developing this theme from the outset, Mooney begins with an extended review of man's efforts to defy nature through flight, focusing on the evolution of the zeppelin. This story culminates in the construction of the Hindenburg, and the Nazis' claims of its indestructibility. Mooney then traces the fateful voyage, advising the reader almost immediately of Spehl's scheme. The book concludes with the airship's explosion.

Mooney acknowledges, in this case, that he consulted Hoehling's book, and that he relied on it for some details. He asserts that he first discovered the "Spehl-as-saboteur" theory when he read [another account of the disaster authored by Dale Titler, and entitled] *Wings of Mystery*. Indeed,

Titler concludes that Spehl was the saboteur, for essentially the reasons stated by Hoehling. Mooney also claims to have studied the complete National Archives and New York Times files concerning the Hindenburg, as well as all previously published material. Moreover, he traveled to Germany, visited Spehl's birthplace, and conducted a number of interviews with survivors.

After Mooney prepared an outline of his anticipated book, his publisher succeeded in negotiations to sell the motion picture rights to appellee Universal City Studios. Universal then commissioned a screen story by writers Levinson and Link, best known for their television series, *Columbo,* in which a somewhat disheveled, but wise detective unravels artfully conceived murder mysteries. In their screen story, Levinson and Link created a Columbo-like character who endeavored to identify the saboteur on board the Hindenburg. Director Robert Wise, however, was not satisfied with this version, and called upon Nelson Gidding to write a final screenplay. Gidding * * * had engaged in preliminary work on a film about the Hindenburg almost twenty years earlier.

The Gidding screenplay follows what is known in the motion picture industry as a "Grand Hotel" formula, developing a number of fictional characters and subplots involving them. This formula has become standard fare in so-called "disaster" movies, which have enjoyed a certain popularity in recent years. In the film, which was released in late 1975, a rigger named "Boerth," who has an anti-Nazi ladyfriend, plans to destroy the airship in an effort to embarrass the Reich. Nazi officials, vaguely aware of sabotage threats, station a Luftwaffe intelligence officer on the zeppelin, loosely resembling a Colonel Erdmann who was aboard the Hindenburg. This character is portrayed as a likable fellow who soon discovers that Boerth is the saboteur. Boerth, however, convinces him that the Hindenburg should be destroyed and the two join forces, planning the explosion for several hours after the landing at Lakehurst, when no people would be on board. In Gidding's version, the airship is delayed by a storm, frantic efforts to defuse the bomb fail, and the Hindenburg is destroyed. The film's subplots involve other possible suspects, including a fictional countess who has had her estate expropriated by the Reich, two fictional confidence men wanted by New York City police, and an advertising executive rushing to close a business deal in America.

Upon learning of Universal's plans to release the film, Hoehling instituted this action against Universal for copyright infringement and common law unfair competition in the district court for the District of Columbia in October 1975. Judge Smith declined to issue an order restraining release of the film in December, and it was distributed throughout the nation.

[In subsequent litigation, the district court granted summary judgment in favor of defendants Universal and Mooney, concluding that all similarities between the plaintiff's and the defendants' works pertained to various categories of non-copyrightable material.]

II.

* * *

A

Hoehling's principal claim is that both Mooney and Universal copied the essential plot of his book i.e., Eric Spehl, influenced by his girlfriend, sabotaged the Hindenburg by placing a crude bomb in Gas Cell 4. In their briefs, and at oral argument, appellees have labored to convince us that their plots are not substantially similar to Hoehling's. While Hoehling's Spehl destroys the airship to please his communist girlfriend, Mooney's character is motivated by an aversion to the technological age. Universal's Boerth, on the other hand, is a fervent anti-fascist who enlists the support of a Luftwaffe colonel who, in turn, unsuccessfully attempts to defuse the bomb at the eleventh hour.

Although this argument has potential merit when presented to a fact finder adjudicating the issue of substantial similarity, it is largely irrelevant to a motion for summary judgment where the issue of substantial similarity has been eliminated by the judge's affirmative assumption. Under Rule 56(c), summary judgment is appropriate only when "there is no genuine issue as to any material fact." Perhaps recognizing this, appellees further argue that Hoehling's plot is an "idea," and ideas are not copyrightable as a matter of law. *See Sheldon v. Metro-Goldwyn Pictures Corp.*, 81 F.2d 49, 54 (2d Cir. 1936).

Hoehling, however, correctly rejoins that while ideas themselves are not subject to copyright, his "expression" of his idea is copyrightable. *Id.* at 54. He relies on Learned Hand's opinion in *Sheldon, supra,* at 50, holding that *Letty Lynton* infringed *Dishonored Lady* by copying its story of a woman who poisons her lover, and Augustus Hand's analysis in *Detective Comics, Inc. v. Bruns Publications, Inc.*, 111 F.2d 432 (2d Cir. 1940), concluding that the exploits of "Wonderman" infringed the copyright held by the creators of "Superman," the original indestructible man. Moreover, Hoehling asserts that, in both these cases, the line between "ideas" and "expression" is drawn, in the first instance, by the fact finder.

Sheldon and *Detective Comics*, however, dealt with works of fiction, where the distinction between an idea and its expression is especially elusive. But, where, as here, the idea at issue is an interpretation of an historical event, our cases hold that such interpretations are not copyrightable as a matter of law. In *Rosemont Enterprises, Inc. v. Random House, Inc.*, 366 F.2d 303 (2d Cir.1966), we held that the defendant's biography of Howard Hughes did not infringe an earlier biography of the reclusive alleged billionaire. Although the plots of the two works were necessarily similar, there could be no infringement because of the "public benefit in encouraging the development of historical and biographical works and their public distribution." *Id.* at 307; *accord, Oxford Book Co. v. College Entrance Book Co.*, 98 F.2d 688 (2d Cir. 1938). To avoid a chilling effect on authors who contemplate tackling an historical issue or event, broad latitude must be granted to subsequent authors who make use of historical subject matter, including theories or plots. Learned Hand counseled in *Myers v. Mail & Express Co.*, 36 C.O.Bull. 478, 479 (S.D.N.Y. 1919), "(t)here cannot be any such thing as copyright in the order of presentation of the facts, nor, indeed, in their selection."

In the instant case, the hypothesis that Eric Spehl destroyed the Hindenburg is based entirely on the interpretation of historical facts, including Spehl's life, his girlfriend's anti-Nazi connections, the explosion's origin in Gas Cell 4, Spehl's duty station, discovery of a dry-cell battery among the wreckage, and rumors about Spehl's involvement dating from a 1938 Gestapo investigation. Such an historical interpretation, whether or not it originated with Mr. Hoehling, is not protected by his copyright and can be freely used by subsequent authors.

B

The same reasoning governs Hoehling's claim that a number of specific facts, ascertained through his personal research, were copied by appellees. The cases in this circuit, however, make clear that factual information is in the public domain. *See, e. g., Rosemont Enterprises, Inc., supra*, 366 F.2d at 309; *Oxford Book Co., supra*, 98 F.2d at 691. Each appellee had the right to "avail himself of the facts contained" in Hoehling's book and to "use such information, whether correct or incorrect, in his own literary work." *Greenbie v. Noble*, 151 F.Supp. 45, 67 (S.D.N.Y. 1957). Accordingly, there is little consolation in relying on cases in other circuits holding that the fruits of original research are copyrightable. *See, e. g., Toksvig v. Bruce Publishing Co.*, 181 F.2d 664, 667 (7th Cir. 1950); *Miller v. Universal City Studios, Inc.*, 460 F.Supp. 984 (S.D. Fla. 1978). Indeed, this circuit has clearly repudiated *Toksvig* and its progeny. In *Rosemont Enterprises, Inc., supra*, 366 F.2d at 310, we refused to "subscribe to the view that an author is absolutely precluded from saving time and effort by referring to and relying upon prior published material. . . . It is just such wasted effort that the proscription against the copyright of ideas and facts. . . . are designed to prevent."

C

The remainder of Hoehling's claimed similarities relate to random duplications of phrases and sequences of events. For example, all three works contain a scene in a German beer hall, in which the airship's crew engages in revelry prior to the voyage. Other claimed similarities concern common German greetings of the period, such as "Heil Hitler," or songs, such as the German National anthem. These elements, however, are merely scenes a faire, that is, "incidents, characters or settings which are as a practical matter indispensable, or at least standard, in the treatment of a given topic." *Alexander, supra*, 460 F.Supp. at 45. Because it is virtually impossible to write about a particular historical era or fictional theme without employing certain "stock" or standard literary devices, we have held that scenes a faire are not copyrightable as a matter of law. *See Reyher v. Children's Television Workshop*, 533 F.2d 87, 91 (2d Cir. 1976).

D

All of Hoehling's allegations of copying, therefore, encompass material that is non-copyrightable as a matter of law, rendering summary judgment entirely appropriate. We are aware, however, that in distinguishing between themes, facts, and scenes a faire on the one hand, and copyrightable expression on the other, courts may lose sight of the forest for the trees. By factoring out similarities based on non-copyrightable elements, a court runs the risk of overlooking wholesale usurpation of a prior author's expression. A verbatim reproduction of another work, of course, even in the realm of nonfiction, is actionable as copyright infringement. *See Wainwright Securities, Inc. v. Wall Street Transcript Corp.*, 558 F.2d 91 (2d Cir. 1977). Thus, in granting or reviewing a grant of summary judgment for defendants, courts should assure themselves that the works before them are not virtually identical. In this case, it is clear that all three authors relate the story of the Hindenburg differently.

In works devoted to historical subjects, it is our view that a second author may make significant use of prior work, so long as he does not bodily appropriate the expression of another. *Rosemont Enterprises, Inc., supra*, 366 F.2d at 310. This principle is justified by the fundamental policy undergirding the copyright laws the encouragement of contributions to recorded knowledge. The "financial reward guaranteed to the copyright holder is but an incident of this general objective, rather than an end in itself." *Berlin v. E. C. Publications, Inc.*, 329 F.2d 541, 543–44 (2d Cir. 1964). Knowledge is expanded as well by granting new authors of historical works a relatively free hand to build upon the work of their predecessors.

III.

Finally, we affirm Judge Metzner's rejection of Hoehling's claims based on the common law of "unfair competition." Where, as here, historical facts, themes, and research have been deliberately exempted from the scope of copyright protection to vindicate the overriding goal of encouraging contributions to recorded knowledge, the states are pre-empted from removing such material from the public domain. *See, e. g., Sears, Roebuck & Co. v. Stiffel Co.*, 376 U.S. 225 (1964); *Compco Corp. v. Day-Brite*

Lighting, Inc., 376 U.S. 234 (1964). "To forbid copying" in this case, "would interfere with the federal policy . . . of allowing free access to copy whatever the federal patent and copyright laws leave in the public domain." *Id.* at 237.

The judgment of the district court is affirmed.

WALT DISNEY PRODUCTIONS V. AIR PIRATES

581 F.2d 751 (9th Cir. 1978), *cert. denied*, 439 U.S. 1132, 99 S.Ct. 1054 (1979).

CUMMINGS, CIRCUIT JUDGE:

This case involves the admitted copying of plaintiff Walt Disney Productions' ("Disney") cartoon characters in defendants' adult "counter-culture" comic books. * * *

* * *

The works protected by the copyrights comprise a series of cartoon drawings ranging from a single page to "book length." The cartoons depict the antics of characters created by plaintiff, with "balloons" over each of the characters' heads containing dialog. Cartoons are drawn to form a narrative. According to plaintiff, defendants infringed Disney copyrights by copying the graphic depiction of over 17 characters. Two of the characters are represented as insects, and the others as animals endowed with human qualities. Each character has a recognizable image. The individual defendants have participated in preparing and publishing two magazines of cartoons entitled "Air Pirates Funnies." The characters in defendants' magazines bear a marked similarity to those of plaintiff. The names given to defendants' characters are the same names used in plaintiff's copyrighted work. However, the themes of defendants' publications differ markedly from those of Disney. While Disney sought only to foster "an image of innocent delightfulness," defendants supposedly sought to convey an allegorical message of significance. Put politely by one commentator, the "Air Pirates" was "an 'underground' comic book which had placed several well-known Disney cartoon characters in incongruous settings where they engaged in activities clearly antithetical to the accepted Mickey Mouse world of scrubbed faces, bright smiles and happy endings." * * *

* * *

The essence of defendants' argument is that characters are never copyrightable and therefore cannot in any way constitute a copyrightable component part. That argument flies in the face of a series of cases dating back to 1914 that have held comic strip characters protectable under the old Copyright Act.

It is true that this Court's opinion in *Warner Brothers Pictures v. Columbia Broadcasting System*, 216 F.2d 945 (9th Cir.1954), lends some support to the position that characters ordinarily are not copyrightable. There the mystery writer Dashiell Hammett and his publisher entered into a 1930 contract with Warner Brothers giving the movie production company copyright and various other rights to a "certain story * * * entitled Maltese Falcon" involving the fictional detective Sam Spade. In 1946, Hammett and other defendants used the Maltese Falcon characters in other writings, causing Warner Brothers to sue for copyright infringement and "unfair use and competition." After pointing out the sophisticated nature of the plaintiff, we construed the contracts between the parties and held:

> "We are of the opinion that since the use of characters and character names are nowhere specifically mentioned in the agreements (including the assignment of copyright instrument), but that other items, including the title, 'The Maltese Falcon', and their use are specifically mentioned as being granted (to Warner Brothers), that the character rights with the names cannot be held to be within the grants, and that under the doctrine of Ejusdem generis, general language cannot be held to include them." (Footnote omitted.)

After so holding, Judge Stephens' opinion considered "whether it was ever intended by the copyright statute that characters with their names should be under its protection." In that context he concluded that such a restriction on Hammett's future use of a character was unreasonable, at least when the characters were merely vehicles for the story and did not "really constitute" the story being told. Judge Stephens' reasons for that conclusion provide an important indication of the applicability of that conclusion to comic book characters as opposed to literary characters. In reasoning that characters "are always limited and always fall into limited patterns," Judge Stephens recognized that it is difficult to delineate distinctively a literary character. *Cf. Nichols v. Universal Pictures Corp.*, 45 F.2d 119 (2d Cir.1930). When the author can add a visual image, however, the difficulty is reduced. Put another way, while many literary characters may embody little more than an unprotected idea (*see Sid & Marty Krofft Television v. McDonald's Corp.*, 562 F.2d 1157 (9th Cir.1977)), a comic book character, which has physical as well as conceptual qualities, is more likely to contain some unique elements of expression. Because comic book characters therefore are distinguishable from literary characters, the Warner Brothers language does not preclude protection of Disney's characters.

* * *

NOTES

1. To what extent, if any, should copyright protect the following characters: Mickey Mouse, Superman, Sam Spade (from "The Maltese Falcon"), James Bond, R2D2 (from "Star Wars"), Austin Powers (International Man of Mystery), or Katniss Everdeen (from "The Hunger Games")? If copyright does not protect a particular character against copying, would protection be available under any other doctrine? *See Rice v. Fox Broadcasting Company*, 330 F.3d 1170 (9th Cir. 2003) (holding that a masked magician who reveals the secrets behind magic tricks was too generic a character to warrant copyright protection).

2. Recall the facts of *Stern Electronics, Inc. v. Kaufman*, 669 F.2d 852 (2d Cir.1982), *supra*. The court discussed the application of the "originality" requirement to the "Scramble" videogame as follows:

> Appellants' claim that the work lacks originality proceeds along two lines. Repeating their attack on fixation, they assert that each play of the game is an original work because of the player's participation. The videotape of a particular play of the game, they assert, secured protection only for that one "original" display. However, the repeated appearance of the same sequence of numerous sights and sounds in each play of the game defeats this branch of the argument. Attacking from the opposite flank, appellants contend that the audiovisual display contains no originality because all of its reappearing features are determined by the previously created computer program. This argument is also without merit. The visual and aural features of the audiovisual display are plainly original variations sufficient to render the display copyrightable even though the underlying written program has an independent existence and is itself eligible for copyright. Nor is copyright defeated because the audiovisual work and the computer program are both embodied in the same components of the game. The same thing occurs when an audio tape embodies both a musical composition and a sound recording. Moreover, the argument overlooks the sequence of the creative process. Someone first conceived what the audiovisual display would look like and sound like. Originality occurred at that point. Then the program was written. Finally, the program was imprinted into the memory devices so that, in operation with the components of the game, the sights and sounds could be seen and heard. The resulting display satisfies the requirement of an original work.
>
> We need not decide at what point the repeating sequence of images would form too insubstantial a portion of an entire display to warrant a copyright, nor the somewhat related issue of whether a sequence of images (e.g., a spaceship shooting down an attacking plane) might contain so little in the way of particularized form of expression as to be only an abstract idea portrayed in

> noncopyrightable form, *see Nichols v. Universal Pictures Corp.*, 45 F.2d 119, 121 (2d Cir.1930). Assessing the entire effect of the game as it appears and sounds, we conclude that its repetitive sequence of images is copyrightable as an audiovisual display.

669 F.2d at 856–57. Consider whether a screen display which displays a black-and-white checkerboard or tic-tac-toe pattern satisfies the *Stern* court's originality test. What about a similar display using two or more colors (*e.g.*, to demarcate the playing spaces or to differentiate the opponents' positions on the board)?

3. Should copyright protection extend more readily to the expression of fictional ideas such as plots and characters than to the expression of more fact-oriented ideas such as bookkeeping methods or scientific theories?

MASON V. MONTGOMERY DATA, INC.

967 F.2d 135 (5th Cir. 1992).

REAVLEY, CIRCUIT JUDGE:

[Plaintiff Mason sued MDI, Landata, and Conroe Title for infringing Mason's copyrights in 233 real estate maps.] We agree with Mason that the maps are copyrightable, so we reverse * * *.

I. Background

* * * [Mason's] maps, which display copyright notices, pictorially portray the location, size, and shape of surveys, land grants, tracts, and various topographical features within the county. Numbers and words on the maps identify deeds, abstract numbers, acreage, and the owners of the various tracts. Mason obtained the information that he included on the maps from a variety of sources. * * * Mason testified that he used substantial judgment and discretion to reconcile inconsistencies among the various sources, to select which features to include in the final map sheets, and to portray the information in a manner that would be useful to the public. * * *

Mason's infringement claims are based on the defendants' use of his maps as part of a geographical indexing system that Landata created to continuously organize and store ever-changing title information on each tract in Montgomery County. To create this system, Landata purchased a set of Mason's maps and reorganized them by cutting and pasting them into 72 map sheets. Landata then attached a transparent overlay to each of the 72 sheets, and depicted on these overlays numerous updates and corrections to the information on Mason's maps. * * *

II. Discussion

A. The Copyrightability of Mason's Maps

1. The Idea Expression Merger Doctrine

The Copyright Act extends copyright protection to "original works of authorship fixed in any tangible medium of expression." 17 U.S.C.A. § 102(a) (West Supp. 1992). The scope of that protection, however, is not unlimited. "In no case does copyright protection for an original work of authorship extend to any *idea*, . . . regardless of the form in which it is described, explained, illustrated, or embodied in such work." *Id.* § 102(b) (emphasis added). Thus, while a copyright bars others from copying an author's original expression of an idea, it does not bar them from using the idea itself. "Others are free to utilize the 'idea' so long as they do not plagiarize its 'expression.' " *Herbert Rosenthal Jewelry Corp. v. Kalpakian*, 446 F.2d 738, 741 (9th Cir. 1971). In some cases, however, it is so difficult to distinguish between an idea and its expression that the two are said to merge. Thus, when there is essentially only one way to express an idea, "copying the 'expression' will not be barred, since protecting the 'expression' in such circumstances would confer a monopoly of the 'idea' upon the copyright owner free of the conditions and limitations imposed by the patent law." *Id.* at 742. By denying protection to an expression that is merged with its underlying idea, we "prevent an author from monopolizing an idea merely by copyrighting a few expressions of it." *Toro Co. v. R & R Products Co.*, 787 F.2d 1208, 1212 (8th Cir. 1986).

The district court applied these principles to the present case and concluded that "the problem with the Hodge Mason maps is . . . that [they] express the only pictorial presentation which could result from a correct interpretation of the legal description and other factual information relied upon by the plaintiffs in producing the maps." The court believed that, to extend copyright protection to the Hodge Mason maps, which resulted from facts essentially in the public domain, would give the plaintiffs a monopoly over the facts. * * * The court thus concluded that "the plaintiffs' idea to create the maps, based on legal and factual public information, is inseparable from its expression embodied within the maps, and hence not subject to copyright protection."

We agree with Mason that the district court erred in applying the merger doctrine in this case. To determine whether the doctrine is applicable in any case, the court must "focus on whether the idea is capable of various modes of expression." *Apple Computer*, [*Inc. v. Franklin Computer Corp.*, 714 F.2d 1240, 1253 (3d Cir. 1983)]. Thus, the court must first identify the idea that the work expresses, and then attempt to distinguish that idea from the author's expression of it. If the court concludes that the idea and its expression are inseparable, then the merger doctrine applies and the expression will not be protected. Conversely, if the court can distinguish the idea from its expression, then the expression will be protected because the fact that one author has copyrighted one expression of that idea will not prevent other authors from creating and copyrighting their own expressions of the same idea. In all cases, "the guiding consideration in drawing the line is the preservation of the balance between competition and protection reflected in the patent and copyright laws." *Herbert Rosenthal Jewelry*, 446 F.2d at 742.

The district court determined that Mason's idea, "which includes drawing the abstract and tract boundaries, indicating the ownership name, the tract size, and the other factual information" on a map of Montgomery County, was "to create the maps, based on legal and factual public information." Mason argues that the court clearly erred in finding that this idea can be expressed in only one or a limited number of ways. We agree. The record in this case contains copies of maps created by Mason's competitors that prove beyond dispute that the idea embodied in Mason's maps is capable of a variety of expressions. Although the competitors' maps and Mason's maps embody the same idea, they differ in the placement, size, and dimensions of numerous surveys, tracts, and other features. The record also contains affidavits in which licensed surveyors and experienced mapmakers explain that the differences between Mason's maps and those of his competitors are the natural result of each mapmaker's selection of sources, interpretation of those sources, discretion in reconciling inconsistencies among the sources, and skill and judgment in depicting the information.

* * * By selecting different sources, or by resolving inconsistencies among the same sources differently, or by coordinating, arranging, or even drawing the information differently, other mapmakers may create—and indeed have created—expressions of Mason's idea that differ from those that Mason created.

Finally, the defendants contend that this court's decision in *Kern River Gas Transmission Co. v. Coastal Corp.*, [899 F.2d 1458 (5th Cir. 1990),] requires application of the merger doctrine in this case. *Kern River* concerned the copyrightability of maps on which Kern River Gas Transmission Company (Kern River) depicted the location that it proposed for construction of a gas pipeline. The idea at issue in *Kern River* was simply the placing on a map of Kern River's certain "proposed location for a prospective pipeline." This court concluded that that idea merged with Kern River's expression because there was only one way to effectively express that idea.

The defendants argue that the merger doctrine applies in this case because drawing lines on a public map is the only way to depict the locations of surveys and boundary lines in Montgomery County, just as it was the only way to depict the location of a pipeline in *Kern River*. But the distinction between *Kern River* and this case is not in the methods available for depicting an object's location on a map, but in the ideas that the maps in the two cases embody. We cannot determine whether an idea is capable of a variety of expressions until we first identify what that idea is. A court's decision whether to apply the merger doctrine often depends on how it defines the author's idea. For this reason, in defining the idea the court should be guided by "the balance between competition and protection reflected in the patent and copyright laws." *Herbert Rosenthal Jewelry*, 446 F.2d at 742.

We focus in this case on an earlier point in the mapping process, a point prior to the selection of information and decisions where to locate tract lines. The idea here was to bring together the available information on boundaries, landmarks, and ownership, and to choose locations and an effective pictorial expression of those locations. That idea and its final expression are separated by Mason's efforts and creativity that are entitled to protection from competitors. The evidence in this case demonstrates that a mapmaker who desires to express the idea of depicting the location and ownership of property in Montgomery County in map form must select information from numerous sources, reconcile inconsistencies among those sources, and depict the information according to the mapmaker's skill and judgment. Although Mason sought to depict the information accurately, the conflicts among the sources and the limitations inherent in the process of representing reality in pictorial map form required him to make choices that resulted in independent expression. Extending protection to that expression will not grant Mason a monopoly over the idea, because other mapmakers can express the same idea differently. The protection that each map receives extends only to its original expression, and neither the facts nor the idea embodied in the maps is protected. "[T]he facts and ideas . . . are free for the taking. . . ." "[T]he very same facts and ideas may be divorced from the context imposed by the author, and restated or reshuffled by second comers, even if the author was the first to discover the facts or to propose the ideas." *Feist*, 111 S.Ct. at 1289.

For these reasons, we conclude that the district court erred by applying the merger doctrine in this case. Because the idea embodied in Mason's maps can be expressed in a variety of ways, the merger doctrine does not render Mason's expression of that idea uncopyrightable.

2. The "Originality" Requirement

Landata contends that, even if the merger doctrine does not apply, Mason's maps are uncopyrightable because they are not "original" under *Feist*. Although the district court applied the merger doctrine to hold that Mason's maps are not copyrightable, it found that "the problem with the Hodge Mason maps is not a lack of originality." We agree that Mason's maps are original. Originality does not require "novelty, ingenuity, or aesthetic merit." H.R.Rep. No. 1476, 94th Cong., 2d Sess. 51 (1976). Instead, originality "means only that the work was independently created by the author (as opposed to copied from other works), and that it possesses at least some minimal degree of creativity." *Feist,* 111 S. Ct. at 1287. The parties do not dispute Mason's claim that he independently created his maps, but Landata contends that they do not possess the degree of creativity necessary to qualify them as original under *Feist.*

Mason's maps pass muster under *Feist* because Mason's selection, coordination, and arrangement of the information that he depicted are sufficiently creative to qualify his maps as original "compilations" of facts. Under the originality standard, bare facts are never copyrightable "because facts do not owe their origin to an act of authorship." *Id.* at 1288. A compilation of facts, however, may be copyrightable if the author made choices as to "which facts to include, in what order to place them, and how to arrange the collected data so that they may be used effectively by readers." *Id.* at 1289. The author's selection, coordination, and arrangement of facts, however, are protected only if they were "made independently . . . and entail a minimal degree of creativity." *Id.*

* * *

But the evidence in this case demonstrates that Mason exercised sufficient creativity when he created his maps. In his deposition and affidavit, Mason explained the choices that he independently made to select information from numerous and sometimes conflicting sources, and to depict that information on his maps. Mason's compilation of the information on his maps involved creativity that far exceeds the required minimum level.

Mason's maps also possess sufficient creativity to merit copyright protection as pictorial and graphic works of authorship. Historically, most courts have treated maps solely as compilations of facts. The Copyright Act, however, categorizes maps not as factual compilations but as "pictorial, graphic, and sculptural works"—a category that includes photographs and architectural plans. 17 U.S.C.A. § 101. Some courts have recognized that maps, unlike telephone directories and other factual compilations, have an inherent pictorial or photographic nature that merits copyright protection. *See, e.g., Rockford Map Publishers, Inc. v. Directory Service Co.,* 768 F.2d 145, 149 (7th Cir.1985) ("Teasing pictures from the debris left by conveyancers is a substantial change in the form of the information. The result is copyrightable. . . ."); *United States v. Hamilton,* 583 F.2d 448, 451 (9th Cir.1978) ("Expression in cartography is not so different from other artistic forms seeking to touch upon external realities that unique rules are needed to judge whether the authorship is original."). We agree with these courts. * * *

Because Mason's maps possess sufficient creativity in both the selection, coordination, and arrangement of the facts that they depict, and as in the pictorial, graphic nature of the way that they do so, we find no error in the district court's determination that Mason's maps are original.

* * *

NOTES

1. The court in *Mason* emphasizes that the differences in the maps of Montgomery County arise from the use of different sources, and the mapmakers' skill and judgment. If a mapmaker were to produce a map that was an indisputably complete and accurate depiction of a geographic area, would the map be copyrightable? What about images from Google Earth?

2. In *Mason* the court states that the mapmaker exercised judgment in reconciling conflicting information. Would it be more accurate to say that this mental effort was expended in acquiring information, or in expressing it? Were the mapmaker's choices "creative"? How does this affect the copyright analysis?

3. In *Kern River Gas Transmission Co. v. Coastal Corp.*, 899 F.2d 1458 (5th Cir. 1990), discussed by the *Mason* court, two contractors were competing for the same contract to build an oil pipeline. The first submitted a proposal which included the location of its proposed pipeline, drawn on USGS topographic maps, after compiling information about the pipeline's route by undertaking independent field work. An environmental consulting group then completed an Environmental Impact Statement (EIS) covering a mile-wide corridor along the proposed route. The second competitor's proposal initially deviated from this mile-wide corridor in several locations. In the process of correcting these deviations, the second competitor copied the center line of the EIS corridor from the first competitor's maps onto their own maps. The first competitor sued for copyright infringement, but the district court and the Fifth Circuit found no infringement by virtue of the merger doctrine:

> [T]he district court held that the idea of the location of the pipeline and its expression embodied in the 1:250,000 maps are inseparable and not subject to protection. We agree. The idea of the proposed location of a prospective pipeline is not copyrightable. The 1:250,000 maps consisted of lines representing the proposed location of the pipeline drawn on maps sold to the general public. Such map markings are certainly the only effective way to convey the idea of the proposed location of a pipeline across 1,000 miles of terrain. To extend protection to the lines would be to grant [plaintiff] Kern River a monopoly of the idea for locating a proposed pipeline in the chosen corridor, a foreclosure of competition that Congress could not have intended to sanction through copyright law, especially given the ALJ's finding in the *Mojave-Kern River* proceedings that the southern

> California enhanced oil recovery market could support only one pipeline. * * *
>
> The district court did find that Kern River conducted expensive and detailed field work to acquire the information needed to formulate mile-by-mile the precise location of their pipeline. Clearly, the consequent placement of locating lines on the 1:24,000 maps met the originality requirement of the Act. The problem for the copyrightability of the resulting maps, however, is not a lack of originality, but rather that the maps created express in the only effective way the idea of the location of the pipeline.

899 F.2d at 1463–64. Does *Kern River* properly apply the merger doctrine? Does *Mason* persuasively distinguish *Kern River*?

4. Is a contract for the sale of goods copyrightable? What about forms containing blanks to be filled in? Rules for a contest? In *Utopia Provider Systems v. Pro-Med Clinical Systems*, 596 F.3d 1313 (11th Cir. 2010), the Eleventh Circuit addressed the copyrightability of blank templates designed for use by emergency room physicians in capturing their encounters with patients. The court held that these blank forms, which do not convey information or images, are not copyrightable subject matter.

5. In each of the following scenarios, consider whether the defendant has copied protected expression:

(a) Plaintiff prepares and administers standardized multiple-choice tests. Defendant acquires a stolen copy of one of plaintiff's tests, and incorporates between 200 and 300 of the questions in a series of practice tests for defendant's students. Many of the questions are copied "verbatim or nearly verbatim." *See Educational Testing Services v. Katzman*, 793 F.2d 533 (3d Cir. 1986).

(b) Plaintiff publishes a list of thousands of medical procedures and assigns to each of them a 5-digit numerical code with a 2-digit modifier. The codes are listed in numerical order, except that the most frequently used numbers, which begin with "99," are listed first. The defendant publishes an improved, pocket-sized version of the plaintiff's work which copies the plaintiff's list of procedures and identifying numbers in the same order, but corrects certain errors. *See Practice Management Information Corp. v. American Medical Ass'n*, 877 F.Supp. 1386 (C.D. Cal. 1994), *aff'd in part and rev'd in part*, 121 F.3d 516 (9th Cir. 1997).

(c) Plaintiff publishes a comprehensive daily listing of called municipal bonds. The list identifies the issuer, the series, the redemption date and price, and the name of the paying agent. Plaintiff obtains this information from "tombstone" ads in newspapers. Defendant, a provider of bond rating and other financial information services, publishes bi-weekly news reports on the municipal bonds which it rates. When preparing a report on a particular bond that has been called, the defendant copies the redemption information published by plaintiff and adds certain additional information of interest to its subscribers. *See Financial Information, Inc. v. Moody's Investors Service, Inc.*, 751 F.2d 501 (2d Cir. 1984).

(d) Plaintiff, the star of a television cooking show, periodically publishes his recipes in paperback compilations for sale to the public. Each compilation contains a dozen or so recipes. Defendant, a cookbook publisher, reproduces three of these recipes, each from a different compilation, in a new cookbook. Defendant copies the ingredients lists virtually verbatim, but rewrites the directions in the simplest terms possible in order to eliminate the plaintiff's distinctive phrasings. *See Publications, Int'l Ltd. v. Meredith Corp.*, 88 F.3d 473 (7th Cir.1996).

(e) Plaintiff, a physician, has prepared "symptom guides," which are lists of symptoms which she has found helpful in diagnosing particular diseases. Defendant, a publishing house, obtains copies of the guides and reproduces them. *See Kregos v. Associated Press*, 937 F.2d 700 (2d Cir.1991).

(f) Plaintiff is the author of two books on trivia. Each consists of a compilation of facts, alphabetically arranged under headings that are followed by explanations of the particular entry. Each book contains 6,000 entries. Plaintiff gathered the information from books, films, and television shows after extensive research. Defendant makes and sells trivia games using many facts copied from plaintiff's books. *See Worth v. Selchow & Righter Co.*, 827 F.2d 569 (9th Cir.1987).

(g) Plaintiff, an amateur videographer, captures footage of a crime in progress. No other footage, and no still photographs, are available which record the event. Defendant wishes to incorporate that footage in a documentary about the crime. *See Time, Inc. v. Bernard Geis Assocs.*, 293 F.Supp. 130 (S.D.N.Y.1968).

(h) An original equipment hardware manufacturer (OEM) uses nine-digit numbers to identify each component of the equipment it manufacturers. Defendant, a supplier of compatible replacement parts, publishes a list of its own replacement parts that cross-references the part numbers used by the OEM. In determining whether the OEM's list of part numbers is copyrightable, does it matter whether (1) the OEM part numbers are arbitrary, or (2) each digit in the OEM part number conveys specific information about the component and the equipment that uses it? *See ATC Distrib. Group, Inc. v. Whatever It Takes Transmission & Parts, Inc.*, 402 F.3d 700 (6th Cir. 2005); *Southco, Inc. v. Kanebridge Corp.*, 390 F.3d 276 (3d Cir. 2004); *Mitel v. Iqtel, Inc.*, 124 F.3d 1366 (10th Cir. 1997); *American Dental Ass'n v. Delta Dental Plans Ass'n*, 126 F.3d 977 (7th Cir. 1997); *Toro Co. v. R & R Prods. Co.*, 787 F.2d 1208 (8th Cir. 1986).

(i) Bikram Choudhury (Choudhury) is the founder of Bikram's Yoga College of India. Choudhury developed a particular sequence of twenty-six yoga poses and two breathing exercises (the Sequence) and incorporated them into a book. Is this sequence copyrightable in itself, or as a compilation, or as a choreographic work? *See Bikram's Yoga College of India L.P. v. Evolation Yoga LLC*, 803 F.3d 1032 (9th Cir. 2015).

6. Some countries have enacted legislation protecting owners of certain databases against unauthorized copying of the information contained in the database, and similar legislation has been proposed (as yet, unsuccessfully) in the United States.

Could Congress enact such a proposal under the Intellectual Property Clause? Under the Commerce Clause or other lawmaking authority? How significantly would such a proposal change the law regarding data compilations? Is such legislation advisable?

ORACLE AMERICA, INC. V. GOOGLE, INC.

750 F.3d 1339 (Fed. Cir. 2014).

O'MALLEY, CIRCUIT JUDGE.

This copyright dispute involves 37 packages of computer source code. The parties have often referred to these groups of computer programs, individually or collectively, as "application programming interfaces," or API packages. * * *

Sun Microsystems, Inc. ("Sun") developed the Java "platform" for computer programming and released it in 1996. The aim was to relieve programmers from the burden of writing different versions of their computer programs for different operating systems or devices. "The Java platform, through the use of a virtual machine, enable[d] software developers to write programs that [we]re able to run on different types of computer hardware without having to rewrite them for each different type." With Java, a software programmer could "write once, run anywhere."

* * *

Sun wrote a number of ready-to-use Java programs to perform common computer functions and organized those programs into groups it called "packages." These packages, which are the application programming interfaces at issue in this appeal, allow programmers to use the pre-written code to build certain functions into their own programs, rather than write their own code to perform those functions from scratch. They are shortcuts. Sun called the code for a specific operation (function) a "method." It defined "classes" so that each class consists of specified methods plus variables and other elements on which the methods operate. To organize the classes for users, then, it grouped classes (along with certain related "interfaces") into "packages." The parties have not disputed the district court's analogy: Oracle's collection of API packages is like a library, each package is like a bookshelf in the library, each class is like a book on the shelf, and each method is like a how-to chapter in a book.

* * *

Every package consists of two types of source code—what the parties call (1) declaring code; and (2) implementing code. Declaring code is the expression that identifies the prewritten function and is sometimes referred to as the "declaration" or "header." As the district court explained, the "main point is that this header line of code introduces the method body and specifies very precisely the inputs, name and other functionality." The expressions used by the programmer from the declaring code command the computer to execute the associated implementing code, which gives the computer the step-by-step instructions for carrying out the declared function.

* * *

With respect to the 37 packages at issue, "Google believed Java application programmers would want to find the same 37 sets of functionalities in the new Android system callable by the same names as used in Java." To achieve this result, Google copied the declaring source code from the 37 Java API packages verbatim, inserting that code into parts of its Android software. In doing so, Google copied the elaborately organized taxonomy of all the names of methods, classes, interfaces, and packages—the "overall system of organized names—covering 37 packages, with over six hundred classes, with over six thousand methods." The parties and district court referred to this taxonomy of expressions as the "structure, sequence, and organization" or "SSO" of the 37 packages. It is undisputed, however, that Google wrote its own implementing code * * *.

For the reasons that follow, we conclude that the declaring code and the structure, sequence, and organization of the 37 Java API packages are entitled to copyright protection. * * *

A. Copyrightability

The Copyright Act provides protection to "original works of authorship fixed in any tangible medium of expression," including "literary works." 17 U.S.C. § 102(a). It is undisputed that computer programs—defined in the Copyright Act as "a set of statements or instructions to be used directly or indirectly in a computer in order to bring about a certain result," 17 U.S.C. § 101—can be subject to copyright protection as "literary works." Indeed, the legislative history explains that "literary works" includes "computer programs to the extent that they incorporate authorship in the programmer's expression of original ideas, as distinguished from the ideas themselves." H.R.Rep. No. 1476, 94th Cong., 2d Sess. 54 (1976).

* * *

It is well established that copyright protection can extend to both literal and non-literal elements of a computer program. The literal elements of a computer program are the source code and object code. Courts have defined source code as "the spelled-out program commands that humans can read." Object code refers to "the binary language comprised of zeros and ones through which the computer directly receives its instructions." * * *

The non-literal components of a computer program include, among other things, the program's sequence, structure, and organization, as well as the program's user interface. As discussed below, whether the non-literal elements of a program "are protected depends on whether, on the particular facts of each case, the component in question qualifies as an expression of an idea, or an idea itself."

In this case, Oracle claims copyright protection with respect to both: (1) literal elements of its API packages—the 7,000 lines of declaring source code; and (2) non-literal elements—the structure, sequence, and organization of each of the 37 Java API packages.

The distinction between literal and non-literal aspects of a computer program is separate from the distinction between literal and non-literal copying. "Literal" copying is verbatim copying of original expression. "Non-literal" copying is "paraphrased or loosely paraphrased rather than word for word." Here, Google concedes that it copied the declaring code verbatim. Oracle explains that the lines of declaring code "embody the structure of each [API] package, just as the chapter titles and topic sentences represent the structure of a novel." As Oracle explains, when Google copied the declaring code in these packages "it also copied the 'sequence and organization' of the packages (i.e., the three-dimensional structure with all the chutes and ladders)" employed by Sun/Oracle in the packages. Oracle also argues that the nonliteral elements of the API packages—the structure, sequence, and organization that led naturally to the implementing code Google created—are entitled to protection. Oracle does not assert "literal" copying of the entire SSO, but, rather, that Google literally copied the declaring code and then paraphrased the remainder of the SSO by writing its own implementing code. It therefore asserts non-literal copying with respect to the entirety of the SSO.

At this stage, it is undisputed that the declaring code and the structure and organization of the Java API packages are original. The testimony at trial revealed that designing the Java API packages was a creative process and that the Sun/Oracle developers had a vast range of options for the structure and organization. * * * The [district] court found, however, that neither the declaring code nor the SSO was entitled to copyright protection under the Copyright Act.

Although the parties agree that Oracle's API packages meet the originality requirement under Section 102(a), they disagree as to the proper interpretation and application of Section 102(b). For its part, Google suggests that there is a two-step copyrightability analysis, wherein Section 102(a) grants copyright protection to original works, while Section 102(b) takes it away if the work has a functional component. To the contrary, however, Congress emphasized that Section 102(b) "in no way enlarges or contracts the scope of copyright protection" and that its "purpose is to restate . . . that the basic dichotomy between expression and idea remains unchanged." *Feist,* 499 U.S. at 356 (quoting H.R.Rep. No. 1476, 94th Cong., 2d Sess. 54 (1976)). "Section 102(b) does not extinguish the protection accorded a particular expression of an idea merely because that expression is embodied in a method of operation." *Mitel, Inc. v. Iqtel, Inc.,* 124 F.3d 1366, 1372 (10th Cir.1997). Section 102(a) and 102(b) are to be considered collectively so that certain expressions are subject to greater scrutiny. In assessing copyrightability, the district court is required to ferret out apparent expressive aspects of a work and then separate protectable expression from "unprotectable ideas, facts, processes, and methods of operation."

Of course, as with many things, in defining this task, the devil is in the details. Circuit courts have struggled with, and disagree over, the tests to be employed when attempting to draw the line between what is protectable expression and what is not. *Compare Whelan Assocs., Inc. v. Jaslow Dental Lab., Inc.,* 797 F.2d 1222, 1236 (3d Cir.1986) (everything not necessary to the purpose or function of a work is expression), *with Lotus,* 49 F.3d at 815 (methods of operation are means by which a user operates something and any words used to effectuate that operation are unprotected expression). When assessing whether the non-literal elements of a computer program constitute protectable expression, the Ninth Circuit has endorsed an "abstraction-filtration-comparison" test formulated by the Second Circuit and expressly adopted by several other circuits. *Sega Enters. Ltd. v. Accolade, Inc.,* 977 F.2d 1510, 1525 (9th Cir.1992) ("In our view, in light of the essentially utilitarian nature of computer programs, the Second Circuit's approach is an appropriate one."). This test rejects the notion that anything that performs a function is necessarily uncopyrightable. *See Mitel,* 124 F.3d at 1372 (rejecting the *Lotus* court's formulation, and concluding that, "although an element of a work may be characterized as a method of operation, that element may nevertheless contain expression that is eligible for copyright protection."). And it also rejects as flawed the *Whelan* assumption that, once any separable idea can be identified in a computer program everything else must be protectable expression, on grounds that more than one idea may be embodied in any particular program.

Thus, this test eschews bright line approaches and requires a more nuanced assessment of the particular program at issue in order to determine what expression is protectable and infringed. As the Second Circuit explains, this test has three steps. In the abstraction step, the court "first break[s] down the allegedly infringed program into its constituent structural parts." *Id.* at 706. In the filtration step, the court "sift[s] out all non-protectable material," including ideas and "expression that is necessarily incidental to those ideas." *Id.* In the final step, the court compares the remaining creative expression with the allegedly infringing program.[4]

In the second step, the court is first to assess whether the expression is original to the programmer or author. The court must then determine whether the particular inclusion of any level of abstraction is dictated by considerations of efficiency, required by factors already external to the program itself, or taken from the public domain—all of which would render the expression unprotectable. These conclusions are to be informed by traditional copyright principles of originality, merger, and scenes a faire.

* * *

Oracle asserts that all of the trial court's conclusions regarding copyrightability are erroneous. Oracle argues that its Java API packages are entitled to protection under the Copyright Act because they are expressive and could have been written and organized in any number of ways to achieve the same functions. Specifically, Oracle argues that the district court erred when it: (1) concluded that each line of declaring code is uncopyrightable because the idea and expression have merged; (2) found the declaring code uncopyrightable because it employs short phrases; (3) found all aspects of the SSO devoid of protection as a "method of operation" under 17 U.S.C. § 102(b); and (4) invoked Google's "interoperability" concerns in the copyrightability analysis. For the reasons explained below, we agree with Oracle on each point.

1. Declaring Source Code

First, Oracle argues that the district court erred in concluding that each line of declaring source code is completely unprotected under the merger and short phrases doctrines. * * *

---

[4] Importantly, this full analysis only applies where a copyright owner alleges infringement of the non-literal aspects of its work. Where "admitted literal copying of a discrete, easily-conceptualized portion of a work" is at issue—as with Oracle's declaring code—a court "need not perform a complete abstraction-filtration-comparison analysis" and may focus the protectability analysis on the filtration stage, with attendant reference to standard copyright principles.

a. Merger

The merger doctrine functions as an exception to the idea/expression dichotomy. It provides that, when there are a limited number of ways to express an idea, the idea is said to "merge" with its expression, and the expression becomes unprotected. * * *

Under the merger doctrine, a court will not protect a copyrighted work from infringement if the idea contained therein can be expressed in only one way. For computer programs, "this means that when specific [parts of the code], even though previously copyrighted, are the only and essential means of accomplishing a given task, their later use by another will not amount to infringement." We have recognized, however, applying Ninth Circuit law, that the "unique arrangement of computer program expression . . . does not merge with the process so long as alternate expressions are available."

* * * Because it is undisputed that Google wrote its own implementing code, the copyrightability of the precise language of that code is not at issue on appeal. Instead, our focus is on the declaring code and structure of the API packages.

On appeal, Oracle argues that the district court: (1) misapplied the merger doctrine; and (2) failed to focus its analysis on the options available to the original author. We agree with Oracle on both points. First, we agree that merger cannot bar copyright protection for any lines of declaring source code unless Sun/Oracle had only one way, or a limited number of ways, to write them. The evidence showed that Oracle had "unlimited options as to the selection and arrangement of the 7000 lines Google copied." * * * Because "alternative expressions [we]re available," there is no merger.

We further find that the district court erred in focusing its merger analysis on the options available to Google at the time of copying. It is well-established that copyrightability and the scope of protectable activity are to be evaluated at the time of creation, not at the time of infringement. The focus is, therefore, on the options that were available to Sun/Oracle at the time it created the API packages. Of course, once Sun/Oracle created "java.lang.Math.max," programmers who want to use that particular package have to call it by that name. But, as the court acknowledged, nothing prevented Google from writing its own declaring code, along with its own implementing code, to achieve the same result. In such circumstances, the chosen expression simply does not merge with the idea being expressed.

* * *

b. Short Phrases

The district court also found that Oracle's declaring code consists of uncopyrightable short phrases. Specifically, the court concluded that, "while the Android method and class names could have been different from the names of their counterparts in Java and still have worked, copyright protection never extends to names or short phrases as a matter of law."

The district court is correct that "[w]ords and short phrases such as names, titles, and slogans" are not subject to copyright protection. 37 C.F.R. § 202.1(a). The court failed to recognize, however, that the relevant question for copyrightability purposes is not whether the work at issue contains short phrases—as literary works often do—but, rather, whether those phrases are creative. And, by dissecting the individual lines of declaring code at issue into short phrases, the district court further failed to recognize that an original combination of elements can be copyrightable.

By analogy, the opening of Charles Dickens' *A Tale of Two Cities* is nothing but a string of short phrases. Yet no one could contend that this portion of Dickens' work is unworthy of copyright protection because it can be broken into those shorter constituent components. The question is not whether a short phrase or series of short phrases can be extracted from the work, but whether the manner in which they are used or strung together exhibits creativity.

Although the district court apparently focused on individual lines of code, Oracle is not seeking copyright protection for a specific short phrase or word. Instead, the portion of declaring code at issue is 7,000 lines, and Google's own "Java guru" conceded that there can be "creativity and artistry even in a single method declaration." Because Oracle "exercised creativity in the selection and arrangement" of the method declarations when it created the API packages and wrote the relevant declaring code, they contain protectable expression that is entitled to copyright protection. *See Atari,* 975 F.2d at 840; *see also* 17 U.S.C. §§ 101, 103 (recognizing copyright protection for "compilations" which are defined as work that is "selected, coordinated, or arranged in such a way that the resulting work as a whole constitutes an original work of authorship"). Accordingly, we conclude that the district court erred in applying the short phrases doctrine to find the declaring code not copyrightable.

c. Scenes a Faire

The scenes a faire doctrine, which is related to the merger doctrine, operates to bar certain otherwise creative expression from copyright protection. It provides that "expressive elements of a work of authorship are not entitled to protection against infringement if they are standard, stock, or common to a topic, or if they necessarily follow from a common theme or setting." Under this doctrine, "when certain commonplace expressions are indispensable and naturally associated with the treatment of a given idea, those expressions are treated like ideas and therefore [are] not protected by copyright." In the computer context, "the scene a faire doctrine denies protection to program elements that are dictated by external factors such as 'the mechanical specifications of the computer on which a particular program is intended to run' or 'widely accepted programming practices within the computer industry.'"

* * *

Google cannot rely on the scenes a faire doctrine as an alternative ground upon which we might affirm the copyrightability judgment of the district court. * * * Google's reliance on the doctrine below and the amici reference to it here are premised on a fundamental misunderstanding of the doctrine. Like merger, the focus of the scenes a faire doctrine is on the circumstances presented to the creator, not the copier. The court's analytical focus must be upon the external factors that dictated Sun's selection of classes, methods, and code—not upon what Google encountered at the time it chose to copy those groupings and that code. It is this showing the trial court found Google failed to make, and Google cites to nothing in the record which indicates otherwise.

For these reasons, the trial court was correct to conclude that the scenes a faire doctrine does not affect the copyrightability of either the declaring code in, or the SSO of, the Java API packages at issue.

2. The Structure, Sequence, and Organization of the API Packages

The district court found that the SSO of the Java API packages is creative and original, but nevertheless held that it is a "system or method of operation . . . and, therefore, cannot be copyrighted" under 17 U.S.C. § 102(b). In reaching this conclusion, the district court seems to have relied upon language contained in a First Circuit decision: *Lotus Development Corp. v. Borland International, Inc.*, 49 F.3d 807 (1st Cir.1995), *aff'd without opinion by equally divided court,* 516 U.S. 233 (1996).

In *Lotus,* it was undisputed that the defendant copied the menu command hierarchy and interface from Lotus 1–2–3, a computer spreadsheet program "that enables users to perform accounting functions electronically on a computer." The menu command hierarchy referred to a series of commands—such as "Copy," "Print," and "Quit"—which were arranged into more than 50 menus and submenus. Although the defendant did not copy any Lotus source code, it copied the menu command hierarchy into its rival program. The question before the court was "whether a computer menu command hierarchy is copyrightable subject matter."

Although it accepted the district court's finding that Lotus developers made some expressive choices in selecting and arranging the command terms, the First Circuit found that the command hierarchy was not copyrightable because, among other things, it was a "method of operation" under Section 102(b). In reaching this conclusion, the court defined a "method of operation" as "the means by which a person operates something, whether it be a car, a food processor, or a computer." Because the Lotus menu command hierarchy provided "the means by which users control and operate Lotus 1–2–3," it was deemed unprotectable. For example, if users wanted to copy material, they would use the "Copy" command and the command terms would tell the computer what to do. According to the *Lotus* court, the "fact that Lotus developers could have designed the Lotus menu command hierarchy differently is immaterial to the question of whether it is a 'method of operation.' " The court further indicated that, "[i]f specific words are essential to operating something, then they are part of a 'method of operation' and, as such, are unprotectable."

* * *

We find * * * that the hard and fast rule set down in *Lotus* and employed by the district court here—i.e., that elements which perform a function can never be copyrightable—is at odds with the Ninth Circuit's endorsement of the abstraction-filtration-comparison analysis discussed earlier. As the Tenth Circuit concluded in expressly rejecting the *Lotus* "method of operation" analysis, in favor of the Second Circuit's abstraction-filtration-comparison test, "although an element of a work may be characterized as a method of operation, that element may nevertheless contain expression that is eligible for copyright protection." *Mitel,* 124 F.3d at 1372. Specifically, the court found that Section 102(b) "does not extinguish the protection accorded a particular expression of an idea merely because that expression is embodied in a method of operation at a higher level of abstraction." *Id.*

Other courts agree that components of a program that can be characterized as a "method of operation" may nevertheless be copyrightable. For example, the Third Circuit rejected a defendant's argument that operating system programs are "per se" uncopyrightable because an operating system is a "method of operation" for a computer. *Apple Computer, Inc. v. Franklin Computer Corp.,* 714 F.2d 1240, 1250–52 (3d Cir.1983). The court distinguished between the "method which instructs the computer to perform its operating functions" and "the instructions themselves," and found that the instructions were copyrightable. In its analysis, the court noted: "[t]hat the words of a program are used ultimately in the implementation of a process should in no way affect their copyrightability." The court focused "on whether the idea is capable of various modes of expression" and indicated that, "[i]f other programs can be written or created which perform the same function as [i]n Apple's operating system program, then that program is an expression of the idea and hence copyrightable." Notably, no other circuit has adopted the First Circuit's "method of operation" analysis.

Courts have likewise found that classifying a work as a "system" does not preclude copyright for the particular expression of that system. *See Toro Co. v. R & R Prods. Co.*, 787 F.2d 1208, 1212 (8th Cir.1986) (rejecting the district court's decision that "appellant's parts numbering system is not copyrightable because it is a 'system' " and indicating that Section 102(b) does not preclude protection for the "particular expression" of that system); *see also Am. Dental Ass'n v. Delta Dental Plans Ass'n*, 126 F.3d 977, 980 (7th Cir.1997) ("A dictionary cannot be called a 'system' just because new novels are written using words, all of which appear in the dictionary. Nor is word-processing software a 'system' just because it has a command structure for producing paragraphs.").

Here, the district court recognized that the SSO "resembles a taxonomy," but found that "it is nevertheless a command structure, a system or method of operation—a long hierarchy of over six thousand commands to carry out pre-assigned functions."[12] In other words, the court concluded that, although the SSO is expressive, it is not copyrightable because it is also functional. The problem with the district court's approach is that computer programs are by definition functional—they are all designed to accomplish some task. Indeed, the statutory definition of "computer program" acknowledges that they function "to bring about a certain result." If we were to accept the district court's suggestion that a computer program is uncopyrightable simply because it "carr[ies] out pre-assigned functions," no computer program is protectable. That result contradicts Congress's express intent to provide copyright protection to computer programs, as well as binding Ninth Circuit case law finding computer programs copyrightable, despite their utilitarian or functional purpose. Though the trial court did add the caveat that it "does not hold that the structure, sequence and organization of all computer programs may be stolen," it is hard to see how its method of operation analysis could lead to any other conclusion.

While it does not appear that the Ninth Circuit has addressed the precise issue, we conclude that a set of commands to instruct a computer to carry out desired operations may contain expression that is eligible for copyright protection. We agree with Oracle that, under Ninth Circuit law, an original work—even one that serves a function—is entitled to copyright protection as long as the author had multiple ways to express the underlying idea. Section 102(b) does not, as Google seems to suggest, automatically deny copyright protection to elements of a computer program that are functional. Instead, as noted, Section 102(b) codifies the idea/expression dichotomy and the legislative history confirms that, among other things, Section 102(b) was "intended to make clear that the expression adopted by the programmer is the copyrightable element in a

[12] This analogy by the district court is meaningful because taxonomies, in varying forms, have generally been deemed copyrightable.

computer program." H.R.Rep. No. 1476, 94th Cong., 2d Sess. 54 (1976). Therefore, even if an element directs a computer to perform operations, the court must nevertheless determine whether it contains any separable expression entitled to protection.

On appeal, Oracle does not—and concedes that it cannot—claim copyright in the idea of organizing functions of a computer program or in the "package-class-method" organizational structure in the abstract. Instead, Oracle claims copyright protection only in its *particular* way of naming and organizing each of the 37 Java API packages. * * *

As the district court acknowledged, Google could have structured Android differently and could have chosen different ways to express and implement the functionality that it copied. Specifically, the court found that "the very same functionality could have been offered in Android without duplicating the exact command structure used in Java." The court further explained that Google could have offered the same functions in Android by "rearranging the various methods under different groupings among the various classes and packages." The evidence showed, moreover, that Google designed many of its own API packages from scratch, and, thus, could have designed its own corresponding 37 API packages if it wanted to do so.

Given the court's findings that the SSO is original and creative, and that the declaring code could have been written and organized in any number of ways and still have achieved the same functions, we conclude that Section 102(b) does not bar the packages from copyright protection just because they also perform functions.

3. Google's Interoperability Arguments are Irrelevant to Copyrightability

Oracle also argues that the district court erred in invoking interoperability in its copyrightability analysis. Specifically, Oracle argues that Google's interoperability arguments are only relevant, if at all, to fair use—not to the question of whether the API packages are copyrightable. We agree.

In characterizing the SSO of the Java API packages as a "method of operation," the district court explained that "[d]uplication of the command structure is necessary for interoperability." The court found that, "[i]n order for at least some of [the pre-Android Java] code to run on Android, Google was required to provide the same java.package.Class.method() command system using the same names with the same 'taxonomy' and with the same functional specifications." And, the court concluded that "Google replicated what was necessary to achieve a degree of interoperability—but no more, taking care, as said before, to provide its own implementations." In reaching this conclusion, the court relied primarily on two Ninth Circuit decisions: *Sega Enterprises v. Accolade, Inc.*, 977 F.2d 1510 (9th Cir.1992), and *Sony Computer Entertainment, Inc. v. Connectix, Corp.*, 203 F.3d 596 (9th Cir.2000).

Both *Sega* and *Sony* are fair use cases in which copyrightability was addressed only tangentially. In *Sega,* for example, * * * the only question was whether Accolade's intermediate copying was fair use. The court never addressed the question of whether Sega's software code, which had functional elements, also contained separable creative expression entitled to protection. Likewise, although the court in *Sony* determined that Sony's computer program had functional elements, it never addressed whether it also had expressive elements. * * *

We disagree with Google's suggestion that *Sony* and *Sega* created an "interoperability exception" to copyrightability. Although both cases recognized that the software programs at issue there contained unprotected functional elements, a determination that some elements are unprotected is not the same as saying that the entire work loses copyright protection. To accept Google's reading would contradict Ninth Circuit case law recognizing that both the literal and non-literal components of a software program are eligible for copyright protection. And it would ignore the fact that the Ninth Circuit endorsed the abstraction-filtration-comparison inquiry in *Sega* itself.

As previously discussed, a court must examine the software program to determine whether it contains creative expression that can be separated from the underlying function. In doing so, the court filters out the elements of the program that are "ideas" as well as elements that are "dictated by considerations of efficiency, so as to be necessarily incidental to that idea; required by factors external to the program itself."

To determine "whether certain aspects of an allegedly infringed software are not protected by copyright law, the focus is on external factors that influenced the choice of the creator of the infringed product." The Second Circuit, for example, has noted that programmers are often constrained in their design choices by "extrinsic considerations" including "the mechanical specifications of the computer on which a particular program is intended to run" and "compatibility requirements of other programs with which a program is designed to operate in conjunction." The Ninth Circuit has likewise recognized that: (1) computer programs "contain many logical, structural, and visual display elements that are dictated by . . . external factors such as compatibility requirements and industry demands"; and (2) "[i]n some circumstances, even the exact set of commands used by the programmer is deemed functional rather than creative for purposes of copyright." *Sega,* 977 F.2d at 1524 (internal citation omitted).

Because copyrightability is focused on the choices available to the plaintiff at the time the computer program was created, the relevant compatibility inquiry asks whether the plaintiff's choices were dictated by a need to ensure that its program worked with existing third-party programs. Whether a defendant later seeks to make its program interoperable with the plaintiff's program has no bearing on whether the software the plaintiff created had any design limitations dictated by external factors. Stated differently, the focus is on the compatibility needs and programming choices of the party claiming copyright protection—not the choices the defendant made to achieve compatibility with the plaintiff's program. Consistent with this approach, courts have recognized that, once the plaintiff creates a copyrightable work, a defendant's desire "to achieve total compatibility . . . is a commercial and competitive objective which does not enter into the . . . issue of whether particular ideas and expressions have merged." *Apple Computer,* 714 F.2d at 1253.

Given this precedent, we conclude that the district court erred in focusing its interoperability analysis on Google's desires for its Android software. Whether Google's software is "interoperable" in some sense with any aspect of the Java platform (although as Google concedes, certainly not with the JVM) has no bearing on the threshold question of whether Oracle's software is copyrightable. It is the interoperability and other needs of Oracle—not those of Google—that apply in the copyrightability context, and there is no evidence that when Oracle created the Java API packages at issue it did so to meet compatibility requirements of other pre-existing programs.

Google maintains on appeal that its use of the "Java class and method names and declarations was 'the only and essential means' of achieving a degree of interoperability with existing programs written in the [Java language]." * * * Although this competitive objective might be relevant to the fair use inquiry, we conclude that it is irrelevant to the copyrightability of Oracle's declaring code and organization of the API packages.

Finally, to the extent Google suggests that it was entitled to copy the Java API packages because they had become the effective industry standard, we are unpersuaded. Google cites no authority for its suggestion that copyrighted works lose protection when they become popular, and we have found none. In fact, the Ninth Circuit has rejected the argument that a work that later becomes the industry standard is uncopyrightable. *See Practice Mgmt. Info. Corp. v. Am. Med. Ass'n,* 121 F.3d 516, 520 n. 8 (9th Cir.1997) (noting that the district court found plaintiff's medical coding system entitled to copyright protection, and that, although the system had become the industry standard, plaintiff's copyright did not prevent competitors "from developing comparative or better coding systems and lobbying the federal government and private actors to adopt them. It simply prevents wholesale copying of an existing system."). Google was free to develop its own API packages and to "lobby" programmers to adopt them. Instead, it chose to copy Oracle's declaring code and the SSO to capitalize on the preexisting community of programmers who were accustomed to using the Java API packages. That desire has nothing to do with copyrightability. For these reasons, we find that Google's industry standard argument has no bearing on the copyrightability of Oracle's work.

* * *

Conclusion

For the foregoing reasons, we conclude that the declaring code and the structure, sequence, and organization of the 37 Java API packages at issue are entitled to copyright protection. * * *

NOTES

1. This portion of the opinion addresses only the question whether the declaring code was copyrightable. The remainder of the opinion considered whether Google's copying was infringement or fair use. The fair use question eventually reached the Supreme Court, and you can read an excerpt from that opinion in Chapter 17.

2. Several courts have observed that neither copyright law nor patent law is well suited to the protection of computer software. *Oracle America* examines some of the reasons related to copyright law. Can you think of others? (The patentability of software is addressed in Chapter 10.)

3. Some courts treat the merger and scene a faire doctrines as part of the copyrightability analysis, while others treat them as relevant only to the question of infringement. Why does it matter, and which is the sounder approach?

3. ORIGINALITY IN DERIVATIVE WORKS

ALFRED BELL & CO. LTD. V. CATALDA FINE ARTS, INC.

191 F.2d 99 (2d Cir. 1951).

FRANK, CIRCUIT JUDGE:

[Plaintiff commissioned mezzotint engravings of well-known public domain paintings. Mezzotint engraving was a difficult, expensive, and time-consuming process, requiring substantial skill and judgment. It produced realistic and fairly accurate reproductions of the original works, although no two engravings of the same work would be identical. Plaintiff sued for copyright infringement when defendants produced and sold color lithographs of plaintiff's mezzotints. The district court found that the copyrights were valid and infringed, and the defendants appealed.]

* * *

1. Congressional power to authorize both patents and copyrights is contained in Article 1, Sec. 8 of the Constitution. In passing on the validity

of patents, the Supreme Court recurrently insists that this constitutional provision governs. On this basis, pointing to the Supreme Court's consequent requirement that, to be valid, a patent must disclose a high degree of uniqueness, ingenuity and inventiveness, the defendants assert that the same requirement constitutionally governs copyrights. As several sections of the Copyright Act—e.g., those authorizing copyrights of "reproductions of works of art," maps, and compilations—plainly dispense with any such high standard, defendants are, in effect, attacking the constitutionality of those sections. But the very language of the Constitution differentiates (a) "authors" and their "writings" from (b) "inventors" and their "discoveries." Those who penned the Constitution, of course, knew the difference. * * *

* * *

The defendants' contention apparently results from the ambiguity of the word "original". It may mean startling, novel or unusual, a marked departure from the past. Obviously this is not what is meant when one speaks of "the original package," or the "original bill," or (in connection with the "best evidence" rule) an "original" document; none of those things is highly unusual in creativeness. "Original" in reference to a copyrighted work means that the particular work "owes its origin" to the "author." No large measure of novelty is necessary. Said the Supreme Court in *Baker v. Selden*, 101 U.S. 99, 102–103: "The copyright of the book, if not pirated from other works, would be valid without regard to the novelty, or want of novelty, of its subject-matter. The novelty of the art or thing described or explained has nothing to do with the validity of the copyright. To give to the author of the book an exclusive property in the art described therein, when no examination of its novelty has ever been officially made, would be a surprise and a fraud upon the public. That is the province of letters-patent, not of copyright. The claim to an invention or discovery of an art or manufacture must be subjected to the examination of the Patent Office before an exclusive right therein can be obtained; and it can only be secured by a patent from the government. * * * "

In *Bleistein v. Donaldson Lithographing Co.*, 188 U.S. 239, 250, 252, the Supreme Court cited with approval *Henderson v. Tompkins*, C.C., 60 F. 758, where it was said, 60 F. at page 764: "There is a very broad distinction between what is implied in the word 'author,' found in the constitution, and the word 'inventor.' The latter carries an implication which excludes the results of only ordinary skill, while nothing of this is necessarily involved in the former. Indeed, the statutes themselves make broad distinctions on this point. So much as relates to copyrights * * * is expressed, so far as this particular is concerned, by the mere words, 'author, inventor, designer or proprietor,' with such aid as may be derived from the words 'written, composed or made,' * * *. But a multitude of books rest safely under copyright, which show only ordinary skill and diligence in their preparation. Compilations are noticeable examples of this fact. With reference to this subject, the courts have not undertaken to assume the functions of critics, or to measure carefully the degree of originality, or literary skill or training involved."

It is clear, then, that nothing in the Constitution commands that copyrighted matter be strikingly unique or novel. Accordingly, we were not ignoring the Constitution when we stated that a "copy of something in the public domain" will support a copyright if it is a "distinguishable variation"; or when we rejected the contention that "like a patent, a copyrighted work must be not only original, but new", adding, "That is not * * * the law as is obvious in the case of maps or compendia, where later works will necessarily be anticipated." All that is needed to satisfy both the Constitution and the statute is that the "author" contributed something more than a "merely trivial" variation, something recognizably "his own." Originality in this context "means little more than a prohibition of actual copying." No matter how poor artistically the "author's" addition, it is enough if it be his own. *Bleistein v. Donaldson Lithographing Co.*, 188 U.S. 239, 250.

On that account, we have often distinguished between the limited protection accorded a copyright owner and the extensive protection granted a patent owner. So we have held that "independent reproduction of a copyrighted * * * work is not infringement", whereas it is *vis a vis* a patent. Correlative with the greater immunity of a patentee is the doctrine of anticipation which does not apply to copyrights: The alleged inventor is chargeable with full knowledge of all the prior art, although in fact he may be utterly ignorant of it. The "author" is entitled to a copyright if he independently contrived a work completely identical with what went before; similarly, although he obtains a valid copyright, he has no right to prevent another from publishing a work identical with his, if not copied from his. A patentee, unlike a copyrightee, must not merely produce something "original"; he must also be "the first inventor or discoverer." "Hence it is possible to have a plurality of valid copyrights directed to closely identical or even identical works. Moreover, none of them, if independently arrived at without copying, will constitute an infringement of the copyright of the others."

* * *

2. We consider untenable defendants' suggestion that plaintiff's mezzotints could not validly be copyrighted because they are reproductions of works in the public domain. Not only does the Act include "Reproductions of a work of art", but—while prohibiting a copyright of "the original text of any work * * * in the public domain"—it explicitly provides for the copyrighting of "translations, or other versions of works in the public domain". The mezzotints were such "versions." They "originated" with

those who make them, and—on the trial judge's findings well supported by the evidence—amply met the standards imposed by the Constitution and the statute. There is evidence that they were not intended to, and did not, imitate the paintings they reproduced. But even if their substantial departures from the paintings were inadvertent, the copyrights would be valid. A copyist's bad eyesight or defective musculature, or a shock caused by a clap of thunder, may yield sufficiently distinguishable variations. Having hit upon such a variation unintentionally, the "author" may adopt it as his and copyright it.

Accordingly, defendants' arguments about the public domain become irrelevant. * * *

* * *

NOTES

1. *L. Batlin & Son v. Snyder*, 536 F.2d 486 (2d Cir. 1976), addressed whether a plastic replica of an antique cast metal "Uncle Sam" bank was eligible for copyright protection. The court found that the minor differences between the plaintiff's replica and the public domain original were insufficient to warrant copyright protection for the replica. One of these "minor" differences was that, in the original, an American eagle clutched arrows in its talons, while in the plaintiff's replica, the eagle's talons clutched a cluster of leaves. If the plaintiff had designed and produced a sculpture depicting only the cluster of leaves, would that sculpture have been copyrightable? Does your answer change when the leaves are placed in the eagle's talons on the replica Uncle Sam bank? Would it matter if the plaintiff chose to depict leaves instead of arrows on the replica only because leaves were easier to reproduce in a smaller-scale plastic replica?

2. In *Alva Studios, Inc. v. Winninger*, 177 F.Supp. 265 (S.D.N.Y. 1965), the district court held that an exact scale-model replica of Rodin's "Hand of God" sculpture was copyrightable even though the only difference between the original and the replica was size. The court explained that "great skill and originality is called for when one seeks to produce a scale reduction of a great work with exactitude." Do you agree with the court's decision?

3. If a musician transposes existing music into a different key, is the result copyrightable as a derivative work? Is a colorized film copyrightable?

SCHROCK V. LEARNING CURVE INTERNATIONAL, INC.

586 F.3d 513 (7th Cir. 2009).

SYKES, CIRCUIT JUDGE.

HIT Entertainment ("HIT") owns the copyright to the popular "Thomas & Friends" train characters, and it licensed Learning Curve International ("Learning Curve") to make toy figures of its characters.

Learning Curve in turn hired Daniel Schrock, a professional photographer, to take pictures of the toys for promotional materials. Learning Curve used Schrock's services on a regular basis for about four years and thereafter continued to use some of his photographs in its advertising and on product packaging. After Learning Curve stopped giving him work, Schrock registered his photos for copyright protection and sued Learning Curve and HIT for infringement.

The district court granted summary judgment for the defendants, holding that Schrock has no copyright in the photos. The court classified the photos as "derivative works" under the Copyright Act—derivative, that is, of the "Thomas & Friends" characters, for which HIT owns the copyright—and held that Schrock needed permission from Learning Curve (HIT's licensee) not only to make the photographs but also to copyright them. Because Schrock had permission to make but not permission to copyright the photos, the court dismissed his claim for copyright infringement.

We reverse. We assume for purposes of this decision that the district court correctly classified Schrock's photographs as derivative works. It does not follow, however, that Schrock needed authorization from Learning Curve to copyright the photos. As long as he was authorized to make the photos (he was), he owned the copyright in the photos to the extent of their incremental original expression. In requiring permission to make *and* permission to copyright the photos, the district court relied on language in *Gracen v. Bradford Exchange*, 698 F.2d 300 (7th Cir. 1983), suggesting that both are required for copyright in a derivative work. We have more recently explained, however, that copyright in a derivative work arises by operation of law—not through authority from the owner of the copyright in the underlying work—although the parties may alter this default rule by agreement. *See Liu v. Price Waterhouse LLP*, 302 F.3d 749, 755 (7th Cir. 2002). Schrock created the photos with permission and therefore owned the copyright to the photos *provided* they satisfied the other requirements for copyright and the parties did not contract around the default rule.

We also take this opportunity to clarify another aspect of *Gracen* that is prone to misapplication. *Gracen* said that "a derivative work must be substantially different from the underlying work to be copyrightable." 698 F.2d at 305. This statement should not be understood to require a heightened standard of originality for copyright in a derivative work. We have more recently explained that "the only 'originality' required for [a] new work to be copyrightable . . . is enough expressive variation from public-domain or other existing works to enable the new work to be readily distinguished from its predecessors." *Bucklew v. Hawkins, Ash, Baptie & Co., LLP*, 329 F.3d 923, 929 (7th Cir. 2003). Here, Schrock's photos of Learning Curve's "Thomas & Friends" toys possessed sufficient incremental original expression to qualify for copyright.

* * *

B. *Originality and Derivative Works*

* * *

Federal courts have historically applied a generous standard of originality in evaluating photographic works for copyright protection. *See, e.g., Ets-Hokin,* 225 F.3d at 1073–77; *SHL Imaging, Inc. v. Artisan House, Inc.,* 117 F.Supp.2d 301, 305 (S.D.N.Y. 2000). In some cases, the original expression may be found in the staging and creation of the scene depicted in the photograph. *See, e.g., Mannion v. Coors Brewing Co.,* 377 F.Supp.2d 444, 452 (S.D.N.Y. 2005). But in many cases, the photographer does not invent the scene or create the subject matter depicted in it. Rather, the original expression he contributes lies in the *rendition* of the subject matter-that is, the effect created by the combination of his choices of perspective, angle, lighting, shading, focus, lens, and so on. *See id.; Rogers v. Koons,* 960 F.2d 301, 307 (2d Cir.1992) ("Elements of originality in a photograph may include posing the subjects, lighting, angle, selection of film and camera, evoking the desired expression, and almost any other variant involved."). Most photographs contain at least some originality in their rendition, *see Mannion,* 377 F.Supp.2d at 452 ("Unless a photograph replicates another work with total or near-total fidelity, it will be at least somewhat original in the rendition."), except perhaps for a very limited class of photographs that can be characterized as "slavish copies" of an underlying work, *Bridgeman Art Library, Ltd. v. Corel Corp.,* 25 F.Supp.2d 421, 427 (S.D.N.Y.1998) (finding no originality in transparencies of paintings where the goal was to reproduce those works exactly and thus to minimize or eliminate any individual expression).

Our review of Schrock's photographs convinces us that they do not fall into the narrow category of photographs that can be classified as "slavish copies," lacking any independently created expression. To be sure, the photographs are accurate depictions of the three-dimensional "Thomas & Friends" toys, but Schrock's artistic and technical choices combine to create a two-dimensional image that is subtly but nonetheless sufficiently his own. This is confirmed by Schrock's deposition testimony describing his creative process in depicting the toys. Schrock explained how he used various camera and lighting techniques to make the toys look more "life like," "personable," and "friendly." He explained how he tried to give the toys "a little bit of dimension" and that it was his goal to make the toys "a little bit better than what they look like when you actually see them on the shelf." The original expression in the representative sample is not particularly great (it was not meant to be), but it is enough under the applicable standard to warrant the limited copyright protection accorded derivative works under § 103(b).

* * *

The defendants' second and more substantial argument is that it is not enough that Schrock's photographs might pass the ordinary test for originality; they claim that as derivative works, the photos are subject to a higher standard of originality. A leading copyright commentator disagrees. The Nimmer treatise maintains that the quantum of originality required for copyright in a derivative work is the same as that required for copyright in any other work. *See* 1 NIMMER ON COPYRIGHT § 3.01, at 3–2, § 3.03[A], at 3–7. More particularly, Nimmer says the relevant standard is whether a derivative work contains a "nontrivial" variation from the preexisting work "sufficient to render the derivative work distinguishable from [the] prior work in any meaningful manner." *Id.* § 3.03[A], at 3–10. The caselaw generally follows this formulation. *See, e.g., Eden Toys, Inc. v. Florelee Undergarment Co.,* 697 F.2d 27, 34–35 (2d Cir.1982) (holding that numerous minor changes in an illustration of Paddington Bear were sufficiently nontrivial because they combined to give Paddington a "different, cleaner 'look' "); *Millworth Converting Corp. v. Slifka,* 276 F.2d 443, 445 (2d Cir.1960) (holding that embroidered reproduction of a public-domain embroidery of Peter Pan was sufficiently distinguishable because the latter gave a "three-dimensional look" to the former embroidery).

Learning Curve and HIT argue that our decision in *Gracen* established a more demanding standard of originality for derivative works. *Gracen* involved an artistic competition in which artists were invited to submit paintings of the character Dorothy from the Metro-Goldwyn-Mayer ("MGM") movie *The Wizard of Oz.* Participating artists were given a still photograph of Dorothy from the film as an exemplar, and the paintings were solicited and submitted with the understanding that the best painting would be chosen for a series of collector's plates. *Gracen,* 698 F.2d at 301. Plaintiff Gracen prevailed in the competition, but she refused to sign the contract allowing her painting to be used in the collector's plates. The competition sponsor commissioned another artist to create a similar plate, and Gracen sued the sponsor, MGM, and the artist for copyright infringement. We held that Gracen could not maintain her infringement suit because her painting, a derivative work, was not "substantially different from the underlying work to be copyrightable." *Id.* at 305.

Gracen drew this language from an influential Second Circuit decision, *L. Batlin & Son, Inc. v. Snyder,* 536 F.2d 486 (2d Cir.1976). Read in context, however, the cited language from *L. Batlin* did not suggest that a heightened standard of originality applies to derivative works. To the contrary, the Second Circuit said only that to be copyrightable a work must " 'contain some substantial, not merely trivial originality.' " *Id.* at 490 (quoting *Chamberlin v. Uris Sales Corp.,* 150 F.2d 512, 513 (2d Cir.1945)). The court explained that for derivative works, as for any other work, "[t]he test of originality is concededly one with a low threshold in that all that is needed is that the author contributed something more than a merely trivial variation, something recognizably his own." *Id.* (internal quotation marks and ellipsis omitted).

The concern expressed in *Gracen* was that a derivative work could be so similar in appearance to the underlying work that in a subsequent infringement suit brought by a derivative author, it would be difficult to separate the original elements of expression in the derivative and underlying works in order to determine whether one derivative work infringed another. The opinion offered the example of artists A and B who both painted their versions of the Mona Lisa, a painting in the public domain. *See Gracen,* 698 F.2d at 304. "[I]f the difference between the original and A's reproduction is slight, the difference between A's and B's reproductions will also be slight, so that if B had access to A's reproductions the trier of fact will be hard-pressed to decide whether B was copying A or copying the Mona Lisa itself." *Id.*

No doubt this concern is valid. But nothing in the Copyright Act suggests that derivative works are subject to a more exacting originality requirement than other works of authorship. Indeed, we have explained since *Gracen* that "the only 'originality' required for [a] new work to by copyrightable . . . is enough expressive variation from public-domain or other existing works to enable the new work to be readily distinguished from its predecessors." *Bucklew,* 329 F.3d at 929. We emphasized in *Bucklew* that this standard does not require a "high degree of [incremental] originality." *Id.*

We think *Gracen* must be read in light of *L. Batlin,* on which it relied, and *Bucklew,* which followed it. And doing so reveals the following general principles: (1) the originality requirement for derivative works is not more demanding than the originality requirement for other works; and (2) the key inquiry is whether there is sufficient nontrivial expressive variation in the derivative work to make it distinguishable from the underlying work in some meaningful way. This focus on the presence of nontrivial "distinguishable variation" adequately captures the concerns articulated in *Gracen* without unduly narrowing the copyrightability of derivative works. It is worth repeating that the copyright in a derivative work is thin, extending only to the incremental original expression contributed by the author of the derivative work. *See* 17 U.S.C. § 103(b).

As applied to photographs, we have already explained that the original expression in a photograph generally subsists in its rendition of the subject matter. If the photographer's rendition of a copyrighted work varies enough from the underlying work to enable the photograph to be distinguished from the underlying work (aside from the obvious shift from three dimensions to two), then the photograph contains sufficient incremental originality to qualify for copyright. Schrock's photos of the "Thomas & Friends" toys are highly accurate product photos but contain minimally sufficient variation in angle, perspective, lighting, and dimension to be distinguishable from the underlying works; they are not "slavish copies." Accordingly, the photos qualify for the limited derivative-work copyright provided by § 103(b). *See SHL Imaging*, 117 F.Supp.2d at 311 (holding that copyright protection in product-accurate photographs was "thin"); *see also*, *Rockford Map Publishers, Inc. v. Directory Serv. Co. of Colo., Inc.*, 768 F.2d 145, 148 (7th Cir.1985) ("Perhaps the smaller the effort the smaller the contribution; if so, the copyright simply bestows fewer rights."). However narrow that copyright might be, it at least protects against the kind of outright copying that occurred here.

* * *

C. Authorization and Derivative Works

To be copyrightable, a derivative work must not be infringing. *See* 17 U.S.C. § 103(a). The owner of the copyright in the underlying work has the exclusive right to "prepare derivative works based upon the copyrighted work," 17 U.S.C. § 106(2), and "it is a copyright infringement to make or sell a derivative work without a license from the owner of the copyright on the work from which the derivative work is derived," *Bucklew*, 329 F.3d at 930. This means the author of a derivative work must have permission to make the work from the owner of the copyright in the underlying work; *Gracen* suggested, however, that the author of a derivative work must *also* have permission to *copyright* it. 698 F.2d at 303–04 ("[T]he question is not whether Miss Gracen was licensed to make a derivative work but whether she was also licensed to exhibit [her] painting and to copyright it. . . . Even if [Gracen] was authorized to exhibit her derivative works, she may not have been authorized to copyright them."). The district court relied on this language from *Gracen* to conclude that Schrock has no copyright in his photos because he was not authorized by Learning Curve to copyright them. This was error.

First, *Gracen*'s language presupposing a permission-to-copyright requirement was dicta; the case was actually decided on nonoriginality grounds. *Id.* at 305. More importantly, the dicta was mistaken; there is nothing in the Copyright Act requiring the author of a derivative work to obtain permission to copyright his work from the owner of the copyright in the underlying work. To the contrary, the Act provides that copyright in a derivative work, like copyright in any other work, arises by operation of law once the author's original expression is fixed in a tangible medium. "Copyright protection subsists . . . in original works of authorship fixed in any tangible medium of expression," 17 U.S.C. § 102(a), and "[t]he subject matter of copyright . . . includes . . . derivative works," *id.* § 103(a). * * * While the author of an original work "may obtain a certificate of copyright, which is '*prima facie* evidence' of its validity," *JCW Invs., Inc. v. Novelty, Inc.*, 482 F.3d 910, 915 (7th Cir. 2007), "copyright protection begins at the moment of creation of 'original works of authorship,'" *id.* at 914. This principle applies with equal force to derivative works.

The leading treatise on copyright law confirms this basic understanding. "[T]he right to claim copyright in a noninfringing derivative work arises by operation of law, not through authority from the copyright owner of the underlying work." 1 NIMMER ON COPYRIGHT § 3.06, at 3–34.34. We have cited Nimmer with approval on this point. *See Liu,* 302 F.3d at 755. As we noted in *Liu,* however, there is an important proviso explained in the treatise: "[I]f the pertinent agreement between the parties affirmatively bars the licensee from obtaining copyright protection even in a licensed derivative work, that contractual provision would appear to govern." 1 NIMMER ON COPYRIGHT § 3.06, at 3–34.34.

* * *

In this case, the evidence submitted with the summary-judgment motion does not establish as a matter of law that the parties adjusted Schrock's rights by contract; * * * it may be a jury question. We say "may" because further development of the record might resolve the remaining liability questions as a matter of law. It is undisputed that Schrock was authorized to photograph the "Thomas & Friends" toys, and as the creator of the photos, Schrock's copyright arose by operation of law. We cannot tell, however, whether the parties altered this default rule in their agreements. * * *

Accordingly, for all the foregoing reasons, we REVERSE the judgment of the district court and REMAND for further proceedings consistent with this opinion.

NOTES

1. Suppose that a writer publishes an unauthorized English-language translation of a copyrighted French novel. Can she claim a copyright in her translation? *See* 17 U.S.C. § 103(a).

2. Suppose that a short story was adapted into a motion picture with the consent of the story's copyright owner. Some years later, the motion picture enters the public domain because the movie studio failed to comply with certain copyright formalities. Does the owner of copyright in the short story have a copyright claim against parties that make and distribute copies of the public domain motion picture? *See Russell v. Price,* 612 F.2d 1123 (9th Cir. 1979). Alternatively, suppose the short story enters the public domain before the motion picture (which would be the more common scenario). Does the owner of the motion picture copyright have a copyright claim against the maker of a second motion picture based on the same story?

4. USEFUL ARTICLES

Statutes: 17 U.S.C. §§ 101, 113

MAZER V. STEIN

347 U.S. 201, 74 S.Ct. 460 (1954).

MR. JUSTICE REED delivered the opinion of the Court.

This case involves the validity of copyrights obtained by respondents for statuettes of male and female dancing figures made of semivitreous china. The controversy centers around the fact that although copyrighted as "works of art," the statuettes were intended for use and used as bases for table lamps, with electric wiring, sockets and lamp shades attached. [The defendant contended that the statuettes were not copyrightable because plaintiff intended to, and did, mass produce them and use them as lamp bases.]

* * *

This Court once essayed to fix the limits of the fine arts. That effort need not be appraised in relation to this copyright issue. It is clear Congress intended the scope of the [1909] copyright statute to include more than the traditional fine arts. Herbert Putnam, Esq., then Librarian of Congress and active in the movement to amend the copyright laws, told the joint meeting of the House and Senate Committees:

> * * * "The term 'works of art' is deliberately intended as a broader specification than 'works of the fine arts' in the present statute with the idea that there is subject-matter (for instance, of applied design, not yet within the province of design patents), which may properly be entitled to protection under the copyright law."

The successive acts, the legislative history of the 1909 Act and the practice of the Copyright Office unite to show that "works of art" and "reproductions of works of art" are terms that were intended by Congress to include the authority to copyright these statuettes. Individual perception of the beautiful is too varied a power to permit a narrow or rigid concept of art. * * *

But petitioners assert that congressional enactment of the design patent laws should be interpreted as denying protection to artistic articles embodied or reproduced in manufactured articles. They say:

> "Fundamentally and historically, the Copyright Office is the repository of what each claimant considers to be a cultural treasure, whereas the Patent Office is the repository of what each applicant considers to be evidence of the advance in industrial and technological fields."

Their argument is that design patents require the critical examination given patents to protect the public against monopoly. Attention is called to *Gorham Mfg. Co. v. White*, 14 Wall. 511, interpreting the design patent law of 1842, 5 Stat. 544, granting a patent to anyone who by "their own industry, genius, efforts, and expense, may have invented or produced any new and original design for a manufacture * * *." A pattern for flat silver was there upheld. The intermediate and present law differs little. "Whoever invents any new, original and ornamental design for an article of manufacture may obtain a patent therefor, . . ." subject generally to the provisions concerning patents for invention. § 171, 66 Stat. 805. As petitioner sees the effect of the design patent law:

> "If an industrial designer can not satisfy the novelty requirements of the design patent laws, then his design as used on articles of manufacture can be copied by anyone."

Petitioner has furnished the Court a booklet of numerous design patents for statuettes, bases for table lamps and similar articles for manufacture, quite indistinguishable in type from the copyrighted statuettes here in issue. Petitioner urges that overlapping of patent and copyright legislation so as to give an author or inventor a choice between patents and copyrights should not be permitted. We assume petitioner takes the position that protection for a statuette for industrial use can only be obtained by patent, if any protection can be given.

As we have held the statuettes here involved copyrightable, we need not decide the question of their patentability. Though other courts have passed upon the issue as to whether allowance by the election of the author or patentee of one bars a grant of the other, we do not. We do hold that the patentability of the statuettes, fitted as lamps or unfitted, does not bar copyright as works of art. Neither the Copyright Statute nor any other says that because a thing is patentable it may not be copyrighted. We should not so hold.

* * * The copyright protects originality rather than novelty or invention—conferring only "the sole right of multiplying copies." Absent copying there can be no infringement of copyright. Thus, respondents may not exclude others from using statuettes of human figures in table lamps; they may only prevent use of copies of their statuettes as such or as incorporated in some other article. [Copyright Office] Regulation § 202.8, *supra*, makes clear that artistic articles are protected in "form but not their mechanical or utilitarian aspects." *See Stein v. Rosenthal*, 103 F.Supp. 227, 231. The dichotomy of protection for the aesthetic is not beauty and utility but art for the copyright and the invention of original and ornamental design for design patents. We find nothing in the copyright statute to support the argument that the intended use or use in industry of an article

eligible for copyright bars or invalidates its registration. We do not read such a limitation into the copyright law.

* * *

"The copyright law, like the patent statutes, makes reward to the owner a secondary consideration." *United States v. Paramount Pictures*, 334 U.S. 131, 158. However, it is "intended definitely to grant valuable, enforceable rights to authors, publishers, etc., without burdensome requirements; 'to afford greater encouragement to the production of literary [or artistic] works of lasting benefit to the world.'" *Washingtonian Co. v. Pearson*, 306 U.S. 30, 36.

The economic philosophy behind the clause empowering Congress to grant patents and copyrights is the conviction that encouragement of individual effort by personal gain is the best way to advance public welfare through the talents of authors and inventors in "Science and useful Arts." Sacrificial days devoted to such creative activities deserve rewards commensurate with the services rendered.

Affirmed.

STAR ATHLETICA, L.L.C. V. VARSITY BRANDS, INC.

580 U.S. 405, 137 S.Ct. 1002 (2017).

JUSTICE THOMAS delivered the opinion of the Court.

Congress has provided copyright protection for original works of art, but not for industrial designs. The line between art and industrial design, however, is often difficult to draw. This is particularly true when an industrial design incorporates artistic elements. Congress has afforded limited protection for these artistic elements by providing that "pictorial, graphic, or sculptural features" of the "design of a useful article" are eligible for copyright protection as artistic works if those features "can be identified separately from, and are capable of existing independently of, the utilitarian aspects of the article." 17 U.S.C. § 101.

We granted certiorari to resolve widespread disagreement over the proper test for implementing § 101's separate-identification and independent-existence requirements. We hold that a feature incorporated into the design of a useful article is eligible for copyright protection only if the feature (1) can be perceived as a two- or three-dimensional work of art separate from the useful article and (2) would qualify as a protectable pictorial, graphic, or sculptural work—either on its own or fixed in some other tangible medium of expression—if it were imagined separately from the useful article into which it is incorporated. Because that test is satisfied in this case, we affirm.

I

Respondents Varsity Brands, Inc., Varsity Spirit Corporation, and Varsity Spirit Fashions & Supplies, Inc., design, make, and sell cheerleading uniforms. Respondents have obtained or acquired more than 200 U.S. copyright registrations for two-dimensional designs appearing on the surface of their uniforms and other garments. These designs are primarily "combinations, positionings, and arrangements of elements" that include "chevrons . . ., lines, curves, stripes, angles, diagonals, inverted [chevrons], coloring, and shapes."

Petitioner Star Athletica, L.L.C., also markets and sells cheerleading uniforms. Respondents sued petitioner for infringing their copyrights in the five designs. The District Court entered summary judgment for petitioner on respondents' copyright claims on the ground that the designs did not qualify as protectable pictorial, graphic, or sculptural works. It reasoned that the designs served the useful, or "utilitarian," function of identifying the garments as "cheerleading uniforms" and therefore could not be "physically or conceptually" separated under § 101 "from the utilitarian function" of the uniform.

The Court of Appeals for the Sixth Circuit reversed. In its view, the "graphic designs" were "separately identifiable" because the designs "and a blank cheerleading uniform can appear 'side by side'—one as a graphic design, and one as a cheerleading uniform." And it determined that the designs were " 'capable of existing independently' " because they could be incorporated onto the surface of different types of garments, or hung on the wall and framed as art.

Judge McKeague dissented. He would have held that, because "identifying the wearer as a cheerleader" is a utilitarian function of a cheerleading uniform and the surface designs were "integral to" achieving that function, the designs were inseparable from the uniforms.

II

* * *

"Works of authorship" include "pictorial, graphic, and sculptural works," § 102(a)(5), which the statute defines to include "two-dimensional and three-dimensional works of fine, graphic, and applied art, photographs, prints and art reproductions, maps, globes, charts, diagrams, models, and technical drawings, including architectural plans," § 101. * * *

The Copyright Act also establishes a special rule for copyrighting a pictorial, graphic, or sculptural work incorporated into a "useful article," which is defined as "an article having an intrinsic utilitarian function that is not merely to portray the appearance of the article or to convey information." *Ibid.* The statute does not protect useful articles as such. Rather, "the design of a useful article" is "considered a pictorial, graphical, or sculptural work only if, and only to the extent that, such design incorporates pictorial, graphic, or sculptural features that can be identified separately from, and are capable of existing independently of, the utilitarian aspects of the article." *Ibid.*

Courts, the Copyright Office, and commentators have described the analysis undertaken to determine whether a feature can be separately identified from, and exist independently of, a useful article as "separability." In this case, our task is to determine whether the arrangements of lines, chevrons, and colorful shapes appearing on the surface of respondents' cheerleading uniforms are eligible for copyright protection as separable features of the design of those cheerleading uniforms.

A

As an initial matter, we must address whether separability analysis is necessary in this case.

1

Respondents argue that "[s]eparability is only implicated when a [pictorial, graphic, or sculptural] work is the 'design of a useful article.'" They contend that the surface decorations in this case are "two-dimensional graphic designs that appear on useful articles," but are not themselves designs of useful articles. Consequently, the surface decorations are protected two-dimensional works of graphic art without regard to any separability analysis under § 101. *See* 2 W. Patry, Copyright § 3:151, p. 3–485 (2016) (Patry) ("Courts looking at two-dimensional design claims should not apply the separability analysis regardless of the three-dimensional form that design is embodied in"). Under this theory, two-dimensional artistic features on the surface of useful articles are "inherently separable."

This argument is inconsistent with the text of § 101. The statute requires separability analysis for any "pictorial, graphic, or sculptural features" incorporated into the "design of a useful article." "Design" refers here to "the combination" of "details" or "features" that "go to make up" the useful article. 3 Oxford English Dictionary 244 (def. 7, first listing) (1933) (OED). Furthermore, the words "pictorial" and "graphic" include, in this context, two-dimensional features such as pictures, paintings, or drawings. *See* 4 *id.*, at 359 (defining "[g]raphic" to mean "[o]f or pertaining to drawing or painting"); 7 *id.*, at 830 (defining "[p]ictorial" to mean "of or pertaining to painting or drawing"). And the statute expressly defines "[p]ictorial, graphical, and sculptural works" to include "two-dimensional . . . works of . . . art." § 101. The statute thus provides that the "design of a useful article" can include two-dimensional "pictorial" and "graphic" features, and separability analysis applies to those features just as it does to three-dimensional "sculptural" features.

* * *

B

We must now decide when a feature incorporated into a useful article "can be identified separately from" and is "capable of existing independently of" "the utilitarian aspects" of the article. This is not a free-ranging search for the best copyright policy, but rather "depends solely on statutory interpretation." *Mazer v. Stein*, 347 U.S. 201 (1954). "The controlling principle in this case is the basic and unexceptional rule that courts must give effect to the clear meaning of statutes as written." *Estate of Cowart v. Nicklos Drilling Co.*, 505 U.S. 469, 476 (1992). We thus begin and end our inquiry with the text, giving each word its "ordinary, contemporary, common meaning." *Walters v. Metropolitan Ed. Enterprises, Inc.*, 519 U.S. 202, 207 (1997) (internal quotation marks omitted). We do not, however, limit this inquiry to the text of § 101 in isolation. "[I]nterpretation of a phrase of uncertain reach is not confined to a single sentence when the text of the whole statute gives instruction as to its meaning." *Maracich v. Spears*, 133 S.Ct. 2191, 2203 (2013). We thus "look to the provisions of the whole law" to determine § 101's meaning. *United States v. Heirs of Boisdore*, 8 How. 113, 122 (1849).

1

The statute provides that a "pictorial, graphic, or sculptural featur[e]" incorporated into the "design of a useful article" is eligible for copyright protection if it (1) "can be identified separately from," and (2) is "capable of existing independently of, the utilitarian aspects of the article." § 101. The first requirement—separate identification—is not onerous. The decisionmaker need only be able to look at the useful article and spot some two- or three-dimensional element that appears to have pictorial, graphic, or sculptural qualities.

The independent-existence requirement is ordinarily more difficult to satisfy. The decisionmaker must determine that the separately identified feature has the capacity to exist apart from the utilitarian aspects of the article. In other words, the feature must be able to exist as its own pictorial, graphic, or sculptural work as defined in § 101 once it is imagined apart from the useful article. If the feature is not capable of existing as a pictorial, graphic, or sculptural work once separated from the useful article, then it was not a pictorial, graphic, or sculptural feature of that article, but rather one of its utilitarian aspects.

Of course, to qualify as a pictorial, graphic, or sculptural work on its own, the feature cannot itself be a useful article or "[a]n article that is normally a part of a useful article" (which is itself considered a useful article). § 101. Nor could someone claim a copyright in a useful article merely by creating a replica of that article in some other medium—for example, a cardboard model of a car. Although the replica could itself be copyrightable, it would not give rise to any rights in the useful article that inspired it.

2

The statute as a whole confirms our interpretation. The Copyright Act provides "the owner of [a] copyright" with the "exclusive righ[t] . . . to reproduce the copyrighted work in copies." § 106(1). The statute clarifies that this right "includes the right to reproduce the [copyrighted] work in or on any kind of article, whether useful or otherwise." § 113(a). Section 101 is, in essence, the mirror image of § 113(a). Whereas § 113(a) protects a work of authorship first fixed in some tangible medium other than a useful article and subsequently applied to a useful article, § 101 protects art first fixed in the medium of a useful article. The two provisions make clear that copyright protection extends to pictorial, graphic, and sculptural works regardless of whether they were created as freestanding art or as features of useful articles. The ultimate separability question, then, is whether the feature for which copyright protection is claimed would have been eligible for copyright protection as a pictorial, graphic, or sculptural work had it originally been fixed in some tangible medium other than a useful article before being applied to a useful article.

3

This interpretation is also consistent with the history of the Copyright Act. In *Mazer*, a case decided under the 1909 Copyright Act, the respondents copyrighted a statuette depicting a dancer. The statuette was intended for use as a lamp base, "with electric wiring, sockets and lamp shades attached." 347 U.S. at 202. Copies of the statuette were sold both as lamp bases and separately as statuettes. The petitioners copied the statuette and sold lamps with the statuette as the base. They defended against the respondents' infringement suit by arguing that the respondents did not have a copyright in a statuette intended for use as a lamp base.

Two of *Mazer*'s holdings are relevant here. First, the Court held that the respondents owned a copyright in the statuette even though it was intended for use as a lamp base. In doing so, the Court approved the Copyright Office's regulation extending copyright protection to works of art that might also serve a useful purpose. *See ibid.* (approving 37 C.F.R. § 202.8(a) (1949) (protecting "works of artistic craftsmanship, in so far as their form but not their mechanical or utilitarian aspects are concerned")).

Second, the Court held that it was irrelevant to the copyright inquiry whether the statuette was initially created as a freestanding sculpture or as a lamp base. 347 U.S., at 218–219 ("Nor do we think the subsequent registration of a work of art published as an element in a manufactured article, is a misuse of copyright. This is not different from the registration of a statuette and its later embodiment in an industrial article"). *Mazer* thus interpreted the 1909 Act consistently with the rule discussed above: If a design would have been copyrightable as a standalone pictorial, graphic, or sculptural work, it is copyrightable if created first as part of a useful article.

Shortly thereafter, the Copyright Office enacted a regulation implementing the holdings of *Mazer*. As amended, the regulation introduced the modern separability test to copyright law:

> "If the sole intrinsic function of an article is its utility, the fact that the article is unique and attractively shaped will not qualify it as a work of art. However, if the shape of a utilitarian article incorporates features, such as artistic sculpture, carving, or pictorial representation, which can be identified separately and are capable of existing independently as a work of art, such features will be eligible for registration." 37 C.F.R. § 202.10(c) (1960).

Congress essentially lifted the language governing protection for the design of a useful article directly from the post-*Mazer* regulations and placed it into § 101 of the 1976 Act. Consistent with *Mazer*, the approach we outline today interprets §§ 101 and 113 in a way that would afford copyright protection to the statuette in *Mazer* regardless of whether it was first created as a standalone sculptural work or as the base of the lamp.

C

In sum, a feature of the design of a useful article is eligible for copyright if, when identified and imagined apart from the useful article, it would qualify as a pictorial, graphic, or sculptural work either on its own or when fixed in some other tangible medium.

Applying this test to the surface decorations on the cheerleading uniforms is straightforward. First, one can identify the decorations as features having pictorial, graphic, or sculptural qualities. Second, if the arrangement of colors, shapes, stripes, and chevrons on the surface of the cheerleading uniforms were separated from the uniform and applied in another medium—for example, on a painter's canvas—they would qualify as "two-dimensional . . . works of . . . art," § 101. And imaginatively removing the surface decorations from the uniforms and applying them in another medium would not replicate the uniform itself. Indeed, respondents have applied the designs in this case to other media of expression—different types of clothing—without replicating the uniform. The decorations are therefore separable from the uniforms and eligible for copyright protection.

The dissent argues that the designs are not separable because imaginatively removing them from the uniforms and placing them in some other medium of expression—a canvas, for example—would create "pictures of cheerleader uniforms." Petitioner similarly argues that the decorations cannot be copyrighted because, even when extracted from the useful article, they retain the outline of a cheerleading uniform.

This is not a bar to copyright. Just as two-dimensional fine art corresponds to the shape of the canvas on which it is painted, two-dimensional applied art correlates to the contours of the article on which it is applied. A fresco painted on a wall, ceiling panel, or dome would not lose copyright protection, for example, simply because it was designed to track the dimensions of the surface on which it was painted. Or consider, for example, a design etched or painted on the surface of a guitar. If that entire design is imaginatively removed from the guitar's surface and placed on an album cover, it would still resemble the shape of a guitar. But the image on the cover does not "replicate" the guitar as a useful article. Rather, the design is a two-dimensional work of art that corresponds to the shape of the useful article to which it was applied. The statute protects that work of art whether it is first drawn on the album cover and then applied to the guitar's surface, or vice versa. Failing to protect that art would create an anomaly: It would extend protection to two-dimensional designs that cover a part of a useful article but would not protect the same design if it covered the entire article. The statute does not support that distinction, nor can it be reconciled with the dissent's recognition that "artwork printed on a t-shirt" could be protected.

To be clear, the only feature of the cheerleading uniform eligible for a copyright in this case is the two-dimensional work of art fixed in the tangible medium of the uniform fabric. Even if respondents ultimately succeed in establishing a valid copyright in the surface decorations at issue here, respondents have no right to prohibit any person from manufacturing a cheerleading uniform of identical shape, cut, and dimensions to the ones on which the decorations in this case appear. They may prohibit only the reproduction of the surface designs in any tangible medium of expression—a uniform or otherwise.

D

Petitioner and the Government raise several objections to the approach we announce today. None is meritorious.

1

Petitioner first argues that our reading of the statute is missing an important step. It contends that a feature may exist independently only if it can stand alone as a copyrightable work and if the useful article from which it was extracted would remain equally useful. In other words, copyright extends only to "solely artistic" features of useful articles. According to petitioner, if a feature of a useful article "advance[s] the utility of the article," then it is categorically beyond the scope of copyright. The designs here are not protected, it argues, because they are necessary to two of the uniforms' "inherent, essential, or natural functions"—identifying the wearer as a cheerleader and enhancing the wearer's physical appearance. Because the uniforms would not be equally useful without the designs, petitioner contends that the designs are inseparable from the "utilitarian aspects" of the uniform.

The Government raises a similar argument, although it reaches a different result. It suggests that the appropriate test is whether the useful article with the artistic feature removed would "remai[n] similarly useful." In the view of the United States, however, a plain white cheerleading uniform is "similarly useful" to uniforms with respondents' designs.

The debate over the relative utility of a plain white cheerleading uniform is unnecessary. The focus of the separability inquiry is on the extracted feature and not on any aspects of the useful article that remain after the imaginary extraction. The statute does not require the decisionmaker to imagine a fully functioning useful article without the artistic feature. Instead, it requires that the separated feature qualify as a nonuseful pictorial, graphic, or sculptural work on its own.

Of course, because the removed feature may not be a useful article—as it would then not qualify as a pictorial, graphic, or sculptural work—there necessarily would be some aspects of the original useful article "left behind" if the feature were conceptually removed. But the statute does not require the imagined remainder to be a fully functioning useful article at all, much less an equally useful one. Indeed, such a requirement would deprive the *Mazer* statuette of protection had it been created first as a lamp base rather than as a statuette. Without the base, the "lamp" would be just a shade, bulb, and wires. The statute does not require that we imagine a nonartistic replacement for the removed feature to determine whether that feature is capable of an independent existence.

Petitioner's argument follows from its flawed view that the statute protects only "solely artistic" features that have no effect whatsoever on a useful article's utilitarian function. This view is inconsistent with the statutory text. The statute expressly protects two- and three-dimensional "applied art." § 101. "Applied art" is art "employed in the decoration, design, or execution of useful objects," Webster's Third New International Dictionary 105 (1976) (emphasis added), or "those arts or crafts that have a primarily utilitarian function, or . . . the designs and decorations used in these arts," Random House Dictionary 73 (1966); *see also* 1 OED 576 (2d ed. 1989) (defining "applied" as "[p]ut to practical use"). An artistic feature that would be eligible for copyright protection on its own cannot lose that protection simply because it was first created as a feature of the design of a useful article, even if it makes that article more useful.

Indeed, this has been the rule since *Mazer*. In holding that the statuette was protected, the Court emphasized that the 1909 Act abandoned any "distinctions between purely aesthetic articles and useful works of art." 347 U.S., at 211. Congress did not enact such a distinction in the 1976 Act. Were we to accept petitioner's argument that the only protectable features are those that play absolutely no role in an article's function, we would effectively abrogate the rule of *Mazer* and read "applied art" out of the statute.

Because we reject the view that a useful article must remain after the artistic feature has been imaginatively separated from the article, we necessarily abandon the distinction between "physical" and "conceptual" separability, which some courts and commentators have adopted based on the Copyright Act's legislative history. *See* H.R. Rep. No. 94–1476, p. 55 (1976). According to this view, a feature is physically separable from the underlying useful article if it can "be physically separated from the article by ordinary means while leaving the utilitarian aspects of the article completely intact." Compendium § 924.2(A). Conceptual separability applies if the feature physically could not be removed from the useful article by ordinary means.

The statutory text indicates that separability is a conceptual undertaking. Because separability does not require the underlying useful article to remain, the physical-conceptual distinction is unnecessary.

2

Petitioner next argues that we should incorporate two "objective" components into our test to provide guidance to the lower courts: (1) "whether the design elements can be identified as reflecting the designer's artistic judgment exercised independently of functional influence," and (2) whether "there is [a] substantial likelihood that the pictorial, graphic, or sculptural feature would still be marketable to some significant segment of the community without its utilitarian function."

We reject this argument because neither consideration is grounded in the text of the statute. The first would require the decisionmaker to consider evidence of the creator's design methods, purposes, and reasons. The statute's text makes clear, however, that our inquiry is limited to how the article and feature are perceived, not how or why they were designed. *See Brandir Int'l, Inc. v. Cascade Pacific Lumber Co.*, 834 F.2d 1142, 1152 (C.A.2 1987) (Winter, J., concurring in part and dissenting in part) (The statute "expressly states that the legal test is how the final article is perceived, not how it was developed through various stages").

The same is true of marketability. Nothing in the statute suggests that copyrightability depends on market surveys. Moreover, asking whether some segment of the market would be interested in a given work threatens to prize popular art over other forms, or to substitute judicial aesthetic preferences for the policy choices embodied in the Copyright Act. *See Bleistein v. Donaldson Lithographing Co.*, 188 U.S. 239, 251 (1903) ("It would be a dangerous undertaking for persons trained only to the law to constitute themselves final judges of the worth of pictorial illustrations, outside of the narrowest and most obvious limits").

3

Finally, petitioner argues that allowing the surface decorations to qualify as a "work of authorship" is inconsistent with Congress' intent to entirely exclude industrial design from copyright. Petitioner notes that Congress refused to pass a provision that would have provided limited copyright protection for industrial designs, including clothing, when it enacted the 1976 Act, *see* S. 22, Tit. II, 94th Cong., 2d Sess., 122 Cong. Rec. 3856–3859 (1976), and that it has enacted laws protecting designs for specific useful articles—semiconductor chips and boat hulls, *see* 17 U.S.C. §§ 901–914, 1301–1332—while declining to enact other industrial design statutes. From this history of failed legislation petitioner reasons that Congress intends to channel intellectual property claims for industrial design into design patents. It therefore urges us to approach this question with a presumption against copyrightability.

We do not share petitioner's concern. As an initial matter, "[c]ongressional inaction lacks persuasive significance" in most circumstances. *Pension Benefit Guaranty Corporation v. LTV Corp.*, 496 U.S. 633, 650 (1990). Moreover, we have long held that design patent and copyright are not mutually exclusive. *See Mazer*, 347 U.S., at 217. Congress has provided for limited copyright protection for certain features of industrial design, and approaching the statute with presumptive hostility toward protection for industrial design would undermine Congress' choice. In any event, as explained above, our test does not render the shape, cut, and physical dimensions of the cheerleading uniforms eligible for copyright protection.

III

We hold that an artistic feature of the design of a useful article is eligible for copyright protection if the feature (1) can be perceived as a two- or three-dimensional work of art separate from the useful article and (2) would qualify as a protectable pictorial, graphic, or sculptural work either on its own or in some other medium if imagined separately from the useful article. Because the designs on the surface of respondents' cheerleading uniforms in this case satisfy these requirements, the judgment of the Court of Appeals is affirmed.

JUSTICE GINSBURG, concurring in the judgment.

I concur in the Court's judgment but not in its opinion. Unlike the majority, I would not take up in this case the separability test appropriate under 17 U.S.C. § 101. Consideration of that test is unwarranted because the designs at issue are not designs of useful articles. Instead, the designs are themselves copyrightable pictorial or graphic works reproduced on useful articles.

* * *

The designs here in controversy are standalone pictorial and graphic works that respondents Varsity Brands, Inc., et al. (Varsity) reproduce on cheerleading uniforms. Varsity's designs first appeared as pictorial and graphic works that Varsity's design team sketched on paper. * * *

In short, Varsity's designs are not themselves useful articles meet for separability determination under § 101; they are standalone PGS works that may gain copyright protection as such, including the exclusive right to reproduce the designs on useful articles.

JUSTICE BREYER, with whom JUSTICE KENNEDY joins, dissenting.

I agree with much in the Court's opinion. But I do not agree that the designs that Varsity Brands, Inc., submitted to the Copyright Office are eligible for copyright protection. Even applying the majority's test, the designs cannot "be perceived as . . . two- or three-dimensional work[s] of art separate from the useful article."

Look at the designs that Varsity submitted to the Copyright Office. *See* Appendix to opinion of the Court, ante. You will see only pictures of cheerleader uniforms. And cheerleader uniforms are useful articles. A picture of the relevant design features, whether separately "perceived" on paper or in the imagination, is a picture of, and thereby "replicate[s]," the underlying useful article of which they are a part. Hence the design features that Varsity seeks to protect are not "capable of existing independently o[f] the utilitarian aspects of the article."

* * *

NOTES

1. In the first appellate opinion to apply *Star Athletica,* the Third Circuit held that the non-utilitarian sculptural features of a full-body banana costume satisfied the Court's two-part test, because they could be separately imagined as a banana sculpture. *Silvertop Assocs. v. Kangaroo Mfg.*, 931 F.3d 215 (3d Cir. 2019).

2. In *Brandir International, Inc. v. Cascade Pacific Lumber Co.*, 834 F.2d 1142 (2d Cir. 1987), the Second Circuit held that the "Ribbon rack" bicycle rack was not eligible for copyright protection. The design originated from a work of sculptural art but was then modified to make it serve functionally as a bike rack. What would be the result today in light of *Star Athletica*? Could the Ribbon Rack be protected by a design patent? A utility patent?

3. In *Pivot Point International Inc. v. Charlene Products Inc.*, 372 F.3d 913 (7th Cir. 2004), the Seventh Circuit applied the *Brandir* analysis to

conclude that a hair-styling mannequin head with the "hungry-look" of a runway model had artistic features that were physically and conceptually separable from its utilitarian aspects, and was therefore copyrightable. What would be the result under *Star Athletica*?

4. Would copyright protect artist Christo's "Running Fence," which consisted of an 18-foot tall "fence" made of white nylon fabric, stretched over 24.5 miles of undulating hillside terrain, where the appearance of the fence was affected by wind and light? Would your answer change if Christo were a property owner who placed his "Running Fence" around his property in order to delineate its boundaries, protect livestock, or discourage trespassers?

5. Consider the copyrightability of the following: A seamstress's mannequin shaped like a male or female torso? A taxidermist's mannequins shaped like a fish, a deer's head, or the full body of a bear? A teddy bear? A toy truck? A board game (*e.g.*, Monopoly)? Theatrical or Halloween costumes? A sofa? A fishing lure? A shovel?

6. Does copyright protect full-size replicas of the Batmobile? A pre-*Star Athletica* case, *DC Comics v. Towle*, 802 F.3d 1012 (9th Cir. 2015), involved replicas of the Batmobile as it appeared in both the 1966 television show and the 1989 Motion Picture. Defendant Towle made and sold these full-size replicas to car collectors as part of his business at "Gotham Garage." The Ninth Circuit held that the Batmobile, as it appeared graphically in comic books, and as a three-dimensional car in television series and motion pictures, was an especially distinctive character entitled to copyright protection and that Towle's production and sale of replicas of the Batmobile infringed the exclusive right to produce derivative works. The court held that the Batmobile was entitled to copyright protection because: (1) it had physical and conceptual qualities because it appeared graphically in comic books, and as a "three-dimensional car in television series and motion pictures;" (2) the Batmobile was "sufficiently delineated" to be recognizable wherever it appeared; and (3) it is "especially distinctive" and contains unique elements of expression because along with its character traits and physical characteristics it had its "unique and highly recognizable name." *Id.* at 1021–22.

7. In *Lamps Plus, Inc. v. Seattle Lighting Fixture Co.*, 345 F.3d 1140 (9th Cir. 2003), the Second Circuit held that merely combining several useful, unprotectable elements does not rise to the level of originality that affords copyright protection, stating:

> Lamps Plus's mechanical combination of four preexisting ceiling-lamp elements with a preexisting table-lamp base did not result in the expression of an original work of authorship as required by § 101. Lamps Plus did not create any of the "design . . . features that can be identified separately from, and are capable of existing independently of, the utilitarian aspects" of any of the lamp's component parts.

345 F.3d at 1147. Would the result be the same under *Star Athletica*?

8. *Sui Generis Protection for Boat Hull Designs:* The Digital Millenium Copyright Act, Pub. L. No. 105–304 (signed Oct. 28, 1998), introduced *sui generis* protection for boat hull designs, to replace the type of state law protection which the Supreme Court held to be preempted in *Bonito Boats, Inc. v. Thunder Craft Boats, Inc.*, 489 U.S. 141 (1989) (*see* Chapter 19.B.2.). Title V of the Act, titled the "Vessel Hull Design Protection Act," adds a new Chapter 13 to Title 17 which gives the owner of an original boat hull design the exclusive right for 10 years to make, import, sell, or distribute articles embodying that design for sale or use in trade, notwithstanding the intrinsic utilitarian function of the design. The new provision imposes a marking requirement, limits infringement liability to cases in which the infringing article was created with knowledge that its design was copied from a protected design, exempts copying that is solely for teaching or evaluative purposes, and requires that a design be registered with the Copyright Office before an infringement suit can be filed. Infringement remedies include injunctions, seizure and destruction of the infringing articles, attorneys' fees, and either damages (including enhanced damages) or the infringer's profits. Issuance of a design patent for a vessel hull design preempts Chapter 13 protection for that design, but Chapter 13 does not preempt either (a) federal or state protection for unregistered designs or (b) trademark or unfair competition laws. The new provision was initially scheduled to expire after two years, but has subsequently been extended.

9. *Fashion Designs:* Because fashion designs (meaning the shape and structure of garments, as opposed to the surface decoration of their fabrics) have generally been denied copyright protection under the useful articles doctrine, sui generis protection has been proposed from time to time. Some of these proposals have been modeled on the Vessel Hull Design Protection Act. Are fashion designs copyrightable after *Star Athletica*? If not, then what, if any, type of protection should be afforded to fashion designs?

5. ARCHITECTURAL WORKS

Prior to 1990, drawings and blueprints depicting architectural works had been copyrightable in the "pictorial, graphic, and sculptural works category." However, it was not clear whether copying such a design from the building itself infringed the copyright. The Architectural Works Copyright Protection Act of 1990 attempted to resolve this issue. It applies to works created on or after December 1, 1990.

ARCHITECTURAL WORKS COPYRIGHT PROTECTION ACT OF 1990

H.R. Rep. No. 101–735.
101st Cong., 2d Sess. 11, 18–21 (1990).

* * *

Article 2(1) of the Berne Convention requires member countries to provide copyright for "works of architecture"—the constructed design of buildings. This category of subject matter is distinct from "illustrations, plans, sketches and three-dimensional works relative to architecture," which are also required to be protected under Article 2(1). The current U.S. Copyright Act expressly includes "diagrams, models, and technical drawings, including architectural plans" as a species of protected "pictorial, graphic, and sculptural work." It does not, however, expressly protect "works of architecture," although this Committee's Report accompanying the 1976 Copyright Act contemplated that at least selected works of architecture—those containing elements physically or conceptually separable from their utilitarian function—would be protected to the extent of their separability. * * *

Section 202. Definitions

Section 202 adds a new definition ("architectural work") to the Copyright Act and amends an existing definition ("Berne Convention work").

Subsection (a) amends section 101 of title 17, United States Code, to provide a definition of the subject matter protected by the bill, "architectural works." * * *

* * * The protected work i[s] the design of a building. The term "design" includes the overall form as well as the arrangement and composition of spaces and elements in the design. The phrase "arrangement and composition of spaces and elements" recognizes that: (1) creativity in architecture frequently takes the form of a selection, coordination, or arrangement of unprotectible elements into an original, protectible whole; (2) an architect may incorporate new, protectible design elements into otherwise standard, unprotectible building features; and (3) interior architecture may be protected.

Consistent with other provis[i]ons of the Copyright Act and Copyright Office regul[a]tions, the definition makes clear that protection does not extend to individual standard features, such as common windows, doors, and other staple building components. A grant of exclusive rights in such features would impede, rather than promote, the progress of architectural innovation. The provision is not, however, intended to ex[c]lude from the copyright in the architectural work any individual features that reflect the [a]rchitect's creativity.

* * *

During the Subcommittee's 1990 hearing, testimony was received that a potential gap in protection may exist where an architectural work has been depicted in plans or drawings, but has not yet been constructed. Since the original definition of architectural work in H.R. 3990 referred only to architectural works "as embodied in" buildings, there was concern that a defendant with access to the plans or drawings could construct an identical building but escape liability so long as the plans or drawings were not copied.

The Register of Copyright disagrees that liability could be avoided in such circumstances, arguing that the witnesses misconstrued the access prong of infringement analysis. The Register's position, based on general principles of copyright law, is that where a three-dimensional work meets the standard for protection, infringement may lie regardless of whether access to the three-dimensional work is obtained from a two-dimensional or three-dimensional depiction thereof.

In order to resolve this debate, subsection 202(a) of title II of H.R. 5498 modifies the definition of architectural work so that a work of architecture may be embodied in the built design—the constructed three-dimensional building—or in plans, drawings, or in "any tangible medium of expression," such as a blueprint or computer disk. Protection for architectural plans, drawings, and models as pictorial, graphic, or sculptural works under section 102(a)(5), title 17, United States Code, is unaffected by this bill.

This change does, however, raise questions regarding the relationship between copyright in the architectural work and copyright in plans and drawings. The bill's intention is to keep these two forms of protection separate. An individual creating an architectural work by depicting that work in plans or drawing will have two separate copyrights, one in the architectural work (section 102(a)(8)), the other in the plans or drawings (section 102(a)(5)). * * *

The Subcommittee made a second amendment in the definition of architectural work: the deletion of the phrase "or three-dimensional structure." This phrase was included in H.R. 3990 to cover cases where architectural works embodied in innovative structures that defy easy classification. Unfortunately, the phrase also could be interpreted as covering interstate highway bridges, cloverleafs, canals, dams, and pedestrian walkways. The Subcommittee examined protection for these works, some of which form important elements of this nation's transportation system, and determined that copyright protection is not necessary to stimulate creativity or prohibit unauthorized reproduction.

The sole purpose of legislating at this time is to place the United States unequivocally in compliance with its Berne Convention obligations. Protection for bridges and related nonhabitable three-dimensional structures is not required by the Berne Convention. Accordingly, the question of copyright protection for these works can be deferred to another day. As a consequence, the phrase "or other three-dimensional structures" was deleted from the definition of architectural work and from all other places in the bill.

This deletion, though, raises more sharply the question of what is meant by the term "building." Obviously, the term encompassed habitable structures such as houses and office buildings. It also covers structures that are used, but not inhabited, by human beings, such as churches, pergolas, gazebos, and garden pavilions.

Subsection (b) amends the definitions of "Berne Convention work" in section 101, title 17, United States Code, to provide a point of attachment for national eligibility purposes. An architectural work is a "Berne Convention work" if the building in which the architectural work is embodied "is erected in a country adhering to the Berne Convention." This amendment is necessitated by United States membership in the Berne Union.

Section 203. Subject Matter of Copyright

* * * By creating a new category of protectible subject matter in new section 102(a)(8), and, therefore, by deliberately not encompassing architectural works as pictorial, graphic, or sculptural works in existing section 102(a)(5), the copyrightability of architectural works shall not be evaluated under the separability test applicable to pictorial, graphic, or sculptural works embodied in useful articles. There is considerable scholarly and judicial disagreement over how to apply the separability test, and the principal reason for not treating architectural works as pictorial, graphic, or sculptural works is to avoid entangling architectural works in this disagreement.

The Committee does not suggest, though, that in evaluating the copyrightability or scope of protection for architectural works, the Copyright Office or the courts should ignore functionality. A two-step analysis is envisioned. First, an architectural work should be examined to determine whether there are original design elements present, including overall shape and interior architecture. If such design elements are present, a second step is reached to examine whether the design elements are functionally required. If the design elements are not functionally required, the work is protectible without regard to physical or conceptual separability. As a consequence, contrary to the Committee's report accompanying the 1976 Copyright Act with respect to industrial products, the aesthetically pleasing overall shape of an architectural work could be protected under this bill.

The proper scope of protection for architectural works is distinct from registrability. Functional considerations may, for example, determine only particular design elements. Protection would be denied for the functionally determined elements, but would be available for the nonfunctionally determined elements. Under such circumstances, the Copyright Office should issue a certificate of registration, letting the courts determine the scope of protection. In each case, the courts must be free to decide the issue upon the facts presented, free of the separability conundrum presented by the useful articles doctrine applicable for pictorial, graphic, and sculptural works. Evidence that there is more than one method of obtaining a given functional result may be considered in evaluating registrability or the scope of protection.

The proposed legislation incorporates the general standards of originality applicable for all other copyrightable subject matter. * * *

NOTES

1. What kinds of architectural design elements are sufficiently nonfunctional to be copyrightable under current law but would not have been copyrightable before the effective date of the 1990 amendments? For a case on the protectability of architectural plans, *see Savant Homes Inc. v. Collins*, 809 F.3d 1133 (10th Cir. 2016) (plaintiff failed to show that the plan included any protectable element or arrangement of elements).

2. At the hearings preceding enactment of the 1990 architectural works provisions, several experts testified that the designs of buildings were already copyrightable under the 1976 Act regardless of whether they were embodied in drawings or in three-dimensional structures, and that further legislation was therefore unnecessary in order to comply with the requirements of the Berne Convention. Do you agree? If so, does copyright already extend to the types of structures that Congress intended to exclude from the definition of "architectural works"? For example, would a design for a bridge or a highway overpass be copyrightable? Does *Star Athletica* affect this analysis? *Should* these designs be copyrightable?

3. Is a garage an architectural work? A treehouse? A doghouse?

4. Most pre-1990 case law indicated that, despite *Baker v. Selden*, copying architectural plans was an infringement even if the purpose of copying them was to construct the building they depicted, *see Imperial Homes Corp. v. Lamont*, 458 F.2d 895 (5th Cir. 1972); *Demetriades v. Kaufmann*, 680 F.Supp. 658 (S.D.N.Y. 1988); *but see Scholz Homes, Inc. v. Maddox*, 379 F.2d 84 (6th Cir. 1967) (applying *Baker* to reach contrary holding). However, the same opinions distinguished the situation where the only copying that took place was the actual construction of the building depicted in the plans, finding that copyright should not exclude others from implementing the ideas revealed in the plans. Do the 1990 amendments overrule this line of cases?

6. UNITED STATES GOVERNMENT WORKS

Statute: 17 U.S.C. § 105

COPYRIGHT ACT OF 1976

H.R. Rep. No. 94–1476.
94th Cong., 2d Sess. 58–59 (1976).

Section 105. U.S. Government Works

Scope of the prohibition

* * *

The general prohibition against copyright in section 105 applies to "any work of the United States Government," which is defined in section 101 as "a work prepared by an officer or employee of the United States Government as part of that person's official duties." Under this definition a Government official or employee would not be prevented from securing copyright in a work written at that person's own volition and outside his or her duties, even though the subject matter involves the Government work or professional field of the official or employee. Although the wording of the definition of "work of the United States Government" differs somewhat from that of the definition of "work made for hire," the concepts are intended to be construed in the same way.

A more difficult and far-reaching problem is whether the definition should be broadened to prohibit copyright in works prepared under U.S. Government contract or grant. As the bill is written, the Government agency concerned could determine in each case whether to allow an independent contractor or grantee to secure copyright in works prepared in whole or in part with the use of Government funds. * * *

The prohibition on copyright protection for United States Government works is not intended to have any effect on protection of these works abroad. Works of the governments of most other countries are copyrighted. There are no valid policy reasons for denying such protection to United States Government works in foreign countries, or for precluding the Government from making licenses for the use of its works abroad.

* * *

NOTES

1. Does section 105 mean that the federal government can never own a copyright? To what extent can a state, local or foreign government own copyrights?

2. Suppose that a federal official writes and delivers a speech at a college graduation, a National Press Club luncheon, an academic conference,

or a trade association gathering. In which case(s), if any, is the speech copyrightable, and by whom?

7. GOVERNMENT EDICTS

GEORGIA V. PUBLIC.RESOURCE.ORG, INC.

___ U.S. ___, 140 S.Ct. 1498 (2020).

CHIEF JUSTICE ROBERTS delivered the opinion of the Court.

The Copyright Act grants potent, decades-long monopoly protection for "original works of authorship." 17 U.S.C. § 102(a). The question in this case is whether that protection extends to the annotations contained in Georgia's official annotated code.

We hold that it does not. Over a century ago, we recognized a limitation on copyright protection for certain government work product, rooted in the Copyright Act's "authorship" requirement. Under what has been dubbed the government edicts doctrine, officials empowered to speak with the force of law cannot be the authors of—and therefore cannot copyright—the works they create in the course of their official duties.

We have previously applied that doctrine to hold that non-binding, explanatory legal materials are not copyrightable when created *by judges* who possess the authority to make and interpret the law. See *Banks v. Manchester*, 128 U.S. 244 (1888). We now recognize that the same logic applies to non-binding, explanatory legal materials created *by a legislative body* vested with the authority to make law. Because Georgia's annotations are authored by an arm of the legislature in the course of its legislative duties, the government edicts doctrine puts them outside the reach of copyright protection.

I

A

The State of Georgia has one official code—the "Official Code of Georgia Annotated," or OCGA. The first page of each volume of the OCGA boasts the State's official seal and announces to readers that it is "Published Under Authority of the State."

The OCGA includes the text of every Georgia statute currently in force, as well as various non-binding supplementary materials. At issue in this case is a set of annotations that appear beneath each statutory provision. The annotations generally include summaries of judicial decisions applying a given provision, summaries of any pertinent opinions of the state attorney general, and a list of related law review articles and similar reference materials. In addition, the annotations often include editor's notes that provide information about the origins of the statutory text, such as whether it derives from a particular judicial decision or resembles an older provision that has been construed by Georgia courts.

The OCGA is assembled by a state entity called the Code Revision Commission. In 1977, the Georgia Legislature established the Commission to recodify Georgia law for the first time in decades. The Commission was (and remains) tasked with consolidating disparate bills into a single Code for reenactment by the legislature and contracting with a third party to produce the annotations. * * * Under the Georgia Constitution, the Commission's role in compiling the statutory text and accompanying annotations falls "within the sphere of legislative authority."

* * *

The annotations in the current OCGA were prepared in the first instance by Matthew Bender & Co., Inc., a division of the LexisNexis Group, pursuant to a work-for-hire agreement with the Commission. The agreement between Lexis and the Commission states that any copyright in the OCGA vests exclusively in "the State of Georgia, acting through the Commission." Lexis and its army of researchers perform the lion's share of the work in drafting the annotations, but the Commission supervises that work and specifies what the annotations must include in exacting detail. Under the agreement, Lexis enjoys the exclusive right to publish, distribute, and sell the OCGA. * * *

[When Public.Resource.Org (PRO) made an unlicensed copy of the OCGA available on the Internet, the Commission filed suit on behalf of the state of Georgia. The district court found PRO liable for copyright infringement, the Eleventh Circuit reversed, and the Supreme Court granted certiorari.]

* * *

II

We hold that the annotations in Georgia's Official Code are ineligible for copyright protection, though for reasons distinct from those relied on by the Court of Appeals. A careful examination of our government edicts precedents reveals a straightforward rule based on the identity of the author. Under the government edicts doctrine, judges—and, we now confirm, legislators—may not be considered the "authors" of the works they produce in the course of their official duties as judges and legislators. That rule applies regardless of whether a given material carries the force of law. And it applies to the annotations here because they are authored by an arm of the legislature in the course of its official duties.

A

We begin with precedent. The government edicts doctrine traces back to a trio of cases decided in the 19th century. In this Court's first copyright case, *Wheaton v. Peters*, 8 Pet. 591 (1834), the Court's third Reporter of Decisions, Wheaton, sued the fourth, Peters, unsuccessfully asserting a copyright interest in the Justices' opinions. In Wheaton's view, the opinions "must have belonged to some one" because "they were new, original," and much more "elaborate" than law or custom required. Wheaton argued that the Justices were the authors and had assigned their ownership interests to him through a tacit "gift." The Court unanimously rejected that argument, concluding that "no reporter has or can have any copyright in the written opinions delivered by this court" and that "the judges thereof cannot confer on any reporter any such right."

That conclusion apparently seemed too obvious to adorn with further explanation, but the Court provided one a half century later in *Banks v. Manchester*, 128 U.S. 244 (1888). That case concerned whether Wheaton's state-court counterpart, the official reporter of the Ohio Supreme Court, held a copyright in the judges' opinions and several non-binding explanatory materials prepared by the judges. The Court concluded that he did not, explaining that "the judge who, in his judicial capacity, prepares the opinion or decision, the statement of the case and the syllabus or head note" cannot "be regarded as their author or their proprietor, in the sense of [the Copyright Act]." Pursuant to "a judicial *consensus*" dating back to *Wheaton*, judges could not assert copyright in "whatever work they perform in their capacity as judges." Rather, "[t]he whole work done by the judges constitutes the authentic exposition and interpretation of the law, which, binding every citizen, is free for publication to all." *Ibid.*

In a companion case decided later that Term, *Callaghan v. Myers*, 128 U.S. 617 (1888), the Court identified an important limiting principle. As in *Wheaton* and *Banks*, the Court rejected the claim that an official reporter held a copyright interest in the judges' opinions. But, resolving an issue not addressed in *Wheaton* and *Banks*, the Court upheld the reporter's copyright interest in several explanatory materials that the reporter had created himself: headnotes, syllabi, tables of contents, and the like. *Callaghan*, 128 U.S. at 645, 647. Although these works mirrored the judge-made materials rejected in *Banks*, they came from an author who had no authority to speak with the force of law. Because the reporter was not a judge, he was free to "obtain[ ] a copyright" for the materials that were "the result of his [own] intellectual labor." 128 U.S. at 647.

These cases establish a straightforward rule: Because judges are vested with the authority to make and interpret the law, they cannot be the "author" of the works they prepare "in the discharge of their judicial duties." *Banks*, 128 U.S. at 253. This rule applies both to binding works (such as opinions) and to non-binding works (such as headnotes and syllabi). It does not apply, however, to works created by government officials (or private parties) who lack the authority to make or interpret the law, such as court reporters.

The animating principle behind this rule is that no one can own the law. "Every citizen is presumed to know the law," and "it needs no argument to show . . . that all should have free access" to its contents. *Nash*, 142 Mass. at 35. Our cases give effect to that principle in the copyright context through construction of the statutory term "author." Rather than attempting to catalog the materials that constitute "the law," the doctrine bars the officials responsible for creating the law from being considered the "author[s]" of "*whatever work* they perform in their capacity" as lawmakers. Because these officials are generally empowered to make and interpret law, their "whole work" is deemed part of the "authentic exposition and interpretation of the law" and must be "free for publication to all."

If judges, acting as judges, cannot be "authors" because of their authority to make and interpret the law, it follows that legislators, acting as legislators, cannot be either. Courts have thus long understood the government edicts doctrine to apply to legislative materials.

Moreover, just as the doctrine applies to "whatever work [judges] perform in their capacity as judges," *Banks*, 128 U.S., at 253, it applies to whatever work legislators perform in their capacity as legislators. That of course includes final legislation, but it also includes explanatory and procedural materials legislators create in the discharge of their legislative duties. In the same way that judges cannot be the authors of their headnotes and syllabi, legislators cannot be the authors of (for example) their floor statements, committee reports, and proposed bills. These materials are part of the "whole work done by [legislators]," so they must be "free for publication to all." *Ibid.*

Under our precedents, therefore, copyright does not vest in works that are (1) created by judges and legislators (2) in the course of their judicial and legislative duties.

B

1

Applying that framework, Georgia's annotations are not copyrightable. The first step is to examine whether their purported author qualifies as a legislator.

As we have explained, the annotations were prepared in the first instance by a private company (Lexis) pursuant to a work-for-hire agreement with Georgia's Code Revision Commission. The Copyright Act therefore deems the Commission the sole "author" of the work. 17 U.S.C. § 201(b). * * *

If there were any doubt about the link between the Commission and the legislature, the Georgia Supreme Court has dispelled it by holding that, under the Georgia Constitution, "the work of the Commission; *i.e.*, selecting a publisher and contracting for and supervising the codification of the laws enacted by the General Assembly, including court interpretations thereof, *is within the sphere of legislative authority.*" *Harrison Co.*, 244 Ga. at 330. * * *

2

The second step is to determine whether the Commission creates the annotations in the "discharge" of its legislative "duties." *Banks*, 128 U.S. at 253. It does. Although the annotations are not enacted into law through bicameralism and presentment, the Commission's preparation of the annotations is under Georgia law an act of "legislative authority," *Harrison Co.*, 244 Ga. at 330, 260 S.E.2d at 34, and the annotations provide commentary and resources that the legislature has deemed relevant to understanding its laws. * * *

In light of the Commission's role as an adjunct to the legislature and the fact that the Commission authors the annotations in the course of its legislative responsibilities, the annotations in Georgia's Official Code fall within the government edicts doctrine and are not copyrightable.

III

Georgia resists this conclusion on several grounds. At the outset, Georgia advances two arguments for why, in its view, excluding the OCGA annotations from copyright protection conflicts with the text of the Copyright Act. Both are unavailing.

First, Georgia notes that § 101 of the Act specifically lists "annotations" among the kinds of works eligible for copyright protection. But that provision refers only to "annotations . . . which . . . represent an original work of *authorship*." 17 U.S.C. § 101. The whole point of the government edicts doctrine is that judges and legislators cannot serve as authors when they produce works in their official capacity. While the reference to "annotations" in § 101 may help explain why supplemental, explanatory materials are copyrightable when prepared by a private party, or a non-lawmaking official like the reporter in *Callaghan*, it does not speak to whether those same materials are copyrightable when prepared by a judge or a legislator. In the same way that judicial materials are ineligible for protection even though they plainly qualify as "[l]iterary works . . . expressed in words," *ibid.*, legislative materials are ineligible for protection even if they happen to fit the description of otherwise copyrightable "annotations."

Second, Georgia draws a negative inference from the fact that the Act excludes from copyright protection "work[s] prepared by an officer or employee of the United States Government as part of that person's official duties" and does not establish a similar rule for the States. § 101; see also § 105. But the bar on copyright protection for federal works sweeps much more broadly than the government edicts doctrine does. That bar applies to works created by all federal "officer[s] or employee[s]," without regard for the nature of their position or scope of their authority. Whatever policy reasons might justify the Federal Government's decision to forfeit copyright protection for its own proprietary works, that federal rule does not suggest an intent to displace the much narrower government edicts doctrine with respect to the States. That doctrine does not apply to non-lawmaking officials, leaving States free to assert copyright in the vast majority of expressive works they produce, such as those created by their universities, libraries, tourism offices, and so on.

* * *

Turning to our government edicts precedents, Georgia insists that they can and should be read to focus exclusively on whether a particular work has "the force of law." * * * But that framing has multiple flaws.

Most obviously, it cannot be squared with the reasoning or results of our cases—especially *Banks*. *Banks*, following *Wheaton* and the "judicial consensus" it inspired, denied copyright protection to judicial opinions without excepting concurrences and dissents that carry no legal force. As every judge learns the hard way, "comments in [a] dissenting opinion" about legal principles and precedents "are just that: comments in a dissenting opinion." *Railroad Retirement Bd. v. Fritz*, 449 U.S. 166, 177, n. 10 (1980). Yet such comments are covered by the government edicts doctrine because they come from an official with authority to make and interpret the law.

Indeed, *Banks* went even further and withheld copyright protection from headnotes and syllabi produced by judges. Surely these supplementary materials do not have the force of law, yet they are covered by the doctrine. The simplest explanation is the one *Banks* provided: These non-binding works are not copyrightable because of who creates them—judges acting in their judicial capacity.

The same goes for non-binding legislative materials produced by legislative bodies acting in a legislative capacity. There is a broad array of such works ranging from floor statements to proposed bills to committee reports. Under the logic of Georgia's "force of law" test, States would own such materials and could charge the public for access to them.

* * *

Georgia minimizes the OCGA annotations as non-binding and non-authoritative, but that description undersells their practical significance. Imagine a Georgia citizen interested in learning his legal rights and duties. If he reads the economy-class version of the Georgia Code available online, he will see laws requiring political candidates to pay hefty qualification fees (with no indigency exception), criminalizing broad categories of consensual sexual conduct, and exempting certain key evidence in criminal trials from standard evidentiary limitations—with no hint that important aspects of those laws have been held unconstitutional by the Georgia Supreme Court. Meanwhile, first-class readers with access to the annotations will be assured that these laws are, in crucial respects, unenforceable relics that the legislature has not bothered to narrow or repeal.

If everything short of statutes and opinions were copyrightable, then States would be free to offer a whole range of premium legal works for those who can afford the extra benefit. A State could monetize its entire suite of legislative history. With today's digital tools, States might even launch a subscription or pay-per-law service.

* * *

Thankfully, there is a clear path forward that avoids these concerns—the one we are already on. Instead of examining whether given material carries "the force of law," we ask only whether the author of the work is a judge or a legislator. If so, then whatever work that judge or legislator produces in the course of his judicial or legislative duties is not copyrightable. That is the framework our precedents long ago established, and we adhere to those precedents today.

NOTES

1. How does the copyright exclusion under the government edicts doctrine compare to the exclusion under section 105? For example, would informational materials related to the influenza vaccine be subject to a different analysis depending on whether they were prepared by the federal government or a state or local government?

2. Does copyright protect a model law or code drafted by a non-governmental entity? What if the model law is later adopted as the governing law of a state or municipality? *See, e.g., Veeck v. Southern Bldg. Code Cong. Int'l, Inc.,* 293 F.3d 791 (5th Cir. 2002) (holding that copyright protected municipal building codes written by a private entity only until cities adopted the codes).

3. The American Medical Association (AMA) developed and published a system of codes for identifying medical procedures, and asserted copyright in the coding system. The federal government later licensed the codes and made their use mandatory for Medicare and Medicaid claims. Does this affect the AMA's copyright? Should the analysis be the same as that which applies to model legal codes? *See Practice Management Information Corp. v. American Medical Ass'n,* 121 F.3d 516 (9th Cir. 1997).

4. Consider the following facts: A state legislature revises its statutes without assigning any section numbers to indicate where in the state code the new provisions should appear. A publisher of state codes determines the proper placement of the new provisions, and identifies them by the section number of

the immediately preceding code section followed by an identifier (such as A or AA) generated by the publisher. To what extent, if any, can the publisher assert a copyright in its compilation of the state laws? Does it matter whether the state adopts that compilation as the "official" code? What if, for all practical purposes, the only sources of the state code to which most persons have access are copyrighted works? *See Texas v. West Pub. Co.*, 882 F.2d 171 (5th Cir.1989).

8. NATIONAL ORIGIN RESTRICTIONS

Statute: 17 U.S.C. § 104

Although United States copyright has extended to works by foreign authors since 1891, some restrictions based on national origin remain. Under current law, copyright in unpublished works exists regardless of the author's nationality or domicile. In the case of published works, however, copyright exists only if the work fits within at least one of the five categories set forth in section 104(b)(1)–(5). Generally speaking, the works that fail this test are works which are first published outside the United States or any other nation that is a member of the Berne Convention or the Universal Copyright Convention (a pre-Berne international copyright convention to which the United States is a signatory), *and* which do not have at least one author that is a stateless person, a national or domiciliary of the United States or a national, domiciliary or sovereign authority of one of our copyright treaty partners. Protection extends to architectural works and pictorial, graphic or sculptural works that are incorporated in buildings located in countries belonging to the Berne Convention, to works first published by the United Nations or the Organization of American States, and to works simultaneously first published in a Berne country and in a non-Berne country. The President is authorized to extend protection to other foreign works only upon finding that the nation of authorship or first publication extends nondiscriminatory protection to United States works. Thus, in general, the United States does not extend its copyright protection to published works originating in countries that fail to provide nondiscriminatory protection to works originating in the United States.

The WIPO Copyright and Performances and Phonograms Treaties Implementation Act of 1998, contained in Title I of the Digital Millennium Copyright Act (DMCA), Pub. L. No. 105–304 (1998), revised the copyright statutes to conform to the requirements of the WIPO Copyright Treaty and the WIPO Performances and Phonograms Treaty. Section 102 of the DMCA revised §§ 101, 104, and 104A of Title 17 to reflect the United States' adherence to those treaties.

CHAPTER 15

OWNERSHIP, ASSIGNMENT, AND LICENSING OF COPYRIGHTS

■ ■ ■

A. INITIAL OWNERSHIP

1. IDENTIFYING THE AUTHOR

Statutes: 17 U.S.C. §§ 101 (as needed), 201–02, 1401

a. Joint Works

CHILDRESS V. TAYLOR

945 F.2d 500 (2d Cir. 1991).

NEWMAN, CIRCUIT JUDGE.

This appeal requires consideration of the standards for determining when a contributor to a copyrighted work is entitled to be regarded as a joint author. The work in question is a play about the legendary Black comedienne Jackie "Moms" Mabley. The plaintiff-appellee Alice Childress claims to be the sole author of the play. Her claim is disputed by defendant-appellant Clarice Taylor, who asserts that she is a joint author of the play. * * *

Facts

[Actress Taylor asked playwright Childress to write her a play based on the life of legendary black comedienne Jackie "Moms" Mabley. While Childress was writing the play, the two spoke regularly about its progress, and Taylor contributed her own research and ideas. Childress registered the script's copyright in her own name, and declined to enter an agreement for co-ownership with Taylor. Taylor then hired another writer, Caldwell, to revise the play without Childress's consent.]

* * *

Taylor identifies the following as her major contributions to the play: (1) she learned through interviews that "Moms" Mabley called all of her piano players "Luther," so Taylor suggested that the play include such a character; (2) Taylor and Childress together interviewed Carey Jordan, "Moms" Mabley's housekeeper, and upon leaving the interview they came to the conclusion that she would be a good character for the play, but Taylor could not recall whether she or Childress suggested it; (3) Taylor informed Childress that "Moms" Mabley made a weekly trip to Harlem to do ethnic food shopping; (4) Taylor suggested a street scene in Harlem with speakers because she recalled having seen or listened to such a scene many times; (5) the idea of using a minstrel scene came out of Taylor's research; (6) the idea of a card game scene also came out of Taylor's research, although Taylor could not recall who specifically suggested the scene; (7) some of the jokes used in the play came from Taylor's research; and (8) the characteristics of "Moms" Mabley's personality portrayed in the play emerged from Taylor's research. Essentially, Taylor contributed facts and details about "Moms" Mabley's life and discussed some of them with Childress. However, Childress was responsible for the actual structure of the play and the dialogue.

* * *

Childress sued Taylor and other defendants alleging violations of the Copyright Act, 17 U.S.C. § 101 et seq. (1988) * * *. Taylor contended that she was a joint author with Childress, and therefore shared the rights to the play. Childress moved for summary judgment, which the District Court granted. The Court concluded that Taylor was not a joint author of Childress's play and that Caldwell's play was substantially similar to and infringed Childress's play. In rejecting Taylor's claim of joint authorship, Judge Haight ruled (a) that a work qualifies as a "joint work" under the definition section of the Copyright Act, 17 U.S.C. § 101, only when both authors intended, at the time the work was created, "that their contributions be merged into inseparable or interdependent parts of a unitary whole," *id.*, and (b) that there was insufficient evidence to permit a reasonable trier to find that Childress had the requisite intent. The Court further ruled that copyright law requires the contributions of both authors to be independently copyrightable, and that Taylor's contributions, which consisted of ideas and research, were not copyrightable.

Discussion

In common with many issues arising in the domain of copyrights, the determination of whether to recognize joint authorship in a particular case requires a sensitive accommodation of competing demands advanced by at least two persons, both of whom have normally contributed in some way to the creation of a work of value. Care must be taken to ensure that true collaborators in the creative process are accorded the perquisites of co-authorship and to guard against the risk that a sole author is denied exclusive authorship status simply because another person rendered some form of assistance. Copyright law best serves the interests of creativity when it carefully draws the bounds of "joint authorship" so as to protect the legitimate claims of both sole authors and co-authors.

* * *

The Copyright Act defines a "joint work" as

> a work prepared by two or more authors with the intention that their contributions be merged into inseparable or interdependent parts of a unitary whole.

17 U.S.C. § 101. As Professor Nimmer has pointed out, this definition is really the definition of a work of joint authorship. *See* 1 NIMMER ON COPYRIGHT § 6.01 (1991). The definition concerns the creation of the work by the joint authors, not the circumstances, in addition to joint authorship, under which a work may be jointly owned, for example, by assignment of an undivided interest. The distinction affects the rights that are acquired. Joint authors hold undivided interests in a work, like all joint owners of a work, but joint authors, unlike other joint owners, also enjoy all the rights of authorship, including the renewal rights applicable to works in which a statutory copyright subsisted prior to January 1, 1978. *See* 17 U.S.C. § 304.

* * *

The legislative history also clarifies other aspects of the statutory definition, but leaves some matters in doubt. Endeavoring to flesh out the definition, the committee reports state:

> [A] work is "joint" if the authors collaborated with each other, or if *each* of the authors prepared his or her contribution with the knowledge and *intention* that it would be merged with the contributions of other authors as "inseparable or interdependent parts of a unitary whole." The touchstone here is the *intention, at the time the writing is done*, that the parts be absorbed or combined into an integrated unit. . . .

House Report at 120; Senate Report at 103 (emphasis added). This passage appears to state two alternative criteria—one focusing on the act of collaboration and the other on the parties' intent. However, it is hard to imagine activity that would constitute meaningful "collaboration" unaccompanied by the requisite intent on the part of both participants that their contributions be merged into a unitary whole, and the case law has read the statutory language literally so that the intent requirement applies to all works of joint authorship. *See, e.g., Weissmann v. Freeman*, 868 F.2d 1313, 1317–19 (2d Cir.1989); *Eckert v. Hurley Chicago Co., Inc.*, 638 F. Supp. 699, 702–03 (N.D.Ill.1986).

A more substantial issue arising under the statutory definition of "joint work" is whether the contribution of each joint author must be copyrightable or only the combined result of their joint efforts must be copyrightable. The Nimmer treatise argues against a requirement of copyrightability of each author's contribution, *see* 1 NIMMER ON COPYRIGHT § 6.07; Professor Goldstein takes the contrary view, *see* 1 PAUL GOLDSTEIN,

COPYRIGHT: PRINCIPLES, LAW AND PRACTICE § 4.2.1.2 (1989), with the apparent agreement of the Latman treatise, *see* WILLIAM F. PATRY, LATMAN'S THE COPYRIGHT LAW 116 (6th ed. 1986). The case law supports a requirement of copyrightability of each contribution. * * * The Register of Copyrights strongly supports this view, arguing that it is required by the statutory standard of "authorship" and perhaps by the Constitution. *See* Moral Rights in Our Copyright Laws: Hearings on S. 1198 and S. 1253 Before the Subcomm. on Patents, Copyrights and Trademarks of the Senate Comm. on the Judiciary, 101st Cong., 1st Sess. 210–11 (1989) (statement of Ralph Oman).

The issue, apparently open in this Circuit, is troublesome. If the focus is solely on the objective of copyright law to encourage the production of creative works, it is difficult to see why the contributions of all joint authors need be copyrightable. An individual creates a copyrightable work by combining a non-copyrightable idea with a copyrightable form of expression; the resulting work is no less a valuable result of the creative process simply because the idea and the expression came from two different individuals. Indeed, it is not unimaginable that there exists a skilled writer who might never have produced a significant work until some other person supplied the idea. The textual argument from the statute is not convincing. The Act surely does not say that each contribution to a joint work must be copyrightable, and the specification that there be "authors" does not necessarily require a copyrightable contribution. "Author" is not defined in the Act and appears to be used only in its ordinary sense of an originator. The "author" of an uncopyrightable idea is nonetheless its author even though, for entirely valid reasons, the law properly denies him a copyright on the result of his creativity. And the Register's tentative constitutional argument seems questionable. It has not been supposed that the statutory grant of "authorship" status to the employer of a work made for hire exceeds the Constitution, though the employer has shown skill only in selecting employees, not in creating protectable expression.

Nevertheless, we are persuaded to side with the position taken by the case law and endorsed by the agency administering the Copyright Act. The insistence on copyrightable contributions by all putative joint authors might serve to prevent some spurious claims by those who might otherwise try to share the fruits of the efforts of a sole author of a copyrightable work, even though a claim of having contributed copyrightable material could be asserted by those so inclined. More important, the prevailing view strikes an appropriate balance in the domains of both copyright and contract law. In the absence of contract, the copyright remains with the one or more persons who created copyrightable material. Contract law enables a person to hire another to create a copyrightable work, and the copyright law will recognize the employer as "author." 17 U.S.C. § 201(b). Similarly, the person with non-copyrightable material who proposes to join forces with a skilled writer to produce a copyrightable work is free to make a contract to disclose his or her material in return for assignment of part ownership of the resulting copyright. *Id.* § 201(d). And, as with all contract matters, the parties may minimize subsequent disputes by formalizing their agreement in a written contract. *Cf.* 17 U.S.C. § 101 ("work made for hire" definition of "specially ordered" or "commissioned" work includes requirement of written agreement). It seems more consistent with the spirit of copyright law to oblige all joint authors to make copyrightable contributions, leaving those with non-copyrightable contributions to protect their rights through contract.

There remains for consideration the crucial aspect of joint authorship—the nature of the intent that must be entertained by each putative joint author at the time the contribution of each was created. The wording of the statutory definition appears to make relevant only the state of mind regarding the unitary nature of the finished work—an intention "that their contributions be merged into inseparable or interdependent parts of a unitary whole." However, an inquiry so limited would extend joint author status to many persons who are not likely to have been within the contemplation of Congress. For example, a writer frequently works with an editor who makes numerous useful revisions to the first draft, some of which will consist of additions of copyrightable expression. Both intend their contributions to be merged into inseparable parts of a unitary whole, yet very few editors and even fewer writers would expect the editor to be accorded the status of joint author, enjoying an undivided half interest in the copyright in the published work. Similarly, research assistants may on occasion contribute to an author some protectable expression or merely a sufficiently original selection of factual material as would be entitled to a copyright, yet not be entitled to be regarded as a joint author of the work in which the contributed material appears. What distinguishes the writer-editor relationship and the writer-researcher relationship from the true joint author relationship is the lack of intent of both participants in the venture to regard themselves as joint authors.

Focusing on whether the putative joint authors regarded themselves as joint authors is especially important in circumstances, such as the instant case, where one person (Childress) is indisputably the dominant author of the work and the only issue is whether that person is the sole author or she and another (Taylor) are joint authors. * * * This concern requires less exacting consideration in the context of traditional forms of collaboration, such as between the creators of the words and music of a song.

In this case, appellant contends that Judge Haight's observation that "Childress never shared Taylor's notion that they were co-authors of the play" misapplies the statutory standard by focusing on whether Childress "intended the legal consequences which flowed from her prior acts." * * *

We do not think Judge Haight went so far. He did not inquire whether Childress intended that she and Taylor would hold equal undivided interests in the play. But he properly insisted that they entertain in their minds the concept of joint authorship, whether or not they understood precisely the legal consequences of that relationship. Though joint authorship does not require an understanding by the co-authors of the legal consequences of their relationship, obviously some distinguishing characteristic of the relationship must be understood in order for it to be the subject of their intent. In many instances, a useful test will be whether, in the absence of contractual agreements concerning listed authorship, each participant intended that all would be identified as co-authors. Though "billing" or "credit" is not decisive in all cases and joint authorship can exist without any explicit discussion of this topic by the parties, consideration of the topic helpfully serves to focus the fact-finder's attention on how the parties implicitly regarded their undertaking.

* * *

Examination of whether the putative co-authors ever shared an intent to be co-authors serves the valuable purpose of appropriately confining the bounds of joint authorship arising by operation of copyright law, while leaving those not in a true joint authorship relationship with an author free to bargain for an arrangement that will be recognized as a matter of both copyright and contract law. Joint authorship entitles the co-authors to equal undivided interests in the work, *see* 17 U.S.C. § 201(a); *Community for Creative Non-Violence v. Reid*, 846 F.2d 1485, 1498 (D.C.Cir.1988), *aff'd without consideration of this point*, 490 U.S. 730 (1989). That equal sharing of rights should be reserved for relationships in which all participants fully intend to be joint authors. The sharing of benefits in other relationships involving assistance in the creation of a copyrightable work can be more precisely calibrated by the participants in their contract negotiations regarding division of royalties or assignment of shares of ownership of the copyright, *see* 17 U.S.C. § 201(d).

In this case, the issue is not only whether Judge Haight applied the correct standard for determining joint authorship but also whether he was entitled to conclude that the record warranted a summary judgment in favor of Childress. We are satisfied that Judge Haight was correct as to both issues. We need not determine whether we agree with his conclusion that Taylor's contributions were not independently copyrightable since, even if they were protectable as expression or as an original selection of facts, we agree that there is no evidence from which a trier could infer that Childress had the state of mind required for joint authorship. As Judge Haight observed, whatever thought of co-authorship might have existed in Taylor's mind "was emphatically not shared by the purported co-author." There is no evidence that Childress ever contemplated, much less would have accepted, crediting the play as "written by Alice Childress and Clarice Taylor."

Childress was asked to write a play about "Moms" Mabley and did so. To facilitate her writing task, she accepted the assistance that Taylor provided, which consisted largely of furnishing the results of research concerning the life of "Moms" Mabley. As the actress expected to portray the leading role, Taylor also made some incidental suggestions, contributing ideas about the presentation of the play's subject and possibly some minor bits of expression. But there is no evidence that these aspects of Taylor's role ever evolved into more than the helpful advice that might come from the cast, the directors, or the producers of any play. A playwright does not so easily acquire a co-author.

* * *

NOTES

1. In *Erickson v. Trinity Theatre, Inc.*, 13 F.3d 1061 (7th Cir. 1994), the Seventh Circuit followed *Childress* in concluding that joint authorship required both separate copyrightability and intent to be co-authors. In finding intent necessary, the court observed:

> [T]he "collaboration alone" standard would frustrate the goal of the Act "to promote the Progress of Science and the useful Arts." U.S. Const. art. I, § 8, cl. 8. Seldom would an author subject his work to preregistration peer review if this were the applicable test. Those seeking copyrights would not seek further refinement that colleagues may offer if they risked losing their sole authorship. * * *

13 F.3d at 1069.

Does *Childress* require that *both* collaborators think of themselves as co-authors in order to create a joint work? Is this requirement appropriate? Supported by the statutes?

2. In *Thomson v. Larson*, 147 F.3d 195 (2d Cir. 1998), the Second Circuit followed *Childress* in affirming a district court's rejection of a dramaturg's claim that she was a co-author of the musical "Rent." Although the plaintiff's contributions appeared to be both copyrightable and substantial, the Second Circuit agreed with the lower court that the musical could not be a joint work because the principal author had never intended to share authorship with her. Is this a reasonable interpretation of the concept of "joint works"? Does it represent sound policy? If not, what legal standard would best distinguish true joint works? Can an editor be a co-author?

3. The *Erickson* court noted that Professor Melville Nimmer rejected the rule that a co-author's contribution must be separately copyrightable:

> Professor Nimmer, the late scholar on copyright, took the position that all that should be required to achieve joint author status is more

> than a de minimis contribution by each author. "De minimis" requires that "more than a word or line must be added by one who claims to be a joint author." NIMMER § 6.07, at 6–21. Professor Nimmer distinguishes his de minimis standard from the standard for copyrightability. *Id.* As an example, Professor Nimmer asserts that if two authors collaborate, with one contributing only uncopyrightable plot ideas and another incorporating those ideas into a completed literary expression, the two authors should be regarded as joint authors of the resulting work. *Id.*

13 F.3d at 1069–70. Does the Goldstein or the Nimmer standard better serve the goals of copyright? If an actor or producer provides detailed character and plot elements to a writer who supplies the dialogue, are they co-authors under Nimmer's standard? Under the Goldstein standard?

The Seventh Circuit modified the separate copyrightability requirement from *Erickson* in *Gaiman v. McFarlane,* 360 F.3d 644 (7th Cir. 2004). Gaiman, a writer, and McFarlane, an illustrator, collaborated on "Spawn" comic books. Jointly, Gaiman and McFarlane created the characters "Medieval Spawn," "Angela," and "Count Nicholas Cogliostro." Based on the nature of comic book creation, the court observed:

> [T]he decisions that say, rightly in the generality of cases, that each contributor to a joint work must make a contribution that if it stood alone would be copyrightable weren't thinking of the case in which it couldn't stand alone because of the nature of the particular creative process that had produced it.

360 F.3d at 659. Therefore, Gaiman's contribution of character traits and dialogue was sufficiently original for him to be considered a joint author.

The Federal Circuit embraced the separate copyrightability requirement (as well as the *Childress* analysis) in *Gaylord v. United States,* 595 F.3d 1364 (Fed. Cir. 2010), holding that government entities were not joint authors of a war memorial where their contributions consisted of general suggestions regarding the appearance and positioning of the sculpted soldiers; accordingly, the sculptor was the sole author of the commissioned work.

4. In *Erickson,* the court repeatedly emphasized that Erickson (whom it ultimately found to be the sole author) had the final say as to which of the other contributors' suggestions would be included in the final work (a play). How is this relevant to the question of joint authorship? How much weight should this factor receive?

5. The Ninth Circuit has adopted a variation on the *Childress* standard, holding in *Aalmuhammed v. Lee,* 202 F.3d 1227, 1234 (9th Cir. 2000), that joint authorship depends on three factors: (1) who exercised control over the creative effort; (2) whether the putative joint authors made "objective manifestations of a shared intent to be coauthors"; and (3) whether "the audience appeal of the work depends on both contributions and 'the share of each in its success cannot be appraised.' " The court added that "[c]ontrol in many cases will be the most

important factor." *Id.* Compared to *Childress*, is this standard more or less likely to achieve a sound result?

6. The legislative history of the 1976 Act includes the following discussion of the rights of co-authors:

> There is also no need for a specific statutory provision concerning the rights and duties of the coowners of a work; court-made law on this point is left undisturbed. Under the bill, as under the present law, coowners of a copyright would be treated generally as tenants in common, with each coowner having an independent right to use or license the use of a work, subject to a duty of accounting to the other coowners for any profits.

H.R. Rep. No. 94–1476, 94th Cong., 2d Sess. 121 (1976). Can one author of a co-authored work give a third party a non-exclusive license in that work? An exclusive license? Can a single co-owner transfer ownership of the copyright? In each case, what are the rights of the non-granting co-author? Of the transferee? Suppose that, for nominal consideration, one of two co-authors grants a third party a nonexclusive license to exploit a work in all media for the duration of the copyright. If these rights were in fact worth a great deal more, what are the rights of the non-licensing co-author?

7. If two co-authors agree between themselves that neither one may license the copyright without the consent of the other, what are the rights of a licensee who receives the consent of only one of the co-authors to exploit the work?

8. If two parties intend to create a joint work, and each makes a separately copyrightable contribution, but one makes a significantly greater contribution than the other, have they created a joint work? If so, what share of the copyright will be owned by each contributor? Is there any way they can alter this result?

9. Suppose one author writes a poem, and a composer later obtains the lyricist's permission to set the poem to music. Who is the author of the resulting song? Would it matter if the first author wrote the poem as a lyric, anticipating that someone eventually might set it to music?

10. If a composer writes the music and lyrics of a song, then later agrees to allow new lyrics to be substituted, is the composer a joint author of the new song?

11. If two authors collaborate on a joint work, and one of them independently creates a derivative work based on the joint work, does the other co-author become a co-author of the derivative work?

12. Suppose that a homeowner hires an architect to design a home, and the homeowner provides the architect with a general description of the desired features. Is the homeowner a joint author of the resulting design? What if the homeowner contributes sketches that illustrate those features?

13. Assuming that the fixation requirement is satisfied, who owns the copyright in an interview? In an on-line "chat"?

14. Under the new sui generis federal protection for pre-1972 sound recordings, codified at 17 U.S.C. § 1401, the initial owner of the rights is "the person that has the exclusive right to reproduce a sound recording under the laws of any State, as of the day before the date of enactment [October 11, 2018]." Because these recordings are not subject to federal copyright, the owners are called "rights owners" rather than "copyright owners."

b. Works Made for Hire

COMMUNITY FOR CREATIVE NON-VIOLENCE V. REID

490 U.S. 730, 109 S.Ct. 2166 (1989).

JUSTICE MARSHALL delivered the opinion of the Court.

In this case, an artist and the organization that hired him to produce a sculpture contest the ownership of the copyright in that work. To resolve this dispute, we must construe the "work made for hire" provisions of the Copyright Act of 1976 (Act or 1976 Act), 17 U.S.C. §§ 101 and 201(b), and in particular, the provision in § 101, which defines as a "work made for hire" a "work prepared by an employee within the scope of his or her employment" (hereinafter § 101(1)).

I

[Petitioners are the Community for Creative Non-Violence ("CCNV"), an organization dedicated to helping the homeless, and Mitch Snyder, a member and trustee of CCNV. CCNV conceived the idea of commissioning, as a Christmastime display, a modern Nativity scene titled "Third World America," which featured a sculpture of a homeless family on a steam grate.]

* * *

Snyder made inquiries to locate an artist to produce the sculpture. He was referred to respondent James Earl Reid, a Baltimore, Maryland, sculptor. In the course of two telephone calls, Reid agreed to sculpt the three human figures. CCNV agreed to make the steam grate and pedestal for the statue. Reid proposed that the work be cast in bronze, at a total cost of approximately $100,000 and taking six to eight months to complete. Snyder rejected that proposal because CCNV did not have sufficient funds, and because the statue had to be completed by December 12 to be included in the pageant. Reid then suggested, and Snyder agreed, that the sculpture would be made of a material known as "Design Cast 62," a synthetic substance that could meet CCNV's monetary and time constraints, could be tinted to resemble bronze, and could withstand the elements. The parties agreed that the project would cost no more than $15,000, not including Reid's services, which he offered to donate. The parties did not sign a written agreement. Neither party mentioned copyright.

After Reid received an advance of $3,000, he made several sketches of figures in various poses. At Snyder's request, Reid sent CCNV a sketch of a proposed sculpture showing the family in a creche like setting: the mother seated, cradling a baby in her lap; the father standing behind her, bending over her shoulder to touch the baby's foot. Reid testified that Snyder asked for the sketch to use in raising funds for the sculpture. Snyder testified that it was also for his approval. Reid sought a black family to serve as a model for the sculpture. Upon Snyder's suggestion, Reid visited a family living at CCNV's Washington shelter but decided that only their newly born child was a suitable model. While Reid was in Washington, Snyder took him to see homeless people living on the streets. Snyder pointed out that they tended to recline on steam grates, rather than sit or stand, in order to warm their bodies. From that time on, Reid's sketches contained only reclining figures.

Throughout November and the first two weeks of December 1985, Reid worked exclusively on the statue, assisted at various times by a dozen different people who were paid with funds provided in installments by CCNV. On a number of occasions, CCNV members visited Reid to check on his progress and to coordinate CCNV's construction of the base. CCNV rejected Reid's proposal to use suitcases or shopping bags to hold the family's personal belongings, insisting instead on a shopping cart. Reid and CCNV members did not discuss copyright ownership on any of these visits.

On December 24, 1985, 12 days after the agreed-upon date, Reid delivered the completed statue to Washington. There it was joined to the steam grate and pedestal prepared by CCNV and placed on display near the site of the pageant. Snyder paid Reid the final installment of the $15,000. * * *

[When a dispute over copyright in the statue arose, both Reid and CCNV filed certificates of copyright registration, and petitioners commenced this action. The District Court held that CCNV owned the copyright under the "work made for hire" doctrine, because Reid had acted as an employee of CCNV.]

The Court of Appeals for the District of Columbia Circuit reversed and remanded, holding that Reid owned the copyright because "Third World America" was not a work for hire. 846 F.2d 1485, 1494 (1988). Adopting what it termed the "literal interpretation" of the Act as articulated by the Fifth Circuit in *Easter Seal Society for Crippled Children & Adults of Louisiana, Inc. v. Playboy Enterprises*, 815 F.2d 323, 329 (1987), the court read § 101 as creating "a simple dichotomy in fact between employees and independent contractors." Because, under agency law, Reid was an independent contractor, the court concluded that the work was not "prepared by an employee" under § 101(1). Nor was the sculpture a "work made for hire" under the second subsection of § 101 (hereinafter § 101(2)): sculpture is not one of the nine categories of works enumerated in that subsection, and the parties had not agreed in writing that the sculpture would be a work for hire. The court suggested that the sculpture nevertheless may have been jointly authored by CCNV and Reid, and remanded for a determination whether the sculpture is indeed a joint work under the Act.

We granted certiorari to resolve a conflict among the Courts of Appeals over the proper construction of the "work made for hire" provisions of the Act. * * * We now affirm.

II

A

The Copyright Act of 1976 provides that copyright ownership "vests initially in the author or authors of the work." 17 U.S.C. § 201(a). As a general rule, the author is the party who actually creates the work, that is, the person who translates an idea into a fixed, tangible expression entitled to copyright protection. § 102. The Act carves out an important exception, however, for "works made for hire." If the work is for hire, "the employer or other person for whom the work was prepared is considered the author" and owns the copyright, unless there is a written agreement to the contrary. § 201(b). Classifying a work as "made for hire" determines not only the initial ownership of its copyright, but also the copyright's duration, § 302(c), and the owners' renewal rights, § 304(a), [and] termination rights, § 203(a) * * *. The contours of the work for hire doctrine therefore carry profound significance for freelance creators—including artists, writers, photographers, designers, composers, and computer programmers—and for the publishing, advertising, music, and other industries which commission their works.

Section 101 of the 1976 Act provides that a work is "for hire" under two sets of circumstances * * *. Petitioners do not claim that the statue satisfies the terms of § 101(2). Quite clearly, it does not. Sculpture does not fit within any of the nine categories of "specially ordered or commissioned" works enumerated in that subsection, and no written agreement between the parties establishes "Third World America" as a work for hire.

The dispositive inquiry in this case therefore is whether "Third World America" is "a work prepared by an employee within the scope of his or her employment" under § 101(1). The Act does not define these terms. In the absence of such guidance, four interpretations have emerged. The first holds that a work is prepared by an employee whenever the hiring party retains the right to control the product. Petitioners take this view. A second, and closely related, view is that a work is prepared by an employee under § 101(1) when the hiring party has actually wielded control with respect to the creation of a particular work. This approach was formulated by the Court of Appeals for the Second Circuit, *Aldon Accessories Ltd. v. Spiegel, Inc.*, 738 F.2d 548 (1984), and adopted by the Fourth Circuit, *Brunswick Beacon, Inc. v. Schock-Hopchas Publishing Co.*, 810 F.2d 410 (1987), the Seventh Circuit, *Evans Newton Inc. v. Chicago Systems Software*, 793 F.2d 889 (1986), and, at times, by petitioners. A third view is that the term "employee" within § 101(1) carries its common-law agency law meaning. This view was endorsed by the Fifth Circuit in *Easter Seal Society for Crippled Children & Adults of Louisiana, Inc. v. Playboy Enterprises*, 815 F.2d 323 (1987), and by the Court of Appeals below. Finally, respondent and numerous amici curiae contend that the term "employee" only refers to "formal, salaried" employees. * * * The Court of Appeals for the Ninth Circuit recently adopted this view. *See Dumas v. Gommerman*, 865 F.2d 1093 (1989).

The starting point for our interpretation of a statute is always its language. The Act nowhere defines the terms "employee" or "scope of employment." It is, however, well established that "[w]here Congress uses terms that have accumulated settled meaning under . . . the common law, a court must infer, unless the statute otherwise dictates, that Congress means to incorporate the established meaning of these terms." *NLRB v. Amax Coal Co.*, 453 U.S. 322, 329 (1981). In the past, when Congress has used the term "employee" without defining it, we have concluded that Congress intended to describe the conventional master-servant relationship as understood by common-law agency doctrine. *See, e.g., Kelley v. Southern Pacific Co.*, 419 U.S. 318, 322–323 (1974); *Baker v. Texas & Pacific R. Co.*, 359 U.S. 227, 228 (1959) (per curiam); *Robinson v. Baltimore & Ohio R. Co.*, 237 U.S. 84, 94 (1915). Nothing in the text of the work for hire provisions indicates that Congress used the words "employee" and "employment" to describe anything other than " 'the conventional relation of employer and employee.' " *Kelley, supra*, at 323, quoting *Robinson, supra*, at 94 * * *.

In past cases of statutory interpretation, when we have concluded that Congress intended terms such as "employee," "employer," and "scope of employment" to be understood in light of agency law, we have relied on the general common law of agency, rather than on the law of any particular State, to give meaning to these terms. This practice reflects the fact that "federal statutes are generally intended to have uniform nationwide application." *Mississippi Band of Choctaw Indians v. Holyfield*, [490 U.S. 30 (1989)] at 43. Establishment of a federal rule of agency, rather than reliance on state agency law, is particularly appropriate here given the Act's express objective of creating national, uniform copyright law by broadly pre-empting state statutory and common-law copyright regulation. *See* 17 U.S.C. § 301(a). We thus agree with the Court of Appeals that the term "employee" should be understood in light of the general common law of agency.

In contrast, neither test proposed by petitioners is consistent with the text of the Act. The exclusive focus of the right to control the product test on the relationship between the hiring party and the product clashes with the language of § 101(1), which focuses on the relationship between the hired and hiring parties. The right to control the product test also would distort the meaning of the ensuing subsection, § 101(2). Section 101 plainly creates two distinct ways in which a work can be deemed for hire: one for works prepared by employees, the other for those specially ordered or commissioned works which fall within one of the nine enumerated categories and are the subject of a written agreement. The right to control the product test ignores this dichotomy by transforming into a work for hire under § 101(1) any "specially ordered or commissioned" work that is subject to the supervision and control of the hiring party. Because a party who hires a "specially ordered or commissioned" work by definition has a right to specify the characteristics of the product desired, at the time the commission is accepted, and frequently until it is completed, the right to control the product test would mean that many works that could satisfy § 101(2) would already have been deemed works for hire under § 101(1). Petitioners' interpretation is particularly hard to square with § 101(2)'s enumeration of the nine specific categories of specially ordered or commissioned works eligible to be works for hire, e.g., "a contribution to a collective work," "a part of a motion picture," and "answer material for a test." The unifying feature of these works is that they are usually prepared at the instance, direction, and risk of a publisher or producer. By their very nature, therefore, these types of works would be works by an employee under petitioners' right to control the product test.

The actual control test, articulated by the Second Circuit in *Aldon Accessories*, fares only marginally better when measured against the language and structure of § 101. Under this test, independent contractors who are so controlled and supervised in the creation of a particular work are deemed "employees" under § 101(1). Thus work for hire status under § 101(1) depends on a hiring party's *actual* control of, rather than *right to* control, the product. Under the actual control test, a work for hire could arise under § 101(2), but not under § 101(1), where a party commissions, but does not actually control, a product which falls into one of the nine enumerated categories. Nonetheless, we agree with the Court of Appeals for the Fifth Circuit that "[t]here is simply no way to milk the 'actual control' test of *Aldon Accessories* from the language of the statute." *Easter Seal Society*, 815 F.2d, at 334. Section 101 clearly delineates between works prepared by an employee and commissioned works. Sound though other distinctions might be as a matter of copyright policy, there is no statutory support for an additional dichotomy between commissioned works that are actually controlled and supervised by the hiring party and those that are not.

We therefore conclude that the language and structure of § 101 of the Act do not support either the right to control the product or the actual control approaches.[8] The structure of § 101 indicates that a work for hire can arise through one of two mutually exclusive means, one for employees and one for independent contractors, and ordinary canons of statutory interpretation indicate that the classification of a particular hired party should be made with reference to agency law.

[The Court also examined the legislative history of the "work made for hire" definition and found no support there for a "control" test of employment status.]

* * *

Finally, petitioners' construction of the work for hire provisions would impede Congress' paramount goal in revising the 1976 Act of enhancing predictability and certainty of copyright ownership. In a "copyright marketplace," the parties negotiate with an expectation that one of them will own the copyright in the completed work. With that expectation, the parties at the outset can settle on relevant contractual terms, such as the price for the work and the ownership of reproduction rights.

To the extent that petitioners endorse an actual control test, CCNV's construction of the work for hire provisions prevents such planning. Because that test turns on whether the hiring party has closely monitored the production process, the parties would not know until late in the process, if not until the work is completed, whether a work will ultimately fall within § 101(1). Under petitioners' approach, therefore, parties would have to predict in advance whether the hiring party will sufficiently control a given work to make it the author. "If they guess incorrectly, their reliance on 'work for hire' or an assignment may give them a copyright interest that they did not bargain for." *Easter Seal Society*, 815 F.2d, at 333.This understanding of the work for hire provisions clearly thwarts Congress' goal of ensuring predictability through advance planning. Moreover, petitioners' interpretation "leaves the door open for hiring parties, who have failed to get a full assignment of copyright rights from independent contractors falling outside the subdivision (2) guidelines, to unilaterally obtain work-made-for-hire rights years after the work has been completed

[8] We also reject the suggestion of respondent and amici that the § 101(1) term "employee" refers only to formal, salaried employees. While there is some support for such a definition in the legislative history, * * * the language of § 101(1) cannot support it. The Act does not say "formal" or "salaried" employee, but simply "employee." Moreover, respondent and those amici who endorse a formal, salaried employee test do not agree upon the content of this test. * * * Even the one Court of Appeals to adopt what it termed a formal, salaried employee test in fact embraced an approach incorporating numerous factors drawn from the agency law definition of employee which we endorse. *See Dumas*, 865 F.2d, at 1104.

as long as they directed or supervised the work, a standard that is hard not to meet when one is a hiring party." Hamilton, *Commissioned Works as Works Made for Hire Under the 1976 Copyright Act: Misinterpretation and Injustice*, 135 U. PA. L. REV. 1281, 1304 (1987).

In sum, we must reject petitioners' argument. Transforming a commissioned work into a work by an employee on the basis of the hiring party's right to control, or actual control of, the work is inconsistent with the language, structure, and legislative history of the work for hire provisions. To determine whether a work is for hire under the Act, a court first should ascertain, using principles of general common law of agency, whether the work was prepared by an employee or an independent contractor. After making this determination, the court can apply the appropriate subsection of § 101.

B

We turn, finally, to an application of § 101 to Reid's production of "Third World America." In determining whether a hired party is an employee under the general common law of agency, we consider the hiring party's right to control the manner and means by which the product is accomplished. Among the other factors relevant to this inquiry are the skill required; the source of the instrumentalities and tools; the location of the work; the duration of the relationship between the parties; whether the hiring party has the right to assign additional projects to the hired party; the extent of the hired party's discretion over when and how long to work; the method of payment; the hired party's role in hiring and paying assistants; whether the work is part of the regular business of the hiring party; whether the hiring party is in business; the provision of employee benefits; and the tax treatment of the hired party. *See* Restatement § 220(2) (setting forth a nonexhaustive list of factors relevant to determining whether a hired party is an employee). No one of these factors is determinative.

Examining the circumstances of this case in light of these factors, we agree with the Court of Appeals that Reid was not an employee of CCNV but an independent contractor. True, CCNV members directed enough of Reid's work to ensure that he produced a sculpture that met their specifications. But the extent of control the hiring party exercises over the details of the product is not dispositive. Indeed, all the other circumstances weigh heavily against finding an employment relationship. Reid is a sculptor, a skilled occupation. Reid supplied his own tools. He worked in his own studio in Baltimore, making daily supervision of his activities from Washington practicably impossible. Reid was retained for less than two months, a relatively short period of time. During and after this time, CCNV had no right to assign additional projects to Reid. Apart from the deadline for completing the sculpture, Reid had absolute freedom to decide when and how long to work. CCNV paid Reid $15,000, a sum dependent on "completion of a specific job, a method by which independent contractors are often compensated." *Holt v. Winpisinger*, 811 F.2d 1532, 1540 (1987). Reid had total discretion in hiring and paying assistants. "Creating sculptures was hardly 'regular business' for CCNV." 846 F.2d, at 1494, n. 11. Indeed, CCNV is not a business at all. Finally, CCNV did not pay payroll or Social Security taxes, provide any employee benefits, or contribute to unemployment insurance or workers' compensation funds.

Because Reid was an independent contractor, whether "Third World America" is a work for hire depends on whether it satisfies the terms of § 101(2). This petitioners concede it cannot do. Thus, CCNV is not the author of "Third World America" by virtue of the work for hire provisions of the Act. However, as the Court of Appeals made clear, CCNV nevertheless may be a joint author of the sculpture if, on remand, the District Court determines that CCNV and Reid prepared the work "with the intention that their contributions be merged into inseparable or interdependent parts of a unitary whole." 17 U.S.C. § 101. In that case, CCNV and Reid would be co-owners of the copyright in the work. *See* § 201(a).

For the aforestated reasons, we affirm the judgment of the Court of Appeals for the District of Columbia Circuit.

NOTES

1. Should the list of commissioned works that can be treated as works made for hire be expanded, and if so, what categories should be included?

2. Based on the facts presented in *Reid*, how strong is CCNV's argument for joint authorship? After the Court's decision in *Reid*, the parties agreed to joint ownership of the copyright, with CCNV as the sole owner of the physical sculpture. Is CCNV required to give Reid access to the sculpture in order to exercise his rights (*e.g.*, by making a mold of the statue so that he could make replicas)? *See Community for Creative Non-Violence v. Reid*, 1991 WL 378209 (D.D.C. Oct. 29, 1991).

3. Should each of the *Reid* factors receive equal weight in any given case? Why or why not?

4. In the entertainment industry—especially the film industry—many creative participants are unionized, meaning that they are treated as employees for purposes of federal labor law. Examples include actors, directors, screenwriters, editors, and cinematographers. Does union membership mean that these participants are employees of the production company for purposes of the work-made-for-hire analysis? *See Horror, Inc. v. Miller,* 15 F.4th 232 (2d Cir. 2003).

5. Where it is unclear that an employment relationship exists for purposes of the work-made-for-hire doctrine, can the parties reduce the resulting legal uncertainties?

6. To ensure work-made-for-hire status under clause (2) of the statutory definition:

(a) Must the work-made-for-hire agreement be executed before the work is produced?

(b) Would a pre-production oral agreement or implied agreement be sufficient if it were reduced to writing after the work was produced?

(c) Must the agreement use the phrase "work made for hire"?

7. When university professors write articles or books, or prepare their classroom lectures, who owns the copyright in these works? Who owns the copyright in material authored by their research assistants? Would a college or university have standing (as a copyright owner) to bring an infringement suit if a company hired students to record professors' lectures and then sold transcripts of those lectures?

8. In *Foraste v. Brown University*, 290 F.Supp.2d 234 (D.R.I. 2003), photographer John Foraste claimed that he held the copyrights of the photographs he took for Brown University, based on a copyright policy written in Brown staff and faculty handbooks, which stated: "*Ownership:* It is the University's position that, as a general premise, ownership of copyrightable property which results from performance of one's University duties and activities will belong to the author or originator. This applies to books, art works, software, etc." The court held that, in order for copyright ownership to be transferred from an employer to an employee in a "work made for hire" situation, the strict requirements of section 201(b) must be met, and even assuming that these requirements were met, the policy set out in the Brown handbooks was too vague to constitute a valid transfer under section 204(a) because none of the particular details about the transfer appeared in the policy. Is this analysis correct?

9. Assume that a greeting card and novelty manufacturer executes a contract with an artist under which the artist agrees to provide artwork to the manufacturer. The manufacturer is free to accept or reject any of the artwork. The parties' contract states that "Any work created by the Artist during the period of this contract shall be the sole property of the Company." Comment on the legal effect of this language.

10. Section 1011(d) of the Satellite Home Viewer Improvement Act of 1999, which was enacted in section 1000(a)(9) of Pub. L. No. 106–113, 106th Cong., 1st Sess. (1999), amended the definition of "work made for hire" in 17 U.S.C. § 101 to add sound recordings to the list of enumerated works which can be works made for hire if created pursuant to a written work made for hire agreement.

Under prior law, it was unclear whether "work made for hire" contract clauses were enforceable against artists performing as independent contractors on sound recordings. The recording industry had taken the position that a sound recording was a "contribution to a collective work," and thus included in the enumerated list even prior to this amendment, but several federal courts have held that sound recordings do not fit the enumerated categories. *E.g., Lulirama Ltd. v. Axcess Broad. Servs., Inc.*, 128 F.3d 872, 878 (5th Cir.1997); *Staggers v. Real Authentic Sound*, 77 F.Supp.2d 57, 62–64 (D.D.C.1999); *Ballas v. Tedesco*, 41 F.Supp.2d 531, 541 (D.N.J.1999). If the works in question are not works made for hire, then they are in most cases joint works. The earliest opportunity for recording artists to terminate their grants to record companies arose in 2013 (for sound recordings created in 1978).

Because most record companies have routinely required recording artists to sign "work made for hire" agreements (as well as copyright transfer agreements) with respect to their recorded performances, it was unclear whether the 1999 amendment might affect authorship determinations with respect to *existing* as well as future recordings, in which case many recording artists would be unable to reclaim their copyrights in existing recordings under the section 203 termination provisions.

Although described in the legislation as a "technical" amendment, the addition of sound recordings to the list of enumerated works was characterized as a substantial change in the law by recording artists and their representatives, as well as by Register of Copyrights Marybeth Peters and many copyright scholars, who criticized Congress for enacting this change with no hearings, debate, or input from musical performers. In response to the outrage expressed by recording artists, in October 2000 Congress retroactively deleted the phrase "as a sound recording" from Section 101(2) of Title 17, and added a lengthy postscript to the statutory definition of a work made for hire, specifically declining to decide whether sound recordings should qualify under this clause. As a result, the question whether sound recordings can be works made for hire under the 1976 Act will have to be resolved by the courts.

11. The Copyright Act of 1909 did not define "works made for hire," and by the 1970s most courts were treating a work as "made for hire" if it was made at the "instance and expense" of another. *See Martha Graham Sch. & Dance Found., Inc. v. Martha Graham*, 380 F.3d 624, 634–35 (2d Cir. 2004) (some, but not all, dances created for school and nonprofit foundation from 1950s through 1970s were works made for hire); *Estate of Burne Hogarth v. Edgar Rice Burroughs, Inc.*, 342 F.3d 149 (2d Cir. 2003) ("Tarzan" graphic novels created in 1970s were works made for hire). For pre-1978 works, this determination affected ownership of the renewal term under 17 U.S.C. § 304(a), and continues to determine the existence of a termination right under 17 U.S.C. § 304(c). Does the "instance and expense" test make it more likely that a pre-1978 sound recording is a work made for hire? *See Fifty-Six Hope Road Music Ltd. v. UMG Recordings, Inc.*, 2010 WL 3564258 (S.D.N.Y. Sept.

10, 2010) (recordings made by musician Bob Marley in 1970s were works made for hire).

In *Marvel Characters, Inc. v. Kirby*, 726 F.3d 119 (2d Cir. 2013), *cert. dismissed,* 573 U.S. 988 (2014), the heirs of Kirby, a writer for Marvel, tried to exercise statutory termination rights under section 304(c)(2) for material written by Kirby while he was working for Marvel. Marvel sued for declaratory relief, and the court held for Marvel, finding that defendants failed to overcome the presumption that the works in question were "works made for hire" without an agreement to the contrary. Applying the applicable standard under the 1909 Act, the court held that the works also met the instance and expense test. The works were made at the publisher's instance because the artist's and publisher's working relationship was close when the artist created the works, the artist created the works pursuant to the publisher's assignments or with them in mind, and the publisher played at least some creative role in the creation of the works. The works were made at the publisher's expense because Kirby was paid a flat rate per page and the publisher could reject his pages without pay, even though it did not pay for Kirby's supplies or give him office space.

In *Gary Friedrich Enters., LLC v. Marvel Characters, Inc.*, 716 F.3d 302 (2d Cir. 2013), the plaintiff was an author who claimed to have conceived and developed the character Ghost Rider, which was then published by defendant beginning in 1972; Marvel claimed it was a work made for hire. The court held that a form work-for-hire agreement between the parties made after Ghost Rider was published (and after the effective date of the 1976 Copyright Act) could not ex-post-facto deem it a work made for hire. The court held that there was a genuine issue of material fact as to whether it was a work made for hire, since Plaintiff showed evidence he was the sole creator, while Marvel showed evidence that the work was a collaborative effort of Marvel's employees.

12. Under the "instance and expense" test used by courts under the 1909 Act, even an autobiography could be a work made for hire. On remand, after the Supreme Court's opinion in *Dastar Corp. v. Twentieth Century Fox Film Corp.,* 539 U.S. 23 (2003) (excerpted in Chapter 4, *supra*), the Ninth Circuit upheld a lower court ruling that the Eisenhower memoir ("Crusade in Europe") was a work-for-hire. *See Twentieth Century Fox Film Corp. v. Entertainment Distributing,* 429 F.3d 869 (9th Cir. 2005). Applying the 1909 Act, the court relied on the fact that the work had been financed by the publisher, which had also exercised substantial editorial control over the completion of the manuscript.

13. Another noteworthy case is *Garcia v. Google, Inc.*, 786 F.3d 733 (9th Cir. 2014), which addresses the work-made-for-hire doctrine in the context of a film. Plaintiff Garcia was cast and filmed for a minor role in what was described to her as an "adventure" film. However, her performance was partially overdubbed and used in an anti-Islamic video that was then put on YouTube.com (owned by the defendant). Plaintiff received death threats for her part in the film, and filed takedown notices under the DMCA.

Judge Kozinski's opinion for the Ninth Circuit panel, 766 F.3d 929 (9th Cir. 2014), reversed the district court's denial of Garcia's motion for preliminary injunction, holding that she had a copyrightable interest in her performance in the film. The "work made for hire" doctrine did not apply, because Garcia did not qualify as a traditional employee (the producer hired her for a specific task, she worked for only three days, and she did not receive traditional employee benefits) and because she did not sign a written work made-for-hire agreement. The plaintiff established a likelihood of success on the merits of her claim that the producer exceeded the scope of a non-exclusive implied license granted by her, because the video radically differed from the film in which she was told she would be appearing. *See also U.S. Auto Parts Network, Inc. v. Parts Geek, LLC*, 692 F.3d 1009 (9th Cir. 2012) (genuine issue of material fact as to whether software was a work made for hire).

On rehearing the case en banc, however, the Ninth Circuit disagreed with Judge Kozinski, and affirmed the district court, holding that Garcia was unlikely to succeed in her claim that she owned the copyright in her performance because (1) a copyright cannot subsist in each individual actor's performance in a film, (2) Garcia did not fix or consent to the fixation of her performance.

Which opinion is more persuasive? Can you suggest a better analysis?

2. FORMALITIES: NOTICE, REGISTRATION, AND DEPOSIT

Statutes: 17 U.S.C. §§ 101 (as needed), 401–12

The Copyright Act of 1909 required copyright owners to take affirmative steps to prevent their published works from entering the public domain. In many cases those steps were not taken, through ignorance, error, or inadvertence, and valuable property rights were forfeited. Beginning with the 1976 Copyright Act, however, the significance of formalities in federal copyright law has been greatly reduced.

a. Notice

Under the 1909 Act, publication marked the dividing line between common law copyright protection and federal copyright protection. Once a work was published, it either enjoyed federal copyright protection or it entered the public domain in the United States. To prevent the work from entering the public domain upon publication, section 10 required the copyright owner to affix copyright notice "to each copy thereof published or offered for sale in the United States by authority of the copyright proprietor."[1] Sections 19 and 20 spelled out the required form, content and

[1] Sections 22 and 23 exempted English-language books and periodicals first published abroad, giving them a 5-year interim copyright (convertible into the full term after publication with notice in the United States) if the author complied with certain deposit and registration requirements.

placement of the copyright notice. The work would enter the public domain if notice were omitted from even a single copy of the work. In some cases, minor deviations from the required form had the same consequence, although courts displayed varying degrees of tolerance where the copyright claimant demonstrated good faith. Where the copyright owner sought to comply with the notice requirement, but notice was omitted from one or more copies "by accident or mistake," section 21 provided that the copyright would not be deemed invalid in an action against an infringer that undertook the infringing conduct after receiving actual notice of the copyright; however, "accident or mistake" was generally interpreted narrowly, including omissions resulting from mechanical failures in the printing process but excluding omissions due to negligence or oversight.

The significance of copyright notice changed dramatically beginning with the 1976 Act, which provided that a copyright owner who failed to affix copyright notice on a published work could avoid forfeiting the copyright by satisfying one of the conditions in 17 U.S.C. § 405(a). For works first published on or after March 1, 1989 (the effective date of the Berne Convention Implementation Act of 1988), omission of notice does not lead to loss of copyright at all. However, notice may still be advisable to preclude a defendant from invoking the "innocent infringement" defense in mitigation of statutory damages under 17 U.S.C. §§ 405(b) and 504(c)(2).

NOTES

1. In *Charles Garnier, Paris v. Andin International, Inc.*, 36 F.3d 1214 (1st Cir. 1994), the First Circuit addressed the copyright notice cure provision, 17 U.S.C. § 405(a)(2), holding that the plaintiff's efforts to remedy its prior failure to affix notice of copyright to its earrings were insufficient to avoid forfeiture of its copyright. What steps are required under section 405(a)(2)?

2. Suppose that the plaintiff, a United States toy manufacturer, acquired the copyright in certain toys from a party that had, between 1978 and 1988, distributed the toys without notice overseas. Assuming that the toys would be otherwise eligible for copyright in the United States, would this omission trigger the forfeiture/cure provisions of the 1976 Act? If so, when should the United States copyright owner be found to have "discovered" the omission? Would the plaintiff's obligation to affix notice (to cure the omission) extend to copies distributed in the United States by a foreign distributor? *See Hasbro Bradley, Inc. v. Sparkle Toys, Inc.*, 780 F.2d 189 (2d Cir. 1985).

3. When the cure provisions of section 405(a) apply and the copyright owner complies with them, does the original omission of notice have any effect on the copyright owner's rights?

4. What year should be included in a copyright notice? What is the effect of an erroneous name or date in the copyright notice affixed to a work distributed after March 1, 1989? Before that date?

5. Suppose that a book was published in 1987 under the authority of the copyright owner but without notice, and the omission was cured by complying with section 405(a)(2). If the work went out of print in 1989, and a second printing of the book (with no alteration of the copyrighted material) commenced in 1994, what would be the legal effect, if any, of omitting copyright notice from the copies published in 1994 and thereafter?

6. In the case of certain foreign works that entered the public domain in the United States due to noncompliance with formalities such as the notice requirement, copyright may be restored pursuant to section 104A. *See* Part B.2 of this chapter, *infra*.

7. Besides the "cure" provisions of section 405(a)(2), the 1976 Act contains two additional exceptions to copyright forfeiture. Application of the section 405(a)(1) exception for omission of copyright notice on a "relatively small" number of copies or phonorecords has led one court to conclude that 1% of publicly distributed copies is relatively small, and another to conclude that 2.4% is too many. (Compare section 21 of the 1909 Act.) Section 405(a)(3) creates a more complex ambiguity: If notice is omitted in violation of an implied or oral condition of publication, is the publication not "by authority of the copyright owner" under section 405(a)? However this question is resolved, should the answer be the same for purposes of unnoticed publication under section 10 of the 1909 Act?

8. If two persons own the copyright in a work, and only one of them authorizes the public distribution of the work without notice, what effect does this have on the work's copyright (a) under the 1909 Act? (b) under the 1976 Act? Would it matter whether the distribution without notice took place in the United States or exclusively overseas? Would it matter whether they each owned undivided interests in the entire copyright, or distinct and separate portions of the copyright?

9. If a compilation was published without notice under the 1909 or 1976 Acts, did the underlying works enter the public domain? *Cf. Shoptalk, Ltd. v. Concorde-New Horizons Corp.*, 168 F.3d 586 (2d Cir. 1999) (dealing with unpublished underlying works).

b. Registration and Deposit

Under the 1909 Act, registration and deposit were essential to statutory copyright protection of unpublished works. While they were not essential to obtaining statutory copyright in published works (since this was accomplished by publication with notice), they were still prerequisites to filing an infringement claim. In addition, registration was a prerequisite to filing a renewal registration. (Renewal registration is discussed in Part B.1. of this chapter, *infra*.)

Registration has taken on a different significance under the 1976 Act. Because statutory copyright now commences with fixation rather than publication, registration is no longer a prerequisite to statutory copyright protection of unpublished works. Except for works published without proper notice between January 1, 1978, and March 1, 1989, which entered the public domain unless they were registered within the five-year window specified by section 405(a)(2), registration under the 1976 Act was, and remains, permissive for all works.

Nonetheless, under section 411 registration (or pre-registration under section 408(f), as discussed below) continues to be a prerequisite to filing an infringement claim, except in the case of (1) foreign works protected by international copyright agreements to which the United States is a party, and (2) certain live transmissions under section 411(c) if they are registered within three months after the initial transmission. In contrast, registration is not a prerequisite to a moral rights claim under section 106A.

The purpose of the section 411(a) registration requirement is to incentivize "prompt registration of copyright claims." *Fourth Estate Public Benefit Corp. v. Wall-Street.com LLC*, ___ U.S. ___, 139 S.Ct. 881 (2019). Although the Supreme Court held in 2010 that registration is not a *jurisdictional* requirement divesting federal courts of the power to hear a case involving unregistered copyrights, *Reed Elsevier, Inc. v. Muchnick,* 559 U.S. 154 (2010), the Court held in *Fourth Estate* that a copyright owner bringing an infringement claim must have filed an application for registration *and* the Copyright Office must have acted by either granting or denying the application. Merely filing the copyright application before instituting the civil action is insufficient—contrary to the case law in some circuits before *Fourth Estate*. If the copyright owner has submitted a properly executed application to register the work, but registration has been refused, the plaintiff may still file an infringement action if notice thereof is served on the Register of Copyrights. The latter then has the option to become a party to the action with respect to the issue of registrability.

Registration, if made before or within five years of initial publication, is also prima facie evidence of a claimant's valid copyright (section 410(c)). Registration has further evidentiary value in helping to establish the date on which a work was created, which can support or rebut circumstantial evidence of copying (see Chapter 18). In addition, section 412 specifies that no statutory damages or attorney's fees can be recovered for a pre-registration infringement of an unpublished work; where a work is infringed after publication, statutory damages and attorney's fees are available for a pre-registration infringement only if the work is registered within three months of publication.

Registration remains important for several additional reasons. In the case of conflicting transfers, a work must be registered in order to establish priority through recordation under section 205. With respect to nondramatic musical works, compulsory license fees under section 115 can be distributed only to the copyright owner(s) identified in the registration or other public records of the Copyright Office. Finally, registration is a prerequisite to obtaining relief against importation of infringing items through the U.S. Customs service under section 603, or in an action before the International Trade Commission, under 19 U.S.C. § 1337(a)(1)(B)(i), (a)(1)(D). Thus, even though the significance of registration has diminished under the 1976 Act, Congress retained certain incentives to encourage copyright owners to register their works.

Copyright registrants are required to deposit one complete copy or phonorecord (two, in the case of published works) under section 408(b). In addition, a separate deposit requirement applies to published works (whether or not registered) under section 407. Although noncompliance with section 407 may lead to a financial penalty, it does not lead to loss of copyright protection. Since 2018, copyright owners of literary monographs and musical compositions have been able to satisfy both the registration deposit and mandatory deposit requirements by submitting one copy of the best edition of the work. 83 Fed. Reg. 2371 (Jan. 17, 2018).

If a copyright applicant knowingly provides inaccurate information in a registration application, and awareness of the inaccuracy would have caused the Copyright Office to refuse the registration, then the resulting copyright registration will be treated as invalid for purposes of infringement actions and remedies. 17 U.S.C. § 411(b). In contrast, the registration will not be considered invalid if the applicant lacked knowledge that the information was inaccurate. In *Unicolors, Inc. v. H&M Nennes & Mauritz, L.P.*, 142 S.Ct. 941 (2022), the Supreme Court held that the same rule applies regardless of whether the inaccuracy relates to a factual matter or a question of law. For a falsehood to lead to invalidation, actual subjective knowledge—or willful blindness—is required. Accordingly, a mere mistake of fact or law will not lead to invalidation.

In 2005, Congress added a new preregistration procedure, codified in section 408(f), which allows preregistration of certain works even before completion. Section 408(f) applies to certain categories of unpublished works that are being prepared for commercial distribution, if the Register of Copyrights determines that works in this category have a history of infringement prior to authorized public distribution—such as motion pictures, software, and sound recordings. A full application for registration, together with a copy of the work, must be submitted within three months after the work's publication. Section 408(f) is intended to enable these copyright owners to initiate infringement actions promptly upon learning of infringement, even if the registration process is not yet complete.

The deposit and registration provisions that apply to copyrighted works do not apply to pre-1972 sound recordings. Because the 2018 Music Modernization Act granted these works sui generis protection rather than copyright protection, they are not eligible for copyright registration. Instead, section 1401 imposes a "filing" requirement as a precondition to recovering attorneys' fees or statutory damages; the filing must include the title, artist, and rights owner, as well as other information determined by the Copyright Office. 17 U.S.C. § 1401(f)(5)(A).

NOTES

1. Is an infringement suit barred if the plaintiff's application to register the work is refused?

2. Suppose a producer plans a live pay-per-view broadcast (with simultaneous fixation) of a major sporting event. Two days before the broadcast, she learns that several sports bars with de-scrambling devices plan to intercept the broadcast for the benefit of their patrons without paying for it. Can she get injunctive relief before the broadcast?

3. Suppose that a composer who resides outside the United States in a country that is a Berne signatory writes a song but does not register it in the United States because she has no thought of exploiting it here. Without her knowledge or consent, her song is recorded by an American record company. The composer learns of this shortly before the record's scheduled release and would like to obtain immediate injunctive relief. What obstacles is the composer likely to encounter in filing her suit? Would your answer change if the infringement took place after she filed her registration papers but before she received her registration certificate?

4. What public purposes are served by registration and deposit?

5. What if a copyright plaintiff wishes to register a work in order to initiate an infringement action, but no longer has access to a copy of the work—for example, because the plaintiff's copy was lost or destroyed, or because the defendant has lawful possession of the only copy?

6. The Copyright Office regulations exempt "secure tests" from the deposit requirement of section 408. 37 C.F.R. § 202.20(c)(2)(vi). A "secure test" is "a nonmarketed test administered under supervision at specified centers on specific dates, all copies of which are accounted for and either destroyed or returned to restricted locked storage following each administration." 37 C.F.R. § 202.20(b)(4). Where a test meets this definition, the registrant need only deposit a portion or description of the test that is sufficient to identify it. *Id.* § 202.20(c)(2)(vi). Does this exemption conflict with any of the policies behind the copyright statutes or the Copyright Clause of the Constitution? Note that the regulations exempt from the deposit requirement of section 407 (but not section 408) several other categories of works—three-dimensional sculptural works, individual contributions to collective works, and most advertisements. *See* 17 U.S.C. § 407(c); 37 C.F.R. § 202.19.

7. In *Raquel v. Education Management Corp.*, 196 F.3d 171 (3d Cir. 1999), *vacated and remanded,* 531 U.S. 952 (2000), the Third Circuit invalidated a copyright registration because it misidentified the registered

work (a song) as an "audiovisual work," but this decision was overturned by the Supreme Court. What types of errors, if any, should invalidate a copyright registration?

8. In *Reed Elsevier, Inc. v. Muchnick*, 559 U.S. 154 (2010), the Supreme Court held that section 411(a)'s requirement of copyright registration as a prerequisite to filing suit does not deprive a federal court of subject matter jurisdiction in a case involving infringement of unregistered works. Accordingly, it rejected the Second Circuit's holding that, in a class action by freelance authors alleging unauthorized digital republication of their works, the district court lacked jurisdiction to certify the class and to approve the settlement, which involved both registered and unregistered copyrights. The Court declined to address whether a district court may or should enforce section 411(a) *sua sponte* by dismissing copyright claims involving unregistered works.

3. THE CHANGED SIGNIFICANCE OF PUBLICATION

INTELLECTUAL PROPERTY AND THE NATIONAL INFORMATION INFRASTRUCTURE

The Report of the Working Group on Intellectual Property Rights, Information Infrastructure Task Force 28–30 (1995).

* * *

Historically, the concept of publication has been a major underpinning of copyright law. Under the dual system of protection which existed until the 1976 Copyright Act took effect, unpublished works were generally protected under state law. Published works, on the other hand, were protected under Federal copyright law.[68] On the effective date of the 1976 Act [January 1, 1978], Federal copyright protection became available for unpublished as well as published works. The concept of publication thus lost its "all-embracing importance" as the threshold to Federal statutory protection.

However, while the importance of publication has been reduced through amendment to the law (e.g., granting Federal protection to unpublished works and removing the notice requirement for published works), the status of a work as either published or unpublished still has significance under the Copyright Act. For example:

> only works that are published in the United States are subject to mandatory deposit in the Library of Congress;[71] deposit requirements for registration with the Copyright Office differ

[68] See *Wheaton v. Peters*, 33 U.S. (8 Pet.) 591, 662–63 (1834).

[71] 117 U.S.C. § 407 (1988). * * * The deposit requirements are not conditions of copyright protection, but failure to deposit copies of a published work may subject the copyright owner to significant fines. *See* 17 U.S.C. § 407(a), (d) (1988).

depending on whether a work is published or unpublished;[72] the scope of the fair use defense may be narrower for unpublished works;[73] unpublished works are eligible for protection without regard to the nationality or domicile of the author;[74] published works must bear a copyright notice if published before March 1, 1989;[75] and certain limitations on the exclusive rights of a copyright owner are applicable only to published works.[76]

* * *

4. THE MEANING OF PUBLICATION

The meaning of "publication" was somewhat different under the 1909 Act than under the 1976 Act. Whether a particular event constitutes "publication" depends in part on which of these Acts was in effect when that event took place. Thus, the uncertainties surrounding the meaning of "publication" under the 1909 Act will remain problematic until all works published before 1978 have entered the public domain.

Because the 1909 Act provided little guidance as to what constituted "publication," defining this term was left largely to the courts.[2] The question whether a work had been published was often a crucial one since, prior to January 1, 1978, publication without proper copyright notice could inject a work into the public domain. In addition, publication was, for most works,[3] a prerequisite to obtaining federal copyright protection under section 10 of the 1909 Act, and thus was necessary if a copyright plaintiff wished to invoke the federal court's subject matter jurisdiction and obtain federal remedies. Therefore, copyright plaintiffs whose disseminated works bore the required copyright notice often sought a ruling that their works had been published. This was known as "investive" publication. In contrast, where a work had been disseminated without notice, the copyright owner would argue that the dissemination was not a publication and that the work therefore retained its perpetual common law copyright under section

[72] *See* 17 U.S.C. § 408(b) (1988) * * *.

[73] The first factor of the fair use analysis—the nature of the copyrighted work—generally weighs against a finding of fair use if the work is unpublished. *See Harper & Row* [*v. Nation Enterprises*, 471 U.S. 539, 105 S. Ct. 2218 (1985)] * * *.

[74] 17 U.S.C. § 104(a) (1988 & Supp. V 1993); House Report at 58, reprinted in 1976 U.S.C.C.A.N. 5671 (Section 104(a) "imposes no qualification of nationality and domicile with respect to unpublished works"); *see also* 17 U.S.C. § 104(b) (1988 & Supp. V 1993) (national origin requirements for published works).

[75] 17 U.S.C. § 405 (1988 & Supp. V 1993).

[76] See generally 17 U.S.C. §§ 107–120 (1988 & Supp. V 1993). See, e.g., 17 U.S.C. § 118 (1988 & Supp. V 1993) (compulsory license is available for the use of certain published works in connection with noncommercial broadcasting).

[2] Section 26 defined the "date of publication" as the date on which copies were first "placed on sale, sold, or publicly distributed" under the copyright owner's authority.

[3] Section 22 provided an exception for certain works not reproduced for sale, provided the author satisfied the registration and deposit requirements of that section.

2 of the 1909 Act. A publication without notice, which caused the work to enter the public domain, was known as a "divestive" publication. Because the last works published under the 1909 Act will not enter the public domain until the end of 2072, in many cases courts are still required to resolve questions of investive or divestive publication.

Although section 101 of the 1976 Act includes an explicit definition of "publication," it does not resolve all of the uncertainties that arose under prior law. The 1976 Act is silent on the question whether, under any circumstances, an unauthorized public distribution can constitute publication; courts interpreting the 1909 Act found publication only where the copyright owner had consented to the distribution. For the most part, the 1976 Act does not reject the case law interpreting "publication" under prior law; thus, those authorities help to define "publication" even under current law. Under both the 1909 and 1976 Acts, for example, a "publication" without notice will not be found where the work is distributed without the authority of the copyright owner. *See, e.g., Twentieth Century-Fox Film Corp. v. Dunnahoo*, 637 F.2d 1338 (9th Cir.1981) (applying 1909 Act); *Midway Manufacturing Co. v. Artic International, Inc.*, 547 F.Supp. 999 (N.D.Ill.1982), *aff'd*, 704 F.2d 1009 (7th Cir.1983) (applying 1976 Act).

According to case law interpreting the 1909 Act, a mere offer to sell or otherwise distribute a work (either the original or copies) to the public, if authorized by the copyright owner, was a publication. This interpretation was at least partially codified in the definition of "publication" contained in section 101 of the 1976 Act; however, because of the ambiguous language of that section, the codified rule appears to be narrower than that adopted by courts applying the 1909 Act, because the codified rule refers only to an offer to distribute "for purposes of further distribution, public performance, or public display," thus creating uncertainty as to the status of offers to distribute works to the public for their private use.

Significant issues in interpreting "publication" under the 1909 Act have included: (1) whether a particular distribution was private or public; (2) whether a public performance or display was a publication; and (3) whether publication of a derivative work (such as a sound recording or a motion picture) constituted publication of the underlying work (a musical composition or a story or screenplay, respectively). Some, but not all, of these questions were addressed in the 1976 Act.

a. General Versus Limited Distributions

Courts interpreting the 1909 Act distinguished general distributions, which constituted publication, from "limited" distributions, which did not. "Limited" distributions were made to "a definitely selected group for a limited purpose, and without the right of diffusion, reproduction, distribution or sale. . . . [T]he circulation must be restricted both as to persons and purpose, or it cannot be called a private or limited publication."

White v. Kimmell, 193 F.2d 744 (9th Cir.1952) (holding that distribution of no more than 20 copies of a manuscript lacking copyright notice to persons author did not know, with no restriction on further distribution, was general publication). The precedents distinguishing limited from general distributions under the 1909 Act continue to be relevant in construing "publication" under the 1976 Act. *See, e.g., Vane v. The Fair, Inc.*, 676 F.Supp. 133 (E.D.Tex.1987).

In general, it appears that courts interpreting the 1909 Act were especially reluctant to find that a distribution constituted divestive publication; indeed, some courts explicitly stated that a broader dissemination was necessary to prove divestive publication than investive publication. *See, e.g., Hirshon v. United Artists Corp.*, 243 F.2d 640 (D.C.Cir.1957); *American Visuals v. Holland*, 239 F.2d 740 (2d Cir.1956).

It is nonetheless difficult to reconcile some of these decisions.

In one notable case, *Academy of Motion Picture Arts & Sciences v. Creative House Promotions, Inc.*, 944 F.2d 1446 (9th Cir.1991), *rev'g in part, aff'g in part, and remanding* 728 F.Supp. 1442 (C.D.Cal.1989), the Ninth Circuit ruled that the Oscar statuette was not injected into the public domain when the Academy distributed 158 Oscars without copyright notice and with no express restriction on further distribution by the recipients; the court went to some trouble to find an "implied" restriction.

In *King v. Mister Maestro*, 224 F.Supp. 101 (S.D.N.Y.1963), the district court found only a "limited" distribution where Martin Luther King gave advance copies of his "I Have a Dream" speech to reporters, with no restriction on further distribution or copying, even though this enabled the media to reproduce and distribute numerous copies to the public. Years later, in *Estate of Martin Luther King, Jr., Inc. v. CBS, Inc.*, 13 F.Supp.2d 1347 (N.D.Ga.1998), a federal district court expressly disagreed with the holding of *King v. Mister Maestro* and granted summary judgment that King's "I Have a Dream" speech entered the public domain because it was publicly distributed without notice during the 1963 March on Washington, but the court of appeals reversed, finding genuine issues of material fact as to whether the alleged instances of distribution were controlled and/or unauthorized. *See Estate of Martin Luther King, Jr. v. CBS, Inc.*, 194 F.3d 1211 (11th Cir.1999). The case was subsequently settled.

There were also sharply conflicting decisions on whether distributing copies of motion pictures and television programs for the purpose of public performance was a publication under the 1909 Act; most courts found only a limited distribution.

b. Public Performances and Displays

In *Ferris v. Frohman*, 223 U.S. 424 (1912), the Supreme Court concluded that public performance of a work did not constitute publication under the 1909 Act. Public displays were the subject of numerous precedents, including one Supreme Court decision that predated the 1909 Act. *See American Tobacco Co. v. Werckmeister,* 207 U.S. 284 (1907) (divestive publication did not occur when a picture was publicly displayed without a copyright notice, because the rules of the exhibition prohibited copying, but such publication might be found where the artist took "no measure to protect" against copying). The courts generally agreed that no publication would be found where a work was publicly displayed without notice, as long as the circumstances evidenced that the author did not intend to forfeit copyright. This was usually established by showing that the viewers were subject to restrictions on copying. *See, e.g., Letter Edged in Black Press, Inc. v. Public Building Commission,* 320 F.Supp. 1303 (N.D.Ill.1970).

The 1976 Act expressly excludes public performances and displays from the definition of "publication" in section 101.

c. Public Distributions of Sound Recordings and Other Derivative Works as Publication of Underlying Work

A persistent question under the 1909 Act was whether public distribution of a sound recording or motion picture (or, for that matter, any other derivative work) amounted to publication of the underlying musical, dramatic or literary composition.[4]

In the case of sound recordings, cases interpreting the 1909 Act reached conflicting conclusions until Congressional action finally resolved the matter in 1997. *Compare Rosette v. Rainbo Record Mfg. Corp.*, 354 F.Supp. 1183 (S.D.N.Y.1973), *aff'd per curiam*, 546 F.2d 461 (2d Cir.1976) (sale of phonograph records did not constitute "publication" of the musical composition, based on the holding in *White-Smith Music Pub. Co. v. Apollo Co.*, 209 U.S. 1, 17–18 (1908), that for copyright purposes only an object from which a musical composition was visually perceptible could be a "copy" of the composition, a decision which Congress did not expressly overrule in the 1909 Act) *with La Cienega Music Co. v. ZZ Top*, 53 F.3d 950 (9th Cir.1995) (expressly rejecting *Rosette*). The consequence of finding publication was highly significant; the phonorecords in question typically bore no copyright notice for the underlying composition; indeed, sound recordings fixed before February 15, 1972 did not bear a copyright notice at all, because they were not eligible for federal copyright. If distribution of the phonorecords published the underlying works, then these works entered the public domain. Otherwise, assuming that the underlying compositions had not also been distributed as sheet music, they retained

[4] Under the 1976 Act, before notice became optional, this question was addressed by requiring notice on "copies" but not on "phonorecords" of musical works. *See* H.R. Rep. No. 1476, 94th Cong., 2d Sess. 145 (1976); 17 U.S.C.A. § 402 (prior to amendment by Berne Convention Implementation Act of 1988); 17 U.S.C.A. § 101 (definition of "copies").

their perpetual common law copyright (until January 1, 1978, at which time unpublished works became subject to the statutory term, as discussed in Part B, *infra*). In 1997, an amendment to the Copyright Act (prompted by the result in *La Cienega*) provided that the distribution of a phonorecord is not a publication of the musical work embodied therein. The U.S. Court of Appeals for the Ninth Circuit has subsequently held that the new section 303(b) applies retroactively because it is not a change in the law, merely a clarification. *See ABKCO Music, Inc. v. LaVere*, 217 F.3d 684 (9th Cir.2000) (reversing a summary judgment, the court held that the legislation explicitly applies to conduct occurring before January 1, 1978). In 2010, section 303(b) was amended to include dramatic works and literary works embodied in phonorecords.

With respect to derivative works other than sound recordings—motion pictures, for example—there is surprisingly little direct authority on the question whether publishing the derivative work also publishes the underlying work. In *Shoptalk Ltd. v. Concorde-New Horizons Corp.*, 168 F.3d 586 (2d Cir.1999), the Second Circuit held that publication in 1960 of a film constituted publication of the previously-unpublished (and unregistered) screenplay, which as a result entered the public domain. The court rejected the argument that section 7 of the 1909 Act preserved common law rights in unpublished works incorporated in derivative works. Should the same result follow in the case of films published between January 1, 1978 and March 1, 1989?

NOTE

If a work is made available to the public only by digital transmission (for example, by posting it on YouTube, a blog, or Facebook, or including it in an electronic library or other database available to the public in general or to participants in a subscriber service), does this constitute publication under current law? Should it?

B. DURATION

Statutes: 17 U.S.C. §§ 101 (as needed), 302–05

1. 1909 AND 1976 ACTS COMPARED

COPYRIGHT ACT OF 1976

H.R. Rep. No. 94–1476.
94th Cong., 2d Sess. 133–35 (1976).

* * *

Section 302. Duration of Copyright in Works Created After Effective Date

In general

The debate over how long a copyright should last is as old as the oldest copyright statute and will doubtless continue as long as there is a copyright law. * * *

Under the present law statutory copyright protection begins on the date of publication (or on the date of registration in unpublished form) and continues for 28 years from that date; it may be renewed for a second 28 years, making a total potential term of 56 years in all cases. The principal elements of this system—a definite number of years, computed from either publication or registration, with a renewal feature—have been a part of the U.S. copyright law since the first statute in 1790. The arguments for changing this system to one based on the life of the author can be summarized as follows:

1. The present 56-year term is not long enough to insure an author and his dependents the fair economic benefits from his works. Life expectancy has increased substantially, and more and more authors are seeing their works fall into the public domain during their lifetimes, forcing later works to compete with their own early works in which copyright has expired.

2. The tremendous growth in communications media has substantially lengthened the commercial life of a great many works. A short term is particularly discriminatory against serious works of music, literature, and art, whose value may not be recognized until after many years.

3. Although limitations on the term of copyright are obviously necessary, too short a term harms the author without giving any substantial benefit to the public. * * * In some cases the lack of copyright protection actually restrains dissemination of the work, since publishers and other users cannot risk investing in the work unless assured of exclusive rights.

4. A system based on the life of the author would go a long way toward clearing up the confusion and uncertainty involved in the vague concept of "publication," and would provide a much simpler, clearer method for computing the term. The death of the author is a definite, determinable event, and it would be the only date that a potential user would have to worry about. All of a particular author's works, including successive revisions of them, would fall into the public domain at the same time, thus avoiding the present problems of determining a multitude of publication dates and of distinguishing "old" and "new" matter in later editions. The bill answers the problems

of determining when relatively obscure authors died, by establishing a registry of death dates and a system of presumptions.

5. One of the worst features of the present copyright law is the provision for renewal of copyright. A substantial burden and expense, this unclear and highly technical requirement results in incalculable amounts of unproductive work. In a number of cases it is the cause of inadvertent and unjust loss of copyright. Under a life-plus-50 system the renewal device would be inappropriate and unnecessary.

6. Under the preemption provisions of section 301 and the single Federal system they would establish, authors will be giving up perpetual, unlimited exclusive common law rights in their unpublished works, including works that have been widely disseminated by means other than publication. A statutory term of life-plus-50 years is no more than a fair recompense for the loss of these perpetual rights.

7. A very large majority of the world's countries have adopted a copyright term of the life of the author and 50 years after the author's death. * * * Without this change, the possibility of future United States adherence to the Berne Copyright Union would evaporate * * *.

* * *

NOTE

Based on sentiments like the ones reflected in the passage excerpted above from the legislative history, Congress enacted the 1976 General Copyright Revision with provisions establishing a statutory term of life plus 50 years for individually authored works, and alternative provisions establishing terms of 75 years from publication or 100 years from creation (whichever occurred first) for all other works, including works for hire as well as anonymous and pseudonymous works.

Meanwhile, most European countries began to move toward providing a copyright term of life plus 70 years—while limiting protection of U.S. works to life plus 50 years because that remained the maximum protection which U.S. law afforded to works originating in those countries. Pressure in the United States to match the European terms mounted accordingly, and Congress finally responded in 1998.

The Sony Bono Copyright Term Extension Act (CTEA), Pub. L. No. 105–298 (signed Oct. 27, 1998), added 20 years to U.S. copyright terms, effective October 27, 1998. Although section 304(b) was amended to grant the additional 20 years of protection to older works whose renewal terms had not yet expired, works whose renewal terms had expired as of that date received no additional term of protection. The new law also amended section 303 to add another 20 years to the minimum copyright terms of works that were created before 1978 and first published between January 1, 1978, and December 31, 2002.

In *Eldred v. Reno*, 74 F. Supp. 2d 1, 3 (D.D.C.1999), the district court refused to hold that the CTEA was invalid under either the "limited times" language of the Intellectual Property Clause or the First Amendment, or that Congress had exceeded its authority under the clause by giving the benefit of the extended term to copyright assignees rather than solely to authors. The D.C. Circuit affirmed the decision in favor of the government. *See Eldred v. Reno*, 239 F.3d 372 (D.C. Cir. 2001) (holding, inter alia, that copyright is "categorically immune" to First Amendment challenges). The Supreme Court then issued the decision excerpted below.

ELDRED V. ASHCROFT

537 U.S. 186, 123 S.Ct. 769 (2003), *rehearing denied* 538 U.S. 916, 123 S.Ct. 1505 (2003).

JUSTICE GINSBURG delivered the opinion of the court.

* * * Under the CTEA, most copyrights now run from creation until 70 years after the author's death. 17 U.S.C. § 302(a). Petitioners do not challenge the "life-plus-70-years" timespan itself * * *. Congress went awry, petitioners maintain, not with respect to newly created works, but in enlarging the term for published works with existing copyrights. The "limited Tim[e]" in effect when a copyright is secured, petitioners urge, becomes the constitutional boundary, a clear line beyond the power of Congress to extend. As to the First Amendment, petitioners contend that the CTEA is a content-neutral regulation of speech that fails inspection under the heightened judicial scrutiny appropriate for such regulations.

* * *

I

A

We evaluate petitioners' challenge to the constitutionality of the CTEA against the backdrop of Congress' previous exercises of its authority under the Copyright Clause. [The Court reviewed the copyright terms under the 1790 Act (14 years plus a 14-year renewal term), the 1831 Act (28 years plus a 14-year renewal term), the 1909 Act (28 years plus a 28-year renewal term), and the 1976 Act (author's life plus 50 years).]

* * *

The measure at issue here, the CTEA, installed the fourth major duration extension of federal copyrights. * * * Retaining the general structure of the 1976 Act, the CTEA enlarges the terms of all existing and future copyrights by 20 years. For works created by identified natural persons, the term now lasts from creation until 70 years after the author's death. 17 U.S.C. § 302(a). This standard harmonizes the baseline United States copyright term with the term adopted by the European Union in 1993. For anonymous works, pseudonymous works, and works made for hire, the term is 95 years from publication or 120 years from creation, whichever expires first. 17 U.S.C. § 302(c).

Paralleling the 1976 Act, the CTEA applies these new terms to all works not published by January 1, 1978. §§ 302(a), 303(a). For works published before 1978 with existing copyrights as of the CTEA's effective date, the CTEA extends the term to 95 years from publication. §§ 304(a) and (b). Thus, in common with the 1831, 1909, and 1976 Acts, the CTEA's new terms apply to both future and existing copyrights. * * *

II

A

We address first the determination of the courts below that Congress has authority under the Copyright Clause to extend the terms of existing copyrights. Text, history, and precedent, we conclude, confirm that the Copyright Clause empowers Congress to prescribe "limited Times" for copyright protection and to secure the same level and duration of protection for all copyright holders, present and future.

The CTEA's baseline term of life plus 70 years, petitioners concede, qualifies as a "limited Tim[e]" as applied to future copyrights. * * * Petitioners contend, however, that existing copyrights extended to endure for that same term are not "limited." Petitioners' argument essentially reads into the text of the Copyright Clause the command that a time prescription, once set, becomes forever "fixed" or "inalterable." The word "limited," however, does not convey a meaning so constricted. * * * Thus understood, a timespan appropriately "limited" as applied to future copyrights does not automatically cease to be "limited" when applied to existing copyrights. And as we observe, *infra*, there is no cause to suspect that a purpose to evade the "limited Times" prescription prompted Congress to adopt the CTEA.

To comprehend the scope of Congress' power under the Copyright Clause, "a page of history is worth a volume of logic." *New York Trust Co. v. Eisner*, 256 U.S. 345, 349 (1921) (Holmes, J.). History reveals an unbroken congressional practice of granting to authors of works with existing copyrights the benefit of term extensions so that all under copyright protection will be governed evenhandedly under the same regime. As earlier recounted, the First Congress accorded the protections of the Nation's first federal copyright statute to existing and future works alike. 1790 Act § 1. Since then, Congress has regularly applied duration extensions to both existing and future copyrights. 1831 Act §§ 1, 16; 1909 Act §§ 23–24; 1976 Act §§ 302–303; 17 U.S.C. §§ 302–304.

* * *

Congress' consistent historical practice of applying newly enacted copyright terms to future and existing copyrights reflects a judgment stated concisely by Representative Huntington at the time of the 1831 Act: "[J]ustice, policy, and equity alike forb[id]" that an "author who had sold his [work] a week ago, be placed in a worse situation than the author who should sell his work the day after the passing of [the] act." 7 Cong. Deb. 424 (1831). The CTEA follows this historical practice by keeping the duration provisions of the 1976 Act largely in place and simply adding 20 years to each of them. Guided by text, history, and precedent, we cannot agree with petitioners' submission that extending the duration of existing copyrights is categorically beyond Congress' authority under the Copyright Clause.

Satisfied that the CTEA complies with the "limited Times" prescription, we turn now to whether it is a rational exercise of the legislative authority conferred by the Copyright Clause. On that point, we defer substantially to Congress. *Sony Corp. of America v. Universal City Studios, Inc.*, 464 U.S. 417, 429 (1984) ("[I]t is Congress that has been assigned the task of defining the scope of the limited monopoly that should be granted to authors . . . in order to give the public appropriate access to their work product.").

The CTEA reflects judgments of a kind Congress typically makes, judgments we cannot dismiss as outside the Legislature's domain. As respondent describes, a key factor in the CTEA's passage was a 1993 European Union (EU) directive instructing EU members to establish a copyright term of life plus 70 years. Consistent with the Berne Convention, the EU directed its members to deny this longer term to the works of any non-EU country whose laws did not secure the same extended term. *See* Berne Conv. Art. 7(8). By extending the baseline United States copyright term to life plus 70 years, Congress sought to ensure that American authors would receive the same copyright protection in Europe as their European counterparts. The CTEA may also provide greater incentive for American and other authors to create and disseminate their work in the United States.

In addition to international concerns, Congress passed the CTEA in light of demographic, economic, and technological changes, and rationally credited projections that longer terms would encourage copyright holders to invest in the restoration and public distribution of their works, *see* H.R.Rep. No. 105–452, p. 4 (1998) (term extension "provide[s] copyright owners generally with the incentive to restore older works and further disseminate them to the public").

In sum, we find that the CTEA is a rational enactment; we are not at liberty to second-guess congressional determinations and policy judgments of this order, however debatable or arguably unwise they may be. Accordingly, we cannot conclude that the CTEA—which continues the unbroken congressional practice of treating future and existing copyrights in parity for term extension purposes—is an impermissible exercise of Congress' power under the Copyright Clause.

B

Petitioners' Copyright Clause arguments rely on several novel readings of the Clause. We next address these arguments and explain why we find them unpersuasive.

* * *

Petitioners dominantly advance a series of arguments all premised on the proposition that Congress may not extend an existing copyright absent new consideration from the author. They pursue this main theme under three headings. Petitioners contend that the CTEA's extension of existing copyrights (1) overlooks the requirement of "originality," (2) fails to "promote the Progress of Science," and (3) ignores copyright's quid pro quo.

Petitioners' "originality" argument draws on *Feist Publications, Inc. v. Rural Telephone Service Co.*, 499 U.S. 340 (1991). * * * *Feist*, however, did not touch on the duration of copyright protection. Rather, the decision addressed the core question of copyrightability, i.e., the "creative spark" a work must have to be eligible for copyright protection at all. Explaining the originality requirement, *Feist* trained on the Copyright Clause words "Authors" and "Writings." *Id.*, at 346–347. The decision did not construe the "limited Times" for which a work may be protected, and the originality requirement has no bearing on that prescription.

More forcibly, petitioners contend that the CTEA's extension of existing copyrights does not "promote the Progress of Science" as contemplated by the preambular language of the Copyright Clause. Art. I, § 8, cl. 8. To sustain this objection, petitioners do not argue that the Clause's preamble is an independently enforceable limit on Congress' power. Rather, they maintain that the preambular language identifies the sole end to which Congress may legislate; accordingly, they conclude, the meaning of "limited Times" must be "determined in light of that specified end." The CTEA's extension of existing copyrights categorically fails to "promote the Progress of Science," petitioners argue, because it does not stimulate the creation of new works but merely adds value to works already created.

As petitioners point out, we have described the Copyright Clause as "both a grant of power and a limitation," *Graham v. John Deere Co. of Kansas City*, 383 U.S. 1, 5 (1966), and have said that "[t]he primary objective of copyright" is "[t]o promote the Progress of Science," *Feist*, 499 U.S., at 349. * * *

We have also stressed, however, that it is generally for Congress, not the courts, to decide how best to pursue the Copyright Clause's objectives. The justifications we earlier set out for Congress' enactment of the CTEA, provide a rational basis for the conclusion that the CTEA "promote[s] the Progress of Science."

On the issue of copyright duration, Congress, from the start, has routinely applied new definitions or adjustments of the copyright term to both future works and existing works not yet in the public domain. Such consistent congressional practice is entitled to "very great weight, and when it is remembered that the rights thus established have not been disputed during a period of [over two] centur[ies], it is almost conclusive." *Burrow-Giles Lithographic Co. v. Sarony*, 111 U.S., at 57. * * *

Closely related to petitioners' preambular argument, or a variant of it, is their assertion that the Copyright Clause "imbeds a quid pro quo." They contend, in this regard, that Congress may grant to an "Autho[r]" an "exclusive Right" for a "limited Tim[e]," but only in exchange for a "Writin[g]." Congress' power to confer copyright protection, petitioners argue, is thus contingent upon an exchange: The author of an original work receives an "exclusive Right" for a "limited Tim[e]" in exchange for a dedication to the public thereafter. Extending an existing copyright without demanding additional consideration, petitioners maintain, bestows an unpaid-for benefit on copyright holders and their heirs, in violation of the quid pro quo requirement.

We can demur to petitioners' description of the Copyright Clause as a grant of legislative authority empowering Congress "to secure a bargain—this for that." *Id.*, at 16; *see Mazer v. Stein*, 347 U.S. 201, 219 (1954) ("The economic philosophy behind the clause empowering Congress to grant patents and copyrights is the conviction that encouragement of individual effort by personal gain is the best way to advance public welfare through the talents of authors and inventors in 'Science and useful Arts.' "). But the legislative evolution earlier recalled demonstrates what the bargain entails. Given the consistent placement of existing copyright holders in parity with future holders, the author of a work created in the last 170 years would reasonably comprehend, as the "this" offered her, a copyright not only for the time in place when protection is gained, but also for any renewal or extension legislated during that time. Congress could rationally seek to "promote . . . Progress" by including in every copyright statute an express guarantee that authors would receive the benefit of any later legislative extension of the copyright term. Nothing in the Copyright Clause bars Congress from creating the same incentive by adopting the same position as a matter of unbroken practice.

* * *

For the several reasons stated, we find no Copyright Clause impediment to the CTEA's extension of existing copyrights.

III

Petitioners separately argue that the CTEA is a content-neutral regulation of speech that fails heightened judicial review under the First Amendment. We reject petitioners' plea for imposition of uncommonly strict scrutiny on a copyright scheme that incorporates its own speech-protective purposes and safeguards. The Copyright Clause and First Amendment were adopted close in time. This proximity indicates that, in the Framers' view, copyright's limited monopolies are compatible with free speech principles. Indeed, copyright's purpose is to promote the creation and publication of free expression. As *Harper & Row* observed: "[T]he Framers intended copyright itself to be the engine of free expression. By establishing a marketable right to the use of one's expression, copyright supplies the economic incentive to create and disseminate ideas." 471 U.S., at 558.

In addition to spurring the creation and publication of new expression, copyright law contains built-in First Amendment accommodations. First, it distinguishes between ideas and expression and makes only the latter eligible for copyright protection. Specifically, 17 U.S.C. § 102(b) provides: "In no case does copyright protection for an original work of authorship extend to any idea, procedure, process, system, method of operation, concept, principle, or discovery, regardless of the form in which it is described, explained, illustrated, or embodied in such work." As we said in *Harper & Row*, this "idea/expression dichotomy strike[s] a definitional balance between the First Amendment and the Copyright Act by permitting free communication of facts while still protecting an author's expression." 471 U.S., at 556. Due to this distinction, every idea, theory, and fact in a copyrighted work becomes instantly available for public exploitation at the moment of publication.

Second, the "fair use" defense allows the public to use not only facts and ideas contained in a copyrighted work, but also expression itself in certain circumstances. Codified at 17 U.S.C. § 107, the defense provides: "[T]he fair use of a copyrighted work, including such use by reproduction in copies . . ., for purposes such as criticism, comment, news reporting, teaching (including multiple copies for classroom use), scholarship, or research, is not an infringement of copyright." The fair use defense affords considerable "latitude for scholarship and comment," *Harper & Row*, 471 U.S., at 560, and even for parody, *see Campbell v. Acuff-Rose Music, Inc.*, 510 U.S. 569 (1994) (rap group's musical parody of Roy Orbison's "Oh, Pretty Woman" may be fair use).

The CTEA itself supplements these traditional First Amendment safeguards. First, it allows libraries, archives, and similar institutions to "reproduce" and "distribute, display, or perform in facsimile or digital form" copies of certain published works "during the last 20 years of any term of copyright . . . for purposes of preservation, scholarship, or research" if the work is not already being exploited commercially and further copies are unavailable at a reasonable price. 17 U.S.C. § 108(h). Second, Title II of the CTEA, known as the Fairness in Music Licensing Act of 1998, exempts small businesses, restaurants, and like entities from having to pay performance royalties on music played from licensed radio, television, and similar facilities. 17 U.S.C. § 110(5)(B).

* * *

The CTEA * * * protects authors' original expression from unrestricted exploitation. Protection of that order does not raise the free speech concerns present when the government compels or burdens the communication of particular facts or ideas. The First Amendment securely protects the freedom to make—or decline to make—one's own speech; it bears less heavily when speakers assert the right to make other people's speeches. To the extent such assertions raise First Amendment concerns, copyright's built-in free speech safeguards are generally adequate to address them. We recognize that the D.C. Circuit spoke too broadly when it declared copyrights "categorically immune from challenges under the First Amendment." 239 F.3d, at 375. But when, as in this case, Congress has not altered the traditional contours of copyright protection, further First Amendment scrutiny is unnecessary. *See Harper & Row*, 471 U.S., at 560.

* * *

As we read the Framers' instruction, the Copyright Clause empowers Congress to determine the intellectual property regimes that, overall, in that body's judgment, will serve the ends of the Clause. *See Graham*, 383 U.S., at 6 (Congress may "implement the stated purpose of the Framers by selecting the policy which *in its judgment* best effectuates the constitutional aim." (emphasis added)). Beneath the facade of their inventive constitutional interpretation, petitioners forcefully urge that Congress pursued very bad policy in prescribing the CTEA's long terms. The wisdom of Congress' action, however, is not within our province to second guess. Satisfied that the legislation before us remains inside the domain the Constitution assigns to the First Branch, we affirm the judgment of the Court of Appeals.

* * *

NOTES

1. Justice Breyer dissented in *Eldred* for a number of reasons, including the economic impact on users of copyrighted works. Due to the length of the copyright term, users will need permission, and will probably have to pay a licensing fee, for many works that are already more than 100 years old. Also, consider the situation of someone who seeks permission to exploit a

copyrighted work. Because copyright notice and registration are now optional (and registration has always been optional for most unpublished works), it may be difficult or impossible to identify or locate the current copyright owner even after a diligent search. This is the problem of "orphan works"—works that are still under copyright but whose owners cannot be identified or located for purposes of obtaining permission to exploit the work. Congress has considered, but not yet enacted, legislation to address this problem.

2. *Eldred* holds that copyright laws are not "categorically immune" from First Amendment challenges, but the CTEA did not violate the First Amendment. What level of scrutiny is the Court applying? Under what circumstances would copyright law implicate the First Amendment in such a way as to trigger heightened scrutiny? For more on this question, *see* the excerpt from *Golan v. Holder* later in this chapter.

3. During the last 20 years of the term in published works, a new subsection 108 privilege (§ 108(h)), added by the CTEA, permits libraries and archives to make, distribute, display or perform copies of the work (in facsimile or digital form) for purposes of preservation, scholarship, or research, under circumstances in which copies cannot otherwise be obtained at a reasonable price. However, the reproduction and distribution privilege does not apply to "musical works, pictorial, graphic or sculptural works, or a motion picture or other audiovisual work other than an audiovisual work dealing with news." Why this limitation? What does it mean in practice?

4. What copyright term applies to works by joint authors? What about a work that is jointly authored by some persons who are acting under work-made-for-hire arrangements and other persons who are not?

5. In the case of manuscripts that were unpublished (and thus theoretically entitled to perpetual copyright under state law) when the 1976 Act took effect, what copyright term now applies under the Act?

6. In the case of a copyright that is measured by the life-plus-seventy term, how can a potential user determine whether a particular author is still living, or what was the author's date of death? Does it matter if the work is unregistered and unpublished?

7. In addition to replacing the initial and renewal copyright terms of the 1909 Act with a single copyright term, the 1976 Act added an additional 19 years to the renewal terms of all copyrights subsisting as of January 1, 1978; this is known as the "extended renewal term." Because Congress passed interim legislation extending the renewal terms of subsisting copyrights during the years preceding enactment of the 1976 Act, any copyright that was timely renewed under the 1909 Act subsisted for a total of at least 75 years. While some of these copyrights entered the public domain after 75 years, any copyrights that were still in force as of 1998 received an additional 20 years of protection under the CTEA.

8. Can trademark law extend protection even beyond the term offered by copyright? *See, e.g., Dastar Corp. v. Twentieth Century Fox Film Corp.*, 539 U.S. 23 (2003), excerpted in Chapter 4.

9. *Klinger v. Conan Doyle Estate, Ltd.*, 755 F.3d 496 (7th Cir. 2014), which involved characters from the *Sherlock Holmes* series of mystery books, addressed the question whether copyright subsists in characters that first appeared in books that have since entered the public domain, if the author continued to develop those characters in subsequent books that are still protected by copyright. The Seventh Circuit held that the characters introduced in the public domain books were now in the public domain; it expressed concern that a contrary ruling would lead to perpetual copyright protection for characters.

10. Based on your understanding of the term of copyright protection under the 1909 Act and the CTEA, what was the original publication year for works that will enter the public domain on January 1 of next year?

11. The 2018 Music Modernization Act granted pre-1972 sound recordings a sui generis form of federal protection under section 1401 that is similar but not identical to copyright. One dissimilarity is the term of protection, which varies based on the recording's initial publication date. In each case, federal protection ends no sooner than 95 years from publication, and for some recordings it lasts longer. However, all of these terms end no later than February 15, 2067. The exact formula is set forth in 17 U.S.C. § 1401(a)(2). Under this formula, if a sound recording was first published in 1955, when will its protection under section 1401 end?

2. RENEWAL RIGHTS UNDER THE 1909 ACT

As discussed earlier, the copyright term for works published prior to January 1, 1978, included an initial term plus a renewal term. Until 1992, renewal was not automatic, and failure to renew the copyright caused the work to enter the public domain—obviously, a serious consequence for the copyright owner. In contrast, if the copyright was properly renewed, the work would receive the full renewal term. (And, in many cases, that meant the copyright was still in force in 1998, and thus got the benefit of the additional 20-year CTEA extension.)

Many of these copyrights were licensed or assigned during their initial terms, in contracts that conveyed both the initial term and the renewal term. However, the Supreme Court held in *Miller Music Corp. v. Charles N. Daniels, Inc.*, 362 U.S. 373 (1960), that a grant of the renewal term was valid only if the author was still living at the time the renewal term vested—that is, at the end of the initial term. In other words, the renewal term was a mere "expectancy," and did not become an actual property right until vesting. If the author died before the vesting date, then the renewal term instead vested in the author's statutory heirs as designated in section 304(a)(1)(C), which gave first priority to the deceased author's surviving spouse and/or children, then to the executor, and then to the next of kin in the absence of a will. In such cases, the contractual grant of rights in the renewal term was void, and the grantee could obtain those rights only by negotiating with the statutory heir(s) in whom the rights had vested. (This complication did not apply, however, to copyrights in works made for hire.)

The Supreme Court further held, in *Stewart v. Abend,* 495 U.S. 207 (1990), that the same rules applied even if the original grant included the right to create a derivative work and the grantee had already created the derivative work before the initial copyright term expired. As a result of this decision, the Hitchcock film *Rear Window* had to be temporarily withdrawn from circulation, because even though the author of the underlying short story had conveyed both the initial and the renewal terms to the film studio, he died before the renewal term vested.

By now, all copyrighted works that were eligible for renewal terms have entered their renewal terms (or the public domain if they were not timely renewed). There is, of course, no such thing as a renewal term for any works created under the 1976 Act, because all such works have a single unitary term (*e.g.,* life plus 70 years). Today, therefore, copyright grantees no longer face the uncertainty of wondering whether they will ever receive the renewal terms for which they bargained.

Why did the 1976 Act finally do away with the renewal term? You can find the answer in the following excerpt from the legislative history of the 1992 amendment in which Congress decided that any remaining renewals should be automatic, so that failure to renew would no longer cause any works to enter the public domain. Note that any works which had already entered the public domain due to non-renewal prior to 1992 received no benefit from this legislation; they remained in the public domain. (But some of them, as we will see shortly, were rescued from the public domain just a few years later.)

COPYRIGHT RENEWAL ACT OF 1992

S.Rep. No. 102–194.
102nd Cong., 1st Sess. 4–7, 21–22 (1991).

Because of its complexities, the Copyright Office, book and music publishers, authors, filmmakers and other copyright organizations criticized the registration renewal provision for being burdensome and unfair to thousands of copyright holders and their heirs. * * *

* * * Witnesses also maintained that the present renewal provisions are even more puzzling for foreign authors, who are even less familiar with this formality because it is unique to U.S. law. * * * The domestic laws of most developed countries contain very few formalities conditioning copyright protection. Compliance with formalities is antithetical to the major international treaty on copyright relations, the Berne Convention for

the Protection of Literary and Artistic Works. In the 1976 general revision, Congress dispensed with many of the formalities contained in the 1909 copyright law, and in 1988, the United States adhered to the Berne Convention (Paris, 1971). However, Congress declined to modify the renewal provision in the Berne Convention Implementation Act (Public Law 100–568) because it felt that the cutting off or altering [of] existing expectancies at that time would be unfair and the safer course would be to allow the renewal provisions to phase out by the year 2005. * * *

Opponents of the bill argue that mandatory registration renewal should be retained because it * * * serves an important public purpose: increasing the volume of works that fall into the public domain, free of copyright protection. This argument is contrary to the real public purpose for copyright protection: our copyright law grants authors exclusive, limited rights to exploit their creations for a sufficient time so they will be encouraged to continue creating works that entertain, educate, and fire our imaginations.

The committee believes that the public domain should consist of works which have enjoyed a full and fair term of protection and should not be enlarged because of an author's error in recordkeeping, or any other innocent failure to comply with overly technical formalities in the copyright law. * * *

The automatic renewal provisions will apply only to those works that are still in their first, 28-year term of protection on the date this bill becomes law. Under the bill, works that acquired a first-term of copyright protection between 1963 and December 31, 1977, and that are eligible for registration renewal between 1991 and 2005, will benefit from the automatic renewal provisions. Consequently, the bill provides only prospective protection; it does not restore protection to works that have already fallen into the public domain, nor extend the term of protection to qualifying works beyond what they are already entitled to receive if a renewal registration is made. The committee concludes that these amendments to the registration renewal provisions will restore a measure of equity and fairness to the copyright law.

3. COPYRIGHT RESTORATION

Statute: 17 U.S.C. § 104A

URUGUAY ROUND AGREEMENTS ACT

S. Rep. No. 103–412.
103d Cong., 2d Sess. 225–26 (1994).

The legislation includes language to restore copyright protection to certain foreign works from countries that are members of the Berne

Convention or WTO that have fallen into the public domain for reasons other than the normal expiration of their term of protection.

The Agreement requires WTO countries to comply with Article 18 of the Berne Convention. While the United States declared its compliance with the Berne Convention in 1989, it never addressed or enacted legislation to implement Article 18 of the Convention. Article 18 requires that the terms of the convention apply to all works that have fallen into the public domain by reasons other than the expiration of its term of protection. (Examples include failure to file a timely renewal application and failure to affix a copyright notice).

The bill would automatically restore copyright protection for qualifying works of authors from Berne or WTO countries one year after the WTO comes into being. In order for the restored copyright to be enforced against a "reliance party," it is necessary for the author or copyright owner (rightholder) of the foreign work to either file a "notice of intent" with the Copyright Office during the 24 months after the effective date of the Uruguay Round Agreement or provide actual notice (for the life of the copyright term) directly by notifying the reliance party. Reliance parties then have one year from publication of the constructive notice or receipt of the actual notice to continue to use or sell off copies of the work that have been restored to a foreign author or rightholder. Reproduction of the work during this period is not permitted. After this period, reliance parties are subject to remedies for infringement, except in certain cases.

Section 104A(d)(3) provides additional protection to a reliance party who used a restored foreign work to create a derivative work because a one year sell off period might be an inadequate period to recoup the investment. In the case of a derivative work that was created based upon a foreign work that was in the public domain but has been restored, the reliance party may continue to sell the derivative work in exchange for providing reasonable compensation to the owner of the restored copyright. In the event that an agreement cannot be reached regarding compensation a district court may determine reasonable compensation, based upon the contribution made by the reliance party as well as the author of the underlying restored work. The court is to take into consideration any damage to the market for the restored work.

* * *

NOTES

1. The Uruguay Round Agreements Act (URAA), Pub.L. 103–465, became law on Dec. 8, 1994. The copyright restoration provisions are contained in section 514 of the URAA, and codified at 17 U.S.C. § 104A. For a work to qualify for copyright restoration: (1) it must be an original work of authorship; (2) its copyright term in its country of origin must not have expired; (3) it must

have entered the public domain in the United States because of lack of national eligibility (*see* 17 U.S.C. § 104), noncompliance with formalities (such as notice, renewal, or the manufacturing clause under 17 U.S.C. § 601), or ineligible subject matter (in the case of a sound recording fixed before February 15, 1972); and (4) at the time the work was created, at least one of its authors or rightholders must have been a national or domiciliary of an eligible country, meaning a country (other than the United States) that is a member of the Berne Convention or the World Trade Organization (WTO), or that is subject to a presidential proclamation extending copyright protection to works of that country based on reciprocal treatment. If the work is published, it must not have been published in the United States within 30 days of first publication in the eligible country. For works from countries which were already WTO members or Berne signatories, the effective date of restoration was January 1, 1996.

According to the Copyright Office, the date on which reliance parties are required to stop reproducing or preparing derivative works based on any restored work is the earlier of (1) the date on which they receive actual notice of the owner's intent to enforce the restored copyright, or (2) the date on which the Copyright Office publishes in the Federal Register a list identifying works as to which notices of intent to enforce have been filed. After receiving either form of notice, reliance parties have a 12-month grace period during which they may sell off existing inventory, publicly perform or display the work, or authorize others to do so. Notices of intent to enforce could be filed beginning January 1, 1996. Beginning in May 1996, and at regular intervals thereafter, the Copyright Office was required to publish lists of those notices of intent.

2. Suppose a reliance party created a derivative work (such as a translation or a motion picture) prior to the restoration of copyright in the underlying work. After the 12-month grace period expires, does the reliance party have any continuing right to exploit the derivative work?

3. Suppose that copyright in a particular work was restored on January 1, 1996. If a company made and sold copies of that work from 1965 to 1984, discontinued those activities from 1984–1996, then resumed them in 1996, is the company a reliance party? How does this determination affect the company's rights? *See Troll Co. v. Uneeda Doll Co.*, 483 F.3d 150 (2d Cir. 2007).

GOLAN V. HOLDER

565 U.S. 302, 132 S.Ct. 873 (2012).

JUSTICE GINSBURG delivered the opinion of the Court.

The Berne Convention for the Protection of Literary and Artistic Works (Berne Convention or Berne), which took effect in 1886, is the principal accord governing international copyright relations. Latecomer to the international copyright regime launched by Berne, the United States joined the Convention in 1989. To perfect U.S. implementation of Berne, and as part of our response to the Uruguay Round of multilateral trade negotiations, Congress, in 1994, gave works enjoying copyright protection abroad the same full term of protection available to U.S. works. Congress did so in § 514 of the Uruguay Round Agreements Act (URAA), which grants copyright protection to preexisting works of Berne member countries, protected in their country of origin, but lacking protection in the United States for any of three reasons: The United States did not protect works from the country of origin at the time of publication; the United States did not protect sound recordings fixed before 1972; or the author had failed to comply with U.S. statutory formalities (formalities Congress no longer requires as prerequisites to copyright protection).

The URAA accords no protection to a foreign work after its full copyright term has expired, causing it to fall into the public domain, whether under the laws of the country of origin or of this country. Works encompassed by § 514 are granted the protection they would have enjoyed had the United States maintained copyright relations with the author's country or removed formalities incompatible with Berne. Foreign authors, however, gain no credit for the protection they lacked in years prior to § 514's enactment. They therefore enjoy fewer total years of exclusivity than do their U.S. counterparts. As a consequence of the barriers to U.S. copyright protection prior to the enactment of § 514, foreign works "restored" to protection by the measure had entered the public domain in this country. To cushion the impact of their placement in protected status, Congress included in § 514 ameliorating accommodations for parties who had exploited affected works before the URAA was enacted.

Petitioners include orchestra conductors, musicians, publishers, and others who formerly enjoyed free access to works § 514 removed from the public domain. They maintain that the Constitution's Copyright and Patent Clause, Art. I, § 8, cl. 8, and First Amendment both decree the invalidity of § 514. Under those prescriptions of our highest law, petitioners assert, a work that has entered the public domain, for whatever reason, must forever remain there.

In accord with the judgment of the Tenth Circuit, we conclude that § 514 does not transgress constitutional limitations on Congress' authority. Neither the Copyright and Patent Clause nor the First Amendment, we hold, makes the public domain, in any and all cases, a territory that works may never exit.

* * *

II

We first address petitioners' argument that Congress lacked authority, under the Copyright Clause, to enact § 514. The Constitution states that "Congress shall have Power . . . [t]o promote the Progress of Science . . . by securing for limited Times to Authors . . . the exclusive Right to their . . .

Writings." Art. I, § 8, cl. 8. Petitioners find in this grant of authority an impenetrable barrier to the extension of copyright protection to authors whose writings, for whatever reason, are in the public domain. We see no such barrier in the text of the Copyright Clause, historical practice, or our precedents.

A

The text of the Copyright Clause does not exclude application of copyright protection to works in the public domain. Petitioners' contrary argument relies primarily on the Constitution's confinement of a copyright's lifespan to a "limited Tim[e]." "Removing works from the public domain," they contend, "violates the 'limited [t]imes' restriction by turning a fixed and predictable period into one that can be reset or resurrected at any time, even after it expires."

Our decision in *Eldred* [*v. Ashcroft,* 537 U.S. 186 (2003)] is largely dispositive of petitioners' limited-time argument. There we addressed the question whether Congress violated the Copyright Clause when it extended, by 20 years, the terms of existing copyrights. Ruling that Congress acted within constitutional bounds, we declined to infer from the text of the Copyright Clause "the command that a time prescription, once set, becomes forever 'fixed' or 'inalterable.'" "The word 'limited,'" we observed, "does not convey a meaning so constricted." * * * The construction petitioners tender closely resembles the definition rejected in *Eldred* and is similarly infirm.

The terms afforded works restored by § 514 are no less "limited" than those the CTEA lengthened. In light of *Eldred,* petitioners do not here contend that the term Congress has granted U.S. authors—their lifetimes, plus 70 years—is unlimited. Nor do petitioners explain why terms of the same duration, as applied to foreign works, are not equally "circumscribed" and "confined." *See Eldred,* 537 U.S., at 199. Indeed, * * * the copyrights of restored foreign works typically last for fewer years than those of their domestic counterparts.

The difference, petitioners say, is that the limited time had already passed for works in the public domain. What was that limited term for foreign works once excluded from U.S. copyright protection? Exactly "zero," petitioners respond. We find scant sense in this argument, for surely a "limited time" of exclusivity must begin before it may end.

* * *

B

Historical practice corroborates our reading of the Copyright Clause to permit full U.S. compliance with Berne. Undoubtedly, federal copyright legislation generally has not affected works in the public domain. Section 514's disturbance of that domain, petitioners argue, distinguishes their suit from Eldred's. In adopting the CTEA, petitioners note, Congress acted in accord with "an unbroken congressional practice" of granting pre-expiration term extensions, 537 U.S., at 200, No comparable practice, they maintain, supports § 514.

On occasion, however, Congress has seen fit to protect works once freely available. Notably, the Copyright Act of 1790 granted protection to many works previously in the public domain. Act of May 31, 1790 (1790 Act), § 1, 1 Stat. 124 (covering "any map, chart, book, or books already printed within these United States"). Before the Act launched a uniform national system, three States provided no statutory copyright protection at all. Of those that did afford some protection, seven failed to protect maps; eight did not cover previously published books; and all ten denied protection to works that failed to comply with formalities. The First Congress, it thus appears, did not view the public domain as inviolate. As we have recognized, the "construction placed upon the Constitution by [the drafters of] the first [copyright] act of 1790 and the act of 1802 . . . men who were contemporary with [the Constitution's] formation, many of whom were members of the convention which framed it, is of itself entitled to very great weight." *Burrow-Giles Lithographic Co. v. Sarony,* 111 U.S. 53, 57 (1884).

Subsequent actions confirm that Congress has not understood the Copyright Clause to preclude protection for existing works. Several private bills restored the copyrights of works that previously had been in the public domain. These bills were unchallenged in court.

* * *

* * * Given the authority we hold Congress has, we will not second-guess the political choice Congress made between leaving the public domain untouched and embracing Berne unstintingly.

C

Petitioners' ultimate argument as to the Copyright and Patent Clause concerns its initial words. Congress is empowered to "promote the Progress of Science and useful Arts" by enacting systems of copyright and patent protection. U.S. Const., Art. I, § 8, cl. 8. Perhaps counterintuitively for the contemporary reader, Congress' copyright authority is tied to the progress of science; its patent authority, to the progress of the useful arts.

The "Progress of Science," petitioners acknowledge, refers broadly to "the creation and spread of knowledge and learning." They nevertheless argue that federal legislation cannot serve the Clause's aim unless the legislation "spur[s] the creation of . . . new works." Because § 514 deals solely with works already created, petitioners urge, it "provides no plausible incentive to create new works" and is therefore invalid.

The creation of at least one new work, however, is not the sole way Congress may promote knowledge and learning. In *Eldred,* we rejected an argument nearly identical to the one petitioners rehearse. * * *

Even were we writing on a clean slate, petitioners' argument would be unavailing. Nothing in the text of the Copyright Clause confines the "Progress of Science" exclusively to "incentives for creation." Evidence from the founding, moreover, suggests that inducing *dissemination*—as opposed to creation—was viewed as an appropriate means to promote science. * * * Our decisions correspondingly recognize that "copyright supplies the economic incentive to create *and disseminate* ideas." *Harper & Row, Publishers, Inc. v. Nation Enterprises,* 471 U.S. 539, 558 (1985) (emphasis added).

Considered against this backdrop, § 514 falls comfortably within Congress' authority under the Copyright Clause. Congress rationally could have concluded that adherence to Berne "promotes the diffusion of knowledge." A well-functioning international copyright system would likely encourage the dissemination of existing and future works. Full compliance with Berne, Congress had reason to believe, would expand the foreign markets available to U.S. authors and invigorate protection against piracy of U.S. works abroad, thereby benefitting copyright-intensive industries stateside and inducing greater investment in the creative process.

The provision of incentives for the creation of new works is surely an essential means to advance the spread of knowledge and learning. We hold, however, that it is not the sole means Congress may use "[t]o promote the Progress of Science." Congress determined that exemplary adherence to Berne would serve the objectives of the Copyright Clause. We have no warrant to reject the rational judgment Congress made.

III

A

We next explain why the First Amendment does not inhibit the restoration authorized by § 514. To do so, we first recapitulate the relevant part of our pathmarking decision in *Eldred.* The petitioners in *Eldred,* like those here, argued that Congress had violated not only the "limited Times" prescription of the Copyright Clause. In addition, and independently, the *Eldred* petitioners charged, Congress had offended the First Amendment's freedom of expression guarantee. The CTEA's 20-year enlargement of a copyright's duration, we held in *Eldred,* offended neither provision.

* * *

Given the "speech-protective purposes and safeguards" embraced by copyright law, we concluded in *Eldred* that there was no call for the heightened review petitioners sought in that case. We reach the same conclusion here. Section 514 leaves undisturbed the "idea/expression" distinction and the "fair use" defense. Moreover, Congress adopted measures to ease the transition from a national scheme to an international copyright regime: It deferred the date from which enforcement runs, and it cushioned the impact of restoration on "reliance parties" who exploited foreign works denied protection before § 514 took effect.

B

* * *

The Tenth Circuit's initial opinion determined that petitioners marshaled a stronger First Amendment challenge than did their predecessors in *Eldred,* who never "possessed unfettered access to any of the works at issue." As petitioners put it in this Court, Congress impermissibly revoked their right to exploit foreign works that "belonged to them" once the works were in the public domain.

To copyright lawyers, the "vested rights" formulation might sound exactly backwards: Rights typically vest at the *outset* of copyright protection, in an author or rightholder. Once the term of protection ends, the works do not revest in any rightholder. Instead, the works simply lapse into the public domain. Anyone has free access to the public domain, but no one, after the copyright term has expired, acquires ownership rights in the once-protected works.

Congress recurrently adjusts copyright law to protect categories of works once outside the law's compass. For example, Congress broke new ground when it extended copyright protection to foreign works in 1891; to dramatic works in 1856; to photographs and photographic negatives in 1865; to motion pictures in 1912; to fixed sound recordings in 1972; and to architectural works in 1990. And on several occasions, as recounted above, Congress protected works previously in the public domain, hence freely usable by the public. If Congress could grant protection to these works without hazarding heightened First Amendment scrutiny, then what free speech principle disarms it from protecting works prematurely cast into the public domain for reasons antithetical to the Berne Convention?[33]

Section 514, we add, does not impose a blanket prohibition on public access. Petitioners protest that fair use and the idea/expression dichotomy "are plainly inadequate to protect the speech and expression rights that Section 514 took from petitioners, or . . . the public"—that is, "the unrestricted right to perform, copy, teach and distribute the *entire* work,

[33] It was the Fifth Amendment's Takings Clause—not the First Amendment—that Congress apparently perceived to be a potential check on its authority to protect works then freely available to the public. The reliance-party protections supplied by § 514 were meant to address such concerns.

for any reason." "Playing a few bars of a Shostakovich symphony," petitioners observe, "is no substitute for performing the entire work."

But Congress has not put petitioners in this bind. The question here, as in *Eldred,* is whether would-be users must pay for their desired use of the author's expression, or else limit their exploitation to "fair use" of that work. Prokofiev's Peter and the Wolf could once be performed free of charge; after § 514 the right to perform it must be obtained in the marketplace. This is the same marketplace, of course, that exists for the music of Prokofiev's U.S. contemporaries: works of Copland and Bernstein, for example, that enjoy copyright protection, but nevertheless appear regularly in the programs of U.S. concertgoers.

Before we joined Berne, domestic works and some foreign works were protected under U.S. statutes and bilateral international agreements, while other foreign works were available at an artificially low (because royalty-free) cost. By fully implementing Berne, Congress ensured that most works, whether foreign or domestic, would be governed by the same legal regime. The phenomenon to which Congress responded is not new: Distortions of the same order occurred with greater frequency—and to the detriment of both foreign and domestic authors—when, before 1891, foreign works were excluded entirely from U.S. copyright protection. Section 514 continued the trend toward a harmonized copyright regime by placing foreign works in the position they would have occupied if the current regime had been in effect when those works were created and first published. Authors once deprived of protection are spared the continuing effects of that initial deprivation; § 514 gives them nothing more than the benefit of their labors during whatever time remains before the normal copyright term expires.

Unlike petitioners, the dissent makes much of the so-called "orphan works" problem. We readily acknowledge the difficulties would-be users of copyrightable materials may face in identifying or locating copyright owners. But as the dissent concedes, this difficulty is hardly peculiar to works restored under § 514. It similarly afflicts, for instance, U.S. libraries that attempt to catalogue U.S. books.

* * *

IV

Congress determined that U.S. interests were best served by our full participation in the dominant system of international copyright protection. Those interests include ensuring exemplary compliance with our international obligations, securing greater protection for U.S. authors abroad, and remedying unequal treatment of foreign authors. The judgment § 514 expresses lies well within the ken of the political branches. It is our obligation, of course, to determine whether the action Congress took, wise or not, encounters any constitutional shoal. For the reasons stated, we are satisfied it does not. The judgment of the Court of Appeals for the Tenth Circuit is therefore

Affirmed.

NOTES

1. Does *Golan*'s interpretation of the "traditional contours" of copyright as referenced in *Eldred* seem like a natural or strained reading of the relevant passage in *Eldred*?

2. Are copyright statutes immune from First Amendment scrutiny after *Eldred* and *Golan*?

3. Does copyright protection really promote greater dissemination of existing works, as the *Golan* majority contends? If so, then should the duration of copyright be extended even further?

4. Justices Breyer and Alito dissented in *Golan*, arguing that section 514 did not incentivize the creation of new works, and inhibited the dissemination of the older works that it removed from the public domain. The dissent highlighted the difficulty of locating copyright owners of older works with restored copyrights in order to secure permission to use those works (which is part of the larger problem of "orphan works"). They also pointed out that the United States could have satisfied Article 18 of Berne without removing works from the public domain. Considering the following language of Article 18, do you agree? If so, does this undermine the majority's analysis?

> (1) This Convention shall apply to all works which, at the moment of its coming into force, have not yet fallen into the public domain in the country of origin through the expiry of the term of protection.
>
> * * *
>
> (3) The application of this principle shall be subject to any provisions contained in special conventions to that effect existing or to be concluded between countries of the Union. In the absence of such provisions, the respective countries shall determine, each in so far as it is concerned, the conditions of application of this principle.

5. Does Congress have the authority to restore copyright protection for works *originating in the United States* that entered the public domain due to failure to comply with formalities? To restore copyright in the works of Shakespeare?

6. In the 2018 Music Modernization Act, Congress for the first time granted federal protection (similar though not identical to copyright) to sound recordings fixed in the United States before February 15, 1972. *See* 17 U.S.C. § 1401. Congress had already done something similar in 1998, when it enacted sui generis protection for boat hull designs in 17 U.S.C. § 1301 *et seq.*, and in 1994, when it invoked its Commerce Clause powers to extend federal protection

to live musical performances in 17 U.S.C. § 1101. Before each of these enactments, the works in question had received protection only under state law, if at all. Did Congress, in effect, remove these works from the public domain? Could Congress do the same thing for fashion designs or other product designs that are currently ineligible for federal copyright protection due to the useful articles doctrine?

C. ALIENABILITY OF COPYRIGHT

1. ASSIGNMENTS AND LICENSES

Statutes: 17 U.S.C. §§ 201–05

COPYRIGHT ACT OF 1976

H.R. Rep. No. 94–1476,
94th Cong., 2d Sess. 123 (1976).

Transfer of ownership

The principle of unlimited alienability of copyright is stated in clause (1) of section 201(d). Under that provision the ownership of a copyright, or of any part of it, may be transferred by any means of conveyance or by operation of law, and is to be treated as personal property upon the death of the owner. * * *

Clause (2) of subsection (d) contains the first explicit statutory recognition of the principle of divisibility of copyright in our law. This provision, which has long been sought by authors and their representatives, and which has attracted wide support from other groups, means that any of the exclusive rights that go to make up a copyright, including those enumerated in section 106 and any subdivision of them, can be transferred and owned separately. The definition of "transfer of copyright ownership" in section 101 makes clear that the principle of divisibility applies whether or not the transfer is "limited in time or place of effect," and another definition in the same section provides that the term "copyright owner," with respect to any one exclusive right, refers to the owner of that particular right.

* * *

EFFECTS ASSOCIATES, INC. V. COHEN

908 F.2d 555 (9th Cir. 1990).

KOZINSKI, CIRCUIT JUDGE.

What we have here is a failure to compensate. Larry Cohen, a low-budget horror movie mogul, paid less than the agreed price for special effects footage he had commissioned from Effects Associates. Cohen then used this footage without first obtaining a written license or assignment of the copyright; Effects sued for copyright infringement. We consider whether a transfer of copyright without a written agreement, an arrangement apparently not uncommon in the motion picture industry, conforms with the requirements of the Copyright Act.

[When Effects orally agreed to provide special effects footage for Cohen's film, the parties never discussed who would own the copyright in the commissioned footage. When Effects sued Cohen for infringement (after Cohen failed to tender full payment), the district court granted summary judgment, holding that Effects had granted Cohen an implied license to use the footage. On appeal, the Ninth Circuit held that Effects (which both parties agree is the initial copyright owner) had not transferred the copyright to Cohen, because an oral transfer of copyright ownership is invalid under 17 U.S.C. § 204(a). However, because a "transfer" of copyright is defined by 17 U.S.C. § 101 to include an exclusive license but not a nonexclusive license, the court then addressed the question whether Cohen had acquired an oral nonexclusive license to use the footage.]

* * *

Discussion

A. Transfer of Copyright Ownership

The law couldn't be clearer: The copyright owner of "a motion picture or other audiovisual work" has the exclusive rights to copy, distribute or display the copyrighted work publicly. 17 U.S.C. § 106 (1988). While the copyright owner can sell or license his rights to someone else, section 204 of the Copyright Act invalidates a purported transfer of ownership unless it is in writing. Here, no one disputes that Effects is the copyright owner of the special effects footage used in "The Stuff," and that defendants copied, distributed and publicly displayed this footage without written authorization.

Cohen suggests that section 204's writing requirement does not apply to this situation, advancing an argument that might be summarized, tongue in cheek, as: Moviemakers do lunch, not contracts. Cohen concedes that "[i]n the best of all possible legal worlds" parties would obey the writing requirement, but contends that moviemakers are too absorbed in developing "joint creative endeavors" to "focus upon the legal niceties of copyright licenses." Thus, Cohen suggests that we hold section 204's writing requirement inapplicable here because "it [i]s customary in the motion picture industry . . . not to have written licenses." To the extent that Cohen's argument amounts to a plea to exempt moviemakers from the normal operation of section 204 by making implied transfers of copyrights "the rule, not the exception," we reject his argument.

Common sense tells us that agreements should routinely be put in writing. This simple practice prevents misunderstandings by spelling out the terms of a deal in black and white, forces parties to clarify their thinking and consider problems that could potentially arise, and encourages them to take their promises seriously because it's harder to backtrack on a written contract than on an oral one. Copyright law dovetails nicely with common sense by requiring that a transfer of copyright ownership be in writing. Section 204 ensures that the creator of a work will not give away his copyright inadvertently and forces a party who wants to use the copyrighted work to negotiate with the creator to determine precisely what rights are being transferred and at what price. Most importantly, section 204 enhances predictability and certainty of copyright ownership—"Congress' paramount goal" when it revised the Act in 1976. *Community for Creative Non-Violence,* 109 S.Ct. at 2177. Rather than look to the courts every time they disagree as to whether a particular use of the work violates their mutual understanding, parties need only look to the writing that sets out their respective rights.

Section 204's writing requirement is not unduly burdensome; it necessitates neither protracted negotiations nor substantial expense. The rule is really quite simple: If the copyright holder agrees to transfer ownership to another party, that party must get the copyright holder to sign a piece of paper saying so. It doesn't have to be the Magna Charta; a one-line pro forma statement will do.

Cohen's attempt to exempt moviemakers from the requirements of the Copyright Act is largely precluded by recent Supreme Court and circuit authority construing the work-for-hire doctrine. * * *

The Supreme Court and this circuit, while recognizing the custom and practice in the industry, have refused to permit moviemakers to sidestep section 204's writing requirement. Accordingly, we find unpersuasive Cohen's contention that section 204's writing requirement, which singles out no particular group, somehow doesn't apply to him. As section 204 makes no special allowances for the movie industry, neither do we.

B. Nonexclusive Licenses

Although we reject any suggestion that moviemakers are immune to section 204, we note that there is a narrow exception to the writing requirement that may apply here. Section 204 provides that all transfers of copyright ownership must be in writing; section 101 defines transfers of ownership broadly, but expressly removes from the scope of section 204 a "nonexclusive license." The sole issue that remains, then, is whether Cohen had a nonexclusive license to use plaintiff's special effects footage.

The leading treatise on copyright law states that "[a] nonexclusive license may be granted orally, or may even be implied from conduct." 3 M. NIMMER & D. NIMMER, NIMMER ON COPYRIGHT § 10.03[A], at 10–36 (1989).

Cohen relies on the latter proposition; he insists that, although Effects never gave him a written or oral license, Effects's conduct created an implied license to use the footage in "The Stuff."

Cohen relies largely on our decision in *Oddo v. Ries*, 743 F.2d 630 (9th Cir.1984). There, we held that Oddo, the author of a series of articles on how to restore Ford F-100 pickup trucks, had impliedly granted a limited non-exclusive license to Ries, a publisher, to use plaintiff's articles in a book on the same topic. We relied on the fact that Oddo and Ries had formed a partnership to create and publish the book, with Oddo writing and Ries providing capital. *Id.* at 632 & n. 1. Oddo prepared a manuscript consisting partly of material taken from his prior articles and submitted it to Ries. *Id.* at 632. Because the manuscript incorporated pre-existing material, it was a derivative work; by publishing it, Ries would have necessarily infringed the copyright in Oddo's articles, unless Oddo had granted him a license. *Id.* at 634. We concluded that, in preparing and handing over to Ries a manuscript intended for publication that, if published, would infringe Oddo's copyright, Oddo "impliedly gave the partnership a license to use the articles insofar as they were incorporated in the manuscript, for without such a license, Oddo's contribution to the partnership venture would have been of minimal value." *Id.*[5]

The district court agreed with Cohen, and we agree with the district court: *Oddo* controls here. Like the plaintiff in *Oddo*, Effects created a work at defendant's request and handed it over, intending that defendant copy and distribute it.[6] To hold that Effects did not at the same time convey a license to use the footage in "The Stuff" would mean that plaintiff's contribution to the film was "of minimal value," a conclusion that can't be squared with the fact that Cohen paid Effects almost $56,000 for this footage. Accordingly, we conclude that Effects impliedly granted nonexclusive licenses to Cohen and his production company to incorporate the special effects footage into "The Stuff" and to New World Entertainment to distribute the film.

Nor can we construe payment in full as a condition precedent to implying a license. Conditions precedent are disfavored and will not be

---

[5] Oddo did nevertheless prevail, but on other grounds. Ries was unhappy with Oddo's manuscript and hired another writer to do the job right. This writer added much new material, but also used large chunks of Oddo's manuscript, thereby incorporating portions of Oddo's pre-existing articles. 743 F.2d at 632. By publishing the other writer's book, Ries exceeded the scope of his implied license to use Oddo's articles and was liable for copyright infringement. *Id.* at 634.

[6] As the district court found, "every objective fact concerning the transaction at issue supports a finding that an implied license existed." Effects's copyright registration certificate states that the footage is to be used in "The Stuff," so does the letter agreement of October 29, 1984, and Effects's President James Danforth agreed at his deposition that this was his understanding. Also, Effects delivered the film negatives to Cohen, never warning him that cutting the negatives into the film would constitute copyright infringement. While delivery of a copy "does not *of itself* convey any rights in the copyrighted work," 17 U.S.C. § 202 (1988) (emphasis added), it is one factor that may be relied upon in determining that an implied license has been granted.

read into a contract unless required by plain, unambiguous language. *Sulmeyer v. United States* (*In re Bubble Up Delaware, Inc.*), 684 F.2d 1259, 1264 (9th Cir.1982). The language of the October 29, 1984, agreement doesn't support a conclusion that full payment was a condition precedent to Cohen's use of the footage. Moreover, Effects's president conceded at his deposition that he never told Cohen that a failure to pay would be viewed as copyright infringement. * * *

Conclusion

We affirm the district court's grant of summary judgment in favor of Cohen and the other defendants. We note, however, that plaintiff doesn't leave this court empty-handed. Copyright ownership is comprised of a bundle of rights; in granting a nonexclusive license to Cohen, Effects has given up only one stick from that bundle—the right to sue Cohen for copyright infringement. It retains the right to sue him in state court on a variety of other grounds, including breach of contract. Additionally, Effects may license, sell or give away for nothing its remaining rights in the special effects footage. * * *

NOTES

1. Is an exclusive license a "transfer" for copyright purposes? What about a nonexclusive license? Which must be in writing to be valid? Why?

2. Suppose that a copyright owner attempts an oral assignment of his rights to a second party. Some time after that, an infringement occurs. Does the second party have standing to sue the infringer? Suppose the parties confirm the transfer in writing after the infringement occurs? *See Barefoot Architect, Inc. v. Bunge*, 632 F.3d 822 (3d Cir. 2011) (collecting cases).

3. What purposes are served by the recording provisions of section 205? What kinds of grants should *always* be recorded?

4. Which party prevails when:

(a) An exclusive licensee fails to record, and the licensor makes a subsequent gift of the entire copyright, which is promptly recorded?

(b) An exclusive license takes place, followed by the licensor's grant of a conflicting nonexclusive license (in a written instrument signed by the licensor)? Assume that the exclusive transferee records within 30 days, but this recordation takes place 5 days *after* the nonexclusive license was granted.

(c) The first exclusive licensee records 90 days after the transfer, and a conflicting transfer for valid consideration occurs 100 days after the first transfer, where the second transferee acts in good faith and is unaware of the prior transfer?

(d) Same facts as (c), but the work was never registered.

5. Section 28 of the 1909 Act required a written instrument for any assignment of a statutory copyright in its entirety, but not for an exclusive license of a statutory copyright, and not for any assignment or license of a common law copyright. What impact, if any, does this have on copyright interests today? Should the 1976 Act be applied retroactively to pre-1978 assignments and exclusive licenses? *See Roth v. Pritikin*, 710 F.2d 934 (2d Cir. 1983).

6. Can an exclusive copyright licensee transfer its rights without the licensor's consent? *Compare Gardner v. Nike, Inc.*, 279 F.3d 774 (9th Cir. 2002) *with Traicoff v. Digital Media, Inc.*, 439 F. Supp. 2d 872 (S.D. Ind. 2006). A 2010 legislative proposal to answer this in the affirmative was not enacted. In 2020, the U.S. Court of Appeals for the First Circuit held that the Copyright Act grants copyright licensees an implied right to sublicense the copyrights. *Photographic Illustrators Corp. v. Orgill Inc.*, 953 F.3d 56 (1st Cir. 2020). This implied right to sublicense can be negated, however, with anti-sublicensing language in the licensing agreement.

7. Does a license to publish an author's work "in book form" extend to e-books? *See Random House, Inc. v. Rosetta Books LLC*, 283 F.3d 490 (2d Cir. 2002).

NEW YORK TIMES CO., INC. V. TASINI

533 U.S. 483, 121 S.Ct. 2381 (2001).

JUSTICE GINSBURG delivered the opinion of the Court.

This copyright case concerns the rights of freelance authors and a presumptive privilege of their publishers. The litigation was initiated by six freelance authors and relates to articles they contributed to three print periodicals (two newspapers and one magazine). Under agreements with the periodicals' publishers, but without the freelancers' consent, two computer database companies placed copies of the freelancers' articles—along with all other articles from the periodicals in which the freelancers' work appeared—into three databases. Whether written by a freelancer or staff member, each article is presented to, and retrievable by, the user in isolation, clear of the context the original print publication presented.

The freelance authors' complaint alleged that their copyrights had been infringed by the inclusion of their articles in the databases. The publishers, in response, relied on the privilege of reproduction and distribution accorded them by § 201(c) of the Copyright Act * * *. Specifically, the publishers maintained that, as copyright owners of collective works, *i.e.*, the original print publications, they had merely exercised "the privilege" § 201(c) accords them to "reproduc[e] and distribut[e]" the author's discretely copyrighted contribution.

In agreement with the Second Circuit, we hold that § 201(c) does not authorize the copying at issue here. The publishers are not sheltered by

§ 201(c), we conclude, because the databases reproduce and distribute articles standing alone and not in context, not "as part of that particular collective work" to which the author contributed, "as part of . . . any revision" thereof, or "as part of . . . any later collective work in the same series." Both the print publishers and the electronic publishers, we rule, have infringed the copyrights of the freelance authors.

I

A

* * * The Authors registered copyrights in each of the[ir] Articles. The Times, Newsday, and Time (Print Publishers) registered collective work copyrights in each periodical edition in which an Article originally appeared. The Print Publishers engaged the Authors as independent contractors (freelancers) under contracts that in no instance secured consent from an Author to placement of an Article in an electronic database.

At the time the Articles were published, all three Print Publishers had agreements with petitioner LEXIS/NEXIS (formerly Mead Data Central Corp.), owner and operator of NEXIS, a computerized database that stores information in a text-only format. NEXIS contains articles from hundreds of journals (newspapers and periodicals) spanning many years. The Print Publishers have licensed to LEXIS/NEXIS the text of articles appearing in the three periodicals. The licenses authorize LEXIS/NEXIS to copy and sell any portion of those texts.

Pursuant to the licensing agreements, the Print Publishers regularly provide LEXIS/NEXIS with a batch of all the articles published in each periodical edition. The Print Publisher codes each article to facilitate computerized retrieval, then transmits it in a separate file. After further coding, LEXIS/NEXIS places the article in the central discs of its database.

Subscribers to NEXIS, accessing the system through a computer, may search for articles by author, subject, date, publication, headline, key term, words in text, or other criteria. * * * Each article appears as a separate, isolated "story"—without any visible link to the other stories originally published in the same newspaper or magazine edition. NEXIS does not contain pictures or advertisements, and it does not reproduce the original print publication's formatting features such as headline size, page placement (*e.g.*, above or below the fold for newspapers), or location of continuation pages.

* * *

We granted certiorari to determine whether the copying of the Authors' Articles in the Databases is privileged by 17 U.S.C. § 201(c). Like the Court of Appeals, we conclude that the § 201(c) privilege does not override the Authors' copyrights, for the Databases do not reproduce and distribute the Articles as part of a collective work privileged by § 201(c). Accordingly, and again like the Court of Appeals, we find it unnecessary to determine whether the privilege is transferable.

II

* * *

Section 201(c) both describes and circumscribes the "privilege" a publisher acquires regarding an author's contribution to a collective work:

> "In the absence of an express transfer of the copyright or of any rights under it, the owner of copyright in the collective work is presumed to have acquired *only* the privilege of reproducing and distributing the contribution as part of that particular collective work, any revision of that collective work, and any later collective work in the same series." (Emphasis added.)

A newspaper or magazine publisher is thus privileged to reproduce or distribute an article contributed by a freelance author, absent a contract otherwise providing, only "as part of" any (or all) of three categories of collective works: (a) "that collective work" to which the author contributed her work, (b) "any revision of that collective work," or (c) "any later collective work in the same series." In accord with Congress' prescription, a "publishing company could reprint a contribution from one issue in a later issue of its magazine, and could reprint an article from a 1980 edition of an encyclopedia in a 1990 revision of it; the publisher could not revise the contribution itself or include it in a new anthology or an entirely different magazine or other collective work." H.R. Rep. 122–123, U.S.Code Cong. & Admin.News 1976, pp. 5659, 5738.

Essentially, § 201(c) adjusts a publisher's copyright in its collective work to accommodate a freelancer's copyright in her contribution. If there is demand for a freelance article standing alone or in a new collection, the Copyright Act allows the freelancer to benefit from that demand; after authorizing initial publication, the freelancer may also sell the article to others. * * * It would scarcely "preserve the author's copyright in a contribution" as contemplated by Congress, H.R. Rep. 122, U.S. Code Cong. & Admin. News 1976, pp. 5659, 5738, if a newspaper or magazine publisher were permitted to reproduce or distribute copies of the author's contribution in isolation or within new collective works. * * *

III

In the instant case, the Authors wrote several Articles and gave the Print Publishers permission to publish the Articles in certain newspapers and magazines. It is undisputed that the Authors hold copyrights and, therefore, exclusive rights in the Articles.[7] It is clear, moreover, that the

---

[7] The Publishers do not claim that the Articles are "work[s] made for hire." 17 U.S.C. § 201(b). As to such works, the employer or person for whom a work was prepared is treated as the

Print and Electronic Publishers have exercised at least some rights that § 106 initially assigns exclusively to the Authors * * *.

Against the Authors' charge of infringement, the Publishers do not here contend the Authors entered into an agreement authorizing reproduction of the Articles in the Databases. * * * Each discrete edition of the periodicals in which the Articles appeared is a "collective work," the Publishers agree. They contend, however, that reproduction and distribution of each Article by the Databases lie within the "privilege of reproducing and distributing the [Articles] as part of . . . [a] revision of that collective work," § 201(c). The Publishers' encompassing construction of the § 201(c) privilege is unacceptable, we conclude, for it would diminish the Authors' exclusive rights in the Articles.

In determining whether the Articles have been reproduced and distributed "as part of" a "revision" of the collective works in issue, we focus on the Articles as presented to, and perceptible by, the user of the Databases. In this case, the three Databases present articles to users clear of the context provided either by the original periodical editions or by any revision of those editions. * * * When the user conducts a search, each article appears as a separate item within the search result. [The] article appears to a user without the graphics, formatting, or other articles with which the article was initially published. * * * [W]e cannot see how the Database perceptibly reproduces and distributes the article "as part of" either the original edition or a "revision" of that edition.

* * *

The Publishers press an analogy between the Databases, on the one hand, and microfilm and microfiche, on the other. We find the analogy wanting. Microforms typically contain continuous photographic reproductions of a periodical in the medium of miniaturized film. Accordingly, articles appear on the microforms, writ very small, in precisely the position in which the articles appeared in the newspaper. * * * True, the microfilm roll contains multiple editions, and the microfilm user can adjust the machine lens to focus only on the Article, to the exclusion of surrounding material. Nonetheless, the user first encounters the Article in context. In the Databases, by contrast, the Articles appear disconnected from their original context. * * * In short, unlike microforms, the Databases do not perceptibly reproduce articles as part of the collective work to which the author contributed or as part of any "revision" thereof.

* * *

---

author. *Ibid.* The Print Publishers, however, neither engaged the Authors to write the Articles as "employee[s]" nor "commissioned" the Articles through "a written instrument signed by [both parties]" indicating that the Articles shall be considered "work[s] made for hire." § 101 (1994 ed., Supp. V) (defining "work made for hire").

IV

The Publishers warn that a ruling for the Authors will have "devastating" consequences. The Databases, the Publishers note, provide easy access to complete newspaper texts going back decades. A ruling for the Authors, the Publishers suggest, will punch gaping holes in the electronic record of history. * * *

Notwithstanding the dire predictions from some quarters, it hardly follows from today's decision that an injunction against the inclusion of these Articles in the Databases (much less all freelance articles in any databases) must issue. The parties (Authors and Publishers) may enter into an agreement allowing continued electronic reproduction of the Authors' works; they, and if necessary the courts and Congress, may draw on numerous models for distributing copyrighted works and remunerating authors for their distribution. In any event, speculation about future harms is no basis for this Court to shrink authorial rights Congress established in § 201(c). Agreeing with the Court of Appeals that the Publishers are liable for infringement, we leave remedial issues open for initial airing and decision in the District Court.

* * *

We conclude that the Electronic Publishers infringed the Authors' copyrights by reproducing and distributing the Articles in a manner not authorized by the Authors and not privileged by § 201(c). We further conclude that the Print Publishers infringed the Authors' copyrights by authorizing the Electronic Publishers to place the Articles in the Databases and by aiding the Electronic Publishers in that endeavor. We therefore affirm the judgment of the Court of Appeals.

It is so ordered.

NOTES

1. In 1997, the National Geographic Magazine published all of its back issues in a CD-ROM compilation, consisting of digitally scanned images of the original magazine pages, two at a time, just as they appeared in the original print version, even separated by a fold down the middle. Freelance writers and photographers then brought a series of suits in the Second and Eleventh Circuits, alleging that their copyrights were infringed by the unauthorized digital compilation. The Second Circuit applied *Tasini* to conclude that the National Geographic compilation was privileged as a "revision" under section 201(c); even if some new elements were added, the compilation was a "revision" of the original collective work rather than a "new" collective work because these changes did not "substantially alter the original context." *Faulkner v. National Geographic Enterprises, Inc.*, 409 F.3d 26, 38 (2d Cir. 2005). Furthermore, the print publishers' section 201(c) privilege was transferable to the electronic publishers. *Id.* at 39. The same analysis applied even to the articles that were

published before 1978, when section 201(c) took effect. On similar facts, the Eleventh Circuit agreed that section 201(c) applied in *Greenberg v. National Geographic Soc'y*, 533 F.3d 1244, 1252, 1255 (11th Cir. 2008) (en banc). However, one of the new elements added—a 25-second montage of National Geographic cover photos—was not privileged under section 201(c), and required further adjudication. *Id.* at 1258.

2. How will *Tasini* affect future practices in the area of copyright licenses and assignments like the ones involved in the case? For existing compilations, can a publisher avoid liability while still including the freelance works in its searchable database?

3. Because copyright protection can restrict the availability of works of authorship, and can limit the ability of users to adapt and improve upon those works, creators have explored various ways to opt out of the traditional copyright regime. Even though copyright attaches automatically to eligible works under section 102, several licensing schemes have been developed which enable creators to ensure that their works—and even modifications of their works—will be freely available to the public. One scheme even allows an author to dedicate a work to the public domain.

Creative Commons: A nonprofit organization called Creative Commons (CC) has drafted a variety of standardized licenses which enable an author to grant a perpetual, worldwide, royalty-free license allowing the general public to use the author's copyrighted work in specified ways. Each CC license requires the user to attribute the work to its author, and each allows copying and distribution of the work. Beyond these common features, authors may choose from a number of CC licenses, depending on the scope of the rights they wish to grant. For example, the license may or may not allow commercial uses; it may or may not allow adaptations; and it may or may not allow a licensee that adapts the work to impose a different set of licensing terms on those who wish to use the adaptation. There is also a public domain tool ("CC0" or "CC Zero") enabling a copyright owner to dedicate his or her work to the public domain even if its copyright term has not expired.

Open source software: A software license is considered "open source" if the source code is made available to the user, and the user is free to copy, modify, and distribute it. Software that is based on open source software includes Linux, Mozilla, Apache, PERL, and PNG. While open source software can be sold, anyone who has a copy is free to copy and distribute it, which means that copies can often be obtained at a low cost or at no cost, because no one can use the leverage of copyright to restrict those activities.

A number of public licenses for open source software are available, of which the best known is the GNU General Public License (GPL). The GNU GPL is a type of "copyleft" license, meaning that it allows the user to copy, distribute, and adapt the software for free, but a user that distributes a modified version of the software (either gratis or for a fee) must allow recipients the same freedom, and must make the source code available to them. The GNU GPL does not place the software in the public domain. Instead, it uses the leverage of copyright to ensure that licensees who modify the work cannot assert exclusive rights in those modifications. It does not, however, prevent them from selling copies of their modified programs; they are still required to make the source code available, and they cannot prevent their purchasers from copying, modifying, and/or distributing the software. All modified versions must carry a copyright notice identifying the author of the modifications.

In the context of open source software licensing, the Federal Circuit has held that a licensor is not limited to contract remedies, and can sue for copyright infringement where a licensee violates conditions of the license, even where the licensor distributed the software for free. *See Jacobsen v. Katzer*, 535 F.3d 1373 (Fed. Cir. 2008).

2. TERMINATION PROVISIONS

Statutes: 17 U.S.C. §§ 203, 304(c)

It is important to distinguish the two termination provisions created by the 1976 Act. The termination provision of section 304(c) applies only to pre-1978 grants of the renewal term for works copyrighted under the 1909 Act. The termination provision of section 203 applies only to grants executed after 1977. Both provisions contain a "derivative works exception."

COPYRIGHT ACT OF 1976

H.R. Rep. No. 94–1476.
94th Cong., 2d Sess. 124–27, 140–41 (1976).

The Problem in General

The provisions of section 203 are based on the premise that the reversionary provisions of the present section on copyright renewal (17 U.S.C. sec. 24) should be eliminated, and that the proposed law should substitute for them a provision safeguarding authors against unremunerative transfers. A provision of this sort is needed because of the unequal bargaining position of authors, resulting in part from the impossibility of determining a work's value until it has been exploited. Section 203 reflects a practical compromise that will further the objectives of the copyright law while recognizing the problems and legitimate needs of all interests involved.

Scope of the Provision

Instead of being automatic, as is theoretically the case under the present renewal provision, the termination of a transfer or license under section 203 would require the serving of an advance notice within specified time limits and under specified conditions. However, although affirmative action is needed to effect a termination, the right to take this action cannot be waived in advance or contracted away. Under section 203(a) the right of termination would apply only to transfers and licenses executed after the effective date of the new statute, and would have no retroactive effect.

The right of termination would be confined to inter vivos transfers or licenses executed by the author, and would not apply to transfers by the author's successors in interest or to the author's own bequests. The scope of the right would extend not only to any "transfer of copyright ownership," as defined in section 101, but also to nonexclusive licenses. The right of termination would not apply to "works made for hire," which is one of the principal reasons the definition of that term assumed importance in the development of the bill.

* * *

When a Grant Can Be Terminated

Section 203 draws a distinction between the date when a termination becomes effective and the earlier date when the advance notice of termination is served. With respect to the ultimate effective date, section 203(a)(3) provides, as a general rule, that a grant may be terminated during the 5 years following the expiration of a period of 35 years from the execution of the grant. As an exception to this basic 35-year rule, the bill also provides that "if the grant covers the right of publication of the work, the period begins at the end of 35 years from the date of publication of the work under the grant or at the end of 40 years from the date of execution of the grant, whichever term ends earlier." * * *

Effect of Termination

Section 203(b) makes clear that, unless effectively terminated within the applicable 5-year period, all rights covered by an existing grant will continue unchanged, and that rights under other Federal, State, or foreign laws are unaffected. * * *

An important limitation on the rights of a copyright owner under a terminated grant is specified in section 203(b)(1). This clause provides that, notwithstanding a termination, a derivative work prepared earlier may "continue to be utilized" under the conditions of the terminated grant; the clause adds, however, that this privilege is not broad enough to permit the preparation of other derivative works. In other words, a film made from a play could continue to be licensed for performance after the motion picture contract had been terminated but any remake rights covered by the contract would be cut off. * * *

Termination of Grants Covering Extended Term

An issue underlying the 19-year extension of renewal terms under both subsections (a) and (b) of section 304 is whether, in a case where their rights have already been transferred, the author or the dependents of the author should be given a chance to benefit from the extended term. The arguments for granting rights of termination are even more persuasive under section 304 than they are under section 203; the extended term represents a completely new property right, and there are strong reasons for giving the author, who is the fundamental beneficiary of copyright under the Constitution, an opportunity to share in it.

Subsection (c) of section 304 is a close but not exact counterpart of section 203. In the case of either a first-term or renewal copyright already subsisting when the new statute becomes effective, any grant of rights covering the renewal copyright in the work, executed before the effective date, may be terminated under conditions and limitations similar to those provided in section 203. Except for transfers and licenses covering renewal copyrights already extended under Public Laws 87–668, 89–142, 90–141, 90–416, 91–147, 91–555, 92–170, 92–566, and 93–573, which would become subject to termination immediately upon the coming into effect of the revised law, the 5-year period during which termination could be made effective would start 56 years after copyright was originally secured.

The bill distinguishes between the persons who can terminate a grant under section 203 and those entitled to terminate a grant covering an extended term under section 304. Instead of being limited to transfers and licenses executed by the author, the right of termination under section 304(c) also extends to grants executed by those beneficiaries of the author who can claim renewal under the present law: his or her widow or widower, children, executors, or next of kin.

* * * [I]n connection with section 203, the bill adopts the principle that, where a transfer or license by the author is involved, termination may be effected by a per stirpes majority of those entitled to terminate, and this principle also applies to the ownership of rights under a termination and to the making of further grants of reverted rights. In general, this principle has also been adopted with respect to the termination of rights under an extended renewal copyright in section 304, but with several differences made necessary by the differences between the legal status of transfers and licenses made after the effective date of the new law (governed by section 203) and that of grants of renewal rights made earlier and governed by section 304(c). * * *

NOTES

1. Note that termination rights apply to grants involving individually or jointly authored works, but not to grants involving works made for hire—another factor to be considered when parties have the opportunity to proceed under either arrangement.

2. Compare the derivative works exceptions in section 203 and 304 with that of section 104A: they have a similar purpose—to protect investments in new creative works that were made in reliance on an underlying work having

a particular legal status. But the section 104A exception protects a party that relied on the underlying work's public domain status at a time when there was little reason to believe that its copyright would someday be restored, whereas the section 203 exception protects reliance on rights acquired under a post-1978 grant even though the possibility of the grant being terminated was foreseeable at the time of the grant (and thus this exception encourages parties to enter into such grants by eliminating the risk of losing their investment in the derivative work); and the section 304 exception protects reliance on a pre-1978 grant which was entered into with the expectation that the underlying work would enter the public domain at the end of 56 years so that continued exploitation of the derivative work after that time would not infringe.

3. Some recording artists have attempted to use the termination provisions to regain the copyright in their sound recordings. Record labels, however, have taken the position that these recordings are ineligible for termination because they were created as works made for hire. Even if that is not the case, do you see any difficulties with recognizing recording artists as "authors" who can exercise termination rights in their recordings?

4. In the 2018 Music Modernization Act, Congress for the first time granted federal protection to pre-1972 sound recordings under newly enacted section 1401. Although the protection resembles copyright, it is not identical. One significant difference is that section 1401 does not provide the authors of the sound recordings with a termination right. Because the termination rights under section 203 and 304 apply only to "copyright" grants, and section 1401 does not grant copyright protection, termination rights do not apply to pre-1972 sound recordings protected by section 1401. Note, however, that a different provision, section 104A, grants copyright protection to pre-1972 sound recordings fixed outside the United States. Therefore, termination rights may be available for those foreign sound recordings. Given the age of those recordings, however, and the conflict of laws issues that arise from trying to identify their "authors," disputes over termination rights in these recordings appear unlikely.

WOODS V. BOURNE CO.

60 F.3d 978 (2d Cir. 1995).

FEINBERG, CIRCUIT JUDGE:

This appeal requires us to address conflicting claims to royalties generated by various uses of the song "When the Red, Red, Robin Comes Bob, Bob, Bobbin' Along" (the Song) during what is known in copyright law as an extended renewal term. Plaintiffs [doing business as Callicoon Music], heirs of song composer Harry Woods, and defendant Bourne, Inc., Woods's music publisher, both claim the right to receive certain royalties generated during this period. Essentially, plaintiffs claim that they are entitled to the royalties because they have exercised their statutory right to terminate the publisher's interests in the Song pursuant to 17 U.S.C.

§ 304(c). Bourne maintains that the royalties belong to it because all the disputed post-termination uses of the Song are attributable to so-called derivative works, which were prepared under its authority prior to termination and which therefore do not revert to the author. 17 U.S.C. § 304(c)(6)(A).

The royalties at issue were generated by several different uses of the Song following termination. These uses include (1) television performances of movies and television programs that incorporate the Song (hereafter sometimes referred to collectively as "audiovisual works"); (2) radio performances of sound recordings of the Song; and (3) sales of reprints of published arrangements. * * *

The district court essentially reached its determination by analyzing whether any of the musical arrangements of the Song contained in the movies, television shows, sound recordings and printed arrangements were sufficiently original to qualify as derivative works. Finding that, with one minor exception, no version of the Song was sufficiently original, the district court granted judgment for the plaintiffs. The district court did not consider it relevant that some of the disputed royalties were generated by performances of audiovisual works, such as movies containing the Song, which are conceded to be original enough to qualify as derivative works.

For reasons set forth below, we hold that when a musical arrangement is contained within an audiovisual work produced under license from a publisher prior to termination, the publisher is entitled to receive royalties from post-termination performances of the audiovisual work under the terms of pre-termination licenses governing performance rights. It is irrelevant to disposition of those royalties whether the musical arrangement in the audiovisual work would qualify independently as a derivative work. * * *

BACKGROUND

* * *

B. The Extended Renewal Term

[In 1926, composer Woods assigned the copyright and renewal term in the Song to music publisher Berlin. During the original and renewal copyright terms, Berlin and its successor Bourne issued "synchronization" (or "synch") licenses authorizing others to incorporate the Song in movies and television programs.]

Under the Copyright Act of 1909, in effect at the time of Woods's grant to Berlin, the original term of a copyright was 28 years, followed by a renewal term of another 28 years. Thus, the grant from Woods to Berlin in the Songwriter's Agreement, which included renewal rights, was to endure for up to 56 years, ending in 1982.

The reason for including a renewal term in the Copyright Act was to permit an author who sold the rights in his work for little consideration, when measured against the work's subsequent success, to enjoy a second opportunity with more bargaining power to reap the full value of the work. Thus, Congress attempted to alleviate the problem of the inability of authors to know the true monetary value of their works prior to commercial exploitation. That purpose, however, was largely eroded by a subsequent Supreme Court decision holding that renewal rights were assignable along with original term rights in a work. *Fisher Music Co. v. M. Witmark & Sons*, 318 U.S. 643 (1943).

When the Copyright Act was thoroughly revised in 1976, Congress attempted to restore a second chance to authors or their heirs. Among other changes, Congress prolonged the duration of copyrights then in the renewal term so that they would continue for an additional 19 years. 17 U.S.C. § 304(b). At the end of the 28th year of the renewal term, the author (if alive) or the author's surviving spouse or children may terminate the rights of a grantee, usually a publisher, to whom the author had transferred rights in the original work. 17 U.S.C. § 304(c)(1)–(3). During the 19-year extended renewal term, a copyrighted work does not enter the public domain but continues to generate royalties. If the author or heirs elect to terminate the publisher's rights, royalties become payable to them rather than to the publisher. 17 U.S.C. § 304(c)(6). The author or heirs thus "recapture" rights in the copyrighted work and may thereby be relieved "of the consequences of ill-advised and unremunerative grants that had been made before the author had a fair opportunity to appreciate the [work's] true value." *Mills Music, Inc. v. Snyder*, 469 U.S. 153, 172–73 (1985).

There is an important exception to the reversion rights of the author or heirs for derivative works produced by an authorized party during the original and renewal copyright terms. The Copyright Act of 1976 provides that

> [a] derivative work prepared under authority of the grant before its termination may continue to be utilized under the terms of the grant after its termination, but this privilege does not extend to the preparation after the termination of other derivative works based upon the copyrighted work covered by the terminated grant.

17 U.S.C. § 304(c)(6)(A) (referred to hereafter as "the Derivative Works Exception" or simply "the Exception"). * * *

The renewal term for Bourne's copyright in the Song came to an end in April 1982, and Callicoon terminated Bourne's rights immediately thereafter.

* * *

D. Performance Rights

* * *

During the original and renewal terms, Bourne received royalties from ASCAP for television broadcasts of movies and television programs containing the Song and radio broadcasts of the Song. A typical synch license issued by Bourne for the production of an audiovisual work required a producer to pay a flat fee but provided that any broadcast entity performing the Song as contained in the audiovisual work must obtain a performance license from ASCAP or Bourne. Thus, for each pre-recorded audiovisual work incorporating the Song, Bourne had two sources of income: royalties from the producer for the right to incorporate the Song in the audiovisual work and royalties from television stations, via ASCAP, for each performance of the Song contained in the work. * * *

The district court determined that Callicoon was entitled to all of the royalties generated by post-termination performances of the Song, including performances contained in pre-termination derivative audiovisual works. The court acknowledged, and the parties do not dispute, that the works in which the Song was incorporated—for example, movies—were by definition derivative. Nevertheless, the court found the controlling issue, as to all categories of performance, to be whether the underlying arrangement of the Song itself is a derivative work. Only then would performance royalties continue to go to Bourne during the extended renewal term. * * *

DISCUSSION

* * *

A. Royalties from Television Performances

We consider first the basis for determining entitlement to royalties from post-termination performances of the Song as contained in pre-termination movies and television programs.

The Derivative Works Exception preserves the right of owners of derivative works to continue to exploit their works during the extended renewal term under previously negotiated terms. Without such an exception, authors might use their reversion rights to extract prohibitive fees from owners of successful derivative works or to bring infringement actions against them.

The goal of keeping derivative works in public circulation does not require that publishers rather than authors receive royalties for their use. As long as the royalties paid by a derivative work user remain unchanged, the user should be indifferent as to whether an author or publisher receives the payment. The royalties generated during the extended renewal term will be a windfall to either authors (and their heirs) or publishers since, at the time the rights at issue were originally established, neither group expected to get royalties for more than 56 years. The question, therefore, is: Who is the beneficiary of this windfall?

1. *The Mills Music Decision*

The answer, according to the decision of the Supreme Court in *Mills Music, Inc. v. Snyder*, is found in the phrase "under the terms of the grant," as used in the Derivative Works Exception. We quote its text again for convenience:

> A derivative work prepared under authority of the grant before its termination may continue to be utilized *under the terms of the grant* after its termination, but this privilege does not extend to the preparation after the termination of other derivative works based upon the copyrighted work covered by the terminated grant.

17 U.S.C. § 304(c)(6)(A) (emphasis supplied).

Mills Music posed circumstances similar to those of the instant case. Snyder, treated for purposes of that case as the sole author of the song "Who's Sorry Now," had assigned renewal rights in the song to a publisher, Mills, in 1940 in exchange for, among other things, a 50% share in mechanical royalties, that is, royalties from sales of copies of sound recordings. Mills in turn licensed record companies to produce copies of sound recordings of the song. Upon termination of the grant from Snyder to Mills, Snyder's heirs claimed the right to 100%, rather than just 50%, of future mechanical royalties. Mills claimed that the sound recordings at issue were derivative works created under the terms of the grant from Snyder to Mills and that, therefore, Mills should continue to share in mechanical royalties according to the terms of that grant.

In the district court, Judge Edward Weinfeld held that the sound recordings produced before termination were derivative works and that the terms of the grant required payment of mechanical royalties to Mills. This court reversed, holding that upon termination only the grant from Mills to the record companies remained in effect. Since the basis for Mills's retention of half the mechanical royalties was the grant from Snyder, and since that grant was now terminated, all mechanical royalties should revert to Snyder's heirs.

The Supreme Court reversed. It found that the phrase "terminated grant," the last two words in the Derivative Works Exception, must refer to the original grant from author to publisher. The Court reasoned that the other two uses of the word "grant" in the single sentence of the Derivative Works Exception must logically refer to the same grant. 469 U.S. at 164–65. The Court noted that "[t]he 1940 grant from Snyder to Mills expressly gave Mills the authority to license others to make derivative works." *Id.* at 165. It then concluded that "a fair construction of the phrase 'under the terms of the grant' as applied to any particular licensee would necessarily encompass both the [original] grant [from author to publisher] and the individual license [to record producers] executed pursuant thereto." *Id.* at 166–67. Because the combination of the two grants directed record companies to pay royalties to Mills, and Mills in turn to pay 50% of the amount collected to Snyder, the Court held that Mills was entitled to retain its 50% share of mechanical royalties on sales of records produced before termination but sold during the extended renewal term.

Mills Music is, of course, binding upon us. *Mills Music* appears to require that where multiple levels of licenses govern use of a derivative work, the "terms of the grant" encompass the original grant from author to publisher and each subsequent grant necessary to enable the particular use at issue. If one of those grants requires payment of royalties by licensees to an intermediary, such as a publisher, then continued utilization of derivative works "under the terms of the grant" requires continued payments to the intermediary. The effect of *Mills Music*, then, is to preserve during the post-termination period the panoply of contractual obligations that governed pre-termination uses of derivative works by derivative work owners or their licensees.

2. Applying the Mills Music Decision

The derivative works involved in *Mills Music* were sound recordings, and the use there was the sale of copies. The concededly derivative works we now address are audiovisual works and the use in question is public performance. We believe that the reasoning of *Mills Music* also applies in this situation.

There is no question that the owners of the copyrights in audiovisual works have the right to perform the works publicly. They typically exercise this right by licensing television stations to broadcast their works. In this case, the terms of the synch licenses issued by Bourne to the producers required the television stations performing the audiovisual works to obtain a second grant from either Bourne or ASCAP, licensing the stations to perform the Song contained in the audiovisual works. In practice, this license is always obtained from ASCAP, which then remits the publisher's share of fees to Bourne pursuant to the agreement between Bourne and ASCAP. Under our reading of *Mills Music*, the "terms of the grant" include the provisions of the grants from Bourne to ASCAP and from ASCAP to television stations. This pair of licenses is contemplated in the grant of the synch licenses from Bourne to film and television producers.

* * *

We therefore reverse the decision of the district court as to royalties from post-termination performances of pre-termination audiovisual works. On remand, the court should enter judgment ordering defendant ASCAP to pay these royalties to Bourne in accordance with the terms of the grants in effect immediately prior to the effective date of Callicoon's termination.

* * *

NOTES

1. In *Fred Ahlert Music Corp. v. Warner/Chappell Music, Inc.*, 155 F.3d 17 (2d Cir. 1998), the Second Circuit held that the scope of the derivative works exception to the termination rights of a music copyright owner depends not only on the scope of the original author-publisher grant, but also on the scope of that publisher's grant to a record company authorizing the creation of a derivative work sound recording. Thus, where the first publisher (Warner) had, prior to termination, granted A & M Records a license to make and distribute *one* recording (the derivative work at issue) utilizing the plaintiff's musical composition, after termination of the original author-publisher grant Warner could not authorize a second record company to include that same recording in a movie soundtrack, and release it on the soundtrack album, because these activities exceeded the scope of the original grant from Warner to A & M, which was limited to using the song on a single recording. Therefore, the publisher's share of royalties from the soundtrack and soundtrack album was payable not to Warner, but to Fred Ahlert Music Co., which had acquired the publishing rights in the song post-termination.

2. Pursuant to the 2018 Music Modernization Act, an organization called the Mechanical Licensing Collective (MLC) administers compulsory licenses (under 17 U.S.C. § 115) that permit digital music providers (like Spotify) to distribute downloads and provide on-demand streaming of the copyrighted musical compositions embodied in sound recordings. The MLC then distributes the royalties to the music publishers that own the distribution rights in the musical compositions. Even after a songwriter lawfully terminates a publishing grant for a particular composition, the MLC continues to send the original publisher any royalties collected for compulsory licenses that were issued before termination, reasoning that the derivative works exception applies. However, in 2022 the Copyright Office proposed a new rule reversing this practice, and requiring the MLC to distribute these royalties to the songwriter (or any new publisher the songwriter chooses). The rationale is that the compulsory license was not executed by the author or the author's heirs (because it is mandated by law), and thus is not subject to termination or to the derivative works exception. Do you agree with the Copyright Office? (For more on the § 115 compulsory license and the MLC, see Chapter 16.B.5.)

3. The Sonny Bono Copyright Term Extension Act, Pub. L. No. 105–298 (signed Oct. 27, 1998), which added 20 years to U.S. copyright terms, also added a new termination right at 17 U.S.C. § 304(d), permitting termination with respect to the new 20-year term extension, but only with respect to pre-1978 grants pertaining to works which were not works made for hire, which were in their renewal term as of Oct. 27, 1998, which had not previously been the subject of a termination under section 304(c), and with respect to which the

section 304(c) termination rights granted under prior law had expired on or before Oct. 27, 1998.

MILNE V. STEPHEN SLESINGER, INC.

430 F.3d 1036 (9th Cir. 2005).

CALLAHAN, CIRCUIT JUDGE:

This copyright action arises from a termination notice sent by the appellant to the appellee, seeking to recapture rights to various characters created by her grandfather, Alan Alexander Milne, who authored the "Winnie-the-Pooh" children's books. Milne originally granted various rights in those works to the appellee in 1930. Then, in 1983, due to a change in copyright law in 1976, Milne's heirs considered terminating the 1930 grant outright, but instead entered into a new agreement that revoked the original grant and re-issued rights in the works to the appellee. The appellant seeks to invalidate the 1983 agreement based on 1998 legislation. The 1998 legislation only authorizes the termination of copyright agreements executed before 1978. Because the 1983 revocation and re-grant were valid, we affirm the district court's decision.

* * *

In the 1920s, Alan Alexander Milne ("the author") created in his classic children's books the characters of the boy Christopher Robin and his stuffed bear, Winnie-the-Pooh, as well as their friends Eeyore, Owl, Piglet, Rabbit, Kanga, Roo, and Tigger. Four of those works are involved in this action: (1) *When We Were Very Young;* (2) *Winnie-the-Pooh;* (3) *Now We Are Six;* and (4) *House at Pooh Corner* (collectively, "Pooh works"). U.S. copyrights in the Pooh works were registered between 1924 and 1928, and renewed between 1952 and 1956.

[In 1930, the author granted exclusive merchandising and other rights in the Pooh works, throughout the U.S. and Canada, to Stephen Slesinger, Inc. (SSI) for the entire period of copyright and any renewal thereof, in exchange for royalties.]

* * *

In 1956, the author passed away and was survived by his widow and their son, Christopher Robin Milne. The author's will bequeathed all beneficial interests in the Pooh works to a trust for the benefit of his widow during her lifetime ("Milne Trust"), and, after her death, to other beneficiaries ("Pooh Properties Trust"), which included his son, Christopher, and Christopher's daughter, Clare. Clare is the author's sole grandchild and the plaintiff-appellant in this case.

In 1961, SSI granted exclusively to Walt Disney Productions ("Disney") the rights it had acquired in the 1930 grant, and Disney agreed to pay certain royalties to SSI. Around the same time, Disney also entered into a similar agreement with the author's widow and the Milne Trust, granting Disney exclusive motion-picture rights, foreign-merchandising rights, and other exclusive rights in the Pooh works in exchange for royalties

In 1971, the author's widow passed away and, in 1972, her beneficial interests under the Milne Trust were assigned to the Pooh Properties Trust in accordance with the author's will. This meant that the Pooh Properties Trust would receive the author's copyright interest in the Pooh works plus the royalties payable under the 1961 Milne-Disney agreement.

* * *

In 1983, faced with the possibility that Christopher might seek to terminate the rights Disney had received in 1961 from SSI, Disney proposed that the parties renegotiate the rights to the Pooh works. Christopher accepted Disney's proposal and, using the bargaining power conferred by his termination right, negotiated and signed on April 1, 1983 a more lucrative deal with SSI and Disney that would benefit the Pooh Properties Trust and its beneficiaries.

The new agreement acknowledged the 1930 grant and the 1961 assignment of rights to Disney, and observed that although ownership of the copyrights had been transferred to the Pooh Properties Trust, there were "disputes[which] had existed[.]" Recognizing that the author's heir, Christopher, may well have a right of termination under the 1976 Copyright Act, the agreement declared that the parties were resolved to "clarify certain aspects of their contractual arrangements and to settle revised agreements." Christopher therefore agreed not to seek termination of the existing arrangements in return for executing the new agreement. The agreement then provided for the revocation of the 1930 and 1961 agreements in favor of the new agreement, followed by the re-granting (on the same page) of the rights in the Pooh works to SSI. In exchange for royalties, SSI turned around and granted Disney the radio, television, motion-picture, and merchandising rights to those works.

One result of the 1983 agreement was an increase of the amounts that the Pooh Properties Trust received over the sums that had been payable under the 1961 Milne-Disney agreement. The Pooh Properties Trust now received double SSI's share of the royalties, compared to about half of SSI's share before the 1983 agreement. Thus, the renegotiations between the parties resulted, by some estimates, in a net gain of hundreds of millions of dollars to the Pooh Properties Trust, which included Clare as a prime beneficiary.

On November 4, 2002, motivated by the recent enactment of the CTEA and its favorable treatment of authors' heirs, Clare set out to recapture the rights to the Pooh works. Toward that end, she served SSI with a notice of termination, which referenced November 5, 2004 as the effective date for termination of the 1930 grant of rights to SSI. The same day that she served the termination notice, Clare entered into an agreement with Disney, assigning the rights expected to revert to her in 2004.

[Clare sought a declaratory judgment that her termination was effective to terminate SSI's rights in the Pooh works. SSI argued that the notice was invalid because the 1930 grant was revoked by the 1983 agreement. The District Court held the notice invalid, and Clare appealed.]

* * *

A. Right of Termination Under the CTEA

Clare argues that she properly terminated SSI's rights in the Pooh works. We hold that the district court's contrary conclusion is correct.

In a copyright case, as in most cases, the language of the statute provides the starting point for our analysis. The CTEA provides in relevant part:

> In the case of any copyright other than a work made for hire, subsisting in its renewal term on the effective date of the Sonny Bono Copyright Term Extension Act [effective October 27, 1998] for which the termination right provided in subsection (c) [of this section] has expired by such date, where the author or owner of the termination right has not previously exercised such termination right, the exclusive or nonexclusive grant of a transfer or license of the renewal copyright or any right under it, *executed before January 1, 1978,* by any of the persons designated in subsection (a)(1)(C) of this section, other than by will, is subject to termination. . . .

17 U.S.C. § 304(d) (emphasis added).

Although Clare's termination notice purports to terminate the 1930 grant under the CTEA (section 304(d)), that statute provides a termination right to only those transfers or licences "executed *before* January 1, 1978[.]" *Id.* (emphasis added). The only pre-1978 grant of rights to SSI, and the only grant to SSI specified in the termination notice, was the 1930 grant made by the author to Slesinger. The 1930 grant, however, was terminated by the beneficiaries of the Pooh Properties Trust upon the execution of the 1983 agreement. Accordingly, there was no pre-1978 grant of rights to SSI in existence when Congress enacted the CTEA in 1998.

The sole grant of rights to SSI, either at the time of the CTEA's enactment or when Clare served her termination notice, was the grant of rights embodied in the 1983 agreement. As the district court correctly explained, however, this grant is not subject to termination under section

304(d) because it was not "executed before January 1, 1978," as the statute expressly requires. 17 U.S.C. § 304(d).

1. "Agreement to the Contrary"

Faced with the reality that she is dealing with a post-1978 agreement, Clare attempts to circumvent the 1983 agreement by claiming that another provision of the CTEA, 17 U.S.C. § 304(c)(5), requires this court to regard the 1983 agreement as an "agreement to the contrary" that does not prevent her from terminating SSI's rights to the Pooh works. Section 304(c)(5) states that a "[t]ermination . . . may be effected notwithstanding any agreement to the contrary, including any agreement to make a will or to make any future grant." 17 U.S.C. § 304(c)(5).

The statute does not define the phrase "agreement to the contrary," although it does provide two examples of agreements that would constitute an "agreement to the contrary": "an agreement to make a will" and an agreement "to make any future grant." *Id.* The undisputed fact that the 1983 agreement does not fall into either category supports the district court's finding that the 1983 agreement is not "an agreement to the contrary."

* * *

Clare also relies on the Second Circuit's decision in *Marvel Characters, Inc. v. Simon,* 310 F.3d 280 (2d Cir.2002), to support her claim that the 1983 agreement is an "agreement to the contrary" under section 304(c)(5). The contract at issue there was a settlement agreement between the parties, which ended a series of lawsuits filed in the 1960s by the creator of a copyrighted work. The creator argued that the settlement agreement should not be given effect because it contractually changed the nature of the copyrighted work, labeling it as a "work made for hire" many years after its creation. The effects of this after-the-fact label were to make the creator an "employee for hire" rather than the author of the copyrighted work, and to foreclose his right to terminate the grant he had made in the copyrighted work. Thus, unlike the issue presented in the case at bar, the issue facing the Second Circuit was "whether § 304(c)(5)'s phrase 'any agreement to the contrary' includes a settlement agreement stating that a work was created for hire[.]" *Id.* at 290.

After examining the legislative history and considering the purpose of section 304(c), the court concluded "that an agreement made subsequent to a work's creation which retroactively deems it a work for hire constitutes an agreement to the contrary under § 304(c)(5) of the 1976 Act." *Id.* at 292. The Second Circuit held that an employer cannot contractually transform a creator or author of a copyrighted work into an "employee for hire." *Id.* The court expressed concern that if it held otherwise, works not satisfying the relationship-based "for hire" test could be coerced by post-facto agreements that designate such works to be something they are not: "works for hire."

The facts, reasoning, and holding of *Marvel* have little relevance to this case because, here, there is no after-the-fact attempt to recharacterize the work or a prior agreement. Instead, the 1983 agreement involves contractual provisions that operated prospectively through the revocation of an existing grant and the making of a new one. As the district court recognized, "[t]he parties in the 1983 [a]greement did not attempt to change or modify the nature of their association with one another, or alter the character of their long-standing author/grantee relationship."

Reinforcing this reasoning are the undisputed facts that the 1930 grant was expressly revoked by the Pooh Properties Trust, which made a new grant of rights to SSI that, *inter alia,* was more lucrative for the author's heirs. The fact that the 1983 agreement was meant to protect the continuing viability of the author's grant of rights to SSI is evident from the agreement itself. In that vein, it is important to note that the parties describe their 1983 agreement as a "new agreement *for the future* which the parties believe would not be subject to any right of termination under 17 U.S.C. Secs. 203 or 304(c)."

Neither *Marvel* nor any other of Clare's cited authority supplies a basis for us to question the district court's decision or to undo the 1983 agreement, which was freely and intelligently entered into by the parties. The beneficiaries of the Pooh Properties Trust were able to obtain considerably more money as a result of the bargaining power wielded by the author's son, Christopher, who was believed to own a statutory right to terminate the 1930 grant under section 304(c) of the 1976 Copyright Act. Although Christopher presumably could have served a termination notice, he elected instead to use his leverage to obtain a better deal for the Pooh Properties Trust. His daughter, Clare, was a beneficiary of this new arrangement, and her current dissatisfaction provides no reason to discredit the validity of the 1983 agreement and the rights conferred thereby.

* * *

After more than 50 years of advancement of the Pooh works in the marketplace, their value was sufficiently demonstrated, and the 1976 Copyright Act provided Christopher a window for termination. The Pooh Properties Trust recognized the perceived right to terminate as a valuable bargaining chip, and used it to obtain an advantageous agreement that doubled its royalty share relative to SSI's share. Thus, the 1983 agreement exemplifies the increased bargaining power that Congress intended to bestow on authors and their heirs by creating the termination right under the 1976 Copyright Act. As the 1983 agreement appears to be the type expressly contemplated and endorsed by Congress, we do not consider it to be a prohibited "agreement to the contrary" under section 304(c)(5).

* * *

III

For the foregoing reasons, the district court correctly declared Clare's termination notice ineffective. The CTEA's termination provision does not apply to post-1978 agreements such as the parties' 1983 agreement, which continues to control the parties' rights and royalty shares in the Pooh works. In addition, Clare is unable to show that the 1983 agreement constitutes an "agreement to the contrary" under section 304(c)(5), and thus the courts cannot disregard the 1983 agreement. Nor are we persuaded by Clare's "moment of freedom" argument. Quite simply, there is no principle of logic, canon of statutory construction, or consideration of fairness that supports Clare's reading of the CTEA. Accordingly, the decision of the district court is AFFIRMED.

NOTES

1. The Second Circuit adopted *Milne*'s reasoning in *Penguin Group (USA), Inc. v. Steinbeck*, 537 F.3d 193 (2d Cir. 2008), concluding that John Steinbeck's widow effectively eradicated his descendants' termination rights under section 304(d) when she renegotiated a 1938 grant in 1994 without ever serving a formal termination notice. (Because Steinbeck was alive when each of his renewal terms vested, he was able to bequeath his renewal terms to his widow exclusively, leaving his sons with no share in his copyrights.) Did his descendants still have a termination right under section 203?

2. The Ninth Circuit distinguished *Milne* in *Classic Media, Inc. v. Mewborn*, 532 F.3d 978 (9th Cir. 2008), which held that the section 304(c) right to terminate an heir's 1976 assignment of certain rights in the *Lassie Come Home* short story and novel (published in 1938 and 1940 respectively) was not eliminated when a new contract for those rights was executed in 1978. The new contract included a broader grant of rights, and provided additional compensation to the heir. *Mewborn* concluded that the 1978 contract was an "agreement to the contrary" under section 304(c), and thus had no effect on the heir's right to terminate the original 1976 grant in 1996. In contrast to *Milne,* where the new grant was executed during the period when the heir was entitled to serve a termination notice, the heir in *Mewborn* executed the 1978 assignment six years before she was entitled to serve notice, and thus "had nothing in hand with which to bargain." *Id.* at 989. According to *Mewborn,* therefore, *Milne* involved a *de facto* exercise of the termination right; the parties simply did not follow the statutory formalities. Furthermore, the new contract in *Milne* expressly revoked the old contract, while the new contract in *Mewborn* merely conveyed additional rights. Finally, the evidence suggested that "Mewborn did not intend to waive her termination rights." *Id.* Are these distinctions persuasive?

In a footnote, the *Mewborn* court added that "it may be possible for an author or heir to transfer the future rights scheduled to revert upon service of a termination notice, subject to surviving until the time such rights vest in the author or heir." 532 F.3d at 986 n.4 (citing *Stewart v. Abend*, 495 U.S. 207, 219–21 (1990)). Do you agree?

3. In *Baldwin v. EMI Feist Catalog, Inc.*, 805 F.3d 18 (2d Cir. 2015), which involved the heirs to the author of the song "Santa Claus is Comin' To Town," the central issue was whether EMI owned its rights in the song under a 1951 agreement or under a contract executed in 1981. The court held that EMI owned its rights under the 1981 agreement, because that agreement clearly manifested the intent to replace and supersede the 1951 Agreement. EMI's ownership of rights under the 1981 agreement was important because section 203 termination rights do not apply to pre-1978 agreements, meaning if EMI owned its rights under the 1951 agreement the heirs would not be able to terminate the copyright agreement. The court concluded that the plaintiffs' 2007 termination notice meant that EMI's rights in the song were terminated as of December 2015.

4. The termination provisions in sections 203 and 304(c) do not explicitly account for one category of works: those which were the subject of an assignment or license executed before 1978, but which were not created until January 1, 1978 or later—in other words, works that were subject to a pre-creation license or assignment agreement such as a recording contract (assuming that the works do not qualify as works made for hire). The Register of Copyrights decided to address this "termination gap" by accepting and recording termination notices with respect to such works under section 203; this approach is reflected in the Copyright Office regulations at 27 C.F.R. § 201.10(f)(1)(ii)(C). The underlying reasoning is that a grant of rights does not take effect until the work has been created; thus, these pre-1978 grants did not actually take effect until after January 1, 1978, which brings them within the scope of section 203. In 2020, a federal district court agreed with the Copyright Office approach. *Waite v. UMG Recordings, Inc.*, 477 F. Supp.3d 265, 274–75 (S.D.N.Y. 2020) (addressing sound recordings).

CHAPTER 16

EXCLUSIVE RIGHTS

■ ■ ■

A. THE SECTION 106 RIGHTS

Statutes: 17 U.S.C. §§ 101 (as needed), 106, 109, 114, 602–03, 1401

1. REPRODUCTION

HORGAN V. MACMILLAN, INC.

789 F.2d 157 (2d Cir. 1986).

FEINBERG, CHIEF JUDGE:

This appeal presents the novel question whether still photographs of a ballet can infringe the copyright on the choreography for the ballet. Barbara Horgan, executrix of the estate of the renowned choreographer George Balanchine, appeals from a judgment of the United States District Court for the Southern District of New York, Richard Owen, J., denying her motion for a preliminary injunction. Appellant Horgan sought to enjoin the publication of a book entitled "The Nutcracker: A Story & a Ballet," which portrays, in text and photographs, the New York City Ballet Company's production of The Nutcracker ballet, choreographed by Balanchine. Defendant Macmillan is the publisher, and defendant Ellen Switzer the author, of the book; defendants Steven Caras and Costas provided the photographs. The district court held that the book did not infringe Balanchine's copyright because choreography is the flow of steps in a ballet, which could not be reproduced from the still photographs in the book. 621 F. Supp. 1169 (S.D.N.Y.1985). * * *

I.

[In 1954, Balanchine choreographed his now-classic version of the ballet The Nutcracker, an adaptation of a folk tale set to music by Tchaikovsky. Balanchine's version of the ballet also incorporates elements of a previous version by Russian choreographer Ivanov. The New York City Ballet Company and other entities pay Balanchine's estate a royalty or other consideration in exchange for a license to publicly perform his copyrighted choreography.]

In December 1981, Balanchine registered his claim to copyright in the choreography of The Nutcracker with the United States Copyright Office.

As part of his claim, he deposited with the Copyright Office a videotape of a New York City Ballet Company dress rehearsal of the ballet. * * *

In early April 1985, appellant Horgan learned for the first time that Macmillan was planning to publish, under its Atheneum imprint, a book about the New York City Ballet/Balanchine version of The Nutcracker. * * *

The book is designed primarily for an audience of young people. The title page displays three black and white photographs of George Balanchine directing a rehearsal of the ballet. The book begins with a 15-page text by defendant Switzer regarding the origins of The Nutcracker as a story and as a ballet. The remainder of the book is introduced by a second title page, as follows:

The Balanchine Ballet

As Performed by the Dancers of the New York City Ballet Company

The principal section of the book consists of 60 color photographs by Caras and Costas of scenes from the New York City Ballet Company production of The Nutcracker, following the sequence of the ballet's story and dances. The photographs are interspersed with Switzer's narration of the story, including those portions not portrayed visually. The final section of the book contains interviews with ten of the dancers, with black and white photographs of them out of costume. Defendants Switzer, Caras and Costas obtained this material through their access to company rehearsals and performances. Switzer is a free lance journalist who was apparently given such access by the press liaison for the Company. Caras and Costas are considered "official photographers" of the New York City Ballet. According to appellant, this means that Balanchine authorized them to take photographs of the Company, some of which might be purchased by the Company for publicity and related purposes.

* * *

On October 11, 1985, Horgan brought suit on behalf of the estate, seeking declaratory relief and both a preliminary and permanent injunction against publication of the book. * * * [T]he judge denied Horgan's motion for a preliminary injunction. The judge stated, in an opinion and order substantially similar to his earlier memorandum, that the book did not infringe the copyright on Balanchine's choreography because

> choreography has to do with the flow of the steps in a ballet. The still photographs in the Nutcracker book, numerous though they are, catch dancers in various attitudes at specific instants of time; they do not, nor do they intend to, take or use the underlying choreography. The staged performance could not be recreated from them.

621 F. Supp. at 1170 [(adding in a footnote: "Just as a Beethoven symphony could not be recreated from a document containing only every twenty-fifth chord of the symphony.")]. * * *

II.

The principal question on appeal, whether still photographs of a ballet can infringe the copyright on the choreography for the ballet, is a matter of first impression. Explicit federal copyright protection for choreography is a fairly recent development, and the scope of that protection is an uncharted area of the law. The 1976 Copyright Act (the Act), 17 U.S.C. § 101 et seq., was the first federal copyright statute expressly to include "choreographic works" as a subject of protection. * * *

The Act does not define choreography, and the legislative reports on the bill indicate only that "social dance steps and simple routines" are not included. *See, e.g.*, H.R. Rep. No. 1476, 94th Cong., 2d Sess. 53–54 (1976). The Compendium of Copyright Office Practices, Compendium II (1984), which is issued by that office, defines choreographic works as follows:

> Choreography is the composition and arrangement of dance movements and patterns, and is usually intended to be accompanied by music. Dance is static and kinetic successions of bodily movement in certain rhythmic and spatial relationships. Choreographic works need not tell a story in order to be protected by copyright.

Section 450.01. Under "Characteristics of choreographic works," Compendium II states that

> Choreography represents a related series of dance movements and patterns organized into a coherent whole.

Section 450.03(a). * * * The Act grants the owner of a copyrighted original work that is "fixed in any tangible medium of expression," 17 U.S.C. § 102(a), the exclusive right "to reproduce the copyrighted work in copies . . .," "to prepare derivative works based upon the copyrighted work" and, "in the case of . . . choreographic works, . . . to display the copyrighted work publicly." 17 U.S.C. § 106(1), (2) & (5). Appellant claims that the Switzer book is a "copy" of Balanchine's copyrighted work because it portrays the essence of the Balanchine Nutcracker, or, in the alternative, that the book is an infringing "derivative work." * * *

In response, appellees assert that the photographs in the Switzer book do not capture the flow of movement, which is the essence of dance, and thus cannot possibly be substantially similar to the choreographic component of the production of the ballet. Appellees rely on the various definitions of choreography in Compendium II, quoted above, to support their position that the central characteristic of choreography is "movement." According to appellees, since each photograph in the book captures only a fraction of an instant, even the combined effect of 60 color photographs does not reproduce the choreography itself, nor provide sufficient details of movement to enable a choreographic work to be reproduced from the photographs.

* * * [T]he district judge took a far too limited view of the extent to which choreographic material may be conveyed in the medium of still photography. A snapshot of a single moment in a dance sequence may communicate a great deal. It may, for example, capture a gesture, the composition of dancers' bodies or the placement of dancers on the stage. Such freezing of a choreographic moment is shown in a number of the photographs in the Switzer book * * *. A photograph may also convey to the viewer's imagination the moments before and after the split second recorded. On page 76–77 of the Switzer book, for example, there is a two-page photograph of the "Sugar Canes," one of the troupes that perform in The Nutcracker. In this photograph, the Sugar Canes are a foot or more off the ground, holding large hoops above their heads. One member of the ensemble is jumping through a hoop, which is held extended in front of the dancer. The dancer's legs are thrust forward, parallel to the stage and several feet off the ground. The viewer understands instinctively, based simply on the laws of gravity, that the Sugar Canes jumped up from the floor only a moment earlier, and came down shortly after the photographed moment. An ordinary observer, who had only recently seen a performance of The Nutcracker, could probably perceive even more from this photograph. The single instant thus communicates far more than a single chord of a Beethoven symphony—the analogy suggested by the district judge.

It may be that all of the photographs mentioned above are of insufficient quantity or sequencing to constitute infringement; it may also be that they do copy but also are protected as fair use. But that is not what the district judge said in denying a preliminary injunction. The judge erroneously held that still photographs cannot infringe choreography. Since the judge applied the wrong test in evaluating appellant's likelihood of success on the preliminary injunction, we believe that a remand is appropriate. * * *

We reverse and remand for further proceedings consistent with this opinion.

WALT DISNEY PRODUCTIONS V. FILMATION ASSOCIATES

628 F.Supp. 871 (C.D. Cal. 1986).

STOTLER, UNITED STATES DISTRICT JUDGE:

Introduction

* * *

[Plaintiff Walt Disney Productions ("Disney") alleges that Filmation Associates ("Filmation") copied cartoon figures from Disney's animated film "Pinocchio" and has begun to use them in producing an animated film entitled "The New Adventures of Pinocchio."]

* * * In the course of production, Filmation has produced a script, "story board," "story reel,"[2] models, and designs, which are said to be tangible and permanent reproductions of characters and scenes, "constituting copies of material" copyrighted by Disney. *Id.*, para. 61.

It is undisputed that Filmation has generated a substantial body of work preliminary to a "finished film." It is also undisputed, however, that it has not completed its film "The New Adventures of Pinocchio." Filmation contends that Count Six is not actionable until it has completed work on its motion picture. Alternatively, Filmation asserts it is entitled to judgment because any articles so far produced are not substantially similar to Disney's copyrighted expressions.

1. Actionable "Copies"

Filmation argues that the materials so far created are only transitory steps en route to a fixed product, and that until its film is completed and ready for distribution, there exists no article that could be said to infringe any of Disney's copyrights.

Filmation's argument is refuted by the provisions of the 1976 Copyright Act, 17 U.S.C. §§ 101–914 (the "Act"). Under the Act, " 'copies' are material objects . . . in which a work is fixed by any method now known or later developed, and from which the work can be perceived, reproduced, or otherwise communicated, either directly or with the aid of a machine or device." 17 U.S.C. § 101. The definition "includes the material object . . . in which the work is first fixed." *Id.* Further, a work is " 'fixed' in a tangible medium of expression when its embodiment in a copy . . . is sufficiently permanent or stable to permit it to be perceived, reproduced, or otherwise communicated for a period of more than transitory duration." *Id.* When the work is "prepared over a period of time, the portion of it that has been fixed at any particular time constitutes the work as of that time, and where the work has been prepared in different versions, each version constitutes a separate work." *Id.* To constitute an actionable copy, therefore, an expression need only be a material object permanently cast in some intelligible form.

---

2 A "story reel" is a working model used to create the final animated product. To create a story reel, Filmation first records a reading of the script. It then creates a "story board" comprising sketches of the various scenes in the film set in the order in which they will be portrayed and "shoots" the sketches to synchronize with the recorded dialogue track and a rough music track. By viewing the reel, the director can get a "feel" for the story line and pacing of the anticipated picture and can begin allocating responsibility for its animation. * * *

The articles created by Filmation in the production of its film, including a script, story board, story reel, and promotional "trailer," satisfy this definition, and thus can constitute copies for purposes of the Act. Because the right of reproduction affords a copyright owner protection against an infringer even if he does not also infringe the § 106(3) right of distribution, *Sony Corp. v. Universal City Studios, Inc.*, 464 U.S. 417, 474 (1984) (Blackmun, J., dissenting); House Report No. 94–1476, 94th Cong., 2d Sess. (1976), p. 61, the fact that the articles may never be published or, indeed, may be prepared only for the use of Filmation's animators, does not obviate the possibility of infringement. *See Harper & Row v. Nation Enterprises,* 471 U.S. 539 (1985) (noting that the Act "eliminated publication 'as a dividing line between common law and statutory protection,' . . . extending statutory protection to all works from the time of their creation"). As explained by Professor Nimmer, "subject to the privilege of fair use, and subject to certain other exemptions, copyright infringement occurs whenever an unauthorized copy . . . is made, even if it is used solely for the private purposes of the reproducer." 2 NIMMER, § 8.02(C), p. 8–26. It is thus irrelevant that Filmation has not concluded or "realized" what it considers to be a final motion picture: the Act prohibits the creation of copies, even if the creator considers those copies mere interim steps toward some final goal.

It is similarly no defense to copying that some of Filmation's expressions may be embodied in a medium different from that of plaintiff's. *Berkic v. Crichton*, 761 F.2d 1289, 1292 (9th Cir.1985) ("in comparing . . . a film with a written work, the proper question . . . is whether the ordinary, reasonable audience would recognize the defendant's work as a 'dramatization' or 'picturization' of the plaintiff's work"). *See also Eden Toys, Inc. v. Florelee Undergarment Co.*, 697 F.2d 27 (2d Cir.1982) (copying from gift wrapping paper to clothing actionable). *But see Sid & Marty Krofft Television v. McDonald's Corp.*, 562 F.2d 1157, 1164 (9th Cir.1977) (observing, in dicta, that a painting of a nude would not infringe a statue of a nude). Thus, Filmation's materials, including scripts and story outlines, can infringe Disney's copyright on "Pinocchio" even though they are not rendered as a motion picture.

This had been the law in the Ninth Circuit even under the Copyright Act of 1909. In *Walker v. University Books, Inc.*, 602 F.2d 859 (9th Cir.1979), plaintiff had copyrighted a set of fortune telling cards. She attempted unsuccessfully to strike a marketing deal with defendants, submitting to them a sample of her deck in the process. Afterward, she assigned her copyright to a third party. Plaintiff subsequently discovered that defendant planned to market a deck of cards similar to the ones she had supplied them in the course of negotiations. She received from defendants "certain blueprints," which were produced before the date of the assignment (*id.* at 863), but could adduce no evidence of a completed deck of cards produced and sold during the period in which she owned the copyright.

On appeal from summary judgment in defendant's favor, the court of appeals rejected defendant's argument that the blueprints were not themselves copies:

> The district court viewed the making of the blueprints as merely a preliminary step or process directed towards the manufacture of [defendants'] finished product, their set of [cards].... However, the fact that an allegedly infringing copy of a protected work may itself be only an inchoate representation of some final product to be marketed commercially does not in itself negate the possibility of infringement.

Walker, 602 F.2d at 864. According to the *Walker* court, the operative question was not whether defendants considered the article a final product, but "whether they unauthorizedly utilized [plaintiff's] work in the manufacture of their blueprints." *Id.*

Finally, the absence of a completed motion picture does not preclude meaningful comparison of Disney's character depictions and film with Filmation's materials. Although Filmation contends that copyright infringement of a cartoon character cannot be based on a mere sketch that is not part of a story, there is no support for this proposition. It is true that courts generally have considered "not only the visual resemblances but also the totality of the characters' attributes and traits," 1 Nimmer § 2.12, p. 175, n. 16.2, and, thus, that the trier of fact would ordinarily evaluate a character in the context of a story. But where the work sued upon is not a "completed" story, but a series of depictions and other works, comparison of the expressions may be made in the form in which they are presented. *Walt Disney Productions v. Air Pirates*, 581 F.2d 751, 756 (9th Cir.1978) (comparison of graphic images of cartoon characters sufficient to allow action for copyright infringement).

* * *

NOTES

1. In *Sega Enterprises Ltd. v. Accolade, Inc.*, 977 F.2d 1510 (9th Cir. 1992), the Ninth Circuit reaffirmed its holding in *Walker v. University Books* that a copyright holder's exclusive rights under section 106 extended to copying undertaken as a preliminary step to creating a non-infringing finished product. *See also DSC Communications Corp. v. DGI Techs., Inc.*, 898 F.Supp. 1183, 1188 (N.D. Tex.1995) (following *Sega*), *aff'd*, 81 F.3d 597 (5th Cir. 1996). Citing *Filmation* with approval, the *Sega* court distinguished several cases which had refused to consider evidence of intermediate copying, noting that in each case the plaintiff had alleged infringement only by the final, publicly distributed

version of the defendant's work. *See, e.g., Walker v. Time Life Films, Inc.*, 784 F.2d 44, 52 (2d Cir. 1986); *See v. Durang*, 711 F.2d 141, 142 (9th Cir. 1983).

In determining whether liability should arise from such intermediate copying, should it matter whether a final version of the defendant's work has been completed or distributed, and whether the final version itself infringes the plaintiff's work? Suppose the defendant abandons or delays the project after the intermediate copying, or, as happened in *Walker v. University Books*, the plaintiff assigns her copyright after the intermediate copy has been made, but before the defendant's final version is completed and distributed? What remedies should be available in a case involving solely intermediate copying?

2. In *Amsinck v. Columbia Pictures Industries*, 862 F.Supp. 1044, 1047–48 (S.D.N.Y. 1994), the district court defined the reproduction right narrowly, refusing to find infringement of that right where the plaintiff's copyrighted mobile was clearly visible in the background of certain scenes in the defendants' motion picture. The court reasoned that the defendant's use of the work did not have "the intent or effect of fulfilling the demand for the original." Is this a correct interpretation of the Copyright Act? Can this be reconciled with *Horgan* and *Filmation*? *See Walker v. University Books, Inc.*, 602 F.2d 859, 863–64 (9th Cir. 1979) ("fixation" in a "copy" means that the work can be perceived from the tangible object); *see also Woods v. Universal City Studios*, 920 F.Supp. 62 (S.D.N.Y. 1996) (holding that drawing of apparatus was reproduced where apparatus was constructed and used as scenery in motion picture). *Cf. Ringgold v. Black Entertainment Television, Inc.*, 126 F.3d 70 (2d Cir. 1997) (defendants' use of copyrighted poster in background of television program was not de minimis).

3. Suppose an artist produces a painting of a model, and then sells the painting and its copyright. Is the exclusive reproduction right infringed where an artist subsequently places the same model in the same pose and thereby produces a nearly identical painting? Does your answer change if it is the same artist? Would it matter if the painting were a landscape, and the artist duplicated it from memory by standing in the same place and waiting for the same lighting conditions?

4. Consider whether the following activities involve "reproduction" of a copyrighted work within the meaning of section 106(1):

(a) Defendant records her performance of a copyrighted musical composition for which she acquired a copy of the sheet music.

(b) Defendant, who is impressed with a low-budget student film, but convinced that in its current form it is not commercially viable, produces a big-budget remake which incorporates all of the plot and character details of the original without using any of the literal dialogue or original footage.

(c) A building is constructed from copyrighted architectural plans.

(d) A tourist photographs a newly constructed historical monument.

(e) On request, a bakery decorates birthday cakes with the same design that appears on the customers' birthday party invitations.

(f) A publisher downloads cases from WESTLAW, then edits out the headnotes and page numbers, as well as any other original content added by West, then publishes the cases (organized by subject matter) in digital and print media for distribution to law students and practitioners.

(g) Plaintiff makes and sells both video game hardware and video games, and defendant wishes to make its video games compatible with plaintiff's hardware. To accomplish this, defendant copies the object code from plaintiff's cartridges, and "reverse engineers" this information to construct its own object code, which provides the compatibility needed without containing any of the plaintiff's code.

5. A passerby who observed the assassination of President John F. Kennedy in 1963 captured the event on film. Because it is the only available film footage of the assassination, and the best-known photographic evidence, it was studied extensively by the FBI and the Warren Commission. A few years later, an author writing a book about the assassination and the investigation was denied permission to reproduce portions of the footage in his book. Instead, he used sketches which accurately depicted the most significant aspects of those individual frames. Assuming that there had been no divestive publication of the footage, did the author of the book make unauthorized copies of a copyrighted work? What remedy should be available to the filmmaker? *See Time, Inc. v. Bernard Geis Associates*, 293 F.Supp. 130 (S.D.N.Y. 1968).

CARTOON NETWORK LP V. CSC HOLDINGS, INC.

536 F.3d 121 (2d Cir. 2008).

JOHN M. WALKER, JR., CIRCUIT JUDGE.

Defendant-Appellant Cablevision Systems Corporation ("Cablevision") wants to market a new "Remote Storage" Digital Video Recorder system ("RS-DVR"), using a technology akin to both traditional, set-top digital video recorders, like TiVo ("DVRs"), and the video-on-demand ("VOD") services provided by many cable companies. Plaintiffs-Appellees produce copyrighted movies and television programs that they provide to Cablevision pursuant to numerous licensing agreements. They contend that Cablevision, through the operation of its RS-DVR system as proposed, would directly infringe their copyrights both by making unauthorized reproductions, and by engaging in public performances, of their copyrighted works. * * *

In the district court, plaintiffs successfully argued that Cablevision's proposed system would directly infringe their copyrights * * *. First, by briefly storing data in the primary ingest buffer and other data buffers integral to the function of the RS-DVR, Cablevision would make copies of protected works and thereby directly infringe plaintiffs' exclusive right of reproduction under the Copyright Act. Second, by copying programs onto the Arroyo Server hard disks (the "playback copies"), Cablevision would again directly infringe the reproduction right. * * * Agreeing with [plaintiffs,] the district court awarded summary declaratory judgment to plaintiffs and enjoined Cablevision from operating the RS-DVR system without obtaining licenses from the plaintiff copyright holders.

As to the buffer data, the district court rejected defendants' arguments 1) that the data were not "fixed" and therefore were not "copies" as defined in the Copyright Act, and 2) that any buffer copying was de minimis because the buffers stored only small amounts of data for very short periods of time. In rejecting the latter argument, the district court noted that the "aggregate effect of the buffering" was to reproduce the entirety of Cablevision's programming, and such copying "can hardly be called de minimis."

* * *

I. The Buffer Data

It is undisputed that Cablevision, not any customer or other entity, takes the content from one stream of programming, after the split, and stores it, one small piece at a time, in the BMR buffer and the primary ingest buffer. As a result, the information is buffered before any customer requests a recording, and would be buffered even if no such request were made. The question is whether, by buffering the data that make up a given work, Cablevision "reproduce[s]" that work "in copies," 17 U.S.C. § 106(1), and thereby infringes the copyright holder's reproduction right.

"Copies," as defined in the Copyright Act, "are material objects . . . in which a work is fixed by any method . . . and from which the work can be . . . reproduced." *Id.* § 101. The Act also provides that a work is " 'fixed' in a tangible medium of expression when its embodiment . . . is sufficiently permanent or stable to permit it to be . . . reproduced . . . *for a period of more than transitory duration.*" *Id.* (emphasis added). We believe that this language plainly imposes two distinct but related requirements: the work must be embodied in a medium, i.e., placed in a medium such that it can be perceived, reproduced, etc., from that medium (the "embodiment requirement"), and it must remain thus embodied "for a period of more than transitory duration" (the "duration requirement"). Unless both requirements are met, the work is not "fixed" in the buffer, and, as a result, the buffer data is not a "copy" of the original work whose data is buffered.

The district court mistakenly limited its analysis primarily to the embodiment requirement. As a result of this error, once it determined that the buffer data was "[c]learly . . . capable of being reproduced," i.e., that the work was embodied in the buffer, the district court concluded that the work was therefore "fixed" in the buffer, and that a copy had thus been made. In doing so, it relied on a line of cases beginning with *MAI Systems Corp. v. Peak Computer Inc.,* 991 F.2d 511 (9th Cir.1993). It also relied on the United States Copyright Office's 2001 report on the Digital Millennium Copyright Act, which states, in essence, that an embodiment is fixed "[u]nless a reproduction manifests itself so fleetingly that *it cannot be copied.*" U.S. Copyright Office, *DMCA Section 104 Report* 111 (Aug.2001) ("*DMCA Report*") (emphasis added).

The district court's reliance on cases like *MAI Systems* is misplaced. In general, those cases conclude that an alleged copy is fixed without addressing the duration requirement; it does not follow, however, that those cases assume, much less establish, that such a requirement does not exist. Indeed, the duration requirement, by itself, was not at issue in *MAI Systems* and its progeny. As a result, they do not speak to the issues squarely before us here: If a work is only "embodied" in a medium for a period of transitory duration, can it be "fixed" in that medium, and thus a copy? And what constitutes a period "of more than transitory duration"?

* * *

The *MAI Systems* court referenced the "transitory duration" language but did not discuss or analyze it. The opinion notes that the defendants "vigorously" argued that the program's embodiment in the RAM was not a copy, but it does not specify the arguments defendants made. This omission suggests that the parties did not litigate the significance of the "transitory duration" language, and the court therefore had no occasion to address it. This is unsurprising, because it seems fair to assume that in these cases the program was embodied in the RAM for at least several minutes.

Accordingly, we construe *MAI Systems* and its progeny as holding that loading a program into a computer's RAM *can* result in copying that program. We do not read *MAI Systems* as holding that, as a matter of law, loading a program into a form of RAM *always* results in copying. Such a holding would read the "transitory duration" language out of the definition, and we do not believe our sister circuit would dismiss this statutory language without even discussing it. It appears the parties in *MAI Systems* simply did not dispute that the duration requirement was satisfied; this line of cases simply concludes that when a program is loaded into RAM, the embodiment requirement is satisfied—an important holding in itself, and one we see no reason to quibble with here.

At least one court, relying on *MAI Systems* in a highly similar factual setting, has made this point explicitly. In *Advanced Computer Services of Michigan, Inc. v. MAI Systems Corp.,* the district court expressly noted that the unlicensed user in that case ran copyrighted diagnostic software "for minutes or longer," but that the program's embodiment in the computer's RAM might be too ephemeral to be fixed if the computer had been shut down "within seconds or fractions of a second" after loading the copyrighted program. 845 F.Supp. 356, 363 (E.D.Va. 1994). We have no quarrel with this reasoning; it merely makes explicit the reasoning that is implicit in the other *MAI Systems* cases. Accordingly, those cases provide no support for the conclusion that the definition of "fixed" does not include a duration requirement. * * *

Nor does the Copyright Office's 2001 DMCA Report, also relied on by the district court in this case, explicitly suggest that the definition of "fixed" does not contain a duration requirement. However, as noted above, it does suggest that an embodiment is fixed "[u]nless a reproduction manifests itself so fleetingly that it cannot be copied, perceived or communicated." *DMCA Report, supra,* at 111. As we have stated, to determine whether a work is "fixed" in a given medium, the statutory language directs us to ask not only 1) whether a work is "embodied" in that medium, but also 2) whether it is embodied in the medium "for a period of more than transitory duration." According to the Copyright Office, if the work is capable of being copied from that medium *for any amount of time,* the answer to both questions is "yes." The problem with this interpretation is that it reads the "transitory duration" language out of the statute.

* * *

In sum, no case law or other authority dissuades us from concluding that the definition of "fixed" imposes both an embodiment requirement and a duration requirement. *Accord CoStar Group Inc. v. LoopNet, Inc.,* 373 F.3d 544, 551 (4th Cir.2004) (while temporary reproductions "may be made in this transmission process, they would appear not to be 'fixed' in the sense that they are 'of more than transitory duration' "). We now turn to whether, in this case, those requirements are met by the buffer data.

Cablevision does not seriously dispute that copyrighted works are "embodied" in the buffer. Data in the BMR buffer can be reformatted and transmitted to the other components of the RS-DVR system. Data in the primary ingest buffer can be copied onto the Arroyo hard disks if a user has requested a recording of that data. Thus, a work's "embodiment" in either buffer "is sufficiently permanent or stable to permit it to be perceived, reproduced," (as in the case of the ingest buffer) "or otherwise communicated" (as in the BMR buffer). 17 U.S.C. § 101. The result might be different if only a single second of a much longer work was placed in the buffer in isolation. In such a situation, it might be reasonable to conclude that only a minuscule portion of a work, rather than "a work" was embodied in the buffer. Here, however, where every second of an entire work is placed, one second at a time, in the buffer, we conclude that the work is embodied in the buffer.

Does any such embodiment last "for a period of more than transitory duration"? *Id.* No bit of data remains in any buffer for more than a fleeting

1.2 seconds. And unlike the data in cases like *MAI Systems,* which remained embodied in the computer's RAM memory until the user turned the computer off, each bit of data here is rapidly and automatically overwritten as soon as it is processed. While our inquiry is necessarily fact-specific, and other factors not present here may alter the duration analysis significantly, these facts strongly suggest that the works in this case are embodied in the buffer for only a "transitory" period, thus failing the duration requirement.

Against this evidence, plaintiffs argue only that the duration is not transitory because the data persist "long enough for Cablevision to make reproductions from them." As we have explained above, however, this reasoning impermissibly reads the duration language out of the statute, and we reject it. Given that the data reside in no buffer for more than 1.2 seconds before being automatically overwritten, and in the absence of compelling arguments to the contrary, we believe that the copyrighted works here are not "embodied" in the buffers for a period of more than transitory duration, and are therefore not "fixed" in the buffers. Accordingly, the acts of buffering in the operation of the RS-DVR do not create copies, as the Copyright Act defines that term. Our resolution of this issue renders it unnecessary for us to determine whether any copies produced by buffering data would be de minimis, and we express no opinion on that question.

II. Direct Liability for Creating the Playback Copies

In most copyright disputes, the allegedly infringing act and the identity of the infringer are never in doubt. These cases turn on whether the conduct in question does, in fact, infringe the plaintiff's copyright. In this case, however, the core of the dispute is over the authorship of the infringing conduct. After an RS-DVR subscriber selects a program to record, and that program airs, a copy of the program—a copyrighted work—resides on the hard disks of Cablevision's Arroyo Server, its creation unauthorized by the copyright holder. The question is *who* made this copy. If it is Cablevision, plaintiffs' theory of direct infringement succeeds; if it is the customer, plaintiffs' theory fails because Cablevision would then face, at most, secondary liability, a theory of liability expressly disavowed by plaintiffs.

Few cases examine the line between direct and contributory liability. Both parties cite a line of cases beginning with *Religious Technology Center v. Netcom On-Line Communication Services,* 907 F.Supp. 1361 (N.D.Cal.1995). In *Netcom,* a third-party customer of the defendant Internet service provider ("ISP") posted a copyrighted work that was automatically reproduced by the defendant's computer. The district court refused to impose direct liability on the ISP, reasoning that "[a]lthough copyright is a strict liability statute, there should still be some element of volition or causation which is lacking where a defendant's system is merely used to create a copy by a third party." *Id.* at 1370. Recently, the Fourth Circuit endorsed the *Netcom* decision, noting that

> to establish *direct* liability under . . . the Act, something more must be shown than mere ownership of a machine used by others to make illegal copies. There must be actual infringing conduct with a nexus sufficiently close and causal to the illegal copying that one could conclude that the machine owner himself trespassed on the exclusive domain of the copyright owner.

CoStar Group, Inc. v. LoopNet, Inc., 373 F.3d 544, 550 (4th Cir.2004).

Here, the district court pigeon-holed the conclusions reached in *Netcom* and its progeny as "premised on the unique attributes of the Internet." *Cablevision I,* 478 F.Supp.2d at 620. While the *Netcom* court was plainly concerned with a theory of direct liability that would effectively "hold the entire Internet liable" for the conduct of a single user, 907 F.Supp. at 1372, its reasoning and conclusions, consistent with precedents of this court and the Supreme Court, and with the text of the Copyright Act, transcend the Internet. Like the Fourth Circuit, we reject the contention that "the *Netcom* decision was driven by expedience and that its holding is inconsistent with the established law of copyright," *CoStar,* 373 F.3d at 549, and we find it "a particularly rational interpretation of § 106," *id.* at 551, rather than a special-purpose rule applicable only to ISPs.

When there is a dispute as to the author of an allegedly infringing instance of reproduction, *Netcom* and its progeny direct our attention to the volitional conduct that causes the copy to be made. There are only two instances of volitional conduct in this case: Cablevision's conduct in designing, housing, and maintaining a system that exists only to produce a copy, and a customer's conduct in ordering that system to produce a copy of a specific program. In the case of a VCR, it seems clear—and we know of no case holding otherwise—that the operator of the VCR, the person who actually presses the button to make the recording, supplies the necessary element of volition, not the person who manufactures, maintains, or, if distinct from the operator, owns the machine. We do not believe that an RS-DVR customer is sufficiently distinguishable from a VCR user to impose liability as a direct infringer on a different party for copies that are made automatically upon that customer's command.

The district court emphasized the fact that copying is "instrumental" rather than "incidental" to the function of the RS-DVR system. *Cablevision I,* 478 F.Supp.2d at 620. While that may distinguish the RS-DVR from the ISPs in *Netcom* and *CoStar,* it does not distinguish the RS-DVR from a VCR, a photocopier, or even a typical copy shop. And the parties do not seem to contest that a company that merely makes photocopiers available to the public on its premises, without more, is not subject to liability for direct infringement for reproductions made by customers using those copiers. They only dispute whether Cablevision is similarly situated to such a proprietor.

The district court found Cablevision analogous to a copy shop that makes course packs for college professors. In the leading case involving such a shop, for example, "[t]he professor [gave] the copyshop the materials of which the coursepack [was] to be made up, and the copyshop [did] the rest." *Princeton Univ. Press v. Mich. Document Servs.*, 99 F.3d 1381, 1384 (6th Cir.1996) (en banc). There did not appear to be any serious dispute in that case that the shop itself was directly liable for reproducing copyrighted works. The district court here found that Cablevision, like this copy shop, would be "doing" the copying, albeit "at the customer's behest." *Cablevision I*, 478 F.Supp.2d at 620.

But because volitional conduct is an important element of direct liability, the district court's analogy is flawed. In determining who actually "makes" a copy, a significant difference exists between making a request to a human employee, who then volitionally operates the copying system to make the copy, and issuing a command directly to a system, which automatically obeys commands and engages in no volitional conduct. In cases like *Princeton University Press*, the defendants operated a copying device and sold the product they made using that device. *See* 99 F.3d at 1383 ("The corporate defendant . . . is a commercial copyshop that reproduced substantial segments of copyrighted works of scholarship, bound the copies into 'coursepacks,' and sold the coursepacks to students. . . ."). Here, by selling access to a system that automatically produces copies on command, Cablevision more closely resembles a store proprietor who charges customers to use a photocopier on his premises, and it seems incorrect to say, without more, that such a proprietor "makes" any copies when his machines are actually operated by his customers. *See Netcom*, 907 F.Supp. at 1369. Some courts have held to the contrary, but they do not explicitly explain why, and we find them unpersuasive. *See, e.g., Elektra Records Co. v. Gem Elec. Distribs., Inc.*, 360 F.Supp. 821, 823 (E.D.N.Y.1973) (concluding that, "regardless" of whether customers or defendants' employees operated the tape-copying machines at defendants' stores, defendant had actively infringed copyrights).

* * *

[The court's analysis of the public performance issue is excerpted in Part A.4. of this chapter.]

NOTE

In the 1976 Act, Congress authorized the creation of a National Commission on New Technological Uses of Copyrighted Works (CONTU) to study copyright questions pertaining to computer software and photocopying.

CONTU's 1978 report to Congress stated that "[t]he text of the new [1976] copyright law makes it clear that the placement of a copyrighted work into a computer * * * is the preparation of a copy," and added, with respect to the "fixation" language in the 1976 House Report:

> Insofar as a contrary conclusion is suggested in one report accompanying the new law, this should be regarded as incorrect and should not be followed, since legislative history need not be perused in the construction of an unambiguous statute.

Final Report of the National Commission on New Technological Uses of Copyrighted Works 55 & n. 131 (July 31, 1978) ("CONTU Report").

In *MAI Systems Corp. v. Peak Computer, Inc.*, 991 F.2d 511 (9th Cir. 1993), the Ninth Circuit concluded that the loading of a program into a computer's random access memory (RAM) was sufficient to constitute reproduction even though the program would be lost when the computer's power was turned off. The *Peak* court relied in part on language in *Apple Computer, Inc. v. Formula Int'l, Inc.*, 594 F.Supp. 617, 622 (C.D. Cal. 1984), which described the loading of a program into RAM as a "temporary fixation." *Accord Stenograph L.L.C. v. Bossard Associates, Inc.*, 144 F.3d 96 (D.C.Cir. 1998); *Triad Systems Corp. v. Southeastern Express Co.*, 64 F.3d 1330 (9th Cir. 1995); *Religious Technology Center v. Netcom On-Line Communication Services, Inc.*, 907 F.Supp. 1361 (N.D. Cal. 1995); *Advanced Computer Services of Michigan, Inc. v. MAI Systems Corp.*, 845 F.Supp. 356 (E.D. Va. 1994). But *see NLFC, Inc. v. Devcom Mid-America, Inc.*, 45 F.3d 231, 236 (7th Cir. 1995) (implying that remote access to a document through a dedicated phone line from a "dumb terminal" does not involve copying the document into the computer's memory).

Congress appears to have acquiesced in the conclusion that loading software into RAM constitutes copying, although it has not addressed the question directly. Title III of the DMCA revised section 117 (discussed *infra* Chapter 18.D.) to permit "the owner or lessee" of a computer to authorize computer repair services to copy software into RAM in the course of activating the computer for servicing. The Conference Report states that such a clarification is "necessary in light of judicial decisions holding that such copying is a 'reproduction' under section 106," and adds that "this section does not in any way alter the law with respect to the scope of the term 'reproduction' as it is used in the Copyright Act." H.R. Rep. No. 105–796, 105th Cong., 2d Sess. (1998).

2. PREPARATION OF DERIVATIVE WORKS

COPYRIGHT ACT OF 1976

H.R. Rep. No. 94–1476.
94th Cong., 2d Sess. 62 (1976).

* * *

Preparation of derivative works.—The exclusive right to prepare derivative works, specified separately in clause (2) of section 106, overlaps the exclusive right of reproduction to some extent. It is broader than that right, however, in the sense that reproduction requires fixation in copies or phonorecords, whereas the preparation of a derivative work, such as a ballet, pantomime, or improvised performance, may be an infringement even though nothing is ever fixed in tangible form.

To be an infringement the "derivative work" must be "based upon the copyrighted work," and the definition in section 101 refers to "a translation, musical arrangement, dramatization, fictionalization, motion picture version, sound recording, art reproduction, abridgment, condensation, or any other form in which a work may be recast, transformed, or adapted." Thus, to constitute a violation of section 106(2), the infringing work must incorporate a portion of the copyrighted work in some form; for example, a detailed commentary on a work or a programmatic musical composition inspired by a novel would not normally constitute infringements under this clause. * * *

MIDWAY MANUFACTURING CO. V. ARTIC INTERNATIONAL, INC.

704 F.2d 1009 (7th Cir. 1983).

CUMMINGS, CHIEF JUDGE:

* * *

[The plaintiff produces video games.] Defendant sells printed circuit boards for use inside video game machines. One of the circuit boards defendant sells speeds up the rate of play—how fast the sounds and images change—of "Galaxian," one of plaintiff's video games, when inserted in place of one of the "Galaxian" machine's circuit boards. * * *

[Although an expert witness concluded that portions of the source code in defendant's speed-up kits had been copied from the plaintiff's Galaxian memory board, *see* 547 F. Supp. 999, 1004 (N.D. Ill. 1982), the district court concluded that "the copyrighted work at issue in this case is the audiovisual display that appears on the video game's screen. The speed-up kit sold by Artic clearly changes that display during the play mode." *Id.* at 1013. The district court concluded that the plaintiff was likely to succeed on the merits of its claim that defendant "induced others to prepare a derivative work" by using the speed-up kits to alter the plaintiff's copyrighted audiovisual displays.]

[Defendant appeals from the district court's order enjoining defendant from making or distributing its speed-up kits, arguing] that selling plaintiff's licensees circuit boards that speed up the rate of play of plaintiff's video games is not an infringement of plaintiff's copyrights. Speeding up the rate of play of a video game is a little like playing at 45 or 78 revolutions per minute ("RPM's") a phonograph record recorded at 33 RPM's. If a discotheque licensee did that, it would probably not be an infringement of the record company's copyright in the record. One might argue by analogy that it is not a copyright infringement for video game licensees to speed up the rate of play of video games, and that it is not a contributory infringement for the defendant to sell licensees circuit boards that enable them to do that.

There is this critical difference between playing records at a faster than recorded speed and playing video games at a faster than manufactured rate: there is an enormous demand for speeded-up video games but there is little if any demand for speeded-up records. Not many people want to hear 33 RPM records played at 45 and 78 RPM's so that record licensors would not care if their licensees play them at that speed. But there is a big demand for speeded-up video games. Speeding up a video game's action makes the game more challenging and exciting and increases the licensee's revenue per game. Speeded-up games end sooner than normal games and consequently if players are willing to pay an additional price-per-minute in exchange for the challenge and excitement of a faster game, licensees will take in greater total revenues. Video game copyright owners would undoubtedly like to lay their hands on some of that extra revenue and therefore it cannot be assumed that licensees are implicitly authorized to use speeded-up circuit boards in the machines plaintiff supplies.

Among a copyright owner's exclusive rights is the right "to prepare derivative works based upon the copyrighted work." 17 U.S.C. § 106(2). If, as we hold, the speeded-up "Galaxian" game that a licensee creates with a circuit board supplied by the defendant is a derivative work based upon "Galaxian," a licensee who lacks the plaintiff's authorization to create a derivative work is a direct infringer and the defendant is a contributory infringer through its sale of the speeded-up circuit board. *See, e.g., Gershwin Publishing Corp. v. Columbia Artists Mgmt., Inc.*, 443 F.2d 1159, 1162 (2d Cir.1971); *Universal City Studios, Inc. v. Sony Corp. of America*, 659 F.2d 963, 975 (9th Cir.1981), *certiorari granted*, 457 U.S. 1116 (1982).

Section 101 of the 1976 Copyright Act defines a derivative work as "a work based upon one or more preexisting works, such as a translation, musical arrangement, dramatization, fictionalization, motion picture version, sound recording, art reproduction, abridgment, condensation, or any other form in which a work may be recast, transformed, or adapted." It is not obvious from this language whether a speeded-up video game is a derivative work. A speeded-up phonograph record probably is not. *Cf. Shapiro, Bernstein & Co. v. Jerry Vogel Music Co.*, 73 F. Supp. 165, 167 (S.D.N.Y.1947) ("The change in time of the added chorus, and the slight variation in the base of the accompaniment, there being no change in the tune or lyrics, would not be 'new work' "); 1 NIMMER ON COPYRIGHT § 3.03 (1982). But that is because the additional value to the copyright owner of having the right to market separately the speeded-up version of the recorded performance is too trivial to warrant legal protection for that right. A speeded-up video game is a substantially different product from the original game. As noted, it is more exciting to play and it requires some creative effort to produce. For that reason, the owner of the copyright on the game should be entitled to monopolize it on the same theory that he is entitled to monopolize the derivative works specifically listed in Section 101. The current rage for video games was not anticipated in 1976, and like any new technology the video game does not fit with complete ease the definition of derivative work in Section 101 of the 1976 Act. But the amount by which the language of Section 101 must be stretched to accommodate speeded-up video games is, we believe, within the limits within which Congress wanted the new Act to operate. * * *

AFFIRMED.

LEWIS GALOOB TOYS, INC. V. NINTENDO OF AMERICA, INC.

964 F.2d 965 (9th Cir. 1992).

FARRIS, CIRCUIT JUDGE:

Nintendo of America appeals the district court's judgment following a bench trial (1) declaring that Lewis Galoob Toys' Game Genie does not violate any Nintendo copyrights and dissolving a temporary injunction and (2) denying Nintendo's request for a permanent injunction enjoining Galoob from marketing the Game Genie. * * * We affirm.

Facts

The Nintendo Entertainment System is a home video game system marketed by Nintendo. To use the system, the player inserts a cartridge containing a video game that Nintendo produces or licenses others to produce. By pressing buttons and manipulating a control pad, the player controls one of the game's characters and progresses through the game. The games are protected as audiovisual works under 17 U.S.C. § 102(a)(6).

The Game Genie is a device manufactured by Galoob that allows the player to alter up to three features of a Nintendo game. For example, the Game Genie can increase the number of lives of the player's character, increase the speed at which the character moves, and allow the character to float above obstacles. The player controls the changes made by the Game Genie by entering codes provided by the Game Genie Programming Manual and Code Book. The player also can experiment with variations of these codes.

The Game Genie functions by blocking the value for a single data byte sent by the game cartridge to the central processing unit in the Nintendo

Entertainment System and replacing it with a new value. If that value controls the character's strength, for example, then the character can be made invincible by increasing the value sufficiently. The Game Genie is inserted between a game cartridge and the Nintendo Entertainment System. The Game Genie does not alter the data that is stored in the game cartridge. Its effects are temporary.

Discussion

1. Derivative work

The Copyright Act of 1976 confers upon copyright holders the exclusive right to prepare and authorize others to prepare derivative works based on their copyrighted works. *See* 17 U.S.C. § 106(2). Nintendo argues that the district court erred in concluding that the audiovisual displays created by the Game Genie are not derivative works. * * *

A derivative work must incorporate a protected work in some concrete or permanent "form." * * *

Our analysis is not controlled by the Copyright Act's definition of "fixed." The Act defines copies as "material objects, other than phonorecords, in which a work is *fixed* by any method." 17 U.S.C. § 101 (emphasis added). The Act's definition of "derivative work," in contrast, lacks any such reference to fixation. *See id.* Further, we have held in a copyright infringement action that "it makes no difference that the derivation may not satisfy certain requirements for statutory copyright registration itself." *Lone Ranger Television v. Program Radio Corp.*, 740 F.2d 718, 722 (9th Cir.1984). *See also* Paul Goldstein, *Derivative Rights and Derivative Works in Copyright*, 30 J. COPYRIGHT SOC'Y U.S.A. 209, 231 n.75 (1983) ("the Act does not require that the derivative work be protectable for its preparation to infringe"). *Cf. Kalem Co. v. Harper Bros.*, 222 U.S. 55, 61 (1911) (finding the movie "Ben Hur" infringed copyright in the book Ben Hur even though Copyright Act did not yet include movies as protectable works). A derivative work must be fixed to be *protected* under the Act, *see* 17 U.S.C. § 102(a), but not to *infringe*.

The argument that a derivative work must be fixed because "[a] 'derivative work' is a work," 17 U.S.C. § 101, and "[a] work is 'created' when it is fixed in a copy or phonorecord for the first time," *id.*, relies on a misapplication of the Copyright Act's definition of "created":

> A work is 'created' when it is fixed in a copy or phonorecord for the first time; where a work is prepared over a period of time, the portion of it that has been fixed at any particular time constitutes the work as of that time, and where the work has been prepared in different versions, each version constitutes a separate work.

Id. The definition clarifies the *time* at which a work is *created*. If the provision were a definition of "work," it would not use that term in such a casual manner. The Act does not contain a definition of "work." Rather, it contains specific definitions: "audiovisual works," "literary works," and "pictorial, graphic and sculptural works," for example. The definition of "derivative work" does not require fixation.

The district court's finding that no independent work is created, see *Galoob*, 780 F. Supp. at 1291, is supported by the record. The Game Genie merely enhances the audiovisual displays (or underlying data bytes) that originate in Nintendo game cartridges. The altered displays do not incorporate a portion of a copyrighted work in some concrete or permanent form. Nintendo argues that the Game Genie's displays are as fixed in the hardware and software used to create them as Nintendo's original displays. Nintendo's argument ignores the fact that the Game Genie cannot produce an audiovisual display; the underlying display must be produced by a Nintendo Entertainment System and game cartridge. Even if we were to rely on the Copyright Act's definition of "fixed," we would similarly conclude that the resulting display is not "embodied," *see* 17 U.S.C. § 101, in the Game Genie. It cannot be a derivative work.

Mirage Editions is illustrative. Albuquerque A.R.T. transferred artworks from a commemorative book to individual ceramic tiles. *See Mirage Editions*, 856 F.2d at 1342. We held that "by borrowing and mounting the preexisting, copyrighted individual art images without the consent of the copyright proprietors . . . [Albuquerque A.R.T.] has prepared a derivative work and infringed the subject copyrights." *Id.* at 1343. The ceramic tiles *physically* incorporated the copyrighted works in a form that could be sold. Perhaps more importantly, sales of the tiles supplanted purchasers' demand for the underlying works. Our holding in *Mirage Editions* would have been much different if Albuquerque A.R.T. had distributed lenses that merely enabled users to view several artworks simultaneously.

Nintendo asserted at oral argument that the existence of a $150 million market for the Game Genie indicates that its audiovisual display must be fixed. We understand Nintendo's argument; consumers clearly would not purchase the Game Genie if its display was not "sufficiently permanent or stable to permit it to be perceived . . . for a period of more than transitory duration." 17 U.S.C. § 101. But, Nintendo's reliance on the Copyright Act's definition of "fixed" is misplaced. Nintendo's argument also proves too much; the existence of a market does not, and cannot, determine conclusively whether a work is an infringing derivative work. For example, although there is a market for kaleidoscopes, it does not necessarily follow that kaleidoscopes create unlawful derivative works when pointed at protected artwork. The same can be said of countless other products that enhance, but do not replace, copyrighted works.

Nintendo also argues that our analysis should focus exclusively on the audiovisual displays created by the Game Genie, i.e., that we should compare the altered displays to Nintendo's original displays. Nintendo emphasizes that " 'audiovisual works' are works that consist of a series of related images . . . *regardless of the nature of the material objects . . . in which the works are embodied.*" 17 U.S.C. § 101 (emphasis added). The Copyright Act's definition of "audiovisual works" is inapposite; the *only* question before us is whether the audiovisual displays created by the Game Genie are "derivative works." The Act does not similarly provide that a work can be a derivative work regardless of the nature of the material objects in which the work is embodied. A derivative work must incorporate a protected work in some concrete or permanent form. We cannot ignore the actual source of the Game Genie's display.

Nintendo relies heavily on *Midway Mfg. Co. v. Artic Int'l, Inc.*, 704 F.2d 1009 (7th Cir. 1983). *Midway* can be distinguished. The defendant in *Midway*, Artic International, marketed a computer chip that could be inserted in Galaxian video games to speed up the rate of play. The Seventh Circuit held that the speeded-up version of Galaxian was a derivative work. *Id.* at 1013–14. Artic's chip substantially copied and replaced the chip that was originally distributed by Midway. Purchasers of Artic's chip also benefited economically by offering the altered game for use by the general public. The Game Genie does not physically incorporate a portion of a copyrighted work, nor does it supplant demand for a component of that work. The court in *Midway* acknowledged that the Copyright Act's definition of "derivative work" "must be stretched to accommodate speeded-up video games." *Id.* at 1014. Stretching that definition further would chill innovation and fail to protect "society's competing interest in the free flow of ideas, information, and commerce." *Sony Corp. of America v. Universal Studios, Inc.*, 464 U.S. 417, 429 (1984).

In holding that the audiovisual displays created by the Game Genie are not derivative works, we recognize that technology often advances by improvement rather than replacement. * * * Some time ago, for example, computer companies began marketing spell-checkers that operate within existing word processors by signalling the writer when a word is misspelled. These applications, as well as countless others, could not be produced and marketed if courts were to conclude that the word processor and spell-checker combination is a derivative work based on the word processor alone. The Game Genie is useless by itself. It can only enhance, and cannot duplicate or recast, a Nintendo game's output. It does not contain or produce a Nintendo game's output in some concrete or permanent form, nor does it supplant demand for Nintendo game cartridges. Such innovations rarely will constitute infringing derivative works under the Copyright Act. * * *

Galoob has not violated the Copyright Act. Nintendo therefore is not entitled to a temporary or permanent injunction.

AFFIRMED.

NOTES

1. *Midway* and *Lewis Galoob Toys* both discuss the impact of the defendant's product on the market for the plaintiff's copyrighted work. Is this the "correct" test for determining whether the plaintiff's right to create derivative works has been infringed? If not, is it perhaps a better test?

2. *Lewis Galoob Toys* states that the infringing work must incorporate the plaintiff's work in a "concrete or permanent" form, but rejects the suggestion that a derivative work must be "fixed." How can a copyrighted work be incorporated in a permanent but unfixed form? How would this analysis apply to a defendant who, in rendering a live performance of a copyrighted work, improvises substantial variations on the original work without the copyright owner's permission?

3. If the altered visual display of the video game in *Lewis Galoob Toys* is processed through the computer's RAM before it appears on the screen, is this a sufficient fixation to constitute a "reproduction" under section 106(1)? (*See* Part A.1. of this chapter, *supra*.) Is it in sufficiently "concrete or permanent form" to be a derivative work under *Lewis Galoob Toys*?

4. The holding in *Lewis Galoob Toys* was later applied in a series of cases involving internet "pop-up" ads on the internet. In *U-Haul International, Inc. v. WhenU.com, Inc.*, 279 F. Supp. 2d 723 (E.D. Va. 2003), and *Wells Fargo & Co. v. WhenU.com, Inc.*, 293 F. Supp. 2d 734 (E.D. Mich. 2003), the courts held that "pop-up" ads did not infringe the copyright of the underlying website because the original website was not altered, but merely placed in the computer's background when the advertisement appeared in the foreground.

LEE V. A.R.T. CO.

125 F.3d 580 (7th Cir. 1997).

EASTERBROOK, CIRCUIT JUDGE.

Annie Lee creates works of art, which she sells through her firm Annie Lee & Friends. Deck the Walls, a chain of outlets for modestly priced art, is among the buyers of her works, which have been registered with the Register of Copyrights. One Deck the Walls store sold some of Lee's notecards and small lithographs to A.R.T. Company, which mounted the works on ceramic tiles (covering the art with transparent epoxy resin in the process) and resold the tiles. Lee contends that these tiles are derivative works, which under 17 U.S.C. § 106(2) may not be prepared without the permission of the copyright proprietor. She seeks both monetary and injunctive relief. Her position has the support of two cases holding that A.R.T.'s business violates the copyright laws. *Munoz v.*

Albuquerque A.R.T. Co., 38 F.3d 1218 (9th Cir.1994), *affirming without published opinion*, 829 F. Supp. 309 (D.Alaska 1993); *Mirage Editions, Inc. v. Albuquerque A.R.T. Co.*, 856 F.2d 1341 (9th Cir.1988). *Mirage Editions*, the only full appellate discussion, dealt with pages cut from books and mounted on tiles; the court of appeals' brief order in Munoz concludes that the reasoning of Mirage Editions is equally applicable to works of art that were sold loose. Our district court disagreed with these decisions and entered summary judgment for the defendant. 925 F.Supp. 576 (N.D.Ill.1996).

Now one might suppose that this is an open and shut case under the doctrine of first sale, codified at 17 U.S.C. § 109(a). A.R.T. bought the work legitimately, mounted it on a tile, and resold what it had purchased. Because the artist could capture the value of her art's contribution to the finished product as part of the price for the original transaction, the economic rationale for protecting an adaptation as "derivative" is absent. An alteration that includes (or consumes) a complete copy of the original lacks economic significance. One work changes hands multiple times, exactly what sec. 109(a) permits, so it may lack legal significance too. But sec. 106(2) creates a separate exclusive right, to "prepare derivative works", and Lee believes that affixing the art to the tile is "preparation," so that A.R.T. would have violated sec. 106(2) even if it had dumped the finished tiles into the Marianas Trench. For the sake of argument we assume that this is so and ask whether card-on-a-tile is a "derivative work" in the first place.

"Derivative work" is a defined term:

> A "derivative work" is a work based upon one or more preexisting works, such as a translation, musical arrangement, dramatization, fictionalization, motion picture version, sound recording, art reproduction, abridgment, condensation, or any other form in which a work may be recast, transformed, or adapted. A work consisting of editorial revisions, annotations, elaborations, or other modifications which, as a whole, represent an original work of authorship, is a "derivative work".

17 U.S.C. § 101. The district court concluded that A.R.T.'s mounting of Lee's works on tile is not an "original work of authorship" because it is no different in form or function from displaying a painting in a frame or placing a medallion in a velvet case. No one believes that a museum violates sec. 106(2) every time it changes the frame of a painting that is still under copyright, although the choice of frame or glazing affects the impression the art conveys, and many artists specify frames (or pedestals for sculptures) in detail. *Munoz* and *Mirage Editions* acknowledge that framing and other traditional means of mounting and displaying art do not infringe authors' exclusive right to make derivative works. Nonetheless,

the Ninth Circuit held, what A.R.T. does creates a derivative work because the epoxy resin bonds the art to the tile. Our district judge thought this a distinction without a difference, and we agree. If changing the way in which a work of art will be displayed creates a derivative work, and if Lee is right about what "prepared" means, then the derivative work is "prepared" when the art is mounted; what happens later is not relevant, because the violation of the sec. 106(2) right has already occurred. If the framing process does not create a derivative work, then mounting art on a tile, which serves as a flush frame, does not create a derivative work. What is more, the Ninth Circuit erred in assuming that normal means of mounting and displaying art are easily reversible. A painting is placed in a wooden "stretcher" as part of the framing process; this leads to some punctures (commonly tacks or staples), may entail trimming the edges of the canvas, and may affect the surface of the painting as well. Works by Jackson Pollock are notoriously hard to mount without damage, given the thickness of their paint. As a prelude to framing, photographs, prints, and posters may be mounted on stiff boards using wax sheets, but sometimes glue or another more durable substance is employed to create the bond.

Lee wages a vigorous attack on the district court's conclusion that A.R.T.'s mounting process cannot create a derivative work because the change to the work "as a whole" is not sufficiently original to support a copyright. Cases such as *Gracen v. The Bradford Exchange, Inc.*, 698 F.2d 300 (7th Cir.1983), show that neither A.R.T. nor Lee herself could have obtained a copyright in the card-on-a-tile, thereby not only extending the period of protection for the images but also eliminating competition in one medium of display. After the Ninth Circuit held that its mounting process created derivative works, A.R.T. tried to obtain a copyright in one of its products; the Register of Copyrights sensibly informed A.R.T. that the card-on-a-tile could not be copyrighted independently of the note card itself. But Lee says that this is irrelevant—that a change in a work's appearance may infringe the exclusive right under sec. 106(2) even if the alteration is too trivial to support an independent copyright. Pointing to the word "original" in the second sentence of the statutory definition, the district judge held that "originality" is essential to a derivative work. This understanding has the support of both cases and respected commentators. *E.g., L. Batlin & Son, Inc. v. Snyder*, 536 F.2d 486 (2d Cir.1976); MELVILLE B. NIMMER & DAVID NIMMER, 1 NIMMER ON COPYRIGHTS sec. 3.03 (1997). Pointing to the fact that the first sentence in the statutory definition omits any reference to originality, Lee insists that a work may be derivative despite the mechanical nature of the transformation. This view, too, has the support of both cases and respected commentators. *E.g., Lone Ranger Television, Inc. v. Program Radio Corp.*, 740 F.2d 718, 722 (9th Cir.1984); PAUL GOLDSTEIN, COPYRIGHT: PRINCIPLES, LAW AND PRACTICE sec. 5.3.1 (2d ed.1996) (suggesting that a transformation is covered by sec. 106(2) whenever it creates a "new work for a different market").

Fortunately, it is not necessary for us to choose sides. Assume for the moment that the first sentence recognizes a set of non-original derivative works. To prevail, then, Lee must show that A.R.T. altered her works in one of the ways mentioned in the first sentence. The tile is not an "art reproduction"; A.R.T. purchased and mounted Lee's original works. That leaves the residual clause: "any other form in which a work may be recast, transformed, or adapted." None of these words fits what A.R.T. did. Lee's works were not "recast" or "adapted". "Transformed" comes closer and gives the Ninth Circuit some purchase for its view that the permanence of the bond between art and base matters. Yet the copyrighted note cards and lithographs were not "transformed" in the slightest. The art was bonded to a slab of ceramic, but it was not changed in the process. It still depicts exactly what it depicted when it left Lee's studio. If mounting works a "transformation," then changing a painting's frame or a photograph's mat equally produces a derivative work. Indeed, if Lee is right about the meaning of the definition's first sentence, then any alteration of a work, however slight, requires the author's permission. We asked at oral argument what would happen if a purchaser jotted a note on one of the note cards, or used it as a coaster for a drink, or cut it in half, or if a collector applied his seal (as is common in Japan); Lee's counsel replied that such changes prepare derivative works, but that as a practical matter artists would not file suit. A definition of derivative work that makes criminals out of art collectors and tourists is jarring despite Lee's gracious offer not to commence civil litigation.

If Lee (and the Ninth Circuit) are right about what counts as a derivative work, then the United States has established through the back door an extraordinarily broad version of authors' moral rights, under which artists may block any modification of their works of which they disapprove. No European version of droit moral goes this far. Until recently it was accepted wisdom that the United States did not enforce any claim of moral rights; even bowdlerization of a work was permitted unless the modifications produced a new work so different that it infringed the exclusive right under sec. 106(2). *Compare WGN Continental Broadcasting Co. v. United Video, Inc.*, 693 F.2d 622 (7th Cir.1982), *with Gilliam v. American Broadcasting Companies, Inc.*, 538 F.2d 14, 24 (2d Cir.1976). The Visual Artists Rights Act of 1990, Pub.L. 101–650, 104 Stat. 5089, 5123–33, moves federal law in the direction of moral rights, but the cornerstone of the new statute, 17 U.S.C. § 106A, does not assist Lee. Section 106A(a)(3)(A) gives an artist the right to "prevent any intentional distortion, mutilation, or other modification of that work which would be prejudicial to his or her honor or reputation". At oral argument Lee's lawyer disclaimed any contention that the sale of her works on tile has damaged her honor or reputation. What is more, sec. 106A applies only to a "work of visual art", a new term defined in sec. 101 to mean either a unique work or part of a limited edition (200 copies or fewer) that has been "signed and consecutively numbered by the author". Lee's note cards and lithographs are not works of visual art under this definition, so she could not invoke sec. 106A even if A.R.T.'s use of her works to produce kitsch had damaged her reputation. It would not be sound to use sec. 106(2) to provide artists with exclusive rights deliberately omitted from the Visual Artists Rights Act. We therefore decline to follow *Munoz* and *Mirage Editions.*

Affirmed.

NOTES

1. In *Mirage Editions, Inc. v. Albuquerque A.R.T. Co.*, 856 F.2d 1341 (9th Cir. 1988), the Ninth Circuit held that infringing derivative works were created where the defendant removed individual pictures from the plaintiff's book of art reproductions, then glued each picture on a black plastic sheet so that a black margin showed on all sides, glued this onto a white ceramic tile, covered it with a transparent plastic film, and then offered the mounted artwork for resale. The court concluded that this activity "recast or transformed" the individual images.

Can *Mirage Editions* and *Lee v. A.R.T.* be reconciled? Suppose that a defendant simply removed pictures from a book and sold them unmounted? Or reassembled them in separate groupings, in a collage, or in a different sequence than they appeared in the plaintiff's book?

2. Would *Lee v. A.R.T.* have reached a different conclusion if the defendant had added hour and minute hands to the front of each mounted notecard, and a battery-powered motor to the back, and sold them as clocks?

3. In *Lone Ranger Television, Inc. v. Program Radio Corp.*, 740 F.2d 718, 721–22 (9th Cir. 1984), the Ninth Circuit adopted Professor Paul Goldstein's distinction between the right to copy and the right to create a derivative work:

> As one commentator distinguishes between such a derivative right and a right to copy: "It is that point at which the contribution of independent expression to an existing work effectively creates a new work for a different market." Goldstein, *Derivative Rights and Derivative Works in Copyright*, 30 J. COPYRIGHT SOC'Y U.S.A. 209, 217 (1983). *Cf. Sony*, 104 S.Ct. at 811 (Blackmun, J., dissenting). * * *
>
> * * *
>
> As *Russell* [*v. Price*, 612 F.2d 1123 (9th Cir.1979)] makes clear, the protection of derivative rights extends beyond mere protection against unauthorized copying to include the right to "make other versions of, perform or exhibit the work." 612 F.2d at 1128 n.16. It makes no difference that the derivation may not satisfy certain requirements for statutory copyright registration itself. *See* Goldstein, *supra*, 30 J. COPYRIGHT SOC'Y U.S.A. at 229–32 & 231 n.75 (discussing 1909 and 1976 Acts collectively) ("the Act does not require that the derivative work be protectable for its preparation to

infringe"); *see also Kalem Co. v. Harper Brothers*, 222 U.S. 55, 61 (1911) (a year before the 1909 Act's 1912 amendment, which specifically included movies as protectable works, * * * the Court found the movie "Ben Hur" infringed the copyright in the book Ben Hur).

Do you agree? Or should the copyright owner who sells copies of a work be required to tolerate certain alterations in those copies? (For example, should the seller of software be required to permit users to customize the software for their needs? *See* 17 U.S.C. § 117).

4. Plaintiff owns the copyrights in a line of baseball cards. Defendant purchases the cards and assembles them in groups of three by using one card as a backdrop, then cutting the players out of two other cards and staggering these cut-outs in front of the rear card, creating a three-dimensional effect. This assemblage is then mounted in a plastic frame and offered for sale. Has the defendant infringed the plaintiff's exclusive right to create derivative works? *See Major League Baseball Players Ass'n v. Dad's Kid Corp.*, 806 F.Supp. 458 (S.D.N.Y. 1992).

5. Would the owner of copyright in a movie have an infringement claim if the film were edited for television broadcasting without the copyright owner's consent? What about the author of the underlying script? *See Gilliam v. American Broadcasting Companies, Inc.*, 538 F.2d 14 (2d Cir. 1976).

3. PUBLIC DISTRIBUTION

COPYRIGHT ACT OF 1976

H.R. Rep. No. 94–1476.
94th Cong., 2d Sess. 62 (1976).

* * *

Public distribution.—Clause (3) of section 106 establishes the exclusive right of publication: The right "to distribute copies or phonorecords of the copyrighted work to the public by sale or other transfer of ownership, or by rental, lease, or lending." Under this provision the copyright owner would have the right to control the first public distribution of an authorized copy or phonorecord of his work, whether by sale, gift, loan, or some rental or lease arrangement. Likewise, any unauthorized public distribution of copies or phonorecords that were unlawfully made would be an infringement. As section 109 makes clear, however, the copyright owner's rights under section 106(3) cease with respect to a particular copy or phonorecord once he has parted with ownership of it.

* * *

WALT DISNEY CO. V. VIDEO 47, INC.

972 F.Supp. 595 (S.D. Fla. 1996).

UNGARO-BENAGES, UNITED STATES DISTRICT JUDGE.

* * *

[Upon learning that defendants' video stores rented to the public unauthorized copies of plaintiffs' copyrighted motion picture videocassettes, plaintiffs filed an action for infringement. Pursuant to a court order, the videotapes were seized and, upon examination, were determined to be counterfeit. The district court then entered a Consent Decree and Final Judgment pursuant to a settlement agreement. Upon learning that the defendants were continuing to rent counterfeit tapes, the plaintiffs filed this action for contempt.]

Findings of Fact

* * *

3. Plaintiffs are the lawful owners of the exclusive right under the United States Copyright Act to reproduce, to distribute and to authorize the reproduction and distribution of thirteen (13) motion picture titles at issue in this action. * * *

4. Plaintiffs are members of the Motion Picture Association of America (MPAA), a trade association whose film security office investigates unlawful duplication and distribution of videocassette tapes whose copyrights are owned by members of the MPAA.

5. Based upon a tip to the MPAA, an investigation of Defendants was conducted from October 10, 1995 to October 11, 1995 as testified to by Robert W. Butler ("Butler"), presently a field representative for the Film Security office of the MPAA and formerly a Special Agent in Charge of the Tampa Office for the Federal Bureau of Investigation ("FBI").

6. The investigation of VIDEO 47 was conducted by Patrick R. Cooney ("Cooney"), a former FBI agent who currently works for the anti-piracy office of the MPAA. Cooney employed a "stringer" from the neighborhood to rent tapes from VIDEO 47. Initially, six (6) tapes were rented and five (5) were counterfeit * * *.

14. Defendants did not produce any documentation that showed any authorization by Plaintiffs or any of their distributors to distribute copies of the Plaintiffs' copyrighted motion pictures.

15. Defendant Eduardo Celorio testified and stated that he * * * purchased tapes from individuals who sold videocassettes from their cars and that he contacted his distributors by beeper.

16. Defendant Eduardo Celorio testified that the 16 videocassettes at issue were not available for rental to the public, whereas Mr. Cooney

testified that these videocassettes were seized from the portion of the store where the videocassettes were available for rental. The Court rejects the testimony of Defendant Eduardo Celorio and accepts the testimony of Mr. Cooney on this factual issue.

* * *

Conclusions of Law

* * * [T]his Court entered a Consent Decree and Final Judgment in this case on or about August 4, 1994, pursuant to which the Defendants were permanently enjoined from infringing or participating in the infringement by others of Plaintiffs' rights in any motion pictures as to which Plaintiffs own the copyrights or other exclusive interests. * * * Plaintiffs now move to hold the Defendants in contempt for violation of such Final Judgment. Therefore, the Court must determine whether Defendants have violated Plaintiffs' rights under the copyright laws, and whether Defendants are liable for contempt for violation of this Court's prior Orders.

1. Copyright

* * * Plaintiffs' copyright registrations give Plaintiffs the exclusive right to reproduce, distribute and sell videocassette tapes of the movie titles at issue in this litigation. 17 U.S.C. § 106. The Court finds that Defendants infringed Plaintiffs' rights in the titles at issue in this litigation by renting counterfeit videocassette tapes without Plaintiffs' authorization to do so. 17 U.S.C. § 501. Plaintiffs need not demonstrate knowledge or intent on the part of the Defendants. * * *

As the Court finds that Defendants have violated Plaintiffs' rights in the motion pictures at issue here, it follows that Defendants are in direct violation of this Court's Consent Decree and Final Judgment dated August 4, 1994, which permanently enjoined Defendants from:

> (a) manufacturing, duplicating or performing publicly, without authorization, any motion picture as to which any Plaintiff holds legal or beneficial ownership of the copyright or other exclusive interest; (b) in any manner infringing or contributing to or participating in the infringement by others of any copyright or other exclusive interest owned by any Plaintiff in, for or to any motion picture; or (c) acting in concert or confederacy with, or aiding or abetting others to infringe in any way any copyright or other exclusive interest owned by any Plaintiff.

* * *

[The court therefore held the defendants in contempt.]

RELIGIOUS TECHNOLOGY CENTER V. NETCOM ON-LINE COMMUNICATION SERVICES, INC.

907 F.Supp. 1361 (N.D. Cal. 1995).

WHYTE, UNITED STATES DISTRICT JUDGE.

* * *

Plaintiffs Religious Technology Center ("RTC") and Bridge Publications, Inc. ("BPI") hold copyrights in the unpublished and published works of L. Ron Hubbard, the late founder of the Church of Scientology ("the Church"). Defendant Dennis Erlich ("Erlich") is a former minister of Scientology turned vocal critic of the Church, whose pulpit is now the Usenet newsgroup alt.religion.scientology ("a.r.s."), an on-line forum for discussion and criticism of Scientology. Plaintiffs maintain that Erlich infringed their copyrights when he posted portions of their works on a.r.s. Erlich gained his access to the Internet through defendant Thomas Klemesrud's ("Klemesrud's") BBS [bulletin board service] "support.com." Klemesrud is the operator of the BBS, which is run out of his home and has approximately 500 paying users. Klemesrud's BBS is not directly linked to the Internet, but gains its connection through the facilities of defendant Netcom On-Line Communications, Inc. ("Netcom"), one of the largest providers of Internet access in the United States.

* * *

Playboy Enterprises, Inc. v. Frena involved a suit against the operator of a small BBS whose system contained files of erotic pictures. 839 F. Supp. 1552, 1554 (M.D.Fla.1993). A subscriber of the defendant's BBS had uploaded files containing digitized pictures copied from the plaintiff's copyrighted magazine, which files remained on the BBS for other subscribers to download. *Id.* The court did not conclude, as plaintiffs suggest in this case, that the BBS is itself liable for the unauthorized reproduction of plaintiffs' work; instead, the court concluded that the BBS operator was liable for violating the plaintiff's right to publicly distribute and display copies of its work. *Id.* at 1556–57.

* * *

Plaintiffs allege that Netcom is directly liable for making copies of their works. They also allege that Netcom violated their exclusive rights to publicly display copies of their works. There are no allegations that Netcom violated plaintiffs' exclusive right to publicly distribute their works. However, in their discussion of direct infringement, plaintiffs insist that Netcom is liable for "maintaining copies of [Erlich's] messages on its server for eleven days for access by its subscribers and 'USENET neighbors'" and they compare this case to the *Playboy* case, which discussed the right of public distribution. Plaintiffs also argued this theory of infringement at oral argument. Because this could be an attempt to argue that Netcom has infringed plaintiffs' rights of public distribution and display, the court will address these arguments.

Playboy concluded that the defendant infringed the plaintiff's exclusive rights to publicly distribute and display copies of its works. 839 F. Supp. at 1556–57. The court is not entirely convinced that the mere possession of a digital copy on a BBS that is accessible to some members of the public constitutes direct infringement by the BBS operator. Such a holding suffers from the same problem of causation as the reproduction argument. Only the subscriber should be liable for causing the distribution of plaintiffs' work, as the contributing actions of the BBS provider are automatic and indiscriminate. Erlich could have posted his messages through countless access providers and the outcome would be the same: anyone with access to Usenet newsgroups would be able to read his messages. There is no logical reason to draw a line around Netcom and Klemesrud and say that they are uniquely responsible for distributing Erlich's messages. Netcom is not even the first link in the chain of distribution—Erlich had no direct relationship with Netcom but dealt solely with Klemesrud's BBS, which used Netcom to gain its Internet access. Every Usenet server has a role in the distribution, so plaintiffs' argument would create unreasonable liability. Where the BBS merely stores and passes along all messages sent by its subscribers and others, the BBS should not be seen as causing these works to be publicly distributed or displayed.

Even accepting the *Playboy* court's holding, the case is factually distinguishable. Unlike the BBS in that case, Netcom does not maintain an archive of files for its users. Thus, it cannot be said to be "supplying a product." In contrast to some of its larger competitors, Netcom does not create or control the content of the information available to its subscribers; it merely provides access to the Internet, whose content is controlled by no single entity. Although the Internet consists of many different computers networked together, some of which may contain infringing files, it does not make sense to hold the operator of each computer liable as an infringer merely because his or her computer is linked to a computer with an infringing file. It would be especially inappropriate to hold liable a service that acts more like a conduit, in other words, one that does not itself keep an archive of files for more than a short duration. Finding such a service liable would involve an unreasonably broad construction of public distribution and display rights. No purpose would be served by holding liable those who have no ability to control the information to which their subscribers have access, even though they might be in some sense helping to achieve the Internet's automatic "public distribution" and the users' "public" display of files.

* * *

NOTES

1. Were the defendants in *Video 47* subjected to a different liability standard than the defendants in *Netcom*? Is this appropriate? If a merchant distributes a work (such as a videocassette) without knowing that it incorporates an infringing component (such as a piece of soundtrack music), is the merchant liable? What if the defendant is a public lending library?

2. Since the decision in *Netcom*, the Digital Millennium Copyright Act introduced limits on the infringement liability of internet service providers. These limits are discussed in Chapter 18.D.1., *infra*.

3. In determining what constitutes an infringing distribution of a work, courts have applied the same criteria that determine whether a work has been "published" for copyright purposes (distinguishing between private and public distributions, for example). *See* Chapter 15.A.4.a., *supra*. In this regard, the 1976 House Report advises:

> Under the definition in section 101, a work is "published" if one or more copies or phonorecords embodying it are distributed to the public—that is, generally to persons under no explicit or implicit restrictions with respect to disclosure of its contents—without regard to the manner in which the copies or phonorecords changed hands. The definition clears up the question of whether the sale of phonorecords constitutes publication, and it also makes plain that any form or dissemination in which a material object does not change hands—performances or displays on television, for example—is not a publication no matter how many people are exposed to the work. On the other hand, the definition also makes clear that, when copies or phonorecords are offered to a group of wholesalers, broadcasters, motion picture theaters, etc., publication takes place if the purpose is "further distribution, public performance, or public display."

H.R. Rep. No. 94–1476, 94th Cong., 2d Sess. 138 (1976). If this legislative history is treated as an authoritative construction of the meaning of "public distribution," should the exclusive distribution right be interpreted to include electronic transmissions?

4. When a teacher distributes materials to students, is this a public distribution?

4. PUBLIC PERFORMANCE AND PUBLIC DISPLAY

COPYRIGHT ACT OF 1976

H.R. Rep. No. 94–1476.
94th Cong., 2d Sess. 62–65 (1976).

* * *

Under the definitions of "perform," "display," "publicly," and "transmit" in section 101, the concepts of public performance and public display cover not only the initial rendition or showing, but also any further act by which that rendition or showing is transmitted or communicated to the public.

* * * A performance may be accomplished "either directly or by means of any device or process," including all kinds of equipment for reproducing or amplifying sounds or visual images, any sort of transmitting apparatus, any type of electronic retrieval system, and any other techniques and systems not yet in use or even invented.

* * *

Under clause (1) of the definition of "publicly" in section 101, a performance or display is "public" if it takes place "at a place open to the public or at any place where a substantial number of persons outside of a normal circle of a family and its social acquaintances is gathered." One of the principal purposes of the definition was to make clear that, contrary to the decision in *Metro-Goldwyn-Mayer Distributing Corp. v. Wyatt*, 21 C.O. Bull. 203 (D. Md. 1932), performances in "semipublic" places such as clubs, lodges, factories, summer camps, and schools are "public performances" subject to copyright control. The term "a family" in this context would include an individual living alone, so that a gathering confined to the individual's social acquaintances would normally be regarded as private. Routine meetings of businesses and governmental personnel would be excluded because they do not represent the gathering of a "substantial number of persons."

Clause (2) of the definition of "publicly" in section 101 makes clear that the concepts of public performance and public display include not only performances and displays that occur initially in a public place, but also acts that transmit or otherwise communicate a performance or display of the work to the public by means of any device or process. The definition of "transmit"—to communicate a performance or display "by any device or process whereby images or sound are received beyond the place from which they are sent"—is broad enough to include all conceivable forms and combinations of wires and wireless communications media, including but by no means limited to radio and television broadcasting as we know them. Each and every method by which the images or sounds comprising a performance or display are picked up and conveyed is a "transmission," and if the transmission reaches the public in [any] form, the case comes within the scope of clauses (4) or (5) of section 106.

Under the bill, as under the present law, a performance made available by transmission to the public at large is "public" even though the recipients are not gathered in a single place, and even if there is no proof that any of the potential recipients was operating his receiving apparatus at the time of the transmission. The same principles apply whenever the potential recipients of the transmission represent a limited segment of the public, such as the occupants of hotel rooms or the subscribers of a cable television service.

* * *

ON COMMAND VIDEO CORPORATION V. COLUMBIA PICTURES INDUSTRIES

777 F.Supp. 787 (N.D. Cal. 1991).

WEIGEL, DISTRICT JUDGE:

Plaintiff seeks a declaratory judgment that its hotel video-movie viewing system does not infringe defendants' copyrights in the movies shown through the system. * * * Plaintiff, the designer and builder of an innovative video viewing system currently installed in a number of hotels, insists that a hotel occupant's viewing of one or more of defendants' movies through its system does not constitute a "public performance" under the 1976 Copyright Act, 17 U.S.C. § 101 et seq. Defendants, seven major United States movie companies, contend that such viewings do constitute public performances and that plaintiff's system therefore violates defendants' exclusive right of public performance under § 106(4) of the Act.

I. Facts

The material facts of this case are not in dispute. On Command has developed a system for the electronic delivery of movie video tapes. The system consists of a computer program, a sophisticated electronic switch, and a bank of video cassette players ("VCPs"), all of which are centrally located in a hotel equipment room. The VCPs are connected to the hotel's guest rooms by wiring. The computer program directs the electronic switches so that a particular VCP will be dedicated to the guest room where a particular movie is requested. Each VCP contains a video tape. When a guest requests a particular movie, the computer identifies the VCP containing that movie, switches the VCP to that particular room, and starts the movie video.

A hotel guest operates the system from his or her room by remote control. After the television is turned on, the screen lists a menu of available movies. The guest selects a movie by entering the appropriate code on the remote control. Once a particular video is selected, that video selection disappears from the menu of available videos displayed on all other television sets in the hotel. The video is seen only in the room where it was selected by the guest. It cannot be seen in any other guest room or in any other location in the hotel. The viewer cannot pause, rewind, or fast-forward the video. When the movie ends, it is automatically rewound and then immediately available for viewing by another hotel guest.

The only components of the system installed in the guest rooms are the hand-held remote control and a microprocessor in the television set.

When a guest checks in to the hotel, the hotel clerk uses a front-desk terminal connected to the On Command computer program to activate movie transmission to the appropriate room. At the guest's request, the clerk can prevent the transmission of adult movies to a room or deactivate service to a room altogether. The apparent advantages On Command's system enjoys over existing closed-circuit hotel video systems with pre-set movie times, such as "Spectravision," are the larger variety of movies available for viewing and the guests' freedom to watch them on their own schedule. On Command's system also eliminates the effort and potential guest embarrassment of in-house hotel video rental programs, in which VCPs are installed in individual rooms and guests must physically rent videos from the hotel staff.

II. Discussion

A copyright owner has the exclusive right "to perform the copyrighted work publicly" or to authorize any such public performance. 17 U.S.C. § 106(4). What constitutes a public performance is defined by the Copyright Act in two clauses. Under clause (1), the "public place" clause, a performance is public if it occurs

> at a place open to the public or at any place where a substantial number of persons outside of a normal circle of a family and its social acquaintances is gathered.

17 U.S.C. § 101. Under clause (2), the "transmit" clause, a performance is public if someone

> transmits or otherwise communicates a performance or display of the work to a place specified by clause (1) or to the public, by means of any device or process.

Id. Under the transmit clause, a performance is public "whether the members of the public capable of receiving the performance or display receive it in the same place or in separate places and at the same time or at different times." *Id.*

Both plaintiff and defendants base their motions for summary judgment on favorable interpretations of these clauses. Both also rely heavily on the Ninth Circuit's decision in *Columbia Pictures v. Professional Real Estate*, 866 F.2d 278 (9th Cir.1989). This Court must therefore determine whether On Command's system results in the public performance of defendants' movies under the statutory clauses and Professional Real Estate.

A. *The Public Place Clause.*

Professional Real Estate held that hotel guest rooms are not "public places" for the purposes of the Copyright Act. Defendants do not challenge this holding. Rather, defendants argue that because On Command's system comprises components dispersed throughout a hotel—i.e., the command center is located in a hotel equipment room, the hotel operator's terminal is in the front lobby, the transmission wiring is installed throughout the walls and ceilings—the relevant place of performance is not the individual hotel rooms but the entire hotel, which defendants contend is a public place under the language of the Act. This argument is unavailing. At least for the purposes of public place analysis, a performance of a work does not occur every place a wire carrying the performance passes through; a performance occurs where it is received. Accepting defendants' argument would eviscerate both the concepts of "performance" and "public place." The Act defines the performance of a motion picture as the "showing of its images in any sequence or to make the sounds accompanying it audible." 17 U.S.C. § 101. A movie video is thus performed only when it is visible and audible. In On Command's system, this viewing and hearing occurs only in an individual guest room. That can be the only relevant place of performance for public place analysis. Since hotel guest rooms are indisputably not public places for copyright purposes, On Command's system results in no public performances under the public place clause.

B. The Transmit Clause.

Public performance of defendants' movies under this clause occurs if On Command "transmits" the movies "to the public." Under the Copyright Act, to "transmit" a performance is

> to communicate it by any device or process whereby images or sounds are received beyond the place from which they are sent.

Id. Plaintiff's argument that On Command's system involves not "transmissions" but "electronic rentals" similar to patrons' physical borrowing of videotapes is without merit. On Command transmits movie performances directly under the language of the definition. The system "communicates" the motion picture "images and sounds" by a "device or process"—the equipment and wiring network—from a central console in a hotel to individual guest rooms, where the images and sounds are received "beyond the place from which they are sent." The fact that hotel guests initiate this transmission by turning on the television and choosing a video is immaterial.

On Command's video transmissions are also "to the public" for the purposes of the transmit clause. Hotel guests watching a video movie in their room through On Command's system are not watching it in a "public place" but they are nonetheless members of "the public." *See Columbia Pictures Industries, Inc. v. Redd Horne*, 568 F.Supp. 494 (W.D.Pa.1983), *aff'd* 749 F.2d 154, 159 (3d Cir.1984) ("the transmission of a performance to members of the public, even in private settings such as hotel rooms . . . constitutes a public performance") (citing H.R. Rep. No. 1476, 94th Cong., 2d Sess. at 64 (1976) ("1976 House Report")); *ESPN Inc. v. Edinburg*

Community Hotel, Inc., 735 F.Supp. 1334, 1340 (S.D.Tex.1986) ("The [1976] House Report . . . on the Copyright Act makes explicit that performances to occupants of hotel rooms fall within the definition of a public performance"). This is because the relationship between the transmitter of the performance, On Command, and the audience, hotel guests, is a commercial, "public" one regardless of where the viewing takes place. The non-public nature of the place of the performance has no bearing on whether or not those who enjoy the performance constitute "the public" under the transmit clause.

A performance may still be public under the transmit clause "whether the members of the public . . . receive it in the same place or in separate places and at the same time or at different times." 17 U.S.C. § 101. A 1967 Report by the House of Representatives reveals that Congress added this language to the transmit clause to cover precisely the sort of single-viewer system developed by plaintiff:

> [This language makes doubly clear that] a performance made available by transmission to the public at large is "public" even though the recipients are not gathered in a single place, and even if there is no direct proof that any of the potential recipients was operating his receiving apparatus at the time of the transmission. The same principles apply whenever the potential recipients of the transmission represent a limited segment of the public, such as the occupants of hotel rooms. . . .; they are also applicable where the transmission is capable of reaching different recipients at different times, as in the case of sounds or images stored in an information system and capable of being performed or displayed at the initiative of individual members of the public.

H.R. Rep. No. 83, 90th Cong., 1st Sess. at 29 (1967). Thus, whether the number of hotel guests viewing an On Command transmission is one or one hundred, and whether these guests view the transmission simultaneously or sequentially, the transmission is still a public performance since it goes to members of the public. *See also Redd Horne*, 749 F.2d at 159 (transmissions of videos to private viewing booths occupied by one to four persons infringing under transmit clause); *Paramount Pictures Corp. v. Labus*, 16 U.S.P.Q. 2d (BNA) 1142, 1147 (W.D. Wisc.1990) (hotel's distribution of unauthorized copies of video cassettes to single guest violated copyright owner's exclusive right to distribute work to "the public"). On Command therefore "publicly performs" defendants' movies under the meaning of the transmit clause.

* * *

NOTES

1. Consider whether a public performance occurs when (a) a state penitentiary shows movies once a week to prisoners in the prison's dining hall; (b) a university shows movies once a week in the recreation room of each dormitory; (c) a corporation shows a movie to employees at the company's annual retreat; (d) movies are shown to military personnel on a military base or on a ship at sea; (e) a movie theatre shows free movies every Friday at midnight; (f) a retail store plays background music for its customers; and (g) a person plays a radio loudly in a street or shopping mall?

2. In order to enforce their public performance rights, owners of copyrighted musical compositions normally designate a performance rights organization to act as their nonexclusive agent for the purpose of licensing and monitoring public performances and collecting the associated royalties. The performance rights organizations operating in the United States are the American Society of Composers, Authors and Publishers (ASCAP), Broadcast Music, Inc. (BMI), Global Music Rights, and SESAC. Performance rights organizations exist in other nations as well.

Television networks, clubs, restaurants and other enterprises that perform large numbers of musical works can, for a fee, obtain a "blanket" license covering the entire catalog of works represented by a particular performance rights organization. Each performing rights organization monitors the frequency with which particular works in its repertoire are performed in order to determine how to allocate its receipts among the various copyright owners it represents. Where a publisher owns the copyright in a work, the organization distributes half of the collected fees to the publisher and half to the composer, unless the contract between those parties calls for a different allocation.

3. Suppose that a nightclub which performed recorded music transformed itself into a private club, allowing people to become members only if they filed an application form, submitted to an interview, and paid an initiation fee and membership dues. How would this affect the "public performance" analysis?

CARTOON NETWORK LP V. CSC HOLDINGS, INC.

536 F.3d 121 (2d Cir. 2008).

JOHN M. WALKER, JR., CIRCUIT JUDGE:

[The facts and background for this case can be found in Part A.1. of this chapter.]

DISCUSSION

* * * [T]he district court found that Cablevision would infringe the public performance right by transmitting a program to an RS-DVR customer in response to that customer's playback request. * * *

* * * The Act grants a copyright owner the exclusive right, "in the case of . . . motion pictures and other audiovisual works, to perform the copyrighted work publicly." 17 U.S.C. § 106(4). Section 101, the definitional section of the Act, explains that

> [t]o perform or display a work "publicly" means (1) to perform or display it at a place open to the public or at any place where a substantial number of persons outside of a normal circle of a family and its social acquaintances is gathered; or (2) to transmit or otherwise communicate a performance or display of the work to a place specified by clause (1) or to the public, by means of any device or process, whether the members of the public capable of receiving the performance or display receive it in the same place or in separate places and at the same time or at different times.

Id. § 101.

The parties agree that this case does not implicate clause (1). Accordingly, we ask whether these facts satisfy the second, "transmit clause" of the public performance definition: Does Cablevision "transmit . . . a performance . . . of the work . . . to the public"? *Id.* No one disputes that the RS-DVR playback results in the transmission of a performance of a work—the transmission from the Arroyo Server to the customer's television set. Cablevision contends that (1) the RS-DVR customer, rather than Cablevision, does the transmitting and thus the performing and (2) the transmission is not "to the public" under the transmit clause.

As to Cablevision's first argument, we note that our conclusion in Part II [*see* excerpt, *supra*, in Part A.1. of this chapter] that the customer, not Cablevision, "does" the copying does not dictate a parallel conclusion that the customer, and not Cablevision, "performs" the copyrighted work. The definitions that delineate the contours of the reproduction and public performance rights vary in significant ways. For example, the statute defines the verb "perform" and the noun "copies," but not the verbs "reproduce" or "copy." *Id.* We need not address Cablevision's first argument further because, even if we assume that Cablevision makes the transmission when an RS-DVR playback occurs, we find that the RS-DVR playback, as described here, does not involve the transmission of a performance "to the public."

The statute itself does not expressly define the term "performance" or the phrase "to the public." It does explain that a transmission may be "to the public . . . whether the members of the public capable of receiving the performance . . . receive it in the same place or in separate places and at the same time or at different times." *Id.* This plain language instructs us that, in determining whether a transmission is "to the public," it is of no moment that the potential recipients of the transmission are in different places, or that they may receive the transmission at different times. The implication from this same language, however, is that it is relevant, in determining whether a transmission is made to the public, to discern who is "capable of receiving" the performance being transmitted. The fact that the statute says "capable of receiving the performance," instead of "capable of receiving the transmission," underscores the fact that a transmission of a performance is itself a performance. *Cf. Buck v. Jewell-La Salle Realty Co.*, 283 U.S. 191, 197–98 (1931).

The legislative history of the transmit clause supports this interpretation. The House Report on the 1976 Copyright Act states that

> [u]nder the bill, as under the present law, a performance made available *by transmission to the public at large* is "public" even though the recipients are not gathered in a single place, and even if there is no proof that any of the *potential recipients* was operating his receiving apparatus at the time of the transmission. The same principles apply whenever the *potential recipients of the transmission* represent a limited segment of the public, such as the occupants of hotel rooms or the subscribers of a cable television service.

H.R.Rep. No. 94–1476, at 64–65 (1976) (emphases added).

* * *

From the foregoing, it is evident that the transmit clause directs us to examine who precisely is "capable of receiving" a particular transmission of a performance. Cablevision argues that, because each RS-DVR transmission is made using a single unique copy of a work, made by an individual subscriber, one that can be decoded exclusively by that subscriber's cable box, only one subscriber is capable of receiving any given RS-DVR transmission. This argument accords with the language of the transmit clause, which, as described above, directs us to consider the potential audience of a given transmission. We are unpersuaded by the district court's reasoning and the plaintiffs' arguments that we should consider a larger potential audience in determining whether a transmission is "to the public."

The district court, in deciding whether the RS-DVR playback of a program to a particular customer is "to the public," apparently considered all of Cablevision's customers who subscribe to the channel airing that program and all of Cablevision's RS-DVR subscribers who request a copy of that program. Thus, it concluded that the RS-DVR playbacks constituted public performances because "Cablevision would transmit the *same program* to members of the public, who may receive the performance at different times, depending on whether they view the program in real time or at a later time as an RS-DVR playback." *Cablevision I*, 478 F.Supp.2d at 623 (emphasis added). In essence, the district court suggested that, in considering whether a transmission is "to the public," we consider not the potential audience of a particular transmission, but the potential audience of the underlying work (i.e., "the program") whose content is being transmitted.

We cannot reconcile the district court's approach with the language of the transmit clause. That clause speaks of people capable of receiving a particular "transmission" or "performance," and not of the potential audience of a particular "work." Indeed, such an approach would render the "to the public" language surplusage. Doubtless the *potential* audience for every copyrighted audiovisual work is the general public. As a result, any transmission of the content of a copyrighted work would constitute a public performance under the district court's interpretation. But the transmit clause obviously contemplates the existence of non-public transmissions; if it did not, Congress would have stopped drafting that clause after "performance."

On appeal, plaintiffs offer a slight variation of this interpretation. They argue that both in its real-time cablecast and via the RS-DVR playback, Cablevision is in fact transmitting the "same performance" of a given work: the performance of the work that occurs when the programming service supplying Cablevision's content transmits that content to Cablevision and the service's other licensees. * * *

Thus, according to plaintiffs, when Congress says that to perform a work publicly means to transmit . . . a performance . . . to the public, they really meant "transmit . . . the 'original performance' . . . to the public." The implication of this theory is that to determine whether a given transmission of a performance is "to the public," we would consider not only the potential audience of that transmission, but also the potential audience of any transmission of the same underlying "original" performance.

Like the district court's interpretation, this view obviates any possibility of a purely private transmission. Furthermore, it makes Cablevision's liability depend, in part, on the actions of legal strangers. Assume that HBO transmits a copyrighted work to both Cablevision and Comcast. Cablevision merely retransmits the work from one Cablevision facility to another, while Comcast retransmits the program to its subscribers. Under plaintiffs' interpretation, Cablevision would still be transmitting the performance to the public, solely because Comcast has transmitted the same underlying performance to the public. Similarly, a hapless customer who records a program in his den and later transmits the recording to a television in his bedroom would be liable for publicly performing the work simply because some other party had once transmitted the same underlying performance to the public.

We do not believe Congress intended such odd results. Although the transmit clause is not a model of clarity, we believe that when Congress speaks of transmitting a performance to the public, it refers to the performance created by the act of transmission. Thus, HBO transmits its own performance of a work when it transmits to Cablevision, and Cablevision transmits its own performance of the same work when it retransmits the feed from HBO.

* * *

Given that each RS-DVR transmission is made to a given subscriber using a copy made by that subscriber, we conclude that such a transmission is not "to the public," without analyzing the contours of that phrase in great detail. No authority cited by the parties or the district court persuades us to the contrary.

* * *

This holding, we must emphasize, does not generally permit content delivery networks to avoid all copyright liability by making copies of each item of content and associating one unique copy with each subscriber to the network, or by giving their subscribers the capacity to make their own individual copies. We do not address whether such a network operator would be able to escape any other form of copyright liability, such as liability for unauthorized reproductions or liability for contributory infringement.

In sum, because we find, on undisputed facts, that Cablevision's proposed RS-DVR system would not directly infringe plaintiffs' exclusive rights to reproduce and publicly perform their copyrighted works, we grant summary judgment in favor of Cablevision with respect to both rights.

* * *

NOTES

1. When someone makes a copyrighted artistic, musical, or audiovisual work available on the internet, does this constitute a public display? A public performance?

2. If a defendant receives a satellite transmission and transmits it to a cable television system, but not directly to the public, does this implicate the public performance right? *Compare Allarcom Pay Television v. General Instrument Corp.*, 69 F.3d 381 (9th Cir. 1995) *with NFL v. Primetime 24 Joint Venture*, 211 F.3d 10 (2d Cir. 2000) *and WGN Continental Broadcasting Co. v. United Video*, 693 F.2d 622 (7th Cir. 1982).

AMERICAN BROADCASTING COS., INC. V. AEREO, INC.

573 U.S. 431, 134 S.Ct. 2498 (2014).

JUSTICE BREYER delivered the opinion of the Court.

The Copyright Act of 1976 gives a copyright owner the "exclusive righ[t]" to "perform the copyrighted work publicly." 17 U.S.C. § 106(4). The Act's Transmit Clause defines that exclusive right as including the right to

> "transmit or otherwise communicate a performance . . . of the [copyrighted] work . . . to the public, by means of any device or process, whether the members of the public capable of receiving the performance . . . receive it in the same place or in separate places and at the same time or at different times." § 101.

We must decide whether respondent Aereo, Inc., infringes this exclusive right by selling its subscribers a technologically complex service that allows them to watch television programs over the Internet at about the same time as the programs are broadcast over the air. We conclude that it does.

I

A

For a monthly fee, Aereo offers subscribers broadcast television programming over the Internet, virtually as the programming is being broadcast. Much of this programming is made up of copyrighted works. Aereo neither owns the copyright in those works nor holds a license from the copyright owners to perform those works publicly.

Aereo's system is made up of servers, transcoders, and thousands of dime-sized antennas housed in a central warehouse. It works roughly as follows: First, when a subscriber wants to watch a show that is currently being broadcast, he visits Aereo's website and selects, from a list of the local programming, the show he wishes to see.

Second, one of Aereo's servers selects an antenna, which it dedicates to the use of that subscriber (and that subscriber alone) for the duration of the selected show. A server then tunes the antenna to the over-the-air broadcast carrying the show. The antenna begins to receive the broadcast, and an Aereo transcoder translates the signals received into data that can be transmitted over the Internet.

Third, rather than directly send the data to the subscriber, a server saves the data in a subscriber-specific folder on Aereo's hard drive. In other words, Aereo's system creates a subscriber-specific copy—that is, a "personal" copy—of the subscriber's program of choice.

Fourth, once several seconds of programming have been saved, Aereo's server begins to stream the saved copy of the show to the subscriber over the Internet. (The subscriber may instead direct Aereo to stream the program at a later time, but that aspect of Aereo's service is not before us.) The subscriber can watch the streamed program on the screen of his personal computer, tablet, smart phone, Internet-connected television, or other Internet-connected device. The streaming continues, a mere few seconds behind the over-the-air broadcast, until the subscriber has received the entire show. *See* A DICTIONARY OF COMPUTING 494 (6th ed. 2008) (defining "streaming" as "[t]he process of providing a steady flow of audio or video data so that an Internet user is able to access it as it is transmitted").

Aereo emphasizes that the data that its system streams to each subscriber are the data from his own personal copy, made from the broadcast signals received by the particular antenna allotted to him. Its system does not transmit data saved in one subscriber's folder to any other subscriber. When two subscribers wish to watch the same program, Aereo's system activates two separate antennas and saves two separate copies of the program in two separate folders. It then streams the show to the subscribers through two separate transmissions—each from the subscriber's personal copy.

B

Petitioners are television producers, marketers, distributors, and broadcasters who own the copyrights in many of the programs that Aereo's system streams to its subscribers. They brought suit against Aereo for copyright infringement in Federal District Court. They sought a preliminary injunction, arguing that Aereo was infringing their right to "perform" their works "publicly," as the Transmit Clause defines those terms.

[The Second Circuit affirmed the District Court's denial of a preliminary injunction, relying on *Cartoon Network* (excerpted earlier in this chapter).] * * * In the Second Circuit's view, Aereo does not perform publicly within the meaning of the Transmit Clause because it does not transmit "to the public." Rather, each time Aereo streams a program to a subscriber, it sends a *private* transmission that is available only to that subscriber. * * *

II

This case requires us to answer two questions: First, in operating in the manner described above, does Aereo "perform" at all? And second, if so, does Aereo do so "publicly"? We address these distinct questions in turn.

Does Aereo "perform"? *See* § 106(4) ("[T]he owner of [a] copyright . . . has the exclusive righ[t] . . . to *perform* the copyrighted work publicly" (emphasis added)); § 101 ("To *perform* . . . a work 'publicly' means [among other things] to transmit . . . a performance . . . of the work . . . to the public

. . ." (emphasis added)). Phrased another way, does Aereo "transmit . . . a performance" when a subscriber watches a show using Aereo's system, or is it only the subscriber who transmits? In Aereo's view, it does not perform. It does no more than supply equipment that "emulate[s] the operation of a home antenna and [digital video recorder (DVR)]." Like a home antenna and DVR, Aereo's equipment simply responds to its subscribers' directives. So it is only the subscribers who "perform" when they use Aereo's equipment to stream television programs to themselves.

Considered alone, the language of the Act does not clearly indicate when an entity "perform[s]" (or "transmit[s]") and when it merely supplies equipment that allows others to do so. But when read in light of its purpose, the Act is unmistakable: An entity that engages in activities like Aereo's performs.

A

History makes plain that one of Congress' primary purposes in amending the Copyright Act in 1976 was to overturn this Court's determination that community antenna television (CATV) systems (the precursors of modern cable systems) fell outside the Act's scope. In *Fortnightly Corp. v. United Artists Television, Inc.*, 392 U.S. 390 (1968), the Court considered a CATV system that carried local television broadcasting, much of which was copyrighted, to its subscribers in two cities. The CATV provider placed antennas on hills above the cities and used coaxial cables to carry the signals received by the antennas to the home television sets of its subscribers. The system amplified and modulated the signals in order to improve their strength and efficiently transmit them to subscribers. A subscriber "could choose any of the . . . programs he wished to view by simply turning the knob on his own television set." The CATV provider "neither edited the programs received nor originated any programs of its own."

Asked to decide whether the CATV provider infringed copyright holders' exclusive right to perform their works publicly, the Court held that the provider did not "perform" at all. The Court drew a line: "Broadcasters perform. Viewers do not perform." And a CATV provider "falls on the viewer's side of the line."

The Court reasoned that CATV providers were unlike broadcasters:

> "Broadcasters select the programs to be viewed; CATV systems simply carry, without editing, whatever programs they receive. Broadcasters procure programs and propagate them to the public; CATV systems receive programs that have been released to the public and carry them by private channels to additional viewers."

Instead, CATV providers were more like viewers, for "the basic function [their] equipment serves is little different from that served by the equipment generally furnished by" viewers. "Essentially," the Court said, "a CATV system no more than enhances the viewer's capacity to receive the broadcaster's signals [by] provid[ing] a well-located antenna with an efficient connection to the viewer's television set." Viewers do not become performers by using "amplifying equipment," and a CATV provider should not be treated differently for providing viewers the same equipment.

In *Teleprompter Corp. v. Columbia Broadcasting System, Inc.*, 415 U.S. 394 (1974), the Court considered the copyright liability of a CATV provider that carried broadcast television programming into subscribers' homes from hundreds of miles away. Although the Court recognized that a viewer might not be able to afford amplifying equipment that would provide access to those distant signals, it nonetheless found that the CATV provider was more like a viewer than a broadcaster. It explained: "The reception and rechanneling of [broadcast television signals] for simultaneous viewing is essentially a viewer function, irrespective of the distance between the broadcasting station and the ultimate viewer."

The Court also recognized that the CATV system exercised some measure of choice over what to transmit. But that fact did not transform the CATV system into a broadcaster. A broadcaster exercises significant creativity in choosing what to air, the Court reasoned. In contrast, the CATV provider makes an initial choice about which broadcast stations to retransmit, but then " 'simply carr[ies], without editing, whatever programs [it] receive[s].' "

B

In 1976 Congress amended the Copyright Act in large part to reject the Court's holdings in *Fortnightly* and *Teleprompter*. *See* H.R. REP. NO. 94–1476, pp. 86–87 (1976) (hereinafter H.R. REP.) (The 1976 amendments "completely overturned" this Court's narrow construction of the Act in *Fortnightly* and *Teleprompter*). Congress enacted new language that erased the Court's line between broadcaster and viewer, in respect to "perform[ing]" a work. The amended statute clarifies that to "perform" an audiovisual work means "to show its images in any sequence or to make the sounds accompanying it audible." § 101; *see ibid.* (defining "[a]udiovisual works" as "works that consist of a series of related images which are intrinsically intended to be shown by the use of machines . . ., together with accompanying sounds"). Under this new language, *both* the broadcaster *and* the viewer of a television program "perform," because they both show the program's images and make audible the program's sounds. *See* H.R. REP., at 63 ("[A] broadcasting network is performing when it transmits [a singer's performance of a song] . . . and any individual is performing whenever he or she . . . communicates the performance by turning on a receiving set").

Congress also enacted the Transmit Clause, which specifies that an entity performs publicly when it "transmit[s] . . . a performance . . . to the public." § 101; see *ibid.* (defining "[t]o 'transmit' a performance" as "to communicate it by any device or process whereby images or sounds are received beyond the place from which they are sent"). Cable system activities, like those of the CATV systems in *Fortnightly* and *Teleprompter*, lie at the heart of the activities that Congress intended this language to cover. The Clause thus makes clear that an entity that acts like a CATV system itself performs, even if when doing so, it simply enhances viewers' ability to receive broadcast television signals.

Congress further created a new section of the Act to regulate cable companies' public performances of copyrighted works. *See* § 111. Section 111 creates a complex, highly detailed compulsory licensing scheme that sets out the conditions, including the payment of compulsory fees, under which cable systems may retransmit broadcasts.

Congress made these three changes to achieve a similar end: to bring the activities of cable systems within the scope of the Copyright Act.

C

This history makes clear that Aereo is not simply an equipment provider. Rather, Aereo, and not just its subscribers, "perform[s]" (or "transmit[s]"). Aereo's activities are substantially similar to those of the CATV companies that Congress amended the Act to reach. *See id.*, at 89 ("[C]able systems are commercial enterprises whose basic retransmission operations are based on the carriage of copyrighted program material"). Aereo sells a service that allows subscribers to watch television programs, many of which are copyrighted, almost as they are being broadcast. In providing this service, Aereo uses its own equipment, housed in a centralized warehouse, outside of its users' homes. By means of its technology (antennas, transcoders, and servers), Aereo's system "receive[s] programs that have been released to the public and carr[ies] them by private channels to additional viewers." *Fortnightly*, 392 U.S., at 400. It "carr[ies] . . . whatever programs [it] receive[s]," and it offers "all the programming" of each over-the-air station it carries. *Id.*, at 392, 400.

Aereo's equipment may serve a "viewer function"; it may enhance the viewer's ability to receive a broadcaster's programs. It may even emulate equipment a viewer could use at home. But the same was true of the equipment that was before the Court, and ultimately before Congress, in *Fortnightly* and *Teleprompter*.

We recognize, and Aereo and the dissent emphasize, one particular difference between Aereo's system and the cable systems at issue in *Fortnightly* and *Teleprompter*. The systems in those cases transmitted constantly; they sent continuous programming to each subscriber's television set. In contrast, Aereo's system remains inert until a subscriber indicates that she wants to watch a program. Only at that moment, in automatic response to the subscriber's request, does Aereo's system activate an antenna and begin to transmit the requested program.

This is a critical difference, says the dissent. It means that Aereo's subscribers, not Aereo, "selec[t] the copyrighted content" that is "perform[ed]," (opinion of SCALIA, J.), and for that reason they, not Aereo, "transmit" the performance. Aereo is thus like "a copy shop that provides its patrons with a library card." A copy shop is not directly liable whenever a patron uses the shop's machines to "reproduce" copyrighted materials found in that library. *See* § 106(1) ("exclusive righ[t] . . . to reproduce the copyrighted work"). And by the same token, Aereo should not be directly liable whenever its patrons use its equipment to "transmit" copyrighted television programs to their screens.

In our view, however, the dissent's copy shop argument, in whatever form, makes too much out of too little. Given Aereo's overwhelming likeness to the cable companies targeted by the 1976 amendments, this sole technological difference between Aereo and traditional cable companies does not make a critical difference here. The subscribers of the *Fortnightly* and *Teleprompter* cable systems also selected what programs to display on their receiving sets. Indeed, as we explained in *Fortnightly,* such a subscriber "could choose any of the . . . programs he wished to view by simply turning the knob on his own television set." The same is true of an Aereo subscriber. Of course, in *Fortnightly* the television signals, in a sense, lurked behind the screen, ready to emerge when the subscriber turned the knob. Here the signals pursue their ordinary course of travel through the universe until today's "turn of the knob"—a click on a website—activates machinery that intercepts and reroutes them to Aereo's subscribers over the Internet. But this difference means nothing to the subscriber. It means nothing to the broadcaster. We do not see how this single difference, invisible to subscriber and broadcaster alike, could transform a system that is for all practical purposes a traditional cable system into "a copy shop that provides its patrons with a library card."

In other cases involving different kinds of service or technology providers, a user's involvement in the operation of the provider's equipment and selection of the content transmitted may well bear on whether the provider performs within the meaning of the Act. * * * We conclude that Aereo is not just an equipment supplier and that Aereo "perform[s]."

III

Next, we must consider whether Aereo performs petitioners' works "publicly," within the meaning of the Transmit Clause. Under the Clause, an entity performs a work publicly when it "transmit[s] . . . a performance . . . of the work . . . to the public." § 101. Aereo denies that it satisfies this definition. It reasons as follows: First, the "performance" it "transmit[s]" is the performance created by its act of transmitting. And second, because each of these performances is capable of being received by one and only one subscriber, Aereo transmits privately, not publicly. Even assuming Aereo's first argument is correct, its second does not follow.

We begin with Aereo's first argument. What performance does Aereo transmit? Under the Act, "[t]o 'transmit' a performance . . . is to communicate it by any device or process whereby images or sounds are received beyond the place from which they are sent." *Ibid.* And "[t]o 'perform' " an audiovisual work means "to show its images in any sequence or to make the sounds accompanying it audible." *Ibid.*

Petitioners say Aereo transmits a *prior* performance of their works. Thus when Aereo retransmits a network's prior broadcast, the underlying broadcast (itself a performance) is the performance that Aereo transmits. Aereo, as discussed above, says the performance it transmits is the *new* performance created by its act of transmitting. That performance comes into existence when Aereo streams the sounds and images of a broadcast program to a subscriber's screen.

We assume *arguendo* that Aereo's first argument is correct. Thus, for present purposes, to transmit a performance of (at least) an audiovisual work means to communicate contemporaneously visible images and contemporaneously audible sounds of the work. *Cf. United States v. American Soc. of Composers, Authors and Publishers,* 627 F.3d 64, 73 (2d Cir. 2010) (holding that a download of a work is not a performance because the data transmitted are not "contemporaneously perceptible"). When an Aereo subscriber selects a program to watch, Aereo streams the program over the Internet to that subscriber. Aereo thereby "communicate[s]" to the subscriber, by means of a "device or process," the work's images and sounds. And those images and sounds are contemporaneously visible and audible on the subscriber's computer (or other Internet-connected device). So under our assumed definition, Aereo transmits a performance whenever its subscribers watch a program.

But what about the Clause's further requirement that Aereo transmit a performance "to the public"? As we have said, an Aereo subscriber receives broadcast television signals with an antenna dedicated to him alone. Aereo's system makes from those signals a personal copy of the selected program. It streams the content of the copy to the same subscriber and to no one else. One and only one subscriber has the ability to see and hear each Aereo transmission. The fact that each transmission is to only one subscriber, in Aereo's view, means that it does not transmit a performance "to the public."

In terms of the Act's purposes, these differences do not distinguish Aereo's system from cable systems, which do perform "publicly." Viewed in terms of Congress' regulatory objectives, why should any of these technological differences matter? They concern the behind-the-scenes way in which Aereo delivers television programming to its viewers' screens. They do not render Aereo's commercial objective any different from that of cable companies. Nor do they significantly alter the viewing experience of Aereo's subscribers. Why would a subscriber who wishes to watch a television show care much whether images and sounds are delivered to his screen via a large multisubscriber antenna or one small dedicated antenna, whether they arrive instantaneously or after a few seconds' delay, or whether they are transmitted directly or after a personal copy is made? And why, if Aereo is right, could not modern CATV systems simply continue the same commercial and consumer-oriented activities, free of copyright restrictions, provided they substitute such new technologies for old? Congress would as much have intended to protect a copyright holder from the unlicensed activities of Aereo as from those of cable companies.

The text of the Clause effectuates Congress' intent. Aereo's argument to the contrary relies on the premise that "to transmit . . . a performance" means to make a single transmission. But the Clause suggests that an entity may transmit a performance through multiple, discrete transmissions. That is because one can "transmit" or "communicate" something through a *set* of actions. Thus one can transmit a message to one's friends, irrespective of whether one sends separate identical e-mails to each friend or a single e-mail to all at once. So can an elected official communicate an idea, slogan, or speech to her constituents, regardless of whether she communicates that idea, slogan, or speech during individual phone calls to each constituent or in a public square.

The fact that a singular noun ("a performance") follows the words "to transmit" does not suggest the contrary. One can sing a song to his family, whether he sings the same song one-on-one or in front of all together. Similarly, one's colleagues may watch a performance of a particular play—say, this season's modern-dress version of "Measure for Measure"—whether they do so at separate or at the same showings. By the same principle, an entity may transmit a performance through one or several transmissions, where the performance is of the same work.

The Transmit Clause must permit this interpretation, for it provides that one may transmit a performance to the public "whether the members of the public capable of receiving the performance . . . receive it . . . at the same time or at different times." § 101. Were the words "to transmit . . . a performance" limited to a single act of communication, members of the public could not receive the performance communicated "at different times." Therefore, in light of the purpose and text of the Clause, we conclude that when an entity communicates the same contemporaneously perceptible images and sounds to multiple people, it transmits a performance to them regardless of the number of discrete communications it makes.

We do not see how the fact that Aereo transmits via personal copies of programs could make a difference. The Act applies to transmissions "by means of any device or process." And retransmitting a television program using user-specific copies is a "process" of transmitting a performance. A "cop[y]" of a work is simply a "material objec[t] . . . in which a work is fixed . . . and from which the work can be perceived, reproduced, or otherwise communicated." *Ibid.* So whether Aereo transmits from the same or separate copies, it performs the same work; it shows the same images and makes audible the same sounds. Therefore, when Aereo streams the same television program to multiple subscribers, it "transmit[s] . . . a performance" to all of them.

* * *

For these reasons, we conclude that Aereo transmits a performance of petitioners' copyrighted works to the public, within the meaning of the Transmit Clause.

IV

Aereo and many of its supporting *amici* argue that to apply the Transmit Clause to Aereo's conduct will impose copyright liability on other technologies, including new technologies, that Congress could not possibly have wanted to reach. We agree that Congress, while intending the Transmit Clause to apply broadly to cable companies and their equivalents, did not intend to discourage or to control the emergence or use of different kinds of technologies. But we do not believe that our limited holding today will have that effect.

* * *

We cannot now answer more precisely how the Transmit Clause or other provisions of the Copyright Act will apply to technologies not before us. We agree with the Solicitor General that "[q]uestions involving cloud computing, [remote storage] DVRs, and other novel issues not before the Court, as to which 'Congress has not plainly marked [the] course,' should await a case in which they are squarely presented." And we note that, to the extent commercial actors or other interested entities may be concerned with the relationship between the development and use of such technologies and the Copyright Act, they are of course free to seek action from Congress.

3

In sum, having considered the details of Aereo's practices, we find them highly similar to those of the CATV systems in *Fortnightly* and *Teleprompter*. And those are activities that the 1976 amendments sought to bring within the scope of the Copyright Act. Insofar as there are differences, those differences concern not the nature of the service that Aereo provides so much as the technological manner in which it provides the service. We conclude that those differences are not adequate to place Aereo's activities outside the scope of the Act.

For these reasons, we conclude that Aereo "perform[s]" petitioners' copyrighted works "publicly," as those terms are defined by the Transmit Clause. We therefore reverse the contrary judgment of the Court of Appeals, and we remand the case for further proceedings consistent with this opinion.

It is so ordered.

JUSTICE SCALIA, with whom JUSTICE THOMAS and JUSTICE ALITO join, dissenting.

This case is the latest skirmish in the long-running copyright battle over the delivery of television programming. * * * The Networks sued Aereo for several forms of copyright infringement, but we are here concerned with a single claim: that Aereo violates the Networks' "exclusive righ[t]" to "perform" their programs "publicly." 17 U.S.C. § 106(4). That claim fails at the very outset because Aereo does not "perform" at all. The Court manages to reach the opposite conclusion only by disregarding widely accepted rules for service-provider liability and adopting in their place an improvised standard ("looks-like-cable-TV") that will sow confusion for years to come.

I. Legal Standard

There are two types of liability for copyright infringement: direct and secondary. As its name suggests, the former applies when an actor personally engages in infringing conduct. *See Sony Corp. of America v. Universal City Studios, Inc.,* 464 U.S. 417, 433 (1984). Secondary liability, by contrast, is a means of holding defendants responsible for infringement by third parties, even when the defendants "have not themselves engaged in the infringing activity." *Id.,* at 435. It applies when a defendant "intentionally induc[es] or encourag[es]" infringing acts by others or profits from such acts "while declining to exercise a right to stop or limit [them]." *Metro-Goldwyn-Mayer Studios Inc. v. Grokster, Ltd.,* 545 U.S. 913, 930 (2005).

Most suits against equipment manufacturers and service providers involve secondary-liability claims. For example, when movie studios sued to block the sale of Sony's Betamax videocassette recorder (VCR), they argued that Sony was liable because *its customers* were making unauthorized copies. Record labels and movie studios relied on a similar theory when they sued Grokster and StreamCast, two providers of peer-to-peer file-sharing software. *See Grokster, supra,* at 920–921, 927.

This suit, or rather the portion of it before us here, is fundamentally different. The Networks claim that Aereo *directly* infringes their public-performance right. Accordingly, the Networks must prove that Aereo "perform[s]" copyrighted works, § 106(4), when its subscribers log in, select a channel, and push the "watch" button. That process undoubtedly results in a performance; the question is *who* does the performing. If Aereo's subscribers perform but Aereo does not, the claim necessarily fails.

The Networks' claim is governed by a simple but profoundly important rule: A defendant may be held directly liable only if it has engaged in volitional conduct that violates the Act. This requirement is firmly grounded in the Act's text, which defines "perform" in active, affirmative terms: One "perform[s]" a copyrighted "audiovisual work," such as a movie or news broadcast, by "show[ing] its images in any sequence" or "mak[ing] the sounds accompanying it audible." § 101. And since the Act makes it unlawful to copy or perform copyrighted works, not to copy or perform in general, *see* § 501(a), the volitional-act requirement demands conduct directed to the plaintiff's copyrighted material. Every Court of Appeals to have considered an automated-service provider's direct liability for copyright infringement has adopted that rule. *See Fox Broadcasting Co. v. Dish Network LLC,* 747 F.3d 1060, 1066–1068 (9th Cir. 2014); *Cartoon Network, supra,* at 130–131 (2d Cir. 2008); *CoStar Group, Inc. v. LoopNet, Inc.,* 373 F.3d 544, 549–550 (4th Cir. 2004). Although we have not opined on the issue, our cases are fully consistent with a volitional-conduct requirement. For example, we gave several examples of direct infringement in *Sony,* each of which involved a volitional act directed to the plaintiff's copyrighted material. *See* 464 U.S., at 437, n. 18.

The volitional-conduct requirement is not at issue in most direct-infringement cases; the usual point of dispute is whether the defendant's conduct is infringing (*e.g.,* Does the defendant's design copy the plaintiff's?), rather than whether the defendant has acted at all (*e.g.,* Did this defendant create the infringing design?). But it comes right to the fore when a direct-infringement claim is lodged against a defendant who does nothing more than operate an automated, user-controlled system. Internet-service providers are a prime example. When one user sends data to another, the provider's equipment facilitates the transfer automatically. Does that mean that the provider is directly liable when the transmission happens to result in the "reproduc[tion]," § 106(1), of a copyrighted work? It does not. The provider's system is "totally indifferent to the material's content," whereas courts require "some aspect of volition" directed at the copyrighted material before direct liability may be imposed. *CoStar,* 373 F.3d, at 550–551.[2] The defendant may be held directly liable only if the defendant *itself*

[2] Congress has enacted several safe-harbor provisions applicable to automated network processes, *see, e.g.,* 17 U.S.C. § 512(a)–(b), but those provisions do not foreclose "any other defense," § 512(*l*), including a volitional-conduct defense.

"trespassed on the exclusive domain of the copyright owner." *Id.*, at 550. Most of the time that issue will come down to who selects the copyrighted content: the defendant or its customers.

A comparison between copy shops and video-on-demand services illustrates the point. A copy shop rents out photocopiers on a per-use basis. One customer might copy his 10-year-old's drawings—a perfectly lawful thing to do—while another might duplicate a famous artist's copyrighted photographs—a use clearly prohibited by § 106(1). Either way, *the customer* chooses the content and activates the copying function; the photocopier does nothing except in response to the customer's commands. Because the shop plays no role in selecting the content, it cannot be held directly liable when a customer makes an infringing copy.

Video-on-demand services, like photocopiers, respond automatically to user input, but they differ in one crucial respect: *They choose the content.* * * * That selection and arrangement by the service provider constitutes a volitional act directed to specific copyrighted works and thus serves as a basis for direct liability.

The distinction between direct and secondary liability would collapse if there were not a clear rule for determining whether *the defendant* committed the infringing act. The volitional-conduct requirement supplies that rule; its purpose is not to excuse defendants from accountability, but to channel the claims against them into the correct analytical track. Thus, in the example given above, the fact that the copy shop does not choose the content simply means that its culpability will be assessed using secondary-liability rules rather than direct-liability rules.

II. Application to Aereo

So which is Aereo: the copy shop or the video-on-demand service? In truth, it is neither. Rather, it is akin to a copy shop that provides its patrons with a library card. Aereo offers access to an automated system consisting of routers, servers, transcoders, and dime-sized antennae. Like a photocopier or VCR, that system lies dormant until a subscriber activates it. When a subscriber selects a program, Aereo's system picks up the relevant broadcast signal, translates its audio and video components into digital data, stores the data in a user-specific file, and transmits that file's contents to the subscriber via the Internet—at which point the subscriber's laptop, tablet, or other device displays the broadcast just as an ordinary television would. The result of that process fits the statutory definition of a performance to a tee: The subscriber's device "show[s]" the broadcast's "images" and "make[s] the sounds accompanying" the broadcast "audible." § 101. The only question is whether those performances are the product of Aereo's volitional conduct.

They are not. Unlike video-on-demand services, Aereo does not provide a prearranged assortment of movies and television shows. Rather, it assigns each subscriber an antenna that—like a library card—can be used to obtain whatever broadcasts are freely available. Some of those broadcasts are copyrighted; others are in the public domain. The key point is that subscribers call all the shots: Aereo's automated system does not relay any program, copyrighted or not, until a subscriber selects the program and tells Aereo to relay it. Aereo's operation of that system is a volitional act and a but-for cause of the resulting performances, but, as in the case of the copy shop, that degree of involvement is not enough for direct liability. *See Grokster,* 545 U.S., at 960 (BREYER, J., concurring) ("[T]he producer of a technology which *permits* unlawful copying does not himself *engage* in unlawful copying").

In sum, Aereo does not "perform" for the sole and simple reason that it does not make the choice of content. And because Aereo does not perform, it cannot be held directly liable for infringing the Networks' public-performance right. That conclusion does not necessarily mean that Aereo's service complies with the Copyright Act. Quite the contrary. The Networks' complaint alleges that Aereo is directly *and* secondarily liable for infringing their public-performance rights (§ 106(4)) *and also* their reproduction rights (§ 106(1)). Their request for a preliminary injunction—the only issue before this Court—is based exclusively on the direct-liability portion of the public-performance claim (and further limited to Aereo's "watch" function, as opposed to its "record" function). Affirming the judgment below would merely return this case to the lower courts for consideration of the Networks' remaining claims.

III. Guilt By Resemblance

The Court's conclusion that Aereo performs boils down to the following syllogism: (1) Congress amended the Act to overrule our decisions holding that cable systems do not perform when they retransmit over-the-air broadcasts; (2) Aereo looks a lot like a cable system; therefore (3) Aereo performs. * * *

* * *

* * * The Court vows that its ruling will not affect cloud-storage providers and cable-television systems, but it cannot deliver on that promise given the imprecision of its result-driven rule. Indeed, the difficulties inherent in the Court's makeshift approach will become apparent in this very case. Today's decision addresses the legality of Aereo's "watch" function, which provides nearly contemporaneous access to live broadcasts. On remand, one of the first questions the lower courts will face is whether Aereo's "record" function, which allows subscribers to save a program while it is airing and watch it later, infringes the Networks' public-performance right. The volitional-conduct rule provides a clear answer to that question: Because Aereo does not select the programs viewed by its users, it does not perform. But it is impossible to say how the

issue will come out under the Court's analysis, since cable companies did not offer remote recording and playback services when Congress amended the Copyright Act in 1976.

I share the Court's evident feeling that what Aereo is doing (or enabling to be done) to the Networks' copyrighted programming ought not to be allowed. But perhaps we need not distort the Copyright Act to forbid it. * * * It is not the role of this Court to identify and plug loopholes. It is the role of good lawyers to identify and exploit them, and the role of Congress to eliminate them if it wishes. * * *

NOTE

After losing at the Supreme Court, Aereo suspended operations while it applied for a compulsory license under 17 U.S.C. § 111, which would enable it to resume retransmitting television signals to its subscribers upon payment of the statutory licensing fee. However, the Copyright Office notified Aereo that it was not eligible for the license. This reflects the Copyright Office's own interpretation of § 111, which the Second Circuit endorsed in *WPIX, Inc. v. ivi*, 691 F.3d 275 (2d Cir. 2012). Aereo later declared bankruptcy and was acquired by TiVo, and a district court rejected its arguments under § 111. *See ABC v. Aereo, Inc.*, 2014 WL 5393867 (S.D.N.Y. Oct. 23, 2014). For several years, New Yorkers with poor antenna reception had to decide whether to forego local broadcasts, invest in high-end digital antennas, or subscribe to conventional cable or satellite services (costing far more than Aereo's $8 a month). One federal district court ruled that an internet retransmission service similar to Aereo was entitled to utilize the cable compulsory license under § 111, but this decision was reversed on appeal. *See Fox Television Stations, Inc. v. AereoKiller*, 115 F.Supp.3d 1152 (C.D. Cal. 2015), *rev'd*, 851 F.3d 1002 (9th Cir. 2017). Consumers now have more options for "cutting the cord," with the advent of numerous online streaming services operating under copyright licenses.

UNITED STATES V. AMERICAN SOCIETY OF COMPOSERS, AUTHORS AND PUBLISHERS

627 F.3d 64 (2d Cir. 2010).

JOHN M. WALKER, JR., CIRCUIT JUDGE:

This case presents two distinct questions that arise from the transmittal of musical works over the Internet: First, whether a download of a digital file containing a musical work constitutes a public performance of that musical work; and, second, whether the district court, acting in its capacity as the rate court, was reasonable in its assessment of the blanket license fees of Yahoo! Inc. and RealNetworks, Inc. (collectively, "the Internet Companies") to publicly perform any of the millions of musical compositions in the American Society of Composers, Authors and Publishers ("ASCAP") repertory.

For the reasons set forth below, we affirm the district court's ruling that a download of a musical work does not constitute a public performance of that work * * *.

I. Public Performance Right as Applied to Downloads

The Copyright Act confers upon the owner of a copyright "a bundle of discrete exclusive rights," each of which may be transferred or retained separately by the copyright owner. *N.Y. Times Co. v. Tasini*, 533 U.S. 483, 495–96 (2001). Section 106 of the Copyright Act sets forth these various rights, including the right "to reproduce the copyrighted work in copies" and the right "to perform the copyrighted work publicly." 17 U.S.C. §§ 106(1), (4). In this case, the Internet Companies offer their customers the ability to download musical works over the Internet. It is undisputed that these downloads create copies of the musical works, for which the parties agree the copyright owners must be compensated. However, the parties dispute whether these downloads are also public performances of the musical works, for which the copyright owners must separately and additionally be compensated. The district court held that these downloads are not public performances, and we agree.

In answering the question of whether a download is a public performance, we turn to Section 101 of the Copyright Act, which states that "[t]o 'perform' a work means to recite, render, play, dance, or act it, either directly or by means of any device or process." 17 U.S.C. § 101. A download plainly is neither a "dance" nor an "act." Thus, we must determine whether a download of a musical work falls within the meaning of the terms "recite," "render," or "play."

* * *

The ordinary sense of the words "recite," "render," and "play" refer to actions that can be perceived contemporaneously. To "recite" is "to repeat from memory or read aloud esp[ecially] before an audience," WEBSTER'S THIRD NEW INTERNATIONAL DICTIONARY 1895 (1981); to "render" is to "say over: recite, repeat," *id.* at 1922; and to "play" is to "perform on a musical instrument," "sound in performance," "reproduce sound of recorded material," or "act on a stage or in some other dramatic medium," *id.* at 1737. All three actions entail contemporaneous perceptibility.

These definitions comport with our common-sense understandings of these words. Itzakh Perlman gives a "recital" of Beethoven's Violin Concerto in D Major when he performs it aloud before an audience. Jimmy Hendrix memorably (or not, depending on one's sensibility) offered a "rendition" of the Star-Spangled Banner at Woodstock when he performed it aloud in 1969. Yo-Yo Ma "plays" the Cello Suite No. 1 when he draws the bow across his cello strings to audibly reproduce the notes that Bach inscribed. Music is neither recited, rendered, nor played when a recording (electronic or otherwise) is simply delivered to a potential listener.

The final clause of the § 101 definition of "to perform" further confirms our interpretation. It states that "[t]o 'perform' . . . a motion picture or other audiovisual work . . . [is] to show its images in any sequence or to make the sounds accompanying it audible." 17 U.S.C. § 101. The fact that the statute defines performance in the audio-visual context as "show[ing]" the work or making it "audible" reinforces the conclusion that "to perform" a musical work entails contemporaneous perceptibility. ASCAP has provided no reason, and we can surmise none, why the statute would require a contemporaneously perceptible event in the context of an audio-visual work, but not in the context of a musical work.

The downloads at issue in this appeal are not musical performances that are contemporaneously perceived by the listener. They are simply transfers of electronic files containing digital copies from an on-line server to a local hard drive. The downloaded songs are not performed in any perceptible manner during the transfers; the user must take some further action to play the songs after they are downloaded. Because the electronic download itself involves no recitation, rendering, or playing of the musical work encoded in the digital transmission, we hold that such a download is not a performance of that work, as defined by § 101.

ASCAP, pointing to the definition of "publicly" in § 101, argues that a download constitutes a public performance. Section 101 defines "[t]o perform or display a work 'publicly' " as follows:

> (1) to perform or display it at a place open to the public or at any place where a substantial number of persons outside of a normal circle of a family and its social acquaintances is gathered; or (2) to transmit or otherwise communicate a performance or display of the work to a place specified by clause (1) or to the public, by means of any device or process, whether the members of the public capable of receiving the performance or display receive it in the same place or in separate places and at the same time or at different times.

Id. § 101. ASCAP argues that downloads fall under clause (2) of this definition because downloads "transmit or otherwise communicate a performance," *id.*, namely the initial or underlying performance of the copyrighted work, to the public. We find this argument unavailing. The definition of "publicly" simply defines the circumstances under which a performance will be considered public; it does not define the meaning of "performance." Moreover, ASCAP's proposed interpretation misreads the definition of "publicly." As we concluded in *Cartoon Network LP v. CSC Holdings, Inc.*, "when Congress speaks of transmitting a performance to the public, it refers to the performance created by the act of transmission," not simply to transmitting a recording of a performance. 536 F.3d 121, 136 (2d Cir.2008). ASCAP's alternative interpretation is flawed because, in disaggregating the "transmission" from the simultaneous "performance" and treating the transmission itself as a performance, ASCAP renders superfluous the subsequent "a performance . . . of the work" as the object of the transmittal. *See Duncan v. Walker*, 533 U.S. 167, 174 (2001) ("It is our duty to give effect, if possible, to every clause and word of a statute."). In contrast, our interpretation in *Cartoon Network* recognizes that a "transmittal of a work" is distinct from a transmittal of "a performance"—the former being a transmittal of the underlying work and the latter being a transmittal that is itself a performance of the underlying work. *See* 536 F.3d at 134 ("The fact that the statute says 'capable of receiving the performance,' instead of 'capable of receiving the transmission,' underscores the fact that a transmission of a performance is itself a performance.").

The Internet Companies' stream transmissions, which all parties agree constitute public performances, illustrate why a download is not a public performance. A stream is an electronic transmission that renders the musical work audible as it is received by the client-computer's temporary memory. This transmission, like a television or radio broadcast, is a performance because there is a playing of the song that is perceived simultaneously with the transmission. In contrast, downloads do not immediately produce sound; only after a file has been downloaded on a user's hard drive can he perceive a performance by playing the downloaded song. Unlike musical works played during radio broadcasts and stream transmissions, downloaded musical works are transmitted at one point in time and performed at another. Transmittal without a performance does not constitute a "public performance." *Cf. Columbia Pictures Indus., Inc., v. Prof'l Real Estate Investors, Inc.*, 866 F.2d 278, 282 (9th Cir.1989) (holding that renting videodiscs to a hotel guest for playback in the guest's room does not constitute the "transmission" of a public performance).

ASCAP misreads our opinion in *NFL v. PrimeTime 24 Joint Venture*, 211 F.3d 10, 11–13 (2d Cir.2000), to hold that the Copyright Act does not, in fact, require a contemporaneously perceptible performance to infringe on the public performance right. In *NFL*, defendant PrimeTime, a satellite television provider, captured protected content in the United States from the NFL, transmitted it from the United States to a satellite ("the uplink"), and then transmitted it from the satellite to subscribers in both the United States and Canada ("the downlink"). PrimeTime had a license to transmit NFL games to its subscribers in the United States but not to Canada. The NFL sought to enjoin the transmissions sent to Canada by arguing that the uplink in the United States constituted unauthorized public performances of the games in the United States. The relevant issue was whether the uplink transmission was a public performance even though the uplink was only to a satellite and could not, itself, be perceived by viewers. We determined that PrimeTime's uplink transmission of signals captured in the United States amounted to a public performance because it was an integral part of the larger process by which the NFL's protected work was delivered to a public audience.

ASCAP seizes on the fact that the uplink to the satellite was not contemporaneously perceptible to argue against a contemporaneous perceptibility requirement in this case. ASCAP's argument, however, fails to accord controlling significance to the fact that the immediately sequential downlink from the satellite to Canadian PrimeTime subscribers was a public performance of the games. *Id.* at 11–13; *see also David v. Showtime/The Movie Channel, Inc.,* 697 F.Supp. 752, 758–60 (S.D.N.Y.1988) (finding that because "Showtime and The Movie Channel both broadcast television programming . . . to cable system operators," which, in turn, "pass[ed] the signal along to their individual customers," the initial transmissions constituted public performances because they were a "step in the process by which a protected work wends its way to its audience"); MELVILLE B. NIMMER & DAVID NIMMER, 2 NIMMER ON COPYRIGHT § 8.14[C][2] at 190.6 & n. 63 (2009) (explaining that when a transmission is made "to cable systems that will in turn transmit directly to the public," the earlier transmission is a public performance despite the absence of any contemporaneous perceptibility). In holding the transmission in *Cartoon Network* not to be a public performance, we distinguished *NFL* on the basis that in that case the final act in the sequence of transmissions was a public performance. That same distinction applies here. Just as in *Cartoon Network,* the Internet Companies transmit a copy of the work to the user, who then plays his unique copy of the song whenever he wants to hear it; because the performance is made by a unique reproduction of the song that was sold to the user, the ultimate performance of the song is not "to the public." *See id.* at 137, 138.

Accordingly, we affirm the district court's grant of partial summary judgment on the basis that downloads do not constitute public performances of the downloaded musical works.

[Discussion of royalty rates omitted.]

* * *

NOTES

1. When a mobile phone company transmits a musical recording as a ringtone to a customer, does a public performance take place? When the phone rings, is there a public performance? *See In re Cellco Partnership*, 663 F. Supp. 2d 363 (S.D.N.Y. 2009).

2. If a transmission originates overseas, but is received in the United States, does this implicate the U.S. public performance right? What about the reverse?

5. THE SCOPE OF EXCLUSIVE RIGHTS IN SOUND RECORDINGS

Statutes: 17 U.S.C. §§ 106(6), 114

In the case of sound recordings, section 114 defines the exclusive rights to reproduce a work and to incorporate it in derivative works more narrowly than in the case of other copyrightable works. In addition, section 114(a) clarifies that there is no exclusive public performance right in sound recordings under section 106(4). Sound recordings are one instance in which the classification of a work under section 102(a) significantly affects the scope of the copyright owner's rights.

Until 1995, the United States did not recognize performance rights in sound recordings at all. However, the Digital Performance Right in Sound Recordings Act, Pub. L. 104–39 (1995), added new section 106(6), giving the owners of copyrights in sound recordings a public performance right limited to performances via transmission by digital subscription services. In 1998, the right was extended to encompass certain nonsubscription services, most notably webcasting. The Act reflected the concern that digital transmissions have the potential to supplant record sales, thus reducing the revenues which those sales previously generated for the owners of sound recording copyrights. In addition, any decrease in record sales will reduce the mechanical royalties payable by record companies to composers, publishers, and performers according to their contracts.

The new law benefits recording artists regardless of whether they own copyright interests in the recordings on which they perform; new section 114(g) allocates a portion of the digital licensing revenues to the recording artists.

Section 114(d)(3) limits the right of the sound recording copyright owner to grant exclusive licenses of the section 106(6) right to interactive subscription services (where the user selects the recording to be performed), in response to the concern expressed by composers and publishers "that the copyright owners of sound recordings might become 'gatekeepers' and limit opportunities for public performances of the musical works embodied in the sound recordings." S. Rep. No. 104–128, 104th Cong., 1st Sess. 25 (1995). No restrictions are imposed on the granting of nonexclusive licenses for section 106(6) rights. New sections 114(e) through (i) establish licensing rules and statutory royalty rates for digital performance rights.

Nations that recognize broader performance rights in sound recordings have in the past refused to allow United States persons owning sound recording copyrights to collect royalties for public performances in those countries, because the United States did not reciprocate. Most nations have continued this practice in spite of the enactment of Pub. L. 104–39, although some nations will remit royalties for digital performances.

NOTES

1. If someone wishes to make a "soundalike" recording that closely imitates an existing recording of a copyrighted musical work, can this be done without seeking the consent of copyright owners? If not, whose consent is required? If a soundalike recording is authorized by section 114, would a featured musician or singer whose "sound" was imitated have a cause of action against the maker of the soundalike recording?

2. Why did Congress define the reproduction right so narrowly in the case of sound recordings?

3. Should Congress revise the copyright laws to recognize a public performance right in sound recordings that is broader than section 106(6)? (Compare Article 15 of the 1996 WIPO Performances and Phonograms Treaty.) All of our treaty partners recognize such a right, but do no remit sound recording performance royalties to U.S. record labels due to the lack of reciprocity.

4. Title IV of the DMCA amended section 114(d)(1) to clarify which transmissions of sound recordings are excluded from section 106(6), and amended section 114(d)(2) to extend the statutory licensing provisions for nonexempt subscription transmissions to include certain eligible nonsubscription transmissions (defined in a new subsection (j)(6) to exclude interactive services and most advertising). The statutory licensing scheme and royalty distribution scheme is thus broadened to include many internet music transmissions.

5. Another type of music license is the "synchronization" license, which allows music to accompany visual images. For example, in *Leadsinger, Inc. v. BMG Music Publishing*, 512 F.3d 522 (9th Cir. 2008), the Ninth Circuit held that a manufacturer of karaoke machines needed a synchronization license in order to display song lyrics while a sound recording of the song played. Would a compulsory mechanical license be needed as well?

6. *Sections 106(6) and 114—Digital Public Performance Right:* In *Arista Records, LLC v. Launch Media, Inc.*, 578 F.3d 148 (2d Cir. 2009), the Second Circuit addressed the definition of an "interactive service" under section 114, under which "interactive" music webcasting services are subject to the digital public performance right in sound recordings and are not eligible for the statutory licensing scheme. The defendant's LAUNCHcast music service provides individualized music "stations" for its listeners. It does so by creating a customized playlist for each user that takes account of the user's expressed preferences. The service allows users to rate specific songs according to their

preferences, to specify their preferred artists and genres, as well as the percentage of new music they would like to hear (that is, music that they have not previously rated), and to indicate whether they wish to exclude music with profane lyrics. The service then uses this information to select, from thousands of possibilities, 50 songs for the user's unique playlist. A new playlist is generated each time the user logs on to the service. A user may elect to become a "DJ" by permitting other users to subscribe to his or her playlist.

In the court's view, the question whether LAUNCHcast is "interactive" within the meaning of section 114 turned on the question whether each customized songlist is "specially created" for the user. *Id.* at 161. Based on a detailed analysis of LAUNCHcast's song selection process, and consideration of Congress's intent to give record companies control over interactive services that compete with record sales, the Second Circuit concluded that the songlists, while unique to each user, were not "specially created" within the meaning of the statute, "because the webcasting service does not provide sufficient control to users such that playlists are so predictable that users will choose to listen to the webcast in lieu of purchasing music, thereby—in the aggregate—diminishing record sales." *Id.* at 162–64.

B. SPECIFIC LIMITATIONS ON THE SECTION 106 RIGHTS

Statutes: 17 U.S.C. §§ 101 (as needed), 108–22, 1001–10, 1401

The exclusive rights of the copyright owner under section 106 are subject to a number of narrowly-tailored limitations and compulsory licenses, which are set forth in sections 108–22 and 1001–10. In addition, all of the rights under section 106 are subject to the more broadly-framed fair use provisions of section 107 (which is the subject of Chapter 17). The limitations under section 114 have already been discussed. Limitations applicable to rights other than those embodied in section 106 are discussed in Part C of this chapter, *infra*.

Under the 2018 Music Modernization Act, pre-1972 sound recordings protected by section 1401 are subject to the same exclusive rights and limitations as copyrighted works, with one additional limitation: Certain noncommercial uses of these recordings are permitted if the rights owner (1) is not commercially exploiting them, and (2) does not "opt out" after the user complies with certain statutory procedures. 17 U.S.C. § 1401(c).

1. SECTION 117: COPYING COMPUTER SOFTWARE

Statute: 17 U.S.C. § 117

VAULT CORP. V. QUAID SOFTWARE LTD.

847 F.2d 255 (5th Cir. 1988).

REAVLEY, CIRCUIT JUDGE:

[Plaintiff Vault manufactured and marketed PROLOK computer diskettes containing Vault's copyrighted copy-protection software, which prevented persons from making fully functional copies of any other computer programs contained on those diskettes. Vault sold its diskettes to software makers who would place their own copyrighted programs on the copy-protected diskettes in order to prevent unauthorized copying. Defendant Quaid manufactured and sold CopyWrite diskettes, which contained software with a feature known as "RAMKEY" that could "unlock" the PROLOK copy protection. Buyers of Copywrite diskettes could use them to make fully functional copies of any software contained in a PROLOK diskette.]

* * * Vault claims that Quaid infringed its copyright under § 501(a) by: (1) directly copying Vault's program into the memory of Quaid's computer; (2) contributing to the unauthorized copying of Vault's program and the programs Vault's customers place on PROLOK diskettes; and (3) preparing derivative works of Vault's program.

Section 117 of the Copyright Act limits a copyright owner's exclusive rights under § 106 by permitting an owner of a computer program to make certain copies of that program without obtaining permission from the program's copyright owner. With respect to Vault's first two claims of copyright infringement, Quaid contends that its activities fall within the § 117 exceptions and that it has, therefore, not infringed Vault's exclusive rights under § 501(a). To appreciate the arguments of the parties, we examine the legislative history of § 117.

A. Background

In 1974 Congress established the National Commission on New Technological Uses of Copyrighted Works (the "CONTU") to perform research and make recommendations concerning copyright protection for computer programs. Before receiving the CONTU's recommendations, Congress amended the Copyright Act in 1976 to include computer programs in the definition of protectable literary works and to establish that a program copied into a computer's memory constitutes a reproduction. * * *

In 1978 the CONTU issued its final report in which it recognized that "the cost of developing computer programs is far greater than the cost of their duplication," CONTU Report at 26, and concluded that "some form of protection is necessary to encourage the creation and broad distribution of computer programs in a competitive market," *id.* at 27. After acknowledging the importance of balancing the interest of proprietors in obtaining "reasonable protection" against the risks of "unduly burdening users of programs and the general public," *id.* at 29, the Report recommended * * * the enactment of a new section 117 which would proscribe the unauthorized copying of computer programs but permit a "rightful possessor" of a program

> to make or authorize the making of another copy or adaptation of that computer program *provided*:
>
> (1) that such a new copy or adaptation is created as an essential step in the utilization of the computer program in conjunction with a machine and that it is used in no other manner, or
>
> (2) that such new copy or adaptation is for archival purposes only and that all archival copies are destroyed in the event that continued possession of the computer program should cease to be rightful.

Id. at 30 (emphasis in original).

Because the act of loading a program from a medium of storage into a computer's memory creates a copy of the program, the CONTU reasoned that "one who rightfully possesses a copy of a program . . . should be provided with a legal right to copy it to that extent which will permit its use by the possessor," and drafted proposed § 117(1) to "provide that persons in rightful possession of copies of programs be able to use them freely without fear of exposure to copyright liability." *Id.* at 31. With respect to proposed section 117(2), the "archival exception," the Report explained that a person in rightful possession of a program should have the right "to prepare archival copies of it to guard against destruction or damage by mechanical or electrical failure. But this permission would not extend to other copies of the program. Thus one could not, for example, make archival copies of a program and later sell some to another while retaining some for use." *Id.*

In 1980, Congress enacted the Computer Software Copyright Act which adopted the recommendations contained in the CONTU Report. Section 117[11] * * * was enacted, and the proposed definition of "computer program" was added to section 101. The Act's legislative history, contained in a short paragraph in a committee report, merely states that the Act, "embodies the recommendations of [the CONTU] with respect to clarifying

---

[11] In enacting the new section 117, Congress adopted the proposed section with only one change. The final version grants "owners," as opposed to "rightful possessors," a limited right to copy and adapt their software. * * *

the law of copyright of computer software." H.R. Rep. No. 1307, 96th Cong., 2d Sess., pt. 1, at 23. The absence of an extensive legislative history and the fact that Congress enacted proposed section 117 with only one change have prompted courts to rely on the CONTU Report as an expression of legislative intent.

B. Direct Copying

In order to develop RAMKEY, Quaid analyzed Vault's program by copying it into its computer's memory. Vault contends that, by making this unauthorized copy, Quaid directly infringed upon Vault's copyright. The district court held that "Quaid's actions clearly fall within [the § 117(1)] exemption. The loading of [Vault's] program into the [memory] of a computer is an 'essential step in the utilization' of [Vault's] program. Therefore, Quaid has not infringed Vault's copyright by loading [Vault's program] into [its computer's memory]." *Vault*, 655 F. Supp. at 758.

Section 117(1) permits an owner of a program to make a copy of that program provided that the copy "is created as an essential step in the utilization of the computer program in conjunction with a machine and that it is used in no other manner." Congress recognized that a computer program cannot be used unless it is first copied into a computer's memory, and thus provided the § 117(1) exception to permit copying for this essential purpose. *See* CONTU Report at 31. Vault contends that, due to the inclusion of the phrase "and that it is used in no other manner," this exception should be interpreted to permit only the copying of a computer program for the purpose of using it for its intended purpose. Because Quaid copied Vault's program into its computer's memory for the express purpose of devising a means of defeating its protective function, Vault contends that § 117(1) is not applicable.

We decline to construe § 117(1) in this manner. Even though the copy of Vault's program made by Quaid was not used to prevent the copying of the program placed on the PROLOK diskette by one of Vault's customers (which is the purpose of Vault's program), and was, indeed, made for the express purpose of devising a means of defeating its protective function, the copy made by Quaid was "created as an essential step in the utilization" of Vault's program. Section 117(1) contains no language to suggest that the copy it permits must be employed for a use intended by the copyright owner, and, absent clear congressional guidance to the contrary, we refuse to read such limiting language into this exception. We therefore hold that Quaid did not infringe Vault's exclusive right to reproduce its program in copies under § 106(1).

* * *

C. Contributory Infringement

Vault contends that, because purchasers of programs placed on PROLOK diskettes use the RAMKEY feature of CopyWrite to make unauthorized copies, Quaid's advertisement and sale of CopyWrite diskettes with the RAMKEY feature violate the Copyright Act by contributing to the infringement of Vault's copyright and the copyrights owned by Vault's customers. Vault asserts that it lost customers and substantial revenue as a result of Quaid's contributory infringement because software companies which previously relied on PROLOK diskettes to protect their programs from unauthorized copying have discontinued their use.

* * *

[The court reviewed the test for contributory copyright infringement (*see* Chapter 18.C.2., *infra*) and determined that Quaid could not be held liable for the infringing acts of RAMKEY customers if RAMKEY also had substantial "commercially significant" noninfringing uses.]

Quaid asserts that RAMKEY serves the legitimate purpose of permitting purchasers of programs recorded on PROLOK diskettes to make archival copies under § 117(2) and that this purpose constitutes a substantial noninfringing use. At trial, witnesses for Quaid testified that software programs placed on floppy diskettes are subject to damage by physical and human mishap and that RAMKEY protects a purchaser's investment by providing a fully functional archival copy that can be used if the original program on the PROLOK protected diskette, or the diskette itself, is destroyed. Quaid contends that an archival copy of a PROLOK protected program, made without RAMKEY, does not serve to protect against these forms of damage because a computer will not read the program into its memory from the copy unless the PROLOK diskette containing the original undamaged program is also in one of its disk drives, which is impossible if the PROLOK diskette, or the program placed thereon, has been destroyed due to physical or human mishap.

Computer programs can be stored on a variety of mediums, including floppy diskettes, hard disks, non-erasable read only memory ("ROM") chips, and a computer's random access memory, and may appear only as printed instructions on a sheet of paper. Vault contends that the archival exception was designed to permit *only* the copying of programs which are subject to "destruction or damage by *mechanical or electrical failure.*" CONTU Report at 31 (emphasis added). While programs stored on all mediums may be subject to damage due to physical abuse or human error, programs stored on certain mediums are not subject to damage by mechanical or electrical failure. Therefore, Vault argues, the medium of storage determines whether the archival exception applies, thus providing only owners of programs, placed on mediums of storage which subject them to damage by mechanical or electrical failure, the right to make back-up copies. To support its construction of § 117(2), Vault notes that one court has held that the archival exception does not apply to the copying of programs stored on ROM chips where there was no evidence that programs stored on this medium were subject to damage by mechanical or electrical failure, *Atari*[, *Inc. v. JS & A Group, Inc.*, 597 F. Supp. 5, 9–10 (N.D.Ill.1983)], and another court has likewise held that the archival exception does not apply to the copying of programs which appear only in the form of printed instructions in a magazine, *Micro-Sparc, Inc. v. Amtype Corp.*, 592 F. Supp. 33, 35–36 (D.Mass.1984).

Vault contends that the district court's finding that programs stored on floppy diskettes are subject to damage by mechanical or electrical failure is erroneous because there was insufficient evidence presented at trial to support it, and, based on this contention, Vault asserts that the archival exception does not apply to permit the unauthorized copying of these programs. Vault performed a trial demonstration to prove that even if a program on an original PROLOK diskette, and Vault's protective program, were completely erased from this diskette, these programs could be restored on the original diskette using a copy made without RAMKEY. Therefore, Vault argues that even if a program recorded on a PROLOK diskette is subject to damage by mechanical or electrical failure, the non-operational copy of a PROLOK protected program made without RAMKEY is sufficient to protect against this type of damage. Vault concludes that, in light of the fact that RAMKEY facilitates the making of unauthorized copies and owners of PROLOK protected programs can make copies to protect against damage by mechanical and electrical failure without RAMKEY, the RAMKEY feature is not capable of substantial noninfringing uses.

*** We read the stated causes of damage [in CONTU] to be illustrative only, and not exclusive. Similarly, the statement follows with the prohibited use of the archival copies which does not include a prohibition against copying for purposes other than to protect against "mechanical or electrical failure." The Report, or Congress, could have easily limited the scope of § 117(2) to authorize the making of archival copies of programs subject to damage, and to guard against, only mechanical or electrical failure. CONTU did not recommend that language, nor did Congress enact it. Congress, following CONTU's advice, provided that an owner of a computer program may make a copy of that program provided that "such new copy . . . is for archival purposes only." 17 U.S.C. § 117(2). Congress did not choose to spell out detailed restrictions on the copying as was done in sections 108 and 112. Congress imposed no restriction upon the purpose or reason of the owner in making the archival copy; only the use made of that copy is restricted. *See* CONTU Report at 31 ("one could not, for example, make archival copies of a program and later sell some to another while retaining some for use"). An owner of a program is entitled, under § 117(2), to make an archival copy of that program in order to guard against all types of risks, including physical and human mishap as well as mechanical and electrical failure.

A copy of a PROLOK protected program made with RAMKEY protects an owner from all types of damage to the original program, while a copy made without RAMKEY only serves the limited function of protecting against damage to the original program by mechanical and electrical failure. Because § 117(2) permits the making of fully functional archival copies, it follows that RAMKEY is capable of substantial noninfringing uses. Quaid's advertisement and sale of CopyWrite diskettes with the RAMKEY feature does not constitute contributory infringement.

* * *

NOTES

1. The enactment of the narrowed version of section 117 led to findings of infringement in cases where the defendant acted under authority of the lawful *possessor*, but not the *owner*, of a copy of the plaintiff's software. *See MAI Systems Corp. v. Peak Computer, Inc.*, 991 F.2d 511, 519 n.5 (9th Cir. 1993) (computer service company infringed when it loaded MAI software into RAM for servicing purposes, where customer was licensee rather than owner of the copy of the software); *accord Triad Systems Corp. v. Southeastern Express Co.*, 64 F.3d 1330 (9th Cir. 1995) (following *MAI*, and rejecting fair use defense); *Advanced Computer Services of Michigan, Inc. v. MAI Systems Corp.*, 845 F.Supp. 356 (E.D. Va. 1994) (similar).

Title III of the DMCA, titled the "Computer Maintenance Competition Assurance Act," amended 17 U.S.C. § 117 to permit an authorized computer repair service to utilize copyrighted software in a computer during servicing. To what extent, if any, does this overrule the *MAI Systems* line of cases?

2. Consider the following scenarios:

(a) Defendant manufactures and sells kits which can be assembled into computers. Plaintiff is a manufacturer of computers and software. Defendant purchases authorized copies of two of the plaintiff's most valuable programs. Defendant then copies these programs, without the plaintiff's consent, onto silicon chips which are included with the computer kits and which enable the computers, when assembled, to utilize the plaintiff's other software. Is the defendant's copying authorized by section 117?

(b) Plaintiff manufactures and sells video games. The game cartridges store the videogame programs in ROM ("read only memory"), a form of memory that can neither be reprogrammed nor erased. However, they could be mechanically destroyed—e.g., by crushing or liquid spillage. Defendant manufactures and sells a device which enables users to copy plaintiff's games. Defendant may be held contributorily liable (*see* Chapter 18.C.2., *infra*) for copyright infringement only if the users' copying infringes the plaintiff's copyright in its games. Does section 117 help the defendant?

3. Suppose a person purchases software for use in a business, but finds it necessary to modify the software to suit the particular characteristics of that business. If this is done without the copyright owner's permission, is this an infringing derivative work? When the business is sold, is the copyright owner's permission required to include the modified software in the sale?

4. As interpreted in *Vault v. Quaid*, does section 117 encourage circumvention of copy protection technology? In 1998, Congress attempted to discourage such activities in the Digital Millenium Copyright Act, as discussed in Chapter 18, *infra*.

2. SECTION 109: THE FIRST SALE RULE

Statutes: 17 U.S.C. §§ 109, 117, 602

a. Sale or License?

VERNOR V. AUTODESK, INC.

621 F.3d 1102 (9th Cir. 2010).

CALLAHAN, CIRCUIT JUDGE:

Timothy Vernor purchased several used copies of Autodesk, Inc.'s AutoCAD Release 14 software from one of Autodesk's direct customers, and he resold the Release 14 copies on eBay. Vernor brought this declaratory judgment action against Autodesk to establish that these resales did not infringe Autodesk's copyright. The district court issued the requested declaratory judgment, holding that Vernor's sales were lawful because of two of the Copyright Act's affirmative defenses that apply to owners of copies of copyrighted works, the first sale doctrine and the essential step defense.

Autodesk distributes Release 14 pursuant to a limited license agreement in which it reserves title to the software copies and imposes significant use and transfer restrictions on its customers. We determine that Autodesk's direct customers are licensees of their copies of the software rather than owners, which has two ramifications. Because Vernor did not purchase the Release 14 copies from an owner, he may not invoke the first sale doctrine, and he also may not assert an essential step defense on behalf of his customers. For these reasons, we vacate the district court's grant of summary judgment to Vernor and remand for further proceedings.

I.

A. Autodesk's Release 14 software and licensing practices

* * *

Since at least 1986, Autodesk has offered AutoCAD to customers pursuant to an accompanying software license agreement ("SLA"), which customers must accept before installing the software. A customer who does not accept the SLA can return the software for a full refund. Autodesk offers SLAs with different terms for commercial, educational institution, and student users. The commercial license, which is the most expensive, imposes the fewest restrictions on users and allows them software upgrades at discounted prices.

The SLA for Release 14 first recites that Autodesk retains title to all copies. Second, it states that the customer has a nonexclusive and nontransferable license to use Release 14. Third, it imposes transfer restrictions, prohibiting customers from renting, leasing, or transferring the software without Autodesk's prior consent and from electronically or physically transferring the software out of the Western Hemisphere. Fourth, it imposes significant use restrictions:

> YOU MAY NOT: (1) modify, translate, reverse-engineer, decompile, or disassemble the Software . . . (3) remove any proprietary notices, labels, or marks from the Software or Documentation; (4) use . . . the Software outside of the Western Hemisphere; (5) utilize any computer software or hardware designed to defeat any hardware copy-protection device, should the software you have licensed be equipped with such protection; or (6) use the Software for commercial or other revenue-generating purposes if the Software has been licensed or labeled for educational use only.

Fifth, the SLA provides for license termination if the user copies the software without authorization or does not comply with the SLA's restrictions. Finally, the SLA provides that if the software is an upgrade of a previous version [then the customer must destroy its copies of the previous version.]

Autodesk takes measures to enforce these license requirements. It assigns a serial number to each copy of AutoCAD and tracks registered licensees. It requires customers to input "activation codes" within one month after installation to continue using the software. * * *

B. Autodesk's provision of Release 14 software to CTA

[Autodesk customer CTA acquired Release 14 and agreed to the terms of the SLA. However, when it later upgraded to Release 15, CTA did not destroy its copies of Release 14 as the SLA required, but sold them to

Vernor along with the activation codes. Vernor acquired an additional copy from another source. While Vernor was aware of the SLA's existence, he never agreed to its terms. Vernor offered his copies for sale on eBay. When Autodesk alleged that these sales were infringing, Vernor sought and obtained a declaratory judgment of non-infringement. Autodesk appealed.]

III.

Copyright is a federal law protection provided to the authors of "original works of authorship," including software programs. 17 U.S.C. §§ 101–103. The Copyright Act confers several exclusive rights on copyright owners, including the exclusive rights to reproduce their works and to distribute their works by sale or rental. *Id.* § 106(1), (3). The exclusive distribution right is limited by the first sale doctrine, an affirmative defense to copyright infringement that allows owners of copies of copyrighted works to resell those copies. The exclusive reproduction right is limited within the software context by the essential step defense, another affirmative defense to copyright infringement that is discussed further *infra.* Both of these affirmative defenses are unavailable to those who are only licensed to use their copies of copyrighted works.

This case requires us to decide whether Autodesk sold Release 14 copies to its customers or licensed the copies to its customers. If CTA owned its copies of Release 14, then both its sales to Vernor and Vernor's subsequent sales were non-infringing under the first sale doctrine.[6] However, if Autodesk only licensed CTA to use copies of Release 14, then CTA's and Vernor's sales of those copies are not protected by the first sale doctrine and would therefore infringe Autodesk's exclusive distribution right.

A. The first sale doctrine

The Supreme Court articulated the first sale doctrine in 1908, holding that a copyright owner's exclusive distribution right is exhausted after the owner's first sale of a particular copy of the copyrighted work. *See Bobbs-Merrill Co. v. Straus,* 210 U.S. 339, 350–51 (1908). In *Bobbs-Merrill,* the plaintiff-copyright owner sold its book with a printed notice announcing that any retailer who sold the book for less than one dollar was responsible for copyright infringement. Plaintiff sought injunctive relief against defendants-booksellers who failed to comply with the price restriction. The Supreme Court rejected the plaintiff's claim, holding that its exclusive distribution right applied only to first sales of copies of the work. The distribution right did not permit plaintiff to dictate that subsequent sales of the work below a particular price were infringing. The Court noted that its decision solely applied to the rights of a copyright owner that distributed

[6] If Autodesk's transfer of Release 14 copies to CTA was a first sale, then CTA's resale of the software in violation of the SLA's terms would be a breach of contract, but would not result in copyright liability.

its work without a license agreement. *Id.* at 350 ("There is no claim in this case of contract limitation, nor license agreement controlling the subsequent sales of the book.").

Congress codified the first sale doctrine the following year. *See* 17 U.S.C. § 41 (1909). In its current form, it allows the "owner of a particular copy" of a copyrighted work to sell or dispose of his copy without the copyright owner's authorization. *Id.* § 109(a) (enacted 1976). The first sale doctrine does not apply to a person who possesses a copy of the copyrighted work without owning it, such as a licensee. *See id.* § 109(d); *cf. Quality King Distribs., Inc. v. L'anza Research Int'l Inc.,* 523 U.S. 135, 146–47 (1998) ("[T]he first sale doctrine would not provide a defense to . . . any non-owner such as a bailee, a licensee, a consignee, or one whose possession of the copy was unlawful.").

B. Owners vs. licensees

We turn to our precedents governing whether a transferee of a copy of a copyrighted work is an owner or licensee of that copy. We then apply those precedents to CTA's and Vernor's possession of Release 14 copies.

1. United States v. Wise, 550 F.2d 1180 (9th Cir.1977)

In *Wise,* a criminal copyright infringement case, we considered whether copyright owners who transferred copies of their motion pictures pursuant to written distribution agreements had executed first sales. The defendant was found guilty of copyright infringement based on his for-profit sales of motion picture prints. The copyright owners distributed their films to third parties pursuant to written agreements that restricted their use and transfer. On appeal, the defendant argued that the government failed to prove the absence of a first sale for each film. If the copyright owners' initial transfers of the films were first sales, then the defendant's resales were protected by the first sale doctrine and thus were not copyright infringement.

To determine whether a first sale occurred, we considered multiple factors pertaining to each film distribution agreement. Specifically, we considered whether the agreement (a) was labeled a license, (b) provided that the copyright owner retained title to the prints, (c) required the return or destruction of the prints, (d) forbade duplication of prints, or (e) required the transferee to maintain possession of the prints for the agreement's duration. * * *

2. *The "MAI trio" of cases*

Over fifteen years after *Wise,* we again considered the distinction between owners and licensees of copies of copyrighted works in three software copyright cases, the "*MAI* trio". *See MAI Sys. Corp. v. Peak Computer, Inc.,* 991 F.2d 511 (9th Cir.1993); *Triad Sys. Corp. v. Se. Express Co.,* 64 F.3d 1330 (9th Cir.1995); *Wall Data, Inc. v. Los Angeles County*

Sheriff's Dep't, 447 F.3d 769 (9th Cir.2006). In the *MAI* trio, we considered which software purchasers were owners of copies of copyrighted works for purposes of a second affirmative defense to infringement, the essential step defense.

The enforcement of copyright owners' exclusive right to reproduce their work under the Copyright Act, 17 U.S.C. § 106(1), has posed special challenges in the software context. In order to use a software program, a user's computer will automatically copy the software into the computer's random access memory ("RAM"), which is a form of computer data storage. Congress enacted the essential step defense to codify that a software user who is the "owner of a copy" of a copyrighted software program does not infringe by making a copy of the computer program, if the new copy is "created as an essential step in the utilization of the computer program in conjunction with a machine and . . . is used in no other manner." 17 U.S.C. § 117(a)(1).

The Copyright Act provides that an "owner of a copy" of copyrighted software may claim the essential step defense, and the "owner of a particular copy" of copyrighted software may claim the first sale doctrine. 17 U.S.C. §§ 109(a), 117(a)(1). The *MAI* trio construed the phrase "owner of a copy" for essential step defense purposes. Neither Vernor nor Autodesk contends that the first sale doctrine's inclusion of the word "particular" alters the phrase's meaning, and we "presume that words used more than once in the same statute have the same meaning throughout." *Moldo v. Matsco, Inc. (In re Cybernetic Servs., Inc.),* 252 F.3d 1039, 1051 (9th Cir.2001). Accordingly, we consider the *MAI* trio's construction of "owner of a copy" controlling in our analysis of whether CTA and Vernor became "owner[s] of a particular copy" of Release 14 software.

In *MAI* and *Triad,* the defendants maintained computers that ran the plaintiffs' operating system software. When the defendants ran the computers, the computers automatically loaded plaintiffs' software into RAM. The plaintiffs in both cases sold their software pursuant to restrictive license agreements, and we held that their customers were licensees who were therefore not entitled to claim the essential step defense. We found that the defendants infringed plaintiffs' software copyrights by their unauthorized loading of copyrighted software into RAM. In *Triad,* the plaintiff had earlier sold software outright to some customers. We noted that these customers were owners who were entitled to the essential step defense, and the defendant did not infringe by making RAM copies in servicing their computers.

In *Wall Data,* plaintiff sold 3,663 software licenses to the defendant. The licenses (1) were non-exclusive; (2) permitted use of the software on a single computer; and (3) permitted transfer of the software once per month, if the software was removed from the original computer. The defendant installed the software onto 6,007 computers via hard drive imaging, which saved it from installing the software manually on each computer. It made an unverified claim that only 3,663 users could simultaneously access the software.

The plaintiff sued for copyright infringement, contending that the defendant violated the license by "over-installing" the software. The defendant raised an essential step defense, contending that its hard drive imaging was a necessary step of installation. * * * Citing *MAI*, we held that the essential step defense does not apply where the copyright owner grants the user a license and significantly restricts the user's ability to transfer the software. Since the plaintiff's license imposed "significant restrictions" on the defendant's software rights, the defendant was a licensee and was not entitled to the essential step defense.

* * *

We read *Wise* and the *MAI* trio to prescribe three considerations that we may use to determine whether a software user is a licensee, rather than an owner of a copy. First, we consider whether the copyright owner specifies that a user is granted a license. Second, we consider whether the copyright owner significantly restricts the user's ability to transfer the software. Finally, we consider whether the copyright owner imposes notable use restrictions. Our holding reconciles the *MAI* trio and *Wise*, even though the *MAI* trio did not cite *Wise*.

* * *

IV.

* * *

A. Analysis

We hold today that a software user is a licensee rather than an owner of a copy where the copyright owner (1) specifies that the user is granted a license; (2) significantly restricts the user's ability to transfer the software; and (3) imposes notable use restrictions. Applying our holding to Autodesk's SLA, we conclude that CTA was a licensee rather than an owner of copies of Release 14 and thus was not entitled to invoke the first sale doctrine or the essential step defense.

Autodesk retained title to the software and imposed significant transfer restrictions: it stated that the license is nontransferable, the software could not be transferred or leased without Autodesk's written consent, and the software could not be transferred outside the Western Hemisphere. The SLA also imposed use restrictions against the use of the software outside the Western Hemisphere and against modifying, translating, or reverse-engineering the software, removing any proprietary marks from the software or documentation, or defeating any copy protection device. Furthermore, the SLA provided for termination of the license upon the licensee's unauthorized copying or failure to comply with other license restrictions. Thus, because Autodesk reserved title to Release 14 copies and imposed significant transfer and use restrictions, we conclude that its customers are licensees of their copies of Release 14 rather than owners.

CTA was a licensee rather than an "owner of a particular copy" of Release 14, and it was not entitled to resell its Release 14 copies to Vernor under the first sale doctrine. 17 U.S.C. § 109(a). Therefore, Vernor did not receive title to the copies from CTA and accordingly could not pass ownership on to others. Both CTA's and Vernor's sales infringed Autodesk's exclusive right to distribute copies of its work. *Id.* § 106(3).

Because Vernor was not an owner, his customers are also not owners of Release 14 copies. Therefore, when they install Release 14 on their computers, the copies of the software that they make during installation infringe Autodesk's exclusive reproduction right because they too are not entitled to the benefit of the essential step defense.[13] 17 U.S.C. §§ 106(1), 117(a)(1).

Although unnecessary to our resolution of the case, we address the legislative history in order to address the arguments raised by the parties and amici. That legislative history supports our conclusion that licensees such as CTA are not entitled to claim the first sale doctrine. The House Report for § 109 underscores Congress' view that the first sale doctrine is available only to a person who has acquired a copy via an "outright sale". H.R.Rep. No. 94–1476, at 79 (1976). The report also asserts that the first sale doctrine does not "apply to someone who merely possesses a copy or phonorecord without having acquired ownership of it." *Id.*

Our conclusion that those who rightfully possess, but do not own, a copy of copyrighted software are not entitled to claim the essential step defense is also supported by the legislative history. Congress enacted § 117 following a report from the National Commission on New Technological Uses of Copyrighted Works ("CONTU") proposing Copyright Act amendments. CONTU's proposed version of § 117 was identical to the version that Congress enacted with one exception. CONTU's version provided, "[I]t is not an infringement for the rightful possessor of a copy of a computer program to make or authorize the making of another copy or adaptation of that program. . . ." *Id.* Without explanation, Congress substituted "owner" for "rightful possessor." This modification suggests

---

[13] It may seem intuitive that every lawful user of a copyrighted software program, whether they own their copies or are merely licensed to use them, should be entitled to an "essential step defense" that provides that they do not infringe simply by using a computer program that they lawfully acquired. However, the Copyright Act confers this defense only on owners of software copies. *See* 17 U.S.C. § 117. In contrast, a licensee's right to use the software, including the right to copy the software into RAM, is conferred by the terms of its license agreement.

that more than rightful possession is required for § 117 to apply—i.e., that Congress did not intend licensees subject to significant transfer and use restrictions to receive the benefit of the essential step defense.

* * *

V.

Although our holding today is controlled by our precedent, we recognize the significant policy considerations raised by the parties and amici on both sides of this appeal.

Autodesk, the Software & Information Industry Association ("SIIA"), and the Motion Picture Association of America ("MPAA") have presented policy arguments that favor our result. For instance, Autodesk argues in favor of judicial enforcement of software license agreements that restrict transfers of copies of the work. Autodesk contends that this (1) allows for tiered pricing for different software markets, such as reduced pricing for students or educational institutions; (2) increases software companies' sales; (3) lowers prices for all consumers by spreading costs among a large number of purchasers; and (4) reduces the incidence of piracy by allowing copyright owners to bring infringement actions against unauthorized resellers. SIIA argues that a license can exist even where a customer (1) receives his copy of the work after making a single payment and (2) can indefinitely possess a software copy, because it is the software code and associated rights that are valuable rather than the inexpensive discs on which the code may be stored. Also, the MPAA argues that a customer's ability to possess a copyrighted work indefinitely should not compel a finding of a first sale, because there is often no practically feasible way for a consumer to return a copy to the copyright owner.

Vernor, eBay, and the American Library Association ("ALA") have presented policy arguments against our decision. Vernor contends that our decision (1) does not vindicate the law's aversion to restraints on alienation of personal property; (2) may force everyone purchasing copyrighted property to trace the chain of title to ensure that a first sale occurred; and (3) ignores the economic realities of the relevant transactions, in which the copyright owner permanently released software copies into the stream of commerce without expectation of return in exchange for upfront payment of the full software price. eBay contends that a broad view of the first sale doctrine is necessary to facilitate the creation of secondary markets for copyrighted works, which contributes to the public good by (1) giving consumers additional opportunities to purchase and sell copyrighted works, often at below-retail prices; (2) allowing consumers to obtain copies of works after a copyright owner has ceased distribution; and (3) allowing the proliferation of businesses.

The ALA contends that the first sale doctrine facilitates the availability of copyrighted works after their commercial lifespan, by *inter alia* enabling the existence of libraries, used bookstores, and hand-to-hand exchanges of copyrighted materials. The ALA further contends that judicial enforcement of software license agreements, which are often contracts of adhesion, could eliminate the software resale market, require used computer sellers to delete legitimate software prior to sale, and increase prices for consumers by reducing price competition for software vendors. It contends that Autodesk's position (1) undermines 17 U.S.C. § 109(b)(2), which permits non-profit libraries to lend software for non-commercial purposes, and (2) would hamper efforts by non-profits to collect and preserve out-of-print software. The ALA fears that the software industry's licensing practices could be adopted by other copyright owners, including book publishers, record labels, and movie studios.

These are serious contentions on both sides, but they do not alter our conclusion that our precedent from *Wise* through the *MAI* trio requires the result we reach. Congress is free, of course, to modify the first sale doctrine and the essential step defense if it deems these or other policy considerations to require a different approach.

* * *

NOTES

1. Software makers often use "shrinkwrap licenses" or "click-through licenses" when distributing copies of software to the public. Consider the following example, which is based on the license employed by the plaintiff in *Vault*:

> [MAKER] IS PROVIDING THE ENCLOSED MATERIALS TO YOU ON THE EXPRESS CONDITION THAT YOU ASSENT TO THIS SOFTWARE LICENSE. BY USING ANY OF THE ENCLOSED DISKETTE(S), YOU AGREE TO THE FOLLOWING PROVISIONS. IF YOU DO NOT AGREE WITH THESE LICENSE PROVISIONS, RETURN THESE MATERIALS TO YOUR DEALER, IN ORIGINAL PACKAGING WITHIN 3 DAYS FROM RECEIPT, FOR A REFUND.
>
> This copy of the [MAKER'S] Software Protection System and this [MAKER'S] Software Protection Diskette (the "Licensed Software") are licensed to you, the end-user, for your own internal use. Title to the Licensed Software and all copyrights and proprietary rights in the Licensed Software shall remain with [MAKER]. You may not transfer, sublicense, rent, lease, convey, copy, modify, translate, convert to another programming language, decompile or disassemble the Licensed Software for any purpose without [MAKER's] prior written consent.

How are the rights of the software user affected by this language?

2. Could similar licenses be enforced against purchasers of other copyrightable works, such as books or DVDs?

3. Suppose that a record company sends radio stations promotional CDs bearing a label which states that the CD is "the property of the record company and is licensed to the intended recipient for personal use only," and which prohibits resale or transfer of possession. If a person finds and purchases these CDs at a flea market, is he or she free to resell them? *See UMG Recordings, Inc. v. Augusto*, 628 F.3d 1175 (9th Cir. 2011).

b. Imported Copies

KIRTSAENG V. JOHN WILEY & SONS, INC.

568 U.S. 519, 133 S.Ct. 1351 (2013).

JUSTICE BREYER delivered the opinion of the Court.

Section 106 of the Copyright Act grants "the owner of copyright under this title" certain "exclusive rights," including the right "to distribute copies . . . of the copyrighted work to the public by sale or other transfer of ownership." 17 U.S.C. § 106(3). These rights are qualified, however, by the application of various limitations set forth in the next several sections of the Act, §§ 107 through 122. Those sections, typically entitled "Limitations on exclusive rights," include, for example, the principle of "fair use" (§ 107), permission for limited library archival reproduction (§ 108), and the doctrine at issue here, the "first sale" doctrine (§ 109).

Section 109(a) sets forth the "first sale" doctrine as follows:

> "Notwithstanding the provisions of section 106(3) [the section that grants the owner exclusive distribution rights], the owner of a particular copy or phonorecord *lawfully made under this title* . . . is entitled, without the authority of the copyright owner, to sell or otherwise dispose of the possession of that copy or phonorecord."

(Emphasis added.)

Thus, even though § 106(3) forbids distribution of a copy of, say, the copyrighted novel Herzog without the copyright owner's permission, § 109(a) adds that, once a copy of Herzog has been lawfully sold (or its ownership otherwise lawfully transferred), the buyer of that copy and subsequent owners are free to dispose of it as they wish. In copyright jargon, the "first sale" has "exhausted" the copyright owner's § 106(3) exclusive distribution right.

What, however, if the copy of Herzog was printed abroad and then initially sold with the copyright owner's permission? Does the "first sale" doctrine still apply? Is the buyer, like the buyer of a domestically manufactured copy, free to bring the copy into the United States and dispose of it as he or she wishes?

To put the matter technically, an "importation" provision, § 602(a)(1), says that

> "[i]mportation into the United States, without the authority of the owner of copyright under this title, of copies . . . of a work that have been acquired outside the United States is an infringement of the exclusive right to distribute copies . . . *under section 106* . . . ."

17 U.S.C. § 602(a)(1) (emphasis added).

Thus § 602(a)(1) makes clear that importing a copy without permission violates the owner's exclusive distribution right. But in doing so, § 602(a)(1) refers explicitly to the § 106(3) exclusive distribution right. As we have just said, § 106 is by its terms "[s]ubject to" the various doctrines and principles contained in §§ 107 through 122, including § 109(a)'s "first sale" limitation. Do those same modifications apply—in particular, does the "first sale" modification apply—when considering whether § 602(a)(1) prohibits importing a copy?

In *Quality King Distributors, Inc. v. L'anza Research Int'l, Inc.*, 523 U.S. 135, 145 (1998), we held that § 602(a)(1)'s reference to § 106(3)'s exclusive distribution right incorporates the later subsections' limitations, including, in particular, the "first sale" doctrine of § 109. Thus, it might seem that, § 602(a)(1) notwithstanding, one who buys a copy abroad can freely import that copy into the United States and dispose of it, just as he could had he bought the copy in the United States.

But *Quality King* considered an instance in which the copy, though purchased abroad, was initially manufactured in the United States (and then sent abroad and sold). This case is like *Quality King* but for one important fact. The copies at issue here were manufactured abroad. That fact is important because § 109(a) says that the "first sale" doctrine applies to "a particular copy or phonorecord lawfully made under this title." And we must decide here whether the five words, "lawfully made under this title," make a critical legal difference.

Putting section numbers to the side, we ask whether the "first sale" doctrine applies to protect a buyer or other lawful owner of a copy (of a copyrighted work) lawfully manufactured abroad. Can that buyer bring that copy into the United States (and sell it or give it away) without obtaining permission to do so from the copyright owner? Can, for example, someone who purchases, say at a used bookstore, a book printed abroad subsequently resell it without the copyright owner's permission?

In our view, the answers to these questions are, yes. We hold that the "first sale" doctrine applies to copies of a copyrighted work lawfully made abroad.

I

A

* * *

* * * [T]here are two essentially equivalent versions of a Wiley textbook, each version manufactured and sold with Wiley's permission: (1) an American version printed and sold in the United States, and (2) a foreign version manufactured and sold abroad. And Wiley makes certain that copies of the second version state that they are not to be taken (without permission) into the United States.

Petitioner, Supap Kirtsaeng, a citizen of Thailand, moved to the United States in 1997 to study mathematics at Cornell University. He paid for his education with the help of a Thai Government scholarship which required him to teach in Thailand for 10 years on his return. Kirtsaeng successfully completed his undergraduate courses at Cornell, successfully completed a Ph.D. program in mathematics at the University of Southern California, and then, as promised, returned to Thailand to teach. While he was studying in the United States, Kirtsaeng asked his friends and family in Thailand to buy copies of foreign edition English-language textbooks at Thai book shops, where they sold at low prices, and mail them to him in the United States. Kirtsaeng would then sell them, reimburse his family and friends, and keep the profit.

B

In 2008 Wiley brought this federal lawsuit against Kirtsaeng for copyright infringement. Wiley claimed that Kirtsaeng's unauthorized importation of its books and his later resale of those books amounted to an infringement of Wiley's § 106(3) exclusive right to distribute as well as § 602's related import prohibition. Kirtsaeng replied that the books he had acquired were " 'lawfully made' " and that he had acquired them legitimately. Thus, in his view, § 109(a)'s "first sale" doctrine permitted him to resell or otherwise dispose of the books without the copyright owner's further permission.

* * *

II

We must decide whether the words "lawfully made under this title" restrict the scope of § 109(a)'s "first sale" doctrine geographically. The Second Circuit, the Ninth Circuit, Wiley, and the Solicitor General (as amicus) all read those words as imposing a form of geographical limitation. The Second Circuit held that they limit the "first sale" doctrine to particular copies "made in territories in which the Copyright Act is law," which (the Circuit says) are copies "manufactured domestically," not "outside of the United States." * * * And the Ninth Circuit has held that those words limit the "first sale" doctrine's applicability (1) to copies lawfully made in the United States, and (2) to copies lawfully made outside the United States but initially sold in the United States with the copyright owner's permission. *Denbicare U.S.A. Inc. v. Toys "R" Us, Inc.*, 84 F.3d 1143, 1149–1150 (1996).

Under any of these geographical interpretations, § 109(a)'s "first sale" doctrine would not apply to the Wiley Asia books at issue here. And, despite an American copyright owner's permission to make copies abroad, one who buys a copy of any such book or other copyrighted work—whether at a retail store, over the Internet, or at a library sale—could not resell (or otherwise dispose of) that particular copy without further permission.

Kirtsaeng, however, reads the words "lawfully made under this title" as imposing a non-geographical limitation. He says that they mean made "in accordance with" or "in compliance with" the Copyright Act. In that case, § 109(a)'s "first sale" doctrine would apply to copyrighted works as long as their manufacture met the requirements of American copyright law. In particular, the doctrine would apply where, as here, copies are manufactured abroad with the permission of the copyright owner.

In our view, § 109(a)'s language, its context, and the common-law history of the "first sale" doctrine, taken together, favor a non-geographical interpretation. We also doubt that Congress would have intended to create the practical copyright-related harms with which a geographical interpretation would threaten ordinary scholarly, artistic, commercial, and consumer activities. We consequently conclude that Kirtsaeng's nongeographical reading is the better reading of the Act.

A

The language of § 109(a) read literally favors Kirtsaeng's nongeographical interpretation, namely, that "lawfully made under this title" means made "in accordance with" or "in compliance with" the Copyright Act. The language of § 109(a) says nothing about geography. The word "under" can mean "[i]n accordance with." 18 OXFORD ENGLISH DICTIONARY 950 (2d ed.1989). And a nongeographical interpretation provides each word of the five-word phrase with a distinct purpose. The first two words of the phrase, "lawfully made," suggest an effort to distinguish those copies that were made lawfully from those that were not, and the last three words, "under this title," set forth the standard of "lawful[ness]." Thus, the nongeographical reading is simple, it promotes a traditional copyright objective (combatting piracy), and it makes word-by-word linguistic sense.

The geographical interpretation, however, bristles with linguistic difficulties. It gives the word "lawfully" little, if any, linguistic work to do. (How could a book be unlawfully "made under this title"?) It imports geography into a statutory provision that says nothing explicitly about it. And it is far more complex than may at first appear.

To read the clause geographically, Wiley, like the Second Circuit and the Solicitor General, must first emphasize the word "under." Indeed, Wiley reads "under this title" to mean "in conformance with the Copyright Act where the Copyright Act is applicable." Wiley must then take a second step, arguing that the Act "is applicable" only in the United States. And the Solicitor General must do the same.

One difficulty is that neither "under" nor any other word in the phrase means "where." *See, e.g.*, 18 OXFORD ENGLISH DICTIONARY, *supra*, at 947–952 (definition of "under"). It might mean "subject to," but as this Court has repeatedly acknowledged, the word evades a uniform, consistent meaning.

A far more serious difficulty arises out of the uncertainty and complexity surrounding the second step's effort to read the necessary geographical limitation into the word "applicable" (or the equivalent). Where, precisely, is the Copyright Act "applicable"? The Act does not instantly protect an American copyright holder from unauthorized piracy taking place abroad. But that fact does not mean the Act is inapplicable to copies made abroad. * * *

The appropriateness of this linguistic usage is underscored by the fact that § 104 of the Act itself says that works "subject to protection under this title" include unpublished works "without regard to the nationality or domicile of the author," and works "first published" in any one of the nearly 180 nations that have signed a copyright treaty with the United States. Thus, ordinary English permits us to say that the Act "applies" to an Irish manuscript lying in its author's Dublin desk drawer as well as to an original recording of a ballet performance first made in Japan and now on display in a Kyoto art gallery.

The Ninth Circuit's geographical interpretation produces still greater linguistic difficulty. As we said, that Circuit interprets the "first sale" doctrine to cover both (1) copies manufactured in the United States and (2) copies manufactured abroad but first sold in the United States with the American copyright owner's permission. *Denbicare U.S.A.*, 84 F.3d, at 1149–1150.

We can understand why the Ninth Circuit may have thought it necessary to add the second part of its definition. As we shall later describe, without some such qualification a copyright holder could prevent a buyer from domestically reselling or even giving away copies of a video game made in Japan, a film made in Germany, or a dress (with a design copyright) made in China, even if the copyright holder has granted permission for the foreign manufacture, importation, and an initial domestic sale of the copy. A publisher such as Wiley would be free to print its books abroad, allow their importation and sale within the United States, but prohibit students from later selling their used texts at a campus bookstore. We see no way, however, to reconcile this half-geographical/half-nongeographical interpretation with the language of the phrase, "lawfully made under this title." As a matter of English, it would seem that those five words either do cover copies lawfully made abroad or they do not.

In sum, we believe that geographical interpretations create more linguistic problems than they resolve. And considerations of simplicity and coherence tip the purely linguistic balance in Kirtsaeng's, nongeographical, favor.

B

Both historical and contemporary statutory context indicate that Congress, when writing the present version of § 109(a), did not have geography in mind. In respect to history, we compare § 109(a)'s present language with the language of its immediate predecessor. That predecessor said:

> "[N]othing in this Act shall be deemed to forbid, prevent, or restrict the transfer of any copy of a copyrighted work *the possession of which has been lawfully obtained.*"

Copyright Act of 1909, § 41, 35 Stat. 1084 (emphasis added). The predecessor says nothing about geography (and Wiley does not argue that it does). So we ask whether Congress, in changing its language implicitly *introduced* a geographical limitation that previously was lacking.

A comparison of language indicates that it did not. The predecessor says that the "first sale" doctrine protects "the transfer of any copy *the possession of which has been lawfully obtained.*" The present version says that "*the owner* of a particular copy or phonorecord lawfully made under this title is entitled to sell or otherwise dispose of the possession of that copy or phonorecord." What does this change in language accomplish?

The language of the former version referred to those who are not owners of a copy, but mere possessors who "lawfully obtained" a copy. The present version covers only those who are owners of a "lawfully made" copy. Whom does the change leave out? Who might have lawfully obtained a copy of a copyrighted work but not owned that copy? One answer is owners of movie theaters, who during the 1970's (and before) often *leased* films from movie distributors or filmmakers. Because the theater owners had "lawfully obtained" their copies, the earlier version could be read as allowing them to sell that copy, *i.e.*, it might have given them "first sale" protection. Because the theater owners were lessees, not owners, of their copies, the change in language makes clear that they (like bailees and other lessees) cannot take advantage of the "first sale" doctrine. * * *

This objective perfectly well explains the new language of the present version, including the five words here at issue. Section 109(a) now makes clear that a lessee of a copy will *not* receive "first sale" protection but one who *owns* a copy *will* receive "first sale" protection, *provided*, of course, that the copy was "*lawfully made*" and not pirated. The new language also takes into account that a copy may be "lawfully made under this title" when the copy, say of a phonorecord, comes into its owner's possession through use of a compulsory license, which "this title" provides for elsewhere, namely, in § 115. * * *

Other provisions of the present statute also support a nongeographical interpretation. For one thing, the statute phases out the "manufacturing clause," a clause that appeared in earlier statutes and had limited importation of many copies (of copyrighted works) printed outside the United States. § 601, 90 Stat. 2588 ("Prior to July 1, 1982 . . . the importation into or public distribution in the United States of copies of a work consisting preponderantly of nondramatic literary material . . . is prohibited unless the portions consisting of such material have been manufactured in the United States or Canada"). The phasing out of this clause sought to equalize treatment of copies manufactured in America and copies manufactured abroad.

The "equal treatment" principle, however, is difficult to square with a geographical interpretation of the "first sale" clause that would grant the holder of an American copyright (perhaps a foreign national) permanent control over the American distribution chain (sales, resales, gifts, and other distribution) in respect to copies printed abroad but not in respect to copies printed in America. And it is particularly difficult to believe that Congress would have sought this unequal treatment while saying nothing about it and while, in a related clause (the manufacturing phase-out), seeking the opposite kind of policy goal. * * *

Finally, we normally presume that the words "lawfully made under this title" carry the same meaning when they appear in different but related sections. But doing so here produces surprising consequences. Consider:

(1) Section 109(c) says that, despite the copyright owner's exclusive right "to display" a copyrighted work (provided in § 106(5)), the owner of a particular copy "lawfully made under this title" may publicly display it without further authorization. To interpret these words geographically would mean that one who buys a copyrighted work of art, a poster, or even a bumper sticker, in Canada, in Europe, in Asia, could not display it in America without the copyright owner's further authorization.

(2) Section 109(e) specifically provides that the owner of a particular copy of a copyrighted video arcade game "lawfully made

under this title" may "publicly perform or display that game in coin-operated equipment" without the authorization of the copyright owner. To interpret these words geographically means that an arcade owner could not ("without the authority of the copyright owner") perform or display arcade games (whether new or used) originally made in Japan.

(3) Section 110(1) says that a teacher, without the copyright owner's authorization, is allowed to perform or display a copyrighted work (say, an audiovisual work) "in the course of face-to-face teaching activities"—unless the teacher knowingly used "a copy that was not lawfully made under this title." To interpret these words geographically would mean that the teacher could not (without further authorization) use a copy of a film during class if the copy was lawfully made in Canada, Mexico, Europe, Africa, or Asia.

(4) In its introductory sentence, § 106 provides the Act's basic exclusive rights to an "owner of a copyright under this title." The last three words cannot support a geographic interpretation.

Wiley basically accepts the first three readings, but argues that Congress intended the restrictive consequences. And it argues that context simply requires that the words of the fourth example receive a different interpretation. Leaving the fourth example to the side, we shall explain in Part II-D why we find it unlikely that Congress would have intended these, and other related consequences.

C

A relevant canon of statutory interpretation favors a nongeographical reading. "[W]hen a statute covers an issue previously governed by the common law," we must presume that "Congress intended to retain the substance of the common law." *Samantar v. Yousuf*, 560 U.S. 305, 319 n. 13 (2010).

The "first sale" doctrine is a common-law doctrine with an impeccable historic pedigree. In the early 17th century Lord Coke explained the common law's refusal to permit restraints on the alienation of chattels. Referring to Littleton, who wrote in the 15th century, Lord Coke wrote:

> "[If] a man be possessed of . . . a horse, or of any other chattell . . . and give or sell his whole interest . . . therein upon condition that the Donee or Vendee shall not alien[ate] the same, the [condition] is voi[d], because his whole interest . . . is out of him, so as he hath no possibilit[y] of a Reverter, and it is against Trade and Traffi[c], and bargaining and contracting betwee[n] man and man: and it is within the reason of our Author that it should ouster him of all power given to him."

1 E. COKE, INSTITUTES OF THE LAWS OF ENGLAND § 360, p. 223 (1628).

A law that permits a copyright holder to control the resale or other disposition of a chattel once sold is similarly "against Trade and Traffi[c], and bargaining and contracting." *Id.*

With these last few words, Coke emphasizes the importance of leaving buyers of goods free to compete with each other when reselling or otherwise disposing of those goods. American law too has generally thought that competition, including freedom to resell, can work to the advantage of the consumer.

The "first sale" doctrine also frees courts from the administrative burden of trying to enforce restrictions upon difficult-to-trace, readily movable goods. And it avoids the selective enforcement inherent in any such effort. Thus, it is not surprising that for at least a century the "first sale" doctrine has played an important role in American copyright law. *See Bobbs-Merrill Co. v. Straus*, 210 U.S. 339 (1908); Copyright Act of 1909, § 41, 35 Stat. 1084.

The common-law doctrine makes no geographical distinctions; nor can we find any in *Bobbs-Merrill* (where this Court first applied the "first sale" doctrine) or in § 109(a)'s predecessor provision, which Congress enacted a year later. Rather, as the Solicitor General acknowledges, "a straightforward application of *Bobbs-Merrill*" would not preclude the "first sale" defense from applying to authorized copies made overseas. And we can find no language, context, purpose, or history that would rebut a "straightforward application" of that doctrine here.

* * *

D

Associations of libraries, used-book dealers, technology companies, consumer-goods retailers, and museums point to various ways in which a geographical interpretation would fail to further basic constitutional copyright objectives, in particular "promot[ing] the Progress of Science and useful Arts." U.S. CONST., ART. I, § 8, cl. 8.

The American Library Association tells us that library collections contain at least 200 million books published abroad (presumably, many were first published in one of the nearly 180 copyright-treaty nations and enjoy American copyright protection under 17 U.S.C. § 104; that many others were first published in the United States but printed abroad because of lower costs; and that a geographical interpretation will likely require the libraries to obtain permission (or at least create significant uncertainty) before circulating or otherwise distributing these books.

How, the American Library Association asks, are the libraries to obtain permission to distribute these millions of books? * * * Are the libraries to stop circulating or distributing or displaying the millions of books in their collections that were printed abroad?

Used-book dealers tell us that, from the time when Benjamin Franklin and Thomas Jefferson built commercial and personal libraries of foreign books, American readers have bought used books published and printed abroad. The dealers say that they have "operat[ed]. . . for centuries" under the assumption that the "first sale" doctrine applies. But under a geographical interpretation a contemporary tourist who buys, say, at Shakespeare and Co. (in Paris), a dozen copies of a foreign book for American friends might find that she had violated the copyright law. The used-book dealers cannot easily predict what the foreign copyright holder may think about a reader's effort to sell a used copy of a novel. And they believe that a geographical interpretation will injure a large portion of the used-book business.

Technology companies tell us that "automobiles, microwaves, calculators, mobile phones, tablets, and personal computers" contain copyrightable software programs or packaging. Many of these items are made abroad with the American copyright holder's permission and then sold and imported (with that permission) to the United States. A geographical interpretation would prevent the resale of, say, a car, without the permission of the holder of each copyright on each piece of copyrighted automobile software. Yet there is no reason to believe that foreign auto manufacturers regularly obtain this kind of permission from their software component suppliers, and Wiley did not indicate to the contrary when asked. Without that permission a foreign car owner could not sell his or her used car.

Retailers tell us that over $2.3 trillion worth of foreign goods were imported in 2011. American retailers buy many of these goods after a first sale abroad. And, many of these items bear, carry, or contain copyrighted "packaging, logos, labels, and product inserts and instructions for [the use of] everyday packaged goods from floor cleaners and health and beauty products to breakfast cereals." The retailers add that American sales of more traditional copyrighted works, "such as books, recorded music, motion pictures, and magazines" likely amount to over $220 billion. A geographical interpretation would subject many, if not all, of them to the disruptive impact of the threat of infringement suits.

Art museum directors ask us to consider their efforts to display foreign-produced works by, say, Cy Twombly, Rene Magritte, Henri Matisse, Pablo Picasso, and others. A geographical interpretation, they say, would require the museums to obtain permission from the copyright owners before they could display the work—even if the copyright owner has already sold or donated the work to a foreign museum. What are the museums to do, they ask, if the artist retained the copyright, if the artist cannot be found, or if a group of heirs is arguing about who owns which copyright?

* * *

Thus, we believe that the practical problems that petitioner and his amici have described are too serious, too extensive, and too likely to come about for us to dismiss them as insignificant—particularly in light of the ever-growing importance of foreign trade to America. The upshot is that copyright-related consequences along with language, context, and interpretive canons argue strongly against a geographical interpretation of § 109(a).

* * *

* * * Wiley and the dissent claim that a nongeographical interpretation will make it difficult, perhaps impossible, for publishers (and other copyright holders) to divide foreign and domestic markets. We concede that is so. A publisher may find it more difficult to charge different prices for the same book in different geographic markets. But we do not see how these facts help Wiley, for we can find no basic principle of copyright law that suggests that publishers are especially entitled to such rights.

* * *

To the contrary, Congress enacted a copyright law that (through the "first sale" doctrine) limits copyright holders' ability to divide domestic markets. And that limitation is consistent with antitrust laws that ordinarily forbid market divisions. Whether copyright owners should, or should not, have more than ordinary commercial power to divide international markets is a matter for Congress to decide. We do no more here than try to determine what decision Congress has taken.

* * *

For these reasons we conclude that the considerations supporting Kirtsaeng's nongeographical interpretation of the words "lawfully made under this title" are the more persuasive. The judgment of the Court of Appeals is reversed, and the case is remanded for further proceedings consistent with this opinion.

It is so ordered.

JUSTICE KAGAN, with whom JUSTICE ALITO joins, concurring.

I concur fully in the Court's opinion. Neither the text nor the history of 17 U.S.C. § 109(a) supports removing first-sale protection from every copy of a protected work manufactured abroad. I recognize, however, that the combination of today's decision and *Quality King Distributors, Inc. v. L'anza Research Int'l, Inc.*, 523 U.S. 135 (1998), constricts the scope of § 602(a)(1)'s ban on unauthorized importation. I write to suggest that any problems associated with that limitation come not from our reading of § 109(a) here, but from *Quality King*'s holding that § 109(a) limits § 602(a)(1). * * * In now holding that copies "lawfully made under this title" include copies manufactured abroad, we unavoidably diminish § 602(a)(1)'s scope—indeed, limit it to a fairly esoteric set of applications.

But if Congress views the shrinking of § 602(a)(1) as a problem, it should recognize *Quality King*—not our decision today—as the culprit. Here, after all, we merely construe § 109(a); *Quality King* is the decision holding that § 109(a) limits § 602(a)(1). Had we come out the opposite way in that case, § 602(a)(1) would allow a copyright owner to restrict the importation of copies irrespective of the first-sale doctrine.[1] That result would enable the copyright owner to divide international markets in the way John Wiley claims Congress intended when enacting § 602(a)(1). But it would do so without imposing downstream liability on those who purchase and resell in the United States copies that happen to have been manufactured abroad. In other words, that outcome would target unauthorized importers alone, and not the "libraries, used-book dealers, technology companies, consumer-goods retailers, and museums" with whom the Court today is rightly concerned. Assuming Congress adopted § 602(a)(1) to permit market segmentation, I suspect that is how Congress thought the provision would work—not by removing first-sale protection from every copy manufactured abroad (as John Wiley urges us to do here), but by enabling the copyright holder to control imports even when the first-sale doctrine applies (as *Quality King* now prevents).[2]

At bottom, John Wiley (together with the dissent) asks us to misconstrue § 109(a) in order to restore § 602(a)(1) to its purportedly rightful function of enabling copyright holders to segment international markets. I think John Wiley may have a point about what § 602(a)(1) was designed to do; that gives me pause about *Quality King*'s holding that the first-sale doctrine limits the importation ban's scope. But the Court today correctly declines the invitation to save § 602(a)(1) from *Quality King* by destroying the first-sale protection that § 109(a) gives to every owner of a copy manufactured abroad. That would swap one (possible) mistake for a much worse one, and make our reading of the statute only less reflective of Congressional intent. If Congress thinks copyright owners need greater power to restrict importation and thus divide markets, a ready solution is

---

[1] Although Quality King concluded that the statute's text foreclosed that outcome, the Solicitor General offered a cogent argument to the contrary. He reasoned that § 109(a) does not limit § 602(a)(1) because the former authorizes owners only to "sell or "dispose" of copies—not to import them: The Act's first-sale provision and its importation ban thus regulate separate, non-overlapping spheres of conduct. That reading remains the Government's preferred way of construing the statute.

[2] * * * I can see no reason why Congress would have conditioned a copyright owner's power to divide markets on outsourcing its manufacturing to a foreign country.

at hand—not the one John Wiley offers in this case, but the one the Court rejected in *Quality King*.

JUSTICE GINSBURG, with whom JUSTICE KENNEDY joins, and with whom JUSTICE SCALIA joins except as to Parts III and V-B-1, dissenting.

"In the interpretation of statutes, the function of the courts is easily stated. It is to construe the language so as to give effect to the intent of Congress." *United States v. American Trucking Assns., Inc.*, 310 U.S. 534, 542 (1940). Instead of adhering to the Legislature's design, the Court today adopts an interpretation of the Copyright Act at odds with Congress' aim to protect copyright owners against the unauthorized importation of low-priced, foreign-made copies of their copyrighted works. * * *

To justify a holding that shrinks to insignificance copyright protection against the unauthorized importation of foreign-made copies, the Court identifies several "practical problems." The Court's parade of horribles, however, is largely imaginary. Congress' objective in enacting 17 U.S.C. § 602(a)(1)'s importation prohibition can be honored without generating the absurd consequences hypothesized in the Court's opinion. I dissent from the Court's embrace of "international exhaustion," and would affirm the sound judgment of the Court of Appeals.

* * *

II

The text of the Copyright Act demonstrates that Congress intended to provide copyright owners with a potent remedy against the importation of foreign-made copies of their copyrighted works. As the Court recognizes this case turns on the meaning of the phrase "lawfully made under this title" in § 109(a). In my view, that phrase is most sensibly read as referring to instances in which a copy's creation is governed by, and conducted in compliance with, Title 17 of the U.S. Code. * * *

Section 109(a), properly read, affords Kirtsaeng no defense against Wiley's claim of copyright infringement. The Copyright Act, it has been observed time and again, does not apply extraterritorially. The printing of Wiley's foreign-manufactured textbooks therefore was not governed by Title 17. The textbooks thus were not "lawfully made under [Title 17]," the crucial precondition for application of § 109(a). And if § 109(a) does not apply, there is no dispute that Kirtsaeng's conduct constituted copyright infringement under § 602(a)(1).

The Court's point of departure is similar to mine. According to the Court, the phrase " 'lawfully made under this title' means made 'in accordance with' or 'in compliance with' the Copyright Act." But the Court overlooks that, according to the very dictionaries it cites, the word "under" commonly signals a relationship of subjection, where one thing is governed or regulated by another. *See* BLACK'S LAW DICTIONARY 1525 (6th ed.1990) ("under "frequently" means "inferior" or "subordinate" (internal quotation marks omitted)); 18 OXFORD ENGLISH DICTIONARY 950 (2d ed.1989) ("under" means, among other things, "[i]n accordance with (some regulative power or principle)" (emphasis added)). Only by disregarding this established meaning of "under" can the Court arrive at the conclusion that Wiley's foreign-manufactured textbooks were "lawfully made under" U.S. copyright law, even though that law did not govern their creation. * * *

* * *

III

The history of § 602(a)(1) reinforces the conclusion I draw from the text of the relevant provisions: § 109(a) does not apply to copies manufactured abroad.

* * *

The current text of § 602(a)(1) was finally enacted into law in 1976. The House and Senate Committee Reports on the 1976 Act demonstrate that Congress understood, as did the Copyright Office, just what that text meant. Both Reports state:

> "Section 602 [deals] with two separate situations: importation of 'piratical' articles (that is, copies or phonorecords made without any authorization of the copyright owner), and unauthorized importation of copies or phonorecords that were lawfully made. The general approach of section 602 is to make unauthorized importation an act of infringement in both cases, but to permit the Bureau of Customs to prohibit importation only of 'piratical' articles."

S. REP. NO. 94–473, p. 151 (1975).

In sum, the legislative history of the Copyright Act of 1976 is hardly "inconclusive." To the contrary, it confirms what the plain text of the Act conveys: Congress intended § 602(a)(1) to provide copyright owners with a remedy against the unauthorized importation of foreign-made copies of their works, even if those copies were made and sold abroad with the copyright owner's authorization.

* * *

V

I turn now to the Court's justifications for a decision difficult to reconcile with the Copyright Act's text and history.

* * *

B

The Court sees many "horribles" following from a holding that the § 109(a) phrase "lawfully made under this title" does not encompass foreign-made copies. If § 109(a) excluded foreign-made copies, the Court fears, then copyright owners could exercise perpetual control over the downstream distribution or public display of such copies. A ruling in Wiley's favor, the Court asserts, would shutter libraries, put used-book dealers out of business, cripple art museums, and prevent the resale of a wide range of consumer goods, from cars to calculators. Copyright law and precedent, however, erect barriers to the anticipated horribles.

1

* * *

Under the logic of *Bobbs-Merrill*, the sale of a foreign-manufactured copy in the United States carried out with the copyright owner's authorization would exhaust the copyright owner's right to "vend" that copy. The copy could thenceforth be resold, lent out, or otherwise redistributed without further authorization from the copyright owner. Although § 106(3) uses the word "distribute" rather than "vend," there is no reason to think Congress intended the word "distribute" to bear a meaning different from the construction the Court gave to the word "vend" in *Bobbs-Merrill*. Thus, in accord with *Bobbs-Merrill*, the first authorized distribution of a foreign-made copy in the United States exhausts the copyright owner's distribution right under § 106(3). After such an authorized distribution, a library may lend, or a used-book dealer may resell, the foreign-made copy without seeking the copyright owner's permission.

For example, if Wiley, rather than Kirtsaeng, had imported into the United States and then sold the foreign-made textbooks at issue in this case, Wiley's § 106(3) distribution right would have been exhausted under the rationale of *Bobbs-Merrill*. Purchasers of the textbooks would thus be free to dispose of the books as they wished without first gaining a license from Wiley.

* * *

2

Other statutory prescriptions provide further protection against the absurd consequences imagined by the Court. For example, § 602(a)(3)(C) permits "an organization operated for scholarly, educational, or religious purposes" to import, without the copyright owner's authorization, up to five foreign-made copies of a non-audiovisual work—notably, a book—for "library lending or archival purposes."

* * *

Limiting § 109(c) to U.S.-made works, however, does not bar art museums from lawfully displaying works made in other countries. Museums can, of course, seek the copyright owner's permission to display a work. Furthermore, the sale of a work of art to a U.S. museum may carry with it an implied license to publicly display the work. Displaying a work of art as part of a museum exhibition might also qualify as a "fair use" under 17 U.S.C. § 107.

The Court worries about the resale of foreign-made consumer goods "contain[ing] copyrightable software programs or packaging." For example, the Court observes that a car might be programmed with diverse forms of software, the copyrights to which might be owned by individuals or entities other than the manufacturer of the car. Must a car owner, the Court asks, obtain permission from all of these various copyright owners before reselling her car?

Although this question strays far from the one presented in this case and briefed by the parties, principles of fair use and implied license (to the extent that express licenses do not exist) would likely permit the car to be resold without the copyright owners' authorization.[25]

* * *

NOTES

1. If the first sale rule applies to copies that are lawfully made anywhere in the world, does this apply to copies made in countries where the work does not enjoy copyright protection? Where the copies are made under a compulsory license? Where the copies are made with the consent of the person who owns the copyright in the country where the copies were made, but not with the consent of the United States copyright owner?

2. In her dissent, Justice Ginsburg argues that, even if the first sale rule did not apply to all lawfully made foreign copies, copyright law would still prevent the "parade of horribles" envisioned in Part II.D. of the majority opinion. How persuasive is this argument? Can Congress grant copyright owners an exclusive importation right without triggering the parade of horribles? How would you draft such a provision?

3. Can copyright owners use contract law to prevent the importation of lawful copies intended only for foreign markets?

---

[25] Principles of fair use and implied license may also allow a U.S. tourist "who buys a copyrighted work of art, a poster, or . . . a bumper sticker" abroad to publicly "display it in America without the copyright owner's further authorization." (The tourist could lawfully bring the work of art, poster, or bumper sticker into the United States under 17 U.S.C. § 602(a)(3)(B), which provides that § 602(a)(1)'s importation ban does not apply to "importation . . . by any person arriving from outside the United States . . . with respect to copies . . . forming part of such person's personal baggage."). * * *

4. Does the first sale rule:

(a) allow the owner of a tangible copy of a work of authorship (*e.g.*, a handwritten manuscript, a film negative, a master sound recording, or an architectural work) to alter, mutilate or destroy that article? (Assume that section 106A, discussed *infra* at Chapter 16.C.2., does not apply to these works.)

(b) permit the owner of a copy of a copyrighted work to display that copy publicly in a museum? on television? on the internet?

(c) permit the owner of a motion picture DVD to publicly perform the DVD?

5. The first sale rule is subject to two important exceptions, applicable to phonorecords and computer software. The phonorecords exception was introduced in the Record Rental Amendment of 1984, Pub. L. 98–450, 98 Stat. 1727 (1984), and the software exception was added several years later by the Computer Software Rental Amendments Act of 1990, Pub. L. 101–650, tit. 8, sec. 802, 104 Stat. 5089, 5134–35 (1990). Those exceptions are codified in section 109(b). Why did Congress carve out exceptions only for commercial rentals of these categories of works, and why is there no comparable exception for motion picture DVDs? Are the current provisions consistent with Article 7 of the 1996 WIPO Copyright Treaty? Do they apply to commercial rental of books on tape/CD? *See Brilliance Audio, Inc. v. Haights Cross Communications, Inc.*, 474 F.3d 365 (6th Cir. 2007).

6. Suppose that a software retailer permits its customers to return software within one week even if the package has been opened, and provides full refunds minus a $5.00 handling fee. Is this activity infringing?

c. Digital First Sale

Does the first sale rule apply to digital copies? In *Capitol Records, LLC v. ReDigi Inc.*, 934 F. Supp. 2d 640 (S.D.N.Y. 2013), *aff'd*, 910 F.3d 649 (2d Cir. 2018), the district court held that the first sale rule did not apply to a service (version 1.0 of ReDigi) that enabled consumers to sell their digital music files without transferring a tangible object such as a CD. The first step in the transaction involved transferring the file to ReDigi's server. Once the file was sold, the buyer could stream or download the file from ReDigi's server, and the seller's access to it was terminated. Although the seller was required to delete any additional copies of the file still in his or her possession, ReDigi did not delete them automatically and could not ensure that the seller had deleted them. The district court held that the first sale rule did not apply, for two reasons: (1) the first sale rule is an exception only to the distribution right, and ReDigi's process involved a reproduction; and (2) the reproduction itself was unlawful, and the first sale rule applies only to "lawfully made" copies.

The Second Circuit affirmed, holding that "each transfer of a digital music file to ReDigi's server and each new purchaser's download of a digital music file to his device creates new phonorecords," *Capitol Records, LLC v. ReDigi, Inc.*, 910 F.3d 649, 657 (2d Cir. 2018), and that ReDigi's actions did not constitute fair use, *id.* at 660–63. The court rejected ReDigi's argument that this holding would eliminate the possibility of secondary markets for digital music files, by requiring owners to sell their computers or hard drives in order to sell their music files:

> A secondary market can readily be imagined for first purchasers who cost-effectively place 50 or 100 (or more) songs on an inexpensive device such as a thumb drive and sell it. *See* U.S. Copyright Office, Library of Cong., Digital Millennium Copyright Act § 104 Report 78 (2001) ("DMCA Report 2001") ("Physical copies of works in a digital format, such as CDs or DVDs, are subject to section 109 in the same way as physical copies of works in analog form."); 4 Patry on Copyright § 13:23 (observing that § 109 permits the sale of an iPod that contains lawfully made digital music files). Furthermore, other technology may exist or be developed that could lawfully effectuate a digital first sale.

Id. at 659. How persuasive is this reasoning? Will digital resale continue to be an important issue in copyright law, or will streaming services and the preference for licenses over sales make the topic obsolete?

3. THE SECTION 110 LIMITATIONS

Statute: 17 U.S.C. § 110

Section 110 exempts a variety of public performances and displays from the reach of section 106. In contrast to the 1909 Act, which treated nonprofit public performances as noninfringing, in section 106 the 1976 Act broadened the public performance right to include nonprofit performances. Section 110 preserves a number of narrowly defined nonprofit exemptions, as well as a few for-profit activities. One of these for-profit exemptions is the "homestyle exemption" of section 110(5).

COPYRIGHT ACT OF 1976

H.R. Rep. No. 94–1476.
94th Cong., 2d Sess. 62–63, 86–87 (1976).

* * *

Right of Public Performance and Display

Performing rights and the "for profit" limitation.—The right of public performance under section 106(4) extends to "literary, musical, dramatic, and choreographic works, pantomimes, and motion pictures and other audiovisual works and sound recordings" and, unlike the equivalent provisions now in effect, is not limited by any "for profit" requirement. The approach of the bill, as in many foreign laws, is first to state the public performance right in broad terms, and then to provide specific exemptions for educational and other nonprofit uses.

This approach is more reasonable than the outright exemption of the 1909 statute. The line between commercial and "nonprofit" organizations is increasingly difficult to draw. Many "non-profit" organizations are highly subsidized and capable of paying royalties, and the widespread public exploitation of copyrighted works by public broadcasters and other noncommercial organizations is likely to grow. In addition to these trends, it is worth noting that performances and displays are continuing to supplant markets for printed copies and that in the future a broad "not for profit" exemption could not only hurt authors but could dry up their incentive to write.

* * *

Mere reception in public

Unlike the first four clauses of section 110, clause (5) is not to any extent a counterpart of the "for profit" limitation of the present statute. It applies to performances and displays of all types of works, and its purpose is to exempt from copyright liability anyone who merely turns on, in a public place, an ordinary radio or television receiving apparatus of a kind commonly sold to members of the public for private use.

The basic rationale of this clause is that the secondary use of the transmission by turning on an ordinary receiver in public is so remote and minimal that no further liability should be imposed. In the vast majority of these cases no royalties are collected today, and the exemption should be made explicit in the statute. This clause has nothing to do with cable television systems and the exemptions would be denied in any case where the audience is charged directly to see or hear the transmission.

On June 17, 1975, the Supreme Court handed down a decision in *Twentieth Century Music Corp. v. Aiken*, 95 S.Ct. 2040, that raised fundamental questions about the proper interpretation of section 110(5). The defendant, owner and operator of a fast-service food shop in downtown Pittsburgh, had "a radio with outlets to four speakers in the ceiling," which he apparently turned on and left on throughout the business day. Lacking any performing license, he was sued for copyright infringement by two ASCAP members. He lost in the District Court, won a reversal in the Third Circuit Court of Appeals, and finally prevailed, by a margin of 7–2, in the Supreme Court.

* * *

Under the particular fact situation in the *Aiken* case, assuming a small commercial establishment and the use of a home receiver with four ordinary loudspeakers grouped within a relatively narrow circumference from the set, it is intended that the performances would be exempt from clause (5). However, the Committee considers this fact situation to represent the outer limit of the exemption, and believes that the line should be drawn at that point. Thus, the clause would exempt small commercial establishments whose proprietors merely bring onto their premises standard radio or television equipment and turn it on for their customers' enjoyment, but it would impose liability where the proprietor has a commercial "sound system" installed or converts a standard home receiving apparatus (by augmenting it with sophisticated or extensive amplification equipment) into the equivalent of a commercial sound system. Factors to consider in particular cases would include the size, physical arrangement, and noise level of the areas within the establishment where the transmissions are made audible or visible, and the extent to which the receiving apparatus is altered or augmented for the purpose of improving the aural or visual quality of the performance for individual members of the public using those areas.

* * *

NOTES

1. The Conference Report on section 110(5) added that "the intent of the conferees [is] that a small commercial establishment of the type involved in *Aiken*, which merely augmented a home-type receiver and which was not of sufficient size to justify, as a practical matter, a subscription to a commercial background music service, would be exempt." H.R. Rep. 1733, 94th Cong., 2d Sess. 75 (1976). Why should small businesses enjoy an exemption from the public performance rules?

2. In determining whether section 110(5) should apply to a particular establishment, courts had difficulty determining which factors to consider, and what relative weights to assign them. Factors that courts considered include: the revenues of the business, the square footage of the establishment, the nature of the receiving apparatus and the speaker system, whether the receiver and speakers are located in different rooms, and whether the business is independent or part of a chain. Representative appellate opinions include *Broadcast Music, Inc. v. Claire's Boutiques, Inc.*, 949 F.2d 1482 (7th Cir. 1991); *Broadcast Music, Inc. v. United States Shoe Corp.*, 678 F.2d 816 (9th Cir. 1982); and *Sailor Music v. Gap Stores, Inc.*, 668 F.2d 84 (2d Cir. 1981), *cert. denied*, 456 U.S. 945 (1982).

The difficulty in applying section 110(5) in its original form led to numerous amendment proposals. Some of these would have broadened the exemption to reach any situation in which music is merely "incidental" to the main purpose of the business, while others would simply have clarified the scope of the exemption—by specifying, for example, the maximum number of speakers permitted, the maximum square footage of the store, or the maximum level of annual revenues.

Title II of the CTEA, titled the "Fairness in Music Licensing Act of 1998," amended section 110(5) by redesignating the existing 110(5) exemption as section 110(5)(A), and adding a new section 110(5)(B) that provides safe harbors for certain establishments that communicate "a transmission embodying a performance or display of a nondramatic musical work intended to be received by the general public." New subsection (B) limits the safe harbor to transmissions that are originated by an FCC-licensed radio or television broadcast station, or, in the case of audiovisual transmissions, by a cable system or satellite carrier. To qualify for the safe harbor, the establishment must either (a) be smaller than 2,000 square feet (except for a food service or drinking establishment, which must be smaller than 3,750 square feet), or (b) use no more than six loudspeakers (with no more than four in one room) for the audio portion of any performances, and no more than four audiovisual devices (with screens no larger than fifty-five inches diagonal, and no more than one such device per room) for any visual component. The exemption does not apply at all if a direct charge is made to see or hear the transmission, if the establishment transmits the performance or display to any other location, or if the transmission was not authorized by the copyright owner of the work performed or displayed therein.

Title II also revised 17 U.S.C. § 504 to double the amount of damages a plaintiff can collect from a defendant that invokes section 110(5) without reasonable grounds for doing so, and broadened the section 110(7) exemption to include in-store public performances of nondramatic musical works for the purpose of selling audiovisual or other devices used for those performances.

Finally, Title II added section 513 to Title 17, providing certain small business owners with an alternative means to resolve their licensing fee disputes with ASCAP and BMI. Whereas the antitrust decree binding those organizations requires that such disputes be adjudicated in the federal district court for the Southern District of New York, the bill permits a small business owner to seek a reasonable license fee determination from a federal district court in the circuit where his or her establishment is located.

In the summer of 2000, a World Trade Organization (WTO) Dispute Panel ruled that the revised version of section 110(5)(B) violated Articles 9.1 and 13 of the TRIPS (Trade-Related Aspects of Intellectual Property Rights) provisions of the WTO Agreement, because it created too broad an exception to the public performance right in musical compositions. Because Congress did not repeal or amend section 110(5)(B) to bring it into compliance with TRIPS, the United States now pays annual reparations to foreign copyright owners injured by this noncompliance.

3. Does section 110(5) permit the playing of tapes, CDs, or DVDs in a small business establishment? Does it permit a restaurant to use a satellite dish to receive transmissions of football games that are blacked out in that vicinity?

4. Under sections 106 and 110(5), is there an infringing public performance where music is played on a radio or CD player in a taxi? Where a store selling television sets turns them on while customers are in the store? Where a store places a television in its window so that passers-by can view the programs? Where a bar plays free or pay-per-view television for its patrons?

5. *Other Section 110 Exemptions:* Section 110 recognizes a number of other specific exemptions, of which most, though not all, are limited to nonprofit uses. Consider whether the actions described below are protected by section 110:

(a) A church choir director makes twenty copies of the sheet music for a Christmas carol, which the choir then performs at the Christmas Eve mass.

(b) A college dormitory director plays DVDs of popular movies for students in one of the dorm's public areas every Friday night, with no admission charge.

(c) A college professor records an episode of a popular television show off the air, plays it for students in his Modern Literature class, and engages those students in a discussion of its theme and dramatic structure.

(d) A civic organization performs a popular song in the course of a musical revue to which admission is charged, and the profits from which are devoted to the organization's civic activities.

(e) A traveling nonprofit theatre troupe performs a play, translated into American Sign Language, at a school for deaf students.

(f) A company distributes software that alters the performance of a commercial motion picture DVD by "bleeping out" any profanity and blurring any nude scenes, without permanently altering the DVD content. Use of this software enables customers to view purchased or rented DVDs without being exposed to material that offends them.

4. SECTION 108: LIBRARY AND ARCHIVAL COPYING

Statute: 17 U.S.C. § 108

Section 108 reflects Congress' decision that libraries and archives should be free to make copies of works for such legitimate purposes as repairing damaged copies, making archival copies of works that would be difficult to replace if lost or damaged, and making interlibrary loans, but not for such purposes as avoiding the cost of purchases or subscriptions. The number of copies made, and the purpose and frequency of copying, must be within the statutory limits. No distribution for direct or indirect commercial advantage is permitted, and to qualify under section 108 the library or archives must be open to the public or to persons conducting research in a specialized field even if not affiliated with the institution of which the library or archives is a part. All copies must bear a copyright notice. Subsections (d) and (e) spell out the limitations on user-initiated copying requests, and require that copyright warnings be placed on self-service copying equipment.

NOTES

1. Does section 108 allow a university library to make copies of reading materials assigned by a professor for a large class, where the library has only one or two copies of each reading? Suppose the professor places the materials on reserve, and the students make their own copies on self-service copiers?

2. Suppose that over a 30-day period seven different patrons enter a university library with a request for a copy of the same article. At what point, if any, does the copying exceed the scope of section 108?

3. Suppose the Bigleaf Tobacco Company has a library of research material relevant to addictive drugs and carcinogens. Does section 108 apply to the library if it is open to the public? Open only to Bigleaf employees? Open only to persons doing research on the health effects of smoking?

4. Does section 108 allow the central branch of the local public library to make copies of certain materials and send them to the other branches so that the branches will not have to purchase those materials?

5. Does section 108 allow a university library to scan a rare book in its entirety and download it so it can be lent to a patron? Can it do so in order to preserve a copy to guard against loss, theft, damage or deterioration?

6. Does section 108 allow a university library to make copies of film footage for a researcher?

7. The 1998 Digital Millennium Copyright Act ("DMCA") broadened the exemptions for libraries and archives found in section 108(a)–(c) to allow digital as well as facsimile copying, and to extend this exemption to a published work when its existing format has become obsolete. The CTEA, which added 20 years to the terms of subsisting copyrights, also revised section 108 to provide that, during the last 20 years of a published work's copyright term, libraries and archives may make, distribute, display, or perform copies of selected works (in facsimile or digital form) for purposes of preservation, scholarship, or research, under circumstances in which copies cannot otherwise be obtained at a reasonable price.

5. SECTION 115: COMPULSORY LICENSING OF MUSICAL COMPOSITIONS FOR REPRODUCTION ON PHONORECORDS

Statute: 17 U.S.C. § 115

The oldest compulsory licensing provision in United States copyright law, section 115 of the 1976 Act, is based on section 1(e) of the 1909 Act. This provision concerns "mechanical licensing" of nondramatic musical works for the manufacture and distribution of phonorecords. Although the term "nondramatic musical works" is nowhere defined in the Copyright Act, it is generally understood to refer to music (together with lyrics, if any) that was not created as part of a dramatic work (*e.g.*, operas and musical theater).

Section 115(a) provides that once a nondramatic musical work has been recorded on phonorecords and these have been distributed to the public in the United States under the authority of the copyright owner, any other persons may record that work on phonorecords for the primary purpose of distributing those recordings to the public for private use, provided that they notify the copyright owner as required by section 115(b), and provided that they pay the royalty specified in section 115(c)(2) on each phonorecord that is made and distributed. Under the Digital Performance Right in Sound Recordings Act of 1995, *see* Part A.5. of this chapter, *supra*, the compulsory licensing provisions now apply to digital phonorecord deliveries as well. A digital phonorecord delivery is defined as "each individual delivery of a phonorecord by digital transmission of a sound recording which results in a specifically identifiable reproduction by and for any transmission recipient of a phonorecord of that sound recording." 17 U.S.C. § 115(d). Thus, for example, sales of recordings on iTunes are eligible for the compulsory license.

The compulsory mechanical license is an alternative to a negotiated mechanical license. In practice, the compulsory royalty rate under section 115 effectively sets a ceiling on negotiated royalties.

While the traditional compulsory licensing system remains in place for record labels, the 2018 Music Modernization Act (MMA) amended § 115 to create a new system for ensuring that songwriters and music publishers receive the mechanical royalties they are owed when sound recordings of their works are performed by interactive music streaming services or made available through digital downloads. First, it clarified that interactive streaming services must obtain mechanical licenses (in addition to public performance licenses) in order to stream copyrighted musical compositions, resolving an issue that was unclear under prior law. Second, it added section 115(d), authorizing the creation of a new Mechanical Licensing Collective (MLC) which now issues blanket compulsory mechanical licenses to digital music services providing downloads or interactive streaming, and collects and distributes those royalties to the copyright owners of the musical compositions. This system replaces the previous compulsory licensing process under which the digital music services (which were at that time subject to the same rules as traditional record labels) typically filed notices of intent with the U.S. Copyright Office for large numbers of musical compositions, but often failed to pay the music publishers the compulsory mechanical royalties they were due.

In contrast to the traditional compulsory mechanical license, under section 115(d) a digital music service does not have to make a new recording of the song—that is, a "cover" recording. Instead, the music service can use the compulsory mechanical license to stream or offer downloads of an existing recording. In order to stream or offer downloads of an existing recording, of course, the service separately needs to obtain the consent of the record label that owns the copyright in the sound recording, because the record label owns the reproduction rights and digital audio transmission rights in its sound recordings. (In the case of pre-1972 sound recordings protected under section 1401 rather than under copyright, the music service would need the consent of the party owning the section 1401 rights in that recording.)

Although the rates for compulsory mechanical licenses will continue to be set by the Copyright Royalty Board, the 2018 amendments also established a new standard that is likely to lead to higher royalty rates than in the past.

NOTES

1. Consider whether the following actions may be undertaken under section 115(a) without seeking the consent of a copyright owner. Except where otherwise indicated, assume that the musical composition for which the compulsory license is sought was originally fixed on phonorecords and distributed to the public in the United States under the authority of the copyright owner, that the requirements of sections 115(b) and (c) are satisfied, and that the musical composition is nondramatic:

(a) recording a musical composition onto the audio track of a motion picture or television program

(b) arranging the music (originally written for a male singer) to accommodate the higher vocal range of a female singer and recording the resulting arrangement for retail sale

(c) recording on phonorecords, for retail sale, an "easy listening" version of a rap song

(d) recording on phonorecords, for retail sale, an instrumental version of a musical composition that was originally written and recorded with lyrics

(e) recording a musical composition, with few alterations, for use as background music at a roller rink

(f) recording on phonorecords, for retail sale, a musical composition that was previously distributed only in Europe and Japan

(g) recording on phonorecords, for retail sale, an instrumental composition first used in the audio track of a motion picture

(h) recording a musical composition, previously distributed on phonorecords, onto a multimedia format which causes a video display of the song's lyrics while the song is being played.

2. If a dramatic musical work is later recorded separately (that is, not as part of the dramatic work itself) on phonorecords, does that work become subject to compulsory licensing under section 115?

3. If the music and lyrics of a song were created separately, rather than as a joint work, does section 115 apply to the song?

4. Do cell phone ringtones qualify for the compulsory license?

6. THE AUDIO HOME RECORDING ACT

Statutes: 17 U.S.C. §§ 1001–10

In the 1980s, the growth of digital audio technology made it possible to make durable, high quality, inexpensive copies of sound recordings. These results could not be obtained through the analog recording technology that was previously available. Music publishers and record companies understandably became concerned that widespread unauthorized copying of their copyrighted works onto digital media would lead to substantial lost revenues. In response to these concerns, Congress enacted the Audio Home Recording Act of 1992 ("AHRA"), a compromise measure that allows home audio taping for private use while providing compensation to copyright owners.

Section 1008 of the AHRA bars any infringement action "based on the noncommercial use by a consumer" of digital audio recording devices or media, or analog recording devices or media, for making digital or analog musical recordings. It also bars infringement actions based on the manufacture, importation, or distribution of such devices or media. However, section 1002 prohibits the manufacture, distribution or importation of any digital audio recording device that fails to incorporate an effective means of preventing serial copying of digital works. *See* 17 U.S.C. § 1001(11) (defining "serial copying"). In addition, section 1003 imposes a royalty, payable to the Register of Copyrights, on each digital audio recording device or medium distributed in the United States. Under sections 1006–07, these royalties are allocated to various funds payable to the parties most likely to be affected by consumer copying—composers, music publishers, performers, and owners of sound recording copyrights. Section 1002 prohibits importing, manufacturing or distributing devices, or offering or performing services, that are designed to circumvent the serial copying controls mandated by that section.

Under section 1009, remedies for violations of section 1002 or 1003 include injunctions, actual or statutory damages, costs, and attorney's fees, and the impounding, remedial modification and/or destruction of the offending devices and recordings; actual damages are also available for violations of section 1002.

In *Recording Industry Association of America v. Diamond Multimedia Systems, Inc.*, 180 F.3d 1072 (9th Cir. 1999), the Ninth Circuit held that the "Rio," a portable device that plays digital music downloaded by a computer from the internet, is not a "digital audio recording device" within the meaning of the AHRA, and thus need not incorporate a Serial Copy Management System. The court reasoned that music on a computer's hard drive is not a "digital musical recording" as that term is used in section 1001(5)(A)–(B). If the *Diamond Multimedia* decision is correct, then how relevant is the AHRA to the unauthorized copying of musical recordings today?

7. SECTION 120: ARCHITECTURAL WORKS

Statute: 17 U.S.C. § 120

Although the Architectural Works Copyright Protection Act of 1990 extended copyright protection to works of architecture in the form of buildings rather than only in the form of drawings, blueprints, or other nonfunctional depictions, the right to reproduce architectural works is limited by section 120.

ARCHITECTURAL WORKS COPYRIGHT PROTECTION ACT OF 1990

H.R Rep. No. 101–735.
101st Cong., 2d Sess. 21–23 (1990).

* * *

Section 204. Scope of Exclusive Rights on Architectural Works

Section 204 creates a new section 120 of title 17, United States Code, limiting the exclusive rights in architectural works.

Subsection (a) of new section 120 permits the unauthorized "making, distributing, or public display of pictures, paintings, photographs, or other pictorial representations of the work, if the building in which the work is embodied is located in or ordinarily visible from a public place." Similar exceptions are found in many Berne member countries, and serve to balance the interests of authors and the public. Architecture is a public art form and is enjoyed as such. Millions of people visit our cities every year and take back home photographs, posters, and other pictorial representations of prominent works of architecture as a memory of their trip. Additionally, numerous scholarly books on architecture are based on the ability to use photographs of architectural works.

These uses do not interfere with the normal exploitation of architectural works. Given the important public purpose served by these uses and the lack of harm to the copyright owner's market, the Committee chose to provide an exemption, rather than rely on the doctrine of fair use, which requires ad hoc determinations. After a careful examination of the provisions of the Berne Convention, the laws of other Berne member countries, and expert opinion, the Committee concluded that this exemption is consistent with our obligations under the Convention.

Subsection (b) provides a limitation on the copyright owner's right—under section 106(2) of title 17, United States Code—to prepare derivative works. Subsection (b) permits the owner of a building embodying a protected architectural work to "make or authorize the making of alterations to such building, and to destroy or authorize the destruction of such building" without the copyright owner's consent. With respect to the right to destroy a building embodying a protected architectural work, the provision is consistent with existing section 109(a) of title 17, United States Code. Section 109(a) permits the owner of a lawfully made copy to "sell or otherwise dispose of the possession of that copy of phonorecord." While the provisions of section 109(a) apply to architectural works, in light of the fact that architectural works represent a new category of protected subject matter, and unlike other forms of subject matter are habitable, the Committee believed it advisable to spell out expressly the limitations contained in section 120(b).

* * *

NOTES

1. Would section 120(a) permit the manufacture and sale of such souvenirs as snow globes, key chains, refrigerator magnets, and small statuettes depicting protected works of architecture?

2. In *Leicester v. Warner Brothers*, 232 F.3d 1212 (9th Cir. 2000) the Ninth Circuit affirmed a lower court decision that the images of sculptural works constituting a building's streetwall that appeared in the defendant's film did not infringe the plaintiff artist's rights. The court concluded that Congress intended public photographing of architectural works to be exempt from protection; this exemption extended to the sculptures because they were a component of the architectural work, even though they were physically separate from the building.

8. SECTION 112: EPHEMERAL RECORDINGS

Statute: 17 U.S.C. § 112

Section 112 allows broadcasters to make temporary fixations, and more limited archival fixations, of their transmissions to the public which embody authorized performances or displays of certain copyrighted works.

In the case of nonprofit or governmental transmissions, subsections 112(b)–(d) permit, under specified conditions, more liberal copying than is allowed under the general rule of section 112(a). Generally speaking, these liberalized copying rules apply to educational transmissions, transmissions of religious music, and transmissions directed to persons with disabilities under section 110(8).

Title IV of the Digital Millenium Copyright Act ("DMCA") broadened the section 112(a) exemption for ephemeral reproduction of sound recordings during radio or television broadcast transmissions so that it now explicitly includes both subscription and nonsubscription digital audio transmissions (thus including FCC-licensed broadcasters as well as subscription music services, internet "webcasters," satellite digital audio radio services and others with statutory licenses to perform sound recordings under section 114(f)). Title IV also added a new section 112(a)(2) exempting transmitting organizations from liability under the new anti-circumvention provisions of section 1201(a)(1) to the extent necessary to exercise their ephemeral recording privilege.

NOTES

1. In *Agee v. Paramount Communications, Inc.*, 59 F.3d 317 (2d Cir. 1995), the Second Circuit ruled that the ephemeral recording exemption of section 112(a) protected individual television stations from liability for certain infringements of copyrighted sound recordings. In this case, the infringement occurred when the producer of a syndicated television program incorporated the sound recordings into its program without the consent of the copyright owner. The producer recorded the program on videotape and then delivered it by satellite feed to the individual stations, which taped the feed for later rebroadcast. Was this a proper application of section 112(a)?

2. Does section 112 permit ephemeral recordings of a transmission embodying a performance or display that was not authorized by the copyright owner but falls within the bounds of fair use?

3. Once a broadcaster has made copies under section 112, how may the copies be used?

9. OTHER SPECIFIC LIMITATIONS ON SECTION 106

Statutes: 17 U.S.C. §§ 111, 113(a)–(c), 116, 118–19, 121–22

(a) *Secondary Transmissions: Exemptions and Compulsory Licenses for Cable Systems and Satellite Carriers (Sections 111, 119, and 122).* Although the growth of cable television and satellite systems has made it possible for more consumers to be served by television broadcasters, it has also raised questions of copyright liability, since allowing cable and satellite systems to carry television programming for free into subscribers' homes would enable them to perform and display copyrighted material to a large audience without compensating the copyright owners. In addition, these retransmitters often compete directly with the broadcasters who have paid to carry the same copyrighted material. However, it would be impracticable to require such simultaneous retransmitters to separately negotiate copyright licensing for all the programming they retransmit. Finding that the provisions of the 1909 Act were inadequate to resolve these problems, Congress enacted, and periodically has revised, the secondary transmission provisions of Title 17, beginning with the enactment of section 111 in the 1976 Act, which exempted certain narrowly-defined retransmissions (*see* § 111(a)–(b)) while subjecting most cable television retransmissions to a compulsory licensing scheme. The emergence of satellite delivery systems during the 1980s led to enactment of the Satellite Home Viewer Act of 1988, which revised section 111 and added section 119 to make the scheme of exemptions and compulsory licensing applicable to satellite systems, permitting them to carry signals from distant stations. To make the satellite industry more competitive with the cable industry, the Satellite Home Viewer Improvement Act of 1999, Pub. L. No. 106–113, 106th Cong., 1st Sess. (1999), created a new section 122 compulsory license permitting satellite retransmission of broadcast signals from *local* stations.

(b) *Sections 113(a)–(c): Useful Articles.* Subsections (a) through (c) of section 113 address the rights of the various interested parties when copyrighted artwork is incorporated in a useful article that is manufactured, displayed, and distributed in commerce, or when a copyrighted work depicts a useful article. Section 113(d) addresses the rights of an author whose work of visual art may be damaged or destroyed in removing it from a building. *See* Part C.2. of this chapter, *infra*.

(c) *Section 116: Jukebox Licenses.* Section 1(e) of the 1909 Act gave jukebox operators an outright exemption from copyright liability unless the establishment charged admission. Intense criticism led Congress to replace this exemption with a compulsory license in the 1976 Act, applicable only to nondramatic musical works. Further change became necessary, however, when the United States joined the Berne Convention, Article 11(1) of which provides that the authors of musical works "shall enjoy the exclusive right of authorizing: (i) the public performance of their works, including such public performance by any means or process." Eventually the compulsory license was replaced by a system of negotiations and administrative proceedings under section 116.

(d) *Section 118: Noncommercial Educational Broadcasting.* The compulsory license under section 118 provides that owners of copyright in published nondramatic musical works and published pictorial, graphic and sculptural works may negotiate with noncommercial educational broadcasters to reach agreement on royalties to be paid for producing and transmitting a program in which such a work is performed or displayed, as well as for reproducing and distributing copies of such a program for the purpose of future qualifying transmissions. If voluntary negotiations fail, the Copyright Royalty Judges will determine the royalty rates and terms. The license also allows a nonprofit or government entity to copy the program during its transmission, and temporarily retain the copies, solely for purposes of a performance or display that meets the requirements of section 110(1).

(e) *Sections 121 and 121A: Special Formats for Persons with Disabilities.* Section 12 permits authorized nonprofit organizations, under specified conditions, to reproduce and distribute, in the U.S., copies of previously published literary and musical works in specialized braille, audio, digitized, and other accessible formats, for persons who are blind or have other disabilities that interfere with reading, without obtaining the copyright owner's consent. Section 121A, which was added in 2018 to comply with the Marrakesh Treaty, creates a limited right to import or export such copies.

C. BEYOND COPYRIGHT: PERFORMERS' RIGHTS, MORAL RIGHTS, AND RESALE ROYALTIES

1. PERFORMERS' RIGHTS

Statutes: 17 U.S.C. §§ 106(6), 114(g), 502–05, 1101; 18 U.S.C. § 2319A

Originally, the 1976 Act gave performers no rights in their performances except to the extent that those performances constituted copyrightable works authored by the performers. Other performers asserting a protectable interest in their performances were, and in many cases still are, limited to remedies under the Lanham Act and state law doctrines such as unfair competition and the right of publicity.

Under the Digital Performance Right in Sound Recordings Act of 1995, discussed in Part A.5. of this chapter, *supra,* musicians and vocalists are entitled to statutory royalties for certain public performances of their recordings through digital transmissions. 17 U.S.C. § 114(g).

Legislation has addressed the problem of unauthorized recording (or "bootlegging") of live musical performances. The United States enacted an anti-bootlegging law in order to meet its obligations under the TRIPS provisions of the Uruguay Round of the General Agreement on Tariffs and Trade (GATT). Sections 512 and 513 of the Uruguay Round Agreements Act of 1994 ("URAA") amended Titles 17 and 18 to impose civil, and in some cases, criminal penalties for unauthorized transmission or recording of live musical performances, and for reproduction and distribution of such unauthorized recordings. The Senate Report notes, however, that "[i]t is intended that the legislation will not apply in cases where First Amendment principles are implicated, such as where small portions of an unauthorized fixation of a sound recording are used without permission in a news broadcast or for other purposes of comment or criticism." S. Rep. No. 412, 103d Cong., 2d Sess. 225 (1994). The federal courts have exclusive jurisdiction over actions arising under section 1101.

Section 1101 applies regardless whether the unauthorized fixation occurred before or after the law's enactment date (Dec. 8, 1994), although liability will arise only for acts taken after enactment. Users of pre-1995 recordings must therefore be mindful of any potential liability.

As you read section 1101, try to answer the following questions:

(a) Do the work-made-for-hire provisions apply to section 1101?

(b) Are the rights assignable?

(c) Where several performers render a single performance, will the consent of one performer, or of a majority of the performers, satisfy section 1101 with respect to the entire performance?

(d) If all performers consent to recording of their performance in return for compensation, how should that compensation be divided among them?

(e) Do section 1101 rights apply to federal government employees rendering performances within the scope of their employment?

(f) Must consent under 1101 be in a signed writing?

(g) What is a "live musical performance"? Where a live performance integrates music, dance, literary, and dramatic elements, does section 1101 apply to the entire performance or only to its musical components?

(h) Whereas the criminal provisions under 18 U.S.C. § 2319A(a) have a scienter requirement, most of the civil remedies under 17 U.S.C. §§ 502–05 are available without regard to the defendant's state of mind. How can persons wishing to reproduce or distribute a musical recording (or a work incorporating such a recording) acquired from another party protect themselves from liability?

(i) How long do a performer's rights endure under section 1101? Can the spouse or children of a deceased performer bring suit under section 1101?

(j) Do sections 1101 and 2319A satisfy our obligations under Article 14 of TRIPS? Do they exceed those obligations? (Also compare Article 6 of the 1996 WIPO Performances and Phonograms Treaty.)

(k) Does section 1101 exceed Congress's authority under the Intellectual Property Clause? If so, is it defensible nevertheless under the Commerce Clause? *Cf. United States v. Martignon*, 492 F.3d 140 (2d Cir. 2007) (addressing § 2319).

(*l*) Is there a "fair use" exception to section 1101?

2. MORAL RIGHTS

Statutes: 17 U.S.C. §§ 101 (as needed), 106A, 113(d), 412, 501(a); 15 U.S.C. § 1125(a)

MASSACHUSETTS MUSEUM OF CONTEMPORARY ART V. BÜCHEL

593 F.3d 38 (1st Cir. 2010).

LIPEZ, CIRCUIT JUDGE.

As one observer has noted, this case, which raises important and unsettled legal issues under the Visual Artists Rights Act ("VARA"), may well serve as "the ultimate how-not-to guide in the complicated world of installation art." Geoff Edgers, *Dismantled*, The Boston Globe, Oct. 21, 2007, at 1N. Artist Christoph Büchel conceived of an ambitious, football-field-sized art installation entitled "Training Ground for Democracy," which was to be exhibited at the Massachusetts Museum of Contemporary Art ("MASS MoCA," or "the Museum"). Unfortunately, the parties never memorialized the terms of their relationship or their understanding of the intellectual property issues involved in the installation in a written agreement. Even more unfortunately, the project was never completed. Numerous conflicts and a steadily deteriorating relationship between the artist and the Museum prevented the completion of "Training Ground for Democracy" in its final form.

In the wake of this failed endeavor, the Museum went to federal court seeking a declaration that it was "entitled to present to the public the materials and partial constructions" it had collected for "Training Ground for Democracy." Büchel responded with several counterclaims under VARA and the Copyright Act, seeking an injunction that would prevent MASS MoCA from displaying the unfinished installation and damages for the Museum's alleged violations of his rights under both VARA and the general Copyright Act.

On cross-motions for summary judgment, the district court assumed that VARA applies to unfinished works of art, but it nonetheless ruled for the Museum in all respects because, even granting VARA's applicability, it found no genuine issues of material fact. *Massachusetts Museum of Contemporary Art Found., Inc. v. Büchel,* 565 F.Supp.2d 245 (D.Mass.2008). Büchel appeals. Because we find that, if VARA applies, genuine issues of material fact would foreclose summary judgment on one of Büchel's VARA claims—that MASS MoCA violated his right of artistic integrity by modifying the installation—we cannot assume that VARA applies to unfinished works but instead must decide its applicability. We conclude that the statute does apply to such works.

* * *

B. Factual Background

* * * [T]he key conflict between MASS MoCA and the artist involved Büchel's dissatisfaction with the way in which the Museum was implementing his instructions and procuring the items necessary for the installation. Büchel himself was not present in North Adams for the first several months of work on the project. Instead, he conducted much of his work on the installation throughout the fall of 2006 remotely, by providing Museum personnel with detailed instructions as to the particular materials he required and their placement within the exhibition space. [Büchel returned in October, 2006, to complete the installation, but he was dissatisfied with the Museum's progress. He departed again in December. During this time there were numerous disputes between the parties, and their relationship deteriorated.]

* * *

As the vitriolic exchanges between the parties continued, and negotiations over the project's eventual completion became hopeless, "Training Ground" languished in its unfinished state. It became clear that Büchel would not complete the installation. On May 22, 2007, MASS MoCA announced the cancellation of "Training Ground," and contemporaneously publicized the opening of a new exhibit entitled "Made at MASS MoCA," which was to be "a documentary project exploring the issues raised in the course of complex collaborative projects between artists and institutions." The press release noted that this lawsuit had been filed the previous day; it also highlighted the Museum's desire to use its "other experiences working with artists" to "provide [its] audience with thought-provoking insights into the complexities of the art-making process." The release further explained that, due to "space constraints imposed by the materials assembled for *Training Ground for Democracy,*" the exhibition would be presented in the Museum's "only remaining available gallery space"; therefore, in order to enter the exhibit, visitors would have to pass through Building 5, "housing the materials and unfinished fabrications that were to have comprised elements of *Training Ground for Democracy.*" The Museum represented that "[r]easonable steps [had] been taken to control and restrict the view of these materials, pending a court ruling."

When "Made at MASS MoCA" opened, many in the art world disagreed with the Museum's handling of its dispute with Büchel, though the parties have different views on whether the Museum's actions ultimately tarnished the artist's reputation. Moreover, the parties differ on whether the "reasonable steps . . . taken to control and restrict the view of the[ ] materials"—the placement of yellow tarpaulins over the unfinished work—actually concealed all of the individual components and vital design elements of "Training Ground," or whether the tarpaulins simply "hid[ ] an elephant behind a napkin," effectively inviting individuals to peek behind the cloth coverings and view the unfinished work. *See* Charles Giuliano, *Christoph Buchel's Tarp Art at Mass MoCA: Crap Under Wrap* (July 31, 2007).

* * *

[Both Büchel and MASS MoCA asked the district court for declaratory judgments of their respective rights in the exhibit.] The court ruled in favor of the Museum, noting that nothing in VARA prevented MASS MoCA from showing the incomplete project. Therefore, MASS MoCA was "entitled to present" the unfinished installation to the public as long as it posted a disclaimer that would "inform anyone viewing the exhibit that the materials assembled in Building 5 constitute an unfinished project that [did] not carry out the installation's original intent." The court correspondingly denied the artist's request for injunctive relief barring public display of the unfinished installation, ruling that he had failed to prove a likelihood of success on the merits of his VARA claim.

II.

Passed in 1990, the Visual Artists Rights Act, 17 U.S.C. § 106A, was an amendment to the Copyright Act that protects the "moral rights" of certain visual artists in the works they create, consistent with Article 6 *bis* of the Berne Convention. *Phillips v. Pembroke Real Estate, Inc.*, 459 F.3d 128, 133 (1st Cir.2006); *Carter v. Helmsley-Spear, Inc.*, 71 F.3d 77, 83 (2d Cir.1995) (citing H.R.Rep. No. 101–514, at 5 (1990) ("House Report")). The "rubric of moral rights encompasses many varieties of rights," but the two most widely recognized are attribution and integrity. *Id.* at 81. We will discuss both of these in detail below, but note briefly now that the right of attribution protects the author's right to be identified as the author of his work and also protects against the use of his name in connection with works created by others. The right of integrity "allows the author to prevent any deforming or mutilating changes to his work." *Id.* Although these moral rights "exist independent[ly] of the economic rights" granted to all authors under the Copyright Act, they are part of the same statutory framework.

* * *

B. VARA

Beyond the Copyright Act's protections of certain economic rights, VARA provides additional and independent protections to authors of works of visual art. A work of visual art is defined to include "a painting, drawing, print, or sculpture, existing in a single copy" or in a limited edition. 17 U.S.C. § 101. The definition specifically excludes a number of works that are otherwise copyrightable, including motion pictures and other audiovisual works, books, posters, periodicals, works made for hire, and merchandising, advertising, promotional, or packaging materials. *Id.*

VARA provides that, in addition to the exclusive rights provided by section 106 of the Copyright Act, but subject to certain limitations, the author of a work of visual art

> (1) shall have the right—
>
> > (A) to claim authorship of that work, and
> >
> > (B) to prevent the use of his or her name as the author of any work of visual art which he or she did not create;
>
> (2) shall have the right to prevent the use of his or her name as the author of the work of visual art in the event of a distortion, mutilation, or other modification of the work which would be prejudicial to his or her honor or reputation; and
>
> (3) subject to the limitations set forth in section 113(d), shall have the right—
>
> > (A) to prevent any intentional distortion, mutilation, or other modification of that work which would be prejudicial to his or her honor or reputation, and any intentional distortion, mutilation, or modification of that work is a violation of that right, and
> >
> > (B) to prevent any destruction of a work of recognized stature, and any intentional or grossly negligent destruction of that work is a violation of that right.

17 U.S.C. § 106A(a).

VARA's passage reflected Congress's belief that the art covered by the Act "meet[s] a special societal need, and [its] protection and preservation serve an important public interest." House Report at 5–6. To encourage the creation of such art, VARA protects the "moral rights" of its creators. These are "rights of a spiritual, non-economic and personal nature" that exist "independently of an artist's copyright in his or her work" and "spring from a belief that an artist in the process of creation injects his spirit into the work and that the artist's personality, as well as the integrity of the work, should therefore be protected and preserved." *Carter*, 71 F.3d at 81. The recognition of moral rights fosters a " 'climate of artistic worth and honor that encourages the author in the arduous act of creation.' " *Id.* at 83 (quoting House Report at 6). Although an artist may not transfer his VARA rights (as they are considered an extension of his personality), he may waive those rights by "expressly agree[ing] to such waiver in a written instrument." 17 U.S.C. § 106A(e)(1). Also, "[a]ll remedies available under copyright law, other than criminal remedies, are available in an action for infringement of moral rights." *Carter,* 71 F.3d at 83 (citing 17 U.S.C. § 506); *see also* 17 U.S.C. § 501(a).

More specifically, by guaranteeing the moral rights of "attribution" and "integrity," VARA " 'protects both the reputations of certain visual artists and the works of art they create.' " *Carter,* 71 F.3d at 83 (quoting House Report at 6). Before discussing the precise contours of these rights, we consider whether, as a threshold matter, the indisputably unfinished "Training Ground for Democracy" was a "work of visual art" within the meaning of VARA.

C. Does VARA Apply to Unfinished Works of Art?

* * *

The text of VARA itself does not state when an artistic project becomes a work of visual art subject to its protections. However, VARA is part of the Copyright Act, and that Act's definition section, which defines "work of visual art," specifies that its definitions, unless otherwise provided, control throughout Title 17. *See* 17 U.S.C. § 101. That general definitional section of the Copyright Act states that a work is "created" when it "is fixed in a copy . . . for the first time." Further, "where a work is prepared over a period of time, *the portion of it that has been fixed at any particular time constitutes the work as of that time.*" 17 U.S.C. § 101 (emphasis added). A work is "fixed" when it has been formed, "by or under the authority of the author," in a way that is "sufficiently permanent or stable to permit it to be perceived, reproduced, or otherwise communicated for a period of more than transitory duration." *Id.*

Not surprisingly, based on section 101's general definitions, courts have held that the Copyright Act's protections extend to unfinished works. * * *

Reading VARA in accordance with the definitions in section 101, it too must be read to protect unfinished, but "fixed," works of art that, if completed, would qualify for protection under the statute. To conclude otherwise would be "contrary to the rule that provisions of a single act should be construed in as harmonious a fashion as possible." *United States v. Maravilla,* 907 F.2d 216, 231 (1st Cir.1990). At least one circuit has previously assumed VARA's applicability to unfinished works. *See Carter,* 71 F.3d at 83–88 (discussing VARA claims stemming from an unfinished, walk-through sculpture being installed in the lobby of a building).

* * *

III.

Given Büchel's right to protection under VARA for his artistic investment in a partially completed artwork, we must now assess the district court's ruling that Büchel failed to raise a genuine issue of material fact with respect to any of his claims. * * *

A. The Scope of VARA's Integrity and Attribution Right

1. The Right of Integrity

VARA's right of integrity, codified at 17 U.S.C. § 106A(a)(3)(A), provides that an artist shall have the right "to prevent any intentional distortion, mutilation, or other modification of [his or her] work which would be prejudicial to his or her honor or reputation, and [that] any intentional distortion, mutilation, or modification of that work is a violation of that right." It thus allows artists to protect their works against intentional modifications that would be prejudicial to their honor or reputations.

There is arguably some uncertainty about the plaintiff's burden of proof in a case such as this because the second part of section (a)(3)(A)—stating that "any intentional distortion, mutilation, or modification of th[e] work is a violation" of the right of integrity—does not explicitly require a showing of prejudice when the alteration already has occurred and damages, rather than injunctive relief, would be the appropriate remedy. * * * [W]e have found no case law discussing a possible difference in the showing required for injunctive relief and damages for right-of-integrity claims.

Some courts, however, have assumed without analysis that the prejudice showing is necessary for both injunctive relief and damages. *See, e.g., Hanrahan v. Ramirez,* No. 2:97–CV–7470, 1998 WL 34369997, at *3 (C.D.Cal. June 3, 1998) (citing 17 U.S.C. § 106A(a)(3)); *Carter v. Helmsley-Spear, Inc.,* 861 F.Supp. 303, 329–30 (S.D.N.Y.1994), *aff'd in part, vacated in part, and rev'd in part by Carter,* 71 F.3d at 77. At least one commentator likewise accepts, without discussion, that the damages remedy requires a showing of prejudice. *See* MELVILLE B. NIMMER, 3–8D NIMMER ON COPYRIGHT § 8D.06[C][1] (noting that "an intentional and prejudicial mutilation is an integrity violation, remediable through not only an injunction, but damages as well"). Interestingly, Nimmer raises, and dismisses, a different imprecision in section (a)(3)(A):

> The statutory language—"distortion, mutilation, or other modification of the work which would be prejudicial to his or her honor or reputation"—is susceptible of a reading whereby the requisite prejudice applies only to "modification," not to the antecedents of "distortion" or "mutilation." Though not without ambiguity, the better view under the Berne Convention, from

which this language is drawn, is that prejudice applies in all three instances.

Id.

We agree with Nimmer's view of the provision, including the application of the prejudice requirement to a claim for damages, and consider that construction soundly grounded in VARA's legislative history. Under the heading "Purpose of the Legislation," the House Report notes that the right of integrity "allows artists to protect their works against modifications and destructions that are prejudicial to their honor or reputations." House Report at 6. The Report also notes that the rights provided by VARA are "analogous to those protected by Article 6bis of the Berne Convention," *id.*, which in turn describes the right of integrity as applicable to "certain modifications and other derogatory actions" that would be prejudicial to the artist's honor or reputation.[14] Given the stated purpose of the legislation and the similar depiction of the integrity right in the Berne Convention, we conclude that Congress intended the prejudice requirement to apply to the right of integrity whether the remedy sought is injunctive relief or damages.

Although VARA does not define the terms "prejudicial," "honor," or "reputation," the House Report recommended that the prejudice inquiry "focus on the artistic or professional honor or reputation of the individual as embodied in the work that is protected," and "examine the way in which a work has been modified and the professional reputation of the author of the work." House Report at 15. Relying on dictionary definitions of prejudice, honor and reputation, the district court in *Carter* concluded that it should "consider whether [the proposed] alteration would cause injury or damage to plaintiffs' good name, public esteem, or reputation in the artistic community." 861 F.Supp. at 323. We think this a useful approach, but emphasize that the focus is on the artist's reputation in relation to the altered work of art; the artist need not have public stature beyond the context of the creation at issue. *See* House Report at 15 ("[A]n author need not prove a pre-existing standing in the artistic community.").

2. The Right of Attribution

VARA's right of attribution grants the author of a work of visual art the right, in part, (1) "to claim authorship of that work"; (2) "to prevent the

---

[14] Article 6*bis* of the Berne Convention, which is titled "Moral Rights," includes a heading that lists among those rights "to object to certain modifications and other derogatory actions." The provision itself states, in relevant part:

> (1) Independently of the author's economic rights, and even after the transfer of the said rights, the author shall have the right . . . to object to any distortion, mutilation or other modification of, or other derogatory action in relation to, the said work, which would be prejudicial to his honor or reputation.

Berne Convention for the Protection of Literary and Artistic Works art. 6 *bis*, Sept. 9, 1986, S. Treaty Doc. No. 99–27, 1161 U.N.T.S. 30.

use of his or her name as the author of any work of visual art which he or she did not create"; and (3) "to prevent the use of his or her name as the author of the work of visual art in the event of a distortion, mutilation, or other modification of the work which would be prejudicial to his or her honor or reputation." 17 U.S.C. § 106A(a)(1),(2). The right "ensures that artists are correctly identified with the works of art they create, and that they are not identified with works created by others." House Report at 6. In addition, if a work of visual art has been distorted or modified (and, unlike the integrity right, the original distortion or modification need not be intentional), associating the author's name with the distorted work against his wishes would violate his right of attribution.

The right of attribution under VARA thus gives an artist a claim for injunctive relief to, inter alia, assert or disclaim authorship of a work. Whether VARA entitles an artist to damages for violation of the right of attribution is a separate question. We find the answer in the difference between the statutory language on the right of integrity and the language on the right of attribution. Subsection (a)(3) of section 106A, which codifies the right of integrity, is further divided into two subsections: (A) confers the right to protect the work against intentional alterations that would be prejudicial to honor or reputation, and (B) confers the right to protect a work of "recognized stature" from destruction.[16] Although both subsections are framed as rights "to prevent" certain conduct, they both also contain an additional clause stating that the occurrence of that conduct is, at least in certain circumstances, "a violation of th[e] right" to prevent the conduct from happening. *See* 17 U.S.C. § 106A(a)(3)(A) ("any intentional distortion, mutilation, or modification of that work is a violation of that right"); *id.* at § 106(a)(3)(B) ("any intentional or grossly negligent destruction of that work is a violation of that right").

No such "violation" clause is included in the sections codifying the right of attribution. *See* NIMMER, *supra,* at § 8D.06[B][1] ("The statute does not make any provision to redress *violation* of any of the foregoing three attribution rights."). The legislative history sheds no light on this difference, but Nimmer speculates as follows:

> Perhaps the implication is that whereas an integrity violation could give rise to a monetary recovery, failure to attribute is remediable solely through injunction. If that conclusion were intended, Congress certainly could have expressed its intent less obliquely.

Id. We agree with Nimmer's surmise that VARA does not provide a damages remedy for an attribution violation. Where the statutory language

---

[16] Section 106A(a)(3) states that the author of a work of visual art shall have the right "(A) to prevent any intentional distortion, mutilation, or other modification of that work which would be prejudicial to his or her honor or reputation" and the right "(B) to prevent any destruction of a work of recognized stature."

is framed as a right "to prevent" conduct, it does not necessarily follow that a plaintiff is entitled to damages once the conduct occurs. The question is whether "doing" the act the artist has a right to prevent also triggers a damages remedy, and the statutory language indicates that Congress answered that question for the attribution right differently from the integrity right.

It is also noteworthy that Congress crafted a damages remedy for the destruction of a work of recognized stature that is narrower than the right to prevent destruction of such works. While an artist may "prevent *any* destruction of a work of recognized stature," only an "intentional or grossly negligent destruction of that work is a violation of that right." 17 U.S.C. § 106A(a)(3)(B) (emphasis added). This narrowing further indicates that Congress did not intend a damages remedy to arise automatically from the right to prevent conduct. In failing to provide a damages remedy for any type of violation of the moral right of attribution, Congress may have concluded that artists could obtain adequate relief for the harms of false attribution by resorting to the Copyright Act and other traditional claims.

B. Büchel's VARA Claims

With this legal framework in mind, we turn to the record before the district court. By dismantling "Training Ground," the Museum prevented the further use of Büchel's name in connection with the work, eliminating any basis for injunctive relief, and we therefore do not address the attribution claim in our VARA analysis. We thus consider the evidence in the light most favorable to Büchel in determining whether there are genuine issues of material fact regarding the alleged violations of his right of integrity.

* * *

Büchel alleges that MASS MoCA violated his right to integrity in three distinct ways: first, by continuing to work on the installation without his authorization, particularly in early 2007, and by then exhibiting the distorted artwork to the public; second, by using tarpaulins to "partially cover[ ]"—and thus modify and distort—the installation, and allowing Museum visitors to see it in that condition; and third, merely by showing Büchel's work in its unfinished state, which he claims was a distortion. Büchel asserts that these actions caused prejudice to his honor or reputation.

As we shall explain, we conclude that summary judgment was improperly granted to MASS MoCA because material disputes of fact exist concerning the first of Büchel's integrity claims—*i.e.,* that MASS MoCA modified "Training Ground" over his objections, to his detriment. We further conclude that the record contains sufficient evidence to allow a jury to find that MASS MoCA's actions caused prejudice to Büchel's honor or reputation. The other integrity claims, however, are unavailing.

1. Continuing Work on "Training Ground"

* * *

Both in his deposition and in his affidavit, Büchel described ways in which he felt the Museum had knowingly disregarded his specific instructions. * * * Indeed, even the Museum, in its August 31, 2007 memorandum of law in support of its motion for summary judgment, admitted that the installation "[m]aterials as they now stand *reflect significant aesthetic and design choices by MASS MoCA personnel,* including with respect to the layout of the [m]aterials, and with respect to the selection and procurement of pre-existing buildings and vehicles that have been modified and incorporated into the [m]aterials." (Emphasis added.)

MASS MoCA argues that the evidence, taken in its entirety, does not add up to a triable issue with respect to a violation of Büchel's right of integrity, but shows only that Museum personnel were attempting to carry out Büchel's vision based on his instructions. * * *

As we have noted, a jury may well accept the Museum's depiction of its intention and its actions. At this juncture, however, the record must be viewed in the light most favorable to Büchel. The evidence we have described would permit a jury to find that the Museum forged ahead with the installation in the first half of 2007 knowing that the continuing construction in Büchel's absence would frustrate—and likely contradict—Büchel's artistic vision. We thus conclude that a jury issue exists as to whether these actions effected an intentional distortion or other modification of "Training Ground" that subjected MASS MoCA to liability under VARA.

The record also contains evidence from which a jury could conclude that the Museum's alterations had a detrimental impact on Büchel's honor or reputation. An article in the Boston Globe reported that, in February, Museum officials had shown the unfinished project to a group of Museum directors and curators who were attending an arts conference in the area. Another journalist reported on observing the unfinished (and still untarped) work. [Another report indicated that the work was shown to several elected officials.]

Although the commentary generated by these visits is not all negative, there was sufficient evidence for a jury to find that the changes to "Training Ground" caused prejudice to Büchel. The New York Times noted that the exhibition would "certainly give people unfamiliar with his obsessive, history-driven aesthetic an inaccurate sense of his art, and this is indeed a form of damage." A critic for the Boston Globe similarly observed that "many people are going to judge [Büchel] and his work on the basis of this experience." One viewer, writing in *Commentary* magazine, observed that "I am not sure that it suffers from being enveiled." A review published in *Berkshire Fine Arts*—subtitled "Crap Under Wrap"—concluded that it would be a "huge mistake" to uncover the installation, which offered "virtually nothing of substance or interest."

The record thus shows that some viewers of the installation reacted unfavorably to the work in its allegedly modified and distorted form. A factfinder might conclude, of course, that it was Büchel's underlying concept (notwithstanding its unfinished state) rather than MASS MoCA's actions that elicited the negative reactions. However, a jury could also reasonably infer that the negative impressions resulted from the Museum's unauthorized modifications to "Training Ground," diminishing the quality of the work and thereby harming Büchel's professional honor or reputation as a visual artist.

* * *

2. Showing "Training Ground" Covered with Tarpaulins

Büchel also claims that MASS MoCA improperly modified and distorted "Training Ground" when it partially covered it with the yellow tarpaulins and displayed it in that condition. * * *

Although the tarpaulins did prevent visitors to the Museum from seeing the entire unfinished installation, the record shows that a number of people were able to form an impression of "Training Ground" despite the partial covering. For example, according to one observer,

> [the tarps] don't reach the floor, and they rise only about two feet above eye level, so they don't cover much. You can easily crouch down to slip your head underneath or peek through the slits between the vinyl sheets. * * *

Thomas Micchelli, *Christoph Büchel Training Ground for Democracy*, The Brooklyn Rail (September 2007). Another critic noted that the installation "under all the tarps is really kind of a conceptual peep show. It doesn't take much effort or imagination to see most of the work. . . . Mass MoCA is hiding an elephant behind a napkin," and called it a "wink, wink, wrap show." Photographs in the record confirm that the covers did not obscure the general path and layout of the installation. Indeed, given the location of "Training Ground," visitors to "Made at MASS MoCA" could not avoid seeing the unfinished "Training Ground" bedecked in tarpaulins.

Nonetheless, although the installation unquestionably looked different with the tarpaulins partially covering it, we agree with the district court that the mere covering of the artwork by the Museum, its host, cannot reasonably be deemed an intentional act of distortion or modification of Büchel's creation. To conclude otherwise would be to say that, even if all had gone well, the Museum would have been subject to a right-of-integrity claim if it had partially covered the work before its formal opening to prevent visitors from seeing it prematurely.

* * *

3. Exhibiting "Training Ground" in Its Unfinished State

Büchel maintains that, even aside from the alleged modifications to "Training Ground," merely exhibiting the work of art in its unfinished state, without the artist's consent, constitutes a distortion. We reject this claim. A separate moral right of disclosure (also known as the right of divulgation) protects an author's authority to "prevent third parties from disclosing [his or her] work to the public without the author's consent," and is not covered by VARA.

Although Büchel proffered an expert who opined that showing an unfinished work without the artist's permission is inherently a distortion, we decline to interpret VARA to include such a claim where a separate moral right of disclosure is widely recognized in other jurisdictions and Congress explicitly limited the statute's coverage to the rights of attribution and integrity. Any right Büchel possesses to withhold display of his artwork must be found outside VARA. * * *

4. Summary of VARA Claims

After careful review of the record, we are persuaded that a reasonable jury could find that Büchel is entitled to relief under VARA based on the Museum's continuing work on "Training Ground" over his objections. Genuine disputes of material fact foreclose summary judgment for either Büchel or MASS MoCA on that claim. We find no merit, however, in Büchel's claim that MASS MoCA intentionally modified or distorted "Training Ground" by covering it with tarpaulins, and we reject as outside the scope of the statute Büchel's claim that the Museum violated VARA by displaying the installation over his objections. We affirm the district court's grant of summary judgment for the Museum on Büchel's right-of-attribution claim, which became moot when MASS MoCA dismantled the installation in 2007.

* * *

V.

We summarize our holdings:

1. VARA's protection of an artist's moral rights extends to unfinished creations that are "works of art" within the meaning of the Copyright Act;

2. The right of integrity under VARA protects artists from distortions, mutilations or modifications of their works that are

prejudicial to their reputation or honor, and prejudice must be shown for both injunctive relief and damages;

3. Büchel has adduced sufficient evidence to raise a genuine issue of material fact as to whether MASS MoCA violated his right of integrity on one of his three asserted bases for liability, namely, by modifying "Training Ground" over his objections in a manner that harmed his honor or reputation. His right-of-integrity claims based on the yellow tarpaulins and the mere display of "Training Ground" lack merit;

4. Büchel's right-of-attribution claim is moot, as VARA provides only injunctive relief to protect the right of attribution and the installation no longer exists;

* * *

We thus remand the case for further proceedings on Büchel's remaining right-of-integrity claim under VARA and his public display claim under section 106 of the Copyright Act.

NOTES

1. Could the *Büchel* dispute have been avoided by contract? Is it possible that Büchel and the Museum were joint authors? If so, how would this affect Buchel's VARA claim?

2. Does VARA apply to works made for hire? Why did Congress make that choice?

3. Did the Museum violate Büchel's exclusive right to create derivative works? His exclusive public display right? *See Büchel*, 593 F.3d at 63–65.

4. Would the dismantling and removal of "Training Ground" require Büchel's consent? More generally, under what circumstances does the destruction of a work of art violate VARA?

5. If a venue operator decides to completely cover up an artist's work, without inflicting any physical damage, does the artist have a moral rights claim? Does it matter whether the work is physically incorporated into the building? *See Kerson v. Vermont Law School*, 2021 WL 4142268 (D. Vt. 2021) (university temporarily covered murals with a tarp, and planned to cover them more permanently with acoustic panels).

6. How can an artist establish that his or her work is "of recognized stature"? *See Martin v. City of Indianapolis*, 192 F.3d 608, 612–13 (7th Cir. 1999); *id.* at 616 (Manion, C.J., concurring in part and dissenting in part); *Carter v. Helmsley-Spear, Inc.*, 861 F.Supp. 303, 324–26 (S.D.N.Y. 1994), *aff'd in part, vacated in part, rev'd in part,* 71 F.3d 77 (2d Cir. 1995).

7. Suppose that an art installation is physically incorporated into a building, or located on public land. Does VARA allow the landowner (or public

authority) to remove it in order to renovate or re-develop the property? What if removal will destroy it? How can the parties address this possibility in advance? *See Martin v. City of Indianapolis*, 192 F.3d 608 (7th Cir. 1999).

8. "Site-specific art" is a type of art in which "one of the component physical objects is the location." *Phillips v. Pembroke Real Estate, Inc.*, 459 F.3d 128, 129 (1st Cir. 2006). Is VARA violated when site-specific art is removed from its original location without the artist's consent? *Compare Phillips*, 459 F.3d at 139–43 (1st Cir. 2006) *with Kelley v. Chicago Park Dist.*, 635 F.3d 290, 306–07 (2011), *cert. denied*, 565 U.S. 934 (2011).

9. Does VARA protect a landscaped garden? *See Kelley*, 635 F.3d at 302–06.

10. When purchasing a work of visual art, can the buyer require the artist to waive or assign his or her rights under VARA? What is the term of protection under VARA?

11. If an office building's management places Christmas wreaths, "Santa" hats, and red ribbons on a sculpture in its lobby, does the sculptor have a claim under section 106A?

12. Would an artist's rights under section 106A be violated if the work were destroyed in (1) a fire caused by someone forgetting to turn off a coffee pot? (2) a fire started for the purpose of collecting insurance on the work?

13. What rights, if any, does VARA give an artist to repair a work of visual art if it begins to deteriorate or suffers accidental damage?

GILLIAM V. AMERICAN BROADCASTING COMPANIES, INC.

538 F.2d 14 (2d Cir. 1976).

LUMBARD, CIRCUIT JUDGE.

[Plaintiffs Gilliam et al., known as the "Monty Python" group, were the authors and copyright owners of certain television scripts which they licensed to BBC for production and public performance. The plaintiffs retained their copyright in the scripts, however, and the licensing agreement expressly reserved to them the right to object to any alterations of the recorded programs. BBC sublicensed the American television rights to Time-Warner. When Time-Warner granted broadcast rights to ABC, ABC edited the programs extensively in order to fit time constraints and insert commercials. After determining that the plaintiffs were likely to succeed on their claim that this unauthorized editing violated the plaintiffs' exclusive right under 17 U.S.C. § 106(2) to create derivative works, the court of appeals addressed the plaintiffs' claims under section 43(a) of the Lanham Act, 15 U.S.C. § 1125(a).]

* * *

Here, the appellants claim that the editing done for ABC mutilated the original work and that consequently the broadcast of those programs as the creation of Monty Python violated the Lanham Act § 43(a), 15 U.S.C. § 1125(a).[10] This statute, the federal counterpart to state unfair competition laws, has been invoked to prevent misrepresentations that may injure plaintiff's business or personal reputation, even where no registered trademark is concerned. It is sufficient to violate the Act that a representation of a product, although technically true, creates a false impression of the product's origin. *See Rich v. RCA Corp.*, 390 F. Supp. 530 (S.D.N.Y.1975) (recent picture of plaintiff on cover of album containing songs recorded in distant past held to be a false representation that the songs were new).

These cases cannot be distinguished from the situation in which a television network broadcasts a program properly designated as having been written and performed by a group, but which has been edited, without the writer's consent, into a form that departs substantially from the original work. "To deform his work is to present him to the public as the creator of a work not his own, and thus makes him subject to criticism for work he has not done." Roeder, *The Doctrine of Moral Right,* 53 HARV. L. REV. 554, 569 (1940). In such a case, it is the writer or performer, rather than the network, who suffers the consequences of the mutilation, for the public will have only the final product by which to evaluate the work. Thus, an allegation that a defendant has presented to the public a "garbled," distorted version of plaintiff's work seeks to redress the very rights sought to be protected by the Lanham Act, 15 U.S.C. § 1125(a), and should be recognized as stating a cause of action under that statute. During the hearing on the preliminary injunction, Judge Lasker viewed the edited version of the Monty Python program broadcast on December 26 and the original, unedited version. After hearing argument of this appeal, this panel also viewed and compared the two versions. We find that the truncated version at times omitted the climax of the skits to which appellants' rare brand of humor was leading and at other times deleted essential elements in the schematic development of a story line. We therefore agree with Judge Lasker's conclusion that the edited version broadcast by ABC impaired the integrity of appellants' work and represented to the public as the product of appellants what was actually a mere caricature of their talents. We believe that a valid cause of action for such distortion exists and that therefore a preliminary injunction may

---

[10] That statute provides in part:

Any person who shall affix, apply, or annex, or use in connection with any goods or services, . . . a false designation of origin, or any false description or representation . . . and shall cause such goods or services to enter into commerce . . . shall be liable to a civil action by any person . . . who believes that he is or is likely to be damaged by the use of any such false description or representation.

issue to prevent repetition of the broadcast prior to final determination of the issues.

* * *

NOTE

Does moral rights protection in the United States comply with Art. 6bis of the Berne Convention? (*See* footnote 14 in *Buchel.*) If not, should it?

3. RESALE ROYALTIES (*DROIT DE SUITE*)

The European doctrine known as *droit de suite* protects an artist's right to share in the revenues from subsequent sales of his or her work. In the United States, however, there is no federal resale royalty provision, and state legislation has been adopted only in California. The California Resale Royalties Act, Cal. Civ. Code § 986, gives the artist a five percent royalty on sales of "fine art" for $1000 or more which take place within California or involve state residents; the right expires 20 years after the artist's death.

What public interests are served by resale royalty legislation? Should Congress enact a federal resale royalty statute? If individual states follow California's lead, what are the potential economic effects of imposing resale royalty obligations only on transactions taking place within certain states or involving state residents? Does California's law frustrate the purposes of the first sale rule?

In *Sam Francis Foundation v. Christies, Inc.*, 784 F.3d 1320 (9th Cir. 2015) (en banc), the Ninth Circuit held that the California provision "regulating sales outside the state of California facially violates the 'dormant' Commerce Clause but that the offending provision is severable from the remainder of the Act." The court remanded for further proceedings.

CHAPTER 17

FAIR USE

■ ■ ■

Statute: 17 U.S.C. § 107

When "fair use" was finally codified in the 1976 Act, this judicially-created concept already had a lengthy history. English courts applying the Statute of Anne of 1710 had recognized that in some instances a "fair abridgement" of a work should not be deemed to infringe the author's rights, and though Congress did not mention fair use in the Copyright Act of 1790, the doctrine was recognized shortly thereafter in two opinions by Justice Story, *Folsom v. Marsh*, 9 F. Cas. 342 (C.C.D. Mass.1841), and *Gray v. Russell*, 10 F. Cas. 1035 (C.C.D. Mass.1839). It received broad judicial acceptance thereafter as an affirmative defense.

Unlike the rights-specific limitations spelled out in sections 108–20 and 1008 of Title 17, section 107 can be applied to limit any of the rights contained in sections 106 and 106A. Reflecting Congress' intent to preserve the historic flexibility of this judge-made doctrine, the codification of fair use in section 107 is remarkably brief. The 1976 House Report lists examples, "by no means exhaustive," of potential fair use activities:

> "Quotation of excerpts in a review or criticism for purposes of illustration or comment; quotation of short passages in a scholarly or technical work, for illustration or clarification of the author's observations; use in a parody of some of the content of the work parodied; summary of an address or article, with brief quotations, in a news report; reproduction by a library of a portion of a work to replace part of a damaged copy; reproduction by a teacher or student of a small part of a work to illustrate a lesson; reproduction of a work in legislative or judicial proceedings or reports; incidental and fortuitous reproduction, in a newsreel or broadcast, of a work located in the scene of an event being reported." * * *

H.R. Rep. No. 94–1476, 94th Cong., 2d Sess. 65 (1976) (quoting p. 24 of 1961 Register of Copyright's Report).

The function of fair use in copyright law was summarized in the House Report accompanying the most recent amendment of section 107:

> * * * As United States District Judge Pierre Leval has written, the purpose of fair use is to "serve the copyright objective of

> stimulating productive thought and public instruction without excessively diminishing the incentives for creativity." * * * Section 107 contains criteria derived from earlier court decisions. The preamble to Section 107 lists six illustrative types of uses that may be analyzed under the doctrine: criticism, comment, news reporting, teaching, scholarship, and research. These uses are not, however, presumptively fair. Instead, the courts are directed to examine the use according to four statutory factors * * *. While all four factors must be considered in each fair use case, additional factors may also be considered in the court's discretion. All claims of fair use must be judged on the totality of the facts in the particular case by balancing all the factors. For this reason, fair use litigation will always be piecemeal: no legislative solution can answer in advance the outcome of a given dispute.

H.R. Rep. No. 102–836, 102d Cong., 2d Sess. 3–4 (1992).

SONY CORP. OF AMERICA V. UNIVERSAL CITY STUDIOS, INC.

464 U.S. 417, 104 S.Ct. 774 (1984).

JUSTICE STEVENS delivered the opinion of the Court.

[Respondents Universal City Studios and Walt Disney Productions, which owned copyrights in various motion pictures broadcast on television, brought this action against petitioner Sony for damages, an accounting and an injunction preventing further manufacture and marketing of its home videotape recorders (Betamax VTRs). Respondents argued that selling the VTRs made Sony a contributory copyright infringer because some of Sony's customers used the devices to record respondents' programs off the air. At trial, the evidence showed that the customers' primary use of their VTRs was for "time-shifting"—that is, recording a television program in order to view it at a later, more convenient, time, and then erasing the tape for reuse. Although the district court ruled in Sony's favor, the Ninth Circuit reversed, holding Sony liable for contributory infringement. On appeal, the Supreme Court held that, by analogy to patent law, Sony could be held liable for contributory copyright infringement only if the VTRs were not capable of any "substantial noninfringing use." (See Chapter 18 for a discussion of contributory copyright infringement.) This led the Court to analyze whether time-shifting was a fair use under § 107.]

* * *

Even unauthorized uses of a copyrighted work are not necessarily infringing. An unlicensed use of the copyright is not an infringement unless it conflicts with one of the specific exclusive rights conferred by the copyright statute. Moreover, the definition of exclusive rights in § 106 of the present Act is prefaced by the words "subject to sections 107 through

118." Those sections describe a variety of uses of copyrighted material that "are not infringements of copyright" "notwithstanding the provisions of section 106." The most pertinent in this case is § 107, the legislative endorsement of the doctrine of "fair use."

That section identifies various factors that enable a court to apply an "equitable rule of reason" analysis to particular claims of infringement. Although not conclusive, the first factor requires that "the commercial or nonprofit character of an activity" be weighed in any fair use decision. If the Betamax were used to make copies for a commercial or profit-making purpose, such use would presumptively be unfair. The contrary presumption is appropriate here, however, because the District Court's findings plainly establish that time-shifting for private home use must be characterized as a noncommercial, nonprofit activity. Moreover, when one considers the nature of a televised copyrighted audiovisual work, *see* 17 U.S.C. § 107(2), and that time-shifting merely enables a viewer to see such a work which he had been invited to witness in its entirety free of charge, the fact that the entire work is reproduced, *see* § 107(3), does not have its ordinary effect of militating against a finding of fair use.

This is not, however, the end of the inquiry because Congress has also directed us to consider "the effect of the use upon the potential market for or value of the copyrighted work." § 107(4). The purpose of copyright is to create incentives for creative effort. Even copying for noncommercial purposes may impair the copyright holder's ability to obtain the rewards that Congress intended him to have. But a use that has no demonstrable effect upon the potential market for, or the value of, the copyrighted work need not be prohibited in order to protect the author's incentive to create. The prohibition of such noncommercial uses would merely inhibit access to ideas without any countervailing benefit.

Thus, although every commercial use of copyrighted material is presumptively an unfair exploitation of the monopoly privilege that belongs to the owner of the copyright, noncommercial uses are a different matter. A challenge to a noncommercial use of a copyrighted work requires proof either that the particular use is harmful, or that if it should become widespread, it would adversely affect the potential market for the copyrighted work. Actual present harm need not be shown; such a requirement would leave the copyright holder with no defense against predictable damage. Nor is it necessary to show with certainty that future harm will result. What is necessary is a showing by a preponderance of the evidence that some meaningful likelihood of future harm exists. If the intended use is for commercial gain, that likelihood may be presumed. But if it is for a noncommercial purpose, the likelihood must be demonstrated.

In this case, respondents failed to carry their burden with regard to home time-shifting. * * *

On the question of potential future harm from time-shifting, the District Court * * * rejected respondents' "fear that persons 'watching' the original telecast of a program will not be measured in the live audience and the ratings and revenues will decrease," by observing that current measurement technology allows the Betamax audience to be reflected. It rejected respondents' prediction "that live television or movie audiences will decrease as more people watch Betamax tapes as an alternative," with the observation that "[there] is no factual basis for [the underlying] assumption." It rejected respondents' "fear that time-shifting will reduce audiences for telecast reruns," and concluded instead that "given current market practices, this should aid plaintiffs rather than harm them." And it declared that respondents' suggestion that "theater or film rental exhibition of a program will suffer because of time-shift recording of that program" "lacks merit."

After completing that review, the District Court [concluded that] "Harm from time-shifting is speculative and, at best, minimal."

The District Court's conclusions are buttressed by the fact that to the extent time-shifting expands public access to freely broadcast television programs, it yields societal benefits. In *Community Television of Southern California v. Gottfried*, 459 U.S. 498, 508, n. 12 (1983), we acknowledged the public interest in making television broadcasting more available. Concededly, that interest is not unlimited. But it supports an interpretation of the concept of "fair use" that requires the copyright holder to demonstrate some likelihood of harm before he may condemn a private act of time-shifting as a violation of federal law.

When these factors are all weighed in the "equitable rule of reason" balance, we must conclude that this record amply supports the District Court's conclusion that home time-shifting is fair use. * * *

NOTES

1. Suppose that *Sony* were decided years later, after pay-per-view and subscription cable and satellite services became a large part of the television market. How should this influence the fair use analysis?

2. How would the fair use analysis apply to each of the following instances of unauthorized copying, assuming that the copy in each case is *retained permanently* for the purpose of noncommercial, personal use:

(a) recording television or radio broadcasts off the air?

(b) copying prerecorded DVDs?

(c) downloading sound recordings off the internet?

3. *A & M Records, Inc. v. Napster, Inc.*, 239 F.3d 1004 (9th Cir. 2001), addressed music file-sharing. Napster argued that its users did not directly infringe plaintiffs' copyrights because the users were engaged in fair use.

Napster identified three specific alleged fair uses: sampling, where users made temporary copies of a work before purchasing; space-shifting, where users accessed a sound recording through Napster that they already owned in CD format; and permissive distribution of recordings by both new and established artists. Was the unauthorized file-sharing in *Napster* different from the scenario in *Sony*?

4. The motion picture industry's dire predictions in *Sony* proved to be unfounded when home video devices created a vast new market for the industry—the sale of films on videotapes, DVDs, and Blu-ray discs—displaced many years later by the market for streaming video.

HARPER & ROW V. NATION ENTERPRISES

471 U.S. 539, 105 S.Ct. 2218 (1985).

JUSTICE O'CONNOR delivered the opinion of the Court.

* * *

I

[Former President Gerald Ford wrote a memoir that included previously unpublished material about the Watergate crisis and Ford's pardon of former President Nixon, and sold the rights to Harper & Row. The latter gave Time magazine an exclusive license to publish excerpts on the eve of the book's publication. Before that could happen, however, The Nation magazine knowingly obtained an unauthorized copy of Ford's manuscript, and published excerpts without a license. As a result, Time exercised its right to cancel the Harper & Row contract. In the ensuing infringement suit, the district court rejected The Nation's fair use defense. A split panel of the Second Circuit reversed, finding that, once uncopyrightable facts and ideas were separated from copyrightable expression, The Nation had copied only 300 words protected by copyright.]

* * *

Examining the four factors enumerated in § 107, the majority found the purpose of the article was "news reporting," the original work was essentially factual in nature, the 300 words appropriated were insubstantial in relation to the 2,250-word piece, and the impact on the market for the original was minimal as "the evidence [did] not support a finding that it was the very limited use of expression per se which led to Time's decision not to print the excerpt." The Nation's borrowing of verbatim quotations merely "[lent] authenticity to this politically significant material . . . complementing the reporting of the facts." The Court of Appeals was especially influenced by the "politically significant" nature of the subject matter and its conviction that it is not "the purpose of the Copyright Act to impede that harvest of knowledge so necessary to a democratic state" or "chill the activities of the press by forbidding a circumscribed use of copyrighted words."

II

We agree with the Court of Appeals that copyright is intended to increase and not to impede the harvest of knowledge. But we believe the Second Circuit gave insufficient deference to the scheme established by the Copyright Act for fostering the original works that provide the seed and substance of this harvest. The rights conferred by copyright are designed to assure contributors to the store of knowledge a fair return for their labors.

* * * The Nation has admitted to lifting verbatim quotes of the author's original language totaling between 300 and 400 words and constituting some 13% of The Nation article. In using generous verbatim excerpts of Mr. Ford's unpublished manuscript to lend authenticity to its account of the forthcoming memoirs, The Nation effectively arrogated to itself the right of first publication, an important marketable subsidiary right. For the reasons set forth below, we find that this use of the copyrighted manuscript, even stripped to the verbatim quotes conceded by The Nation to be copyrightable expression, was not a fair use within the meaning of the Copyright Act.

III

A

Fair use was traditionally defined as "a privilege in others than the owner of the copyright to use the copyrighted material in a reasonable manner without his consent." H. BALL, LAW OF COPYRIGHT AND LITERARY PROPERTY 260 (1944). The statutory formulation of the defense of fair use in the Copyright Act reflects the intent of Congress to codify the common-law doctrine. Section 107 requires a case-by-case determination whether a particular use is fair, and the statute notes four nonexclusive factors to be considered. This approach was "intended to restate the [pre-existing] judicial doctrine of fair use, not to change, narrow, or enlarge it in any way." H. R. Rep. No. 94–1476, p. 66 (1976) (hereinafter House Report).

"[The] author's consent to a reasonable use of his copyrighted works [had] always been implied by the courts as a necessary incident of the constitutional policy of promoting the progress of science and the useful arts, since a prohibition of such use would inhibit subsequent writers from attempting to improve upon prior works and thus . . . frustrate the very ends sought to be attained." BALL 260. Professor Latman, in a study of the doctrine of fair use commissioned by Congress for the revision effort, summarized prior law as turning on the "importance of the material copied or performed from the point of view of the reasonable copyright owner. In other words, would the reasonable copyright owner have consented to the use?" A. LATMAN, FAIR USE OF COPYRIGHTED WORKS (1958).

As early as 1841, Justice Story gave judicial recognition to the doctrine in a case that concerned the letters of another former President, George Washington.

> "[A] reviewer may fairly cite largely from the original work, if his design be really and truly to use the passages for the purposes of fair and reasonable criticism. On the other hand, it is as clear, that if he thus cites the most important parts of the work, with a view, not to criticise, but to supersede the use of the original work, and substitute the review for it, such a use will be deemed in law a piracy." *Folsom v. Marsh*, 9 F.Cas. 342, 344–345 (C.C.Mass.)

As Justice Story's hypothetical illustrates, the fair use doctrine has always precluded a use that "[supersedes] the use of the original." *Ibid.*

* * * [I]t has never been seriously disputed that "the fact that the plaintiff's work is unpublished . . . is a factor tending to negate the defense of fair use." 3 NIMMER § 13.05, at 13–62, n. 2. Publication of an author's expression before he has authorized its dissemination seriously infringes the author's right to decide when and whether it will be made public, a factor not present in fair use of published works. Respondents contend, however, that Congress, in including first publication among the rights enumerated in § 106, which are expressly subject to fair use under § 107, intended that fair use would apply in pari materia to published and unpublished works. The Copyright Act does not support this proposition.

* * *

Though the right of first publication, like the other rights enumerated in § 106, is expressly made subject to the fair use provision of § 107, fair use analysis must always be tailored to the individual case. The right of first publication implicates a threshold decision by the author whether and in what form to release his work. First publication is inherently different from other § 106 rights in that only one person can be the first publisher; as the contract with Time illustrates, the commercial value of the right lies primarily in exclusivity. Because the potential damage to the author from judicially enforced "sharing" of the first publication right with unauthorized users of his manuscript is substantial, the balance of equities in evaluating such a claim of fair use inevitably shifts.

The Senate Report confirms that Congress intended the unpublished nature of the work to figure prominently in fair use analysis. In discussing fair use of photocopied materials in the classroom the Committee Report states:

> "A key, though not necessarily determinative, factor in fair use is whether or not the work is available to the potential user. If the

work is 'out of print' and unavailable for purchase through normal channels, the user may have more justification for reproducing it. . . . The applicability of the fair use doctrine to unpublished works is narrowly limited since, although the work is unavailable, this is the result of a deliberate choice on the part of the copyright owner. Under ordinary circumstances, the copyright owner's 'right of first publication' would outweigh any needs of reproduction for classroom purposes." Senate Report, at 64.

* * *

B

Respondents, however, contend that First Amendment values require a different rule under the circumstances of this case. The thrust of the decision below is that "[t]he scope of [fair use] is undoubtedly wider when the information conveyed relates to matters of high public concern." Respondents advance the substantial public import of the subject matter of the Ford memoirs as grounds for excusing a use that would ordinarily not pass muster as a fair use—the piracy of verbatim quotations for the purpose of "scooping" the authorized first serialization. Respondents explain their copying of Mr. Ford's expression as essential to reporting the news story it claims the book itself represents. In respondents' view, not only the facts contained in Mr. Ford's memoirs, but "the precise manner in which [he] expressed himself [were] as newsworthy as what he had to say." * * * Respondents argue that the public's interest in learning this news as fast as possible outweighs the right of the author to control its first publication.

The Second Circuit noted, correctly, that copyright's idea/expression dichotomy "strike[s] a definitional balance between the First Amendment and the Copyright Act by permitting free communication of facts while still protecting an author's expression." No author may copyright his ideas or the facts he narrates. 17 U.S.C. § 102(b). * * *

Respondents' theory, however, would expand fair use to effectively destroy any expectation of copyright protection in the work of a public figure. Absent such protection, there would be little incentive to create or profit in financing such memoirs, and the public would be denied an important source of significant historical information. The promise of copyright would be an empty one if it could be avoided merely by dubbing the infringement a fair use "news report" of the book.

Nor do respondents assert any actual necessity for circumventing the copyright scheme with respect to the types of works and users at issue here. Where an author and publisher have invested extensive resources in creating an original work and are poised to release it to the public, no legitimate aim is served by pre-empting the right of first publication. The fact that the words the author has chosen to clothe his narrative may of themselves be "newsworthy" is not an independent justification for unauthorized copying of the author's expression prior to publication. * * *

In our haste to disseminate news, it should not be forgotten that the Framers intended copyright itself to be the engine of free expression. By establishing a marketable right to the use of one's expression, copyright supplies the economic incentive to create and disseminate ideas. This Court stated in *Mazer v. Stein,* 347 U.S. 201, 209 (1954):

> "The economic philosophy behind the clause empowering Congress to grant patents and copyrights is the conviction that encouragement of individual effort by personal gain is the best way to advance public welfare through the talents of authors and inventors in 'Science and useful Arts.' "

* * *

It is fundamentally at odds with the scheme of copyright to accord lesser rights in those works that are of greatest importance to the public. Such a notion ignores the major premise of copyright and injures author and public alike. * * *

In view of the First Amendment protections already embodied in the Copyright Act's distinction between copyrightable expression and uncopyrightable facts and ideas, and the latitude for scholarship and comment traditionally afforded by fair use, we see no warrant for expanding the doctrine of fair use to create what amounts to a public figure exception to copyright. Whether verbatim copying from a public figure's manuscript in a given case is or is not fair must be judged according to the traditional equities of fair use.

IV

Fair use is a mixed question of law and fact. *Pacific & Southern Co. v. Duncan,* 744 F.2d 1490, 1495, n. 8 (C.A.11 1984). Where the district court has found facts sufficient to evaluate each of the statutory factors, an appellate court "need not remand for further factfinding . . . [but] may conclude as a matter of law that [the challenged use] do[es] not qualify as a fair use of the copyrighted work." *Id.*, at 1495. Thus whether The Nation article constitutes fair use under § 107 must be reviewed in light of the principles discussed above. The factors enumerated in the section are not meant to be exclusive: "[S]ince the doctrine is an equitable rule of reason, no generally applicable definition is possible, and each case raising the question must be decided on its own facts." House Report, at 65. The four factors identified by Congress as especially relevant in determining whether the use was fair are: (1) the purpose and character of the use; (2) the nature of the copyrighted work; (3) the substantiality of the portion used in relation to the copyrighted work as a whole; (4) the effect on the potential market for or value of the copyrighted work. We address each one separately.

Purpose of the Use. The Second Circuit correctly identified news reporting as the general purpose of The Nation's use. News reporting is one of the examples enumerated in § 107 to "give some idea of the sort of activities the courts might regard as fair use under the circumstances." Senate Report, at 61. This listing was not intended to be exhaustive, *see ibid.*; § 101 (definition of "including" and "such as"), or to single out any particular use as presumptively a "fair" use. The drafters resisted pressures from special interest groups to create presumptive categories of fair use, but structured the provision as an affirmative defense requiring a case-by-case analysis. *See* H. R. Rep. No. 83, 90th Cong., 1st Sess., 37 (1967). "[W]hether a use referred to in the first sentence of section 107 is a fair use in a particular case will depend upon the application of the determinative factors, including those mentioned in the second sentence." Senate Report, at 62. The fact that an article arguably is "news" and therefore a productive use is simply one factor in a fair use analysis.

We agree with the Second Circuit that the trial court erred in fixing on whether the information contained in the memoirs was actually new to the public. * * * The Nation has every right to seek to be the first to publish information. But The Nation went beyond simply reporting uncopyrightable information and actively sought to exploit the headline value of its infringement, making a "news event" out of its unauthorized first publication of a noted figure's copyrighted expression.

The fact that a publication was commercial as opposed to nonprofit is a separate factor that tends to weigh against a finding of fair use. "[E]very commercial use of copyrighted material is presumptively an unfair exploitation of the monopoly privilege that belongs to the owner of the copyright." *Sony Corp. of America v. Universal City Studios, Inc.*, 464 U.S., at 451. In arguing that the purpose of news reporting is not purely commercial, The Nation misses the point entirely. The crux of the profit/nonprofit distinction is not whether the sole motive of the use is monetary gain but whether the user stands to profit from exploitation of the copyrighted material without paying the customary price.

In evaluating character and purpose we cannot ignore The Nation's stated purpose of scooping the forthcoming hardcover and Time abstracts. The Nation's use had not merely the incidental effect but the *intended purpose* of supplanting the copyright holder's commercially valuable right of first publication. Also relevant to the "character" of the use is "the propriety of the defendant's conduct." 3 NIMMER § 13.05[A], at 13–72. "Fair use presupposes 'good faith' and 'fair dealing.'" *Time Inc. v. Bernard Geis Associates*, 293 F.Supp. 130, 146 (S.D.N.Y.1968). The trial court found that The Nation knowingly exploited a purloined manuscript. Unlike the typical claim of fair use, The Nation cannot offer up even the fiction of consent as justification. Like its competitor newsweekly, it was free to bid for the right of abstracting excerpts from "A Time to Heal." Fair use "distinguishes between 'a true scholar and a chiseler who infringes a work for personal profit.'" *Wainwright Securities Inc. v. Wall Street Transcript Corp.*, 558 F.2d, at 94.

Nature of the Copyrighted Work. Second, the Act directs attention to the nature of the copyrighted work. "A Time to Heal" may be characterized as an unpublished historical narrative or autobiography. The law generally recognizes a greater need to disseminate factual works than works of fiction or fantasy. *See* Gorman, *Fact or Fancy? The Implications for Copyright*, 29 J. COPYRIGHT SOC. 560, 561 (1982).

> "[E]ven within the field of fact works, there are gradations as to the relative proportion of fact and fancy. One may move from sparsely embellished maps and directories to elegantly written biography. The extent to which one must permit expressive language to be copied, in order to assure dissemination of the underlying facts, will thus vary from case to case." *Id.*, at 563.

Some of the briefer quotes from the memoirs are arguably necessary adequately to convey the facts; for example, Mr. Ford's characterization of the White House tapes as the "smoking gun" is perhaps so integral to the idea expressed as to be inseparable from it. But The Nation did not stop at isolated phrases and instead excerpted subjective descriptions and portraits of public figures whose power lies in the author's individualized expression. Such use, focusing on the most expressive elements of the work, exceeds that necessary to disseminate the facts.

The fact that a work is unpublished is a critical element of its "nature." Our prior discussion establishes that the scope of fair use is narrower with respect to unpublished works. While even substantial quotations might qualify as fair use in a review of a published work or a news account of a speech that had been delivered to the public or disseminated to the press, the author's right to control the first public appearance of his expression weighs against such use of the work before its release. The right of first publication encompasses not only the choice whether to publish at all, but also the choices of when, where, and in what form first to publish a work.

In the case of Mr. Ford's manuscript, the copyright holders' interest in confidentiality is irrefutable; the copyright holders had entered into a contractual undertaking to "keep the manuscript confidential" and required that all those to whom the manuscript was shown also "sign an agreement to keep the manuscript confidential." While the copyright holders' contract with Time required Time to submit its proposed article seven days before publication, The Nation's clandestine publication afforded no such opportunity for creative or quality control. It was hastily patched together and contained "a number of inaccuracies." A use that so clearly infringes the copyright holder's interests in confidentiality and creative control is difficult to characterize as "fair."

Amount and Substantiality of the Portion Used. Next, the Act directs us to examine the amount and substantiality of the portion used in relation to the copyrighted work as a whole. In absolute terms, the words actually quoted were an insubstantial portion of "A Time to Heal." The District Court, however, found that "[T]he Nation took what was essentially the heart of the book." We believe the Court of Appeals erred in overruling the District Judge's evaluation of the qualitative nature of the taking. A Time editor described the chapters on the pardon as "the most interesting and moving parts of the entire manuscript." The portions actually quoted were selected by Mr. Navasky as among the most powerful passages in those chapters. He testified that he used verbatim excerpts because simply reciting the information could not adequately convey the "absolute certainty with which [Ford] expressed himself," or show that "this comes from President Ford," or carry the "definitive quality" of the original. In short, he quoted these passages precisely because they qualitatively embodied Ford's distinctive expression.

As the statutory language indicates, a taking may not be excused merely because it is insubstantial with respect to the *infringing* work. As Judge Learned Hand cogently remarked, "no plagiarist can excuse the wrong by showing how much of his work he did not pirate." *Sheldon v. Metro-Goldwyn Pictures Corp.*, 81 F.2d 49, 56 (CA2 1936). Conversely, the fact that a substantial portion of the infringing work was copied verbatim is evidence of the qualitative value of the copied material, both to the originator and to the plagiarist who seeks to profit from marketing someone else's copyrighted expression.

Stripped to the verbatim quotes, the direct takings from the unpublished manuscript constitute at least 13% of the infringing article. The Nation article is structured around the quoted excerpts which serve as its dramatic focal points. In view of the expressive value of the excerpts and their key role in the infringing work, we cannot agree with the Second Circuit that the "magazine took a meager, indeed an infinitesimal amount of Ford's original language."

Effect on the Market. Finally, the Act focuses on "the effect of the use upon the potential market for or value of the copyrighted work." This last factor is undoubtedly the single most important element of fair use. "Fair use, when properly applied, is limited to copying by others which does not materially impair the marketability of the work which is copied." 1 NIMMER § 1.10[D], at 1–87. The trial court found not merely a potential but an actual effect on the market. Time's cancellation of its projected serialization and its refusal to pay the $12,500 were the direct effect of the infringement. * * *

More important, to negate fair use one need only show that if the challenged use "should become widespread, it would adversely affect the *potential* market for the copyrighted work." *Sony Corp. of America v. Universal City Studios, Inc.*, 464 U.S., at 451. This inquiry must take account not only of harm to the original but also of harm to the market for derivative works. "If the defendant's work adversely affects the value of any of the rights in the copyrighted work (in this case the adaptation [and serialization] right) the use is not fair." 3 NIMMER § 13.05[B], at 13–77–13–78.

* * * [A] a fair use doctrine that permits extensive prepublication quotations from an unreleased manuscript without the copyright owner's consent poses substantial potential for damage to the marketability of first serialization rights in general. "Isolated instances of minor infringements, when multiplied many times, become in the aggregate a major inroad on copyright that must be prevented."

V

The Court of Appeals erred in concluding that The Nation's use of the copyrighted material was excused by the public's interest in the subject matter. It erred, as well, in overlooking the unpublished nature of the work and the resulting impact on the potential market for first serial rights of permitting unauthorized prepublication excerpts under the rubric of fair use. Finally, in finding the taking "infinitesimal," the Court of Appeals accorded too little weight to the qualitative importance of the quoted passages of original expression. In sum, the traditional doctrine of fair use, as embodied in the Copyright Act, does not sanction the use made by The Nation of these copyrighted materials. Any copyright infringer may claim to benefit the public by increasing public access to the copyrighted work. But Congress has not designed, and we see no warrant for judicially imposing, a "compulsory license" permitting unfettered access to the unpublished copyrighted expression of public figures.

The Nation conceded that its verbatim copying of some 300 words of direct quotation from the Ford manuscript would constitute an infringement unless excused as a fair use. Because we find that The Nation's use of these verbatim excerpts from the unpublished manuscript was not a fair use, the judgment of the Court of Appeals is reversed, and the case is remanded for further proceedings consistent with this opinion.

It is so ordered.

NOTES

1. After the Supreme Court's decision in *Harper & Row*, the Second Circuit issued two opinions which, to many observers, appeared to conclude that *Harper & Row* had established a *per se* rule that there could be no fair use of an unpublished work. *See Salinger v. Random House, Inc.*, 811 F.2d 90 (2d Cir. 1987); *New Era Publications Int'l v. Henry Holt & Co.*, 873 F.2d 576 (2d Cir. 1989). Although the Second Circuit later appeared to retreat from this position, the intense concern sparked by these two decisions led Congress in 1992 to disavow such a *per se* rule by adding what is now the final sentence of section 107: "The fact that a work is unpublished shall not itself bar a finding of fair use if such finding is made upon consideration of all the above factors." Is the unpublished nature of a work still relevant to the fair use analysis?

2. In evaluating the amount of copyrighted expression that was taken, the quantitative analysis asks what percentage of the plaintiff's copyrighted work was taken. But how should the "work" be defined? Suppose the plaintiff owns the copyright in a series of photographs or short stories, which are compiled in a single book? What about individual chapters in a nonfiction text, or entries in an encyclopedia?

CAMPBELL V. ACUFF-ROSE MUSIC, INC.

510 U.S. 569, 114 S.Ct. 1164 (1994).

JUSTICE SOUTER delivered the opinion of the Court.

We are called upon to decide whether 2 Live Crew's commercial parody of Roy Orbison's song, "Oh, Pretty Woman," may be a fair use within the meaning of the Copyright Act of 1976, 17 U.S.C. § 107. Although the District Court granted summary judgment for 2 Live Crew, the Court of Appeals reversed, holding the defense of fair use barred by the song's commercial character and excessive borrowing. Because we hold that a parody's commercial character is only one element to be weighed in a fair use enquiry, and that insufficient consideration was given to the nature of parody in weighing the degree of copying, we reverse and remand.

I

In 1964, Roy Orbison and William Dees wrote a rock ballad called "Oh, Pretty Woman" and assigned their rights in it to respondent Acuff-Rose Music, Inc. Acuff-Rose registered the song for copyright protection.

[Many years later, the rap music group 2 Live Crew wrote and recorded a song called "Pretty Woman," which one member of the group later described as intended, "through comical lyrics, to satirize the original work." Although the group requested permission to use the Orbison/Dees song, offering to pay for it and to afford appropriate credit to the authors and publisher, Acuff-Rose refused. 2 Live Crew released the recording anyway, accompanied by the promised credits, on a collection of songs entitled "As Clean As They Wanna Be." When Acuff-Rose sued for infringement, the district court found that the defendants' song was a parody of the original, and held that it was a fair use. The Sixth Circuit reversed, stating that the defendants' use, even if a parody, was commercial, that they had copied "the heart of the original," and that, according to *Sony*, market harm must be presumed in the case of commercial uses. The Supreme Court granted certiorari.]

* * *

II

It is uncontested here that 2 Live Crew's song would be an infringement of Acuff-Rose's rights in "Oh, Pretty Woman," under the Copyright Act of 1976 but for a finding of fair use through parody. From the infancy of copyright protection, some opportunity for fair use of copyrighted materials has been thought necessary to fulfill copyright's very purpose, "to promote the Progress of Science and useful Arts. . . ." U.S. Const., Art. I, § 8, cl. 8. For as Justice Story explained, "in truth, in literature, in science and in art, there are, and can be, few, if any, things, which in an abstract sense, are strictly new and original throughout. Every book in literature, science and art, borrows, and must necessarily borrow, and use much which was well known and used before." *Emerson v. Davies*, 8 F. Cas. 615, 619 (No. 4,436) (CCD Mass. 1845). * * *

In *Folsom v. Marsh*, Justice Story distilled the essence of law and methodology from the earlier cases: "look to the nature and objects of the selections made, the quantity and value of the materials used, and the degree in which the use may prejudice the sale, or diminish the profits, or supersede the objects, of the original work." 9 F. Cas. 342, 348 (CCD Mass. 1841). Thus expressed, fair use remained exclusively judge-made doctrine until the passage of the 1976 Copyright Act, in which Story's summary is discernible[.] * * * Congress meant § 107 "to restate the present judicial doctrine of fair use, not to change, narrow, or enlarge it in any way" and intended that courts continue the common law tradition of fair use adjudication. H. R. Rep. No. 94–1476, p. 66 (1976) (hereinafter House Report); S. Rep. No. 94–473, p. 62 (1975) (hereinafter Senate Report). The fair use doctrine thus "permits [and requires] courts to avoid rigid application of the copyright statute when, on occasion, it would stifle the very creativity which that law is designed to foster." *Stewart v. Abend*, 495 U.S. 207, 236 (1990).

The task is not to be simplified with bright-line rules, for the statute, like the doctrine it recognizes, calls for case-by-case analysis. The text employs the terms "including" and "such as" in the preamble paragraph to indicate the "illustrative and not limitative" function of the examples given, § 101, which thus provide only general guidance about the sorts of copying that courts and Congress most commonly had found to be fair uses. Nor may the four statutory factors be treated in isolation, one from another. All are to be explored, and the results weighed together, in light of the purposes of copyright.

A

The first factor in a fair use enquiry is "the purpose and character of the use, including whether such use is of a commercial nature or is for nonprofit educational purposes." § 107(1). This factor draws on Justice Story's formulation, "the nature and objects of the selections made." *Folsom v. Marsh,* 9 F. Cas., at 348. The enquiry here may be guided by the examples given in the preamble to § 107, looking to whether the use is for criticism, or comment, or news reporting, and the like, *see* § 107. The central purpose of this investigation is to see, in Justice Story's words, whether the new work merely "supersedes the objects" of the original creation, or instead adds something new, with a further purpose or different character, altering the first with new expression, meaning, or message; it asks, in other words, whether and to what extent the new work is "transformative." Although such transformative use is not absolutely necessary for a finding of fair use,[11] the goal of copyright, to promote science and the arts, is generally furthered by the creation of transformative works. Such works thus lie at the heart of the fair use doctrine's guarantee of breathing space within the confines of copyright, and the more transformative the new work, the less will be the significance of other factors, like commercialism, that may weigh against a finding of fair use.

This Court has only once before even considered whether parody may be fair use, and that time issued no opinion because of the Court's equal division. *Benny v. Loew's Inc.,* 239 F.2d 532 (C.A.9 1956), *aff'd sub nom. Columbia Broadcasting System, Inc. v. Loew's Inc.,* 356 U.S. 43 (1958). Suffice it to say now that parody has an obvious claim to transformative value, as Acuff-Rose itself does not deny. Like less ostensibly humorous forms of criticism, it can provide social benefit, by shedding light on an earlier work, and, in the process, creating a new one. We thus line up with the courts that have held that parody, like other comment or criticism, may claim fair use under § 107. *See, e.g., Fisher v. Dees,* 794 F.2d 432 (C.A.9 1986) ("When Sonny Sniffs Glue," a parody of "When Sunny Gets Blue," is fair use); *Elsmere Music, Inc. v. National Broadcasting Co.,* 482 F. Supp. 741 (S.D.N.Y.), *aff'd,* 623 F.2d 252 (C.A.2 1980) ("I Love Sodom," a "Saturday Night Live" television parody of "I Love New York" is fair use); *see also* House Report, p. 65; Senate Report, p. 61 ("Use in a parody of some of the content of the work parodied" may be fair use).

The germ of parody lies in the definition of the Greek parodeia, quoted in Judge Nelson's Court of Appeals dissent, as "a song sung alongside

[11] The obvious statutory exception to this focus on transformative uses is the straight reproduction of multiple copies for classroom distribution.

another." Modern dictionaries accordingly describe a parody as a "literary or artistic work that imitates the characteristic style of an author or a work for comic effect or ridicule," or as a "composition in prose or verse in which the characteristic turns of thought and phrase in an author or class of authors are imitated in such a way as to make them appear ridiculous." For the purposes of copyright law, the nub of the definitions, and the heart of any parodist's claim to quote from existing material, is the use of some elements of a prior author's composition to create a new one that, at least in part, comments on that author's works. If, on the contrary, the commentary has no critical bearing on the substance or style of the original composition, which the alleged infringer merely uses to get attention or to avoid the drudgery in working up something fresh, the claim to fairness in borrowing from another's work diminishes accordingly (if it does not vanish), and other factors, like the extent of its commerciality, loom larger.[14] Parody needs to mimic an original to make its point, and so has some claim to use the creation of its victim's (or collective victims') imagination, whereas satire can stand on its own two feet and so requires justification for the very act of borrowing.[15]

The fact that parody can claim legitimacy for some appropriation does not, of course, tell either parodist or judge much about where to draw the line. Like a book review quoting the copyrighted material criticized, parody may or may not be fair use, and petitioner's suggestion that any parodic use is presumptively fair has no more justification in law or fact than the equally hopeful claim that any use for news reporting should be presumed fair, *see Harper & Row*, 471 U.S., at 561. The Act has no hint of an evidentiary preference for parodists over their victims, and no workable presumption for parody could take account of the fact that parody often shades into satire when society is lampooned through its creative artifacts, or that a work may contain both parodic and non-parodic elements. Accordingly, parody, like any other use, has to work its way through the relevant factors, and be judged case by case, in light of the ends of the copyright law.

Here, the District Court held, and the Court of Appeals assumed, that 2 Live Crew's "Pretty Woman" contains parody, commenting on and criticizing the original work, whatever it may have to say about society at

---

[14] A parody that more loosely targets an original than the parody presented here may still be sufficiently aimed at an original work to come within our analysis of parody. If a parody whose wide dissemination in the market runs the risk of serving as a substitute for the original or licensed derivatives (see *infra*, discussing factor four), it is more incumbent on one claiming fair use to establish the extent of transformation and the parody's critical relationship to the original. By contrast, when there is little or no risk of market substitution, whether because of the large extent of transformation of the earlier work, the new work's minimal distribution in the market, the small extent to which it borrows from an original, or other factors, taking parodic aim at an original is a less critical factor in the analysis, and looser forms of parody may be found to be fair use, as may satire with lesser justification for the borrowing than would otherwise be required.

[15] Satire has been defined as a work "in which prevalent follies or vices are assailed with ridicule," or are "attacked through irony, derision, or wit."

large. As the District Court remarked, the words of 2 Live Crew's song copy the original's first line, but then "quickly degenerate into a play on words, substituting predictable lyrics with shocking ones . . . [that] derisively demonstrate how bland and banal the Orbison song seems to them." Judge Nelson, dissenting below, came to the same conclusion, that the 2 Live Crew song "was clearly intended to ridicule the white-bread original" and "reminds us that sexual congress with nameless streetwalkers is not necessarily the stuff of romance and is not necessarily without its consequences. The singers (there are several) have the same thing on their minds as did the lonely man with the nasal voice, but here there is no hint of wine and roses." Although the majority below had difficulty discerning any criticism of the original in 2 Live Crew's song, it assumed for purposes of its opinion that there was some.

We have less difficulty in finding that critical element in 2 Live Crew's song than the Court of Appeals did, although having found it we will not take the further step of evaluating its quality. The threshold question when fair use is raised in defense of parody is whether a parodic character may reasonably be perceived. Whether, going beyond that, parody is in good taste or bad does not and should not matter to fair use. As Justice Holmes explained, "it would be a dangerous undertaking for persons trained only to the law to constitute themselves final judges of the worth of [a work], outside of the narrowest and most obvious limits. At the one extreme some works of genius would be sure to miss appreciation. Their very novelty would make them repulsive until the public had learned the new language in which their author spoke." *Bleistein v. Donaldson Lithographing Co.*, 188 U.S. 239, 251 (1903).

While we might not assign a high rank to the parodic element here, we think it fair to say that 2 Live Crew's song reasonably could be perceived as commenting on the original or criticizing it, to some degree. 2 Live Crew juxtaposes the romantic musings of a man whose fantasy comes true, with degrading taunts, a bawdy demand for sex, and a sigh of relief from paternal responsibility. The later words can be taken as a comment on the naivete of the original of an earlier day, as a rejection of its sentiment that ignores the ugliness of street life and the debasement that it signifies. It is this joinder of reference and ridicule that marks off the author's choice of parody from the other types of comment and criticism that traditionally have had a claim to fair use protection as transformative works.

The Court of Appeals, however, immediately cut short the enquiry into 2 Live Crew's fair use claim by confining its treatment of the first factor essentially to one relevant fact, the commercial nature of the use. The court then inflated the significance of this fact by applying a presumption ostensibly culled from *Sony*, that "every commercial use of copyrighted material is presumptively . . . unfair. . . ." *Sony*, 464 U.S., at 451. In giving virtually dispositive weight to the commercial nature of the parody, the Court of Appeals erred.

The language of the statute makes clear that the commercial or nonprofit educational purpose of a work is only one element of the first factor enquiry into its purpose and character. Section 107(1) uses the term "including" to begin the dependent clause referring to commercial use, and the main clause speaks of a broader investigation into "purpose and character." As we explained in *Harper & Row*, Congress resisted attempts to narrow the ambit of this traditional enquiry by adopting categories of presumptively fair use, and it urged courts to preserve the breadth of their traditionally ample view of the universe of relevant evidence. 471 U.S., at 561; House Report, p. 66. Accordingly, the mere fact that a use is educational and not for profit does not insulate it from a finding of infringement, any more than the commercial character of a use bars a finding of fairness. If, indeed, commerciality carried presumptive force against a finding of fairness, the presumption would swallow nearly all of the illustrative uses listed in the preamble paragraph of § 107, including news reporting, comment, criticism, teaching, scholarship, and research, since these activities "are generally conducted for profit in this country." Congress could not have intended such a rule, which certainly is not inferable from the common-law cases, arising as they did from the world of letters in which Samuel Johnson could pronounce that "no man but a blockhead ever wrote, except for money." 3 BOSWELL'S LIFE OF JOHNSON 19.

Sony itself called for no hard evidentiary presumption. There, we emphasized the need for a "sensitive balancing of interests," noted that Congress had "eschewed a rigid, bright-line approach to fair use," and stated that the commercial or nonprofit educational character of a work is "not conclusive," but rather a fact to be "weighed along with others in fair use decisions." The Court of Appeals' elevation of one sentence from *Sony* to a per se rule thus runs as much counter to *Sony* itself as to the long common-law tradition of fair use adjudication. Rather, as we explained in *Harper & Row*, *Sony* stands for the proposition that the "fact that a publication was commercial as opposed to nonprofit is a separate factor that tends to weigh against a finding of fair use." But that is all, and the fact that even the force of that tendency will vary with the context is a further reason against elevating commerciality to hard presumptive significance. The use, for example, of a copyrighted work to advertise a product, even in a parody, will be entitled to less indulgence under the first factor of the fair use enquiry, than the sale of a parody for its own sake, let alone one performed a single time by students in school.[18]

---

[18] Finally, regardless of the weight one might place on the alleged infringer's state of mind, compare *Harper & Row*, 471 U.S., at 562 (fair use presupposes good faith and fair dealing), with *Folsom v. Marsh*, 9 F.Cas. 342, 349 (No. 4,901) (CCD Mass. 1841) (good faith does not bar a finding

B

The second statutory factor, "the nature of the copyrighted work," § 107(2), draws on Justice Story's expression, the "value of the materials used." This factor calls for recognition that some works are closer to the core of intended copyright protection than others, with the consequence that fair use is more difficult to establish when the former works are copied. *See, e.g., Stewart v. Abend*, 495 U.S., at 237–238 (contrasting fictional short story with factual works); *Harper & Row*, 471 U.S., at 563–564 (contrasting soon-to-be-published memoir with published speech); *Sony*, 464 U.S., at 455, n. 40 (contrasting motion pictures with news broadcasts); *Feist*, 499 U.S., at 348–351 (contrasting creative works with bare factual compilations). We agree with both the District Court and the Court of Appeals that the Orbison original's creative expression for public dissemination falls within the core of the copyright's protective purposes. This fact, however, is not much help in this case, or ever likely to help much in separating the fair use sheep from the infringing goats in a parody case, since parodies almost invariably copy publicly known, expressive works.

C

The third factor asks whether "the amount and substantiality of the portion used in relation to the copyrighted work as a whole," § 107(3), are reasonable in relation to the purpose of the copying. Here, attention turns to the persuasiveness of a parodist's justification for the particular copying done, and the enquiry will harken back to the first of the statutory factors, for, as in prior cases, we recognize that the extent of permissible copying varies with the purpose and character of the use. *See Sony*, 464 U.S., at 449–450 (reproduction of entire work "does not have its ordinary effect of militating against a finding of fair use" as to home videotaping of television programs); *Harper & Row*, 471 U.S., at 564 ("Even substantial quotations might qualify as fair use in a review of a published work or a news account of a speech" but not in a scoop of a soon-to-be-published memoir). The facts bearing on this factor will also tend to address the fourth, by revealing the degree to which the parody may serve as a market substitute for the original or potentially licensed derivatives.

The District Court considered the song's parodic purpose in finding that 2 Live Crew had not helped themselves overmuch. The Court of Appeals disagreed, stating that "while it may not be inappropriate to find that no more was taken than necessary, the copying was qualitatively substantial. . . . We conclude that taking the heart of the original and

---

of infringement); *Leval* 1126–1127 (good faith irrelevant to fair use analysis), we reject Acuff-Rose's argument that 2 Live Crew's request for permission to use the original should be weighed against a finding of fair use. Even if good faith were central to fair use, 2 Live Crew's actions do not necessarily suggest that they believed their version was not fair use; the offer may simply have been made in a good faith effort to avoid this litigation. If the use is otherwise fair, then no permission need be sought or granted. Thus, being denied permission to use a work does not weigh against a finding of fair use.

making it the heart of a new work was to purloin a substantial portion of the essence of the original." 972 F.2d, at 1438.

The Court of Appeals is of course correct that this factor calls for thought not only about the quantity of the materials used, but about their quality and importance, too. In *Harper & Row*, for example, the Nation had taken only some 300 words out of President Ford's memoirs, but we signalled the significance of the quotations in finding them to amount to "the heart of the book," the part most likely to be newsworthy and important in licensing serialization. We also agree with the Court of Appeals that whether "a substantial portion of the infringing work was copied verbatim" from the copyrighted work is a relevant question, for it may reveal a dearth of transformative character or purpose under the first factor, or a greater likelihood of market harm under the fourth; a work composed primarily of an original, particularly its heart, with little added or changed, is more likely to be a merely superseding use, fulfilling demand for the original.

Where we part company with the court below is in applying these guides to parody, and in particular to parody in the song before us. Parody presents a difficult case. Parody's humor, or in any event its comment, necessarily springs from recognizable allusion to its object through distorted imitation. Its art lies in the tension between a known original and its parodic twin. When parody takes aim at a particular original work, the parody must be able to "conjure up" at least enough of that original to make the object of its critical wit recognizable. What makes for this recognition is quotation of the original's most distinctive or memorable features, which the parodist can be sure the audience will know. Once enough has been taken to assure identification, how much more is reasonable will depend, say, on the extent to which the song's overriding purpose and character is to parody the original or, in contrast, the likelihood that the parody may serve as a market substitute for the original. But using some characteristic features cannot be avoided.

We think the Court of Appeals was insufficiently appreciative of parody's need for the recognizable sight or sound when it ruled 2 Live Crew's use unreasonable as a matter of law. It is true, of course, that 2 Live Crew copied the characteristic opening bass riff (or musical phrase) of the original, and true that the words of the first line copy the Orbison lyrics. But if quotation of the opening riff and the first line may be said to go to the "heart" of the original, the heart is also what most readily conjures up the song for parody, and it is the heart at which parody takes aim. Copying does not become excessive in relation to parodic purpose merely because the portion taken was the original's heart. If 2 Live Crew had copied a significantly less memorable part of the original, it is difficult to see how its parodic character would have come through.

This is not, of course, to say that anyone who calls himself a parodist can skim the cream and get away scot free. In parody, as in news reporting, context is everything, and the question of fairness asks what else the parodist did besides go to the heart of the original. It is significant that 2 Live Crew not only copied the first line of the original, but thereafter departed markedly from the Orbison lyrics for its own ends. 2 Live Crew not only copied the bass riff and repeated it,[19] but also produced otherwise distinctive sounds, interposing "scraper" noise, overlaying the music with solos in different keys, and altering the drum beat. This is not a case, then, where "a substantial portion" of the parody itself is composed of a "verbatim" copying of the original. It is not, that is, a case where the parody is so insubstantial, as compared to the copying, that the third factor must be resolved as a matter of law against the parodists.

Suffice it to say here that, as to the lyrics, we think the Court of Appeals correctly suggested that "no more was taken than necessary," but just for that reason, we fail to see how the copying can be excessive in relation to its parodic purpose, even if the portion taken is the original's "heart." As to the music, we express no opinion whether repetition of the bass riff is excessive copying, and we remand to permit evaluation of the amount taken, in light of the song's parodic purpose and character, its transformative elements, and considerations of the potential for market substitution sketched more fully below.

D

The fourth fair use factor is "the effect of the use upon the potential market for or value of the copyrighted work." § 107(4). It requires courts to consider not only the extent of market harm caused by the particular actions of the alleged infringer, but also "whether unrestricted and widespread conduct of the sort engaged in by the defendant . . . would result in a substantially adverse impact on the potential market" for the original. The enquiry "must take account not only of harm to the original but also of harm to the market for derivative works." *Harper & Row, supra,* at 568.

Since fair use is an affirmative defense, its proponent would have difficulty carrying the burden of demonstrating fair use without favorable evidence about relevant markets. In moving for summary judgment, 2 Live Crew left themselves at just such a disadvantage when they failed to address the effect on the market for rap derivatives, and confined themselves to uncontroverted submissions that there was no likely effect on the market for the original. They did not, however, thereby subject themselves to the evidentiary presumption applied by the Court of Appeals.

[19] This may serve to heighten the comic effect of the parody, as one witness stated; *see also Elsmere Music, Inc. v. National Broadcasting Co.*, 482 F. Supp. 741, 747 (S.D.N.Y.1980) (repetition of "I Love Sodom"), or serve to dazzle with the original's music, as Acuff-Rose now contends.

In assessing the likelihood of significant market harm, the Court of Appeals quoted from language in *Sony* that " 'if the intended use is for commercial gain, that likelihood may be presumed. But if it is for a noncommercial purpose, the likelihood must be demonstrated.' " The court reasoned that because "the use of the copyrighted work is wholly commercial, . . . we presume a likelihood of future harm to Acuff-Rose exists." In so doing, the court resolved the fourth factor against 2 Live Crew, just as it had the first, by applying a presumption about the effect of commercial use, a presumption which as applied here we hold to be error.

No "presumption" or inference of market harm that might find support in *Sony* is applicable to a case involving something beyond mere duplication for commercial purposes. *Sony*'s discussion of a presumption contrasts a context of verbatim copying of the original in its entirety for commercial purposes, with the non-commercial context of *Sony* itself (home copying of television programming). In the former circumstances, what *Sony* said simply makes common sense: when a commercial use amounts to mere duplication of the entirety of an original, it clearly "supersedes the objects" of the original and serves as a market replacement for it, making it likely that cognizable market harm to the original will occur. But when, on the contrary, the second use is transformative, market substitution is at least less certain, and market harm may not be so readily inferred. Indeed, as to parody pure and simple, it is more likely that the new work will not affect the market for the original in a way cognizable under this factor, that is, by acting as a substitute for it ("superseding [its] objects"). This is so because the parody and the original usually serve different market functions.

We do not, of course, suggest that a parody may not harm the market at all, but when a lethal parody, like a scathing theater review, kills demand for the original, it does not produce a harm cognizable under the Copyright Act. Because "parody may quite legitimately aim at garroting the original, destroying it commercially as well as artistically," B. KAPLAN, AN UNHURRIED VIEW OF COPYRIGHT 69 (1967), the role of the courts is to distinguish between "biting criticism [that merely] suppresses demand [and] copyright infringement[, which] usurps it." *Fisher v. Dees*, 794 F.2d at 438.

This distinction between potentially remediable displacement and unremediable disparagement is reflected in the rule that there is no protectable derivative market for criticism. The market for potential derivative uses includes only those that creators of original works would in general develop or license others to develop. Yet the unlikelihood that creators of imaginative works will license critical reviews or lampoons of their own productions removes such uses from the very notion of a potential licensing market. "People ask . . . for criticism, but they only want praise." S. MAUGHAM, OF HUMAN BONDAGE 241. Thus, to the extent that the opinion below may be read to have considered harm to the market for parodies of "Oh, Pretty Woman," the court erred.[22]

In explaining why the law recognizes no derivative market for critical works, including parody, we have, of course, been speaking of the later work as if it had nothing but a critical aspect (i.e., "parody pure and simple"). But the later work may have a more complex character, with effects not only in the arena of criticism but also in protectable markets for derivative works, too. In that sort of case, the law looks beyond the criticism to the other elements of the work, as it does here. 2 Live Crew's song comprises not only parody but also rap music, and the derivative market for rap music is a proper focus of enquiry. Evidence of substantial harm to it would weigh against a finding of fair use, because the licensing of derivatives is an important economic incentive to the creation of originals. Of course, the only harm to derivatives that need concern us, as discussed above, is the harm of market substitution. The fact that a parody may impair the market for derivative uses by the very effectiveness of its critical commentary is no more relevant under copyright than the like threat to the original market.

Although 2 Live Crew submitted uncontroverted affidavits on the question of market harm to the original, neither they, nor Acuff-Rose, introduced evidence or affidavits addressing the likely effect of 2 Live Crew's parodic rap song on the market for a non-parody, rap version of "Oh, Pretty Woman." * * * [I]t is impossible to deal with the fourth factor except by recognizing that a silent record on an important factor bearing on fair use disentitled the proponent of the defense, 2 Live Crew, to summary judgment. The evidentiary hole will doubtless be plugged on remand.

III

It was error for the Court of Appeals to conclude that the commercial nature of 2 Live Crew's parody of "Oh, Pretty Woman" rendered it presumptively unfair. No such evidentiary presumption is available to address either the first factor, the character and purpose of the use, or the fourth, market harm, in determining whether a transformative use, such as parody, is a fair one. The court also erred in holding that 2 Live Crew had necessarily copied excessively from the Orbison original, considering the parodic purpose of the use. We therefore reverse the judgment of the Court of Appeals and remand for further proceedings consistent with this opinion.

It is so ordered.

---

[22] We express no opinion as to the derivative markets for works using elements of an original as vehicles for satire or amusement, making no comment on the original or criticism of it.

NOTES

1. The *Campbell* majority distinguishes between parody and satire for purposes of the fair use analysis. Is this distinction persuasive? Practicable? How should the court resolve the question reserved in footnote 22? Consider the following specific examples in your response:

(a) Defendant, a professional political humorist, writes and performs a humorous song, containing pointed social commentary about the United States military establishment, which uses the music and some of the lyrics of the well-known Marine Corps Hymn.

(b) Defendant writes a song that is intended as a parody but is not perceived as one because the consumers who purchase the sound recording of the parody are either unfamiliar with the original version (and simply want to listen to the parodic version for its own sake), or else simply do not perceive the intended criticism of the original.

(c) Defendant writes a song that is intended simply as a humorous or irreverent variation on another work but is perceived by at least some listeners as a parody or criticism.

2. Compare *Sony*, *Harper & Row*, and *Campbell* in answering the following: (a) In a fair use case, which party bears the burden of establishing the presence or absence of injury to the market for the plaintiff's work? (b) Once injury to the market for the plaintiff's work has been established, which party must prove the cause of the injury—that is, must the defendant prove that the injury was caused by factors other than substitution of the defendant's work for the plaintiff's work, or must the plaintiff prove that no other factors caused the injury?

3. The *Campbell* majority defines the "market" for a work narrowly for purposes of evaluating the fourth factor: "The market for potential derivative uses includes only those that creators of original works would in general develop or license others to develop." Is this akin to a "reasonable copyright owner" standard? Is it circular? Does—and should—the standard take account of different levels of entrepreneurship between different copyright owners? Does this standard make allowance for future technological and market developments? (Consider, for example, whether the market for articles in a daily financial newspaper should be considered to include the use of those articles as teaching materials in a business school, or the use of excerpts from those materials in a blog.)

4. In *American Geophysical Union v. Texaco, Inc.*, 60 F.3d 913, 926 (2d Cir. 1994), the Second Circuit observed:

> Prior to *Campbell*, the Supreme Court had characterized the fourth factor as "the single most important element of fair use," *Harper & Row*, 471 U.S. at 566. However, *Campbell*'s discussion of the fourth factor conspicuously omits this phrasing. Apparently abandoning the

> idea that any factor enjoys primacy, *Campbell* instructs that "all [four factors] are to be explored, and the results weighed together, in light of the purposes of copyright." 114 S.Ct. at 1171.

Do you agree with the Second Circuit's interpretation of *Campbell*? Does such a shift in emphasis improve the fair use analysis?

5. In *Suntrust Bank v. Houghton Mifflin Co.*, 268 F.3d 1257 (11th Cir. 2001), the Eleventh Circuit addressed a lawsuit by the trustee of the Mitchell Trust, which holds the copyright to Margaret Mitchell's novel, *Gone With the Wind* ("GWTW"), against the publisher of Alice Randall' novel, *The Wind Done Gone* ("TWDG"). Randall characterized her novel as a critique of GWTW's depiction of slavery and the Civil-War era American South. To carry out this goal, she used the characters, plot, and major scenes from GWTW in the first half of TWDG. Was this a fair use?

6. If a derivative work's unauthorized use of preexisting material constitutes a fair use, and the derivative work contains sufficient originality, can its author claim copyright protection for her original creative contributions? *See Keeling v. Hars*, 809 F.3d 43 (2d Cir. 2015) (case involving "Point Break Live," a theatrical parody of the 1991 movie Point Break).

GOOGLE LLC V. ORACLE AMERICA, INC.

__ U.S. __, 141 S.Ct. 1183 (2021).

JUSTICE BREYER delivered the opinion of the Court.

Oracle America, Inc., is the current owner of a copyright in Java SE, a computer program that uses the popular Java computer programming language. Google, without permission, has copied a portion of that program, a portion that enables a programmer to call up prewritten software that, together with the computer's hardware, will carry out a large number of specific tasks. The lower courts have considered (1) whether Java SE's owner could copyright the portion that Google copied, and (2) if so, whether Google's copying nonetheless constituted a "fair use" of that material, thereby freeing Google from copyright liability. The Federal Circuit held in Oracle's favor (*i.e.*, that the portion is copyrightable and Google's copying did not constitute a "fair use"). In reviewing that decision, we assume, for argument's sake, that the material was copyrightable. But we hold that the copying here at issue nonetheless constituted a fair use. Hence, Google's copying did not violate the copyright law.

* * *

VI

We turn now to the basic legal question before us: Was Google's copying of the Sun Java API, specifically its use of the declaring code and organizational structure for 37 packages of that API, a "fair use." In answering this question, we shall consider the four factors set forth in the fair use statute as we find them applicable to the kind of computer programs before us. * * * For expository purposes, we begin with the second.

A. "The Nature of the Copyrighted Work"

The Sun Java API is a "user interface." It provides a way through which users (here the programmers) can "manipulate and control" task-performing computer programs "via a series of menu commands." * * *

[W]e can think of the technology as having three essential parts. First, the API includes "implementing code," which actually instructs the computer on the steps to follow to carry out each task. * * *

Second, the Sun Java API associates a particular command, called a "method call," with the calling up of each task. * * *.

Third, the Sun Java API contains computer code that will associate the writing of a method call with particular "places" in the computer that contain the needed implementing code. This is the declaring code. The declaring code both labels the particular tasks in the API and organizes those tasks, or "methods," into "packages" and "classes." We have referred to this organization, by way of rough analogy, as file cabinets, drawers, and files. Oracle [claims] that Google's use of the Sun Java API's declaring code violates its copyrights.

The declaring code at issue here resembles other copyrighted works in that it is part of a computer program. Congress has specified that computer programs are subjects of copyright. It differs, however, from many other kinds of copyrightable computer code. It is inextricably bound together with a general system, the division of computing tasks, that no one claims is a proper subject of copyright. It is inextricably bound up with the idea of organizing tasks into what we have called cabinets, drawers, and files, an idea that is also not copyrightable. It is inextricably bound up with the use of specific commands known to programmers, known here as method calls (such as java.lang.Math.max, etc.), that Oracle does not here contest. And it is inextricably bound up with implementing code, which is copyrightable but was not copied.

* * *

These features mean that, as part of a user interface, the declaring code differs to some degree from the mine run of computer programs. Like other computer programs, it is functional in nature. But unlike many other programs, its use is inherently bound together with uncopyrightable ideas (general task division and organization) and new creative expression (Android's implementing code). Unlike many other programs, its value in significant part derives from the value that those who do not hold copyrights, namely, computer programmers, invest of their own time and effort to learn the API's system. And unlike many other programs, its value lies in its efforts to encourage programmers to learn and to use that system so that they will use (and continue to use) Sun-related implementing programs that Google did not copy.

Although copyrights protect many different kinds of writing, we have emphasized the need to "recogni[ze] that some works are closer to the core of [copyright] than others," *Campbell*, 510 U.S., at 586. In our view, for the reasons just described, the declaring code is, if copyrightable at all, further than are most computer programs (such as the implementing code) from the core of copyright. That fact diminishes the fear, expressed by both the dissent and the Federal Circuit, that application of "fair use" here would seriously undermine the general copyright protection that Congress provided for computer programs. And it means that this factor, "the nature of the copyrighted work," points in the direction of fair use.

B. "The Purpose and Character of the Use"

In the context of fair use, we have considered whether the copier's use "adds something new, with a further purpose or different character, altering" the copyrighted work "with new expression, meaning or message." Commentators have put the matter more broadly, asking whether the copier's use "fulfill[s] the objective of copyright law to stimulate creativity for public illumination." In answering this question, we have used the word "transformative" to describe a copying use that adds something new and important. An " 'artistic painting' " might, for example, fall within the scope of fair use even though it precisely replicates a copyrighted " 'advertising logo to make a comment about consumerism.' " Or, as we held in *Campbell*, a parody can be transformative because it comments on the original or criticizes it, for "[p]arody needs to mimic an original to make its point."

* * *

Here Google's use of the Sun Java API seeks to create new products. It seeks to expand the use and usefulness of Android-based smartphones. Its new product offers programmers a highly creative and innovative tool for a smartphone environment. To the extent that Google used parts of the Sun Java API to create a new platform that could be readily used by programmers, its use was consistent with that creative "progress" that is the basic constitutional objective of copyright itself.

The jury heard that Google limited its use of the Sun Java API to tasks and specific programming demands related to Android. It copied the API (which Sun created for use in desktop and laptop computers) only insofar as needed to include tasks that would be useful in smartphone programs. And it did so only insofar as needed to allow programmers to call upon those tasks without discarding a portion of a familiar programming language and learning a new one. * * *

The record here demonstrates the numerous ways in which reimplementing an interface can further the development of computer programs. The jury heard that shared interfaces are necessary for different programs to speak to each other. ("We have to agree on the APIs so that the application I write to show a movie runs on your device"). It heard that the reimplementation of interfaces is necessary if programmers are to be able to use their acquired skills. ("If the API labels change, then either the software wouldn't continue to work anymore or the developer . . . would have to learn a whole new language to be able to use these API labels"). It heard that the reuse of APIs is common in the industry. It heard that Sun itself had used pre-existing interfaces in creating Java. And it heard that Sun executives thought that widespread use of the Java programming language, including use on a smartphone platform, would benefit the company.

* * *

These and related facts convince us that the "purpose and character" of Google's copying was transformative—to the point where this factor too weighs in favor of fair use.

There are two other considerations that are often taken up under the first factor: commerciality and good faith. The text of § 107 includes various noncommercial uses, such as teaching and scholarship, as paradigmatic examples of privileged copying. There is no doubt that a finding that copying was not commercial in nature tips the scales in favor of fair use. But the inverse is not necessarily true, as many common fair uses are indisputably commercial. For instance, the text of § 107 includes examples like "news reporting," which is often done for commercial profit. So even though Google's use was a commercial endeavor—a fact no party disputed—that is not dispositive of the first factor, particularly in light of the inherently transformative role that the reimplementation played in the new Android system.

As for bad faith, our decision in *Campbell* expressed some skepticism about whether bad faith has any role in a fair use analysis. We find this skepticism justifiable, as "[c]opyright is not a privilege reserved for the well-behaved." We have no occasion here to say whether good faith is as a general matter a helpful inquiry. We simply note that given the strength of the other factors pointing toward fair use and the jury finding in Google's favor on hotly contested evidence, that factbound consideration is not determinative in this context.

C. "The Amount and Substantiality of the Portion Used"

If one considers the declaring code in isolation, the quantitative amount of what Google copied was large. Google copied the declaring code for 37 packages of the Sun Java API, totaling approximately 11,500 lines of code. Those lines of code amount to virtually all the declaring code needed to call up hundreds of different tasks. On the other hand, if one considers the entire set of software material in the Sun Java API, the quantitative amount copied was small. The total set of Sun Java API computer code, including implementing code, amounted to 2.86 million lines, of which the copied 11,500 lines were only 0.4 percent.

The question here is whether those 11,500 lines of code should be viewed in isolation or as one part of the considerably greater whole. We have said that even a small amount of copying may fall outside of the scope of fair use where the excerpt copied consists of the " 'heart' " of the original work's creative expression. *Harper & Row*, 471 U.S., at 564–565. On the other hand, copying a larger amount of material can fall within the scope of fair use where the material copied captures little of the material's creative expression or is central to a copier's valid purpose. * * *

Several features of Google's copying suggest that the better way to look at the numbers is to take into account the several million lines that Google did not copy. For one thing, the Sun Java API is inseparably bound to those task-implementing lines. Its purpose is to call them up. For another, Google copied those lines not because of their creativity, their beauty, or even (in a sense) because of their purpose. It copied them because programmers had already learned to work with the Sun Java API's system, and it would have been difficult, perhaps prohibitively so, to attract programmers to build its Android smartphone system without them. Further, Google's basic purpose was to create a different task-related system for a different computing environment (smartphones) and to create a platform—the Android platform—that would help achieve and popularize that objective. The "substantiality" factor will generally weigh in favor of fair use where, as here, the amount of copying was tethered to a valid, and transformative, purpose.

* * *

D. Market Effects

The fourth statutory factor focuses upon the "effect" of the copying in the "market for or value of the copyrighted work." Consideration of this factor, at least where computer programs are at issue, can prove more complex than at first it may seem. It can require a court to consider the amount of money that the copyright owner might lose. * * *

But a potential loss of revenue is not the whole story. We here must consider not just the amount but also the source of the loss. As we pointed out in *Campbell*, a "lethal parody, like a scathing theatre review," may "kil[l] demand for the original." Yet this kind of harm, even if directly translated into foregone dollars, is not "cognizable under the Copyright Act."

Further, we must take into account the public benefits the copying will likely produce. * * *

As to the likely amount of loss, the jury could have found that Android did not harm the actual or potential markets for Java SE. * * * First, evidence at trial demonstrated that, regardless of Android's smartphone technology, Sun was poorly positioned to succeed in the mobile phone market. * * *

Second, the jury was repeatedly told that devices using Google's Android platform were different in kind from those that licensed Sun's technology. * * * Taken together, the evidence showed that Sun's mobile phone business was declining, while the market increasingly demanded a new form of smartphone technology that Sun was never able to offer.

Finally, the jury also heard evidence that Sun foresaw a benefit from the broader use of the Java programming language in a new platform like Android, as it would further expand the network of Java-trained programmers. In other words, the jury could have understood Android and Java SE as operating in two distinct markets. And because there are two markets at issue, programmers learning the Java language to work in one market (smartphones) are then able to bring those talents to the other market (laptops). See 4 Nimmer on Copyright § 13.05[A][4] (explaining that factor four asks what the impact of "widespread conduct of the sort engaged in by the defendant" would be on the market for the present work).

* * *

On the other hand, Google's copying helped Google make a vast amount of money from its Android platform. And enforcement of the Sun Java API copyright might give Oracle a significant share of these funds. It is important, however, to consider why and how Oracle might have become entitled to this money. When a new interface, like an API or a spreadsheet program, first comes on the market, it may attract new users because of its expressive qualities, such as a better visual screen or because of its superior functionality. As time passes, however, it may be valuable for a different reason, namely, because users, including programmers, are just used to it. They have already learned how to work with it.

The record here is filled with evidence that this factor accounts for Google's desire to use the Sun Java API. This source of Android's profitability has much to do with third parties' (say, programmers') investment in Sun Java programs. It has correspondingly less to do with Sun's investment in creating the Sun Java API. We have no reason to believe that the Copyright Act seeks to protect third parties' investment in learning how to operate a created work. Cf. *Campbell*, 510 U.S., at 591–592 (discussing the need to identify those harms that are "cognizable under the Copyright Act").

Finally, given programmers' investment in learning the Sun Java API, to allow enforcement of Oracle's copyright here would risk harm to the public. Given the costs and difficulties of producing alternative APIs with similar appeal to programmers, allowing enforcement here would make of the Sun Java API's declaring code a lock limiting the future creativity of new programs. * * * To that extent, the lock would interfere with, not further, copyright's basic creativity objectives. * * *

The uncertain nature of Sun's ability to compete in Android's market place, the sources of its lost revenue, and the risk of creativity-related harms to the public, when taken together, convince that this fourth factor—market effects—also weighs in favor of fair use.

* * *

We reach the conclusion that in this case, where Google reimplemented a user interface, taking only what was needed to allow users to put their accrued talents to work in a new and transformative program, Google's copying of the Sun Java API was a fair use of that material as a matter of law. * * *

NOTES

1. After *Google,* does the fourth fair use factor now require courts to consider any *benefits* that a copyright owner might receive as a result of the unauthorized copying (or which might result if the unauthorized copying became widespread)?

2. How much weight did the Court give to the factual finding that Sun/Oracle was poorly positioned to enter the market in which Google exploited the unauthorized copies? How should this consideration affect other fair use cases in which an accused infringer is better positioned than the copyright owner to profit from exploiting the copyrighted work? Is there a risk that this approach will favor "Goliath" defendants over "David" plaintiffs?

3. The *Google* opinion reiterated the Court's holding in *Harper & Row* that fair use is a mixed question of law and fact, in which factual determinations are a necessary part of assessing each of the fair use factors, while the ultimate question is a legal one. How should this affect the standard of review?

4. In *Atari Games Corp. v. Nintendo*, 975 F.2d 832, 843–44 (Fed. Cir. 1992), the Federal Circuit held that fair use did not apply where the defendant made false statements to the Copyright Office in order to obtain a copy of plaintiff's source code as an aid to "reverse engineering" those portions of plaintiff's object code that were needed to make defendant's videogames compatible with plaintiff's videogame console. Comment on the following proposition, which the court derived from *Harper & Row*: "To invoke the fair use exception, an individual must possess an authorized copy of a literary

work." (Note that *Atari Games* predated the Supreme Court's decision in *Google*).

5. To what extent does the use of copyrighted images for illustrative purposes constitute fair use? Consider the case of *Bill Graham Archives v. Dorling Kindersley Ltd.*, 448 F.3d 605 (2d Cir. 2006), which involved concert posters reproduced in reduced size (with captions identifying the events) on the pages of a biography of the musical group, the Grateful Dead. The court found that reproduction of seven images in the 480-page book was fair use, concluding that:

> [U]se of concert posters and tickets as historical artifacts of Grateful Dead performances is transformatively different from the original expressive purpose of BGA's copyrighted images. While the second factor favors BGA because of the creative nature of the images, its weight is limited because DK did not exploit the expressive value of the images. Although BGA's images are copied in their entirety, the third factor does not weigh against fair use because the reduced size of the images is consistent with the author's transformative purpose. Finally, we conclude that DK's use does not harm the market for BGA's sale of its copyrighted artwork, and we do not find market harm based on BGA's hypothetical loss of license revenue from DK's transformative market.

Id. at 615. How useful is this ruling to future biographers, given that each image used in the book took up 1/8 of a page or less?

6. Evaluate the strength of a fair use argument in the following scenarios:

(a) A former member of a controversial church wishes to discredit the church by revealing the contents of its secret "scriptures"—various training documents instructing church ministers in the indoctrination of new members—and therefore scans the documents electronically and posts them on a blog. Various newspapers download them and publish substantial excerpts in related news stories. The former church member, the blogger, and the newspapers are all named as defendants. (Would it matter whether the documents in question were obtained from official court records or from sources within the church?) *See Religious Technology Center v. Netcom On-Line Communication Services, Inc.*, 907 F.Supp. 1361 (N.D. Cal. 1995).

(b) Defendant, a contemporary artist, finds a postcard with a black-and-white photo of a smiling husband and wife seated on a bench and holding a litter of cute puppies. The artist produces a sculpture duplicating the photograph in precise detail, except that it leaves out the original copyright notice. The artist includes this sculpture in a collection of his works which he calls "Banality," and which features sculptures depicting various commodities and images that, in his view, reflect something about modern American culture. The literature accompanying the exhibit describes the puppy sculpture as a "satire or parody" of society at large and as "social criticism," reflecting his belief that there has been an aesthetic decline in American culture. He describes himself as belonging to an artistic tradition traceable to Cubism, Dadaism, and the work of Marcel Duchamp. This tradition incorporates manufactured objects into works of art as a critical commentary both on the incorporated object and on the political and economic system that created it. *See Rogers v. Koons*, 960 F.2d 301 (2d Cir. 1992); *compare Blanch v. Koons*, 467 F.3d 244 (2d Cir. 2006) (finding fair use where same artist used elements of a copyrighted fashion photograph in a collage painting).

(c) Defendants, members of a city council, surreptitiously record adult films being shown at plaintiff's theatre in order to obtain evidence for determining whether the plaintiff's theatre is a public nuisance. *See Jartech, Inc. v. Clancy*, 666 F.2d 403 (9th Cir. 1982).

(d) Defendant, a religious and political figure, is the subject of an obscene satire in plaintiff's magazine. He makes numerous copies of the satire and sends them to his supporters with a request for contributions to defray the cost of his defamation suit. *See Hustler Magazine, Inc. v. Moral Majority, Inc.*, 796 F.2d 1148 (9th Cir. 1986).

(e) Defendant, a college professor, copies plaintiff's copyrighted music videos off of television and edits clips of the videos together into a video, which he narrates, analyzing the depiction of women as sex objects in rock music videos. He also offers the video for sale to colleges, libraries, and individuals.

(f) Defendant makes an unauthorized copy of a physically deteriorating motion picture or sound recording for preservation purposes. Would it matter if the defendant exhibited the resulting works in restored form in order to recoup the expenses of restoration? *See* H.R. Rep. No 94–1476, at 73.

(g) Defendant uses short excerpts and individual frames of an audiovisual work for purposes of criticism or commentary in an educational broadcast. *See* H.R. Rep. No. 94–1476 at 72.

(h) Defendant runs a news clipping subscription service, which collects newspapers and magazines, and records television and radio broadcasts, sorting out the news items and sending copies to the clients to whom each item pertains. The original publishers and broadcasters do not provide a comparable service. *Cf. Pacific & Southern Co. v. Duncan*, 744 F.2d 1490 (11th Cir. 1984).

(i) Plaintiff's copyrighted artwork is visible in the background of a scene in defendant's motion picture. *Cf. Amsinck v. Columbia Pictures Industries*, 862 F.Supp. 1044 (S.D.N.Y. 1994).

(j) An artist produces a series of photographs depicting naked Barbie dolls being attacked by vintage kitchen appliances. *See Mattel, Inc. v. Walking Mountain Prods.*, 353 F.3d 792 (9th Cir. 2003).

7. *Copying for Research Purposes:* Suppose that an organization subscribes to various professional or scientific journals. Without seeking permission from the journals, the institution makes copies of articles at the request of its employees, who use the articles in their research. Is this fair use? Does it matter whether obtaining a license to copy the articles is cumbersome or prohibitively expensive? Does it matter whether the institution is operated for profit—for example, a pharmaceutical company or a law firm?

8. Defendant, a computer servicing company, is sued for copyright infringement by the manufacturer of the computers serviced by the defendant. The plaintiff licenses its software to purchasers of its computers under a licensing agreement that bars customers from letting any other parties copy the software for any purpose, including maintenance of the computers. Defendant is not licensed by the manufacturer to copy its software, but necessarily does so in the course of servicing the computers. Defendant services plaintiff's computers at a lower cost to customers than does the plaintiff, and many of the plaintiff's customers would not have bought the plaintiff's computers if they did not have access to the defendant's lower-cost service. If defendant can prove that plaintiff's revenues have in fact been enhanced as a result of defendant's unauthorized copying, does the fourth fair use factor favor the defendant? *See Triad Systems Corp. v. Southeastern Express Co.*, 64 F.3d 1330 (9th Cir. 1995).

9. Defendant writes a biography of a deceased novelist, and includes excerpts from the novelist's letters, unpublished manuscripts, and private journals (to which defendant had access through a university library), as well as from published novels. In an infringement suit by the novelist's estate, what facts would be important in determining the strength of the defendant's fair use argument? *Compare Salinger v. Random House, Inc.*, 811 F.2d 90 (2d Cir. 1987) *with Wright v. Warner Books*, 953 F.2d 731 (2d Cir. 1991). Recall that Congress amended section 107 in 1992, adding the last sentence to that section particularly in response to the opinion in *Salinger*.

10. Does "fair use" apply to section 1101? Should it?

11. *Fair Use and Section 106A:* The legislative history of the Visual Artists Rights Act of 1990 makes the following comment on fair use:

> Fair Use.—Section 7 of the bill amends 17 U.S.C.A. § 107, and states that section 107's fair use provisions apply to violations of new section 106A as well as to violations of section 106. The Committee does not want to preclude fair use claims in this context. However, it recognizes that it is unlikely that such claims will be appropriate given the limited number of works covered by the Act, and given that the modification of a single copy or limited edition of a work of visual

art has different implications for the fair use doctrine than does an act involving a work reproduced in potentially unlimited copies.

H.R. Rep. 101–514, 101st Cong., 2d Sess. 22 (1990).

12. A professional football team failed to obtain an artist's consent to use his drawing as the team's logo, which the team used on its uniforms and other items for two seasons. After being held liable for infringement, the team adopted a new logo for future seasons, but the old logo was still visible on the team uniforms in videos and photographs from their prior seasons. Which of the following depictions, if any, should be treated as fair use of the artwork?

(a) Videos relating stories from the history of the team and the NFL (including careers of particular players).

(b) Season highlight films.

(c) A short video shown on a large screen in the stadium during home games.

(d) Photographs and a highlight reel that were included in a historical display at the team's stadium.

Compare Bouchat v. Baltimore Ravens Ltd. Partnership, 737 F.3d 932 (4th Cir. 2013) *with Bouchat v. Baltimore Ravens Ltd. Partnership,* 619 F.3d 301 (4th Cir. 2010).

13. *Educational Copying:* In drafting the 1976 Act, Congress chose not to enact a specific exemption for educational copying. H.R. Rep. 1476, 94th Cong., 2d Sess. 66–67 (1976). In an effort to provide greater certainty with regard to copying for classroom use, the House Report incorporates a set of guidelines which resulted from negotiations among the Ad Hoc Committee of Educational Institutions and Organizations on Copyright Law Revision, the Authors League of America, Inc., and the Association of American Publishers, Inc. *See* Agreement on Guidelines for Classroom Copying in Not-For-Profit Educational Institutions, in H.R. Rep. 1476, 94th Cong., 2d Sess. 68–70 (1976). The House Report also incorporates a separate set of guidelines for educational copying of musical works (not limited to photocopying), developed as a result of negotiations between representatives of music publishers, music teachers, and music schools. However, in each case the guidelines note that their purpose is to state the minimum, rather than the maximum, standards of educational fair use. *Id.* at 68–72.

In *Cambridge University Press v. Patton*, 769 F.3d 1232, 1283–84 (11th Cir. 2014), publishers of nonfiction works sued various officials at Georgia State University (GSU) for injunctive relief, alleging that GSU infringed their copyrights by copying, storing, and distributing excerpts of their works in coursepacks made available to students through its electronic reserves system. The district court concluded that GSU's activity was a fair use, but the Eleventh Circuit reversed, based on the following analysis: GSU's use was nontransformative although noncommercial and educational. With respect to the nature of the copyrighted work, even nonfiction works may deserve strong copyright protection, depending on their content. As to the amount copied, while the district court was correct to give little weight to the Classroom Guidelines, it should not have applied a rigid quantitative standard (ten percent or one chapter). Finally, the district court should have given more weight to the market substitution effect, which was "severe," because the copying was nontransformative and GSU used the works for one of the very purposes for which they were marketed.

The scope of "fair use" with respect to classroom photocopying has been litigated on only a few other occasions. *See Princeton University Press v. Michigan Document Services*, 99 F.3d 1381 (6th Cir. 1996) (en banc) (holding commercial copy center liable for infringement where it exceeded the House Report's guidelines in preparing course packs for university professors), *rev'g* 74 F.3d 1512 (6th Cir. 1996); *Basic Books, Inc. v. Kinko's Graphics Corp.*, 758 F.Supp. 1522 (S.D.N.Y. 1991) (similar); *Addison-Wesley Publishing v. New York University,* 1983 Copyright L. Dec. (CCH) para. 25,544 (S.D.N.Y. 1983) (consent decree requiring defendant university to follow House Report's guidelines in future).

Under what circumstances should unauthorized copying of materials for teaching purposes be considered fair use? While the cases above involved photocopying—in some cases by commercial copy shops rather than universities—today's educational uses typically involve uploading, downloading, streaming, or printing digitized works. Should it matter whether the copyright owners participate in the Copyright Clearance Center or a similar arrangement whereby permission can be obtained promptly, without negotiation, at a reasonable price?

Is there an argument for adopting a bright-line test for identifying permissible educational uses of copyrighted works? (See, for example, the educational exemption for certain performances and displays in 17 U.S.C. §§ 110(1)–(2).) Alternatively, should Congress adopt a compulsory licensing scheme?

14. In *Cariou v. Prince*, 714 F.3d 694 (2d Cir. 2013), an "appropriation artist" altered the plaintiff's photographs and incorporated them in a series of paintings and collages. The Second Circuit held that such a use can be transformative even if it does not comment on the original or on popular culture, if the "composition, presentation, scale, color palette, and media are fundamentally different and new compared to the photographs." *Id.* at 706. In this case, the defendant's work "manifest[ed] an entirely different aesthetic." Furthermore, the court's determination was not governed by defendant's stated intent: "we instead examine how the artworks 'may reasonably be perceived' to assess their transformative nature." *Id.* at 707. While the court found that most of the defendant's works were transformative, the court remanded as to five works with the fewest alterations, finding that these presented a closer question.

15. Does fair use permit the reproduction of copyrighted materials in connection with a government proceeding? Publishers of scientific journals

have brought infringement suits against law firms that reproduce journal articles in the course of preparing and prosecuting a patent application. Initially the plaintiffs argued that submitting the copies to the PTO (as evidence of prior art) was an infringement. Even after they amended their complaints to focus only on the copying and distribution of the articles in connection with preparing the application, two federal district courts have held that these activities are protected by fair use. *See American Institute of Physics v. Schwegman Lundberg & Woessner P.A.*, 2013 WL 4666330 (D. Minn. Aug. 30, 2013), *appeal dismissed*, (8th Circ. 13–3351) (Feb 19, 2014); *American Institute of Physics v. Winstead PC*, 2013 WL 6242843 (N.D. Tex. Dec. 3, 2013). Do you agree? To what other proceedings might the same analysis apply?

ANDY WARHOL FOUNDATION V. GOLDSMITH

11 F.4th 26 (2d Cir. 2021).

GERARD E. LYNCH, CIRCUIT JUDGE:

This case concerns a series of silkscreen prints and pencil illustrations created by the visual artist Andy Warhol based on a 1981 photograph of the musical artist Prince that was taken by Defendant-Appellant Lynn Goldsmith in her studio, and in which she holds copyright. In 1984, Goldsmith's agency, Defendant-Appellant Lynn Goldsmith, Ltd. ("LGL"), then known as Lynn Goldsmith, Inc., licensed the photograph to Vanity Fair magazine for use as an artist reference. Unbeknownst to Goldsmith, that artist was Warhol. Also unbeknownst to Goldsmith (and remaining unknown to her until 2016), Warhol did not stop with the image that Vanity Fair had commissioned him to create, but created an additional fifteen works, which together became known as the Prince Series.

[Upon learning of the Prince Series in 2016, Goldsmith sent a notice of infringement. When the Andy Warhol Foundation [AWF] brought a declaratory judgement action, the district court granted summary judgment to AWF on the ground of fair use. Goldsmith appealed.]

* * *

As the Supreme Court has held, fair use presents a holistic, context-sensitive inquiry "not to be simplified with bright-line rules[.] . . . All [four statutory factors] are to be explored, and the results weighed together, in light of the purposes of copyright." *Campbell*, 510 U.S. at 577–78. Indeed, the Supreme Court has explained that courts must "apply [fair use] in light of the sometimes conflicting aims of copyright law" and that "copyright's protection may be stronger where the copyrighted material . . . serves an artistic rather than a utilitarian function." *Google*, 141 S. Ct. at 1197.

With those competing goals in mind, we consider each factor to determine whether AWF can avail itself of the fair-use defense in this case. We hold that it cannot.

A. The Purpose and Character of The Use

This factor requires courts to consider the extent to which the secondary work is "transformative," as well as whether it is commercial. We address these considerations separately below.

1. Transformative Works and Derivative Works

Following the Supreme Court's decision in *Campbell*, our assessment of this first factor has focused chiefly on the degree to which the use is "transformative," *i.e.*, "whether the new work merely supersedes the objects of the original creation, or instead adds something new, with a further purpose or different character, altering the first with new expression, meaning, or message." 510 U.S. at 579 . * * *

Although the most straightforward cases of fair use * * * involve a secondary work that comments on the original in some fashion, in *Cariou v. Prince*, we rejected the proposition that a secondary work *must* comment on the original in order to qualify as fair use. *See* 714 F.3d at 706. In that case, we considered works of appropriation artist Richard Prince that incorporated, among other materials, various black-and-white photographs of Rastafarians taken by Patrick Cariou. After concluding that the district court had imposed a requirement unsupported by the Copyright Act, we conducted our own examination of Prince's works and concluded that twenty-five of the thirty at issue were transformative of Cariou's photographs as a matter of law. In reaching this conclusion, we observed that Prince had incorporated Cariou's "serene and deliberately composed portraits and landscape photographs" into his own "crude and jarring works . . . [that] incorporate[d] color, feature[d] distorted human and other forms and settings, and measure[d] between ten and nearly a hundred times the size of the photographs." Thus, we concluded that these works "used [Cariou's photographs] as raw material, transformed in the creation of new information, new aesthetics, new insights and understandings," and were transformative within the meaning of this first factor.

* * *

As discussed *supra*, both the Supreme Court and this Court have emphasized that fair use is a context-sensitive inquiry that does not lend itself to simple bright-line rules. Notwithstanding, the district court appears to have read *Cariou* as having announced such a rule, to wit, that any secondary work is *necessarily* transformative as a matter of law "[i]f looking at the works side-by-side, the secondary work has a different character, a new expression, and employs new aesthetics with [distinct] creative and communicative results." Although a literal construction of certain passages of *Cariou* may support that proposition, such a reading stretches the decision too far.

Of course, the alteration of an original work "with 'new expression, meaning, or message,'" whether by the use of "new aesthetics," by placing the work "in a different context," or by any other means is the *sine qua non* of transformativeness. It does not follow, however, that any secondary work that adds a new aesthetic or new expression to its source material is necessarily transformative.

Consider the five works at issue in *Cariou* that we did *not* conclude were transformative as a matter of law. Though varying in degree both amongst themselves and as compared to the works that we did adjudge transformative, each undoubtedly imbued Cariou's work with a "new aesthetic" as that phrase might be colloquially understood. Prince's *Canal Zone (2007)* is a collage of thirty-six of Cariou's photographs, most of which Prince altered by, for example, painting over the faces and bodies of Cariou's subjects, in some instances altering them significantly. In *Graduation*, Prince added blue "lozenges" over the eyes and mouth of Cariou's subject and pasted an image of hands playing a blue guitar over his hands. Both of these works certainly imbued the originals from which they derive with a "new aesthetic;" notwithstanding, we could not "confidently . . . make a determination about their transformative nature as a matter of law."

Moreover, there exists an entire class of secondary works that add "new expression, meaning, or message" to their source material, *Campbell*, 510 U.S. at 579, but may nonetheless fail to qualify as fair use: derivative works. There is some inherent tension in the Copyright Act between derivative works, reserved to the copyright holder, which are defined in part as works that "recast[ ], *transform*[ ], or adapt[ ]" an original work, 17 U.S.C. § 101 (emphasis added), and "transformative" fair uses of the copyrighted work by others. Thus, as we have previously observed, an overly liberal standard of transformativeness, such as that employed by the district court in this case, risks crowding out statutory protections for derivative works.

We addressed derivative works in *Cariou*, characterizing them as secondary works that merely present "the same material but in a new form" without "add[ing] something new." While that description may be a useful shorthand, it is likewise susceptible to misapplication if interpreted too broadly. Indeed, many derivative works that "add something new" to their source material would *not* qualify as fair use.

Consider, for example, a film adaptation of a novel. Such adaptations frequently add quite a bit to their source material: characters are combined, eliminated, or created out of thin air; plot elements are simplified or eliminated; new scenes are added; the moral or political implications of the original work may be eliminated or even reversed, or plot and character elements altered to create such implications where the original text eschewed such matters. And all of these editorial modifications are filtered through the creative contributions of the screenwriter, director, cast, camera crew, set designers, cinematographers, editors, sound engineers, and myriad other individuals integral to the creation of a film. It is for that reason that we have recognized that "[w]hen a novel is converted to a film . . . [t]he invention of the original author combines with the cinematographic interpretive skills of the filmmaker to produce something that neither could have produced independently." Despite the extent to which the resulting movie may transform the aesthetic and message of the underlying literary work, film adaptations are identified as a paradigmatic example of derivative works.

In evaluating the extent to which a work is transformative in the fair use context, we consider the "purpose and character" of the primary and secondary works. In *Bill Graham Archives v. Dorling Kindersley Ltd.*, for example, we held that the reproduction in a book about the Grateful Dead of images of posters originally created to advertise Grateful Dead concerts was transformative because that use was "plainly different from the original purpose for which they were created." 448 F.3d 605, 609–10 (2d Cir. 2006). Likewise, in *HathiTrust* we held that the defendants' creation of a searchable "digital corpus" comprising scanned copies of tens of millions of books that enabled researchers, scholars, and others to pinpoint the exact page of any book in the catalogue on which the searched term was used was a "quintessentially transformative use." 755 F.3d at 97. In *Authors Guild*, we reached the same conclusion when faced with a larger digital corpus complete with tools that enabled researchers to track how a specific word or phrase has been used throughout the development of the English language, despite the fact that, unlike the database in *Hathitrust*, Google's database also permitted the searcher to view a "snippet" from the original text showing the context in which the word or phrase had appeared. 804 F.3d at 216–17. And most recently, in *Google*, the Supreme Court held that fair use protected Google's "precise[ ]" copying of certain computer programming language in part because Google sought "to create new products . . . [and] expand the use and usefulness of . . . smartphones" with it. *Google*. Thus, the Supreme Court concluded, "the 'purpose and character' of Google's copying was transformative."

But purpose is perhaps a less useful metric where, as here, our task is to assess the transformative nature of works of visual art that, at least at a high level of generality, share the same overarching purpose (*i.e.*, to serve as works of visual art). While this is not the first time we have had to conduct this inquiry, our cases on such works are considerably fewer in number, and a brief review of them yields conflicting guidance. In *Blanch v. Koons*, for example, we adjudged transformative a Jeff Koons painting that incorporated a copyrighted photograph drawn from a fashion magazine where Koons had testified that he intended to "us[e] Blanch's image as fodder for his commentary on the social and aesthetic consequences of mass media." 467 F.3d at 253. Some time earlier, however, in *Rogers v. Koons*, we denied Koons's fair-use defense as applied to a three-dimensional sculpture recreating a photograph, notwithstanding his claim that he intended his sculpture to serve as a commentary on modern society. 960 F.2d 301, 309–11 (2d Cir. 1992). And, in *Cariou*, we held twenty-five of Richard Prince's works transformative as a matter of law even though Prince had testified that he "was not 'trying to create anything with a new meaning or a new message.' "

Matters become simpler, however, when we compare the works at issue in each case against their respective source materials. The sculpture at issue in *Rogers* was a three-dimensional colorized version of the photograph on which it was based. In *Blanch*, however, Koons used Blanch's photograph, depicting a woman's legs in high-heeled shoes, as part of a larger work in which he set it alongside several other similar photographs with "changes of its colors, the background against which it is portrayed, the medium, the size of the objects pictured, [and] the objects' details." In so doing, Koons used Blanch's photograph "as raw material for an entirely different type of art . . . that comment[ed] on existing images by juxtaposing them against others." *Id.* at 262 (Katzmann, J., concurring). And in *Cariou*, the copyrighted works found to have been fairly used were, in most cases, juxtaposed with other photographs and "obscured and altered to the point that Cariou's original [was] barely recognizable." The works that were found potentially infringing in *Cariou*, however, were ones in which the original was altered in ways that did not incorporate other images and that superimposed other elements that did not obscure the original image and in which the original image remained, as in the Koons sculpture at issue in *Rogers*, a major if not dominant component of the impression created by the allegedly infringing work.

A common thread running through these cases is that, where a secondary work does not obviously comment on or relate back to the original or use the original for a purpose other than that for which it was created, the bare assertion of a "higher or different artistic use," *Rogers*, 960 F.2d at 310, is insufficient to render a work transformative. Rather, the secondary work itself must reasonably be perceived as embodying a distinct artistic purpose, one that conveys a new meaning or message separate from its source material. While we cannot, nor do we attempt to, catalog all of the ways in which an artist may achieve that end, we note that the works that have done so thus far have themselves been distinct works of art that draw from numerous sources, rather than works that simply alter or recast a single work with a new aesthetic.

Which brings us back to the Prince Series. The district court held that the Prince Series works are transformative because they "can reasonably be perceived to have transformed Prince from a vulnerable, uncomfortable person to an iconic, larger-than-life figure." That was error.

Though it may well have been Goldsmith's subjective intent to portray Prince as a "vulnerable human being" and Warhol's to strip Prince of that humanity and instead display him as a popular icon, whether a work is transformative cannot turn merely on the stated or perceived intent of the artist or the meaning or impression that a critic—or for that matter, a judge—draws from the work. Were it otherwise, the law may well "recogniz[e] any alteration as transformative." 4 Melville B. Nimmer & David Nimmer, *Nimmer on Copyright* § 13.05(B)(6).

In conducting this inquiry, however, the district judge should not assume the role of art critic and seek to ascertain the intent behind or meaning of the works at issue. That is so both because judges are typically unsuited to make aesthetic judgments and because such perceptions are inherently subjective. As Goldsmith argues, her own stated intent notwithstanding, "an audience viewing the [Goldsmith] [P]hotograph today, across the vista of the singer's long career, might well see him in a different light than Goldsmith saw him that day in 1981." We agree; it is easy to imagine that a whole generation of Prince's fans might have trouble seeing the Goldsmith Photograph as depicting anything other than the iconic songwriter and performer whose musical works they enjoy and admire.

Instead, the judge must examine whether the secondary work's use of its source material is in service of a "fundamentally different and new" artistic purpose and character, such that the secondary work stands apart from the "raw material" used to create it. *Cariou*, 714 F.3d at 706. Although we do not hold that the primary work must be "barely recognizable" within the secondary work, as was the case with the works held transformative in *Cariou*, the secondary work's transformative purpose and character must, at a bare minimum, comprise something more than the imposition of another artist's style on the primary work such that the secondary work remains both recognizably deriving from, and retaining the essential elements of, its source material.

With this clarification, viewing the works side-by-side, we conclude that the Prince Series is not "transformative" within the meaning of the first factor. That is not to deny that the Warhol works display the distinct aesthetic sensibility that many would immediately associate with Warhol's signature style—the elements of which are absent from the Goldsmith photo. But the same can be said, for example, of the Ken Russell film, from a screenplay by Larry Kramer, derived from D.H. Lawrence's novel, *Women in Love*: the film is as recognizable a "Ken Russell" as the Prince Series are recognizably "Warhols." But the film, for all the ways in which it transforms (that is, in the ordinary meaning of the word, which indeed is used in the very definition of derivative works, *see* 17 U.S.C. § 101) its source material, is also plainly an adaptation of the Lawrence novel.

As in the case of such paradigmatically derivative works, there can be no meaningful dispute that the overarching purpose and function of the two works at issue here is identical, not merely in the broad sense that they are created as works of visual art,[5] but also in the narrow but essential sense that they are portraits of the same person. *See Gaylord v. United States*, 595 F.3d 1364, 1372–73 (Fed. Cir. 2010) (photograph of Korean War Memorial used on stamp not transformative despite "different expressive character" brought about by subdued lighting and snow since sculpture and stamp shared purpose of "honor[ing] veterans of the Korean War"). Although this observation does not *per se* preclude a conclusion that the Prince Series makes fair use of the Goldsmith Photograph, the district court's conclusion rests significantly on the transformative character of Warhol's work. But the Prince Series works can't bear that weight.

Warhol created the series chiefly by removing certain elements from the Goldsmith Photograph, such as depth and contrast, and embellishing the flattened images with "loud, unnatural colors." Nonetheless, although we do not conclude that the Prince Series works are necessarily *derivative* works as a matter of law, they are much closer to presenting the same work in a different form, that form being a high-contrast screenprint, than they are to being works that make a transformative use of the original. Crucially, the Prince Series retains the essential elements of the Goldsmith Photograph without significantly adding to or altering those elements.

Indeed, the differences between the Goldsmith Photograph and the Prince Series here are in many respects less substantial than those made to the five works that we could not find transformative as a matter of law in *Cariou*. Unlike the Prince Series, those works unmistakably deviated from Cariou's original portraiture in a manner that suggested an entirely distinct artistic end; rather than recasting those photographs in a new medium, Richard Prince added material that pulled them in new directions. *See, e.g., Cariou*, 714 F.3d at 711 ("Where [Cariou's] photograph presents someone comfortably at home in nature, [Prince's] *Graduation* combines divergent elements to present a sense of discomfort."). Nevertheless, we could not confidently determine whether those modest alterations "amount[ed] to a substantial transformation of the original work[s] of art such that the new work[s] were transformative," and remanded the case to the district court to make that determination in the first instance.

---

[5] The fact that the Goldsmith Photograph and the Prince Series were both created for artistic purposes makes this a different case from, for example, "[a]n artistic painting . . . precisely replicat[ing] a copyrighted advertising logo to make a comment about consumerism" (such as Warhol's well-known depictions of Campbell's soup cans), which "might . . . fall within the scope of fair use." *Google*, 141 S. Ct. at 1203.

In contrast, the Prince Series retains the essential elements of its source material, and Warhol's modifications serve chiefly to magnify some elements of that material and minimize others. While the cumulative effect of those alterations may change the Goldsmith Photograph in ways that give a different impression of its subject, the Goldsmith Photograph remains the recognizable foundation upon which the Prince Series is built.

Finally, we feel compelled to clarify that it is entirely irrelevant to this analysis that "each Prince Series work is immediately recognizable as a 'Warhol.'" Entertaining that logic would inevitably create a celebrity-plagiarist privilege; the more established the artist and the more distinct that artist's style, the greater leeway that artist would have to pilfer the creative labors of others. But the law draws no such distinctions; whether the Prince Series images exhibit the style and characteristics typical of Warhol's work (which they do) does not bear on whether they qualify as fair use under the Copyright Act. As Goldsmith notes, the fact that Martin Scorsese's recent film *The Irishman* is recognizably "a Scorsese" "do[es] not absolve [him] of the obligation to license the original book" on which it is based.

In reaching this conclusion, we do not mean to discount the artistic value of the Prince Series itself. As used in copyright law, the words "transformative" and "derivative" are legal terms of art that do not express the simple ideas that they carry in ordinary usage. We do not disagree with AWF's contention that the cumulative effect of Warhol's changes to the Goldsmith Photograph is to produce a number of striking and memorable images. And our conclusion that those images are closer to what the law deems "derivative" (and not "transformative") does not imply that the Prince Series (or Warhol's art more broadly) is "derivative," in the pejorative artistic sense, of Goldsmith's work or of anyone else's. As Goldsmith succinctly puts it, "[t]here is little doubt . . . that the Prince Series reflects Andy Warhol's talent, creativity, and distinctive aesthetic." Appellants' But the task before us is not to assess the artistic worth of the Prince Series nor its place within Warhol's oeuvre; that is the domain of art historians, critics, collectors, and the museum-going public. Rather, the question we must answer is simply whether the law permits Warhol to claim it as his own, and AWF to exploit it, without Goldsmith's permission. And, at least as far as this aspect of the first factor is concerned, we conclude that the answer to that question is "no."

2. Commercial Use

The statutory language of the first factor also specifically directs courts to consider "whether [the] use is of a commercial nature or is for nonprofit educational purposes." 17 U.S.C. § 107(1). Although finding that a secondary use is commercial "tends to weigh against" finding that it is fair, we apply the test with caution since "nearly all of the illustrative uses listed in the preamble paragraph of § 107 . . . are generally conducted for profit in this country." *Campbell*, 510 U.S. at 584–85. And, since "[t]he crux of the profit/nonprofit distinction is . . . whether the user stands to profit from exploitation of the copyrighted material without paying the customary price," *Harper & Row Publishers, Inc. v. Nation Enters.*, 471 U.S. 539, 562 (1985), the commercial nature of a secondary use is of decreased importance when the use is sufficiently transformative such that the primary author should not reasonably expect to be compensated.

We agree with the district court that the Prince Series works are commercial in nature, but that they produce an artistic value that serves the greater public interest. We also agree that, although more relevant to the character of the *user* than of the *use*, the fact that AWF's mission is to advance the visual arts, a mission that is doubtless in the public interest, may militate against the simplistic assertion that AWF's sale and licensing of the Prince Series works necessarily derogates from a finding of fair use. Nevertheless, just as we cannot hold that the Prince Series is transformative as a matter of law, neither can we conclude that Warhol and AWF are entitled to monetize it without paying Goldsmith the "customary price" for the rights to her work, even if that monetization is used for the benefit of the public.

* * *

B. The Nature of the Copyrighted Work

The second factor directs courts to consider the nature of the copyrighted work, including (1) whether it is "expressive or creative . . . or more factual, with a greater leeway being allowed to a claim of fair use where the work is factual or informational, and (2) whether the work is published or unpublished, with the scope of fair use involving unpublished works being considerably narrower." *Blanch*, 467 F.3d at 256.

The district court correctly held that the Goldsmith Photograph is both unpublished and creative but nonetheless concluded that the second factor should favor neither party because LGL had licensed the Goldsmith Photograph to Vanity Fair and because the Prince Series was highly transformative. That was error. That Goldsmith, through LGL, made the Goldsmith Photograph available for a single use on limited terms does not change its status as an unpublished work nor diminish the law's protection of her choice of "when to make a work public and whether to withhold a work to shore up demand." Further, though we have previously held that this factor "may be of limited usefulness where the creative work is being used for a transformative purpose," *Bill Graham Archives*, 448 F.3d at 612, this relates only to the weight assigned to it, not whom it favors.

Having recognized the Goldsmith Photograph as both creative and unpublished, the district court should have found this factor to favor

Goldsmith irrespective of whether it adjudged the Prince Series works transformative within the meaning of the first factor. And, because we disagree that the Prince Series works are transformative, we would accord this factor correspondingly greater weight.

C. *The Amount and Substantiality of the Use*

The third factor considers "the amount and substantiality of the portion used in relation to the copyrighted work as a whole." 17 U.S.C. § 107(3). "In assessing this factor, we consider not only 'the quantity of the materials used' but also 'their quality and importance' " in relation to the original work. * * *

In this case, AWF argues, and the district court concluded, that this factor weighs in its favor because, by cropping and flattening the Goldsmith Photograph, thereby removing or minimizing its use of light, contrast, shading, and other expressive qualities, Warhol removed nearly all of its copyrightable elements. We do not agree.

We begin with the uncontroversial proposition that copyright does not protect ideas, but only "the original or unique way that an author expresses those ideas, concepts, principles, or processes." *Rogers*, 960 F.2d at 308. As applied to photographs, this protection encompasses the photographer's "posing the subjects, lighting, angle, selection of film and camera, evoking the desired expression, and almost any other variant involved." *Id.* at 307. The cumulative manifestation of these artistic choices—and what the law ultimately protects—is the image produced in the interval between the shutter opening and closing, *i.e.*, the photograph itself. This is, as we have previously observed, the photographer's "particular expression" of the idea underlying her photograph. *Leibovitz*, 137 F.3d at 115–16.

It is thus easy to understand why AWF's contention misses the mark. The premise of its argument is that Goldsmith cannot copyright Prince's face. True enough. Were it otherwise, nobody else could have taken the man's picture without either seeking Goldsmith's permission or risking a suit for infringement. But while Goldsmith has no monopoly on Prince's face, the law grants her a broad monopoly on its image as it appears in her photographs of him, including the Goldsmith Photograph. And where, as here, the secondary user has used the photograph itself, rather than, for example, a similar photograph, the photograph's specific depiction of its subject cannot be neatly reduced to discrete qualities such as contrast, shading, and depth of field that can be stripped away, taking the image's entitlement to copyright protection along with it.

With that in mind, we readily conclude that the Prince Series borrows significantly from the Goldsmith Photograph, both quantitatively and qualitatively. While Warhol did indeed crop and flatten the Goldsmith Photograph, the end product is not merely a screenprint identifiably based on a photograph of Prince. Rather it is a screenprint readily identifiable as deriving from a *specific* photograph of Prince, the Goldsmith Photograph. A comparison of the images in the Prince Series makes plain that Warhol did not use the Goldsmith Photograph simply as a reference or *aide-mémoire* in order to accurately document the physical features of its subject. Instead, the Warhol images are instantly recognizable as depictions or images of the Goldsmith Photograph itself.

* * *

The district court, reasoning that Warhol had taken only the unprotected elements of the Goldsmith Photograph in service of a transformative purpose, held that this factor strongly favored AWF. Because we disagree on both counts, we conclude that this factor strongly favors Goldsmith.

D. The Effect of the Use on the Market for the Original

The fourth factor asks "whether, if the challenged use becomes widespread, it will adversely affect the potential market for the copyrighted work." *Bill Graham Archives*, 448 F.3d at 613. "Analysis of this factor requires us to balance the benefit the public will derive if the use is permitted and the personal gain the copyright owner will receive if the use is denied." *Wright v. Warner Books, Inc.*, 953 F.2d 731, 739 (2d Cir. 1991). * * *

We agree with the district court that the primary market for the Warhol Prince Series (that is, the market for the original works) and the Goldsmith Photograph do not meaningfully overlap, and Goldsmith does not seriously challenge that determination on appeal. * * *

We are unpersuaded, however, by the district court's conclusion that the Prince Series poses no threat to Goldsmith's *licensing* markets. While Goldsmith does not contend that she has sought to license the Goldsmith Photograph itself, the question under this factor is not solely whether the secondary work harms an *existing* market for the specific work alleged to have been infringed. Rather, we must also consider whether "unrestricted and widespread conduct of the sort engaged in by [AWF] would result in a substantially adverse impact on the potential market" for the Goldsmith Photograph.

As an initial matter, we note that the district court erred in apparently placing the burden of proof as to this factor on Goldsmith. While our prior cases have suggested that the rightsholder bears some initial burden of identifying relevant markets, we have never held that the rightsholder bears the burden of showing actual market harm. Nor would we so hold. Fair use is an affirmative defense; as such, the ultimate burden of proving that the secondary use does not compete in the relevant market is appropriately borne by the party asserting the defense: the secondary user. *See Campbell*, 510 U.S. at 590.

In any case, whatever the scope of Goldsmith's initial burden, she satisfied it here. * * * [T]here is no material dispute that both Goldsmith and AWF have sought to license (and indeed have successfully licensed) their respective depictions of Prince to popular print magazines to accompany articles about him. As Goldsmith succinctly states: "both [works] are illustrations of the same famous musician with the same overlapping customer base." Contrary to AWF's assertions, that is more than enough. And, since Goldsmith has identified a relevant market, AWF's failure to put forth any evidence that the availability of the Prince Series works poses no threat to Goldsmith's actual or potential revenue in that market tilts the scales toward Goldsmith.

Further, the district court entirely overlooked the potential harm to Goldsmith's derivative market, which is likewise substantial. * * * And here, that market is established both by Goldsmith's uncontroverted expert testimony that photographers generally license others to create stylized derivatives of their work in the vein of the Prince Series, and by the genesis of the Prince Series: a licensing agreement between LGL and Vanity Fair to use the Goldsmith Photograph as an artist reference.

We also must consider the impact on this market if the sort of copying in which Warhol engaged were to become a widespread practice. That harm is also self-evident. There currently exists a market to license photographs of musicians, such as the Goldsmith Photograph, to serve as the basis of a stylized derivative image; permitting this use would effectively destroy that broader market, as, if artists "could use such images for free, there would be little or no reason to pay for [them]." *Barcroft Media, Ltd. v. Coed Media Grp., LLC*, 297 F. Supp. 3d 339, 355 (S.D.N.Y. 2017). This, in turn, risks disincentivizing artists from producing new work by decreasing its value—the precise evil against which copyright law is designed to guard.

Finally, our analysis of the fourth factor also "take[s] into account the public benefits the copying will likely produce." *Google*, 141 S. Ct. at 1206. AWF argues that weighing the public benefit cuts in its favor because "[d]enying fair-use protection to works like Warhol's will chill the creation of art that employs pre-existing imagery to convey a distinct message." We disagree. Nothing in this opinion stifles the creation of art that may reasonably be perceived as conveying a new meaning or message, and embodying a new purpose, separate from its source material. * * * Moreover, what encroaches on Goldsmith's market is AWF's commercial licensing of the Prince Series, not Warhol's original creation. Thus, art that is not turned into a commercial replica of its source material, and that otherwise occupies a separate primary market, has significantly more "breathing space" than the commercial licensing of the Prince Series. *Campbell*, 510 U.S. at 579.

Thus, although the primary market for the Goldsmith Photograph and the Prince Series may differ, the Prince Series works pose cognizable harm to Goldsmith's market to license the Goldsmith Photograph to publications for editorial purposes and to other artists to create derivative works based on the Goldsmith Photograph and similar works. Further, the public benefit of the copying at issue in this case does not outweigh the harm identified by Goldsmith. Accordingly, the fourth factor favors Goldsmith.

E. Weighing the Factors

"[T]his court has on numerous occasions resolved fair use determinations at the summary judgment stage where there are no genuine issues of material fact." As no party contends that there exist any issues of material fact in this case, we believe it appropriate to exercise that discretion here.

Having considered each of the four factors, we find that each favors Goldsmith. Further, although the factors are not exclusive, AWF has not identified any additional relevant considerations unique to this case that we should take into account. Accordingly, we hold that AWF's defense of fair use fails as a matter of law.

NOTES

1. In a concurring opinion, Judge Jacobs emphasized that the court's analysis of the "market harm" factor applied only to the commercial licensing of Warhol's Prince Series, and not to Warhol's creation of the original artwork itself. Would the majority have reached a different conclusion as to the latter?

2. Does the concept of a "transformative use" require further clarification? In 2022, the Supreme Court granted certiorari in *Warhol Foundation*, and a decision can be expected in the 2022–2023 term.

3. Although the Supreme Court has not yet addressed the issue, a number of appellate courts have considered whether reproducing copyrighted material in a online database in order to facilitate internet searches constitutes fair use. Consider whether a fair use defense should succeed in the following examples:

(a) Defendant's for-profit service records television broadcasts and collects them into a text-searchable database. Clients can search the database for items of interest, and watch an unlimited number of ten-minute clips of the relevant recordings. *See Fox News Network, LLC v. Tveyes, Inc.*, 883 F.3d 169 (2d Cir. 2018).

(b) Defendant digitally scans entire library collections of books, and compiles the scans into a searchable database available to users at no charge. (Does it matter whether the service allows users to view "snippets" of the actual books showing the passages where their search terms appear, or merely identifies the book and page numbers where those terms appear?) *See Authors Guild v. Google, Inc.*, 804

F.3d 202 (2d Cir. 2015); *Authors Guild, Inc. v. HathiTrust*, 755 F.3d 87 (2d Cir. 2014).

(c) Defendant is a search engine that provides small "thumbnail" versions of copyrighted images in response to internet queries. Clicking on the thumbnail takes the user to the photographer's website where the full-sized image appears. *See Perfect 10, Inc. v. Amazon.com, Inc.*, 508 F.3d 1146, 1168 (9th Cir. 2007); *Kelly v. Arriba Soft Corp.*, 336 F.3d 811 (9th Cir. 2003).

CHAPTER 18

INFRINGEMENT, DEFENSES, AND REMEDIES

■ ■ ■

Statutes: 17 U.S.C. §§ 101 (as needed), 411, 501–11, 602–03, 1001–10, 1401

A. THE CONCEPT OF INFRINGEMENT

Copyright infringement is the unauthorized exercise of one or more of the exclusive rights reserved to the copyright owner under sections 106 and 106A, unless the activity in question falls within the limitations and exceptions set forth in sections 107–122 and 1008. A suit for unauthorized use of a pre-1972 sound recording in violation of section 1401 is governed by principles similar to copyright infringement, including the aforementioned limitations and exceptions. (Throughout this chapter, therefore, references to copyright infringement include section 1401 actions, except as otherwise indicated.)

Courts frequently use the term "copying" as shorthand for the exercise of any of the exclusive rights described in section 106. In some infringement cases, there is no doubt that the defendant used the plaintiff's work, and the sole issue is whether the defendant's *activity* is of a type proscribed by section 106 or 106A. (For example, was the defendant's performance of the plaintiff's work public or private?) In other cases, the parties may dispute the threshold question of whether the material exploited by the defendant incorporated the plaintiff's copyrighted material in the first place. In the latter case, absent direct evidence of copying (such as a witness or an admission), a prima facie case of copying may be established by circumstantial evidence.

Copying that amounts to infringement may be either literal or nonliteral. Copying is literal (or "verbatim") when the defendant copies a portion of the actual language of a text or, in the case of software, an actual code sequence. If the copying is nonliteral, this means that the defendant has copied other elements of the plaintiff's creative expression—such as plot, character, structure, theme, mood, setting, sequencing, organization, or "total concept and feel."

In cases involving nonliteral copying, it can be difficult to determine whether the defendant has copied the plaintiff's copyrightable expression or merely uncopyrightable ideas. Judge Learned Hand offered a classic statement of this problem in *Nichols v. Universal Pictures Corp.*, 45 F.2d 119 (2d Cir. 1930), an infringement case involving two works—a play and a motion picture—each of which depicted two families who opposed the marriage of their respective children. In one case, the respective families were Jewish and Catholic; in the other, they were Jewish and Irish. After conducting a detailed review of the plot and characters of each work, Judge Hand explained:

> It is of course essential to any protection of literary property, whether at common-law or under the statute, that the right cannot be limited literally to the text, else a plagiarist would escape by immaterial variations. That has never been the law, but, as soon as literal appropriation ceases to be the test, the whole matter is necessarily at large, so that, as was recently well said by a distinguished judge, the decisions cannot help much in a new case. When plays are concerned, the plagiarist may excise a separate scene, or he may appropriate part of the dialogue. Then the question is whether the part so taken is "substantial," and therefore not a "fair use" of the copyrighted work; it is the same question [as] arises in the case of any other copyrighted work. But when the plagiarist does not take out a block in suit, but an abstract of the whole, decision is more troublesome. Upon any work, and especially upon a play, a great number of patterns of increasing generality will fit equally well, as more and more of the incident is left out. The last may perhaps be no more than the most general statement of what the play is about, and at times might consist only of its title; but there is a point in this series of abstractions where they are no longer protected, since otherwise the playwright could prevent the use of his "ideas," to which, apart from their expression, his property is never extended. Nobody has ever been able to fix that boundary, and nobody ever can. In some cases the question has been treated as though it were analogous to lifting a portion out of the copyrighted work, but the analogy is not a good one, because, though the skeleton is a part of the body, it pervades and supports the whole. In such cases we are rather concerned with the line between expression and what is expressed. As respects plays, the controversy chiefly centers upon the characters and sequence of incident, these being the substance.
>
> We did not in *Dymow v. Bolton*, 11 F.(2d) 690, hold that a plagiarist was never liable for stealing a plot * * *. We found the plot of the second play was too different to infringe, because the most detailed pattern, common to both, eliminated so much from each that its content went into the public domain; and for this reason we said, "this mere subsection of a plot was not susceptible

> of copyright." But we do not doubt that two plays may correspond in plot closely enough for infringement. How far that correspondence must go is another matter. Nor need we hold that the same may not be true as to the characters, quite independently of the "plot" proper, though, as far as we know such a case has never arisen. If Twelfth Night were copyrighted, it is quite possible that a second comer might so closely imitate Sir Toby Belch or Malvolio as to infringe, but it would not be enough that for one of his characters he cast a riotous knight who kept wassail to the discomfort of the household, or a vain and foppish steward who became amorous of his mistress. These would be no more than Shakespeare's "ideas" in the play, as little capable of monopoly as Einstein's Doctrine of Relativity, or Darwin's theory of the Origin of Species. It follows that the less developed the characters, the less they can be copyrighted; that is the penalty an author must bear for marking them too indistinctly.

Id. at 121.

WARNER BROS. INC. V. AMERICAN BROADCASTING COMPANIES, INC.

654 F.2d 204 (2d Cir. 1981).

MESKILL, CIRCUIT JUDGE:

This is an appeal from an order entered in the United States District Court for the Southern District of New York, Motley, J., which denied a motion made by plaintiffs, Warner Bros. Inc., Film Export, A.G., and DC Comics, Inc., for a preliminary injunction and temporary restraining order to enjoin the defendant, American Broadcasting Companies, Inc. (ABC), from (1) broadcasting certain promotional television spots relating to its series entitled "The Greatest American Hero" (*Hero*); (2) broadcasting the premiere of *Hero*; and (3) broadcasting any episode of *Hero* prior to affording the plaintiffs an adequate opportunity to examine the work and to seek appropriate relief. Plaintiffs alleged that ABC's *Hero* and related promotional campaign infringed their copyrights in the popular character Superman in violation of 17 U.S.C. s 501(b) (1976). * * *

BACKGROUND

Plaintiffs are the owners of the copyrights and other rights in the character Superman and the works embodying him, including comic books depicting the cartoon character Superman; television series depicting Superman in animated and unanimated features; and the motion picture "Superman, The Movie." The plaintiffs have enjoyed remarkable commercial success for over forty years; they have derived substantial revenue from both domestic and international commercial exploitation of Superman.

The character "evolved" over the years in comic strips, cartoons, television shows, and motion pictures under the ostensible protection of copyright. A glance at the record, for example, reveals that originally Superman was only capable of leaping in the position of a hurdler over tall buildings, while in a recent film version, "Superman, The Movie," the character is shown demonstrating an apparently later-acquired power of self-propelled flight; Superman assumes a more sophisticated and streamlined style, flying in the prone position, with arms extended in front of him and red cape billowing in the wind.

The entire fictional biographical account of Superman is retold in "Superman, The Movie." The character is depicted as a superhuman being from a fictional planet, Krypton, who was sent to earth to escape the fatal consequences of the imminent destruction of his planet. Superman is found by the Kents, a midwestern couple, who name the boy Clark and raise him as their son in a bucolic setting. The Kents instill in Clark a strong sense of moral conviction and faith in the "American way," and counsel the boy not to reveal his superhuman powers to anyone. Clark matures into a tall, well-built, dark-haired, and strikingly handsome young man. Ultimately, Clark leaves his pastoral home, finding himself drawn by a mysterious force to a place where he encounters the image of his deceased father, Jor-El. There, Jor-El informs him of his true identity and instructs him to use his superpowers to protect the world from evil. Clark emerges from his fantastic encounter with Jor-El wearing for the first time his Superman costume a skin-tight blue leotard with red briefs, boots and cape, and a large "S" emblazoned in red and gold upon the chest and cape.

Clark subsequently obtains a position as a reporter for the Daily Planet, but reveals his true identity to no one, assuming instead the appearance of a shy, bumbling, but well-intentioned young man. There he soon meets and becomes infatuated with a beautiful colleague, Lois Lane. Later he appears clad in his Superman regalia to perform amazing feats of strength and courage which immediately attract wide attention, acclaim, and the amorous interest of Lois Lane.

Superman is continually confronted by villains in all of his adventures, but eventually overcomes all evil opponents by exploiting his superpowers of self-propelled flight, imperviousness to bullets, blinding speed, X-ray vision, fantastic hearing, and seemingly immeasurable strength. He fights for "TRUTH, JUSTICE AND THE AMERICAN WAY" and is often described as "FASTER THAN A SPEEDING BULLET," "MORE POWERFUL THAN A LOCOMOTIVE," and "ABLE TO LEAP TALL BUILDINGS IN A SINGLE BOUND." For decades, startled pedestrians in comic strips have shouted, "LOOK, UP IN THE SKY . . . IT'S A BIRD . . . IT'S A PLANE . . . IT'S 'SUPERMAN'!"

In January 1981, defendant ABC issued press releases and began to run promotional spots for the premiere of *Hero*. * * *

The protagonist in *Hero*, Ralph Hinkley, is portrayed as a young high school teacher who is trying to cope with a recent divorce, a resultant dispute over the custody of his son, and the strain that his domestic problems place upon his work and his relationship with an attractive girlfriend. Hinkley's physical attributes are far from extraordinary; he is of medium height, and has a scrawny build and curly blond hair. According to the testimony of his creator, Hinkley is intended to typify the "ordinary guy."

In the premiere episode of *Hero*, Hinkley's van breaks down en route to a high school field trip in the desert. While walking along a road in search of help, Hinkley is nearly run over by an out-of-control automobile driven by Bill Maxwell, an American undercover agent. Maxwell has been searching the desert for his missing FBI partner who, unbeknownst to Maxwell, has been murdered by a band of extremists. Maxwell and Hinkley are suddenly approached by a brightly glowing spaceship from which descends the image of Maxwell's deceased partner. Hinkley is handed a magical caped costume a red leotard with a tunic top, no boots, and a black cape which, when worn, endows him with fantastic powers. Unfortunately, however, Hinkley loses the instruction book that accompanied the intergalactic gift and is left only with the verbal instruction that he should use his powers to save the world from self-destruction. Hinkley grudgingly accepts the mission after being importuned to do so by Maxwell.

While in the privacy of his bedroom the next day, Hinkley holds the suit in front of himself before a mirror and says, "IT'S A BIRD! IT'S A PLANE! IT'S RALPH HINKLEY!" Shortly thereafter he states cynically, "What the world needs is another flying superhero." Hinkley later reveals his newly acquired powers to his girlfriend and begs her understanding. Eventually, he uses his powers to overcome a villain's plan to destroy a portion of southern California.

Although Hinkley ultimately wins the battle with his evil opponent, he does not achieve this goal with the majestic grace, strength, skill, and panache characteristic of Superman. For example, when flying he hollers in fright, and invariably crash-lands, rather than landing with the aplomb of Superman. On one occasion while flying, Hinkley crashes into a building, is nearly knocked unconscious, and then is unceremoniously arrested for vagrancy. And though his magical costume renders him impervious to bullets, when being shot at by villains Hinkley cringes and cowers. Finally, after winning the day in his first adventure, Hinkley shakes the hand of his partner, Maxwell, but unfortunately fractures it, neglecting to restrain his super strength.

On March 16, 1981, two days before the scheduled broadcast of the premiere of *Hero,* plaintiffs filed their complaint seeking the injunctive relief previously described. Judge Motley viewed the promotional spots, the premiere episode of *Hero,* and "Superman, The Movie." The district judge also heard testimony concerning the creation and production of *Hero* and the promotional spots, and the characteristics of the superhero genre. Judge Motley concluded that the parties' works were not substantially similar * * * . Thus, the defendant was permitted to televise the premiere of *Hero* on March 18, 1981 as scheduled.

DISCUSSION

To establish a claim for copyright infringement, a plaintiff "must show ownership of a valid copyright and copying by the defendant." Plaintiffs' copyrights and their validity were not contested for the purposes of the preliminary injunction motion, leaving only the issue of copying to be determined.

* * * "(T)he determination of the extent of similarity which will constitute a substantial and hence infringing similarity presents one of the most difficult questions in copyright law, and one which is the least susceptible of helpful generalizations." The general test for determining substantial similarity is "whether an average lay observer would recognize the alleged copy as having been appropriated from the copyrighted work." In the case of literary works, it is axiomatic that copyright protection only extends to the expression of the author's idea, not to the idea itself. Thus, in determining whether two such works are so substantially similar as to reveal an infringement of one by the other, courts must decide whether the similarities shared by the works are something more than mere generalized ideas or themes. * * *

This is not the first occasion we have been called upon to decide this issue in an action involving the copyrights in the famous character Superman. *See* Detective Comics, Inc. v. Bruns Publications, Inc., 111 F.2d 432 (2d Cir. 1940). In *Bruns,* we held that while "the pictorial representations and verbal descriptions of 'Superman'" presented more than "a benevolent Hercules" and thus constituted "proper subjects of copyright," we cautioned that the owners of the Superman copyrights were not "entitled to a monopoly of the mere character of a 'Superman' who is a blessing to mankind." This admonition was, of course, consistent with our earlier decisions in *Nichols* and Sheldon v. Metro-Goldwyn Pictures Corp., 81 F.2d 49 (2d Cir. 1936), in which this Court ruled that generalized themes and ideas lie in the public domain and are not copyrightable. In deciding in *Bruns* that the defendant's "Wonderman" comic character infringed the plaintiff's copyrighted Superman works, the Court reviewed the parties' works, identified the similarities between them and concluded that the "only real difference between them is that 'Superman' wears a blue uniform and 'Wonderman' a red one." The Court concluded that the defendants "used more than general types and ideas and . . . appropriated the pictorial and literary details embodied in the complainant's copyrights." * * *

After reviewing the parties' works in this case, Judge Motley concluded that "(a) comparison of the characters Ralph Hinkley and Superman and their respective stories reveals . . . that they are so dissimilar as to preclude a finding of substantial similarity." The plaintiffs contend that Judge Motley's statement betrays a fundamental misunderstanding of copyright law. They assert that Judge Motley incorrectly focused upon the differences rather than the similarities between the works. The plaintiffs further claim that, in placing undue emphasis upon the disparities, Judge Motley disregarded what otherwise would be deemed substantial similarity between the works. We disagree.

While the works of plaintiffs and defendant share common ideas, themes, and general imagery, we believe that the similarities are not sufficiently particular and concrete so as to represent an appropriation of the protected expression of the plaintiffs' works. In arriving at this determination we also conclude that Judge Motley properly considered the great differences between the works in analyzing whether the parties' works were substantially similar.

Plaintiffs offer an extensive list of similarities between their works and those of the defendants to establish substantial similarity; for example, both superheroes are shown performing feats of miraculous strength; both wear tight acrobatic costumes; both do battle with villains; both fly with their arms extended in front of them and cape billowing behind; both are impervious to bullets; both have X-ray type vision; both have fantastic hearing and sight; both fly gracefully in the night sky past a city's lit skyscrapers; both lift a car with one hand; both lead a double life; both heroes' power emanates from another planet; and both are drawn to a mysterious spot to meet an extraterrestrial being. We find it unnecessary to recount several other purported similarities between the works suggested by the plaintiffs, since a close examination of the items already listed reveals the fallacy of their argument.

Though it is true that both heroes perform feats of miraculous strength, that is too common and general a characteristic or theme to even approach the degree of concreteness and particularity deserving of copyright protection. In any event, the expression of the general idea of a hero with miraculous strength in *Hero* and *Superman* substantially differs. In *Hero*, Ralph Hinkley derives his power exclusively from his magic suit, whereas in *Superman*, the hero's strength is a natural attribute of his extraterrestrial physical makeup. Additionally, Superman's exploitation of his strength is controlled, whereas Ralph Hinkley struggles at times to conjure it up and at other times to contain it. As to the common use of tight-fitting acrobatic costumes, the defendants convincingly established below that such garb is common in the superhero genre rather than unique to Superman. Moreover, while Superman wears a blue leotard with red briefs, boots and cape, Ralph Hinkley's costume is a red leotard with a tunic top, no boots, and a black cape. The plaintiffs suggest similarity between the works in that both heroes fight wealthy megalomaniacal villains; however, this suggested similarity concerns something hardly more specific or particular than the classic theme of good versus evil. With respect to the two heroes' common power of self-propelled flight, the defendants demonstrated satisfactorily that several comic strip superheroes possess the power of self-propelled flight and fly with their arms extended in front of them and capes billowing behind. But more important in this regard, the style of flying employed by Superman and Ralph Hinkley hardly could be more different. Superman has mastered the art of self-propelled flight and accomplishes the feat with grace and verve. Ralph Hinkley, on the other hand, seems to be terrified when flying and each time, without fail, crash-lands. Concededly both heroes at some point are shown lifting a car with one hand, but this display would seem to constitute a stereotypical means of demonstrating great strength, within the scenes a faire doctrine. The latter notwithstanding, the scenes in each work in which a car is lifted differ substantially; in *Superman*, an infant lifts a pickup truck revealing fantastic strength to the Kents, his future step-parents, whereas in *Hero*, Ralph Hinkley lifts up an automobile to reveal and prove his supernatural strength to his girlfriend. As to the heroes' imperviousness to bullets, while the trait is shared, the expression of the concept differs dramatically. Ralph Hinkley cringes and cowers in the face of gunfire, whereas Superman boldly holds his ground when being fired upon. With respect to the plaintiffs' claim that both heroes share X-ray vision, Ralph Hinkley experiences holographic visions, whereas Superman sees through objects. Nor does the fact that both heroes lead double lives persuade us that the works are substantially similar. The defendants demonstrated below that other personages in the superhero genre lead double lives, their heroic side being kept in deep secrecy. And even more important, the expression of this classic literary idea differs between the two works in this case. In *Superman*, Clark Kent never reveals his true identity, whereas in *Hero*, Ralph Hinkley voluntarily discloses his part-time superhero status to his girlfriend. With respect to the scenes in which both heroes are shown flying at night with a lit city skyline in the background, the impact of the scene in *Superman* is majestic whereas the impact of the scene in *Hero* is humorous. Superman is shown flying gracefully; Ralph Hinkley flies holding a skylight in one hand for balance. Finally, the scenes in which the hero of each work is drawn mysteriously to a spot to meet an extraterrestrial being are hardly similar in expression. Superman encounters his deceased father's image at some polar icecap location; Ralph Hinkley encounters an unidentified flying object while sitting in an automobile with his future sidekick, Bill Maxwell, and is greeted by Maxwell's deceased partner.

* * *

Finally, plaintiffs cannot seriously contend that the pattern of scenes, sequence of incident, principal characters, or the general theme between *Hero* and "Superman, The Movie," for example, are substantially similar. Quite to the contrary, * * * the "total concept and feel" of the two works greatly differ. The *Superman* works portray a benevolent superhuman who seeks to achieve noble goals through the exercise of innate superpowers while at the same time trying to maintain the secrecy of his true identity in order to occupy a position in society as an ordinary person. *Hero* on the other hand, is a "mirror image" of the Superman character. *Hero* depicts a typical, young American man with common everyday problems who attempts to cope with the impact upon his life caused by the superhuman powers that are foisted upon him by unidentified alien beings. We conclude that plaintiffs have attempted to demonstrate substantial similarity between the parties' works "by an analysis which alters the actual sequence or construction of plaintiff(s') work in order to achieve a juxtaposition that makes for greater similarity with defendant(s') work." 3 Nimmer, *supra*, s 13.03(E)(3) at 13–48.

* * *

The order of the district court is affirmed * * * .

NOTES

1. On the facts of this case, do you agree that the defendants copied only abstract ideas about Superman and not the plaintiffs' specific expression of Superman?

2. For those of you who have studied unfair competition law, could the facts of this support a colorable claim under section 43(a) of the Lanham Act?

3. Nonliteral copying has been analyzed extensively in cases involving literary works, including software, as well as motion pictures that bring plots and characters to life through audiovisual expression. How meaningful or useful is the concept of nonliteral copying in such contexts as pictorial, graphic, and sculptural works, choreography, architectural works, or musical works?

B. THE PRIMA FACIE CASE

"A prima facie case of infringement consists of ownership of the right asserted and unauthorized appropriation by the defendant of a material amount of expression. The copying of facts or of a de minimis amount of expression will not support a prima facie case of infringement." H.R. Rep. No. 102–836, 102nd Cong., 2nd Sess. 3 (1992). A plaintiff may establish appropriation of a copyrighted work either by presenting direct evidence of copying or by demonstrating (through circumstantial or direct evidence) (1) the defendant's access to the plaintiff's work plus (2) some similarity between that work and the defendant's work.

These attempts at proof ordinarily raise questions of fact. Given adequate proof of appropriation, the materiality of the appropriation—in other words, its ultimate actionability—is a separate, additional issue of fact. Summary disposition is generally disfavored in infringement practice, but a defendant who is confronted with no evidence of either access or appropriation may move successfully to dismiss the complaint or for summary judgment. Conversely, striking similarity between the works is sometimes accepted as equivalent to proof of both access and appropriation, and may even be sufficient to justify summary judgment or a directed verdict for the plaintiff. In theory and practice alike, however, the existence of similarity (even striking similarity) may be misleading: it is entirely possible that the defendant may have created a work like the plaintiff's, either without copying at all or without copying from the *plaintiff*. As to the latter possibility, if the defendant copied from a third party's copyrighted work, the third party may have an infringement action. Alternatively, if the third party's work is in the public domain, there can be no copyright action at all.

ARNSTEIN V. PORTER

154 F.2d 464 (2d Cir. 1946).

FRANK, CIRCUIT JUDGE:

* * *

[Plaintiff alleged that several of defendant's musical compositions were copied from plaintiff's works, of which some, but not all, had been published, publicly performed on the radio, or distributed to a limited group. Plaintiff offered no direct evidence that defendant had ever seen or heard these compositions, and defendant denied having any acquaintance with them. The district court granted the defendant's motion for summary judgment, and the plaintiff appealed.]

The principal question on this appeal is whether the lower court * * * properly deprived plaintiff of a trial of his copyright infringement action. The answer depends on whether 'there is the slightest doubt as to the facts.' In applying that standard here, it is important to avoid confusing two separate elements essential to a plaintiff's case in such a suit: (a) that defendant copied from plaintiff's copyrighted work and (b) that the copying (assuming it to be proved) went so far as to constitute improper appropriation.

As to the first—copying—the evidence may consist (a) of defendant's admission that he copied or (b) of circumstantial evidence—usually evidence of access—from which the trier of the facts may reasonably infer copying. Of course, if there are no similarities, no amount of evidence of access will suffice to prove copying. If there is evidence of access and similarities exist, then the trier of the facts must determine whether the similarities are sufficient to prove copying. On this issue, analysis ("dissection") is relevant, and the testimony of experts may be received to aid the trier of the facts. If evidence of access is absent, the similarities must be so striking as to preclude the possibility that plaintiff and defendant independently arrived at the same result.

If copying is established, then only does there arise the second issue, that of illicit copying (unlawful appropriation). On that issue (as noted more in detail below) the test is the response of the ordinary lay hearer; accordingly, on that issue, "dissection" and expert testimony are irrelevant.

In some cases, the similarities between the plaintiff's and defendant's work are so extensive and striking as, without more, both to justify an inference of copying and to prove improper appropriation. But such double-purpose evidence is not required; that is, if copying is otherwise shown, proof of improper appropriation need not consist of similarities which, standing alone, would support an inference of copying.

Each of these two issues—copying and improper appropriation—is an issue of fact. If there is a trial, the conclusions on those issues of the trier of the facts—of the judge if he sat without a jury, or of the jury if there was a jury trial—bind this court on appeal, provided the evidence supports those findings, regardless of whether we would ourselves have reached the same conclusions. But a case could occur in which the similarities were so striking that we would reverse a finding of no access, despite weak evidence of access (or no evidence thereof other than the similarities); and similarly as to a finding of no illicit appropriation.

We turn first to the issue of copying. After listening to the compositions as played in the phonograph recordings submitted by defendant, we find similarities; but we hold that unquestionably, standing alone, they do not compel the conclusion, or permit the inference, that defendant copied. The similarities, however, are sufficient so that, if there is enough evidence of access to permit the case to go to the jury, the jury may properly infer that the similarities did not result from coincidence.

Summary judgment was, then, proper if indubitably defendant did not have access to plaintiff's compositions. Plainly that presents an issue of fact. On that issue, the district judge, who heard no oral testimony, had before him the depositions of plaintiff and defendant. The judge characterized plaintiff's story as "fantastic"; and, in the light of the references in his opinion to defendant's deposition, the judge obviously accepted defendant's denial of access and copying. Although part of plaintiff's testimony on deposition * * * does seem "fantastic," yet plaintiff's credibility, even as to those improbabilities, should be left to the jury. * * *

But even if we were to disregard the improbable aspects of plaintiff's story, there remain parts by no means "fantastic." On the record now before us, more than a million copies of one of his compositions were sold; copies of others were sold in smaller quantities or distributed to radio stations or band leaders or publishers, or the pieces were publicly performed. If, after hearing both parties testify, the jury disbelieves defendant's denials, it can, from such facts, reasonably infer access. It follows that, as credibility is unavoidably involved, a genuine issue of material fact presents itself. * * *

With all that in mind, we cannot now say—as we think we must say to sustain a summary judgment—that at the close of a trial the judge could properly direct a verdict.

* * *

Assuming that adequate proof is made of copying, that is not enough; for there can be "permissible copying," copying which is not illicit. Whether (if he copied) defendant unlawfully appropriated presents, too, an issue of fact. The proper criterion on that issue is not an analytic or other comparison of the respective musical compositions as they appear on paper or in the judgment of trained musicians. The plaintiff's legally protected interest is not, as such, his reputation as a musician but his interest in the potential financial returns from his compositions which derive from the lay public's approbation of his efforts. The question, therefore, is whether defendant took from plaintiff's works so much of what is pleasing to the ears of lay listeners, who comprise the audience for whom such popular music is composed, that defendant wrongfully appropriated something which belongs to the plaintiff.

Surely, then, we have an issue of fact which a jury is peculiarly fitted to determine. * * *

We should not be taken as saying that a plagiarism case can never arise in which absence of similarities is so patent that a summary judgment for defendant would be correct. Thus suppose that Ravel's "Bolero" or Shostakovitch's "Fifth Symphony" were alleged to infringe "When Irish Eyes Are Smiling." But this is not such a case. For, after listening to the playing of the respective compositions, we are, at this time, unable to conclude that the likenesses are so trifling that, on the issue of misappropriation, a trial judge could legitimately direct a verdict for defendant.

At the trial, plaintiff may play, or cause to be played, the pieces in such manner that they may seem to a jury to be inexcusably alike, in terms of the way in which lay listeners of such music would be likely to react. The plaintiff may call witnesses whose testimony may aid the jury in reaching its conclusion as to the responses of such audiences. Expert testimony of musicians may also be received, but it will in no way be controlling on the issue of illicit copying, and should be utilized only to assist in determining the reactions of lay auditors. The impression made on the refined ears of musical experts or their views as to the musical excellence of plaintiff's or defendant's works are utterly immaterial on the issue of misappropriation; for the views of such persons are caviar to the general—and plaintiff's and defendant's compositions are not caviar.

* * *

SHAW V. LINDHEIM

919 F.2d 1353 (9th Cir. 1990).

ALARCON, CIRCUIT JUDGE.

Lou Shaw and Eastbourne Productions, Inc. (Shaw) appeal from a grant of summary judgment in favor of Richard Lindheim, Michael Sloan, and three entertainment corporations (defendants). On appeal, Shaw argues that the district court erred in finding that, as a matter of law, there was no substantial similarity between his script entitled "The Equalizer" and defendants' pilot script for their "Equalizer" television series. Because a reasonable trier of fact could have found that the two works are substantially similar, Shaw argues, the district court erred in dismissing his copyright * * * claims on summary judgment. We reverse and remand.

* * *

Discussion

I. *Copyright Claim*

Copyright law protects an author's expression; facts and ideas within a work are not protected. To establish a successful copyright infringement claim, Shaw must show that he owns the copyright and that defendant copied protected elements of the work. Because, in most cases, direct evidence of copying is not available, a plaintiff may establish copying by showing that the infringer had access to the work and that the two works are substantially similar. The defendants conceded Shaw's ownership of the original Equalizer script and their access to the script for purposes of the summary judgment motion. As a result, the only issue before the district court on the copyright claim was whether defendants' version of the Equalizer is substantially similar to Shaw's original script.

Any test for substantial similarity is necessarily imprecise:

> "Upon any work, and especially upon a play, a great number of patterns of increasing generality will fit equally well, as more and more of the incident is left out. The last may perhaps be no more than the most general statement of what the play is about and at

times might consist of only its title; but there is a point in this series of abstractions where they are no longer protected, since otherwise the playwright could prevent the use of his 'ideas,' to which, apart from their expression, his property is never extended."

Sid & Marty Krofft Television Prods., Inc. v. McDonald's Corp., 562 F.2d 1157, 1163 (9th Cir.1977) (quoting *Nichols v. Universal Pictures Corp.*, 45 F.2d 119, 121 (2d Cir.1930)). It is thus impossible to articulate a definitive demarcation that measures when the similarity between works involves copying of protected expression; decisions must inevitably be ad hoc.

A. The Krofft Framework

The Ninth Circuit employs a two-part test for determining whether one work is substantially similar to another. Established in *Sid & Marty Krofft Television Prods., Inc. v. McDonald's Corp.*, 562 F.2d 1157, 1164 (9th Cir.1977), the test permits a finding of infringement only if a plaintiff proves both substantial similarity of general ideas under the "extrinsic test" and substantial similarity of the protectable expression of those ideas under the "intrinsic test."

1. Scope of the Krofft Tests

Krofft defined the extrinsic test as a "test for similarity of ideas" under which "analytic dissection and expert testimony are appropriate." The intrinsic test, according to *Krofft*, should measure "substantial similarity in expressions ... depending on the response of the ordinary reasonable person.... It does not depend on the type of external criteria and analysis which marks the extrinsic test." In decisions under the intrinsic test, "analytic dissection and expert testimony are not appropriate."

Relying on this language, panels applying *Krofft* to literary works have included a lengthy list of concrete elements under the extrinsic test. Whereas *Krofft* listed "the type of artwork involved, the materials used, the subject matter, and the setting for the subject" as criteria for consideration under the extrinsic test, a series of opinions beginning with the district court opinion in *Jason v. Fonda*, 526 F.Supp. 774 (C.D.Cal.1981), *aff'd and incorporated by reference*, 698 F.2d 966 (9th Cir.1982), have listed "plot, themes, dialogue, mood, setting, pace, and sequence" as extrinsic test criteria. 526 F.Supp. at 777; *see also Narell v. Freeman*, 872 F.2d 907, 912 (9th Cir. 1989) (adding "characters" to the list and transforming "sequence" into "sequence of events").

Now that it includes virtually every element that may be considered concrete in a literary work, the extrinsic test as applied to books, scripts, plays, and motion pictures can no longer be seen as a test for mere similarity of ideas. Because the criteria incorporated into the extrinsic test encompass all objective manifestations of creativity, the two tests are more sensibly described as objective and subjective analyses of expression, having strayed from *Krofft*'s division between expression and ideas. *See Narell*, 872 F.2d at 912 (referring to an objective, extrinsic test and a subjective, intrinsic test). Indeed, a judicial determination under the intrinsic test is now virtually devoid of analysis, for the intrinsic test has become a mere subjective judgment as to whether two literary works are or are not similar.

2. The District Court's Application of Krofft

An example of how the absence of legal analysis may frustrate appellate review of the intrinsic test is the district court's order in this matter. The district court found, after extensive analysis, that reasonable minds might conclude that plaintiffs' and defendants' works were substantially similar as to the objective characteristics of theme, plot, sequence of events, characters, dialogue, setting, mood, and pace. Nevertheless, the court made a subjective determination under the intrinsic test that no reasonable juror could determine that the works had a substantially similar total concept and feel. * * *

The district court's decision to grant summary judgment solely on a subjective assessment under *Krofft*'s intrinsic test conflicts with the prescriptions of *Krofft*. In *Krofft*, this court stated that the outcome of the extrinsic test "may often be decided as a matter of law." 562 F.2d at 1164. In contrast "[i]f there is substantial similarity in ideas, then *the trier of fact* must decide [under the intrinsic test] whether there is substantial similarity in the expressions of the ideas so as to constitute infringement." *Id.* (emphasis added); *see also id.* at 1166 ("[T]he intrinsic test for expression is uniquely suited for determination by *the trier of fact*." (emphasis added)). Professor Nimmer has also noted that "the second step in the [*Krofft*] analytic process requires that *the trier of fact* then decide 'whether there is substantial similarity in the expressions of the ideas so as to constitute infringement.'" 3 M. NIMMER, NIMMER ON COPYRIGHT § 13.03[E][3], at 62.14 (1989).

3. Krofft and the Summary Judgment Standard

* * *

We must determine in this matter whether a party that demonstrates a triable issue of fact under the extrinsic test has made a sufficient showing of substantial similarity to defeat a summary judgment motion. As noted above, the extrinsic test focuses on "specific similarities between the plot, theme, dialogue, mood, setting, pace, characters, and sequence of events. . . . 'the actual concrete elements that make up the total sequence of events and the relationships between the major characters.'" These are the measurable, objective elements that constitute a literary work's expression. Because these elements are embodied in the extrinsic test, we hold that it is improper for a court to find, as the district court did, that there is no substantial similarity as a matter of law after a writer has satisfied the extrinsic test. To conclude otherwise would allow a court to base a grant of summary judgment on a purely subjective determination of similarity. * * *

The rule we announce today—that satisfaction of the extrinsic test creates a triable issue of fact in a copyright action involving a literary work—is in harmony with our prior decisions. Although various panels of this circuit have affirmed grants of summary judgment on the issue of substantial similarity between books, scripts, films, or plays, none of these decisions have rested on application of the intrinsic test alone. * * *

* * * A comparison of literary works * * * generally requires the reader or viewer to engage in a two-step process. The first step involves the objective comparison of concrete similarities; the second employs the subjective process of comprehension, reasoning, and understanding. The imagery presented in a literary work may also engage the imagination of the audience and evoke an emotional response. Because each of us differs, to some degree, in our capability to reason, imagine, and react emotionally, subjective comparisons of literary works that are objectively similar in their expression of ideas must be left to the trier of fact.

For these reasons, a showing of substantial similarity with reference to the eight objective components of expression in the extrinsic test applied to literary works creates a genuine issue for trial. If a district court concludes, after analyzing the objective criteria under the extrinsic test, that reasonable minds might differ as to whether there is substantial similarity between the protected expression of ideas in two literary works, and the record supports the district court's conclusion, there is a triable issue of fact that precludes summary judgment. This rule is necessary because our expansion of the extrinsic test as applied to literary works has incorporated all objective elements of expression, leaving a mere subjective assessment of similarity for the intrinsic test. Because such an assessment may not properly be made as a matter of law, it is for the trier of fact to determine whether the intrinsic test is satisfied. Accordingly, our decision in this matter turns on whether Shaw has raised a triable issue of fact under *Krofft*'s extrinsic test.

B. The Extrinsic Test

1. Role of Access

Although access was not an issue before the district court for purposes of the defendants' summary judgment motion, we must consider defendants' access to Shaw's script in determining substantial similarity. * * * Thus, defendants' admission that they had access to Shaw's script is a factor to be considered in favor of Shaw.

* * *

3. *The Extrinsic Test Applied*

[The appellate court then applied the extrinsic text to determine the extent of objective similarities in the plot, theme, dialogue, mood, setting, pace, characters, and sequence of events in each of the two works.] * * *

4. *Conclusion*

We conclude that Shaw has satisfied the extrinsic test for literary works and thus has presented a triable issue of fact regarding substantial similarity of protected expression. "Even if a copied portion be relatively small in proportion to the entire work, if qualitatively important, the finder of fact may properly find substantial similarity." *Baxter v. MCA, Inc.*, 812 F.2d 421, 425 (9th Cir.1987). A reasonable trier of fact could find that the similarity between Shaw's script and defendants' pilot is not so general as to be beyond the protections of copyright law. Because Shaw has produced a triable issue of fact under the extrinsic test, we reverse the district court's grant of summary judgment on Shaw's copyright claim.

* * *

LEIGH V. WARNER BROTHERS, INC.

212 F.3d 1210 (11th Cir. 2000).

KRAVITCH, SENIOR CIRCUIT JUDGE.

This appeal concerns the scope of a photographer's copyright and trademark rights in his work, the role of the court in determining whether images are "substantially similar" for purposes of copyright, and the power of the court to rule on dispositive motions without first allowing broad discovery. Jack Leigh took the now-famous photograph of the Bird Girl statue in Savannah's Bonaventure Cemetery that appears on the cover of the best-selling novel *Midnight in the Garden of Good and Evil.* Warner Brothers made a film version of the novel and used images of the Bird Girl both in promotional materials and in the movie itself. Leigh sued Warner Brothers, asserting that it infringed his copyright and trademark rights in the Bird Girl photograph. The district court granted summary judgment for Warner Brothers on all claims, except one that the parties now have settled, and Leigh appeals.

The district court correctly ascertained the elements of Leigh's photograph protected by copyright and determined that the Warner Brothers film sequences are not substantially similar to those protected elements. Copyright infringement is generally a question of fact for the jury to decide, however, and the court erred in holding as a matter of law that no reasonable jury could find that the Warner Brothers promotional single-frame images were substantially similar to the aspects of Leigh's work protected by copyright.

* * *

I. Background

In 1993, Random House commissioned Jack Leigh to take a photograph for the cover of *Midnight in the Garden of Good and Evil* ("*Midnight*"), a novel by John Berendt. After reading a manuscript of the novel, Leigh explored appropriate settings in Savannah and ultimately selected a photograph of a sculpture in the Bonaventure Cemetery known as the Bird Girl. Sylvia Shaw Judson had sculpted the Bird Girl in 1938, and she produced three copies of the statue. The Trosdal family had purchased one of the statues and placed it in their plot at Bonaventure Cemetery. The novel does not mention the Bird Girl statue. Leigh granted Random House permission to use the photo, but retained ownership and registered his claim of copyright.

In 1997, Warner Brothers produced a movie based on *Midnight* and decided to use the Bird Girl statue on promotional materials and at the beginning and end of the movie. Because the Trosdals had removed the statue from their cemetery plot after the book's publication, Warner Brothers made a replica of the Bird Girl with the permission of Sylvia Shaw Judson's heir. The company then took photographs and film footage of the replica in a new location in Bonaventure Cemetery. Those images are the subject of this lawsuit.

Three segments of film footage depict the Bird Girl statue. One is a promotional clip, and the others appear at the beginning and end of the Warner Brothers movie. Six still images feature the Bird Girl: a promotional photograph and nearly identical picture on the "goodandevil" web site, a movie poster, a newspaper advertisement, the cover for the movie's soundtrack, and an internet icon. Leigh alleges that these images infringed his copyright and trademark rights in his Bird Girl photograph. The district court * * * granted summary judgment for Warner Brothers on all claims except a copyright claim pertaining to the internet icon. The parties subsequently settled all claims pertaining to that internet icon.

We review the district court's grant of summary judgment *de novo*, construing all evidence in the light most favorable to the non-moving party. * * *

II. Leigh's Copyright Claims

To establish a claim of copyright infringement, a plaintiff must prove, first, that he owns a valid copyright in a work and, second, that the defendant copied original elements of that work. *See Feist Publications, Inc. v. Rural Tel. Serv. Co.*, 499 U.S. 340, 361 (1991). The plaintiff can prove copying either directly or indirectly, by establishing that the defendant had access, and produced something "substantially similar," to the copyrighted work. *See Original Appalachian Artworks, Inc. v. Toy Loft, Inc.*, 684 F.2d 821, 829 (11th Cir.1982). Substantial similarity, in this sense, "exists where an average lay observer would recognize the alleged copy as having been appropriated from the copyrighted work." *Id.* (internal quotation omitted).

"Substantial similarity" also is important in a second, more focused way. No matter how the copying is proved, the plaintiff also must establish specifically that the allegedly infringing work is substantially similar to the plaintiff's work *with regard to its protected elements.* Even in the rare case of a plaintiff with direct evidence that a defendant attempted to appropriate his original expression, there is no infringement unless the defendant succeeded to a meaningful degree.

For the purposes of its motion for summary judgment and this appeal, Warner Brothers does not contest Leigh's ownership of a valid copyright in the Bird Girl photograph. Leigh, on the other hand, takes issue both with the district court's view of the scope of his copyright and with the court's analysis of the similarities between the Bird Girl images.

Leigh's copyright does not cover the appearance of the statue itself or of Bonaventure Cemetery, for Leigh has no rights in the statue or its setting. Nor does the copyright protect the association of the statue with the *Midnight* story. Leigh may have been the first to think of the statue as evocative of the novel's mood and as an appropriate symbol of the book's themes, but copyright law protects only original expression, not ideas.

Thus, the district court correctly identified the elements of artistic craft protected by Leigh's copyright as the selection of lighting, shading, timing, angle, and film. Leigh suggests that the court also should have considered the overall combination of these protected elements as well as the mood they convey. The court determined that the "eerie," "spiritual" mood was *scenes a faire,* expression commonly associated with the subject matter (cemeteries) and thus non-original and unprotectable. Leigh contests the notion that cemeteries are typically portrayed in an eerie, spiritual manner, but there is no need to determine whether *scenes a faire* applies in this case.

Analyzing relatively amorphous characteristics of the picture as a whole (such as the "mood" or "combination of elements") creates a danger of unwittingly extending copyright protection to unoriginal aspects of the work. This danger is especially acute in a case such as this, in which the unprotected elements of the plaintiff's work—the haunting pose and expression of the Bird Girl and the cemetery setting—are so significant.

Although some cases have evaluated the "mood" of a work independently, in this case it is safest to focus on the more concrete elements of the photographer's craft. Even as Leigh describes it, the mood is not so much an independent aspect of his photograph protected by copyright, as the effect created by the lighting, shading, timing, angle, and film. The same holds true for the overall combination of elements in the photograph. As long as the analysis is not overly detached and technical, it can adequately address both the effect of the protected, original elements of Leigh's photograph on the viewer and the contribution of those elements to the work as a whole.

In its order granting summary judgment, the court methodically and accurately details a number of differences in the compositional elements between Leigh's photograph and the Warner Brothers images. This circuit has noted, however, that lists of similarities between works are inherently subjective and unreliable, and the same can be true of lists of distinguishing characteristics.

The court was correct to hold as a matter of law that the film sequences featuring the Bird Girl statue are not substantially similar to the protected elements of Leigh's photograph. In one sequence, the cemetery is shrouded in fog, revealing only the Bird Girl and a Celtic cross, a decoration absent from Leigh's photograph. The camera frame also crops the head of the Bird Girl statue. A second sequence is shot at least partly in color and in broad daylight. The statue's plinth is never shown, and as the camera pans up it shows only the upper portions of the statue on the left side of the screen. In the final sequence, the camera rotates around the statue, beginning with a side shot, and captures only the head and shoulders before panning back to show the Bird Girl's torso. Again, the statue is on the left side of the screen and the sequence is shot in daylight. The film sequences were not shot in the same section of the Bonaventure Cemetery as Leigh's photograph, so the surrounding gravestones and greenery are different. These film sequences have nothing substantial in common with Leigh's photograph except the statue itself.

The same cannot be said for Warner Brothers' photographic images. There are, undeniably, significant differences between the pictures. The statue is smaller and more distant in most of the Warner Brothers pictures than in Leigh's photograph, and as a result the vegetation and headstones in the foreground are more prominent. The Bird Girl is approximately the same size only on the soundtrack cover. Although both the Leigh photograph and the soundtrack cover have diffuse light that "glows" about the statue, the lighting contrast is more extreme in most of the Warner Brothers pictures, with beams of light piercing the tree canopy like spotlights. The shafts of light and surrounding shadows obscure details of the statue and the cemetery setting. Finally, Warner Brothers has added elements to some of its images that are absent from Leigh's photo: some have a green or orange tint; some prominently feature a Celtic cross and tree; and the movie poster includes pictures of the cast along its left side.

Although it may be easy to identify differences between the Warner Brothers still shots and Leigh's photograph, however, the Warner Brothers images also have much in common with the elements protected by Leigh's copyright. All of the photographs are taken from a low position, angled up slightly at the Bird Girl so that the contents of the bowls in her hands remain hidden. Hanging Spanish moss borders the tops of all the photographs except the soundtrack cover. The statue is close to centered in all of the pictures except one newspaper advertisement for the movie, which places the Bird Girl in the left third of the frame. Light shines down and envelopes the statue in all of the images, leaving the surrounding cemetery in relative darkness. All of the photographs are monochromatic.

These expressive elements all make the pictures more effective. The Spanish moss provides a top border to the images. The location of the statue and the lighting in the pictures together draw the viewer's attention. The lighting also lends a spiritual air to the Bird Girl. Finally, by keeping the contents of the Bird Girl's bowls hidden, the angle contributes to the mystery and symbolic meaning of the images.

A jury ultimately may conclude that the similarities between the protected elements of the Leigh photograph and the Warner Brothers still shots are not "substantial." The similarities are significant enough, however, to preclude summary judgment. "Substantial similarity" is a question of fact, and summary judgment is only appropriate if no reasonable jury could differ in weighing the evidence. * * *

V. Conclusion

We AFFIRM the grant of summary judgment for the Defendant on Leigh's trademark claims and the copyright claim as it relates to the film sequences. We REVERSE the grant of summary judgment for the Defendant on Leigh's copyright claim as it relates to Warner Brothers' single-frame images, and we REMAND for proceedings consistent with this decision.

NOTES

1. "Striking similarity" refers to a degree of similarity "so striking that the possibilities of independent creation, coincidence and prior common source are, as a practical matter, precluded." *Selle v. Gibb*, 741 F.2d 896, 901 (7th Cir. 1984). Striking similarity might be found, for example, where two works have the same errors or the same highly idiosyncratic or whimsical elements. Where such similarities are found, could a finding of infringement be proper even if the evidence showed that access was highly improbable?

2. Does the presence of the plaintiff's copyrighted materials on the internet, on a public website, by itself justify an inference that the defendant had access to those materials? *See Design Basics, LLC v. Lexington Homes, Inc.*, 858 F.3d 1093 (7th Cir. 2017).

3. In some cases, a defendant is found to have copied the plaintiff's work unconsciously; in other cases, the defendant has copied a work in the erroneous belief that it is in the public domain. Is the defendant's state of mind relevant to the question of infringement liability? Should it be?

4. *Litchfield v. Spielberg*, 736 F.2d 1352, 1357 (9th Cir. 1984) held that the substantial similarity test applies to infringement claims involving the right to create derivative works under section 106(2), and not just those claims involving the right to reproduce under section 106(1), noting that "[a] work will be considered a derivative work *only if it would be considered an infringing work if* the material which it has derived from a prior work had been taken without the consent of a copyright proprietor of such prior work." *Id.*

5. In *Sandoval v. New Line Cinema Corp.*, 147 F.3d 215 (2d Cir. 1998), the court found no substantial similarity between the plaintiff's photographs and scenes from the defendant's movie, in which the photographs were used as set decoration, because the copying was "de minimis." The photos that appeared in the film were never in focus, were seen at a distance, and were often obstructed by actors or props in the foreground. The Second Circuit held that it was error to undertake a fair use analysis without first determining whether the defendant's use of the plaintiff's copyrighted work was so minimal as to be "de minimis as a matter of law" and therefore not actionable. *Id.* at 217. The court thus approved its previous dicta in *Ringgold v. Black Entertainment Television, Inc.*, 126 F.3d 70, 76 (2d Cir. 1997), that where "the allegedly infringing work makes such a quantitatively insubstantial use of the copyrighted work as to fall below the threshold required for actionable copying, it makes more sense to reject the claim on that basis and find no infringement, rather than undertake an elaborate fair use analysis."

6. In *Scholastic, Inc. v. Stouffer*, 221 F. Supp. 2d 425 (S.D.N.Y. 2002), *aff'd*, 81 Fed. Appx. 396 (2d Cir. 2003), a declaratory judgment action, defendant Stouffer, author of *Larry Potter and His Best Friend Lilly*, alleged that the cover illustrations of the *Harry Potter* books, authored by J.K. Rowling, infringed the copyrights on an illustration in the Larry Potter story. The Larry Potter stories were published nine years before the first Harry Potter book. Ruling for the plaintiff, the court found that the similarities in the character illustrations (young boys with dark hair and glasses) involved generic elements which are not copyrightable. Protectable elements of the Larry Potter drawing (facial features, eyeglass shape and color, and hair-style) were absent in plaintiff's illustrations. Since the allegedly copied elements were not protectable, the court did not analyze whether the illustrations were substantially similar. The court noted that there was no proof that Rowling or her illustrator had access to the defendant's work.

7. The Fourth Circuit has held that when a copyrighted work has a targeted audience, the substantial similarity inquiry must focus on the perspective of that particular audience. *See Lyons Partnership, L.P. v. Morris Costumes, Inc.*, 243 F.3d 789 (4th Cir. 2001) (analysis of Barney the purple dinosaur and similar costumes must consider the perspective of the intended

audience of children, rather than the adult purchaser). Is this the best approach to copyrighted children's products?

8. Under the 1909 Act, registration of a musical work required deposit of the sheet music; deposits of sound recordings were not permitted. In two high-profile cases involving infringement of musical works published under the 1909 Act, the Ninth Circuit upheld district court rulings that prevented jurors from hearing commercial sound recordings of the plaintiffs' works, on the ground that the sound recordings might include elements not present in the sheet music. In addition, both cases involved extensive expert testimony by musicologists. *See Skidmore v. Led Zeppelin*, 952 F.3d 1051 (9th Cir.) (upholding jury finding that Led Zeppelin's "Stairway to Heaven" did not infringe Spirit's "Taurus"), *cert. denied,* 141 S.Ct. 453 (2020); *Williams v. Gaye*, 895 F.3d 1106 (9th Cir. 2018) (upholding jury finding that the song "Blurred Lines," by Robin Thicke and Pharrell Williams infringed Marvin Gaye's "Got to Give It Up").

9. Until recently, the Ninth Circuit followed the "inverse ratio" rule for proving infringement, under which proof of a high degree of access justified a lower standard of proof of similarity. However, the Ninth Circuit abrogated this rule, and expressly overruled its prior case law, in *Skidmore v. Led Zeppelin*, 952 F.3d 1051 (9th Cir. 2020), *cert. denied,* 141 S.Ct. 453 (2020), thus aligning itself with the majority of circuits.

10. *Digital Music Sampling:* Music sampling has become a source of some controversy. Sampling is the practice of copying a previously released portion of a musical recording, digitally altering it (through pitch, repetition or other variances), and then using it in a new sound recording; it is omnipresent in today's music, and is particularly common in hip-hop.

In *Bridgeport Music, Inc. v. Dimension Films*, 410 F.3d 792, 798 (6th Cir. 2005), the Sixth Circuit held that neither the substantial similarity standard nor the concept of de minimis copying applies to digital sampling of a sound recording. In other words, *any* copying from a sound recording infringes, absent fair use. In the Sixth Circuit's view, this "bright-line" rule is dictated by the literal language of section 114(b), and also represents sound policy. *Id.* at 801–04. However, the Ninth Circuit squarely rejected this view in *VMG Salsoul, LLC v. Ciccone,* 824 F.3d 871 (9th Cir. 2016). Which position is more persuasive?

11. If the copyright owner of a sound recording copyright consents to sampling, is the consent of the owner of the copyright in the musical composition needed as well? This scenario arose in *Newton v. Diamond*, 349 F.3d 591 (9th Cir. 2003), where the Ninth Circuit held that the Beastie Boys' sampling of a three-note sequence from a musical composition was *de minimis,* and therefore affirmed summary judgment of non-infringement. Because the amount sampled was very small and was a very common three-note sequence, it did not meet the substantial similarity requirement necessary for a finding of infringement.

12. Federal courts have exclusive jurisdiction over actions "arising under" federal laws relating to copyrights, 28 U.S.C. § 1338(a), except that the Court of Federal Claims has exclusive jurisdiction over copyright infringement actions brought against the United States government or a person acting on its behalf, 28 U.S.C. § 1498(b). In contrast, the statutes are silent on whether federal courts have exclusive jurisdiction over section 1401 claims.

13. In most cases, section 411(a) makes copyright registration (or preregistration, for certain eligible works) a prerequisite to bringing suit for copyright infringement. This requirement does not apply, however, to (1) moral rights actions under section 106A, (2) actions alleging infringement of foreign works protected under copyright treaties, or (3) actions under section 1401 for unauthorized use of pre-1972 sound recordings.

14. For small claims, Congress in 2020 authorized creation of a voluntary alternative to litigation in federal district courts—the Copyright Claims Board (CCB), which is a three-member tribunal within the Copyright Office. The CCB, which began operating in 2022, is authorized to hear civil infringement disputes as well as claims involving misrepresentations in DMCA take-down notices. Discovery is limited, parties have the option to proceed without attorneys, and hearings are conducted electronically. There are no jury trials, the maximum damages award is $30,000, and injunctive relief requires the consent of both parties. CCB decisions can be appealed to the Register of Copyrights, and from there, under very limited circumstances, to a federal court.

C. THE PROPER PARTIES

Statute: 17 U.S.C. § 501

1. PLAINTIFF: STANDING TO SUE

COPYRIGHT ACT OF 1976

H.R. Rep. No. 94–1476.
94th Cong., 2d Sess. 123, 158–59 (1976).

* * *

[Under section 201(d)(2)] any of the exclusive rights that go to make up a copyright, including those enumerated in section 106 and any subdivision of them, can be transferred and owned separately. The definition of "transfer of copyright ownership" in section 101 makes clear that the principle of divisibility applies whether or not the transfer is "limited in time or place of effect," and another definition in the same section provides that the term "copyright owner," with respect to any one exclusive right, refers to the owner of that particular right. The last sentence of section 201(d)(2) adds that the owner, with respect to the particular exclusive right he or she owns, is entitled "to all of the protection and remedies accorded to the copyright owner by this title." It is thus clear, for example, that a local broadcasting station holding an exclusive license to transmit a particular work within a particular geographic area and for a particular period of time, could sue, in its own name as copyright owner, someone who infringed that particular exclusive right. * * *

The principle of the divisibility of copyright ownership, established by section 201(d), carries with it the need in infringement actions to safeguard the rights of all copyright owners and to avoid a multiplicity of suits. Subsection (b) of section 501 enables the owner of a particular right to bring an infringement action in that owner's name alone, while at the same time insuring to the extent possible that the other owners whose rights may be affected are notified and given a chance to join the action.

The first sentence of subsection (b) empowers the "legal or beneficial owner of an exclusive right" to bring suit for "any infringement of that particular right committed while he or she is the owner of it." A "beneficial owner" for this purpose would include, for example, an author who had parted with legal title to the copyright in exchange for percentage royalties based on sales or license fees.

* * *

NOTES

1. Different standing rules apply to infringement cases that do not involve rights under section 106. Under section 106A, the plaintiff is the artist whose right of attribution or integrity has been violated, even if the artist no longer owns any interest in the copyright. Under section 1101, the plaintiff is the live musical performer whose performance has been unlawfully exploited.

Who would be the plaintiff in a posthumous cause of action under section 106A(d)(2)? Could there be a posthumous cause of action under section 1101, and if so, who would be the plaintiff?

2. Under sections 111(c) and 501(c)–(e), the general rule for standing to bring an infringement claim is broadened in the case of secondary cable or satellite transmissions which fail to comply with the section 111 requirements for compulsory licensing. In some cases, the plaintiff can be a broadcaster that does not have an exclusive license, or even a nonexclusive license, to broadcast the work in question in the local broadcast area where the infringing secondary transmission occurred.

3. Can the assignee of a copyright bring suit for an infringement that preceded the assignment? Can the accrued infringement claim be assigned without the underlying copyright? *See Silvers v. Sony Pictures Entertainment, Inc.*, 402 F.3d 881 (9th Cir. 2005); *ABKCO Music, Inc. v. Harrisongs Music, Ltd.*, 944 F.2d 971 (2d Cir. 1991).

4. Does a stock photography agency, which is a non-exclusive licensing agency, have standing to sue parties who have copied copyrighted images from its collection? *See DRK Photo v. McGraw-Hill Global Education Holdings, LLC,* 870 F.3d 978 (9th Cir. 2017).

2. DEFENDANT: DIRECT AND SECONDARY LIABILITY FOR INFRINGEMENT

Statute: 17 U.S.C. § 501

FONOVISA, INC. V. CHERRY AUCTION, INC.

76 F.3d 259 (9th Cir. 1996).

SCHROEDER, CIRCUIT JUDGE:

This is a copyright and trademark enforcement action against the operators of a swap meet, sometimes called a flea market, where third-party vendors routinely sell counterfeit recordings that infringe on the plaintiff's copyrights and trademarks. The district court dismissed on the pleadings, holding that the plaintiffs, as a matter of law, could not maintain any cause of action against the swap meet for sales by vendors who leased its premises. * * * We reverse.

Background

The plaintiff and appellant is Fonovisa, Inc., a California corporation that owns copyrights and trademarks to Latin/Hispanic music recordings. Fonovisa filed this action in district court against defendant-appellee, Cherry Auction, Inc., and its individual operators (collectively "Cherry Auction"). For purposes of this appeal, it is undisputed that Cherry Auction operates a swap meet in Fresno, California, similar to many other swap meets in this country where customers come to purchase various merchandise from individual vendors. The vendors pay a daily rental fee to the swap meet operators in exchange for booth space. Cherry Auction supplies parking, conducts advertising and retains the right to exclude any vendor for any reason, at any time, and thus can exclude vendors for patent and trademark infringement. In addition, Cherry Auction receives an entrance fee from each customer who attends the swap meet.

There is also no dispute for purposes of this appeal that Cherry Auction and its operators were aware that vendors in their swap meet were selling counterfeit recordings in violation of Fonovisa's trademarks and copyrights. Indeed, it is alleged that in 1991, the Fresno County Sheriff's Department raided the Cherry Auction swap meet and seized more than 38,000 counterfeit recordings. The following year, after finding that vendors at the Cherry Auction swap meet were still selling counterfeit recordings, the Sheriff sent a letter notifying Cherry Auction of the on-going sales of infringing materials, and reminding Cherry Auction that they had agreed to provide the Sheriff with identifying information from each vendor. In addition, in 1993, Fonovisa itself sent an investigator to the Cherry Auction site and observed sales of counterfeit recordings.

* * * Although the Copyright Act does not expressly impose liability on anyone other than direct infringers, courts have long recognized that in certain circumstances, vicarious or contributory liability will be imposed. * * *

Vicarious Copyright Infringement

The concept of vicarious copyright liability was developed in the Second Circuit as an outgrowth of the agency principles of respondeat superior. The landmark case on vicarious liability for sales of counterfeit recordings is *Shapiro Bernstein and Co. v. H. L. Green Co.*, 316 F.2d 304 (2d Cir.1963). In *Shapiro*, the court was faced with a copyright infringement suit against the owner of a chain of department stores where a concessionaire was selling counterfeit recordings. Noting that the normal agency rule of respondeat superior imposes liability on an employer for copyright infringements by an employee, the court endeavored to fashion a principle for enforcing copyrights against a defendant whose economic interests were intertwined with the direct infringer's, but who did not actually employ the direct infringer.

The *Shapiro* court looked at the two lines of cases it perceived as most clearly relevant. In one line of cases, the landlord-tenant cases, the courts had held that a landlord who lacked knowledge of the infringing acts of its tenant and who exercised no control over the leased premises was not liable for infringing sales by its tenant. In the other line of cases, the so-called "dance hall cases," the operator of an entertainment venue was held liable for infringing performances when the operator (1) could control the premises and (2) obtained a direct financial benefit from the audience, who paid to enjoy the infringing performance.

From those two lines of cases, the *Shapiro* court determined that the relationship between the store owner and the concessionaire in the case before it was closer to the dance-hall model than to the landlord-tenant model. It imposed liability even though the defendant was unaware of the infringement. *Shapiro* deemed the imposition of vicarious liability neither unduly harsh nor unfair because the store proprietor had the power to cease the conduct of the concessionaire, and because the proprietor derived an obvious and direct financial benefit from the infringement. The test was more clearly articulated in a later Second Circuit case as follows: "even in the absence of an employer-employee relationship one may be vicariously liable if he has the right and ability to supervise the infringing activity and also has a direct financial interest in such activities." *Gershwin Publishing Corp. v. Columbia Artists Management, Inc.*, 443 F.2d 1159, 1162 (2d Cir.1971). * * *

The district court in this case agreed with defendant Cherry Auction that Fonovisa did not, as a matter of law, meet either the control or the financial benefit prong of the vicarious copyright infringement test articulated in *Gershwin*. Rather, the district court concluded that based on the pleadings, "Cherry Auction neither supervised nor profited from the vendors' sales." In the district court's view, with respect to both control and financial benefit, Cherry Auction was in the same position as an absentee landlord who has surrendered its exclusive right of occupancy in its leased property to its tenants.

This analogy to absentee landlord is not in accord with the facts as alleged in the district court and which we, for purposes of appeal, must accept. The allegations below were that vendors occupied small booths within premises that Cherry Auction controlled and patrolled. According to the complaint, Cherry Auction had the right to terminate vendors for any reason whatsoever and through that right had the ability to control the activities of vendors on the premises. In addition, Cherry Auction promoted the swap meet and controlled the access of customers to the swap meet area. In terms of control, the allegations before us are strikingly similar to those in *Shapiro* and *Gershwin*.

In *Shapiro*, for example, the court focused on the formal licensing agreement between defendant department store and the direct infringer-concessionaire. There, the concessionaire selling the bootleg recordings had a licensing agreement with the department store (H. L. Green Company) that required the concessionaire and its employees to "abide by, observe and obey all regulations promulgated from time to time by the H. L. Green Company," and H. L. Green Company had the "unreviewable discretion" to discharge the concessionaires' employees. In practice, H. L. Green Company was not actively involved in the sale of records and the concessionaire controlled and supervised the individual employees. Nevertheless, H. L. Green's ability to police its concessionaire—which parallels Cherry Auction's ability to police its vendors under Cherry Auction's similarly broad contract with its vendors—was sufficient to satisfy the control requirement.

In *Gershwin*, the defendant lacked the formal, contractual ability to control the direct infringer. Nevertheless, because of defendant's "pervasive participation in the formation and direction" of the direct infringers, including promoting them (i.e. creating an audience for them), the court found that defendants were in a position to police the direct infringers and held that the control element was satisfied. As the promoter and organizer of the swap meet, Cherry Auction wields the same level of control over the direct infringers as did the *Gershwin* defendant.

The district court's dismissal of the vicarious liability claim in this case was therefore not justified on the ground that the complaint failed to allege sufficient control.

We next consider the issue of financial benefit. The plaintiff's allegations encompass many substantive benefits to Cherry Auction from the infringing sales. These include the payment of a daily rental fee by each of the infringing vendors; a direct payment to Cherry Auction by each customer in the form of an admission fee, and incidental payments for parking, food and other services by customers seeking to purchase infringing recordings.

Cherry Auction nevertheless contends that these benefits cannot satisfy the financial benefit prong of vicarious liability because a commission, directly tied to the sale of particular infringing items, is required. They ask that we restrict the financial benefit prong to the precise facts presented in *Shapiro*, where defendant H. L. Green Company received a 10 or 12 per cent commission from the direct infringers' gross receipts. Cherry Auction points to the low daily rental fee paid by each vendor, discounting all other financial benefits flowing to the swap meet, and asks that we hold that the swap meet is materially similar to a mere landlord. The facts alleged by Fonovisa, however, reflect that the defendants reap substantial financial benefits from admission fees, concession stand sales and parking fees, all of which flow directly from customers who want to buy the counterfeit recordings at bargain basement prices. The plaintiff has sufficiently alleged direct financial benefit.

Our conclusion is fortified by the continuing line of cases, starting with the dance hall cases, imposing vicarious liability on the operator of a business where infringing performances enhance the attractiveness of the venue to potential customers. In *Polygram Int'l Pub., Inc. v. Nevada/TIG, Inc.*, for example, direct infringers were participants in a trade show who used infringing music to communicate with attendees and to cultivate interest in their wares. 855 F.Supp. 1314, 1332 (D. Mass. 1994). The court held that the trade show participants "derived a significant financial benefit from the attention" that attendees paid to the infringing music. *Id.*; *See also Famous Music Corp. v. Bay State Harness Horse Racing and Breeding Ass'n*, 554 F.2d 1213, 1214 (1st Cir.1977) (race track owner vicariously liable for band that entertained patrons who were not "absorbed in watching the races"); *Shapiro*, 316 F.2d at 307 (dance hall cases hold proprietor liable where infringing "activities provide the proprietor with a source of customers and enhanced income"). In this case, the sale of pirated recordings at the Cherry Auction swap meet is a "draw" for customers, as was the performance of pirated music in the dance hall cases and their progeny.

Plaintiffs have stated a claim for vicarious copyright infringement.

Contributory Copyright Infringement

Contributory infringement originates in tort law and stems from the notion that one who directly contributes to another's infringement should be held accountable. *See* 1 NEIL BOORSTYN, BOORSTYN ON COPYRIGHT § 10.06[2], at 10–21 (1994) ("In other words, the common law doctrine that one who knowingly participates in or furthers a tortious act is jointly and severally liable with the prime tortfeasor, is applicable under copyright law"). Contributory infringement has been described as an outgrowth of enterprise liability, and imposes liability where one person knowingly contributes to the infringing conduct of another. The classic statement of the doctrine is in *Gershwin*, 443 F.2d 1159, 1162: "One who, with knowledge of the infringing activity, induces, causes or materially contributes to the infringing conduct of another, may be held liable as a 'contributory' infringer."

There is no question that plaintiff adequately alleged the element of knowledge in this case. The disputed issue is whether plaintiff adequately alleged that Cherry Auction materially contributed to the infringing activity. We have little difficulty in holding that the allegations in this case are sufficient to show material contribution to the infringing activity. Indeed, it would be difficult for the infringing activity to take place in the massive quantities alleged without the support services provided by the swap meet. These services include, inter alia, the provision of space, utilities, parking, advertising, plumbing, and customers.

Here again Cherry Auction asks us to ignore all aspects of the enterprise described by the plaintiffs, to concentrate solely on the rental of space, and to hold that the swap meet provides nothing more. Yet Cherry Auction actively strives to provide the environment and the market for counterfeit recording sales to thrive. Its participation in the sales cannot be termed "passive," as Cherry Auction would prefer.

The district court apparently took the view that contribution to infringement should be limited to circumstances in which the defendant "expressly promoted or encouraged the sale of counterfeit products, or in some manner protected the identity of the infringers." Given the allegations that the local sheriff lawfully requested that Cherry Auction gather and share basic, identifying information about its vendors, and that Cherry Auction failed to comply, the defendant appears to qualify within the last portion of the district court's own standard that posits liability for protecting infringers' identities. Moreover, we agree with the Third Circuit's analysis in *Columbia Pictures Industries, Inc. v. Aveco, Inc.*, 800 F.2d 59 (3d Cir.1986) that providing the site and facilities for known infringing activity is sufficient to establish contributory liability.

* * *

SONY CORP. OF AMERICA V. UNIVERSAL CITY STUDIOS, INC.

464 U.S. 417, 104 S.Ct. 774 (1984).

[Plaintiffs/respondents, the owners of copyrights in various recorded programs shown on television, brought suit against Sony, the maker of Betamax videotape recorders (VTRs), alleging that Sony was liable for contributory copyright infringement because it sold VTRs to television viewers who used the VTRs to make infringing recordings of those works. They did not, however, bring suit against the television viewers that used the VTRs.]

* * *

III

The Copyright Act does not expressly render anyone liable for infringement committed by another. In contrast, the Patent Act expressly brands anyone who "actively induces infringement of a patent" as an infringer, 35 U.S.C. § 271(b), and further imposes liability on certain individuals labeled "contributory" infringers, § 271(c). The absence of such express language in the copyright statute does not preclude the imposition of liability for copyright infringements on certain parties who have not themselves engaged in the infringing activity. For vicarious liability is imposed in virtually all areas of the law, and the concept of contributory infringement is merely a species of the broader problem of identifying the circumstances in which it is just to hold one individual accountable for the actions of another.

* * * The only contact between Sony and the users of the Betamax that is disclosed by this record occurred at the moment of sale. The District Court expressly found that "no employee of Sony * * * had either direct involvement with the allegedly infringing activity or direct contact with purchasers of Betamax who recorded copyrighted works off-the-air." And it further found that "there was no evidence that any of the copies made by Griffiths or the other individual witnesses in this suit were influenced or encouraged by [Sony's] advertisements."

* * *

If vicarious liability is to be imposed on Sony in this case, it must rest on the fact that it has sold equipment with constructive knowledge of the fact that its customers may use that equipment to make unauthorized copies of copyrighted material. There is no precedent in the law of copyright for the imposition of vicarious liability on such a theory. The closest analogy is provided by the patent law cases to which it is appropriate to refer because of the historic kinship between patent law and copyright law.

In the Patent Act both the concept of infringement and the concept of contributory infringement are expressly defined by statute. The prohibition against contributory infringement is confined to the knowing sale of a component especially made for use in connection with a particular patent. There is no suggestion in the statute that one patentee may object to the sale of a product that might be used in connection with other patents. Moreover, the Act expressly provides that the sale of a "staple article or commodity of commerce suitable for substantial noninfringing use" is not contributory infringement. 35 U.S.C. § 271(c).

When a charge of contributory infringement is predicated entirely on the sale of an article of commerce that is used by the purchaser to infringe a patent, the public interest in access to that article of commerce is necessarily implicated. A finding of contributory infringement does not, of course, remove the article from the market altogether; it does, however, give the patentee effective control over the sale of that item. Indeed, a finding of contributory infringement is normally the functional equivalent of holding that the disputed article is within the monopoly granted to the patentee.[21]

For that reason, in contributory infringement cases arising under the patent laws the Court has always recognized the critical importance of not allowing the patentee to extend his monopoly beyond the limits of his specific grant. These cases deny the patentee any right to control the distribution of unpatented articles unless they are "unsuited for any commercial noninfringing use." Unless a commodity "has no use except through practice of the patented method," the patentee has no right to claim that its distribution constitutes contributory infringement. * * *

We recognize there are substantial differences between the patent and copyright laws. But in both areas the contributory infringement doctrine is grounded on the recognition that adequate protection of a monopoly may require the courts to look beyond actual duplication of a device or publication to the products or activities that make such duplication possible. The staple article of commerce doctrine must strike a balance between a copyright holder's legitimate demand for effective—not merely symbolic—protection of the statutory monopoly, and the rights of others freely to engage in substantially unrelated areas of commerce. Accordingly, the sale of copying equipment, like the sale of other articles of commerce, does not constitute contributory infringement if the product is widely used for legitimate, unobjectionable purposes. Indeed, it need merely be capable of substantial noninfringing uses.

[21] It seems extraordinary to suggest that the Copyright Act confers upon all copyright owners collectively, much less the two respondents in this case, the exclusive right to distribute VTR's simply because they may be used to infringe copyrights. That, however, is the logical implication of their claim. * * *

IV

The question is thus whether the Betamax is capable of commercially significant noninfringing uses. In order to resolve that question, we need not explore all the different potential uses of the machine and determine whether or not they would constitute infringement. Rather, we need only consider whether on the basis of the facts as found by the District Court a significant number of them would be noninfringing. Moreover, in order to resolve this case we need not give precise content to the question of how much use is commercially significant. For one potential use of the Betamax plainly satisfies this standard, however it is understood: private, noncommercial time-shifting in the home. It does so both (A) because respondents have no right to prevent other copyright holders from authorizing it for their programs, and (B) because the District Court's factual findings reveal that even the unauthorized home time-shifting of respondents' programs is legitimate fair use.

A. Authorized Time-Shifting

Each of the respondents owns a large inventory of valuable copyrights, but in the total spectrum of television programming their combined market share is small. The exact percentage is not specified, but it is well below 10%. If they were to prevail, the outcome of this litigation would have a significant impact on both the producers and the viewers of the remaining 90% of the programming in the Nation. No doubt, many other producers share respondents' concern about the possible consequences of unrestricted copying. Nevertheless the findings of the District Court make it clear that time-shifting may enlarge the total viewing audience and that many producers are willing to allow private time-shifting to continue, at least for an experimental time period.

* * * [The District Court found] that the evidence concerning "sports, religious, educational and other programming" was sufficient to establish a significant quantity of broadcasting whose copying is now authorized, and a significant potential for future authorized copying. That finding is amply supported by the record. * * *

* * *

If there are millions of owners of VTR's who make copies of televised sports events, religious broadcasts, and educational programs such as Mister Rogers' Neighborhood, and if the proprietors of those programs welcome the practice, the business of supplying the equipment that makes such copying feasible should not be stifled simply because the equipment is used by some individuals to make unauthorized reproductions of respondents' works. The respondents do not represent a class composed of all copyright holders. Yet a finding of contributory infringement would inevitably frustrate the interests of broadcasters in reaching the portion of their audience that is available only through time-shifting.

Of course, the fact that other copyright holders may welcome the practice of time-shifting does not mean that respondents should be deemed to have granted a license to copy their programs. Third-party conduct would be wholly irrelevant in an action for direct infringement of respondents' copyrights. But in an action for contributory infringement against the seller of copying equipment, the copyright holder may not prevail unless the relief that he seeks affects only his programs, or unless he speaks for virtually all copyright holders with an interest in the outcome. In this case, the record makes it perfectly clear that there are many important producers of national and local television programs who find nothing objectionable about the enlargement in the size of the television audience that results from the practice of time-shifting for private home use. The seller of the equipment that expands those producers' audiences cannot be a contributory infringer if, as is true in this case, it has had no direct involvement with any infringing activity.

B. *Unauthorized Time-Shifting*

[The Court undertook a fair use analysis under section 107 and concluded that "private noncommercial time-shifting in the home" was a non-infringing use. For the Court's discussion of this aspect of the case, see Chapter 17, *supra*.]

* * *

In summary, the record and findings of the District Court lead us to two conclusions. First, Sony demonstrated a significant likelihood that substantial numbers of copyright holders who license their works for broadcast on free television would not object to having their broadcasts time-shifted by private viewers. And second, respondents failed to demonstrate that time-shifting would cause any likelihood of nonminimal harm to the potential market for, or the value of, their copyrighted works. The Betamax is, therefore, capable of substantial noninfringing uses. Sony's sale of such equipment to the general public does not constitute contributory infringement of respondents' copyrights.

NOTES

1. Plaintiff manufactures and sells computer video game systems. The software for plaintiff's games is contained in "Read Only Memory" ("ROM") chips which can neither be reprogrammed nor erased. The cartridges sell for around $40. Defendant sells a device the sole function of which is to copy video games that are compatible with the plaintiff's system. The device sells for $119, and blank cartridges cost $10 each. At the same time defendant began selling its copying device, the defendant also began selling a small number of video games that are compatible with the plaintiff's system. Defendant expressly

gives its customers permission to copy its own games. Is defendant contributorily liable for its customers' copying of plaintiff's copyrighted games?

2. Suppose that the defendant ships copyrighted DVDs from the United States to a recipient overseas, where the DVDs are unavailable. If the defendant knows that the recipient intends to make and distribute unauthorized copies, is the defendant contributorily liable for infringement? Does it matter whether the unauthorized copies are distributed in the United States or only overseas?

METRO-GOLDWYN-MAYER STUDIOS, INC. V. GROKSTER, LTD.

545 U.S. 913, 125 S.Ct. 2764 (2005).

JUSTICE SOUTER delivered the opinion of the Court.

The question is under what circumstances the distributor of a product capable of both lawful and unlawful use is liable for acts of copyright infringement by third parties using the product. We hold that one who distributes a device with the object of promoting its use to infringe copyright, as shown by clear expression or other affirmative steps taken to foster infringement, is liable for the resulting acts of infringement by third parties.

I

A

Respondents, Grokster, Ltd., and StreamCast Networks, Inc., defendants in the trial court, distribute free software products that allow computer users to share electronic files through peer-to-peer networks, so called because users' computers communicate directly with each other, not through central servers. The advantage of peer-to-peer networks over information networks of other types shows up in their substantial and growing popularity. Because they need no central computer server to mediate the exchange of information or files among users, the high-bandwidth communications capacity for a server may be dispensed with, and the need for costly server storage space is eliminated. Since copies of a file (particularly a popular one) are available on many users' computers, file requests and retrievals may be faster than on other types of networks, and since file exchanges do not travel through a server, communications can take place between any computers that remain connected to the network without risk that a glitch in the server will disable the network in its entirety. Given these benefits in security, cost, and efficiency, peer-to-peer networks are employed to store and distribute electronic files by universities, government agencies, corporations, and libraries, among others.

Other users of peer-to-peer networks include individual recipients of Grokster's and StreamCast's software, and although the networks that they enjoy through using the software can be used to share any type of digital file, they have prominently employed those networks in sharing copyrighted music and video files without authorization. A group of copyright holders (MGM for short, but including motion picture studios, recording companies, songwriters, and music publishers) sued Grokster and StreamCast for their users' copyright infringements, alleging that they knowingly and intentionally distributed their software to enable users to reproduce and distribute the copyrighted works in violation of the Copyright Act. MGM sought damages and an injunction.

* * *

The Court of Appeals * * * read *Sony Corp. of America v. Universal City Studios, Inc.*, 464 U.S. 417 (1984), as holding that distribution of a commercial product capable of substantial noninfringing uses could not give rise to contributory liability for infringement unless the distributor had actual knowledge of specific instances of infringement and failed to act on that knowledge. * * *

The Ninth Circuit also considered whether Grokster and StreamCast could be liable under a theory of vicarious infringement. The court held against liability because the defendants did not monitor or control the use of the software, had no agreed-upon right or current ability to supervise its use, and had no independent duty to police infringement. We granted certiorari.

II

A

MGM and many of the amici fault the Court of Appeals's holding for upsetting a sound balance between the respective values of supporting creative pursuits through copyright protection and promoting innovation in new communication technologies by limiting the incidence of liability for copyright infringement. The more artistic protection is favored, the more technological innovation may be discouraged; the administration of copyright law is an exercise in managing the trade-off.

The tension between the two values is the subject of this case, with its claim that digital distribution of copyrighted material threatens copyright holders as never before, because every copy is identical to the original, copying is easy, and many people (especially the young) use file-sharing software to download copyrighted works. This very breadth of the software's use may well draw the public directly into the debate over copyright policy, and the indications are that the ease of copying songs or movies using software like Grokster's and Napster's is fostering disdain for copyright protection. As the case has been presented to us, these fears are said to be offset by the different concern that imposing liability, not only on infringers but on distributors of software based on its potential for unlawful use, could limit further development of beneficial technologies.

The argument for imposing indirect liability in this case is, however, a powerful one, given the number of infringing downloads that occur every day using StreamCast's and Grokster's software. When a widely shared service or product is used to commit infringement, it may be impossible to enforce rights in the protected work effectively against all direct infringers, the only practical alternative being to go against the distributor of the copying device for secondary liability on a theory of contributory or vicarious infringement.

One infringes contributorily by intentionally inducing or encouraging direct infringement, and infringes vicariously by profiting from direct infringement while declining to exercise a right to stop or limit it. Although "[t]he Copyright Act does not expressly render anyone liable for infringement committed by another," *Sony Corp. v. Universal City Studios*, 464 U.S., at 434, these doctrines of secondary liability emerged from common law principles and are well established in the law.

B

* * *

The parties and many of the amici in this case think the key to resolving it is the *Sony* rule and, in particular, what it means for a product to be "capable of commercially significant noninfringing uses." *Sony Corp. v. Universal City Studios, supra*, at 442. MGM advances the argument that granting summary judgment to Grokster and StreamCast as to their current activities gave too much weight to the value of innovative technology, and too little to the copyrights infringed by users of their software, given that 90% of works available on one of the networks was shown to be copyrighted. Assuming the remaining 10% to be its noninfringing use, MGM says this should not qualify as "substantial," and the Court should quantify to the extent of holding that a product used "principally" for infringement does not qualify. As mentioned before, Grokster and StreamCast reply by citing evidence that their software can be used to reproduce public domain works, and they point to copyright holders who actually encourage copying. Even if infringement is the principal practice with their software today, they argue, the noninfringing uses are significant and will grow.

We agree with MGM that the Court of Appeals misapplied *Sony*, which it read as limiting secondary liability quite beyond the circumstances to which the case applied. *Sony* barred secondary liability based on presuming or imputing intent to cause infringement solely from the design or distribution of a product capable of substantial lawful use, which the distributor knows is in fact used for infringement. The Ninth Circuit has read *Sony*'s limitation to mean that whenever a product is capable of substantial lawful use, the producer can never be held contributorily liable for third parties' infringing use of it; it read the rule as being this broad, even when an actual purpose to cause infringing use is shown by evidence independent of design and distribution of the product, unless the distributors had "specific knowledge of infringement at a time at which they contributed to the infringement, and failed to act upon that information." Because the Circuit found the StreamCast and Grokster software capable of substantial lawful use, it concluded on the basis of its reading of *Sony* that neither company could be held liable, since there was no showing that their software, being without any central server, afforded them knowledge of specific unlawful uses.

This view of *Sony*, however, was error, converting the case from one about liability resting on imputed intent to one about liability on any theory. Because *Sony* did not displace other theories of secondary liability, and because we find below that it was error to grant summary judgment to the companies on MGM's inducement claim, we do not revisit *Sony* further, as MGM requests, to add a more quantified description of the point of balance between protection and commerce when liability rests solely on distribution with knowledge that unlawful use will occur. It is enough to note that the Ninth Circuit's judgment rested on an erroneous understanding of *Sony* and to leave further consideration of the *Sony* rule for a day when that may be required.

C

Sony's rule limits imputing culpable intent as a matter of law from the characteristics or uses of a distributed product. But nothing in *Sony* requires courts to ignore evidence of intent if there is such evidence, and the case was never meant to foreclose rules of fault-based liability derived from the common law. Thus, where evidence goes beyond a product's characteristics or the knowledge that it may be put to infringing uses, and shows statements or actions directed to promoting infringement, *Sony's* staple-article rule will not preclude liability.

The classic case of direct evidence of unlawful purpose occurs when one induces commission of infringement by another, or "entic[es] or persuad[es] another" to infringe, as by advertising. Thus at common law a copyright or patent defendant who "not only expected but invoked [infringing use] by advertisement" was liable for infringement "on principles recognized in every part of the law."

The rule on inducement of infringement as developed in the early cases is no different today. Evidence of "active steps . . . taken to encourage direct infringement," *Oak Industries, Inc. v. Zenith Electronics Corp.*, 697 F.Supp. 988, 992 (N.D.Ill.1988), such as advertising an infringing use or instructing how to engage in an infringing use, show an affirmative intent that the product be used to infringe, and a showing that infringement was encouraged overcomes the law's reluctance to find liability when a defendant merely sells a commercial product suitable for some lawful use, *see, e.g., Water Technologies Corp. v. Calco, Ltd.*, 850 F.2d 660, 668 (C.A.Fed.1988) (liability for inducement where one "actively and knowingly aid[s] and abet[s] another's direct infringement" (emphasis omitted)); *Fromberg, Inc. v. Thornhill*, 315 F.2d 407, 412–413 (C.A.5 1963) (demonstrations by sales staff of infringing uses supported liability for inducement). * * *

For the same reasons that *Sony* took the staple-article doctrine of patent law as a model for its copyright safe-harbor rule, the inducement rule, too, is a sensible one for copyright. We adopt it here, holding that one who distributes a device with the object of promoting its use to infringe copyright, as shown by clear expression or other affirmative steps taken to foster infringement, is liable for the resulting acts of infringement by third parties. We are, of course, mindful of the need to keep from trenching on regular commerce or discouraging the development of technologies with lawful and unlawful potential. Accordingly, just as *Sony* did not find intentional inducement despite the knowledge of the VCR manufacturer that its device could be used to infringe, mere knowledge of infringing potential or of actual infringing uses would not be enough here to subject a distributor to liability. Nor would ordinary acts incident to product distribution, such as offering customers technical support or product updates, support liability in themselves. The inducement rule, instead, premises liability on purposeful, culpable expression and conduct, and thus does nothing to compromise legitimate commerce or discourage innovation having a lawful promise.

III

A

The only apparent question about treating MGM's evidence as sufficient to withstand summary judgment under the theory of inducement goes to the need on MGM's part to adduce evidence that StreamCast and Grokster communicated an inducing message to their software users. The classic instance of inducement is by advertisement or solicitation that broadcasts a message designed to stimulate others to commit violations. MGM claims that such a message is shown here. It is undisputed that StreamCast beamed onto the computer screens of users of Napster-compatible programs ads urging the adoption of its OpenNap program, which was designed, as its name implied, to invite the custom of patrons of Napster, then under attack in the courts for facilitating massive infringement. Those who accepted StreamCast's OpenNap program were offered software to perform the same services, which a factfinder could conclude would readily have been understood in the Napster market as the ability to download copyrighted music files. Grokster distributed an electronic newsletter containing links to articles promoting its software's ability to access popular copyrighted music. And anyone whose Napster or free file-sharing searches turned up a link to Grokster would have understood Grokster to be offering the same file-sharing ability as Napster, and to the same people who probably used Napster for infringing downloads; that would also have been the understanding of anyone offered Grokster's suggestively named Swaptor software, its version of OpenNap. And both companies communicated a clear message by responding affirmatively to requests for help in locating and playing copyrighted materials.

In StreamCast's case, of course, the evidence just described was supplemented by other unequivocal indications of unlawful purpose in the internal communications and advertising designs aimed at Napster users ("When the lights went off at Napster . . . where did the users go?"). Whether the messages were communicated is not to the point on this record. The function of the message in the theory of inducement is to prove by a defendant's own statements that his unlawful purpose disqualifies him from claiming protection (and incidentally to point to actual violators likely to be found among those who hear or read the message). * * * Proving that a message was sent out, then, is the preeminent but not exclusive way of showing that active steps were taken with the purpose of bringing about infringing acts, and of showing that infringing acts took place by using the device distributed. Here, the summary judgment record is replete with other evidence that Grokster and StreamCast, unlike the manufacturer and distributor in *Sony*, acted with a purpose to cause copyright violations by use of software suitable for illegal use. * * *

Three features of this evidence of intent are particularly notable. First, each company showed itself to be aiming to satisfy a known source of demand for copyright infringement, the market comprising former Napster users. StreamCast's internal documents made constant reference to Napster, it initially distributed its Morpheus software through an OpenNap program compatible with Napster, it advertised its OpenNap program to Napster users, and its Morpheus software functions as Napster did except that it could be used to distribute more kinds of files, including copyrighted movies and software programs. Grokster's name is apparently derived from Napster, it too initially offered an OpenNap program, its software's function is likewise comparable to Napster's, and it attempted to divert queries for Napster onto its own Web site. Grokster and StreamCast's efforts to supply services to former Napster users, deprived of a mechanism to copy and distribute what were overwhelmingly infringing files, indicate a principal, if not exclusive, intent on the part of each to bring about infringement.

Second, this evidence of unlawful objective is given added significance by MGM's showing that neither company attempted to develop filtering tools or other mechanisms to diminish the infringing activity using their software. While the Ninth Circuit treated the defendants' failure to develop such tools as irrelevant because they lacked an independent duty to monitor their users' activity, we think this evidence underscores Grokster's and StreamCast's intentional facilitation of their users' infringement.

Third, there is a further complement to the direct evidence of unlawful objective. It is useful to recall that StreamCast and Grokster make money by selling advertising space, by directing ads to the screens of computers employing their software. As the record shows, the more the software is used, the more ads are sent out and the greater the advertising revenue becomes. Since the extent of the software's use determines the gain to the distributors, the commercial sense of their enterprise turns on high-volume use, which the record shows is infringing. This evidence alone would not justify an inference of unlawful intent, but viewed in the context of the entire record its import is clear. The unlawful objective is unmistakable.

B

In addition to intent to bring about infringement and distribution of a device suitable for infringing use, the inducement theory of course requires evidence of actual infringement by recipients of the device, the software in this case. As the account of the facts indicates, there is evidence of infringement on a gigantic scale, and there is no serious issue of the adequacy of MGM's showing on this point in order to survive the companies' summary judgment requests. Although an exact calculation of infringing use, as a basis for a claim of damages, is subject to dispute, there is no question that the summary judgment evidence is at least adequate to entitle MGM to go forward with claims for damages and equitable relief.

NOTES

1. Judge Posner's approach from *In re Aimster Copyright Litigation*, 334 F.3d 643 (7th Cir. 2003), another file-sharing case, focused on a cost-benefit analysis:

> [W]hen a supplier is offering a product or service that has noninfringing as well as infringing uses, some estimate of the respective magnitudes of these uses is necessary for a finding of contributory infringement. The Court's action in striking the cost-benefit tradeoff in favor of *Sony* came to seem prescient when it later turned out that the principal use of video recorders was to allow people to watch at home movies that they bought or rented rather than to tape television programs. * * * An enormous new market thus opened for the movie industry—which by the way gives point to the Court's emphasis on potential as well as actual noninfringing uses. But the balancing of costs and benefits is necessary only in a case in

which substantial noninfringing uses, present or prospective, are demonstrated.

Id. at 649–50. What are some possible substantial noninfringing uses of a file-sharing system?

2. BitTorrent file-sharing technology allows users to obtain a complete copy of a work by obtaining small portions of it from each of a large number of suppliers. Should courts allow copyright plaintiffs to join all of the suppliers—whose identities are typically unknown until the discovery phase—as defendants?

D. DISCRETE ISSUES AFFECTING LIABILITY UNDER THE DMCA

1. SAFE HARBORS UNDER SECTION 512

Before the Digital Millennium Copyright Act (DMCA) was enacted in 1998, it was unclear whether, and under what circumstances, an internet service provider (ISP) should be held directly, contributorily, or vicariously liable for the infringing acts of its users. Some courts reached conflicting conclusions. For example, *Religious Technology Center v. Netcom On-Line Communication Services, Inc.*, 907 F.Supp. 1361 (N.D. Cal. 1995), held that an ISP was not directly liable for storing infringing copies that users posted on its system, if the service functioned *only* as a passive conduit for the users' activities. In contrast, *Playboy Enterprises, Inc. v. Frena*, 839 F.Supp. 1552 (M.D. Fla. 1993), held an ISP liable for storing infringing material uploaded by users without ever considering whether the ISP played an active or passive role in posting the material or making it available to others. The *Frena* approach placed many ISPs at risk.

In most cases, claims for contributory and vicarious liability against ISPs were analyzed under the familiar principles of *Gershwin* and *Shapiro*. Thus, most courts held that ISPs were not contributorily liable for their users' infringing activities unless they actively induced those activities or had specific knowledge of those infringements and failed to take action. *See A&M Records, Inc. v. Napster, Inc.*, 239 F.3d 1004, 1020 (9th Cir. 2001); *Netcom, supra,* at 1374. With respect to vicarious liability, an ISP had the "right and ability to supervise the infringing activity" if it had the ability to block an infringing user's access to its services. *Napster, supra,* at 1023; *Netcom, supra,* at 1375–76. Since many, if not most, ISPs had such ability, and knowledge of a specific infringing activity was not a requirement for imposing vicarious liability, many ISPs faced potential liability under this standard.

Congress attempted to clarify the legal position of ISPs—and avoid "breaking the internet"—by enacting Title II of the DMCA, the "Online Copyright Infringement Liability Limitation Act," which added section 512 to Title 17. Section 512 addresses the liability of ISPs and (1) creates safe harbors within which ISPs are exempt from monetary damages and (2) limits the availability and scope of injunctive relief against ISPs. The liability limitations apply only if the ISP (1) accommodates standard technical measures used by copyright owners to identify or protect their works, and (2) implements a policy of terminating the use of its services by repeat infringers. Under those circumstances, an ISP enjoys limited liability for:

1) serving as a mere conduit for the infringing transmission;

2) temporary storage, through "system caching," of infringing material, provided that the caching incorporates prescribed features which protect the rights of the copyright owner;

3) storing infringing material, provided that (a) the ISP either is unaware of the infringing activity or promptly removes or disables access to the material after becoming aware of the infringing activity, (b) where the ISP has the right and ability to control the infringing activity, it derives no financial benefit from this activity, and (c) the ISP acts promptly to remove or disable access to the infringing material upon receiving notification of the claimed infringement that conforms with the statutory requirements; and

4) using information location tools to refer or link users to a site containing infringing material, provided that (a) the ISP either is unaware of the infringement or promptly removes or disables access to the material upon becoming aware of the infringement, (b) where the ISP has the right and ability to control the infringing activity, it derives no financial benefit therefrom, and (c) the ISP acts promptly to remove or disable access to the infringing material upon receiving notice that conforms with the statutory requirements.

Section 512 also limits the injunctive relief available against nonprofit educational institutions acting as ISPs, and spells out the circumstances under which such institutions will *not* have imputed to them the knowledge or activities of faculty or graduate student-employees engaged in teaching or research activities.

COSTAR GROUP, INC. V. LOOPNET, INC.

373 F.3d 544 (4th Cir. 2004).

NIEMEYER, CIRCUIT JUDGE:

[When CoStar's copyrighted photographs were posted on LoopNet's website by LoopNet's subscribers, CoStar brought an infringement action against LoopNet, alleging strict liability under § 106 even though, as a web hosting service, LoopNet's role was passive. Relying on *Religious Technology Center v. Netcom On-Line Communication Services, Inc.*, 907 F.Supp. 1361 (N.D.Cal.1995), the district court entered summary judgment in favor of LoopNet. CoStar appealed.]

* * *

CoStar contends principally that the district court erred in providing LoopNet "conclusive immunity," as a " 'passive' provider of Internet" services, from strict liability for its hosting of CoStar's copyrighted pictures on LoopNet's website. The district court based its decision on the reasoning of *Religious Technology Center v. Netcom On-Line Communication Services, Inc.*, 907 F.Supp. 1361 (N.D.Cal.1995) ("*Netcom*"), which held that an ISP serving as a passive conduit for copyrighted material is not liable as a direct infringer. CoStar asserts that LoopNet is strictly liable for infringement of CoStar's rights protected by § 106 of the Copyright Act. According to CoStar, any immunity for the passive conduct of an ISP such as LoopNet must come from the safe harbor immunity provided by the Digital Millennium Copyright Act ("DMCA"), if at all, because the DMCA codified and supplanted the *Netcom* holding. Because Loop-Net could not meet the conditions for immunity under the DMCA as to many of the copyrighted photographs, LoopNet accordingly would be liable under CoStar's terms for direct copyright infringement for hosting web pages containing the infringing photos.

Stated otherwise, CoStar argues (1) that the *Netcom* decision was a pragmatic and temporary limitation of traditional copyright liability, which would otherwise have held ISPs strictly liable, and that in view of the enactment of the DMCA, *Netcom*'s limitation is no longer necessary; (2) that Congress considered *Netcom* in enacting the DMCA, codifying its principles and thereby supplanting and preempting *Netcom* as the only exemption from liability for direct infringement; and (3) that because LoopNet cannot satisfy the conditions of the DMCA, it remains strictly liable for direct infringement under §§ 106 and 501 of the Copyright Act. * * *

CoStar rests its position * * * on the assertion that the DMCA rendered *Netcom* no longer necessary—indeed, even codified and preempted *Netcom*—by imposing an exclusive safe harbor for ISPs that fulfill the conditions of the DMCA. CoStar argues that because the DMCA supplanted *Netcom*, LoopNet must rely for its defense exclusively on the immunity conferred by the DMCA. This argument, however, is belied by the plain language of the DMCA itself.

The DMCA was enacted as § 512 of the Copyright Act. The relevant subsection of § 512 provides limitations on liability "for infringement of copyright by reason of the storage at the direction of a user of material that resides on a system or network controlled or operated by or for the service for the [Internet] service provider" if the ISP lacks scienter about a copyright violation by a user, does not profit directly from the violation, and responds expeditiously to a proper notice of the violation. *See* 17 U.S.C. § 512(c)(1). In order to enjoy the safe harbor provided by § 512(c), the ISP must also fulfill other conditions imposed by the DMCA. *See id.* § 512(c), (i). Even though the DMCA was designed to provide ISPs with a safe harbor from copyright liability, nothing in the language of § 512 indicates that the limitation on liability described therein is exclusive. Indeed, another section of the DMCA provides explicitly that the DMCA is *not* exclusive:

> *Other defenses not affected.*—The failure of a service provider's conduct to qualify for limitation of liability under this section shall not bear adversely upon the consideration of a defense by the service provider that the service provider's conduct is not infringing under this title or any other defense.

Id. § 512(*l*). Thus the statute specifically provides that despite a failure to meet the safe-harbor conditions in § 512(c) and (i), an ISP is still entitled to all other arguments under the law—whether by way of an affirmative defense or through an argument that conduct simply does not constitute a prima facie case of infringement under the Copyright Act.

Given that the statute declares its intent not to "bear adversely upon" any of the ISP's defenses under law, including the defense that the plaintiff has not made out a prima facie case for infringement, it is difficult to argue, as CoStar does, that the statute in fact precludes ISPs from relying on an entire strain of case law holding that direct infringement must involve conduct having a volitional or causal aspect. Giving such a construction to the DMCA would in fact "bear adversely upon the consideration" of this defense, in direct contravention of § 512(*l*). We conclude that in enacting the DMCA, Congress did not preempt the decision in *Netcom* nor foreclose the continuing development of liability through court decisions interpreting §§ 106 and 501 of the Copyright Act.

* * *

CoStar's argument that the DMCA supplanted and preempted *Netcom* is further undermined by the DMCA's legislative history. Congress actually expressed its intent that the courts would continue to determine how to apply the Copyright Act to the Internet and that the DMCA would merely create a floor of protection for ISPs. After citing the conflicting decisions in *Netcom* and *Frena*, the Senate Committee on the Judiciary explained that "rather than embarking upon a wholesale clarification of these doctrines, the Committee decided to leave current law in its evolving state and, instead, to create a series of 'safe harbors,' for certain common activities of service providers." S.Rep. No. 105–190, at 19 (1998). The Ninth Circuit has found this language persuasive, citing it in finding that "[t]he DMCA did not simply rewrite copyright law for the on-line world." *Ellison v.*

Robertson, 357 F.3d 1072, 1077 (9th Cir.2004). Furthermore, the final conference report supports this passage, stating:

> As provided in subsection (*l*), Section 512 is not intended to imply that a service provider is or is not liable as an infringer either for conduct that qualifies for a limitation of liability or for conduct that fails to so qualify. Rather, the limitations of liability apply if the provider is found to be liable under existing principles of law.

H.R. Conf. Rep. No. 105–796, at 73 (1998). Thus the DMCA was intended not to change the "evolving" doctrines on ISP liability for copyright infringement, which included *Netcom* and *Frena,* but to offer a certain safe harbor for ISPs. Courts were left free to continue to construe the Copyright Act in deciding the scope and nature of prima facie liability. The legislative "compromise" repeatedly invoked by CoStar and its *amici* was that Congress would not end the debate by importing and fixing copyright infringement liability in the form articulated by *Netcom,* but rather would provide a limited safe harbor immediately necessary to ISPs, and allow the courts to continue defining what constitutes a prima facie case of copyright infringement against an ISP.

* * *

It is clear that Congress intended the DMCA's safe harbor for ISPs to be a floor, not a ceiling, of protection. Congress said nothing about whether passive ISPs should ever be held strictly liable as direct infringers or whether plaintiffs suing ISPs should instead proceed under contributory theories. The DMCA has merely added a second step to assessing infringement liability for Internet service providers, after it is determined whether they are infringers in the first place under the preexisting Copyright Act. Thus, the DMCA is irrelevant to determining what constitutes a prima facie case of copyright infringement.

At bottom, we hold that ISPs, when passively storing material at the direction of users in order to make that material available to other users upon their request, do not "copy" the material in direct violation of § 106 of the Copyright Act. Agreeing with the analysis in *Netcom,* we hold that the automatic copying, storage, and transmission of copyrighted materials, when instigated by others, does not render an ISP strictly liable for copyright infringement under §§ 501 and 106 of the Copyright Act. An ISP, however, can become liable indirectly upon a showing of additional involvement sufficient to establish a contributory or vicarious violation of the Act. In that case, the ISP could still look to the DMCA for a safe harbor if it fulfilled the conditions therein.

III

CoStar contends that even under *Netcom*'s construction of copyright infringement liability for ISPs, LoopNet's conduct in this case is more than passive, in that LoopNet screens photographs posted by its subscribers. In CoStar's opinion, this screening process renders LoopNet liable for direct copyright infringement.

LoopNet, like other ISPs, affords its subscribers an Internet-based facility on which to post materials, but the materials posted are of a type and kind selected by the subscriber and at a time initiated by the subscriber. Similarly, users who wish to access a subscriber's information may do so without intervention from LoopNet. A subscriber seeking to post a listing on LoopNet's website containing only *text* fills out a form and agrees to LoopNet's "Terms and Conditions," which include the obligation to respect others' copyrights. Once the subscriber has filled out the form and agreed to the "Terms and Conditions," an identification number is automatically assigned to the listing, and a web page containing the listing and the identification number is automatically created. The web page is then hosted on LoopNet's website to be viewed by users who request the listing. CoStar does not contend that LoopNet's activity in signing up subscribers with *only* textual property listings is anything other than passive.

To argue that LoopNet loses its status as a passive ISP and therefore becomes liable for direct copyright infringement, CoStar focuses on LoopNet's gatekeeping practice with respect to photographs. To add a photograph to a listing, the subscriber must fill out another form and again agree to the "Terms and Conditions." After expressly warranting that he has "all necessary rights and authorizations from the . . . copyright owner of the photographs," the subscriber uploads the photograph into a folder in LoopNet's system. The photograph is then transferred to the RAM of one of LoopNet's computers for review. A LoopNet employee reviews the photo for two purposes: (1) to block photographs that do not depict commercial real estate, and (2) to block photographs with obvious signs that they are copyrighted by a third party. If the photograph carries a copyright notice or represents subject matter other than commercial real estate, the employee deletes the photograph; otherwise, she clicks a button marked "accept," and LoopNet's system automatically associates the photograph with the subscriber's web page for the property listing, making it available for use. Unless a question arises, this entire process takes "a few seconds."

Although LoopNet engages in volitional conduct to block photographs measured by two grossly defined criteria, this conduct, which takes only seconds, does not amount to "copying," nor does it add volition to LoopNet's involvement in storing the copy. The employee's look is so cursory as to be insignificant, and if it has any significance, it tends only to lessen the possibility that LoopNet's automatic electronic responses will inadvertently enable others to trespass on a copyright owner's rights. In performing this gatekeeping function, LoopNet does not attempt to search out or select photographs for duplication; it merely *prevents* users from duplicating certain photographs. To invoke again the analogy of the shop with the copy machine, LoopNet can be compared to an owner of a copy machine who has stationed a guard by the door to turn away customers who are attempting to duplicate clearly copyrighted works. LoopNet has not by this screening process become engaged as a "copier" of copyrighted works who can be held liable under §§ 501 and 106 of the Copyright Act.

To the extent that LoopNet's intervention in screening photographs goes further than the simple gatekeeping function described above, it is because of CoStar's complaints about copyright violations. Whenever CoStar has complained to LoopNet about a particular photograph, LoopNet has removed the photograph, and the property listing with which the photograph was associated has been marked. The next time the user tries to post a photograph to accompany that listing, LoopNet conducts a manual side-by-side review to make sure that the user is not reposting the infringing photograph. CoStar and other copyright holders benefit significantly from this type of response. If they find such conduct by an ISP too active, they can avoid it by adding a copyright notice to their photographs, which CoStar does not do. CoStar can hardly request LoopNet to prevent its users from infringing upon particular unmarked photographs and then subsequently seek to hold LoopNet liable as a direct infringer when Loop-Net complies with CoStar's request.

In short, we do not conclude that LoopNet's perfunctory gatekeeping process, which furthers the goals of the Copyright Act, can be taken to create liability for LoopNet as a direct infringer when its conduct otherwise does not amount to direct infringement.

For the reasons given, we affirm the judgment of the district court.

NOTE

Other courts have shared the *CoStar* court's concern that an overly broad concept of "volitional" conduct would discourage ISPs from voluntary efforts to eliminate infringing content. *See BWP Media USA, Inc. v. T&S Software Associates, Inc.*, 852 F.3d 436 (5th Cir. 2017). Accordingly, courts have held that the "right and ability to control the infringing activity" is not established by the mere fact that the ISP (1) has, in the past, removed some infringing material; (2) has engaged in limited monitoring of its website for apparent infringements; and (3) has the ability to block users' access to its site. In contrast, the dissenting judge in *CoStar* argued that LoopNet's review of photographs prior to posting was volitional conduct sufficient to support strict liability for direct infringement. The majority's holding, he suggested, "expands the non-volitional defense well beyond *Netcom* and subsequent holdings, and gives direct infringers in the commercial cybersphere far greater protections than they would be accorded in print and other more traditional media." 373 F.3d at 557 (Gregory, J., dissenting). Which argument is more persuasive?

PERFECT 10, INC. V. CCBILL LLC

488 F.3d 1102 (9th Cir. 2007).

MILAN D. SMITH, JR., CIRCUIT JUDGE.

Perfect 10, the publisher of an adult entertainment magazine and the owner of the subscription website perfect10.com, alleges that CCBill and CWIE violated copyright, trademark, and state unfair competition, false advertising and right of publicity laws by providing services to websites that posted images stolen from Perfect 10's magazine and website. Perfect 10 appeals the district court's finding that CCBill and CWIE qualified for certain statutory safe harbors from copyright infringement liability under the Digital Millennium Copyright Act ("DMCA"), 17 U.S.C. § 512 * * *.

DISCUSSION

I. SECTION 512 SAFE HARBORS

The DMCA established certain safe harbors to "provide protection from liability for: (1) transitory digital network communications; (2) system caching; (3) information residing on systems or networks at the direction of users; and (4) information location tools." These safe harbors limit liability but "do not affect the question of ultimate liability under the various doctrines of direct, vicarious, and contributory liability," and "nothing in the language of § 512 indicates that the limitation on liability described therein is exclusive." *CoStar Group, Inc. v. LoopNet, Inc.*, 373 F.3d 544, 552 (4th Cir.2004).

A. Reasonably Implemented Policy: § 512(i)(1)(A)

To be eligible for any of the four safe harbors at §§ 512(a)–(d), a service provider must first meet the threshold conditions set out in § 512(i), including the requirement that the service provider:

> [H]as adopted and reasonably implemented, and informs subscribers and account holders of the service provider's system or network of, a policy that provides for the termination in appropriate circumstances of subscribers and account holders of the service provider's system or network who are repeat infringers.

Section 512(i)(1)(A). The statute does not define "reasonably implemented." We hold that a service provider "implements" a policy if it has a working notification system, a procedure for dealing with DMCA-compliant notifications, and if it does not actively prevent copyright owners from collecting information needed to issue such notifications. The statute permits service providers to implement a variety of procedures, but an implementation is reasonable if, under "appropriate circumstances," the service provider terminates users who repeatedly or blatantly infringe copyright. *See* 17 U.S.C. § 512(i).

1. *"Implementation"*

Perfect 10 argues that there is a genuine issue of material fact whether CCBill and CWIE prevented the implementation of their policies by failing to keep track of repeatedly infringing webmasters. The district court found that there was not, and we agree.

In *Ellison,* Stephen Robertson posted copies of Harlan Ellison's copyrighted short stories on Internet newsgroups available through USENET servers. 357 F.3d at 1075. Ellison asserted that America Online, Inc. ("AOL") had infringed his copyright by providing access to the USENET servers. Based on evidence that AOL changed its contact email address for copyright infringement notices from copyright@aol.com to aolcopyright@aol.com in the fall of 1999, but neglected to register the change with the U.S. Copyright Office until April 2000, we held that the district court erred in concluding on summary judgment that AOL satisfied the requirements of § 512(i). Even though Ellison did not learn of the infringing activity until after AOL had notified the U.S. Copyright Office of the correct email address, we found that "AOL allowed notices of potential copyright infringement to fall into a vacuum and go unheeded; that fact is sufficient for a reasonable jury to conclude that AOL had not reasonably implemented its policy against repeat infringers." *Id.* at 1080.

Similarly, the *Aimster* cases hold that a repeat infringer policy is not implemented under § 512(i)(1)(A) if the service provider prevents copyright holders from providing DMCA-compliant notifications. In *Aimster,* the district court held that Aimster did not reasonably implement its stated repeat infringer policy because "the encryption on Aimster renders it impossible to ascertain which users are transferring which files." 252 F.Supp.2d at 659. The court found that "[a]dopting a repeat infringer policy and then purposely eviscerating any hope that such a policy could ever be carried out is not an 'implementation' as required by § 512(i)." *Id.* The Seventh Circuit affirmed, finding that Aimster did not meet the requirement of § 512(i)(1)(A) because, in part, "by teaching its users how to encrypt their unlawful distribution of copyrighted materials [Aimster] disabled itself from doing anything to prevent infringement." *In re Aimster Copyright Litig.,* 334 F.3d 643, 655 (7th Cir.2003).

Based on *Ellison* and the *Aimster* cases, a substantial failure to record webmasters associated with allegedly infringing websites may raise a genuine issue of material fact as to the implementation of the service provider's repeat infringer policy. In this case, however, the record does not reflect such a failure. * * *

Unlike *Ellison* and *Aimster,* where the changed email address and the encryption system ensured that *no* information about the repeat infringer was collected, it is undisputed that CCBill and CWIE recorded most webmasters. The district court properly concluded that the DMCA Log does not raise a triable issue of fact that CCBill and CWIE did not implement a repeat infringer policy.

2. Reasonableness

A service provider reasonably implements its repeat infringer policy if it terminates users when "appropriate." Section 512(i) itself does not clarify when it is "appropriate" for service providers to act. It only requires that a service provider terminate users who are "repeat infringers."

To identify and terminate repeat infringers, a service provider need not affirmatively police its users for evidence of repeat infringement. Section 512(c) states that "[a] service provider shall not be liable for monetary relief" if it does not know of infringement. A service provider is also not liable under § 512(c) if it acts "expeditiously to remove, or disable access to, the material" when it (1) has actual knowledge, (2) is aware of facts or circumstances from which infringing activity is apparent, or (3) has received notification of claimed infringement meeting the requirements of § 512(c)(3). Were we to require service providers to terminate users under circumstances other than those specified in § 512(c), § 512(c)'s grant of immunity would be meaningless. This interpretation of the statute is supported by legislative history. *See* H.R. Rep., at 61 (Section 512(i) is not intended "to undermine the . . . knowledge standard of [§ 512](c).").

Perfect 10 claims that CCBill and CWIE unreasonably implemented their repeat infringer policies by tolerating flagrant and blatant copyright infringement by its users despite notice of infringement from Perfect 10, notice of infringement from copyright holders not a party to this litigation and "red flags" of copyright infringement.

a. Perfect 10's Claimed Notice of Infringement

Perfect 10 argues that CCBill and CWIE implemented their repeat infringer policy in an unreasonable manner because CCBill and CWIE received notices of infringement from Perfect 10, and yet the infringement identified in these notices continued. The district court found that Perfect 10 did not provide notice that substantially complied with the requirements of § 512(c)(3), and thus did not raise a genuine issue of material fact as to whether CCBill and CWIE reasonably implemented their repeat infringer policy. We agree.

Compliance is not "substantial" if the notice provided complies with only some of the requirements of § 512(c)(3)(A). * * *

* * *

Taken individually, Perfect 10's communications do not substantially comply with the requirements of § 512(c)(3). Each communication contains more than mere technical errors; often one or more of the required elements are entirely absent. In order to substantially comply with § 512(c)(3)'s requirements, a notification must do more than identify infringing files. The DMCA requires a complainant to declare, under penalty of perjury, that he is authorized to represent the copyright holder, and that he has a good-faith belief that the use is infringing. This requirement is not superfluous. Accusations of alleged infringement have drastic consequences: A user could have content removed, or may have his access terminated entirely. If the content infringes, justice has been done. But if it does not, speech protected under the First Amendment could be removed. We therefore do not require a service provider to start potentially invasive proceedings if the complainant is unwilling to state under penalty of perjury that he is an authorized representative of the copyright owner, and that he has a good-faith belief that the material is unlicensed.

* * *

Since Perfect 10 did not provide effective notice, knowledge of infringement may not be imputed to CCBill or CWIE based on Perfect 10's communications. Perfect 10's attempted notice does not raise a genuine issue of material fact that CCBill and CWIE failed to reasonably implement a repeat infringer policy within the meaning of § 512(i)(1)(A).

b. Non-Party Notices

Perfect 10 also cites to notices of infringement by other copyright holders, and argues that CCBill and CWIE did not reasonably implement their repeat infringer policies because they continued to provide services for websites that infringed non-party copyrights. The district court expressly declined to consider evidence of notices provided by any party other than Perfect 10 on the basis that these notices were irrelevant to Perfect 10's claims. We disagree.

CCBill and CWIE's actions towards copyright holders who are not a party to the litigation are relevant in determining whether CCBill and CWIE reasonably implemented their repeat infringer policy. Section 512(i)(1)(A) requires an assessment of the service provider's "policy," not how the service provider treated a particular copyright holder. Thus, CCBill and CWIE's response to adequate non-party notifications is relevant in determining whether they reasonably implemented their policy against repeat infringers.

A policy is unreasonable only if the service provider failed to respond when it had knowledge of the infringement. The district court in this case did not consider any evidence relating to copyright holders other than Perfect 10. We remand for determination of whether CCBill and/or CWIE implemented its repeat infringer policy in an unreasonable manner with respect to any copyright holder other than Perfect 10.

c. *Apparent Infringing Activity*

In importing the knowledge standards of § 512(c) to the analysis of whether a service provider reasonably implemented its § 512(i) repeat infringer policy, Congress also imported the "red flag" test of § 512(c)(1)(A)(ii). Under this section, a service provider may lose immunity if it fails to take action with regard to infringing material when it is "aware of facts or circumstances from which infringing activity is apparent." § 512(c)(1)(A)(ii). Notice that fails to substantially comply with § 512(c)(3), however, cannot be deemed to impart such awareness. §§ 512(c)(3)(B)(i) & (ii).

Perfect 10 alleges that CCBill and CWIE were aware of a number of "red flags" that signaled apparent infringement. Because CWIE and CCBill provided services to "illegal.net" and "stolencelebritypics.com," Perfect 10 argues that they must have been aware of apparent infringing activity. We disagree. When a website traffics in pictures that are titillating by nature, describing photographs as "illegal" or "stolen" may be an attempt to increase their salacious appeal, rather than an admission that the photographs are actually illegal or stolen. We do not place the burden of determining whether photographs are actually illegal on a service provider.

* * *

In addition, Perfect 10 argues that password-hacking websites, hosted by CWIE, also obviously infringe. While such sites may not directly infringe on anyone's copyright, they may well contribute to such infringement. The software provided by Grokster in *Metro-Goldwyn-Mayer Studios Inc. v. Grokster, Ltd.*, 545 U.S. 913 (2005), also did not itself infringe, but did enable users to swap infringing files. *Grokster* held that "instructing [users] how to engage in an infringing use" could constitute contributory infringement. Similarly, providing passwords that enable users to illegally access websites with copyrighted content may well amount to contributory infringement.

However, in order for a website to qualify as a "red flag" of infringement, it would need to be apparent that the website instructed or enabled users to infringe another's copyright. We find that the burden of determining whether passwords on a website enabled infringement is not on the service provider. The website could be a hoax, or out of date. The owner of the protected content may have supplied the passwords as a short-term promotion, or as an attempt to collect information from unsuspecting users. The passwords might be provided to help users maintain anonymity without infringing on copyright. There is simply no way for a service provider to conclude that the passwords enabled infringement without trying the passwords, and verifying that they enabled illegal access to copyrighted material. We impose no such investigative duties on service providers. Password-hacking websites are thus not *per se* "red flags" of infringement.

Perfect 10 also alleges that "red flags" raised by third parties identified repeat infringers who were not terminated. Because the district court did not consider potential red flags raised by third parties, we remand to the district court to determine whether third-party notices made CCBill and CWIE aware that it provided services to repeat infringers, and if so, whether they responded appropriately.

* * *

C. Transitory Digital Network Communications: § 512(a)

Section 512(a) provides safe harbor for service providers who act as conduits for infringing content. In order to qualify for the safe harbor of § 512(a), a party must be a service provider under a more restrictive definition than applicable to the other safe harbors provided under § 512:

> As used in subsection (a), the term "service provider" means an entity offering the transmission, routing, or providing of connections for digital online communications, between or among points specified by a user, of material of the user's choosing, without modification to the content of the material as sent or received.

Section 512(k)(1)(A). The district court held that CCBill [a credit card payment processor] met the requirements of § 512(k)(1)(A) by "provid[ing] a connection to the material on its clients' websites through a system which it operates in order to provide its clients with billing services." We reject Perfect 10's argument that CCBill is not eligible for immunity under § 512(a) because it does not itself transmit the infringing material. A service provider is "an entity offering the transmission, routing, or providing of connections for digital online communications." § 512(k)(1)(A). There is no requirement in the statute that the communications must themselves be infringing, and we see no reason to import such a requirement. It would be perverse to hold a service provider immune for transmitting information that was infringing on its face, but find it contributorily liable for transmitting information that did not infringe.

Section 512(a) provides a broad grant of immunity to service providers whose connection with the material is transient. When an individual clicks on an Internet link, his computer sends a request for the information. The company receiving that request sends that request on to another computer, which sends it on to another. After a series of such transmissions, the request arrives at the computer that stores the information. The requested information is then returned in milliseconds, not necessarily along the same path. In passing the information along, each intervening computer makes a short-lived copy of the data. A short time later, the information is displayed on the user's computer.

Those intervening computers provide transient cónnections among users. The Internet as we know it simply cannot exist if those intervening computers must block indirectly infringing content. We read § 512(a)'s grant of immunity exactly as it is written: Service providers are immune for transmitting all digital online communications, not just those that directly infringe.

* * *

D. Information Location Tools: § 512(d)

After CCBill processes a consumer's credit card and issues a password granting access to a client website, CCBill displays a hyperlink so that the user may access the client website. CCBill argues that it falls under the safe harbor of § 512(d) by displaying this hyperlink at the conclusion of the consumer transaction. We disagree. Section 512(d) reads:

> A service provider shall not be liable for monetary relief, or, except as provided in subsection (j), for injunctive or other equitable relief, for infringement of copyright by reason of the provider referring or linking users to an online location containing infringing material or infringing activity, by using information location tools, including a directory, index, reference, pointer, or hypertext link.

Even if the hyperlink provided by CCBill could be viewed as an "information location tool," the majority of CCBill's functions would remain outside of the safe harbor of § 512(d). Section 512(d) provides safe harbor only for "infringement of copyright *by reason of* the provider referring or linking users to an online location containing infringing material or infringing activity." (Emphasis added). Perfect 10 does not claim that CCBill infringed its copyrights by providing a hyperlink; rather, Perfect 10 alleges infringement through CCBill's performance of other business services for these websites. Even if CCBill's provision of a hyperlink is immune under § 512(n), CCBill does not receive blanket immunity for its other services.

E. Information Residing on Systems or Networks at the Direction of Users: § 512(c)

Section 512(c) "limits the liability of qualifying service providers for claims of direct, vicarious, and contributory infringement for storage at the direction of a user of material that resides on a system or network controlled or operated by or for the service provider." H.R. Rep., at 53. A service provider qualifies for safe harbor under § 512(c) if it meets the requirements of § 512(i) and:

(A)(i) does not have actual knowledge that the material or an activity using the material on the system or network is infringing;

(ii) in the absence of such actual knowledge, is not aware of facts or circumstances from which infringing activity is apparent; or

(iii) upon obtaining such knowledge or awareness, acts expeditiously to remove, or disable access to, the material;

(B) does not receive a financial benefit directly attributable to the infringing activity, in a case in which the service provider has the right and ability to control such activity; and

(C) upon notification of claimed infringement as described in paragraph (3), responds expeditiously to remove, or disable access to, the material that is claimed to be infringing or to be the subject of infringing activity.

Section 512(c)(1). As discussed above, Perfect 10 did not provide CWIE [a webhosting service] with knowledge or awareness within the standard of § 512(c)(1)(A), and Perfect 10 did not provide notice that complies with the requirements of § 512(c)(3).

The remaining question is whether Perfect 10 raises a genuine issue of material fact that CWIE does not qualify for safe harbor under § 512(c) because it fails to meet the requirements of § 512(c)(1)(B), namely, that a service provider not receive a direct financial benefit from the infringing activity if the service provider also has the right and ability to control the infringing activity.

Based on the "well-established rule of construction that where Congress uses terms that have accumulated settled meaning under common law, a court must infer, unless the statute otherwise dictates, that Congress means to incorporate the established meaning of these terms," we hold that "direct financial benefit" should be interpreted consistent with the similarly-worded common law standard for vicarious copyright liability. Thus, the relevant inquiry is "whether the infringing activity constitutes a draw for subscribers, not just an added benefit." In *Ellison*, the court held that "no jury could reasonably conclude that AOL received a direct financial benefit from providing access to the infringing material" because "[t]he record lacks evidence that AOL attracted or retained subscriptions because of the infringement or lost subscriptions because of AOL's eventual obstruction of the infringement." *Id.*

In this case, Perfect 10 provides almost no evidence about the alleged direct financial benefit to CWIE. Perfect 10 only alleges that "CWIE 'hosts' websites for a fee." This allegation is insufficient to show that the infringing activity was "a draw" as required by *Ellison*. Furthermore, the legislative history expressly states that "receiving a one-time set-up fee and flat, periodic payments for service from a person engaging in infringing activities would not constitute receiving a 'financial benefit directly attributable to the infringing activity.'" H.R. Rep., at 54. Perfect 10 has not raised a genuine issue of material fact that CWIE receives a direct financial benefit from infringing activity. Because CWIE does not receive a direct financial benefit, CWIE meets the requirements of § 512(c).

If the district court finds that CWIE meets the threshold requirements of § 512(i), CWIE is entitled to safe harbor under § 512(c).

* * *

CONCLUSION

We remand to the district court for a determination of whether CCBill and CWIE reasonably implemented a policy under § 512(i)(1)(A) based on its treatment of non-party copyright holders. Because § 512(i)(1)(A) is a threshold determination, we remand the remaining issues under § 512 for further proceedings consistent with this opinion.

NOTES

1. In its pursuit of copyright infringers, the record industry at one time attempted to get the names of internet users through their ISPs, using the DMCA's subpoena provision, section 512(h). Two circuits held that section 512(h) applies only to ISPs that are engaged in storing infringing content for users; it does not apply to an ISP that acts solely as a conduit for the infringing transmission. *Recording Indus. Ass'n v. Charter Comm'ns, Inc. (In re Charter Comm'ns, Inc., Subpoena Enforcement Matter),* 393 F.3d 771, 778 (8th Cir. 2005); *Recording Indus. Ass'n v. Verizon Internet Servs., Inc.*, 351 F.3d 1229, 1233 (D.C. Cir. 2003). The D.C. Circuit explained:

> We are not unsympathetic either to the RIAA's concern regarding the widespread infringement of its members' copyrights, or to the need for legal tools to protect those rights. It is not the province of the courts, however, to rewrite the DMCA in order to make it fit a new and unforeseen internet architecture, no matter how damaging that development has been to the music industry or threatens being to the motion picture and software industries.

Verizon Internet Services, 351 F.3d at 1238.

2. *Take-Down Notices:* To qualify for the section 512 safe harbor, an ISP that stores copyrighted material at the direction of users (*e.g.*, YouTube or a web-hosting service) is subject to section 512(c), which requires, *inter alia,* that the ISP remove or disable access to infringing material upon learning that the material infringes. A copyright owner may trigger this obligation by sending the ISP a take-down notice that substantially complies with section 512(c)(3). As noted in *Perfect 10 v. CCBill,* a take-down notice must include a statement asserting, under penalties of perjury, (1) authorization to represent the copyright owner, and (2) a good faith belief that the use is infringing. In *Lenz*

v. Universal Music Corp., 815 F.3d 1145 (9th Cir. 2015), the Ninth Circuit held that the DMCA required copyright holders to consider whether the potentially infringing material was fair use before issuing a take-down notice, and that fact issues remained as to whether the copyright owner had a subjective good faith belief that the posting was not fair use in the case at bar, which involved a posting of a video of the defendant's young child dancing to the Prince song, "Let's Go Crazy."

Any person who has posted material that becomes the subject of a take-down notice can respond to the notice by sending the ISP a counter-notification under section 512(g). Sending either a take-down notice or a counter-notification with knowledge that it contains a material and false representation is actionable under section 512(f).

3. File-sharing sites such as Aimster and Napster have been unsuccessful in their attempts to invoke the section 512 safe harbor. *See In Re Aimster*, 334 F.3d 643 (7th Cir. 2003); *A & M Records, Inc. v. Napster, Inc.*, 239 F.3d 1004 (9th Cir. 2001). Why do you think this is so?

4. Even if an ISP establishes a repeat infringer policy and communicates that policy to users, it will be ineligible for the safe harbor if it fails to implement that policy in any consistent or meaningful way. *See BMG Rights Management v. Cox Communications Inc.*, 881 F.3d 293 (4th Cir. 2018) (safe harbor did not protect internet access provider that failed to terminate repeat infringers even after numerous violations).

5. Would the section 512 safe harbor apply to a "music locker" cloud storage service for downloaded music recordings? *See Capitol Records v. MP3tunes LLC*, 821 F. Supp. 2d 627 (S.D.N.Y. 2011).

6. Are independent contractors equivalent to "users" for purposes of the Section 512 safe harbor? *See BWP Media USA, Inc. v. Clarity Digital Group, LLC*, 820 F.3d 1175 (10th Cir. 2016).

VIACOM INTERNATIONAL, INC. V. YOUTUBE, INC.

676 F.3d 19 (2d Cir. 2012).

JOSÉ A. CABRANES, CIRCUIT JUDGE:

[Viacom sued YouTube and Google for direct and secondary copyright infringement based on the public performance, display, and reproduction of approximately 79,000 audiovisual "clips" that appeared on YouTube between 2005 and 2008. The District Court held that the defendants were protected from liability by the section 512(c) safe harbor because they lacked knowledge of specific and identifiable infringements, and did not have the right and ability to control the infringing activity. Viacom appealed.]

* * *

A. Actual and "Red Flag" Knowledge: § 512(c)(1)(A)

The first and most important question on appeal is whether the DMCA safe harbor at issue requires "actual knowledge" or "aware[ness]" of facts or circumstances indicating "specific and identifiable infringements," *Viacom,* 718 F.Supp.2d at 523. We consider first the scope of the statutory provision and then its application to the record in this case.

1. The Specificity Requirement

"As in all statutory construction cases, we begin with the language of the statute," *Barnhart v. Sigmon Coal Co.,* 534 U.S. 438, 450 (2002). Under § 512(c)(1)(A), safe harbor protection is available only if the service provider:

> (i) does not have actual knowledge that the material or an activity using the material on the system or network is infringing;
>
> (ii) in the absence of such actual knowledge, is not aware of facts or circumstances from which infringing activity is apparent; or
>
> (iii) upon obtaining such knowledge or awareness, acts expeditiously to remove, or disable access to, the material. . . .

17 U.S.C. § 512(c)(1)(A). As previously noted, the District Court held that the statutory phrases "actual knowledge that the material . . . is infringing" and "facts or circumstances from which infringing activity is apparent" refer to "knowledge of specific and identifiable infringements." *Viacom,* 718 F.Supp.2d at 523. For the reasons that follow, we substantially affirm that holding.

* * * [T]he basic operation of § 512(c) requires knowledge or awareness of specific infringing activity. Under § 512(c)(1)(A), knowledge or awareness alone does not disqualify the service provider; rather, the provider that gains knowledge or awareness of infringing activity retains safe-harbor protection if it "acts expeditiously to remove, or disable access to, the material." 17 U.S.C. § 512(c)(1)(A)(iii). Thus, the nature of the removal obligation itself contemplates knowledge or awareness of specific infringing material, because expeditious removal is possible only if the service provider knows with particularity which items to remove. * * *

On appeal, the plaintiffs dispute this conclusion by drawing our attention to § 512(c)(1)(A)(ii), the so-called "red flag" knowledge provision. In their view, the use of the phrase "facts or circumstances" demonstrates that Congress did not intend to limit the red flag provision to a particular type of knowledge. The plaintiffs contend that requiring awareness of specific infringements in order to establish "aware[ness] of facts or circumstances from which infringing activity is apparent," 17 U.S.C. § 512(c)(1)(A)(ii), renders the red flag provision superfluous, because that provision would be satisfied only when the "actual knowledge" provision is also satisfied. For that reason, the plaintiffs urge the Court to hold that the red flag provision "requires less specificity" than the actual knowledge provision.

This argument misconstrues the relationship between "actual" knowledge and "red flag" knowledge. * * * The phrase "actual knowledge," which appears in § 512(c)(1)(A)(i), is frequently used to denote subjective belief. By contrast, courts often invoke the language of "facts or circumstances," which appears in § 512(c)(1)(A)(ii), in discussing an objective reasonableness standard.

The difference between actual and red flag knowledge is thus not between specific and generalized knowledge, but instead between a subjective and an objective standard. In other words, the actual knowledge provision turns on whether the provider actually or "subjectively" knew of specific infringement, while the red flag provision turns on whether the provider was subjectively aware of facts that would have made the specific infringement "objectively" obvious to a reasonable person. The red flag provision, because it incorporates an objective standard, is not swallowed up by the actual knowledge provision under our construction of the § 512(c) safe harbor. Both provisions do independent work, and both apply only to specific instances of infringement.

The limited body of case law interpreting the knowledge provisions of the § 512(c) safe harbor comports with our view of the specificity requirement. Most recently, a panel of the Ninth Circuit addressed the scope of § 512(c) in *UMG Recordings, Inc. v. Shelter Capital Partners LLC*, 667 F.3d 1022 (9th Cir.2011), a copyright infringement case against Veoh Networks, a video-hosting service similar to YouTube. As in this case, various music publishers brought suit against the service provider, claiming direct and secondary copyright infringement based on the presence of unauthorized content on the website, and the website operator sought refuge in the § 512(c) safe harbor. The Court of Appeals affirmed the district court's determination on summary judgment that the website operator was entitled to safe harbor protection. With respect to the actual knowledge provision, the panel declined to "adopt[ ] a broad conception of the knowledge requirement," holding instead that the safe harbor "[r]equir[es] specific knowledge of particular infringing activity." The Court of Appeals "reach [ed] the same conclusion" with respect to the red flag provision, noting that "[w]e do not place the burden of determining whether [materials] are actually illegal on a service provider." Although *Shelter Capital* contains the most explicit discussion of the § 512(c) knowledge provisions, other cases are generally in accord. *See, e.g., Capitol Records, Inc. v. MP3tunes, LLC*, 821 F.Supp.2d 627 (S.D.N.Y. 2011) ("Undoubtedly, MP3tunes is aware that some level of infringement occurs. But, there is no genuine dispute that MP3tunes did not have specific 'red flag' knowledge with respect to any particular link. . . . "); *UMG Recordings, Inc. v. Veoh*

Networks, Inc., 665 F.Supp.2d 1099, 1108 (C.D.Cal.2009) ("*UMG II*") ("[I]f investigation of 'facts and circumstances' is required to identify material as infringing, then those facts and circumstances are not 'red flags.' "). While we decline to adopt the reasoning of those decisions *in toto*, we note that no court has embraced the contrary proposition—urged by the plaintiffs—that the red flag provision "requires less specificity" than the actual knowledge provision.

Based on the text of § 512(c)(1)(A), as well as the limited case law on point, we affirm the District Court's holding that actual knowledge or awareness of facts or circumstances that indicate specific and identifiable instances of infringement will disqualify a service provider from the safe harbor.

* * *

i. Specific Knowledge or Awareness

The plaintiffs argue that, even under the District Court's construction of the safe harbor, the record raises material issues of fact regarding YouTube's actual knowledge or "red flag" awareness of specific instances of infringement. To that end, the plaintiffs draw our attention to various estimates regarding the percentage of infringing content on the YouTube website. For example, Viacom cites evidence that YouTube employees conducted website surveys and estimated that 75–80% of all YouTube streams contained copyrighted material. The class plaintiffs similarly claim that Credit Suisse, acting as financial advisor to Google, estimated that more than 60% of YouTube's content was "premium" copyrighted content—and that only 10% of the premium content was authorized. These approximations suggest that the defendants were conscious that significant quantities of material on the YouTube website were infringing. But such estimates are insufficient, standing alone, to create a triable issue of fact as to whether YouTube actually knew, or was aware of facts or circumstances that would indicate, the existence of particular instances of infringement.

Beyond the survey results, the plaintiffs rely upon internal YouTube communications that do refer to particular clips or groups of clips. The class plaintiffs argue that YouTube was aware of specific infringing material because, *inter alia*, YouTube attempted to search for specific Premier League videos on the site in order to gauge their "value based on video usage." In particular, the class plaintiffs cite a February 7, 2007 e-mail from Patrick Walker, director of video partnerships for Google and YouTube, requesting that his colleagues calculate the number of daily searches for the terms "soccer," "football," and "Premier League" in preparation for a bid on the global rights to Premier League content. On another occasion, Walker requested that any "clearly infringing, official broadcast footage" from a list of top Premier League clubs—including

Liverpool Football Club, Chelsea Football Club, Manchester United Football Club, and Arsenal Football Club—be taken down in advance of a meeting with the heads of "several major sports teams and leagues." YouTube ultimately decided not to make a bid for the Premier League rights—but the infringing content allegedly remained on the website.

The record in the *Viacom* action includes additional examples. For instance, YouTube founder Jawed Karim prepared a report in March 2006 which stated that, "[a]s of today[,] episodes and clips of the following well-known shows can still be found [on YouTube]: Family Guy, South Park, MTV Cribs, Daily Show, Reno 911, [and] Dave Chapelle [sic]." Karim further opined that, "although YouTube is not legally required to monitor content . . . and complies with DMCA takedown requests, we would benefit from *preemptively* removing content that is blatantly illegal and likely to attract criticism." He also noted that "a more thorough analysis" of the issue would be required. At least some of the TV shows to which Karim referred are owned by Viacom. A reasonable juror could conclude from the March 2006 report that Karim knew of the presence of Viacom-owned material on YouTube, since he presumably located specific clips of the shows in question before he could announce that YouTube hosted the content "[a]s of today." A reasonable juror could also conclude that Karim believed the clips he located to be infringing (since he refers to them as "blatantly illegal"), and that YouTube did not remove the content from the website until conducting "a more thorough analysis," thus exposing the company to liability in the interim.

Furthermore, in a July 4, 2005 e-mail exchange, YouTube founder Chad Hurley sent an e-mail to his co-founders with the subject line "budlight commercials," and stated, "we need to reject these too." Steve Chen responded, "can we please leave these in a bit longer? another week or two can't hurt." Karim also replied, indicating that he "added back in all 28 bud videos." Similarly, in an August 9, 2005 e-mail exchange, Hurley urged his colleagues "to start being *diligent* about rejecting copyrighted/ inappropriate content," noting that "there is a cnn clip of the shuttle clip on the site today, if the boys from Turner would come to the site, they might be pissed?" Again, Chen resisted:

> but we should just keep that stuff on the site. i really don't see what will happen. what? someone from cnn sees it? he happens to be someone with power? he happens to want to take it down right away. he gets in touch with cnn legal. 2 weeks later, we get a cease & desist letter. we take the video down.

And again, Karim agreed, indicating that "the CNN space shuttle clip, I like. we can remove it once we're bigger and better known, but for now that clip is fine."

Upon a review of the record, we are persuaded that the plaintiffs may have raised a material issue of fact regarding YouTube's knowledge or awareness of specific instances of infringement. The foregoing Premier League e-mails request the identification and removal of "clearly infringing, official broadcast footage." The March 2006 report indicates Karim's awareness of specific clips that he perceived to be "blatantly illegal." Similarly, the Bud Light and space shuttle e-mails refer to particular clips in the context of correspondence about whether to remove infringing material from the website. On these facts, a reasonable juror could conclude that YouTube had actual knowledge of specific infringing activity, or was at least aware of facts or circumstances from which specific infringing activity was apparent. *See* § 512(c)(1)(A)(i)–(ii). Accordingly, we hold that summary judgment to YouTube on all clips-in-suit, especially in the absence of any detailed examination of the extensive record on summary judgment, was premature.

[The plaintiffs also argued that YouTube was "willfully blind" to specific infringing activity.] * * * A person is "willfully blind" or engages in "conscious avoidance" amounting to knowledge where the person " 'was aware of a high probability of the fact in dispute and consciously avoided confirming the fact.' "

* * * [W]e hold that the willful blindness doctrine may be applied, in appropriate circumstances, to demonstrate knowledge or awareness of specific instances of infringement under the DMCA. [The court instructed the district court on remand to consider whether the defendants made a "deliberate effort to avoid guilty knowledge."]

* * *

B. Control and Benefit: § 512(c)(1)(B)

Apart from the foregoing knowledge provisions, the § 512(c) safe harbor provides that an eligible service provider must "not receive a financial benefit directly attributable to the infringing activity, in a case in which the service provider has the right and ability to control such activity." 17 U.S.C. § 512(c)(1)(B). The District Court addressed this issue in a single paragraph, quoting from § 512(c)(1)(B), the so-called "control and benefit" provision, and concluding that "[t]he 'right and ability to control' the activity requires knowledge of it, which must be item-specific." For the reasons that follow, we hold that the District Court erred by importing a specific knowledge requirement into the control and benefit provision, and we therefore remand for further fact-finding on the issue of control.

1. "Right and Ability to Control" Infringing Activity

On appeal, the parties advocate two competing constructions of the "right and ability to control" infringing activity. Because each is fatally flawed, we reject both proposed constructions in favor of a fact-based inquiry to be conducted in the first instance by the District Court.

The first construction, pressed by the defendants, is the one adopted by the District Court, which held that "the provider must know of the particular case before he can control it." *Viacom,* 718 F.Supp.2d at 527. The Ninth Circuit recently agreed, holding that "until [the service provider] becomes aware of specific unauthorized material, it cannot exercise its 'power or authority' over the specific infringing item. In practical terms, it does not have the kind of ability to control infringing activity the statute contemplates." *UMG Recordings, Inc. v. Shelter Capital Partners LLC,* 667 F.3d 1022, 1041 (9th Cir.2011). The trouble with this construction is that importing a specific knowledge requirement into § 512(c)(1)(B) renders the control provision duplicative of § 512(c)(1)(A). Any service provider that has item-specific knowledge of infringing activity and thereby obtains financial benefit would already be excluded from the safe harbor under § 512(c)(1)(A) for having specific knowledge of infringing material and failing to effect expeditious removal. No additional service provider would be excluded by § 512(c)(1)(B) that was not already excluded by § 512(c)(1)(A). Because statutory interpretations that render language superfluous are disfavored, we reject the District Court's interpretation of the control provision.

The second construction, urged by the plaintiffs, is that the control provision codifies the common law doctrine of vicarious copyright liability. The common law imposes liability for vicarious copyright infringement "[w]hen the right and ability to supervise coalesce with an obvious and direct financial interest in the exploitation of copyrighted materials—even in the absence of actual knowledge that the copyright monopoly is being impaired." *Shapiro, Bernstein & Co. v. H.L. Green Co.,* 316 F.2d 304, 407 (2d Cir.1963). To support their codification argument, the plaintiffs rely on a House Report relating to a preliminary version of the DMCA: "The 'right and ability to control' language . . . codifies the second element of vicarious liability. . . . Subparagraph (B) is intended to preserve existing case law that examines all relevant aspects of the relationship between the primary and secondary infringer." H.R.Rep. No. 105–551(I), at 26 (1998). In response, YouTube notes that the codification reference was omitted from the committee reports describing the final legislation, and that Congress ultimately abandoned any attempt to "embark[ ] upon a wholesale clarification" of vicarious liability, electing instead "to create a series of 'safe harbors' for certain common activities of service providers." S.Rep. No. 105–190, at 19.

Happily, the future of digital copyright law does not turn on the confused legislative history of the control provision. The general rule with respect to common law codification is that when "Congress uses terms that have accumulated settled meaning under the common law, a court must infer, unless the statute otherwise dictates, that Congress means to incorporate the established meaning of those terms." Under the common law vicarious liability standard, "[t]he ability to block infringers' access to a particular environment for any reason whatsoever is evidence of the right and ability to supervise." *Arista Records LLC v. Usenet.com, Inc.,* 633 F.Supp.2d 124, 157 (S.D.N.Y.2009). To adopt that principle in the DMCA context, however, would render the statute internally inconsistent. Section 512(c) actually presumes that service providers have the ability to "block . . . access" to infringing material. *Id.* at 157. Indeed, a service provider who has knowledge or awareness of infringing material or who receives a takedown notice from a copyright holder is *required* to "remove, or disable access to, the material" in order to claim the benefit of the safe harbor. 17 U.S.C. §§ 512(c)(1)(A)(iii) & (C). But in taking such action, the service provider would—in the plaintiffs' analysis—be admitting the "right and ability to control" the infringing material. Thus, the prerequisite to safe harbor protection under §§ 512(c)(1)(A)(iii) & (C) would at the same time be a disqualifier under § 512(c)(1)(B).

Moreover, if Congress had intended § 512(c)(1)(B) to be coextensive with vicarious liability, "the statute could have accomplished that result in a more direct manner." *Shelter Capital,* 667 F.3d at 1045.

> It is conceivable that Congress . . . intended that [service providers] which receive a financial benefit directly attributable to the infringing activity would not, under any circumstances, be able to qualify for the subsection (c) safe harbor. But if that was indeed their intention, it would have been far simpler and much more straightforward to simply say as much.

Id.

In any event, the foregoing tension—elsewhere described as a "predicament" and a "catch22"—is sufficient to establish that the control provision "dictates" a departure from the common law vicarious liability standard. Accordingly, we conclude that the "right and ability to control" infringing activity under § 512(c)(1)(B) "requires something more than the ability to remove or block access to materials posted on a service provider's website." *MP3tunes, LLC,* 2011 WL 5104616, at *14. The remaining—and more difficult—question is how to define the "something more" that is required.

To date, only one court has found that a service provider had the right and ability to control infringing activity under § 512(c)(1)(B).[13] In *Perfect 10, Inc. v. Cybernet Ventures, Inc.,* 213 F.Supp.2d 1146 (C.D.Cal.2002), the

---

[13] Other courts have suggested that control may exist where the service provider is "actively involved in the listing, bidding, sale and delivery" of items offered for sale, *Hendrickson v. eBay, Inc.,* 165 F.Supp.2d 1082, 1094 (C.D.Cal.2001), or otherwise controls vendor sales by previewing products prior to their listing, editing product descriptions, or suggesting prices, *Corbis Corp.,* 351 F.Supp.2d at 1110. Because these cases held that control did *not* exist, however, it is not clear that the practices cited therein are individually sufficient to support a finding of control.

court found control where the service provider instituted a monitoring program by which user websites received "detailed instructions regard[ing] issues of layout, appearance, and content." The service provider also forbade certain types of content and refused access to users who failed to comply with its instructions. Similarly, inducement of copyright infringement under *Metro-Goldwyn-Mayer Studios Inc. v. Grokster, Ltd.*, 545 U.S. 913 (2005), which "premises liability on purposeful, culpable expression and conduct," might also rise to the level of control under § 512(c)(1)(B). Both of these examples involve a service provider exerting substantial influence on the activities of users, without necessarily—or even frequently—acquiring knowledge of specific infringing activity.

In light of our holding that § 512(c)(1)(B) does not include a specific knowledge requirement, we think it prudent to remand to the District Court to consider in the first instance whether the plaintiffs have adduced sufficient evidence to allow a reasonable jury to conclude that YouTube had the right and ability to control the infringing activity and received a financial benefit directly attributable to that activity.

C. "By Reason of" Storage: § 512(c)(1)

The § 512(c) safe harbor is only available when the infringement occurs "by reason of the storage at the direction of a user of material that resides on a system or network controlled or operated by or for the service provider." 17 U.S.C. § 512(c)(1). In this case, the District Court held that YouTube's software functions fell within the safe harbor for infringements that occur "by reason of" user storage, noting that a contrary holding would "confine[ ] the word 'storage' too narrowly to meet the statute's purpose." For the reasons that follow, we affirm that holding with respect to three of the challenged software functions—the conversion (or "transcoding") of videos into a standard display format, the playback of videos on "watch" pages, and the "related videos" function. We remand for further fact-finding with respect to a fourth software function, involving the third-party syndication of videos uploaded to YouTube.

As a preliminary matter, we note that "the structure and language of [§ 512] indicate that service providers seeking safe harbor under [§]512(c) are not limited to merely storing material." The structure of the statute distinguishes between so-called "conduit only" functions under § 512(a) and the functions addressed by § 512(c) and the other subsections. Most notably, [§ 512] contains two definitions of "service provider." 17 U.S.C. § 512(k)(1)(A)–(B). The narrower definition, which applies only to service providers falling under § 512(a), is limited to entities that "offer[ ] the transmission, routing or providing of connections for digital online communications, between or among points specified by a user, of material of the user's choosing, *without modification to the content of the material* as sent or received." *Id.* § 512(k)(1)(A) (emphasis added). No such limitation appears in the broader definition, which applies to service providers—including YouTube—falling under § 512(c). Under the broader definition, "the term 'service provider' means a provider of online services or network access, or the operator of facilities therefor, and includes an entity described in subparagraph (A)." *Id.* § 512(k)(1)(B). In the absence of a parallel limitation on the ability of a service provider to modify user-submitted material, we conclude that § 512(c) "is clearly meant to cover more than mere electronic storage lockers." *UMG Recordings, Inc. v. Veoh Networks, Inc.*, 620 F.Supp.2d 1081, 1088 (C.D.Cal.2008) ("*UMG I*").

The relevant case law makes clear that the § 512(c) safe harbor extends to software functions performed "for the purpose of facilitating access to user-stored material." Two of the software functions challenged here—transcoding and playback—were expressly considered by our sister Circuit in *Shelter Capital,* which held that liability arising from these functions occurred "by reason of the storage at the direction of a user." 17 U.S.C. § 512(c). Transcoding involves "[m]aking copies of a video in a different encoding scheme" in order to render the video "viewable over the Internet to most users." The playback process involves "deliver[ing] copies of YouTube videos to a user's browser cache" in response to a user request. The District Court correctly found that to exclude these automated functions from the safe harbor would eviscerate the protection afforded to service providers by § 512(c).

A similar analysis applies to the "related videos" function, by which a YouTube computer algorithm identifies and displays "thumbnails" of clips that are "related" to the video selected by the user. The plaintiffs claim that this practice constitutes content promotion, not "access" to stored content, and therefore falls beyond the scope of the safe harbor. * * * But even if the plaintiffs are correct that § 512(c) incorporates a principle of proximate causation—a question we need not resolve here—the indexing and display of related videos retain a sufficient causal link to the prior storage of those videos. The record makes clear that the related videos algorithm "is fully automated and operates solely in response to user input without the active involvement of YouTube employees." Furthermore, the related videos function serves to help YouTube users locate and gain access to material stored at the direction of other users. Because the algorithm "is closely related to, and follows from, the storage itself," and is "narrowly directed toward providing access to material stored at the direction of users," we conclude that the related videos function is also protected by the § 512(c) safe harbor.

The final software function at issue here—third-party syndication—is the closest case. In or around March 2007, YouTube transcoded a select number of videos into a format compatible with mobile devices and "syndicated" or licensed the videos to Verizon Wireless and other companies. The plaintiffs argue—with some force—that business transactions do not occur at the "direction of a user" within the meaning of § 512(c)(1) when they involve the manual selection of copyrighted material for licensing to a third party. The parties do not dispute, however, that none of the clips-in-suit were among the approximately 2,000 videos provided to Verizon Wireless. In order to avoid rendering an advisory opinion on the outer boundaries of the storage provision, we remand for fact-finding on the question of whether any of the clips-in-suit were in fact syndicated to any other third party.

* * *

NOTES

1. In *Columbia Pictures Indus. v. Fung*, 96 U.S.P.Q.2d (BNA) 1620, *aff'd in relevant part*, 710 F.3d 1020 (9th Cir. 2013), the court held that a peer-to-peer file sharing service utilizing BitTorrent had "red flag" knowledge of infringement, and was therefore ineligible for the DMCA safe harbor, because (1) the defendant had used his own service to download infringing content, (2) 90–95% of the material available through the service was copyrighted, and (3) the defendant's website displayed updated lists of popular content, including numerous copyrighted works.

2. Is section 512 superior to the conventional analysis of secondary liability (under such cases as *Netcom* and *Fonovisa*) in striking a balance between the interests of service providers and their clients, on the one hand, and copyright owners on the other?

3. Much has changed since section 512 was enacted in 1998, and copyright owners as well as users have become dissatisfied with its operation. Copyright owners are frustrated by the difficulty of proving actual or "red flag" knowledge and by the burden of constantly sending takedown notices only to find that someone has simply reposted the infringing content. Users are frustrated by the overzealous (and frequently automated) use of takedown notices targeting content that is either fair use or otherwise non-infringing. Updating the DMCA safe harbors is therefore high on Congress's agenda for the next revision of Title 17. One possible option is to impose on ISPs an affirmative duty to monitor and filter material posted by users, a policy that is already being implemented in the European Union. What are the arguments for and against this approach?

2. CIRCUMVENTING ANTI-COPYING TECHNOLOGY OR ALTERING COPYRIGHT MANAGEMENT INFORMATION

In order to bring the United States into compliance with the 1996 WIPO treaties, Congress also included in the DMCA new provisions establishing liability for circumventing anti-copying technology. Title I of the DMCA, the "WIPO Copyright and Performances and Phonograms Treaties Implementation Act of 1998," created a new Chapter 12 of Title

17 which prohibits circumvention of anti-copying technology (17 U.S.C. § 1201) and also prohibits falsification, removal, or alteration of "copyright management information" that identifies a copyrighted work on computer networks (17 U.S.C. § 1202). The anti-circumvention provisions are subject to narrow limitations and exemptions applicable to reverse engineering, lawful government investigations, encryption research, security testing, investigations relating to personal privacy, activities of nonprofit libraries, archives, educational institutions, and (with respect to remedies only) "innocent" violations. The prohibitions of Title I are enforced by civil remedies as well as criminal penalties (17 U.S.C. §§ 1203 and 1204, respectively).

MDY INDUS., LLC V. BLIZZARD ENTERTAINMENT, INC.

629 F.3d 928 (9th Cir. 2010).

CALLAHAN, CIRCUIT JUDGE:

Blizzard Entertainment, Inc. ("Blizzard") is the creator of World of Warcraft ("WoW"), a popular multiplayer online role-playing game in which players interact in a virtual world while advancing through the game's 70 levels. MDY Industries, LLC and its sole member Michael Donnelly ("Donnelly") (sometimes referred to collectively as "MDY") developed and sold Glider, a software program [or "bot"] that automatically plays the early levels of WoW for players.

* * *

In November 2004, Blizzard created WoW, a "massively multiplayer online role-playing game" in which players interact in a virtual world. WoW has ten million subscribers, of which two and a half million are in North America. The WoW software has two components: (1) the game client software that a player installs on the computer; and (2) the game server software, which the player accesses on a subscription basis by connecting to WoW's online servers. WoW does not have single-player or offline modes.

WoW players roleplay different characters, such as humans, elves, and dwarves. A player's central objective is to advance the character through the game's 70 levels by participating in quests and engaging in battles with monsters. As a player advances, the character collects rewards such as in-game currency, weapons, and armor. WoW's virtual world has its own economy, in which characters use their virtual currency to buy and sell items directly from each other, through vendors, or using auction houses. * * *

In September 2005, Blizzard launched Warden, a technology that it developed to prevent its players who use unauthorized third-party software, including bots, from connecting to WoW's servers. Warden was able to detect Glider, and Blizzard immediately used Warden to ban most Glider users. MDY responded by modifying Glider to avoid detection * * *.

[The District Court held that MDY was liable under DMCA § 1201(a)(2) and (b)(1), because it programmed Glider to avoid detection by Warden. This appeal followed.]

B. The Digital Millenium Copyright Act

Congress enacted the DMCA in 1998 to conform United States copyright law to its obligations under two World Intellectual Property Organization ("WIPO") treaties, which require contracting parties to provide effective legal remedies against the circumvention of protective technological measures used by copyright owners. In enacting the DMCA, Congress sought to mitigate the problems presented by copyright enforcement in the digital age. The DMCA contains three provisions directed at the circumvention of copyright owners' technological measures. The Supreme Court has yet to construe these provisions, and they raise questions of first impression in this circuit.

The first provision, 17 U.S.C. § 1201(a)(1)(A), is a general prohibition against "circumventing a technological measure that effectively controls access to a work protected under [the Copyright Act]." The second prohibits trafficking in technology that circumvents a technological measure that "effectively controls access" to a copyrighted work. 17 U.S.C. § 1201(a)(2). The third prohibits trafficking in technology that circumvents a technological measure that "effectively protects" a copyright owner's right. 17 U.S.C. § 1201(b)(1).

* * *

D. Construction of § 1201

One of the issues raised by this appeal is whether certain provisions of § 1201 prohibit circumvention of access controls when access does not constitute copyright infringement. To answer this question and others presented by this appeal, we address the nature and interrelationship of the various provisions of § 1201 in the overall context of the Copyright Act.

We begin by considering the scope of DMCA § 1201's three operative provisions, §§ 1201(a)(1), 1201(a)(2), and 1201(b)(1). * * *

1. *Text of the operative provisions*

* * * Section 1201(a)(1)(A) prohibits "circumvent[ing] a technological measure that effectively controls access to a work protected under this title." Sections 1201(a)(2) and (b)(1) provide that "[n]o person shall manufacture, import, offer to the public, provide, or otherwise traffic in any technology, product, service, device, component, or part thereof, that—

§ 1201(a)(2)	§1201(b)(2)
(A) is primarily designed or produced for the purpose of **circumventing a technological measure** that effectively controls access to**a work protected under this title**;	(A) is primarily designed or produced for the purpose of **circumventing protection afforded by a technological measure** that effectively protects **a right of a copyright owner**;
(B) has only limited commercially significant purpose or use other than to circumvent a technological measure that effectively controls access to a work protected under this title;	(B) has only limited commercially significant purpose or use other than to circumvent protection afforded by a technological measure that effectively protects a right of a copyright owner under this title in a work or a portion thereof;
(C) is marketed by that person or another acting in concert with that person with that person's knowledge for use in circumventing a technological measure that effectively controls access to a work protected under this title.	(C) is marketed by that person or another acting in concert with that person with that person's knowledge for use in circumventing protection afforded by a technological measure that effectively protects a right of a copyright owner under this title in a work or a portion thereof."

(emphasis added).

2. *Our harmonization of the DMCA's operative provisions*

For the reasons set forth below, we believe that § 1201 is best understood to create two distinct types of claims. First, § 1201(a) prohibits the circumvention of any technological measure that effectively controls access to a protected work and grants copyright owners the right to enforce that prohibition. Second, and in contrast to § 1201(a), § 1201(b)(1) prohibits trafficking in technologies that circumvent technological measures that effectively protect "a right of a copyright owner." Section 1201(b)(1)'s prohibition is thus aimed at circumventions of measures that protect the copyright itself: it entitles copyright owners to protect their existing exclusive rights under the Copyright Act. Those exclusive rights are reproduction, distribution, public performance, public display, and creation of derivative works. Historically speaking, preventing "access" to a protected work in itself has not been a right of a copyright owner arising from the Copyright Act.

Our construction of § 1201 is compelled by the four significant textual differences between § 1201(a) and (b). First, § 1201(a)(2) prohibits the circumvention of a measure that "effectively controls access to a *work protected under this title*," whereas § 1201(b)(1) concerns a measure that "effectively protects *a right of a copyright owner under this title in a work or portion thereof*." (emphasis added). We read § 1201(b)(1)'s language—"right of a copyright owner under this title"—to reinforce copyright owners' traditional exclusive rights under § 106 by granting them an additional cause of action against those who traffic in circumventing devices that facilitate infringement. Sections 1201(a)(1) and (a)(2), however, use the term "work protected under this title." Neither of these two subsections explicitly refers to traditional copyright infringement under § 106. Accordingly, we read this term as extending a new form of protection, i.e., the right to prevent circumvention of access controls, broadly to works protected under Title 17, i.e., copyrighted works.

Second, as used in § 1201(a), to "circumvent a technological measure" means "to descramble a scrambled work, to decrypt an encrypted work, or otherwise to avoid, bypass, remove, deactivate, or impair a technological measure, without the authority of the copyright owner." 17 U.S.C. § 1201(a)(3)(A). These two specific examples of unlawful circumvention under § 1201(a)—descrambling a scrambled work and decrypting an encrypted work—are acts that do not necessarily infringe or facilitate infringement of a copyright.[6] Descrambling or decrypting only enables someone to watch or listen to a work without authorization, which is not necessarily an infringement of a copyright owner's traditional exclusive rights under § 106. Put differently, descrambling and decrypting do not necessarily result in someone's reproducing, distributing, publicly performing, or publicly displaying the copyrighted work, or creating derivative works based on the copyrighted work.

The third significant difference between the subsections is that § 1201(a)(1)(A) prohibits circumventing an effective access control measure, whereas § 1201(b) prohibits trafficking in circumventing devices, but does not prohibit circumvention itself because such conduct was already outlawed as copyright infringement. The Senate Judiciary Committee explained:

> This . . . is the reason there is no prohibition on conduct in 1201(b) akin to the prohibition on circumvention conduct in 1201(a)(1). The prohibition in 1201(a)(1) is necessary because prior to this Act, the conduct of circumvention was never before made unlawful. The device limitation on 1201(a)(2) enforces this new prohibition on conduct. The copyright law has long forbidden copyright infringements, so no new prohibition was necessary.

S.Rep. No. 105–90, at 11 (1998). This difference reinforces our reading of § 1201(b) as strengthening copyright owners' traditional rights against copyright infringement and of § 1201(a) as granting copyright owners a new anti-circumvention right.

Fourth, in § 1201(a)(1)(B)–(D), Congress directs the Library of Congress ("Library") to identify classes of copyrighted works for which "noninfringing uses by persons who are users of a copyrighted work are, or are likely to be, adversely affected, and the [anti-circumvention] prohibition contained in [§ 1201(a)(1)(A)] shall not apply to such users with respect to such classes of works for the ensuing 3-year period." There is no

[6] Perhaps for this reason, Congress did not list descrambling and decrypting as circumventing acts that would violate § 1201(b)(1). *See* 17 U.S.C. § 1201(b)(2)(A).

analogous provision in § 1201(b). We impute this lack of symmetry to Congress' need to balance copyright owners' new anti-circumvention right with the public's right to access the work. * * * Sections 1201(a)(1)(B)–(D) thus promote the public's right to access by allowing the Library to exempt circumvention of effective access control measures in particular situations where it concludes that the public's right to access outweighs the owner's interest in restricting access[7] * * *

Our reading of § 1201(a) and (b) ensures that neither section is rendered superfluous. A violation of § 1201(a)(1)(A), which prohibits circumvention itself, will not be a violation of § 1201(b), which does not contain an analogous prohibition on circumvention. A violation of § 1201(a)(2), which prohibits trafficking in devices that facilitate circumvention of *access* control measures, will not always be a violation of § 1201(b)(1), which prohibits trafficking in devices that facilitate circumvention of measures that protect against *copyright infringement.* Of course, if a copyright owner puts in place an effective measure that both (1) controls access and (2) protects against copyright infringement, a defendant who traffics in a device that circumvents that measure could be liable under both § 1201(a) and (b). Nonetheless, we read the differences in structure between § 1201(a) and (b) as reflecting Congress's intent to address distinct concerns by creating different rights with different elements.

3. *Our construction of the DMCA is consistent with the legislative history*

Although the text suffices to resolve the issues before us, we also consider the legislative history in order to address the parties' arguments concerning it. Our review of that history supports the view that Congress created a new anticircumvention right in § 1201(a)(2) independent of traditional copyright infringement and granted copyright owners a new weapon against copyright infringement in § 1201(b)(1). For instance, the Senate Judiciary Committee report explains that § 1201(a)(2) and (b)(1) are "not interchangeable": they were "designed to protect two distinct rights and to target two distinct classes of devices," and "many devices will be subject to challenge only under one of the subsections." S.Rep. No. 105–190, at 12 (1998). That is, § 1201(a)(2) "is designed to protect access to a copyrighted work," while § 1201(b)(1) "is designed to protect the traditional copyright rights of the copyright owner." *Id.* Thus, the Senate Judiciary Committee understood § 1201 to create the following regime:

> [I]f an effective technological protection measure does nothing to prevent access to the plain text of the work, but is designed to

[7] For instance, pursuant to § 1201(a), the Library of Congress recently approved circumvention of the technological measures contained on the iPhone and similar wireless phone handsets known as "smartphones," in order to allow users to install and run third-party software applications on these phones.

> prevent that work from being copied, then a potential cause of action against the manufacturer of a device designed to circumvent the measure lies under § 1201(b)(1), but not under § 1201(a)(2). Conversely, if an effective technological protection measure limits access to the plain text of a work only to those with authorized access, but provides no additional protection against copying, displaying, performing or distributing the work, then a potential cause of action against the manufacturer of a device designed to circumvent the measure lies under § 1201(a)(2), but not under § 1201(b).

Id. The Senate Judiciary Committee proffered an example of § 1201(a) liability with no nexus to infringement, stating that if an owner effectively protected access to a copyrighted work by use of a password, it would violate § 1201(a)(2)(A).

> [T]o defeat or bypass the password and to make the means to do so, as long as the primary purpose of the means was to perform this kind of act. This is roughly analogous to making it illegal to break into a house using a tool, the primary purpose of which is to break into houses.

Id. at 12. The House Judiciary Committee similarly states of § 1201(a)(2), "The act of circumventing a technological protection measure put in place by a copyright owner to control access to a copyrighted work is the electronic equivalent of breaking into a locked room in order to obtain a copy of a book." *See* H.R.Rep. No. 105–551, pt. 1, at 17 (1998). We note that bypassing a password and breaking into a locked room in order to read or view a copyrighted work would not infringe on any of the copyright owner's exclusive rights under § 106.

We read this legislative history as confirming Congress's intent, in light of the current digital age, to grant copyright owners an independent right to enforce the prohibition against circumvention of effective technological access controls.[9] In § 1201(a), Congress was particularly concerned with encouraging copyright owners to make their works available in digital formats such as "on-demand" or "pay-per-view," which allow consumers effectively to "borrow" a copy of the work for a limited time or a limited number of uses. As the House Commerce Committee explained:

> [A]n increasing number of intellectual property works are being distributed using a "client-server" model, where the work is effectively "borrowed" by the user (e.g., infrequent users of expensive software purchase a certain number of uses, or viewers

[9] Indeed, the House Commerce Committee proposed, albeit unsuccessfully, to move § 1201 out of Title 17 altogether "because these regulatory provisions have little, if anything, to do with copyright law. The anticircumvention provisions (and the accompanying penalty provisions for violations of them) would be separate from, and cumulative to, the existing claims available to copyright owners." H.R.Rep. No. 105–551 (1998), pt. 2, at 23–24.

> watch a movie on a pay-per-view basis). To operate in this environment, content providers will need both the technology to make new uses possible and the legal framework to ensure they can protect their work from piracy.

See H.R.Rep. No. 105–551 pt. 2, at 23 (1998).

Our review of the legislative history supports our reading of § 1201: that section (a) creates a new anticircumvention right distinct from copyright infringement, while section (b) strengthens the traditional prohibition against copyright infringement.[10] We now review the decisions of the Federal Circuit that have interpreted § 1201 differently.

4. *The Federal Circuit's decisions*

The Federal Circuit has adopted a different approach to the DMCA. In essence, it requires § 1201(a) plaintiffs to demonstrate that the circumventing technology infringes or facilitates infringement of the plaintiff's copyright (an "infringement nexus requirement"). *See Chamberlain Group, Inc. v. Skylink Techs., Inc.,* 381 F.3d 1178, 1203 (Fed.Cir.2004).

The seminal decision is *Chamberlain.* In *Chamberlain,* the plaintiff sold garage door openers ("GDOs") with a "rolling code" security system that purportedly reduced the risk of crime by constantly changing the transmitter signal necessary to open the door. Customers used the GDOs' transmitters to send the changing signal, which in turn opened or closed their garage doors.

Plaintiff sued the defendant, who sold "universal" GDO transmitters for use with plaintiff's GDOs, under § 1201(a)(2). The plaintiff alleged that its GDOs and transmitters both contained copyrighted computer programs and that its rolling code security system was a technological measure that controlled access to those programs. Accordingly, plaintiff alleged that the defendant—by selling GDO transmitters that were compatible with plaintiff's GDOs—had trafficked in a technology that was primarily used for the circumvention of a technological measure (the rolling code security system) that effectively controlled access to plaintiff's copyrighted works.

The Federal Circuit rejected the plaintiff's claim, holding that the defendant did not violate § 1201(a)(2) because, *inter alia,* the defendant's universal GDO transmitters did not infringe or facilitate infringement of the plaintiff's copyrighted computer programs. The linchpin of the *Chamberlain* court's analysis is its conclusion that DMCA coverage is limited to a copyright owner's rights under the Copyright Act as set forth

---

[10] The Copyright Office has also suggested that § 1201(a) creates a new access control right independent from copyright infringement, by expressing its view that the fair use defense to traditional copyright infringement does not apply to violations of § 1201(a)(1). U.S. Copyright Office, The Digital Millennium Copyright Act of 1998: U.S. Copyright Office Summary 4 (1998).

in § 106 of the Copyright Act. Thus, it held that § 1201(a) did not grant copyright owners a new anti-circumvention right, but instead, established new causes of action for a defendant's unauthorized access of copyrighted material when it infringes upon a copyright owner's rights under § 106. Accordingly, a § 1201(a)(2) plaintiff was required to demonstrate a nexus to infringement—i.e., that the defendant's trafficking in circumventing technology had a "reasonable relationship" to the protections that the Copyright Act affords copyright owners. The Federal Circuit explained:

> Defendants who traffic in devices that circumvent access controls in ways that facilitate infringement may be subject to liability under § 1201(a)(2). Defendants who use such devices may be subject to liability under § 1201(a)(1) whether they infringe or not. Because all defendants who traffic in devices that circumvent rights controls necessarily facilitate infringement, they may be subject to liability under § 1201(b). Defendants who use such devices may be subject to liability for copyright infringement. *And finally, defendants whose circumvention devices do not facilitate infringement are not subject to § 1201 liability.*

381 F.3d at 1195 (emphasis added). *Chamberlain* concluded that § 1201(a) created a new cause of action linked to copyright infringement, rather than a new anti-circumvention right separate from copyright infringement, for six reasons.

First, *Chamberlain* reasoned that Congress enacted the DMCA to balance the interests of copyright owners and information users, and an infringement nexus requirement was necessary to create an anti-circumvention right that truly achieved that balance. Second, *Chamberlain* feared that copyright owners could use an access control right to prohibit exclusively fair uses of their material even absent feared foul use. Third, *Chamberlain* feared that § 1201(a) would allow companies to leverage their sales into aftermarket monopolies, in potential violation of antitrust law and the doctrine of copyright misuse. Fourth, *Chamberlain* viewed an infringement nexus requirement as necessary to prevent "absurd and disastrous results," such as the existence of DMCA liability for disabling a burglary alarm to gain access to a home containing copyrighted materials.

Fifth, *Chamberlain* stated that an infringement nexus requirement might be necessary to render Congress's exercise of its Copyright Clause authority rational. The Copyright Clause gives Congress "the task of defining the scope of the limited monopoly that should be granted to authors . . . in order to give the public appropriate access to their work product." *Id.* at 1196. Without an infringement nexus requirement, Congress arguably would have allowed copyright owners in § 1201(a) to deny all access to the public by putting an effective access control measure in place that the public was not allowed to circumvent.

Finally, the *Chamberlain* court viewed an infringement nexus requirement as necessary for the Copyright Act to be internally consistent. It reasoned that § 1201(c)(1), enacted simultaneously, provides that "nothing in this section shall affect rights, remedies, limitations, or defenses to copyright infringement, including fair use, under this title." The *Chamberlain* court opined that if § 1201(a) creates liability for access without regard to the remainder of the Copyright Act, it "would clearly affect rights and limitations, if not remedies and defenses." *Id.*

Accordingly, the Federal Circuit held that a DMCA § 1201(a)(2) action was foreclosed to the extent that the defendant trafficked in a device that did not facilitate copyright infringement. *Id.*

5. *We decline to adopt an infringement nexus requirement*

While we appreciate the policy considerations expressed by the Federal Circuit in *Chamberlain,* we are unable to follow its approach because it is contrary to the plain language of the statute. In addition, the Federal Circuit failed to recognize the rationale for the statutory construction that we have proffered. Also, its approach is based on policy concerns that are best directed to Congress in the first instance, or for which there appear to be other reasons that do not require such a convoluted construction of the statute's language.

i. Statutory inconsistencies

Were we to follow *Chamberlain* in imposing an infringement nexus requirement, we would have to disregard the plain language of the statute. Moreover, there is significant textual evidence showing Congress's intent to create a new anticircumvention right in § 1201(a) distinct from infringement. As set forth *supra,* this evidence includes: (1) Congress's choice to link only § 1201(b)(1) explicitly to infringement; (2) Congress's provision in § 1201(a)(3)(A) that descrambling and decrypting devices can lead to § 1201(a) liability, even though descrambling and decrypting devices may only enable non-infringing access to a copyrighted work; and (3) Congress's creation of a mechanism in § 1201(a)(1)(B)–(D) to exempt certain non-infringing behavior from § 1201(a)(1) liability, a mechanism that would be unnecessary if an infringement nexus requirement existed.

Though unnecessary to our conclusion because of the clarity of the statute's text, we also note that the legislative history supports the conclusion that Congress intended to prohibit even non-infringing circumvention and trafficking in circumventing devices. Moreover, in mandating a § 1201(a) nexus to infringement, we would deprive copyright owners of the important enforcement tool that Congress granted them to make sure that they are compensated for valuable non-infringing access—for instance, copyright owners who make movies or music available online, protected by an access control measure, in exchange for direct or indirect payment.

The *Chamberlain* court reasoned that if § 1201(a) creates liability for access without regard to the remainder of the Copyright Act, it "would clearly affect rights and limitations, if not remedies and defenses." This perceived tension is relieved by our recognition that § 1201(a) creates a new anti-circumvention right distinct from the traditional exclusive rights of a copyright owner. It follows that § 1201(a) does not limit the traditional framework of exclusive rights created by § 106, or defenses to those rights such as fair use.[12] We are thus unpersuaded by *Chamberlain's* reading of the DMCA's text and structure.

ii. Additional interpretive considerations

Though we need no further evidence of Congress's intent, the parties, citing *Chamberlain,* proffer several other arguments, which we review briefly in order to address the parties' contentions. *Chamberlain* relied heavily on policy considerations to support its reading of § 1201(a). As a threshold matter, we stress that such considerations cannot trump the statute's plain text and structure. Even were they permissible considerations in this case, however, they would not persuade us to adopt an infringement nexus requirement. *Chamberlain* feared that § 1201(a) would allow companies to leverage their sales into aftermarket monopolies, in tension with antitrust law and the doctrine of copyright misuse.[13] Concerning antitrust law, we note that there is no clear issue of anti-competitive behavior in this case because Blizzard does not seek to put a direct competitor who offers a competing role-playing game out of business and the parties have not argued this issue. If a § 1201(a)(2) defendant in a future case claims that a plaintiff is attempting to enforce its DMCA anti-circumvention right in a manner that violates antitrust law, we will then consider the interplay between this new anti-circumvention right and antitrust law.

Chamberlain also viewed an infringement nexus requirement as necessary to prevent "absurd and disastrous results," such as the existence of DMCA liability for disabling a burglary alarm to gain access to a home containing copyrighted materials. In addition, the Federal Circuit was concerned that, without an infringement nexus requirement, § 1201(a) would allow copyright owners to deny all access to the public by putting an effective access control measure in place that the public is not allowed to circumvent. Both concerns appear to be overstated, but even accepting

[12] Like the *Chamberlain* court, we need not and do not reach the relationship between fair use under § 107 of the Copyright Act and violations of § 1201. *Chamberlain,* 381 F.3d at 1199 n. 14. MDY has not claimed that Glider use is a "fair use" of WoW's dynamic non-literal elements. Accordingly, we too leave open the question whether fair use might serve as an affirmative defense to a prima facie violation of § 1201. *Id.*

[13] Copyright misuse is an equitable defense to copyright infringement that denies the copyright holder the right to enforce its copyright during the period of misuse. Since we have held that § 1201(a) creates a right distinct from copyright infringement, we conclude that we need not address copyright misuse in this case.

them, *arguendo,* as legitimate concerns, they do not permit reading the statute as requiring the imposition of an infringement nexus. As § 1201(a) creates a distinct right, it does not disturb the balance between public rights and the traditional rights of owners of copyright under the Copyright Act. Moreover, § 1201(a)(1)(B)–(D) allows the Library of Congress to create exceptions to the § 1201(a) anticircumvention right in the public's interest. If greater protection of the public's ability to access copyrighted works is required, Congress can provide such protection by amending the statute.

In sum, we conclude that a fair reading of the statute (supported by legislative history) indicates that Congress created a distinct anti-circumvention right under § 1201(a) without an infringement nexus requirement. Thus, even accepting the validity of the concerns expressed in *Chamberlain,* those concerns do not authorize us to override congressional intent and add a non-textual element to the statute. Accordingly, we reject the imposition of an infringement nexus requirement. We now consider whether MDY has violated § 1201(a)(2) and (b)(1).

E. Blizzard's § 1201(a)(2) claim

1. *WoW's literal elements and individual non-literal elements*

We agree with the district court that MDY's Glider does not violate DMCA § 1201(a)(2) with respect to WoW's literal elements and individual non-literal elements, because Warden does not effectively control access to these WoW elements. First, Warden does not control access to WoW's literal elements because these elements—the game client's software code—are available on a player's hard drive once the game client software is installed. Second, as the district court found:

> [WoW's] individual nonliteral components may be accessed by a user without signing on to the server. As was demonstrated during trial, an owner of the game client software may use independently purchased computer programs to call up the visual images or the recorded sounds within the game client software. For instance, a user may call up and listen to the roar a particular monster makes within the game. Or the user may call up a virtual image of that monster.

Since a player need not encounter Warden to access WoW's individual non-literal elements, Warden does not effectively control access to those elements.

Our conclusion is in accord with the Sixth Circuit's decision in *Lexmark International v. Static Control Components,* 387 F.3d 522 (6th Cir.2004). In *Lexmark,* the plaintiff sold laser printers equipped with an authentication sequence, verified by the printer's copyrighted software, that ensured that only plaintiff's own toner cartridges could be inserted into the printers. The defendant sold microchips capable of generating an authentication sequence that rendered other manufacturers' cartridges compatible with plaintiff's printers.

The Sixth Circuit held that plaintiff's § 1201(a)(2) claim failed because its authentication sequence did not effectively control access to its copyrighted computer program. Rather, the mere purchase of one of plaintiff's printers allowed "access" to the copyrighted program. Any purchaser could read the program code directly from the printer memory without encountering the authentication sequence. The authentication sequence thus blocked only one form of access: the ability to make use of the printer. However, it left intact another form of access: the review and use of the computer program's literal code. * * *

Here, a player's purchase of the WoW game client allows access to the game's literal elements and individual non-literal elements. Warden blocks one form of access to these elements: the ability to access them while connected to a WoW server. However, analogously to the situation in *Lexmark,* Warden leaves open the ability to access these elements directly via the user's computer. We conclude that Warden is not an effective access control measure with respect to WoW's literal elements and individual non-literal elements, and therefore, that MDY does not violate § 1201(a)(2) with respect to these elements.

2. *WoW's dynamic non-literal elements*

We conclude that MDY meets each of the six textual elements for violating § 1201(a)(2) with respect to WoW's dynamic non-literal elements [i.e., those elements of the game that a player can access only when connected to the WoW server]. That is, MDY (1) traffics in (2) a technology or part thereof (3) that is primarily designed, produced, or marketed for, or has limited commercially significant use other than (4) circumventing a technological measure (5) that effectively controls access (6) to a copyrighted work.

The first two elements are met because MDY "traffics in a technology or part thereof"—that is, it sells Glider. The third and fourth elements are met because Blizzard has established that MDY *markets* Glider for use in circumventing Warden, thus satisfying the requirement of § 1201(a)(2)(C). Indeed, Glider has no function other than to facilitate the playing of WoW. The sixth element is met because, as the district court held, WoW's dynamic non-literal elements constitute a copyrighted work. *See, e.g., Atari Games Corp. v. Oman,* 888 F.2d 878, 884–85 (D.C.Cir.1989) (the audiovisual display of a computer game is copyrightable independently from the software program code, even though the audiovisual display generated is partially dependent on user input).

The fifth element is met because Warden is an effective access control measure. To "effectively control access to a work," a technological measure must "in the ordinary course of its operation, require[ ] the application of information, or a process or a treatment, with the authority of the copyright owner, to gain access to the work." 17 U.S.C. § 1201(a)(3)(B). Both of Warden's two components "require[ ] the application of information, or a process or a treatment . . . to gain access to the work." For a player to connect to Blizzard's servers which provide access to WoW's dynamic non-literal elements, scan.dll must scan the player's computer RAM and confirm the absence of any bots or cheats. The resident component also requires a "process" in order for the user to continue accessing the work: the user's computer must report portions of WoW code running in RAM to the server. Moreover, Warden's provisions were put into place by Blizzard, and thus, function "with the authority of the copyright owner." Accordingly, Warden effectively controls access to WoW's dynamic non-literal elements. We hold that MDY is liable under § 1201(a)(2) with respect to WoW's dynamic non-literal elements. Accordingly, we affirm the district court's entry of a permanent injunction against MDY to prevent future § 1201(a)(2) violations.

F. Blizzard's § 1201(b)(1) claim

Blizzard may prevail under § 1201(b)(1) only if Warden "effectively protect[s] a right" of Blizzard under the Copyright Act. Blizzard contends that Warden protects its reproduction right against unauthorized copying. We disagree.

First, although WoW players copy the software code into RAM while playing the game, Blizzard's [Terms of Use (ToU)] authorize all licensed WoW players to do so. * * * ToU § 4(B)'s bot prohibition is a license covenant rather than a condition. Thus, a Glider user who violates this covenant does not infringe by continuing to copy code into RAM. Accordingly, MDY does not violate § 1201(b)(1) by enabling Glider users to avoid Warden's interruption of their *authorized* copying into RAM.

Second, although WoW players can theoretically record game play by taking screen shots, there is no evidence that Warden detects or prevents such allegedly infringing copying. This is logical, because Warden was designed to reduce the presence of cheats and bots, not to protect WoW's dynamic non-literal elements against copying. We conclude that Warden does not effectively protect any of Blizzard's rights under the Copyright Act, and MDY is not liable under § 1201(b)(1) for Glider's circumvention of Warden.

* * * The district court's decision is VACATED and the case is REMANDED to the district court for further proceedings consistent with this opinion.

NOTES

1. Which interpretation of section 1201(a) is more persuasive—that of the Federal Circuit in *Chamberlain* or the Ninth Circuit in *Blizzard*? Is your answer based on the statutory language, the legislative history, or policy considerations?

2. In addition to the statutory exemptions set forth in sections 1201(d)–(j), the DMCA authorizes the Librarian of Congress to promulgate regulations that exempt entire classes of works from the anti-circumvention rules if those rules would adversely affect users' ability to make non-infringing uses of such works. 17 U.S.C. § 1201(a)(1)(C). These regulations, which are updated every three years to reflect new uses and technologies, appear at 37 C.F.R. § 201.40.

UNIVERSAL CITY STUDIOS, INC. V. CORLEY

273 F.3d 429 (2d Cir. 2001).

NEWMAN, CIRCUIT JUDGE.

When the Framers of the First Amendment prohibited Congress from making any law "abridging the freedom of speech," they were not thinking about computers, computer programs, or the Internet. But neither were they thinking about radio, television, or movies. Just as the inventions at the beginning and middle of the 20th century presented new First Amendment issues, so does the cyber revolution at the end of that century. This appeal raises significant First Amendment issues concerning one aspect of computer technology—encryption to protect materials in digital form from unauthorized access. The appeal challenges the constitutionality of the Digital Millennium Copyright Act ("DMCA"), 17 U.S.C. § 1201 *et seq.* (Supp. V 1999) and the validity of an injunction entered to enforce the DMCA. * * *

[Defendant Corley wrote, and posted on his website, an article explaining how the DeCSS code could be used to circumvent anti-copying protection on DVDs. The article included a copy of the DeCSS code, as well as links to other websites where the code could be found. Corley] argues primarily that: (1) the DMCA oversteps limits in the Copyright Clause on the duration of copyright protection; (2) the DMCA as applied to his dissemination of DeCSS violates the First Amendment because computer code is "speech" entitled to full First Amendment protection and the DMCA fails to survive the exacting scrutiny accorded statutes that regulate "speech"; and (3) the DMCA violates the First Amendment and the Copyright Clause by unduly obstructing the "fair use" of copyrighted materials. * * *

III. CONSTITUTIONAL CHALLENGES BASED ON THE FIRST AMENDMENT

[This part of the court's analysis concluded that computer code, and computer programs, can constitute speech eligible for First Amendment protection, but that the scope of that protection depended, in part, on whether the relevant DMCA provisions were a "content neutral" speech regulation. The fact that computer code has both speech and non-speech (that is, functional) components was also relevant to the First Amendment analysis.]

B. First Amendment Challenge

The District Court's injunction applies the DMCA to the Defendants by imposing two types of prohibition, both grounded on the anti-trafficking provisions of the DMCA. The first prohibits posting DeCSS or any other technology for circumventing CSS on any Internet web site. The second prohibits knowingly linking any Internet web site to any other web site containing DeCSS. The validity of the posting and linking prohibitions must be considered separately.

1. Posting

The initial issue is whether the posting prohibition is content-neutral, since, as we have explained, this classification determines the applicable constitutional standard. The Appellants contend that the anti-trafficking provisions of the DMCA and their application by means of the posting prohibition of the injunction are content-based. They argue that the provisions "specifically target . . . scientific expression based on the particular topic addressed by that expression—namely, techniques for circumventing CSS." We disagree. The Appellants' argument fails to recognize that the target of the posting provisions of the injunction—DeCSS—has both a nonspeech and a speech component, and that the DMCA, as applied to the Appellants, and the posting prohibition of the injunction target only the nonspeech component. Neither the DMCA nor the posting prohibition is concerned with whatever capacity DeCSS might have for conveying information to a human being, and that capacity, as previously explained, is what arguably creates a speech component of the decryption code. The DMCA and the posting prohibition are applied to DeCSS solely because of its capacity to instruct a computer to decrypt CSS. That functional capability is not speech within the meaning of the First Amendment. * * * This type of regulation is therefore content-neutral, just as would be a restriction on trafficking in skeleton keys identified because of their capacity to unlock jail cells, even though some of the keys happened to bear a slogan or other legend that qualified as a speech component.

As a content-neutral regulation with an incidental effect on a speech component, the regulation must serve a substantial governmental interest, the interest must be unrelated to the suppression of free expression, and the incidental restriction on speech must not burden substantially more speech than is necessary to further that interest. The Government's interest in preventing unauthorized access to encrypted copyrighted material is unquestionably substantial, and the regulation of DeCSS by the posting prohibition plainly serves that interest. Moreover, that interest is unrelated to the suppression of free expression. The injunction regulates the posting of DeCSS, regardless of whether DeCSS code contains any information comprehensible by human beings that would qualify as speech. Whether the incidental regulation on speech burdens substantially more speech than is necessary to further the interest in preventing unauthorized access to copyrighted materials requires some elaboration.

Posting DeCSS on the Appellants' web site makes it instantly available at the click of a mouse to any person in the world with access to the Internet, and such person can then instantly transmit DeCSS to anyone else with Internet access. Although the prohibition on posting prevents the Appellants from conveying to others the speech component of DeCSS, the Appellants have not suggested, much less shown, any technique for barring them from making this instantaneous worldwide distribution of a decryption code that makes a lesser restriction on the code's speech component. It is true that the Government has alternative means of prohibiting unauthorized access to copyrighted materials. For example, it can create criminal and civil liability for those who gain unauthorized access, and thus it can be argued that the restriction on posting DeCSS is not absolutely necessary to preventing unauthorized access to copyrighted materials. But a content-neutral regulation need not employ the least restrictive means of accomplishing the governmental objective. It need only avoid burdening "substantially more speech than is necessary to further the government's legitimate interests." The prohibition on the Defendants' posting of DeCSS satisfies that standard.

2. Linking

* * *

In applying the DMCA to linking (via hyperlinks), Judge Kaplan recognized, as he had with DeCSS code, that a hyperlink has both a speech and a nonspeech component. It conveys information, the Internet address of the linked web page, and has the functional capacity to bring the content of the linked web page to the user's computer screen (or, as Judge Kaplan put it, to "take one almost instantaneously to the desired destination."). As he had ruled with respect to DeCSS code, he ruled that application of the DMCA to the Defendants' linking to web sites containing DeCSS is content-neutral because it is justified without regard to the speech component of the hyperlink. The linking prohibition applies whether or not the hyperlink contains any information, comprehensible to a human being, as to the

Internet address of the web page being accessed. The linking prohibition is justified solely by the functional capability of the hyperlink.

Applying the * * * requirements for content-neutral regulation, Judge Kaplan then ruled that the DMCA, as applied to the Defendants' linking, served substantial governmental interests and was unrelated to the suppression of free expression. We agree. He then carefully considered the "closer call," as to whether a linking prohibition would satisfy the narrow tailoring requirement. In an especially carefully considered portion of his opinion, he observed that strict liability for linking to web sites containing DeCSS would risk two impairments of free expression. Web site operators would be inhibited from displaying links to various web pages for fear that a linked page might contain DeCSS, and a prohibition on linking to a web site containing DeCSS would curtail access to whatever other information was contained at the accessed site.

To avoid applying the DMCA in a manner that would "burden substantially more speech than is necessary to further the government's legitimate interests," Judge Kaplan adapted the standards of *New York Times Co. v. Sullivan,* 376 U.S. 254, 283 (1964), to fashion a limited prohibition against linking to web sites containing DeCSS. He required clear and convincing evidence that those responsible for the link (a) know at the relevant time that the offending material is on the linked-to site, (b) know that it is circumvention technology that may not lawfully be offered, and (c) create or maintain the link for the purpose of disseminating that technology. He then found that the evidence satisfied his three-part test by his required standard of proof.

* * *

Mindful of the cautious approach to First Amendment claims involving computer technology expressed in *Name.Space, Inc. v. Network Solutions, Inc.,* 202 F.3d 573, 584 n. 11 (2d Cir. 2000), we see no need on this appeal to determine whether a test as rigorous as Judge Kaplan's is required to respond to First Amendment objections to the linking provision of the injunction that he issued. It suffices to reject the Appellants' contention that an intent to cause harm is required and that linking can be enjoined only under circumstances applicable to a print medium. As they have throughout their arguments, the Appellants ignore the reality of the functional capacity of decryption computer code and hyperlinks to facilitate instantaneous unauthorized access to copyrighted materials by anyone anywhere in the world. Under the circumstances amply shown by the record, the injunction's linking prohibition validly regulates the Appellants' opportunity instantly to enable anyone anywhere to gain unauthorized access to copyrighted movies on DVDs.

* * *

IV. CONSTITUTIONAL CHALLENGE BASED ON CLAIMED RESTRICTION OF FAIR USE

Asserting that fair use "is rooted in and required by both the Copyright Clause and the First Amendment," the Appellants contend that the DMCA, as applied by the District Court, unconstitutionally "*eliminates* fair use" of copyrighted materials. We reject this extravagant claim.

Preliminarily, we note that the Supreme Court has never held that fair use is constitutionally required, although some isolated statements in its opinions might arguably be enlisted for such a requirement. In *Stewart v. Abend,* 495 U.S. 207 (1990), cited by the Appellants, the Court merely noted that fair use " 'permits courts to avoid rigid application of the copyright statute when, on occasion, it would stifle the very creativity which that law is designed to foster,' " *id.*; *see also Harper & Row, Publishers, Inc. v. Nation Enterprises,* 471 U.S. 539, 560 (1985) (noting "the First Amendment protections already embodied in the Copyright Act's distinction between copyrightable expression and uncopyrightable facts and ideas, and the latitude for scholarship and comment traditionally afforded by fair use"). In *Campbell v. Acuff-Rose Music, Inc.,* 510 U.S. 569 (1994), the Court observed, "From the infancy of copyright protection, some opportunity for fair use of copyrighted materials has been thought necessary to fulfill copyright's very purpose, '[t]o promote the Progress of Science and useful Arts. . . .' " *Id.* at 575.

We need not explore the extent to which fair use might have constitutional protection, grounded on either the First Amendment or the Copyright Clause, because whatever validity a constitutional claim might have as to an application of the DMCA that impairs fair use of copyrighted materials, such matters are far beyond the scope of this lawsuit for several reasons. In the first place, the Appellants do not claim to be making fair use of any copyrighted materials, and nothing in the injunction prohibits them from making such fair use. They are barred from trafficking in a decryption code that enables unauthorized access to copyrighted materials.

Second, as the District Court properly noted, to whatever extent the anti-trafficking provisions of the DMCA might prevent others from copying portions of DVD movies in order to make fair use of them, "the evidence as to the impact of the anti-trafficking provision[s] of the DMCA on prospective fair users is scanty and fails adequately to address the issues." *Universal I,* 111 F.Supp.2d at 338 n. 246.

Third, the Appellants have provided no support for their premise that fair use of DVD movies is constitutionally required to be made by copying the original work in its original format. Their examples of the fair uses that they believe others will be prevented from making all involve copying in a digital format those portions of a DVD movie amenable to fair use, a copying that would enable the fair user to manipulate the digitally copied portions. One example is that of a school child who wishes to copy images from a DVD movie to insert into the student's documentary film. We know of no authority for the proposition that fair use, as protected by the Copyright Act, much less the Constitution, guarantees copying by the optimum method or in the identical format of the original. Although the Appellants insisted at oral argument that they should not be relegated to a "horse and buggy" technique in making fair use of DVD movies,[35] the DMCA does not impose even an arguable limitation on the opportunity to make a variety of traditional fair uses of DVD movies, such as commenting on their content, quoting excerpts from their screenplays, and even recording portions of the video images and sounds on film or tape by pointing a camera, a camcorder, or a microphone at a monitor as it displays the DVD movie. The fact that the resulting copy will not be as perfect or as manipulable as a digital copy obtained by having direct access to the DVD movie in its digital form, provides no basis for a claim of unconstitutional limitation of fair use. A film critic making fair use of a movie by quoting selected lines of dialogue has no constitutionally valid claim that the review (in print or on television) would be technologically superior if the reviewer had not been prevented from using a movie camera in the theater, nor has an art student a valid constitutional claim to fair use of a painting by photographing it in a museum. Fair use has never been held to be a guarantee of access to copyrighted material in order to copy it by the fair user's preferred technique or in the format of the original. * * *

NOTES

1. The *Corley* court also considered, but dismissed, the argument that the absence of any durational limitation in section 1201(a) could lead to *de facto* perpetual protection for technologically-protected works even after their copyright expires, in violation of the "limited times" language of the Copyright Clause. Did the court properly reject that argument? (Consider this: Which of its constitutional powers do you think Congress was exercising when it enacted section 1201(a)?)

2. Several of the issues raised in *Corley* resurfaced in *Green v. U.S. Department of Justice*, 392 F.Supp.3d 68 (D.D.C. 2019), a declaratory judgment action brought by a security researcher who wanted to circumvent certain security systems in order to publish a book explaining how such circumvention was possible, and an engineer who wanted to circumvent protections that restrict the viewing of HDMI signals so that his company could develop, use, and market a device (the "NeTVCR") that would enable users to edit their digital video streams. Although none of the plaintiffs' proposed activities involved copyright infringement, they were concerned about potential civil

[35] In their supplemental papers, the Appellants contend, rather hyperbolically, that a prohibition on using copying machines to assist in making fair use of texts could not validly be upheld by the availability of "monks to scribe the relevant passages."

and/or criminal liability for violating the anti-circumvention and anti-trafficking provisions of section 1201(a).

The district court agreed with *Corley* that section 1201(a) is a content-neutral speech regulation that is subject to intermediate scrutiny, and held that the government had failed to meet its burden of proving that section 1201(a), as applied to the plaintiffs' specific activities, "does not burden substantially more speech than is necessary to further the government's legitimate interests." *Id.* at 96. The government's concerns—that the proposed book and the NeTVCR device might be used by third parties to engage in circumvention for infringing purposes—were simply not supported by any facts in the record. *Id.* However, the court dismissed the plaintiffs' broader claim—that section 1201(a) is *facially invalid* as a violation of the First Amendment because (1) it interferes with third parties' ability to engage in fair uses of copyrighted works, and (2) fair use is a First Amendment right. Thus, the court refused to hold that section 1201(a) is unconstitutional on its face.

The plaintiffs have appealed the latter ruling. How should the Federal Circuit rule? Specifically: Does section 1201(a) interfere with the public's right to make fair use of copyrighted works? If so, is this a First Amendment concern, or can Congress lawfully decide to allow such impairment? Is the burden on free speech greater than necessary to further the government's legitimate interests? Are there less burdensome ways to further those interests?

3. Section 1202 of the DMCA prohibits falsifying any "copyright management information" that accompanies a copy of a copyrighted work, or distributing such altered copies, with the intent to induce, enable, facilitate or conceal infringement. It also prohibits intentionally removing or altering such information, and distributing or publicly performing works with the knowledge that their copyright management information has been unlawfully removed or altered. Copyright management information includes, *inter alia*, the title of the work as well as information about the author and the copyright owner. This information is especially important in the case of digitized works disseminated on the internet, where potential users may find it difficult to determine the copyright status of a work in the absence of such information. Many claims brought under 1202 have failed, however, because the plaintiffs could not prove the requisite knowledge or intent.

E. AFFIRMATIVE DEFENSES

A copyright infringement defendant may attack the validity of the plaintiff's copyright or ownership claim, may argue that the challenged use falls within one of the specific limitations on the exclusive rights discussed in Chapter 16, may assert rights under an assignment or license, or may raise the affirmative defense of fair use, discussed in Chapter 17. Other affirmative defenses include copyright misuse, abandonment, the statute of limitations, the Eleventh Amendment (in cases involving a state defendant), and such equitable defenses as laches, estoppel and unclean hands (including fraudulent registration).

APPLE, INC. V. PSYSTAR CORP.

658 F.3d 1150 (9th Cir. 2011).

SCHROEDER, CIRCUIT JUDGE:

[Apple sold its Mac line of computers with the Mac OS X operating system preinstalled. It also distributed stand-alone copies of Mac OS X at retail to enable existing customers to upgrade to the latest version. The Software License Agreement (SLA) that accompanied this software required that Mac OS X be used only on Apple computers. Nonetheless, Psystar, a small computer manufacturer, figured out how to install it on non-Apple computers, and offered such systems for sale. When Apple sued for infringement, Psystar argued that Apple's copyright was unenforceable, because the SLA restriction constituted copyright misuse. The district court rejected the copyright misuse defense, and this appeal followed.]

* * *

Psystar's main contention of misuse is aimed at Apple's requirement that licensees of Mac OS X run their copies only on Apple computers. The relevant section of Apple's SLA for Mac OS X provides,

> This License allows you to install, use and run one (1) copy of the Apple Software on a single-Apple-labeled computer at a time. You agree not to install, use or run the Apple Software on any non-Apple labeled computer, or to enable others to do so.

Psystar contends that this language barring use of the Apple software on non-Apple computers impermissibly extends the reach of Apple's copyright and constitutes misuse. We conclude that the district court correctly ruled that Apple had not engaged in copyright misuse. As we will explain, this is principally because its licensing agreement was intended to require the operating system to be used on the computer it was designed to operate, and it did not prevent others from developing their own computer or operating systems. These licensing agreements were thus appropriately used to prevent infringement and control use of the copyrighted material.

A. Software licensing agreements, rather than sales, have become ubiquitous in the software industry because they enable the licensor to control the use of the copyrighted material.

To understand why license agreements, rather than sales, have become the predominate form of the transfer of rights to use copyrighted software material, it is necessary to understand the legal principle that applies when copyrighted works are not licensed, but sold: the "first sale doctrine." The first sale doctrine allows owners of copies of copyrighted works to resell their copies without restriction.

[Here the court reviewed the case law interpreting section 109(a), in particular its recent decision in *Vernor v. Autodesk*, 621 F.3d 1102 (9th Cir.

2010), excerpted in Chapter 16 *supra*, which held that section 109(a) did not apply to copies of software that were licensed rather than sold.]

It is this distinction between sales and licenses that has caused the use of software licensing agreements to flourish and become the preferred form of software transactions.

* * *

B. Licensees have reacted to the proliferation of software licensing agreements by asking the courts to apply copyright misuse defense to limit the scope of such agreements.

Copyright misuse is a judicially crafted affirmative defense to copyright infringement, derived from the long-standing existence of such a defense in patent litigation. The patent misuse defense was originally recognized by the Supreme Court in 1942, in holding that the owner of the patent on a salt tablet machine could not require licensees to use only unpatented salt tablets sold by the patent owner. *Morton Salt Co. v. G.S. Suppiger Co.,* 314 U.S. 488 (1942). The Court held that this improper tying of a patented product and an unpatented product constituted misuse, and prohibited the patent holder from maintaining infringement actions until the patent holder ceased misuse of the patent. *Id.* at 493 ("Where the patent is used as a means of restraining competition with the patentee's sale of an unpatented product . . . [e]quity may rightly withhold its assistance from such a use of the patent by declining to entertain a suit for infringement [until] the improper practice has been abandoned and [the] consequences of the misuse of the patent have been dissipated.").

In 1990, the Fourth Circuit became the first federal circuit to extend the misuse rationale to copyrights. *See Lasercomb Am., Inc. v. Reynolds,* 911 F.2d 970, 972 (4th Cir.1990). In *Lasercomb,* a software manufacturer required its customers to agree to a licensing agreement that barred the licensee from creating any competing software. *Id.* at 978 ("Each time Lasercomb sells its Interact program to a company . . . the company is required to forego utilization of the creative abilities of all its officers, directors and employees in the area of CAD/CAM die-making software."). Drawing on patent misuse jurisprudence, the Fourth Circuit concluded that Lasercomb's licensing agreement was an "egregious" anticompetitive restraint, which amounted to copyright misuse. *Id.* at 979. It was aimed at preventing the creation of competing software.

Subsequently, our court recognized the existence of a copyright misuse doctrine. *See, e.g., Practice Mgmt. Info. Corp. v. Am. Med. Ass'n,* 121 F.3d 516, 521 (9th Cir.1997), *amended by* 133 F.3d 1140 (9th Cir.1998). * * *

Our decision in *Practice Management* is the only case in which we upheld a copyright misuse defense. We did so because the copyright licensor in that case prevented the licensee from using any other competing product. In *Practice Management,* a publisher and distributor of medical books was using a coding system developed by the American Medical Association ("AMA") to enable physicians and others to identify particular medical procedures with precision. *Id.* Practice Management sued the AMA for a declaratory judgment that the AMA's copyright in its coding system, the Physician's Current Procedural Terminology ("CPT"), was not valid. The CPT had become an industry standard, and the AMA had a licensing agreement that allowed the Health Care Financing Administration ("HCFA") to use the AMA system. The agreement provided, however, that HCFA use only the AMA system. *Id.* at 520–21 (the agreement required "HCFA to use the AMA's copyrighted coding system and prohibit[ed] HCFA from using any other.").

We held this was copyright misuse, because the AMA was not entitled to use the license agreement to prevent the use of all competitor's products. *Id.* at 521 ("Conditioning the license on HCFA's promise not to use competitors' products constituted a misuse of the copyright by the AMA."). In recognizing clear abuse of the copyright, we observed that the AMA's misuse was its limitation on the HCFA's right to decide whether or not to use other systems as well. It was not necessary to decide whether the limitation, in the antitrust context, would have been reasonable or not. We said that "a defendant in a copyright infringement suit need not prove an antitrust violation to prevail on a copyright misuse defense."

* * *

C. Psystar's Misuse Defense fails because it is an attempt to apply the First Sale Doctrine to a valid licensing agreement.

[Applying the distinction between sales and licenses, the court concluded that when Apple sold its customers a retail-packaged DVD containing Mac OS X software, the buyers merely "purchased the disc," not a copy of the software. Apple's SLA made clear that the customers "were licensees, not owners, of the software."]

* * *

Contrary to Psystar's assertion, such licensing arrangements are also firmly rooted in the history of copyright law. While copyright owners may choose to simply exclude others from their work, i.e. not to transfer their rights, courts have long held that copyright holders may also use their limited monopoly to leverage the right to use their work on the acceptance of specific conditions, *see, e.g., Metro-Goldwyn-Mayer Distrib. Corp. v. Bijou Theatre Co.,* 59 F.2d 70, 77 (1st Cir.1932) (holding that if a motion picture license is subject to the condition that its exhibition must occur at specified times and places, the licensee's exhibitions at other times and places is without authority from the licensor and therefore constitutes copyright infringement).

D. The Fifth Circuit's Decision in Alcatel Unlike This Case Involved Restrictions Aimed At Stifling Competition.

The copyright misuse doctrine does not prohibit using conditions to control use of copyrighted material, but it does prevent copyright holders from using the conditions to stifle competition. Psystar relies on the Fifth Circuit's opinion in *Alcatel USA, Inc. v. DGI Techs., Inc.*, 166 F.3d 772 (5th Cir. 1999). This reliance is inapposite. In *Alcatel,* the license conditions prevented development of competing products, and thus constituted copyright misuse.

In *Alcatel,* the plaintiff and copyright holder (formerly known as DSC) manufactured telephone switching systems consisting of copyrighted operational software and numerous non-copyrighted components. The software license agreement provided that the software was "licensed to customers to be used only in conjunction with DSC-manufactured hardware," and such hardware included expansion cards. To develop compatible cards, the defendant had to download and copy the software for testing and development purposes. This would have been a breach of the licensing agreement. The Fifth Circuit held, however, that the restrictive terms of the licensing agreement constituted copyright misuse.

Unlike the licensing agreement in *Alcatel,* Apple's SLA does not restrict competitor's ability to develop their own software, nor does it preclude customers from using non-Apple components with Apple computers. Instead, Apple's SLA merely restricts the use of Apple's own software to its own hardware. As the district court properly concluded, Apple's SLA has "not prohibited others from independently developing and using their own operating systems." Psystar produces its own computer hardware and it is free to develop its own computer software.

* * *

Alcatel appears to be more like our decision in *Practice Management* where we found an anti-competitive license condition. In *Practice Management,* the agreement prohibited the licensee from using any competing system. In *Alcatel,* the agreement effectively prohibited the licensee from using any competing expansion cards. Therefore, Apple's SLA, like the one we reviewed in *Triad,* represents the legitimate exercise of a copyright holder's right to conditionally transfer works of authorship, and does not constitute copyright misuse.

* * *

NOTES

1. The relationship between copyright misuse and antitrust violations was examined in *Lasercomb America, Inc. v. Reynolds*, 911 F.2d 970 (4th Cir. 1990), where the Fourth Circuit observed:

> [W]hile it is true that the attempted use of a copyright to violate antitrust law probably would give rise to a misuse of copyright defense, the converse is not necessarily true—a misuse need not be a violation of antitrust law in order to comprise an equitable defense to an infringement action. The question is not whether the copyright is being used in a manner violative of antitrust law (such as whether the licensing agreement is "reasonable"), but whether the copyright is being used in a manner violative of the public policy embodied in the grant of a copyright.

Id. at 978. The Seventh Circuit reached a similar conclusion in *Assessment Technologies of WI, LLC v. WIREdata, Inc.*, 350 F.3d 640 (7th Cir. 2003), noting:

> The argument for applying copyright misuse beyond the bounds of antitrust, besides the fact that confined to antitrust the doctrine would be redundant, is that for a copyright owner to use an infringement suit to obtain property protection, here in data, that copyright law clearly does not confer, hoping to force a settlement or even achieve an outright victory over an opponent that may lack the resources or the legal sophistication to resist effectively, is an abuse of process.

Id. at 647.

2. Where a finding of copyright misuse is based on a licensing restriction, it makes the copyright unenforceable for so long as the misuse continues. Thus, the defense is not limited to the licensees who were subject to the restriction; it can be invoked by any party alleged to have infringed the same copyrighted work while the restriction was still in place. *Lasercomb*, 911 F.2d at 979. Accordingly, even a party that chooses not to enter the restrictive licensing agreement may use copyright misuse as a defense to an infringement claim, until the improper restriction is lifted.

3. Consider the shrinkwrap license reproduced in Note 1 following *Vernor v. Autodesk*, in Chapter 16.B.2.a., *supra*. Could the imposition of such a license constitute copyright misuse? Can you think of other actions that might constitute copyright misuse? Consider these examples:

(a) A motion picture studio grants an internet service a license to provide short trailers of the studio's films to online movie retailers for use as "previews" available to potential purchasers. One condition of the license is that the licensee must not allow negative comments about the licensor to appear on any of the websites where the trailers are used. *See Video Pipeline, Inc. v. Buena Vista Home Entertainment, Inc.*, 342 F.3d 191 (3d Cir. 2003).

(b) County tax assessors use licensed database software to organize and store real estate data. One condition of the license forbids the licensee counties from extracting the raw data and making it available to third parties, such as the Multiple Listing Service. *Cf.*

Assessment Technologies of WI, LLC v. WIREdata, Inc., 350 F.3d 640 (7th Cir. 2003).

4. *Unclean Hands:* Courts sometimes use the terms "copyright misuse" and "unclean hands" interchangeably; however, in addition to antitrust violations and other conventionally anticompetitive behavior, activity supporting an unclean hands defense can include misleading conduct or bad faith in dealing with the defendant, and fraud or failure to disclose required information in the copyright application.

5. *Statute of Limitations:* Section 507 bars civil and criminal copyright actions unless initiated within three years of the infringing activity. Although section 507(a) (the criminal provision) refers to the date on which the cause of action "arose" and section 507(b) (the civil provision) refers to the date on which the claim "accrued," the reason for this different terminology is unclear. Courts disagree on whether infringing activities preceding this three-year period can be included in an infringement action as part of a "continuing wrong." *Compare Taylor v. Meirick*, 712 F.2d 1112 (7th Cir. 1983) (copying which preceded the limitations period actionable in combination with distribution which took place during that period), *with Roley v. New World Pictures, Ltd.*, 19 F.3d 479 (9th Cir. 1994) (rejecting *Taylor*) *and Stone v. Williams*, 970 F.2d 1043 (2d Cir. 1992) (rejecting *Taylor*). A defendant may be estopped from raising the statute of limitations defense if the defendant misleads the plaintiff into believing that litigation is unnecessary. The statute may be tolled in cases of fraudulent concealment, duress, or coercion. It has also been tolled when the plaintiff could not reasonably have been expected to discover the infringement within the limitations period. *Taylor v. Meirick*, 712 F.2d at 1117–18.

6. *Abandonment:* Abandonment differs from forfeiture of copyright, which could occur under pre-1989 law as a result of publication without notice. Abandonment, in contrast, requires intent to surrender copyright. Most courts impose the additional requirement of an overt act evidencing that intent, such as an explicit statement renouncing all claims to copyright. As noted earlier (see Chapter 15.C.1.), the Creative Commons has introduced a public domain tool ("CC0" or "CC Zero") that enables a copyright owner to dedicate his or her work to the public domain. Thus far, no courts have recognized a defense of partial abandonment (*e.g.*, abandonment in a particular region or medium).

7. *Laches:* The Supreme Court addressed the laches defense in *Petrella v. MGM, Inc.*, 572 U.S. 663 (2014). The plaintiff inherited her father's copyright interest and renewal rights in the screenplay, copyrighted in 1963, for the film *Raging Bull*, which MGM released and copyrighted in 1980. In 1991, plaintiff renewed her copyright in the screenplay. Seven years later, she informed MGM that its continued exploitation of *Raging Bull* violated her copyright. Nine years after that notice, she filed suit seeking injunctive relief and damages incurred as a result of acts occurring in the past three years. MGM invoked the doctrine of laches, but the Court held that it did not apply because the copyright statute of limitations already takes account of delays in filing suit. The Court stated that the laches defense could potentially have relevance to

plaintiff's claim for injunctive relief, though on the facts of this case the Court expressed doubt that the delay would be dispositive on remand even as to injunctive relief.

8. *Equitable Estoppel:* Traditional principles of equitable estoppel preclude copyright relief for a plaintiff where (1) the plaintiff knows of the defendant's infringing activity, (2) the plaintiff's conduct with respect to the infringing activity is such that the defendant has a right to rely on that conduct, (3) the defendant is unaware of the truth, and (4) the defendant detrimentally relies on the plaintiff's conduct. Suppose that a defendant creates a derivative work incorporating non-literal portions of a plaintiff's copyrighted work which the plaintiff had represented as factual. In a subsequent infringement action, however, the plaintiff asserts that these portions of the work were fictional. Who should prevail, and why?

9. *Innocent Infringement:* If an infringer relies in good faith on a purported transfer or license from a person wrongly identified in the copyright notice as the owner of the copyright in the work, and if that copy was publicly distributed by authority of the copyright owner before March 1, 1989, the infringer has a complete defense unless, before the infringement took place, either (1) the work was registered by the copyright owner, or (2) a document showing the ownership of the copyright had been executed by the person named in the notice, and had been recorded. 17 U.S.C. § 406(a).

Two other "innocent infringement" defenses, in sections 405(b) and 504(c), affect only the availability of certain damages remedies, not the underlying question of liability. How do sections 401 and 402 affect the availability of these defenses? Why?

10. You now know that a defendant may be liable for direct infringement even if he or she had no reason to know that the activity was infringing. What planning techniques can a copyright licensee use to protect itself from liability if the licensed material turns out to include infringing content?

11. *Eleventh Amendment:* Prior to 1990, Congress had not addressed the question whether the Eleventh Amendment precluded copyright infringement suits against the states; most courts had concluded that it did. In the Copyright Remedy Clarification Act of 1990, Congress amended section 501(a) and added section 511 to abrogate the states' Eleventh Amendment immunity from such suits. In 2020, however, the Supreme Court held that that the 1990 amendments were unconstitutional, thus restoring the states' immunity. *Allen v. Cooper*, ___ U.S. ___, 140 S.Ct. 994 (2020). This ruling was not unexpected, considering that, in a pair of 1999 decisions, the Supreme Court had already invalidated Congress's attempts to abrogate the states' Eleventh Amendment immunity from suits for false advertising under the Lanham Act and for patent infringement. *Florida Prepaid Postsecondary Educ. Expense Bd. v. College Savings Bank*, 527 U.S. 627 (1999); *College Savings Bank v. Florida Prepaid Postsecondary Educ. Expense Bd.*, 527 U.S. 666 (1999). Because federal courts have exclusive jurisdiction over copyright infringement suits (under 28 U.S.C. § 1338), this means that the states are immune from damages liability for

copyright infringement. However, under the doctrine of *Ex parte Young*, 209 U.S. 123 (1908), a copyright plaintiff can still seek injunctive relief against the individual state officer engaging in the infringing activity.

12. *First Amendment:* Courts have generally resisted the argument that copyright law, either on its face or as applied to a specific infringement claim, violates the First Amendment; but as we have seen the question is by no means free from doubt. Some important recent cases—including *Suntrust Bank* (the *Wind Done Gone* case) and *Corley*—have supposed that the First Amendment does apply to copyright in some fashion. The Supreme Court's opinions in *Eldred v. Ashcroft* and *Golan v. Holder* suggest that a majority of the Court believes that copyright, "as traditionally configured," does not violate the First Amendment. As you read the next section, ask yourself whether First Amendment considerations should ever affect the choice of infringement *remedies*.

F. REMEDIES

Statutes: 17 U.S.C. §§ 412, 502–06, 18 U.S.C. §§ 2318–19C

1. INJUNCTIONS

Although section 502(a) of the 1976 Act authorizes a court to "grant temporary and final injunctions on such terms as it may deem reasonable to prevent or restrain infringement of a copyright," it does not mandate injunctive relief. *See* H.R. Rep. No. 94–1476, 94th Cong., 2d Sess. 160 (1976) ("Section 502(a) reasserts the discretionary power of courts to grant injunctions and restraining orders, whether 'preliminary,' 'temporary,' 'interlocutory,' 'permanent,' or 'final,' to prevent or stop infringements of copyright."). Note, however, that injunctive relief against the United States is barred by 28 U.S.C. § 1498.

Prior to the Supreme Court's decision in *eBay v. MercExchange*, 547 U.S. 388 (2006) (a patent case, *see supra* Chapter 12), courts and commentators often stated that a permanent injunction should issue against the defendant when liability for copyright infringement has been established and there is a threat of continuing violations, and this was the common practice. In *eBay*, however, the Court held that a patent infringement plaintiff is not entitled to a permanent injunction unless the plaintiff proves that (1) it has suffered irreparable injury; (2) the remedies available at law, such as damages, are inadequate to compensate for that injury; (3) considering the balance of hardships between the parties, an equitable remedy is warranted; and (4) the public interest would not be disserved by a permanent injunction. *eBay*, 547 U.S. at 391. The Supreme Court later announced a similar test for preliminary injunctions, modifying the "injury" factor to require proof that the plaintiff is "likely" to suffer irreparable harm in the absence of injunctive relief. *Winter v. Natural Resources Defense Council, Inc.*, 555 U.S. 7 (2008).

Most circuits agree that *eBay* and *Winter* apply also to copyright infringement cases, and that successful infringement plaintiffs no longer have a presumptive entitlement to preliminary or permanent injunctive relief. *See, e.g., Perfect 10, Inc. v. Google, Inc.*, 653 F.3d 976 (9th Cir. 2011); *Salinger v. Colting*, 607 F.3d 68 (2d Cir. 2010). (Although the Trademark Modernization Act of 2020 reinstated the presumption of irreparable harm for Lanham Act claims, it has no effect on copyright or patent cases.) Therefore, before awarding injunctive relief in copyright cases, courts must consider each of the equitable factors outlined by the Supreme Court.

Even before the *eBay* decision, however, a number of authorities had suggested that equitable considerations—including the public interest—might sometimes require courts to withhold injunctive relief. For example, in *Abend v. MCA, Inc.*, 863 F.2d 1465 (9th Cir. 1988), *aff'd sub nom. Stewart v. Abend*, 495 U.S. 207 (1990), the Ninth Circuit adopted a commentator's suggestion that "where great public injury would be worked by an injunction, the courts might . . . award damages or a continuing royalty instead of an injunction in such special circumstances." *Id.* at 1479 (quoting 3 M. NIMMER, NIMMER ON COPYRIGHT § 14.06[B] (1988)). It found such circumstances to exist where the defendant's continued exploitation of its motion picture, a derivative work prepared during the initial copyright term of the underlying short story, infringed the story's copyright during the renewal term, because the short story's author died before the renewal term could vest, thus invalidating the author's previous grant of renewal term rights to the defendant:

> The "Rear Window" film resulted from the collaborative efforts of many talented individuals other than Cornell Woolrich, the author of the underlying story. The success of the movie resulted in large part from factors completely unrelated to the underlying story, "It Had To Be Murder." It would cause a great injustice for the owners of the film if the court enjoined them from further exhibition of the movie. An injunction would also effectively foreclose defendants from enjoying legitimate profits derived from exploitation of the "new matter" comprising the derivative work, which is given express copyright protection by section 7 of the 1909 Act. Since defendants could not possibly separate out the "new matter" from the underlying work, their right to enjoy the renewal copyright in the derivative work would be rendered meaningless by the grant of an injunction. We also note that an injunction could cause public injury by denying the public the opportunity to view a classic film for many years to come.

863 F.2d at 1479.

In *Campbell v. Acuff-Rose*, 510 U.S. 569 (1994), the Supreme Court suggested in a footnote that it agreed with the Ninth Circuit's approach:

> Because the fair use enquiry often requires close questions of judgment as to the extent of permissible borrowing in cases involving parodies (or other critical works), courts may also wish to bear in mind that the goals of the copyright law, "to stimulate the creation and publication of edifying matter," are not always best served by automatically granting injunctive relief when parodists are found to have gone beyond the bounds of fair use.

510 U.S. at 578 n.10 (citing *Abend*, 863 F.2d at 1479).

NOTES

1. In determining whether to grant injunctive relief, consider how much weight, if any, should be given to each of the following: (1) the defendant's creative contribution to, or financial investment in, the infringing work; (2) the omission of copyright notice on the plaintiff's work; (3) the defendant's efforts to locate the copyright owner in order to obtain consent; (4) other evidence of the defendant's good faith, such as crediting the copyright owner.

2. Consider the appropriateness of injunctive relief where:

(a) the copyright in an architectural design is infringed by construction of a building;

(b) a defendant copies protectible elements of the plaintiff's work as a preliminary step in creating a finished work from which all infringing material has been expunged.

3. Would unauthorized file-sharing be an appropriate scenario for awarding continuing damages (such as a compulsory royalty) in place of injunctive relief? *See A & M Records, Inc. v. Napster, Inc.*, 239 F.3d 1004, 1028–29 (9th Cir. 2001).

4. Would denial of injunctive relief be consistent with the United States' obligations under Arts. 8–14bis of the Berne Convention? *Cf.* Art. 6bis.

5. Courts often issue permanent injunctions that extend to works which the defendant has not yet infringed, and even those which the plaintiff has not yet created. *See, e.g., Walt Disney Co. v. Powell*, 897 F.2d 565, 568 (D.C. Cir. 1990) (collecting authorities). Can this approach be reconciled with the requirement that a copyright be registered as a prerequisite to an infringement suit?

6. *Preliminary Injunctions:* Should a plaintiff's delay in bringing suit be relevant to the equitable analysis under *eBay* and *Winter*?

7. *Infringement by the United States:* Under 28 U.S.C. § 1498(b), the exclusive remedy for copyright infringement by the United States or its contractors is a suit in the Court of Federal Claims for reasonable compensation, including statutory damages under section 504(c). Injunctive relief is unavailable.

2. ACTUAL DAMAGES AND PROFITS

FRANK MUSIC CORP. V. METRO-GOLDWYN-MAYER, INC.

772 F.2d 505 (9th Cir. 1985).

FLETCHER, CIRCUIT JUDGE:

This copyright infringement suit arises out of defendants' use of five songs from plaintiffs' dramatico-musical play *Kismet* in a musical revue staged at defendant MGM Grand Hotel in 1974–76. After a bench trial, the district court found infringement and awarded the plaintiffs $22,000 as a share of defendants' profits. Plaintiffs appeal and defendants cross-appeal. We affirm in part, reverse in part, and remand.

I. Facts

[The original version of *Kismet* was a dramatic play by Edward Knoblock; its copyright expired in 1967. A musical adaptation of that play was copyrighted in 1953 and 1954, and in 1954 the musical's authors licensed a predecessor of MGM to produce a motion picture version of the musical. The plaintiffs in this action are the authors and assignee of the copyright in the musical stage play.]

* * *

On April 26, 1974, defendant MGM Grand Hotel premiered a musical revue entitled *Hallelujah Hollywood* in the hotel's Ziegfield Theatre. The show was staged, produced, and directed by defendant Donn Arden. It featured ten acts of singing, dancing, and variety performances. Of the ten acts, four were labeled as "tributes" to MGM motion pictures of the past, and one was a tribute to the "Ziegfield Follies." The remaining acts were variety numbers, which included performances by a live tiger, a juggler, and the magicians, Siegfried and Roy.

* * *

Act IV of *Hallelujah Hollywood*, the subject of this lawsuit, was entitled "Kismet," and was billed as a tribute to the MGM movie of that name. Comprised of four scenes, it was approximately eleven and one-half minutes in length. It was set in ancient Baghdad, as was plaintiffs' play, and the characters were called by the same or similar names to those used in plaintiffs' play. Five songs were taken in whole or in part from plaintiffs' play. No dialogue was spoken during the act, and, in all, it contained approximately six minutes of music taken directly from plaintiffs' play.

The total running time of *Hallelujah Hollywood* was approximately 100 minutes, except on Saturday nights when two acts were deleted, shortening the show to 75 minutes. The show was performed three times on Saturday evenings, twice on the other evenings of the week.

* * *

1. *Actual Damages*

"Actual damages" are the extent to which the market value of a copyrighted work has been injured or destroyed by an infringement. In this circuit, we have stated the test of market value as "what a willing buyer would have been reasonably required to pay to a willing seller for plaintiffs' work."

The district court declined to award actual damages. The court stated that it was "unconvinced that the market value of plaintiffs' work was in any way diminished as a result of defendant's infringement." * * *

Plaintiffs contend the district court's finding is clearly erroneous in light of the evidence they presented concerning the royalties *Kismet* could have earned in a full Las Vegas production. Plaintiffs did offer evidence of the royalties *Kismet* had earned in productions around the country. They also introduced opinion testimony, elicited from plaintiff Lester and from *Kismet*'s leasing agent, that a full production of *Kismet* could have been licensed in Las Vegas for $7,500 per week. And they introduced other opinion testimony to the effect that *Hallelujah Hollywood* had destroyed the Las Vegas market for a production of plaintiffs' *Kismet.*

In a copyright action, a trial court is entitled to reject a proffered measure of damages if it is too speculative. Although uncertainty as to the amount of damages will not preclude recovery, uncertainty as to the fact of damages may. It was the *fact* of damages that concerned the district court. The court found that plaintiffs "failed to establish *any* damages attributable to the infringement." This finding is not clearly erroneous.

Plaintiffs offered no disinterested testimony showing that *Hallelujah Hollywood* precluded plaintiffs from presenting *Kismet* at some other hotel in Las Vegas. It is not implausible to conclude, as the court below apparently did, that a production presenting six minutes of music from *Kismet,* without telling any of the story of the play, would not significantly impair the prospects for presenting a full production of that play.[7] Based

[7] Another panel of this court considered a similar problem recently in *Cream Records, Inc. v. Jos. Schlitz Brewing Co.*, 754 F.2d 826 (9th Cir.1985) (interpreting the 1976 Act). In *Cream Records*, the jury found that Schlitz and its advertising agency infringed Cream's copyright in "The Theme from Shaft", by using a ten-note ostinato from the song in a television commercial. The district court awarded $12,000 as actual damages for loss of licensing fees. We concluded that the award was insufficient, stating:

> The only evidence before the court was that unauthorized use of the Shaft theme music in Schlitz's commercial ended Cream's opportunity to license the music for this purpose. There was no evidence that Schlitz sought, or Cream was willing to grant, a license for use of less than the entire copyrighted work, that a license limited to the portion used in the commercial would have had less value, or that use limited to this portion would have had a less devastating effect upon Cream's opportunity to license to another. Since defendants' unauthorized use destroyed the value of the copyrighted work for this purpose, plaintiff was entitled to recover that value as damages.

on the record presented, the district court was not clearly erroneous in finding that plaintiffs' theory of damages was uncertain and speculative.

2. *Infringer's Profits*

As an alternative to actual damages, a prevailing plaintiff in an infringement action is entitled to recover the infringer's profits to the extent they are attributable to the infringement. In establishing the infringer's profits, the plaintiff is required to prove only the defendant's sales; the burden then shifts to the defendant to prove the elements of costs to be deducted from sales in arriving at profit. Any doubt as to the computation of costs or profits is to be resolved in favor of the plaintiff. If the infringing defendant does not meet its burden of proving costs, the gross figure stands as the defendant's profits.

The district court, following this approach, found that the gross revenue MGM Grand earned from the presentation of *Hallelujah Hollywood* during the relevant time period was $24,191,690. From that figure, the court deducted direct costs of $18,060,084 and indirect costs (overhead) of $3,641,960, thus arriving at a net profit of $2,489,646.

* * * Plaintiffs claim the district court erred in allowing deductions for overhead expenses for two reasons: because the infringement was "conscious and deliberate," and because defendants failed to show that each item of claimed overhead assisted in the production of the infringement. Plaintiffs also contend the court erred in not including in gross profits some portion of MGM's earnings on its hotel and gaming operations.

A portion of an infringer's overhead properly may be deducted from gross revenues to arrive at profits, at least where the infringement was not willful, conscious, or deliberate. Plaintiffs argue that the infringement here was conscious and deliberate, but the district court found to the contrary. The court's finding is not clearly erroneous. Defendants believed their use of *Kismet* was protected under MGM Grand's ASCAP license. Although their contention ultimately proved to be wrong, it was not implausible. Defendants reasonably could have believed that their production was not infringing plaintiffs' copyrights, and, therefore, the district court was not clearly erroneous in finding that their conduct was not willful.

Id. at 827–28.

In *Cream Records*, the evidence showed that another advertiser had approached Cream for a license for the song, but withdrew when the Schlitz commercial was aired. "There was testimony that use of a well-known popular song in a commercial destroys its value to other advertisers for that purpose."

The evidence concerning the effect of defendants' infringement is far less convincing in our case. Plaintiffs did introduce testimony that the infringement had destroyed the Las Vegas market for a full production of *Kismet*, but that testimony came from *Kismet*'s leasing agent, not a disinterested party. We agree with the district court's characterization of this evidence as "meager," and we cannot conclude that the court clearly erred in discrediting it.

We find more merit in plaintiffs' second challenge to the deduction of overhead costs. They argue that defendants failed to show that each item of claimed overhead assisted in the production of the infringement. The evidence defendants introduced at trial segregated overhead expenses into general categories, such as general and administrative costs, sales and advertising, and engineering and maintenance. Defendants then allocated a portion of these costs to the production of *Hallelujah Hollywood* based on a ratio of the revenues from that production as compared to MGM Grand's total revenues. The district court adopted this approach.

* * *

We do not doubt that some of defendants' claimed overhead contributed to the production of *Hallelujah Hollywood.* The difficulty we have, however, is that defendants offered no evidence of what costs were included in general categories such as "general and administrative expenses," nor did they offer any evidence concerning how these costs contributed to the production of *Hallelujah Hollywood.* The defendants contend their burden was met when they introduced evidence of their total overhead costs allocated on a reasonable basis. The district court apparently agreed with this approach. That is not the law of this circuit. Under *Kamar International,* a defendant additionally must show that the categories of overhead actually contributed to sales of the infringing work. We can find no such showing in the record before us. Therefore, we conclude the district court's finding that "defendants have established that these items of general expense [the general categories of claimed overhead] contributed to the production of '*Hallelujah Hollywood*'" was clearly erroneous.

Plaintiffs next challenge the district court's failure to consider MGM Grand's earnings on hotel and gaming operations in arriving at the amount of profits attributable to the infringement. The district court received evidence concerning MGM Grand's total net profit during the relevant time period, totaling approximately $395,000,000, but its memorandum decision does not mention these indirect profits and computes recovery based solely on the revenues and profits earned on the production of *Hallelujah Hollywood* (approximately $24,000,000 and $2,500,000 respectively). We surmise from this that the district court determined plaintiffs were not entitled to recover indirect profits, but we have no hint as to the district court's reasons.

Whether a copyright proprietor may recover "indirect profits" is one of first impression in this circuit. We conclude that under the 1909 Act indirect profits may be recovered.

The 1909 Act provided that a copyright proprietor is entitled to "all the profits which the infringer shall have made from such infringement. . . ." The language of the statute is broad enough to permit recovery of indirect as well as direct profits. At the same time, a court may deny recovery of a defendant's profits if they are only remotely or speculatively attributable to the infringement. *See, e.g., Roy Export Co. v. Columbia Broadcasting System, Inc.*, 503 F.Supp. 1137, 1156–57 (S.D.N.Y.1980) (profits from an infringing unsponsored television broadcast could not be ascertained since benefit received by CBS "consists of unmeasurable good-will with affiliates and increased stature and prestige vis-a-vis competitors."), *aff'd*, 672 F.2d 1095 (2d Cir. 1982).

The allowance of indirect profits was considered in *Sid & Marty Krofft Television Productions, Inc. v. McDonald's Corp.*, 1983 Copyright L. Rep. (CCH) P25,572 at 18,381 (C.D. Cal. 1983) (*Krofft II*), on remand from 562 F.2d 1157 (9th Cir.1977), a case involving facts analogous to those presented here. The plaintiffs, creators of the "H.R. Pufnstuf" children's television program, alleged that they were entitled to a portion of the profits McDonald's earned on its food sales as damages for the "McDonaldland" television commercials that infringed plaintiffs' copyright. The district court rejected as speculative the plaintiffs' formula for computing profits attributable to the infringement. However, the court's analysis and award of in lieu damages indicate that it considered indirect profits recoverable. The court stated, in awarding $1,044,000 in statutory damages, that "because a significant portion of defendants' profits made from the infringement are not ascertainable, a higher award of [statutory] in lieu damages is warranted."

Like the television commercials in *Krofft II*, *Hallelujah Hollywood* had promotional value. Defendants maintain that they endeavor to earn profits on all their operations and that *Hallelujah Hollywood* was a profit center. However, that fact does not detract from the promotional purposes of the show—to draw people to the hotel and the gaming tables. MGM's 1976 annual report states that "the hotel and gaming operations of the MGM Grand—Las Vegas continue to be materially enhanced by the popularity of the hotel's entertainment[, including] 'Hallelujah Hollywood', the spectacularly successful production revue. . . ." Given the promotional nature of *Hallelujah Hollywood*, we conclude indirect profits from the hotel and gaming operations, as well as direct profits from the show itself, are recoverable if ascertainable.

3. *Apportionment of Profits*

How to apportion profits between the infringers and the plaintiffs is a complex issue in this case. Apportionment of direct profits from the production as well as indirect profits from the hotel and casino operations are involved here, although the district court addressed only the former at the first trial.

When an infringer's profits are attributable to factors in addition to use of plaintiff's work, an apportionment of profits is proper. The burden of proving apportionment, (i.e., the contribution to profits of elements other than the infringed property), is the defendant's. We will not reverse a district court's findings regarding apportionment unless they are clearly erroneous.

After finding that the net profit earned by *Hallelujah Hollywood* was approximately $2,500,000, the district court offered the following explanation of apportionment:

> While no precise mathematical formula can be applied, the court concludes in light of the evidence presented at trial and the entire record in this case, a fair approximation of the profits of Act IV attributable to the infringement is $22,000.

The district court was correct that mathematical exactness is not required. However, a reasonable and just apportionment of profits is required.

Arriving at a proper method of apportionment and determining a specific amount to award is largely a factual exercise. Defendants understandably argue that the facts support the district court's award. They claim that the infringing material, six minutes of music in Act IV, was an unimportant part of the whole show, that the unique features of the Ziegfield Theater contributed more to the show's success than any other factor. This is proved, they argue, by the fact that when the music from *Kismet* was removed from *Hallelujah Hollywood* in 1976, the show suffered no decline in attendance and the hotel received no complaints.

Other evidence contradicts defendants' position. For instance, defendant Donn Arden testified that *Kismet* was "a very important part of the show" and "[he] hated to see it go." Moreover, while other acts were deleted from the shortened Saturday night versions of the show, Act IV "*Kismet*" never was.

We reject defendants' contention that the relative unimportance of the *Kismet* music was proved by its omission and the show's continued success thereafter. *Hallelujah Hollywood* was a revue, comprised of many different entertainment elements. Each element contributed significantly to the show's success, but no one element was the sole or overriding reason for that success. Just because one element could be omitted and the show goes on does not prove that the element was not important in the first instance and did not contribute to establishing the show's initial popularity.

The difficulty in this case is that the district court has not provided us with any reasoned explanation of or formula for its apportionment. We know only the district court's bottom line: that the plaintiffs are entitled to $22,000. Given the nature of the infringement, the character of the infringed property, the success of defendants' show, and the magnitude of the defendants' profits, the amount seems to be grossly inadequate. It amounts to less than one percent of MGM Grand's profits from the show, or roughly $13 for each of the 1700 infringing performances.

On remand, the district court should reconsider its apportionment of profits, and should fully explain on the record its reasons and the resulting method of apportionment it uses. Apportionment of indirect profits may be a part of the calculus. If the court finds that a reasonable, nonspeculative formula cannot be derived, or that the amount of profits a reasonable formula yields is insufficient to serve the purposes underlying the statute, then the court should award statutory damages. * * *

NOTES

1. Although *Frank Music* was decided under the 1909 Act, courts follow the same principles today in applying 17 U.S.C. § 504.

2. In calculating a damages award based on defendant's profits, should an infringer be permitted to subtract taxes paid on those profits? Should an infringer's profits be reduced by the cost of infringing inventory that has not been sold?

3. Some courts have permitted copyright infringers to deduct overhead expenses in calculating an award of the defendant's profits. *See Hamil America, Inc. v. GFI*, 193 F.3d 92 (2d Cir. 1999) (requiring a "nexus" between the overhead category and the infringing item); *ZZ Top v. Chrysler Corp.*, 70 F. Supp. 2d 1167 (W.D. Wash. 1999) (allowing willful infringer to deduct overhead, finding this an open question in the Ninth Circuit, and rejecting contrary authorities from other circuits).

4. In *Los Angeles News Service v. Reuters Television Int'l*, 149 F.3d 987 (9th Cir. 1998), the Ninth Circuit held that a copyright owner could recover infringement damages "flowing from" overseas exploitation of the defendant's domestic infringements. The court adopted the reasoning of the Second Circuit in *Sheldon v. Metro-Goldwyn Pictures Corp.*, 106 F.2d 45 (2d Cir. 1939), *aff'd*, 309 U.S. 390 (1940), which allowed recovery of damages from infringing uses abroad where a domestic infringing act made the foreign exploitation possible. The court distinguished cases such as *Subafilms, Ltd. v. MGM-Pathe Communications Co.*, 24 F.3d 1088, 1094 (9th Cir. 1994) (en banc), and *Allarcom Pay Television, Ltd. v. General Instrument Corp.*, 69 F.3d 381, 387 (9th Cir. 1995), in which no *liability* was found because there was no direct infringement in the United States. In 2003, the Ninth Circuit again looked at the issue of damages and profits from overseas infringing activity in *Los Angeles News Service v. Reuters Television Int'l*, 340 F.3d 926 (9th Cir. 2003). The court narrowed its previous holding, stating that the Copyright Act does not provide recovery of actual damages resulting from overseas infringement, but only the profits that the infringer derived from these infringements.

5. As an alternative to lost profits, actual damages may be based on the fair market value of a hypothetical license fee. *See, e.g., Gaylord v. United States*, 678 F.3d 1339 (Fed. Cir. 2012); *Polar Bear Prods., Inc. v. Timex Corp.*,

384 F.3d 700 (9th Cir. 2004); *On Davis v. The Gap, Inc.*, 246 F.3d 152 (2d Cir. 2001).

3. ADDITIONAL REMEDIES

a. Statutory Damages and Attorneys' Fees

Although a plaintiff may elect to recover statutory damages in place of actual damages and profits, in most cases involving infringement of exclusive rights under section 106, section 412 precludes an award of statutory damages or attorneys' fees for infringements which precede registration of the copyright in the infringed work. This rule does not apply to moral rights claims, because these are brought under section 106A, not section 106.

Even in the case of infringements under section 106, the rule is subject to a number of exceptions: First, it does not apply to claims brought under section 411(c). Second, it does not apply to *published* works that are registered within three months of publication, but which are infringed *between* publication and registration. 17 U.S.C. § 412(2). Third, the rule does not apply to works that are pre-registered under section 408(f) before the infringement occurs, and which have an effective registration date no later than three months after publication or one month after the copyright owner learns of the infringement.

A slightly different rule applies to pre-1972 sound recordings protected by section 1401. While copyright registration is not required (or even possible), a rights owner seeking to recover attorneys' fees or statutory damages for unauthorized activities must file a schedule with the Copyright Office identifying the title, artist, and rights owner of the recording, along with any other information specified in Copyright Office regulations; even then, attorneys' fees or statutory damages may be recovered only for unauthorized uses that take place at least 90 days after the filing becomes a public record.

In *Feltner v. Columbia Pictures Television, Inc.*, 523 U.S. 340, 355 (1998), the Supreme Court held that, while section 504(c) itself does not provide a right to a jury trial on the question of statutory damages, the Seventh Amendment "provides a right to a jury trial on all issues pertinent to an award of statutory damages under § 504(c) of the Copyright Act, including the amount itself."

Amount of Statutory Damages Recoverable: Section 504(c) establishes a wide range of discretion in the amount that a judge or jury may award, but permits only a *single* award of statutory damages for *each work* infringed by the defendant, regardless of how many acts of infringement took place. *See Venegas-Hernandez v. Sonolux Records*, 370 F.3d 183 (1st Cir. 2004). For statutory damages purposes, section 504 provides that all parts of a compilation or derivative work are considered a single work. However, some courts have departed from this rule where the individual components of a compilation have different copyright owners.

The amounts recoverable as statutory damages have increased substantially since 1976. Under the general rule, the minimum statutory damages award is $750 per work, and the maximum statutory damages award is $30,000 per work. However, a court may reduce the minimum award to $200 where the infringer was not aware, and had no reason to believe, that his or her acts constituted infringement. In contrast, if the infringement was willful, the court may increase the statutory damages award to $150,000. Infringement is considered willful if it is carried out with knowledge that the conduct is infringing. While willfulness is ultimately a question of fact, a 2004 amendment to section 504(c)(3)(A) creates a rebuttable presumption of willfulness where the violator (or a person acting in concert with the violator) knowingly provided materially false contact information in connection with registering, maintaining or renewing a domain name used in connection with the infringement.

Statutory damages are remitted altogether in the case of certain activities by nonprofit entities and public broadcasters if they believed their actions constituted fair use. This rule overrides the provisions of section 401 and 402 which make the innocent infringement defense unavailable with respect to works bearing a copyright notice.

During a period when the record industry brought a number of high-profile lawsuits based on unauthorized file-sharing by ordinary individuals, juries were remarkably generous in their statutory damages awards, to the dismay of both defendants and judges. In several cases, judges reduced these jury awards as excessive, even though the awards fell within the range allowed under section 504(c). In one case, the district judge called the jury's award of $1,920,000 for downloading 24 songs for personal use "shocking," and remitted the award to $54,000. A new trial on the same facts (on defendant's motion) produced a jury award of $1.5 million, which the district judge again remitted to $54,000. *See Capitol Records, Inc. v. Thomas-Rasset,* 799 F.Supp.2d 999 (2011). Many observers have expressed concern that section 504(c) permits statutory damages awards that seem grossly disproportionate to the actual harm suffered by the plaintiffs.

Under section 405(b), if copyright notice was omitted from copies distributed before March 1, 1989 (the effective date of the Berne Convention Implementation Act), an infringer who reasonably and in good faith believed that his or her conduct was noninfringing, and who was misled by the omission of notice, will incur no liability for actual or statutory damages for infringing acts undertaken before receiving actual notice of the copyright registration. Note, however, that section 405(b) permits a court to award other remedies, such as the defendant's profits, a reasonable royalty, or injunctive relief.

Standards for Awarding Attorneys' Fees: Section 505 permits a court at its discretion to award "full costs" and "a reasonable attorney's fee" to the prevailing party in infringement litigation. In *Fogerty v. Fantasy, Inc.*, 510 U.S. 517 (1994), the Supreme Court addressed a split of authority on whether the same standards should apply to prevailing plaintiffs as to prevailing defendants, or whether fees should be awarded to prevailing plaintiffs as a matter of course and to prevailing defendants only if the suit was frivolous or brought in bad faith. The Court held that the 1976 Act requires an "evenhanded" approach, finding no support in section 505 or its legislative history for treating plaintiffs and defendants differently.

Noting that there was "no precise rule or formula" for determining when an award was appropriate, the *Fogerty* Court nonetheless took note of certain nonexclusive factors that had been applied by courts in following the evenhanded approach:

> These factors include "frivolousness, motivation, objective unreasonableness (both in the factual and in the legal components of the case) and the need in particular circumstances to advance considerations of compensation and deterrence." We agree that such factors may be used to guide courts' discretion, so long as such factors are faithful to the purposes of the Copyright Act and are applied to prevailing plaintiffs and defendants in an evenhanded manner.

Id. at 534 n.19. Although bad faith is not a statutory prerequisite, in practice most courts have awarded attorneys' fees in copyright actions only against a party that has demonstrated some culpability, such as willful infringement or bad faith litigation.

NOTES

1. Why is copyright registration not required for an award of statutory damages or attorneys' fees for violations of sections 106A and 411(c)?

2. In a case involving continuing infringements of a plaintiff's copyrighted maps, where the infringements commenced before registration of most of those works and continued after registration, the Fifth Circuit held that a plaintiff could not recover, for the *same* infringed work, both actual damages for pre-registration infringements and statutory damages and attorneys' fees for post-registration infringements by the same defendant. *Mason v. Montgomery Data, Inc.*, 967 F.2d 135 (5th Cir. 1992). Note, however, that where a single action involves infringement of some unregistered and some registered works, the plaintiff may elect actual damages for the unregistered works and statutory damages (plus attorneys' fees) for the registered works.

3. In a suit for infringement of an unregistered work under section 106, section 412 provides that (subject to the various exceptions described earlier), prevailing plaintiffs may not recover attorneys' fees or statutory damages. This can make it difficult for authors of such works to retain legal counsel to represent them in infringement actions. Consider also whether this rule is appropriate in the case of works that have only been published abroad. (Most foreign countries do not require registration as a condition for copyright protection or remedies.)

b. Impounding, Importation Relief, Prejudgment Interest, and Costs

Impounding: A prevailing copyright plaintiff may obtain a court order impounding and ordering the disposition of the infringing copies as well as any articles that may be used to reproduce them. Typically the court will order that the items be turned over to the plaintiff, although outright destruction may also be ordered. 17 U.S.C. § 503.

Importation Relief: Under section 337 of the Tariff Act of 1930, a copyright owner may bring an action before the International Trade Commission to obtain an order barring importation of infringing goods, provided that the plaintiff's copyright has been registered. *See* 19 U.S.C. § 1337. Exclusion of goods that infringe registered copyrights is also available under 17 U.S.C. § 603.

Prejudgment Interest: Although the copyright statutes are silent on the availability of prejudgment interest, a number of courts have allowed it. *See, e.g., William A. Graham Co. v. Haughey*, 646 F.3d 138 (3d Cir. 2011).

Costs: Section 505 permits a court to award "full costs" to any party "other than the United States or an officer thereof," but provides no guidelines for the exercise of this discretion. In practice, most courts have awarded costs only against a party that demonstrates some degree of culpability.

c. Criminal Penalties

Under section 506, some instances of copyright infringement (as well as certain acts other than infringement, as specified in section 506(c)–(f)) may give rise to criminal prosecution and penalties. The penalties, which may include fines and/or imprisonment, are set forth in 18 U.S.C. §§ 2319–2319C. Criminal prosecution is also possible for certain violations of section 1101 (which prohibits bootlegging of live musical performances), *see* 18 U.S.C. § 2319A, as well as the DMCA's provisions on circumvention and copyright management information, *see* 17 U.S.C. § 1204. In contrast, moral rights violations do not give rise to criminal prosecution.

Prior to 1997, criminal penalties for infringement under section 506 applied only where the infringement was both willful and "for purposes of commercial advantage or private financial gain." 17 U.S.C. § 506(a). In *United States v. LaMacchia*, 871 F.Supp. 535 (D. Mass. 1994), the "commercial advantage" requirement prevented the government from prosecuting a defendant for criminal copyright infringement where he made internet sites available for others to receive and transmit copyrighted commercial software. The result under *LaMacchia* prompted concerns that malicious copiers could flood the internet with unauthorized copies of valuable works, causing serious harm to copyright owners, yet could avoid criminal prosecution if they were not seeking profits. *See* Information Infrastructure Task Force, Intellectual Property and the National Information Infrastructure, The Report of the Working Group on Intellectual Property Rights 228–29 (1995).

In 1997, Congress responded to these concerns by enacting the No Electronic Theft Act, which defined "private financial gain" to include the receipt of anything of value, including other copyrighted works, and also revised section 506(a) to reach willful copying or distribution with a total retail value of $1,000 or more within a 6-month period, even if the actions were not undertaken for commercial advantage or private financial gain.

Section 506(a) was broadened further by the Family Entertainment and Copyright Act of 2005, which expanded criminal infringement to include the unauthorized distribution of a work being prepared for commercial distribution, by making it available on a publicly-accessible computer network, by a person who knew or should have known that the work was intended for commercial distribution.

More recently, the Protect Lawful Streaming Act of 2020 added 18 U.S.C. § 2319C, making it a felony to willfully, and for the purpose of commercial advantage or private financial gain, offer to the public a digital transmission service that (1) is primarily designed to publicly perform copyrighted works unlawfully, (2) has no commercially significant purpose or use other than to publicly perform copyrighted works unlawfully, or (3) is intentionally marketed to promote its use in publicly performing copyrighted works unlawfully. Penalties for felony streaming include fines (under 18 U.S.C. § 3571) and/or imprisonment for (1) up to 3 years, or (2) up to 5 years if the defendant knew or should have known that the work was being prepared for commercial public performance, or (3) up to 10 years for a second or subsequent offense under either § 2319C or § 2319(a).

PART 7

PREEMPTION

■ ■ ■

CHAPTER 19

PREEMPTION OF STATE LAW BY FEDERAL PATENT AND COPYRIGHT LAW

■ ■■ ■

State laws protecting various forms of intellectual property will in some cases be unenforceable because they interfere with the functioning of the federal copyright or patent regime. Under the Supremacy Clause of the Constitution, federal law must prevail when such a conflict arises; this is called "conflict preemption." Because it is not always clear whether the operation of a particular state doctrine contravenes the intent of Congress, in section 301 of the Copyright Act of 1976 Congress specified certain conditions under which state laws would be preempted by federal copyright law. A comparable provision appears in the Semiconductor Chip Protection Act of 1984. *See* 17 U.S.C. § 912(c). In patent law, by contrast, there is no statutory preemption standard.

A. STATUTORY COPYRIGHT PREEMPTION: SECTION 301

Statute: 17 U.S.C.A. § 301

In the excerpt from H.Rep. No. 94–1476 which follows, note that the specific examples cited from 17 U.S.C. § 301(b)(3) of the 1976 Act were deleted prior to its passage. *See* H.R. Rep. No. 94–1733, 94th Cong., 2d Sess. 79 (1976). What impact does this have on your analysis of the scope of preemption under section 301?

COPYRIGHT ACT OF 1976

H.R. Rep. No. 94–1476.
94th Cong., 2d Sess. 129–33 (1976).

* * *

Section 301, one of the bedrock provisions of the bill, would accomplish a fundamental and significant change in the present law. Instead of a dual system of "common law copyright" for unpublished works and statutory copyright for published works, which has been the system in effect in the United States since the first copyright statute in 1790, the bill adopts a single system of Federal statutory copyright from creation. * * *

By substituting a single Federal system for the present anachronistic, uncertain, impractical, and highly complicated dual system, the bill would greatly improve the operation of the copyright law and would be much more effective in carrying out the basic constitutional aims of uniformity and the promotion of writing and scholarship. * * *

> * * * One of the fundamental purposes behind the copyright clause of the Constitution, as shown in Madison's comments in The Federalist, was to promote national uniformity and to avoid the practical difficulties of determining and enforcing an author's rights under the differing laws and in the separate courts of the various States. Today, when the methods for dissemination of an author's work are incomparably broader and faster than they were in 1789, national uniformity in copyright protection is even more essential than it was then to carry out the constitutional intent. * * *

Preemption of State law

The intention of section 301 is to preempt and abolish any rights under the common law or statutes of a State that are equivalent to copyright and that extend to works coming within the scope of the Federal copyright law. The declaration of this principle in section 301 is intended to be stated in the clearest and most unequivocal language possible, so as to foreclose any conceivable misinterpretation of its unqualified intention that Congress shall act preemptively, and to avoid the development of any vague borderline areas between State and Federal protection.

* * * Regardless of when the work was created and whether it is published or unpublished, disseminated or undisseminated, in the public domain or copyrighted under the Federal statute, the States cannot offer it protection equivalent to copyright. * * * The preemptive effect of section 301 is limited to State laws; as stated expressly in subsection (d) of section 301, there is no intention to deal with the question of whether Congress can or should offer the equivalent of copyright protection under some constitutional provision other than the patent-copyright clause of article 1, section 8.

As long as a work fits within one of the general subject matter categories of sections 102 and 103, the bill prevents the States from protecting it even if it fails to achieve Federal statutory copyright because it is too minimal or lacking in originality to qualify, or because it has fallen into the public domain. * * * [U]nfixed works are not included in the specified "subject matter of copyright." They are therefore not affected by the preemption of section 301, and would continue to be subject to protection under State statute or common law until fixed in tangible form.

The preemption of rights under State law is complete with respect to any work coming within the scope of the bill, even though the scope of exclusive rights given the work under the bill is narrower than the scope of common law rights in the work might have been.

* * *

In a general way subsection (b) of section 301 represents the obverse of subsection (a). It sets out, in broad terms and without necessarily being exhaustive, some of the principal areas of protection that preemption would not prevent the States from protecting. Its purpose is to make clear, consistent with the 1964 Supreme Court decisions in *Sears, Roebuck & Co. v. Stiffel Co.*, 376 U.S. 225, and *Compco Corp. v. Day-Brite Lighting, Inc.*, 376 U.S. 234, that preemption does not extend to causes of action, or subject matter outside the scope of the revised Federal copyright statute.

* * *

The examples in clause (3), while not exhaustive, are intended to illustrate rights and remedies that are different in nature from the rights comprised in a copyright and that may continue to be protected under State common law or statute. The evolving common law rights of "privacy," "publicity," and trade secrets, and the general laws of defamation and fraud, would remain unaffected as long as the causes of action contain elements, such as an invasion of personal rights or a breach of trust or confidentiality, that are different in kind from copyright infringement. Nothing in the bill derogates from the rights of parties to contract with each other and to sue for breaches of contract; however, to the extent that the unfair competition concept known as "interference with contract relations" is merely the equivalent of copyright protection, it would be preempted.

The last example listed in clause (3)—"deceptive trade practices such as passing off and false representation"—represents an effort to distinguish between those causes of action known as "unfair competition" that the copyright statute is not intended to preempt and those that it is. Section 301 is not intended to preempt common law protection in cases involving activities such as false labeling, fraudulent representation, and passing off even where the subject matter involved comes within the scope of the copyright statute.

"Misappropriation" is not necessarily synonymous with copyright infringement, and thus a cause of action labeled as "misappropriation" is not preempted if it is in fact based neither on a right within the general scope of copyright as specified by section 106 nor on a right equivalent thereto. For example, state law should have the flexibility to afford a remedy (under traditional principles of equity) against a consistent pattern of unauthorized appropriation by a competitor of the facts (i.e., not the literary expression) constituting "hot" news, whether in the traditional mold of *International News Service v. Associated Press*, 248 U.S. 215 (1918), or in the newer form of data updates from scientific, business, or financial data bases. Likewise, a person having no trust or other relationship with the proprietor of a computerized data base should not be immunized from sanctions against electronically or cryptographically breaching the proprietor's security arrangements and assessing proprietor's data. The unauthorized data access which should be remediable might also be achieved by the intentional interception of data transmissions by wire, microwave or laser transmissions, or by the common unintentional means of "crossed" telephone lines occasioned by errors in switching.

The proprietor of data displayed on the cathode ray tube of a computer terminal should be afforded protection against unauthorized printouts by third parties (with or without improper access), even if the data are not copyrightable. For example, the data may not be copyrighted because they are not fixed in a tangible medium of expression (i.e., the data are not displayed for a period [of] * * * more than transitory duration).

Nothing contained in section 301 precludes the owner of a material embodiment of a copy or a phonorecord from enforcing a claim of conversion against one who takes possession of the copy or phonorecord without consent.

* * *

COMPUTER ASSOCIATES INTERNATIONAL, INC. V. ALTAI, INC.

982 F.2d 693 (2d Cir. 1992).

[Plaintiff Computer Associates (CA) alleged that defendant Altai had copied portions of its ADAPTER software in creating Altai's competing OSCAR software; CA's complaint charged both copyright infringement and misappropriation of its trade secrets. The portion of the opinion addressing the copyright cause of action appears in Chapter 14.C.4., *supra*.]

* * *

II. Trade Secret Preemption

In its complaint, CA alleged that Altai misappropriated the trade secrets contained in the ADAPTER program. Prior to trial, while the proceedings were still before Judge Mishler, Altai moved to dismiss and for summary judgment on CA's trade secret misappropriation claim. Altai argued that section 301 of the Copyright Act preempted CA's state law cause of action. Judge Mishler denied Altai's motion, reasoning that " 'the elements of the tort of appropriation of trade secrets through the breach of contract or confidence by an employee are not the same as the elements of a claim of copyright infringement.' "

The parties addressed the preemption issue again, both in pre- and post-trial briefs. Judge Pratt then reconsidered and reversed Judge

Mishler's earlier ruling. The district court concluded that CA's trade secret claims were preempted because "CA—which is the master of its own case—has pleaded and proven facts which establish that one act constituted both copyright infringement and misappropriation of trade secrets [namely, the] copying of ADAPTER into OSCAR 3.4. . . ."

In our original opinion, we affirmed Judge Pratt's decision. * * * Upon reconsideration, we have granted the petition for rehearing, withdrawn our initial opinion, and conclude in this amended opinion that the district court's preemption ruling on CA's trade secret claims should be vacated. We accordingly vacate the judgment of the district court on this point and remand CA's trade secret claims for a determination on the merits.

A. *General Law of Copyright Preemption Regarding Trade Secrets and Computer Programs*

Congress carefully designed the statutory framework of federal copyright preemption. In order to insure that the enforcement of these rights remains solely within the federal domain, section 301(a) of the Copyright Act expressly preempts

> all legal or equitable rights that are equivalent to any of the exclusive rights within the general scope of copyright as specified by section 106 in works of authorship that are fixed in a tangible medium of expression and come within the subject matter of copyright as specified by sections 102 and 103. . . .

17 U.S.C. § 301(a). This sweeping displacement of state law is, however, limited by section 301(b), which provides, in relevant part, that

> nothing in this title annuls or limits any rights or remedies under the common law or statutes of any State with respect to . . . activities violating legal or equitable rights that are not equivalent to any of the exclusive rights within the general scope of copyright as specified by section 106. . . .

17 U.S.C. § 301(b)(3). * * *

Section 301 thus preempts only those state law rights that "may be abridged by an act which, in and of itself, would infringe one of the exclusive rights" provided by federal copyright law. *See Harper & Row, Publishers, Inc. v. Nation Enters.*, 723 F.2d 195, 200 (2d Cir.1983), *rev'd on other grounds*, 471 U.S. 539 (1985). But if an "extra element" is "required instead of or in addition to the acts of reproduction, performance, distribution or display, in order to constitute a state-created cause of action, then the right does not lie 'within the general scope of copyright,' and there is no preemption." 1 NIMMER § 1.01[B], at 1–14–15.

A state law claim is not preempted if the "extra element" changes the "nature of the action so that it is qualitatively different from a copyright infringement claim." *Mayer v. Josiah Wedgwood & Sons, Ltd.*, 601 F.Supp. 1523, 1535 (S.D.N.Y.1985); *see Harper & Row, Publishers, Inc.*, 723 F.2d at 201. To determine whether a claim meets this standard, we must determine "what plaintiff seeks to protect, the theories in which the matter is thought to be protected and the rights sought to be enforced." 1 ROGER M. MILGRIM, MILGRIM ON TRADE SECRETS § 2.06A[3], at 2–150 (1992) (hereinafter "MILGRIM"). An action will not be saved from preemption by elements such as awareness or intent, which alter "the action's scope but not its nature. . . ." *Mayer*, 601 F.Supp. at 1535.

Following this "extra element" test, we have held that unfair competition and misappropriation claims grounded solely in the copying of a plaintiff's protected expression are preempted by section 301. *See, e.g., Walker v. Time Life Films, Inc.*, 784 F.2d 44, 53 (2d Cir. 1986); *Warner Bros. Inc. v. American Broadcasting Cos.*, 720 F.2d 231, 247 (2d Cir.1983); *Durham Indus., Inc. v. Tomy Corp.*, 630 F.2d 905, 919 & n. 15 (2d Cir.1980). We also have held to be preempted a tortious interference with contract claim grounded in the impairment of a plaintiff's right under the Copyright Act to publish derivative works. *See Harper & Row, Publishers, Inc.*, 723 F.2d at 201.

However, many state law rights that can arise in connection with instances of copyright infringement satisfy the extra element test, and thus are not preempted by section 301. These include unfair competition claims based upon breach of confidential relationship, breach of fiduciary duty and trade secrets.

Trade secret protection, the branch of unfair competition law at issue in this case, remains a "uniquely valuable" weapon in the defensive arsenal of computer programmers. *See* 1 MILGRIM § 2.06A[5][c], at 2–172.4. Precisely because trade secret doctrine protects the discovery of ideas, processes, and systems which are explicitly precluded from coverage under copyright law, courts and commentators alike consider it a necessary and integral part of the intellectual property protection extended to computer programs.

* * *

Trade secret claims often are grounded upon a defendant's breach of a duty of trust or confidence to the plaintiff through improper disclosure of confidential material. The defendant's breach of duty is the gravamen of such trade secret claims, and supplies the "extra element" that qualitatively distinguishes such trade secret causes of action from claims for copyright infringement that are based solely upon copying.

B. Preemption in this Case

The district court stated that:

> Were CA's [trade secret] allegations premised on a theory of illegal acquisition of a trade secret, a charge that might have been alleged against Arney [its former employee who used the trade secrets in his new position working for defendant], who is not a defendant in this case, the preemption analysis might be different, for there seems to be no corresponding right guaranteed to copyright owners by § 106 of the copyright act.

Computer Assocs., 775 F.Supp. at 565. However, the court concluded that CA's trade secret claims were not grounded in a theory that Altai violated a duty of confidentiality to CA. Rather, Judge Pratt stated that CA proceeded against Altai solely "on a theory that the misappropriation took place by Altai's use of ADAPTER—the same theory as the copyright infringement count." *Id.* The district court reasoned that "the right to be free from trade secret misappropriation through 'use', and the right to exclusive reproduction and distribution of a copyrighted work are not distinguishable." *Id.* Because he concluded that there was no qualitative difference between the elements of CA's state law trade secret claims and a claim for federal copyright infringement, Judge Pratt ruled that CA's trade secret claims were preempted by section 301.

We agree with CA that the district court failed to address fully the factual and theoretical bases of CA's trade secret claims. The district court relied upon the fact that Arney—not Altai—allegedly breached a duty to CA of confidentiality by stealing secrets from CA and incorporating those secrets into OSCAR 3.4. However, under a wrongful acquisition theory based on RESTATEMENT (FIRST) OF TORTS § 757 (1939), Williams and Altai may be liable for violating CA's right of confidentiality. Section 757 states in relevant part:

> One who discloses or uses another's trade secret, without a privilege to do so, is liable to another if. . . . (c) he learned the secret from a third person with notice of the fact that it was a secret and that the third person discovered it by improper means or that the third person's disclosure of it was otherwise a breach of his duty to the other. . . .

Actual notice is not required for such a third party acquisition claim; constructive notice is sufficient. A defendant is on constructive notice when, "from the information which he has, a reasonable man would infer [a breach of confidence], or if, under the circumstances, a reasonable man would be put on inquiry and an inquiry pursued with reasonable intelligence and diligence would disclose the [breach]." *Id.*, comment 1 * * *.

We agree with the district court that New Jersey's governing governmental interest choice of law analysis directs the application of Texas law to CA's trade secret misappropriation claim. Texas law recognizes trade secret misappropriation claims grounded in the reasoning of Restatement section 757(c), and the facts alleged by CA may well support such a claim.

It is undisputed that, when [Altai employee, and former CA employee,] Arney stole the ADAPTER code and incorporated it into his design of OSCAR 3.4, he breached his confidentiality agreement with CA. The district court noted that while such action might constitute a valid claim against Arney, CA is the named defendant in this lawsuit. Additionally, the district court found, as a matter of fact, that "no one at Altai, other than Arney, knew that Arney had the ADAPTER code. . . ." *Computer Assocs.*, 775 F.Supp. at 554. However, the district court did not consider fully Altai's potential liability for improper trade secret acquisition. It did not consider the question of Altai's trade secret liability in connection with OSCAR 3.4 under a constructive notice theory, or Altai's potential liability under an actual notice theory in connection with OSCAR 3.5.

* * *

In response to CA's complaint, Altai rewrote OSCAR 3.4, creating OSCAR 3.5. While we agree with the district court that OSCAR 3.5 did not contain any expression protected by copyright, it may nevertheless still have embodied many of CA's trade secrets that Arney brought with him to Altai. Since Altai's rewrite was conducted with full knowledge of Arney's prior misappropriation, in breach of his duty of confidentiality, it follows that OSCAR 3.5 was created with actual knowledge of trade secret violations. Thus, with regard to OSCAR 3.5, CA has a viable trade secret claim against Altai that must be considered by the district court on remand. This claim is grounded in Altai's alleged use of CA's trade secrets in the creation of OSCAR 3.5, while on actual notice of Arney's theft of trade secrets and incorporation of those secrets into OSCAR 3.4. The district court correctly stated that a state law claim based solely upon Altai's "use", by copying, of ADAPTER's non-literal elements could not satisfy the governing "extra element" test, and would be preempted by section 301. However, where the use of copyrighted expression is simultaneously the violation of a duty of confidentiality established by state law, that extra element renders the state right qualitatively distinct from the federal right, thereby foreclosing preemption under section 301.

* * *

Accordingly, we vacate the judgment of the district court and remand for reconsideration of those aspects of CA's trade secret claims related to Altai's alleged constructive notice of Arney's theft of CA's trade secrets and incorporation of those secrets into OSCAR 3.4. We note, however, that CA may be unable to recover damages for its trade secrets which are embodied in OSCAR 3.4 since Altai has conceded copyright liability and damages for its incorporation of ADAPTER into OSCAR 3.4. CA may not obtain a double recovery where the damages for copyright infringement and trade secret misappropriation are coextensive.

* * *

NATIONAL BASKETBALL ASS'N V. MOTOROLA, INC.

105 F.3d 841 (2d Cir. 1997).

WINTER, CIRCUIT JUDGE:

Motorola, Inc. and Sports Team Analysis and Tracking Systems ("STATS") appeal from a permanent injunction entered by Judge Preska. The injunction concerns a handheld pager sold by Motorola and marketed under the name "SportsTrax," which displays updated information of professional basketball games in progress. The injunction prohibits appellants, absent authorization from the National Basketball Association and NBA Properties, Inc. (collectively the "NBA"), from transmitting scores or other data about NBA games in progress via the pagers, STATS's site on America On-Line's computer dial-up service, or "any equivalent means."

The crux of the dispute concerns the extent to which a state law "hot-news" misappropriation claim based on *International News Service v. Associated Press*, 248 U.S. 215 (1918) ("*INS*"), survives preemption by the federal Copyright Act and whether the NBA's claim fits within the surviving INS-type claims. We hold that a narrow "hot-news" exception does survive preemption. However, we also hold that appellants' transmission of "real-time" NBA game scores and information tabulated from television and radio broadcasts of games in progress does not constitute a misappropriation of "hot news" that is the property of the NBA.

* * *

I. Background

The facts are largely undisputed. Motorola manufactures and markets the SportsTrax paging device while STATS supplies the game information that is transmitted to the pagers. The product became available to the public in January 1996, at a retail price of about $200. SportsTrax's pager has an inch-and-a-half by inch-and-a-half screen and operates in four basic modes: "current," "statistics," "final scores" and "demonstration." It is the "current" mode that gives rise to the present dispute. In that mode, SportsTrax displays the following information on NBA games in progress: (i) the teams playing; (ii) score changes; (iii) the team in possession of the ball; (iv) whether the team is in the free-throw bonus; (v) the quarter of the game; and (vi) time remaining in the quarter. The information is updated every two to three minutes, with more frequent updates near the end of the first half and the end of the game. There is a lag of approximately two or three minutes between events in the game itself and when the information appears on the pager screen.

SportsTrax's operation relies on a "data feed" supplied by STATS reporters who watch the games on television or listen to them on the radio. The reporters key into a personal computer changes in the score and other information such as successful and missed shots, fouls, and clock updates. The information is relayed by modem to STATS's host computer, which compiles, analyzes, and formats the data for retransmission. The information is then sent to a common carrier, which then sends it via satellite to various local FM radio networks that in turn emit the signal received by the individual SportsTrax pagers.

* * *

II. The State Law Misappropriation Claim

A. *Summary of Ruling*

Because our disposition of the state law misappropriation claim rests in large part on preemption by the Copyright Act, our discussion necessarily goes beyond the elements of a misappropriation claim under New York law, and a summary of our ruling here will perhaps render that discussion—or at least the need for it—more understandable.

The issues before us are ones that have arisen in various forms over the course of this century as technology has steadily increased the speed and quantity of information transmission. Today, individuals at home, at work, or elsewhere, can use a computer, pager, or other device to obtain highly selective kinds of information virtually at will. *International News Service v. Associated Press*, 248 U.S. 215 (1918) ("*INS*") was one of the first cases to address the issues raised by these technological advances, although the technology involved in that case was primitive by contemporary standards. *INS* involved two wire services, the Associated Press ("AP") and International News Service ("INS"), that transmitted news stories by wire to member newspapers. INS would lift factual stories from AP bulletins and send them by wire to INS papers. INS would also take factual stories from east coast AP papers and wire them to INS papers on the west coast that had yet to publish because of time differentials. The Supreme Court held that INS's conduct was a common-law misappropriation of AP's property.

With the advance of technology, radio stations began "live" broadcasts of events such as baseball games and operas, and various entrepreneurs began to use the transmissions of others in one way or another for their own profit. In response, New York courts created a body of misappropriation law, loosely based on *INS*, that sought to apply ethical standards to the use by one party of another's transmissions of events.

Federal copyright law played little active role in this area until 1976. Before then, it appears to have been the general understanding—there being no case law of consequence—that live events such as baseball games were not copyrightable. Moreover, doubt existed even as to whether a recorded broadcast or videotape of such an event was copyrightable. In 1976, however, Congress passed legislation expressly affording copyright protection to simultaneously-recorded broadcasts of live performances such as sports events. *See* 17 U.S.C. § 101. Such protection was not extended to the underlying events.

The 1976 amendments also contained provisions preempting state law claims that enforced rights "equivalent" to exclusive copyright protections when the work to which the state claim was being applied fell within the area of copyright protection. *See* 17 U.S.C. § 301. Based on legislative history of the 1976 amendments, it is generally agreed that a "hot-news" *INS*-like claim survives preemption. H.R. No. 94–1476 at 132 (1976). However, much of New York misappropriation law after *INS* goes well beyond "hot-news" claims and is preempted.

We hold that the surviving "hot-news" *INS*-like claim is limited to cases where: (i) a plaintiff generates or gathers information at a cost; (ii) the information is time-sensitive; (iii) a defendant's use of the information constitutes free-riding on the plaintiff's efforts; (iv) the defendant is in direct competition with a product or service offered by the plaintiffs; and (v) the ability of other parties to free-ride on the efforts of the plaintiff or others would so reduce the incentive to produce the product or service that its existence or quality would be substantially threatened. We conclude that SportsTrax does not meet that test.

B. *Copyrights in Events or Broadcasts of Events*

The NBA asserted copyright infringement claims with regard both to the underlying games and to their broadcasts. The district court dismissed these claims, and the NBA does not appeal from their dismissal. Nevertheless, discussion of the infringement claims is necessary to provide the framework for analyzing the viability of the NBA's state law misappropriation claim in light of the Copyright Act's preemptive effect.

1. *Infringement of a Copyright in the Underlying Games*

In our view, the underlying basketball games do not fall within the subject matter of federal copyright protection because they do not constitute "original works of authorship" under 17 U.S.C. § 102(a). Section 102(a) lists eight categories of "works of authorship" covered by the act, including such categories as "literary works," "musical works," and "dramatic works." The list does not include athletic events, and, although the list is concededly non-exclusive, such events are neither similar nor analogous to any of the listed categories.

Sports events are not "authored" in any common sense of the word. There is, of course, at least at the professional level, considerable preparation for a game. However, the preparation is as much an expression of hope or faith as a determination of what will actually happen. Unlike movies, plays, television programs, or operas, athletic events are competitive and have no underlying script. Preparation may even cause mistakes to succeed, like the broken play in football that gains yardage because the opposition could not expect it. Athletic events may also result in wholly unanticipated occurrences, the most notable recent event being in a championship baseball game in which interference with a fly ball caused an umpire to signal erroneously a home run.

What "authorship" there is in a sports event, moreover, must be open to copying by competitors if fans are to be attracted. If the inventor of the T-formation in football had been able to copyright it, the sport might have come to an end instead of prospering. Even where athletic preparation most resembles authorship—figure skating, gymnastics, and, some would uncharitably say, professional wrestling—a performer who conceives and executes a particularly graceful and difficult—or, in the case of wrestling, seemingly painful—acrobatic feat cannot copyright it without impairing the underlying competition in the future. A claim of being the only athlete to perform a feat doesn't mean much if no one else is allowed to try.

For many of these reasons, NIMMER ON COPYRIGHT concludes that the "far more reasonable" position is that athletic events are not copyrightable. 1 M. NIMMER & D. NIMMER, NIMMER ON COPYRIGHT § 2.09[F] at 2–170.1 (1996). Nimmer notes that, among other problems, the number of joint copyright owners would arguably include the league, the teams, the athletes, umpires, stadium workers and even fans, who all contribute to the "work." Concededly, case law is scarce on the issue of whether organized events themselves are copyrightable, but what there is indicates that they are not. *See Prod. Contractors, Inc. v. WGN Continental Broadcasting Co.*, 622 F.Supp. 1500 (N.D.Ill.1985) (Christmas parade is not a work of authorship entitled to copyright protection). In claiming a copyright in the underlying games, the NBA relied in part on a footnote in *Baltimore Orioles, Inc. v. Major League Baseball Players Assn.*, 805 F.2d 663, 669 n. 7 (7th Cir.1986), which stated that the "players' performances" contain the "modest creativity required for copyrightability." However, the court went on to state, "Moreover, even if the players' performances were not sufficiently creative, the players agree that the cameramen and director contribute creative labor to the telecasts." *Id.* This last sentence indicates that the court was considering the copyrightability of telecasts—not the underlying games, which obviously can be played without cameras.

We believe that the lack of case law is attributable to a general understanding that athletic events were, and are, uncopyrightable. Indeed, prior to 1976, there was even doubt that broadcasts describing or depicting such events, which have a far stronger case for copyrightability than the events themselves, were entitled to copyright protection. Indeed, as described in the next subsection of this opinion, Congress found it necessary to extend such protection to recorded broadcasts of live events. The fact that Congress did not extend such protection to the events themselves confirms our view that the district court correctly held that appellants were not infringing a copyright in the NBA games.

2. Infringement of a Copyright in the Broadcasts of NBA Games

As noted, recorded broadcasts of NBA games—as opposed to the games themselves—are now entitled to copyright protection. The Copyright Act was amended in 1976 specifically to insure that simultaneously-recorded transmissions of live performances and sporting events would meet the Act's requirement that the original work of authorship be "fixed in any tangible medium of expression." 17 U.S.C. § 102(a). Accordingly, Section 101 of the Act, containing definitions, was amended to read:

> A work consisting of sounds, images, or both, that are being transmitted, is "fixed" for purposes of this title if a fixation of the work is being made simultaneously with its transmission.

17 U.S.C. § 101. Congress specifically had sporting events in mind:

> The bill seeks to resolve, through the definition of "fixation" in section 101, the status of live broadcasts—sports, news coverage, live performances of music, etc.—that are reaching the public in unfixed form but that are simultaneously being recorded.

H.R. No. 94–1476 at 52.

The House Report also makes clear that it is the broadcast, not the underlying game, that is the subject of copyright protection. In explaining how game broadcasts meet the Act's requirement that the subject matter be an "original work[ ] of authorship," 17 U.S.C. § 102(a), the House Report stated:

> When a football game is being covered by four television cameras, with a director guiding the activities of the four cameramen and choosing which of their electronic images are sent out to the public and in what order, there is little doubt that what the cameramen and the director are doing constitutes "authorship."

H.R. No. 94–1476 at 52.

Although the broadcasts are protected under copyright law, the district court correctly held that Motorola and STATS did not infringe NBA's copyright because they reproduced only facts from the broadcasts, not the expression or description of the game that constitutes the broadcast. The "fact/expression dichotomy" is a bedrock principle of copyright law that "limits severely the scope of protection in fact-based works." *Feist Publications, Inc. v. Rural Tel. Service Co.*, 499 U.S. 340, 350 (1991). " 'No author may copyright facts or ideas. The copyright is limited to those aspects of the work—termed 'expression'—that display the stamp of the author's originality.' " *Id.* (quoting *Harper & Row, Inc. v. Nation Enterprises*, 471 U.S. 539, 547–48 (1985)).

We agree with the district court that the "defendants provide purely factual information which any patron of an NBA game could acquire from the arena without any involvement from the director, cameramen, or others who contribute to the originality of a broadcast." 939 F.Supp. at 1094. Because the SportsTrax device and AOL site reproduce only factual information culled from the broadcasts and none of the copyrightable expression of the games, appellants did not infringe the copyright of the broadcasts.

C. *The State-Law Misappropriation Claim*

The district court's injunction was based on its conclusion that, under New York law, defendants had unlawfully misappropriated the NBA's property rights in its games. The district court reached this conclusion by holding: (i) that the NBA's misappropriation claim relating to the underlying games was not preempted by Section 301 of the Copyright Act; and (ii) that, under New York common law, defendants had engaged in unlawful misappropriation. We disagree.

1. *Preemption Under the Copyright Act*

a) Summary

When Congress amended the Copyright Act in 1976, it provided for the preemption of state law claims that are interrelated with copyright claims in certain ways. Under 17 U.S.C. § 301, a state law claim is preempted when: (i) the state law claim seeks to vindicate "legal or equitable rights that are equivalent" to one of the bundle of exclusive rights already protected by copyright law under 17 U.S.C. § 106—styled the "general scope requirement"; and (ii) the particular work to which the state law claim is being applied falls within the type of works protected by the Copyright Act under Sections 102 and 103—styled the "subject matter requirement."

The district court concluded that the NBA's misappropriation claim was not preempted because, with respect to the underlying games, as opposed to the broadcasts, the subject matter requirement was not met. The court dubbed as "partial preemption" its separate analysis of misappropriation claims relating to the underlying games and misappropriation claims relating to broadcasts of those games. The district court then relied on a series of older New York misappropriation cases involving radio broadcasts that considerably broadened *INS*. We hold that where the challenged copying or misappropriation relates in part to the copyrighted broadcasts of the games, the subject matter requirement is met as to both the broadcasts and the games. We therefore reject the partial preemption doctrine and its anomalous consequence that "it is possible for a plaintiff to assert claims both for infringement of its copyright in a broadcast and misappropriation of its rights in the underlying event." We do find that a properly-narrowed *INS* "hot-news" misappropriation claim survives preemption because it fails the general scope requirement, but that the broader theory of the radio broadcast cases relied upon by the district court were preempted when Congress extended copyright protection to simultaneously-recorded broadcasts.

b) "Partial Preemption" and the Subject Matter Requirement

The subject matter requirement is met when the work of authorship being copied or misappropriated "falls within the ambit of copyright protection." *Harper & Row, Inc. v. Nation Enterprises*, 723 F.2d 195, 200 (1983), *rev'd on other grounds*, 471 U.S. 539 (1985). We believe that the subject matter requirement is met in the instant matter and that the concept of "partial preemption" is not consistent with Section 301 of the Copyright Act. Although game broadcasts are copyrightable while the underlying games are not, the Copyright Act should not be read to distinguish between the two when analyzing the preemption of a misappropriation claim based on copying or taking from the copyrightable work. We believe that:

> Once a performance is reduced to tangible form, there is no distinction between the performance and the recording of the performance for the purposes of preemption under § 301(a). Thus, if a baseball game were not broadcast or were telecast without being recorded, the Players' performances similarly would not be fixed in tangible form and their rights of publicity would not be subject to preemption. By virtue of being videotaped, however, the Players' performances are fixed in tangible form, and any rights of publicity in their performances that are equivalent to the rights contained in the copyright of the telecast are preempted.

Baltimore Orioles, 805 F.2d at 675 (citation omitted).

Copyrightable material often contains uncopyrightable elements within it, but Section 301 preemption bars state law misappropriation claims with respect to uncopyrightable as well as copyrightable elements. In *Harper & Row*, for example, we held that state law claims based on the copying of excerpts from President Ford's memoirs were preempted even with respect to information that was purely factual and not copyrightable. We stated:

> The [Copyright] Act clearly embraces "works of authorship," including "literary works," as within its subject matter. The fact that portions of the Ford memoirs may consist of uncopyrightable material . . . does not take the work as a whole outside the subject matter protected by the Act. Were this not so, states would be free to expand the perimeters of copyright protection to their own liking, on the theory that preemption would be no bar to state protection of material not meeting federal statutory standards.

723 F.2d at 200 (citation omitted). The legislative history supports this understanding of Section 301(a)'s subject matter requirement. * * *

Adoption of a partial preemption doctrine—preemption of claims based on misappropriation of broadcasts but no preemption of claims based on misappropriation of underlying facts—would expand significantly the reach of state law claims and render the preemption intended by Congress unworkable. It is often difficult or impossible to separate the fixed copyrightable work from the underlying uncopyrightable events or facts. Moreover, Congress, in extending copyright protection only to the broadcasts and not to the underlying events, intended that the latter be in the public domain. Partial preemption turns that intent on its head by allowing state law to vest exclusive rights in material that Congress intended to be in the public domain and to make unlawful conduct that Congress intended to allow. This concern was recently expressed in *ProCD, Inc. v. Zeidenberg*, 86 F.3d 1447 (7th Cir.1996), a case in which the defendants reproduced non-copyrightable facts (telephone listings) from plaintiffs' copyrighted software. In discussing preemption under Section 301(a), Judge Easterbrook held that the subject matter requirement was met and noted:

> ProCD's software and data are "fixed in a tangible medium of expression", and the district judge held that they are "within the subject matter of copyright". The latter conclusion is plainly right for the copyrighted application program, and the judge thought that the data likewise are "within the subject matter of copyright" even if, after *Feist*, they are not sufficiently original to be copyrighted. *Baltimore Orioles, Inc. v. Major League Baseball Players Ass'n*, 805 F.2d 663, 676 (7th Cir.1986), supports that conclusion, with which commentators agree. . . . One function of § 301(a) is to prevent states from giving special protection to works of authorship that Congress has decided should be in the public domain, which it can accomplish only if "subject matter of copyright" includes all works of a type covered by sections 102 and 103, even if federal law does not afford protection to them.

ProCD, 86 F.3d at 1453 (citation omitted). We agree with Judge Easterbrook and reject the separate analysis of the underlying games and broadcasts of those games for purposes of preemption.

c) The General Scope Requirement

Under the general scope requirement, Section 301 "preempts only those state law rights that 'may be abridged by an act which, in and of itself, would infringe one of the exclusive rights' provided by federal copyright law." *Computer Assoc. Int'l, Inc. v. Altai, Inc.*, 982 F.2d 693, 716 (2d Cir.1992). However, certain forms of commercial misappropriation otherwise within the general scope requirement will survive preemption if an "extra-element" test is met. As stated in *Altai*:

> But if an "extra element" is "required instead of or in addition to the acts of reproduction, performance, distribution or display, in order to constitute a state-created cause of action, then the right does not lie 'within the general scope of copyright,' and there is no preemption."

Id.

ProCD was in part an application of the extra-element test. Having held the misappropriation claims to be preempted, Judge Easterbrook went on to hold that the plaintiffs could bring a state law contract claim. The court held that the defendants were bound by the software's shrink-wrap licenses as a matter of contract law and that the private contract rights were not preempted because they were not equivalent to the exclusive rights granted by copyright law. In other words, the contract right claims were not preempted because the general scope requirement was not met. *ProCD*, 86 F.3d at 1455.

We turn, therefore, to the question of the extent to which a "hot-news" misappropriation claim based on *INS* involves extra elements and is not the equivalent of exclusive rights under a copyright. Courts are generally agreed that some form of such a claim survives preemption. *Financial Information, Inc. v. Moody's Investors Service, Inc.*, 808 F.2d 204, 208 (2d Cir.1986) ("*FII*"). This conclusion is based in part on the legislative history of the 1976 amendments. The House Report stated:

> "Misappropriation" is not necessarily synonymous with copyright infringement, and thus a cause of action labeled as "misappropriation" is not preempted if it is in fact based neither on a right within the general scope of copyright as specified by section 106 nor on a right equivalent thereto. For example, state law should have the flexibility to afford a remedy (under traditional principles of equity) against a consistent pattern of unauthorized appropriation by a competitor of the facts (i.e., not the literary expression) constituting "hot" news, whether in the

> traditional mold of *International News Service v. Associated Press*, 248 U.S. 215 (1918), or in the newer form of data updates from scientific, business, or financial data bases.

H.R. No. 94–1476 at 132 (footnote omitted). The crucial question, therefore, is the breadth of the "hot-news" claim that survives preemption.

* * *

The theory of the New York misappropriation cases relied upon by the district court is considerably broader than that of *INS*. For example, the district court quoted at length from *Metropolitan Opera Ass'n v. Wagner-Nichols Recorder Corp.*, 101 N.Y.S.2d 483 (N.Y.Sup.Ct.1950), *aff'd*, 107 N.Y.S.2d 795 (1st Dep't 1951). *Metropolitan Opera* described New York misappropriation law as standing for the "broader principle that property rights of commercial value are to be and will be protected from any form of commercial immorality"; that misappropriation law developed "to deal with business malpractices offensive to the ethics of [ ] society"; and that the doctrine is "broad and flexible." 939 F.Supp. at 1098–1110 (quoting *Metropolitan Opera*, 101 N.Y.S.2d at 492, 488–89). However, we believe that *Metropolitan Opera*'s broad misappropriation doctrine based on amorphous concepts such as "commercial immorality" or society's "ethics" is preempted. Such concepts are virtually synonymous for wrongful copying and are in no meaningful fashion distinguishable from infringement of a copyright. The broad misappropriation doctrine relied upon by the district court is, therefore, the equivalent of exclusive rights in copyright law.

Indeed, we said as much in *FII*. That decision involved the copying of financial information by a rival financial reporting service and specifically repudiated the broad misappropriation doctrine of *Metropolitan Opera*. We explained:

> We are not persuaded by FII's argument that misappropriation is not "equivalent" to the exclusive rights provided by the Copyright Act. . . . Nor do we believe that a possible exception to the general rule of preemption in the misappropriation area—for claims involving "any form of commercial immorality," . . . quoting *Metropolitan Opera Ass'n v. Wagner-Nichols Recorder Corp.*, 101 N.Y.S.2d 483, . . .—should be applied here. We believe that no such exception exists and reject its use here. Whether or not reproduction of another's work is "immoral" depends on whether such use of the work is wrongful. If, for example, the work is in the public domain, then its use would not be wrongful. Likewise, if, as here, the work is unprotected by federal law because of lack of originality, then its use is neither unfair nor unjustified.

FII, 808 F.2d at 208. In fact, *FII* only begrudgingly concedes that even narrow "hot news" *INS*-type claims survive preemption. *Id.* at 209.

Moreover, *Computer Associates Intern., Inc. v. Altai Inc.* indicated that the "extra element" test should not be applied so as to allow state claims to survive preemption easily. 982 F.2d at 717. "An action will not be saved from preemption by elements such as awareness or intent, which alter 'the action's scope but not its nature'. . . . Following this 'extra element' test, we have held that unfair competition and misappropriation claims grounded solely in the copying of a plaintiff's protected expression are preempted by section 301." *Id.* (citation omitted).

In light of cases such as *FII* and *Altai* that emphasize the narrowness of state misappropriation claims that survive preemption, most of the broadcast cases relied upon by the NBA are simply not good law. Those cases were decided at a time when simultaneously-recorded broadcasts were not protected under the Copyright Act and when the state law claims they fashioned were not subject to federal preemption. For example, *Metropolitan Opera*, 101 N.Y.S.2d 483, involved the unauthorized copying, marketing, and sale of opera radio broadcasts. As another example, in *Mutual Broadcasting System v. Muzak Corp.*, 30 N.Y.S.2d 419 (N.Y.Sup. Ct. 1941), the defendant simultaneously retransmitted the plaintiff's baseball radio broadcasts onto telephone lines. As discussed above, the 1976 amendments to the Copyright Act were specifically designed to afford copyright protection to simultaneously-recorded broadcasts, and *Metropolitan Opera* and *Muzak* could today be brought as copyright infringement cases. Moreover, we believe that they would have to be brought as copyright cases because the amendments affording broadcasts copyright protection also preempted the state law misappropriation claims under which they were decided.

Our conclusion, therefore, is that only a narrow "hot-news" misappropriation claim survives preemption for actions concerning material within the realm of copyright.[7]

In our view, the elements central to an *INS* claim are: (i) the plaintiff generates or collects information at some cost or expense, *see FII*, 808 F.2d at 206; *INS*, 248 U.S. at 240; (ii) the value of the information is highly time-

---

[7] Quite apart from Copyright Act preemption, *INS* has long been regarded with skepticism by many courts and scholars and often confined strictly to its facts. In particular, Judge Learned Hand was notably hostile to a broad reading of the case. He wrote:

> We think that no more was covered than situations substantially similar to those then at bar. The difficulties of understanding it otherwise are insuperable. We are to suppose that the court meant to create a sort of common-law patent or copyright for reasons of justice. Either would flagrantly conflict with the scheme which Congress has for more than a century devised to cover the subject-matter.

Cheney Bros. v. Doris Silk Corp., 35 F.2d 279, 280 (2d Cir.1929), cert. denied, 281 U.S. 728 (1930). *See also* Restatement (Third) of Unfair Competition § 38 cmt. c (1995):

> The facts of the *INS* decision are unusual and may serve, in part, to limit its rationale. . . . The limited extent to which the *INS* rationale has been incorporated into the common law of the states indicate that the decision is properly viewed as a response to unusual circumstances rather than as a statement of generally applicable principles of common law. Many subsequent decisions have expressly limited the *INS* case to its facts.

sensitive, *see FII*, 808 F.2d at 209; *INS*, 248 U.S. at 231; RESTATEMENT (THIRD) UNFAIR COMPETITION, § 38 cmt. c.; (iii) the defendant's use of the information constitutes free-riding on the plaintiff's costly efforts to generate or collect it, *see FII*, 808 F.2d at 207; *INS*, 248 U.S. at 239–40; RESTATEMENT § 38 at cmt. c.; MCCARTHY, § 10:73 at 10–139; (iv) the defendant's use of the information is in direct competition with a product or service offered by the plaintiff, *FII*, 808 F.2d at 209, *INS*, 248 U.S. at 240; (v) the ability of other parties to free-ride on the efforts of the plaintiff would so reduce the incentive to produce the product or service that its existence or quality would be substantially threatened, *FII*, 808 F.2d at 209; RESTATEMENT, § 38 at cmt. c.; *INS*, 248 U.S. at 241 ("[INS's conduct] would render [AP's] publication profitless, or so little profitable as in effect to cut off the service by rendering the cost prohibitive in comparison with the return.").

INS is not about ethics; it is about the protection of property rights in time-sensitive information so that the information will be made available to the public by profit-seeking entrepreneurs. If services like AP were not assured of property rights in the news they pay to collect, they would cease to collect it. The ability of their competitors to appropriate their product at only nominal cost and thereby to disseminate a competing product at a lower price would destroy the incentive to collect news in the first place. The newspaper-reading public would suffer because no one would have an incentive to collect "hot news."

We therefore find the extra elements—those in addition to the elements of copyright infringement—that allow a "hot news" claim to survive preemption are: (i) the time-sensitive value of factual information, (ii) the free-riding by a defendant, and (iii) the threat to the very existence of the product or service provided by the plaintiff.

2. *The Legality of SportsTrax*

We conclude that Motorola and STATS have not engaged in unlawful misappropriation under the "hot-news" test set out above. To be sure, some of the elements of a "hot-news" *INS* claim are met. The information transmitted to SportsTrax is not precisely contemporaneous, but it is nevertheless time-sensitive. Also, the NBA does provide, or will shortly do so, information like that available through SportsTrax. It now offers a service called "Gamestats" that provides official play-by-play game sheets and half-time and final box scores within each arena. It also provides such information to the media in each arena. In the future, the NBA plans to enhance Gamestats so that it will be networked between the various arenas and will support a pager product analogous to SportsTrax. SportsTrax will of course directly compete with an enhanced Gamestats.

However, there are critical elements missing in the NBA's attempt to assert a "hot-news" *INS*-type claim. As framed by the NBA, their claim compresses and confuses three different informational products. The first product is generating the information by playing the games; the second product is transmitting live, full descriptions of those games; and the third product is collecting and retransmitting strictly factual information about the games. The first and second products are the NBA's primary business: producing basketball games for live attendance and licensing copyrighted broadcasts of those games. The collection and retransmission of strictly factual material about the games is a different product: e.g., box-scores in newspapers, summaries of statistics on television sports news, and real-time facts to be transmitted to pagers. In our view, the NBA has failed to show any competitive effect whatsoever from SportsTrax on the first and second products and a lack of any free-riding by SportsTrax on the third.

With regard to the NBA's primary products—producing basketball games with live attendance and licensing copyrighted broadcasts of those games—there is no evidence that anyone regards SportsTrax or the AOL site as a substitute for attending NBA games or watching them on television. In fact, Motorola markets SportsTrax as being designed "for those times when you cannot be at the arena, watch the game on TV, or listen to the radio . . ."

The NBA argues that the pager market is also relevant to a "hot-news" *INS*-type claim and that SportsTrax's future competition with Gamestats satisfies any missing element. We agree that there is a separate market for the real-time transmission of factual information to pagers or similar devices, such as STATS's AOL site. However, we disagree that SportsTrax is in any sense free-riding off Gamestats.

An indispensable element of an *INS* "hot-news" claim is free-riding by a defendant on a plaintiff's product, enabling the defendant to produce a directly competitive product for less money because it has lower costs. SportsTrax is not such a product. The use of pagers to transmit real-time information about NBA games requires: (i) the collecting of facts about the games; (ii) the transmission of these facts on a network; (iii) the assembling of them by the particular service; and (iv) the transmission of them to pagers or an on-line computer site. Appellants are in no way free-riding on Gamestats. Motorola and STATS expend their own resources to collect purely factual information generated in NBA games to transmit to SportsTrax pagers. They have their own network and assemble and transmit data themselves.

To be sure, if appellants in the future were to collect facts from an enhanced Gamestats pager to retransmit them to SportsTrax pagers, that would constitute free-riding and might well cause Gamestats to be unprofitable because it had to bear costs to collect facts that SportsTrax did not. If the appropriation of facts from one pager to another pager service were allowed, transmission of current information on NBA games to pagers or similar devices would be substantially deterred because any potential transmitter would know that the first entrant would quickly encounter a lower cost competitor free-riding on the originator's transmissions.

However, that is not the case in the instant matter. SportsTrax and Gamestats are each bearing their own costs of collecting factual information on NBA games, and, if one produces a product that is cheaper or otherwise superior to the other, that producer will prevail in the marketplace. This is obviously not the situation against which *INS* was intended to prevent: the potential lack of any such product or service because of the anticipation of free-riding.

For the foregoing reasons, the NBA has not shown any damage to any of its products based on free-riding by Motorola and STATS, and the NBA's misappropriation claim based on New York law is preempted.

* * *

NOTES

1. One of the cases cited in *NBA v. Motorola*, above, is *Baltimore Orioles, Inc. v. Major League Baseball Players Ass'n*, 805 F.2d 663 (7th Cir. 1986). In a footnote, the *Baltimore Orioles* court had rejected the players' argument that copyright law does not preempt the right of publicity "because the work that it protects—a public figure's persona—cannot be fixed in a tangible medium of expression," finding that "a performance is fixed in tangible form when it is recorded." 805 F.2d at 677 n.26. It also rejected the argument that the right of publicity is not the equivalent of any right under section 106 because it requires an "extra element" other than the "reproduction, performance, distribution or display of a copyrighted work," adding:

> [T]he right of publicity does not require an invasion of personal privacy to make out a cause of action. It is true that the rights of publicity and of privacy evolved from similar origins; however, whereas the right of privacy protects against intrusions on seclusion, public disclosure of private facts, and casting an individual in a false light in the public eye, the right of publicity protects against the unauthorized exploitation of names, likenesses, personalities, and performances that have acquired value for the very reason that they are known to the public.

Id. Was the court correct to reject these arguments?

2. Suppose that an organization representing professional athletes brings a right of publicity claim against fantasy sports providers that utilize the athletes' names, biographical data, and playing statistics in games offered to the public via the internet. Should this claim be preempted? *Cf. C.B.C. Distrib. & Marketing v. MLB Advanced Media*, 505 F.3d 818 (8th Cir. 2007). *See also Dryer v. NFL*, 814 F.3d 938, 943 (8th Cir. 2016) (finding right of publicity claims preempted by the Copyright Act because the claims brought

by former NFL players against the NFL were based on use of video footage within the subject matter of copyright and sought to control dissemination of the footage, which was equivalent to copyright's exclusive rights).

3. The plaintiff is a brokerage that conducts research on publicly traded securities as well as overall market conditions. Each morning before the markets open, the plaintiff delivers its reports and recommendations exclusively to clients and potential clients. This practice encourages investors to utilize the plaintiff's brokerage services, thus generating commissions. The defendant is a subscription-based news service which, through some unknown means, has been able to acquire and disseminate the plaintiff's recommendations each morning before they are released, thus eliminating the informational advantage of the plaintiff's clients, and making them less likely to place trades through the plaintiff's brokerage. If the plaintiff brings a misappropriation claim under New York law, alleging that defendant's actions have injured its business, should the defendant's preemption defense succeed? *See Barclays Capital, Inc. v. Theflyonthewall.com, Inc.*, 650 F.3d 876 (2d Cir. 2011).

4. In *Lowry's Reports, Inc. v. Legg Mason, Inc.*, 271 F. Supp. 2d 737 (D. Md. 2003), the district court held that Legg Mason's broadcast of Lowry's stock market numbers to its employees constituted a "public performance," which is an exclusive right of the copyright holder. Therefore, the court held that Lowry's "hot news" claim was preempted. Did the court reach the right conclusion?

5. Suppose that a well-known singer with a distinctive voice and performance style records a hit song. An advertising agency obtains permission from the owner of the copyright in the music and lyrics of the song to use the song in a television commercial, but the record company refuses to license the actual recording, and the singer refuses to perform the song for the commercial. The agency hires a "sound-alike" singer to imitate the original recording as closely as possible. On these facts, if state law gives the original singer a cause of action for infringement of her right of publicity, would that claim be preempted by section 301?

6. Under a state's commercial code, a security interest in mortgaged property can be perfected only by filing a UCC–1 filing statement with the secretary of state. Where the property in question is an exclusive interest in a copyright, section 205 of the 1976 Copyright Act allows recording security interests with the Copyright Office. Suppose a creditor has a security interest in all the assets of a corporation, including several copyrights. Under section 301, if the creditor records the mortgage only with the secretary of state, has the security interest been perfected?

7. Computer software is often sold subject to a click-through or shrink-wrap license which states that, by opening the package or by downloading the software, the purchaser agrees to certain limitations in exchange for the privilege of using that copy of the software. (For example, consider the license excerpted in Note 1 following the *Vernor v. Autodesk* case in Chapter 16,

supra.) These licenses may prohibit the licensee from engaging in activities that would otherwise be permissible under the copyright statutes (*e.g.*, copying that is permitted by section 117, or reverse engineering that constitutes fair use) Assuming the license is enforceable under state law, is enforcement barred under section 301? *Compare ProCD v. Zeidenberg,* 86 F.3d 1447 (7th Cir. 1996) (permitting enforcement) *and Bowers v. Baystate Techs., Inc.,* 320 F.3d 1317 (Fed. Cir. 2003) (similar) *with Vault Corp. v. Quaid Software Ltd.*, 847 F.2d 255 (5th Cir. 1988) (finding enforcement preempted).

8. Would section 301 preempt:

(a) a state law protecting data compilations against unauthorized copying of their informational content (as opposed to their arrangement)?

(b) a state resale royalty law?

(c) a state law allowing minors or incompetent persons to disaffirm written assignments of copyright?

(d) a state law enforcing oral transfers of copyright?

(e) a state law requiring film distributors to provide free screenings when requested by theatrical exhibitors prior to bidding on the right to exhibit those films?

(f) a state law unfair competition claim against a publisher for producing a work without properly crediting its author?

9. In *Rodrigue v. Rodrigue*, 218 F.3d 432, 436 (5th Cir. 2000), the Fifth Circuit held that state community property laws are not preempted by copyright law, noting that "even though the author's copyright arises at the moment of creation of the work, the Act explicitly allows for subsequent vesting in non-authors, either jointly with the author or subsequent to him by virtue of transfer of all or lesser portions of the copyright."

10. Note that § 301(b)(4) preserves laws regarding state and local landmarks, as well as preservation, zoning, or building codes relating to architectural works. This provision was added in 1995 as part of the Architectural Works Protection Act (AWPA). Would preemption under section 301 necessarily have followed the AWPA in the absence of subsection (4)?

11. *Statutory Preemption of Moral Rights Laws:* The Visual Artists Rights Act of 1990 (VARA), which became effective June 1, 1991, added section 301(f) preempting state laws providing equivalent rights. Consider the following questions:

(a) Would section 301 preempt a state law giving an artist a cause of action where the artist's name was removed from a work of visual art without his or her consent?

(b) Would section 301 preempt a state law granting creators of works of visual art a right of integrity, if the state law allowed that right to be exercised by a deceased artist's estate?

(c) Would section 301 preempt a state law granting novelists a right of integrity?

WRENCH LLC V. TACO BELL CORP.

256 F.3d 446 (6th Cir. 2001).

GRAHAM, DISTRICT JUDGE.

This case raises a question of first impression in this circuit regarding the extent to which the Copyright Act preempts state law claims based on breach of an implied-in-fact contract.

* * *

I. Background

Appellants Thomas Rinks and Joseph Shields are creators of the "Psycho Chihuahua" cartoon character which they promote, market, and license through their wholly-owned Michigan limited liability company, Wrench LLC. The parties have described Psycho Chihuahua as a clever, feisty dog with an attitude; a self-confident, edgy, cool dog who knows what he wants and will not back down.

In June 1996, Shields and Rinks attended a licensing trade show in New York City, where they were approached by two Taco Bell employees, Rudy Pollak, a vice president, and Ed Alfaro, a creative services manager. Pollak and Alfaro expressed interest in the Psycho Chihuahua character, which they thought would appeal to Taco Bell's core consumers, males aged eighteen to twenty-four. Pollak and Alfaro obtained some Psycho Chihuahua materials to take with them back to Taco Bell's headquarters in California.

Upon returning to California, Alfaro began promoting the Psycho Chihuahua idea within Taco Bell. Alfaro contacted Rinks and asked him to create art boards combining Psycho Chihuahua with the Taco Bell name and image. Rinks and Shields prepared the art boards and sent them to Alfaro along with Psycho Chihuahua T-shirts, hats, and stickers for Alfaro to use in promoting the character. Because Alfaro was not part of the marketing group at Taco Bell, he first sought to gain support for Psycho Chihuahua from top executives outside of the marketing department. After several meetings with non-marketing executives, Alfaro showed the Psycho Chihuahua materials to Vada Hill, Taco Bell's vice president of brand management, as well as to Taco Bell's then-outside advertising agency, Bozell Worldwide. Alfaro also tested the Psycho Chihuahua marketing concept with focus groups to gauge consumer reaction to the designs submitted by Rinks and Shields.

During this time period, Rinks told Alfaro that instead of using the cartoon version of Psycho Chihuahua in its television advertisements, Taco

Bell should use a live dog, manipulated by computer graphic imaging, with the personality of Psycho Chihuahua and a love for Taco Bell food. Rinks and Alfaro also discussed what it was going to cost for Taco Bell to use appellants' character, and although no specific numbers were mentioned, Alfaro understood that if Taco Bell used the Psycho Chihuahua concept, it would have to pay appellants.

In September 1996, Rinks and Shields hired Strategy Licensing ("Strategy"), a licensing agent, to represent Wrench in its dealings with Taco Bell. Representatives from Strategy contacted Alfaro about Taco Bell's interest in the Psycho Chihuahua concept, and presented him with additional materials for presentation to Taco Bell's advertising agency. These materials described Psycho Chihuahua as "irreverent," "edgy," and "spicy," with an "over-the-top" attitude and an "insatiable craving" for Taco Bell food. * * *

On November 18, 1996, Strategy representatives forwarded a licensing proposal to Alfaro. The proposal provided that Taco Bell would pay Wrench a fee based upon a percentage of the money spent on advertising; a percentage of Taco Bell's retail licensing sales; and a percentage of the cost of premiums, such as toys sold at Taco Bell restaurants. Taco Bell did not accept this proposal, although it did not explicitly reject it or indicate that it was ceasing further discussions with Wrench.

On December 5, 1996, Alfaro met with Hill, who had been promoted to the position of chief marketing officer, and others, to present various licensing ideas, including Psycho Chihuahua. On February 6, 1997, Alfaro again met with appellants and representatives of Strategy to review and finalize a formal presentation featuring Psycho Chihuahua that was to be given to Taco Bell's marketing department in early March 1997. At this meeting, appellants exhibited examples of possible Psycho Chihuahua promotional materials and also orally presented specific ideas for television commercials featuring a live dog manipulated by computer graphics imaging. These ideas included a commercial in which a male dog passed up a female dog in order to get to Taco Bell food. While Alfaro was meeting with appellants, another marketing firm, TLP Partnership ("TLP"), was also promoting appellants' Psycho Chihuahua to Taco Bell marketing executives. TLP presented several ideas, including the Psycho Chihuahua concept, to Taco Bell in anticipation of an upcoming summer promotion. TLP had discovered Psycho Chihuahua at a trade show in New York and had received Strategy's consent to use the image in its presentation. Alfaro was not aware of TLP's presentation. Following the presentation, Taco Bell conducted a series of focus groups to research the reaction to TLP's proposals. Psycho Chihuahua was received positively by consumers, but Taco Bell decided not to use any of TLP's ideas.

Alfaro was unable to arrange a meeting with the marketing department during March 1997 to present the Psycho Chihuahua materials. On April 4, 1997, however, Strategy made a formal presentation to Alfaro and his group using samples of uniform designs, T-shirts, food wrappers, posters, and cup designs based on the ideas discussed during the February 6, 1997, meeting. Alfaro and his group were impressed with Strategy's presentation.

On March 18, 1997, Taco Bell hired a new advertising agency, TBWA Chiat/Day ("Chiat/Day"). * * * Chuck Bennett and Clay Williams were designated as the creative directors of Taco Bell's account.

On June 2, 1997, Bennett and Williams proposed a commercial to Taco Bell in which a male Chihuahua would pass up a female Chihuahua to get to a person seated on a bench eating Taco Bell food. Bennett and Williams say that they conceived of the idea for this commercial one day as they were eating Mexican food at a sidewalk cafe and saw a Chihuahua trotting down the street, with no master or human intervention, "on a mission." Bennett and Williams contend that this image caused them jointly to conceive of the idea of using a Chihuahua as a way of personifying the intense desire for Taco Bell food. Williams subsequently wrote an advertisement script using a Chihuahua, which Taco Bell decided to produce as a television commercial.

When, in June 1997, Alfaro learned that Chiat/Day was planning to use a Chihuahua in a commercial, he contacted Hill again about the possibility of using Psycho Chihuahua. Hill passed Alfaro on to Chris Miller, a Taco Bell advertising manager and the liaison between Taco Bell's marketing department and Chiat/Day. On June 27, 1997, Alfaro gave Psycho Chihuahua materials to Miller along with a note suggesting that Taco Bell consider using Psycho Chihuahua as an icon and as a character in its advertising. Miller sent these materials to Chiat/Day, which received them sometime between June 28 and July 26.

Taco Bell aired its first Chihuahua commercial in the northeastern United States in July 1997, and received a very positive consumer reaction. On that basis, Taco Bell decided that the Chihuahua would be the focus of its 1998 marketing efforts, and launched a nationwide advertising campaign featuring Chihuahua commercials in late December 1997.

Appellants brought suit in January 1998, alleging breach of implied-in-fact contract as well as various tort and statutory claims under Michigan and California law. * * * Although the district court dismissed appellants' unjust enrichment, conversion, and dilution claims on the basis that they were preempted by the Copyright Act, the court held that appellants' misappropriation and unfair competition claims were not preempted because they required appellants to prove an "extra element" not required for a copyright infringement claim, namely, the existence of a legal relationship arising from an implied contract. * * * The district court also granted appellants leave to amend their conversion claim so that it might survive preemption.

* * *

A. Preemption

* * *

1. Subject Matter Requirement

Appellants contend that the district court erred in finding that their claims fell within the subject matter provisions of the Copyright Act. Appellants argue that their state law claims are based on ideas and concepts that were conveyed to Taco Bell in both tangible and intangible form. They conclude that their claims do not come within the subject matter of copyright, and are thus not preempted, because § 102(b) expressly excludes intangible ideas and concepts from the subject matter of copyright.

In *Wrench I*, the district court found that appellants' claims fell within the subject matter of copyright "because they are premised upon ideas and concepts fixed in a tangible medium of expression, namely, 'storyboards' and 'presentation materials' furnished by Plaintiffs." The district court reasoned that appellants' state law claims depended substantially upon works subject to the copyright protection, and did not arise solely out of intangible concepts that were orally conveyed to Taco Bell.

In reaching this conclusion, the district court relied on the Fourth Circuit's decision in [*United States ex rel. Berge v. Board of Trustees of the Univ. of Ala.*, 104 F.3d 1453 (4th Cir.1997)], in which a plaintiff brought a state law conversion action claiming that defendants had used ideas and methods contained in plaintiff's dissertation without her permission. The plaintiff contended that because ideas and methods are excluded from copyright protection under § 102, her state law claims could not be preempted under § 301. The court rejected this argument on the ground that the scope of protection afforded under copyright law is not the same as the scope of preemption. Rather, the court concluded that "the shadow actually cast by the Act's preemption is notably broader than the wing of its protection."

Appellants urge this court to reject this conclusion for the same reason urged by the plaintiff in *Berge*. Specifically, appellants argue that *Berge* does not comport with a literal reading of § 102(b), which expressly excludes ideas and other intangible forms of expression from copyright protection. Appellants rely on several district court cases which have held that because ideas and concepts are not afforded copyright protection, they are not within the subject matter of copyright. The appellate courts that have addressed this question have disagreed with the reasoning of the decisions cited by appellants, however. The Second, Fourth, and Seventh Circuits have held that the scope of the Copyright Act's subject matter extends beyond the tangible expressions that can be protected under the Act to elements of expression which themselves cannot be protected. *See, e.g., National Basketball Ass'n*, 105 F.3d at 849–850 (holding that subject matter of copyright under § 301 includes "uncopyrightable" as well as "copyrightable" elements); *Berge*, 104 F.3d at 1463 (finding that "scope and protection are not synonyms," and holding that uncopyrightable ideas that make up copyrightable works are within subject matter of copyright); *ProCD, Inc. v. Zeidenberg*, 86 F.3d 1447, 1453 (7th Cir.1996) (finding that uncopyrightable data underlying a copyrightable computer program are within subject matter of copyright). As the Second Circuit reasoned, the fact that copyrightable material contains uncopyrightable expressions should not remove the work from the subject matter of copyright under § 301, because otherwise "states would be free to expand the perimeters of copyright protection to their own liking, on the theory that preemption would be no bar to state protection of material not meeting federal statutory standards." *Harper & Row*, 723 F.2d at 200 (quoting H.R. Rep. No. 94–1476 at 130 (1976)).

We join our sister circuits in holding that the scope of the Copyright Act's subject matter is broader than the scope of the Act's protections. The record demonstrates that appellants expended considerable effort preparing and presenting tangible expressions of their Psycho Chihuahua concept for appellee, which expressions included storyboards, scripts, drawings, clothing designs, and packaging. The position now urged by appellants would require us to separate out appellants' intangible ideas from these tangible expressions, and would afford appellants a state law claim in the face of clear congressional intent to preempt such action. As the Seventh Circuit has noted, "[o]ne function of § 301(a) is to prevent states from giving special protection to works of authorship that Congress has decided should be in the public domain, which it can accomplish only if 'subject matter of copyright' includes all works of a type covered by sections 102 and 103, even if federal law does not afford protection to them." *Zeidenberg*, 86 F.3d at 1453. Thus, we conclude that the district court did not err with respect to the subject matter prong of its preemption analysis.

2. *Equivalency Requirement*

The second prong of the preemption analysis—the so-called "equivalency" or "general scope" requirement—augments the subject matter inquiry by asking whether the state common law or statutory action at issue asserts rights that are the same as those protected under § 106 of the Copyright Act. Under § 301(a), even if appellants' state law claims concern works within the subject matter of copyright, such claims will only be preempted if they assert rights that are "equivalent to any of the exclusive rights within the general scope of copyright as specified by section 106[.]" 17 U.S.C. § 301(a).

Equivalency exists if the right defined by state law may be abridged by an act which in and of itself would infringe one of the exclusive rights. *See Harper & Row*, 723 F.2d at 200. Conversely, if an extra element is required instead of or in addition to the acts of reproduction, performance, distribution or display in order to constitute a state-created cause of action, there is no preemption, provided that the extra element changes the nature of the action so that it is qualitatively different from a copyright infringement claim. *See id.*; *Rosciszewski v. Arete Associates, Inc.*, 1 F.3d 225, 230 (4th Cir.1993); *National Car Rental Sys., Inc. v. Computer Assocs. Intn'l, Inc.*, 991 F.2d 426, 431 (8th Cir.1993). We find that appellants' state law implied-in-fact contract claim survives preemption under these rules.

Under Michigan law, "[a]n implied contract, like other contracts, requires mutual assent and consideration." *Spruytte v. Dep't of Corr.*, 266 N.W.2d 482, 483 (Mich. Ct. App. 1978). Michigan draws a clear distinction between contracts implied in fact and contracts implied in law:

> The first does not exist, unless the minds of the parties meet, by reason of words or conduct. The second is quasi or constructive, and does not require a meeting of minds, but is imposed by fiction of law[.]

The gist of appellants' state law implied-in-fact contract claim is breach of an actual promise to pay for appellants' creative work. It is not the use of the work alone but the failure to pay for it that violates the contract and gives rise to the right to recover damages. Thus, the state law right is not abridged by an act which in and of itself would infringe one of the exclusive rights granted by § 106, since the right to be paid for the use of the work is not one of those rights.

An extra element is required instead of or in addition to the acts of reproduction, performance, distribution or display, in order to constitute the state-created cause of action. The extra element is the promise to pay. This extra element does change the nature of the action so that it is qualitatively different from a copyright infringement claim. The qualitative difference includes the requirement of proof of an enforceable promise and a breach thereof which requires, inter alia, proof of mutual assent and consideration, as well as proof of the value of the work and appellee's use thereof.

This qualitative difference is further reflected by the difference in the remedy afforded by the state law claim. Under Michigan law, a plaintiff's remedy for breach of an implied-in-fact contract includes recovery of the reasonable value of the services rendered, considering factors such as the general practice of the industry. * * *

Under the Copyright Act, remedies for infringement are limited to injunctions; impounding and destruction of infringing articles; recovery of the copyright owner's actual damages and any additional profits of the infringer or statutory damages; and costs and attorneys fees. *See* 17 U.S.C. §§ 502, 503, 504 and 505. The remedies available under copyright law do not include damages for the reasonable value of the defendants' use of the work. *See Business Trends Analysts, Inc. v. Freedonia Group, Inc.*, 887 F.2d 399, 406–07 (2d Cir.1989).

The proposition that a state law breach of contract claim based upon a promise to pay for the use of the work is not preempted is supported by an eminent authority on copyright law. *See* 1 NIMMER ON COPYRIGHT § 1.01[B][1][a] at 1–15 to 1–16, which states:

> [a] Breach of Contract. Adverting first to contract rights, an author's right to royalties under a publication contract may be conditioned upon the publisher's acts of reproduction and distribution of copies of the work, but there is also another crucial act that stands as a condition to the publisher's liability: the publisher's promise to pay the stated royalty. Without a promise there is no contract, while a promise on the part of one who engages in unlicensed reproduction or distribution is not required in order to constitute him a copyright infringer. Certainly, preemption should be denied, to the extent that a breach of contract cause of action alleges more than reproduction, adaptation, etc. simplicter of a copyrighted work.

Here, as in the example given in NIMMER ON COPYRIGHT, there is another crucial act that stands as a condition to the appellee's liability, to wit: its promise to pay for the use of the work. Thus, this is a case in which the breach of contract cause of action alleges more than reproduction, adaptation, etc., simplicter.

In finding that appellants' state law contract claim is not preempted, we do not embrace the proposition that all state law contract claims survive preemption simply because they involve the additional element of promise. *See, e.g., Zeidenberg*, 86 F.3d at 1454; *Taquino v. Teledyne Monarch Rubber*, 893 F.2d 1488, 1501 (5th Cir.1990) (appendix). Under that rationale, a contract which consisted only of a promise not to reproduce the copyrighted work would survive preemption even though it was limited to one of the exclusive rights enumerated in 17 U.S.C. § 106. If the promise amounts only to a promise to refrain from reproducing, performing, distributing or displaying the work, then the contract claim is preempted. The contrary result would clearly violate the rule that state law rights are preempted when they would be abridged by an act which in and of itself would infringe one of the exclusive rights of § 106. As the authors note in 1 NIMMER ON COPYRIGHT § 1.01[B][1][a] at 1–22: "Although the vast majority of contract claims will presumably survive scrutiny . . . nonetheless preemption should continue to strike down claims that, though denominated 'contract,' nonetheless complain directly about the reproduction of expressive materials."

* * *

For the purpose of the preemption analysis, there is a crucial difference between a claim based on quasi-contract, i.e., a contract implied in law, and a claim based upon a contract implied in fact. In the former, the action depends on nothing more than the unauthorized use of the work. Thus, an action based on a contract implied in law requires no extra element in addition to an act of reproduction, performance, distribution or display, whereas an action based on a contract implied in fact requires the extra element of a promise to pay for the use of the work which is implied from the conduct of the parties. * * *

Here, appellants' implied-in-fact contract claim contains the essential element of expectation of compensation which is an element not envisioned by § 106. *See Cascaden*, 225 N.W. at 511–12 ("Plaintiffs cannot recover on the theory of a contract implied in fact, for the work was not done . . . under circumstances authorizing plaintiffs to entertain an expectation of pay from defendants.").

We conclude that the district court erred with respect to the equivalency prong of the preemption analysis and find that appellants' state law implied-in-fact contract claim is not preempted by the Copyright Act.

* * *

NOTES

1. In *Utopia Provider Systems v. Pro-Med Clinical Systems*, 596 F.3d 1313 (11th Cir. 2010), the court held that a state law claim for breach of a license agreement included additional elements—the existence and breach of a contract—which precluded preemption. *Cf. R.W. Beck, Inc. v. E3 Consulting*, 577 F.3d 1133 (10th Cir. 2009) (unfair competition and unjust enrichment claims for alleged copying of engineering reports preempted). In *ATC Distribution Group, Inc. v. Whatever It Takes Transmissions & Parts, Inc.*, 402 F.3d 700 (6th Cir. 2005), an automobile transmission parts seller's claims against a competitor for unfair competition, unjust enrichment, and misappropriation, based on copying of the seller's parts catalog, were preempted by federal copyright law. Even though the catalog was found to be insufficiently original to warrant copyright protection, the catalog was nevertheless within the scope of copyrightable subject matter.

2. Preemption cases under Section 301 abound, and their outcomes are not always consistent. Among the more interesting cases are: *Montz v. Pilgrim*

Films & Television, Inc., 649 F.3d 975 (9th Cir. 2011) (en banc) (breach of implied contract and breach of confidence claims by writers arising from use of their ideas not preempted); *Sturdza v. United Arab Emirates,* 281 F.3d 1287 (D.C. Cir. 2002) (claims in architectural concepts not preempted); *Lipscher v. LRP Publications, Inc.*, 266 F.3d 1305 (11th Cir. 2001) (claims challenging use of published jury verdict reports preempted); *Archie Comic Publications, Inc. v. DeCarlo*, 141 F. Supp. 2d 428 (S.D.N.Y. 2001) (claims for rights in comic book characters preempted); *Design Art Inc. v. National Football League Properties Inc.*, 2000 WL 33151646 (S.D. Cal. 2000) (claims challenging use of logo preempted); *Chicago Style Productions, Inc. v. Chicago Sun Times, Inc.*, 728 N.E.2d 1204 (2000) (law claim for theft of an idea preempted).

In *GlobeRanger Corp. v. Software AG*, 691 F.3d 702 (5th Cir. 2012), the plaintiff developed RFID software. After losing to defendant on a bid for a government contract, plaintiff brought several state claims including conversion of plaintiff's software, conspiracy, tortious interference, and unfair competition. The court held that most of the state claims were not preempted under the Copyright Act because the plaintiff plausibly pled more than a copying of material that would be protected subject matter under the Copyright Act and because the claims did not protect rights equivalent to the exclusive rights of a federal copyright. The conversion claim related to intangible property, however, and thus could be preempted by the Copyright Act.

In *Tire Eng'g and Distr'n, LLC v. Shandong Linglong Rubber Co., Ltd.*, 682 F.3d 292 (4th Cir. 2012), a domestic tire producer brought suit against two foreign corporations, alleging they conspired to steal tire blueprints, produce infringing tires, and resell them. Plaintiff brought a number of claims, including federal copyright claims and state claims. The court affirmed the defendant's liability under the Copyright Act and for conversion under Virginia law, but it dismissed the other theories of liability. A claim for conspiracy to infringe copyrights was preempted by the Copyright Act since the core of the two claims are the same; the extra element of agreement in a conspiracy claim did not prevent the claims from being equivalent. The Virginia claims of conversion and conspiracy to convert were held to be not preempted by the Copyright Act (the latter was set aside for other reasons), because both claims involved an extra element of defendant's unlawful retention of physical objects from plaintiff, and they were thus not equivalent to a Copyright Act claim.

Finally, in *Forest Park Pictures v. Universal Television Network, Inc.*, 683 F.3d 424 (2d Cir. 2012), the plaintiffs developed an idea for a TV series and created a writing that embodied it. They submitted the idea to defendant, who then appropriated it. Plaintiffs brought a claim for breach of contract, alleging defendant made an implied promise to pay reasonable compensation if defendant used the idea. The court held that the plaintiff had adequately alleged the breach of contract claim. It further held that because that claim was based on rights that are not equivalent to those protected by the Copyright Act (*i.e.* contract rights against an individual as opposed to rights against the public at large), the state contract claim was not preempted by the Copyright Act.

3. Has Congress achieved its stated goal of establishing clear and unequivocal rules regarding preemption under section 301?

4. Until 2018, federal law did not protect pre-1972 sound recordings. and thus did not preempt state law protection for those recordings. Accordingly, many states provided copyright-like protection to those recordings under statutes or judge-made law. As discussed in Chapter 14, however, the Music Modernization Act of 2018 added section 1401 to Title 17, which extends to those recordings a sui generis form of federal protection that is similar though not identical to copyright. In making this change, Congress also changed the rules on preemption.

Until 2018, § 301(c) stated that state laws protecting sound recordings fixed before February 15, 1972 would not be preempted by federal copyright law until February 15, 2067. However, the Music Modernization Act amended § 301(c) to state that federal preemption under § 301(a) applies to activities involving pre-1972 sound recordings, effective October 11, 2018. Although the statutory language is far from clear, it appears that Congress intended federal law to preempt state laws providing those recordings with protection equivalent to that of section 1401. This appears to encompass state laws recognizing exclusive rights of reproduction, distribution, adaptation, and digital audio transmissions with respect to pre-1972 sound recordings. Beyond that, the scope and effect of the new preemption rule are unclear.

B. CONFLICT PREEMPTION

1. THE SEARS/COMPCO DECISIONS

SEARS, ROEBUCK & CO. V. STIFFEL COMPANY

376 U.S. 225, 84 S.Ct. 784 (1964).

MR. JUSTICE BLACK delivered the opinion of the Court.

The question in this case is whether a State's unfair competition law can, consistently with the federal patent laws, impose liability for or prohibit the copying of an article which is protected by neither a federal patent nor a copyright. The respondent, Stiffel Company, secured design and mechanical patents on a "pole lamp"—a vertical tube having lamp fixtures along the outside, the tube being made so that it will stand upright between the floor and ceiling of a room. Pole lamps proved a decided commercial success, and soon after Stiffel brought them on the market Sears, Roebuck & Company put on the market a substantially identical lamp, which it sold more cheaply, Sears' retail price being about the same as Stiffel's wholesale price. Stiffel then brought this action against Sears in the United States District Court for the Northern District of Illinois, claiming in its first count that by copying its design Sears had infringed Stiffel's patents and in its second count that by selling copies of Stiffel's lamp Sears had caused confusion in the trade as to the source of the lamps and had thereby engaged in unfair competition under Illinois law. There was evidence that identifying tags were not attached to the Sears lamps although labels appeared on the cartons in which they were delivered to customers, that customers had asked Stiffel whether its lamps differed from Sears', and that in two cases customers who had bought Stiffel lamps had complained to Stiffel on learning that Sears was selling substantially identical lamps at a much lower price.

The District Court, after holding the patents invalid for want of invention, went on to find as a fact that Sears' lamp was "a substantially exact copy" of Stiffel's and that the two lamps were so much alike, both in appearance and in functional details, "that confusion between them is likely, and some confusion has already occurred." On these findings the court held Sears guilty of unfair competition, enjoined Sears "from unfairly competing with [Stiffel] by selling or attempting to sell pole lamps identical to or confusingly similar to" Stiffel's lamp, and ordered an accounting to fix profits and damages resulting from Sears' "unfair competition."

The Court of Appeals affirmed. That court held that, to make out a case of unfair competition under Illinois law, there was no need to show that Sears had been "palming off" its lamps as Stiffel lamps; Stiffel had only to prove that there was a "likelihood of confusion as to the source of the products"—that the two articles were sufficiently identical that customers could not tell who had made a particular one. Impressed by the "remarkable sameness of appearance" of the lamps, the Court of Appeals upheld the trial court's findings of likelihood of confusion and some actual confusion, findings which the appellate court construed to mean confusion "as to the source of the lamps." The Court of Appeals thought this enough under Illinois law to sustain the trial court's holding of unfair competition, and thus held Sears liable under Illinois law for doing no more than copying and marketing an unpatented article. We granted certiorari to consider whether this use of a State's law of unfair competition is compatible with the federal patent law.

* * * [T]he patent system is one in which uniform federal standards are carefully used to promote invention while at the same time preserving free competition. Obviously a State could not, consistently with the Supremacy Clause of the Constitution,[8] extend the life of a patent beyond its expiration date or give a patent on an article which lacked the level of invention required for federal patents. To do either would run counter to the policy of Congress of granting patents only to true inventions, and then only for a limited time. Just as a State cannot encroach upon the federal patent laws directly, it cannot, under some other law, such as that forbidding unfair competition, give protection of a kind that clashes with the objectives of the federal patent laws.

[8] U.S. Const., Art. VI.

In the present case the "pole lamp" sold by Stiffel has been held not to be entitled to the protection of either a mechanical or a design patent. An unpatentable article, like an article on which the patent has expired, is in the public domain and may be made and sold by whoever chooses to do so. What Sears did was to copy Stiffel's design and to sell lamps almost identical to those sold by Stiffel. This it had every right to do under the federal patent laws. That Stiffel originated the pole lamp and made it popular is immaterial. "Sharing in the goodwill of an article unprotected by patent or trade-mark is the exercise of a right possessed by all—and in the free exercise of which the consuming public is deeply interested." *Kellogg Co. v. National Biscuit Co.*, 305 U.S. 111, 122 (1938). To allow a State by use of its law of unfair competition to prevent the copying of an article which represents too slight an advance to be patented would be to permit the State to block off from the public something which federal law has said belongs to the public. The result would be that while federal law grants only 14 or 17 years' protection to genuine inventions, *see* 35 U. S. C. §§ 154, 173, States could allow perpetual protection to articles too lacking in novelty to merit any patent at all under federal constitutional standards. This would be too great an encroachment on the federal patent system to be tolerated.

Sears has been held liable here for unfair competition because of a finding of likelihood of confusion based only on the fact that Sears' lamp was copied from Stiffel's unpatented lamp and that consequently the two looked exactly alike. Of course there could be "confusion" as to who had manufactured these nearly identical articles. But mere inability of the public to tell two identical articles apart is not enough to support an injunction against copying or an award of damages for copying that which the federal patent laws permit to be copied. Doubtless a State may, in appropriate circumstances, require that goods, whether patented or unpatented, be labeled or that other precautionary steps be taken to prevent customers from being misled as to the source, just as it may protect businesses in the use of their trademarks, labels, or distinctive dress in the packaging of goods so as to prevent others, by imitating such markings, from misleading purchasers as to the source of the goods. But because of the federal patent laws a State may not, when the article is unpatented and uncopyrighted, prohibit the copying of the article itself or award damages for such copying. The judgment below did both and in so doing gave Stiffel the equivalent of a patent monopoly on its unpatented lamp. That was error, and Sears is entitled to a judgment in its favor.

Reversed.

NOTE

Simultaneously with *Sears*, the Supreme Court decided *Compco Corp. v. Day-Brite Lighting, Inc.*, 376 U.S. 234 (1964), which involved a claim under the same Illinois unfair competition law, again based on the copying of a lamp design—specifically, "a reflector having cross-ribs claimed to give both strength and attractiveness to the fixture" for which a design patent had been issued. Although the district court found the plaintiff's design patent invalid, it also found that the design was distinctive and was not the only one available to the defendant, and that defendant's copying was likely to confuse the public. The court of appeals upheld the award of an injunction and damages. The Supreme Court reversed, noting that even if there was a likelihood of confusion, the state law could not be enforced on these facts:

> Notwithstanding the thinness of the evidence to support findings of likely and actual confusion among purchasers, we do not find it necessary in this case to determine whether there is "clear error" in these findings. They, like those in *Sears, Roebuck & Co. v. Stiffel Co., supra,* were based wholly on the fact that selling an article which is an exact copy of another unpatented article is likely to produce and did in this case produce confusion as to the source of the article. Even accepting the findings, we hold that the order for an accounting for damages and the injunction are in conflict with the federal patent laws. Today we have held in *Sears, Roebuck & Co. v. Stiffel Co., supra,* that when an article is unprotected by a patent or a copyright, state law may not forbid others to copy that article. To forbid copying would interfere with the federal policy, found in Art. I, § 8, cl. 8, of the Constitution and in the implementing federal statutes, of allowing free access to copy whatever the federal patent and copyright laws leave in the public domain. Here Day-Brite's fixture has been held not to be entitled to a design or mechanical patent. Under the federal patent laws it is, therefore, in the public domain and can be copied in every detail by whoever pleases. It is true that the trial court found that the configuration of Day-Brite's fixture identified Day-Brite to the trade because the arrangement of the ribbing had, like a trademark, acquired a "secondary meaning" by which that particular design was associated with Day-Brite. But if the design is not entitled to a design patent or other federal statutory protection, then it can be copied at will.
>
> As we have said in *Sears*, while the federal patent laws prevent a State from prohibiting the copying and selling of unpatented articles, they do not stand in the way of state law, statutory or decisional, which requires those who make and sell copies to take precautions to identify their products as their own. A State of course has power to impose liability upon those who, knowing that the public is relying upon an original manufacturer's reputation for quality and integrity, deceive the public by palming off their copies as the original. That an article copied from an unpatented article could be made in some other way, that the design is "nonfunctional" and not essential to the use of either article, that the configuration of the article copied may have a "secondary meaning" which identifies the

maker to the trade, or that there may be "confusion" among purchasers as to which article is which or as to who is the maker, may be relevant evidence in applying a State's law requiring such precautions as labeling; however, and regardless of the copier's motives, neither these facts nor any others can furnish a basis for imposing liability for or prohibiting the actual acts of copying and selling. And of course a State cannot hold a copier accountable in damages for failure to label or otherwise to identify his goods unless his failure is in violation of valid state statutory or decisional law requiring the copier to label or take other precautions to prevent confusion of customers as to the source of the goods.

Compco, 376 U.S. at 237–39. Do *Sears* and *Compco* invalidate state unfair competition laws that provide a cause of action for copying nonfunctional design elements that acquire secondary meaning?

2. DEVELOPMENTS AFTER SEARS/COMPCO

GOLDSTEIN V. CALIFORNIA

412 U.S. 546, 93 S.Ct. 2303 (1973).

MR. CHIEF JUSTICE BURGER delivered the opinion of the Court.

[Petitioners were convicted of violating California's "record piracy" law, Calif. Penal Code § 653h, which forbids making unauthorized copies of any musical recordings, regardless of the age of the recording. Although, after this case commenced, Congress amended the copyright statutes to grant copyright protection to sound recordings fixed on or after February 15, 1972, all of the recordings at issue in this case were fixed prior to that date.]

* * *

Petitioners' attack on the constitutionality of § 653h has many facets. First, they contend that the statute establishes a state copyright of unlimited duration, and thus conflicts with Art. I, § 8, cl. 8, of the Constitution. Second, petitioners claim that the state statute interferes with the implementation of federal policies inherent in the federal copyright statutes. According to petitioners, it was the intention of Congress, as interpreted by this Court in *Sears, Roebuck & Co. v. Stiffel Co.*, 376 U.S. 225 (1964), and *Compco Corp. v. Day-Brite Lighting*, 376 U.S. 234 (1964), to establish a uniform law throughout the United States to protect original writings. As part of the federal scheme, it is urged that Congress intended to allow individuals to copy any work which was not protected by a federal copyright. Since § 653h effectively prohibits the copying of works which are not entitled to federal protection, petitioners contend that it conflicts directly with congressional policy and must fall under the Supremacy Clause of the Constitution. * * *

II

Petitioners' first argument rests on the premise that the state statute under which they were convicted lies beyond the powers which the States reserved in our federal system. If this is correct, petitioners must prevail, since the States cannot exercise a sovereign power which, under the Constitution, they have relinquished to the Federal Government for its exclusive exercise.

A

* * * The clause of the Constitution granting to Congress the power to issue copyrights does not provide that such power shall vest exclusively in the Federal Government. Nor does the Constitution expressly provide that such power shall not be exercised by the States.

* * *

The question whether exclusive federal power must be inferred is not a simple one, for the powers recognized in the Constitution are broad and the nature of their application varied. * * * We must also be careful to distinguish those situations in which the concurrent exercise of a power by the Federal Government and the States or by the States alone may possibly lead to conflicts and those situations where conflicts will necessarily arise. "It is not . . . a mere possibility of inconvenience in the exercise of powers, but an immediate constitutional repugnancy that can by implication alienate and extinguish a pre-existing right of [state] sovereignty." The Federalist No. 32, p. 243 (B. Wright ed. 1961).

* * *

The objective of the Copyright Clause was clearly to facilitate the granting of rights national in scope. * * *

Although the Copyright Clause thus recognizes the potential benefits of a national system, it does not indicate that all writings are of national interest or that state legislation is, in all cases, unnecessary or precluded. * * * [I]t is unlikely that all citizens in all parts of the country place the same importance on works relating to all subjects. Since the subject matter to which the Copyright Clause is addressed may thus be of purely local importance and not worthy of national attention or protection, we cannot discern such an unyielding national interest as to require an inference that state power to grant copyrights has been relinquished to exclusive federal control.

The question to which we next turn is whether, in actual operation, the exercise of the power to grant copyrights by some States will prejudice the interests of other States. As we have noted, a copyright granted by a particular State has effect only within its boundaries. If one State grants such protection, the interests of States which do not are not prejudiced since their citizens remain free to copy within their borders those works which may be protected elsewhere. * * * We do not see here the type of prejudicial conflicts which would arise, for example, if each State exercised a sovereign power to impose imposts and tariffs; nor can we discern a need for uniformity such as that which may apply to the regulation of interstate shipments.

Similarly, it is difficult to see how the concurrent exercise of the power to grant copyrights by Congress and the States will necessarily and inevitably lead to difficulty. At any time Congress determines that a particular category of "writing" is worthy of national protection and the incidental expenses of federal administration, federal copyright protection may be authorized. Where the need for free and unrestricted distribution of a writing is thought to be required by the national interest, the Copyright Clause and the Commerce Clause would allow Congress to eschew all protection. In such cases, a conflict would develop if a State attempted to protect that which Congress intended to be free from restraint or to free that which Congress had protected. However, where Congress determines that neither federal protection nor freedom from restraint is required by the national interest, it is at liberty to stay its hand entirely. Since state protection would not then conflict with federal action, total relinquishment of the States' power to grant copyright protection cannot be inferred.

As we have seen, the language of the Constitution neither explicitly precludes the States from granting copyrights nor grants such authority exclusively to the Federal Government. The subject matter to which the Copyright Clause is addressed may at times be of purely local concern. No conflict will necessarily arise from a lack of uniform state regulation, nor will the interest of one State be significantly prejudiced by the actions of another. No reason exists why Congress must take affirmative action either to authorize protection of all categories of writings or to free them from all restraint. We therefore conclude that, under the Constitution, the States have not relinquished all power to grant to authors "the exclusive Right to their respective Writings."

* * *

III

Our conclusion that California did not surrender its power to issue copyrights does not end the inquiry. We must proceed to determine whether the challenged state statute is void under the Supremacy Clause. No simple formula can capture the complexities of this determination; the conflicts which may develop between state and federal action are as varied as the fields to which congressional action may apply. "Our primary function is to determine whether, under the circumstances of this particular case, [the state] law stands as an obstacle to the accomplishment and execution of the full purposes and objectives of Congress." *Hines v. Davidowitz*, 312 U.S. 52, 67 (1941). * * *

[The Court reviewed the historical context and legislative history of the 1909 Act and concluded that Congress in enacting those provisions had not decided to deny copyright protection to sound recordings, but had simply not considered the question.]

Petitioners' argument does not rest entirely on the belief that Congress intended specifically to exempt recordings of performances from state control. Assuming that no such intention may be found, they argue that Congress so occupied the field of copyright protection as to pre-empt all comparable state action. * * *

Sears and *Compco*, on which petitioners rely, do not support their position. In those cases, the question was whether a State could, under principles of a state unfair competition law, preclude the copying of mechanical configurations which did not possess the qualities required for the granting of a federal design or mechanical patent. * * *

In regard to mechanical configurations, Congress had balanced the need to encourage innovation and originality of invention against the need to insure competition in the sale of identical or substantially identical products. The standards established for granting federal patent protection to machines thus indicated not only which articles in this particular category Congress wished to protect, but which configurations it wished to remain free. The application of state law in these cases to prevent the copying of articles which did not meet the requirements for federal protection disturbed the careful balance which Congress had drawn and thereby necessarily gave way under the Supremacy Clause of the Constitution. No comparable conflict between state law and federal law arises in the case of recordings of musical performances. In regard to this category of "Writings," Congress has drawn no balance; rather, it has left the area unattended, and no reason exists why the State should not be free to act.

IV

* * *

In sum, we have shown that § 653h does not conflict with the federal copyright statute enacted by Congress in 1909. Similarly, no conflict exists between the federal copyright statute passed in 1971 and the present application of § 653h, since California charged petitioners only with copying recordings fixed prior to February 15, 1972. Finally, we have concluded that our decisions in *Sears* and *Compco*, which we reaffirm today, have no application in the present case, since Congress has indicated neither that it wishes to protect, nor to free from protection, recordings of musical performances fixed prior to February 15, 1972.

We conclude that the State of California has exercised a power which it retained under the Constitution, and that the challenged statute, as applied in this case, does not intrude into an area which Congress has, up to now, pre-empted. Until and unless Congress takes further action with respect to recordings fixed prior to February 15, 1972, the California statute may be enforced against acts of piracy such as those which occurred in the present case.

Affirmed.

NOTE

Goldstein was decided under the 1909 Act. Although the general principles discussed in *Goldstein* remain good law, the question of whether and to what extent federal law preempts state law protection for pre-1972 sound recordings became a matter of statutory interpretation under the 1976 Act. As discussed in Note 4 following *Wrench v. Taco Bell*, *supra*, section 301(c) of the 1976 Act (most recently amended in 2018) specifically addresses federal preemption of state laws protecting those recordings.

KEWANEE OIL CO. V. BICRON CORP.

416 U.S. 470, 94 S.Ct. 1879 (1974).

MR. CHIEF JUSTICE BURGER delivered the opinion of the Court.

We granted certiorari to resolve a question on which there is a conflict in the courts of appeals: whether state trade secret protection is pre-empted by operation of the federal patent law. In the instant case the Court of Appeals for the Sixth Circuit held that there was pre-emption. The Courts of Appeals for the Second, Fourth, Fifth and Ninth Circuits have reached the opposite conclusion.

I

[Petitioner's Harshaw division developed a synthetic crystal using a variety of processes that it considered to be trade secrets. Several of Harshaw's employees, who had executed confidentiality agreements as a condition of their employment, subsequently left Harshaw and went to work for Bicron, which thereafter began producing the same crystal. When petitioner brought an action for misappropriation of its trade secrets, the district court awarded injunctive relief.]

The Court of Appeals for the Sixth Circuit held that the findings of fact by the District Court were not clearly erroneous, and that it was evident from the record that the individual Respondents appropriated to the benefit of Bicron secret information on processes obtained while they were employees at Harshaw. Further, the Court of Appeals held that the District Court properly applied Ohio law relating to trade secrets. Nevertheless, the Court of Appeals reversed the District Court, finding Ohio's trade secret law to be in conflict with the patent laws of the United States. The Court of Appeals reasoned that Ohio could not grant monopoly protection to processes and manufacturing techniques that were appropriate subjects for consideration under 35 U.S.C. § 101 for a federal patent but which had been in commercial use for over one year and so were no longer eligible for patent protection under 35 U.S.C. § 102(b).

We hold that Ohio's law of trade secrets is not preempted by the patent laws of the United States, and, accordingly, we reverse.

II

Ohio has adopted the widely relied-upon definition of a trade secret found at RESTATEMENT OF TORTS § 757, comment b (1939). According to the RESTATEMENT, "(a) trade secret may consist of any formula, pattern, device or compilation of information which is used in one's business, and which gives him an opportunity to obtain an advantage over competitors who do not know or use it. It may be a formula for a chemical compound, a process of manufacturing, treating or preserving materials, a pattern for a machine or other device, or a list of customers."

The subject of a trade secret must be secret, and must not be of public knowledge or of a general knowledge in the trade or business. This necessary element of secrecy is not lost, however, if the holder of the trade secret reveals the trade secret to another "in confidence, and under an implied obligation not to use or disclose it." *Cincinnati Bell Foundry Co. v. Dodds*, 10 Ohio Dec.Reprint 154, 156, 19 Weekly Law Bull. 84 (Super.Ct.1887). These others may include those of the holder's "employees to whom it is necessary to confide it, in order to apply it to the uses for which it is intended." *National Tube Co. v. Eastern Tube Co, supra*, 3 Ohio Cir.Ct.R., N.S., at 462. Often the recipient of confidential knowledge of the subject of a trade secret is a licensee of its holder. *See Lear, Inc. v. Adkins*, 395 U.S. 653 (1969).

The protection accorded the trade secret holder is against the disclosure or unauthorized use of the trade secret by those to whom the secret has been confided under the express or implied restriction of nondisclosure or nonuse. The law also protects the holder of a trade secret against disclosure or use when the knowledge is gained, not by the owner's volition, but by some "improper means," RESTATEMENT OF TORTS § 757(a), which may include theft, wiretapping, or even aerial reconnaissance. A trade secret law, however, does not offer protection against discovery by fair and honest means, such as by independent invention, accidental disclosure, or by so-called reverse engineering, that is by starting with the known product and working backward to divine the process which aided in its development or manufacture.

Novelty, in the patent law sense, is not required for a trade secret, *W. R. Grace & Co. v. Hargadine*, 392 F.2d, at 14. "Quite clearly discovery is something less than invention." *A. O. Smith Corp. v. Petroleum Iron Works Co.*, 73 F.2d 531, 538 (C.A.6 1934), *modified to increase scope of injunction*, 74 F.2d 934 (1935). However, some novelty will be required if merely because that which does not possess novelty is usually known; secrecy, in the context of trade secrets, thus implies at least minimal novelty.

The subject matter of a patent is limited to a "process, machine, manufacture, or composition of matter, or . . . improvement thereof," 35 U.S.C. § 101, which fulfills the three conditions of novelty and utility as articulated and defined in 35 U.S.C. §§ 101 and 102, and nonobviousness, as set out in 35 U.S.C. § 103. If an invention meets the rigorous statutory tests for the issuance of a patent, the patent is granted, for a period of 17 years, giving what has been described as the "right of exclusion," R. ELLIS, PATENT ASSIGNMENTS AND LICENSES § 4, p. 7 (2d ed. 1943). This protection goes not only to copying the subject matter, which is forbidden under the Copyright Act, 17 U.S.C. § 1 *et seq.*, but also to independent creation.

III

The first issue we deal with is whether the States are forbidden to act at all in the area of protection of the kinds of intellectual property which may make up the subject matter of trade secrets.

Article I, § 8, cl. 8, of the Constitution grants to the Congress the power "(t)o promote the Progress of Science and useful Arts, by securing for limited Times to Authors and Inventors the exclusive Right to their respective Writings and Discoveries . . ." In the 1972 Term, in *Goldstein v. California*, 412 U.S. 546 (1973), we held that the cl. 8 grant of power to Congress was not exclusive and that, at least in the case of writings, the States were not prohibited from encouraging and protecting the efforts of those within their borders by appropriate legislation. * * *

Just as the States may exercise regulatory power over writings so may the States regulate with respect to discoveries. States may hold diverse viewpoints in protecting intellectual property to invention as they do in protecting the intellectual property relating to the subject matter of copyright. The only limitation on the States is that in regulating the area of patents and copyrights they do not conflict with the operation of the laws in this area passed by Congress, and it is to that more difficult question we now turn.

IV

The question of whether the trade secret law of Ohio is void under the Supremacy Clause involves a consideration of whether that law "stands as an obstacle to the accomplishment and execution of the full purposes and objectives of Congress." *Hines v. Davidowitz*, 312 U.S. 52, 67 (1941). We stated in *Sears, Roebuck & Co. v. Stiffel Co.*, 376 U.S. 225, 229 (1964), that when state law touches upon the area of federal statutes enacted pursuant to constitutional authority, "it is 'familiar doctrine' that the federal policy 'may not be set at naught, or its benefits denied' by the state law. *Sola Elec. Co. v. Jefferson Elec. Co.*, 317 U.S. 173, 173 (1942). This is true, of course, even if the state law is enacted in the exercise of otherwise undoubted state power."

The laws which the Court of Appeals in this case held to be in conflict with the Ohio law of trade secrets were the patent laws passed by the Congress in the unchallenged exercise of its clear power under Art. I, § 8, cl. 8, of the Constitution. The patent law does not explicitly endorse or forbid the operation of trade secret law. However, as we have noted, if the scheme of protection developed by Ohio respecting trade secrets "clashes with the objectives of the federal patent laws," *Sears, Roebuck & Co. v. Stiffel Co., supra*, 376 U.S., at 231, then the state law must fall. To determine whether the Ohio law "clashes" with the federal law it is helpful to examine the objectives of both the patent and trade secret laws.

The stated objective of the Constitution in granting the power to Congress to legislate in the area of intellectual property is to "promote the Progress of Science and useful Arts." The patent laws promote this progress by offering a right of exclusion for a limited period as an incentive to inventors to risk the often enormous costs in terms of time, research, and development. The productive effort thereby fostered will have a positive effect on society through the introduction of new products and processes of manufacture into the economy, and the emanations by way of increased employment and better lives for our citizens. In return for the right of exclusion—this "reward for inventions," *Universal Oil Co. v. Globe Co.*, 322 U.S. 471, 484 (1944)—the patent laws impose upon the inventor a requirement of disclosure. To insure adequate and full disclosure so that upon the expiration of the 17-year period "the knowledge of the invention [illegible] are thus enabled without restriction to practice it and profit by its use," *United States v. Dubilier Condenser Corp.*, 289 U.S. 178, 187 (1933), the patent laws require that the patent application shall include a full and clear description of the invention and "of the manner and process of making and using it" so that any person skilled in the art may make and use the invention. 35 U.S.C. § 112. When a patent is granted and the information contained in it is circulated to the general public and those especially skilled in the trade, such additions to the general store of knowledge are of such importance to the public weal that the Federal Government is willing to pay the high price of 17 years of exclusive use for its disclosure, which disclosure, it is assumed, will stimulate ideas and the eventual development of further significant advances in the art. The Court has also articulated another policy of the patent law: that which is in the public domain cannot be removed therefrom by action of the States.

* * *

The maintenance of standards of commercial ethics and the encouragement of invention are the broadly stated policies behind trade secret law. "The necessity of good faith and honest, fair dealing, is the very life and spirit of the commercial world." *National Tube Co. v. Eastern Tube Co.*, 3 Ohio Cir.Cr.R., N.S. at 462. In *A. O. Smith Corp. v. Petroleum Iron Works Co.*, 73 F.2d, at 539, the Court emphasized that even though a discovery may not be patentable, that does not "destroy the value of the discovery to one who makes it, or advantage the competitor who by unfair means, or as the beneficiary of a broken faith, obtains the desired knowledge without himself paying the price in labor, money, or machines expended by the discover." In *Wexler v. Greenberg*, 399 Pa. 569, 578–579, 160 A.2d 430, 434–435 (1960), the Pennsylvania Supreme Court noted the importance of trade secret protection to the subsidization of research and development and to increased economic efficiency within large companies through the dispersion of responsibilities for creative developments.

Having now in mind the objectives of both the patent and trade secret law, we turn to an examination of the interaction of these systems of protection of intellectual property—one established by the Congress and the other by a State—to determine whether and under what circumstances the latter might constitute "too great an encroachment on the federal patent system to be tolerated." *Sears, Roebuck & Co. v. Stiffel Co.*, 376 U.S., at 232.

As we noted earlier, trade secret law protects items which would not be proper subjects for consideration for patent protection under 35 U.S.C. § 101. As in the case of the recordings in *Goldstein v. California*, Congress, with respect to nonpatentable subject matter, "has drawn no balance; rather, it has left the area unattended, and no reason exists why the State should not be free to act." *Goldstein v. California, supra*, 412 U.S., at 570 (footnote omitted).

Since no patent is available for a discovery, however useful, novel, and nonobvious, unless it falls within one of the express categories of patentable subject matter of 35 U.S.C. § 101, the holder of such a discovery would have no reason to apply for a patent whether trade secret protection existed or not. Abolition of trade secret protection would, therefore, not result in increased disclosure to the public of discoveries in the area of nonpatentable subject matter. Also, it is hard to see how the public would be benefited by disclosure of customer lists or advertising campaigns; in fact, keeping such items secret encourages businesses to initiate new and individualized plans of operation, and constructive competition results. This, in turn, leads to a greater variety of business methods than would otherwise be the case if privately developed marketing and other data were passed illicitly among firms involved in the same enterprise.

Congress has spoken in the area of those discoveries which fall within one of the categories of patentable subject matter of 35 U.S.C. § 101 and which are, therefore, of a nature that would be subject to consideration for a patent. Processes, machines, manufactures, compositions of matter and improvements thereof, which meet the tests of utility, novelty, and nonobviousness are entitled to be patented, but those which do not, are not. The question remains whether those items which are proper subjects for consideration for a patent may also have available the alternative protection accorded by trade secret law.

Certainly the patent policy of encouraging invention is not disturbed by the existence of another form of incentive to invention. In this respect the two systems are not and never would be in conflict. Similarly, the policy that matter once in the public domain must remain in the public domain is not incompatible with the existence of trade secret protection. By definition a trade secret has not been placed in the public domain.

The more difficult objective of the patent law to reconcile with trade secret law is that of disclosure, the quid pro quo of the right to exclude. We are helped in this stage of the analysis by Judge Henry Friendly's opinion in *Painton & Co. v. Bourns, Inc.*, 442 F.2d 216 (C.A.2 1971). There the Court of Appeals thought it useful, in determining whether inventors will refrain because of the existence of trade secret law from applying for patents, thereby depriving the public from learning of the invention, to distinguish between three categories of trade secrets: "(1) the trade secret believed by its owner to constitute a validly patentable invention; (2) the trade secret known to its owner not to be so patentable; and (3) the trade secret whose valid patentability is considered dubious." *Id.*, at 224. Trade secret protection in each of these categories would run against breaches of confidence—the employee and licensee situations—and theft and other forms of industrial espionage.

As to the trade secret known not to meet the standards of patentability, very little in the way of disclosure would be accomplished by abolishing trade secret protection. With trade secrets of nonpatentable subject matter, the patent alternative would not reasonably be available to the inventor. "There can be no public interest in stimulating developers of such (unpatentable) knowhow to flood an overburdened Patent Office with applications (for) what they do not consider patentable." *Ibid.* The mere filing of applications doomed to be turned down by the Patent Office will bring forth no new public knowledge or enlightenment, since under federal statute and regulation patent applications and abandoned patent applications are held by the Patent Office in confidence and are not open to public inspection.

Even as the extension of trade secret protection to patentable subject matter that the owner knows will not meet the standards of patentability will not conflict with the patent policy of disclosure, it will have a decidedly beneficial effect on society. Trade secret law will encourage invention in areas where patent law does not reach, and will prompt the independent innovator to proceed with the discovery and exploitation of his invention. Competition is fostered and the public is not deprived of the use of valuable, if not quite patentable, invention.

Even if trade secret protection against the faithless employee were abolished, inventive and exploitive effort in the area of patentable subject matter that did not meet the standards of patentability would continue, although at a reduced level. Alternatively with the effort that remained, however, would come an increase in the amount of self-help that innovative companies would employ. Knowledge would be widely dispersed among the employees of those still active in research. Security precautions necessarily would be increased, and salaries and fringe benefits of those few officers or employees who had to know the whole of the secret invention would be fixed in an amount thought sufficient to assure their loyalty. Smaller companies would be placed at a distinct economic disadvantage, since the costs of this kind of self-help could be great, and the cost to the public of the use of this invention would be increased. The innovative entrepreneur with limited resources would tend to confine his research efforts to himself and those few he felt he could trust without the ultimate assurance of legal protection against breaches of confidence. As a result, organized scientific and technological research could become fragmented, and society, as a whole, would suffer.

Another problem that would arise if state trade secret protection were precluded is in the area of licensing others to exploit secret processes. The holder of a trade secret would not likely share his secret with a manufacturer who cannot be placed under binding legal obligation to pay a license fee or to protect the secret. The result would be to hoard rather than disseminate knowledge. * * * The detrimental misallocation of resources and economic waste that would thus take place if trade secret protection were abolished with respect to employees or licensees cannot be justified by reference to any policy that the federal patent law seeks to advance.

Nothing in the patent law requires that States refrain from action to prevent industrial espionage. In addition to the increased costs for protection from burglary, wire-tapping, bribery, and the other means used to misappropriate trade secrets, there is the inevitable cost to the basic decency of society when one firm steals from another. A most fundamental human right, that of privacy, is threatened when industrial espionage is condoned or is made profitable; the state interest in denying profit to such illegal ventures is unchallengeable.

The next category of patentable subject matter to deal with is the invention whose holder has a legitimate doubt as to its patentability. The risk of eventual patent invalidity by the courts and the costs associated with that risk may well impel some with a good-faith doubt as to patentability not to take the trouble to seek to obtain and defend patent protection for their discoveries, regardless of the existence of trade secret protection. Trade secret protection would assist those inventors in the more efficient exploitation of their discoveries and not conflict with the patent law. In most cases of genuine doubt as to patent validity the potential rewards of patent protection are so far superior to those accruing to holders of trade secrets, that the holders of such inventions will seek patent protection, ignoring the trade secret route. For those inventors "on the line" as to whether to seek patent protection, the abolition of trade secret protection might encourage some to apply for a patent who otherwise would not have done so. For some of those so encouraged, no patent will be granted and the result "will have been an unnecessary postponement in the divulging of the trade secret to persons willing to pay for it. If (the patent does issue), it may well be invalid, yet many will prefer to pay a modest royalty than to contest it, even though *Lear* allows them to accept a license and pursue the contest without paying royalties while the fight goes on. The result in such a case would be unjustified royalty payments from many who would prefer not to pay them rather than agreed fees from one or a few who are entirely willing to do so." *Painton & Co. v. Bourns, Inc.*, 442 F.2d, at 225. The point is that those who might be encouraged to file for patents by the absence of trade secret law will include inventors possessing the chaff as well as the wheat. Some of the chaff—the nonpatentable discoveries—will be thrown out by the Patent Office, but in the meantime society will have been deprived of use of those discoveries through trade secret-protected licensing. Some of the chaff may not be thrown out. This Court has noted the difference between the standards used by the Patent Office and the courts to determine patentability. *Graham v. John Deere Co.*, 383 U.S. 1, 18 (1966). In *Lear, Inc. v. Adkins*, 395 U.S. 653 (1969), the Court thought that an invalid patent was so serious a threat to the free use of ideas already in the public domain that the Court permitted licensees of the patent holder to challenge the validity of the patent. Better had the invalid patent never issued. More of those patents would likely issue if trade secret law were abolished. * * * There is no conflict, then, between trade secret law and the patent law policy of disclosure, at least insofar as the first two categories of patentable subject matter are concerned.

The final category of patentable subject matter to deal with is the clearly patentable invention, i.e., that invention which the owner believes to meet the standards of patentability. It is here that the federal interest in disclosure is at its peak; these inventions, novel, useful and nonobvious, are "the things which are worth to the public the embarrassment of an exclusive patent." *Graham v. John Deere Co., supra,* at 9 (quoting Thomas Jefferson). The interest of the public is that the bargain of 17 years of exclusive use in return for disclosure be accepted. If a State, through a system of protection, were to cause a substantial risk that holders of patentable inventions would not seek patents, but rather would rely on the state protection, we would be compelled to hold that such a system could not constitutionally continue to exist. In the case of trade secret law no reasonable risk of deterrence from patent application by those who can reasonably expect to be granted patents exists.

Trade secret law provides far weaker protection in many respects than the patent law. While trade secret law does not forbid the discovery of the trade secret by fair and honest means, e.g., independent creation or reverse engineering, patent law operates "against the world," forbidding any use of the invention for whatever purpose for a significant length of time. The holder of a trade secret also takes a substantial risk that the secret will be passed on to his competitors, by theft or by breach of a confidential relationship, in a manner not easily susceptible of discovery or proof. Where patent law acts as a barrier, trade secret law functions relatively as a sieve. The possibility that an inventor who believes his invention meets the standards of patentability will sit back, rely on trade secret law, and after one year of use forfeit any right to patent protection, 35 U.S.C. § 102(b), is remote indeed.

Nor does society face much risk that scientific or technological progress will be impeded by the rare inventor with a patentable invention who chooses trade secret protection over patent protection. The ripeness-of-time concept of invention, developed from the study of the many independent multiple discoveries in history, predicts that if a particular individual had not made a particular discovery others would have, and in probably a relatively short period of time. If something is to be discovered at all very likely it will be discovered by more than one person. *Singletons and Multiples in Science* (1961), in R. MERTON, THE SOCIOLOGY OF SCIENCE 343 (1973); J. COLE & S. COLE, SOCIAL STRATIFICATION IN SCIENCE 12–13, 229–230 (1973); Ogburn & Thomas, *Are Inventions Inevitable*?, 37 POL.SCI.Q. 83 (1922).[19] Even were an inventor to keep his discovery completely to himself, something that neither the patent nor trade secret laws forbid, there is a high probability that it will be soon independently developed. If the invention, though still a trade secret, is put into public use, the competition is alerted to the existence of the inventor's solution to the problem and may be encouraged to make an extra effort to independently find the solution thus known to be possible. The inventor faces pressures not only from private industry, but from the skilled scientists who work in

[19] *See* J. WATSON, THE DOUBLE HELIX (1968). If Watson and Crick had not discovered the structure of DNA it is likely that Linus Pauling would have made the discovery soon. Other examples of multiple discovery are listed at length in the Ogburn and Thomas article.

our universities and our other great publicly supported centers of learning and research.

We conclude that the extension of trade secret protection to clearly patentable inventions does not conflict with the patent policy of disclosure. Perhaps because trade secret law does not produce any positive effects in the area of clearly patentable inventions, as opposed to the beneficial effects resulting from trade secret protection in the areas of the doubtfully patentable and the clearly unpatentable inventions, it has been suggested that partial pre-emption may be appropriate, and that courts should refuse to apply trade secret protection to inventions which the holder should have patented, and which would have been, thereby, disclosed. However, since there is no real possibility that trade secret law will conflict with the federal policy favoring disclosure of clearly patentable inventions partial pre-emption is inappropriate. Partial pre-emption, furthermore, could well create serious problems for state courts in the administration of trade secret law. As a preliminary matter in trade secret actions, state courts would be obliged to distinguish between what a reasonable inventor would and would not correctly consider to be clearly patentable, with the holder of the trade secret arguing that the invention was not patentable and the misappropriator of the trade secret arguing its undoubted novelty, utility, and nonobviousness. Federal courts have a difficult enough time trying to determine whether an invention, narrowed by the patent application procedure and fixed in the specifications which describe the invention for which the patent has been granted, is patentable. Although state courts in some circumstances must join federal courts in judging whether an issued patent is valid, it would be undesirable to impose the almost impossible burden on state courts to determine the patentability—in fact and in the mind of a reasonable inventor—of a discovery which has not been patented and remains entirely uncircumscribed by expert analysis in the administrative process. Neither complete nor partial pre-emption of state trade secret law is justified.

Our conclusion that patent law does not pre-empt trade secret law is in accord with prior cases of this Court. Trade secret law and patent law have co-existed in this country for over one hundred years. Each has its particular role to play, and the operation of one does not take away from the need for the other. Trade secret law encourages the development and exploitation of those items of lesser or different invention than might be accorded protection under the patent laws, but which items still have an important part to play in the technological and scientific advancement of the Nation. Trade secret law promotes the sharing of knowledge, and the efficient operation of industry; it permits the individual inventor to reap the rewards of his labor by contracting with a company large enough to develop and exploit it. Congress, by its silence over these many years, has seen the wisdom of allowing the States to enforce trade secret protection.

Until Congress takes affirmative action to the contrary, States should be free to grant protection to trade secrets.

* * *

MR. JUSTICE MARSHALL, concurring in the result.

Unlike the Court, I do not believe that the possibility that an inventor with a patentable invention will rely on state trade secret law rather than apply for a patent is "remote indeed." State trade secret law provides substantial protection to the inventor who intends to use or sell the invention himself rather than license it to others, protection which in its unlimited duration is clearly superior to the 17-year monopoly afforded by the patent laws. I have no doubt that the existence of trade secret protection provides in some instances a substantial disincentive to entrance into the patent system, and thus deprives society of the benefits of public disclosure of the invention which it is the policy of the patent laws to encourage. This case may well be such an instance.

But my view of sound policy in this area does not dispose of this case. Rather, the question presented in this case is whether Congress, in enacting the patent laws, intended merely to offer inventors a limited monopoly in exchange for disclosure of their invention, or instead to exert pressure on inventors to enter into this exchange by withdrawing any alternative possibility of legal protection for their inventions. I am persuaded that the former is the case. State trade secret laws and the federal patent laws have co-existed for many, many years. During this time, Congress has repeatedly demonstrated its full awareness of the existence of the trade secret system, without any indication of disapproval. Indeed, Congress has in a number of instances given explicit federal protection to trade secret information provided to federal agencies. *See, e.g.*, 5 U.S.C. § 552(b)(4); 18 U.S.C. § 1905. Because of this, I conclude that there is "neither such actual conflict between the two schemes of regulation that both cannot stand in the same area, nor evidence of a congressional design to pre-empt the field." *Florida Lime & Avocado Growers v. Paul*, 373 U.S. 132 (1963). I therefore concur in the result reached by the majority of the Court.

MR. JUSTICE DOUGLAS, with whom MR. JUSTICE BRENNAN concurs, dissenting.

Today's decision is at war with the philosophy of *Sears, Roebuck & Co. v. Stiffel Co.*, 376 U.S. 225 and *Compco Corp. v. Day-Brite Lighting, Inc.*, 376 U.S. 234. * * *

The product involved in this suit, sodium iodide synthetic crystals, was a product that could be patented but was not. Harshaw the inventor apparently contributed greatly to the technology in that field by developing processes, procedures, and techniques that produced much larger crystals than any competitor. These processes, procedures, and techniques were also patentable; but no patent was sought. Rather Harshaw sought to protect its trade secrets by contracts with its employees. And the District Court found that, as a result of those secrecy precautions, "not sufficient disclosure occurred so as to place the claimed trade secrets in the public domain"; and those findings were sustained by the Court of Appeals.

The District Court issued a permanent injunction against respondents, ex-employees, restraining them from using the processes used by Harshaw. By a patent which would require full disclosure Harshaw could have obtained a 17-year monopoly against the world. By the District Court's injunction, which the Court approves and reinstates, Harshaw gets a permanent injunction running into perpetuity against respondents. In *Sears*, as in the present case, an injunction against the unfair competitor issued. We said: "To allow a State by use of its law of unfair competition to prevent the copying of an article which represents too slight an advance to be patented would be to permit the State to block off from the public something which federal law has said belongs to the public. The result would be that while federal law grants only 14 or 17 years' protection to genuine inventions, *see* 35 U.S.C. §§ 154, 173, States could allow perpetual protection to articles too lacking in novelty to merit any patent at all under federal constitutional standards. This would be too great an encroachment on the federal patent system to be tolerated." 376 U.S., at 231–232.

* * *

BONITO BOATS, INC. V. THUNDER CRAFT BOATS, INC.

489 U.S. 141, 109 S.Ct. 971 (1989).

JUSTICE O'CONNOR delivered the opinion of the Court.

We must decide today what limits the operation of the federal patent system places on the States' ability to offer substantial protection to utilitarian and design ideas which the patent laws leave otherwise unprotected.* * *

I

[Bonito Boats, Inc., sued respondent Thunder Craft Boats, Inc., for using the direct molding process to duplicate the hull design of Bonito's Model 5VBR fiberglass recreational boat, and selling the duplicates, in violation of Florida Statute § 559.94 (1987), which made it unlawful "to use the direct molding process to duplicate for the purpose of sale any manufactured vessel hull or component part of a vessel made by another" or to "knowingly sell" such an unlawfully duplicated hull or component. The trial court dismissed the suit on the ground that the Florida statute was invalid under *Sears, Roebuck & Co. v. Stiffel Co.*, 376 U.S. 225 (1964) and *Compco Corporation v. Day-Brite Lighting, Inc.*, 376 U.S. 234 (1964), because it impermissibly interfered with the scheme of the federal patent laws. The state court of appeal affirmed.]

* * *

On appeal, a sharply divided Florida Supreme Court agreed with the lower courts' conclusion that the Florida law impermissibly interfered with the scheme established by the federal patent laws. The majority read our decisions in *Sears* and *Compco* for the proposition that "when an article is introduced into the public domain, only a patent can eliminate the inherent risk of competition and then but for a limited time." * * * [T]he three dissenting judges argued that the Florida antidirect molding provision "does not prohibit the copying of an unpatented item. It prohibits one method of copying; the item remains in the public domain."

II

* * * [O]ur past decisions have made clear that state regulation of intellectual property must yield to the extent that it clashes with the balance struck by Congress in our patent laws. The tension between the desire to freely exploit the full potential of our inventive resources and the need to create an incentive to deploy those resources is constant. Where it is clear how the patent laws strike that balance in a particular circumstance, that is not a judgment the States may second-guess. We have long held that after the expiration of a federal patent, the subject matter of the patent passes to the free use of the public as a matter of federal law. Where the public has paid the congressionally mandated price for disclosure, the States may not render the exchange fruitless by offering patent-like protection to the subject matter of the expired patent. * * *

The pre-emptive sweep of our decisions in *Sears* and *Compco* has been the subject of heated scholarly and judicial debate. Read at their highest level of generality, the two decisions could be taken to stand for the proposition that the States are completely disabled from offering any form of protection to articles or processes which fall within the broad scope of patentable subject matter. Since the potentially patentable includes "anything under the sun that is made by man," *Diamond v. Chakrabarty*, 447 U.S. 303, 309 (1980) (citation omitted), the broadest reading of *Sears* would prohibit the States from regulating the deceptive simulation of trade dress or the tortious appropriation of private information.

That the extrapolation of such a broad pre-emptive principle from *Sears* is inappropriate is clear from the balance struck in *Sears* itself. The *Sears* Court made it plain that the States "may protect businesses in the use of their trademarks, labels, or distinctive dress in the packaging of goods so as to prevent others, by imitating such markings, from misleading purchasers as to the source of the goods." *Sears, supra*, at 232. Trade dress is, of course, potentially the subject matter of design patents. Yet our decision in *Sears* clearly indicates that the States may place limited regulations on the circumstances in which such designs are used in order to prevent consumer confusion as to source. Thus, while *Sears* speaks in absolutist terms, its conclusion that the States may place some conditions on the use of trade dress indicates an implicit recognition that all state regulation of potentially patentable but unpatented subject matter is not ipso facto pre-empted by the federal patent laws.

What was implicit in our decision in *Sears*, we have made explicit in our subsequent decisions concerning the scope of federal pre-emption of state regulation of the subject matter of patent. Thus, in *Kewanee Oil Co. v. Bicron Corp.*, 416 U.S. 470 (1974), we held that state protection of trade secrets did not operate to frustrate the achievement of the congressional objectives served by the patent laws. Despite the fact that state law protection was available for ideas which clearly fell within the subject matter of patent, the Court concluded that the nature and degree of state protection did not conflict with the federal policies of encouragement of patentable invention and the prompt disclosure of such innovations.

* * *

At the heart of *Sears* and *Compco* is the conclusion that the efficient operation of the federal patent system depends upon substantially free trade in publicly known, unpatented design and utilitarian conceptions. In *Sears*, the state law offered "the equivalent of a patent monopoly," 376 U.S., at 233, in the functional aspects of a product which had been placed in public commerce absent the protection of a valid patent. While, as noted above, our decisions since *Sears* have taken a decidedly less rigid view of the scope of federal pre-emption under the patent laws, *e. g.*, *Kewanee*, *supra*, at 479–480, we believe that the *Sears* Court correctly concluded that the States may not offer patent-like protection to intellectual creations which would otherwise remain unprotected as a matter of federal law. Both the novelty and the nonobviousness requirements of federal patent law are grounded in the notion that concepts within the public grasp, or those so obvious that they readily could be, are the tools of creation available to all. They provide the baseline of free competition upon which the patent system's incentive to creative effort depends. A state law that substantially interferes with the enjoyment of an unpatented utilitarian or design conception which has been freely disclosed by its author to the public at large impermissibly contravenes the ultimate goal of public disclosure and use which is the centerpiece of federal patent policy. Moreover, through the creation of patent-like rights, the States could essentially redirect inventive efforts away from the careful criteria of patentability developed by Congress over the last 200 years. We understand this to be the reasoning at the core of our decisions in *Sears* and *Compco*, and we reaffirm that reasoning today.

III

We believe that the Florida statute at issue in this case so substantially impedes the public use of the otherwise unprotected design and utilitarian ideas embodied in unpatented boat hulls as to run afoul of the teaching of our decisions in *Sears* and *Compco*. It is readily apparent that the Florida statute does not operate to prohibit "unfair competition" in the usual sense that the term is understood. The law of unfair competition has its roots in the common-law tort of deceit: its general concern is with protecting consumers from confusion as to source. * * *

In contrast to the operation of unfair competition law, the Florida statute is aimed directly at preventing the exploitation of the design and utilitarian conceptions embodied in the product itself. * * * Like the patentee, the beneficiary of the Florida statute may prevent a competitor from "making" the product in what is evidently the most efficient manner available and from "selling" the product when it is produced in that fashion. *Compare* 35 U. S. C. § 154. The Florida scheme offers this protection for an unlimited number of years to all boat hulls and their component parts, without regard to their ornamental or technological merit. Protection is available for subject matter for which patent protection has been denied or has expired, as well as for designs which have been freely revealed to the consuming public by their creators.

In this case, the Bonito 5VBR fiberglass hull has been freely exposed to the public for a period in excess of six years. For purposes of federal law, it stands in the same stead as an item for which a patent has expired or been denied: it is unpatented and unpatentable. *See* 35 U.S.C. § 102(b). Whether because of a determination of unpatentability or other commercial concerns, petitioner chose to expose its hull design to the public in the marketplace, eschewing the bargain held out by the federal patent system of disclosure in exchange for exclusive use. Yet, the Florida statute allows petitioner to reassert a substantial property right in the idea, thereby constricting the spectrum of useful public knowledge. Moreover, it does so without the careful protections of high standards of innovation and limited monopoly contained in the federal scheme. We think it clear that such protection conflicts with the federal policy "that all ideas in general circulation be dedicated to the common good unless they are protected by a valid patent." *Lear, Inc. v. Adkins*, 395 U.S., at 668.

That the Florida statute does not remove all means of reproduction and sale does not eliminate the conflict with the federal scheme. In essence, the Florida law prohibits the entire public from engaging in a form of reverse engineering of a product in the public domain. * * * Reverse engineering of chemical and mechanical articles in the public domain often leads to significant advances in technology. If Florida may prohibit this particular method of study and recomposition of an unpatented article, we fail to see the principle that would prohibit a State from banning the use of chromatography in the reconstitution of unpatented chemical compounds, or the use of robotics in the duplication of machinery in the public domain.

Moreover, as we noted in *Kewanee*, the competitive reality of reverse engineering may act as a spur to the inventor, creating an incentive to develop inventions that meet the rigorous requirements of patentability. The Florida statute substantially reduces this competitive incentive, thus eroding the general rule of free competition upon which the attractiveness of the federal patent bargain depends. The protections of state trade secret law are most effective at the developmental stage, before a product has been marketed and the threat of reverse engineering becomes real. During this period, patentability will often be an uncertain prospect, and to a certain extent, the protection offered by trade secret law may "dovetail" with the incentives created by the federal patent monopoly. In contrast, under the Florida scheme, the would-be inventor is aware from the outset of his efforts that rights against the public are available regardless of his ability to satisfy the rigorous standards of patentability. Indeed, it appears that even the most mundane and obvious changes in the design of a boat hull will trigger the protections of the statute. *See* Fla. Stat. § 559.94(2) (1987) (protecting "any manufactured vessel hull or component part"). Given the substantial protection offered by the Florida scheme, we cannot dismiss as hypothetical the possibility that it will become a significant competitor to the federal patent laws, offering investors similar protection without the quid pro quo of substantial creative effort required by the federal statute. The prospect of all 50 States establishing similar protections for preferred industries without the rigorous requirements of patentability prescribed by Congress could pose a substantial threat to the patent system's ability to accomplish its mission of promoting progress in the useful arts.

Finally, allowing the States to create patent-like rights in various products in public circulation would lead to administrative problems of no small dimension. The federal patent scheme provides a basis for the public to ascertain the status of the intellectual property embodied in any article in general circulation. Through the application process, detailed information concerning the claims of the patent holder is compiled in a central location. *See* 35 U. S. C. §§ 111–114. The availability of damages in an infringement action is made contingent upon affixing a notice of patent to the protected article. 35 U. S. C. § 287. The notice requirement is designed "for the information of the public," *Wine Railway Appliance Co. v. Enterprise Railway Equipment Co.*, 297 U.S. 387, 397 (1936), and provides a ready means of discerning the status of the intellectual property embodied in an article of manufacture or design. The public may rely upon the lack of notice in exploiting shapes and designs accessible to all. *See Devices for Medicine, Inc. v. Boehl,* 822 F. 2d 1062, 1066 (C.A.Fed.1987)

("Having sold the product unmarked, [the patentee] could hardly maintain entitlement to damages for its use by a purchaser uninformed that such use would violate [the] patent").

The Florida scheme blurs this clear federal demarcation between public and private property. One of the fundamental purposes behind the Patent and Copyright Clauses of the Constitution was to promote national uniformity in the realm of intellectual property. *See* The Federalist No. 43, p. 309 (B. Wright ed. 1961). * * * This purpose is frustrated by the Florida scheme, which renders the status of the design and utilitarian "ideas" embodied in the boat hulls it protects uncertain. Given the inherently ephemeral nature of property in ideas, and the great power such property has to cause harm to the competitive policies which underlay the federal patent laws, the demarcation of broad zones of public and private right is "the type of regulation that demands a uniform national rule." *Ray v. Atlantic Richfield Co.*, 435 U.S. 151, 179 (1978). Absent such a federal rule, each State could afford patent-like protection to particularly favored home industries, effectively insulating them from competition from outside the State.

* * *

Our decisions since *Sears* and *Compco* have made it clear that the Patent and Copyright Clauses do not, by their own force or by negative implication, deprive the States of the power to adopt rules for the promotion of intellectual creation within their own jurisdictions. *See Aronson*, 440 U.S., at 262; *Goldstein v. California*, 412 U.S. 546, 552–561 (1973); *Kewanee*, 416 U.S., at 478–479. Thus, where "Congress determines that neither federal protection nor freedom from restraint is required by the national interest," *Goldstein, supra*, at 559, the States remain free to promote originality and creativity in their own domains.

Nor does the fact that a particular item lies within the subject matter of the federal patent laws necessarily preclude the States from offering limited protection which does not impermissibly interfere with the federal patent scheme. As *Sears* itself makes clear, States may place limited regulations on the use of unpatented designs in order to prevent consumer confusion as to source. In *Kewanee*, we found that state protection of trade secrets, as applied to both patentable and unpatentable subject matter, did not conflict with the federal patent laws. In both situations, state protection was not aimed exclusively at the promotion of invention itself, and the state restrictions on the use of unpatented ideas were limited to those necessary to promote goals outside the contemplation of the federal patent scheme. Both the law of unfair competition and state trade secret law have coexisted harmoniously with federal patent protection for almost 200 years, and Congress has given no indication that their operation is inconsistent with the operation of the federal patent laws.

Indeed, there are affirmative indications from Congress that both the law of unfair competition and trade secret protection are consistent with the balance struck by the patent laws. Section 43(a) of the Lanham Act, 60 Stat. 441, 15 U. S. C. § 1125(a), creates a federal remedy for making "a false designation of origin, or any false description or representation, including words or other symbols tending falsely to describe or represent the same. . . ." Congress has thus given federal recognition to many of the concerns that underlie the state tort of unfair competition, and the application of *Sears* and *Compco* to nonfunctional aspects of a product which have been shown to identify source must take account of competing federal policies in this regard. Similarly, as Justice Marshall noted in his concurring opinion in *Kewanee*: "State trade secret laws and the federal patent laws have co-existed for many, many, years. During this time, Congress has repeatedly demonstrated its full awareness of the existence of the trade secret system, without any indication of disapproval. Indeed, Congress has in a number of instances given explicit federal protection to trade secret information provided to federal agencies." *Kewanee, supra,* at 494 (concurring in result) (citation omitted). The case for federal pre-emption is particularly weak where Congress has indicated its awareness of the operation of state law in a field of federal interest, and has nonetheless decided to "stand by both concepts and to tolerate whatever tension there [is] between them." *Silkwood v. Kerr-McGee Corp.*, 464 U.S. 238, 256 (1984). The same cannot be said of the Florida statute at issue here, which offers protection beyond that available under the law of unfair competition or trade secret, without any showing of consumer confusion, or breach of trust or secrecy.

The Florida statute is aimed directly at the promotion of intellectual creation by substantially restricting the public's ability to exploit ideas that the patent system mandates shall be free for all to use. Like the interpretation of Illinois unfair competition law in *Sears* and *Compco*, the Florida statute represents a break with the tradition of peaceful coexistence between state market regulation and federal patent policy. The Florida law substantially restricts the public's ability to exploit an unpatented design in general circulation, raising the specter of state-created monopolies in a host of useful shapes and processes for which patent protection has been denied or is otherwise unobtainable. It thus enters a field of regulation which the patent laws have reserved to Congress. The patent statute's careful balance between public right and private monopoly to promote certain creative activity is a "scheme of federal regulation . . . so pervasive as to make reasonable the inference that Congress left no room for the States to supplement it." *Rice v. Santa Fe Elevator Corp.*, 331 U.S. 218, 230 (1947).

Congress has considered extending various forms of limited protection to industrial design either through the copyright laws or by relaxing the restrictions on the availability of design patents. *See generally* Brown, *Design Protection: An Overview*, 34 UCLA L. REV. 1341 (1987). Congress explicitly refused to take this step in the copyright laws, *see* 17 U. S. C. § 101; H. R. Rep. No. 94–1476, p. 55 (1976), and despite sustained criticism for a number of years, it has declined to alter the patent protections presently available for industrial design. *See* Report of the President's Commission on the Patent System, S. Doc. No. 5, 90th Cong., 1st Sess., 20–21 (1967). It is for Congress to determine if the present system of design and utility patents is ineffectual in promoting the useful arts in the context of industrial design. By offering patent-like protection for ideas deemed unprotected under the present federal scheme, the Florida statute conflicts with the "strong federal policy favoring free competition in ideas which do not merit patent protection." *Lear, Inc.*, 395 U.S., at 656. We therefore agree with the majority of the Florida Supreme Court that the Florida statute is preempted by the Supremacy Clause, and the judgment of that court is hereby affirmed.

It is so ordered.

NOTE

The DMCA introduced *sui generis* protection for boat hull designs, to replace the type of state law protection which the Supreme Court held to be preempted in *Bonito Boats*. Title V of the Act, titled the "Vessel Hull Design Protection Act," added a new Chapter 13 to Title 17 which gives the owner of an original boat hull design the exclusive right for 10 years to make, import, sell, or distribute articles embodying that design for sale or use in trade, notwithstanding the intrinsic utilitarian function of the design. The provision imposes a marking requirement, limits infringement liability to cases in which the infringing article was created with knowledge that its design was copied from a protected design, exempts copying that is solely for teaching or evaluative purposes, and requires that a design be registered with the Copyright Office before an infringement suit can be filed. Infringement remedies include injunctions, seizure and destruction of infringing articles, attorneys' fees, and either damages (including enhanced damages) or the infringer's profits. Issuance of a design patent for a vessel hull design precludes Chapter 13 protection for that design, but Chapter 13 does not preempt either (a) federal or state protection for unregistered designs or (b) trademark or unfair competition laws. How does this federal protection compare with the Florida law in *Bonito Boats*? Section 5005 of the Satellite Home Viewer Improvement Act of 1999, Pub. L. No. 106–113, 106th Cong., 1st Sess. (1999), removed the sunset date of the vessel hull design protection provisions, 17 U.S.C. § 1301 *et seq.*, and revised the definition of "vessel" in section 1301(b)(3).

BALADEVON, INC. V. ABBOTT LABORATORIES, INC.

871 F.Supp. 89 (D. Mass. 1994).

SARIS, DISTRICT JUDGE:

This case marks the crossroads of patent and contract law. Plaintiff seeks to enforce an agreement which assigned patent, trademark and other non-patent rights in a device which was potentially patentable, but not yet patented. When the patents which subsequently issued on the device became generally recognized as invalid, defendant terminated payment of the royalties due under the assignment, but continued manufacturing the device and exercising other non-patent rights, notably trademark rights.

Both sides have filed cross-motions for summary judgment. After hearing, the Court ALLOWS plaintiff's motion in part, and DENIES defendant's motion.

Background

* * *

[Radiologists Sacks and Vine invented an "enteral feeding device," used for feeding patients directly through the stomach. Plaintiff Baladevon, Inc. is a corporation owned by the Sacks family and is the assignee of Dr. Vine's claims. While an application for one patent on the device was still pending, and before the application for a second patent had been filed, Baladevon and Vine assigned to Microvasive, Inc. (a division of Boston Scientific, Inc.) the following rights of the two inventors:]

> any rights they may have to [the device and the method for using it which were conceived and developed by Microvasive with their help], to any improvements therein, to the use of the names "Sacks" and "Vine" with respect thereto and to any other rights they may have with respect to the manufacture, use or sale of products that incorporate such concepts, developments or improvements.

In return, Baladevon and Dr. Vine were each to receive 2.5% in royalties through the end of the decade, with the amount to be renegotiated six months before the beginning of 1990, or sooner in the case of certain enumerated events. Most notably, if "a device of comparable design is sold in direct competition," Baladevon and Vine agreed to "consider a reasonable reduction in royalty in order to share the burdens of such events and ensure that Microvasive may continue to sell products without a competitive disadvantage." For the period January 1, 1990 to December 31, 1990, the parties agreed to negotiate over a royalty no less than 1 1/4 percent or more than 3 3/4 percent, taking into account, among other things, "devices which are of comparable design and operation and sold in direct competition with products." Any disputes were to be resolved by binding arbitration.

The agreement gave Microvasive the right, but not the legal obligation, to seek and enforce patents for the inventions and improvements, and gave it the "perpetual royalty free" right to use the names Sacks or Vine as a trademark. Microvasive agreed to pay all costs and expenses incurred in connection with all United States and foreign patent applications and patents. The agreement explicitly applies to inventions and improvements "whether patentable or not."

This litigation hinges on the termination provision, article 9(a), which provides as follows:

> This Agreement shall be terminable in whole *or in part* by Microvasive by giving written notice thereof and by assigning to Baladevon and Vine any patents included in Subject Patent Rights which pertain to the part of the Agreement being terminated and neither party shall thereafter have further obligations to the other party with respect to such part of the Agreement. (Emphasis added).

The term of the agreement was August 1, 1984 to December 31, 1994. On August 13, 1987, the defendant, Abbott Laboratories, Inc., entered the picture for the first time. On that day, the Ross Laboratories division of Abbott acquired the enteral feeding device product line from the Microvasive division of Boston Scientific. In the process, defendant acquired all of the original assignee's rights and obligations under the agreement.

The initial patent application resulted in the issuance of a patent in July, 1988. Defendant also applied for a second patent, which issued. Baladevon and Vine (the assignors) did not own or have any interest in the patents; rather Boston Scientific's employees and Dr. Sacks (who is not a party to the agreement) were the inventors listed in the patent application. Then the unexpected occurred. It came to light that Dr. Sacks had published an article containing the ideas embodied in the enteral feeding device over a year before the first application, a fact that rendered both patents invalid per se. *See* 35 U.S.C. § 102(b). Competitive devices appeared on the market.

On July 14, 1989, defendant notified plaintiff by letter of its intent to "terminate *in part*" (emphasis added) and to assign the patents back under the agreement's termination clause, citing concerns "regarding the validity and enforceability of these patents." Defendant continued to produce and sell enteral feeding devices under the names "Sacks" and "Vine," without paying plaintiff any royalties. Abbott's registration of the Sacks-Vine trademark became effective on September 26, 1989, two months after Abbott terminated the agreement "in part."

Plaintiff filed suit in this court under a variety of contract theories. A cogent memorandum, issued by Judge Woodlock on July 6, 1992, dismissed all claims except those for breach of contract and for an accounting. With regard to the remaining claims, the court found that two key provisions of the contract are ambiguous: those governing trademark rights and termination rights. The court concluded that, because these two provisions, read in context, were each susceptible of different reasonable interpretations, they presented questions of fact that could not be resolved on a motion to dismiss.

Discussion

* * * Defendant argues that plaintiff's interpretation of the termination clause—which would obligate defendant, upon termination, to either cease production of the enteral feeding device or pay royalties to plaintiff, despite the invalidity of the patents—is fatally inconsistent with patent law policy.

2. Lear and its Family

The seminal case is *Lear, Inc. v. Adkins,* 395 U.S. 653 (1969). There, the inventor sued the licensee for using his invention after ceasing royalty payments; the licensee filed a counterclaim for patent invalidity. Two landmark holdings resulted. First, in allowing the licensee to challenge the validity of the patent, the *Lear* Court abolished the state law doctrine of licensee estoppel. Second, the *Lear* Court held that the licensee was not liable for royalties on invalid patents from the moment it challenged their validity.

The *Lear* court characterized the question presented as "whether federal patent law policy bars a State from enforcing a contract regulating access to an unpatented secret idea." 395 U.S. at 672. With respect to royalties accruing after the patent issued, the answer was "yes," because "federal law requires that all ideas in general circulation be dedicated to the common good unless they are protected by a valid patent." 395 U.S. at 668. More specifically, the Court reasoned that the relegation of unpatentable ideas to the public domain was necessary to ensure that inventors did not reap benefits from an invalid patent; and the only way to put such ideas where they belonged was to give licensees the incentive to make validity challenges. However, the Court declined to address the claim to royalties before the patent issued "since it squarely raises the question whether, and to what extent, the States may protect the owners of unpatented inventions who are willing to disclose their ideas to manufacturers only upon payments of royalties." 395 U.S. at 674.

Lear is conventionally grouped with two other Supreme Court cases that grappled with conflicts between patent law and contract law. In *Brulotte v. Thys Co.*, 379 U.S. 29, 32 (1964), the Court held that a contract requiring a licensee to pay royalties after a patent expired was per se unlawful because the patent owner had abused the leverage of the monopoly to project royalties into the period after expiration.

A different principle is embodied in *Aronson v. Quick Point Pencil Co.*, 440 U.S. 257, 259 (1979), a case decided ten years after *Lear*. In *Quick Point*, which involved a royalty agreement covering patent rights and trade secrets, the Court considered "whether federal patent law preempts state contract law so as to preclude enforcement of a contract to pay royalties to a patent applicant, on sales of articles embodying the putative invention, for so long as the contracting party sells them, if a patent is not granted." Pointing out that the parties contracted with "full awareness of both the pendency of a patent application and the possibility that a patent might not issue," it held:

> Commercial agreements traditionally are the domain of state law. State law is not displaced merely because the contract relates to intellectual property which may or may not be patentable; the states are free to regulate the use of such intellectual property in any manner not inconsistent with federal law.

440 U.S. at 261–262. The Court found no merit in the contention that enforcement of the agreement withdrew any idea from the public domain because the design, although not patentable, entered the public domain as a result of the manufacture and sale of the design under the contract. The Court also pointed out that the agreement set two different royalty fees, depending on whether or not the patent issued. Although a pending patent application gives the applicant some additional bargaining power, the court stated the "amount of leverage depends on how likely the parties consider it to be that a valid patent will issue." 440 U.S. at 265.

The Court distinguished *Lear* as not controlling "when no patent has issued, and no ideas have been withdrawn from the market place." 440 U.S. at 264. *Brulotte* was distinguished on the grounds that the patent owner in *Quick Point* had not attempted to use her monopoly as leverage during negotiation of the licensing contract. The Court concluded that federal patent law is not a barrier to enforcement of "contractual obligations, freely undertaken in arm's-length negotiation and with no fixed reliance on a patent or a probable patent grant." 440 U.S. at 266.

The Federal Circuit has been leery of a blind application of *Lear*. In an extensive discussion, the court essentially confined the case to its facts:

> *Lear* . . . precluded the award of royalties to the licensor under the facts of *that case* from the date the patent issued if the patent were later held invalid. *Lear* does not in fact . . . deal with a licensor's right to terminate or rescind a license agreement, or dictate what *must* be held a breach of contract, or what damages *must* be awarded for a breach, or under what circumstances, if any, a licensee can recover royalties paid. Those questions continue to be

> matters dependent on particular fact situations, contract provisions and state contract law, albeit they must be resolved in harmony with general principles discernible from *Lear*.

RCA Corp. v. Data General Corp., 887 F.2d 1056, 1064 (Fed.Cir.1989) (emphasis in original). Thus, the public policy expressed in *Lear* is not so overpowering that it may overcome the especially strong countervailing policy in favor of enforcing contracts that take the form of judicial settlements or consent judgments. It is also possible, at least by some means, to contract around the *Lear* doctrine. *See Sun Studs, Inc. v. ATA Equipment Leasing, Inc.*, 872 F.2d 978, 991–93 (Fed.Cir.1989) (holding that *Lear* policy of encouraging challenges to patent validity does not require court to void contract provision obligating assignee to protect, defend and enforce the patent and to preserve the confidentiality of information).

3. *Hybrid Royalty Agreements*

Defendant argues that the agreement here is unenforceable after *Lear*. Four Circuits have struggled with the question of the enforceability of "hybrid royalty agreements"—agreements, such as the one before the court, that exchange royalties for a mix of patent and non-patent rights—after *Lear*, *Brulotte* and *Quick Point*. A consensus has emerged. Where a licensing agreement fails to distinguish between patent and non-patent rights in royalty payments, and a patent is invalidated, *Lear* precludes enforcement of the contract according to its terms but does not preclude compensation for the non-patent rights. *Chromalloy v. Fischmann*, 716 F.2d 683, 685 (9th Cir.1983) (where a royalty agreement was part of a sale of ongoing business, seller was not entitled to compensation for royalty payments on the invalid patent although court could award compensation on transfer and use of non-patent assets); *Span-Deck, Inc. v. Fab-Con, Inc.*, 677 F.2d 1237, 1246–1249 (8th Cir. 1982) (although hybrid royalty agreement was unenforceable because there was no allocation of the percentage of royalties attributable to trade secrets and know-how, licensor was entitled to compensation for non-patent rights to prevent unjust enrichment); *St. Regis Paper Co. v. Royal Inds.*, 552 F.2d 309, 315 (9th Cir. 1977) (although court could not enforce royalty agreement which failed to distinguish between patent rights and non-patent rights such as know-how, it could award compensation for non-patent rights).

Moreover, two federal courts have suggested that agreements which specifically provide for separate allocation of payments of royalties for patent and non-patent rights may well survive after expiration or invalidity of the patents despite the *Brulotte* rule of per se invalidity. *See Boggild v. Kenner Prods. Div.*, 776 F.2d 1315, 1319 (6th Cir.1985) (holding that *Brulotte* rule of per se invalidity precludes enforcement of license agreement which was developed in "clear contemplation" of patent protection, which requires royalty payments for use, sale or manufacture of patented item for twenty five years, and which "contains neither provisions for reduction of royalties in the event valid patents never issued nor terms for reduction of post-expiration royalties"); *Pitney Bowes, Inc. v. Mestre*, 701 F.2d 1365, 1372 (11th Cir.1983) (holding *Brulotte* was applicable to hybrid agreements concerning patent and trade secret rights, and that non-issuance of the pending patent precluded enforcement where there was no allocation in the agreement between trade secrets and patent rights).

Neither the First Circuit nor the Supreme Court has ever addressed the question whether a hybrid agreement in which patents issue can ever survive the expiration or invalidation of the patents where there is a provision for allocation of payments between patent and non-patent rights.

4. *The Application of Lear to this Case*

There are two crucial factors which support enforceability of this hybrid royalty agreement under this line of cases. First, the contract here took the form of an assignment rather than a licensing arrangement. Second, the assignment agreement provided a mechanism for reducing the royalties to reflect competition in the marketplace should the patent not issue or prove invalid.

a. The assignment

No party disputes that the agreement is, both in form and substance, an assignment. An assignment is a conveyance of a complete bundle of rights, including title to the invention and the right to sue infringers. *See CMS Indus. Inc. v. L.P.S. Int'l, Ltd.*, 643 F.2d 289, 294 (5th Cir.1981) (defining an assignment as a conveyance which "effectively transfers the entire bundle of common law rights presiding in a patent"). An agreement which grants the "exclusive right to make, use and vend the invention" is an assignment, not a license. *Waterman v. Mackenzie*, 138 U.S. 252, 255–56 (1891).

A license "merely grants a party permission to do something which would otherwise be unlawful; it grants immunity from suit rather than a proprietary interest in the patent." *Public Varieties of Mississippi, Inc. v. Sun Valley Seed Co.*, 734 F.Supp. 250, 252 (N.D.Miss.1990).

Outside of licensee estoppel, which is commonly understood to have been abolished by *Lear*, the status of estoppel doctrines in patent law has not been definitively settled. The weight of authority holds that the doctrine of assignee estoppel survived *Lear*. *See Sybron*, 770 F.Supp. at 811 ("the policy reasons which justify allowing a licensee to assert patent invalidity against the licensor and to escape the duty to pay royalties do not justify allowing an assignee to avoid its contractual duty to the assignor to make full payment for what it has received"); *Roberts v. Sears, Roebuck*

& Co., 573 F.2d 976, 982 (7th Cir.1978) ("the primary evil that the Court in *Lear* sought to end, that the public might have to pay tribute to a 'would-be monopolist' is completely irrelevant to this case [involving a complete assignment of rights])"; *Coast Metals*, 205 U.S.P.Q. (BNA) 154 (applying assignee estoppel where assignee got the benefit of the bargain). *See also Diamond Scientific Co. v. Ambico, Inc.*, 848 F.2d 1220, 1224–25 (Fed.Cir. 1988) ("if an assignee of a patent were allowed to challenge the patent, it would be placed in the legally awkward position of simultaneously attacking and defending the validity of the same patent"). On the other hand, some courts have refused to apply assignor estoppel. *See, e.g., Interconnect Planning Corp. v. Feil*, 543 F.Supp. 610 (S.D.N.Y.1982) (rejecting assignor-inventor estoppel when assignee sues assignor for infringement). Whether estoppel should be applied in a particular case, the Federal Circuit has suggested, should be determined by balancing the equities. *See Diamond Scientific*, 848 F.2d at 1224–25 (justifying application of the generally disfavored doctrine of assignor estoppel).

The equities strongly favor the application of estoppel in this case. There is no evidence that plaintiff exercised the increased leverage of an anticipated patent monopoly based on the parties' expectation of a high likelihood that valid patents would issue. *Contrast Boggild*, 776 F.2d at 1321. To the contrary, the undisputed evidence is that the issuance of the patents was not a significant factor in the agreement. Moreover, the terms of the agreement reflect an equality of bargaining power; for example, there is a provision that plaintiff's fees would be reduced in the event of a challenge to the patent or market competition. Finally, the agreement does not purport to extend a royalty agreement beyond the life of the patent.

Furthermore, neither of the two policy rationales supporting the abrogation of estoppel in *Lear* are relevant to the weighing of equities in this case. The two concerns, it will be recalled, were that a patent's validity might go unchallenged, and that the public would continue to pay tribute for an invalid patent. By the time of defendant's termination in this case, the patents had already been widely revealed as invalid and competitive products were on the market. Thus, there is obviously no concern, as there was in *Lear*, that the patent monopoly would continue to be honored lest the defendant be given an incentive to challenge patent validity.

A little thought about the nature of assignments reveals that the other concern of *Lear* is equally invalid here. Royalties in a licensing agreement are an ongoing obligation, continually exchanged for an ongoing right. By contrast, royalties in an assignment agreement are properly conceived as deferred consideration for the original conveyance of rights, with the amount of consideration pegged to the commercial success of the product.

At the time of the agreement in this case, the assigned bundle of rights included the rights to use and sell an invention that was potentially but not certainly patentable. It also included the right to use Sachs' and Vine's names and to obtain trademark registration for these names. In return, the assignors received payment in the form of royalties. Under plaintiff's interpretation of the agreement, Baladevon would be entitled to some amount of royalties throughout the contract term as long as the defendant continued to manufacture—regardless of whether the inventions or improvements were "patentable," regardless of whether patents issued or not, regardless of the patents' validity, regardless of whether defendant retained ownership of the patents or chose to return them under the termination clause. Unlike those barred by *Lear*, the payments plaintiff demands would not be benefits derived from ownership of invalid patents. Rather, they would be deferred, contingent consideration for the commercially useful, potentially patentable ideas that a sophisticated, self-interested firm contracted to buy in 1986, in order to get the right to be first in the market and in order to use the names of Sacks and Vine. This court concludes that the defendant should in this case be estopped from challenging the enforceability of the agreement based on patent invalidity.

b. The royalty renegotiation clause

There is a second, even more significant, distinction between this case and the line of cases extending *Lear* to the context of hybrid royalty agreements. In each of those cases, the court was compelled to invalidate the whole agreement, because it was impossible to disentangle the consideration given for the invalid patent from the consideration given for nonpatent rights. Each court recognized, however, that the plaintiff was still entitled, on the theory of unjust enrichment, to that portion of the consideration (if any) that was designed to compensate it for non-patent rights. *See Chromalloy*, 716 F.2d at 685; *Span-Deck*, 677 F.2d at 1247; *St. Regis*, 552 F.2d at 315.

In this case, as in *Quick Point*, the parties anticipated that the device might not be patentable by providing for renegotiation of the royalty if a competitive product entered the marketplace, and mandatory arbitration if the parties failed to agree. Although the contract itself does not set forth distinct royalty rates depending on the validity of the patent, it takes the more flexible, and equally valid approach, of requiring the parties to renegotiate a fee depending on the validity of the patent. If this court were to invalidate the assignment agreement, then it would be obliged—under the logic of the hybrid royalty cases—to award plaintiff relief tantamount to the renegotiation mechanism provided by the agreement. The assignment contract in this case is not a classic hybrid agreement—it is not an agreement wherein patent and non-patent consideration are hopelessly entangled. On the contrary, the contract fixes the value of the non-patent rights precisely, at the amount of the royalty rate that would be renegotiated in the event of patent invalidity. This court concludes that

Lear does not bar enforcement of the agreement as interpreted by plaintiffs.

* * *

[The court rejected the plaintiff's claim for a 7.5 percent royalty, but granted an accounting.]

NOTES

1. Consider the notes following the § 301 preemption cases, *supra.* Would any of the state laws in question which were *not* preempted under § 301 nevertheless be preempted on the ground that they are fundamentally incompatible with federal copyright policy?

2. Plaintiff agrees to license a copyright to defendant, on a nonexclusive basis, in return for a royalty. The contract does not specify the duration of the license. Under the applicable state law, a contract that is silent as to duration is terminable at will. The plaintiff terminates the contract after 8 years. The defendant, however, contends that the license is not terminable for at least 35 years, under 17 U.S.C. § 203, and continues to exercise the rights specified in the license. Plaintiff sues for copyright infringement. The court rules, however, that the plaintiff's termination of the license was invalid because the state law permitting termination-at-will is preempted by section 203. Is this ruling correct?

3. Where Congress has enacted statutory provisions defining the scope of federal preemption of state law, such as 17 U.S.C. §§ 301, 912(c), should this be interpreted as an acquiescence to state laws which are not preempted by those provisions but might be deemed preempted under a constitutional preemption analysis?

4. When a copyrighted work that contains a person's likeness (such as a film) enters the public domain, can the person depicted therein bring a cause of action for infringement of the right of publicity against a person who exploits the public domain work? What about the title of a copyrighted work that enters the public domain—could an unfair competition suit be premised on use of the title, assuming it has acquired secondary meaning?

5. Do the same standards apply to preemption of state laws by both patent and copyright laws? How can one determine whether Congress made a deliberate choice to deny protection to a particular kind of work, or simply left the area unattended?

6. If Congress chose to withdraw all federal copyright or patent legislation, would the Supremacy Clause bar states from enacting equivalent statutes on their own?

7. Would the Supremacy Clause permit a state to offer exclusive protection to an idea that was not expressed in a copyrightable or patentable form? To a fixed work that was neither novel nor original? What about a database or other noncopyrightable factual compilation?

8. Although federal copyright law preempts some state law unfair competition claims, it does not preempt unfair competition claims brought under the federal Lanham Act, 15 U.S.C. §§ 1051–1127. *See, e.g., Alameda Films SA de CV v. Authors Rights Restoration Corp. Inc.*, 331 F.3d 472 (5th Cir.2003). However, in *Dastar Corp. v. Twentieth Century Fox Film Corp.*, 539 U.S. 23 (2003) (excerpted in Chapter 4, *supra*), the Supreme Court refused to interpret federal unfair competition law in a manner that would provide a substitute for copyright claims or remove a work from the public domain.

9. In *Dow Chemical Co. v. Exxon Corp.*, 139 F.3d 1470 (Fed.Cir.1998), the Federal Circuit held that federal patent law did not preempt state tort claims for intentional interference with actual and prospective contractual relations. The patentee had threatened the plaintiff's customers with infringement suits, even though its patent was invalid due to inequitable conduct in the Patent Office. The court explained:

> Under the standard mandated by the Supreme Court, the state law cause of action at issue here does not present an "obstacle" to the execution and accomplishment of the patent laws. None of the three factors identified in *Kewanee* are implicated by a state tort remedy for intentional interference with actual and prospective contractual relations in instances where the tortfeasor's threats to sue were based upon infringement of a patent obtained by inequitable conduct. It is difficult to fathom how such a state law cause of action could have any discernible effect on the incentive to invent, the full disclosure of ideas, or the principle that ideas in the public domain remain in the public domain. Indeed, it seems most improbable that an inventor would choose to forfeit the benefits of patent protection because of fear of the risk of being found tortiously liable based upon attempting to enforce a patent obtained by inequitable conduct. Moreover, a key purpose behind this tort is the protection of the integrity of commercial contracts which, as noted above, "traditionally are the domain of state law." *Aronson*, 440 U.S. at 262; *see generally*, W. PAGE KEETON ET AL., PROSSER AND KEETON ON THE LAW OF TORTS 978 (1984) ("The law of interference with contract is thus one part of a larger body of tort law aimed at protection of relationships, some economic and some personal." (footnotes omitted)). The tort plainly does not seek to offer patent-like protection to intellectual property inconsistent with the federal scheme.
>
> * * *
>
> Nor do we agree with Exxon that the disputed cause of action is an impermissible alternative state law remedy for inequitable conduct before the PTO as prohibited by *Abbott Laboratories v. Brennan*, 952 F.2d 1346 (Fed.Cir.1991). In *Abbott Laboratories*, we held that a state tort action for abuse of process could not "be invoked as a remedy for inequitable or other unsavory conduct of parties to proceedings in the Patent and Trademark Office." *Id.* at 1355. Such

a tort claim "would be an inappropriate collateral intrusion on the regulatory procedures of the PTO . . . and is contrary to Congress' preemptive regulation in the area of patent law." *Id.* at 1357 (citation omitted). However unlike the common law abuse of process claim at issue in *Abbott*, the tort claim asserted here for intentional interference with actual and prospective contractual relations is not an alternative or additional remedy for inequitable conduct before the PTO. In *Abbott*, the abuse of process claim at issue was based entirely upon bad faith misconduct before the PTO. Indeed, the wrong alleged and for which state law tort damages were sought was no more than bad faith misconduct before the PTO. However, the tort claim at issue here is not premised upon bad faith misconduct in the PTO, but rather is premised upon bad faith misconduct in the marketplace. Unlike the abuse of process claim in dispute in *Abbott*, a tort claim for intentional interference with contractual relations requires elements entirely different to those required for inequitable conduct before the PTO. Thus, for example, it requires that the tortfeasor have knowledge of the contractual relationship with which he is interfering and that he commit an act of intentional inducement to harm that relationship. *See* RESTATEMENT (SECOND) OF TORTS § 766, cmts. h, i. These required elements take place in the marketplace, not before the PTO. Indeed, the tort can be made out without there being any misconduct whatsoever in the PTO. Thus, for example, a holder of a valid and enforceable patent who knowingly brings baseless infringement actions against a competitor's customers might also be subject to such tort liability. Accordingly, because it requires entirely different elements to establish a prima facie state tort action for intentional interference with contractual relations, it plainly is not a preempted alternative or additional state law remedy for inequitable conduct. Rather it is a long-established independent tort remedy for improprieties in the marketplace.

* * *

Any argument that this state law cause of action provides a duplication of federal remedies that could lead to conflicting results is similarly unfounded. The tort of intentional interference with contractual relations is a remedy of money damages for improper behavior by competitors in the marketplace. The tort at issue covers all types of commercial actors and does not single out patent-holders for either increased deference or additional scrutiny. Inequitable conduct, however, provides a defense to those accused by a patent-holder whose patent was obtained by improper conduct in the PTO and provides the specific relief of making the patent unenforceable. Far from being a duplication of remedies, the state tort and the federal defense address entirely different wrongs and also provide different forms of relief. In addition, given that, as discussed earlier, it is well-established that issues of validity and enforceability may be adjudicated in licensing disputes governed by state law and thus yield conflicting results, it seems somewhat unpersuasive to suggest that the possibility of conflicting results raised by this case is an adequate ground for preemption.

Exxon, 139 F.3d at 1475–78 (footnotes omitted).

10. Does patent law preempt a state law regulating the price of patented prescription drugs? *See Biotechnology Industry Org. v. District of Columbia*, 496 F.3d 1362 (Fed. Cir. 2007).

INDEX

References are to Pages

UNCLEAN HANDS

UNFAIR COMPETITION